CADOGANguides

TUSCANY, UMBRIA & THE MARCHES

'Few landscapes are more ancient or more civilized than that of Tuscany; Umbria is more dishevelled and rustic, and celebrated for its green, the 'mystical' colour to suit its mystical, saintly nature.'

Dana Facaros and Michael Pauls

About the Guide

The **full-colour introduction** gives the authors' overview of the region, together with suggested **itineraries** and a regional **'where to go' map** and **feature** to help you plan your trip.

Illuminating and entertaining **cultural chapters** on history, food and drink, art and architecture give you a rich flavour of the region.

Planning Your Trip covers the basics of **getting there** and **getting around**, plus entry formalities. The **Practical A–Z** deals with all the **essential information** and **contact details** that you may need, including a section for disabled travellers.

The **regional chapters** are arranged in a loose touring order, with plenty of public transport and driving information. The authors' top **'Don't Miss'** **sights** are highlighted at the start of each chapter.

A short **language guide**, a **glossary** of cultural terms, ideas for **further reading** and a comprehensive **index** can be found at the end of the book.

Although everything we list in this guide is **personally recommended**, our authors inevitably have their own favourite places to eat and stay. Whenever you see this **Authors' Choice** icon beside a listing, you will know that it is a little bit out of the ordinary.

Hotel Price Guide

Luxury	€€€€€	€230 and above
Very Expensive	€€€€	€150–230
Expensive	€€€	€100–150
Moderate	€€	€60–100
Inexpensive	€	€60 and under

Restaurant Price Guide

Very Expensive	€€€€	€60 and above
Expensive	€€€	€40–60
Moderate	€€	€25–40
Inexpensive	€	€25 and under

About the Authors

Dana Facaros and Michael Pauls, now based in southwest France, spent three years in a tiny Italian village, where they suffered massive overdoses of food, art and wine. They have written more than 40 guides for Cadogan.

10th Edition Published 2007

01 INTRODUCING TUSCANY, UMBRIA & THE MARCHES

Above: Cypress trees, Urbino, The Marches, p.587

A glass of wine before dinner on the terrace, olives glinting in the last flash of the setting sun as geometric vineyards lose their rigid order in the melting darkness and only the black daggers of cypresses stand out against the first stars of the evening – where could you be but Tuscany? It almost needs no introduction, this famous twilit land where 500 years ago Titans of art mimicked and then outdid nature, while nature utters a gentle retort by rivalling art. Neighbouring Umbria is most familiar as the land of St Francis of Assisi, converting many with its mystical eloquence; a land that, as the nun on the bus put it, 'speaks in silences'. Umbria has much in common with Tuscany – wine, art and lavish natural beauty, and a remarkable sense of continuity, of a land and people in perfect agreement. Long overshadowed, the Marches nevertheless share many of the region's best features: transcendant Renaissance art, ageless hilltowns, sandy beaches, as well as a few surprises, all traditionally free of mass tourism. Though no longer a best-kept secret, the Marches still offer a seductive slice of central Italian gentility.

Travellers have been flocking to central Italy since the Middle Ages, to learn, see and understand. Most have come with their Baedekers in hand, and even today it is hard to escape the generations of worthy opinions or avoid treading on those same old grapes of purple prose. After all, most of what we call Western civilization was either rediscovered or invented here, leaving works that have lost none of the power; at times it seems the artists of the early 1400s descended from space with their secret messages

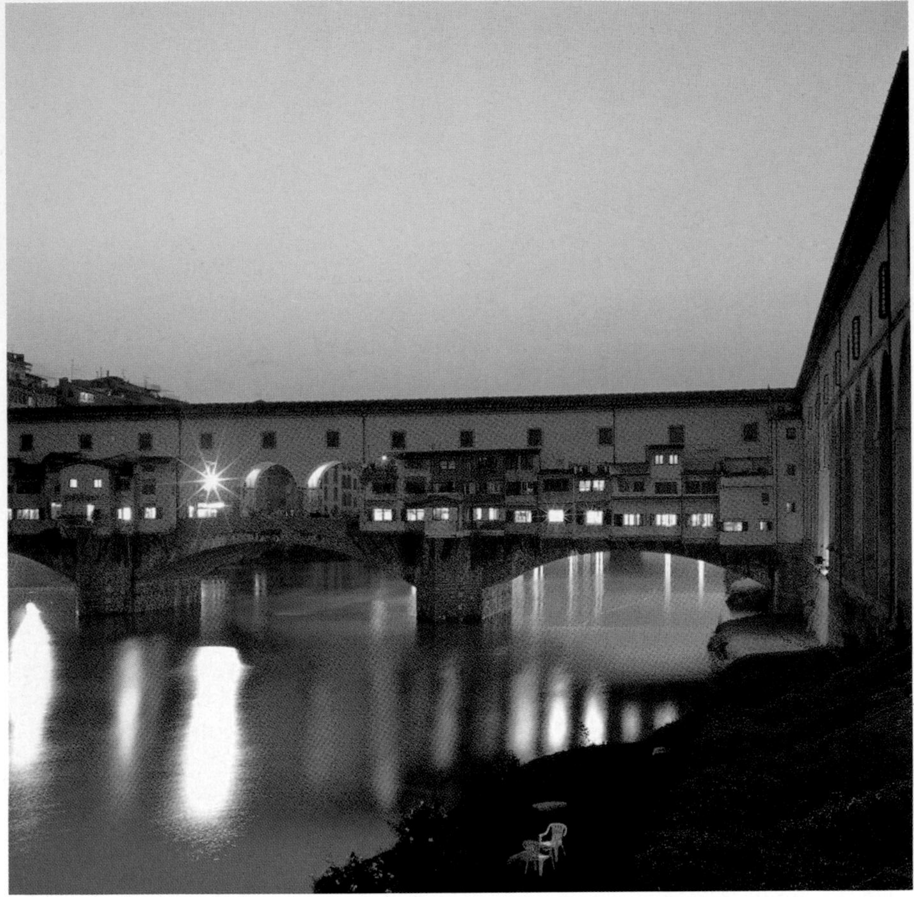

Above: Ponte Vecchio, Florence, p.128

Opposite: San Galgano, west of Siena, p.370

for the imagination. To the mass of accumulated opinion we now add ours, for better or worse, but mostly in the hope of provoking some of your own.

But in times that seem to be changing faster than we can or care to, the enduring charm of Tuscany, Umbria and the Marches is in that dreamy glass of wine, in those hills that look exactly as they did when Piero painted them, in the bartender who's a dead ringer for Lorenzo de' Medici, in those bewitching Etruscan smiles that might have been smiled only yesterday. Things have stayed the same not by accident, or economic reason, or by decree of some Tuscan National Trust, but because that's the way people like them. They make as few concessions to the 21st century as possible, and their Brigadoon may not be for everyone. They're not catching up with the world; the world's catching up with them.

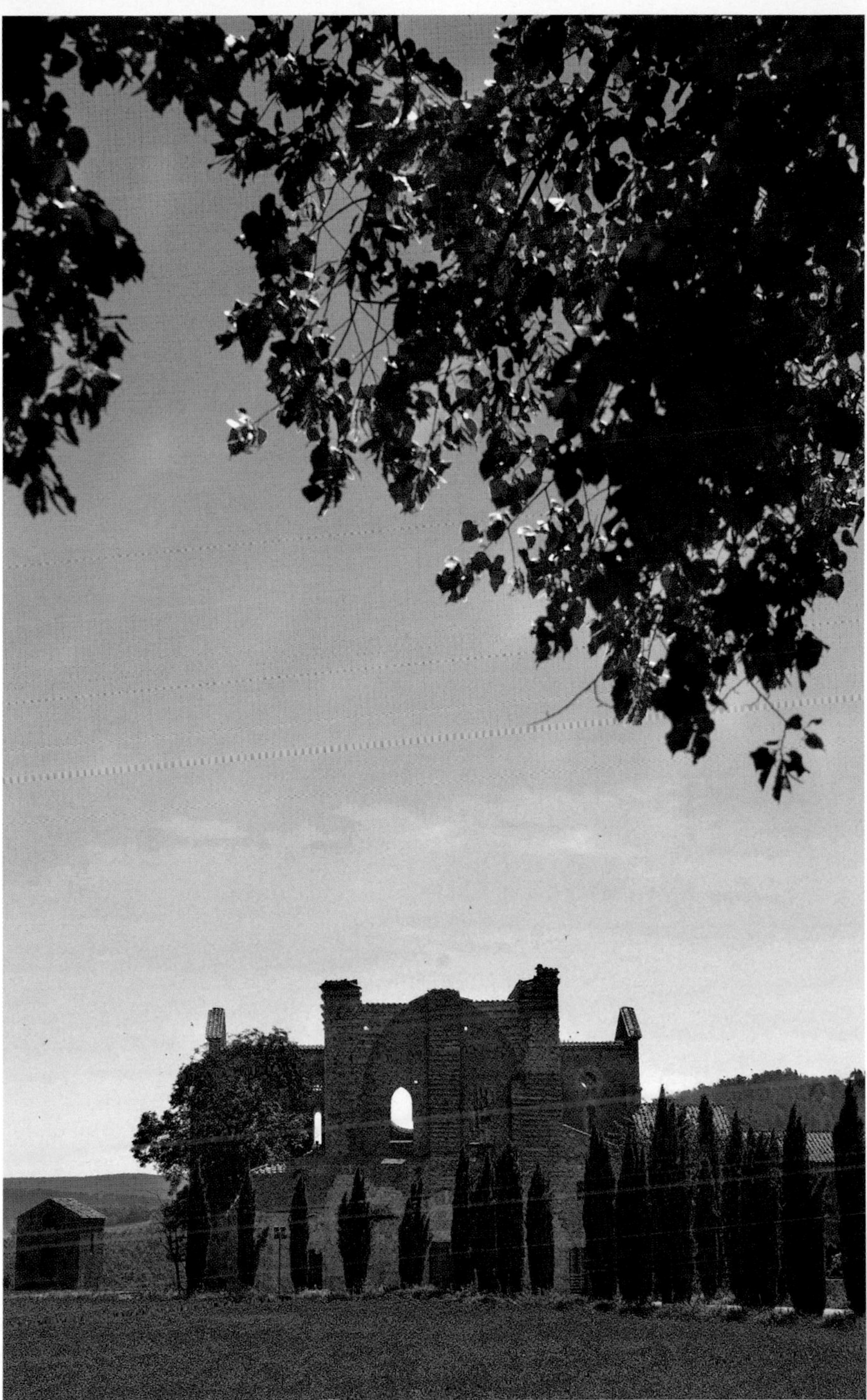

Where to Go

The largest section of this book is devoted to **Tuscany**, starting in the treasure-house of **Florence** and then moving out to the delights of the surrounding countryside with its villages and hilltowns, and other major art centres, including Pisa, Siena and Arezzo.

South and north of Florence, **Chianti** and the **Mugello** are world-famous and obscure respectively, with little in the way of towns, monuments and art but plenty of rolling hills, vineyards and stone farmhouses to enchant you. Next we accompany you through the Arno valley (**The Valdarno**, **Prato** and **Pistoia**), taking in a sprinkling of cities and Florentine towns. Then comes **Lucca**, the **Garfagnana** and **Lunigiana**, Tuscany's northernmost corner, and one full of treats, from the birthplace of Puccini to secretive mountainous micro-regions.

The **Tuscan Coast** is mostly flat and dull, but its archipelago of seven islands, including rugged **Elba**, offers clean, pretty beaches, the port of **Livorno** is famous for its seafood, **Carrara** can teach you about marble, and **Pisa**... well, Pisa needs no introduction.

Tuscany's loveliest city, **Siena**, draped on its three hills, gets a chapter to itself; to the west of it, hilltowns include **San Gimignano** and **Volterra** with remarkable works of art and **Massa Marittima** with one of the best cathedrals in Italy, while the **Metal Hills** present their curious sulphurous pits. More hilltowns abound in **Southern Tuscany** with its charming landscape of farms and pastureland, untainted by tourist hordes. Last stop before Umbria is the province of **Arezzo**, a delightful region that produced many famous artists.

Umbria, 'the green heart of Italy', boasts peaceful landscapes and lovely towns. **Perugia**, the atmospheric capital, is one of the country's greatest art cities; its citizens also enjoy their own 'riviera' at nearby **Lake Trasimeno**. Within view of Perugia is lovely pink and cream **Assisi**, home of St Francis and a very fine art collection. **Northern Umbria** boasts some of Italy's most sparsely populated countryside, full of tobacco farms and olive groves, but frescoes and hilltowns hold your attention, as does a splendid natural park. The magnificent, sun-drenched **Valle d'Umbra** has some of the world's loveliest countryside and many of Umbria's most beautiful hilltowns.

The **Tiber Valley**, the corner of Umbria closest to Rome, has its own distinctive character, much of it concentrated in historically rich Orvieto with its majestic cathedral. Rounding off Umbria is the **Valnerina**, much of which remains an Italian secret, protected as a natural park.

We end with a section on **The Marches** – less well known, but one of the most civilized corners of Italy, containing Renaissance **Urbino** and **Ascoli Piceno** and scores of other fine old towns in the valleys leading up to the **Sibilline mountains**.

Chapter Divisions

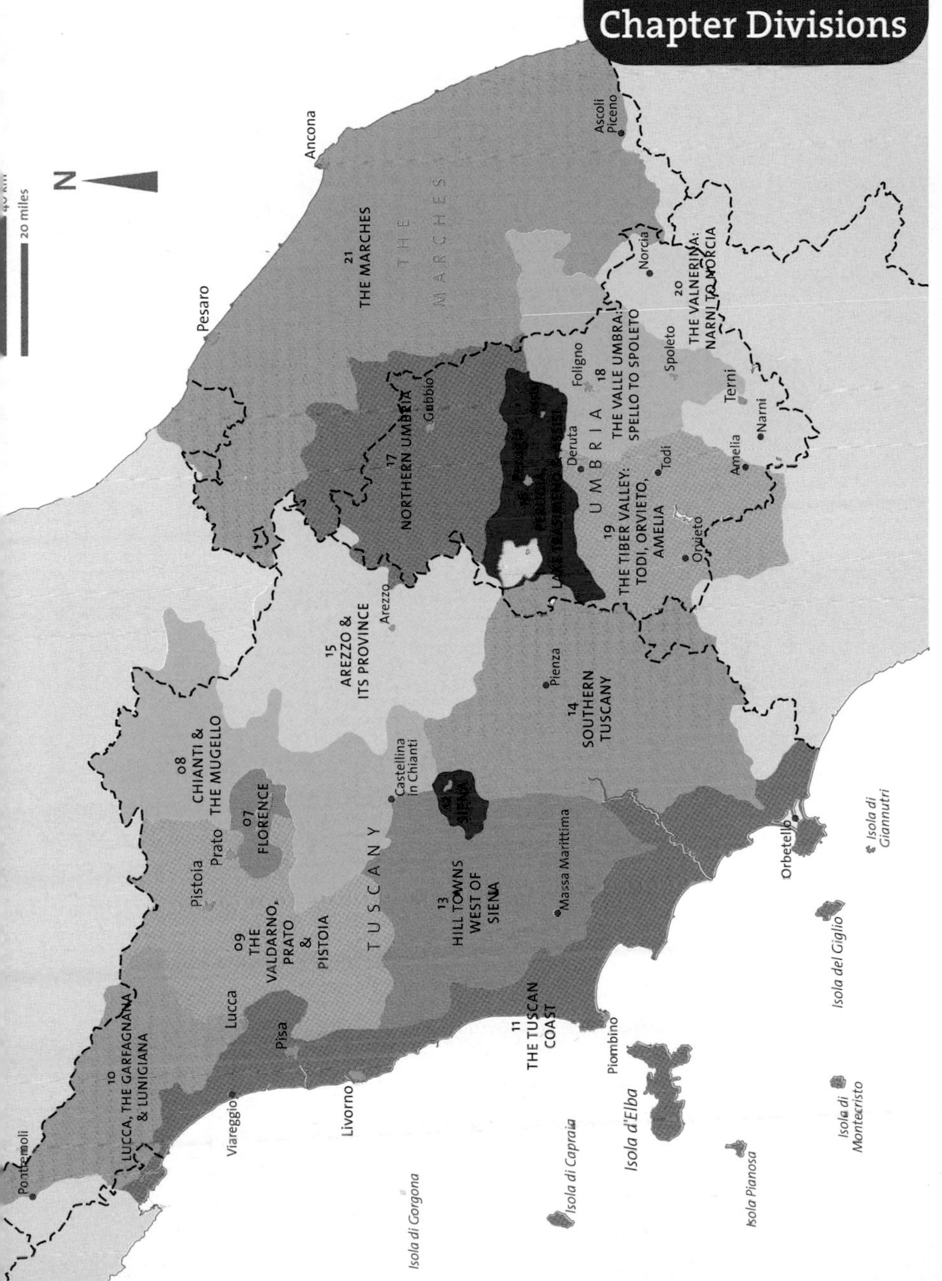

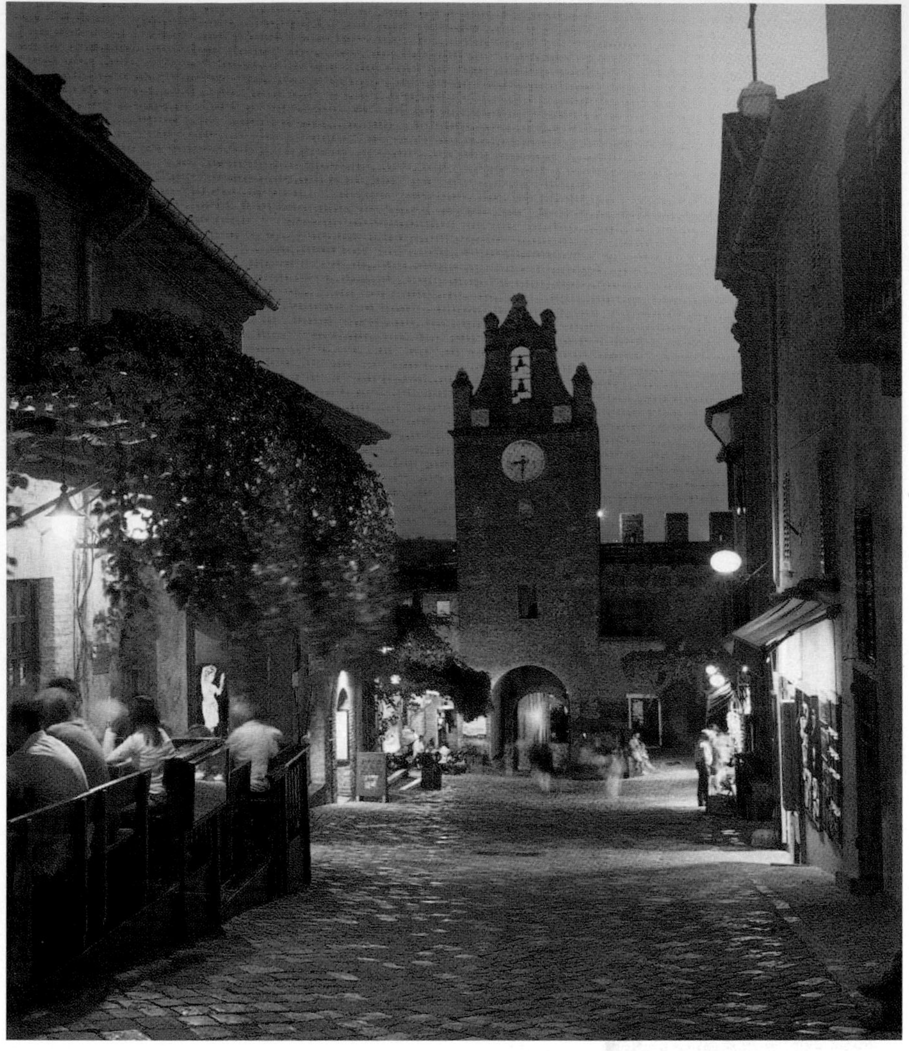

Above: Gradara, The Marches: street illuminated at dusk, p.582

Campanilismo

Which means, in brief, the firm belief that your town's belltower is better than anybody else's belltower. Local feeling and civic pride are built deeply into the Italian character, and nowhere more than here. These cities and towns had their finest hours as free republics in the Middle Ages, trading blows with their neighbours on the battlefield while they contended to outdo them with great buildings and works of art. Thanks to *campanilismo*, you won't just be admiring individual creations in your travels but seeing the whole – large or small, a community loaded with character, personality and individual quirks, one you'll enjoy getting to know.

The Discreet Charm of the Etruscans

You'll see them in their thousands in the archaeological museums. Stone effigies, husband and wife together, lounging on the lids of their own sarcophagi and smiling over some pleasantry spoken 2,500 years ago. No one in all archaeology can smile as winsomely as a dead Etruscan. What's the joke? We'll never know, but brushes with this enigmatic and talented lost civilization will be one of the pleasures of your trip. The Etruscans taught the ancient Romans everything they knew, and then seemingly faded away; you'll find reminders of them not only in Tuscan strongholds such as Volterra, but also in the Umbrian cities they founded, including Perugia and Orvieto.

From top: Etruscan sculpture, Siena, p.321; Etruscan doorway, Chianti, p.201

A Simple Kitchen

Just over the borders, the Romans and the Bolognese may sometimes sniff just a little at the cooking down here. It always comes as a surprise to learn that Tuscany, for all its airs and graces in the arts, doesn't really have an elaborate cuisine to match. That's a lesson. Back in the days of the Medici, the hard-nosed Tuscans prided themselves on their peasant roots, and today a forgotten rustic dish such as spelt soup can be resurrected to become a trendy favourite. There's more to it than country soups and stewed boar: Umbrian truffles and river crayfish, stuffed olives from the Marches, Livornese fish soup, Brunello di Montalcino and Montepulciano wines. The bottom line: you eat as well here as anywhere on the planet.

Above: cheeses; grape harvest; prosciutto

Previous page: truffles; fresh vegetables

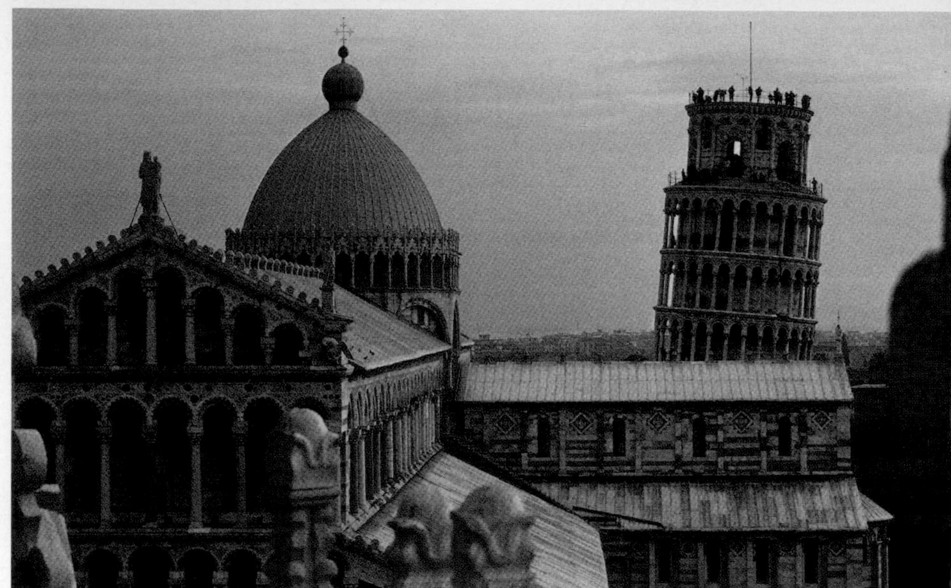

Above: Pisa, p.281

The Real Renaissance

There's the Uffizi and the Bargello, Michelangelo and Leonardo... who needs a guidebook? But even if you've never cared that much for art, this part of Italy will draw you in to a whole universe of delights behind the big names. No one would argue; there are simply more beautiful works of art in this region than anywhere else in the world. Every corner has its own styles and favourite sons, and the most humble village may be concealing something transcendant by someone you've never heard of. Chances are you'll be hooked. Stay long enough and you'll know who Gentile da Fabriano and Benozzo Gozzoli are; you might even be able to tell a Taddeo di Bartolo from a Bartolo di Fredi – and wonder how you ever got along without them.

Nature Rivalling Art

Some people spend months here staring at frescoes and climbing up hilltowns, and never really notice that one of Europe's biggest mountain ranges, the Apennines, is running right through the middle of the region. The works of humankind grab all the attention, and no one thinks of Tuscany and its little sisters as places in which to experience nature. That's a mistake. Tuscans keep their beloved countryside pristine and pretty; beyond the villas and vines there's a sea-coast, with a touch of blue-tinted Mediterranean exoticism in the wild Maremma national park and on the islands of Giglio and Capraia. The Apennines themselves offer hiking and skiing, and scenery that can dazzle, as on the flower-strewn Piano Grande di Norcia.

From top: Giglio Island; p.318, Umbrian landscape

Above: Palio, Siena, p.330

Public Pageantry

No one puts on a show like the Italians – this land of compulsive exhibitionists lays on spectacles to make your eyes pop. Some of the best are known around the world, such as Siena's great city-centre horse-race, the Palio. That one's so popular you might not get in, but there are plenty more. Often it's a contest: a tug-of war on a Pisan bridge, or Florence's Piazza della Signoria covered in soil for a roughhouse medieval football match. It could be a holy procession of giant candles, or a comical donkey race, or even a joust, like the magical Giostra della Quintana in Ascoli Piceno. You'll always be welcome, but the best thing about these festivals is that they're not just put on for the benefit of tourists, they're part of a town's life.

Itineraries

A Renaissance Loop outside Florence: 13 Days

Day 1 Impruneta (Collegiata), Certosa di Galluzzo, Lastra a Signa (Alberti's church) and Poggio a Caiano, the archetypal Renaissance villa.

Day 2 Prato (Santa Maria delle Carceri, Filippo Lippi's fresco cycle in the cathedral, Donatello and Michelozzo's pulpit).

Day 3 Lucca, for the sculpture of Matteo Civitali and Jacopo della Quercia.

Day 4 San Gimignano, which has much of the best painting outside Florence, by Gozzoli, Ghirlandaio, Sodoma and more.

Day 5 Siena, for the Sienese side of the Renaissance (cathedral, especially pavements, tombs, Piccolomini Library and Pinacoteca).

Days 6–7 The exquisite monastic complex and frescoes at Monte Oliveto Maggiore, on the way to Pius II's planned city of Pienza; nearby Montepulciano for the best of classic Renaissance temples, Sangallo's San Biagio, as well as other churches and palaces.

Day 8 Orvieto (cathedral frescoes by Angelico and Signorelli) and Città della Pieve (Perugino).

Day 9 Perugia (Pinacoteca, San Bernardino and others).

Day 10 Cortona (two Renaissance temples, Signorelli and Fra Angelico) and Monte San Savino.

Day 11 Arezzo (Piero della Francesca's frescoes and S. Maria delle Grazie).

Day 12 More Pieros in Monterchi and Sansepolcro.

Day 13 La Verna (Andrea della Robbia) and over the Passo di Consuma to Florence.

The Best of Tuscan and Umbrian DOC Wines (and Ravishing Scenery): 15 Days

Day 1 Florence to Carmignano, Cerreto Guidi and Vinci (wines: Carmignano and Chianti).

Day 2 Montecatini Alta, Collodi and Montecarlo (wines: Bianco della Valdinievole and Montecarlo).

Day 3 South of the Arno to San Miniato and environs, and Certaldo (wines: Bianco Pisano di S. Torpè and Chianti).

Day 4 San Gimignano and Colle di Val d'Elsa (wines: Vernaccia di San Gimignano and Chianti Colli Senesi).

Day 5 Barberino Val d'Elsa and San Casciano to the Florence–Siena wine route, the Chiantigiana and Greve in Chianti (wines: Chianti, Chianti Colli Fiorentini and Chianti Classico).

Day 6 Panzano and Radda in Chianti (wine: Chianti Classico).

Day 7 Gaiole in Chianti, Castello di Brolio and Siena, with a stop at the Enoteca Nazionale (wines: Chianti Classico and Chianti Colli Senesi).

Day 8 Montalcino (wine: Brunello).

Day 9 Montepulciano (wine: Vino Nobile).

Day 10 Cortona (wine: Bianco Vergine della Valdichiana).

Day 11 Tuoro and Passignano on Lake Trasimeno, to Perugia (wines: Colli del Trasimeno and Colli Perugini).

Day 12 Torgiano and its wine museum, Bevagna and Montefalco (wines: Torgiana, Montefalco and Sagrantino).

Day 13 Orvieto (wine: Orvieto Classico).

Day 14 Sovana, Pitigliano, Saturnia (wines: Morellino di Scansano and Bianco di Pitigliano).

Day 15 Check in at the spa at Chianciano Terme for liver repairs!

Discover the Marches: 9 Days

Days 1–2 A day in Urbino to see the Palazzo Ducale and the town, another day exploring outlying villages: Urbania, Fermignano or San Leo.

Day 3 To Fossombrone, with a look at the nearby Gola del Furlo.

Day 4 A drive south through the mountains too see Fabriano, and Genga's caves and Romanesque church, ending up in Jesi.

Day 5 Ancona, and a rest on the beaches around Monte Conero.

Day 6 Art at Loreto and accordions in Castelfidardo.

Day 7 Inland again for pretty towns and picture galleries: Tolentino, Camerino and San Severino Marche.

Day 8 A scenic drive south along the flank of the Monti Sibillini.

Day 9 Ascoli Piceno.

Below: Monti Sibillini, The Marches, *p.637*

CONTENTS

Reference

Maps and Plans

Contents

History and Art

02

Historical Outline

At times, the history of Tuscany and Umbria has been a small part of a bigger story – that of Rome, or modern Italy. However, the crucial eras of the Middle Ages and the Renaissance provide a tremendous chronicle of contending city states, each with a complex history of its own.

For this reason, we have included detailed histories of the most important towns – Florence, Siena, Pisa and Perugia – and covered the rest to a lesser extent. What follows is a brief historical outline for the region as a whole.

The Etruscans

Neolithic cultures seem to have occupied this region of Italy since about 4500 BC without distinguishing themselves artistically or politically. The dawn of history within these parts comes with the arrival of the **Etruscans**, though where they came from and precisely when they arrived remains one of the major mysteries of early Mediterranean history. According to their traditions, the Etruscans migrated from western Anatolia *c.* 900 BC. Some Classical authors believed the migration theory, others saw the Etruscans as the indigenous inhabitants of west-central Italy. Their language remains murky to modern scholars, but the discovery of Etruscan inscriptions on the Greek island of Lemnos, along with other clues, tends to support the Etruscan story.

They were a talented people, and the great wealth they derived from intensive agriculture, manufacturing, and above all mining (Elba and the Metal Hills) allowed these talents to blossom into opulence by the 7th century BC. Though they gave their name to modern Tuscany, the real centre of Etruscan civilization lay to the south; roughly the coast from Orbetello to Cervéteri (Caere) in Lazio and around lakes Bolsena and Trasimeno. Never a unified nation, the Etruscans preferred the general Mediterranean model of the independent city state; the 12 greatest dominated central Italy in a federation called the **Dodecapolis**. Which cities were members is uncertain, but the 14 possibilities include *Veii*, *Cervéteri*, *Tarquinia* and *Vulci* (in Lazio), *Roselle*, *Vetulonia* and *Populonia* (on or near the Tuscan coast), *Volterra*, *Fiesole*, *Arezzo*, *Chiusi*, *Orvieto*, *Cortona* and *Perugia*.

The Etruscans always maintained extremely close trade and cultural ties with classical Greece. They sold Elban iron and bought Greek culture wholesale; the veritable artistic thieving magpies of antiquity, they adapted every style of Greek art, from the Minoan-style frescoes at Tarquinia to the classical bronzes that you can now admire in Florence's archaeology museum, and created something of their very own. When it came to expressive portrait sculpture, however, they surpassed even the Greeks.

A considerable mythology has grown up around the Etruscans. Some historians and poets celebrate them as a nation of free peoples, devoted to art, good food and easy living. A less sentimental view depicts a slave society run for the benefit of a military, aristocratic elite. Whichever, the art they left behind gives them a place as the most enigmatic, vivid and fascinating people of early Italy. Echoes of their culture are clearly visible in everything that has happened in this part of Italy for the last 2,000 years.

The Romans

Etruscan kings once ruled in Rome, but after the establishment of the Republic this precocious city proved the end of the Etruscan world. All of southern Etruria was swallowed up by 358 BC, and internal divisions between the Etruscan cities allowed the Romans to push their conquest inevitably northwards. After the conquest of an Etruscan city, Roman policy was often diabolically clever; by establishing veterans' colonies in new towns nearby to draw off trade, Rome was able to ensure the withering of Etruscan culture and the slow extinction of many of Etruria's greatest cities.

Four other cultures from this time deserve a mention; first the **Umbrii**, a peaceful, pastoral people indigenous to eastern Umbria and parts of the Marches, who adopted the Etruscan alphabet but never had much to say in it – the only surviving inscription in Umbrian is in the Museo Civico in Gubbio. These earliest Umbrians had the sense to avoid antagonizing Rome, and often allied themselves with the city in wars against other Italian tribes. The more war-like **Piceni**, most important of the tribes that occupied what is today the Marches, proved more antagonistic; in fact they played a leading role in the Social Wars of 92–89 BC, the last doomed attempt of the Italians to fight free of Roman imperialism. The wandering **Celts**, who occupied all northern Italy, often made themselves at home in the Apennines and northern Etruria; their influence on the region's culture is slight. Finally, there was the unnamed culture of the rugged **Lunigiana**, around Pontremoli, a people who carried their Neolithic customs and religion (*see* the statue-*steles* in the Museo delle Statue-stele Lunigania, p.269) well into the modern era.

Under the empire, Etruria and Umbria were separate provinces, with the Tiber for a border. Both were relatively quiet, though the region experienced a north/south economic split to mirror the bigger one beginning across Italy. Southern Etruria, the old Etruscan heartland, shrivelled and died under Roman misrule, never to recover. The north became more prosperous, and important new cities appeared: Lucca, Pisa, Florence and, to a lesser extent, Assisi, Gubbio and Siena.

The Dark Ages

Later Italians' willingness to create fanciful stories about the 'barbarian invasions' makes it hard to define what did happen in this troubled time. The first (5th-century) campaigns of the **Goths** in Italy did not seem to cause too much damage, but the curtain finally came down on Roman civilization with the Greek-Gothic wars of 536–563, when Eastern Emperor Justinian and his generals Belisarius and Narses attempted to recapture Italy for Byzantium. The chronicles of many cities record the devastation of the Gothic King, Totila (the sack of Florence, and a seven-year siege of Perugia), though the Imperial aggressors were undoubtedly just as bad. In any case, the damage to an already weakened society was fatal, and the wars opened the way for the conquest of much of Italy by the terrible **Lombards** (568), who established the duchy of Spoleto, with loose control over much of central Italy. Lucca, the late Roman and Gothic capital of Etruria, alone managed to keep the Lombards out. By this time, low-lying cities such as Florence had practically disappeared, while the remnants of the other towns survived under the control of local barons, or occasionally under their bishops. Feudal warfare and marauding became endemic. In the 800s even a band of Arabs came looting and pillaging up the Valnerina, almost in the centre of the peninsula.

By the 10th century things were looking up. Florence had re-established itself, and built its famous baptistry. The old counts of Lucca extended their power to become counts of Tuscany, under the Attoni family, lords of Canossa. As the leading power in the region, they made themselves a force to be reckoned with in European affairs. In 1077, the great Countess Matilda, allied with the Pope, humbled Emperor Henry IV at Canossa – the famous 'penance in the snow' – during the struggles over investiture. Perhaps most important of all was the growth of the maritime city of **Pisa**, which provided Tuscany with a new window on the world, building substantial wealth through trade and inviting new cultural influences from France, Byzantium and the Muslim world.

Medieval Tuscany

By 1000, with the new millennium, all northern Italy was poised to rebuild the civilization lost centuries before. In Tuscany and Umbria, as elsewhere, increasing trade had initiated a rebirth of towns, each doing its best to establish its independence from local nobles or bishops, and to increase its influence at the expense of its neighbours. Thus a thousand minor squabbles were played out against the background of the major issues of the day; first the conflict over investiture in the 11th century, evolving into the endless factional struggles of **Guelphs** and **Ghibellines** after 1215 (*see* p.41). Throughout, the cities were forced to choose sides between the partisans of the popes and those of the emperors. The Ghibellines' brightest hours came with the reigns of strong Hohenstaufen emperors **Frederick I Barbarossa** (1152–90) and his grandson **Frederick II** (1212–50), both of whom spent much time in Tuscany. An early Guelph wave came with the papacy of **Innocent III** (1198–1216), most powerful of the medieval pontiffs, and the Guelphs would come back to dominate Tuscany after the invasion of Charles of Anjou in 1261. Florence, Perugia, Arezzo and Lucca were the mainstays of the Guelphs; Pisa, Pistoia and Siena usually supported the Ghibellines.

In truth, it was every city for itself. By 1200, most towns had become free *comuni*; their imposing public buildings can be seen in almost every corner of Tuscany and Umbria. All the trouble they caused fighting each other (at first with citizen militias, later increasingly with the use of hired *condottieri*) never troubled the booming economy. Florence and Siena became bankers to all Europe; great buildings went up, beginning with the Pisa cathedral complex in the 1100s, and the now tamed and urbanized nobles built fantastical skyscraper skylines of tower-fortresses in the towns. Above all, it was a great age for culture, the age of Dante (b. 1265) and Giotto (b. 1266). Another feature of the time was the 13th-century religious revival, dominated by the figure of **St Francis of Assisi**.

Background of the Renaissance

Florence, biggest and richest of the Tuscan cities, increased its influence all through the 1300s, gaining Prato and Pistoia, and finally winning a seaport with the capture of declining Pisa in 1406. This set the stage for the relative political

Know Your Medici

The powerful Medici family (*see* p.24) started out, perhaps, as doctors or pharmacists (hence the name, which may derive from *medico*, denoting a medical trade), made it big as bankers, and ended up as grand dukes and even popes. From Giovanni de' Medici, the political boss who first took total control of a fractious urban republic, to the senile Gian Gastone, for more than 300 years the Medici *were* Florence. Along the way they patronized artists, from Donatello to Michelangelo, and did more than anyone else to finance the Renaissance.

Here's a little chart to help you to keep them all straight.

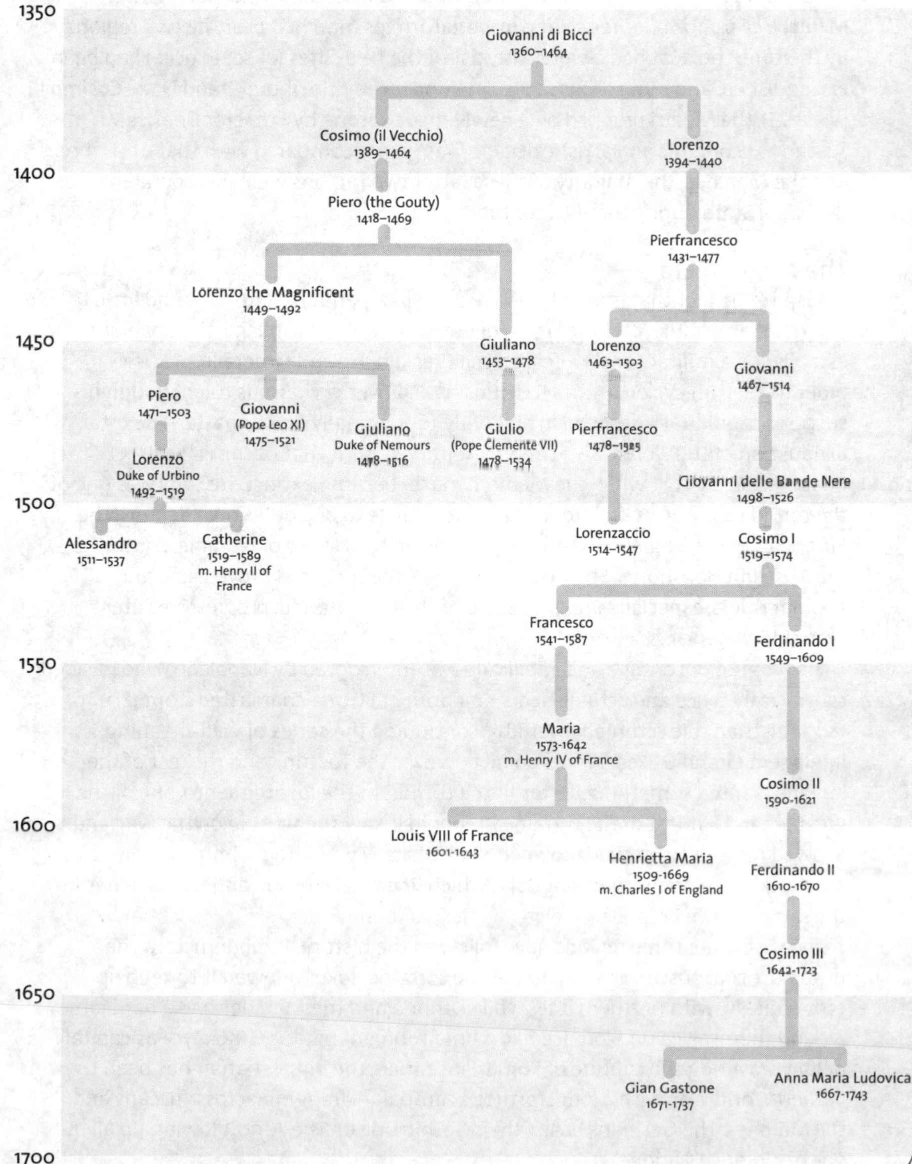

equilibrium of Tuscany during the early Renaissance, which was the height of the region's wealth and artistic achievement. Many Umbrian cities, notably Perugia, participated in both, though Umbria as a whole could not keep up. The popes, newly established in Rome, sent Cardinal Albornoz across the territory in the 1360s with the aim of binding the region more closely to the Papal State; he built a score of fortresses across Umbria.

The **Wars of Italy**, beginning in 1494, put an end to Renaissance tranquillity. Florence was once more lost in its internal convolutions, twice expelling the **Medici** (*see* p.23) while French and Imperial armies marched over the two regions. By the time the dust had cleared, the last of the free cities (except Lucca) had been extinguished, and most of Tuscany came under the rule of the Grand Duke **Cosimo I** (1537–74), the Medici propped on a newly made throne by Emperor Charles V. Tuscany's economic and artistic decline was gentle compared with that of Umbria and the Marches; the majority of these latter two regions were incorporated into the Papal State during the 16th century.

The Modern Era

Despite the fact that it maintained relative independence, Tuscany had little to say in Italian affairs. After the treaty of Cateau-Cambrésis in 1559, the Spaniards established a military enclave, called the Presidio, around Orbetello, precisely in order to keep an eye on central Italy. Cosimo I proved a vigorous ruler, though his successors gradually declined in ability. By 1600 it really didn't matter. The total exhaustion of the Florentine economy kept pace with that of the Florentine imagination. By 1737, when the Medici dynasty became extinct, Tuscany was one of the torpid backwaters of Europe. It had no chance to decide its own destiny; the European powers agreed to bestow Tuscany on the House of Lorraine, cousins to the Austrian Habsburgs. Surprisingly enough, the Lorraines proved able and popular rulers, especially under the rule of the enlightened, progressive Peter Leopold (1765–90).

The languor of Lorraine and Papal rule was interrupted by Napoleon, who invaded central Italy twice and established a Kingdom of Etruria that lasted from 1801 to 1807. Austrian rule returned after 1815, continuing the series of well-meaning, intelligent Grand Dukes. By this point, however, the Tuscans and the rest of the Italians wanted something better. In the tumult of the Risorgimento, one of the greatest and kindest of the Lorraines, Leopold II, saw the writing on the wall and allowed himself to be overthrown in 1859. Tuscany was almost immediately annexed to the new Italian kingdom, which liberated Umbria and the Marches in the same year.

Since then, the three regions have followed the history of modern Italy. The headstart that Tuscany gained under the Lorraine dukes allowed it to keep up economically with northern Italy, while Umbria and the Marches had a hard job picking themselves up. Florence had a brief moment of glory (1865–70) as capital of Italy, awaiting the capture of Rome. Since then, the biggest affair has been the Second World War, with a long, tortuous campaign dragging across Tuscany and the Marches. The Germans based their Gothic Line on the Arno, blowing up all but one of Florence's bridges.

Art and Architecture

Etruscans

We have no way of knowing what life was like for the average person in Camars or Velathrii, but their tomb sculptures and paintings convince us that they were a talented, likeable people. Almost all their art derives from the Greek; the Etruscans built classical temples (of wood, with terracotta embellishments, so little survives), carved sarcophagi decorated with scenes from Homer, and painted pottery red and black after the latest styles from Athens or Corinth. They excelled at portrait sculpture, and had a remarkable gift for capturing personality, sometimes seriously, though never heroically, often with an entirely intentional humour, and the serene smiles of people who truly enjoyed life.

Etruscan art in museums is often maddening; some works are among the finest productions of antiquity, others – from the same time and city – are awkward and childish. Their talent for portraiture, among much else, was carried on by the Romans, and they bequeathed their love of fresco painting to artists of the Middle Ages and Renaissance, who of course weren't even aware of the debt.

Romans and Dark Ages

After destroying the Etruscan nation, the Romans also began the extinction of its artistic tradition; by the time of the Empire there was almost nothing left that could be called distinctively Etruscan. All of Tuscany, Umbria and the Marches contributed little under the Empire. In the chaos that followed, there was little room for art. What painting survived followed styles current in Byzantium.

Middle Ages

In both architecture and sculpture, the first main influence came from the north. Lombard masons filled Tuscany and Umbria with simple Romanesque churches; the first follow the northern style, although it wasn't long before two distinctive Tuscan forms emerged: the Pisan style, characterized by blind rows of colonnades, black and white zebra stripes, and lozenge-shaped designs; and the 'Tuscan Romanesque' that developed around Florence, notable for its use of dark and light marble patterns and simple geometric patterns, often with intricate mosaic floors to match (the baptistry and San Miniato in Florence are the chief examples). In the cities between – Lucca, Arezzo and Pistoia – are interesting variations on the two styles, often carrying an element such as stripes or arcades to remarkable extremes. The only real example of French Gothic in Tuscany is San Galgano, built by Cistercians in the 1200s, although the style never caught on here or anywhere else in Italy.

From the large pool of talent working on Pisa's great cathedral complex in the 13th century emerged Italy's first great sculptor, **Nicola Pisano**, whose baptistry pulpit, with its realistic figures, was derived from ancient reliefs. His even more remarkable son, **Giovanni Pisano**, prefigures Donatello in the expressiveness of his statues and the vigour of his pulpits; his façade of Siena cathedral, though altered, is a unique work of art. **Arnolfo di Cambio**, a student of Nicola Pisano, became chief sculptor-architect of Florence during its building boom in the 1290s, designing its cathedral and Palazzo Vecchio with a hitherto unheard-of scale and grandeur, before moving on to embellish Orvieto with statues and tombs. Orvieto, however, hired the more imaginative **Lorenzo Maitani** in the early 1300s to create a remarkable cathedral façade as individualistic as Siena's, a unique combination of reliefs and mosaics.

Painting at first lagged behind the new realism and more complex composition of sculpture. The first to depart from Byzantine stylization, at least according to Vasari's *Lives of the Artists* (*see* p.38), was **Cimabue**, in the late 1200s, who forsook Greek forms for a more 'Latin' or 'natural' way of painting. Cimabue found his greatest pupil, **Giotto**, as a young shepherd chalk-sketching sheep on a piece of slate. Brought to Florence, Giotto soon eclipsed his master's fame (artistic celebrity being a recent Florentine invention) and achieved the greatest advances on the road to the new painting with a plain, rather severe approach that shunned Gothic prettiness while exploring new ideas in composition and expressing psychological depth in his subjects.

Even more importantly, Giotto, through his intuitive grasp of perspective, was able to go further than any previous artist in representing his subjects as actual figures in space. In a sense Giotto actually invented space; it was this, despite his often awkward and graceless draughtsmanship, that so astounded his contemporaries. His followers, **Taddeo and Agnolo Gaddi** (father and son), **Giovanni da Milano** and **Maso di Banco**, filled Florence's churches with their own interpretations of the master's style. In the latter half of the 1300s, however, **Andrea Orcagna**, regarded as the most important Florentine sculptor, painter and architect of his day, appeared. Inspired by the more elegant style of **Andrea Pisano**'s baptistry doors, Orcagna broke away from simple Giottoesque forms to assume a more elaborate, detailed style in his sculpture, while the fragments of his frescoes that survive have a vivid dramatic power that must owe something to the time of the Black Death and the social upheavals ongoing as they were painted.

Siena never produced a Vasari to chronicle its accomplishments, though they were considerable; in the 13th and 14th centuries, Siena's Golden Age, the city's artists, like its soldiers, rivalled and often surpassed those of Florence. For whatever reason, it seemed purposefully to seek inspiration in different directions from Florence; at first from central Italian styles around Spoleto and then, with prosperity and the advent of **Guido da Siena** in the early 1200s, from the more elegant line and colour of Byzantium. Guido's work paved the way for the pivotal figure of **Duccio di Buoninsegna**, who founded the essentials of Sienese art by uniting the beauty of Byzantine line and colour with the sweet finesse of western Gothic art. With Duccio's great followers **Pietro and Ambrogio Lorenzetti** and **Simone Martini**, the Sienese produced an increasingly elegant and rarefied art, almost oriental in its refined stylization. They were less innovative than the Florentines, though they brought the 'International Gothic' style – flowery and ornate, with the bright tones of May – to its highest form in Italy. Simone Martini introduced the Sienese manner to Florence in the early 1400s, where it influenced, most notably, the work of **Lorenzo Monaco**, **Masolino** and of the young goldsmith and sculptor **Ghiberti**. The Umbrian artists of the trecento, most of them anonymous, were also heavily influenced by the Sienese, using just as much colour, if less sophistication.

The Renaissance

Under the assaults of historians and critics, the term 'Renaissance' has become a vague, controversial word. Yet, however you choose to interpret this rebirth of the arts, and whatever dates you assign to it, Florence inescapably takes the credit. This is no small claim. Combining art, science and humanist scholarship to shape a visual revolution that often seemed pure sorcery to their contemporaries, a handful of Florentine geniuses taught the Western eye a new way of seeing. Perspective seems a simple enough trick to us now, but its discovery determined everything that followed, not only in art but in science and philosophy as well.

Leading what scholars used to call the 'Early Renaissance' are geniuses Brunelleschi, Donatello and Masaccio. **Brunelleschi**, neglecting his considerable talents in sculpture in favour of architecture and science, not only built the majestic dome of Florence cathedral but threw the Pandora's box of perspective wide open by mathematically codifying the principles of foreshortening. Brunelleschi's friend **Donatello**, the greatest sculptor since the ancient Greeks, inspired a new generation of sculptors and painters to explore new horizons in portraiture and 3D representation. The first painter to incorporate Brunelleschi and Donatello's lessons of spatiality, perspective and expressiveness was young prodigy **Masaccio**, who, along with his master Masolino, painted the Brancacci chapel in the Carmine, studied by nearly all Florentine artists right up to Michelangelo.

The new science of architecture, sculpture and painting introduced by this triumvirate ignited an explosion of talent unequalled before or since: a score of masters, most Tuscan, following the dictates of their genius to create a remarkable range of themes and styles. Among the most prominent are **Lorenzo Ghiberti**, who followed Donatello's advice on his second set of baptistry doors to cause a Renaissance revolution; **Leon Battista Alberti**, who took Brunelleschi's ideas to their most classical extreme in architecture, creating new forms; provocative **Paolo Uccello**, who according to Vasari drove himself mad with the study of perspective and the possibilities of illusionism; **Piero della Francesca** of Sansepolcro, who explored the limits of perspective and geometrical forms to create the most compelling, haunting images of the quattrocento; **Fra (now Beato) Angelico**, who combined Masaccio's innovations, International Gothic colours and his own deep faith to create the most purely spiritual art of his time; and **Andrea del Castagno**, who made use of perspective to create monumental, if often restless, figures.

Some of Donatello's gifted followers were **Agostino di Duccio**, **Benedetto da Maiano**, **Desiderio da Settignano**, **Antonio and Bernardo Rossellino**, **Mino da Fiesole** and, perhaps most famously, **Luca della Robbia**, inventor of the coloured terracottas spread by his family through Tuscany. There are still more: **Benozzo Gozzoli**, whose spring colours and delight in detail are a throwback to International Gothic; **Antonio and Piero Pollaiuolo**, sons of a poultry-man, whose dramatic use of line and form, often violent and writhing, would be echoed in Florentine Mannerism; **Fra Filippo Lippi**, a monk like Fra Angelico but far more earthly, the master of lovely Madonnas and teacher of his talented son **Filippino Lippi**; **Domenico Ghirlandaio**, whose easy charm and flawless technique made him society's favoured fresco painter; **Andrea del Verrocchio**, who cast in bronze, painted or carved with perfect detail; **Luca Signorelli**, who achieved apocalyptic grandeur in Orvieto cathedral;

Masters and Students: The Progress of the Renaissance

The purpose of this chart is to show who learned from whom – an insight into 300 years of artistic continuity.

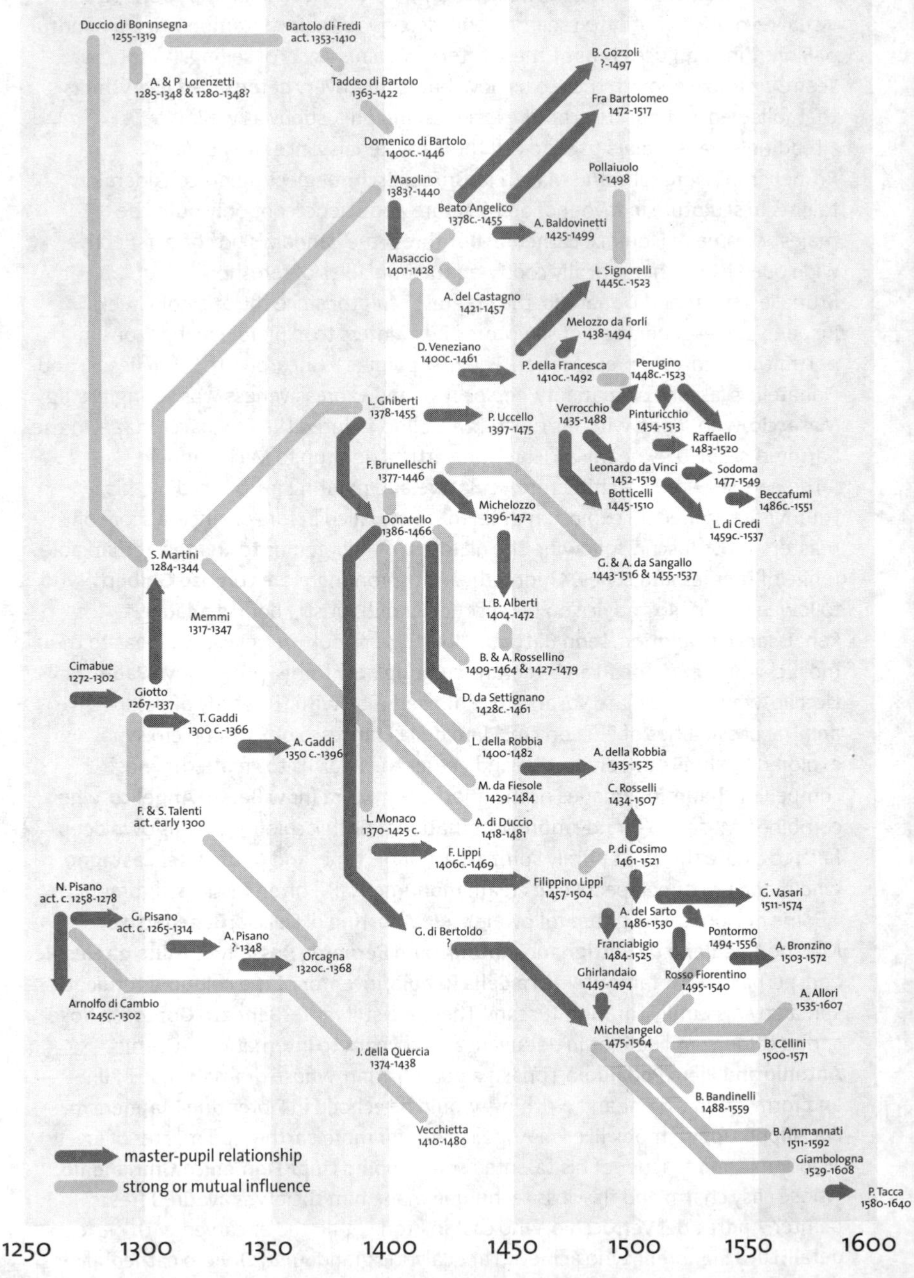

Perugino (Pietro Vannucci) of Umbria, who painted the stillness of his native region into his landscapes and taught young **Raphael** of Urbino; and **Sandro Botticelli**, whose intellectual but melancholy, mythological paintings are in a class of their own.

The 'Early Renaissance' came to a close near the end of the 1400s with the advent of **Leonardo da Vinci**, whose unique talent in painting challenged the certainty of naturalism with a subtlety and chiaroscuro that approaches magic. One sole passion, however, obsessed the other great figure of the 'High Renaissance', **Michelangelo Buonarroti**: the human body, graceful and serene as in most of his Florentine works and later contorted and anguished after he left for Rome.

Mannerism

Michelangelo left in Florence the seeds of the bold, neurotic avant-garde art that has come to be known as Mannerism. This first conscious 'movement' in Western art can be seen as a last fling amidst the growing intellectual and spiritual exhaustion of 1530s Florence, conquered once and for all by the Medici. The Mannerists' calculated exoticism and exaggerated, tortured poses, together with the brooding self-absorption of Michelangelo, are a prelude to Florentine art's abrupt turn into decadence, and prophesy its final extinction.

Foremost among Mannerist painters are **Jacopo Pontormo** and **Rosso Fiorentino**, strange characters not in such great demand as the coldly classical **Andrea del Sarto** and **Bronzino**. There were also charming reactionaries, especially **Il Sodoma** and **Pinturicchio**; both left their best works in Siena. In sculpture **Giambologna** and, to a lesser extent, **Bartolommeo Ammannati** specialized in virtuoso contrapposto figures, each more impossible than the last. With their contemporary **Giorgio Vasari**, Florentine art became a virtuoso style of interior decoration perfectly adaptable to saccharine holy pictures, portraits of new dukes, or absurd, mythological fountains and ballroom ceilings. In the cinquecento, with money to spend and a long Medici tradition of patronage to uphold, this tendency got out of hand. Under the reign of Cosimo I, collector of *pietra dura* tables, silver and gold gimcracks, and stuffed animals, Florence gave birth to the artistic phenomenon modern critics call 'kitsch'.

The Rest Compressed

In the long, dark night of later Tuscan art a few artists stand out – the often whimsical architect and engineer, **Buontalenti**; **Pietro Tacca**, Giambologna's pupil; and the charming Baroque fresco master **Pietro da Cortona**. Most of Tuscany, particularly Florence, chose to sit out the Baroque – almost by choice, it seems, and we can race up to the 19th century to reach the often delightful 'Tuscan Impressionists' or Macchiaioli ('Splatterers'; the best collection is in the modern art section of the Pitti Palace); and in the 20th century, **Modigliani** (from Livorno) of the oval faces; Futurist **Gino Severini** (from Cortona); and **Alberto Burri**, one of the first to use junk as a medium (from Città di Castello, where there's a museum). There is an exceptionally good collection of contemporary Italian art at Macerata in the Marches; others include a museum dedicated to sculptor **Marino Marini** in Florence, and another to **Manzù**, in Orvieto. Newest and most entertaining of all is the late French artist **Niki de Saint-Phalle**'s Tarot Garden south of Orbetello.

Architects, Painters and Sculptors of Tuscany, Umbria and the Marches

The works listed are far from exhaustive, but we have tried to include only the best and most representative works that you'll find in these regions.

Agostino di Duccio (Florentine, 1418–81). A precocious and talented sculptor; his best work is in the Malatesta Temple at **Rimini** – he was exiled from Florence after being accused of theft (**Perugia**, S. Bernardino; **Florence**, Bargello; **Pontremoli**, S. Francesco).

Alberti, Leon Battista (Florentine, b. Genoa, 1404–72). Architect, theorist, writer, sculptor, painter. His greatest contribution was recycling the classical orders and the principles of Vitruvius into Renaissance architecture; he was a consultant to the architecture-loving Duke of Urbino. (**Florence**, Palazzo Rucellai, façade of S. Maria Novella, SS. Annunziata; **Lastra a Signa**, S. Martino).

Allori, Alessandro (1535–1607). Florentine Mannerist painter, prolific follower of Michelangelo and Bronzino (**Florence**, SS. Annunziata, S. Spirito, Spedale degli Innocenti).

L'Alunno (Niccolò di Liberatore, *c.* 1430–1502). Painter from Foligno; genuine Renaissance polish without much to challenge the imagination (**Assisi**, cathedral museum; **Deruta**, Pinacoteca; **Foligno**, S. Niccolò; **Nocera Umbra**, Pinacoteca).

Ammannati, Bartolommeo (Florentine, 1511–92). Restrained, elegant architect (**Florence**, S. Trínita bridge, courtyard of Pitti Palace); neurotic, twisted Mannerist sculptor (**Florence**, Fountain of Neptune, Villa di Castello).

Andrea del Castagno (*c.* 1423–57). Precise, dry Florentine painter, one of the first and greatest slaves of perspective. Died of the plague (**Florence**, Uffizi, S. Apollonia, SS. Annunziata).

Angelico, Fra (or **Beato**) (Giovanni da Fiesole, *c.* 1387–1455). Monk, and one of the great visionary artists of the Renaissance (**Florence**, S. Marco – spectacular *Annunciation* and many more; **Cortona**, cathedral museum; **Fiesole**, S. Domenico; **Perugia**, Galleria Nazionale).

Antonio da Fabriano (active *c.* 1450). One of the school of painters from the little Marches town of **Fabriano**; works there and in **Matelica**.

Arnolfo di Cambio (b. Colle di Val d'Elsa; *c.* 1245–1302). Architect and sculptor, pupil of Nicola Pisano and a key figure in his own right. Much of his best sculpture is in Rome, but he changed the face of Florence as main architect to the city's greatest building programme of the 1290s (**Florence**, cathedral and Palazzo Vecchio; **Orvieto**, Museo Civico, S. Domenico).

Baldovinetti, Alesso (Florentine, 1425–99). Delightful student of Fra Angelico who left few tracks; most famous for fresco work in **Florence** (SS. Annunziata, Uffizi, S. Niccolò sopr'Arno, S. Miniato).

Bandinelli, Baccio (1488–1559). Florence's comic relief of the late Renaissance, so awful it hurts; he was court sculptor to Cosimo I (**Florence**, Piazza della Signoria and SS. Annunziata).

Barna da Siena (active mid–late 1300s). One of the chief followers of Simone Martini, more dramatic and vigorous than the usual ethereal Sienese (**San Gimignano**, Collegiata).

Barocci, Federico (*c.* 1535–1612). Intense proto-Baroque painter of Urbino, inexplicably influential and popular in his time (**Urbino**, Palazzo Ducale and Duomo).

Bartolo di Fredi (Sienese, active *c.* 1353–1410). Student of Ambrogio Lorenzetti, a genuine pre-Raphaelite soul, entirely at home in the Sienese trecento; employs colours never before seen on this planet (**Montepulciano**, Duomo; **San Gimignano**, Collegiata).

Bartolommeo, Fra (*c.* 1472–1517). Florentine painter, master of the High Renaissance style (**Florence**, S. Marco, Pitti Palace).

Beccafumi, Domenico (*c.* 1486–1551). Sienese painter; odd mixture of Sienese conservatism and Florentine Mannerism (**Siena**, Pinacoteca, Palazzo Pubblico, cathedral pavement).

Benedetto da Maiano (Florentine, 1442–97). Sculptor, specialist in narrative reliefs (**Florence**, S. Croce, Strozzi Palace, Bargello; he also designed the loggia of S. Maria delle Grazie, **Arezzo**).

Berruguete, Pedro (*c.* 1450–1504). Spanish Renaissance painter who worked for the Duke of Urbino for many years and painted one of his most celebrated portraits (Palazzo Ducale, **Urbino**).

Bigarelli, Guido (13th century). Talented travelling sculptor from Como, who excelled in elaborate and sometimes bizarre pulpits (**Barga; Pistoia**, S. Bartolomeo; and **Pisa** baptistry).

Bonfigli, Benedetto (Perugia, *c.* 1420–96). Meticulous Umbrian painter, known for his painted banners in many **Perugia** churches; best works, especially the Cappella dei Priori frescoes, are in that city's Galleria Nazionale.

Botticelli, Sandro (Florentine, 1445–1510). Technically excellent, a master of line and colour. Above every other quattrocento artist, his works reveal the imaginative soul of the Florentine Renaissance, particularly his great series of mythological paintings (**Florence**, Uffizi). Later, a little deranged and under the spell of Savonarola, he reverted to intense, though conventional, religious paintings. Many of his best works are probably lost (**Florence**, Accademia; **Montelupo**, S. Giovanni Evangelista).

Bronzino, Agnolo (1503–72). Virtuoso Florentine Mannerist with a cool, glossy, hyper-elegant style, at his best in portraiture (**Florence**, Palazzo Vecchio, Uffizi, S. Lorenzo, SS. Annunziata).

Brunelleschi, Filippo (1377–1446). Florentine architect, credited in his time with restoring the ancient Roman manner of building but deserving more credit for developing a brilliant approach of his own (**Florence**, Duomo cupola, Spedale degli Innocenti, S. Spirito, S. Croce's Pazzi chapel, S. Lorenzo). He was also a sculptor (he lost the competition for the baptistry doors to Ghiberti), and one of the first theorists on perspective.

Buontalenti, Bernardo (1536–1608). The late Florentine Mannerist architect and planner of the new city of Livorno, better known for his Medici villas (**Artimino**, as well as the fascinating grotto in **Florence**'s Boboli Gardens, and, also in Florence, Belvedere Fort and Uffizi Tribuna).

Cellini, Benvenuto (1500–71). Goldsmith and sculptor from Florence who spent much time in Rome. In 1545 he came to work for Cosimo I and to torment Bandinelli (Perseus, Loggia dei Lanzi; also works in the Bargello). He is as famed for his catty *Autobiography* as for his sculpture.

Cimabue (*c*. 1240–1302). Florentine painter credited by Vasari with initiating the 'rebirth of the arts', one of the first painters to depart from the stylization of the Byzantine style (**Florence**, mosaics in baptistry, Crucifix in S. Croce; **Pisa**, cathedral mosaic; whatever is left in the upper church of S. Francesco in **Assisi**).

Civitali, Matteo (Lucca, *c*. 1435–1501). Sweet, imaginative sculptor, apparently self-taught, who would be better known if all his works weren't in **Lucca** (cathedral, Museo Nazionale Guinigi).

Cola dell'Amatrice (1489–1559). Architect and painter, a follower of Carlo Crivelli; worked mainly in **Ascoli Piceno** (cathedral façade and town hall).

Coppo di Marcovaldo (Florentine, active *c*. 1261–75). Another very early painter, as good as Cimabue if not as well known (**San Gimignano**; **Pistoia**, cathedral).

Crivelli, Carlo (1430–95). A refugee from Venice who painted all over the Marches; obsessively precise and something of an eccentric: fond of painting fruit and cucumbers above some of the most spiritual Madonnas and saints ever created (**Corridonia**, **Ancona**, **Ascoli Piceno**, **Macerata**). His brother **Vittore Crivelli** (d. 1501) copied him closely.

Daddi, Bernardo (active 1290–*c*. 1349). Florentine master of delicate altarpieces (**Florence**, Orsanmichele, S. Maria Novella's Spanish chapel).

De Magistris, Simone (active 1560–1600). Little-known Marches painter, one of the last to keep up something of the style and individuality of the Renaissance (**Sarnano**, **San Ginesio**, **Camerino**, **Osimo**, **Ascoli Piceno**).

Desiderio da Settignano (Florentine, 1428/31–61). Sculptor, follower of Donatello (**Florence**, S. Croce, Bargello, S. Lorenzo).

Dolci, Carlo (Florentine, 1616–86). Unsurpassed Baroque master of the 'whites of their eyes' school of religious art (**Florence**, Palazzo Corsini; **Prato**, Museo del Duomo).

Domenico di Bartolo (Sienese, *c*. 1400–46). Interesting painter well out of the Sienese mainstream; the unique naturalism of his art is a Florentine influence (Spedale di S. Maria della Scala, Pinacoteca in **Siena**).

Domenico Veneziano (Florentine 1404–61). Painter, teacher of Piero della Francesca; master of perspective with few surviving works (**Florence**, Uffizi).

Donatello (Florentine, 1386–1466). The greatest Renaissance sculptor, appearing at the beginning of Florence's quattrocento. Never equalled in technical ability, expressiveness, nor imaginative content, his works influenced Renaissance painters as much as sculptors (**Florence**, Bargello – the greatest works, including the original St George from Orsanmichele, David and Cupid-Atys, plus the great pulpits, the masterpiece of his old age in S. Lorenzo; other works in Palazzo Vecchio, and the cathedral museum; **Siena**, cathedral, baptistry).

Duccio di Buoninsegna (d. 1319). One of the first and greatest Sienese painters, to Sienese art what Giotto was to Florence; ignored by Vasari, though his contributions to the new visual language of the Renaissance are comparable to Giotto's (**Siena**, parts of the great Maestà in the cathedral museum, also Pinacoteca; **Florence**, altarpiece in the Uffizi; Massa Marittima, cathedral; **Castelfiorentino**, Pinacoteca).

Francesco di Giorgio Martini (Sienese, 1439–1502). Architect – mostly of fortresses – sculptor and painter, with works scattered all over Italy (**Siena**, cathedral, Pinacoteca; **Cortona**, S. Maria di Calcinaio; elegant castles at **San Leo**, **Mondavio** and a score of other towns in the Marches).

Franciabigio (Florentine, 1482–1525). Most temperamental of Andrea del Sarto's pupils but only mildly Mannerist (**Florence**, Poggio a Caiano and SS. Annunziata).

Gaddi, Taddeo (Florentine; *c.* 1300–*c.* 1366). Most important of the followers of Giotto. He and his son **Agnolo** (d. 1396) contributed some of the finest trecento fresco cycles (**Florence**, notably at S. Croce, and S. Ambrogio; **Prato**, cathedral).

Gentile da Fabriano (*c.* 1360–1427). Master nonpareil of the International Gothic style, from Fabriano in the Marches. Most of his work is lost (**Florence**, Uffizi).

Ghiberti, Lorenzo (1378–1455). Goldsmith, sculptor, and the first artist to write an autobiography (naturally, a Florentine). He would probably be better known had he not spent most of his career working on the doors for the **Florence** baptistry after winning the famous competition of 1401 (also **Florence**, statues at Orsanmichele; **Siena**, baptistry).

Ghirlandaio, Domenico (Florentine, *c.* 1448–94). Painter of the quattrocento establishment, master of colourful, lively fresco cycles (with the help of a big workshop) featuring all the Medici and Florence's banking elite. A great portraitist (**Florence**, Ognissanti, S. Maria Novella, S. Trínita, Spedale degli Innocenti; **San Gimignano**, Collegiata; also **Narni** , Pinacoteca).

Giambologna (1529–1608). A Fleming, born Jean Boulogne; court sculptor to the Medici after 1567 and master of Mannerist virtuosity (**Florence**, Loggia dei Lanzi, Bargello, Villa la Petraia; **Pratolino**, the Appennino).

Giotto (*c.* 1266–1337). Shepherd boy of the Mugello (discovered by Cimabue) and the first great Florentine painter, most important for his revolutionary treatment of space and of the human figure. (**Florence**, S. Croce, cathedral campanile, Horne Museum, S. Maria Novella; **Assisi**, lower church frescoes at S. Francesco; attribution of the great upper church to him or his followers is the longest-running battle in art history).

Giovanni da Milano (14th century). An innovative Lombard inspired by Giotto (**Florence**, S. Croce; **Prato**, cathedral museum).

Giovanni di Paolo (d. 1483). One of the best quattrocento Sienese painters, a colourful, often eccentric, reactionary who continued the traditions of the Sienese trecento (**Siena**, Pinacoteca).

Giovanni di San Giovanni (1592–1633). One of Tuscany's more prolific but likeable Baroque fresco painters (**Florence**, Pitti Palace, Villa la Petraia).

Girolamo di Giovanni (*c.* 1420–73). Refined painter from **Camerino** (in the Marches), little known because his best works are still there.

Gozzoli, Benozzo (Florentine, d. 1497). The most lighthearted, colourful quattrocento artist, who created enchanting frescoes; he earned his trade from Fra Angelico but few artists could have less in common (**Florence**, Medici chapel; **San Gimignano**, S. Agostino; **Pisa**, Camposanto; **Montefalco**, S. Francesco; **Castelfiorentino**, Visitation Chapel; **Narni**, Pinacoteca).

Guido da Siena (13th century). One of the founders of Sienese painting, still heavily Byzantine in style; little is known about his life (**Siena**, Palazzo Pubblico, Pinacoteca; **Grosseto**, Pinacoteca).

Laurana, Luciano (*c.* 1420–79). Dalmatian architect who worked for the court of Urbino, designing much of the Palazzo Ducale, one of the masterpieces of the Renaissance.

Leonardo da Vinci (1452–1519). Florence's 'universal genius', who spent so much time on science and building fortifications that his artistic output was largely unfinished (or lost). All that is left in Tuscany is the *Annunciation* (**Florence**, Uffizi) and models of gadgets at his birthplace, **Vinci**.

Lippi, Filippino (Florentine, 1457–1504). Son and artistic heir of Fra Filippo, often appearing as a neurotic Gozzoli, or at least one of the most thoughtful and serious artists of the quattrocento (**Florence**, S. Maria Novella, S. Maria del Carmine, Badia, Uffizi).

Lippi, Fra Filippo (Florentine, d. 1469). A monk and painter of exquisite, ethereal Madonnas, one of whom he ran off with (the model, at least: a nun). The pope forgave them both. A key figure in the increasingly complex, detailed painting of the middle 1400s (**Florence**, Uffizi; **Prato**, cathedral and Galeria Comunale; **Spoleto**, Duomo).

Lorenzetti, Ambrogio (Sienese, d. 1348). A great innovator in subject matter and landscapes who could also crank out golden Madonnas as well as any Sienese painter. He created the first and greatest of secular frescoes, the *Allegories of Good and Bad Government* in **Siena**'s Palazzo Pubblico. His last known work, the 1344 *Annunciation* in **Siena**'s Pinacoteca, is one of the 14th century's most revolutionary treatments of perspective (also **Massa Marittima**, Pinacoteca).

Lorenzetti, Pietro (Sienese, d. 1348). Ambrogio's big brother, also an innovator, one of the precursors of the Renaissance's new treatment of space (**Assisi**, S. Francesco; **Siena**, S. Spirito; **Arezzo**, Pieve di S. Maria; **Cortona**, cathedral museum).

Lorenzo di Credi (1439–1537). One of the most important followers of Leonardo da Vinci, technically perfect if occasionally vacuous (**Florence**, Uffizi).

Lorenzo Monaco (b. Siena; 1370–1425). A monk at S. Maria degli Angeli in Florence and a brilliant colourist, forming an uncommon connection between the Gothic style of Sienese painting and the new developments in early Renaissance Florence (**Florence**, Uffizi, S. Trínita).

Lotto, Lorenzo (*c.* 1480–1556). Venetian pupil of Giovanni Bellini, best known there as one of the first great portraitists. He spent his declining years in the Marches, where he left a considerable amount of uninspired or magnificent religious work (**Jesi**, **Ancona**, **Recanati**, **Loreto**).

Maitani, Lorenzo (d. 1330). Sienese sculptor and architect whose reputation rests almost entirely on the great façade of **Orvieto** cathedral, where he spent most of his life as master of works.

Manetti, Rutilio (1571–1639). Quirky but likeable Baroque painter, the last artist of any standing produced by Siena (**Massa Marittima**, cathedral).

Margarito d'Arezzo (Arezzo, 13th century, also called **Margaritone**). A near contemporary of Giotto who stuck firmly to his Byzantine guns (**Arezzo**, Museo d'Arte).

Martini, Simone (Sienese, d. 1344). A possible pupil of Giotto who took the Sienese version of International Gothic to an almost metaphysical perfection, creating luminous, lyrical altarpieces and frescoes perhaps unsurpassed in the trecento (**Assisi**, S. Francesco; **Siena**, Palazzo Pubblico; **Pisa**, Museo S. Matteo; **Florence**, Uffizi; **Orvieto**, Museo Civico).

Masaccio (Florentine, 1401–*c.* 1428). The precocious 'shabby Tom' who died young and left little behind but inaugurated the Renaissance in painting by translating Donatello and Brunelleschi's perspective on to a flat surface. He was also revolutionary in his use of light and shadow, and in expressing emotion (**Florence**, S. Maria del Carmine, S. Maria Novella; **Pisa**, Museo S. Matteo).

Maso di Banco (Florentine, active 1340s). One of the more colourful and original followers of Giotto (**Florence**, S. Croce).

Masolino (Florentine, d. 1447). 'Little Tom', perhaps deserving much of the credit, with Masaccio, for the new advances in art at the Carmine in Florence; art historians dispute endlessly how to attribute the frescoes. This brilliant painter left little other work behind to prove his case (**Empoli**, Museo della Collegiata; **Todi**, S. Fortunato; also attributed **Pistoia**, Tau chapel).

Matteo da Gualdo (*c.* 1430–1503). Umbrian painter, perhaps more representative of the lot than Perugino. He created conventional, colourful works, and probably never heard of Florence (works in his home town, **Gualdo Tadino**).

Matteo di Giovanni (Sienese, 1435–95). One Sienese quattrocento painter who could keep up with the Florentines; a contemporary described him as 'Simone Martini come to life again' (**Siena**, Pinacoteca, cathedral pavement, S. Agostino, S. Maria delle Neve; **Grosseto**, Pinacoteca).

Melozzo da Forli (b. Forlí, in the Romagna; 1438–1494). An artist famous for his perspectives and illusionism; of the little of his work that survives, the best preserved (outside **Rome**) is the S. Marco sacristy in **Loreto** (also **Urbino**, Palazzo Ducale).

Memmi, Lippo (Sienese, 1317–47). Brother-in-law and assistant of Simone Martini (**Siena**, S. Spirito; **San Gimignano**, Museo Civico).

Michelangelo Buonarroti (Florentine, 1475–1564). Artist born in Caprese (now called Caprese Michelangelo) into a Florentine family of the minor nobility come down in the world. His early years and artistic training are obscure; he was apprenticed to Ghirlandaio but, showing a preference for sculpture, was sent to the court of Lorenzo de' Medici. Nicknamed Il Divino in his lifetime, he was a complex, difficult character, who seldom got along with mere mortals, popes,or patrons. What he couldn't express by means of the male nude in paint or marble, he did in his beautiful but difficult sonnets. In many ways he was the first modern artist, unsurpassed in technique but also the first genius to go over the top (**Florence**, Medici tombs and library in S. Lorenzo, three works in the Bargello, the *Pietà* in the Museo del Duomo, the *David* in the Accademia, Casa Buonarroti, and his only oil painting, in the Uffizi).

Michelozzo di Bartolomeo (Florentine, 1396–1472). Sculptor who worked with Donatello (**Prato**, pulpit of the Holy Girdle, and the tomb in **Florence**'s baptistry), but better known as the classicizing architect favoured by the elder Cosimo de' Medici (**Florence**, Medici Palace, Chiostro of SS. Annunziata, library of S. Marco; villas at **Trebbio** and **Cafaggiolo**; **Montepulciano**, S. Agostino; **Impruneta**, Tempietto).

Mino da Fiesole (Florentine, 1429–84). Sculptor of portrait busts and tombs; like the Della Robbias, a representative of the Florentine 'sweet style' (**Fiesole**, cathedral; **Empoli**, Museo della Collegiata; **Volterra**, cathedral; **Florence**, Badia, Sant'Ambrogio; **Prato**, cathedral).

Nanni di Banco (1384–1421). Florentine sculptor at the dawn of the Renaissance (**Florence**, Orsanmichele, Porta della Mandorla).

Nelli, Ottaviano (*c.* 1375–*c.* 1440). Typical, often charming representative of the early Umbrian school; most of his work is in his home town, **Gubbio**.

Orcagna, Andrea (Florence, d. 1368). Sculptor, painter and architect who dominated the middle 1300s in Florence, though greatly disparaged by Vasari, who destroyed much of his work. Some believe he is the 'Master of the Triumph of Death' of **Pisa**'s Camposanto (**Florence**, Orsanmichele, S. Croce, S. Maria Novella, *Crucifixion* in refectory of S. Spirito, also often given credit for the Loggia dei Lanzi).

Perugino (Pietro Vannucci, Perugia, *c.* 1450–1523). Perhaps the most distinctive of the Umbrian painters, creator of some works of genius, along with countless idyllic nativity scenes, each with its impeccably sweet Madonna and blue-green tinted background. Some of his later works are awful, though he may not always be responsible: in his cynical old age he let his workshop sign his name to anything (**Città della Pieve**, S. Maria dei Bianchi; **Perugia**, Pinacoteca, Collegio del Cambio; **Trevi**, Madonna delle Lacrime; **Florence**, Uffizi, S. Maddalena dei Pazzi, Cenacolo di Foligno; also in **Fano**).

Piero della Francesca (b. Sansepolcro; *c.* 1415–92). One of the really unique artists of the quattrocento, a leading light in the famous court of Urbino, who wrote two of the most important theoretical works on perspective then illustrated them with a lifetime's work reducing painting to the bare essentials: geometry, light and colour. In his best work his reduction creates nothing dry or academic but dreamlike, almost eerie scenes similar to those of Uccello. And, like Uccello or Botticelli, his subjects are often archetypes of immense psychological depth that no one will ever be able to fully explain (**Arezzo**, S. Francesco and cathedral; **Urbino**, Palazzo Ducale; **Sansepolcro**, Museo Civico; **Monterchi**; **Florence**, Uffizi; **Perugia**, Galleria Nazionale).

Piero di Cosimo (Florentine, 1462–1521). Painter better known for his personal eccentricities than for his art, which in itself is pretty odd. He lived on hard-boiled eggs, which he boiled with his glue (**Florence**, Uffizi; **Fiesole**, S. Francesco).

Pietro da Cortona (Cortona, 1596–1669). The most charming of Tuscan Baroque painters. His best work is in **Rome**, but there are some florid ceilings in the Pitti Palace, **Florence** (works in **Cortona**; also **Perugia**, Galleria Nazionale).

Pinturicchio (Perugia, 1454–1513). A painter who achieved his renown for the gold and rich colours that he employed. Though he was never an innovator, as an absolute virtuoso in colour, style and grace, no one could surpass him. He was another establishment artist, one who was especially favoured by the popes and one who, like Perugino, he was slandered most vilely by Georgio Vasari (**Siena**, Piccolomini library; **Spello**, S. Maria Maggiore; **Perugia**, Galleria Nazionale).

Pisano, Andrea (b. Pontedera; *c.* 1290–1348). Artistic heir of Giovanni and Nicola Pisano and teacher of Orcagna; probably a key figure in introducing new artistic ideas to **Florence** (baptistry, south doors). He was not related to the other Pisani.

Pisano, Nicola (active *c.* 1258–78). The first great medieval Tuscan sculptor really came from down south in Puglia, then enjoying a flowering of classically orientated art under Emperor Frederick II. He created a little Renaissance all his own when he adapted the figures and composition of ancient reliefs to make his wonderful pulpit reliefs in **Siena** and in **Pisa**'s baptistry. His son **Giovanni Pisano** (active *c.* 1265–1314) carried on the tradition, notably in the façade sculptures at **Siena** cathedral (also **Perugia**, S. Domenico, Fontana Maggiore; great relief pulpits in **Pisa** cathedral, Sant'Andrea, **Pistoia**).

Pollaiuolo, Antonio (Florentine, d. 1498). A sculptor, painter and goldsmith whose fame rests on his brilliant, unmistakable line; he occasionally worked with his less gifted brother **Piero** (**Florence**, Uffizi and Bargello).

Pontormo, Jacopo (Florentine; b. Pontormo, 1494–1556). Determined Mannerist eccentric; you haven't seen pink and orange until you've seen his work. After the initial shock, you'll meet an artist of real genius, one whose use of the human body as the sole means for communicating ideas is equal to Michelangelo's (**Florence**, S. Felicità – his *Deposition* – and Uffizi; **Poggio a Caiano; Carmignano**).

Quercia, Jacopo della (Sienese, 1374–1438). Sculptor who learned his style from Pisano's cathedral pulpit; an unsuccessful contestant for the Florence baptistry doors. He may have been Siena's greatest sculptor, though his most celebrated work, the city's Fonte Gaia, is ruined (**Lucca**, cathedral tomb of Ilaria del Carretto; **San Gimignano**, Collegiata; **Siena**, baptistry; **Volterra**, cathedral).

Raphael (Raffaello Sanzio, b. Urbino; 1483–1520). Artist who spent time in Città di Castello, Perugia and Florence before establishing himself in Rome. Only a few of the best works of this High Renaissance master remain in the region in the Pitti Palace and Uffizi, **Florence**, and in **Perugia**'s San Severo; there's also a lovely portrait in the Palazzo Ducale in **Urbino**.

Robbia, Luca della (Florentine, 1400–82). Greatest of the famous family of sculptors, who invented the coloured glaze for terracottas that we associate with the Della Robbias but was also a first-rate relief sculptor (the *cantorie* in **Florence**'s cathedral museum; **Impruneta**, Collegiata). His nephew **Andrea della Robbia** (1435–1525; best works in convent of **La Verna** and the Tempietto at **Montevarchi**) and Andrea's son **Giovanni** (1469–1529; best work in **Pistoia**, Ospedale del Ceppo) carried on the sweet blue-and-white terracotta style in innumerable buildings across Tuscany.

Rosselli, Cosimo (Florentine, 1434–1507). Competent middle-of-the-road Renaissance painter who occasionally excelled (**Florence**, S. Ambrogio).

Rossellino, Bernardo (1409–64). Florentine, planner and architect of the new town of **Pienza**. Also a sculptor (**Florence**, S. Croce, S. Miniato; **Empoli**, Pinacoteca). His brother **Antonio Rossellino** (1427–79) was also a talented sculptor (**Florence**, S. Croce).

Rossi, Vicenzo de' (1525–87). Florentine Mannerist sculptor of chunky male nudes (**Florence**, Palazzo Vecchio).

Rosso Fiorentino (Giovanni Battista di Jacopo, 1494–1540). Florentine Mannerist painter who makes a fitting complement to Jacopo Pontormo, both for his tortured soul and for the exaggerations of form and colour that he used in order to create his gripping, dramatic effects. Fiorentino fled Italy after the Sack of Rome and worked for Francis I at Fontainebleau. (**Volterra** Pinacoteca has his masterpiece, the *Deposition*; **Florence**, Uffizi and S. Lorenzo; **Città di Castello**, Duomo).

Salimbeni, Iacopo (d. about 1427) and **Lorenzo** (d. 1420). Brothers from the Marches, charming masters of detail on the threshold of the Renaissance (**Urbino**, Oratorio di San Giovanni; **San Severino Marche**, Pinacoteca).

Salviati, Francesco (Florentine, 1510–63). Friend of Vasari and a similar sort of painter, though much more talented. He created odd perspectives and decoration, and often bizarre imagery (**Florence**, Palazzo Vecchio and Uffizi).

Sangallo, Antonio da (brother of Giuliano, 1455–1537). Architect at his best in palaces and churches in the monumental style: notably at the temple of S. Biagio, **Montepulciano**; his son, **Antonio da Sangallo the Younger**, also an architect, the family's best, practised mainly in **Rome**.

Sangallo, Giuliano da (Florentine, 1443–1516). Architect of humble origins who later became favourite of Lorenzo de' Medici. He was often tripped up by an obsession, inherited from Alberti, with making architecture conform to philosophical principles (**Poggio a Caiano**; **Florence**, S. Maddalena dei Pazzi; **Prato**, S. Maria delle Carceri).

Il Sassetta (Stefano di Giovanni; active *c.* 1390–1450). One of the great Sienese quattrocento painters, though still working in a style the Florentines would have found hopelessly reactionary; an artist who studied Masaccio but preferred the Gothic elegance of Masolino. His masterpiece, the Borgo Sansepolcro polyptych, is dispersed through half the museums of Europe.

Signorelli, Luca (Cortona, d. 1523). A rarefied Umbrian painter and important influence on Michelangelo. His imaginative, forceful compositions combine geometrical rigour with a touch of unreality, much like his master Piero della Francesca (*The Last Judgement* in **Orvieto** cathedral; **Cortona**, Museo dell'Accademia Etrusca and Museo Diocesano; **Monte Oliveto Maggiore**; **Sansepolcro**, Museo Civico; **Urbino**, Palazzo Ducale).

Il Sodoma (Giovanni Antonio Bazzi, b. Piedmont; 1477–1549). A Sienese by choice, probably not the libertine that his nickname, and Giorgio Vasari's biography, suggest. An endearing artist who eschewed Mannerist distortion, he grew wealthy through his work, then blew it all on feeding his exotic menagerie and died in the poorhouse (**Monte Oliveto Maggiore**; **Siena**, Pinacoteca and S. Domenico).

Spinello Aretino (Arezzo, late 14th century–1410). A link between Giotto and the International Gothic style, imaginative and colourful in his compositions (**Florence**, S. Miniato; **Siena**, Palazzo Pubblico; **Arezzo**, Museo d'Arte). His son **Parri di Spinello** created many fine works, all around **Arezzo** (S. Maria delle Grazie).

Tacca, Pietro (b. Carrara; 1580–1640). A pupil of Giambologna and one of the best of the early Baroque sculptors (**Livorno**, Quattro Mori; **Florence**, Piazza SS. Annunziata fountains; **Prato**, Piazza del Comune).

Taddeo di Bartolo (Volterra, 1363–1422). The greatest Sienese painter of the late 1300s, and the least conventional; never a consummate stylist, he often shows a remarkable imagination in composition and treatment of subject matter (**Siena**, Palazzo Pubblico, S. Spirito; **Perugia**, Pinacoteca; **Volterra**, Pinacoteca; **San Gimignano**, Museo Civico).

Talenti, Francesco (early 14th century). Chief architect of **Florence** cathedral and campanile after Arnolfo di Cambio and Giotto; his son **Simone** made the beautiful windows in Orsanmichele (and perhaps the Loggia dei Lanzi) in **Florence**.

Torrigiano, Pietro (1472–1528). Florentine portrait sculptor, famous for his work in Westminster Abbey and for breaking Michelangelo's nose (**Siena**, cathedral).

Uccello, Paolo (Florentine, 1397–1475). Artist more obsessed than any other with the possibilities of artificial perspective. Like Piero della Francesca, he used the new technique to create a magical world of his own, contemplation of which made him increasingly eccentric in his later years. His provocative, visionary subjects (*Noah* fresco in S. Maria Novella, and *Battle of San Romano* in the Uffizi and cloister of San Miniato, **Florence**) put him up with Piero della Francesca and Botticelli as the most intellectually stimulating of quattrocento artists (also attributed frescoes, **Prato** cathedral, and a painting in the Palazzo Ducale, **Urbino**).

Vasari, Giorgio (Arezzo, 1511–74). Florentine sycophant, writer and artist, and a pretty good architect (**Florence**, Uffizi, Corridoio, and Fish Loggia; also **Città di Castello**, palace).

Il Vecchietta (Lorenzo di Pietro, 1412–80). Sienese painter and sculptor, dry and linear, part Sienese Pollaiuolo and part Donatello. One wonders what he did to acquire his nickname, 'Little Old Woman' (**Siena**, Loggia della Mercanzia, baptistry; **Pienza**, cathedral).

Verrocchio, Andrea del (1435–88). Florentine sculptor who worked in bronze, and spent his life trying to outdo Donatello. He was also a painter, a mystic alchemist in his spare time, and interestingly enough the master of both Botticelli and Leonardo (**Florence**, Uffizi, S. Lorenzo, Orsanmichele, Palazzo Vecchio and Bargello).

Topics

03

The First Professional Philistine

Many who have seen Vasari's work in Florence will wonder how such a mediocre painter should rate so much attention. Ingratiating companion of the rich and famous, workman-like overachiever and tireless self-promoter, Vasari was the perfect man for his time. He was born in Arezzo, in 1511; a fortunate introduction to Cardinal Silvio Passerini gave him the chance of an education in Florence with the young Medici heirs, Ippolito and Alessandro. In his early years he became a fast and reliable frescoist who gained a reputation for customer satisfaction. In the 1530s, after various commissions around Italy, he returned to Florence just when Cosimo I was beginning his plans to remake the city. Vasari became Cosimo's court painter and architect, the most prolific fresco machine, painting over countless good frescoes from the 1300s.

But more than for his paintings, Vasari lives on through his book, *Lives of the Painters, Sculptors and Architects*, a series of exhaustive, gossipy biographies of artists. Beginning with Cimabue, Vasari traces the rise of art out of Byzantine and Gothic barbarism, through Giotto and his followers, towards an ever-improving naturalism, culminating in the great age of Leonardo, Raphael, and Michelangelo, who not only mastered nature but outdid her. His book, being the first of its kind, and containing a mine of valuable information on dozens of Renaissance artists, has had a tremendous influence on all subsequent criticism.

Much of Vasari's world seems quaint to us now: the idea of the artist striving for Virtue and Glory, the slavish worship of anything that survived from ancient Rome, artistic 'progress' and the conviction that art's purpose was to imitate nature. But many of Vasari's opinions have had a long career in the world of ideas. His blind disparagement of everything medieval lived on until the 1800s. His dismissal of Sienese, Umbrian and northern artists has not been entirely corrected even today. Vasari believed in a nice, tidy art that went by the book. With his interior decorator's concept of Beauty, he created a style of criticism in which virtuosity, not imagination, became the standard by which art was to be judged; history offers few more instructive examples of the stamina and resilience of dubious ideas.

Flora and Fauna

Tuscany has been cultivated so long and so intensively that wildlife is pushed to the fringes. Nevertheless, a great variety of birds and beasts complement the diversity of the landscape. Leaving aside Tuscany (*see* p.41–42), this region divides neatly into three: the coastal zone, the central hills and the mountains.

For nature-lovers, the coast will be by far the most interesting; the malaria mosquito kept much of the southern Maremma undeveloped for centuries, leaving it inhabited by vast stretches of pine forest, cork oak and holm oak, thriving wildlife (including wild horses) and marshlands. Its protected nesting grounds (*see* 'Monti dell'Uccellina' p.313, Orbetello's lagoons, p.316, and Lago di Burano, p.320) are Italy's greatest stopovers for migrating waterfowl. Deforested land beyond the marshes is covered with the characteristic Mediterranean maquis (*macchia*, in Italian):

macchia alta with shrub versions of pines, oaks, beech, cypress and laurel; and the *macchia bassa* in drier regions, consisting of thick patches of broom, heather, lentisk and fragrant plants.

As for the **animals**, the viper is the only really unpleasant thing you may meet; proliferating amid abandoned farmland, they're brownish-grey, about 45cm long, and have a vaguely diamond-shaped head. Vipers object to being stepped on. If one bites you, you've got 30 minutes to get hold of the serum – you can buy it in any pharmacy and keep it in the fridge (or your coolbox).

The region's other trademark animal, the boar, is shy but flourishes everywhere, despite the Italians' best efforts to turn him into salami. There are also hares and rabbits, foxes and weasels, polecats, badgers and porcupines in the wilder areas. A few wolves, lynxes and deer survive in the higher reaches of the Apennines, and deer have also been reintroduced in the Maremma coastal parks. You can find all of these, and even wildcats, in the Val di Farma north of Roccastrada, in Tuscany. The only mountain goats are found on the island of Montecristo.

Many writers on this part of Italy comment on the absence of **birdsong**. They're exaggerating. Italian hunters shoot anything that flies, but there are still thrushes, starlings, wrens, and such, along with the white doves, ubiquitous in Umbria, that make you think of Assisi and St Francis. Cuckoos announce the spring, pheasants lie low during the hunting season, and an occasional owl can be heard. Nightingales are rare, though there are supposedly some round Lago di Massaciuccoli and the northern coasts – in the evening you're far more likely to see bats.

The **insect** world is well represented: lovely butterflies and moths; rather forbidding black bullet bees and wasps that resemble vintage fighter planes. The beetles reach disproportionate sizes – you may see a *diavolo*, a large black or red beetle with long, gracefully curving antlers that sing when you trap it; Leonardo drew one in his notebooks. There are enough mosquitoes, midges and little biting flies to be a nuisance in summer, and, perhaps most alarming at first, the shiny black scorpion, who may crawl inside through the window or up drains (keep the plugs in) or come in with the firewood. Once inside they head for dark places such as beds or shoes. One thwack with a shoe will do in even the largest scorpion. Getting stung is painful but not deadly, though you should visit the doctor, mainly to guard against infection or allergic reaction.

As for the **forests**, oaks, chestnuts and beeches predominate, along with tall, upright poplars ('Lombardy' type), pines, willows (not the weeping variety) and a few maples – with rounded leaves, not pointed as in northern Europe and America. Cypress trees are common; the tidier ones have been planted, shaggier ones are the wild variety. Parasol or umbrella pines, that most characteristic Italian tree, make a grand sight isolated on a hillcrest, or in groves along the Maremma. At higher altitudes there are beeches, pines and firs – beautiful silver firs grow around Monte Amiata, while in the Casentino near Camaldoli is a vast stretch of old beech and pine forest. The Garfagnana's Parco Naturale dell'Orecchiella includes an ancient chestnut forest.

Many of the **wildflowers** are close cousins to those seen in northern Europe and America. There are a million varieties of buttercup, usually the tiny *ranuncolo* and *bottoncini d'oro*, and of bluebell, often called *campanella* or *campanellina*.

Many of the common five-petalled pink blossoms in spring fields are wild geraniums (*geranio*), with pointed leaves like the anemone, and you'll see quite a few varieties of violet (*violette*) with round or spade-shaped leaves (a few are yellow). Daisies (*margherita*) come in all sizes. Tiniest of all are the wild pink and blue forget-me-nots (*non ti scordar di me*). Large swatches of lavender are among the charms of the Chianti hills.

The real star here is the bright red poppy. Dandelions and wild mustard are also plentiful, along with white, umbrella-like bunches of florets called *tragosellino* or *podragraria*, similar to Queen Anne's Lace. On a more exotic note, there are wild orchids, rhododendrons (in mountainous areas), five-petalled wild roses and water lilies in the coastal Maremma. The best wildflowers are in the Sibillini mountains; in early summer, the Piano Grande blooming is an unforgettable sight.

There are various other **plants** worth looking out for; a dozen kinds of greens that go into somewhat bitter salads – anise, fennel, mint, rosemary and sage are common. The Italians beat the bushes with fervour every spring looking for wild asparagus and repeat the performance in autumn searching for truffles and *porcini* (boletus) mushrooms.

A Florentine Puzzle

In a city as visually restrained as Florence, every detail of decoration stands out. In the Middle Ages and Renaissance, Florentine builders combined their passion for geometry with their love of making a little go a long way; they embellished buildings with simple geometrical designs. Though nothing special in themselves, they stand out like mystic hieroglyphs, symbols upon which to meditate while contemplating old Florence's remarkable journey through the western mind.

The city is full of them, incorporated into façades, mosaics, windows and friezes. Here are eight of them, providing a little exercise for the eye while tramping the hard pavements of Florence. Your job is to find them. Some are really obvious, others obscure. For No.6 you should be able to find at least three examples (two across the street from each other), and if you're clever you'll find not only No.5, a rather late addition to the cityscape, but also the medieval work that inspired it. Don't worry too much about the last one. But if you're an art historian or a Florentinophile, it's only fair that you seek out this hard one too.

For the answers, *see* p.48.

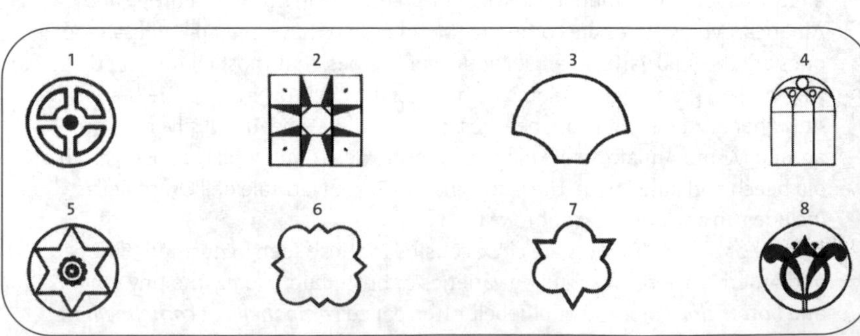

Guelphs and Ghibellines

One medieval Italian writer claimed that the factional strife began with two brothers of Pistoia, Guelf and Gibel. One murdered the other, starting the seemingly endless troubles that to many seemed a God-sent plague to punish the proud and wealthy Italians for their sins. However, most historians trace the roots of this party conflict to two great German houses, *Welf* and *Waiblingen*.

Chroniclers pinpoint the outbreak of the troubles to 1215, when a politically prominent Florentine noble, Buondelmonte dei Buondelmonti, was assassinated by his enemies while crossing the Ponte Vecchio. This ignited a smouldering quarrel all over Italy, particularly in Tuscany. The atmosphere of city-states, each with its own internal struggles between nobles, the rich merchant class and the commoners, crystallized rapidly into parties. Initially the Guelphs, largely a creation of the newly wealthy bourgeois, were all for free trade and the rights of the free cities; the Ghibellines were the party of the German emperors, nominal overlords of Italy. Naturally, the Guelphs found their protector in the emperors' bitter temporal rivals, the popes, which brought a religious angle into the story.

Before long, the labels Guelph and Ghibelline ceased to have any meaning. In the 13th and 14th centuries, the emperors and their Ghibelline allies helped the church root out heretical movements such as the Patarenes, while the popes schemed to destroy the liberty of good Guelph cities, especially in Umbria, and incorporate them into the Papal State. In cities such as Florence, where the Guelphs won a final victory, they themselves split into parties, battling with the same barbaric gusto. Black was the Ghibelline colour, white the Guelph, and cities arranged themselves like squares on a chessboard. When one suffered a revolution and changed from Guelph to Ghibelline, or vice versa, its nearest enemies would soon change the other way. Often the public buildings give us a clue as to the loyalties of a city in any given time. Simple, squared crenellations are Guelph (as in the Palazzo dei Priori in Perugia); ornate 'swallowtail' crenellations (as in Frederick II's castle in Prato) are the mark of the Ghibelline.

The English looked on with bewilderment. Edmund Spenser, in his *Shepheardes' Calendar* (1579), wrote this fanciful etymology: 'when all Italy was distraicte into the Factions of the Guelfes and the Gibelins, being two famous houses in Florence, the name began through their great mischiefes and many outrages, to be so odious or rather dreadfull in the peoples eares, that if theyr children at any time were frowarde and wanton, they would say to them the Guelfe or the Gibeline came. Which words nowe from them (as may thinge els) be come into our usage, and for Guelfes and Gibelines, we say *Elfes* and *Goblins*.'

Landscapes

There may be other regions in Italy that are lusher, others with taller mountains and more fertile valleys, and others that support more varied flora and enjoy a more temperate climate. Yet it is the landscapes of Tuscany and Umbria that exert the most lasting charm. In the paintings of the Renaissance, the rolling hills, cypresses, poplars and parasol pines, vineyards and winding lanes of the background are often more beautiful than the nominally religious subject in the foreground. As early as Giotto, artists took care to relate the figures in their composition to the architecture and the landscape around them, epitomized in the paintings of Leonardo da Vinci, where each tree and rock takes on an almost mystic significance.

The tidy geometry and clipped hedges of an Italian garden are a perfect example of the Italian urge to order nature, and you'll find good examples in the Boboli Gardens and the Medici villas at Castello and Collodi. The Tuscans, in the vanguard of Italy in so many ways, were the first to order their entire territory. The vicious wars of the Middle Ages devastated the countryside (as is visible in the harsh, barren brown and grey hills of trecento painting); the Black Death in the 1300s depopulated the cultivated areas, giving the Tuscans the unique opportunity to arrange things just so. Not entirely by coincidence, the late 14th century was the time when the elite, weary of city strife, discovered the joys of the country and building villas, playing the country squire and gentleman farmer whenever possible. And they planted everything in its place according to elegance and discipline, each tree with its own purpose; to act as a boundary marker, to offer shade, or to support a vine. Cypresses and parasol pines often stand strikingly along the crest of hills, not for aesthetics or as a study in perspective but as a windbreak. Strongest is the sense that nothing has changed for centuries, that in the quattrocento Gozzoli and Fra Angelico painted the same scene you see today. Few landscapes anywhere are more ancient, or more civilized.

The countryside of Umbria is more dishevelled and rustic; its hills steeper, and its valleys narrower, planted with little evidence of elegant Tuscan precision. It is celebrated for its green, the 'mystical' colour to suit its mystical, saintly nature; in autumn and winter, mists swirl romantically through the mountains. One feature, however, is just as artful as Tuscany – its tidy hilltowns of pinkish grey stone. From some spots you can see several at a time, like an archipelago of islands crowned with villages, one behind the other, vanishing into the bluish haze of the horizon.

St Francis of Assisi

Francesco Bernardone was one of the most remarkable men who ever lived. Now patron saint of all Italy, he remained closely attached to his native Umbria, in life as well as death; nearly every town in the region seems to have a legend about him, or at least a Franciscan church founded in the early days of his movement. His gentle spiritual revolution occurred amidst the sound and the fury of the 13th century. Francis taught that the natural world was a beautiful place, and that there was tremendous joy in living an ordinary humble life in it, in imitation of Christ.

Francis was born in 1182 to a merchant, Pietro Bernardone, and his Provençal wife, Madonna Pica. Some say Pietro was the richest man in Assisi; he travelled often through the south of France, trading fine cloth, and though he named his son Giovanni at the font he always called him Francesco after the country he loved. At one point Francis accompanied his father through Provence and up the Rhône to Bruges and Ghent, but most of all he used his father's wealth to finance a merry and dissipated youth; according to his first biographer, Tommaso da Celano, he was 'the first instigator of every evil, and behind none in foolishness'. He was also a poet in the troubadour tradition. His Francophile upbringing gave him an early taste for the cult of chivalry and mystic love, by 1200 all the rage among young Italians.

His conversion to saintliness did not happen overnight. In 1202, he joined the cavalry of Assisi in one of its many wars against Perugia but was captured and spent a dismal year in a Perugian prison. He also suffered a long, severe illness. The two events made him stop and think; he yearned for something more than the carefree life he had been living. Thinking it might be chivalry, he joined a band riding to the Fourth Crusade. He got as far as Spoleto when he fell ill again. He took this as a warning that he was on the wrong track and changed his allegiance from a temporal lord to a spiritual one.

Francis began to spend his time alone in the countryside around Assisi, reflecting on the world's vanity. A revelation came to him while attending Mass one Sunday in 1205, as the priest read the words of the Gospel: '...and as ye go, preach, saying, the kingdom of Heaven is at hand. Heal the sick, cleanse the lepers, raise the dead, cast out devils: freely have ye received, freely give.' Francis took this message literally: he would live like Christ, in poverty and humility.

The story goes that he took his final decision before the crucifix in the little church of San Damiano outside Assisi, which spoke to him, saying, 'Repair my house, which you see is in ruins.' Francis sold his father's packhorse and merchandise in Foligno to do just that; when his angry father hauled him before the bishop of Assisi and reproached him, Francis stripped off his rich clothes and declared that henceforth his only father was his father in heaven.

It has been commented that much of Franciscan legend comes in exemplary packages too tidy to be taken as a literal truth, but there is no doubt that this merchant's son who called himself 'God's Fool', kissing lepers and preaching to the world's outcasts, struck a chord in the hearts of many thirsting for something beyond the carrot and stick fare offered by the medieval Church. Although at first he was chased and stoned, Francis soon attracted a band of followers who lived with him in the Porziuncola, a chapel on the plain below Assisi, and wandered the area preaching, doing odd jobs to support themselves or begging their bread.

His visit in 1210 to Pope Innocent III is part of Franciscan legend. Innocent was perhaps chiefly responsible for the new worldly and militant direction of the Church, and he had little time for reformers or critics of its ambitions and corruption (the previous year he had declared the Albigensian crusade against the otherworldly Cathars in southern France). His court scoffed at the shabby Umbrian holy man, but that night Innocent dreamt that his church of St John Lateran – then the seat of the popes – was collapsing, and that this same Francis came along to hold up its walls.

Dream or not, it did not occur to the pope that he might be able to harness such spiritual renewal within the institutions of the Church; unlike the Cathars and other heretics, Francis never attacked the papal hierarchy, explicitly at any rate, although his beliefs that a person could live by the Gospel in the 13th century and that the love of money was the root of all evil were harder to fit in the current scheme. Innocent nevertheless confirmed his First Rule for a simple lay order based on poverty, which Francis called the Frati Minori. As the movement quickly grew and the roads filled with begging friars, the Church tried to convince Francis to impose on it the discipline of a monastic rule. Francis resisted this, having no interest in organization; he never even took holy orders.

In the meantime, Francis spent his time travelling and preaching, mostly in Umbria, where many villages can show a humble stone in a cave where he rested his head, or tell a legend of his sway over the birds and beasts. In 1219, he went further afield, first in a vain attempt to reach Morocco, then to the Holy Land and Egypt with the Crusaders. At Damietta, on the Nile, he preached to Sultan Malik el Kamil. The story goes that Francis was on an apostolic mission to convert the infidels, but it's just as likely he went to learn from them, especially from the Sufi mystics. One of the more intriguing parallels was a Sufi brotherhood similar to the Friars Minor, founded some 60 years before Francis' birth by a holy man named Najmuddin Kubra, a wandering preacher with an uncanny influence over birds and animals.

Drawing on his troubadour days, Francis composed some of the first and finest vernacular verse in Italy, including the *Canticle of the Sun*, a poem in his native Umbrian dialect on the unity of all creation. His poetry became the foundation of a literary movement, based on Christian devotion: Tommaso da Celano, one of Francis's first followers and his biographer, composed the powerful *Dies Irae*, followed later by Jacopone da Todi (*see* p.523), after Dante, the greatest poet of his century.

By 1221 Francis' extraordinary character and sanctity had inspired a movement of spiritual renewal that had spread across Italy and beyond. Unwilling to manage the growing organization, he turned the vicarship of the Friars Minor to Pieto Catani, who soon died, then to Brother Elias. 'Henceforth I am dead to you,' he declared to the friars, and went to live in retreat with his early followers. But he wasn't quite dead; realizing the movement was slipping away from his intentions, he wrote a second Rule (1223) under Pope Honorius III that created the Franciscan order based on poverty as a supreme good, and confirmed it in his testament, urging his friars to remain 'wayfarers and pilgrims in this world'. At Christmas the same year, he reconstructed a manger scene in Greccio (a village just south of Umbria), to emphasize the humble, human, child side of Christ as opposed to the stern arbitrator of the Last Judgement. The Italians were charmed and have been making their Christmas *presepi* ever since.

In the last three years of his life, Francis spent most of his time at the sanctuary of La Verna in Tuscany, where in 1225 he received the stigmata, seeming to confirm his life as a parallel of Christ's. Increasingly frail, he returned to Assisi a year later to meet his good Sister Death at age 44.

Within two years he was canonized by Gregory IX, who as Cardinal Ugolino had been his friend and one of the Order's first protectors. Gregory also did much to diffuse Francis' dangerous legacy by declaring that his testament was not binding, and by directing the Franciscans down the path of the other new preaching order of the 13th century, the Dominicans. Huge churches, urban convents, university education, rich donations to be 'used' by the property-less friars soon came into being, explained away as being necessary for the times. The Order split into the 'Conventuals', who agreed, and the 'Spirituals', who wanted to hold on to their founder's prescription of poverty, the extremists going off on paths of esoteric mysticism that might have appalled Francis as much as his order's prosperity.

For the average Italian in the streets, though, these intermural disputes took nothing away from the humane Christianity of love and charity exemplified by Francis and preached by his friars. His native Assisi quickly became a place of pilgrimage, and his native land was well on its way to becoming *Umbria mistica*.

Trends in Taste

I took a quick walk through the city to see the Duomo and the Battistero. Once more, a completely new world opened up before me, but I did not wish to stay long. The location of the Boboli Gardens is marvellous. I hurried out of the city as quickly as I entered it.

Goethe, on Florence in *Italian Journey*

Goethe, father of the Italian Grand Tour, en route from Venice to Rome, had little time for the city that likes to call itself 'the Capital of Culture'. Like most travellers in the 18th and early 19th centuries, he knew nothing of Giotto, Masaccio, Botticelli or Piero della Francesca; it was Roman statues that wowed him, the very same ones the modern visitor to the Uffizi passes without a second glance. Shelley filled pages on his visits to the museum without mentioning a single painting.

Some Tuscan attractions never change – the Leaning Tower, Michelangelo's *David*, the villas, gardens and cheap wine. Others have gone through an amazing rise or fall in popularity, thanks in part to John Ruskin, whose *Mornings in Florence* brought to light the charms of the Romanesque architecture, Giotto, and the masters of the trecento; he considered Orcagna the master of them all (but in the 18th century, the Giottos in Santa Croce were whitewashed, while many works of Orcagna had been destroyed earlier, by Vasari). Botticelli went from total obscurity in the 18th century to become the darling of the Victorians. Livorno and Viareggio on the coast, and Bagni di Lucca near the Garfagnana, once hosted thriving English colonies.

But Tuscany itself was very different then; it was where they played *pallone*, somewhere between lawn tennis and *jai alai*; where a herd of 150 camels, introduced by Grand Duke Ferdinand II in 1622, roamed the Pisan park of San Rossore; where, as Robert and Elizabeth Browning found, the rent for a *palazzo* was laughably cheap.

But it's the story of the Venus de' Medici that is perhaps most instructive. The statue is a pleasant, if unremarkable, Greek work of the 2nd century BC, but for two centuries it was Florence's chief attraction; visitors rushed to gaze upon her; those prone to write gushed rapturously of her perfect beauty. Napoleon kidnapped her for France, asking the great neoclassical sculptor Canova to sculpt a replacement; later she was one of the things Florence managed to reclaim, though her reign was soon undermined – Ruskin called her an 'uninteresting little person'. Since then she has stood forlornly in the Uffizi's Tribunale, unnoticed and unloved.

Some things don't change. More than 100 years after Goethe's tour, Aldous Huxley had no time for Florence, either: 'We came back through Florence and the spectacle of that second-rate provincial town with its repulsive Gothic architecture and its acres of Christmas card primitives made me almost sick. The only points about Florence are the country outside it, the Michelangelo tombs, Brunelleschi's dome, and a few rare pictures. The rest is simply dung when compared to Rome.'

Tuscany on Wheels

Tuscans have always loved a parade, and to the casual reader of Renaissance history, it seems they're forever proceeding somewhere or another, even to their own detriment – during outbreaks of plague, holy companies would parade through an afflicted area, invoking divine mercy, while in effect aiding the spread of the pestilence. They also had a great weakness for allegorical parade floats. During the centuries of endless war, each Tuscan city rolled out its *carroccio*, invented by a Milanese bishop in the 11th century. Drawn by six white oxen, this was a kind of holy ship of state in a haycart; a mast held up a crucifix while a battle standard flew from the yardarm, there was an altar for priests to say Mass during the battle and a large bell with which to send signals over the din to the armies. The worst possible outcome of a battle was to lose one's *carroccio* to the enemy, as Fiesole did to Florence. One, in Siena, is still in operation, rumbling out twice a year for the Palio.

Medieval clerical processions, by the time of Dante, became melded with the idea of the Roman 'triumph' (*trionfo*); in Purgatory, the poet finds Beatrice triumphing with a cast of characters from the Apocalypse. Savonarola wrote of a *Triumph of the Cross*; Petrarch and Boccaccio wrote allegorical triumphs of virtues, love and death. More interesting are the secular Roman-style Triumphs staged by the Medici, especially at Carnival (the name, according to Burckhardt, comes from a cart, the pagan *carrus navalis*, the ship of Isis, launched every 5 March to symbolize the reopening of navigation). You can get a hint of their splendour from the frescoes at Poggio a Caiano; the best artists of the day were commissioned to design the decorations. The last relics of these parades are the huge satirical carnival floats at Viareggio. A lovely memory of Florence's processions remains in Gozzoli's fairytale frescoes in the chapel of the Medici palace, of the annual procession staged by the Compagnia de' Re Magi, the most splendid and aristocratic of pageants.

Umbria's Totem Tubers

Umbria's most valuable cash crop has neither seeds nor a planting season, and adamantly refuses to grow in straight rows. An aura of mystery surrounds its very nature; according to legend, it is spawned by lightning bolts flickering among the oaks. Truffles – *tartufi* – are the crop, and although they look a lot like granulated mud on your pasta, these earthy, aromatic and aphrodisiac tubers, actually a weird type of fungi, are the most prized gourmet delicacy in Italy.

Even in their natural state they aren't much to look at, bulbous lumps from the size of a pea to a baby's fist, and they're very picky about where they grow. Umbria is one of their favourite spots – here are the proper calcareous soils, oak and beech forests and exposures, especially around Spoleto, Norcia, and particularly in the Valnerina around Scheggino. This is the realm of the highest-quality black truffle (*tuber melangosporum Vittadini*); within Europe, they grow here, around Périgord in France, and almost nowhere else. The rarer white truffle (*tuber magnatum Pico*), mostly from Piedmont, deigns to grow around Gubbio, and is avidly sought from October to December. The black truffle season is longer, extending into March.

Out of season you can find them bottled in oil (never buy fresh except in season), but they are absolutely heavenly when fresh from the ground and offer a perfectly legitimate reason for visiting Umbria in the off season (serious fans might want to aim for the gastronomic February fair in Norcia).

Except for saffron, truffles are the most expensive comestible in the world. Prices for a good white truffle can reach a staggering €2,700 a kilo; the black truffles are half as much but still make a dent in the pocketbook. Not only do they stubbornly resist cultivation, they're fiendishly hard to track down. The vast majority are still brought to market by secretive truffle hunters and their trained hounds, who learn to love the scent as pups because of the truffle juice rubbed around their mother's teats. They are gathered at night, when the truffles smell strongest, or perhaps because the best truffles are always on someone else's land. Truffle-hunting requires a dog, a special digging implement (*vanghetta*) and a licence. And competition can be deadly – the 1997 season was marred in Umbria by a psycho truffle-dog poisoner. Fortunately, a little *tartufo* goes a long way, and Italians will travel far to look, dreamy-eyed, at glass jars of them at Umbria's truffle fairs.

Profits are such that imitations have made considerable headway. Beware of synthesized truffle aromas, which are nothing like the real thing, or cheap low-grade black truffles imported from China that lack the pungent, aromatic intensity of the Umbrian-grown. And you'd do well to steer clear of one local truffle product – the nubby black bottles of Tartufo liqueur, which tastes as vile as it looks.

After the Earthquakes: Art versus People

According to geologists, the quakes that jolted Umbria and the Marches twice on 26 September 1997, killing 11 and wounding many more, and the aftershocks that continued through 1998, were merely part of a million-year-old trend as the Apennines adjust to fit their crust. The 100,000 people in Umbria and the Marches whose homes were rendered uninhabitable didn't find much comfort in this long-range scientific perspective. Luckily, the government responded quickly, and by Christmas 1997 everyone was housed as close to their villages as possible, in rental accommodation, prefab housing or, as a last resort, shipping containers fitted with doors, windows, room dividers, and soon with electricity and plumbing. People got on with their lives relatively quickly, and soon the skylines of the hilltowns were dominated by cranes and scaffolding.

Quakes are not uncommon in the region, but this one grabbed the world's attention because it gravely damaged one of Italy's most precious and best-loved treasures: the Basilica di San Francesco in Assisi. Billions of lire poured in from the state, charities and other sources to restore art, with priority given to a 'Jubilee list' of art and monuments on the official pilgrimage route, but nearly a third of the 1998 budget went to the big basilica; in Assisi everyone vowed it would reopen by Christmas 1999 and it did – an impressive feat.

Yet even by mid 2000, some people in Assisi were still living in a 'container village' on the outskirts. Less famous towns sometimes had two or three container villages; the worst-hit places were all but abandoned. Plenty of money was available for restoration, but a huge amount (in some cases, half of a town's allotted sum) went to pay for the countless permits, licences and opinions by state experts required even before the real work could begin.

According to the Regione Umbria report (*www.regione.umbria.it/ricostruzione*), the containers are now all gone, and 85% of inhabitants of the region are back in their houses, including buildings badly damaged by the quake. The rest live in replacement flats provided by the government or related institutions, or in independently found accommodation.The second phase of reconstruction, still to be completed and involving 'non-priority interventions', still requires funds, most of which will be spent on private housing.

So was art given precedence over people in Umbria? In many cases the answer is yes, though the result isn't as cold and heartless as it may sound. Tourism is a major source of income in Umbria, and 1998 was an economic disaster for the area because tourists kept away, mainly because so many sights were closed. Repairing and reopening major attractions benefited everybody. And all kinds of restoration projects on buildings not directly damaged by the quakes have been undertaken, on buildings and art that otherwise would have been left to slowly crumble. Local authorities have benefited from the influx of expert restorers and money, and from a heightened focus of attention on 'Art' in Umbria. Many things are in a much better state than they would have been had the quake never happened. Assisi is a particular example: the restoration has been so spectacular that those buildings will be in better condition than for hundreds of years. Even the priceless frescoes inside the Basilica di San Francesco may shine again. On that note, at least in the long-range view of things, the disaster may have been a blessing in disguise.

Answers to 'A Florentine Puzzle' (p.40)

1 **Façade of San Miniato**
2 **Baptistry, interior apse**
3 **Windows at rear of San Iacopo sopr'Arno, visible from Santa Trínita**
4 **Windows, Orsanmichele**
5 **Façade, Santa Croce (inspired by Orcagna's tabernacle in Orsanmichele)**
6 **Baptistry doors (Pisano's and Ghiberti's first set); portico of the Bigallo, interior apse, S. Croce**
7 **Loggia dei Lanzi**
8 **Rucellai Chapel, San Pancrazio**

Food and Drink

04

Eating and drinking are two of the great delights of travelling in central Italy, with plenty of variety and excellent prime ingredients. Regional traditions in Tuscany, Umbria and the Marches are strong, to the point where you you sometimes wish they weren't – especially in the case of bread, which they resolutely refuse to add salt to. Tuscans are the *mangiafagioli*, or bean-eaters of Italy; some say this is part of their austere character, others another sign of the Tuscany's alleged miserliness. Umbria and the Marches, historically poor areas, never had a choice, but it's their very *cucina povera* that is so good for you, generally using only a little meat, fresh vegetables, grains and pulses, prepared with some of the best olive oil in the world.

Regional Specialities

Tuscany

Genuine Tuscan cooking is on the whole simple – calculated, as Tuscans will tell you, to bring out the glories of their wine. For *primo*, the Tuscan relies mostly on soups. Perhaps most traditional is *ribollita* ('reboiled'), made with chunks of yesterday's bread, beans, black cabbage and other vegetables.

In summer look for *pappa al pomodoro*, another bread-based soup with tomatoes, basil and olive oil, and *panzanella*. a 'bread salad' of soaked stale bread, tomatoes, onions, basil, garlic and olive oil. Originally a one-course meal, *acqua cotta* is made by adding boiling water and tomatoes to sautéed veg, eggs and *pecorino* cheese; Livorno is famous for *cacciucco*, a heavenly fish soup. Other first courses include *pappardelle alla lepre* (wide egg noodles with a sauce of stewed hare) and *pici* (thick spaghetti), often served '*all'aglione*' – with a garlic and tomato sauce. In Lucca look for *tortelli* – golden pasta parcels filled with spicy meat and topped with a rich *ragù*.

Tuscan bean classics include *fagioli al fiasco* (with oil and black pepper simmered in an earthenware pot), *fagioli all'uccelletto* (with garlic and tomatoes), and *zuppa di farro* (borlotti bean soup with spelt, a form of wheat going back to the Etruscans, now popular throughout all three regions). Tuscany's tastiest cheese is ewe's milk *pecorino*; the best is from around Pienza, grated over pasta dishes when aged.

Restaurant Generalities

Breakfast (*colazione*) is no lingering affair but an early-morning wake-up shot to the brain: a *cappuccino*, a *caffè latte*, or a *caffè lungo*, accompanied by a croissant (*cornetto*) or similar. This essential caffeine and sugar fuel can be consumed in any bar and repeated as often as necessary.

Lunch (*pranzo*), served around 1pm, is the most important meal of the day in rural areas, with a minimum of a first course (both or either *antipasti* or *primo piatto* – pasta dish, soup or risotto), a second (*secondo piatto* – meat or fish, plus a *contorno* or side dish), followed by fruit or dessert. In towns, however, where office workers (and tourists) don't want to spend a couple of hours at the table, bars serve simple first courses or *panini*.

Dinner (*cena*) is usually eaten from 8pm onwards, although many Italians wouldn't dream of showing up before 10pm.

The old hierarchy of **restaurants** – *ristorante*, *trattoria*, *osteria* and *vino e cucina* – has been confused of late, though on the whole a *ristorante* is the most formal, a *vino e cucina* the most simple. Many offer a *menu turistico* – full, set meals of usually meagre inspiration for a reasonable price; others, with culinary ambitions, often offer a set-price *menu degustazione* – a 'tasting menu' of the chef's specialities.

Deluxe Virgins

Some day, on a trip to one of the fancier Italian food shops, you may pause near the section devoted to condiments and wonder at the beautiful display of bottles of unusually dark whiskies and wines, with corks and elegant labels – why, some is even DOC, though much is far more costly than the usual DOC vintages. A closer look reveals these precious bottles to be full of nothing but olive oil. Admittedly, *olio extra vergine di oliva* from Tuscany and Umbria makes a fine salad dressing – according to those in the know, the oil of the Chianti brooks few rivals, Italian or otherwise. Its delicate, fruity fragrance derives from the excellent quality of the ripe olive and the low acidity extracted from the fruit without any refinements. The finest, Extra Virgin, must have less than 1% acidity (the best has 0.5% acidity). Other designations are Soprafino Virgin, Fine Virgin, and Virgin (each may have up to 4% acidity) in descending order of quality.

As any Italian will tell you, it's good for you – and it had better be, because Tuscan or Umbrian chefs have put it in nearly every dish for centuries. The only difference is that it now comes in a fancy package at a fancy price, a victim of the Italian designer label syndrome and Tuscan preciosity. Not only does the oil have corks, but the trend in the early 1990s was for some of the smarter restaurants to offer an olive oil list similar to a wine list – one restaurant in Tuscany even had an oil sommelier. Many of these, perhaps fortunately, seem to have gone out of business.

Grilled meats, salad and roast potatoes are typical *secondi*, reaching an epiphany in the *bistecca alla fiorentina*, a large thick steak on the bone, cut from loin of beef and cooked over coals, served charred on the outside and pink inside, seasoned with salt and black pepper. Adventurous souls in Florence can try *cibreo* (cockscombs with chicken livers, beans and egg yolks). Tuscan tempura, *fritto misto*, can be divine: the classic version uses lamb chops, liver, sweetbreads, artichokes and courgettes. Other specialities are *arista di maiale* (pork loin with rosemary and garlic), *francesina* (meat, onion and tomato stewed in Vernaccia di San Gimignano), and *anatra* (duck).

It's fairly easy to find seafood as far inland as Florence – one traditional dish is *seppie in zimino*, or cuttlefish simmered with beets. Good Tuscan vegetable dishes are *piselli alla fiorentina*, peas cooked with olive oil, parsley and diced bacon; *tortino di carciofi*, a delicious omelette with fried artichokes; and *spinaci saltati* – fresh spinach sautéed with garlic and olive oil.

Typical sweets include Siena's *panforte* (a dense cake full of nuts and candied fruit), *castagnaccio* (chestnut cake,with pine nuts, raisins and rosemary), Florentine *zuccotto* (a cake of chocolate, nuts and candied fruits) and *biscottini di Prato* (almond biscuits).

Umbria

Umbrian cooking stands out from the Tuscan for its generous use of its black truffles (*tartufi*). In season (Oct–Feb), these are delicious when grated fresh on pasta and meat dishes, or when cooked with eggs, which requires expert timing. Umbrian pork butchers, especially those from Norcia, are considered the best in Italy, and are celebrated for their *salumi* (dried meats such as *pancetta*, *coppa* and *prosciutto* of pork or wild boar), salami, *capocollo* and so on, sold in shops across Umbria called *norcineria*. A platter of *salumi* forms a perfect starter, served with *torta al testa*, traditional flat bread cooked over the fire on a *testa*, an old fashioned disc-shaped griddle; you can also find *torta al testa* stuffed with cheese, olives, spinach, rocket or ham. On the subject of pork, at some point try the classic Umbrian snack, available in markets and at roadside stands – a hard roll filled with fat slices of *porchetta* (roast whole pig stuffed with fennel and garlic).

Umbrians love their pasta. The local favourite is fat, home-made spaghetti (*ciriole* or *pici* or *strangozzi*) with various sauces, with wild asparagus holding pride of place in spring and *porcini* mushrooms and truffles in autumn. In northern Umbria look for *baggiana*, a soup of fava beans, tomatoes and basil, and *strascinati*, home-made macaroni served with sausage, eggs and cheese. The region is famous for its tiny multicoloured lentils, grown in and around Castelluccio, which are quite meaty and tasty and feature in delicious soups. Grilled lamb chops (*scorttaditta* – 'burn the fingers') is a classic trattoria *secondo*; in season pigeon and boar dishes are worth a try as well. In Umbria seafood is rare, although you can usually get trout and crayfish, and lake fish near Trasimeno.

Popular Umbrian sweets you might sample include *crostate* (fruit tarts), a *gelato ai Baci* (ice cream made with Perugia's famous hazelnut chocolates) and the lovely light biscuits known as *brutti ma buoni* ('ugly but good'). In Assisi, many shops sell *rocciata*, a spicy strudel filled with a mixture of almonds, walnuts, prunes, figs, raisins and honey.

The Marches

The Marches, once the breadbox of Rome, is a great pasta region. A classic holiday dish is *vincigrassi*, a kind of lasagne with chicken giblets, sweetbreads, mushrooms and Parmesan. Ascoli Piceno is famous for its *olive all'ascolane* – big green olives stuffed with Parmesan and veal and deep-fried, sold across Italy but best here.

By the coast, look for lobster, oysters, mussels, spider crabs and more. Specialities include *brodetto*, a stew with a dozen types of fish; *ravioli ai filetti di sogliola* (ravioli filled with ricotta, with a sauce of sole, white wine and tomatoes), and *stoccafisso*, cod dried on Norway's coast and mixed with potatoes – Ancona is famous for it.

Like Umbria, the Marches are proud of their *salumi* and also of *ciasuscolo*, a kind of pâté made with fennel, garlic and orange zest. Classic *secondi* include *anatra in porchetta* (stuffed duck) and *pollo in potacchio* (chicken braised in white wine). White truffles grow in the north around Urbino, where natives make *casciotta* cheese (yellow, with tiny holes, tasty with a slice of grilled polenta) and *formaggio di fossa*, a rich amber cheese matured in stone pits for three months, originally to hide it from the marauding armies that passed through; it's delicious with honey.

Wine

The first person to really celebrate Tuscan wines was naturalist Francesco Redi in the 1600s. Like many of us he made a wine tour of the region, then he composed a dithyrambic eulogy, *Bacchus in Tuscany*. Modern Bacchuses in Tuscany, Umbria and the Marches will find treats in the vineyards, cellars and *enoteche* (wine shops/bars).

Tuscany

Tuscany means Sangiovese (or Brunello), the main varietal in nearly all its DOC wines, including some of Italy's noblest reds: Brunello di Montalcino and Vino Nobile di Montepulciano, and Chianti Classico, in which Sangiovese Piccolo (or Sangioveto) is the main varietal in the blend, which also includes white malvasia.

The biggest development has been Super Tuscans – reds that don't follow the DOC rules and yield ripe., full-bodied (and very expensive) wines that have caused a sensation (*see* p.203). Try Flaccianello (Fontodi), a true Tuscan wine.

Some of the most spectacular vineyards in Italy are planted with an indigenous Tuscan grape from Massa, Masseretta (or Barsaglina Nera) that grows on terraces cut into the Apuan Alps where no tractors can reach. Currently an IGT wine, it ages well in oak and is considered one of the most promising in the region.

Lesser-known DOC reds include a dry, bright red, Rosso delle Colline Lucchesi, from the hills north of Lucca; the hearty Pomino Rosso, from Rufina in the Mugello; Carmignano, a ruby red produced just west of Florence; and Morellino di Scansano, from the hills south of Grosseto. The three other DOC reds from the coast are Parrina Rosso, from Parrina near Orbetello, Montescudaio Rosso, and Elba Rosso, a happy island wine, little of which makes it to the mainland.

Of the Tuscan whites, the most notable is Vernaccia di San Gimignano (also a *Riserva*), dry and golden in colour, the perfect complement to seafood; others are dry Montecarlo from the hills east of Lucca, and Candia dei Colli Apuani, a light wine from mountains of marble near Carrara. From the coast comes Bolgheri, while Cortona and its valley produce Bianco Vergine Valdichiana, a fresh and lively wine; from the hills around Montecatini comes the golden, dry Bianco della Valdinievole. Bianco di Pitigliano is a celebrated accompaniment to lobster.

Umbria

Umbria has been a wine region ever since the Etruscans planted the first cuttings from the Greeks. Its most famous wine is probably Orvieto and Orvieto Classico, a delicate wine, dry with a slightly bitter aftertaste; Orvieto Classico comes from the zona around the Paglia river. The area around Montefalco also produces three fine reds: Rosso (made from Sangiovese), inky-dark native Umbrian Sagrantino, with the aroma of blackberries (considered by many Umbria's top wine), and the sweet but increasingly rare Sagrantino Passito, made from raisins.

The other DOC wines of Umbria come in all three shades and are grown on the western hills of the region: the Colli del Trasimeno; Colli Perugini; Colli Amerini (Amelia region); and Colli Altotiberini. Those of Torgiano, made of Montepulciano

Wine Speak

Italian wines are named after the grape and district they come from. DOC (*Denominazione di Origine Controllata*) means that the wine comes from a defined area and was produced according to a certain traditional method; DOCG (the G stands for *Garantita*) means a high quality is also guaranteed. A new classification, IGT (*Indicazione Geografica Tipica*), was invented for the quality Super Tuscans (*see* p.203), but some of these producers still prefer to be labelled *vino da tavola* (VDT), which can refer to either a simple quaffing wine or a great wine that doesn't follow the rules. *Classico* means that a wine comes from the oldest part of the zone of production; *Riserva*, or *Superiore*, means a wine has been aged longer.

Tuscans and Umbrians also make lush, perfumed *vinsanto* from semi-dried white grapes that they press in February and age for a minimum of three years but often a lot longer, creating a dessert wine that can be honeylike or almost dry. Traditionally a wine made in small quantities in very old casks coated with generations of wild yeasts (the *madre*), it was 'the wine of hospitality' that a family would serve to guests; now you can buy it in shops, but it doesn't come cheap.

grapes and the central Italian varietal Ciliegolo, are dry, full-bodied reds that can take years of ageing, and a light and lively *bianco*. One of the more unusual wines is the red dessert wine Vernaccia di Cannara.

The Marches

The hills of the Marches conveniently produce a range of DOC white wines to accompany the day's catch. The dry and delicate Verdicchio from the Jesi district and Matelica is the best known, and pale enough to mistake for water; the best is Verdicchio dei Castelli di Jesi Classico. Falerio dei Colli Ascolani is a dry Trebbiano Toscano wine, as is the pleasant Bianco dei Colli Maceratesi. Pinkish-gold Biancame grapes form the base for Bianchello del Metauro, from the coast of Pesaro and hills along the Metauro river.

The red wines from the Marches include the fruity ruby Lacrima di Morro D'Alba, Sangiovese dei Colli Pesaresi, wonderful Rosso Conero (made from Montepulciano and Sangiovese) and Rosso Piceno, a Sangiovese wine produced above Ascoli Piceno. If you can find it, try Vernaccia di Serrapetrona, a naturally sparkling red wine that is grown in a tiny area near Serrapetrona.

Italian Menu Reader

General

aceto (***balsamico***) vinegar (balsamic)
affumicato smoked
aglio garlic
alla brace on embers
bicchiere glass
burro butter
cacciagione game
costoletta/cotoletta chop
coltello knife
cucchiaio spoon
forchetta fork
forno oven
fritto fried
ghiaccio ice
griglia grill
in bianco without tomato
magro lean meat/pasta without meat
marmellata jam
menta mint
miele honey
mostarda candied mustard sauce
olio oil
pane bread
panna cream
pepe pepper
piatto plate
prezzemolo parsley
ripieno stuffed
rosmarino rosemary
sale salt
salmi wine marinade
salvia sage
senape mustard
tavola table
tazza cup
tovagliolo napkin
umido cooked in sauce
uovo egg
zucchero sugar

Antipasti

bresaola dried raw meat
bruschetta toast with toppings
carciofi (***sott'olio***) artichokes (in oil)
carpaccio thinly sliced raw beef
crostini toast spread with chicken liver paste
funghi (***trifolati***) mushrooms (with anchovies, garlic and lemon)
mozzarella (***in carrozza***) mozzarella cheese (fried with bread in batter)
prosciutto (***con melone***) raw ham (with melon)
salumi cured sausages, salami, etc.

Minestre (Soups) and Pasta

agnolotti ravioli with meat
cacciucco spiced fish soup
cappelletti small ravioli, often in broth
crespelle crêpes
frittata omelette
gnocchi potato dumplings
minestra di verdura thick vegetable soup
minestrone with meat, vegetables and pasta
pappardelle alla lepre pasta with hare sauce
pastina in brodo tiny pasta in broth
spaghetti al pomodoro with tomato sauce
spaghetti al sugo/ragù with meat sauce
spaghetti alle vongole with clam sauce
stracciatella broth with eggs and cheese
zuppa di farro spelt and bean soup

Carne (Meat)

abbacchio milk-fed lamb
agnello lamb
anatra duck
animelle sweetbreads
arista pork loin
arrosto misto mixed roast meats
bistecca beef steak
bollito misto stew of boiled meats
braciola chop
brasato di manzo braised beef with veg
capretto kid
capriolo roebuck
carne di castrato/suino mutton/pork
cassoeula pork stew with cabbage
cervello brains
cervo venison
cinghiale boar
coniglio rabbit
cotoletta veal cutlet
  alla Milanese fried in breadcrumbs
fagiano pheasant
faraona guinea fowl
lepre (***in salmi***) hare (marinated in wine)
lombo di maiale pork loin
lumache snails
maiale (***al latte***) pork (cooked in milk)
manzo beef
osso buco braised veal knuckle
pernice partridge
petto di pollo chicken breast
piccione pigeon
pizzaiola beef steak in tomato and oregano
pollo chicken
polpette meatballs
quaglie quails
rognoni kidneys
salsicce sausages
scaloppine thin slices of veal sautéed in butter
spezzatino pieces of beef/veal, usually stewed
spiedino meat on a skewer/stick
stufato beef and vegetables braised in wine
tacchino turkey
tagliata steak slices, served with rocket and Parmesan
trippa tripe
uccelletti small birds on a skewer
vitello veal

Pesce (Fish)

acciughe or ***alici*** anchovies
anguilla eel
aragosta lobster
baccalà dried salt cod
bonito small tuna
branzino seabass
calamari squid
capesante scallops
cefalo grey mullet
coda di rospo angler fish
cozze mussels
datteri di mare razor (or date) mussels
dentice dentex (perch-like fish)
dorato gilthead
fritto misto mixed fried delicacies, mainly fish
gamberetti shrimp
gamberi (***di fiume***) prawns (crayfish)
granchio crab
insalata di mare seafood salad
merluzzo cod
orata bream
ostriche oysters
pesce azzurro various small fish
pesce di San Pietro John Dory
pesce spada swordfish
polipi/polpi octopus
rombo turbot
sarde sardines
seppie cuttlefish
sgombro mackerel
sogliola sole
stoccafisso wind-dried cod
tonno tuna
triglia red mullet (rouget)
trota trout
trota salmonata salmon trout
vongole small clams
zuppa di pesce fish soup or stew

Contorni (Side Dishes, Vegetables)

asparagi asparagus
carciofi (***alla giudea***) artichokes (deep-fried)
cardi cardoons/thistles
carote carrots
cavolfiore cauliflower
cavolo (***nero***) cabbage (Tuscan kale)
ceci chickpeas (garbanzo beans)
cetriolo cucumber
cipolla onion
fagioli white beans
fagiolini French (green) beans
fave broad beans (fava beans)
finocchio fennel
funghi (***porcini***) mushrooms (boletus)
insalata (***mista/verde***) salad (mixed/green)
lattuga lettuce
lenticchie lentils
melanzane aubergine (eggplant)
patate (***fritte***) potatoes (fried)
peperoncini hot chilli peppers
peperoni sweet peppers
piselli (***al prosciutto***) peas (with ham)
pomodoro(***i***) tomato(es)
porri leeks
radicchio red chicory
radice radish
rucola rocket (arugula)

sedano celery
spinaci spinach
tartufi truffles
verdure greens
zucca pumpkin
zucchini courgettes

Formaggio (Cheese)

cacio/caciocavallo pale yellow, sharp cheese
caprino goats' cheese
gorgonzola soft blue cheese
groviera mild cheese (Gruyère)
pecorino sheeps' cheese
provolone sharp, tangy;
dolce is less strong

Frutta (Fruit, Nuts)

albicocche apricots
ananas pineapple
arance oranges
banane bananas
cachi persimmon
ciliege cherries
cocomero watermelon
datteri dates
fichi figs
fragole strawberries
lamponi raspberries
limone lemon
macedonia di frutta fruit salad
mandarino tangerine
mandorle almonds
melagrana pomegranate
mele apples
mirtilli bilberries
more blackberries
nespola medlar fruit
nocciole hazelnuts
noci walnuts
pera pear
pesca peach
pesca noce nectarine
pinoli pine nuts
pompelmo grapefruit
prugna/susina prune plum
uva grapes

Dolci (Desserts)

amaretti macaroons
crema caramella crème caramel
crostata fruit tart
gelato ice cream
monte bianco chestnut pudding with cream
panettone sponge cake with dried fruit
panforte dense cake of chocolate, almonds and preserved fruit
semifreddo heavily chilled mousse cake
sorbetto sorbet
torrone nougat
torta cake/tart
zabaglione eggs whisked with Marsala wine
zuppa inglese trifle

Bevande (Beverages)

acqua minerale mineral water
con/senza gas sparkling/still
aranciata orange soda
birra (***alla spina***) beer (draught)
caffè (***freddo***) coffee (iced)
cioccolata chocolate
gassosa lemon-flavoured soda
latte (***intero/scremato***) milk (whole/skimmed)
succo di frutta fruit juice
tè tea

Planning Your Trip

05

When to Go

Climate

The climate in Tuscany, Umbria and the Marches is temperate along the coasts and in the valleys, and cooler up in the mountains; the higher Apennines and Monte Amiata have enough snow for **skiing** until April. **Summers** are hot and humid; in August Italians head for the sea or mountains. **Spring**, especially May, when it rains less, is pleasantly warm. **Autumn**, too, is a classic time to visit; in October and November, before the rains, while the air is clear, the colours of the scenery are brilliant and rare. The hills of Tuscany and Umbria are never less than beautiful but in October they're extraordinary – and it's the **truffle season**. **Winter** can be agreeable for visiting indoor city attractions without the crowds, particularly in Florence, where it seldom snows but may rain for days at a time.

Umbria is not called the 'Green Heart of Italy' for nothing: it can be hung over with mists for weeks on end, which, depending on how one looks at it, can be terribly romantic or a big bore. The mountains, especially the Apuan Alps along the coast, also get a lot of rain (80–120mm a year).

Average Maximum Temperatures in °C/°F

	April	July	Oct
Ancona	14/56)	25/77	17/62
Florence	13/55	25/77	16/60
Livorno	5/59	24/75	15/59
Siena	12/54	25/77	15/59
Perugia	11/52	24/75	13/55
Terni	13/55	25/77	15/59

Average Monthly Rainfall in Millimetres (Inches)

	April	July	Oct
Ancona	57/2	28/1	101/4
Florence	74/3	23/1	96/4
Livorno	62/3	7/0.25	110/4
Siena	61/3	21/1	112/4
Perugia	70/3	30/1	115/4
Terni	85/3	43/2	123/5

Festivals

Some festivals in Tuscany, Umbria and the Marches are clearly meant to pull the tourists in, or are just an excuse to hang out under the stars, but this doesn't make them any less fun. The several exceptions to this rule will generally add a note of pageantry or culture to your holiday. Some are great costume affairs, with roots dating back to the Middle Ages, and there are quite a few music festivals, antiques fairs, and most of all, festivals devoted to food and drink. The box below has a calendar of the major events. There are countless others, especially in summer months; look out for banners and ask around when you arrive.

National Holidays

See p.74.

Calendar of Events

January

1st Sun of month Feast of the Gift, the mayor's donation of gold, frankincense and myrrh, Castiglione di Garfagnana.

24 Feast of San Feliciano, procession with a traditional fair, Foligno.

27 Feast of Sant'Emiliano, with a procession of lights, Trevi (Perugia).

February

Carnival is fêted in private parties nearly everywhere; Viareggio has a huge public one with floats, music and parades. Fano, on the Adriatic, has a contemporary carnival with music, dancing and costume parades, while traditional celebrations take place in Ascoli Piceno. In Bibbiena, the last day of Carnival is celebrated with a grand dance and massive bonfire. On the penultimate Sunday of Carnival, Spello has a bruschetta festival with an olive-pickers' parade and garlic toast feast.

5 Procession of Sant'Agata, San Marino: a celebration of independence regained in 1740.

14 St Valentine's Day, with a fair, fireworks and music, Terni (plus romantic concerts all month).

March

18–19 Pancake festival, Montefioralle, near Greve-in-Chianti; San Giuseppe (with rice fritters) and Torrita di Siena (donkey race tournament), Siena.

Mar–April International Assembly of Church Choirs, Loreto.

March or April

Holy Week Religious rites, torchlight processions and so forth, Assisi, Loreto and many others; Umbria jazz, gospel and soul festival, Terni.

Holy Thursday Trial of Jesus and re-enactment of Christ's Passion, **Good Friday**, Sigillo (Perugia).

Good Friday Way of the Cross procession, Grassina, near Florence; procession of the Dead Christ, Gubbio, and Bevagna (Perugia).

Easter Easter morning, *Scoppio del Carro*, 11am explosion of the cart in Florence (*see* p.167); Mary's girdle displayed from Prato's pulpit.

1st Sun after Easter Kite Festival, San Miniato.

April

2 Palio of the Golden Frog, Fermignano (Pesaro), with a race, flag-tossing and costumed parade.

First 3wks Huge antiques fair, Todi.**April–May** Cantamaggio, parade of illuminated floats, Terni.

April–May Corso dell'Anello, medieval Tournament of the Ring, Narni.

Early May Calendimaggio, Assisi.

30 April–5 May Feast of San Pelligrino, Gualdo Tadino (Perugia).

Late April/May

Ascension Day Cricket Festival, with floats and crickets sold in little cages, Florence.

May

All month Iris festivals, Florence, San Polo Robbiana (Chianti).

1st Sun Donkey *palio*, Querceta, near Lucca

1st–3rd wk Sword derring-do and *palio*, Camerino (Macerata).

15 Corsa dei Ceri, race of tower shrines, Gubbio.

4th Sun Historical parade and crossbow tournament, Massa Marittima.

Last Sun Crossbow competition vs Sansepolcro, Gubbio; crossbow competition, wine festival and cart processions at Montespertoli.

May and June Maggio Musicale Fiorentino music festival, Florence.

May or June

Pentecost Festival of the Piceni, celebrating the history of the Marches, Monterubbiano (Ascoli Piceno); La Palombella, Orvieto.

June

2 Festa della Repubblica.

Early June Corpus Domini processions, Orvieto; flower carpets in the streets, Spello; street parade on sawdust designs, Camaiore (Lucca).

2nd Sun Bruschetta festival, Montecatini Terme.

Mid-June–Aug Estate Fiesolana – music, films, ballet and theatre, Fiesole.

Mid-June Giostro della Quintana, medieval joust, Foligno.

16–17 Festa di San Ranieri – lights festival and historic regatta in Pisa.

3rd Sun Festa del Barbarossa, celebrating the meeting of the pope and emperor, with ballet, archery, snails, beans and *pici*, San Quirico d'Orcia.

3rd Sun Palio di Rioni, neighbourhood horserace, Castiglion Fiorentina.

24 St John the Baptist's Day, with fireworks, Florence; Calcio in Costume, Renaissance football game, Florence (2 other games this month).

Last Sun Gioco del Ponte, a traditional tug-of-war on a bridge, with a cart in the middle, Pisa.

Last Sun La Bruscellata, a week of dancing and singing old love songs around a flowering tree, San Donato in Poggio (Florence province).

Last wk Mercato delle Gaite, a medieval fair with archery, Bevagna.

End of June Festival of Two Worlds, Spoleto.

July

All month Umbria Jazz Festival, Perugia.

Every weekend Festa Medioevale, Palazzuolo sul Senio.

1 Versilian Historical Trophy, Querceta (Lucca).

2 Palio, the famous horse race, Siena (also 16 Aug).

2nd Sun Archery contest, Fivizzano (Massa).

3rd Sun Feast of San Paolino, Lucca, a torchlight parade and crossbow contest.

25 Joust of the Bear, Pistoia.

Last wk Elban Wine Festival, Le Ghiaie.

Late July Medieval Festival, Monteriggione, near Siena.

End July–mid-Aug Palio dei Colombi, with costumed crossbowmen freeing doves, Amelia.

July–Aug Concert and theatre festival, San Gimignano; opera, ballet and concerts at the Sferisterio, Macerata; Puccini Opera Festival, Torre del Lago.

August

All month Folklore, religious festivals, Assisi.

Aug–Sept festival of chamber music, Città di Castello.

1st weekend Torneo della Quintana, a 15th-century pageant/joust, Ascoli Piceno; Thanksgiving festival for San Sisto, Pisa.

2nd weekend Battle for the Pail, with four teams in medieval costume trying to get a ball into a well, Sant'Elpidio a Mare (Ascoli Piceno).

2nd Sun Crossbow tournament, Massa Marittima.

14 Palio dei quartieri, flag-tossing and crossbow contest, Gubbio.

15 Beefsteak Festival, Cortona; Palio dell' Assunta, a re-enactment of an 1182 event, with a horserace, Fermo (Asoli Piceno).

16 Palio, dating from 1147, Siena.

2nd Sun Palio Marinaro, boat races, Livorno.

2nd and 3rd wk Rossini Opera Festival, with big-name performers, Pesaro.

15–30 International choir contest, Arezzo.

September

1st Sun Saracen's Joust, Arezzo; Palio dei Cerri between neighbourhoods and Renaissance processions, Cerreto Guidi; lantern festival, Florence.

2nd Sun Giostra della Quintana, jousting, Foligno; crossbow contest with Gubbio, Sansepolcro.

14 Holy Procession in honour of the Volto Santo by torchlight, Lucca.

Mid-Sept Sagra Musicale Umbra, Perugia.

3rd Sun Wine festival, Impruneta; donkey race, Carmignano.

Last weekend Gioche delle Porti, donkey rides and costumed re-enactment of witch-burning, Gualdo Tadino (Perugia).

October

All month Wine/*tartufo* festivals, the Marches.

1st Sun Palio dei Terzieri, historical parade and cart race, Trevi (Perugia).

3–4 Feast of San Francesco, religious and civic rites in honour of Italy's patron saint, Assisi.

November

1–5 All Souls' Fair, Perugia.

11 San Martino, with wine and chestnuts, Sigillo (Perugia).

22 Concerts in honour of Santa Cecilia, Siena.

24 Offering of candles, with processions in 14th-century costume, Amelia (near Terni).

December

8 Fair of the Immaculate Conception, Bagni di Lucca.

9–10 Festa della Venuta, Loreto, celebrating the airborne arrival of the Holy House, with bonfires, religious ceremonies, and a procession.

24 Christmas cribs and Franciscan rites, Assisi; evergreen bonfire, Camporgiano (Lucca).

25–26 St Stephen's feast and display of the holy girdle, Prato.

End Dec–early Jan Umbria Jazz Winter, Orvieto.

Tourist Information

The city/provincial tourist offices (given in the area chapters) often have websites and usually provide lists of villas and farmhouses for rent, plus B&Bs and *agriturismi* (*see* p.68).

For information before you travel, contact the Italian National Tourist Office (*www.italiantourism.com*) in your own country.

Italian Tourist Offices Abroad

UK: Italian State Tourist Board, 1 Princes St, London W1R 8AY, **t** (020) 7408 1254; Italian Embassy, 14 Three King's Yard, Davies St, London W1Y 2EH, **t** (020) 7312 2200, *www.embitaly.org.uk*.

USA: 630 Fifth Ave, Suite 1565, New York, NY 10111, **t** (212) 245 4822; 12400 Wilshire Blvd, Suite 550, Los Angeles, CA 90025, **t** (310) 820 1898; 500 N. Michigan Ave, Suite 2240, Chicago 1 IL 60611, **t** (312) 644 0996.

Australia, Level 4, 46 Market St, Sydney NSW 2000, **t** (02) 92 621666.

Canada: 175 Bloor St East Suite 907, South Tower, Toronto, Ontario, M4W 3R8, **t** (416) 925 4882, *www.italiantourism.com*.

New Zealand: c/o Italian Embassy, 34 Grant Rd, Thorndon, Wellington, **t** (044) 947170.

Information may also be available from **Alitalia** (the national airline) or **CIT** (the state-run travel agency) offices in some countries.

Embassies and Consulates

For a list of **Italian embassies abroad**, see *www.embassyworld.com*.

If you have a choice, use the consulate in Florence if you're staying in Tuscany or the Marches; in Umbria, use the one in Rome.

UK: Via XX Settembre 80a, Rome, **t** 06 4220 0001; Lungarno Corsini 2, Florence, **t** 055 284133.

Ireland: Piazza Campitelli 3, Rome, **t** 06 697 9121.

USA: Via Vittorio Veneto 119a, Rome, **t** 06 46741; Lungarno Amerigo Vespucci 38, Florence, **t** 055 2669 5232.

Canada: Via Zara 30, Rome, **t** 06 445981.

Australia: Via Alessandria 215, Rome, **t** 06 852721.

New Zealand: Via Zara 28, Rome, **t** 06 441 7171.

Entry Formalities

Passports and Visas

To get into Italy you need a valid passport. **EU citizens** do not need visas. Nationals from the **USA**, **Canada**, **Australia** and **New Zealand** do not need visas for stays of up to 90 days. For longer, you must get a *permesso di soggiorno*. For this you need to state your reason for staying and prove both a source of income and medical insurance.

The Italian law states you must register with the police within 8 days of arrival. If you check into a hotel this is done automatically; otherwise you should go to the local police station (in practice few people do this). If you need advice on the forms, call the Rome Police Office for visitors, **t** (06) 4686, ext. 2987.

Customs

EU nationals over 17 can import an unlimited quantity of goods for personal use. Arrivals from non-EU countries have to pass through Italian customs, which are usually benign, unless you're carrying more than 150 cigarettes or 75 cigars, 1 litre of hard liquor or 3 bottles of wine, a couple of cameras, one movie camera, 10 rolls of film for each, one tape-recorder, one radio, one record-player, one canoe less than 5.5m and one TV (though you'll have to pay for a licence for it), or sports equipment not for personal use. Pets must have a bilingual Certificate of Health from your vet. US citizens may return with $400 worth of merchandise – keep your receipts.

There are no limits to the amount of money you may bring into Italy, and no one is likely to check how much you leave with.

Disabled Travellers

Access-for-all laws in Italy have improved the once-dire situation: the number of ramps and stairlifts has increased dramatically in the past decade, and nearly every hotel has one or two rooms with facilities for the disabled, though older ones may not have a lift, or not one large enough for a wheelchair.

Service stations on the *autostrade* have equipped restrooms, but you could get very stuck in the middle of a city – Florence, visited by zillions of tourists, lacks accessible loos. Local tourist offices (listed in the text) are helpful, and may even find someone to give you a hand, while the national tourist office (*see* p.60) can offer tips for difficult hilltowns.

Italian churches are a problem, with their long flights of steps in front.

Disability Organizations

In Italy

Centro Studi Consulenza Invalidi, Via Gozzadini 7, 20148 Milan, **t** 02 4030 8339. Ask for the annual accommodation guide, *Vacanze per Disabili*.

CO.IN (Consorzio Cooperative Integrate), Via Enrico Giglili 54a, 00169 Rome, **t** 800 271027, **t** 06 2326 7504, *www.coinsociale.it/turismo*. The tourist information centre (Mon–Fri 9–5) offers advice and information on accessibility.

In the UK and Ireland

Holiday Care Service, Enham Place, Enham Alamein, Andover SP11 6JS, **t** 0845 124 9971, *www.holidaycare.org.uk*. Information on accommodation, transport, equipment hire, services, tour operators and contacts.

Irish Wheelchair Association, Blackheath Drive, Clontarf, Dublin 3, **t** (01) 818 6400, *www.iwa.ie*. This publishes travel advice guides.

RADAR, 12 City Forum, 250 City Rd, London, EC1V 8AF, **t** (020) 7250 3222, *www.radar.org.uk*. Information and books.

RNIB (Royal National Institute of the Blind), 105 Judd St, London WC1H 9NE, *www.rnib.org.uk*. The mobility unit has a 'Plane Easy' audio-tape with advice for visually impaired flyers, and also advises on finding accommodation.

In the USA and Canada

American Foundation for the Blind, 11 Penn Plaza, Suite 300, New York, NY 10001, **t** (212) 502 7600, *www.afb.org*. Info for visually impaired travellers.

Federation for the Handicapped, 211 West 14th St, New York, NY 10011, **t** (212) 747 4262. Summer tours for members.

SATH (Society for Accessible Travel and Hospitality), 347 5th Ave, Suite 610, New York, NY 10016, **t** (212) 447 7284, *www.sath.org*. Travel and access information. The website has good links and a list of online publications.

Internet Sites

Access-Able Travel Source, *www.access-able.com*. Information for older and disabled travellers.

Access Ability, *www.access-ability.org/travel.html*. Information on travel agencies.

Emerging Horizons, *www.emerginghorizons.com*. An online newsletter for disabled travellers.

Insurance and EHIC Cards

National health services in the UK and Australia have **reciprocal healthcare agreements** with Italy (you need a European Health Insurance or **EHIC card**, which has replaced the old EIII forms; see *www.dh.gov.uk* or pick up a form at a post office), but this only allows for state-provided 'necessary' care, you should also take out your own insurance to cover the gap.

Those from elsewhere should check their current policies to see if they're covered abroad for mishaps such as cancelled flights and lost baggage, and under what circumstances, and judge whether they need an additional policy. Travel agencies sell policies, as well as insurance companies, but they are not cheap. First check whether your credit card company or bank account gives you some kind of cover.

See also **Health and Emergencies**, p.73.

Money

The **euro** is divided into 100 **cents**. There are banknotes in denominations of 5, 10, 20, 50, 100, 200 and 500, and coins in denominations of 1 and 2 euros, and 1, 2, 5, 10, 20 and 50 cents.

You can withdraw cash from most **ATMs**/cash dispensers with any of the common debit or credit cards; your bank may charge a small fee, but it won't work out any more expensive than normal commission rates. It's worth having a backup (e.g. traveller's cheques) in case your card is rejected; bring some euros for when you arrive too..

Credit and debit cards are accepted by most hotels, resort-area restaurants, shops and car-hire firms, although some may take exception to American Express. Italians are wary of plastic, though, and you may be asked for some ID when paying by card.

American Express, Florence: Via Dante Alighieri 22R, off Piazza della Repubblica, **t** 055 50981.

For **banking hours**, *see* p.74.

Getting There

By Air from the UK and Ireland

At the time of writing there are a huge variety of flights from the UK and Ireland to Tuscany, Umbria and the Marches or cities handy for them, many run by low-cost carriers.

From **London Heathrow**, Alitalia and British Airways (BA) fly to Milan Linate, Milan Malpensa and Rome (Fiumicino), and BA also flies to Pisa. From **London Gatwick** Meridiana flies to Florence, BA and Thomsonfly to Pisa, BA and Ethiopian Airlines to Rome (Fiumicino), and easyJet to Rome (Ciampino), Milan Linate and Malpensa. From **London Stansted** Ryanair services Ancona, Bologna (Forlì), Genoa, Parma, Pescara, Pisa, Rome (Ciampino) and Milan (Bergamo).

From **Manchester** My Travel flies to Milan (Bergamo) and Rimini, Alitalia and BA to Milan (Malpensa), Thomsonfly to Pisa, and jet2.com to Pisa and Rome (Fiumicino). From **Leeds/Bradford** jet2.com goes to Milan (Bergamo), Pisa and Rome (Fiumicino). From **Newcastle** Ryanair goes to Milan (Bergamo), jet2.com to Pisa, and easyJet to Rome (Ciampino)

From **Edinburgh** you can get to Pisa with with jet2.com and Rome (Fiumicino) with FlyGlobespan; from **Aberdeen** you can get to Pisa with jet2.com and to Rome (Fiumicino) with British Airways and FlyGlobespan.

From **Dublin**, Aer Lingus flies to Bologna, Milan (Bergamo), Milan (Linate), Rome (Fiumicino), Alitalia to Milan (Malpensa) and Rome (Fiumicino), Ryanair to Milan (Bergamo), Pisa and Rome (Ciampino). Aer Lingus also flies from **Cork** to Rome (Fiumicino).

When this guide went to press, Alitalia and BA return fares started at £150 if booked well ahead, and both airlines offered cheaper tickets on some flights for students and under-26s. Ryanair and easyJet can be much cheaper if booked well in advance on their websites (*see* opposite). It might also save you money to buy via UK **flight websites** such as *www.cheapflights.co.uk*, *www.ebookers.com*, *www.flightline.co.uk*, *www.airflights.co.uk*, *www.flights4less.co.uk* and *www.flightsdirect.com*, and keep your eyes open for bargains and charters in the papers.

Alitalia often has **promotional perks** such as car hire or discounts on domestic flights, hotels or tours within Italy. BA does a fly-drive package to Pisa and Florence.

By Air from the USA and Canada

From the USA, Alitalia flies to Rome or Milan from various destinations, and BA has a New York–London Gatwick–Pisa service. A travel agent may be able to find a much

Direct Flights from the UK and Ireland

Aer Lingus, Ireland **t** 0818 365 000; UK **t** 0845 084 4444, *www.aerlingus.com*.

Alitalia, **t** 0870 544 8259; *www.alitalia.co.uk*.

British Airways, UK **t** 0870 850 9850; Ireland **t** 0845 890 626 747, *www.ba.com*.

Ethiopian Airlines, **t** (020) 8987 7000, *www.ethiopianairlines.com*.

Low-cost Carriers

easyJet, **t** 0905 821 0905, *www.easyJet.com*.

jet2.com, **t** 0870 737 8282, *www.jet2.com*.

FlyGlobespan, **t** 08705 561522, *www.flyglobespan.com*.

Meridiana, **t** 920 7839 2222, *www.meridiana.it*.

My Travel, **t** 0870 241 5333, *www.mytravel.com*

Ryanair, UK **t** 0871 246 0000, Ireland **t** 0818 303030, *www.ryanair.com*.

Thomsonfly, **t** 0870 1900 737, *www.thomsonfly.com*.

Direct Flights from the USA and Canada

Alitalia, US **t** 800 223 5730, *www.alitaliausa.com*.

British Airways, **t** 800 AIRWAYS, *www.ba.com*

Discounts and Youth Fares

From the UK and Ireland

Budget Travel, 134 Lower Baggot St, Dublin 2, **t** (01) 631 1079, *www.budgettravel.ie*.

Italflights, 125 High Holborn, London WC1V 6QA, **t** (020) 7405 6771.

Trailfinders, 215 Kensington High St, London W8, **t** (020) 7937 1234; 4–5 Dawson St, Dublin 2, **t** (01) 677 7888, *www.trailfinders.co.uk*; plus branches in other major UK cities.

United Travel, 2 Old Dublin Rd, Stillorgan, Co. Dublin, **t** (01) 215 9300, *www.unitedtravel.ie*

Besides saving 25% on regular flights, under-26s can fly on on special discount charters. Contact:

STA, 6 Wright's Lane, London W8 6TA, **t** 0870 630026, *www.statravel.co.uk*. There are several other branches in London, and many in other major UK towns and cities.

USIT Now, 19–21 Aston Quay, Dublin 2, **t** (01) 602 1904, *www.usitnow.ie*. Ireland's no.1 specialist student travel agent, with other branches around the country.

From the USA and Canada

It's also worth looking at the websites *www.xfares.com* (carry-on luggage only) and *www.smarterliving.com*

Airhitch, 481 Eighth Ave, Suite 1771, New York, NY 10001-1820, **t** (212) 247 4482 or **t** 1 877 AIRHITCH, *www.air-hitch.org*.

Now Voyager, 74 Varick St, Suite 307, New York, NY 10013, **t** (212) 431 1616, *www.nowvoyager.com*. Courier flights.

STA, **t** 800 781 4040, *www.statravel.com*. There are branches at most universities and at 205 East 42nd St, New York, NY 10017, **t** (212) 822 2700, and ASUC Building, 1st Floor, University of California, Berkeley, CA 94720, **t** (510) 642 3000.

TFI Tours, 34 West 32nd St, New York, NY 10001, **t** (212) 736 1140 or **t** (800) 745 8000, *www.lowestairprice.com*.

The Last Minute Club, 1300 Don Mills Rd, Toronto, Ontario M3B 2W6, **t** (416) 449 5400.

Travel Cuts, 187 College St, Toronto, Ontario M5T 1P7, t (866) 246 9762, *www.travelcuts.com*. Canada's largest student agency, with branches in most provinces.

cheaper fare from your home airport to your Italian airport via London, Brussels, Paris, Frankfurt or Amsterdam. From Canada, only Alitalia flies direct to Italy (from Toronto/Montreal to Rome/Milan).

For **Apex fares**, you need fixed arrival and departure dates and to spend at least a week in Italy but no more than 90 days. Some Apex fares must be purchased at least 14 days (sometimes 21) in advance, and there are penalties if you change dates. At the time of writing the lowest midweek Apex between New York and Rome in the off-season was around $700, rising to about $900 in summer; from Canada, low-season fares are about $900–1,250. Some carriers, including Alitalia, offer **promotions** that might include car hire or discounts on hotels, domestic flights or excursions; ask a travel agent for details. Under-2s usually travel free, and both BA and Alitalia offer cheaper tickets on some flights for students and under-26s.

It may be worth catching a cheap flight to London (New York–London fares are always competitive) then flying on using a British low-cost carriers such as easyJet and Ryanair (*see* box above). Prices are rather more from Canada, so it's best to fly from the USA.

For **discounted flights**, check the small ads in newspaper travel pages (e.g. *New York Times, Chicago Tribune, Toronto Globe & Mail*). Numerous travel clubs and agencies also specialize in discount fares but may require annual membership. You could also try some of the US **cheap flight websites** including: *www.priceline.com* (bid for tickets), *www.expedia.com, www.hotwire.com, www.bestfares.com, www.travelocity.com, www.cheaptrips.com, www.courier.org* (courier flights) and *www.ricksteves.com*. Other websites are listed in the box on p.63.

By Train

By Eurostar to France then onward train from London. the journey time to Florence is about 17hrs. Services run daily and return fares cost around £225. The journey involves changing trains and stations in Paris; sleepers or couchettes are available on the evening train from there.

Eurostar tickets, booking for onward journeys to destinations in Italy, and tickets and passes within Italy, can be bought with:

Rail Europe, **t** 08708 371371, *www.raileurope.co.uk* (in the States **t** 877 257 2887, in Canada **t** 800 361 RAIL, *www.raileurope.com*).

In an age of low-cost airlines, rail travel is not much of an economy unless you can take advantage of student, youth, family and young children or senior citizen discounts, although it is less environmentally harmful. **Interail** (UK) or **Eurail** (USA/Canada) passes offer unlimited travel for all ages throughout Europe for a variety of timeframes. Various youth fares and inclusive rail passes are also available within Italy if you're planning on doing a lot of train travel solely in Italy, organize these before leaving home with:

Rail Choice, **t** 0870 165 7300, *www.railchoice.co.uk*.

The **Trenitalia Pass**, available to non Italian residents, allows 1st- or 2nd-class travel on all Trenitalia trains for 4–10 days (consecutive or non-consecutive) within a 2-month period. It can be obtained at main Italian stations, or in travel agencies abroad. The versions are: Basic for over-26s, Youth for under-26s, and Saver for groups of 2–5. Prices for Basic 2nd-class tickets are £174 for 4 days, £282 for 10 days. You need to pay supplements if you take an Italian Eurostar (*see* opposite), book a couchette or bed on an overnight train, or take an Artesia train.

For more passes and discounts, contact **Rail Europe** or **Rail Choice** (for both, *see* above).

By Coach

The coach is the last refuge of aerophobic bargain-hunters. The journey time from London to Florence is around 30hrs; the return full fare is around £115. There are discounts for students, senior citizens and children as well as off-peak travel.

National Express/Eurolines, **t** 0870 580 8080, *www.nationalexpress.com/eurolines*.

By Car

Driving to Italy from the UK is a lengthy and expensive proposition. No matter how you cross the Channel, it is a good two-day drive – about 1,600km from Calais to Rome. If you're only staying a short time, compare costs against Alitalia's or other airlines' **fly-drive schemes** (some low-cost airlines – *see* p.63 – offer discounted car hire via their websites).

Eurotunnel trains shuttle cars and passengers through the Channel Tunnel from Folkestone to Calais on a drive-on-drive-off system (journey time 35mins) 24hrs a day year-round (at least once an hour through the night). Standard return fares range from £124 to £398, but special offers can bring them as low as £98.

Eurotunnel, **t** 08705 353535, *www.eurotunnel.com*.

A good source of information on the many **ferry routes** is *www.ferrybooker.com*, which also offers discounts on bookings.

You can cut many of the costly **French motorway tolls** by going to Calais, driving to Basle, Switzerland, and from there through the Alps via the toll-free Gotthard Tunnel. In summer you can save the expensive tunnel tolls, and see some marvellous scenery, by taking one of the **mountain passes** instead.

Current motorway tunnel toll charges (one way) are:

Fréjus Tunnel, *www.tunneldufrejus.com*, Modane (France) to Bardonecchia. From €31.20.

Gran San Bernardo, *www.sitrasb.it*, Bourg St Pierre (Switzerland) to Aosta. From €22.40.

Mont Blanc Tunnel, *www.tunnelmb.com*. €31.90.

To **bring your car into Italy**, you need your registration document, a valid driving licence and valid insurance (a Green Card, obtained from your insurer, is not necessary unless you go through Switzerland but is advisable). Make sure everything is in excellent working order; it's not uncommon to be stopped, checked and fined by the police, and **spare parts** for some non-Italian cars are hard to come by. For peace of mind, take out breakdown insurance from the well-reputed **Europ Assistance** (**t** 0870 737 5720, *www.europ-assistance.co.uk*).

Getting Around

The republic has an excellent network of airports, railways, highways and byways, and you'll find getting around fairly easy – unless one union or another goes on strike (*sciopero*, pronounced SHO-PER-O). There's always a day or two's notice of one, and they usually last only 12 or 24 hrs, but this is long enough to throw a spanner in the works if you have to catch a plane, so keep your eyes and ears open for advance warnings. That said, they rarely happen in the main holiday season.

By Train

FS information from anywhere in Italy:
t 892021, *www.trenitalia.com*.

Italy's national railway, the FS (**Ferrovie dello Stato**) is well run and often a pleasure to ride. There are also several private rail lines around cities and in rural districts. We have tried to list them all in the Getting Around sections of the area chapters in this book. Some of these private companies don't accept Interail or Eurail passes.

Train fares have increased greatly over the last five years or so and only those without extra supplements can still be called cheap. Possible FS unpleasantnesses you may encounter, besides a strike, are delays and crowding (especially at weekends and in summer). **Reserve seats** in advance (*fare una prenotazione*); the fee is small and can save you hours of standing. For upper echelon trains (Italian Eurostars and some Intercities), reservations are mandatory. Check when you buy your ticket in advance that the date is correct; tickets are only valid the day they're purchased unless you specify otherwise.

Tickets are sold at stations and many travel agents (and some also online); it's wise to buy in advance as queues can be long. Make sure you ask which platform (*binario*) your train leaves from; the big permanent boards posted in the stations are not always correct.

Always **stamp your ticket** (*convalidare* or *obliterare*) in the not-very-obvious machine at the head of the platform before boarding – failure to do so may result in a fine. If you get on a train without a ticket you can buy one from the conductor, for an added 20%. You can also pay a conductor to move up to first class as long if places are available.

There is a strict **hierarchy of trains**. ***Regionales*** travel short-ish distances, and tend to stop at all stations. There are only a few ***Espressi*** left and they are in poor condition; most serve the long runs from the south of Italy. ***Intercity*** trains link Italian cities, with minimum stops. Some carry an obligatory seat reservation requirement (free); all require a supplement. The 'Kings of the Rails' are the swish, super-fast (Florence–Rome 90mins) ***Eurostars***. These make very few stops, offer 1st- and 2nd-class carriages, and carry a supplement that includes an obligatory seat reservation. For the **Trenitalia pass** for non-residents, *see* p.64.

Refreshments on routes of any great distance are provided by buffet cars or trolleys; you can usually get sandwiches and coffee from vendors along the tracks at intermediary stops. Station bars often have a good variety of takeaway travellers' fare. Bring a bottle of mineral water, as there's no drinking water on the trains.

Major stations have an *albergo diurno* ('day hotel', where you can shower, get a shave and haircut, etc.), information offices, currency exchanges open at weekends (not at the best rates), hotel reservation services, kiosks with foreign papers, restaurants, etc. You can also book a hire car to pick up at your destination, through Avis, Hertz or Maggiore (listed where relevant in the area chapters).

By Coach and Bus

Intercity coach travel is often quicker than train travel and a bit more expensive. You will find regular coach links only where there's no train to offer competition. In many regions, buses are the only means of public transport and are well used, with frequent departures.

Coaches almost always depart from near the train station, and tickets usually need to be bought before boarding. Country bus lines are based in provincial capitals: we've done our best to explain the connections even for the most out-of-the-way routes, as well as listing coach companies in the relevant areas.

City bus routes are well labelled; all charge flat fees for rides within the city limits and immediate suburbs (around €1). Tickets must be purchased before you get on, either from a tobacconist's, a newspaper kiosk, many bars, or ticket machines near the main stops. Once you are on, you must '*obliterate*' (punch) your ticket in the machines at the front or back of the bus; controllers stage random checks, with fines for cheats about €40.

By Car

The advantages of driving in Tuscany, Umbria and the Marches generally outweigh the disadvantages. Before you bring your own car or hire one, consider the kind of holiday you're planning. If it's a tour of major art cities, you're best off not driving: parking is impossible, traffic impossible, deciphering one-way streets, signals and signs impossible. In nearly every other case, a car gives you the freedom of making your way through Italy's delightful open countryside and stopping at smaller towns and villages.

Be prepared to encounter some of the highest **fuel costs** in Europe, to spend a very long time looking for a **parking place** in any town bigger than a peanut, and to face drivers who look at motoring as if it were a video game. No matter how fast you trip along on the *autostrade* (Italy's toll motorways, with an official speed limit 130km/80miles per hr), someone will pass you going twice as fast.

If you aren't intimidated, buy a good **road map** of Italy or a detailed one of the region you're travelling in (the Italian Touring Club produces excellent ones; *see* also p.74 for specialist travel bookshops selling maps). Most **petrol stations** close for lunch, and few stay open late at night, though you may find a 'self-service' one where machines accept nice, smooth banknotes. *Autostrada* **tolls** are high – *www.autostrade.it* helps calculate journey costs. Rest stops and petrol stations along motorways open 24hrs. Other roads are free.

Italians are good at signposting, and roads are almost all excellently maintained. Beware that you may be fined on the spot for speeding, a burnt-out headlamp, etc; if you're especially unlucky you may be slapped with a *super multa*, or superfine, of €130–260 or more. You may even be fined for not having a portable **warning triangle** (these can be bought when you cross the Channel, at the border or from an ACI office). It is now law a) to keep **headlights dipped** on the *autostrada* and in rural areas at all times and b) to carry a bright **orange fluorescent jacket** in the car at all times and put it on if you break down.

The **Automobile Club of Italy** (ACI) (Via Marsala 8, Rome, **t** 064477, *www.aci.it*) is a good friend to the foreign motorist. Besides proffering useful info and tips, they can be reached from anywhere by calling **t** 116 – which is also the number to call if you have an accident, need an ambulance, or simply have to find the nearest service station. If you need **major repairs**, the ACI makes sure the prices charged are according to their guidelines.

Hiring a car is fairly simple if not particularly cheap (an average of €85/day or €500/wk for a smallish car). Italian car-hire firms are called *autonoleggi*. There are large international firms through which you can reserve a car in advance, and local agencies that often have lower prices; we've listed suggestions in the area chapters were relevant. Air or rail travellers should check out possible **discount packages**. Low-cost airlines (*see* p.63) often offer deals through their websites.

Most rental companies require a **deposit** amounting to the estimated cost of the hire, and there is 19% VAT added to the final cost. Rates become more advantageous if you take the car for a week with unlimited mileage. If you need a car for more than 3wks, **leasing** is a more economic alternative. The National Tourist Office (*see* p.60) has a list of firms in Italy that let **caravans** (trailers) and **campers**.

By Taxi

Taxi tariffs from town to town start at €2.33; then add €0.78 per km (there is a minimum charge of €4.50). Each piece of baggage will cost you an extra €1.04, and there are surcharges for trips outside the city limits, between 10pm and 6am, and on Sundays and holidays.

By Motorbike and Bicycle

The transport of choice for many Italians, motorbikes, mopeds and Vespas can be a delightful way to get between cities and see the countryside. You should only consider this, however, if you've ridden them before – Italy's hills and traffic make it no place to learn. Helmets are compulsory. A *motorino* (moped) costs from about €30/day to hire; scooters are somewhat more (from about €50).

Italians are keen cyclists, racing drivers up the steepest hills; if you're not training for the Tour de France, consider the hilliness of the region before planning a bicycling tour – especially in summer months. Bikes can be transported by train in Italy, either with you or within a couple of days; apply at the luggage office (*ufficio bagagli*). Hire prices range from about €10/day; to buy one, think upwards of €150, either in a bike shop or through local classified ads. If you bring your own bike, check with your airline first about their policies on transporting them.

Where to Stay

Hotels

Tuscany, Umbria and the Marches are well endowed with hotels (*alberghi*) of every description. These are rated by the government's tourism bureaucracy, on a 5-star scale. Ratings take into account such features as a restaurant on the premises, plumbing, air-con, etc, but not character, style or charm. And hotels may stay at a lower rating than they've earned, so a three-star could be as comfy as a four-star.

Breakfast is often included in the room rate. You might find that **half- or full-board** is obligatory, particularly in high season at hotels in seaside, lake or mountain resorts, spas or country villas.

Prices

In general, the further south you go in Italy, the cheaper the rates. In **Florence**, prices are slightly higher (*see* box above). Prices are by law listed on the door of each room and printed in hotel lists available from local tourist offices. They may cost up to 50% less in the **low season**. In resorts, hotels may close down for several months of the year.

Hotel Price Ranges

Categories are based on a standard double room (en suite where available) in high season.

In Florence

luxury	€€€€€	€250+
very expensive	€€€€	€180–250
expensive	€€€	€130–180
moderate	€€	€75–130
inexpensive	€	– €75

Elsewhere in the Region

luxury	€€€€€	€230+
very expensive	€€€€	€150–230
expensive	€€€	€100–150
moderate	€€	€60–100
inexpensive	€	– €60

For a **single**, count on paying two-thirds of a double; to add an extra bed in a double adds 35% to the rate. Taxes and service charges are included in rates. **Non-en suite rooms** (i.e. sharing toilets and bathrooms in the hall) are about 20–30% cheaper.

A booking is valid once a **deposit** has been paid; different establishments have different policies about **cancellation charges** after a certain time. If you come In summer without reservations, call around for a place in the morning or put yourself at the mercy of one of the tourist office **hotel-finding services** (we've listed these in the area chapters).

The National Tourist Office (*see* p.60) has lists and booking information for motels and 5- and 4-star hotels and chains. Besides classic hotels, there are an increasing number of alternatives, nearly always in historic buildings, which in Umbria are classified as *residenza d'epoca* or country houses.

Inexpensive Accommodation

Bargains are few and far between in Italy. Most cheaper places are around railway stations. In small towns the tourist office may have a list of *affittacamere* (**rooms to rent**), which vary from basic accommodation in someone's house to more upmarket places.

Besides youth hostels (*see* p.68), there are **city-run hostels** with dorm-style rooms, open to all. In some cities **religious institutions** let extra rooms. Rural monasteries and convents sometimes take guests (bring a letter of introduction from your local priest or pastor).

Youth and Student Hostels

You'll find hostels in Florence, Lucca, Perugia, Tavarnelle Val di Pesa (Chianti), Abetone, Cortona, San Gimignano, Assisi, Foligno, Marina di Massa e Carrara, Ascoli Piceno and Pesaro. You can nearly always buy an **IYHF card** on the spot. There are no age limits, and senior citizens are often given added discounts. Accommodation – usually a bunk in a single-sex room, plus breakfast – costs around €10/day. Curfews are common, and you usually can't check in before 5 or 6pm. Avoid spring, when noisy school groups descend on hostels for field trips.

The **Centro Turistico Studentesco e Giovanile** (CTS; *www.cts.it*), with offices in most Italian cities (and one in London), can also book cheap accommodation for students.

Self-catering Holidays: Villas, Farmhouses and Flats

Renting a villa, farmhouse, cottage or flat has always been the choice way to visit Tuscany, and is becoming increasingly so in Umbria as well. The **Internet** has made finding a place easier than ever, with companies providing detailed listings and photos. Another place to look is the Sunday papers; or, if you're set on a particular area, write to its tourist office (or see its website) for a list of local rental agencies. These should provide photos; make sure all pertinent details are in your rental agreement to avoid misunderstandings later.

In general **minimum lets** are a week; rental **prices** (generally per week) usually include insurance, water and electricity, sometimes linen and maid service. Common problems are water shortages, insects (*see* p.39) and low kilowatts. Most companies offer **packages** with flights and car-hire. Book as far in advance as possible for summer.

Rural Self-catering or *Agriturismo*

For a breath of rural seclusion, gregarious Italians head for **working farms**, offering accommodation (sometimes self-catering) that often approximates French *gîtes*. The real pull may be cooking by the hosts, using home-grown produce. In Tuscany hundreds of *agriturismo* farms offer rooms, varying enormously in standard and price, from quite modest to extremely upmarket. In general, prices, compared with overhyped 'Tuscan villas', are still reasonable.

This branch of the Italian tourist industry is run by **Agriturist** (*www.agriturist.it*), which has several offices in each region. Local tourist offices have information on such accommodation in their areas, or contact:

Associazione Regionale Agriturist, Via Degli Alfani 67, 50120 Florence, **t** 055 287838.

Azienda di Promozione Turistica dell'Umbria, Via Mazzini 21, Perugia, **t** 075 575951, *www.umbria2000.it*.

Solemar, Via G Modena 19, Florence, **t** 055 552131, *www.solemar.it*.

Turismo Verde, Via Jacopo Nardi 41, Florence, **t** 055 23389, *www.turismoverde.it*.

Alternatively, contact the individual provincial Agriturist offices (UPA) directly, as listed on the websites:

Tuscany: *www.agriturist.toscana.it*.

Umbria: *www.agrituristumbria.com*.

The Marches: *www.agriturist.marche.it*.

Alpine Refuges

Rifugi alpini – mountain huts in the Apennines – vary from basic to grand; some are exclusively for hikers and climbers, others are reached by *funivie*, used by skiers in winter and holidaymakers in summer. Rates are about €10–28 a night, depending on whether you are a CAI member, but rise by 20% Dec–April. The clubs has a list of huts, dates available, and booking information.

Club Alpino Italiano: Via E Petrella 19, Milan, **t** 02 205 7231, *www.cai.it*.

Camping

Most official campsites are near the sea, mountains or lakes; there is usually one within commuting distance of major tourist centres. Prices vary enormously. Details are published in the Italian Touring Club's *Campeggi e Villaggi Turistici*, sold in Italian bookshops (€20), or ask for a free abbreviated list from:

Centro Internazionale Prenotazioni Federcampeggio, Casella Postale 23, 50041, Calenzano (Florence), **t** 055 882391, *www.federcampeggio.it*.

You can camp outside an official site with the landowner's permission.

Specialist Tour Operators

For **specialist holidays and courses for foreigners**, *see* p.76.

In Italy

Corymbus Viaggi, Via Massetana Romana 56, 53100 Siena, **t** 0577 271654, *www.corymbus.it*. Etruscan tours, wine tours, art and cookery in Umbria and Tuscany, painting and stencil classes, and mountainbike tours of Chianti.

In the UK

Abercrombie & Kent, St George's House, Ambrose St, Cheltenham, Glos GL0 3LG, **t** 0845 070 0610, *www.abercrombiekent.co.uk*. City breaks in all major cities.

Ace Study Tours, Babraham, Cambridge CB2 4AP, **t** (01223) 835055, *www.study-tours.org*. Cultural tours through Tuscany and Umbria.

Alternative Travel, 69–71 Banbury Rd, Oxford OX2 6PE, **t** (01865) 315678, *www.atg-oxford.co.uk*. Walking, wildflower, garden and cycling tours – 'Piero della Francesca', 'The Palio in Siena' and 'Renaissance Tuscany' – plus truffle hunts and painting courses.

Arblaster & Clarke Wine Tours, Farnham Rd, West Liss, Petersfield, Hants GU33 6JQ, **t** (01730) 893344, *www.arblasterandclarke.com*. Tuscan wine tours, truffle hunts and cooking tours.

Bellini Travel, 7 Barb Mews, London W6 7PA, **t** (020) 7437 8918, *www.bellinitravel.com*. Tailor-made tours to Tuscany and other parts of Italy, including access to villas and gardens not usually open to the public.

British Museum Traveller, 38 Russell Square, London WC1B 3QQ, **t** 0800 085 0864, *www.britishmuseumtraveller.co.uk*. Occasional Tuscan art and architecture tours.

Carrier Travel, London Rd, Alderley Edge, Cheshire SK9 7IT, **t** (0161) 491 7650, *www.carrier.co.uk*. An awardwinning holiday firm with lots of choice in the region.

Citalia Holidays, Atrium, London Rd, Crawley, West Sussex, RH10 9SR, **t** 0870 837 1371, *www.citalia.co.uk*. A wide range of escorted or independent holidays throughout Italy.

Fine Art Travel, 15 Savile Row, London W1X 1AE, **t** (020) 7437 8553, *www.finearttravel.co.uk*. Cultural, art and historical tours.

hush!, No.1 Lakeside, Cheadle SK8 3GW, **t** (0161) 492 1392, *www.hush-italy.com*. 'Authentic' holidays in Tuscany, Umbria and elsewhere.

Inntravel, near Castle Howard, York YO60 7JU, **t** (01653) 617945, *www.inntravel.co.uk*. Another awardwinning firm particularly strong on walking holidays, including Tuscany.

Inscape Fine Art Study Tours, 1 Farley Lane, Stonesfield, Witney, Oxfordshire OX29 8HB, **t** (01993) 891726, *www.inscapetours.co.uk*. Escorted art 'study' tours with guest lecturers in Florence, Siena and southern Tuscany.

JMB Travel Consultants, 3 Powick Mills, Old Rd, Worcester, WR2 4BU, **t** (01905) 422282, *www.jmb-travel.co.uk*. Opera in Macerata and Pesaro.

Italiatour, 9 Whyteleafe Business Village, Whyteleafe, Surrey CR3 0AT, **t** (01883) 621900, *www.italiatour.co.uk*. Resort holidays, city breaks, self-catering accommodation, watercolour and cookery courses, and horseriding in Umbria.

Kirker, 4 Waterloo Court, 10 Theed St, London SE1 8ST, **t** 0870 112 3333. *www.kirkerholidays.com*. City breaks and tailor-made tours.

Magic of Italy, 227 Shepherds Bush Rd, London W14 7AS, **t** 0870 888 0228, *www.magictravelgroup.co.uk*. Tailor-made city breaks and villa holidays.

Magnum, 7 Westleigh Park, Blaby, Leicester, **t** (0116) 277 7123. Holidays in Florence especially suitable for elderly visitors.

Martin Randall Travel, Voysey House, Barley Mow Passage, Chiswick, London W4 4PH, **t** (020) 8742 3355, *www.martinrandall.com*. Imaginative cultural tours with expert guides – art, archaeology, history, architecture, music, 'Medici Villas and Gardens', and opera in Macerata and Pesaro.

Prospect Cultural, 94–104 John Wilson Park, Whitstable, Kent, CT5 3QZ, **t** (01227) 773 545, *www.prospecttours.com*. Art tours in Florence, Urbino and Umbria, and specialist holidays devoted to local cultural figures such as Dante and Piero della Francesca.

Ramblers, Box 43, Welwyn Garden City, Hertfordshire AL8 7TR, **t** (01707) 331133, *www.ramblersholidays.co.uk*. Walking holidays.

Real Holidays Ltd, 66–68 Essex Rd, London N1 8LR, **t** (020) 7359 3938, *www.realhols.co.uk*. Quirky holidays.

Sherpa Expeditions, 131a Heston Rd, Hounslow, Middlesex, TW5 0RF, **t** (020) 8577 2717, *www.sherpa-walking-holidays.co.uk*. Walking and cycling holidays in Tuscany and Umbria.

Simply Tuscany & Umbria, Kings Place, Wood Street, Kingston-upon-Thames, Surrey KT1 1SG, **t** (020) 8541 2222, *www.simplytravel.com*. Accommodation, from opulent villas with pools to country house hotels, plus cookery and painting courses.

Specialtours, 2 Chester Row, London SW1 9SH, **t** (020) 7730 2297, *www.specialtours.co.uk*. Various cultural tours of Tuscany, Umbria and the Marches.

Tasting Places, Unit 40, Buspace Studios, Conlan St, London W10 5AP, **t** (020) 8964 5333, *www.tastingplaces.com*. Cookery courses near Orvieto and Arezzo.

Travelsphere, Compass House, Rockingham Rd, Market Harborough, Leics LE16 7QD, **t** 0870 240 2428, *www.travelsphere.co.uk*. Coach tours of the Tuscan coast.

Waymark, 44 Windsor Rd, Slough, **t** 0870 950 9800, *www.waymarkholidays.co.uk*. Walking tours of San Gimignano, Tuscany and the Marches.

In the USA/Canada

Abercrombie & Kent, Suite 212, 1520 Kensington Rd, Oak Brook, IL 60523 2156, **t** 800 323 7308, *www.abercrombiekent.com*. City breaks and walking holidays.

Archaeological Tours Inc., Suite 904, 271 Madison Ave, New York, NY 10016, **t** 1-800 554 7016, **t** (212) 986 3054, *archtours@aol.com*. Tours of Etruscan sites.

Bike Riders' Tours, PO Box 130254, Boston, MA 02113, **t** 800 473 7040, *www.bikeriderstours.com*. Cycling tours with stopovers at elegant hotels.

CIT Tours, 875 Third Ave, New York, NY 10022, **t** 1-800 CIT-TOUR, *www.cittours.travel*; 7007 Islington Ave, Suite 205, Woodbridge, Ontario L4L 4T5, **t** 800 387 0711. Customized tours.

Europe Train, 2485 Jennings Rd, Olin, NC 28660, *www.etttours.com*. Escorted tours by train and car.

Italiatour, 666 Fifth Ave, New York, NY 10103, **t** 800 845 3365 (US) and **t** 888 515 5245 (Canada), *www.italiatourusa.com*. Fly-drive holidays and sightseeing tours organized by flight operator Alitalia.

Maupintour, 2688 South Rainbow Bd, Las Vegas, NV 89146, *www.maupintour.com*. Escorted packages.

Travel Concepts, 307 Princeton, MA 01541, **t** (978) 464 0411. Gourmet wine and food holidays.

Self-catering Operators

In Italy

The Best in Italy, Via Ugo Foscolo 72, Florence, **t** 055 223064, *www.thebestinitaly.com*.

Solo Affitti, Via Oberdan 33, Grosseto, **t** 0564 416743.

Toscana Vacanze, Piazza Silvio Pellico 1, 52047 Marciano della Chiana, **t** 0575 845348.

Toscanamare Villas, Via W della Gheradesca 5, Castagneto Carducci (LI), **t** 0565 744012, *www.toscanamare.it*.

Vela, Via Colombo 16, Castiglione della Pescaia, **t** 0564 933495, *www.lavelaimmobiliare.it*.

In the UK

Accommodation Line, 46 Maddox St, London W1R 9PB, **t** (020) 7499 4433.

The Apartment Service, 5–6 Francis Grove, London SW19 4DT, **t** (020) 8944 1444, *www.apartmentservice.com*.

Citalia, *see* p.69.

CV Travel, Thames Wharf Studios, Rainville Rd, London, W6 9HA, **t** (020) 7384 5897, *www.cvtravel.net*.

The Individual Travellers, Spring Mill, Earby, Barnoldswick, Lancs BB94 0AA, **t** 08700 780193.

Inghams, 10–18 Putney Hill, London SW15 6AX, **t** (020) 8780 4400/4433, *www.inghams.co.uk*.

Interhome, 383 Richmond Rd, Twickenham, Middx TW1 2EF, **t** (020) 8891 1294, *www.interhome.co.uk*.

Magic of Italy, **t** 0870 8748 7575, *www.magictravelgroup.co.uk*.

Simply Travel, Wigmore Lane, Luton LU2 9TN, **t** 0870 166 4979, *www.simply-travel.co.uk*.

Thomson Villas, *www.thomson.co.uk* (check website to find your nearest branch)

Topflight, 3rd Floor, Jervis House, Jervis St, Dublin 2, **t** (01) 240 1700, *www.topflight.ie*.

Travel à la Carte, The White House, Drove Lane, Cold Ash, Thatcham, RG18 9NL, **t** (01635) 201250, *www.anotheritaly.co.uk*.

In the USA

At Home Abroad, 405 East 56th St 6H, New York, NY 10022-2466, **t** (212) 421 9165, *www.athomeabroadinc.com*.

CIT North America Ltd, **t** (800) CIT-TOUR, 15 West 44th St, New York, NY 10173; in Canada, 7007 Islington Ave, Suite 205, Woodbridge, Ontario, L4L 4T5, **t** 905 264 0158; *www.cit-tours.com*.

Hideaways International, 767 Islington St, Portsmouth, NH 03801, **t** (603) 430 4433 or **t** 877 843 4433, *www.hideaways.com*.

Homebase Abroad, 29 Mary's Lane, Scituate, MA 02006, **t** (781) 545 5112, *www.homebase-abroad*. com.

Italianvillas.com, *www.italianvillas.com*.

Rentals in Italy (and Elsewhere!), 700 E Main St, Ventura, CA 93001, **t** 1-800 726 6702, *www.rentvillas.com*.

Practical A–Z

06

Conversions: Imperial–Metric

Length (multiply by)
Inches to centimetres: 2.54
Centimetres to inches: 0.39
Feet to metres: 0.3
Metres to feet: 3.28
Yards to metres: 0.91
Metres to yards: 1.09
Miles to kilometres: 1.61
Kilometres to miles: 0.62

Area (multiply by)
Inches square to centimetres square: 6.45
Centimetres square to inches square: 0.15
Feet square to metres square: 0.09
Metres square to feet square: 10.76
Miles square to kilometres square: 2.59
Kilometres square to miles square: 0.39
Acres to hectares: 0.40
Hectares to acres: 2.47

Weight (multiply by)
Ounces to grams: 28.35
Grammes to ounces: 0.035
Pounds to kilograms: 0.45
Kilograms to pounds: 2.2
Stones to kilograms: 6.35
Kilograms to stones: 0.16
Tons (UK) to kilograms: 1,016
Kilograms to tons (UK): 0.0009
1 UK ton (2,240lbs) = 1.12 US tonnes (2,000lbs)

°C	°F
40	104
35	95
30	86
25	77
20	68
15	59
10	50
5	41
-0	32
-5	23
-10	14
-15	5

Volume (multiply by)
Pints (UK) to litres: 0.57
Litres to pints (UK): 1.76
Quarts (UK) to litres: 1.13
Litres to quarts (UK): 0.88
Gallons (UK) to litres: 4.55
Litres to gallons (UK): 0.22
1 UK pint/quart/gallon = 1.2 US pints/quarts/ gallons

Temperature
Celsius to Fahrenheit: multiply by 1.8 then add 32

Fahrenheit to Celsius: subtract 32 then multiply by 0.55

Italy Information

Time Differences
Country: + 1hr GMT; + 6hrs EST

Daylight saving from last weekend in March to end of October

Dialling Codes
Italy country code 39

To Italy from: UK, Ireland, New Zealand 00 / USA, Canada 011 / Australia 0011 then dial 39 and the full number including the initial zero

From Italy to: UK 00 44; Ireland 00 353; USA, Canada 001; Australia 00 61; New Zealand 00 64 then the number without the initial zero

Directory enquiries: 12

International directory enquiries: 176

Emergency Numbers
Police: 112/113
Ambulance: 118
Fire: 115
Car breakdown: 116

Embassy Numbers in Italy
UK: (06) 422 0001; **Ireland** (06) 697 9121; **USA**: (055) 2669 5232; **Canada** (06) 445 981; **Australia** (06) 852 721; **New Zealand** (06) 441 7171

Shoe Sizes

Europe	UK	USA
35	2½ / 3	4
36	3 / 3½	4½ / 5
37	4	5½ / 6
38	5	6½
39	5½ / 6	7 / 7½
40	6 / 6½	8 / 8½
41	7	9 / 9½
42	8	9½ / 10
43	9	10½
44	9½ / 10	11
45	10½	12
46	11	12½ / 13

Women's Clothing

Europe	UK	USA
34	6	2
36	8	4
38	10	6
40	12	8
42	14	10
44	16	12

Children

Children are the royalty of Italy: often spoiled, probably more fashionably dressed than you, and never allowed to get dirty. If you're bringing your own *bambini* to Italy, they'll be warmly received. Many **hotels** offer advantageous rates and have play areas, and most larger cities have permanent **Luna Parks** (funfairs). Other attractions young kids enjoy are the **Bomarzo Monster Park** in Lazio, close to the Umbrian border, **Pinocchio Park** in Collodi, near Pisa, **Città della Domenica** in Perugia, **Pistoia Zoo** and the **Nature Park** in Cavriglia in the Valdarno. If a **circus** visits town, you're in for a treat; it will either be a showcase of daredevil skill or a family-run modern version of Fellini's *La Strada*.

Crime and the Police

Police/Emergency, t 113

Cities attract a fair amount of petty crime – pickpocketing, white-collar thievery (check your change) and car break-ins – but violent crime is rare. Stay on the inside of the pavement and hold on to your property; pickpockets most often strike in crowds; don't carry too much cash and don't keep what you have in one place; be extra careful in stations, don't leave valuables in hotel rooms, and park in garages, guarded car parks, or well-lit streets, with any temptations out of sight.

Purchasing small quantities of cannabis is legal, but 'small quantity' isn't specified and if the police dislike you already, it may be enough to get you into big trouble.

Eating Out

When you leave a restaurant you will be given a receipt (*ricevuta fiscale*) that, according to Italian law, you must take with you out of the door and carry for at least 300m. If you aren't given one, the restaurant is probably fudging its taxes and thus offering you lower prices. There is a slim chance the tax police may have their eye on both you and the restaurant; if you don't have a receipt they could slap you with a heavy fine.

When you eat out, mentally add to the bill (*conto*) the bread and cover charge (*pane e coperto*, €1–3), and a 15% service charge. This is often included in the bill (*servizio compreso*); if not, it will say *servizio non compreso*. Extra tipping is at your own discretion; *see* also p.78.

For further information about eating in Italy and a menu vocabulary, *see* pp.49–56.

Restaurant Price Categories

Categories are based on an average complete meal, Italian-style with house wine, for one.

very expensive	€€€€	€60 +
expensive	€€€	€40–60
moderate	€€	€25–40
inexpensive	€	– €25

Electricity

For electric appliances you need a 220AC adaptor with two round prongs on the plug. American appliances need transformers too.

Health and Emergencies

Health Emergencies, t 118

Minor illnesses and problems that crop up in Italy will usually be handled free of charge in a public hospital **walk-in clinic** (*ambulatorio*). If you need minor aid, Italian **pharmacists** are highly trained and can probably diagnose your problem; look for a *farmacia* (all have a list in the window detailing which are open during the night and holidays). Extreme cases should head for the Pronto Soccorso **(A&E)** of the nearest hospital.

Italian doctors are not always great linguists; contact your embassy or consulate (*see* p.60) for an **English-speaking doctor**.

For **insurance and EHIC cards**, *see* p.62.

Internet

Internet access has become much more widespread in Italy in recent years. Nearly all hotels and B&Bs now their own website, which simplifies booking, and offer free internet access (increasingly Wifi) for guests.

Most resorts and towns have at least one internet point of some kind; ask for a list at the tourist office. Costs vary widely: in some cities there is free access for those under 26 or for students.

Maps and Publications

The maps throughout this guide are for orientation only; it is worth investing in a good, up-to-date regional map before you arrive in Italy, ideally from one of the following bookshops:

Stanford's, 12–14 Long Acre, London WC2 9LP, **t** (020) 7836 1321, *www.stanfords.co.uk*. There are also branches in Bristol and Manchester.

The Travel Bookshop, 13 Blenheim Crescent, London W11 2EE, **t** (020) 7229 5260.

The Complete Traveller, 199 Madison Ave, New York, NY 10016, **t** (212) 685 9007.

Excellent touring maps produced by Touring Club Italiano, Michelin and the Istituto Geografico de Agostini are available at major bookshops in Italy or sometimes on newsstands. Italian tourist offices can often supply good area maps and town plans.

Books are more expensive in Italy than the UK, but some excellent shops stock English-language books. A few useful ones are:

Edison, Piazza della Repubblica 27r, Florence, **t** 055 213110

Feltrinelli, Via Cavour 12–20r, Florence, **t** 055 219524.

The Paperback Exchange, Via Fiesolana 31r, Florence, **t** 055 247 8154.

National Holidays

Most museums, banks and shops are closed on the following national holidays:

1 January New Year's Day (*Capodanno*).

6 January Epiphany; better known to Italians as the day of *La Befana* – a kindly witch who brings *bambini* the toys that Santa Claus or *Babbo Natale* somehow forgot.

Easter Monday

25 April Liberation Day.

1 May Labour Day – lots of parades, speeches, picnics, music and drinking.

2 June *Festa della Repubblica*.

15 August Assumption (*Ferragosto*); the biggest holiday of all – woe to the innocent traveller on the road or train!

1 November All Saints (*Ognissanti*).

8 December Immaculate Conception of the Virgin Mary.

25 December Christmas Day.

26 December Santo Stefano.

Opening Hours

Don't be surprised if you find anywhere in Italy unexpectedly closed (or open for that matter), whatever its official stated hours.

Most of Italy closes down at 1pm until 3 or 4pm to eat and digest the main meal of the day. Afternoon hours are 4–7, or often 5–8 in summer. Bars are often the only places open early afternoon.

Museums and Galleries

Most major museums open 9am–7pm; Sun afternoons and Mon they often close. Where possible we have given opening hours for individual museums; but note that they can change at short notice, particularly in summer.

With two works of art per inhabitant, Italy has a hard time financing the preservation of its national heritage; it's as well to enquire at the tourist office as to what is open and what is 'temporarily' closed before setting off on a wild-goose chase.

Entrance charges vary wildly; expect to pay €2–5 for museum entrance; expensive ones can be as high as €9.50 if there is a special exhibition. State museums and monuments are free to under-18s and over-60s (bring ID). One week a year – usually in late spring – all state museums are free of charge for the *Settimana dei Berri Culturali*.

Banks and Shops

Banks are open Mon–Fri 8.30–1/1.20 and 3–4 or 4–5 except local and national holidays (*see* left). For **post offices**, *see* opposite.

Shops are generally open Mon–Sat 8–1 and 3.30–7.30. In bigger towns some supermarkets and department stores now open all day, but this varies from region to region. Food shops shut on Wed afternoons in winter, and Sat afternoons end June–beginning Sept; Sun opening is becoming more usual, particularly in the centre of town.

Churches

Italy's churches have always been a prime target for art thieves and as a consequence are usually locked when there isn't a sacristan or caretaker. All churches, except the really important cathedrals and basilicas, close in the afternoon at the same hours as shops, and the little ones tend to stay closed.

Don't do your visiting during services, and don't come to see paintings and statues in churches the week preceding Easter – you will probably find them covered with mourning shrouds.

Always have a pocketful of coins for light machines in churches.

Photography

Film and developing are very expensive in Italy, so a digital camera is handy.

You are not allowed to take pictures in most museums, or some of the churches.

Post Offices

t 803160, *www.poste.it*.

City post offices usually open Mon–Sat 8.10–6; elsewhere it's Mon–Sat 8.10–1.25.

First-class mail, *posta prioritaria* (€0.60), is supposed to get to an address in Italy within 24hrs and to EU countries within 36. You can use registered delivery, *raccomandata*, for a €2.80 supplement. Stamps (*francobolli*) may also be purchased at tobacconists (*tabacchi*, identified by blue signs with a white T). Airmail letters to and from North America can quite often take up to 2 weeks.

Mail can be sent to you care of your hotel or addressed *Fermo Posta* (*poste restante*: general delivery) to the central post office where you are staying. When you go to pick up mail at the *Fermo Posta* window, take your passport as proof of ID. You will need to pay a nominal charge.

Sports and Activities

Birdwatching

The islands, and coastal parks near the Argentario, are great places to twitch; eco-friendly Giglio offers nature appreciation and classes for Italian speakers, based at the hotel Pardiui's Hermitage, **t** 0564 809034. The bird park at Lago Burano near Capalbio, **t** 0564 898829, is another good spot.

Boats and Sailing

The sailing is beautiful among the coves of the Tuscan archipelago and around the Argentario; there's a good sailing school in Torre del Lago Puccini, **t** 0584 351211.

You can bring your boat by car to Italy for 6 months without paperwork; if you arrive by sea you must report to the authority of your first port to show passports and receive your *constituto*, which identifies you and allows you to purchase fuel tax-free. Boats with engines require a numberplate, and insurance if over 3 horsepower. To leave your boat in Italy for an extended period, you must have a Navigation Licence; after a year you have to start paying taxes on it. All yachts must pay a daily berthing fee in Italian ports.

The National Tourist office (see p.60) has a list of ports that charter yachts in Tuscan ports.

Clubs

Sports clubs are usually private and open only to members. The best (cleanest) swimming is on the islands, especially on beaches that look away from the mainland.

Fishing

Fishing in the sea is possible from the shore or boats, or underwater (not with an aqualung) without a permit, though the Tyrrhennian has been so thoroughly fished commercially that the government declares 2- and 3-month moratoria on all fishing to give fish a break.

Artificial lakes and streams are well stocked, and if you're more interested in the eating than the sport, there are trout farms where you can almost pick the fish out of the water with your hands. To fish in fresh water you need a licence for foreigners (type D; about €40 for 3 months), available from the Federazione Italiana della Pesca Sportiva. Its offices in every province can inform you about local conditions and restrictions. Bait and equipment are readily available.

Gliding

Gliding and hang-gliding are big in Umbria, where hills provide the necessary updraughts; the centre for the sport is at Sigillo, near Gualdo Tadino, **t** 0759 220693. The little airports at Foligno, **t** 0742 670201, and Perugia, S Egidio, **t** 075 592141, also offer gliding.

Golf

There are courses in Florence, Montecatini Terme, Punta Ala, Tirrenia, Orbetello and Portoferraio on Elba. In Umbria there's one near Lake Trasimeno at Ellera.

Horseriding and Horse-racing

Horseriding is popular; Agriturist (*see* p.68) offers villa and riding holidays in Tuscany.

Umbria's riding centre at Corciano, near Lake Trasimeno, offers day and longer excursions; for information, write directly to the local Agriturist office.

There are race and trotting courses in Florence and Montecatini Terme.

Hunting

The most controversial sport in Italy pits avid enthusiasts against a burgeoning number of environmentalists who oppose it.

The Apennines, especially in Umbria, are boar territory, and in the autumn months the woods are full of hunters. Pathetically tiny birds, as well as ducks and pigeons, are the other principal game.

Specialist Holidays and Courses for Foreigners

The **Italian Institute**, 39 Belgrave Square, London SW1X 8NX, **t** (020) 7235 1461, *www.icilondon.esteri.it*, or 686 Park Ave, New York, NY 10021, *t* (212) 879 4242, *www.iicnewyork.esteri.it*, is the main source of information on courses for foreigners in Italy, including Italian state scholarships and language courses for business students. Graduate students should also contact their nearest Italian consulate to find out about scholarships – many go unused each year because no one knows about them.

Worldwide Classroom, *www.worldwide.edu*, also has a database of educational organizations around the world.

Language Courses

One obvious course to take in the linguistically pure land of Dante is Italian language and culture: there are summer classes at the Scuola Lingua e Cultura per Stranieri of the University of Siena, in Cortona, Viareggio (run by the University of Pisa), Urbino (at the University of Urbino, Via Saffi 2, Urbino), and, unsurprisingly, in Florence (sometimes there seem to be more US students than Florentines in the city).

The following offer courses year-round:

British Institute, Piazza Strozzi 2, Florence, **t** 055 267781, *www.britishinstitute.it*. Florentine art and history, Dante, opera and language.

Centro Fiorenza, Via di Santo Spirito 14, Florence, **t** 055 239 8274, *www.centrofiorenza.com*. History, literature and art at basic and advanced levels, plus cooking courses.

Centro Lingulstico Italiano Dante Alighieri, Piazza Repubblica 5, Florence, **t** 055 210808, *www.clida.it*. Language courses.

Scuola Lorenzo de' Medici, Via Alloro 14r, **t** 055 283142, *www.lorenzodemedici.it*. Classes in language and art.

Scuola Macchiavelli, Piazza Santo Spirito 4, Florence, **t** 055 239 6966, *www.centromachiavelli.it*. A small school run by a cooperative of teachers, with a personal approach. There are classes in Italian (including commercial Italian), art history, art and crafts, food and drink, and opera singing.

Università per Stranieri, Ufficio Relazioni con lo Studente, Palazzo Gallenga, Piazza Fortebraccio 4, Perugia, **t** 075 57461, *www.unistrapg.it*. Month-long courses in Italian year-round, attracting up to 4,000 students a year.

Art Courses

There are courses on medieval art and the history of art, restoration and design at Florence's Università Internazionale dell'Arte, Villa Tornabuoni, Via Incontri 3, and workshops in art restoration at Florence's Istituto per l'Arte e il Restauro, Palazzo Spinelli, Borgo Santa Croce 10. In Spoleto, the Centro Italiano Studi di Alto Medioevo, in the Palazzo Ancaiani, offers classes on medieval art in April. Perugia's Accademia delle Belle Arti Pietro Vanucci, Piazza San Francesco al Prato 5, has painting and sculpture courses.

Music Courses

Music courses complement the numerous music festivals: Certaldo's medieval music society, Ars Nova, sponsors a seminar in July. Siena's Accademia Musicale Chigiana, Via di Città, offers masterclasses for instrumentalists and conductors; and in July and August Barga holds an International Opera workshop.

Cookery Courses

Capezzana Wine and Culinary Centre, Via Cappezana 100, 59011 Loc. Seano, Carmignano, 30km from Florence, **t** 055 870 6005, *www.cappezzana.it*. A wine- and olive oil-producing estate running courses for food professionals, skilled cooks and all those involved with food and wine. Accommodation is available in a wing of the villa.

A Taste of Florence, Via Taddea 31, Florence, **t** 055 292578, *www.divinacucina.com*. Courses run by a longtime US expat from her home near the central market in Florence, starting with shopping sessions. Groups are limited to six, and day or week courses are offered.

Medieval Sports

Some ancient sports such as the *palios* (two in Siena and one in Pesaro) are still popular, with rivalries between neighbourhoods and cities intense.

The Florentines play three games of Renaissance football (*calcio in costume*) a year; Sansepolcro and Gubbio stage two annual crossbow matches; while in Lucca archers compete from different city quarters.

Arezzo, Narni, Foligno, Pistoia and Ascoli Piceno have annual jousts; in Pisa there's a medieval tug-of-war.

Potholing

Spelunkers can find Tuscan caves to explore around Montecatini Alta, Monsummano and Sarteano. Monte Cucco near Gualdo Tadino has the most important caves in Umbria.

The Centro Nazionale di Speleologia Monte Cucco is in Costacciaro, **t** 075 917 0400.

Rowing

Umbria's Lake Piediluco earns top billing for its international rowing championship. When there's enough water, you can try your skills in the Arno (*see* p.170).

The annual rowing race between the four old maritime republics of Venice, Amalfi, Genoa and Pisa, alternates between the cities.

Skiing

Tuscany has major ski resorts at Abetone, north of Pistoia, and Monte Amiata.

In Umbria there's skiing in the Monti Sibillini, along the border of the Marches; many people also head south into Lazio to Terminillo, east of Rieti.

Tennis

Each *comune* has at least one or two courts that you can hire by the hour, and many hotels have them too.

Walking

Hiking and signed trails are best-developed in Tuscany; April–Oct is the best and safest time to go. There are several scenic routes through the mountains: the 4-day High Trail of the Apuan Alps, beginning from the Rifugio Carrara, above Carrara (for info call **t** 0585 841972, or the Italian Alpine Club/CAI, Via Giorgi, Carrara, **t** 0585 776782). A second trail, the Grand Apennine Excursion from Lake Scaffaiolo, goes along the mountain ridge that separates Tuscany from Emilia-Romagna, departing from Pracchia (info: **t** 0187 625154). There's a circular trail through the Garfagnana, from Castelnuovo di Garfagnana; contact the Comunità Montana Garfagnana, **t** 0583 644911. In southern Tuscany, trails cover Monte Amiata from Abbadia San Salvatore (Comunità Montana dell'Amiata, **t** 0564 969611).

Other fine day trails are in the Casentino, from Badia Prataglia or Stia, or in the nature parks of Monti dell'Uccellina from Alberese or the Maremma. Maremmagica (**t** 0564 20298) organizes trekking and walking tours with guides. For UK operators specializing in walks, *see* pp.69–70.

In Florence, you can get information from CAI, Via Mezzetta 2, **t** 055 612 0467. In Umbria, local CAI offices can suggest routes: in Perugia, at Via della Gabbia 9; in Spoleto, Vicolo Pianciani 4; in Terni, Via Fratelli Cervi 31; in the Marches, Macerata, Piazza Vittorio Veneto 14, and in most smaller mountain towns and villages.

Telephones

Public phones for **international calls** may be found in the offices of Telecom Italia, Italy's telephone company. They are the only places where you can make **reverse-charge (collect)** calls (*a erre*). but be prepared for a wait, as they go through the operator in Rome. **Rates** for long-distance calls are among the highest in Europe (they're lowest after 11pm).

Direct international calls may be made by dialling the **international prefix** (for the UK 0044, Ireland 00353, USA and Canada 001, Australia 0061, New Zealand 0064).

Calls within Italy are cheapest after 10pm. Most phone booths now take only **phonecards** (*schede telefoniche*) available in €3, €5 and €10 denominations at tobacconists and newsstands – you will have to snap off the small perforated corner to use them. Avoid telephoning from hotels, which often add 25% to the bill.

You now have to dial the full **town prefix**, including the zero, to call anywhere in Italy, even the town you are in. In this book we have given all phone numbers with the full town prefix. To **call Italy from abroad**, dial **t** 0039 followed by the area prefix, including the initial zero, e.g. 0039 06 for Rome.

Note that **mobile phone** numbers do NOT begin with an '0'.

Time

Italy is one hour ahead of UK time and six hours ahead of North American EST. Italian summer time runs from the last Sunday in March to the last Sunday in October; clocks change on those days.

Tipping

If you're in a **bar**, leave the small change in the form of the copper-coloured coins if you are standing, and around 30-50 cents if you sat down. In **restaurants**, service is usually included (if not, leave 10%) but it's nice to reward good service with a few euros.

For **taxis**, 10% is the norm.

Toilets

Don't get confused by Italian plurals: *signori* (gents), *signore* (ladies).

There are very few holes in the ground left in Italy, but public loos only exist in places such as train and bus stations and bars; the latter are legally obliged to let you use their *bagno* without buying a drink. Stations, motorway stops and smarter cafés have toilet attendants who expect a small tip.

Florence

Unless you come with the right attitude, initially Florence can be disenchanting. It only blossoms if you apply your mind as well as your vision, if you go slowly and do not let the art bedazzle until your eyes glaze over in dizzy excess (a common complaint, known in medical circles as the Stendhal syndrome). You will come to realize that loving and hating Florence at the same time may be the only rational response. It is the capital of contradiction; you begin to like it because it goes out of its way to annoy.

07

Don't miss

1. **Italy's best picture gallery**
   The Uffizi p.120
2. **The mystic egg that hatched the Renaissance**
   The Baptistry p.104
3. **Florence's pride, and symbol**
   Brunelleschi's dome p.107
4. **The greatest Renaissance sculpture**
   The Bargello p.129
5. **The finest of frescoes**
   Santa Maria Novella p.137

See map overleaf

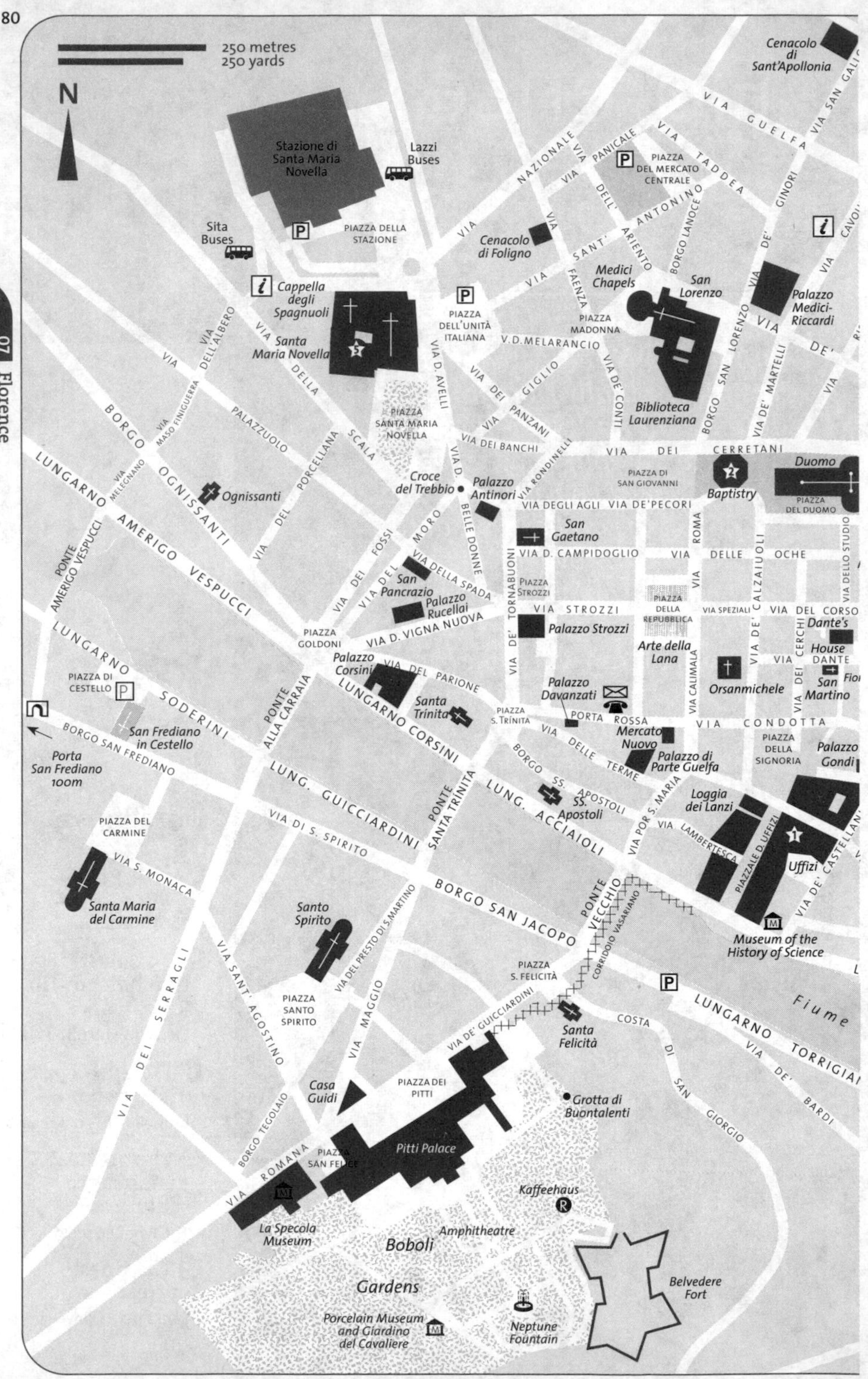
250 metres
250 yards
N
Cenacolo di Sant'Apollonia
Stazione di Santa Maria Novella
Lazzi Buses
Sita Buses
PIAZZA DELLA STAZIONE
PIAZZA DEL MERCATO CENTRALE
VIA GUELFA
VIA SAN GALLO
VIA NAZIONALE
VIA PANICALE
VIA TADDEA
VIA DELL' ARIENTO
VIA SANT' ANTONINO
BORGO LANOCE
VIA GINORI
VIA DE' GINORI
VIA CAVOUR
Cenacolo di Foligno
VIA FAENZA
Medici Chapels
San Lorenzo
Palazzo Medici-Riccardi
Cappella degli Spagnuoli
Santa Maria Novella
PIAZZA DELL'UNITÀ ITALIANA
PIAZZA MADONNA
V.D.MELARANCIO
VIA DE' CONTI
VIA DEL GIGLIO
VIA DEI PANZANI
Biblioteca Laurenziana
BORGO SAN LORENZO
VIA DE' MARTELLI
VIA DELL'ALBERO
VIA DELLA SCALA
VIA MASO FINIGUERRA
VIA PALAZZUOLO
VIA D. AVELLI
PIAZZA SANTA MARIA NOVELLA
BORGO OGNISSANTI
VIA MELEGNANO
VIA DEL PORCELLANA
VIA DEI BANCHI
VIA DEI CERRETANI
VIA RONDINELLI
PIAZZA DI SAN GIOVANNI
Duomo
PIAZZA DEL DUOMO
Baptistry
LUNGARNO AMERIGO VESPUCCI
Ognissanti
Croce del Trebbio
Palazzo Antinori
VIA D. MORO
VIA DEI FOSSI
VIA D. BELLE DONNE
VIA DEGLI AGLI
VIA DE'PECORI
San Gaetano
VIA D. CAMPIDOGLIO
VIA DELLE OCHE
VIA ROMA
VIA DEI CALZAIUOLI
VIA DELLO STUDIO
PONTE AMERIGO VESPUCCI
VIA DEL SOLE
VIA DELLA SPADA
San Pancrazio
Palazzo Rucellai
VIA DE' TORNABUONI
PIAZZA STROZZI
PIAZZA DELLA REPUBBLICA
VIA STROZZI
VIA SPEZIALI
VIA DEL CORSO
Dante's House
VIA DANTE
PIAZZA GOLDONI
VIA D. VIGNA NUOVA
Palazzo Strozzi
Arte della Lana
VIA CALIMALA
Orsanmichele
VIA DEI CERCHI
San Martino
LUNGARNO
PIAZZA DI CESTELLO
Palazzo Corsini
VIA DEL PARIONE
Palazzo Davanzati
PONTE ALLA CARRAIA
LUNGARNO CORSINI
Santa Trìnita
PIAZZA S. TRÌNITA
PORTA ROSSA
VIA CONDOTTA
LUNGARNO SODERINI
San Frediano in Cestello
BORGO SAN FREDIANO
Porta San Frediano 100m
VIA DELLE TERME
Mercato Nuovo
Palazzo di Parte Guelfa
PIAZZA DELLA SIGNORIA
Palazzo Gondi
LUNG. GUICCIARDINI
PONTE SANTA TRÌNITA
BORGO SS. APOSTOLI
SS. Apostoli
LUNG. ACCIAIOLI
VIA POR S. MARIA
Loggia dei Lanzi
VIA LAMBERTESCA
PIAZZALE D. UFFIZI
Uffizi
VIA DE' CASTELLANI
PIAZZA DEL CARMINE
VIA DI S. SPIRITO
VIA S. MONACA
Santa Maria del Carmine
BORGO SAN JACOPO
PONTE VECCHIO
CORRIDOIO VASARIANO
Museum of the History of Science
Santo Spirito
VIA DEL PRESTO DI S.MARTINO
PIAZZA S. FELICITÀ
VIA DEI SERRAGLI
VIA SANT' AGOSTINO
PIAZZA SANTO SPIRITO
VIA MAGGIO
VIA DE' GUICCIARDINI
Santa Felicità
COSTA DI SAN GIORGIO
LUNGARNO TORRIGIANI
VIA DE' BARDI
Fiume
Casa Guidi
PIAZZA DEI PITTI
Grotta di Buontalenti
BORGO TEGOLAIO
VIA ROMANA
PIAZZA SAN FELICE
Pitti Palace
Kaffeehaus
La Specola Museum
Amphitheatre
Boboli Gardens
Belvedere Fort
Porcelain Museum and Giardino del Cavaliere
Neptune Fountain

07 Florence

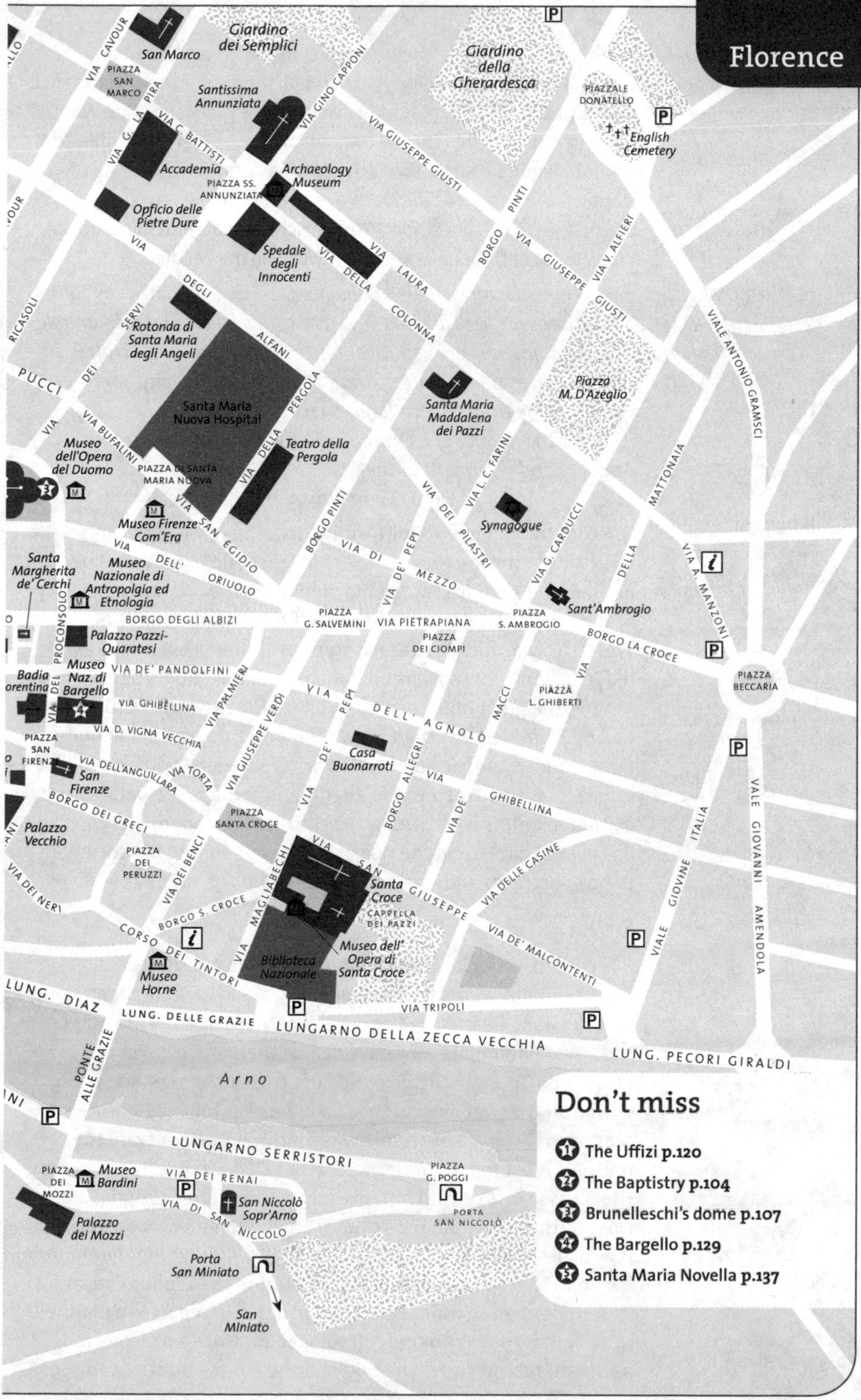

Giardino dei Semplici
San Marco
Piazza San Marco
Via Cavour
Via G. La Pira
Santissima Annunziata
Via Gino Capponi
Giardino della Gherardesca
Piazzale Donatello
English Cemetery
Via C. Battisti
Accademia
Archaeology Museum
Piazza SS. Annunziata
Opficio delle Pietre Dure
Via Giuseppe Giusti
Spedale degli Innocenti
Via della Colonna
Via Laura
Borgo Pinti
Via Giuseppe Giusti
Via V. Alfieri
Via Ricasoli
Via degli Servi
Via degli Alfani
Rotonda di Santa Maria degli Angeli
Viale Antonio Gramsci
Piazza M. D'Azeglio
Via Pucci
Santa Maria Nuova Hospital
Via della Pergola
Santa Maria Maddalena dei Pazzi
Via Bufalini
Museo dell'Opera del Duomo
Teatro della Pergola
Piazza di Santa Maria Nuova
Via L. C. Farini
Mattonaia
Synagogue
Museo Firenze Com'Era
Via San Egidio
Borgo Pinti
Via dei Pilastri
Via G. Carducci
Via della Mattonaia
Via A. Manzoni
Santa Margherita de' Cerchi
Museo Nazionale di Antropolgia ed Etnologia
Via dell' Oriuolo
Via di Mezzo
Via de' Pepi
Sant'Ambrogio
Borgo degli Albizi
Piazza G. Salvemini
Via Pietrapiana
Piazza S. Ambrogio
Palazzo Pazzi-Quaratesi
Piazza dei Ciompi
Borgo La Croce
Via del Proconsolo
Museo Naz. di Bargello
Via de' Pandolfini
Badia Fiorentina
Via Ghibellina
Via Palmieri
Via Macci
Piazza Beccaria
Piazza L. Ghiberti
Via dell' Agnolo
Via D. Vigna Vecchia
Via Giuseppe Verdi
Via de' Pepi
Piazza San Firenze
Via dell'Anguillara
Via Torta
Casa Buonarroti
San Firenze
Borgo Allegri
Via Ghibellina
Vale Giovanni Amendola
Borgo dei Greci
Piazza Santa Croce
Via de' Macci
Palazzo Vecchio
Piazza dei Peruzzi
Via dei Benci
Via Magliabechi
Via San Giuseppe
Via delle Casine
Viale Giovine Italia
Via dei Neri
Santa Croce
Cappella dei Pazzi
Borgo S. Croce
Museo dell' Opera di Santa Croce
Via de' Malcontenti
Corso dei Tintori
Museo Horne
Biblioteca Nazionale
Via Tripoli
Lung. Diaz
Lung. delle Grazie
Lungarno della Zecca Vecchia
Lung. Pecori Giraldi
Ponte alle Grazie
Arno
Lungarno Serristori
Piazza dei Mozzi
Museo Bardini
Via dei Renai
Piazza G. Poggi
Palazzo dei Mozzi
Via di San Niccolò
San Niccolò Sopr'Arno
Porta San Niccolò
Porta San Miniato
San Miniato

Don't miss

1. The Uffizi p.120
2. The Baptistry p.104
3. Brunelleschi's dome p.107
4. The Bargello p.129
5. Santa Maria Novella p.137

Fine balm let Arno be;
The walls of Florence all of silver rear'd,
And crystal pavements in the public way…

14th-century madrigal by Lapo Gianni

'Magari!' – 'If only!' – the modern Florentine would add to Gianni's vision, to this city of art and birthplace of the Renaissance, built by bankers and merchants whose sole preoccupation was making more florins. The precocious capital of Tuscany began to slip into legend back in the 14th century, during the lifetime of Dante; it was noted as *different* even before the Renaissance, before Boccaccio, Masaccio, Brunelleschi, Donatello, Leonardo da Vinci, Botticelli, Michelangelo, Machiavelli, the Medici…

> *This city of Florence is well populated, its good air a healthy tonic; its citizens are well dressed, and its women lovely and fashionable, its buildings are very beautiful, and every sort of useful craft is carried on in them, more so than any other Italian city. For this many come from distant lands to see her, not out of necessity, but for the quality of its manufactures and arts, and for the beauty and ornament of the city.*
>
> Dino Compagni in his *Chronicle* of 1312

According to the tourist office, in 1997, 685 years after Dino, more than 7 million tourists spent at least one night in a Florentine hotel. Some, perhaps, had dental appointments. A large percentage of the others came to inhale the rarefied air of the cradle of Western civilization, to gaze at some of the loveliest things ever made by mortal hands and minds, to walk the streets of new Athens, the great humanist 'city built to the measure of man'. Calling Florence's visitors 'tourists', however, doesn't seem quite right; 'tourism' implies pleasure, a principle alien to this dour, intellectual, measured town. 'Pilgrims' is perhaps the better word, cultural pilgrims who throng the Uffizi, the Accademia, the Bargello to gaze upon the holy mysteries of our secular society, to buy postcards and replicas, the holy cards of our day.

History

The identity of Florence's first inhabitants is a matter of dispute. There seems to have been some kind of settlement along the Arno long before the Roman era, perhaps as early as 1000 BC; the original founders may have been either native Italics or Etruscans. Throughout the period of Etruscan dominance, the village on the river lived in the shadow of Faesulae – Florence's present-day suburb of Fiesole was then an important city, the northernmost member of the Etruscan Dodecapolis. The Arno river cuts across central Italy like a wall. This narrow stretch of it, close to the mountain pass over to Emilia, was always the most logical place for a bridge.

Roman Florence can claim no less a figure than **Julius Caesar** for its founder. Like so many other Italian cities, it began as a planned urban enterprise in an underdeveloped province – a colony for army veterans in 59 BC. The origin of the name – so suggestive of

Florentine Duality

Dante's *Vita Nuova*, the autobiography of his young soul, was only the beginning of Florentine analysis; Petrarch, the introspective 'first modern man', was a Florentine born in exile; Ghiberti was the first artist to write an autobiography; Cellini wrote one of the most readable; Alberti invented art criticism; Vasari invented art history; Michelangelo's personality, in his letters and sonnets, looms as large as his art. In many ways Florence broke away from the medieval idea of community and invented the modern concept of the individual, most famously expressed by Lorenzo de' Medici's friend, Pico della Mirandola, whose *Oration on the Dignity of Man* tells us what the God on the Sistine Chapel ceiling was saying when he created Adam: '...And I have created you neither celestial nor terrestrial, neither mortal nor immortal, so that, like a free and able sculptor and painter of yourself, you may mould yourself entirely in the form of your choice.'

To attempt to understand Florence, remember one historical constant: no matter what the issue, the city always takes both sides, vehemently and often violently, especially in the Punch and Judy days of Guelphs and Ghibellines. In the 1300s this was explained by the fact that the city was founded under the sign of Mars, the war god; but in medieval astronomy Mars is also connected with Aries, another Florentine symbol and the sign of the time of spring blossoms. (The Annunciation, at the beginning of spring, was Florence's most important festival.) One of the city's oldest symbols is the lily (or iris), flying on its oldest gonfalons. Perhaps even older is its *Marzocco*, originally an equestrian statue of Mars on the Ponte Vecchio, later replaced by Donatello's grim lion.

Whatever dispute rocked the streets, Great-Aunt Florence often expressed her schizophrenia in art – floral Florence versus stone Florence, epitomized by the irreconcilable differences between the two most famous works of art: Botticelli's graceful *Primavera* and Michelangelo's cold, perfect *David*. The 'city of flowers' seems a joke; it has nary a real flower, nor even a tree, in its stone streets; indeed, all effort has gone into keeping nature at bay, surpassing it with geometry and art. And yet the Florentines were perhaps the first since the Romans to discover the joys of the countryside. The rusticated stone palaces, like fortresses or prisons, hide charms as delightful as Gozzoli's frescoes in the Palazzo Medici-Riccordi. Luca della Robbia's dancing children and floral wreaths are contemporary with the naked, violent warriors of the Pollaluolo brothers; the writhing, quarrelsome statuary in the Piazza della Signoria is sheltered by one of the most delicate *loggie* imaginable.

After 1500, all the good, bad and ugly symptoms of the Renaissance peaked in the mass fever of Mannerism. Then, drifting into a debilitating twilight, Florence gave birth to the artistic phenomenon known as kitsch – the Medici Princes' chapel is an early kitsch classic. Since then, worn out perhaps, or embarrassed, this city built by merchants has kept its own counsel, expressing its argumentative soul in overblown controversies about traffic, art restoration and the undesirability of fast-food counters and cheap *pensioni*. We who find her fascinating hope she some day comes to remember her proper role, bearing the torch of culture instead of merely collecting tickets for the culture torture.

springtime and flowers – is another mystery. First it was *Florentia*, then *Fiorenza* in the Middle Ages, and finally *Firenze*. One guess is that its foundation took place in April, when the Romans were celebrating the games of the Floralia.

The original street plan of Florentia can be seen today in the neat rectangle of blocks between Via Tornabuoni and Via del Proconsolo, between the Duomo and Piazza della Signoria. Its forum occupied roughly the site of the modern Piazza della Repubblica, and the outline of its amphitheatre can be traced in the oval of streets just west of Piazza Santa Croce. Roman Florentia never really imposed itself on the historian. One writer mentions it as a major town and river crossing along the Via Cassia, connected to Rome and the thriving new cities of northern Italy, such as Bononia and

Getting to Florence

Florence is the central transport node for Tuscany and harder to avoid than to reach.

By Air

Florence's **Vespucci airport** was lengthened in 1996, and now bustles with at least as much international traffic as Pisa. It is 4km out at Peretola, *www.aeroporto.firenze.it*, flight information **t** 055 306 1300 (recorded message in Italian and English). There is a regular **bus** to Florence, terminating at Santa Maria Novella station (15mins). A **taxi** to the centre will cost €20–25.

Alitalia: Lungarno Acciaioli 10/12r, **t** 055 278 8231 (reservations, **t** 06 2222), *www.alitalia.it*.
British Airways: **t** 199 712266 or contact Pisa office, **t** 050 501838, *www.ba.com*.
Meridiana (for London Gatwick): Peretola Airport 28r, **t** 892 928, *www.meridiana.it*.

By Train

The central station is **Santa Maria Novella**; call **t** 892021 for information, *www.trenitalia.com*. Many long-distance trains arriving at night use **Campo di Marte** station, bus nos.12 or 91.

By Bus

It's possible to reach nearly every city, town and village in Tuscany from Florence – once you know which of several bus companies to patronize. The tourist office has a complete list, but here are some of the most popular:

SITA, near station, Via S. Caterina da Siena 15, **t** 055 294955, **t** 800 373760, *www.sitabus.it*: towns in the Val d'Elsa, Chianti, Val di Pesa, Mugello and Casentino; Anghiari, Arezzo, Bibbiena, Castelfiorentino, Certaldo, Città di Castello, Consuma, Figline Valdarno, Firenzuola, Marina di Grosseto, Montevarchi, Poggibonsi (for San Gimignano and Volterra), Pontassieve, Poppi, Pratovecchio, Sansepolcro, Scarperia, Siena, Stia and Vallombrosa.

LAZZI, Piazza Stazione 47r, **t** 055 351061 Mon–Fri, *www.lazzi.it*: along the Arno to the coast, including Calenzano, Cerreto Guidi, Empoli, Forte dei Marmi, Livorno, Lucca, Marina di Carrara, Marina di Massa, Montecatini Terme, Montelupo, Montevarchi, Pescia, Pisa, Pistoia, Pontedera, Prato, Signa, Tirrenia, Torre del Lago, Viareggio.

CAP, Ligo Fili Alimani 9, **t** 055 214637, *www.capautolinee.it*: Borgo S. Lorenzo, Impruneta, Pistoia, Prato.

Blubus, Ligo Fili Alimani 11, **t** 055 214637, *www.blubus.it*: Abetone, Cerreto Guidi, Pistoia, Poggio a Caiano, and Vinci.

GRIFORAMA, Lazzi station, **t** 0564 475111, *www.griforama.it*: Grosseto.

Getting around Florence

Florence is a relatively easy city to get around, because nearly everything you'll want to see is within easy walking distance, and large areas in the centre are pedestrian zones. In addition, there are no hills to climb, and it's hard to lose your way for very long.

Just to make life complicated, however, Florence has two sets of **address numbers** on every street – red ones for business, blue or black for residences; your hotel could be either. However, there has been some improvement in recent years: every major *piazza*, landmark or monument now has a plaque offering relevant background information, and helpful maps have been posted in strategic positions throughout the city.

By Bus

City buses (**ATAF**; *www.ataf.net*) can whizz or inch you across Florence, and are an excellent means of reaching sights on the periphery. Most useful lines begin at Santa Maria Novella station and pass by Piazza del Duomo or Piazza San Marco.

ATAF supply a comprehensive booklet, including a clear map, with details of all bus routes, available at the information/ticket booth at the station, tourist offices, some bars, and at ATAF's central office in Piazza della Stazione, **t** 800 424 500. **Ticket prices**: €1 for 60mins, €1.80 for 3hrs, €4.50 for 24hrs, €16 for a week.

The most useful buses for visitors are:

6 Via Rondinella–Piazza San Marco–Duomo–Stazione–Soffiano.
7 Stazione –Duomo–San Domenico–Fiesole.
10 Stazione –Duomo–San Marco–Ponte a Mensola–Settignano.
11 Viale Calatafimi–San Marco–Piazza Indipendenza–Stazione–Porta Romana–Poggio Imperiale.

11a Viale Calatafimi–Duomo–Porta Romana–Poggio Imperiale.
13 Stazione –Ponte Rosso–Parterre (car park)–Piazza Libertà–Viale Mazzini–Campo di Marte–Piazzale Michelangelo–Porta Romana.
14c Rovezzano–Duomo–Stazione–Careggi (hospital).
17 Cascine–Stazione–Duomo–Via Lamarmora–Salviatino (for the youth hostel).
25 Stazione–San Marco–Piazza Libertà–Via Bolognese–Pratolino.
28 Stazione–Via R Giuliani–Castello–Sesto Fiorentino.
37 Stazione–Ponte alla Carraia–Porta Romana–Certosa del Galluzzo.
38 Porta Romana–Pian del Giullari (you need to book this one from the telephone near the bus stop at Porta Romana, **t** 800 541200 toll free).

As part of the continuing campaign against city smog, a fleet of Lilliputian **electric buses**, routes A, B and D, have recently been introduced. These mainly serve the centre, often taking circuitous routes 'round the houses', and are a good way of seeing some of the sights if you've had enough walking. Details of routes can be found on the ATAF maps. A tram system is currently under construction.

By Taxi

Taxis in Florence don't cruise; you'll find them in ranks at the station and in the major *piazze*, or else ring for a **radio taxi**, **t** 055 4798 or 4242. Taxi meters start at €2.64 plus extras, adding €0.85 per km. There is a minimum charge of €4.30.

By Car

Until the late 1980s, Florence had the most carcinogenic traffic problems in Italy. But in 1988, with great fanfares and accompanied by howls of protest, the city tried to do something about the cars that were choking it to death, by enlarging the limited access zone, the *zona di traffico limitato* (**ZTL**). Within the ZTL, only buses, taxis and cars belonging to residents are permitted; otherwise, you are permitted to pay to park in one of the city's **car parks** (there's the underground car park at the station, or the cheaper, big park at the Parterre, near Piazza Libertà; see *www.firenzeparcheggi.it* for a full list) or take your chances on a sidestreet or on metered parking areas as shown on the maps at the beginning of this chapter.

This new regulation was then followed by whole areas, especially around Piazza della Signoria and the Duomo, becoming totally traffic-free zones. The only danger is the odd ambulance or police car, the speeding mopeds (all of which you can easily hear), and the deadly silent bicycle.

Bicycle, Scooter and Golf Cart Hire

Hiring a **bike** can save you tramping time and angst but it's not risk-free. Watch out for cars and pedestrians. Electric **golf carts** holding up to 4 people have access to pedestrian zones. For both, try **Biancaneve**, **t** 055 7139270.

You can hire a **motorbike** at:
Alinari, Via Guelfa 85r, **t** 055 280500.
Motorent, Via S. Zanobi 9r, **t** 055 490113.
Florence by Bike, Via S. Zanobi 120/122r, **t** 055 488992, *www.florencebybike.it*.

Between 8am and 7.30pm, visitors can now take advantage of one of the (almost) **free bicycles** supplied by the *comune* of Florence. There are various pick-up points around town, the most central being the Fortezza, the Parterre (for the car parks), Piazza Strozzi, Piazza Stazione, Piazza San Marco, the central market and Porta Romana. They cost about €1 for a day.

Car Hire

When you can't take any more art, hire a car and escape into the ravishing countryside. Most rental firms are within easy walking distance of the station.
Avis, Borgo Ognissanti 128r, **t** 055 213629, *www.avisautonoleggio.it*.
Europcar, Borgo Ognissanti 53r, **t** 800 014410, *www.europcar.it*.
Hertz, Via M Finiguerra 33, **t** 199 112211, **t** 055 239 8205, *www.hertz.it*.
Italy by Car, Borgo Ognissanti 134r, **t** 055 287161, *www.Italybycar.it*.
Maggiore-Budget, Via M. Finiguerra 31r, **t** 055 210238, *www.maggiore.it*.
Program, Borgo Ognissanti 135, **t** 055 282916.

Mediolanum (Bologna and Milan). At the height of the empire, the municipal boundaries had expanded out to Via de' Fossi, Via S. Egidio, and Via de' Benci. Nevertheless, Florentia did not play a significant role either in the Empire's heyday or in its decline.

After the fall of Rome, Florence weathered its troubles comparatively well. We hear of it withstanding sieges by the Goths around the year 400, when it was defended by the famous imperial general Stilicho, and again in 541, during the campaigns of Totila and Belisarius; all through the Greek-Gothic wars Florence seems to have taken the side of Constantinople. The Lombards arrived around 570; under their rule Florence was the seat of a duchy subject to the then Tuscan capital of Lucca. The next mention in the chronicles refers to Charlemagne spending Christmas with the Florentines in the year 786. Like the rest of Italy, Florence had undoubtedly declined; a new set of walls went up under Carolingian rule, about 800, enclosing an area that was scarcely larger than the original Roman settlement of 59 BC. Most likely throughout the Dark Ages the city was gradually increasing its relative importance and strength at the expense of its neighbours. The famous baptistry, which was erected some time between the 6th and 9th centuries, is the only important building from that troubled age in all Tuscany.

By the 1100s, Florence was the leading city of the County of Tuscany. **Countess Matilda**, ally of Pope Gregory VII against the emperors, oversaw the construction of a new set of walls in 1078, coinciding with the widest Roman-era boundaries. The city had recovered all the ground lost during the Dark Ages, and the momentum of growth did not abate. New walls again in the 1170s enclosed what was becoming one of the largest cities in Europe. In this period, Florence owed its growth and prosperity largely to the textile industry – weaving and 'finishing' cloth not only from Tuscany but wool shipped from as far afield as Spain and England. The capital gain from this trade, managed by the Calimala and the Arte della Lana, Florence's richest guilds, led naturally to an even more profitable business – banking and finance.

The Florentine Republic Battles with the Barons

In 1125, Florence once and for all conquered its ancient rival Fiesole. Wealth and influence brought with them increasing political responsibilities; the city often found itself at war with its neighbours. Since Countess Matilda's death in 1115, Florence had become a self-governing *comune*, largely independent of the emperor and local barons. The new city republic's hardest problems, however, were closer to home. The nobles of the county, encouraged in their anachronistic feudal behaviour by representatives of the imperial government, proved irreconcilable enemies to the new merchant republic, and Florence spent most of the 12th century trying to keep them in line. Often the city actually declared war on a noble clan, as with the Alberti, or the counts of Guidi, and razed their castles whenever they captured one. To complicate the situation, nobles attracted by the stimulation of urban life – along with the opportunities for making money – often moved their families into Florence itself.

They brought their country habits with them: a boyish eagerness to brawl with their neighbours on the slightest pretext, and a complete disregard for the laws of the *comune*. Naturally, they couldn't feel secure without a little urban castle of their own, and before long Florence's skyline, like that of any prosperous Italian city of the Middle Ages, featured hundreds of tower-fortresses, built as much for status as for defence. Many were more than 60m in height. It wasn't uncommon for the honest citizen to come home from work hoping for a little peace and quiet, only to find siege engines in front of the house and a company of bowmen in the children's bedroom.

But just as Florence was able to break the power of the rural nobles, those in the town also eventually had to succumb. The last tower-fortresses were chopped down to size in the early 1300s. But even without the nobles raising all manner of hell, the Florentines managed to find brand new ways to keep the pot boiling. The rich merchants who dominated the government, familiarly known as the *popolari grossi*, resorted to every sort of murder and mayhem to beat down the demands of the lesser guilds, the *popolari minuti*, for a fair share of the wealth; the two only managed to settle their differences when confronted by murmurs of discontent from what was then one of Europe's largest urban proletariats. But even beyond simple class issues, the city born under the fiery sign of Mars always found a way to make trouble. Not only did Florentines pursue the Guelph-Ghibelline conflict with greater zest than almost any Tuscan city; according to chronicles, they started it. In 1215, men of the Amidei family murdered a prominent citizen named Buondelmonte dei Buondelmonti over a broken wedding engagement; this was the spark that ignited the factionalist struggles first in Florence, then quickly throughout Italy.

Guelphs and Ghibellines

In the 13th century there was never a dull moment in Florence. Guelphs and Ghibellines, often more involved with some feud between powerful families than with real political issues, cast each other into exile and confiscated each other's property with every change of the wind. Religious strife occasionally pushed politics off the front page. In the 1240s, a curious foreshadowing of the Reformation saw Florence wrapped up in the **Patarene heresy**.

This sect, closely related to the Albigensians of southern France, was as obsessed with the presence of Evil in the world as John Calvin – or Florence's own future fire-and-brimstone preacher, Savonarola. Exploiting a streak of religious eccentricity that has always seemed present in the Florentine psyche, the Patarenes thrived in the city, even electing their own bishop. The established Church was up to the challenge; St Peter Martyr, a bloodthirsty Dominican, led his armies of axe-wielding monks to the assault in 1244, exterminating almost the entire Patarene community.

In 1248, with help from Emperor Frederick II, Florence's Ghibellines booted out the Guelphs – once and for all, they thought – but two years later the Guelphs were back, and it was the Ghibellines' turn to leave. The new Guelph regime, called the *primo popolo*, was for the first time completely in the control of the bankers and merchants. It passed the first measures to control the privileges of the turbulent, largely Ghibelline nobles, and forced them all to chop the tops off their tower-fortresses. The next decades witnessed a series of wars with the Ghibelline cities of Tuscany – Siena, Pisa and Pistoia, not just by coincidence Florence's habitual enemies. Usually the Florentines were the aggressors, and more often than not fortune favoured them. In 1260, however, the Sienese, reinforced by Ghibelline exiles from Florence and a few imperial cavalry, destroyed an invading Florentine army at the **battle of Montaperti**. Florence was at the Ghibellines' mercy. Only the refusal of Farinata degli Uberti, the leader of the exiles, to allow the city's destruction kept the Sienese from torching it – a famous episode recounted by Dante in the *Inferno*. (In a typical Florentine gesture of gratitude, Dante found a home for Uberti in one of the lower circles of hell.)

In Florence, a Ghibelline regime under Count Guido Novello made life rough for the wealthy Guelph bourgeoisie. As luck would have it, though, only a few years later the Guelphs were back in power, and Florence was winning on the battlefield again. The new Guelph government, the *secondo popolo*, earned a brief respite from factional strife. In 1289, Florence won a great victory over another old rival, Arezzo. This was the **battle of Campaldino**, where the Florentine citizen army included young Dante Alighieri. In 1282, and again in 1293, Florence tried to clean up an increasingly corrupt government with a series of reforms. The 1293 Ordinamenti della Giustizia once and for all excluded the nobles from the important political offices. By now, however, the real threat to the Guelph merchants' rule did not come so much from the nobility, which had been steadily falling behind in wealth and power for two centuries, but from the lesser guilds, which had been excluded from a share of the power, and also from the growing working class employed in the textile mills and the foundries.

Despite all the troubles, the city's wealth and population grew tremendously throughout the 1200s. Its trade contacts spread across Europe, and crowned heads from London to Constantinople found Florentine bankers ready to float them a loan. About 1235 Florence minted modern Europe's first gold coin, the florin, which soon became a standard currency across the continent. By 1300 Florence counted more than 100,000 souls, making it a little cramped, even inside the vast circuit of walls built by the *comune* in the 1280s. It was not only one of the largest cities in Europe but also one of the richest. Besides banking, the wool trade was also booming: by 1300 the wool guild, the Arte della Lana, had more than 200 large workshops in the city alone. Naturally, this opulence created new possibilities for culture and art. Florence's golden age began perhaps in the 1290s, when the *comune* started its tremendous programme of public buildings – including the Palazzo della Signoria and the cathedral; important religious structures, such as Santa Croce, were under way at the same time. Cimabue was the artist of the day; Giotto was just beginning, and his friend Dante was hard at work on the *Commedia*.

As in so many other Italian cities, Florence developed its republican institutions slowly and painfully. At the beginning of the *comune* in 1115, the leaders were a class called the *boni homines*, which was made up mostly of nobles. Only a few decades later, these were calling themselves *consules*, evoking a memory of the ancient Roman republic. When the Ghibellines took over, the leading official was a *podestà* appointed by the emperor. Later, under the Guelphs, the *podestà* and a new officer called the *capitano del popolo* were both elected by the citizens. With the reforms of the 1290s Florence's republican constitution was perfected – though it satisfied only a few citizens and guaranteed future trouble. Power was invested in the council of the richer guilds, the *Signoria*; the new Palazzo della Signoria was designed expressly as a symbol of their authority, replacing the old Bargello, which had been the seat of the *podestà*. The most novel feature of the government, designed to avoid the violent factionalism of the past, was the selection of officials by lot from among the guild members. In effect, politics was to be abolished.

Business as Usual: Riot, War, Plagues and Revolution

Despite the reforms of the Ordinamenti, Florence found little peace in the new century. As if following some strange and immutable law of city-state behaviour, no sooner had the Guelphs established total control than they themselves split into new factions. The radically anti-imperial **Blacks** and the more conciliatory **Whites** fought each other through the early 1300s with the same fervour that both had once exercised against the

Ghibellines. The Whites, who included Dante among their partisans, came out losers when the Blacks conspired with the pope to bring Charles of Valois' French army into Florence; almost all the losing faction were forced into exile in 1302. Some of them must have sneaked back, for the chronicles of 1304 record the Blacks trying to burn them out of their houses with incendiary bombs, resulting in a fire that consumed a quarter of the city.

Beginning in 1313, Florence was involved in a constant series of inconclusive wars waged with Pisa, Lucca and Arezzo, among others. In 1325, the city was defeated and nearly destroyed by the great Lucchese general **Castruccio Castracani** (*see* p.238). Castruccio died of a common cold while the siege was already underway, in another instance of Florence's famous good luck, unfortunately one of the last. The factions may have been suppressed, but fate had found some more novel disasters for the city. One far-off monarch did more damage to Florence than its Italian enemies had ever managed – King Edward III of England, who in 1339 found it expedient to repudiate his foreign debts. Florence's two biggest banks, the Bardi and the Peruzzi, immediately went bust, and the city's standing as the centre of international finance was gravely damaged.

One constant throughout the history of the republic was the oppression of the poor. The ruling bankers and merchants exploited the labour of the masses and gave them only the bare minimum in return. In the 14th century, undernourishment, overcrowding and a large population of rats made Florence's poorer neighbourhoods a breeding ground for epidemics. Famine, plagues and riots became common in the 1340s, causing a severe political crisis. At one point, in 1342, the Florentines gave over their government to a foreign dictator, Walter de Brienne, the French-Greek 'Duke of Athens'. He lasted only for a year before a popular revolt ended the experiment. The **Black Death** of 1348, which provided the background for Boccaccio's *Decameron*, carried off perhaps one-half of the population. Coming on the heels of a serious depression, it was a blow from which Florence would never really manage to recover.

In the next two centuries, when the city was to stake its position as the great innovator in Western culture, it was already in relative decline, a politically decadent republic with a stagnant economy, barely holding its own among the changes in trade and diplomacy. For the time being, however, things didn't look too bad. Florence bought control of Prato, in 1350, and was successful in a defensive war against expansionist Milan in 1351. War was almost continuous for the last half of the century, constituting a strain on the exchequer but not usually a threat to the city's survival; this was the heyday of the mercenary companies, led by *condottieri* such as

Sir John Hawkwood (Giovanni Acuto), immortalized in Florence's cathedral. Before the Florentines made him a better offer, Hawkwood was often in the employ of their enemies.

Through the century, the Guelph party had steadily tightened its grip over the republic's affairs. Despite the selection of officials by lot, by the 1370s party organization bore an uncanny resemblance to some of the big-city political machines common not so long ago in America. The merchants and the bankers who ran the party used it to turn the Florentine republic into a profit-making business. With the increasingly limited opportunities for making money in trade and finance, the Guelph ruling class tried to make up the difference by soaking the poor. Wars and taxes stretched Florentine tolerance to breaking point, and finally, in 1378, came revolution. The **Ciompi revolt** (*ciompi* were wage labourers in the textile industries) began in July, when a mob of workers seized the Bargello. Under the leadership of wool-carder Michele di Lando, they executed a few Guelph bosses and announced a new, reformed constitution. They were also foolish enough to believe the Guelph magnates when they promised to abide by the new arrangement if only the *ciompi* would go home. Before long Di Lando was in exile and the ruling class firmly back in the seat of power, more than ever determined to eliminate the last vestiges of democracy from the republic.

The Rise of the Medici

In 1393 Florentines celebrated the 100th anniversary of the great reform of the Ordinamenti, while watching their republic descend into oligarchy. In that year **Maso degli Albizzi** became *gonfaloniere* (the head of the Signoria) and served as virtual dictator for many years afterwards. The ruling class of merchants, more than a bit paranoid after the Ciompi Revolt, were relieved to see power concentrated in strong hands. In an atmosphere of repression and conspiracy, the Signoria's secret police hunted down malcontents while Florentine exiles plotted against the republic in foreign courts. Florence was almost constantly at war. In 1398 it defeated an attempt at conquest by Giangaleazzo Visconti of Milan. The imperialist policy of the Albizzi and their allies resulted in some important territorial gains, including the conquest of Pisa in 1406, and the purchase of Livorno from the Genoese in 1421, but unsuccessful wars against Lucca finally disenchanted the Florentines with Albizzi rule. An emergency *parlamento* (the infrequent popular assembly usually called when a coming change of rulers was obvious) in 1434 decreed the recall from exile of the head of the popular opposition, **Cosimo de' Medici**.

Perhaps it was something that could only have happened in Florence – the darling of the plebeians, the great hope for reform, was also the head of Florence's biggest bank. The Medici family had their roots in the Mugello region north of Florence. Their name seems to suggest that they once were pharmacists (later enemies would jibe at the balls on the family arms as 'the pills'). For two centuries they had been active in Florentine politics; many had acquired reputations as troublemakers; their names turned up often in the lists of exiles and records of lawsuits. None of the Medici had ever been particularly rich until **Giovanni di Bicci de' Medici** (1360–1429) parlayed his wife's dowry into the founding of a bank. Good fortune – and a temporary monopoly on the handling of the pope's finances – made the Medici Bank Florence's biggest.

Giovanni had been content to stay on the fringe of politics; his son, **Cosimo** (known in Florentine history as '**Il Vecchio**', the 'old man'), took good care of the bank's affairs but aimed his sights much higher. His strategy was as old as Julius Caesar – the patrician reformer, cultivating the best men, winning the favour of the poor with largesse and gradually, carefully forming a party under a system specifically designed to prevent such things. In 1433 Rinaldo degli Albizzi had him exiled, but it was too late; continuing discontent forced his return only a year later, and for the next 35 years Cosimo would be the unchallenged ruler of Florence. Throughout this period, Cosimo occasionally held public office – this was done by lottery, with the electoral lists manipulated to ensure a majority of Medici supporters at all times. Nevertheless, he received ambassadors at the new family palace (built in 1444), entertained visiting popes and emperors, and made all the important decisions. A canny political godfather and usually a gentleman, Cosimo was also a useful patron to the great figures of the early Renaissance – including Donatello and Brunelleschi. His father had been one of the judges in the famous competition for the baptistry doors, and Cosimo was a member of the commission that picked Brunelleschi to design the cathedral dome.

Under Cosimo's leadership Florence began Europe's first progressive income tax, and invented the concept of the national debt – endlessly rolling over bonds to keep the republic afloat and creditors happy. The poor, with fewer taxes to pay, were also happy, and the ruling classes were positively delighted; never in Florence's history had any government so successfully muted class conflict and the desire for a genuine democracy. Wars were few, and the internal friction negligible. Cosimo died in August 1464; his tomb in San Lorenzo bears the inscription *Pater patriae*, and no dissent was registered when his 40-year-old son **Piero** took up the boss's role.

Lorenzo il Magnifico

Piero didn't quite have the touch of his masterful father, but he survived a stiff political crisis in 1466, when he outmanoeuvred a new faction led by wealthy banker Luca Pitti. In 1469 he succumbed to the Medici family disease, gout, and his 20-year-old son **Lorenzo** succeeded him in an equally smooth transition. He was to last for 23 years. As he was not necessarily more 'magnificent' than other contemporary princes, or other Medici, Lorenzo's honorific reveals something of the myth that was to grow up around him in later centuries. His long reign corresponded with the height of the Florentine Renaissance. It was a relatively peaceful time, and in the light of the disasters that were to follow, Florentines could not help looking back on it as a golden age.

As a ruler, Lorenzo showed many virtues. Still keeping up the pretence of being a private citizen, he lived relatively simply, always accessible to the concerns of his fellow citizens, who would often see him walking the city streets. In the field of foreign policy he was indispensable to Florence and indeed all Italy; he did more than anyone to keep the precarious peninsular balance of power from disintegrating. The most dramatic affair of his reign was the **Pazzi conspiracy**, an attempt to assassinate Lorenzo plotted by Pope Sixtus IV and the wealthy Pazzi family, the pope's bankers and ancient rivals of the Medici. In 1478, two of the Pazzi attacked Lorenzo and his brother Giuliano during mass at the cathedral. Giuliano was killed but Lorenzo managed to escape into the sacristy. The botched murder aborted the planned revolt; the Florentines showed little interest in the Pazzis' call to arms, and before nightfall most of the conspirators were dangling from the cornice of the Palazzo Vecchio.

Apparently, Lorenzo had angered the pope by starting a syndicate to mine for alum in Volterra, threatening the papal monopoly. Since Sixtus failed to murder Lorenzo, he had to settle for excommunicating him, and declaring war in alliance with King Ferrante of Naples. The war went badly for Florence and, in the most memorable act of his career, Lorenzo walked into the lion's cage, travelling to negotiate with the terrible Neapolitan, who had already murdered more than one important guest. As it turned out, Ferrante was only too happy to dump his papal entanglements; Florence found itself at peace once more, and Lorenzo returned home to a hero's welcome.

In other affairs, both foreign and domestic, Lorenzo was more a lucky ruler than a skilled one. Florence's economy was entering a long, slow decline, but for the moment the banks and mills were churning out just enough profit to keep up the accustomed level of opulence. The Medici Bank was on the ropes. Partly because of Lorenzo's neglect, it came close to collapsing on several occasions – and it seems that Lorenzo blithely made up the losses with public funds. Culturally, he was fortunate to be the nabob of Florence at its most artistically creative period; later historians and Medici propagandists gave him a reputation as an art patron that is entirely undeserved. His own tastes tended towards bric-a-brac, jewellery, antique statues and vases; there is little evidence that he appreciated the extraordinary talents of the great artists around him. Perhaps because he was too nearsighted to see anything clearly, he did not commission a single important canvas or fresco in Florence (except for Luca Signorelli's mysterious *Pan*, which was lost in Berlin during the last war). His favourite architect was the hack Giuliano da Sangallo.

Lorenzo was brought up with some of the leading humanist scholars of Tuscany for tutors and his real interests were literary. His well-formed lyrics and winsome pastorals have earned him a place among Italy's greatest 15th-century poets; they neatly reflect the private side of Lorenzo, the retiring, scholarly family man who enjoyed life better in one of the many rural Medici villas than in the busy city. In this he was perfectly in tune with his class and his age. Plenty of Florentine bankers were learning the joys of country life, reading Horace or Catullus in their geometrical gardens and pestering their tenant farmers with well-meant advice.

Back in town they had thick, new walls of rusticated sandstone between them and the bustle of the streets. The late 15th century was the great age of palace-building in Florence. Following the example of Cosimo de' Medici, the bankers and merchants erected dozens of palaces (some of the best can be seen around Via Tornabuoni), each with blank walls and iron-barred windows to the street. Historians always note a turning inward, a 'privatization' of Florentine life in this period. In a city that had become a republic only in name, civic interest and public life ceased to matter so much. The rich began to assume the airs of an aristocracy, and did everything they could to distance themselves from their fellow citizens. Ironically, just at the time when Florence's artists were creating their greatest achievements, the republican ethos, the civic soul that had made Florence great, began to disintegrate.

Savonarola

Lorenzo's death, in 1492, was followed by another apparently smooth transition of power to his son **Piero**. But after 58 years of Medicean quiet and stability, the city was ready for a change. The opportunity came soon enough, when the timid and inept Piero allowed the invading king of France, **Charles VIII**, to occupy Pisa and the Tuscan coast. A spontaneous revolt chased Piero and the rest of the Medici into exile, while a mob sacked the family's palace. A new regime, under **Piero Capponi**, dealt sternly with the French and tried to pump new life into the dormant republican constitution.

The Florence that threw out the Medici was a city in the mood for some radical reform. Already, the dominating figure on the political stage was an intense Dominican friar from Ferrara named

Girolamo Savonarola. Perhaps unsurprisingly, this oversophisticated and overstimulated city was also in the mood to be told how wicked and decadent it was, and Savonarola was happy to oblige. A spellbinding revival preacher with a touch of erudition, Savonarola packed as many as 10,000 into the Duomo to hear his weekly sermons, which were laced with political sarcasm and social criticism. Though an insufferable prig, he was also a sincere democrat. There is a story that the dying Lorenzo called Savonarola to his bedside for the last rites, and that the friar refused him absolution unless he 'restored the liberty of the Florentines', a proposal that only made the dying despot sneer with contempt.

Savonarola also talked Charles VIII into leaving Florence in peace. Pisa, however, took advantage of the confusion to revolt, and the restored republic's attempts to recapture it were in vain. Things were going badly. Piero Capponi's death in 1496 left Florence without an able leader, and Savonarolan extremists became ever more influential. The French invasion and the incessant wars that followed cost the city dearly in trade, while the Medici, now in Rome, intrigued to destroy the republic. Worst of all, Savonarola's attacks on clerical corruption made him another bitter enemy in Rome – **Pope Alexander VI**, the most corrupt cleric ever – who scraped together a league of allies to make war on Florence in 1497.

This war proceeded without serious reverses for either side but Savonarola was able to exploit it brilliantly, convincing the Florentines that they were on a moral crusade against the hated and dissolute Borgias, Medici, French, Venetians and Milanese. The year 1497 was undoubtedly the high point of Savonarola's career. The good friar's spies – mostly children – kept a close eye on any Florentines who were suspected of enjoying themselves, and collected books, fancy clothes and works of art for the famous **Bonfire of Vanities**. It was a climactic moment in the history of Florence's delicate psyche. Somehow the spell had been broken; like the deranged old Michelangelo, taking a hammer to his own work, the Florentines gathered the objects that had once been their greatest pride and put them to the torch. The bonfire was held in the centre of the Piazza della Signoria; a visiting Venetian offered to buy the whole lot, but the Florentines had someone sketch his portrait and threw that on the flames, too.

One vanity the Florentines could not quite bring themselves to part with was their violent factionalism. On one side were the *Piagnoni* ('weepers') of Savonarola's party, on the other the party of the *Arrabbiati* ('the angry'), including the gangs of young delinquents who would demonstrate their opposition to piety and holiness by sneaking into the cathedral and filling Savonarola's pulpit with cow dung. A Medicean party was also gathering strength, a sort of fifth column sowing discontent within the city and undermining the war effort. Three times, unsuccessfully, the exiled Medici attempted to seize the city with bands of mercenaries. The Pisan revolt continued, and Pope Alexander had excommunicated Savonarola and was threatening to place all Florence under an interdict. In the long hangover after the Bonfire of Vanities, the Florentines were growing weary of their preacher. When the Arrabbiati won the elections of 1498, his doom was sealed. A kangaroo court found the new scapegoat guilty of heresy and treason. After some gratuitous torture and public mockery, the very spot where the Bonfire of Vanities had been held now witnessed a bonfire of Savonarola.

Pope Alexander still wasn't happy. He sent an army under his son, Cesare Borgia, to menace the city. Florence weathered this threat, and the relatively democratic 'Savonarolan' constitution of 1494 seemed to be working out well. Under a new and innovative idea, borrowed from Venice and designed to circumvent party strife, a public-spirited gentleman named **Piero Soderini** was elected *gonfaloniere* for life in 1502. With the help of his friend and adviser **Niccolò Machiavelli**, Soderini managed to keep the ship of state on an even keel. Pisa finally surrendered in 1509. Serious trouble returned in 1512, and once more the popes were behind it. As France's only ally in Italy, Florence ran foul of Julius II. Papal and Spanish armies invaded Florentine territory and, after their gruesome sack of Prato, designed specifically to overawe Florence, the frightened and politically apathetic city was ready to submit to the pope's conditions – the expulsion of Soderini, a change of alliance and the return of the Medici.

The End of the Republic

At first, the understanding was that the Medici would live in Florence as private citizens. But **Giuliano de' Medici**, son of Lorenzo and current leader, soon united the upper classes for a rolling back of Savonarolan democracy. With hired soldiers to intimidate the populace, a rigged *parlamento* in September 1512 restored Medici control. The democratic Grand Council was abolished; its new meeting hall in the Palazzo Vecchio (where Leonardo and Michelangelo were to have their 'Battle of the Frescoes') became apartments for soldiers. Soldiers were everywhere, and the Medicean restoration took on the aspect of a police state. Hundreds of political prisoners were tortured in the Palazzo Vecchio's dungeons, among them Machiavelli.

Giuliano died in 1516, succeeded by his nephew **Lorenzo, Duke of Urbino**, a snotty young sport with a tyrant's bad manners. Nobody mourned much when syphilis carried him off in 1519, but the family paid Michelangelo to give both Lorenzo and Giuliano fancy tombs. Ever since Giuliano's death, however, the real Medici boss had been not Lorenzo, but his uncle Giovanni, who in that year became **Pope Leo X**. The Medici, original masters of nepotism, had been planning this for years. Back in the 1470s, Lorenzo il Magnifico realized that the surest way of maintaining the family fortunes would be to get a Medici on the papal throne. He had little Giovanni ordained at the age of eight, purchased him a cardinal's hat at 13, and used bribery and diplomacy to help him accumulate dozens of benefices all over France and Italy. For his easy-going civility (as exemplified in his famous quote: 'God has given us the papacy so let us enjoy it'), and his patronage of scholars and artists, Leo became one of the best-remembered Renaissance popes. On the other side of the coin was his criminal mismanagement of the Church. Upper-class Florentines descended on Rome like a plague of locusts, occupying all the important sinecures and rapidly emptying the papal treasury. Their rapacity, plus the tremendous expenses involved in building the new St Peter's, caused Leo to step up the sale of indulgences all over Europe – disgusting reformers such as Luther and greatly hastening the onset of the Reformation.

Back in Florence, Lorenzo Duke of Urbino's successor Giulio, bastard son of Lorenzo Il Magnifico's murdered brother Giuliano, was little more than a puppet; Leo found enough time between banquets to manage the city's affairs. Giulio himself became pope in 1523, as **Clement VII**, thanks to the newfound financial interdependence between Florence and Rome, and now the Medici presence in Florence was reduced to two more unattractive young bastards, Ippolito and Alessandro, under the guardianship of Cardinal Silvio Passerini. Clement attempted to run the city from Rome as Leo had done, but high taxes and the lack of a strong hand made the new Medici regime increasingly precarious; its end followed after the sack of Rome in 1527. With Clement a prisoner in the Vatican and unable to intervene, a delegation of Florentine notables informed Cardinal Passerini and the Medicis that it was time to go. For the third time in less than a century, Florence had succeeded in getting rid of the Medici.

The new republic, though initiated by the disillusioned wealthy classes, soon found radical Savonarolan democrats gaining the upper hand. The Grand Council met and extended the franchise to include most of the citizens. Vanities were cursed again, books were banned and carnival parades forbidden; the council officially pronounced Jesus Christ 'King of the Florentines', just as it had done in the heyday of the Savonarolan camp meetings. In an intense atmosphere of republican virtue and pious crusade, Florence rushed headlong into the apocalyptic climax of its history. This time it did not take the Medici long to recover. In order to get Florence back, the witless Clement became allied to his former enemy, **Emperor Charles V**, a sordid deal that would eventually betray all Italy to Spanish control. Imperial troops were to help subdue Florence, and Clement's illegitimate son Alessandro was to wed Charles' illegitimate daughter. Charles' troops put Florence under siege in December 1529. The city had few resources for the struggle, and no friends at all, but a heroic resistance kept the imperialists at bay all through the winter and spring. Citizens gave up their gold and silver to be minted into the republic's last coins. The councillors debated seizing little Catherine de' Medici, future Queen of France, but then a prisoner of the republic, and dangling her from the walls to give the enemy a good target. Few artists were left in Florence, but Michelangelo stayed to help with his city's fortifications (by night he was working on the Medici tombs in San Lorenzo; both sides gave him safe passage when he wanted to leave Florence).

In August of 1530, the Florentines' skilful commander, Francesco Ferruccio, was killed in a skirmish near Pistoia; at about the same time the republic realized that its mercenary captain within the walls, Malatesta Baglioni, had sold them out to the pope and emperor. When they tried to arrest him, Baglioni only laughed, and directed his men to turn their artillery on the city. The inevitable capitulation came on 12 August; after almost 400 years, the Florentine republic had breathed its last.

At first, this third Medici return appeared to be just another dreary round of history repeating itself. Again, a packed *parlamento* gutted the constitution and legitimized the Medici takeover. Again the family and its minions combed the city, taking back every penny's worth of property that had been confiscated from them. This time, however, was to be different. Florence had gone from being a large fish in a small Italian pond to being a minuscule but hindersome nuisance in the pan-European world of papal and imperial politics. Charles V didn't much like republics, or disorderly politicking, or indeed anyone who might conceivably say no to him. The orders came down from the emperor in Brussels; it was to be Medici for ever.

Cosimo I: the Medici as Grand Dukes

At first little was changed; the shell of the republican constitution was maintained, but with the 20-year-old illegitimate **Alessandro** as 'Duke of the Florentine Republic'; the harsh reality was under construction above the city's west end – the Fortezza da Basso, with its Spanish garrison, demanded by Charles V as insurance that Florence would never again be able to assert its independence. If any further symbolism was necessary, Alessandro ordered the great bell to be removed from the tower of the Palazzo Vecchio – the bell that had always summoned the citizens to political assemblies and the mustering of the army. In 1537, Alessandro was treacherously murdered by his jealous cousin Lorenzaccio de' Medici. With no legitimate heirs in the direct line Florence was in danger of falling under direct imperial rule, as had happened to Milan two years earlier, upon the extinction of the Sforza dukes. The assassination was kept secret while the Medici and the diplomats angled for a solution. The only reasonable choice turned out to be 18-year-old **Cosimo de' Medici**, heir of the family's cadet branch. This son of a famous mercenary commander, Giovanni of the Black Bands, had grown up on a farm; both the elder statesmen of the family and the imperial representatives thought they would easily be able to manipulate him.

It soon became very clear that they had picked the wrong boy. Right from the start, young Cosimo had a surprisingly complete idea of the ways in which he meant to rule Florence, and also the will and strength of personality to see that his commands were carried out. No one ever admitted to liking him; his puritanical court dismayed even the old partisans of Savonarola, and Florentines enjoyed grumbling over his high taxes, going to support 'colonels, spies, Spaniards, and women to serve Madame' (his Spanish consort Eleanor of Toledo). More surprising, when bowing and scraping Italians were everywhere else losing their liberty, Cosimo held his own against both pope and Spaniard. To back up his growing independence, Cosimo put his domains on an almost permanent war footing. New fortresses were built, a big fleet was begun, and a paid standing army took the place of mercenaries and citizen levies. The skeleton of the old republic was revamped into a modern bureaucratic state.

Early in his reign Cosimo defeated the last-ditch effort of the republican exiles, unreconstructed oligarchs led by the banker Filippo Strozzi, at the **battle of Montemurlo**, the last threat ever to Medici rule. Cosimo's master stroke came in 1557, when with the help of an imperial army he took the entire Republic of Siena. Now the Medicis controlled roughly the boundaries of modern Tuscany; Cosimo was able to cap off his reign in 1569 by purchasing the title of Grand Duke of Tuscany.

Knick-knacks and Tedium: the Later Medici

For all Cosimo's efforts, Florence was entering a very evident decline. Banking and trade did well throughout the late 16th century, which was a prosperous time for almost all of Italy, but there were few opportunities for growth. More than ever, wealth was going into land, palaces and government bonds; the tradition of mercantile venture was becoming a thing of the past. In terms of culture and art, Cosimo's reign turned out to be a disaster. It wasn't what he intended; indeed the Duke brought to the field his accustomed energy and compulsion to improve and organize.

Academies were founded, and research underwritten. Cosimo's emphasis on art as political propaganda helped change the Florentine artist from a guild artisan to a flouncing courtier, ready to roll over at his master's command. The city had as great an influence in its age of decay as in its age of greatness. The cute, well-educated Florentine pranced across Europe, praised as the paragon of culture and refinement. Even in England – though that honest nation soon found him out:

A little Apish hatte, couched fast to the Pate, like an Oyster,
French Camarick Ruffes, deepe with a witnesse,
starched to the purpose,
Delicate in speach, queynte in arraye: conceited in all poyntes:
In Courtyly guyles, a passing singular odde man...

Mirror of Tuscanism, Gabriel Harvey, 1580

Michelangelo, despite frequent entreaties, always refused to work for Cosimo. Most of the other talented Florentine artists eventually left for Rome or for places further afield, leaving lapdogs such as **Giorgio Vasari** to carry on the grand traditions of Florentine art. Vasari, with help from such artists as Ammannati and Bandinelli, transformed much of the city – especially the interiors of its churches and public buildings. Florence began to fill up with equestrian statues of Medici, pageants and plaster triumphal arches displaying the triumphs of the Medici, sculptural allegories (including Cellini's *Perseus*) reminding us of the inevitability of the Medici and, best of all, portraits of semi-divine Medici floating in the clouds along with little Cupids and Virtues. It was all the same to Cosimo and his successors, whose personal tastes tended more to engraved jewels, exotic taxidermy and sculptures made of seashells. But it helped to hasten the extinction of Florentine culture.

Cosimo grew ill, abdicating most responsibility to his son Francesco from 1564 to his death 10 years later. **Francesco**, the genuine oddball among the Medici, was a moody, melancholic sort who cared little for government, preferring to lock himself up in the family palaces to pursue his passion for alchemy, as well as occasional researches into such subjects as perpetual motion and poisons – he received consignments of crates of scorpions every now and then. Despite his lack of interest, Francesco was a capable ruler, best known for his founding of Livorno.

Later Medici followed the general course established by other great families, such as the Habsburgs and Bourbons – each one was worse than the last. Francesco's death in 1587 gave the throne to his brother, **Ferdinando I**, founder of the Medici Chapels at San Lorenzo and another indefatigable collector of bric-a-brac. Next came **Cosimo II** (1609–21), a sickly nonentity who eventually succumbed to tuberculosis, and **Ferdinando II** (1621–70), whose long and uneventful reign oversaw the impoverishment of Florence and most of Tuscany. For this the Medici do not deserve much blame. A long string of bad harvests, beginning in the 1590s, plagues that recurred with terrible frequency as late as the 1630s, and general trade patterns that redistributed wealth and power from the Mediterranean to northern Europe, all set the stage for the collapse of the Florentine economy. The fatal blow came in the 1630s, when the long-deteriorating wool trade collapsed with sudden finality. Banking was going too, partly a victim of the age's continuing inflation, partly of high taxes and lack of worthwhile investments. Florence, by the mid century, found itself with no prospects at all, a pensioner city drawing a barely respectable income from its glorious past.

With **Cosimo III** (1670–1723), the line of the Medici crossed over into the ridiculous. A religious crank and anti-Semite, this Cosimo temporarily wiped out free thought within the universities, allowed Tuscany to fill up with nuns and Jesuits, and decreed fantastical laws such as the one that forbade any man to enter a house in which an unmarried woman resided. In order to support his lavish court and pay the big tributes that were demanded by Spain and Austria (something earlier Medici would have scorned) Cosimo taxed what was left of the Florentine economy into an early grave. His heir, **Gian Gastone** (1723–37), was an obese drunkard, senile and slobbering at the age of 50. He had to be carried up and down stairs on the rare occasions that he got out of bed (mainly to disprove rumours that he was dead); on the one occasion he appeared in public, the chronicles report him vomiting out of the carriage window.

As a footnote on the Medici there is Gian Gastone's perfectly sensible sister, **Anna Maria Ludovica**. As the very last surviving Medici, it fell to her to dispose of the family's vast wealth and hoards of art. When she died, in 1743, her will revealed that the whole bundle was to become the property of the future rulers of Tuscany – whoever they should be – with the provision that not one bit of it should ever, ever, be moved outside Florence. Without her, the great collections of the Uffizi and the Bargello might long ago have been packed away to Vienna or to Paris.

Post-Medici Florence

When Gian Gastone died in 1737, Tuscany's fate had already been decided by the powers of Europe. The Grand Duchy would fall to **Francis Stephen**, Duke of Lorraine and husband-to-be of the Austrian Empress Maria Theresa; his troops had been installed in the Fortezza da Basso a year before. For most of the next century, Florence slumbered under benign Austrian rule. Already the first

Grand Tourists were arriving on their way to Rome and Naples, sons of the Enlightenment such as Goethe, who didn't stop because 'nothing in Florence could interest him', or relics such as the Pretender Charles Edward Stuart, 'Bonnie Prince Charlie', who stayed two years. Napoleon's men occupied the city for most of two decades without making much impression.

After the Napoleonic Wars, the Habsburg restoration brought back the Lorraine dynasty. Between 1824 and 1859 Florence and Tuscany were ruled by **Leopold II**, that most likeable of all grand dukes. This was when Florence first became popular among the northern Europeans and was the time when the Brownings, Dostoevsky, Leigh Hunt and dozens of other artists and writers took up residence, rediscovering the glories of the city and of the early Renaissance. Grand Duke Leopold was decent enough to let himself be overthrown in 1859, during the tumults of the Risorgimento. In 1865, when only the Papal State remained to be incorporated into the Kingdom of Italy, Florence briefly became the new nation's capital. King **Vittorio Emanuele** installed himself in the Pitti Palace, and the Italian Parliament held meetings in the great hall of the Palazzo Vecchio.

It was not meant to last. When the Italian troops entered Rome in 1870, Florence's brief hour as a major capital came to an end, but it had given the staid old city a jolt towards the modern world. In an unusual flurry of exertion, Florence finally threw up a façade for its cathedral, and levelled the picturesque though squalid market area and Jewish ghetto in order to construct the dolorous Piazza della Repubblica. Fortunately, the city regained its senses before too much damage was done. Throughout the 20th century, Florence's role as a museum city was confirmed with each passing year. The Second World War allowed the city to resume briefly its ancient delight in black-and-white political epic. In 1944 and 1945 Florence offered some of the most outrageous spectacles of Fascist fanaticism, and also some of the most courageous stories of the Resistance – including that of the German consul Gerhard Wolf, who used his position to protect Florentines from the Nazi terror, often at great risk.

In August 1944, the Allied armies were poised to advance through northern Tuscany. For the Germans, the Arno made a convenient defensive line, a fact requiring that all the bridges of Florence be demolished. They all were, except for the Ponte Vecchio, which was saved in a last-minute deal, though the buildings on either side of it were destroyed in order to provide piles of rubble around the bridge approaches. After the war, all of them were repaired; the city had the Ponte della Trínita rebuilt stone by stone exactly as it was. No sooner was the war damage redeemed, however, than a greater disaster attacked Florence's heritage. The flood of 1966, when water reached a level of 6.5m, did more damage than Nazis or Napoleons; an international effort was raised to preserve and restore the city's art and monuments.

Since then the Arno has been deepened under the Ponte Vecchio and 5.5m earthen walls have been erected around Ponte Amerigo Vespucci; video screens and computers monitor every fluctuation in the water level. Should another flood occur, Florence will have plenty of time to protect itself. Far more insoluble a threat is terrorism, which touched the city in May 1993, when a bomb killed a family, destroyed the Gregoriophilus library opposite the Uffizi, and damaged the Vasari Corridor. Florence, which was shocked by this intrusion from the outside world into its holy of holies, repaired most of the damage in record time with funds that were raised by national subscription.

Careful planning has saved the best of Florence's immediate countryside from post-war suburbanization, but much of the other territory around the city has been coated by a suburban sprawl

Highlights of Florence

Florence's museums, palaces and churches contain more good art than perhaps any city in Europe, and to see it all without hardship to your eyes, feet and sensibilities would take at least three weeks. If you have only a few days to spend, the highlights will easily take up all of your time – the cathedral and baptistry, the paintings in the Uffizi (preferably not all in the same day) and the sculptures in the Bargello, which is more worthy of your brief time than the Accademia, where the rubbernecks pile in to see Michelangelo's *David*. Stop in for a look at the eccentric Orsanmichele, and see the Arno from the Ponte Vecchio, taking in some of the oldest streets in the city.

If your heart leans towards the graceful lyricism of the 1400s, don't miss the **cathedral museum** and the Fra Angelicos in **San Marco**; if the lush virtuosity of the 1500s is your cup of tea, visit the Pitti Palace's **Galleria Palatina**. Two churches on the edges of the centre, **Santa Maria Novella** and **Santa Croce**, are galleries in themselves; **Santa Maria del Carmine** has the restored frescoes of Masaccio. Devotees of the Michelangelo cult won't want to miss the Medici Chapels and library at **San Lorenzo**. Or head for the oasis of the **Boboli Gardens**. Finally, climb up to **San Miniato**, for the beautiful medieval church and enchanting view over the city.

Florence's 'secondary' sights are just as interesting. You could spend a day walking around old **Fiesole**, or 15 minutes looking at Gozzoli's charming fresco in the **Palazzo Medici-Riccardi**. The **Palazzo Vecchio** has more, but less charming, Medici frescoes. You can see how a wealthy medieval Tuscan merchant lived at the **Palazzo Davanzati**, while the **Museum of the History of Science** will tell you about the scientific side of the Florentine Renaissance; **Santa Trínita**, **Santo Spirito**, **Ognissanti** and the **Annunziata** all contain famous works from the Renaissance. **Casa Buonarroti** has some early sculptures of Michelangelo; the **Museo Archeologico** has even earlier ones by the Etruscans, Greeks and Egyptians; the Pitti Palace's **Museo degli Argenti** overflows with Medici jewellery and trinkets. Take a bus or car out to Lorenzo il Magnifico's villa at **Poggio a Caiano**, or to the other Medici garden villas: **La Petraia** and **Castello**, or **Villa Demidoff** at Pratolino.

There are two museums with 19th- and 20th-century collections to bring you back to the present: the recently expanded **Galleria d'Arte Moderna** in the Pitti Palace, and the **Collezione Alberto della Ragione**. There are two museums founded by Englishmen: the **Horne Museum**, with Renaissance art, and the eccentric **Stibbert Museum**, with everything but the kitchen sink. Strangest of all are the museums in **La Specola**, featuring stuffed animals and wax figures.

Most of the important museums, excluding the Palazzo Vecchio, are run by the State and can be pre-booked; call **t** 055 294883.

that is not exactly attractive. A new airport extension was built, which the Florentines hope will help make up some of the economic ground they've lost to Milan, and buildings on the marshland northwest of the city have been demolished, the land flattened and a project for housing, shops, leisure facilities, a new law court and a new Fiat factory (Fiat along with the insurance group, La Fondiaria, are the sponsors) is underway.

Meanwhile Florence works hard to preserve what it already has. Although new measures to control the city's bugbear – the traffic problems of a city of 500,000 people that receives a staggering 7 million visitors a year – have been enacted to protect the historic centre, pollution from nearby industry continues to eat away at monuments; Donatello's statue of St Mark at Orsanmichele, which was perfectly intact 50 years ago, is now a mutilated leper. Private companies, banks and even individuals finance 90% of the art restoration that takes place in Florence, with techniques invented by the city's innovative Institute of Restoration. Increasingly, copies are made to replace original works. Naturally, half the city is for them, and the other half against.

Piazza del Duomo

Tour groups circle the three great spiritual monuments of medieval Florence like sharks around their prey. Postcard vendors prey on and sax players play to a human carnival from countless countries, who mill about the cathedral good-naturedly while ambulances of a medieval brotherhood dedicated to first aid stand at the ready in case anyone swoons from ecstasy or art-glut.

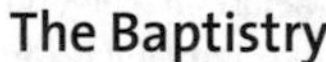

The Baptistry

27 Battistero di San Giovanni
open Mon–Sat 12–7, Sun 8.30–2; bring small change for adm

To begin to understand what magic made the Renaissance first bloom by the Arno, look here; this ancient, mysterious building is the egg from which Florence's golden age was hatched. By the quattrocento, Florentines firmly believed their baptistry was originally a Roman temple to Mars, a touchstone linking them to a legendary past. Scholarship sets its date of construction between the 6th and 9th centuries, in the darkest Dark Ages, which makes it even more remarkable; it may as well have dropped from heaven. Its distinctive dark-green and white marble facing, the tidily classical pattern of arches and rectangles that deceived Brunelleschi and Alberti, was probably added around the 11th century. The masters who built it remain unknown but their strikingly original exercise in geometry provided the model for all Florence's great church façades. When it was new, there was nothing remotely like it in Europe; to visitors from outside the city it must have seemed almost miraculous.

Every 21 March, New Year's Day on the old Florentine calendar, all the children that had been born over the last 12 months would be brought here for a great communal baptism – a habit that helped make the baptistry not merely a religious monument but a civic symbol, in fact the oldest and fondest symbol of the republic. As such, the Florentines never tired of embellishing it. Under the octagonal cupola, the glittering 13th- and 14th-century gold-ground mosaics show a strong Byzantine influence, perhaps laid by mosaicists from Venice. The decoration is divided into concentric strips: over the apse, dominated by a 8.5m figure of Christ, is a *Last Judgement*, while the other bands, from the inside out, portray the *Hierarchy of Heaven*, *Story of Genesis*, *Life of Joseph*, *Life of Christ* and *Life of St John the Baptist*, the last band believed to be the work of Cimabue. The equally beautiful mosaics over the altar and in the vault are the earliest, signed by a monk named Iacopo in the early 1200s. Lighting installed in recent years has vastly improved visitors' view of the ceiling.

To match the mosaics, there is an intricate tessellated marble floor, decorated with signs of the zodiac; the octagonal space in the centre was formerly occupied by the huge font. The green and white patterned walls of the interior are remarkable, combining influences from the ancient world and modern inspiration for something new, the perfect source that architects of the Middle Ages and Renaissance would strive to match. Much of the best design work is in the **galleries**, partially visible from the floor. The baptistry is hardly cluttered; besides a 13th-century Pisan-style baptismal font, only the **tomb of Anti-Pope John XXIII** by Donatello and Michelozzo stands out. This funerary monument, with marble draperies softening its classical lines, is one of the prototypes of the Early Renaissance. But how did Anti-Pope John, deposed by the Council of Constance in 1415, earn the privilege of a tomb here? Why, it was thanks to him that Giovanni di Bicci de' Medici made a fortune as head banker to the Curia.

The Gates of Paradise

Historians used to pinpoint the beginning of the 'Renaissance' as the year 1401, when the merchants' guild, the Arte di Calimala, sponsored a competition for the baptistry's North Doors. The **South Doors** (the main entrance) had already been completed by Andrea Pisano in 1330 in the style of the day. Their 28 panels in quatrefoil frames depict scenes from the life of St John the Baptist and the seven Cardinal and Theological Virtues – formal and elegant works in the best Gothic manner. The celebrated competition of 1401 – perhaps the first ever held in the annals of art – pitted the seven greatest sculptors of the day against one another. Judgement was based on trial panels of the *Sacrifice of Isaac*, and in a dead heat at the end of the day were the two by Brunelleschi and Lorenzo Ghiberti, now displayed in the Bargello. Ghiberti's more classical-style figures were eventually judged the better, and he devoted nearly the rest of his life to creating the most beautiful bronze doors in the world while Brunelleschi, disgusted by his defeat, went on to build the most perfect dome.

Ghiberti's first efforts, the **North Doors** (1403–24), are contained, like Pisano's, in 28 quatrefoil frames. In their scenes on the *Life of Christ*, the *Evangelists*, and the *Doctors of the Church*, you can trace Ghiberti's progress over the 20 years he worked in the increased depth of his compositions, not only visually but dramatically; classical backgrounds begin to fill the frames, ready to break out of their Gothic confines. Ghiberti also designed the floral frame of the doors; the three statues, of *John the Baptist*, the *Levite* and the *Pharisee*, by Francesco Rustici, were based on a design by Leonardo da Vinci and added in 1511.

Ghiberti's work pleased the Arte di Calimala, and they set him loose on another pair of portals, the **East Doors** (1425–52) – his masterpiece and one of the most awesome achievements of the age. Here Ghiberti (perhaps under the guidance of Donatello) dispensed with the small Gothic frames and instead cast 10 large panels that depict the Old Testament in Renaissance high gear, reinterpreting the forms of antiquity with a depth and drama that have never been surpassed. Michelangelo declared them 'worthy to be the Gates of Paradise'. The doors (they're actually copies – eight of the original panels, restored after flood damage, are on display in the Museo dell' Opera del Duomo) have been cleaned and stand in gleaming contrast to the others. In 1996, copies of Andrea Sansovino's marble statues of Christ and John the Baptist (1502) and an 18th-century angel were installed over the doors. The originals had begun to fall to bits in 1974; they too are now housed in the Museo dell'Opera.

Ghiberti wasn't exactly slow to toot his own horn; according to himself, he planned and designed the Renaissance on his own. His unabashedly conceited *Commentarii* was the first attempt at art history and autobiography by an artist, and was a work as revolutionary as his doors in its presentation of the creative God-like powers of the artist. In a typical exhibition of Florentine pride he also put busts of his friends among the prophets and sibyls that adorn the frames of the East Doors. Near the centre, the balding figure with arched eyebrows and a little smile is Ghiberti himself.

Duomo (Cattedrale di Santa Maria del Fiore)
www.duomofirenze.it or www.operaduomo.firenze.it; open Mon–Wed and Fri 10–5, Thurs 10–3.30, Sat 10–4.45 (or 1st Sat of month 10–3.30), Sun 1.30–4.45

The Duomo

For all its importance and prosperity, Florence was one of the last cities to plan a great cathedral. Work began in the 1290s, with the sculptor Arnolfo di Cambio in charge, and from the beginning the

Florentines attempted to make up for their delay with sheer audacity. 'It will be so magnificent in size and beauty,' said a decree of 1296, 'as to surpass anything built by the Greeks and Romans.' In response, Arnolfo planned what in its day was the largest church in Catholicism; he confidently laid the foundations for an enormous octagonal crossing 44.5m in diameter, then died before working out a way to cover it, leaving behind the job of designing the biggest dome in the world.

Beyond its presumptuous size, the cathedral of Santa Maria del Fiore shows little interest in contemporary innovations and styles; a visitor from France or England in the 1400s would certainly have found it somewhat drab and architecturally primitive. Visitors today often circle confusedly around its grimy, ponderous bulk. Instead of the striped bravura of Siena or the elegant colonnades of Pisa, they behold an astonishingly eccentric green, white and red pattern of marble rectangles and flowers – like Victorian wallpaper, or, as one critic expressed it, 'a cathedral wearing pyjamas'. In the sun, the cathedral under its sublime dome sports festively above the dullish dun and ochre sea of Florence; in dismal weather it sprawls morosely across its *piazza* like a beached whale tarted up with a lace doily front.

The fondly foolish **façade** cannot be blamed on Arnolfo. His original design, which was only one-quarter completed, was taken down in a late 16th-century Medici rebuilding programme that never got off the ground. The Duomo turned a blank face to the world until the present neogothic extravaganza was added in 1888. Walk around to the north side to take a look at what many consider a more fitting door, the **Porta della Mandorla**, crowned with an *Assumption of the Virgin* in an almond-shaped frame (hence 'Mandorla'), made by Nanni di Banco in 1420.

Brunelleschi's Dome

open Mon–Fri 8.30–7, Sat 8.30–5.40 (1st Sat of month 8.30–4); adm

Brunelleschi's dome, more than any landmark, makes Florence Florence. Many have noted how the dome repeats the rhythm of the surrounding hills, echoing them with its height and beauty; from those city streets fortunate enough to have a clear view, it rises among the clouds with all the confident mastery, proportions and perfect form that characterize the highest aspirations of the Renaissance. But if it seems miraculous, it certainly isn't divine; unlike the dome of the Hagia Sophia, suspended from heaven by a golden chain, Florence's was made by man.

Losing the competition for the baptistry doors was a bitter disappointment to Filippo Brunelleschi. His reaction was typically a Florentine one: not content with being the second-best sculptor, he turned his talents to a field where he thought no one could beat him, launching himself into a study of architecture and engineering, visiting Rome and probably Ravenna to snatch secrets from the ancients. When proposals were solicited for the dome in 1418, he was ready with a brilliant *tour de force*. Not only would he build the biggest, most beautiful dome of the time, but he would do it without any expensive supports while work was in progress, making use of a cantilevered system of bricks that could support itself while it ascended.

Brunelleschi studied then surpassed the technique of the ancients. To the Florentines, who could have invented the slogan 'form follows function' for their own tastes in building, it must have come as a revelation: the most logical way of covering the space was a work of perfect beauty. Brunelleschi's dome put a crown on the achievements of Florence. After 500 years it is still the city's pride and symbol.

The best way to appreciate Brunelleschi's genius is by touring inside the two concentric shells of the dome (*see* opposite), but before entering note the eight marble ribs that define its octagonal shape; hidden inside are the three huge stone chains that bind them together. Work on the balcony around the base of the dome, designed by Giuliano da Sangallo, was halted in 1515 after Michelangelo commented that it resembled a cricket's cage. As for the lantern, the Florentines were famous for their fondness and admiration for Doubting Thomas, and here they showed why. Even though they marvelled at the dome, they still doubted that Brunelleschi could construct a proper lantern, and forced him to submit to yet another competition. He died before it was begun, and it was completed to his design by Michelozzo.

The Interior

After the façade, the austerity of the Duomo interior is startling. There is plenty of room – contemporary writers mention 10,000 souls packed inside to hear Savonarola's sermons. But, the Duomo hardly seems a religious building – more a *Florentine* building, with simple arches and counterpoint of grey stone and white plaster, full of old familiar Florentine things. Near the entrance, on the righthand side, are busts of Brunelleschi and Giotto. On the left wall, posed inconspicuously, are the two most conspicuous monuments to private individuals ever erected by the Florentine Republic. The one on the right, is to **Sir John Hawkwood**, the English *condottiere* whose name the Italians mangled to Giovanni Acuto, a commander who served Florence for many years and is perhaps best known to English speakers as the hero of *The White Company* by Sir Arthur Conan Doyle. Hawkwood had the Florentines' promise to build him an equestrian statue after his death; it was a typical Florentine trick to pinch pennies and cheat a dead man, but they hired the greatest master of perspective, Paolo

Uccello, to make a fresco that looked like a statue (1436). Twenty years later, they pulled the same trick again, commissioning Andrea del Castagno to paint the non-existent equestrian statue of another *condottiere*, Niccolò da Tolentino.

A little further down, Florence commemorates its own secular scripture with Michelino's well-known fresco of Dante, a vision of the poet and his *Paradiso* outside the walls of Florence. Two singular icons of Florence's fascination with science stand at opposite ends of the building: behind the west front, a bizarre clock painted by Uccello, and in the pavement of the left apse a gnomon fixed by the astronomer Toscanelli in 1475. A beam of sunlight strikes it every year at the summer solstice.

Resti di Santa Reparata
open Sun–Wed and Fri 10–5, Thurs 10–3.30, Sat 10–4.45 (exc. 1st Sat of month 10–3.30); adm

For building the great dome, Brunelleschi was accorded a special honour – he is one of the few Florentines to be buried in the cathedral. His **tomb** may be viewed in the **excavations of Santa Reparata** (the stairway descending on the right of the nave). Arnolfo di Cambio's cathedral was constructed on the ruins of the ancient church of Santa Reparata, which lay forgotten until 1965. Excavations have revealed not only the palaeo-Christian church and its several reconstructions, but also the remains of its Roman predecessor – a rather confusing muddle of walls that have been tidied up in an ambience that resembles an archaeological shopping centre. A coloured model helps explain what is what, and glass cases display items found in the dig, including the spurs of Giovanni de' Medici, who was buried here in 1351. In the ancient crypt of Santa Reparata are 13th-century tomb slabs, and in another section is a fine pre-Romanesque mosaic pavement.

There is surprisingly little religious art – the Florentines for reasons of their own have carted most of it off into the cathedral museum (*see* p.111). Under the dome are the entrances to the two sacristies, with terracotta lunettes over the doors by Luca della Robbia; the scene of the Resurrection over the north sacristy is one of his earliest and best works. He also did the bronze doors beneath it, with tiny portraits on the handles of Lorenzo il Magnifico and his brother Giuliano de' Medici, targets of the Pazzi conspiracy in 1478. In the middle apse is a beautiful bronze urn by Ghiberti containing relics of the Florentine St Zenobius. The only conventional religious decorations are the frescoes some 60m up in the dome, mostly by Vasari. As you stand squinting at them, try not to think that the cupola weighs around 25,000 tons.

A door on the lefthand aisle near the Dante fresco leads up into the **dome** (*see* p.107). The complicated network of stairs and walks between the inner and outer domes (not too difficult, if occasionally claustrophobic and vertiginous) was designed by Brunelleschi, and offers an insight on how thoroughly the architect thought out the problems of the dome's construction, even inserting hooks to hold up scaffolding for future cleaning or repairs; Brunelleschi installed restaurants to save workers the trouble of descending for meals. There is also no better place to get an idea of the dome's scale; the walls of the inner dome are 4m thick, and those of the outer dome 1.8m. These give the dome enough support to preclude the need for further buttressing.

From the gallery of the dome you can get a good look at the lovely **stained glass** by Uccello, Donatello, Ghiberti and Castagno, in the seven circular windows, or *occhi*, made during the construction of the dome, which are being restored one by one. Further up, the views through the small windows offer tantalizing hints of the breathtaking panorama from the marble lantern at the top. The bronze ball at the very top was added by Verrocchio, and can hold almost a dozen people when open.

Giotto's Campanile

The dome steals the show, putting one of Italy's most beautiful belltowers in the shade both figuratively and literally. The dome's great size – 111.5m to the bronze ball – makes the campanile look small, though 85m is not exactly tiny. Giotto was made director of the cathedral works in 1334, and his basic design was completed after his death (1337) by Andrea Pisano and Francesco Talenti. It is difficult to say whether they were entirely faithful to the plan; Giotto was an artist, not an engineer. After he died, his successors realized the thing, then only 12m high, was about to tumble over – a problem they overcame by doubling the thickness of the walls.

Besides its lovely form, the green, pink and white campanile's major fame rests with Pisano and Talenti's **sculptural reliefs** – a veritable encyclopaedia of the medieval world view with prophets, saints and sibyls, allegories of the planets, virtues and sacraments, the liberal arts and industries (the artist's craft is fittingly symbolized by a winged figure of Daedalus). All of these are copies of the originals now in the cathedral museum. If you can take another 400 steps or so, the **terrace** on top offers a slightly different view of Florence and of the cathedral itself.

Campanile terrace
open daily 8.30–7.30; adm

Loggia del Bigallo

The most striking secular building on the Piazza del Duomo is the Loggia del Bigallo, south of the baptistry near the beginning of Via de' Calzaiuoli. This 14th-century porch was built for one of Florence's great charitable confraternities, the Misericordia, which still has its HQ across the street and operates the ambulances parked in front; during the 13th and 14th centuries members courageously nursed and buried victims of the plague. The Loggia itself originally served as a 'lost and found' office for children; if unclaimed after three days, they were sent to foster homes.

To the east of the Loggia del Bigallo is a stone bench labelled the 'Sasso di Dante' – **Dante's Stone** – where the poet would sit and take the air, observing his fellow citizens and watching the construction of the cathedral.

Museo dell'Opera del Duomo

Museo dell'Opera del Duomo
www.duomofirenze.it; open Mon–Sat 9–7.30, Sun 9–1.45; adm

The cathedral museum (Piazza del Duomo 9, near the central apse) is one of Florence's finest museums, housing both relics from the construction of the cathedral and the masterpieces that once adorned it. The 2007 work completes a major restructuring to improve the layout and make it more visitor-friendly: there is now full disabled access, better information, a more logical layout, in a more or less chronological order, and greatly increased floor space. The courtyard has been covered by a glass roof and turned into an exhibition room; and there are long-term plans to incorporate a neighbouring 18th-century theatre into the museum, which has been closed for several centuries and was most recently used as a garage. When the restoration work is finished the museum will have doubled in size.

The entrance leads into the new ticket hall – which is pristine in marble and stone, the same materials that were used in the Duomo's construction – and past the bookshop. Just after the entrance are several fragments of Roman reliefs, then two anterooms containing restored statues or bits of statues that once adorned the façade of the Duomo.

The first hall is devoted to the cathedral's sculptor-architect Arnolfo di Cambio and contains the statues he made to adorn it: the unusual Madonna with the glass eyes, Florence's old patron saints Reparata and Zenobius, and nasty old Boniface VIII, who sits stiffly on his throne like an Egyptian god. There are the four Evangelists, including a *St John* by Donatello, and a small collection of ancient works – Roman sarcophagi and an Etruscan *cippus* carved with dancers. Note the 16th-century 'Libretto', a fold-out display case of saintly odds and ends. The Florentines were never enthusiastic about the worship of relics, and long ago they shipped San Girolamo's jawbone, John the Baptist's index finger and St Philip's arm across the street to this museum.

A nearby room contains a collection of altarpieces, triptychs and paintings of saints, including Giovanni del Biondo's *St Sebastian*. Also here are a series of marble relief panels by Baccio Bandinelli from the altarpiece of the cathedral. A small room next to this contains a section (several fragments pieced together) of the door known as the 'Porta della Mandorla' on the north side of the Duomo. This is an intricately carved marble relief, including a small figure of Hercules with his stick, significant in that it was the first representation of the adult male nude and a taste of things to come – more of a statue than a relief. Also in this room are two statues known as the *Profetini*, which once stood over the door and are attributed to the young Donatello.

On the landing of the stairs is the *Pietà* Michelangelo intended for his own tomb. The artist, increasingly cantankerous in old age, became exasperated with this complex work and took a hammer to Christ's arm, in the first known instance of an artist vandalizing his own work. His assistant repaired the damage and finished part of the figures of Christ and Mary Magdalene. According to Vasari, the hooded figure of Nicodemus is a self-portrait.

Upstairs, the first room is dominated by the two **Cantorie**, two marble choir balconies with exquisite bas-reliefs, made in the 1430s by Luca della Robbia and Donatello. Both rank among the Renaissance's greatest works. Della Robbia's delightful horde of children dancing, singing and playing instruments is a truly angelic choir, Apollonian in its calm and beauty. It is perhaps the most charming work ever to be inspired by the forms of antiquity. Donatello's *putti*, by contrast, dance, or rather race, through their quattrocento decorative motifs with fiendish Dionysian frenzy. Grey and weathered prophets by Donatello and others stand along the white walls. These originally adorned the façade of the campanile. According to Vasari, while carving the most famous of these, *Habbakuk* (better known as *lo Zuccone*, or 'baldy'), Donatello would mutter under his breath 'Speak, damn you. Speak!' The next room contains the original panels on the *Spiritual Progress of Man* from Giotto's campanile, made by Andrea Pisano.

The first thing you see as you enter the last room is Donatello's statue *Mary Magdalene*, surely one of the most jarring figures ever sculpted, ravaged by her own piety and penance, her sunken eyes fixed on a point beyond this vale of tears. This room is dedicated to works removed from the baptistry, especially the lavish silver altar (14th–15th-century), made by Florentine goldsmiths, portraying scenes from the life of John the Baptist. Antonio Pollaiuolo used the same subject to design the 27 needlework panels that once were part of the priest's vestments. There are two 12th-century Byzantine mosaic miniature masterpieces, and a St Sebastian triptych by Giovanni del Biondo that may well win the record for arrows; the poor saint looks like a hedgehog.

A ramp leads into the new part of the museum from the room containing the panels from the campanile. Cases on either side display the collection of pulleys and instruments that were used in the construction of the cathedral. At the bottom of the ramp on the left is Brunelleschi's death mask, facing a model of the lantern, which he was never to see. A window behind this model cleverly gives a close-up view of the cupola itself, which is topped by that self-same lantern.

A series of rooms off a long corridor contain bits and pieces brought out of storage, including the four carved façades, artists' models for the design of the cricket's-cage pattern round the base of the cupola. The corridor leads into a room with walls filled with drawings of the Duomo from the 1875 competition to design the façade. From here, a staircase leads down into the courtyard where eight of Ghiberti's panels from the *Gates of Paradise* are on display. The plan is still to reconstruct the doors and their cornice once the latter and the last two panels are restored. It will have been placed in the new space next door to the museum by late 2007.

Via de' Calzaiuoli and Piazza della Repubblica

Of all the streets that radiate from the Piazza del Duomo, it's the straight, pedestrian-only Via de' Calzaiuoli that most people almost intuitively turn down – the Roman street that became the main thoroughfare of medieval Florence, linking the city's religious centre with the Piazza della Signoria. The widening of this 'Street of the Shoemakers' in the 1840s has destroyed much of its medieval character, and the only shoe shops to be seen are designer-label. Its fate seems benign, though, compared with what happened to the Mercato Vecchio, in the fit of post-Risorgimento 'progress' that converted it into the **Piazza della Repubblica**, located a block to the right along Via Speziali.

On the map, it's easy to pick out the small rectangle of narrow, straight streets around Piazza della Repubblica; these remain unchanged from the little *castrum* of Roman days. At its centre, the old forum deteriorated through the Dark Ages into a shabby market square and the Jewish ghetto, a densely populated quarter known as the **Mercato Vecchio** – the epitome of the picturesque for 19th-century tourists but an eyesore for the movers and shakers of the new Italy, who tore it down. They erected a triumphal arch to themselves and proudly blazoned it with the inscription 'THE ANCIENT CITY CENTRE RESTORED TO NEW LIFE FROM THE SQUALOR OF CENTURIES'. The sad result, the Piazza della Repubblica, is one of the most ghastly squares in Italy, a brash intrusion of ponderous 19th-century buildings. Just the same, it is popular with locals and tourists alike, closed to traffic and full of outdoor cafés, something of an oasis among the narrow, stern streets of medieval Florence.

From Piazza della Repubblica the natural flow of street life will sweep you down to the **Mercato Nuovo**, the old strawmarket, bustling under a beautiful loggia built by Grand Duke Cosimo in the 1500s. Nowadays vendors hawk purses, stationery, toys, clothes, umbrellas and knick-knacks. In medieval times this was the merchants' exchange, where any merchant who committed the crime of bankruptcy was publicly spanked before being carted off to prison; in times of peace it sheltered Florence's battle-stained *carroccio*. Florentines often call the market the '*Porcellino*' (piglet) after the large bronze boar erected in 1612. The current boar was put in place in 1999 – a copy of a copy of the ancient statue in the Uffizi. The drool spilling from the side of its mouth reminds us that Florence is no splashy city of springs and fountains. Rub the piglet's snout, and supposedly destiny will one day bring you back to Florence. The pungent aroma of the tripe sandwiches sold nearby may give you second thoughts.

Orsanmichele

Orsanmichele
in theory open daily 8.15–12 and 4–6; closed 1st and last Mon of month; however, closed most of time due to lack of staff or redecoration (exc for summer concerts)

There is a wonderfully eccentric church on Via de' Calzaiuoli that looks like no other in the world: Orsanmichele, rising in a tall, neat three-storey rectangle. It was built on the site of ancient San Michele ad Hortum (popularly reduced to 'Orsan-michele'), a 9th-century church located near a vegetable garden, which the *comune* destroyed in 1240 to erect a grainmarket; after a fire in 1337 the current market building (by Francesco Talenti and others) was erected, with a loggia on the ground floor and emergency storehouses on top where grain was kept against a siege.

The original market had a pilaster with a painting of the Virgin that became increasingly celebrated for performing miracles. The area around the Virgin became known as the Oratory, and when Talenti reconstructed the market, his intention was to combine both its secular and religious functions; each pilaster of the loggia was assigned to a guild to adorn with an image of its patron saint. In 1380, when the market was relocated, the entire ground floor was given over to the functions of the church, and Francesco Talenti's son Simone was given the task of closing in the arcades with lovely Gothic windows, later bricked in.

The church is most famous as a showcase of 15th-century Florentine sculpture; displaying the stylistic innovations through the decades. Each guild sought to outdo the others, commissioning the finest artists of the day to carve their patron saints and create elaborate niches to hold them. The first statue to the left of the door is one of the oldest; Ghiberti's bronze *St John the Baptist*, erected in 1416 for the Arte di Calimala, was the first life-sized Renaissance statue cast in bronze. Continue to the left on Via de' Lamberti to compare it with Donatello's *St Mark*, patron of linen dealers and used-cloth merchants. Finished in 1411, this is thought to be the first freestanding marble statue of the Renaissance.

The niches continue around Via dell'Arte della Lana, named after the Wool Merchants' Guild, the richest after that of the Bankers. Their headquarters, the **Palazzo dell'Arte della Lana**, is linked by an overhead arch with Orsanmichele; built in 1308, it was restored in 1905 in a William Morris style of medieval picturesque. The first statue on this façade of Orsanmichele is *St Eligio*, patron of smiths, by Nanni di Banco (1415), with a niche embellished with the guild's emblem (black pincers) and a bas-relief below showing one of this rather obscure saint's miracles – apparently he shod a horse by cutting off its hoof, shoeing it, then sticking it back on the leg. The other two statues on this street are bronzes by Ghiberti, the Wool Guild's *St Stephen* (1426) and the Exchange Guild's *St Matthew* (1422), the latter an especially fine work.

On the Via Orsanmichele façade stands a copy of Donatello's famous *St George* (the original now in the Bargello) done in 1417 for the Armourers' Guild, with a dramatic predella of the saint slaying the dragon, also by Donatello, that is one of the first known works making use of perspective; next are the Stonecutters' and Carpenters' Guild's *Four Crowned Saints* (1415, by Nanni di Banco), inspired by Roman statues. Nanni also contributed the Shoemakers' *St Philip* (1415), while the next figure, *St Peter*, is commonly attributed to Donatello (1413). Around the corner on Via de' Calzaiuoli stands the bronze *St Luke*, patron of the Judges and Notaries, by Giambologna, a work of 1602 in a 15th-century niche, and the *Doubting of St Thomas* by Andrea del Verrocchio (1484), made not for a guild but for the Tribunal of Merchandise, who like St Thomas wanted to be certain before making a judgement. In the rondels above some of the niches are terracottas of the guilds' symbols by Luca della Robbia.

Orsanmichele's dark **interior**, if you are lucky enough to find it open, is ornate and cosy, with more of the air of a guildhall than a church. It makes a picturebook medieval setting for one of the masterpieces of the trecento: Andrea Orcagna's beautiful Gothic **Tabernacle**, a large, exquisite work in marble, bronze and coloured glass framing a contemporary painting of the *Madonna* (either by Bernardo Daddi or Orcagna himself), replacing the miraculous one, lost in a fire. The Tabernacle was commissioned by survivors of the 1348 Black Death. On the walls and pilasters are faded 14th-century frescoes of saints, placed as if members of the congregation; if you look at the pilasters on the left as you enter and along the right wall, you can see the old chutes used to transfer grain.

Piazza della Signoria

Now that this big medieval *piazza* is car-free, it serves as a great corral for tourists, endlessly snapping pictures of the Palazzo Vecchio or strutting in circles like pigeons. In the old days it would be full of Florentines, as the stage set for the tempestuous life of their republic. The public assemblies met here, and at times of danger the bells would ring and the *piazza* would fill with citizen militias, assembling under the banners of the quarters and guilds. Savonarola held his Bonfire of Vanities here, and only a few years later the disenchanted Florentines ignited their Bonfire of Savonarola on the same spot. (You can see a painting of the event at San Marco.) Today the *piazza* is still the city's favoured spot for hosting political rallies.

The three graceful arches of the **Loggia dei Lanzi**, next to the Palazzo Vecchio, were the reviewing stand for city officials during assemblies and celebrations. Florentines often call it the Loggia dell'Orcagna, after the architect who designed it in the 1370s. In its simple classicism the Loggia anticipates the architecture of Brunelleschi and all those who came after him. The city has made it an outdoor sculpture gallery, with some of the best-known works in Florence: Cellini's triumphant *Perseus*, radiant after recent restoration, and Giambologna's *Rape of the Sabines*, other works by Giambologna, and a chorus of Roman-era Vestal Virgins along the back wall. Cosimo himself stands imperiously at the centre of the *piazza*, a bronze equestrian statue also by Giambologna.

All the statues in the *piazza* are dear to the Florentines for one reason or another. Some are fine works of art; others have only historical associations. Michelangelo's *David*, a copy of which stands in front of the *palazzo* near the spot the artist intended for it, was meant as a symbol of republican virtue and Florentine excellence. At the opposite extreme, Florentines are taught almost from birth to ridicule the **Neptune fountain**, a pompous monstrosity with a giant marble figure of the god. Ammannati, the sculptor, thought he would upstage Michelangelo, though the result is derisively known as *Il Biancone* ('Big Whitey'). Bandinelli's statue of *Hercules and Cacus* is almost as big and just as awful, according to Cellini looking like a 'sack of melons'.

Palazzo Vecchio

Palazzo Vecchio
open Mon–Wed and Fri–Sun 9–7, Thurs 9–2; adm, joint ticket available with Cappella Brancacci

When Goethe made his blitz-tour of Florence, the Palazzo Vecchio (or Palazzo della Signoria) helped pull the wool over his eyes. 'Obviously,' thought the great poet, 'the people...enjoyed a lucky succession of good governments' – a remark which, as Mary McCarthy wrote, could make the angels in heaven weep. But none of Florence's chronic factionalism mars Arnolfo di Cambio's temple of civic aspirations, part council hall, part fortress. In many ways, the Palazzo Vecchio is the ideal of stone Florence: rugged and imposing, with a rusticated façade that inspired many of the city's private palaces, yet designed according to the proportions of the Golden Section of the ancient Greeks. Its dominant feature, the 94m tower, is a typical piece of Florentine bravado.

The Palazzo Vecchio occupies the site of the old Roman theatre and the medieval Palazzo dei Priori. In the 13th century this earlier palace was flattened along with the Ghibelline quarter interred under the *piazza*, and in 1299 the now-ascendant Guelphs called upon Arnolfo di Cambio, master builder of the cathedral, to design the most impressive 'Palazzo del Popolo' (as the building was originally called) possible. The palace's unusual trapezoidal shape is often, but rather dubiously, explained as Guelph care not to have any of the building touch land once owned by Ghibellines. One doubts that even in the 13th century property realities allowed such delicacy of sentiments; nor does the theory explain why the tower has swallowtail Ghibelline crenellations, as opposed to the square Guelph ones on the palace itself. Later additions to the rear of the palace have obscured its shape even more, although the façade is essentially as Arnolfo built it, except for the bet-hedging monogram over the door hailing Christ the King of Florence, put up in the nervous days of 1529, when the Imperial army of Charles V was on its way to destroy the last Florentine republic; the inscription replaces an earlier one left by Savonarola. The room at the top of the tower was used as a prison for famous people and dubbed the *alberghetto*; inmates in 'the little hotel' included Cosimo il Vecchio before his brief exile, and Savonarola, who spent his last months, between torture sessions, enjoying a superb view of the city before his execution in the *piazza* below.

Inside the Palazzo Vecchio

Today the Palazzo Vecchio serves as Florence's city hall, but nearly all its historic rooms are open to the public. With few exceptions, the interior decorations date from the time of Cosimo I, when he moved his Grand Ducal self from the Medici Palace in 1540. To politically 'correct' its acres of walls and ceilings in the shortest amount of time, he turned to his court artist Giorgio Vasari, who was famed more for the speed at which he could execute a commission than for its quality. On the ground floor of the *palazzo*, before you buy your ticket, you can take a look at some of Vasari's more elaborate handiwork in the **courtyard**, redone for the occasion of Francesco I's unhappy marriage to the plain and stupid Habsburg Joanna of Austria in 1565.

Vasari's suitably grand staircase takes you up to the vast **Salone dei Cinquecento**, which was added by Savonarola for meetings of the 500-strong Consiglio Maggiore, the reformed republic's democratic assembly. Leonardo da Vinci and Michelangelo were commissioned in 1503 to paint the two long walls of the *salone*, in a kind of Battle of the Brushes. Unfortunately, neither completed the project: Michelangelo only finished the cartoons of *The Battle of Cascina* before being summoned to Rome by Julius II, who required the sculptor of the *David* to pander to his own personal megalomania. Leonardo went back to Milan, but not before completing the central group of *The Battle of Angiari*, a seminal work in depicting motion and violence.

In 1563, Vasari was commissioned to fresco scenes of Cosimo's military triumphs over Pisa and Siena, with an apotheosis of the Grand Duke on the ceiling – busy scenes with all the substance of cooked pasta. But art detective Maurizio Seracini (the same who appears in *The Da Vinci Code*) is convinced that Vasari couldn't bear to destroy Leonardo's masterpiece, and hid it in a cavity behind the Medici fluff – one clue is the words Vasari himself wrote on his equestrian battle scene: '*Cerca Trova*' ('He who Seeks, Finds'). Currently a committee is studying how to reveal the work without ruining Vasari's frescoes.

The sculptural groups lining the walls of this large room (the Italian parliament sat here from 1865 to 1870 when Florence was the capital) are only slightly more stimulating; even Michelangelo's *Victory*, on the wall opposite the entrance, is more virtuosity than vision: a vacuous young idiot posing with one knee atop a defeated old man still half-submerged in stone, said to be a self-portrait of the sculptor. Its neighbour, a muscle-bound *Hercules and Diomedes* by Vicenzo de' Rossi, probably was inevitable in this city obsessed by the possibilities of the male nude.

Beyond the *salone*, behind a modern glass door, is a much more intriguing room the size of a closet. This is the **Studiolo of Francesco I**, designed by Vasari in 1572 for Cosimo's melancholic and reclusive son, where he would escape to brood over his real interests in natural curiosities and alchemy. The little study, windowless and more than a little claustrophobic, has been restored to its original appearance, lined with allegorical paintings by Vasari, Bronzino and Allori, and bronze statuettes by Giambologna and Ammannati, their refined, polished and erotic mythological subjects part of a carefully thought-out 16th-century programme on Man and Nature. The lower row of paintings conceals Francesco's secret cupboards where he kept his most precious belongings, his pearls and crystals and gold.

After the *salone* a certain fuzziness begins to set in. Cosimo I's propaganda machine, in league with Vasari's fresco factory, produced room after room of self-glorifying Medicean puffery. The first series of rooms, known as the **Quartiere di Leone X**, carry ancestor-worship to extremes, each chamber dedicated to a different Medici: in the first, Cosimo il Vecchio returns from exile amid tumultuous acclaim; in the second Lorenzo il Magnifico receives the ambassadors in the company of a dignified giraffe; the third and fourth are dedicated to the Medici popes, while the fifth, naturally, is for Cosimo I, who gets the most elaborate treatment.

Upstairs the next series of rooms, known as the **Quartiere degli Elementi**, contains more works of Vasari and his studio, depicting allegories of the elements. In a small room, the **Terrazzo di Giunone**, is the original of Verrocchio's boy with the dolphin, from the courtyard fountain. A balcony across the Salone dei Cinquecento leads to the **Quartiere di Eleonora di Toledo**, Mrs Cosimo I's private apartments. Her chapel is one of the masterpieces of Bronzino, who seemed to relish the opportunity to paint something else besides Medici portraits. The **Sala dell'Udienza**, found beyond the second chapel, has a magnificent quattrocento coffered ceiling by Benedetto and Giuliano da Maiano, and walls painted by Mannerist Francesco Salviati (1550–60).

The last room, the **Sala dei Gigli** ('of the lilies') boasts another fine ceiling by the Da Maiano brothers; it also contains Donatello's restored bronze *Judith and Holofernes*, a late and rather gruesome work dating back to 1455; the warning to tyrants that is inscribed on its base was added when the statue was abducted from the Medici Palace and placed in the Piazza della Signoria.

Off the Sala dei Gigli are two small rooms of interest: the **Guardaroba**, or unique 'wardrobe', adorned with 57 maps painted by Fra Egnazio Danti in 1563, depicting all the world known at the time. The **Cancelleria** was Machiavelli's office from 1498 to 1512, when he served the republic as a secretary and diplomat. He is commemorated with a bust and a portrait. Poor Machiavelli would probably be amazed to learn that his very name had become synonymous with cunning, amoral intrigue. After losing his job upon the return of the Medici, and at one point being tortured and imprisoned on false suspicion of conspiracy, Machiavelli was forced to live in idleness in the country, where he wrote his political works and two fine plays, feverishly trying to return to favour. His concern throughout had been to advise realistically, without mincing words, the fractious and increasingly weak Italians on how to create a strong state. His evil reputation came from openly stating what rulers do, rather than what they would like other people to think they do.

The **Collezione Loeser**, a fine assortment of Renaissance art left to the city in 1928 by Charles Loeser, the Macy's department-store heir, is also housed in the Palazzo Vecchio, in the mezzanine before you exit the museum.

Collezione Alberto della Ragione

Collezione Alberto della Ragione
open by request; adm

After the pomposity of the Palazzo Vecchio and a Campari cure at the Piazza della Signoria's Café Rivoire, you may be in the mood to reconsider the 20th and 21st centuries in Florence's only museum of modern art, the Collezione Alberto della Ragione at Piazza della Signoria 5. There are typical still lifes by De Pisis, equally still landscapes by Carlo Carrà, mysterious baths by De Chirico, Tuscan landscapes by Mario Mafai, Antonio Donghi and Ottone Rosai, a speedy Futurist horse by Fortunato Depero and a window with doves by Gino Severini, a number of richly coloured canvases by Renato Guttuso, paintings after Tintoretto by Emilio Vedova, and many others.

The Uffizi

11 Uffizi
www.polomuseale.firenze.it/uffizi; open Tues–Sun 8.15–6.50; adm exp; long queues very common in summer, so try to arrive early; you can pre-book by phone on **t** *055 294883, and pay at door when you pick up your ticket*

Florence has the most fabulous art museum in Italy, and as usual we have the Medici to thank for that; for the building that holds these treasures, however, credit has to to Grand Duke Cosimo's much-maligned court painter. Poor Giorgio Vasari! His roosterish boastfulness and the conviction that his was the best of all possible artistic worlds, set next to his very modest talents, have made him a comic figure in most art criticism. On one of the rare occasions when he tried his hand as an architect, though, he gave Florence something to be proud of.

The Uffizi ('offices') were built as Cosimo's secretariat, incorporating the old mint (producer of the first gold florins in 1252), the archives and the large church of San Pier Scheraggio, with plenty of room for the bureaucrats who were needed to run Cosimo's efficient, modern state. The matched pair of arcaded buildings have coldly elegant façades that conceal Vasari's surprising innovation: iron reinforcements that make the enormous amount of window area possible and that keep the building stable on the soft, sandy ground. It was a trick that would be almost forgotten until the Crystal Palace and the first American skyscrapers. Almost from the start the Medici began to store some of their huge collection in parts of the building. There are galleries in the world with more works of art – the Uffizi counts some 1,800 – but the Uffizi overwhelms by the fact that everything in it is worth looking at.

The Uffizi has undergone major reorganization in the last few years. Some of this involved the restoration of remaining damage after the bomb of 1993 (all but a very few paintings are now back on display), but improvements have also been made on a practical level. Major restoration of the vaulted rooms on the ground floor has resulted in a vastly improved space; there are now three entrances (for individuals, for groups and for those with pre-paid tickets), bookshops, cloakrooms, video and computer facilities and information desks.

If you are particularly keen on seeing a certain painting, note that rooms may be temporarily closed when you visit; this often seems to depend on staff availability. There is a list of these closures at the ticket counters. Some works are still hung out of chronological order, and the rooms containing work by Caravaggio and Rubens are closed until further notice (although two of the Caravaggios are at present hung in Room 16).

From the ticket counter you can take the lift or sweeping grand staircase up to the second floor, where the Medici once had a huge theatre, now home to the **Cabinet of Drawings and Prints**. Although the bulk of this extensive and renowned collection is only open to scholars with special permission, a roomful of tempting samples gives a hint at what they have a chance to see.

Nowadays one thinks of the Uffizi as primarily a gallery of paintings, but when it first opened visitors came for the fine collection of Hellenistic and Roman marbles. Most of these were collected in Rome by Medici cardinals, and not a few were sources of Renaissance inspiration. The **Vestibule** at the top of the stairs contains some of the best, together with Flemish and Tuscan tapestries made for Cosimo I and his successors. **Room 1**, usually shut, contains excellent early Roman sculpture.

Rooms 2–6: 13th and 14th Centuries

The Uffizi's paintings are arranged in chronological order, the better to educate its visitors on trends in Italian art. The roots of the Early Renaissance are most strikingly revealed in **Room 2**, dedicated to the three great **Maestà** altarpieces by the masters of the 13th century. All portray the same subject of the Madonna and Child enthroned with angels. The one on the right, by Cimabue, was painted around 1285 and represents a breaking away from the flat, stylized Byzantine tradition. To the left is the so-called *Rucellai Madonna*, painted around the same period by the Sienese Duccio di Buoninsegna for Santa Maria Novella. It resembles Cimabue's in many ways but has a more advanced technique for creating depth, and the bright colouring that characterizes the Sienese school. Giotto's altarpiece, painted some 25 years later, takes a great leap forward, not only in his use of perspective but in the arrangement of the angels, standing naturally, and in the portrayal of the Virgin, gently smiling, with real fingers and breasts.

To the left, **Room 3** contains representative Sienese works of the 14th century, with a beautiful Gothic *Annunciation* (1333) by Simone Martini and the brothers Pietro and Ambrogio Lorenzetti. **Room 4** is dedicated to 14th-century Florentines: Bernardo Daddi, Nardo di Cione, and the delicately coloured *San Remigio Pietà* by Giottino. **Rooms 5 and 6** portray Italian contributions to the International Gothic school, most dazzlingly Gentile da Fabriano's *Adoration of the Magi* (1423), two good works by Lorenzo Monaco, and the *Thebaid* of Gherardo Starnina, depicting the rather unusual activities of the 4th-century monks of St Pancratius of Thebes, in Egypt.

Rooms 7–9: Early Renaissance

In the Uffizi, at least, it's but a few short steps from the superbly decorative International Gothic to the masters of the early Renaissance. **Room 7** contains minor works by Fra Angelico, Masaccio and Masolino, and three masterpieces. Domenico Veneziano's pastel *Madonna and Child with Saints* (1448) is one of the rare pictures by this Venetian master, who died a pauper in Florence. It is a new departure not only for its soft colours but for the subject matter, unifying the enthroned Virgin and saints in one panel, in what is known as a *Sacra Conversazione*. Piero della Francesca's famous *Double Portrait of the Duke Federigo da Montefeltro and his Duchess Battista Sforza of Urbino* (1465) depicts one of Italy's noblest Renaissance princes – and surely the one with the most distinctive nose. Piero's ability to create perfectly still, timeless worlds is even more evident in the allegorical 'Triumphs' of the Duke and Duchess painted on the back of their portraits.

A similar stillness and fascination floats over into the surreal in Uccello's *Rout of San Romano* (1456), or at least the third of it still present (the other two panels are in the Louvre and London's National Gallery; all three once decorated the bedroom of Lorenzo il Magnifico in the Medici palace). Both Piero and Uccello were deep students of perspective, but Uccello went half-crazy; the application of his principles to a violent battle scene has left us one of the most provocative works of all time – a vision of warfare in suspended animation, with pink, white and blue toy horses, robot-like knights, and rabbits bouncing in the background.

Room 8 is devoted to the works of the rascally romantic Fra Filippo Lippi, whose ethereally lovely Madonnas were modelled after his brown-eyed nun. In his *Coronation of the Virgin* (1447) she kneels in the foreground with two children, while the artist, dressed in a brown habit, looks dreamily towards her; in his celebrated *Madonna and Child with Two Angels* (1445) she plays the lead before the kind of mysterious landscape Leonardo would later perfect. Lippi taught the art of enchanting Madonnas to his student Botticelli, who has some lovely works in this room and the next; Alesso Baldovinetti, a pupil of the far more holy Fra Angelico, painted the room's beautiful *Annunciation* (1447).

Room 9 has two small scenes from the *Labours of Hercules* (1470) by Antonio Pollaiuolo, whose interest in anatomy, muscular expressiveness and violence presages a strain in Florentine art that culminated in the great Mannerists. He worked with his younger brother Piero on the refined *SS. Vincent, James and Eustace*, brought here from San Miniato. This room also contains the Uffizi's best-known forgery: *The Young Man in a Red Hat* or self-portrait of Filippino Lippi, believed to have been the work of an 18th-century English art dealer who palmed it off on the grand dukes.

Rooms 10–14: Botticelli

To accommodate the bewitching art of 'Little Barrels' and his 20th-century admirers, the Uffizi converted four small rooms into one great Botticellian shrine. Although his masterpieces displayed here have become almost synonymous with the Florentine Renaissance at its most spring-like and charming, they were not publicly displayed until the beginning of the 19th century, nor given much consideration outside Florence until the early 20th century. Botticelli's best works date from his days as a darling of the Medici – family members crop up most noticeably in the *Adoration of the Magi* (1476), where you can pick out Cosimo il Vecchio, Lorenzo il Magnifico and Botticelli himself (in the right foreground, in a yellow robe, gazing at the spectator). His *Annunciation* is a graceful, cosmic dance between the Virgin and the Angel Gabriel. In the *Tondo of the Virgin of the Pomegranate* the lovely melancholy goddess who was to become his Venus makes her first appearance.

Botticelli is best known for his sublime mythological allegories, nearly all painted for the Medici and inspired by the Neo-Platonic, humanistic and hermetic currents that pervaded the intelligentsia of the late 15th century. Perhaps no painting has been debated so fervently as *La Primavera* (1478). This hung for years in the Medici villa at Castello, and it is believed that the subject of the allegory of spring was suggested by Marsilio Ficino, one of the great natural magicians of the Renaissance, and that the figures represent the 'beneficial' planets able to dispel sadness. *Pallas and the Centaur* has been called another subtle allegory of Medici triumph – the rings of Athena's gown are supposedly a family symbol. Other interpretations see the taming of the sorrowful centaur as a melancholy comment on reason and civilization.

Botticelli's last great mythological painting, *The Birth of Venus*, was commissioned by Lorenzo di Pierfrancesco and inspired by a poem by Poliziano, Lorenzo il Magnifico's Latin and Greek scholar, who described how Zephyr and Chloris blew the newborn goddess to shore on a scallop shell, while Hora hastened to robe her – a scene Botticelli portrays once again with dance-like rhythm and delicacy of line. Yet the goddess of love floats towards the spectator with an expression of wistfulness – perhaps reflecting the artist's own feelings of regret. For artistically, the poetic, decorative style he perfected in this painting would be disdained and forgotten in his own lifetime. Spiritually, Botticelli also turned a corner after creating this haunting, uncanny beauty – his and Florence's farewell to a road not taken. Although Vasari's biography of Botticelli portrays a prankster rather than a sensitive soul, the painter absorbed more than any other artist the *fin-de-siècle* neuroticism that beset the city with the rise of Savonarola. So thoroughly did he reject his Neo-Platonism that he would only accept commissions of sacred subjects or supposedly edifying allegories such as his *Calumny*, a small but disturbing work, and a fitting introduction to the dark side of the quattrocento psyche.

This large room also contains works by Botticelli's contemporaries. There are two paintings of the *Adoration of the Magi*, one by Ghirlandaio and one by Filippino Lippi, that show the influence of Leonardo's unfinished but radical work in pyramidal composition (in the next room); Leonardo himself got the idea from the large *Portinari Altarpiece* (1471), at the end of the room, a work by Hugo Van der Goes that was brought back from Bruges by Medici agent Tommaso Portinari.

Rooms 15–24: More Renaissance

Room 15 is dedicated to the Florentine works of Leonardo da Vinci's early career. Here are works by his master Andrea Verrocchio, including the *Baptism of Christ*, in which Leonardo painted the angel on the left. Art critics believe the *Annunciation* (1475) is almost entirely by Leonardo – the soft faces, botanical details, and misty, watery background would become his trademarks. Most influential was his unfinished *Adoration of the Magi* (1481), an unconventional composition that Leonardo abandoned when he left Florence for Milan. Although at first glance it's hard to make out much more than a mass of reddish chiaroscuro, the longer you stare, the better you'll see the serene Madonna and Child surrounded by anxious, troubled humanity, with an exotic background of ruins, trees and horsemen.

Other artists in Room 15 include Leonardo's peers: Lorenzo di Credi, whose religious works have eerie garden-like backgrounds, and the nutty Piero di Cosimo, whose dreamy *Perseus Liberating Andromeda* includes an endearing mongrel of a dragon that gives even the most reserved Japanese tourist fits of giggles. Tuscan maps adorn **Room 16**, as well as scenes by Hans Memling. Temporarily housed here, away from their normal home in Room 43, are Caravaggio's *Bacchus* and *The Head of Medusa*, believed to be self-portraits. In its day the fleshy, heavy-eyed *Bacchus*, half portrait and half still life, was considered highly iconoclastic.

The octagonal **Tribuna** (**Room 18**), with its mother-of-pearl dome and *pietra dura* floor and table, was built by Buontalenti in 1584 for Francesco I and, like the Studiolo in the Palazzo Vecchio, was designed to hold Medici treasures. For centuries the best-known of these was the *Venus de' Medici*, a 2nd-century BC Greek sculpture, farcically claimed as a copy of Praxiteles' celebrated *Aphrodite of Cnidos*, the most erotic statue in antiquity. In the 18th century, amazingly, this rather ordinary girl was considered the greatest sculpture in Florence; today most visitors walk right by without a second glance. Other antique works include the *Wrestlers* and the *Knife Grinder*, both copies of Pergamese originals, the *Dancing Faun*, the *Young Apollo*, and the *Sleeping Hermaphrodite* in the adjacent room, which is usually curtained off.

The real stars of the Tribuna are the Medici court portraits, many of them by Bronzino, who was not only able to catch the likeness of Cosimo I, Eleanor of Toledo and their children, but could also aptly portray the spirit of the day – these are people who took themselves very seriously indeed. They have for company Vasari's posthumous portrait of *Lorenzo il Magnifico* and Pontormo's *Cosimo il Vecchio*, Andrea del Sarto's *Girl with a Book by Petrarch*, and Rosso Fiorentino's *Angel Musician*, an enchanting work entirely out of place in this stodgy temple.

Two followers of Piero della Francesca, Perugino and Luca Signorelli, hold pride of place in **Room 19**; Perugino's *Portrait of a Young Man* is believed to have been modelled on his pupil Raphael. Signorelli's *Tondo of the Holy Family* was to become the inspiration for Michelangelo's (*see* below). The room also contains Lorenzo di Credi's *Venus*, inspired by Botticelli.

The Germans appear in **Room 20**: Dürer's earliest known work, the *Portrait of his Father* (1490), done at age 19, and *The Adoration of the Magi* (1504). Also here are Lucas Cranach's Teutonic *Adam and Eve* and his *Portrait of Martin Luther* (1543), not someone you'd necessarily expect to see in Florence. **Room 21** is dedicated to the great Venetians, most famously Bellini and his uncanny *Sacred Allegory* (1490s), the meaning of which has never been satisfactorily explained. There are two minor works by the elusive Giorgione, and a typically weird *St Dominic* by Cosmè Tura.

Later Flemish and German artists appear in **Room 22**, works by Gerard David and proto-Romantic Albrecht Altdorfer, and a portrait attributed to Hans Holbein of *Sir Thomas More*. **Room 23** is dedicated to non-Tuscans Correggio of Parma and Mantegna of the Veneto, as well as Boltraffio's strange *Narcissus*.

Rooms 25–27: Mannerism

The window-filled South Corridor, with its views over the city and its fine display of antique sculpture, marks only the halfway point in the Uffizi but nearly the end of Florence's contribution. In the first three rooms, however, local talent rallies to produce a brilliantly coloured twilight in Florentine Mannerism. By most accounts, Michelangelo's only completed oil painting, the *Tondo Doni* (1506), was the spark that ignited Mannerism's flaming orange and turquoise hues. Michelangelo was 30 when he painted this unconventional work, in a medium he disliked (sculpture and fresco being the only fit occupations for a man, he believed). It's a typical Michelangelo story that when the purchaser complained the artist was asking too much for it, Michelangelo promptly doubled the price. As shocking as the colours are the spiralling poses of the Holy Family, sharply delineated against a background of five nude, slightly out-of-focus young men of uncertain purpose (are they pagans? angels? boyfriends? or just fillers?) – an ambiguity that was to become a hallmark of Mannerism; as the *Ignudi* they later appear on the Sistine Chapel ceiling. In itself, the *Tondo Doni* is more provocative than immediately appealing; the violent canvas in Room 27, Rosso Fiorentino's *Moses Defending the Children of Jethro*, was painted some 20 years later and at least in its intention to shock the viewer puts a cap on what Michelangelo began.

Room 26 is dedicated mainly to Raphael, who was in and out of Florence from 1504 to 1508. Raphael was the sweetheart of the High Renaissance. His Madonnas, like *The Madonna of the Goldfinch*, have a tenderness that was soon to be overpopularized by others and turned into holy cards, a cloying sentimentality added over the centuries. It's easier, perhaps, to see Raphael's genius in non-sacred subjects, such as *Leo X with Two Cardinals*, a perceptive portrait study of the first Medici pope with his nephew Giulio de' Medici, later Clement VII. The same room contains Andrea del Sarto's most original work, the fluorescent *Madonna of the Harpies* (1517), named after the figures on the Virgin's pedestal. Of the works by Pontormo, the best is in **Room 27**, *Supper at Emmaus* (1525), a strange canvas with the Masonic symbol of the Eye of God hovering over Christ's head.

Rooms 28–45

The Uffizi fairly bristles with masterpieces from other parts of Italy and from abroad. Titian's delicious nudes, especially the voluptuous *Venus of Urbino*, raise the temperature in **Room 28**; Parmigianino's hyperelegant *Madonna with the Long Neck* (1536), displayed in **Room 29**, is a fascinating Mannerist evolutionary dead end. **Room 31** holds Paolo Veronese's *Holy Family with St Barbara*, bathed in a golden Venetian light, with a gorgeously opulent Barbara. Sebastiano del Piombo's *Death of Adonis*, in **Room 32**, is notable for its melancholy, autumn atmosphere, and Venus's annoyed look. Tintoretto's shadowy *Leda* languidly pretends to restrain the lusty swan.

Room 41 is a Flemish domain, with brand-name art by Rubens and Van Dyck; the former's *Baccanale* may be the most grotesque canvas in the whole of Florence. **Room 42**, the Sala della Niobe, was reopened in December 1998 after the bomb damage was repaired. A series of statues, *Niobe and her Sons* (18th-century copies of Hellenic works), are housed in the high, arched-ceilinged room, which is covered in pristine plaster and gold leaf. **Room 43** houses striking Caravaggios.

Room 44 has three portraits by Rembrandt, including two self-portraits, and landscapes by Ruysdael. **Room 45**'s fine 18th-century works include portraits by Chardin, Goya and Longhi, and Venetian landscapes by Guardi and Canaletto. Even more welcome by this time is the **bar**, with a summer terrace.

Contini Bonacossi Collection
visits by appointment, **t** *055 265 4321; Uffizi ticket is also valid for this*

The **Contini Bonacossi collection**, once housed in the Meridiana Pavilion at Palazzo Pitti, was moved to the Uffizi in 1999. There is a separate entrance in Via Lambertesca. This recent bequest includes works of Cimabue, Duccio and Giovanni Bellini, some sculpture and china, and also paintings by El Greco, Goya and Velázquez – the last represented by an exceptional work, *The Water Carrier of Seville*.

Corridoio Vasariano

Corridoio Vasariano
open for very limited periods of year, though now open to individual researchers not just groups; call **t** *055 265 4321 for info and bookings (obligatory); adm exp*

In 1565, when Francesco I married Joanna of Austria, the Medici commissioned Vasari to link their new digs in the Pitti Palace with the Uffizi and the Palazzo Vecchio in such a manner that the archdukes could make their rounds without rubbing elbows with their subjects. With a patina of 400 years, it seems that Florence wouldn't look quite right without this covered catwalk, leap-frogging on rounded arches from the back of the Uffizi, over the Ponte Vecchio, daintily skirting a medieval tower, and darting past the façade of Santa Felicità to the Pitti Palace.

The Corridoio not only offers interesting views of Florence: it has been hung with a celebrated collection of artists' self-portraits, beginning, reasonably, with Vasari himself before continuing in chronological order, past the Gaddis and Raphael to Rembrandt, Van Dyck, Velázquez, Hogarth, Reynolds, Delacroix and Corot.

Museo di Storia della Scienza

Museo di Storia della Scienza
open summer Mon and Wed–Fri 9.30–5, Tues and Sat 9.30–1; winter Mon and Wed–Sat 9.30–5, Tues 9.30–1, 2nd Sun of month 10–1; adm

For all that Florence and Tuscany contributed to the birth of science, it is only fitting to have the **museum of the history of science** in the centre of the city, behind the Uffizi in Piazza Giudici. Much of the first floor is devoted to instruments measuring time and distance: Arabian astrolabes and pocket sundials, Tuscan sundials in the shape of Platonic solids, enormous elaborate armillary spheres and a small reliquary holding the bone of Galileo's finger, erect, like a final gesture to the city that until 1737 denied him a Christian burial. Here, too, are two of his original telescopes and the lens with which he discovered the four moons of Jupiter. Other scientific instruments come from the Accademia del Cimento (of 'trial' or 'experiment'), which was founded in 1657 by Cardinal Leopoldo de' Medici, the world's first scientific organization, dedicated to Galileo's principle of enquiry and proof by experimentation. 'Try and try again' was its motto. Upstairs is a large room filled with machines used to demonstrate principles of physics, which the women who run the museum will operate if you ask. Two unusual ones are the 18th-century automatic writer and the instrument of perpetual motion. The rooms on medicine have a collection of 18th-century wax anatomical models, designed to teach budding obstetricians about unfortunate foetal positions, as well as a fine display of surgical instruments from the period.

Ponte Vecchio and Ponte Santa Trínita

Bent bridges seeming to strain like bows
And tremble with arrowy undertide...
Elizabeth Barrett Browning, 'Casa Guidi Windows'

Often at sunset the Arno becomes a stream of molten gold – that is, during those months when it has a respectable flow of water. But even in the torrid days of August, when the Arno shrivels into muck and spittle, its two famous bridges retain their distinctive beauty. The most famous of these, the **Ponte Vecchio** or 'Old Bridge', crosses the Arno at its narrowest point; the present bridge, with its three stone arches, was built in 1345 to replace a wooden construction from the 970s, which in turn was the successor to a span that may well have dated back to the Romans. On this wooden bridge, at the foot of the *Marzocco*, or statue of Mars, Buondelmonte dei Buondelmonti was murdered in 1215, setting off the wars of the Guelphs and Ghibellines. The original *Marzocco* was washed away in a 14th-century flood, and Donatello's later version has been carted off to the Bargello.

Like old London Bridge, the Ponte Vecchio is covered with shops and houses. By the 1500s it had become the street of hog butchers, although after Vasari built Cosimo's secret passage on top, the Grand Duke evicted the butchers and replaced them with goldsmiths. They have been there ever since, and shoppers from around the world descend on it each year to scrutinize the traditional Florentine talent for jewellery – not a few of the city's great artists began their careers as goldsmiths, beginning with Ghiberti and Donatello and ending with Cellini, whose bust adorns the middle of the bridge. In the 1966 flood the shops did not prove as resilient as the Ponte Vecchio itself, and a fortune of gold was washed down the Arno.

In the summer of 1944, the river briefly became a German defensive line during the slow painful retreat across Italy. Before leaving Florence, the Nazis blew up every one of the city's bridges, saving only, on Hitler's special orders, the Ponte Vecchio, though they blasted a large number of ancient buildings on each side of the span in order to create piles of rubble to block the approaches. Florence's most beautiful span, the **Ponte Santa Trínita**, was the most tragic victim. Immediately after the war the Florentines set about replacing the bridges exactly as they were: for Santa Trínita, old quarries had to be reopened to duplicate the stone, and old methods revived to cut it (modern power saws would have done it too cleanly). The graceful curve of the three arches was a problem;

they could not be constructed geometrically, and considerable speculation went on over how the architect (Ammannati, in 1567) did it. Finally, recalling that Michelangelo had advised Ammannati on the project, someone noticed that the same form of arch could be seen on the decoration of the tombs in Michelangelo's Medici Chapel, constructed most likely by pure artistic imagination. Fortune lent a hand in the reconstruction; of the original statues of the 'Four Seasons', almost all the pieces were fished out of the Arno and rebuilt. Spring's head was eventually found by divers completely by accident in 1961.

Dante's Florence

Badia Fiorentina
cloister open Mon 3–6; church open Mon 3–6, Tues–Sat 6.30–6

Dante would contemplate his Beatrice, the story goes, at Mass in the **Badia Fiorentina**, a Benedictine church on Via del Proconsolo across from the Bargello (entrance on Via Dante Alighieri), with a lovely Gothic spire to grace this corner of the Florentine skyline. The church has undergone many rebuildings since Willa, widow of a Margrave of Tuscany, began it in around 990, but there is still a monument to Ugo, the 'Good Margrave' mentioned in Dante, and a painting of the Madonna appearing to St Bernard by Filippo Lippi.

Casa di Dante
t 055 219416; open Tues–Sat 10–5, 1st Sun of month 10–4, 2nd and 3rd Sun of month 10–1; adm

Between the Badia and Via de' Calzaiuoli, a little corner of medieval Florence has survived the changes of centuries. In these quiet, narrow streets you can visit the **Casa di Dante**, which was actually built in 1911 over the ruins of an amputated towerhouse, although scholars all agree that the Alighieri lived somewhere in the vicinity. Since 1960 this museum dedicated to Dante has made a game attempt to evoke Dante's life and times, in spite of neglect. Near the entrance is an edition of *The Divine Comedy*, all printed in tiny letters on a poster by a mad Milanese. Upstairs are copies of Botticelli's beautiful line illustrations for the *Commedia*.

Nearby, the stout medieval **Torre del Castagna** is all that remains of the original Palazzo del Popolo, residence of the *priori*, the governors of the city, before the construction of the Palazzo Vecchio. Dante himself was a *priore* once, and he would have spent his two-month term of office living here, as the law required.

San Martino del Vescovo
open Mon–Sat 10–12 and 3–5

After giving up on Beatrice, Dante married Gemma Donati, in **Santa Margherita** church on the same block. Another church nearby, **San Martino del Vescovo**, has a fine set of frescoes from the workshop of Ghirlandaio.

4 Museo Nazionale del Bargello
open daily 8.15–1.50; closed 1st and 3rd Sun and 2nd and 4th Mon of month; adm

Museo Nazionale del Bargello

Across from the Badia Fiorentina looms the Bargello, a battlemented urban fortress, well proportioned yet of forbidding grace; for centuries it served as Florence's prison. Today its only inmates are men of marble, gathered together to form Italy's finest collection of sculpture – a fitting complement to the paintings in the Uffizi. The Bargello is 'stone Florence' squared to the sixth degree, rugged and austere *pietra forte*, the model for the even grander Palazzo Vecchio. Even the treasures it houses are hard, definite, certain – and almost unremittingly masculine. The Bargello offers the best insight that is available into Florence's golden age, and it was a man's world indeed.

Completed in 1255, the Bargello was intended as Florence's Palazzo del Popolo, although by 1271 it served instead as the residence of the foreign *podestà*, or chief magistrate, who was installed by Guelph leader Charles of Anjou. The Medici made it the headquarters of the captain of police (the *Bargello*), the city jail and torture chamber, a function it served until 1859. In the Renaissance it was the peculiar custom to paint portraits of the condemned on the exterior walls of the fortress; Andrea del Castagno was so good at it that he was nicknamed Andrea of the Hanged Men. All of these ghoulish souvenirs have long since disappeared, as have the torture instruments – they were burned in 1786, when Grand Duke Peter Leopold abolished torture and the death sentence in Tuscany, only a few months after the Venetians led the way. Today the Gothic **courtyard**, the former site of the gallows and chopping block, is a delightful place, owing much to an imaginative restoration in the 1860s. The encrustation of centuries of *podestà* armorial devices and plaques in a wild vocabulary of symbols, the shadowy arcades and stately stairs combine to create one of Florence's most romantic corners.

The **main ground-floor gallery** is dedicated to Michelangelo and his century, although it must be said that the Michelangelo of the Bargello somewhat lacks the angst and ecstasy that one is accustomed to. The real star of the room is Benvenuto Cellini, who was, besides a good many other things, an exquisite craftsman and a daring innovator.

The stairway from the courtyard leads up to the shady **Loggia**, which has been converted into an aviary for Giambologna's charming bronze birds, created for the animal grotto at the Medici's Villa di Castello.

The **Salone del Consiglio Generale**, formerly the courtroom of the *podestà*, contains the greatest masterpieces of early Renaissance sculpture. When Michelangelo's maudlin self-absorption and the Mannerists' empty virtuosity begin to seem tiresome, a visit to this room will prove a welcome antidote. Donatello's originality and vision are strikingly modern – and mysterious. On the wall hang the two famous trial reliefs for the second set of baptistry doors, by Ghiberti and Brunelleschi, both depicting the *Sacrifice of Isaac*. The remainder of the first floor houses fascinating collections of decorative arts that were donated to the Bargello.

Some of the most interesting items are in the next rooms, especially works in the **ivory collection** – Carolingian and Byzantine diptychs, an 8th-century whalebone coffer from Northumbria adorned with runes, medieval French miniatures chronicling 'The Assault on the Castle of Love', 11th-century chess pieces, and more.

A stairway from the ivory collection leads up to the **second floor**. It houses some of the finest enamelled terracottas of the Della Robbia family workshop, a room of portrait busts, works by Antonio Pollaiuolo and Verrocchio, including his *David* and lovely *Young Lady with a Nosegay*. There is also a collection of armour, and the most important collection of small Renaissance bronzes in Italy.

Piazza San Firenze to the Duomo

The strangely shaped square that the Badia and the Bargello call home is named after the large church of **San Firenze**, now partially used as Florence's law courts. At the corner of the square and Via Gondi, the **Palazzo Gondi** is a fine Renaissance palace built for a merchant by Giuliano da Sangallo in 1489; it's not easy to pick out the discreet 19th-century additions. A block from the square on Via Ghibellina, the **Palazzo Borghese** (No.110) is one of the finest neoclassical buildings in the city, erected in 1822 for a party in honour of Habsburg Grand Duke Ferdinand III. The host was one of the wealthiest men of his day, the Roman prince Camillo Borghese, husband of Pauline Bonaparte and the man responsible for shipping many of Italy's art treasures off to the Louvre.

From Piazza San Firenze, Via del Proconsolo leads straight to the Piazza del Duomo, passing by way of the **Palazzo Pazzi-Quaratesi** (No.10), which was the 15th-century headquarters of the banking family that organized the conspiracy against Lorenzo and Giuliano de' Medici. No.12, the Palazzo Nonfinito – begun in 1593 but, as its name suggests, never completed – is now the home of the **Museo Nazionale di Antropologia ed Etnologia**, founded in 1869 and he first ethnological museum in Italy, with an interesting collection of Peruvian mummies, musical instruments collected by Galileo Chini (who decorated the Liberty-style extravaganzas at Viareggio), some lovely and unusual items of Japan's Ainu and Pakistan's Kafiri, and a large number of skulls from all over the world.

Museo Nazionale di Antropologia ed Etnologia
open Mon, Tues, Thurs and Fri 9–1, Sat 9–5; adm

Florence As It Was

Borgo degli Albizi, the fine old street passing in front of the Palazzo Nonfinito, was in ancient times the Via Cassia, linking Rome with Bologna, and it deserves a leisurely stroll for its palaces (especially No.18, the cinquecento **Palazzo Valori**, nicknamed 'Funny Face Palace' for its surreal, semi-relief herm-busts of Florentine immortals on three floors of the façade). If Borgo degli Albizi, too,

Museo di Firenze Com'Era
open Mon and Tues 9–2, Sat 9–7, plus Wed in winter 9–2; adm

fails to answer to the Florence you've been seeking, take Via dell'Oriuolo (just to the left at Piazza G Salvemini) to reach the **Museum of Florence As It Was**, located at the big garden at No.24. The jewel of this museum is right out in front – the nearly room-sized *Pianta della Catena*, most beautiful of the early views of Florence. It is a copy; the original, made in 1490 by an unknown artist – that handsome fellow pictured in the lower right-hand corner – was lost during the last war in a Berlin museum. This fascinating painting captures Florence at the height of the Renaissance – a city of buildings in bright white, pink and tan; the great churches are without their façades, the Uffizi and Medici chapels have not yet appeared, and the Medici and Pitti palaces are without their later extensions.

The museum is not large. At present it contains only a number of plans and maps, as well as a collection of amateurish watercolours of Florence's sights dating from the last century, and paintings of the city's surroundings by Ottone Rosai, a local favourite who died in 1957. Today's Florentines seem much less interested in the Renaissance than in the city of their grandparents. For further evidence of this, look around the corner of **Via Sant'Egidio**, where some recent remodelling has uncovered posters over the street from 1925, announcing plans for paying the war debt and a coming visit of the *Folies Bergère* – the Florentines have restored them and put them under glass.

From Via dell'Oriuolo, Via Folco Portinari takes you to Florence's main hospital, **Santa Maria Nuova**, which was founded in 1286 by the father of Dante's Beatrice, Folco Portinari. A tomb in the hospital's church, Sant'Egidio, is all that remains of the family. Readers of Iris Origo's *The Merchant of Prato* will recognize it as the workplace of the good notary, Ser Lapo Mazzei. The portico, by Buontalenti, was finished in 1612.

Medieval Streets North of the Arno

Just to the west of Via Por S. Maria, the main street leading down to the Ponte Vecchio, you'll find some of the oldest and best-preserved lanes in all Florence. Near the **Mercato Nuovo** at the top of the street (*see* pp.113–14) stands the **Palazzo di Parte Guelfa**, the 13th-century headquarters of the Guelph party, and often the real seat of power in the city, which was paid for by property confiscated from the Ghibellines; in the 15th century Brunelleschi added a hall on the top floor and an extension.

Next door is the guildhall of the silk-makers, the 14th-century **Palazzo dell'Arte della Seta**, still bearing its bas-relief emblem, or *stemma*, of a closed door, the age-old guild symbol. It's worth continuing around the Guelph Palace to Via Pellicceria to see the fine ensemble of medieval buildings on the tiny square near Via delle Terme, named after the old Roman baths.

Palazzo Davanzati

Palazzo Davanzati
partly closed for restoration; ground-floor exhibition open 2nd and 4th Mon of month and 1st, 3rd and 5th Sun of month 8.15–1.50

To get an idea of what life was like inside these sombre palaces some 600 years ago, stroll over to nearby Via Porta Rossa, site of the elegant Palazzo Davanzati, now the **Museo della Casa Fiorentina Antica**. One of the city's most delightful museums, it offers a chance to step back into domestic life of yore. Originally built in the mid-14th century for the Davizzi family, the house was purchased by merchant Bernardo Davanzati in 1578 and stayed in the family until the 1900s. Restored by an antique-collector in 1904, it is the best-preserved medieval-Renaissance house in Florence.

Piazza Santa Trínita

Three old Roman roads – Via Porta Rossa, Via delle Terme and Borgo SS. Apostoli – lead into the irregularly shaped Piazza Santa Trínita. Borgo SS. Apostoli is named after one of Florence's oldest churches, Romanesque **Santi Apostoli** (11th century), in the sunken Piazzetta del Limbo, former cemetery of unbaptized babies.

Piazza Santa Trínita itself boasts an exceptionally fine architectural ensemble, grouped around the 'Column of Justice' from the Roman baths of Caracalla, which was given by Pius IV to Cosimo I, and later topped with a red statue of Justice by Francesco del Tadda. Its pale granite is set off by the palaces of the *piazza*: the High Renaissance-Roman **Palazzo Bartolini-Salimbeni** by Baccio d'Agnolo (1520) on the corner of Via Porta Rossa, formerly the fashionable Hôtel du Nord where Herman Melville stayed; the medieval **Palazzo Buondelmonti**, with a 1530 façade by Baccio d'Agnolo, once home to the reading room and favourite haunt of such literati in the 19th century as Dumas, Browning, Manzoni and Stendhal; and the magnificent curving **Palazzo Spini-Ferroni**, the largest medieval palace in Florence, built in 1289 and retaining its original battlements. This is now home to the heirs of the Florentine designer Ferragamo and houses a retail outlet and a fascinating small **museum of Ferragamo's life and work**, including some of the most beautiful shoes in the world.

Museo Salvatore Ferragamo
www.salvatoreferragamo.it; open Mon–Fri 9–1 and 2–6 by appt only, **t** *055 336 0456*

Santa Trínita

Santa Trínita
open daily 7–12 and 4–7

The church of Santa Trínita has stood here, in one form or another, since the 12th century; its unusual accent on the first syllable (from the Latin *trinitas*) is considered proof of its ancient foundation. Although the pedestrian façade that was added by Buontalenti in 1593 isn't especially welcoming, step into its shadowy 14th-century interior for several artistic treats, beginning with the **Bartolini-Salimbeni Chapel** (the fourth on the right), frescoed in 1422 by the Sienese Lorenzo Monaco; his *Marriage of the Virgin* takes place in a Tuscan fantasy backdrop of pink towers. He also painted the chapel's graceful, ethereally coloured altarpiece, the *Annunciation*.

In the choir, the **Sassetti Chapel** is one of the masterpieces of Domenico Ghirlandaio, completed in 1495 for wealthy merchant Francesco Sassetti and dedicated to the Life of St Francis, but also to the life of Francesco Sassetti, the city and his Medici circle: the scene above the altar, of Francis receiving the Rule of the Order, is transferred to the Piazza della Signoria, watched by Sassetti (to the right, with the fat purse) and Lorenzo il Magnifico; on the steps stands the great Latinist Poliziano with Lorenzo's three sons. The *Death of St Francis* pays homage to Giotto's similar composition in Santa Croce. The altarpiece, the *Adoration of the Shepherds* (1485), is one of Ghirlandaio's best-known works, often described as the archetypal Renaissance painting, with a contrived but charming classical treatment; the Magi arrive through a triumphal arch, a Roman sarcophagus is used as manger and a ruined temple functions as a stable – all matched by the sibyls on the vault; the sibyl on the outer arch is the one who supposedly announced the birth of Christ to Augustus.

Santa Trínita is a Vallombrosan church, and the first chapel to the right of the altar holds the Order's holy of holies, a painted crucifix formerly in San Miniato. The story goes that on a Good Friday, a young noble named Giovanni Gualberto was on his way to Mass when he met the man who had recently murdered his brother. Rather than take his revenge, Gualberto pardoned the assassin in honour of the holy day. When he arrived at church to pray, this crucifix nodded in approval of his mercy. Giovanni was so impressed that he went on to found the Vallombrosan order in the Casentino. The **sanctuary** was frescoed by Alesso Baldovinetti, though only four Old Testament figures survive. In the second chapel to the left the marble **tomb of Bishop Benozzo Federighi** (1454) is by Luca della Robbia. In the fourth chapel, a detached fresco by Neri di Bicci portrays San Giovanni Gualberto and his fellow Vallombrosan saints.

West of Piazza della Repubblica

The streets to the west of Piazza della Repubblica have always been the choicest district of Florence, and **Via de' Tornabuoni** has always been the smartest shopping street in the city. These days you won't find many innovations here, however: Milan's current status as the headquarters of Italy's fashion industry is a sore point with Florence.

In the bright and ambitious 1400s, however, when Florence was the centre of European high finance, Via de' Tornabuoni and its environs was the area the new merchant elite chose for their palaces. Today's bankers build great skyscrapers for the firm and settle for modest mansions for themselves; in Florence's heyday, things were reversed. Bankers and wool tycoons really owned their businesses. While their places of work were quite simple, their homes were imposing city palaces, all built in the same conservative style and competing with each other in size like some Millionaires' Row in 19th-century America.

The champion was the **Palazzo Strozzi**, a long block up Via de' Tornabuoni from Piazza Trinita. This rusticated stone cube of fearful dimensions squats in its *piazza*, radiating almost visible waves of megalomania. There are few architectural innovations in the Palazzo Strozzi, but here the typical Florentine palace is blown up to the level of the absurd: there are three storeys like other palaces, but each floor is as tall as three or four normal ones, and the rings to tie up horses could hold elephants. Like Michelangelo's *David*, Florence's other beautiful monster, it emits the unpleasant sensation of what Mary McCarthy called the 'giganticism of the human ego' – the will to surpass not only antiquity but nature herself. Nowadays, at least, the Strozzi palace is moderately useful as a space for temporary exhibitions.

Palazzo Rucellai

There are two other exceptional palaces in the quarter. At the north end of Via de' Tornabuoni stands the beautiful golden **Palazzo Antinori** (1465, by an unknown architect), which has Florence's grandest Baroque façade, **San Gaetano** (1648, by Gherardo Silvani), as its equally golden companion, despite being decorated with statues that would look right at home in Rome but have the appearance of bad actors in Florence.

The second important palace, Florence's most celebrated example of domestic architecture, is the **Palazzo Rucellai**, in Via della Vigna Nuova. Its original owner, Giovanni Rucellai, was a quattrocento tycoon like Filippo Strozzi, but an intellectual too, whose *Zibaldone*, or 'commonplace book', is one of the best sources available on the life and tastes of the educated Renaissance merchant. In 1446 Rucellai chose Leon Battista Alberti to design his palace. Actually built by Bernardo Rossellino, it follows Alberti's precepts and theories in its use of the three classical orders; instead of the usual rusticated stone, the façade has a far more delicate decoration of incised irregular blocks and a frieze – elements influential in subsequent Italian architecture, though far more noticeably in Rome than Florence itself. Originally the palace was only five bays wide, and when another two bays were added later the edge was left ragged, unfinished – a nice touch, as if the builders could return at any moment and pick up where they left off. The frieze, like that on Santa Maria Novella, portrays the devices of the Medici and Rucellai families, whose alliance was fêted in the **Loggia dei Rucellai** across the street, also designed by Alberti.

Piazza Goldoni and Ognissanti

Before taking leave of old Florence's west end, head back to the Arno and **Piazza Goldoni**, named after the great comic playwright from Venice. The bridge here, the Ponte alla Carraia, is new and nondescript, but its 1304 version played a leading role in that year's most memorable disaster: a company staging a water pageant of the *Inferno*, with monsters, devils and tortured souls, attracted such a large crowd that the bridge collapsed, and all were drowned.

The most important building on the *piazza*, the **Palazzo Ricasoli**, was built in the 15th century but bears the name of one of unified Italy's first prime ministers, Bettino 'Iron Baron' Ricasoli. Just to the east on Lungarno Corsini looms the enormous **Palazzo Corsini**, the city's most prominent piece of Roman Baroque extravagance, begun in 1650 and crowned with a bevy of statues. The Corsini, the most prominent family of 17th- and 18th-century Florence, were reputedly so wealthy that they could ride from Florence to Rome entirely on their own property. The **Galleria Corsini** (enter on Via del Parione) houses paintings by Giovanni Bellini, Signorelli, Filippino Lippi and Pontormo, and *Muses* from the ducal palace of Urbino, painted by Raphael's first master, Timoteo Viti. It also has the rarest of Florentine amenities: a garden, a 17th-century oasis of box hedges, Roman statues, lemon trees and tortoises. Further east on Lungarno Corsini stood the Libreria Orioli, which caused a scandal when it published the first edition of *Lady Chatterley's Lover* in 1927.

Galleria Corsini
open by appt, call **t** *055 218994 (Mon, Wed or Fri 9.30–12.30)*

To the west of Piazza Goldoni lies the old neighbourhood of the only Florentine to have a continent named after him. Amerigo Vespucci (1451–1512) was a Medici agent in Seville, and made two voyages from there to America on the heels of Columbus. His parish church, **Ognissanti** (All Saints), is set back from the river behind a Baroque façade, on property donated in 1256 by the Umiliati, a religious order that specialized in wool-working. The Vespucci family tomb is below the second altar to the right, and Amerigo himself is said to be pictured next to the Madonna in the fresco of the *Madonna della Misericordia*. Also buried in Ognissanti was the Filipepi family, one of whom was Botticelli.

Ognissanti
open 8–12.30 and 5–7.30

The best art is to be found in the **convent**, just to the left of the church at No.42. Frescoed in the refectory is the great *Last Supper*, or *Cenacolo*, painted by Domenico Ghirlandaio in 1480. It's hard to think of a more serene and elegant *Last Supper*, akin to a garden party with its background of fruit trees and exotic birds; a peacock

Convent
open Sat, Mon and Tues 9–12 (you may have to ring the bell)

sits in the window, cherries and peaches litter the lovely tablecloth. On either side of the fresco are two scholarly saints moved from the church itself; Ghirlandaio's *St Jerome* and, on the right, young Botticelli's *St Augustine*.

Santa Maria Novella

Santa Maria Novella
open Mon–Thurs and Sat 9–5; Sun (exc. Aug) 9–2; adm

As in so many other Italian cities, the two churches of the preaching orders – the Dominicans' Santa Maria Novella and the Franciscans' Santa Croce – became the largest and most prestigious in the city, where wealthy families vied to create the most beautiful chapels and tombs. In Florence, by some twitch of city planning, both of these sacred art galleries dominate broad, stale squares that do not invite you to linger; in the irregular **Piazza Santa Maria Novella** you may find yourself looking over your shoulder for the ghosts of the carriages that once raced madly around the two stout obelisks set on turtles, just as in a Roman circus, in the fashionable carriage races of the 1700s. The arcade on the south side, the **Loggia di San Paolo**, is much like Brunelleschi's Spedale degli Innocenti, although it suffers somewhat from its use as a busy bus shelter; the lunette over the door, by Andrea della Robbia, is the *Meeting of SS. Francis and Dominic*.

Santa Maria Novella redeems the anomie of its square with its stupendous black and white marble **façade**, the finest in Florence. The lower part, with its looping arcades, is Romanesque work in the typical Tuscan mode, finished before 1360. In 1456 Giovanni Rucellai commissioned Alberti to complete it – a remarkably fortunate choice. Alberti's half not only perfectly harmonizes with the original but perfects it with geometrical harmonies to create what appears to be a kind of Renaissance Sun temple. The original builders started it off by orientating the church to the south instead of west, so that at noon the sun streams through the 14th-century rose window. The only symbol Alberti put on the façade is a blazing sun; the unusual sundials, over the arches on the extreme right and left, were added by Cosimo I's court astronomer Egnazio Danti. The base of the façade is also the base of an equilateral triangle, with Alberti's sun at the apex. The beautiful frieze depicts the Rucellai emblem (a billowing sail), as on the Palazzo Rucellai. The wall of Gothic recesses to the right, enclosing the old cemetery, are *avelli*, or family tombs.

The **interior** is vast, lofty and more 'Gothic' in feel than any other church in Florence – no thanks to Vasari, who was set loose to remodel the church to 16th-century taste, painting over the original frescoes, removing the rood screen and Dominicans' choir from the nave and remodelling the altars; in the 1800s restorers did their best to de-Vasari Santa Maria with neo-Gothic details.

Neither party, however, could touch two of the interior's most distinctive features – the striking stone vaulting of the nave and the perspective created by the columns marching down the aisles, each pair placed a little closer together as they approach the altar.

Over the portal at the entrance is a fresco lunette by Botticelli that has recently been restored. One of Santa Maria Novella's best-known pictures has also recently been restored and is at the second altar on the left: Masaccio's *Trinità*, painted around 1425, one of the revolutionary works of the Renaissance. Masaccio's use of architectural elements and perspective gives his composition both physical and intellectual depth. The flat wall becomes a deeply recessed Brunelleschian chapel, calm and classical, enclosed in a coffered barrel vault; at the foot of the fresco a bleak skeleton decays in its tomb, bearing a favourite Tuscan reminder: 'I was that which you are, you will be that which I am.'

Above this morbid suggestion of physical death kneel the two donors; within the celestially rational inner sanctum the Virgin and St John stand at the foot of the Cross, humanity's link with the mystery of the Trinity. In the nearby pulpit, designed by Brunelleschi, Galileo was first denounced by the Inquisition for presuming to believe that the Earth went around the Sun.

There is little else to detain you in the aisles, but the first chapel in the left transept, the raised **Cappella Strozzi**, is one of the most evocative corners of 14th-century Florence, frescoed entirely by Nardo di Cione and his brother, Andrea Orcagna; on the vault pictures of *St Thomas Aquinas* and the *Virtues* are echoed in Andrea's lovely altarpiece *The Redeemer Donating the Keys to St Peter and the Book of Wisdom to St Thomas Aquinas*; on the left wall is a crowded scene of *Paradise*, with the righteous lined up in a medieval school class photograph. On the right, Nardo painted a striking view of Dante's *Inferno*, with all of a Tuscan's special attention to precise map-like detail. Dramatically in the centre of the **nave** hangs Giotto's *Crucifix* (*c.* 1300), one of the artist's first works. In the **Gondi Chapel** hangs another famous *Crucifix*, carved in wood by Brunelleschi, which, according to Vasari, so astonished his friend Donatello that he dropped the eggs he was carrying in his apron for their lunch when he first saw it.

The charming fresco cycle in the **sanctuary** (1485–90), painted by Domenico Ghirlandaio, is the *Lives of the Virgin, St John the Baptist and the Dominican Saints* portrayed in magnificent architectural settings; little Michelangelo was among the students who helped him complete it. Nearly all of the bystanders are portraits of Florentine quattrocento VIPs, including the artist himself (in the red hat, in the *Expulsion of St Joachim from the Temple*), but most prominent are the ladies and gentlemen of the Tornabuoni house. More excellent frescoes adorn the **Filippo Strozzi Chapel**, the finest

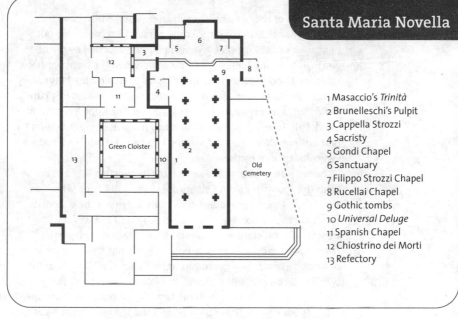

1 Masaccio's *Trinità*
2 Brunelleschi's Pulpit
3 Cappella Strozzi
4 Sacristy
5 Gondi Chapel
6 Sanctuary
7 Filippo Strozzi Chapel
8 Rucellai Chapel
9 Gothic tombs
10 *Universal Deluge*
11 Spanish Chapel
12 Chiostrino dei Morti
13 Refectory

work ever to come from the brush of Filippino Lippi, painted in 1502 near the end of his life; the exaggerated, dark and violent scenes portray the lives of St Philip (his crucifixion and his subduing of the dragon before the Temple of Mars, which creates such a stench that it kills the heathen prince) and of St John the Evangelist (raising Drusiana from the dead and being martyred in boiling oil). The chapel's beautifully carved tomb of Filippo Strozzi is by Benedetto da Maiano. The **Rucellai Chapel** contains a marble statue of the *Madonna and Child* by Nino Pisano and a fine bronze tomb by Ghiberti, which makes an interesting comparison with the three Gothic tombs nearby in the right transept. One of these contains the remains of the Patriarch of Constantinople, who died in here after the failure of the Council of Florence in 1439 to reunite the Western and Eastern Churches.

The Green Cloister and Spanish Chapel

Santa Maria Novella's cloisters
open Mon–Thurs and Sat 9–5, Sun 9–2; adm

More great frescoes, restored after the flood, await the visitor in Santa Maria Novella's cloisters, open as a city museum (entrance just to the left of the church). The first, the so-called **Green Cloister**, one of the masterpieces of Paolo Uccello and his assistants, is named for the *terraverde* or green earth pigment used by the artist, which lends the scenes from Genesis their eerie, ghostly quality. Much damaged by time and neglect, they are nevertheless striking for their two Uccellian obsessions – perspective and animals. Best known, and in better condition than the others, is Uccello's surreal *Universal Deluge*, a composition framed by the steep walls of two arks, before and after views, which have the uncanny effect of making the scene appear to come racing out of its own vanishing point, a vanishing point touched by divine wrath in a searing bolt of lightning. In between the claustrophobic walls the flood rises, tossing up a desperate ensemble of humanity, waterlogged bodies, naked men bearing clubs, crowded in a jam of flotsam and jetsam in the dark waters. In the right foreground, amidst all the panic, stands a tall robed man, seemingly a visionary, perhaps even Noah himself, looking heavenward while a flood victim seizes him by the ankles.

The **Spanish Chapel** at the far end of the cloisters takes its name from the Spanish court followers of Eleonora di Toledo who worshipped here; the Inquisition had earlier made the chapel its headquarters in Florence. The chapel is, again, famous for its frescoes, the masterpiece of a little-known 14th-century artist named Andrea di Buonaiuto, whose subject was the Dominican cosmology, beautifully portrayed so that even the 'Hounds of the Lord' (a pun on the Order's name, the *Domini canes*) on the right wall seem more like pets than militant bloodhounds sniffing out unorthodox beliefs. The church behind the scene with the hounds is a fairy-pink confection of what Buonaiuto imagined the Duomo would look like when finished; it may well be Arnolfo di Cambio's original conception. Famous Florentines, including Giotto, Dante, Boccaccio and Petrarch, stand to the right of the dais supporting the pope, emperor and various sour-faced hierophants. Off to the right the artist has portrayed four urbane Vices with dancing girls, while the Dominicans lead stray sheep back to the fold. On the left wall, St Thomas Aquinas dominates the *Contemplative Life*, surrounded by Virtues and Doctors of the Church.

The oldest part of the monastery, the **Chiostrino dei Morti** (1270s), contains some 14th-century frescoes, while the **great cloister** beyond is now off limits, the property of the *Carabinieri*, the new men in black charged with keeping the Italians orthodox. Off the Green Cloister, the **refectory** is a striking hall with cross vaulting and frescoes by Alessandro Allori, now a museum.

Around Santa Maria Novella

Just behind, but a world apart, another large, amorphous square detracts from one of Italy's finest modern buildings – the **Stazione Centrale**, designed by Michelucci in 1935. Adorned by only a glass block canopy at the entrance (and an early model of that great Italian invention, the digital clock), the station is nevertheless remarkable for its clean lines and impeccable practicality.

Leading south from Piazza Santa Maria Novella, **Via delle Belle Donne** was once known for its excellent brothels. Today it is worth a short stroll to see one of the very few crossroads in Italy that is marked by a cross, a Celtic custom that never really caught on here. According to legend, the **Croce del Trebbio** (from a corruption of '*trivium*') marks the spot where a massacre of Patarene heretics took place in the 1240s, after the masses had been excited by a sermon given by the fire-eating Inquisitor St Peter Martyr from the pulpit of Santa Maria Novella.

San Lorenzo and the Medici Chapels

San Lorenzo
www.basilicadisanlorenzo.it; open Mon–Sat 10–5.30; adm

The lively quarter just east of Santa Maria Novella has been associated with the Medici ever since Giovanni di Bicci de' Medici commissioned Brunelleschi to rebuild the ancient church of San Lorenzo in 1420; subsequent members of the dynasty lavished bushels of florins on its decoration and Medici pantheon, and on several projects commissioned from Michelangelo. The mixed result of all their efforts could be held up as an archetype of the Renaissance, described by Walter Pater as 'great rather by what it designed or aspired to do, than by what it actually achieved'. San Lorenzo's façade of corrugated brick was the most *non-finito* of all of Michelangelo's unfinished projects; commissioned by Medici Pope Leo X in 1516, the project never got further than a scale model, which may be seen in the Casa Buonarroti. To complete the church's dingy aspect, the *piazza* in front contains a universally detested 19th-century statue of Cosimo I's dashing father, Giovanni delle Bande Nere, who died at the age of 28 of wounds received fighting against Emperor Charles V.

The **interior**, completed after Brunelleschi's death to his design, is classically calm in good grey *pietra serena*. Of the artistic treasures it contains, most riveting are **Donatello's pulpits**, the sculptor's last works, completed by his pupils after his death in 1466. Cast in bronze, the pulpits were commissioned by Donatello's friend and patron Cosimo il Vecchio. Little in Donatello's previous work prepares the viewer for these scenes of Christ's Passion and Resurrection with their rough and impressionistic details, their unbalanced, emotional and overcrowded compositions, more reminiscent of Rodin than anything Florentine. Off the left transept, the **old sacristy** is a beautiful vaulted chamber with calmer sculptural decoration by Donatello. Just beyond the Bronzino a door leads into the 15th-century **cloister**, and from there a stair leads up to Michelangelo's **Biblioteca Laurenziana**.

Biblioteca Laurenziana
open Mon, Fri and Sat 8–2, Tues, Wed and Thurs 9–5

The Medici Chapels

Capelli Medici
open Mon–Sat 8.15–4.50, Sun 8.15–6.50; closed 2nd and 4th Sun and 1st, 3rd and 5th Mon of month; adm

San Lorenzo is most famous, however, for the Medici Chapels, which lie outside and behind the church. The entrance leads through the crypt, a dark and austere place where many of the Medici are actually buried.

Their main monument, the family obsession, located just up the steps, has long been known as the **Chapel of the Princes** – it's a stupefying, costly octagon of death that, as much as the grand dukes fussed over it, lends their memory an unpleasant aftertaste of bric-a-brac that grew and grew. Perhaps only a genuine Medici could love its trashy opulence; all Grand Duke Cosimo's descendants worked like beavers to finish it according to the plans left by Cosimo's illegitimate son, Giovanni de' Medici. Yet even today it is only partially completed, the *pietre dure* extending just part of the way up the walls. The 19th-century frescoes in the cupola are a poor substitute for the originally planned 'Apotheosis of the Medici' in lapis lazuli, and the two statues in gilded bronze in the niches over the sarcophagi are nothing like the intended figures to be carved in semi-precious stone. The most interesting feature is the inlaid *pietra dura* arms of Tuscan towns and the large Medici arms above, with their familiar six red boluses. (The balls probably derive from the family's origins as pharmacists or *medici*, and opponents called them 'the pills'. Medici supporters, however, made them their battle cry in street fights: 'Balls! Balls!')

A passageway leads to Michelangelo's **New Sacristy**, commissioned by Leo X to occupy an unfinished room originally built to balance Brunelleschi's Old Sacristy. Michelangelo's first idea was to turn it into a new version of his unfinished Pope Julius Tomb – an idea quickly quashed by his Medici patrons, who requested instead four wall tombs. Michelangelo only worked on two of the monuments but managed to finish the New Sacristy itself, creating a silent and gloomy mausoleum, closed in and grey, a chilly cocoon calculated to depress even the most chatty tour groups.

Nor are the famous tombs guaranteed to cheer. Both honour nonentities: *Night and Day* belongs to Lorenzo il Magnifico's son, the Duke of Nemours, and symbolizes the Active Life, while the *Dawn and Dusk* is of Giuliano's nephew, Lorenzo, Duke of Urbino (and dedicatee of *The Prince*), who symbolizes the Contemplative Life (true to life in one respect – Lorenzo was a disappointment to Machiavelli and everyone else, passively obeying the dictates of his uncle Pope Leo X). Idealized statues of the two men, in Roman patrician gear, represent these states of mind, while draped on their sarcophagi are Michelangelo's four allegorical figures of the *Times of Day*, so heavy with weariness and grief that they seem ready to slide off on to the floor. The most finished figure, *Night*, has always impressed the critics; she is almost a personification of despair, the mouthpiece of Michelangelo's most bitter verse:

Sweet to me is sleep, and even more to be like stone
While wrong and shame endure;
Not to see, nor to feel, is my good fortune.
Therefore, do not wake me; speak softly here.

Both statues of the dukes look towards the back wall, where a large double tomb for Lorenzo il Magnifico and his brother Giuliano was originally planned, to be decorated with river gods. The only part of this tomb ever completed is the statue of the *Madonna and Child* now in place, accompanied by the Medici patron saints, the doctors Cosmas and Damian.

In 1975, charcoal drawings were discovered on the walls of the little room off the altar – ask at the cash desk for a permit, as only 12 people can enter at once. They were attributed to Michelangelo, who may have hidden here in 1530, when the Medici had regained Florence and apparently would only forgive the artist for aiding the republican defence if he would finish their tombs. But Michelangelo had had enough of their ducal pretences and went off to Rome, never to return to Florence.

Mercato Centrale and Perugino

San Lorenzo street market
open Tues–Sat, plus Mon in summer

Mercato Centrale
open Mon–Fri 7–2; some stalls also open Sat pm

Convento delle Terziarie Francescane della Beata Angelina da Foligno
open Mon, Tues and Sat 9–12; ring bell; donation requested

What makes the neighbourhood around San Lorenzo so lively is its **street market**, which the Florentines run with an almost Neapolitan flamboyance. Stalls selling clothes and leather extend from the square up Via dell'Ariento (nicknamed 'Shanghai') towards the **Mercato Centrale**, Florence's main food market, a cast-iron and glass confection of the 1870s, brimful of fresh fruit and vegetables, leering boars' heads and mounds of tripe.

Beyond the market, at Via Faenza 42, is the entrance to Perugino's *Cenacolo di Foligno* fresco, housed in the **ex-convent of the Tertiary Franciscans of Foligno**. This 1490s Umbrian version of the *Last Supper* was discovered in the 1850s and has recently been restored.

Palazzo Medici-Riccardi

A block from San Lorenzo and the Piazza del Duomo stands the palace that held Florence's unofficial court, where ambassadors would call, kings would lodge, and important decisions would be made. Built in 1444 by Michelozzo for Cosimo il Vecchio, it was the principal address of the Medici for 100 years, until Cosimo I abandoned it for larger quarters in the Palazzo Vecchio and the Pitti Palace. In 1659 the Riccardi purchased the palace, added to it and did everything to keep it glittering until Napoleon and his debts drove them to bankruptcy in 1809.

Cappella dei Magi
*open Thurs–Tues 9–7; adm; only a few people allowed in at a time; in summer you can book, **t** 055 276 0340*

The palace is now used as the city's prefecture. In its day, though, it was the largest private address in the city, where the family lived with the likes of Donatello's *David* and *Judith and Holofernes*, Uccello's *Battle of San Romano* and other masterpieces now in the Uffizi and Bargello. Frescoes are much harder to move, however, and the Palazzo Medici is worth visiting to see the most charming one in Italy, Benozzo Gozzoli's 1459 *Procession of the Magi*, located in the **Cappella dei Magi** upstairs.

Painting in a delightful, decorative manner more reminiscent of International Gothic than the awakening Renaissance style of his contemporaries, Gozzoli took a religious subject and turned it into a merry, brilliantly coloured pageant of beautifully dressed kings, knights and pages, accompanied by greyhounds and a giraffe, who travel through a springtime landscape of jewel-like trees and castles. This is a largely secular painting, representing less the original Three Kings than the annual pageant of the Compagnia dei Magi, Florence's richest confraternity. The scene is wrapped around three walls of the small chapel – you feel as if you have walked straight into a glowing fairytale world. Most of the faces are those of the Medici and other local celebrities; Gozzoli certainly had no qualms about putting himself among the crowd of figures on the right wall, with his name written on his red cap. In the foreground, note the black man carrying a bow. Black people, as well as Turks, Circassians, Tartars and others, were common enough in Renaissance Florence, originally brought as slaves. By the 1400s, however, contemporary writers mention them as artisans, fencing masters, soldiers and one famous archery instructor, who may be the man pictured here. For an extraordinary contrast pop into the **gallery** (up the second set of stairs) with its 17th-century ceiling by Neapolitan Luca Giordano, showing the last, unspeakable Medici floating around in marshmallow clouds. In a small adjoining room is a lovely *Madonna and Child* by Filippo Lippi, placed here a couple of years ago after restoration.

San Marco

San Marco
***convent** open Mon–Fri 8.15–1.50, Sat and Sun 8.15–6.50; closed 1st, 3rd and 5th Sun of month and 2nd and 4th Mon of month; bring small change for adm; **church** open daily 7–12 and 4–7*

Despite all the others who contributed to this Dominican monastery and church, it has always been best known for the work of its most famous resident. Fra Angelico lived here from 1436 until his death in 1455, spending the time turning Michelozzo's simple **cloister** into a complete exposition of his own deep faith, expressed in bright colours and angelic pastels. Fra Angelico painted the frescoes in the corners of the cloister, and on the first floor there is a small museum of his work, collected from Florentine churches, as well as several early-15th-century portraits by Fra Bartolommeo, capturing some of the most sincere spirituality of the age. The *Last Supper* in the refectory is by Ghirlandaio. Other works by Fra Angelico include the *Life of Christ* series, in which the Saved are well-dressed Italians holding hands. The Bad (mostly princes and prelates) are stripped to receive their interesting tortures.

Right at the top of the stairs to the monks' dormitory, your eyes meet the Angelic Friar's masterpiece, a miraculous *Annunciation* that offers an intriguing comparison with Leonardo's *Annunciation* in the Uffizi. The subject was a favourite with Florentine artists, not only because it was a severe artistic test – expressing a divine revelation with a composition of strict economy – but because the Annunciation, falling near the spring equinox, was New Year's Day for Florence until the Medici adopted the pope's calendar in the 17th century. In each of the monks' cells, Fra Angelico and students painted the *Crucifixion*, all the same but for some slight differences in pose; glancing in the cells down the corridor in turn gives the impression of a cartoon. One of the cells belonged to Savonarola, who was the prior here during his period of dominance in Florence; it has the simple furniture of the period and a portrait of Savonarola by Fra Bartolommeo. In a nearby corridor, you can see an anonymous painting of the monk and two of his followers being led to the stake on Piazza della Signoria. **Michelozzo's library**, located off the main corridor, is as light and airy as the cloisters below; in it is displayed a collection of choir books, one of which was illuminated by Fra Angelico.

Museo di Geologia e Paleontologia
open Sun–Tues and Thurs–Fri 9–1, Sat 9–5; adm

Museo di Mineralogia et Litologia
open Sun–Tues and Thurs–Fri 9–1, Sat 9–5; adm

Museo di Botanica
open by request, t 055 275 7462

Giardino dei Semplici
open Sun–Tues and Thurs–Fri 9–1, Sat 9–5; adm

Near San Marco, at Via G La Pira 4, the University of Florence runs several small museums; nearly all the collections were begun by the indefatigable Medici. The **geology and palaeontology museum** has one of Italy's best collections of fossils, many of which were uncovered in Tuscany. The **mineralogy and lithology museum** houses a collection of strange and beautiful rocks, especially from Elba. The **botanical museum** is of less interest to the casual visitor, though it houses one of the most extensive herbariums in the world; most impressive here are the exquisite wax models of plants made in the early 1800s.

Also on Via La Pira is the entrance to the University's **Giardino dei Semplici**, the botanical garden created for Cosimo I, with medicinal herbs, Tuscan plants, flowers and tropical plants in its greenhouses.

Sant'Apollonia and the Scalzo

Sant'Apollonia
open daily 8.15–1.50; closed 2nd and 4th Mon and 1st, 3rd and 5th Sun of month

Cenacoli, or frescoes of the Last Supper, became almost *de rigueur* in monastic refectories; in several of these the *Last Supper* is all that remains of a convent. Until 1860, the Renaissance **convent of Sant'Apollonia**, situated off Piazza San Marco at Via XXVII Aprile 1, was the abode of cloistered nuns, and the *cenacolo* within their refectory was a secret. When the convent was suppressed, and the painting discovered under the whitewash, the critics believed it to be the work of Paolo Uccello; it is only lately that is has been unanimously attributed to Andrea del Castagno, who painted it in from 1445 to 1450. The other walls have *sinopie* of the *Crucifixion*, *Entombment* and *Resurrection* by Castagno; in the vestibule are good works by Neri di Bicci and Paolo Schiavo.

Chiostro dello Scalzo
open Mon, Thurs and Sat 8.15–1.50; ring bell

Not far away you can enter a radically different artistic world in the **Chiostro dello Scalzo**, again off Piazza San Marco, at Via Cavour 69. Formerly part of the Confraternity of San Giovanni Battista, this cloister is all that has survived, frescoed (1514–24) with scenes of the life of St John the Baptist by Andrea del Sarto and his pupil Franciabigio. Del Sarto, Browning's 'perfect painter', painted these in monochrome *grisaille*, and while the *Baptism of Christ* is beautiful, some of the other panels are the most unintentionally funny things in Florence – the scene of Herod's banquet is reduced to a meagre breakfast where the king and queen look up indignantly at the man bringing in the platter of the Baptist's head as if he were a waiter who has made a mistake with their order.

Galleria dell'Accademia

Galleria dell' Accademia
open Tues–Sun 8.15–6.50; adm

From Piazza San Marco, Via Ricasoli makes a beeline for the Duomo, but on most days the view is obstructed by the crowds milling around No.60; in the summer the queues are as long as those at the Uffizi, everyone anxious to get a look at *David*. Just over 100 years ago Florence decided to take this precocious symbol of republican liberty out of the rain and install it, with much pomp, in a specially built classical *exedra* in this gallery.

Michelangelo completed the *David* for the city in 1504, when he was 29, and it was the work that established the overwhelming reputation he had in his own time. The monstrous block of marble – 4.8m high but unusually shallow – had been quarried 40 years earlier by the cathedral works and spoiled by other hands. The block was offered around to several other artists, including Leonardo da Vinci, before young Michelangelo decided to take up the challenge of carving the largest statue since Roman times. And it is the dimensions of the *David* that remain the biggest surprise in these days of endless reproductions. Certainly as a political symbol of the Republic he is excessive – the irony of a David the size of a Goliath is disconcerting – but as a symbol of the artistic and intellectual aspirations of the Renaissance he is unsurpassed.

And it's hard to deny, after gazing at this enormous nude, that these same Renaissance aspirations by the 1500s began snuggling uncomfortably close to the frontiers of kitsch. Disproportionate size is one symptom; the calculated intention to excite a strong emotional response is another. In the *David*, virtuosity eclipses vision and commits the even deadlier kitsch sin of seeking the sterile empyrean of perfect beauty – most would argue that Michelangelo here achieves it, perhaps capturing his own feelings about the work in the *David*'s chillingly vain, self-satisfied expression. This is also one of the few statues to have actually injured someone: during a political disturbance in the Piazza della Signoria, its arm broke off and fell on a farmer's toe. In 1991 it was *David*'s toe that fell victim when a madman chopped it off. Since then, the rest of his anatomy has been shielded by glass.

In the Galleria next to the *David* you will find Michelangelo's famous *nonfiniti*, the four *Prisoners* or *Slaves*, which were worked on between 1519 and 1536, sculpted for Pope Julius' tomb and left in various stages of completion, although it is endlessly argued whether this is by design or through lack of time. Whatever the case, they illustrate Michelangelo's view of sculpture as a prisoner in stone just as the soul is a prisoner of the body. When he left them, the Medici snapped them up to decorate Buontalenti's Grotta fountain in the Boboli Gardens.

The Galleria was founded by Grand Duke Pietro Leopold in 1784 to provide Academy students with examples of art from every period. The big busy Mannerist paintings around the *David* are by Michelangelo's contemporaries, among them Pontormo's *Venus and Cupid*, with a Michelangelesque Venus among theatre masks. Other rooms contain a good selection of quattrocento painting, including the *Madonna del Mare* by Botticelli, a damaged Baldovinetti, the *Thebaid* by a follower of Uccello, and Perugino's *Deposition*. The painted frontal of the **Adimari chest** shows a delightful wedding scene of the 1450s with the baptistry in the background that has been reproduced in half the books that have ever been written about the Renaissance.

The hall off to the left of the *David* was formerly the women's ward of a hospital, depicted in a greenish painting by Pontormo. Now it is used as a gallery of plaster models by 19th-century members of the Accademia.

The excellent **collection of old musical instruments** once housed in the Palazzo Vecchio has moved to the Accademia. The collection of some 150 exhibits, including several violins and cellos by Cremona greats such as Stradivarius and Guarneri, is on display in a room on the ground floor, well organized and labelled.

Piazza Santissima Annunziata

This lovely square, the only Renaissance attempt at a unified ensemble in Florence, is surrounded on three sides by arcades. In its centre, gazing down the splendid vista of Via dei Servi towards the Duomo, is the equestrian statue of Ferdinand I (1607) by Giambologna and his pupil, Pietro Tacca, made of bronze from Turkish cannons captured during the battle of Lepanto. More fascinating than Ferdinand are the pair of bizarre Baroque fountains, also by Tacca, that share the square. Though of a nominally marine theme, they resemble tureens of bouillabaisse any ogre would be proud to serve, topped by grinning winged monkeys.

Spedale degli Innocenti
open Mon–Sat 8.30–2, Sun 8.30–7; adm

In the 1420s Filippo Brunelleschi struck the first blow for classical calm in this *piazza* when he built the celebrated **Spedale degli Innocenti** and its famous portico – an architectural landmark, but also a monument to Renaissance Italy's long, hard and ultimately unsuccessful struggle towards some kind of social consciousness. Even in the best of times, Florence's poor were treated like dirt; if any enlightened soul had been so bold as to propose even a modern conservative 'trickle-down' theory to the Medici and the banking elite, their first thought would have been how to stop the leaks. Babies, at least, were treated a little better – the Spedale degli Innocenti was the first hospital for foundlings not only in Italy but in the world. At the left end of the loggia you can still see the original window-wheel where babies were anonymously abandoned until 1875. Today it is a nursery school.

The Spedale was Brunelleschi's first completed work and demonstrates his use of geometrical proportions adapted to traditional Tuscan Romanesque architecture. His lovely portico is adorned with the famous blue and white *tondi* of infants in swaddling clothes by Andrea della Robbia, added as an appeal to charity in the 1480s after several children died of malnutrition. Brunelleschi also designed the two beautiful cloisters of the convent; the **Chiostro delle Donne**, which was reserved for the hospital's nurses (located up the ramp on the right at No.13), is especially fine. Upstairs, the **Museo dello Spedale** contains a number of detached frescoes from Ognissanti and other churches, among them an unusual series of red and orange prophets by Alessandro Allori; other works include a *Madonna and Saints* by Piero di Cosimo, a *Madonna and Child* by Luca della Robbia, and the brilliant *Adoration of the Magi* (1488) that was painted by Domenico Ghirlandaio for the hospital's church – a crowded, colourful composition featuring portraits of members of the Arte della Lana, who funded the Spedale.

Santissima Annunziata

To complement Brunelleschi's arches, the old church of Santissima Annunziata was rebuilt and given a broad arcaded portico by Michelozzo facing the street. Behind the portico the architect added the **Chiostrino dei Voti**, a porch that was decorated with a collection of early-16th-century frescoes, including two by Andrea del Sarto. The best of these, faded as it is, is a finely detailed *Nativity* by Alessio Baldovinetti, one of the quattrocento's underappreciated masters. The church itself is the gaudiest in Florence; its freshly gilded elliptical dome, its unusual polygonal tribune around the sanctuary and megatons of *pietra dura* have helped it become the city's high-society parish, where even funerals are major social events.

The huge candlelit chapel in the rear is the **Tempietta**, which is also by Michelozzo, sheltering a miraculous painting of the *Annunciation*. The church's **cloister** was long used by the Institute of Miltary Geography, but in 2005 restorers made an extremely interesting discovery off a secret staircase: Leonardo's Florentine studio, decorated with frescoes of birds, in which he painted at least one version of the *Virgin and Child with St Anne,* and perhaps also the *Mona Lisa*.

Museo Archeologico

Museo Archeologico
www.firenzemusei.it/archeologico; open Mon 2–7, Tues and Thurs 8.30–7, Wed and Fri–Sun 8.30–2; adm

From Piazza SS. Annunziata, Via della Colonna takes you to Florence's archaeology museum, which is housed in the 17th-century Palazzo della Crocetta, originally built for Grand Duchess Maria Maddalena of Austria. Like nearly every other museum in Florence, this impressive collection was begun by the Medici, beginning with Cosimo il Vecchio and accelerating with the insatiable Cosimo I and his heirs. The Medici were especially fond of Etruscan things, while the impressive Egyptian collection was begun by Leopold II during the 1830s.

The **Etruscan collection** on the first floor includes the famous bronze *Chimera*, a remarkable beast with the three heads of a lion, goat and snake. This 5th-century BC work, dug up near Arezzo in 1555 and immediately snatched by Cosimo I, had a great influence on Mannerist artists. There is no Mannerist fancy about its origins, though; like all such composite monsters, it is a religious icon, a calendar beast symbolizing the three seasons of the ancient Mediterranean agricultural year. In the same corridor stand the *Arringatore*, or Orator, a monumental bronze of the Hellenistic period, a civic-minded and civilized-looking gentleman, dedicated to Aulus Metellus, and the statue of *Minerva*. Also to be found in this section are some other Etruscan bronzes, large and small. The cases here are full of wonderful objects – anything from tiny animals to jewellery, carved mirrors and household objects such as plates and even a strainer. All these show just how skilled the Etruscans were in casting bronze.

The beautifully lit **Egyptian collection**, which is also located on the first floor, has been expanded and modernized. It includes some interesting small statuettes, mummies, Canopic vases, and a unique wood and bone chariot, nearly completely preserved, found in a 14th-century BC tomb in Thebes.

On the second floor there is plenty of Greek art; Etruscan noble families were wont to buy up all they could afford. The beautiful Hellenistic horse's head once adorned the Palazzo Medici-Riccardi. The *Idolino*, a bronze of a young athlete, is believed to be a Roman copy of a 5th-century BC Greek original. There is an excellent *Kouros*, a young man in the archaic style from 6th-century BC Sicily. An unusual, recent find, the silver *Baratti Amphora*, was made in the 4th century BC in Antioch and covered with scores of small medallions showing mythological figures. Scholars believe that the images and their arrangement may encode an entire system of belief, the secret teaching of one of the mystic-philosophical cults common in Hellenistic times, and they hope some day to decipher it. There's a vast collection of Greek pottery (including the massive François vase in Room 2), and large Greek, Roman and Renaissance bronzes, recently brought out of storage. There are also several fabulous Greek marble sculptures dating from *c.* 500 BC.

Tombe Etrusche
open Sat 8.30–2

There is virtually nothing displayed on the ground floor now, although temporary exhibitions are held there. In the garden are several reconstructed **Etruscan tombs**. The fabulous collection of precious stones, coins and, most notably, cameos (amassed by the Medici) is now permanently on display in the corridor which runs between the museum and the church of Santissima Annunziata.

South of Piazza Santissima Annunziata

Santa Maria Maddalena dei Pazzi and the Synagogue

Santa Maria Maddalena dei Pazzi
open Mon–Sat 9.30–12 and 5–7; Sun 9.30–11 and 5–7

To the east of the archaeological museum, Via della Colonna becomes one of Florence's typical straight, boring Renaissance streets. It's well worth taking a detour down Borgo Pinti, to No.58, to visit one of the city's least-known but most intriguing churches, **Santa Maria Maddalena dei Pazzi**, which provides a fine example of architectural syncretism. The church itself was founded in the 13th century and rebuilt in the classically Renaissance style by Giuliano da Sangallo, then given a full dose of Baroque when the church was rededicated to the Counter-Reformation saint of the Pazzi family. Inside it's all high theatre, with a gaudy trompe-l'œil ceiling, paintings by Luca Giordano, florid chapels, and a wild marble chancel. From the sacristy a door leads down into a crypt to the chapterhouse, which contains a frescoed *Crucifixion* (1496), one of Perugino's masterpieces. Despite the symmetry and quiet, contemplative grief of the five figures at the foot of the Cross and the stillness of the luminous Tuscan-Umbrian landscape, the fresco has a powerful impact, giving the viewer the uncanny sensation of being able to walk right into the scene. The fresco has never been restored; during the 1966 flood, the water came within 11cm of it, and then stopped.

Sinagoga
open April, May, Sept and Oct Sun–Thurs 10–5 and Fri 10–2; June–Aug Sun–Thurs 10–6 and Fri 10–2; Nov–Mar Sun–Thurs 10–3; adm

Florence's Jewish community, although today a mere 1,200 strong, has long been one of the most important in Italy, invited to Florence by the republic in 1430 but repeatedly exiled and readmitted until Cosimo I founded Florence's **Ghetto** in 1551. When the Ghetto was opened up in 1848 and demolished soon after, a new **synagogue** (1874–82) was built in Via L C Farini: a tall, charming, Mozarabic Pre-Raphaelite hybrid inspired by the Hagia Sophia and the Transito Synagogue of Toledo. Although seriously

Museo Ebraico
t 055 245252/3; same opening hrs as for synagogue

damaged by the Nazis in August 1944, as well as by the Arno in 1966, it has since been lovingly restored. There's a small **Jewish museum** upstairs, with a documentary history of Florentine Jews.

Sant'Ambrogio and the Flea Market

The streets of Sant'Ambrogio are among the most dusty and piquant in the city centre, a neighbourhood where tourists seldom tread. Life revolves around the church in **Sant'Ambrogio** and its neighbouring food market made of cast iron in 1873; the church (rebuilt in the 13th century, with a 19th-century façade) is of interest for its works of art: the second chapel on the right has a lovely fresco of the *Madonna Enthroned with Saints* by Orcagna (or his school), and the **Cappella del Miracolo**, just left of the high altar, contains Mino da Fiesole's celebrated marble tabernacle (1481) and his own tomb. The chapel has a fresco of a procession by Cosimo Rosselli, especially interesting for its depiction of 15th-century celebrities, including Pico della Mirandola and Rosselli himself (in a black hat, in the group on the left). Andrea Verrocchio is buried in the fourth chapel on the left; on the wall by the second altar is a *Nativity* by Baldovinetti. The fresco of an atypical *St Sebastian* in the first chapel on the left is by Agnolo Gaddi.

From Sant'Ambrogio, take Via Pietrapiana to the bustling **Piazza dei Ciompi**, named after the wool-workers' revolt of 1378. In the morning, Florence's fleamarket or **mercatino** takes place here – it's the best place in town to buy that 1940s radio or outdated ballgown you've always wanted. One side of the square is graced with the **Loggia del Pesce**, which was built by Vasari in 1568 for the fishmongers of the Mercato Vecchio; when that was demolished, the loggia was salvaged and re-erected here.

Casa Buonarroti

Casa Buonarroti
t 055 241752, www.casabuonarroti.it; open Wed–Mon 9.30–2; adm

Michelangelo never lived in this house at Via Ghibellina 70, although he purchased it in 1508. That wasn't the point, especially to an artist who had no thought for his own personal comfort, or anyone else's – he never washed and never took off his boots, even in bed. Real estate was an obsession of his, as he struggled to restore the status of the semi-noble but impoverished Buonarroti family. His nephew Leonardo inherited the house and several works of art in 1564; later he bought the two houses next door to create a memorial to his uncle, hiring artists to paint scenes from Michelangelo's life. In the mid 19th century, the house was opened to the public as a Michelangelo museum.

The ground floor is dedicated to mostly imaginary portraits of the artist, and works of art collected by his nephew's descendants, including an eclectic Etruscan and Roman collection. The main attractions, however, are upstairs, beginning with Michelangelo's earliest known work, the beautiful bas-relief *The Madonna of the Steps* (1490–91), the precocious work of a 16-year-old influenced by Donatello and studying in the household of Lorenzo il Magnifico; the relief of a battle scene, inspired by classical models, dates from the same period. Small models and drawings of potential projects line the walls; there's the wooden model for the façade of San Lorenzo, with designs for some of the statuary Michelangelo intended to fill in its austere blank spaces – as was often the case, his ideas were far too grand for his patron's purse and patience.

The next four rooms were painted in the 17th century to illustrate Michelangelo's life, virtues and apotheosis, depicting a polite, deferential and pleasant Michelangelo hobnobbing with popes. Those who know the artist best from *The Agony and the Ecstasy* may think they painted the wrong man by mistake. One of the best sections is a frieze of famous Florentines in the library. Other exhibits include a painted wooden *Crucifix* discovered in Santo Spirito in 1963 and believed by most scholars to be a documented one by Michelangelo, long thought to be lost; the *contrapposto* position of the slender body, and the fact that only Michelangelo would carve a nude Christ, weigh in favour of the attribution.

Santa Croce

Santa Croce
open Mon–Sat 9.30–5.30, Sun 1–5.30; adm (includes museum)

No place in Florence so feeds the urge to dispute as the church of Santa Croce, Tuscany's 'Westminster Abbey', the largest Franciscan basilica in Italy and a must-see for every tour group. It was here that Stendhal gushed, 'I had attained to that supreme degree of sensibility where the divine intimations of art merge with the impassioned sensuality of emotion. As I emerged from the port of Santa Croce, I was seized with a fierce palpitation of the heart; I walked in constant fear of falling to the ground.' But don't be put off; most people manage to emerge without tripping over.

The contradictions begin in the **Piazza Santa Croce**, which has its interesting points – the row of medieval houses with projecting upper storeys, supported by stone brackets; the faded bloom of dancing nymphs on the **Palazzo dell'Antella**; the curious 14th-century **Palazzo Serristori-Cocchi**, opposite the church; a grim 19th-century **statue of Dante** (if Dante really looked like that, it's no wonder Beatrice married someone else). Because this *piazza* is the lowest-lying in the city, it suffered the worst in the 1966 flood, when 6m of oily water poured in; note the plaque marking the waterline on the corner of Via Verdi.

Dominant over all is Santa Croce's neogothic façade, which was built in 1857–63 and financed by Sir Francis Sloane, whose Sloane Square in London has more admirers than this black and white design, derived from Orcagna's Tabernacle in Orsanmichele.

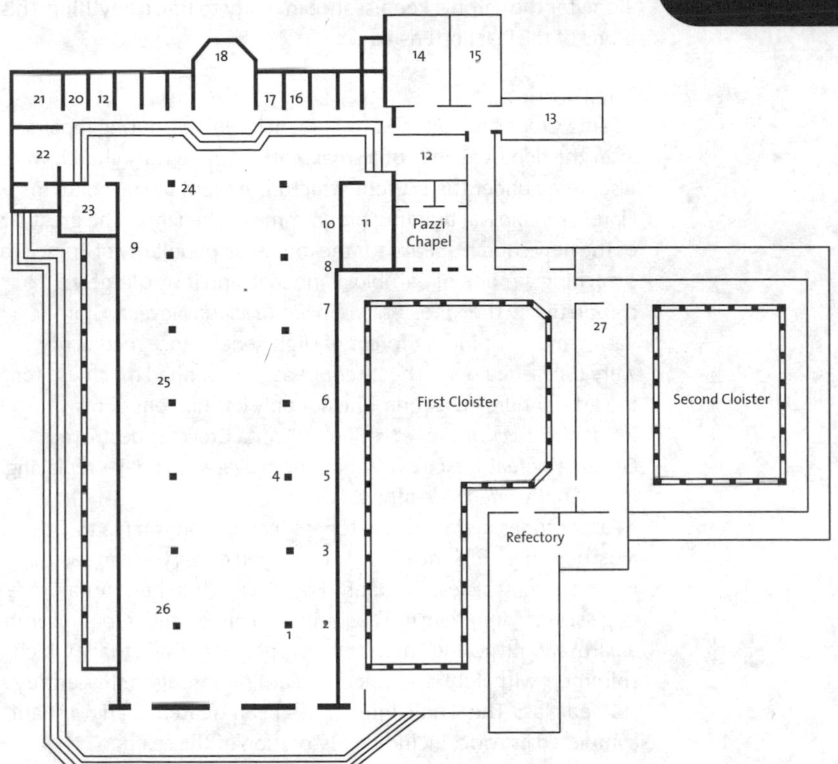

1 *Madonna del Latte*
2 Tomb of Michaelangelo
3 Monument to Dante
4 Benedetto da Maiano's Pulpit
5 Vittorio Alfieri's Tomb
6 Tomb of Machiavelli
7 Donatello's *Annunciation*
8 Tomb of Leonardo Bruni
9 Tomb of Carlo Malaspini
10 Tomb of Rossini
11 Castellani Chapel
12 Baroncelli Chapel
13 Medici Chapel
14 Sacristy
15 Rinuccini Chapel
16 Peruzzi Chapel
17 Bardi Chapel
18 Sanctuary
19 Bardi di Libertà Chapel
20 Bardi di Vernio Chapel
21 Niccolini Chapel
22 Bardi Chapel
23 Salviati Chapel
24 Monument to Alberti
25 Tomb of Lorenzo Ghiberti
26 Galileo's Tomb
27 Museo dell'Opera di Santa Croce

Yet of all the modern façades that were built on Italy's churches to atone for the chronic Renaissance inability to finish anything, this is one of the least offensive.

The Interior

Santa Croce was founded by St Francis himself; during repairs after the flood, vestiges of a small, early-13th-century church were discovered under the present structure. It went by the board in Florence's colossal building programme of the 1290s. The great size of the new church speaks for the immense popularity of Franciscan preaching. Arnolfo di Cambio planned it, and it was largely completed by the 1450s but, as in Santa Maria Novella, Giorgio Vasari and the blinding forces of High Renaissance mediocrity were unleashed upon the interior. Vasari never had much use for the art of Andrea Orcagna – he not only left him out of his influential *Lives of the Artists* but in Santa Croce he destroyed Orcagna's great fresco cycle that once covered the nave, replacing it with uninspired side altars.

For centuries it was the custom to install monuments to illustrious men in Santa Croce and, as you enter, you can see them lining the long aisles. Like many Franciscan churches, Santa Croce's large size, its architectural austerity and open timber roof resemble a barn, but at the end there's a lovely polygonal sanctuary, which shimmers with light and colour streaming through 14th-century stained glass. The whole interior has been treated to an overhaul, completed in 2000, including restoration of the ceiling.

Perversely, the greater the person buried in Santa Croce, the uglier their memorial. A member of the Pazzi conspiracy, Francesco Nori, is buried by the first pillar in the right aisle, and graced by one of the loveliest works of art, the *Madonna del Latte* (1478), a bas-relief by Antonio Rossellino, while the **tomb of Michelangelo** (1570, the first in the right aisle) by Vasari is one of the least attractive. Michelangelo died in Rome in 1564, refusing for 35 years to return to Florence while alive but agreeing to give the city his corpse. Dante has fared even worse, with an 1829 neoclassical monument that's as disappointing as the fact (to the Florentines, anyway) that Dante is buried in Ravenna, where he died in exile in 1321.

Facing the nave, Benedetto da Maiano's marble **pulpit** (1476) is one of the most beautiful the Renaissance ever produced. Behind it, the **Vittorio Alfierl Monument** (1809) was sculpted by neoclassical master Antonio Canova and paid for by his lover, the Countess of Albany. Next is the nondescript 18th-century **monument of Niccolò Machiavelli**, then Donatello's *Annunciation* (1430s), a tabernacle in gilded limestone, the angel wearing a remarkably sweet expression as he gently breaks the news to a grave, thoughtful Madonna. Bernardo Rossellino's **tomb of Leonardo Bruni** (1447), another masterpiece of the Renaissance, is perhaps the one monument that best fits the man it honours. Bruni was a Greek scholar, a humanist, and the author of the first major historical work of the period, *The History of Florence*, a copy of which his effigy holds. The tomb, with its Brunelleschian setting, proved a great inspiration to other artists, most obviously Desiderio da Settignano and his equally beautiful **tomb of Carlo Marsuppini** (1453) directly across the nave, and the less inspired, more imitative **monument to Rossini** crowded in to the left. The last tomb in the aisle belongs to poet and patriot Ugo Foscolo.

Santa Croce is rich in trecento frescoes, providing a unique opportunity to compare the work of Giotto with his followers. The south transept's **Castellani Chapel** has some of the later, more decorative compositions by Agnolo Gaddi (*Scenes from the Lives of Saints*, 1380s). The beautiful **Baroncelli Chapel** was painted with scenes from the *Life of the Virgin* by Agnolo's father Taddeo, Giotto's assistant in the 1330s and includes a bright, gilded altarpiece, the *Coronation of the Virgin* by Giotto and his workshop. *The Annunciation to the Shepherds* by Taddeo, left of the window, is thought to be the first nocturnal scene in the history of Western art.

Medici Chapel
open for Mass at 6pm

The next portal gives on to a corridor and the **Medici Chapel**, both designed by Michelozzo, containing one of Andrea della Robbia's finest altarpieces and a 19th-century fake Donatello, a relief of the *Madonna and Child* that fooled the experts for decades. From the corridor a door leads to the **sacristy**, its walls frescoed by Taddeo Gaddi (*The Crucifixion*), Spinello Aretino and Niccolò di Pietro Gerini. Behind the 14th-century grille, the **Rinuccini Chapel** was frescoed by one of Giotto's most talented followers, the Lombard Giovanni da Milano, in the 1360s.

Giotto's Chapels

The frescoes in the two chapels right of the sanctuary, the **Peruzzi Chapel** and **Bardi Chapel**, were painted by the legendary Giotto in the 1330s, towards the end of his life when he returned from Padua and his work in the Arena chapel. The frescoes have not fared well during the subsequent 660 years. Firstly Giotto painted large parts of the walls *a secco* (on dry plaster) instead of *affresco* (on wet plaster), presenting the same kind of preservation problems that bedevil Leonardo's *Last Supper*; secondly, the 18th century thought so little of the frescoes that they were whitewashed over as eyesores. Rediscovered some 150 years later and finally restored in 1959, the frescoes now, even though fragmentary, may be seen more or less as Giotto painted them. The Peruzzi Chapel contains scenes from the *Lives of St John the Evangelist and the Baptist*. In the Bardi Chapel is the *Life of St Francis*, which makes an interesting comparison with the frescoes in Assisi. The contrast

The Legend of the True Cross

This popular medieval story begins with Noah's son, Seth, as an old man, asking for the essence of mercy. The Angel Gabriel replies by giving Seth a branch, saying that 5,000 years must pass before mankind may know true redemption. Seth plants the branch over Adam's grave on Mount Sinai, and it grows into a magnificent tree. King Solomon orders the tree cut, but as it is too large to move the trunk stays where it is and is used as the main beam of a bridge. The Queen of Sheba is about to cross the bridge when she has a vision that the saviour of the world will be suspended from its wood, and that his death will mark the end of the Kingdom of the Jews. She refuses to cross the bridge and writes of her dream to Solomon, who has the beam buried deep underground. Nevertheless, it is dug up and used to make the cross of Christ.

The cross next appears in the dream of Emperor Constantine before the battle of Milvan Bridge, when he hears a voice saying that under this sign he will conquer. When it proves true, he sends his mother Helen to find the cross in Jerusalem. There she meets Judas Cyriacus, a pious Jew who knows where Golgotha is but won't tell until Helen has him thrown in a well and nearly starved to death. When at last he agrees to dig, a sweet scent fills the air, and Judas Cyriacus is immediately converted. To discover which of the three crosses they find is Christ's, each is held over the coffin of a youth; the True Cross brings him back to life. After all this trouble in finding it, Helen leaves the cross in Jerusalem, where it is stolen by the Persians. Their King Chosroes thinks its power will bring him a great victory, but instead he loses the battle, and Persia, to Emperor Heraclius, who decides to return the holy relic to Jerusalem. But the gate is blocked by the Angel Gabriel, who reminds the proud Heraclius that Jesus entered the city humbly, on the back of an ass. And so, in a similar manner, the emperor returns the cross to Jerusalem.

between Giotto's frescoes and the chapel's 13th-century altarpiece, also showing the *Life of St Francis*, is a fair yardstick for measuring the breadth of the Giottesque revolution. Agnolo Gaddi designed the stained glass around the sanctuary, as well as the fascinating series of frescoes on the *Legend of the True Cross*.

Further left are two more chapels frescoed by followers of Giotto: the fourth, the **Bardi di Libertà Chapel**, by Bernardo Daddi, and the last, the **Bardi di Vernio Chapel**, by Maso di Banco, one of the most innovative and mysterious artists of the trecento. They illustrate the little-known *Life of St Sylvester* – his baptism of Emperor Constantine, the resurrection of the bull, the closing of the dragon's mouth and resurrection of two sorcerers; on the other wall of the chapel are a *Dream of Constantine* and *Vision of SS. Peter and Paul*. In the corner of the transept, the richly marbled **Niccolini Chapel** offers a Mannerist-Baroque change of pace, built by Antonio Dossi in 1584 and decorated with paintings by Allori. Next, the second **Bardi Chapel** houses the famous crucifix by Donatello that Brunelleschi disdainfully called 'a peasant on the Cross'. The last funeral monuments, near the door, are of Lorenzo Ghiberti and Galileo, the latter an 18th-century work. For running foul of the Inquisition, Galileo was not permitted a Christian burial until 1737.

Pazzi Chapel
open Mon–Sat 9.30–5.30, Sun 1–5.30; entrance through Santa Croce; adm

Pazzi Chapel

This chapel is well worth a visit. Brunelleschi, who could excel on the monumental scale of the cathedral dome, saved some of his best work for small places. To make sense of the Pazzi Chapel, you need to have some knowledge of the architect and the austere religious tendencies of the Florentines; it is a Protestant reformation in architecture unlike anything that preceded it. The 'vocabulary' is essential Brunelleschi, the geometric forms emphasized by the simplicity of the decoration: *pietra serena* pilasters and rosettes on white walls, arches, 12 terracotta *tondi* of the *Apostles* by Luca della Robbia, coloured rondels of the *Evangelists* in the pendentives by Donatello, and a small, stained-glass window by Baldovinetti. Even so, that is enough. The contemplative repetition of elements makes for an aesthetic that posed a direct challenge to the International Gothic of the time.

Leaving the Pazzi Chapel (make sure you check out Luca della Robbia's terracotta decorations on the portico), you'll see a doorway on the left of the cloister that leads to Brunelleschi's **Second Cloister**, designed with the same subtlety and forming one of the quietest spots in Florence.

Museo dell'Opera di Santa Croce
open Mon–Sat 9.30–5.30, Sun 1–5.30; adm

The old monastic buildings off the first cloister now house the **Museo dell'Opera di Santa Croce**, where you can see Cimabue's celebrated *Crucifix*, devastated by the flood and partly restored after one of Florence's perennial restoration controversies. The refectory wall has another fine fresco by Taddeo Gaddi, of the *Tree of the Cross* and the *Last Supper*; fragments of Orcagna's frescoes salvaged from Vasari's obliteration offer powerful, nightmarish vignettes of *The Triumph of Death* and *Hell*. Donatello's huge, gilded bronze statue *St Louis of Toulouse* (1423) – a flawed work representing a flawed character, according to Donatello – was made for the façade of Orsanmichele. The museum also contains works by Andrea della Robbia, and a painting of Mayor Bargellini with a melancholy Santa Croce submerged in the 1966 flood for a backdrop; under the colonnade is a statue of Florence Nightingale, born in and named after the city in 1820.

Around Santa Croce: the Horne Museum

The east end of Florence, made up of a rambling district packed with artisans and small manufacturers, traditionally served as the artists' quarter in Renaissance times. It is still one of the livelier neighbourhoods, with a few lingering artists lodged in the upper storeys, hoping to breathe inspiration from the very stones where Michelangelo walked. It is a good place to observe the workaday Florence behind the glossy façade.

Museo Horne
www.museohorne.it; open Mon–Sat 9–1; adm

From Santa Croce, the pretty Borgo Santa Croce takes you towards the Arno and the delightful **Horne Museum**, which is housed in a Renaissance palace, at Via de' Benci 6. Herbert Percy Horne (1844–1916) was an English art historian, the biographer of Botticelli and a Florentinophile, who bequeathed his collection to the nation when he died.

North Bank Peripheral Attractions

The Cascine

The newer sections of the city are, by and large, irredeemably dull. Much of Florence's traffic problem is channelled through its ring of avenues, or *viali*, laid out in the 1860s by Giuseppe Poggi to replace the demolished walls. On and along them are scattered points of interest, including some of the old city gates; the distances involved and danger of carbon monoxide poisoning on the *viali* make the idea of walking insane.

Bus 17C from the station or Duomo will take you through the congestion to the **Cascine**, the long (3.5km), narrow public park lining this bank of the Arno, originally used as the Medici's dairy farm or *cascina*, and later as a grand ducal hunting park and theatre for public spectacles. A windy autumn day here in 1819 inspired Shelley to compose his 'Ode to the West Wind'. Three years later Shelley's drowned body was burnt on a pyre in Viareggio, by his friend Trelawny; curiously, a similar incineration took place in the Cascine in 1870 when the Maharaja of Kohlapur died in Florence. According to ritual his body had to be burned near the confluence of two rivers, in this case, the Arno and Mugnone at the far end of the park, on a spot now marked by the Maharaja's equestrian statue. Florentines come to the Cascine by day to play; it contains a riding school, race tracks, a small amusement park and zoo for children, tennis courts, and a pool. At night they come to ogle the transvestites strutting their stuff on the *viale*.

Beyond the train station, cars and buses hurtle around and around the **Fortezza da Basso**, an enormous bulk built by Antonio da Sangallo on orders from Alessandro de' Medici in 1534. It immediately became the most hated symbol of Medici tyranny. Ironically, the duke who built the Fortezza da Basso was one of very few to meet his end within its ramparts – stabbed by his relative and bosom companion 'Lorenzaccio' de' Medici. As a fortress, the place never saw any action as thrilling or vicious as the Pitti fashion shows that take place behind the walls in its 1978 aluminium exhibition hall.

Just east of the Fortezza, at the corner of Via Leone X and Viale Milton, there's an unexpected sight rising above the sleepy residential neighbourhood – the five graceful onion domes of the **Russian church**, made even more exotic by the palm tree tickling its side. In the 19th century Florence was a popular winter retreat for Russians who could afford it, among them Dostoevsky and Maxim Gorky. Completed by Russian architects in 1904, it is a pretty jewel box of brick and majolica decoration, open on the third Sunday of the month, when the priest comes from Nice to hold a morning service in Russian.

Stibbert Museum

Museo Stibbert
www.museostibbert.it; open Mon–Wed 10–2, Fri–Sun 10–6; adm

From Piazza della Libertà, walk 1km north along dull Via Vittorio Emanuele to reach Via Stibbert and the Stibbert Museum (alternatively, take bus 31 or 32 from the station). Those who make the journey to see the lifetime's accumulations of Frederick Stibbert (1838–1906), who fought with Garibaldi and hobnobbed with Queen Victoria, can savour not only Florence's most bizarre museum but also one of the city's most pleasant small parks, which was laid out by Stibbert, with a mouldering Egyptian temple sinking in a pond; just try to obey the sign on the door: 'Comply with the Forbidden Admittances!'

Stibbert's Italian mother left him a 14th-century house, which he joined to another house to create a Victorian's sumptuous version of what a medieval Florentine house should have looked like – 64 rooms to contain a pack-rat's treasure hoard of all things brilliant and useless, from an attributed Botticelli to snuff boxes and what a local guide intriguingly describes as 'brass and silver basins, used daily by Stibbert'.

Stibbert's serious passion, however, was armour, and he amassed a magnificent collection from all times and places. The best pieces are not arranged in dusty cases, but with a touch of Hollywood, on grim knightly mannequins ranked ready for battle.

The Oltrarno

Over the Ponte Vecchio, a different Florence reveals itself: greener, quieter, and less burdened with traffic. The Oltrarno is not a large district: a chain of hills squeezes it against the river, and their summits afford some of the best views over the city.

Across the Arno, the Medici's catwalk becomes part of the upper façade of **Santa Felicità**, one of Florence's most ancient churches, believed to have been founded by the Syrian Greek traders who introduced Christianity to the city and established the first Christian cemetery in the small square in front of the church.

Rebuilt in the 18th century, it has one compelling reason to enter – here, in the first chapel on the right, is the *ne plus ultra* of Mannerism: Pontormo's weirdly luminous *Deposition* (1528), painted in jarring pinks, oranges and blues that cut through the darkness of the little chapel. The composition itself is highly unconventional, with an effect that derives entirely from the use of figures in unusual, exaggerated poses; there is no sign of a cross, the only background is a single cloud. Sharing the chapel is Pontormo's *Annunciation* fresco, a less idiosyncratic work, as well as four *tondi* of the Evangelists in the cupola, partly the work of Pontormo's pupil and adopted son, Bronzino.

Pitti Palace

Palazzo Pitti
www.palazzopitti.it

As the Medici consolidated their power in Florence, they made a point of buying up the most important properties of their former rivals, especially their proud family palaces. The most spectacular example of this was Cosimo I's acquisition of the Pitti Palace, built in 1457 by a powerful banker named Luca Pitti who seems to have had vague ambitions of toppling the Medici and becoming the big boss himself. The palace, with its extensive grounds, now the Boboli Gardens, was much more pleasant than the medieval Palazzo Vecchio, and in the 1540s Cosimo I and his wife Eleanor of Toledo moved in for good.

The palace remained the residence of the Medici, and later the House of Lorraine, until 1868. The original building, said to have been designed by Brunelleschi, was only as wide as the seven central windows of the façade. Succeeding generations found it too small for their burgeoning hoards of bric-a-brac, and added several stages of symmetrical additions, resulting in a long, bulky profile, resembling a rusticated Stalinist ministry, but a landscaped one, ever since the 1996 European Summit.

There are eight separate **museums in the Pitti**; the ticket office for them all is in the far right corner of the forecourt. They are a tribute to Medici acquisitiveness in the centuries of decadence, from which, in the words of Mary McCarthy, 'flowed a torrent of bad taste that has not yet dried up... if there had been Toby jugs and Swiss weather clocks available, the Grand Dukes would certainly have collected them'. For the visitor who wants to see everything, the Pitti is pitiless; it is impossible to see all in one day.

Galleria Palatina

Galleria Palatina
open Tues–Sun 8.15–6.50; adm, combined ticket with Galleria d'Arte Moderna

The Pitti museum most people visit is the Galleria Palatina, with the grand dukes' famous collection of 16th–18th-century paintings, stacked on the walls in huge gilt frames under the berserk opulence of frescoed ceilings celebrating planets, mythology and, of course, the ubiquitous Medici. The gallery is on the first floor of the right half of the palace; the ticket office is on the ground floor, off Ammannati's exaggerated rustic courtyard, a Mannerist masterpiece.

After the entrance to the Galleria is the neoclassical **Sala Castagnoli**, with the *Tavola delle Muse* in its centre, itself an excellent introduction to the Florentine 'decorative arts'; the table, a paragon of the intricate art of *pietra dura*, was made In the 1870s. The Galleria's best paintings are in the five former reception rooms off to the left, with colourful ceilings painted in the 1640s by Pietro da Cortona, one of the most interesting Italian Baroque artists.

However, the set route takes you through the other part of the palace beforehand starting with the adjacent **Sala di Prometeo** with Filippo Lippi's lovely *Tondo of the Madonna and Child* and

Baldassare Peruzzi's unusual *Dance of Apollo*. Next door you can peek into the **Sala di Bagni**, the Empire bathroom of Elisa Baciocchi, Napoleon's sister, who ruled the *Département de l'Arno* between 1809 and 1814, and seemingly spent much of those years redecorating the Pitti. Caravaggio's *Sleeping Cupid* is a couple of rooms up, in the **Sala dell'Educazione di Giove**. The next room to this is the pretty **Sala della Stufa**, frescoed with the *Four Ages of the World* by Pietro da Cortona.

The first of the reception rooms, the **Sala dell'Iliade** (which was frescoed in the 19th century), has some fine portraits by the Medici court painter and Rubens' friend, Justus Sustermans. Two *Assumptions* by Andrea del Sarto, *Philip II* by Titian and a Velàzquez equestrian portrait of Philip IV share the room with one of the most unusual residents of the gallery, *Queen Elizabeth*, who seems uncomfortable in such company.

The **Sala di Giove**, which was used as the Medici throne room, contains one of Raphael's best-known portraits, the lovely and serene *Donna Velata* (1516). The small painting *The Three Ages of Man* is usually attributed to Giorgione. Salviati, Perugino, Fra Bartolommeo and Andrea del Sarto are also represented. The **Sala di Marte** has two works by Rubens, *The Four Philosophers* and *The Consequences of War*, as well as some excellent portraits by Tintoretto and Van Dyck (*Cardinal Bentivoglio*). The newly restored *Annunciation of San Godenzo*, by Andrea del Sarto, is now back in place after a long absence, and there is also Titian's rather dashing *Cardinal Ippolito de' Medici* in Hungarian costume. Ippolito, despite being destined for the Church, was one of the more high-spirited Medici.

In the **Sala di Apollo** there's more Titian – his *Portrait of a Grey-eyed Gentleman*, evoking the perfect 16th-century English gentleman, and his more sensuous than penitent *Mary Magdalene* – as well as works by Andrea del Sarto and Van Dyck. The last reception room is the **Sala di Venere**, with several works by Titian, including his early *Concert*, believed to have been partly painted by Giorgione and a powerful *Portrait of Pietro Aretino*, Titian's close and caustic friend, who complained to the artist that it was all too accurate and gave it to Cosimo I. There are two beautiful landscapes by Rubens, painted at the end of his life, and an uncanny self-portrait, *La Menzogna* ('The Falsehood') by Neapolitan Salvator Rosa. The centrepiece statue, the *Venus Italica*, was commissioned by Napoleon from neoclassical master Antonio Canova in 1812 to replace the *Venus de' Medici*, which he 'centralized' off to Paris – a rare case of the itchy-fingered Corsican trying to pay for something.

The **Sala di Saturno**, with its restored ceiling, has several paintings from Raphael's Florence days. These include the *Maddalena and Agnolo Doni* (1506) and the *Madonna 'del Granduca'*, influenced by the paintings of Leonardo. Some 10 years later, Raphael had found his own style, which is beautifully evident in his famous *Madonna della Seggiola* ('of the chair') – perhaps the most popular work that the artist ever painted, and one that is far more complex and subtle than it first appears. The rounded, intertwining figures of the Madonna and Child are seen as if through a slightly convex mirror, bulging out – this is one of the first examples of conscious illusionism in the Renaissance.

Some of the more interesting paintings to ferret out in the remainder of the gallery include Filippino Lippi's *Death of Lucrezia* and Raphael's *Madonna dell'Impannata*, both in the **Sala di Ulisse**.

The right half of the Pitti also contains the **State apartments** (included as part of the visit to the Galleria Palatina). These were last redone in the 19th century by the dukes of Lorraine, with touches by the kings of Savoy.

Galleria d'Arte Moderna

Galleria d'Arte Moderna
open Mon–Sat 8.30–6.50, Sun 8.30–1.50; closed 2nd and 4th Sun and 1st, 3rd and 5th Mon of month; adm exp, combined ticket with Galleria Palatina; tickets from main ticket office on ground floor

The second floor above the Galleria Palatina is where you will find Florence's modern – read late-18th–20th-century – art museum. Though the monumental stair may leave you breathless (the Medici negotiated it with sedan chairs and strong-shouldered servants), consider a visit for some sunny painting of the Italy of your great-grandparents. The Galleria was reopened after a major reorganization in 1999 and now consists of more 30 rooms. The most recent paintings on display are those in the last rooms, which cover the years 1900–23. There are plans eventually to open 13 more rooms covering 1923–45.

The 'Splatterers' or *Macchiaioli* (Tuscan Impressionists) illuminate Room 16 and the rest of the museum, forming an excellent introduction to the works by Silvestro Lega, Giovanni Fattori, Nicolo Cannicci, Francesco Gioli, Federigo Zandomeneghi and Telemaco Signorini, with an interval of vast Risorgimento battle scenes. What comes as a shock, especially if you've been touring Florence for a while now, is that the marriage between painting and sculpture that characterizes most of Italian art history seems to have resulted in a nasty divorce in the late 1800s: while the canvases radiate light, statuary becomes disturbingly kitsch, obsessed with death and beauty.

Museo degli Argenti

Museo degli Argenti
open April, May, Sept and Oct daily 8.15–6.30; June–Aug daily 8.15–7.30; Nov–Feb daily 8.15–4.30; Mar daily 8.15–5.30; exc 1st and last Mon of month; adm (combined ticket with Boboli Gardens, porcelain museum and museum of costumes)

The ground floor on the left side of the Pitti was used as the Medici summer apartments and now contains the family's remarkable collection of jewellery, vases, trinkets and pricey curiosities. The Grand Duke's guests would be received in four of the most delightfully frescoed rooms to be found anywhere in Florence, beginning with the **Sala di Giovanni di San Giovanni**, named after the artist who painted it in the 1630s. The theme is the usual Medicean self-glorification – but nowhere does such dubious material achieve such flamboyant treatment. Here the Muses, chased from Paradise, find refuge with Lorenzo il Magnifico; Lorenzo smiles as he studies a bust of Pan by Michelangelo. His real passion, a collection of antique vases carved of semi-precious stones or crystal, is displayed in a room off to the left; the vases were dispersed with the rise of Savonarola, but Lorenzo's nephew Cardinal Giulio had no trouble in locating them, as Lorenzo had his initials LAUR.MED. incised into each. The three **reception rooms** were painted in shadowy blue **trompe l'œil** by two masterful Bolognese illusionists, Agostino Michele and Angelo Colonna.

The grand dukes' treasure hoard is up on the mezzanine. These golden toys are only a fraction of what the Medici had accumulated; despite the terms of Anna Maria's will, leaving everything to Florence, the Lorraines sold off the most valuable pieces and jewels to finance Austria's wars. Among the leftovers here, however, is a veritable apoplexy of fantastical bric-a-brac.

More Pitti Museums

Galleria del Costume/Museo delle Porcellane/ Giardino di Boboli
open April, May, Sept and Oct daily 8.15–6.30; June–Aug daily 8.15–7.30; Nov–Feb daily 8.15–4.30; Mar daily 8.15–5.30; exc 1st and last Mon of month; adm (combined ticket with Museo degli Argenti)

The **museum of costumes** is housed on the second floor of the Palace, near to the Galleria d'Arte Moderna. The highlight, perhaps, is the reconstructed dress that Eleanor of Toledo was buried in – the same one that she wears in Bronzino's famous portrait. The **porcelain museum** is housed in the casino of Cosimo III, which is located out in the Giardino del Cavaliere in the Boboli Gardens (follow the signs). It contains 18th- and 19th-century examples of chinaware from Sèvres, Meissen and Vienna.

Stretching back invitingly from the Pitti, the shady green of the **Boboli Gardens**, which is Florence's largest (and only) central public garden, provides an irresistible oasis in the middle of a stone-hard city. Originally laid out by Buontalenti, the Boboli reigns as queen of all formal Tuscan gardens, the most elaborate and theatrical – a Mannerist-Baroque co-production of Nature and Artifice laid out over a steep hill, full of shady nooks and pretty walks, and beautifully kept. The park is populated by a platoon of statuary; many of them are Roman works, others are absurd Mannerist pieces. There are three entrances and exits to the gardens: through the main courtyard of the Pitti Palace, from Via Romana and in Porta Romana. The main route, from the Pitti Palace, starts at the **amphitheatre**, which ascends in regular tiers from the palace, and was designed like a small Roman circus to hold Medici court spectacles. It has a genuine obelisk, of Rameses II from Heliopolis, which was snatched by the ancient Romans and shipped here by the Medici branch in Rome. The granite basin, which is large enough to submerge an elephant, came from the Roman baths of Caracalla. Straight up the terrace is the **Neptune fountain**; a signposted path leads from there to the pretty **Kaffeehaus**, a boat-like pavilion with a prow and deck offering a fine view of Florence; you can enjoy drinks here in the summer months. From here the path continues up to the **Belvedere Fort** (*see* p.185). Other signs from the Neptune fountain point the way up to the secluded **Giardino del Cavaliere**, located on a bastion on Michelangelo's fortifications. Cosimo III built the **casino** here in order to escape the heat in the Pitti Palace; the view over the ancient villas, vineyards and olives is pure Tuscan enchantment. This is where the porcelain museum (*see* p.163) resides.

Grotta di Buontalenti
open April, May, Sept and Oct daily 8.15–6.30; June–Aug daily 8.15–7.30; Nov–Feb daily 8.15–4.30; Mar daily 8.15–5.30; exc 1st and last Mon of month; adm; combined ticket with Galleria Palatina

At the bottom righthand corner of the garden you will find the remarkable **Grotta di Buontalenti**, one of the architect's most imaginative works, anticipating Gaudí with his dripping, stalactite-like stone, from which fantastic limestone animals struggle to emerge. Casts of Michelangelo's *non-finiti Slaves* in the corners replace the originals put there by the Medici; back in the shadowy depths stands a luscious statue of Venus coming from her bath by Giambologna. The Grotta di Buontalenti has been restored but the fountains are not working yet due to technical problems.

Casa Guidi

Casa Guidi
open April–Nov Mon, Wed and Fri 3–6; donations expected

In the old days the neighbourhood around the Pitti was a fashionable address, but in the 19th century rents for a furnished palace were incredibly low. Shortly after their secret marriage, the Brownings settled in one of these, the Casa Guidi at Piazza San Felice 8; during their 13 years here they wrote their most famous poetry. The house is now owned by the Browning Institute. Dostoevsky wrote *The Idiot* while living nearby, at No.21 Piazza Pitti.

Stuffed Animals and Wax Cadavers

Museo La Specola
open Thurs–Tues 9–1, Sat 9–5; adm

Past the Pitti, at Via Romana 17, is one of Florence's great oddball attractions, the **La Specola museum**. Its **zoological section** has a charmingly old-fashioned collection of nearly everything that walks, flies or swims, from the humble seaworm to the rare Madagascar aye-aye or the swordfish, with an accessory case of different blades. The real horror show stuff, however, is kept hidden away in the **museum of waxes**. Dotty, prudish old Cosimo III was a hypochondriac and morbidly obsessed with diseases, which his favourite artist, a Sicilian priest named Gaetano Zumbo, was able to portray with revolting realism. His macabre anatomIcal models were one of the main sights for Grand Tourists in the 1700s.

Santo Spirito

Santo Spirito
open Mon–Sat 8.30–12 and 3.45–6, Sun and hols 8.30–12 and 3.45–5

Piazza Santo Spirito, the centre of the Oltrarno, is home to a small market on Monday to Saturday mornings under the plane trees, as well as a quiet café or two. In the evening it changes face and the bars fill with people, who meet and chat in the *piazza* and on the church steps until the early hours of the morning. At the southern end, a plain 18th-century façade hides Brunelleschi's last and perhaps greatest church. He designed Santo Spirito in 1440 and lived to see only one column erected, but subsequent architects were faithful to his elegant plan for the interior. This is done in the architect's favourite pale grey and *pietra serena* articulation, a rhythmic forest of columns with semicircular chapels is gracefully recessed into the transepts and the three arms of the crossing. The effect is unfortunately spoiled by the ornate 17th-century *baldacchino*, which sits in this enchanted garden of architecture like a 19th-century bandstand.

The art in the chapels is meagre, as most of the good paintings were sold off over the years. The best include Filippino Lippi's beautiful, restored *Madonna and Saints* in the right transept and Verrocchio's jewel-like *St Monica and Nuns* in the opposite transept. To the left of the church, in the **refectory** of the vanished 14th-century convent, are the scanty remains of a *Last Supper* and a well-preserved, highly dramatic *Crucifixion* by Andrea Orcagna.

Refectory
open Tues–Sat 10–1.30, Sun and hols 10–12.30; adm

Santa Maria del Carmine and the Cappella Brancacci

There is little to say about the surroundings, the *piazza*-cum-car park, the rough stone façade, or the interior of the Oltrarno's other great church, **Santa Maria del Carmine**, which burned down in 1771 and was reconstructed shortly after. Miraculously, the **Cappella Brancacci**, a landmark in Florentine art, survived both the flames and attempts by the authorities to replace it with something more fashionable. Three artists worked on the Brancacci's frescoes: Masolino, who began them in 1425, and who designed the cycle; his pupil Masaccio, who worked on them alone for a year before following his master to Rome, where he died at the age of 27; and Filippino Lippi, who finished them 50 years later. Filippino took care to imitate Masaccio as closely as possible, and the frescoes have an appearance of stylistic unity. Between 1981 and 1988 they were subject to one of Italy's most publicized restorations, cleansed of 550 years of dirt and overpainting, enabling us to see what so thrilled the painters of the Renaissance.

Cappella Brancacci
open 10–5 (last adm 4.45), Sun and hols 1–5; adm, combined ticket available with Palazzo Vecchio; 30 people admitted at a time, for 15mins; booking required, ***t*** *055 276 8224*

Masaccio in his day was a revolution and a revelation in his solid, convincing naturalism; his figures stand in space, without any fussy ornamentation or Gothic grace, very much inspired by Donatello's sculptures. Masaccio conveyed emotion with broad, quick brushstrokes and with his use of light, most obvious in the *Expulsion of Adam and Eve*, one of the most memorable and harrowing images created in the Renaissance. In *The Tribute Money*, the young artist displays his mastery of artificial perspective and light effects. The three episodes in the fresco show an official demanding tribute from the city, St Peter fetching it on Christ's direction from the mouth of a fish, and, lastly, his handing over of the money to the official. Other works by 'Shabby Tom' include *St Peter Baptizing* on the upper register, and *St Peter Healing with his Shadow* and *St Peter Enthroned and Resurrecting the Son of the King of Antioch*, the right half of which was finished by Filippino Lippi. The elegant Masolino is responsible for the remainder, except for the lower register's *Release of St Peter from Prison*, *St Peter Crucified* and *St Paul Visiting St Peter in Prison*, all by Filippino Lippi, based on Masaccio's sketches.

Among the detached frescoes displayed in the cloister and refectory is a good one by Filippino's dad, Fra Filippo Lippi, who was born nearby in Via dell'Ardiglione.

(i) Florence >
Piazza Beccaria, Via Manzoni 16, t 055 23320, www.firenzeturismo.it; closed afternoons and weekends

Via Camillo Cavour 1r, t 055 290832; closed Sun afternoon

Borgo Santa Croce 29r, t 055 234 0444; closed April–Oct Sun and hol afternoons; Nov–Mar Sun

Piazza della Stazione, t 055 212245, www.comune.firenze.it; closed Sun afternoon

Airport, t 055 315874

Tourist Information in Florence

Florence becomes more tourist-friendly all the time and there is now a genuine effort on the part of the city administration to provide helpful tourist information. The *comune* publishes a leaflet listing bars and cafés that 'offer their clients a welcoming reception, politeness and, should they need it, bathroom facilities...'; believe it or not, finding a loo you could use in a bar or café used to be difficult. In addition, there are two guides for the disabled, both available at the tourist office. The more comprehensive is in Italian, but it has a good map and covers access to sites and restaurants, etc.

The **main tourist office** is a bit out of the way, near Piazza Beccaria. There are other branches around town, and on the south side of the **station** in Piazza della Stazione. There is an office at the **airport**. In the summer, look out for the temporary mobile '**Tourist Help Points**' run by the Vigili Urbani (the traffic police), in the centre of town.

Florence Practical A–Z

American Express: Via Dante Alighieri 22r, just off Piazza della Repubblica, **t** 055 50981.

Central post office: Via Pellicceria, near Piazza della Repubblica, **t** 055 273 6481; call **t** 160 for info. *Closed Sun*.

Internet: You can send e-mails, use the Internet or fax from all over the city nowadays; one such service is **Internet Train**, Piazza Stazione 14/38, **t** 055 239 9720, *www.internettrain.it*, or Via Guelfa 54–6, **t** 055 2645146 (opening hours differ from branch to branch); they are also agents for the Swiss Post International if you want to avoid the bureaucratic slowpokes in the Posta Italiana. Mac users might try **Intotheweb**, Via de' Conti 23r, **t** 055 264 5628, *www.intotheweb.it*, which is open daily until 11pm.

Libraries: British Institute Library, Lungarno Guicciardini 9, **t** 055 2677 8270; *closed Sat and Sun*. **American Library**, Via S. Gallo 10; *closed afternoons and weekends*. There are so many other libraries in Florence that one, the **Biblioteca del Servizio Beni Librari**, Via G. Modena 13, **t** 055 438 2655, does nothing but dispense information on the others.

Lost property: in Italian is *Oggetti smarriti* or *Oggetti ritrovati*. The office is in Via Circondaria 17b, **t** 055 328 3942.

Medical: For an ambulance or first aid, **Misericordia**, Piazza del Duomo 20, **t** 055 212222. **Doctor's night service**, **t** 055 287788. For general medical emergencies call **t** 118. The general **Hospital Santa Maria Nuova**, in Piazza S. M. Nuova, **t** 055 27581, is the most convenient. **Tourist Medical Service** (24hrs a day) is staffed by English- and French-speaking physicians at Via Lorenzo il Magnifico 59; ring first on **t** 055 475411. If you find yourself hospitalized while in Florence, the **AVO** (Association of Hospital Volunteers) has volunteer interpreters, **t** 055 425 0126/**t** 055 234 4567.

Pharmacies: Open 24hrs every day in S. Maria Novella station, also **Molteni**, Via Calzaiuoli 7r and **Taverna**, Piazza S. Giovanni 20r, by the baptistry.

Police: emergency **t** 113. The Ufficio Stranieri, in the Questura, Via Zara 2, **t** 055 49771 (*closed afternoons and weekends*) handles most foreigners' problems. Go there for residents' permits, etc.

Tourist aid police: Via Pietrapiana 50, **t** 055 203911; *closed Sat afternoon and Sun.* Interpreters are available to help you report thefts or resolve other problems.

Towed-away cars: There is one car pound (open 24hrs) if your car gets towed away, in the Ponte a Greve car park, near the Ponte al Indiano in the west of the city (bus 44), **t** 055 783882.

Festivals and Events in Florence

Traditional festivals in Florence date back centuries.

Scoppio del Carro (Explosion of the Cart), Easter Sunday. A commemoration of Florentine participation in the First Crusade, which took place in 1096. The Florentines were led by Pazzino de' Pazzi, who was the first over the walls of Jerusalem and who, upon returning home, received the special custody of the flame of Holy Saturday, with which the Florentines traditionally relit their family hearths. To make the event more colourful, the Pazzi constructed a decorated wooden ox cart to carry the flame. They lost the job after the Pazzi conspiracy in 1478, and since then the city has taken over the responsibility. In the morning, a firework-filled wooden float is pulled by white oxen from Il Prato to the cathedral, where, at 11am, during the singing of the Gloria, it is ignited by an iron 'dove' that descends on a wire from the high altar.

Maggio Musicale Fiorentino, Teatro del Maggio Musicale Fiorentino, Corso Italia 12 (off Lungarno Vespucci), **t** 199 112 112 from Italy, **t** 00 39 0424 600458 from abroad, *www.maggiofiorentino.com* (ticket information), late April–early July. The city's big music festival, bringing in big-name concert and opera stars. Some performances may also be held at Teatro della Pergola, or other venues.

Flower and Plant Show, Giardino di Orticoltura, Via Vittorio Emanuele 4, late April. A huge show, a must for horticulture fans, centred around a 19th-century glasshouse.

International Iris Festival, Piazzale Michelangelo, May.

Festa del Grillo (cricket festival), Cascine, Ascension Day, May/June. Michelangelo was thinking of the festival's little wooden cricket cages when he mocked Ammannati's gallery on the cathedral dome.

Calcio Storico in Costume, Piazza Santa Croce, June. Four matches of historical football played in 16th-century costume by 27-man teams from Florence's four quarters, in memory of a defiant football match played there in 1530, during the siege by Charles V. It's great fun, with flag-throwing and a parade in historical costume as part of the pre-game ceremonies. The only fixed date is 24 June; dates for the other matches are pulled out of a hat on Easter Sunday.

Festa di San Giovanni, 24 June. The festival of Florence's patron saint, marked by a big firework display near Piazzale Michelangelo at 10pm.

Estate Fiesolana, late June–Sept. One of the annual cultural events generally adored by Florentines. The old Roman theatre is made the venue for concerts, dance, theatre and films, for reasonable prices.

Summer concerts, Piazza Signoria, summer months. The *piazza* occasionally plays host to concerts and other events during the summertime. Countless smaller-scale concerts are also given, often outdoors or in cloisters, churches and villas. Look out for posters or ask at the tourist office.

Maggio Musicale festival closing concert, late June–early July. A free-for-all heralding the end of the annual music festival.

MaggioDanza ballet company, late June–early July. An evening of dance, held annually, also a free-for-all.

Florence Dance Festival, **t** 055 289276, *www.florencedance.com*, July. An interesting combination of classical and contemporary dance performances, usually held in Fiesole's Roman Theatre.

Festa della Rificolona, 6–7 Sept. A children's festival: Florentine kids gather in the evening in Piazza SS. Annunziata and along the river armed with paper lanterns, and then, after dark, they parade singing around the streets.

Shopping in Florence

Fashion

Though central Florence sometimes seems like one solid boutique, the city is no longer the queen of Italian fashion – the long lack of a central airport, more than anything else, sent most of the big designers to Milan. Even so, the big fashion names of the 1960s and '70s, and the international chain stores, are well represented in smart **Via Tornabuoni**, **Via Calzaiuoli** and around the **Duomo**.

Leather

Via della Vigna Nuova. Leather is something Florence is still known for, and you'll see plenty of it in this central street. Also try **Piazza Santa Croce** and surrounding streets.

The Leather School, entrance at Piazza Santa Croce 16 or Via S. Giuseppe 5r. An unusual institution, occupying part of Santa Croce's cloister, with less expensive goods.

Jewellery

Ponte Vecchio. Florence is famous for jewellery. The shops on, and around, the bridge are forced, by the nature of their location, into wide-open competition. Good prices for Florentine brushed gold (although much of it is made in Arezzo these days) and antique jewellery are more common than you may think. Elsewhere, there are two other stores worth seeking out.

Il Gatto Bianco, Borgo SS. Apostoli 12r. Modern designs crafted on the premises in silver, gold and a variety of other metals with pearls and precious stones.

Pepita Studio, Borgo degli Albizi 23r. Fun, chunky, young designs in plexiglass, wood and glass, at very reasonable prices.

Marbled Paper

Florence is one of the few places in the world that makes marbled paper, an art brought from the Orient in the 12th century. Each sheet is hand-dipped to create a delicate, lightly coloured clouded design; no two sheets are alike. The following shops (and many others) also carry Florentine paper with its colourful Gothic patterns.

Giulio Giannini e Figlio, Piazza Pitti 36r. The oldest manufacturer.

Il Papiro, three shops at: Via Cavour 55r; Piazza del Duomo 24r; and Lung. Acciaiuoli 42r.

La Bottega Artigiana del Libro, Lungarno Corsini 40r.

Il Torchio, Via dei Bardi 17, **t** 055 234 2862. A shop with the workbench in the shop so you can see the artisans in action.

Books

Bookworms fare much better in Florence than in most Italian cities, and prices of books in English seem to have come down in recent years, so there are a fair number of places in which to browse.

The Paperback Exchange, Via Fiesolana 31r. A wide selection of books in English, including many volumes about Florence.

Seeber, Via Tornabuoni 70r. A good selection.

Feltrinelli, Via Cavour 12–20r. Books in English and an excellent range of art books.

BM Bookshop, Borgo Ognissanti 4r. A similar proposition to Feltrinelli.

Franco Maria Ricci, Via delle Belle Donne 41r. A fabulous collection of art books.

Edition, Piazza della Repubblica 27r. Florence's biggest bookshop, with plenty in English, travel guides and maps (also in English), Internet points, video services and a café.

Antiques and Art Galleries

Borgo Ognissanti and the various **Lungarni** are the places to look. Also check out **Piazza dei Ciompi's** fleamarket and the monthly fleamarket (2nd Sun of month) that is held in **Piazza Santo Spirito**.

P. Bazzanti e Figli, Lungarno Corsini 44. A place to pick up an exact replica of the bronze boar in the Mercato Nuovo.

Atelier Alice, Via Faenza 72r. Italian carnival masks (easier to carry than bronze boars) and more. For those who are keen to learn more about the art of the mask, the shop runs 5-lesson courses (ring Professor Dessi on **t** 055 215961 for details).

Via Maggio. A street full of upmarket antique shops.

Serious collectors may want to check Florence's busy auction houses:

Casa d'Aste Pandolfini, Borgo degli Albizi 26, **t** 055 234 0888.

Casa d'Aste Pitti, Via Maggio 15, **t** 055 239 6382.

Sotheby's Italia, Via G Capponi 26, **t** 055 247 9021 (*call for appt*).

Cloth

Casa dei Tessuti, Via de' Pecori 20–24r, **t** 055 215961. A place keeping Florence's ancient cloth trade alive with it lovely linens, silks and woollens. During the lunch break, you might catch a lecture on the history of Florence with special reference to the textile industry.

Silver, Crystal and Porcelain

A Poggi, Via Calzaiuoli 105r and 116r. One of the city's widest selections.

Children's Toys and Clothes

Anichini, Via di Parione 59r. The oldest kids' clothes shop in Florence, with exquisitely produced dresses (made in store), silk party dresses, romper suits, christening robes and playwear.

Città del Sole, Via Cimatori 21r. The best toyshop in Florence.

Cirri, Via Por S. Maria 38–40r. A fairytale selection of dresses.

Wine and Food

Gastronomia di G. Tassini, Borgo SS. Apostoli 24. A good place for items such as truffle cream.

La Bottega del Brunello, Via Ricasoli 81r. A two-part establishment: one for display and one for tasting the wine and specialities on sale.

Casa del Vino, Via dell'Ariento 16r. Wine tastings plus snacks in the San Lorenzo street market.

Enoteca dei Giraldi, Via Giraldi. Tuscan wines from lesser known producers, with more than 140 labels (you can also eat here).

Enoteca Murgia, Via dei Banchi 57, off Piazza S. Maria Novella. A good place for wines and spirits in general.

Marchesi de' Frescobaldi, Via di S. Spirito 11. One of the largest wine suppliers in Italy; visit their ancient cellars.

Mercato Centrale. The central market, housing some speciality food shops.

Millesimi, Borgo Tegolaio 33r. One of the best wine shops in town. Tastings are available by appointment.

Pitti Gola e Cantina, Piazza Pitti 16. A good selection of wines, oils and vinegars, and cookery books (in both English and Italian).

La Porta del Tartufo, Borgo Ognissanti 133r. A place specializing almost exclusively in different types of truffles or 'truffled' foods, ranging from grappa to salmon paste.

Il Procacci, Via Tornabuoni 64r. A high-quality *alimentari* (food shop) selling regional specialities as well as foreign foods. It's most famous as the venue for a lunchtime Prosecco and *panino tartufato*, a glass of sparkling white wine and a truffle-filled sandwich. It's also a bar.

Le Volpi e L'Uva, Piazza de' Rossi 1. A place situated behind the Ponte Vecchio on the square, stocking lesser-known labels.

Markets

Florence's lively street markets offer good bargains, fake designer glad-rags and even some authentic labels.

San Lorenzo. The largest and most boisterous market, selling food (*Mon–Sat 7–2*) and clothes and party gifts (*Tues–Sun 9–7.30, daily in summer*).

Sant'Ambrogio. A bustling and colourful food market.

Mercato Nuovo (Strawmarket). The most touristy market.

Piazza Santo Spirito. Different markets on different days: food, clothes and shoes (small) Mon–Sat; craft and bric-a-brac (big) 2nd Sun of month.

Cascine, along the river, Tues 7–2. A weekly market where many Florentines come to buy their clothes. Here you may easily find some designer clothes off the back of a lorry, shoes and lots more.

Mercato delle Pulci (fleamarket), Piazza dei Ciompi, Tues–Sun 9–7.30 (daily in summer). Perhaps the most fun market, offering desirable junk.

Sports and Activities in Florence

On the Water

The one activity most summertime visitors begin to crave after tramping through the sights is a dip in a pool.

Piscina le Pavoniere, Cascine, **t** 055 362233. The prettiest in Florence. *Open June–Sept daily 10–6.30.*

Bellariva, up the Arno at Lungarno Colombo 2. *Open June–Sept daily 11–5.*

Amici del Nuoto, Via del Romito 38, **t** 055 483951. *Open all year.*

Costoli, Via Paoli, near Campo di Marte, **t** 055 623 6027. *Open all year.*

If there's enough water in the Arno, you can try rowing or canoeing:

Società Canottieri Comunali, Lungarno Ferrucci 6, **t** 055 681 2151.

Società Canottieri Firenze, Lungarno dei Medici 8, **t** 055 238 1010 (membership only).

Horseracing and -riding

Ippodromo Il Visarno, Cascine, **t** 055 360549. Florence's flat race course.

Ippodromo della Mulina, Cascine, **t** 055 422 6069.

Maneggio Marina Horse, Via di Macia 21, **t** 055 887 8066. The nearest place to go riding in the Tuscan hills.

Centro Ippico Ugolino, Via Oliveta 12, Impruneta, **t** 055 230 1289.

Golf

Golf Club Ugolino, on Chiantigiana, **t** 055 230 1009, *www.golfugolino.it*. The nearest 18-hole golf course to Florence, in Grassina, 7km southeast of the city. It's a lovely course.

Squash and Tennis

Centro Squash, Via Empoli 16, **t** 055 732 3055.

Circolo Tennis Firenze, Viale Visarno, **t** 055 354326.

Where to Stay in Florence

Florence ✉ 50100

Florence has some lovely hotels, and not all of them at grand ducal prices, although base rates are the highest in Tuscany. As in any city, the higher cost of living means you won't find much inexpensive accommodation. Florence, Venice and Rome are the most expensive places to stay in Italy, and you should count on having to pay around 25% more for a room here than you would anywhere else.

Historic old palace-hotels are the rule rather than the exception; those listed below are some of the more atmospheric and charming, but to be honest, few are secrets, so reserve as far in advance as possible. Note that many hotels will try to lay down a heavy breakfast charge that is supposed to be optional.

There are almost 400 hotels in Florence, yet that's not enough for anyone who arrives in June and September without a booking (Easter is even more busy). But don't despair; there are several hotel consortia that can help you find a room in nearly any price range for a small commission. If you're arriving by car or train, the most useful will be ITA.

ITA, Santa Maria Novella station, **t** 055 282893, *open daily 8.30–7*. Bookings can be made by phone and a booking fee of between €3 and €8 is charged, according to the category of hotel.

Florence Promhotels, Viale A. Volta 72, **t** 055 553941, toll free **t** 800 866022, *www.promhotels.it*. A free service.

For *agriturismo* or farmhouse accommodation in the surrounding countryside (self-catering or otherwise), contact: **Agriturist Toscana**, Via degli Alfani 67, **t** 055 287838, *www.agriturist.it*; or **Turismo Verde Toscana**, Via Jacopo Nardi 41, **t** 055 23389, *www.turismoverde.it*.

Besides hotels, a number of institutions and private homes let rooms – there's a complete list in the back of the annual provincial hotel book. Many take women only, and fill up with students in the spring.

A cheaper option can be a **bed and breakfast** (*affittacamere*). Ask for a list at the tourist office, or contact the **Bed & Breakfast Association**, Via P. Mastri 26, **t** 055 6540860, *www.abbafirenze.it*.

Luxury (€€€€€)

*******Excelsior**, Piazza Ognissanti 3, **t** 055 27151, *www.westin.com/excelsiorflorence*. The most luxurious option in the city, in the former Florentine address of Napoleon's sister, Caroline. With lots of marble, it's neoclassically plush, lush and green with plants and immaculately staffed, with decadently luxurious bedrooms, many with river views (for a price). The restaurant serves innovative Mediterranean cuisine.

*******Helvetia & Bristol**, Via dei Pescioni 2, **t** 055 26651, *www.royaldemeure.it*. Luxury on a smaller scale, opposite Palazzo Strozzi, with 52 exquisitely furnished bedrooms, each one different but all with rich fabrics adorning windows, walls and beds; Stravinsky, Bertrand Russell and Pirandello stayed here. Additional attractions are the restaurant and the winter garden.

*******Savoy**, Piazza della Repubblica 7, **t** 055 27351, *www. hotelsavoy.it*. A crumbling old place that reopened in spring 2000 under the Forte Group and now strikes a minimalist tone with decor in shades of cream, beige and grey. It has a bar and restaurant, **L'Incontro**, where you can sit out on the *piazza* in fine weather, plus a spa and fitness centre.

*******Villa La Vedetta**, Viale Michelangiolo 78, **t** 055 658 0237, *www.villalavedettahotel.com*. A luxury hotel occupying an elegant villa in a superb position near Piazzale Michelangelo, with panoramic views over the city from its terraces and some of the rooms. Downstairs, cool grey and white marble prevail; the bedrooms are sumptuously – but not ostentatiously – done out in silks. The superb restaurant, **Onice**, which was awarded a Michelin star just one year after opening, serves creative gourmet fare; in summer you can eat outside on the terrace overlooking the city lights.

******Astoria**, Via del Giglio 9, **t** 055 681631, *www.boscolohotels.com*. A recently refurbished grand 16th-century *palazzo* near San Lorenzo market, where Milton wrote *Paradise Lost*. It boasts more character than many hotels that are located near the station. The public rooms are impressive, as are some of the bedrooms – avoid those on the lower floors by the street.

******Gallery Hotel Art**, Vicolo dell'Oro 2, **t** 055 27263, *www.lungarnohotels.it*. Florence's most exciting hotel, and a shrine to contemporary interior design, although it's by no means stark. Its position (a mere two minutes from the Ponte Vecchio) is superb. It has a comfortable library, a smart bar and a restaurant serving trendy fusion food.

******J.K. Place**, Piazza Santa Maria Novella 7, **t** 055 2645181, *www.jkplace.com*. A tall, elegant townhouse on smartened-up Piazza Santa Maria Novella, offering rooms that overlook Alberti's glorious church façade. The interior is luxuriously designer-chic (and attracts the fashion crowd), but manages to be warm and welcoming at the same time. Some of the bedrooms are on the small side, but they are equipped with every mod con; there is a wonderful rooftop terrace and bar. Breakfast is served at a large communal table in a glassed-in courtyard, and a selection of complimentary soft drinks and snacks is available to guests.

******Kraft**, Via Solferino 2, **t** 055 284273, *www.krafthotel.it*. A place frequently used by upmarket tour groups, handy in the opera season (it is 2mins' walk from the Teatro del Maggio Musicale Fiorentino) and with the added advantage of a small rooftop pool. Bedrooms are light and sunny, comfortably furnished with cheerful fabrics, and fitted with Wifi. The suites on the top floor have great views. There is a restaurant.

******Lungarno**, Borgo San Jacopo 14, **t** 055 27261, *www.lungarnohotels.com*. A discreet hotel enjoying a marvellous location on the river, only 2mins' walk from the Ponte Vecchio. The ground-floor sitting/breakfast room and bar, and the new restaurant, which specializes in fish, look out on to the water. The building is modern, but incorporates a medieval tower, and has recently been refurbished; the smallish bedrooms are decorated in smart blue and cream. The best have balconies with 'The View'. Book ahead for these. There are also some self-catering apartments.

******Monna Lisa**, Borgo Pinti 27, **t** 055 247 9751, *www.monnalisa.it*. A Renaissance palace, now owned by the descendants of sculptor Giovanni Dupré, with have a stern façade and, it is said, staff to match. However, it is also one of the loveliest small hotels in Florence – well preserved and filled with family heirlooms and works of art. Rooms vary wildly; try to reserve one that overlooks the garden. There's private parking.

******Villa Carlotta**, Via Michele di Lando 3, **t** 055 233 6134, *www.hotelvillacarlotta.it*. A Tuscan-Edwardian building in a quiet residential district in the upper Oltrarno, close to the Porta Romana, with 32 sophisticated rooms that have been tastefully refurnished and have every mod con. There's a garden and glassed-in veranda, where the large breakfasts are served; a restaurant; and a private garage offering safe parking.

*****Beacci Tornabuoni**, Via Tornabuoni 3, **t** 055 212645, *www.tornabuonihotels.com*. Another excellent small hotel that puts you in the centre of fashionable Florence, on the top three floors of an elegant Renaissance palace. The rooms are comfortable, air-conditioned and equipped with minibars, though It's more fun to sit over your drink or meal on the panoramic roof terrace.

*****Calzaiuoli**, Via Calzaiuoli 6, **t** 055 212456, *www.calzaiuoli.it*. A comfy hotel a few steps from Piazza Signoria and on a traffic-free street, with modern, pleasantly decorated rooms, an American bar, parking, and wonderful views from the top floor.

Relais Santa Croce, Via Ghibellina 87, **t** 055 234 2230, *www.relaisantacroce.com*. The latest in sumptuous Florentine swish, in the exquisitely restored early-18th-century palace of a papal treasurer, with a grand salon and music room, and 24 plush rooms with all mod cons, plus two royal suites with butler service. It shares *piano nobile* lobbies with the fabled Enoteca Pinchiorri (*see* p. 177).

Very Expensive (€€€€)

******Villa Belvedere**, Via Benedetto Castelli 3, **t** 055 222501, *www.villabelvedere.com*. Not the most interesting building in this part of peripheral Florence (1km above Porta Romana), but a pleasant alternative to central accommodation, with a beautiful garden, tennis court, a decent little outdoor pool and good views. Rooms are modern and comfortable with lots of wood and plenty of space. For trips into town, you can leave your car and catch a nearby bus. Light meals are served in the restaurant. It's excellent value.

*****Aprile**, Via della Scala 6, **t** 055 216237, *www.hotelaprile.it*. An old Medici palace convenient for the station and recently given a facelift, with a bust of Cosimo I above the door. Vaulted ceilings and frescoes remain intact, and the bedrooms all have period furniture although some are on the gloomy side; there's a shady courtyard.

*****Hermitage**,Vicolo Marzio 1, **t** 055 287216, *www.hermitagehotel.com*. A little hotel tucked away behind the Ponte Vecchio on the north side of the river, built upside-down – the lift takes you to the fifth floor with its ravishing roof garden, reception and elegant blue and yellow sitting room. The bedrooms below are on the small side but are charmingly furnished with antiques and tasteful fabrics. Some have river views.

*****Loggiato dei Serviti**, Piazza SS. Annunziata 3, **t** 055 289592, *www. loggiatodeiservitihotel.it*. A delightful hotel located on Florence's most beautiful square (now traffic-free), with front rooms overlooking Brunelleschi's famous portico. The 16th-century building was originally a convent, and many of the architectural features remain. Rooms are furnished with antiques and tasteful fabrics; each is very different from the next.

*****Morandi alla Crocetta**, Via Laura 50, **t** 055 234 4747, *www.hotelmorandi.it*. A small but popular choice, with 10 rooms in the university area northeast of Piazza San Marco. The building was a convent in the 16th century, and some of the comfortable and pleasant rooms still have the odd fresco. Two rooms have private terraces.

*****Torre Guelfa**, Borgo SS. Apostoli 8, **t** 055 239 6338, *www.hoteltorreguelfa.com*. A hotel boasting the tallest privately owned tower in Florence, in the middle of the *centro storico*. There's a grand double salon, a sunny breakfast room, and stylish bedrooms in pastel shades with wrought-iron and hand-painted furniture. You can sip your *aperitivo* while contemplating the 360° view.

Casa Howard, Via della Scala 18, **t** 06 6992 4555 (reservations made through Rome), *www.casahoward.com*. An elegant guesthouse following in the footsteps of the two very popular Casa Howards in Rome, only a stone's throw from the train station. It offers 11 individually decorated rooms (there is one for kids, one with a library in it, and one for dogs) at remarkably reasonable prices in a home-from-home atmosphere. All rooms have tea- and coffee-making facilities and some have a private terrace. There's also a Turkish hammam.

Davanzati, Via Porta Rossa 5, **t** 055 286 666, *www.hoteldavanzati.it*. A gem of a hotel in a 15th-century *palazzo*, right next to the Palazzo Davanzati, with wonderful, comfy, bright and airy rooms, friendly staff-owners, and Wifi. Breakfast is included. Book early.

Expensive (€€€)

*****Classic Hotel**, Viale Machiavelli 25, **t** 055 229351, *www.classichotel.it*. A good alternative in a very pleasant location just above Porta Romana on the way to Piazzale Michelangelo, a five-minute walk to a bus stop for the centre. The pink-washed villa stands in a shady garden (a welcome respite from the heat of the city), and breakfast is served in the conservatory in summer. There's private parking.

*****Hotel delle Arti**, Via dei Servi 38/A, **t** 055 267 8553, *www.hoteldellearti.it*. A nine-bedroom hotel under the same ownership as the Loggiato dei Serviti (*see* opposite), with a simpler, more rustic look than its big sister up the road. The stylish bedrooms are decorated in restful shades of green and cream and have wooden floors; a couple have pine four-posters. The three corner rooms are particularly spacious and light, and there is a pretty breakfast room on the top floor, with a wraparound terrace.

*****Silla**, Via dei Renai 5, **t** 055 234 2888, *www.hotelsilla.it*. An old-fashioned *pensione* 10mins' walk east of the Ponte Vecchio on the south bank of the river, in a quiet, quite green neighbourhood. It's on the first floor of a 16th-century *palazzo*, and the spacious breakfast terrace has great views over the Arno and beyond. There's an American bar and Wifi access.

****Alessandra**, Borgo SS. Apostoli 17, **t** 055 283438, *www.hotelalessandra.com*. A modest hotel in a *palazzo* designed by Michelangelo's pupil, Baccio d'Agnolo, on a central but quiet backstreet, with 25 rooms of varying standards. Not all have private baths; the best have waxed parquet floors and antiques and overlook the Arno.

****Belletini**, Via de' Conti 7, **t** 055 213561, *www.hotelbelletini.com*. A friendly place near the Medici chapels, decorated in traditional Florentine style; a couple of rooms have stunning views of the nearby domes. There's a good, generous breakfast. An annexe around the corner houses an additional six stylishly furnished rooms, slightly more expensive. There's TV, air-con, cots, and nearby parking.

****Casci**, Via Cavour 13, **t** 055 211686, *www.hotelcasci.com*. A 15th-century *palazzo* (once home to Rossini) run in a relaxed and cheerful way. The reception area is full of helpful information, the breakfast room has a frescoed ceiling, and the recently refurbished rooms are bright and modern. The choice few look on to a garden at the back.

La Scaletta, Via Guicciardini 13, **t 055 283028, *www.lascaletta.com*. A friendly *pensione* between the Ponte Vecchio and the Pitti Palace, with a roof garden and great views into Boboli. The 12 bedrooms (not all with bathrooms; and some sleeping up to four) are decently furnished, the best with some antique pieces. Moderately priced dinners are available.

Antica Dimora, Via San Gallo 72n, **t** 055 462 7296, *www.anticadimora firenze.it*. A delightful new guesthouse, situated 10mins' walk north of the Duomo, with six beautifully furnished rooms and the warm atmosphere of an elegant private apartment. The four-posters are hung with fine linens and silks, and all rooms have DVDs.

Relais Uffizi, Chiasso de' Baroncelli/ Chiasso del Buco 16, **t** 055 267 6239, *www.relaisuffizi.it*. The only hotel that overlooks Piazza della Signoria, hidden down a series of narrow lanes. The 13 rooms of varying shapes and sizes are decorated and furnished with style, and the overall atmosphere is informal. You can relax in the sitting room and watch the ever-changing *piazza* below.

★ Residenza il Villino >

Residenza il Villino, Via della Pergola, **t** 055 200 1116, *www.ilvillino.it*. A handsome 19th-century Tuscan complex near the Duomo, built around a courtyard and renovated to preserve all its original features. It has lovely owners and serene, spacious rooms (rates include a buffet breakfast; the garage is extra). It's essential to book well in advance.

Tourist House Ghiberti, Via M. Buffani 1, **t** 055 261 171, *www.touristhouseghiberti.com*. Five arty B&B rooms near the Duomo, equipped with original paintings and mosaics, and all the mod cons of a five-star hotel, including a sauna and Jacuzzi.

Moderate (€€)

★ Locanda degli Artisti >

***Locanda degli Artisti, Via Faenza 56, **t** 055 213806, *www.hotelazzi.it*. A hotel a stone's throw from the San Lorenzo market and the train station, with pleasant rooms and an arty, alternative feel to it. On the ground floor, bedrooms are a little more sophisticated (there are even a couple of suites); upstairs, rooms are clean but quite spartan. There's a sauna, a sunny terrace and a breakfast room where dishes made from organic produce are served, plus a free Internet access point.

Boboli, Via Romana 63, **t 055 229 8645, *www.hotelboboli.com*. A modest hotel located near the back entrance of the Boboli gardens. The brightest rooms are right at the top of the four-storey building; a lift has recently been installed. If you want quiet (Via Romana is quite noisy), go for a room on the inner courtyard. Breakfast is served on a little terrace in summer.

Residenza Johanna Cinque Giornate, Via Cinque Giornate 12, **t 055 473377, *www.johanna.it*. A villa representing good value for money in a city where bargains are few and far between, located some way from the centre (near Fortezza da Basso). It stands in its own garden and offers six comfortable rooms, each equipped with a breakfast tray and kettle, as well as a sitting room with plenty of reading material. Facilities are of a three-star standard, and parking is available. The staff are discreet.

*Bavaria, Borgo degli Albizi 26, **t** 055 234 0313, *www.hotelbavariafirenze.it*. A once-crummy hotel in a grand, 16th-century *palazzo* with a façade said to be frescoed by Vasari, recently given a facelift. While only a handful of rooms have private baths, the rooms are stylish, and some have splendid views of the city.

*Maxim, Via del Calzainoli 11b 4, **t** 055 217474, *www.hotelmaximfirenze.it*. A centrally located hotel that has recently had a facelift. The reception area is bright and elegant, and the bedrooms (which sleep two or three) are well furnished and modern. All are ensuite and one even has a Jacuzzi. There's air-conditioning, parking nearby, and a free Internet point.

*Orchidea, Borgo degli Albizi 11, **t** 055 248 0346, *www.hotelorchideaflorence.it*. A hotel in a 12th-century building where Dante's in-laws once lived, run by an Anglo-Italian family. One of the seven cheerful rooms has a private shower; the best of the rest look on to a garden at the back.

★**Sorelle Bandini**, Piazza Santo Spirito 9, **t** 055 215308. A perenially popular choice despite its state of disrepair and relatively high prices, partly due to the romantic loggia along one side of the fourth-storey hotel but also to its location on Piazza Santo Spirito, bustling by day and lively (and noisy) at night. Expect uncomfortable beds, cavernous rooms, heavy Florentine furniture and a certain shabby charm.

Dei Mori B&B, Via Dante Alighieri 12, **t** 055 211 438, *www.bnb.it/deimori*. One of the friendliest and best-value B&Bs in Florence, with pretty rooms (up a fair amount of stairs), many overlooking the courtyard, in a great location between the Duomo and Piazza della Signoria.

Residenza Johanna, Via Bonifacio Lupi 14, **t** 055 481896, *www.johanna.it*. A building identified only by a tiny brass plaque over the bell, just north of Piazza San Marco. There are no TVs or phones in the rooms, no doorman, and not all rooms have private baths, but the furnishings are comfortable, the bedrooms are prettily decorated and there's lots of reading material to hand. Breakfast is on a do-it-yourself tray in each room, and there are kettles out in the corridor.

Residenza Johlea, Via San Gallo 80, **t** 055 463 3292, *www.johanna.it*. Another small hotel a few doors from the Johanna (*see* above), with which it shares ownership. Situated 10mins' walk north of the central market, it has comfortable rooms furnished with taste and style, with excellent bathrooms. Breakfast is supplied on trays in the rooms. On the top floor you'll can enjoy use of a small sitting room and a roof terrace affording 360° views of the city. If all the rooms are full, ask the receptionist about the sister *residenza* (the **Johlea Due**) a few doors down.

Ungherese, Via G.B. Amici 8, **t** 055 573 474, *www.hotelungherese.it*. A wonderfully hospitable little hotel with a lovely garden terrace for *alfresco* drinks or breakfast. It's located outside the ZTL in the San Gervaso quarter (10mins from the centre by frequent bus); you can park on the street for a small fee. Triples and quads are available.

Inexpensive (€)

★**Dali**, Via dell'Oriuolo 17, **t** 055 234 0706, *www.hoteldali.com*. A little hotel a few minutes' walk from the Duomo, run by a genuinely friendly young couple who have decorated the rooms with care and attention to detail in spite of the low prices. Only three of the 10 rooms have ensuite bathrooms, but all are bright and homely and have a small fridge. There's free parking in the internal courtyard but no breakfasts.

★**Scoti**, Via de' Tornabuoni 7, **t** 055 292128, *www.hotelscoti.com*. A simple and cheap *pensione* with a surprisingly upmarket address – the ideal spot if you would rather splurge on the wonderful clothes in the surrounding shops. A recent facelift means that all the simple rooms are now ensuite; luckily the atmosphere has not been spoilt, and there are still wonderful faded floor-to-ceiling frescoes in the sitting room. The owners are friendly and there is a restaurant and bar.

Istituto Gould, Via dei Serragli 49, **t** 055 212576, *www.istitutogould.it*. An excellent budget choice near Santo Spirito, run by the Valdese church. Rooms vary in size from singles (just a couple) to quads and not all have their own bathrooms; you need to book early to secure singles or doubles. The best rooms have access to a terrace, the noisiest are on Via dei Serragli. No smoking is allowed throughout the building and you have to check in during office hours (*Mon–Fri 8.45–1 and 3–7.30, Sat 8.45–1 and 3–6*).

Youth Hostels

Archi Rossi, Via Faenza 94r, **t** 055 290804, *www.hostelarchirossi.com*. The nearest hostel to the station, purposebuilt, fully wheelchair-accessible and well equipped. You can book a place anytime after 6am and occupy your room from 2.30pm. Phone bookings are accepted and there is a 12.30am curfew. There's a restaurant, a bar and Internet access.

Ostello Europa Villa Camerata, Viale A Righe 2/4 (bus from station), **t** 055 601451, *www.ostellionline.org*. Five hundred beds for IYHF card-holders.

Located in an old *palazzo* with gardens, it is a popular place, and you'd be wise to show up at 2pm to get a spot in the summer. The maximum stay is three days.

Ostello Santa Monaca, Via Santa Monaca 6, **t** 055 268338, *www.ostello.it*. Just over 100 beds near the Carmine church, in a 15th-century convent; sign up for a place in the morning. Credit cards are accepted.

Camping

There are a few campsites within easy striking distance of Florence. *See* also Fiesole, p.197.

Camping Internazionale, Via S. Cristofano 2, **t** 055 237 4704, *www.florencecamping.com*. A choice south of the city in Bottai Tavarnuzze, near the A1 exit *autostrada* Firenze–Certosa.

Camping Michelangelo, Viale Michelangelo 80, **t** 055 681 1977, *www.ecvacanze.it*. Fine views over the city and free hot showers; arrive early to get a spot. On the other hand, there's no shade and the disco goes on until 1am. Bus 13 will get you here from the station.

Mugello Verde International Camping, Via Masso Rondinaio 2, in San Piero a Sieve, 25km north of Florence on road to Bologna, **t** 055 848511, *www.florence camping.com*. An option with a very pleasant setting among hills and forests, and frequent buses down to Florence.

Eating Out in Florence

Like any sophisticated city with many visitors, Florence has plenty of fine restaurants; even in cheaper places, standards are high, and if you don't care for anything fancier, there will be lots of good red Chianti to wash down your meal. By popular demand, the city centre is full of *tavole calde*, pizzerias and snackbars where you can grab a sandwich or a salad instead of a full sit-down meal (one of the best pizza-by-the-slice places can be found just across from the Medici Chapels).

You are advised to call ahead and reserve, even a day or two in advance, for the best places, many of which close for all or part of August.

Very Expensive (€€€€)

Alle Murate, Via del Proconsolo 16r, **t** 055 240618. A 'creative traditional' restaurant close to the Bargello, elegant but relaxed, serving two set menus. Ask for the 'Creative Menu': the modern take on Tuscan cuisine will amaze you. Highlights are veal rolls stuffed with aubergine, and octopus with potato purée. Book ahead. *Closed Mon and lunch.*

Angiolino, Via Santo Spirito 36l, **t** 055 239 8976. A reliable place to eat Tuscan standards, though it has lost some of its character after renovation. The vegetable *antipasti* are especially good, and the simple *pollastrina sulla griglia* (grilled spring chicken) is succulent and tasty. *Closed Mon.*

Antico Ristoro di Cambi, Via Sant' Onofrio 1r, **t** 055 217134. A place in the Oltrarno, some way to the west of the centre, that's very popular with the Florentine intelligenzia. The food is genuinely Florentine, the classic soups – *ribollita* and *pappa al pomodoro* – are tasty and warming, as is the penne with pumpkin flowers. *Closed Sun.*

Beccofino, Piazza degli Scarlatti, **t** 055 290076. A trendy restaurant on the river under the British Institute. Inside you could almost be in London or New York, but the food is decidedly Italian. Dishes are enhanced with creative touches and elegantly presented. Both fish and meat dishes are excellent; the menu changes on a monthly basis but you might enjoy scallops with bitter greens, risotto with pears and *pecorino* cheese, and chestnut, potatoes and horseradish tart, or a fabulous *bistecca alla fiorentina*. You can also eat a light meal in the wine bar, where prices are considerably lower. *Closed Mon, and Tues–Sat lunch.*

Buca Lapi, Via del Trebbio 1r, **t** 055 213768. A restaurant open since 1880 in the old wine cellar of the lovely Palazzo Antinori, serving traditional favourites, from *polenta al cinghiale* (with boar) to a *bistecca alla fiorentina con fagioli* that is hard to beat, downed with a wide selection of Tuscan wines. *Closed Sun, Aug, and Mon–Sat lunch.*

Cibreo, Via dei Macci 118r, **t** 055 234 1100. One of the most Florentine of Florentine restaurants, situated close to the market of Sant' Ambrogio. The decor is simple yet elegant, but food is the main concern, and all of it is market-fresh. You can go native and order cold tripe salad, cockscombs and kidneys or rosemary-flavoured grilled baby goat chops, or you can play it safe with *prosciutto* from the Casentino, a fragrant soup (no pasta here) of tomatoes, mussels and bell peppers, and polenta with Parmesan and fresh herbs, topped off with a delicious lemon *crostata*, cheesecake or a chocolate cake that will answer every chocaholic's dream. Advance reservations are essential. *Closed Sun, Mon, Aug and 1st wk Jan.*

Don Chisciotte, Via C Ridolfi 4r, **t** 055 475430. A small place located between the Fortezza Basso and Piazza dell'Indipendenza, serving inventive Italian food with a particular emphasis on fish and vegetables. Let yourself be tempted by the likes of squid filled with ricotta and Sardinian cheese, or tagliatelle with prawns and asparagus. *Closed Aug.*

Enoteca Pinchiorri, Via Ghibellina 87, near Casa Buonarroti, **t** 055 242777. One of the finest gourmet restaurants in all Italy, boasting two Michelin stars. The owners inherited the wine shop that it occupies and converted it into this beautifully appointed restaurant, with meals served in a garden court in the summer months. The cellars contain some 80,000 bottles of the best wines that Italy and France have to offer. The cooking, a mixture of *nouvelle cuisine* and traditional Tuscan, wins prizes every year. Italians tend to complain about the minute portions. A meal will set you back more than €200 excluding wine; the sky's the limit if you go for a more interesting bottle. *Closed Sun, Mon–Wed lunch, and Aug.*

Oliviero, Via delle Terme 51r, **t** 055 212421. A place five minutes from the Piazza della Signoria, with somewhat passé decor and a slightly bizarre clientele but excellent food. You can try such seasonal curiosities such as *gnudi di fiori di zucchini e ricotta* (ravioli stripped of its pasta coating with ricotta cheese and courgette flowers) and boned pigeon stuffed with chestnuts. Try the soufflé. *Closed lunch and Sun.*

Pane e Vino, Via San Niccolò 70r (Oltrarno, just in from Ponte alla Grazie), **t** 055 247 6956. A pleasant and informal place with a superb wine list and very knowledgeable staff to go with it. The *menu degustazione* changes daily but always offers seven small courses; if you're lucky, you'll get to try the spaghetti with octopus or *tortelli* filled with cheese and honey. *Closed Sun and Aug.*

Ristorante Ricchi, Piazza S. Spirito 8r, **t** 055 280830. A small fish restaurant with tables on magical Piazza Santo Spirito. Inside, the decor is both contemporary and elegant, with tables lined up against the walls. The generous plate of *antipasti* is good; main courses include ravioli fillled with *burrata* cheese, lasagne with yellow pumpkin or radish, or fillet of pink tuna with carrots. There are a few meat dishes too. *Closed Sun (exc. 2nd Sun of month, when arts and crafts market takes place), last 2wks Aug, and Feb.*

Targa, Lungarno C Colombo 7, **t** 055 677377. A restaurant that has risen from the rather dated ashes of Caffè Concerto, with a revamped, more casual menu and a fresh approach to eating out. The space (a delightfully warm wood-and-glass room on the Arno) has not changed, but the food on offer is simpler (and a bit cheaper), while still providing a creative take on regional dishes. Try the *garmugia ai tre caci*, with vegetables and typical Luccese cheeses, or a mixture of artichokes and Chinese cabbage with mussels. Make sure to room for the sinful hot chocolate soufflé, and choose a wine from the formidable list, which includes labels from all of Italy and beyond. *Closed Sun and 1st 3wks Aug.*

Taverna del Bronzino, Via delle Ruote 25–27r, **t** 055 495220. An elegant, traditional restaurant located to the north of the Duomo, featuring plenty of Tuscan dishes – the *bistecca alla fiorentina* is succulent and tender – and delights such as ricotta and spinach-stuffed pasta in tomato sauce and seabass in white wine; there are several seafood choices for each course. *Closed Sun and 3wks Aug.*

Expensive (€€€)

Antico Fattore, Via Lambertesca 1/3r, **t** 055 288975. A traditional Florentine trattoria, popular with locals and tourists alike, that suffered serious damage in the 1993 Uffizi bomb but is now back in business, serving excellent and reasonably priced local dishes. Try pappardelle with wild boar or deer sauce, *Il Fritto* (deep-fried rabbit, chicken and brains) or grilled pigeon. *Closed Sun and 2wks Aug.*

Baldovino, Via Giuseppe 22r (Piazza S. Croce), **t** 055 241773. An excellent trattoria/pizzeria where you can eat anything from a big salad, filled *focaccia* or pizza (from a wood-burning oven), *ribollita* or *bistecca alla fiorentina* and delicious home-made cakes. Nearby, at 18r, the **Enoteca Baldovino** offers a great list of wines. *Closed Mon.*

Buca Mario, Palazzo Niccolini, Piazza degli Ottaviani 16r, **t** 055 214179. One of Florence's traditional 'cellar restaurants', accessed via steep stairs. It's a place oozing with Florentine atmosphere, with a menu to match. The typical Tuscan cuisine includes home-made pasta and exquisite grilled meat. Standout dishes include home-made fettuccine with artichokes, *ribollita*, and tuna with beans and onions. *Closed Tues lunch, Wed lunch, and 3wks Aug.*

Cavolo Nero, Via dell'Ardiglione 22, **t** 055 294744, *www.cavolonero.it*. A little restaurant tucked away in a sidestreet near Piazza del Carmine, with quite a following among Florentine trendies. The interior is white on yellow, and as many tables as possible are crowded into the attractive room, though there's a pretty rear garden. The food is mainly Mediterranean with a twist (think gnocchi with tomato and *burrata* cheese, or risotto with clams and shrimp; seabass fillet with artichokes and sweet onion sauce or fried lamb fillet with stewed cabbage), but there are also plenty of local standards. Book ahead. *Closed Sun and 2wks Aug.*

Coco Lezzone, Via del Parioncino 26r (off Lungarno Corsini), **t** 055 287178. A restaurant with a name that means, in old Florentine dialect, 'big, smelly cook', but don't let this put you off. The atmosphere is informal and the food is classic Tuscan, with dishes featuring the highest-quality fresh ingredients, particularly meat. *Closed Sun and Aug.*

Il Latini, Via dei Palchetti 6r (by Palazzo Rucellai), **t** 055 210916. A place that's something of an institution in Florence – crowded (prepare to queue; they don't accept bookings) and noisy but great fun. You eat huge portions of Florentine classics at long tables – try one of the hearty soups followed by the *bistecca*, or, for a change, the *gran pezzo* – a vast rib-roast of beef. The house wine is good; try a *riserva*. *Closed Mon and Aug.*

Osteria Santo Spirito, Piazza Santo Spirito 16r, **t** 055 238 2383. A good (much cheaper) alternative to Borgo Antico (see p.179), a short hop walk across the *piazza*. You can sit outside and enjoy a choice of cold dishes, pastas (try the *orecchiette Santo Spirito*), vegetarian dishes, fillet of beef with truffles and more. The decor is unusual for Florence – warm red paintwork with modern lighting.

Sostanza, Via della Porcellana 25r, **t** 055 212691. One of the last authentic Florentine trattorias, just west of Santa Maria Novella, and known as Il Troia. It's a good place to eat *bistecca*, but one of its most famous dishes is the simple but delectable *petto di pollo al burro* – chicken breast sautéed in butter. No credit cards are taken, and booking is strongly advised. *Closed Sat, Sun and Aug.*

Zibibbo, Via di Terzollina 3r, **t** 055 433383. A wonderful restaurant serving traditional Tuscan fare but in a stylish, un-Tuscan setting (pink-varnished floorboards, contemporary furniture). Plenty of choice between meat and fish dishes; worth the trip up to the northernmost extremes of town. *Closed Sun.*

Moderate (€€)

Aquacotta, Via dei Pilastri 51r, **t** 055 242907. A restaurant north of Piazza Sant'Ambrogio, named for the simple but delicious bread soup that is one of its specialities; you could follow that by deepfried rabbit accompanied by crisply fried courgette flowers. It also serves *acquacotta* ('cooked water'), a Maremman vegetable soup with onions, tomatoes and mushrooms. *Closed Sun and Aug*.

Coquinarius, Via delle Oche 15r, **t** 055 230 2153. A café/wine bar/restaurant where you can eat or drink just about anything. It is a useful stopoff for a light meal or a snack in the centre of tourist-land. Snacks include a series of hot *crostoni* (toasted Tuscan bread with various toppings) and various salads, but you can also order a pasta dish or a meat *carpaccio*. Wines are available by the bottle or the glass. *Closed Sun May–Aug*.

Finisterrae, Via de' Pepi 5–7r, **t** 055 2638675. A great place to come if you are tired of *ribollita* and the typical trattoria look, offering food from a range of Mediterranean countries, from southern Italy and France to Greece, Turkey, Tunisia and Spain. The standard of the food is not always what it might be, but the atmosphere is wonderful – there are a series of rooms decorated In the style of the various countries concerned. While you wait for your table, you can sip an *aperitivo* in the Moroccan-style bar and feast on the excellent nibbles that are provided.

La Casalinga >>

La Vecchia Bettola, Viale Ariosto 32–34r, **t** 055 224158. A noisy trattoria located to the west of the Carmine, with great food; the menu changes daily, but you will nearly always find their classic *tagliolini con funghi porcini* on offer. Try the *bistecca* too. The ice cream comes from Vivoli. *Closed Sun and Mon*.

Trattoria Cibreo (Cibreino) >

Trattoria Cibreo (Cibreino), Via dei Macci 114, **t** 055 234 1100. A little annexe to smart Cibreo (*see* p.177), constituting one of the best deals in town; the food is the same (excluding the odd more extravagant dish) but it's served in a rusticated setting on cheaper porcelain – with the result that your bill will be a third that of those who are dining around the corner. No reservations are taken, so make sure to come early to get a table. *Closed Sun and Aug*.

There aren't many **vegetarian restaurants** as such in Florence, though non-meat eaters will find plenty of choice (pastas, risotto, etc.) to tempt them. Specifically vegetarian restaurants in this range include:

Ruth's, Via Farini 2/A, **t** 055 248 0888. A new, bright and modern kosher vegetarian restaurant next to the synagogue, serving fish and Middle Eastern dishes. Try a *brik*, a savoury pastry filled with fish, potatoes or cheese that tastes better than it sounds. *Closed Fri eve and Sat lunch*.

Il Vegetariano, Via delle Ruote 30r, **t** 055 47030. A self-service place located to the west of San Marco; with excellent fresh food, including a wide choice of soups, salads and more substantial dishes. *Closed Sat lunch, Sun lunch, 3wks Aug*.

Inexpensive (€)

Borgo Antico, Piazza Santo Spirito 62, **t** 055 210437. Popular with a young trendy crowd, so you may have to wait for a table, especially in summer for the terrace. Inside, the music can be unbearably loud, but the pizza is decent, and there are plenty of other choices – Interesting pastas, big salads and more substantial meat and fish dishes. *Closed Mon*.

La Casalinga, Via Michelozzi 9r, **t** 055 218624. A family-run trattoria, also near Piazza Santo Spirito, and always busy, which is not surprising given the quality of the simple home cooking (the name means 'the housewife') and the low prices. Try the ravioli in rabbit sauce, *bollito misto*, and Limoncello sorbet for dessert. *Closed Sun, 1wk Jan, 3wks Aug*.

Da Mario, Via della Rosina 2r, **t** 055 218550. Mario's trattoria, located at the back of the central market, is always buzzing, and there is usually a queue for the few rather cramped tables; don't expect to get a table to yourself. The food is pure Tuscan, excellent and cheap; *ribollita*, *tortelli* stuffed with potatoes, roasted rabbit and tripe. Note that only cash is accepted. *Closed eves, plus Sun, hols and first 3wks Aug*.

Il Pizzaiuolo, Via dei Macci 113r, near Sant'Ambrogio market, **t** 055 241171. One of the best restaurants in the city, boasting a real Neapolitan pizza-maker, whose creations are puffy and light. There's lots of other dishes to choose from, but beware the long queues. Book for evenings. *Closed Sun and Aug.*

Da Ruggero, Via Senese 89r, **t** 055 220542. A tiny, family-run trattoria a little way from the centre of town; it's always full, so make sure to book ahead. The traditional food is home cooked; try the excellent *pappardelle alla lepre* (with hare sauce) and good puddings. *Closed Tues and Wed, and 3wks July/Aug.*

Sabatino, Via Pisana 2r, **t** 055 225955. A simple, family-run trattoria just outside the old city gate of San Frediano, which feels as if it has always been this way. The cooking methods, too, are old-fashioned and suitably rustic. Highlights are the bread and tomato soup, cabbage soup, Florentine tripe and *bistecca alla fiorentina*. Prices are similarly retro. *Closed Sat, Sun and Aug.*

★ Santa Lucia ›

Santa Lucia, Via Ponte alle Mosse 102r, **t** 055 353255. A genuine Neapolitan pizzeria north of the Cascine. It's a noisy, steamy and unromantic place but it makes up for its lack of glamour by serving what is possibly the best pizza in Florence, topped with the sweetest tomatoes and the creamiest *mozzarella di buffala*. Note that payment is by cash only. *Closed Wed and Aug.*

Al Tranvai, near Carmine in Piazza Torquato Tasso 14r, **t** 055 225197. A cheerful little place with two rows of tables that are always full, meaning that you may not get much elbow room. The menu changes daily, but the *crostini misti* are always on offer, and there are lots of offal dishes. *Closed lunch and Sun.*

★ Trattoria del Carmine ›

Trattoria del Carmine, Piazza del Carmine 18r, **t** 055 218601. A traditional, bustling trattoria situated within the San Frediano district, and often full. The long menu includes such staples as *ribollita*, *pasta e fagioli* and roast pork, but also features seasonal dishes such as risotto with asparagus or mushrooms, pasta with wild boar sauce, *osso buco* and fish dishes. *Closed Sun and 3wks Aug.*

Cafés and *Gelaterie*

Caffè Italiano, Via Condotta 12, **t** 055 289020. A popular lunchtime stop for locals, right in the centre of town; they crowd in for the excellent hot and cold dishes. It's on two levels: downstairs there's standing at the bar, upstairs you can sit down. The atmosphere is old-fashioned, particularly in the tearoom upstairs. Newspapers are on offer for browsing.

Caffè Ricchi, Piazza Santo Spirito 8r–9r, **t** 055 215864. A local institution that continues to serve excellent light lunches and wonderful ice cream. The outside tables enjoy the benefit of one of the most beautiful *piazzas* in Florence, though this comes at a price. At *aperitivo* time (6–8pm) there's a great spread of 'free' nibbles to go with your Campari.

Capocaccia, Lungarno Corsini 12r, **t** 055 2345458. A place popular as a nightspot as well as a daytime bar and café, enjoying a great location on the river beside the British Consulate. It opens at lunchtime (earlier at weekends, when it does a brisk brunch trade) for light meals, and is also a great spot for an *aperitivo* with 'free' nibbles in the evening or as an evening venue for music and drinks. *Closed Mon.*

Dolce Vita, Piazza del Carmine, **t** 055 284595. The place where fashionable young Florentines strut their latest togs – a favourite pastime since the 14th century. Live music accompanies *aperitivos* on Wednesday and Thursday evenings. *Closed Mon and 2wks Aug.*

Dolci e Dolcezze, Piazza Cesare Beccaria 8r, **t** 055 234 5438. A place east of Sant'Ambrogio market, with the most delicious cakes, pastries and jams in the city – the *crostate*, *torte* and *bavarese* are expensive but worth every euro. It now has another shop at Via del Corso 41r. *Closed Mon.*

Festival del Gelato, Via del Corso 75r. More than 100 variations of ice cream.

Gelateria de' Ciompi, Via dell'Agnolo 121r. A traditional Florentine ice-cream parlour tucked around the corner from Santa Croce, priding itself on its authentic home-made recipes, some of which are more than 50 years old.

Gilli, Piazza della Repubblica 36–39r, **t** 055 213896. One of of Florence's old grand cafés dating back further than most, to 1733, when the Mercato Vecchio still occupied this area; Its two panelled back rooms are especially pleasant in winter. *Closed Tues.*

Giubbe Rosse, Piazza della Repubblica 13–14r, **t** 055 212280. A place famous as the rendezvous of Florence's literati at the turn of the 19th century, with a chandelier-lit interior that has changed little since.

Il Granduca, Via dei Calzaiuoli 57r. Yet another *gelato* option, with creamy concoctions that challenge those of nearby rival Perché No (*see* below). *Closed Wed.*

Hemingway, Piazza Piattellina 9r, **t** 055 284781. A beautifully appointed bar done out in pale blues with rattan furniture. You can enjoy teas and coffees, as well as cocktails and interesting light meals. The owner is a chocaholic, so the hand-made chocolates and puddings are a dream. Try the *sette veli* chocolate cake. Reservations are recommended. *Closed lunch and Sun.*

L'Oasi, Via dell'Oriuolo 5r, near Duomo. Sophisticated ice-cream flavours, and a good choice of cakes.

Perché No ('Why Not'), Via Tavolini 194. Arctic heaven near Via Calzaiuoli, with wonderful ice cream served in 1940s surroundings.

Rivoire, Piazza della Signoria 5r. Florence's most elegant and classy watering hole, with a marble-detailed interior as lovely as the Piazza della Signoria itself, plus a terrace on the square for fine weather.

Il Triangolo delle Bermude, Via Nazionale 61r. A superb choice of ice cream.

La Via del' Tè, Piazza Ghiberti 22r. A place looking on to the Sant' Ambrogio food market, offering a huge range of teas to choose from plus sweet and savoury snacks.

Vivoli, Via Isola delle Stinche 7r, between Bargello and S. Croce. A place serving decadent confections and rich *semifreddi* that are partially responsible for Florence's claim to be the ice-cream capital of the world. *Closed Mon.*

Wine Bars

Cantinetta dei Verrazzano, Via dei Tavolini 18–20r, **t** 055 268590. Part bakery (selling delicious bread and cakes), part winebar, centrally located and belonging to the Verrazzano wine estate – it serves its own very good wine exclusively. You can sip it with a plate of mixed *crostini* at hand.

Enoteca Baldovino, Via San Giuseppe 18r, **t** 055 234 7220. A bright and cheerful winebar located down the northern side of Santa Croce, offering a range of snacks and pasta dishes. There is a comprehensive wine list and plenty of wines by the glass. *Closed Mon in winter.*

Enoteca dei Giraldi, Via dei Giraldi 4r, **t** 055 216518. A place near the Bargello, hosting art exhibitions and running wine-tasting courses as well as supplying excellent food and drink.

I Fratellini, Via dei Cimatori 38r. A hole in the wall, one of the last of its kind in Florence, where you can join the locals standing on the street, glass and *crostino* in hand. *Closed Sun.*

Frescobaldi Wine Bar, Vicolo dei Gondi (off Via della Condotta), **t** 055 284724. A pleasant little wine bar recently opened by one of Tuscany's best-known wine-growing families, forming annexe to a full-blown (and very elegant) restaurant. The wines on offer are, naturally, all Frescobaldis produced on their estates in Tuscany and the rest of Italy; some are the result of joint ventures in California and Chile. Delicious snacks include cheeses and cold meats, or you can pop next door for dinner. *Closed Sun, and Mon lunch.*

Fuori Porta, Via Monte alle Croci 10r, **t** 055 234 2483. Possibly Florence's most famous winebar of all, where there are some 600 labels on the wine list plus dozens of whiskies and *grappas*. Among the snacks and hot dishes that are on offer, make sure to try one of the *crostoni* – huge slabs of local bread topped with something delicious and heated under the grill. *Closed Sun.*

Pitti Gola e Cantina, Piazza Pitti 16, **t** 055 212704. A delightful little place situated bang opposite the Palazzo

Pitti, with a good choice of wines from Tuscany and beyond, snacks and other more substantial dishes, as well as a few outside tables. *Closed Mon.*

Le Volpi e l'Uva, Piazza dei Rossi 1, **t** 055 239 8132, *www.levolpieluva.com.* A place run by knowledgeable and helpful owners who specialize in relatively unknown labels. Snacks include a marvellous selection of French and Italian cheeses. *Closed Sun.*

Entertainment and Nightlife in Florence

Nightlife with Great-Aunt Florence is still awaiting its Renaissance; according to the Florentines she's conservative, somewhat deaf and retires early – 1am is late in this city. However, there are plenty of people who wish it weren't so, and slowly, slowly, Florence by night is beginning to mean more than the old *passeggiata* over the Ponte Vecchio and an ice cream, and perhaps a late trip up to Fiesole to contemplate the lights.

Look out for listings of concerts and events in Florence's daily, *La Nazione*. The tourist office's free *Florence Today* contains bilingual monthly information and a calendar, as does a booklet called *Florence Concierge Information*, which is available in hotels and tourist offices.

The monthly *Firenze Spettacolo*, which is sold at newsstands, contains a brief section on events in English, but the comprehensive listings (including anything from ecology and trekking events, film societies, clubs, live music, opera and concerts) are easy to understand even in Italian. The annual *Guida locali di Firenze* also gives listings. For all current films that are being shown in Florence, look in the local paper.

Box Office, Via Alamanni 39, **t** 055 210804, *www.boxoffice.it*, is a central ticket agency for all the major events in Tuscany and beyond, including classical, rock, jazz, etc.

Performance Arts

Florence's opera and ballet season runs from September to Christmas, and there are concerts from January to April at the **Teatro del Maggio Musicale Fiorentino**, and in the ***Maggio Musicale* festival**, which features all three, running from mid-April to the end of June. There is usually more opera in July.

Classical Concerts

Concerts are held mainly in the following venues:

Teatro del Maggio Musicale Fiorentino, Via del Corso 16, **t** 055 211158, *www.maggiofiorentino.com.* Florence's municipal opera house, hosting symphony concerts, recitals, opera and ballet.

Teatro della Pergola, Via della Pergola 12–32, **t** 055 226 4316, *www.amicimusica.fi.it.* A stunning 18th-century theatre hosting an excellent chamber-music series promoted by the Amici della Musica.

Teatro Verdi, Via Ghibellina 99, **t** 055 212320, *www.teqtroverdifirenze.it.* A red and gold theatre that's home to Tuscany's regional orchestra, who perform here on a regular basis from late Nov to May.

Many smaller events take place year-round in churches, cloisters and villas, and there are plenty of outdoor concerts in the summer months. Look out for posters: such events are not always well publicized.

Rock and Jazz Concert Venues

Auditorium Flog, Via M Mercati 24b, **t** 055 487145, *www.flog.it.* One of the best places in Florence to hear live music year-round, often hosting ethnic music events. Look out for the Musica dei Popoli festival in October. *Closed July and Aug.*

Palasport, Viale Paoli, **t** 055 678841, *www.boxoffice.it.* A venue in Campo di Marte, seating 7,000 people. Big-name rock and jazz bands nearly always play here.

Saschall, Lungarno Aldo Moro 3, **t** 055 650 4112, *www.saschall.it.* A 3,000-seat venue risen from the ashes (not literally) of the old Teatro Tenda, hosting to all kinds of music (including musicals).

Teatro Verdi, *see* above.

Tenax, Via Pratese 46, **t** 055 308160, *www.tenax.org.* A spacious venue on the outskirts of town, which is very popular and so usually gets crowded.

It stages lots of live rock concerts, with bands ranging from international names to local groups. DJs take over after the live music stops.

In the summer months lots of live music venues spring up all over the city, many of them free, for when the Florentines move outdoors in order to cool off.

Musicus Concentus, Piazza del Carmine 14, **t** 055 287347, *www.musicusconcentus.com*. A venue that attracts big-name jazz performers to Florence.

Cinemas

Summer is a great time to catch the latest films. English-language films are shown throughout the summer three evenings a week at the **Odeon** in Piazza Strozzi, and open-air screens are erected in several venues within Florence, showing two different films in Italian each evening from mid-June until mid-Sept. Details appear in the local newspapers.

The following show original language (usually English) films:

Odeon Cinehall, Piazza Strozzi, **t** 055 214068, *www.cinehall.it*. The latest releases on Mon, Tues and Thurs. *Closed Aug*.

Spazio Uno, Via del Sole 10, **t** 055 215634. Occasional original-language films.

Clubs

Many clubs have themed evenings; keep an eye out for posters or handouts or buy the listings magazine *Firenze Spettacolo*. Places are somewhat seasonal as well.

Caffè Decò, Piazza della Libertà 45–46r, **t** 055 571135. Elegant Art Deco surroundings, where Florence's swells put on the dog, often hosting live jazz. *Closed Mon*.

Caffè La Torre, Lungarno Cellini 65r, **t** 055 680643, *www.caffelatorre.it*. A small club that hosts regular jazz and Latin events.

Central Park, Parco delle Cascine, **t** 055 353505. Possibly the trendiest place in Florence during the summer months, full to bursting point with serious clubbers strutting their stuff to live music on three dancefloors. *Closed Sun and Mon*.

'Ex-Mud', Corso dei Tintori 4, **t** 055 263 8583, *www.exmud.it*. The old Mood club, revamped and given an appropriate new name. Still a cool venue, it is located below ground in a cavernous basement with a bar and a decent dance space. *Closed Mon and Tues*.

Girasol, Via del Romito 1, **t** 055 474948, *www.girasol.it*. The place for those into Latin sounds, north of the city, offering live bands and DJs who supply a good mix of Cuban, Flamenco, Brazilian, Caribbean and salsa rhythms. The space is small, so be sure to arrive early. *Closed Mon*.

Jazz Club, Via Nuova de' Caccini 3, **t** 055 247 9700. A small club with regular live jazz.

Lido, Lungarno Pecori Giraldi 1, **t** 055 234 2726. A small place in a pretty setting on the Arno, playing a wide variety of music to a mixed crowd. *Closed Mon*.

Mago Merlino, Via dei Pilastri 31r, **t** 055 242970. A relaxed tearoom and bar hosting live music, theatre, shows and games.

Maracanà, Via Faenza 4, **t** 055 210298, *www.maracana.it*. The place to come for live music with a Latin feel – samba, mambo and bossanova. *Closed June–Aug*.

Maramao, Via dei Macci 79r, **t** 055 244341. A slick and cool joint where the music played ranges from acid jazz to hip-hop and house. *Closed Mon*.

Rex Café, Via Fiesolana 23r, **t** 055 248 0331, *www.rexcafe.it*. The number one winter hotspot until Universale opened its doors, featuring an unusual decor, tapas, music and dancing. *Closed June–Aug*.

Rio Grande, Viale degli Olmi 1, **t** 055 331371, *www.riogrande.it*. A huge and hugely popular venue with an outside dancefloor in summer. The music is mostly Latin. *Closed Mon exc winter*.

Soulciety, Via San Zanobi 114b, **t** 055 830 3513. A relatively little-known dance venue popular with Florence's Senegalese community. It's a good alternative to the city's run-of-the-mill clubs and, with its rococo decor, has an exotic feel to it. *Closed Mon and June–Sept*.

Universale, Via Pisana 77r, *www. universalefirenze.it*
A vast ex-cinema, with designer decor, a restaurant, several bars and a pizzeria, all accompanied by live music and a giant cinema screen. Chic, sleek surroundings for a chic, sleek crowd, this is fast becoming the hottest hangout in town. *Closed Mon–Wed*.

Yab, Via Sassetti 5r, **t** 055 215160, *www.yab.it*. A place that has been around for a long time, as have some of the punters who hang out here – it is favoured by a decidedly older crowd. It has recently been completely redesigned and has a vast dance space and a great sound system. *Closed mid-June–Aug*.

Pubs

Irish pubs are big in Florence, and you will also find the odd English and Scottish version too.

The Fiddler's Elbow, Piazza Santa Maria Novella 7r, **t** 055 215056. One of the original pubs in Florence, with some live music and an expat atmosphere. It's a handy place to wait for a train and has a terrace on the *piazza*, but otherwise it's a bit grim.

James Joyce, Lungarno B. Cellini 1r, **t** 055 658 0856. An Irish pub with literary pretensions, the James Joyce enjoys a pleasant location with a big garden near the river. Books and magazines are on hand for browsing.

JJ Cathedral Pub, Piazza San Giovanni 44r, **t** 055 280260. A pub sitting in the shadow of the Duomo, with an almost authentic atmosphere. The single table on the tiny terrace overlooking the cathedral itself is much sought-after.

The Lion's Fountain, Borgo degli Albizi 34r, **t** 055 234 4412. A pleasant place that serves food until late.

Il Rifrullo, Via S. Niccolò 55r, **t** 055 234 2621. An older pub/wine bar; probably the most popular of all, and certainly one of the first to attract people to the Oltrarno. There's no word for 'cosy' in Italian, but the Rifrullo does the best it can.

Gay Clubs

There are a few gay clubs in Florence, including:

Crisco, Via Sant'Egidio 43r, **t** 055 248 0580. *Closed Tues*.

Il Piccolo Café, Borgo Santa Croce 23, **t** 055 200 1057. A minuscule, friendly, arty bar.

Silver Stud, Via della Fornace 9, **t** 055 688466, *www.silverstud.it*. A new bar in the Oltrano. *Closed Sun*.

Tabasco, Piazza Santa Cecilia 3r, **t** 055 213000, *www.tabascogay.it*. Italy's first gay bar, going since the 1970s.

Summer Venues

A torrid Florentine summer evening is no time to sit indoors (unless there's air-conditioning), and in summer, nightlife in Florence moves out of doors, with a series of venues opening up between late May and mid-Sept in some of the city's squares and open spaces. These venues usually offer food and drink and some kind of live entertainment. Admission is usually free.

Le Murate, Via dell'Agnolo, **t** 338 506 0253. A venue taking over the courtyard of a former prison, offering music and dancing, food, drink, film and live music.

Parterre, Piazza della Libertà. A club and live music venue.

Piazza Santissima Annunziata. Live music and dance, plus a bar and pizzeria, against the incomparable backdrop of Brunelleschi's loggia.

Le Rime Rampanti. A great spot overlooking the river above Piazza Poggi, with a bar, snacks and live music and dancing.

Nightclubs

Auditorium Flog, Via M Mercanti 24b, **t** 055 490437, *www.flog.it*. A favourite venue among students, usually packed to the gills.

Jackie O, Via dell'Erta Canina 24, **t** 055 234 2442. An old favourite for the 30ish crowd, including a piano bar. *Closed Mon, Tues and Wed*.

Space Electronic, Via Palazzuolo 37, **t** 055 293082, *www.spaceelectronic.net*. A high-tech noise box.

Tenax, Via Pratese 46, **t** 055 308160, *www.tenax.org*. An ultra-trendy spot hosting live music out near the airport. *Closed Sun–Wed and mid-May–Sept*.

A City with a View

Great-Aunt Florence, with her dour complexion and severe, lined face, never was much of a looker from street level, but she improves with a bit of distance – either mental or from one of her hilltop balconies: the Belvedere Fort, San Miniato, Piazzale Michelangelo, Bellosguardo, Fiesole or Settignano.

Belvedere Fort and Arcetri

One of Florence's best and closest balconies is the newly restored **Belvedere Fort**, a graceful, six-point star designed by Buontalenti and built in 1590–95, not so much for the sake of defence but to remind any remaining Florentine republicans who was boss. Since 1958 it has been used for special exhibitions, but you can usually enjoy unforgettable views of Florence and the surrounding countryside from its ramparts. Leading up to it is one of Florence's prettiest streets, **Costa San Giorgio**, which begins in Piazza Santa Felicità, just beyond the Ponte Vecchio.

In this part of Florence, the countryside, a rolling landscape of villas and gardens, olives and cypresses, begins right at the city wall. Via San Leonardo winds its way out towards Arcetri; a 10-minute walk will take you to the 11th-century **San Leonardo in Arcetri**. There is a wonderful 13th-century pulpit here, originally built for San Pier Scheraggio, and a small rose window, which was made according to legend from a wheel of Fiesole's *carroccio*, captured by Florence in 1125.

San Leonardo in Arcetri
usually open Sun mornings

Half a kilometre further, past the Viale Galileo crossroads, Via San Leonardo changes its name to Via Viviani, where it passes the **astrophysical observatory** and **Torre del Gallo**. Another 1km further on, Via Viviani reaches the settlement of **Pian de' Giullari**, where Galileo spent the last years of his life, in the 16th-century **Villa il Gioiello**, virtually under house arrest after his encounter with the Inquisition in 1631. Milton is believed to have visited him here.

San Miniato

San Miniato
open Mon–Sat 8–7, Sun 8–12.30 and 2–7

From Porta San Miniato you can walk up to San Miniato church on the stepped Via di San Salvatore al Monte, complete with the Stations of the Cross, or take the less pious bus 13 up the scenic Viale dei Colli from the station or Via de Benci, near Ponte alle Grazie. High on its monumental steps, San Miniato's beautiful, distinctive façade can be spotted from almost anywhere in the city, although relatively few visitors take the time to actually visit what is in fact one of the finest Romanesque churches in Italy.

San Miniato was built in 1015, over an earlier church that marked the spot where the head of St Minias, a 3rd-century Roman soldier, bounced when the Romans axed it off. Despite its distance from the centre, San Miniato has always been one of the churches dearest to Florentines' hearts. The remarkable geometric pattern of green, black and white marble that adorns its façade was begun in 1090, though funds only permitted the embellishment of the lower, simpler half of the front; the upper half, full of curious astrological symbolism (someone has written a whole book about it), was added in the 12th century, paid for by the Arte di Calimala, the guild that made a fortune buying bolts of fine wool, dyeing them a deep red or scarlet that no one else in Europe could imitate, then selling them back for twice the price; their proud gold eagle stands at the top of the roof. The glittering mosaic of Christ, the Virgin and St Minias, came slightly later.

The Calimala was also responsible for decorating the interior, an unusual design with a raised choir built over the crypt. As the Calimala became richer, so did the fittings; the delicate intarsia marble floor of animals and zodiac symbols dates from 1207. The lower walls were frescoed in the 14th and 15th centuries, including an enormous St Christopher. At the end of the nave stands Michelozzo's unique, free-standing **Cappella del Crocifisso**, built in 1448 to hold the crucifix that spoke to St John Gualberto (now in Santa Trínita); it is magnificently carved and adorned with terracottas by Luca della Robbia. Off the left nave is one of Florence's Renaissance showcases, the **chapel of the Cardinal of Portugal** (1461–6). The 25-year-old cardinal, a member of the Portuguese royal family, died in Florence at an auspicious moment, when the Medici couldn't spend enough money on publicly prominent art, and when some of the greatest artists of the quattrocento were at the height of their careers. The chapel was designed by Manetti, Brunelleschi's pupil; the ceiling exquisitely decorated with enamelled terracotta and medallions by Luca della Robbia; the Cardinal's tomb beautifully carved by Antonio Rossellino; the frescoed *Annunciation* charmingly painted by Alesso Baldovinetti; the altarpiece *Three Saints* is a copy of the original by Piero Pollaiuolo.

Up the steps of the choir more treasures await. The marble transenna and pulpit were carved in 1207, with art and a touch of medieval humour. Playful geometric patterns frame the mosaic in the apse, *Christ between the Virgin and St Minias*, made in 1297 by artists imported from Ravenna, and later restored by Baldovinetti. The colourful **sacristy** on the right was entirely frescoed by Spinello Aretino in 1387 but made rather flat by subsequent restoration. In the **crypt** an 11th-century altar holds the relics of St Minias; the columns are topped by ancient capitals. The **cloister** has frescoes of the Holy Fathers by Paolo Uccello, remarkable works in painstaking and fantastical perspective, rediscovered in 1925. The monks sing magical Gregorian chant every afternoon at about 4pm.

Florence Environs

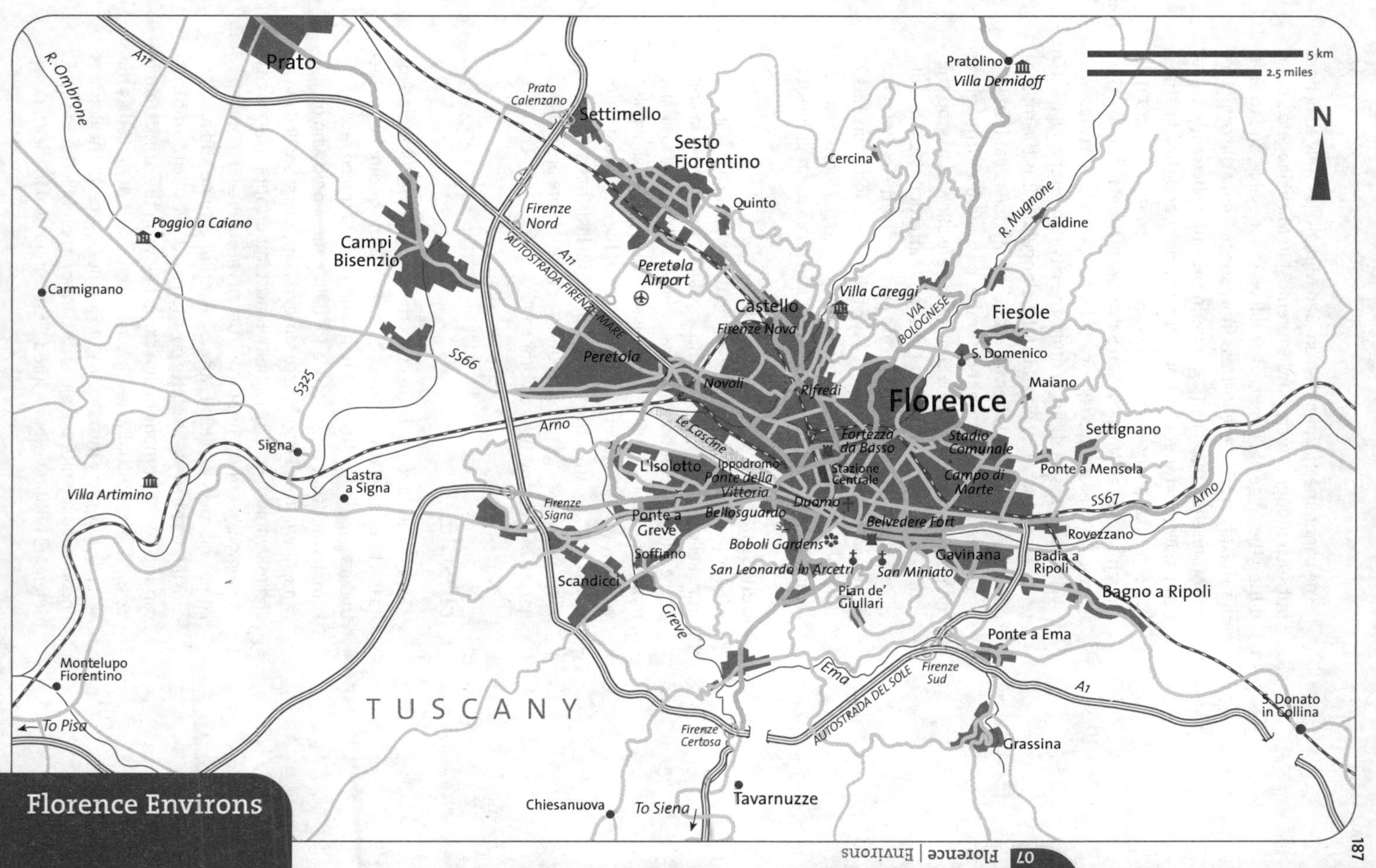

The panorama of Florence from San Miniato is lovely to behold, but such thoughts were hardly foremost in Michelangelo's mind during the Siege of Florence. The hill was vulnerable, and to defend it he hastily erected the fortress (now surrounding the cemetery left of the church), placed cannons in the unfinished 16th-century campanile (built to replace one that fell over), and shielded the tower from artillery with mattresses. He grew fond of the small church below San Miniato, **San Salvatore al Monte**, built by Cronaca in the late 1400s; he called it his 'pretty country lass'.

With these associations in mind, the city named the vast, square terrace car park below **Piazzale Michelangelo**; this is the most popular viewpoint only because it's the only one capable of accommodating an unlimited number of tour buses (though now there are restrictions on the time buses are allowed to stop, the situation has improved a bit). On Sunday afternoons, crowds of Florentines habitually make a stop here during their afternoon *passeggiata*. Besides another copy of the *David* and a fun, tacky carnival atmosphere rampant with souvenirs, balloons and ice cream, the Piazzale offers views that can reach as far as Pistoia.

Bellosguardo

Many people would argue that the finest view over Florence is from Bellosguardo, located almost straight up from Porta Romana at the end of the Boboli Gardens or Piazza Torquato Tasso. Non-mountaineers may want to take a taxi; the famous viewpoint, from where you can see every church façade in the city, is just before Piazza Bellosguardo. The area is a peaceful little oasis of superb villas and houses gathered round a square – there are no shops, bars or indeed anything commercial.

Fiesole

Florence liked to regard itself as the daughter of Rome, and in its fractious heyday explained its quarrelsome nature by the fact that its population from the beginning was of mixed race, of Romans and 'that ungrateful and malignant people who of old came down from Fiesole', according to Dante. First settled in the 2nd millennium BC, it became the most important Etruscan city in the region. Yet from the start Etruscan Faesulae's relationship with Rome was rocky, especially after sheltering Catiline and his conspirators in 65 BC. Its lofty position made Fiesole too difficult to capture, so the Romans built a camp below on the Arno to cut off its supplies. Eventually Fiesole was taken, and it dwindled as the camp below grew into the city of Florence – growth the Romans encouraged to spite the old Etruscans on their hill. This easily defended hill, however, ensured Fiesole's survival in the Dark Ages.

When times became safer, families moved back down to the Arno to rebuild Florence. They returned to smash up most of Fiesole after defeating it in 1125; since then the little town has remained aloof, letting Florence dominate and choke in its own juices far, far below.

But ever since the days of the *Decameron*, whose storytellers retreated to its garden villas to escape the plague, Fiesole has played the role of Florence's aristocratic suburb; its cool breezes, beautiful landscapes and belvedere views make it the perfect refuge from the torrid Florentine summers. There's no escaping the tourists, however; we foreigners have been tramping up and down Fiesole's hill since the days of Shelley. A day-trip has become an obligatory part of a stay in Florence, and although Fiesole has proudly retained its status as an independent *comune*, you can make the 20-minute trip up on Florence city bus 7 from the station or Piazza San Marco. If you have the time, walk up (or perhaps better, down) the old lanes bordered with villas and gardens to absorb some of the world's most civilized scenery.

Around Piazza Mino

The long sloping stage of Piazza Mino is Fiesole's centre, with the bus stop, the local tourist office, the cafés and the **Palazzo Pretorio**, its loggia and façade emblazoned with coats of arms. The square is named after a favourite son, the quattrocento sculptor Mino da Fiesole, whom Ruskin preferred to all others. An example of his work may be seen in the **Duomo**, with its plain façade dominating the north side of the *piazza*. Built in 1028, it was the only building spared by the vindictive Florentines in 1125. It was subsequently enlarged and given a scouring 19th-century restoration, leaving the tall, crenellated campanile its sole distinguishing feature. Still, the interior has an austere charm, with a raised choir over the crypt similar to San Miniato. Up the steps to the right are two works by Mino da Fiesole: the tomb of Bishop Leonardo Salutati and an altar front. The main altarpiece in the choir, *Madonna and Saints*, is by Lorenzo di Bicci, from 1440. Note the two saints frescoed on the columns; it was a north Italian custom to paint holy people as if they were members of the congregation. The crypt, with the remains of Fiesole's patron, St Romulus, is supported by columns bearing doves, spirals and other early Christian symbols.

Museo Bandini
t 055 59477; closed for restoration at time of writing

Located on Via Dupré, the **Bandini Museum** contains sacred works, including Della Robbia terracottas and trecento paintings by Lorenzo Monaco, Neri di Bicci and Taddeo Gaddi.

Archaeological Zone

Area archeologica
www.fiesolemusei.it

Behind the cathedral and museum is the entrance to what remains of Faesulae. Because Fiesole avoided trouble in the Dark Ages, its Roman monuments have survived in much better shape than those of Florence; although hardly spectacular, the ruins are charmingly set amid olive groves and cypresses. The small **Roman theatre** has survived well enough to host plays and concerts in the summer; Fiesole would like to remind you that in ancient times it had the theatre and plays while Florence had the amphitheatre and wild beast shows. Close by are the rather confusing remains of two superimposed temples, the baths and an impressive stretch of Etruscan walls (best seen from Via delle Mure Etrusche, below) that proved their worth against Hannibal's siege.

Teatro Romano
open summer daily 9.30–7; winter Wed–Mon 9.30–6; adm

The **archaeology museum**, in a small 20th-century Ionic temple, has early bronze figurines with flapper wing arms, Etruscan urns and stelae, including the 'stele Fiesolana' with a banquet scene.

Museo Archeologici
open summer daily 9.30–7; winter Wed–Mon 9.30–6

Walking around Fiesole

From Piazza Mino, Via S. Francesco ascends steeply (at first) to the hill that served as the Etruscan and Roman acropolis. Halfway up is a terrace with extraordinary views of Florence and the Arno sprawl, with a monument to the three *carabinieri* who gave themselves up to be shot by the Nazis in 1944 to prevent them from taking civilian reprisals. The church nearby, the **Basilica di Sant'Alessandro**, was constructed over an Etruscan/Roman temple in the 6th century, reusing its lovely *cipollino* (onion marble) columns and Ionic capitals, one still inscribed with an invocation to Venus.

At the top of the hill, square on the ancient acropolis, stands the monastery of **San Francesco**, its church containing a famous early cinquecento *Annunciation* by Raffaellino del Garbo and an *Immaculate Conception* by Piero di Cosimo. A grab-bag of odds and ends collected from the four corners of the world, especially Egypt and China, is displayed in the quaint **Franciscan missionary museum** in the cloister; it also has an Etruscan collection.

Museo Etnologico Missionario
open Tues–Fri 10–12 and 3–5, Sat and Sun 3–5

There are much longer walks to be had along the hill behind the Palazzo Pretorio. Panoramic Via Belvedere leads back to Via Adriano Mari, and in a couple of kilometres to the bucolic **Montececeri**, a wooded park where Leonardo da Vinci performed his flight experiments, and where Florentine architects once quarried their dark *pietra serena* from quarries now abandoned but open for exploration. In Borgunto, as this part of Fiesole is called, there are two 3rd-century BC **Etruscan tombs** on Via Bargellino; east of Borgunto, scenic Via Francesco Ferrucci and Via di Vincigliata pass by Fiesole's castles, the **Castel di Poggio**, site of summer concerts, and the **Castel di Vincigliata**, dating back to 1031. Further down is American critic Bernard Berenson's famous **Villa I Tatti**, which he left, along with a collection of Florentine art, to Harvard University as the Centre of Italian Renaissance Studies.

The road continues down towards **Ponte a Mensola** (6km from Fiesole) and Settignano, with buses back to Florence.

San Domenico di Fiesole

San Domenico is a pleasant walk from Fiesole towards Florence down Via Vecchia Fiesolana, a steep, narrow road that passes the privately owned **Villa Medici** (Via Beato Angelico 2), constructed by Michelozzo for Cosimo il Vecchio; Lorenzo and his friends of the Platonic Academy would come here to escape the world within its lovely gardens; it was also the childhood home of Iris Origo.

Villa Medici
open by appt, t 055 59417

San Domenico, at the bottom of the lane, is where Fra Angelico first entered his monkish world. The church of **San Domenico** (15th century) contains his *Madonna with Angels and Saints*, in a chapel on the left, and a photograph of his *Coronation of the Virgin*, which the French snapped up in 1809 and sent to the Louvre. Across the nave there's a *Crucifixion* by the school of Botticelli, an unusual composition of verticals highlighted by the cypresses in the background. In the chapterhouse of the monastery (ring the bell at No.4) Fra Angelico left a fine fresco *Crucifixion* and a *Madonna and Child*, which is shown with its sinopia, before moving down to Florence and San Marco.

Badia Fiesolana
open Mon–Fri 9–5, Sat 9–12

The lane in front of San Domenico leads to the **Badia Fiesolana**, Fiesole's cathedral, which was constructed in the 9th century by Fiesole's bishop, an Irishman named Donatus, and offers a fine view over the rolling countryside and Florence beyond. Although it was later enlarged, it preserves its original elegant façade, providing a charming example of the geometric black and white marble inlay decoration that characterizes Tuscan Romanesque churches, while the interior is adorned with *pietra serena* in the style of Brunelleschi. The ex-convent next door now houses the European University Institute.

Settignano

The least touristy hill above Florence is beneath the village of Settignano (bus 10 from the station or Piazza San Marco). The road passes **Ponte a Mensola**, Boccaccio's childhood home; it is believed he set scenes of the *Decameron* at the Villa Poggio Gherardo. A Scottish Benedictine named Andrew founded its church of **San Martino a Mensola** in the 9th century and was later canonized. The church was rebuilt in the 1400s, it has three trecento works: Taddeo Gaddi's *Triptych*, his son Agnolo's paintings on St Andrew's casket, and high altar triptych by the school of Orcagna. Quattrocento works include Neri di Bicci's *Madonna and Saints* and an *Annunciation* by a follower of Beato Angelico.

Settignano is one of Tuscany's great cradles of sculptors, having produced Desiderio da Settignano and Antonio and Bernardo Rossellino; Michelangelo too spent his childhood here, at the

Villa Buonarroti. The curious thing is that they left behind no work as a reminder; the good art in **Santa Maria** church is by Andrea della Robbia (an enamelled terracotta *Madonna and Child*) and Buontalenti (the pulpit). However, there are more splendid views to be had from **Piazza Desiderio**, and a couple of decent places to quaff a glass of Chianti.

Medici Villas

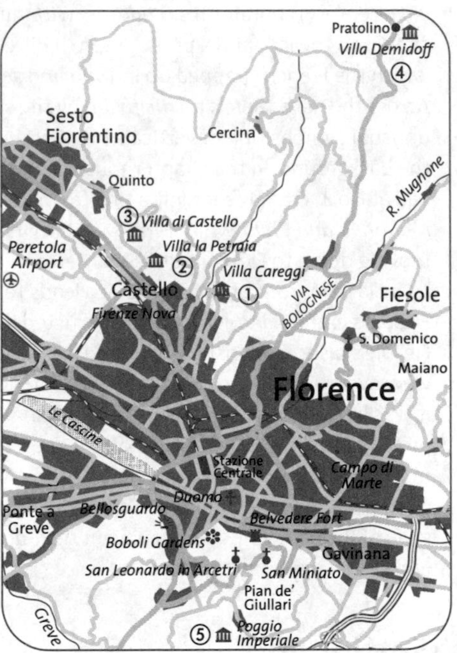

Like their Bourbon cousins in France, the Medici dukes whiled their time away acquiring new palaces for themselves, less as self-exaltation than as property speculation; they always thought generations ahead. As a result the countryside around Florence is littered with Medici villas, most now privately owned, though some are at least partly open to the public.

Villa Careggi

Villa Careggi
Viale Pieraccini 17, (bus 14C from station); open by appt, **t** *055 427 9755*

Perhaps the best-known of the villas is **Careggi** ①, originally a fortified farmhouse but enlarged for Cosimo il Vecchio by Michelozzo in 1434. In the 1460s this villa became synonymous with the birth of humanism. The greatest Latin and Greek scholars of the day, Ficino, Poliziano, Pico della Mirandola and Argyropoulos, would sometimes meet here with Lorenzo il Magnifico and hold philosophical discussions in imitation of a Platonic symposium, calling their informal society the Platonic Academy. It fizzled out when Lorenzo died. Cosimo il Vecchio and Piero had both died at Careggi and, when he felt the end was near, Lorenzo had himself carried out to the villa, with Poliziano and Pico della Mirandola as company. After Lorenzo died, the villa was burned down by Florentine republicans, though Cosimo I later had it rebuilt, and Francis Sloane had it restored.

Villa la Petraia

Villa la Petraia
Open April, May and Sept daily 8.15–6.30; June–Aug daily 8.15–7.30; Nov–Feb daily 8.15–4.30; Mar and Oct daily 8.15–5.30; exc 2nd and 3rd Mon of month. It's hard to reach: if you don't have a car, take a taxi or, if you are adventurous, bus 28 from the station, and get off after the wastelands, by Via Reginaldo Giuliano

Further west, amid the almost continuous conurbation of power lines and industrial landscapes that blight the Prato road, **Villa la Petraia** ② remained Arcadian on its steeply sloping hill. It was bought by Grand Duke Ferdinando I in 1557 and rebuilt by Buontalenti, keeping the tower of the original castle intact. Unfortunately Vittorio Emanuele II liked it as much as the Medici, and redesigned it to suit his relentlessly bad taste. Still, the interior is worthwhile for its ornate Baroque court, frescoed with a pastel history of the Medici by 17th-century masters Volterrano and Giovanni di San Giovanni; Vittorio Emanuele II added the glass roof to use the space as a ballroom. Of the remainder, you're most likely to remember the Chinese painting of Canton and the games room, with billiard tables as large as football fields and perhaps the world's first pinball machine, made of wood. A small room contains a most endearing statue by Giambologna, *Venus Wringing Water from Her Hair*. La Petraia's beautiful gardens and grounds, shaded by ancient cypresses, are open in the afternoon.

Villa di Castello

Villa di Castello
From La Petraia, turn right at Via di Castello and walk about 450m. Open (gardens only) April, May and Sept daily 8.15–6.30; June–Aug daily 8.15–7.30; Nov–Feb daily 8.15–4.30; Mar and Oct daily 8.15–5.30; exc 2nd and 3rd Mon of month

One of Tuscany's most famous gardens is down from La Petraia, at **Villa di Castello** ③, bought in 1477 by Lorenzo di Pierfrancesco and Giovanni de' Medici, cousins of Lorenzo Il Magnifico and Botticelli's best patrons, who hung it with his great mythological paintings now in the Uffizi. The villa was sacked in the 1530 siege then restored by Cosimo I; today it is the HQ of the Accademia della Crusca, dedicated to the study of the Italian language. The garden was laid out for Cosimo I by Tribolo, who also designed the fountain in the centre, with a statue, *Hercules and Antenaeus*, by Ammannati. Behind it is an artificial cavern, the **Grotto degli Animali**, filled by Ammannati and Giambologna with marvellous statues of every known creature, and lined with mosaics of pebbles and shells. The terrace above offers the best view over the garden's geometric patterns; a large statue by Ammannati of January, or *Gennaio*, emerges shivering from a pool among the trees.

A 20-minute walk north from Villa di Castello to **Quinto** are two unusual 7th-century BC **Etruscan tombs**. Neither has any art, but the chambers under their 7.5m artificial hills bear an odd relationship with ancient cultures elsewhere in the Med – domed *tholos* tombs as in Mycenaean Greece, corbelled passages like the *navetas* of Majorca, and entrances that look like the sacred wells of Sardinia.

Sesto Fiorentino

Change gear again by heading out a little further in the sprawl to Sesto Fiorentino, a suburb that since 1954 has been home to the famous Richard-Ginori china and porcelain firm. Founded in Doccia

Museo di Doccia
Via Pratese 31 (signposted); open Sept–July Wed–Sat 10–1 and 2–6; other days by appt; adm

in 1735, the firm offers a neat chronological exhibition of its production of Doccia ware, including many Medici commissions (a ceramic *Venus de' Medici*), fine painted porcelain, and some pretty Art Nouveau works, at the **Doccia Museum**.

Villa Demidoff at Pratolino

Villa Demidoff
Bus 25 leaves about every 20mins from Florence station; open April–Sept Thurs–Sun 10–7.30; Mar and Oct Sun 10–6; adm April–Sept Sat and Sun

It was to the village of Pratolino 12km north of Florence along Via Bolognese that Duke Francesco I bought the **Villa Demidoff** ④ in 1568 as a gift to his mistress, the Venetian Bianca Cappello. He commissioned Buontalenti – artist, architect and hydraulics engineer – to design the vast gardens, making Pratolino the marvel of its day, full of water tricks, ingenious automata and a famous menagerie. Sadly, none of Buontalenti's delights have survived, but the largest ever example of this play between art and environment has – Giambologna's massive *Appennino*, a giant rising from stone, part stalactite, part fountain himself, conquering the dragon, said to be symbolic of the Medici's origins in the Mugello just north of here. The rest of the park, made into an English garden by the Lorena family and named for Prince Paolo Demidoff who bought it in 1872 and restored Francesco's servants' quarters as his villa, is an invitingly cool refuge from a Florentine summer afternoon.

Poggio a Caiano

Poggio a Caiano
CAP buses go past every 30mins, departing from in front of McDonald's on north side of Florence station; open April, May and Sept daily 8.15–5.30; June–Aug daily 8.15–6.30; Nov–Feb daily 8.15–3.30; Mar and Oct daily 8.15–4.30; exc 2nd and 3rd Mon of month; adm

Of all the Medici villas, Poggio a Caiano is the most evocative of the country idylls so delightfully described in the verses of Lorenzo il Magnifico; this was not only his favourite retreat but is generally considered the very first Italian Renaissance villa. Lorenzo bought a farmhouse here in 1480, and commissioned Giuliano da Sangallo to rebuild it in a classical style. It was Lorenzo's sole architectural commission, and its classicism matched the mythological nature poems he composed here, most famously 'L'Ambra', inspired by the stream Ombrone that flows nearby.

Sangallo designed the villa according to Alberti's description of the perfect country house in a style that presages Palladio, and added a classical frieze on the façade, sculpted with the assistance of Andrea Sansovino (now replaced with a copy). Some of the other features – the clock, the curved stair and central loggia – were later additions. In the interior Sangallo designed an airy, two-storey *salone*, which the two Medici popes had frescoed by 16th-century masters Pontormo, Andrea del Sarto, Franciabigio and Allori. The subject, as usual, is Medici self-glorification, and the frescoes depict family members dressed as Romans in historical scenes that parallel events in their lives. In the right lunette, around a large circular window, Pontormo painted the lovely *Vertumnus and Pomona* (1521), a languid summer scene under a willow tree, beautifully coloured. In another room, Francesco I and Bianca

Cappello, his wife, died in 1587, only 11 hours apart; Francesco was always messing with poisons but in fact a nasty virus was the probable killer. In the grounds are fine old trees and a 19th-century statue celebrating Lorenzo's 'L'Ambra'.

Carmignano and Villa Artimino

San Michele
open daily 7.30–5 (until 6 in summer)

A local bus continues 5km southwest of Poggio a Caiano to the village of **Carmignano**, which has, in its **church of San Michele**, Pontormo's uncanny painting *The Visitation* (1530s), a masterpiece of Florentine Mannerism. There are no concessions to naturalism here – the four soulful, ethereal women, draped in Pontormo's customary startling colours, barely touch the ground, standing before a scene as substantial as a stage backdrop. The result is one of the most unforgettable images produced in the 16th century.

Tomba di Montefortini
open summer Fri and Sat 9–6; winter Mon–Sat 8–2

Also to the south, at **Comeana** (3km, signposted), is the well-preserved Etruscan **Tomba di Montefortini**, a 7th-century BC burial mound, 10.5m high and 79m in diameter, covering two chambers. A long hall leads to the vestibule and tomb chamber, both covered with false vaulting; the latter preserves a shelf most probably used for gifts for the afterlife. Nearby, the equally impressive **Tomba dei Boschetti** was seriously damaged over centuries by local farmers.

Villa Artimino
***villa** open for guided tours Tues, **t** 055 871 8124; **museum** open Feb–Oct Mon, Tues and Thurs–Sat 9.30–12.30, Sun 10–12, Wed by appt; Nov–Jan Sun 10–12, plus Thurs–Sat by appt; adm*

The Etruscan city of **Artimino**, 4km to the west, was destroyed by the Romans and is now the site of a small town and another Medici property, the **Villa Artimino** ('La Ferdinanda'), built as hunting lodge for Ferdinando I by Buontalenti. Its semi-fortified air with buttresses was aimed to fit its sporting purpose, but the total effect is simple and charming, with the long roofline punctuated by innumerable chimneys and a graceful stair, added in the 19th century from a drawing by the architect in the Uffizi. There is an **Etruscan archaeological museum** in the basement, containing findings from the tombs; among them a unique censer with two basins and a boat, bronze vases, and a red figured krater painted with initiation scenes, found in a 3rd-century tomb.

Also in Artimino is an attractive Romanesque church, **San Leonardo**, built of stones salvaged from earlier buildings.

Poggio Imperiale and the Certosa del Galluzzo

Villa di Poggio Imperiale
*open Sept–July Wed by request, **t** 055 220151*

One last villa open for visits, the **Villa di Poggio Imperiale** ⑤, lies south of Florence, at the summit of Viale del Poggio Imperiale, which leaves Porta Romana with a stately escort of cypress sentinels. Cosimo I grabbed this huge villa from the Salviati family in 1565, and it remained a ducal property until there were no longer any dukes to duke. Its neoclassical façade was added in 1808, and the audience chamber was decorated in the 17th century by the underrated Rutilio Manetti and others. Much of the villa is now used as a girls' school.

Certosa del Galluzzo
open summer Tues–Sun 9–11 and 3–6; winter Tues–Sun 9–11 and 3–5

The **Certosa del Galluzzo** (also known as the Certosa di Firenze) lies further south, scenically located on a hill off the Siena road (take bus 36 or 37 from the station). Founded as a Carthusian monastery by 14th-century tycoon Niccolò Acciaiuoli, it has been inhabited since 1958 by Cistercians; there are 12 now living there, one of whom takes visitors around. The Certosa has a fine 16th-century courtyard and an uninteresting church, though the crypt-chapel of the lay choir contains some impressive tombs. The **Chiostro Grande**, surrounded by the monks' cells, is decorated with 66 majolica *tondi* of prophets and saints by Giovanni della Robbia and assistants; one cell is opened for visits, and it seems almost cosy. The Gothic **Palazzo degli Studi**, intended by the founder as a school, contains five lunettes by Pontormo, painted while he and his pupil Bronzino hid out here from the plague in 1522.

Where to Stay around Florence

ⓘ Fiesole > *Via Portigiani 3, t 055 598720 or t 055 597 8373, www.comune.fiesole.fi.it*

★ Villa San Michele >

Fiesole ✉ 50014

Many frequent visitors to Florence wouldn't stay anywhere else: it's cooler and quieter here, and at night the city far below twinkles as if made of fairylights.

*******Villa San Michele**, Via Doccia 4, **t** 055 567 8200 (€€€€€). A hotel built as a monastery in the 15th century, and an unbeatable choice if money happens to be no object, set in a breathtaking location just below Fiesole, with a façade and loggia reputedly designed by Michelangelo himself. After suffering bomb damage during the Second World War, it was carefully reconstructed to create one of the most beautiful hotels in Italy, set in a lovely Tuscan garden, complete with a pool. Each of its 46 rooms is richly and elegantly furnished and air-conditioned; the more plush suites have Jacuzzis. The food is delicious, and the reasons to go down to Florence begin to seem insignificant; a stay here is complete in itself. Paradise, however, comes at a price. *Closed 19 Nov–21 Mar.*

******Villa Aurora**, Piazza Mino 38, **t** 055 59368, toll free **t** 800 980613 *www.villaaurora.net* (€€€€). An agreeable 19th-century villa right on Fiesole's famous *piazza*, from where the no.7 bus whisks you down to central Florence in 20mins. The 25 air-conditioned bedrooms have rustic antiques and splendid views over the city, but some of the bathrooms are poky. There is a restaurant – on a terrace overlooking Florence in the summer – and the bar next door (noisy at times) is under the same ownership. There's parking too.

*****Villa Fiesole**, Via Beato Angelico 35, **t** 055 597252, *www.villafiesole.it* (€€€€). A new hotel that was once part of the San Michele convent, and shares part of its driveway with the hotel of the same name. The smart, neoclassical-style interiors are variations on a fresh blue and yellow colour scheme. Light meals are served in a sunny dining room or on the terrace, and there is a fabulous pool with views. The facilities (and prices) here are decidedly four-star.

*****Pensione Bencistà**, Via Benedetto di Maiano 4, **t** 055 59163, *www.bencista.com* (€€€). Another former monastery with views from its flower-decked terrace that are every bit as good as those at Villa San Michele; the welcome is more friendly. The bedrooms, each different from the next, are all comfortably furnished with solid antiques. The three little sitting rooms are inviting in cooler weather when fires are lit. Half- and full-board is available for a reasonable price. Credit cards aren't accepted.

Le Cannelle, Via Gramsci 52–6, **t** 055 597 8336, *www.lecannelle.com* (€€). A friendly new B&B run by two sisters on the main street. Rooms are comfortably rustic and there is a pretty breakfast room.

*__Villa Baccano__, Via Bosconi 4, **t** 055 59341, *www.villabaccano.it* (€). A villa in the hills 2km out of the centre of Fiesole, in a lovely garden setting.

*__Villa Sorriso__, Via Gramsci 21, **t** 055 59027, *www.albergovillasorriso.com* (€). An unpretentious, comfortable hotel in the centre of Fiesole, with a terrace overlooking Florence.

Camping Panoramico Fiesole, Via Peramonda 1, **t** 055 599069, *www.florencecamping.com*. A beautifully situated campsite just above Fiesole on a hill with fabulous views over Florence, but packed and expensive in summer.

Villas in the Florentine Hills

If you're driving, you may consider lodging outside the city, where parking is hassle-free and the summer heat is less intense.

Luxury (€€€€€)

*****__Grand Hotel Villa Cora__, Viale Machiavelli 18–20, **t** 055 229 8451, *www.villacora.it*. An opulent 19th-century mansion set in a beautiful formal garden overlooking the Oltrarno, near Piazzale Michelangelo. Built by Baron Oppenheim, it later served as the residence of the wife of Napoleon III, Empress Eugénie. Its conversion to a hotel has dimmed little of its splendour; some of the bedrooms boast frescoed ceilings and lavish 19th-century furnishings, and all are air-conditioned and have *frigo-bars*, and there's a pretty swimming pool. In the summer, meals are served in the garden, and there's a fine view of Florence from the roof terrace. Wifi access is available.

*****__Villa La Massa__, Via La Massa 6, **t** 055 62611, *www.villalamassa.com*. A lovely choice, up the Arno some 6km from Florence at Candeli. This is the former 15th-century villa of Count Giraldi, and it retains the old dungeon (which now houses one of the two restaurants), the family chapel (now a bar), and other early Renaissance amenities, with modern features such as tennis courts, a swimming pool, a beauty salon and air-con. The recently refurbished interiors are fit for a Renaissance princeling, and there's dining and dancing by the Arno in the summer, a shady garden, and a hotel bus to whizz you into the city. The food is excellent.

****__Torre di Bellosguardo__, Via Roti Michelozzi 2, **t** 055 229 8145, *www.torrebellosguardo.com*. A tower built at Bellosguardo in the 15th century, plus a villa added later, enjoying one of the most breathtaking views over the city. The tower was purchased by the Cavalcanti, friends of Dante, and the villa added below it; after that, Cosimo I confiscated it, the Michelozzi purchased it from the Medici, Elizabeth Barrett Browning wrote about it, and finally, in 1988, it opened its doors as a small hotel. There are frescoes by Baroque master Poccetti in the entrance hall, and fine antiques adorn the rooms, each of which is unique and fitted out with a modern bath. The large, beautiful terraced garden has a pool. For a splurge, reserve the two-level tower suite, with fabulous views in four directions. Superb formal gardens look down to the city below, and lunch is served around the pool. Food and wine courses are also organized.

Very Expensive (€€€€)

****__Paggeria Medicea__, Viale Papa Giovanni XXIII, Artimino, near Carmignano, **t** 055 871 8081, *www.artimino.com*. The refurbished outbuildings of Grand Duke Ferdinand's villa, where you can play the Medici. It offers some unusual amenities – a hunting reserve and a lake stocked with fish, and a farm producing oil and wine. There's also a pool and tennis court, and many of the pleasant modern rooms have balconies (all are air-conditioned). There are some apartments. A short walk across the gardens brings you to the restaurant **Biagio Pignatta**, which specializes in Medici dishes, in the former butcher's quarters.

***__Villa Le Rondini__, Via Vecchia Bolognese 224, **t** 055 400081, *www.villalerondini.it*. Several buildings in a pleasant setting 7km north of Florence, surrounded by olive and cypress trees. The most interesting rooms are in the 16th-century villa. There is a very pleasant swimming pool. Full and half board are available; the restaurant specializes in central Italian recipes.

*****Villa Villoresi**, Via Campi 2, Colonnata di Sesto Fiorentino, **t** 055 443212, *www.villavilloresi.it*. Contessa Cristina Villoresi's family home, forming a lovely oasis in the middle of one of Florence's more un-lovely suburb. It hasn't been too pristinely restored, retaining much of its slightly faded appeal as well as its frescoed ceilings, antiques and chandeliers. The villa boasts the longest loggia in Tuscany, to which five of the grandest bedrooms have direct access. Other rooms are a good deal plainer and somewhat cheaper. There is a pool and a restaurant serving Tuscan cuisine.

Villa Poggio San Felice, Via S. Matteo Arcetri 24, **t** 055 220016, *www.villapoggiosanfelice.com*. A delightful alternative to city hotels –a 15th-century villa on a hill just south of Porta Romana, near the observatory, offering bed and breakfast. It was once owned by a Swiss hotel magnate, whose descendants have restored the house and gardens (designed by Porcinaie) and opened them up to guests. There are five double bedrooms, all furnished with family antiques, and all with stunning views. There is also a small pool, and a bus service to and from Florence. *Closed Dec–Feb*.

Expensive (€€€)

*****Hermitage**, Via Gineparia 112, Bonistallo, **t** 055 877040, *www. hotel hermitageprato.it*. A fine, quiet, affordable choice for families, several miles from Florence, near Poggio a Caiano. There's a pool in the grounds and air-conditioned rooms.

Eating Out around Florence

Bibé, Via delle Bagnese 1r, **t** 055 204 9085 (€€€€). An old farmhouse with a lovely garden a couple of kilometres south of Porta Romana. Try the *pappardelle* with rabbit sauce, *ribollita*, lasagne with artichokes and *caciocavallo* cheese; grilled guinea fowl; or grilled chicken. Desserts here are creative and divine. They also sell local products. *Closed Wed, Thurs lunch, 3wks Nov, 3wks Feb*.

Biagio Pignatta, Artimino, near Carmignano, **t** 055 875 1406, (€€€). A place near the Medici villa in Artimino, named after a celebrated Medici chef, serving Tuscan dishes with a Renaissance flavour, using products directly from the farm. The terrace overlooks vines and olives. Book ahead. *Closed Wed, and Thurs lunch in winter, plus 3wks Nov*.

Centanni, Via di Centanni, Bagno a Ripoli, **t** 055 630122 (€€€). A spot east of Florence, set in an olive grove, with a lovely terrace. Dishes are along traditional lines – home-made pasta with pigeon or wild boar sauce, *bistecca*, chicken or brains – and there is an excellent 400-strong wine list. *Closed Sat and Sun eve, and Mon*.

Da Delfina, Via della Chiesa, Artimino, near Carmignano, **t** 055 871 8074, (€€€). A place worth the drive out for its enchanting surroundings, lovely views, charming atmosphere and sublime Tuscan cooking, including home-made tagliatelle with a sauce made from greens, risotto with vegetables, and rabbit with olives and pine nuts. There's outdoor seating. Only cash is accepted, and booking is advisable. *Closed Mon, and 3wks Aug*.

Omero, Via Pian de' Giuliari 11r, **t** 055 220053 (€€€). A rustic restaurant a 10min taxi ride from the centre of town, the main attraction of which is the wonderful view from the picture windows, over hills dotted with elegant villas, olive groves and cypresses – make sure you get a table in the top room. The typically Tuscan food is reliable without being exceptional, and the atmosphere is old-fashioned. *Closed Tues*.

Entertainment around Florence

Scuola di Musica di Fiesole, Villa la Torraccia, San Domenico, Fiesole, **t** 055 597851, *www. scuolamusica.fiesole.fi.it*. One of the best-known music schools in Italy, which promotes a series of chamber music concerts.

Chianti and the Mugello

Chianti to the south and the Mugello to the north of Florence, one world-famous region and one obscure, are delightfully rural and endowed with every Tuscan charm. No Brunelleschi could have designed the grand stone farmhouses that crown every hill, offering endless variations of arches, loggias and towers, amidst an equally endless variety of rolling hills, vineyards, olives and cypresses. Towns are few, monuments scattered and of minor interest, paintings and sculpture very rare. But you'll find few places more enchanting to explore – by car, by bicycle, by foot – in a day or a lifetime.

08

Don't miss

1. Wine-tasting
Around Greve in Chianti p.209

2. Quattrocento charms
Castellina in Chianti p.209

3. The Iron Baron's castle
Castello di Brolio p.212

4. Breathtaking views
Passo della Futa p.215

5. A Florentine outpost in the Mugello
Scarperia p.216

See map overleaf

Chianti and the Mugello
N
10 km
5 miles
Roncobilaccio
Firenzuola
Montecarelli
Barberino di Mugello
Scarperia
S. Piero a Sieve
Borgo S. Lorenzo
Vaiano
R. Bisenzio
Monti d. Calvana
A1
S65
S503
S302
R. Lamone
Marradi
S551
S67
S. Godenzo
Alpe di San Benedetto
M. Senario
Prato
Sesto Fiorentino
Pratolino
R. Mugnone
A11
Campi Bisenzio
Florence
Fiesole
S325
Signa
Scandicci
Pontassieve
R. Sieve
M. Falterona
Pso. d. Calla
S310
Stia
Pratovecchio
Casentino
Poppi
Bibbiena
M. Penna
E45
M. Secchieta
Pratomagno
S. Donato in Collina
S. Polo in Chianti
Incisa in Val d'A.
Strada in Chianti
R. Pesa
Cerbaia
S. Casciano in Val di Pesa
Mercatale in Val di Pesa
R. Greve
S222
TUSCANY
Castelfranco di Sopra
Greve in Chianti
S69
Tavarnelle in Val di Pesa
Barberino Val d'Elsa
S. Donato in Poggio
S. Giovanni Valdarno
Monti del Chianti
Montevarchi
Castiglion Fibocchi
Subbiano
R. Arno
S71
Caprese Michelangelo
S429
R. Elsa
S2
Pietrafitta
Radda in Chianti
Badia Coltibuono
Poggibonsi
Castellina in Chianti
Arezzo
S73
Foce di Scopetone
Colle di Val d'Elsa
R. Arbia
S484
Cast. di Brolio
Ambra
Civitella in Val Chiana
Monteriggioni
S408
Siena
Dovadola
Predappio
Predappio Alta
Rocca San Casciano
Portico di Romagna
EMILIA-ROMAGNA
Santa Sofia
Bagno di Romagna
Badia Prataglia
p.220
p.352
p.372
p.396
SLOVENIA
CROATIA
BOSNIA-HERZ.
FRANCE
Corsica
Sardinia
Sicily
Don't miss
1 Greve in Chianti p.209
2 Castellina in Chianti p.209
3 Castello di Brolio p.212
4 Passo della Futa p.215
5 Scarperia p.216

Chianti

From good Chianti, an aged wine, majestic and imperious, that passes through my heart and chases away without trouble every worry and grief...
Francesco Redi, *Bacchus in Tuscany*

In the 17th century, naturalist and poet Francesco Redi was the first to note the virtues of 'Florentine red' from Chianti; since then Italians have invested a lot of worry into defining what 'Chianti' means. The name apparently derives from an Etruscan family named Clanti; geographically it refers, roughly, to the hilly region between Florence and Siena, bordered by the Florence–Siena Superstrada del Palio and the A1 from Florence to Arezzo. The part within Siena province is known as *Chianti Storico* or *Chianti Geografico*, once the territories of the Lega del Chianti, a consortium of barons formed in 1385 to protect their interests (and their wine).

But Chianti is an oenological name as well as a geographical one, and, as such, first became official in 1716, when Grand Duke Cosimo III defined which parts of Tuscany could call their vintage Chianti, in effect making wine history – it was the first time a wine had its production area delimited. The Lorraine grand dukes promoted advances in wine-making techniques and the export of Chianti.

Yet the Chianti as we know it had yet to be developed, and it was largely the creation of one man – the 'Iron Baron', Bettino Ricasoli, briefly the second PM of unified Italy. The baron was very wealthy but not handsome, and Luigi Barzini, in *The Italians*, recounts how jealous he became when his new bride was asked to dance at a ball. Without ado, he ordered her into their carriage and told the driver to take her to the ancient family seat at Brolio in the Monti del Chianti – an isolated castle the poor woman rarely left ever after.

To pass the time the baron began to experiment with different vines and processes, eventually hitting upon a pleasing mix of red Sangiovese and Canaiolo grapes, with a touch of white Malvasia. Meanwhile, the famous dark green flask , the *strapeso*, was invented, with its straw covering woven by local women. The end product took the Paris Exhibition of 1878 by storm; imitators soon appeared and, in 1924, the boundaries of Chianti Storico were more than doubled to create Chianti Classico, drawn by local producers to protect the wine's name, adopting the now familiar black cockerel as its symbol. In 1967 Chianti Classico, with Tuscany's six other Chianti vinicultural zones, was given its *denominazione di origine* status. Production soared, but quality and sales declined. To improve it, the Chianti Classico Consortium was upscaled to a DOCG rating to guarantee that all wines bearing the black cockerel would be tested and approved by a panel of judges.

But it was tales of Elizabeth Barrett Browning quaffing Chianti and finding her inspiration in its ruby splendour, as well as the sunny rural elegance of the region, that attracted first the English and Dutch, then Swiss, Americans, French and Germans, especially in the 1960s and 1970s; they form one of Italy's densest foreign

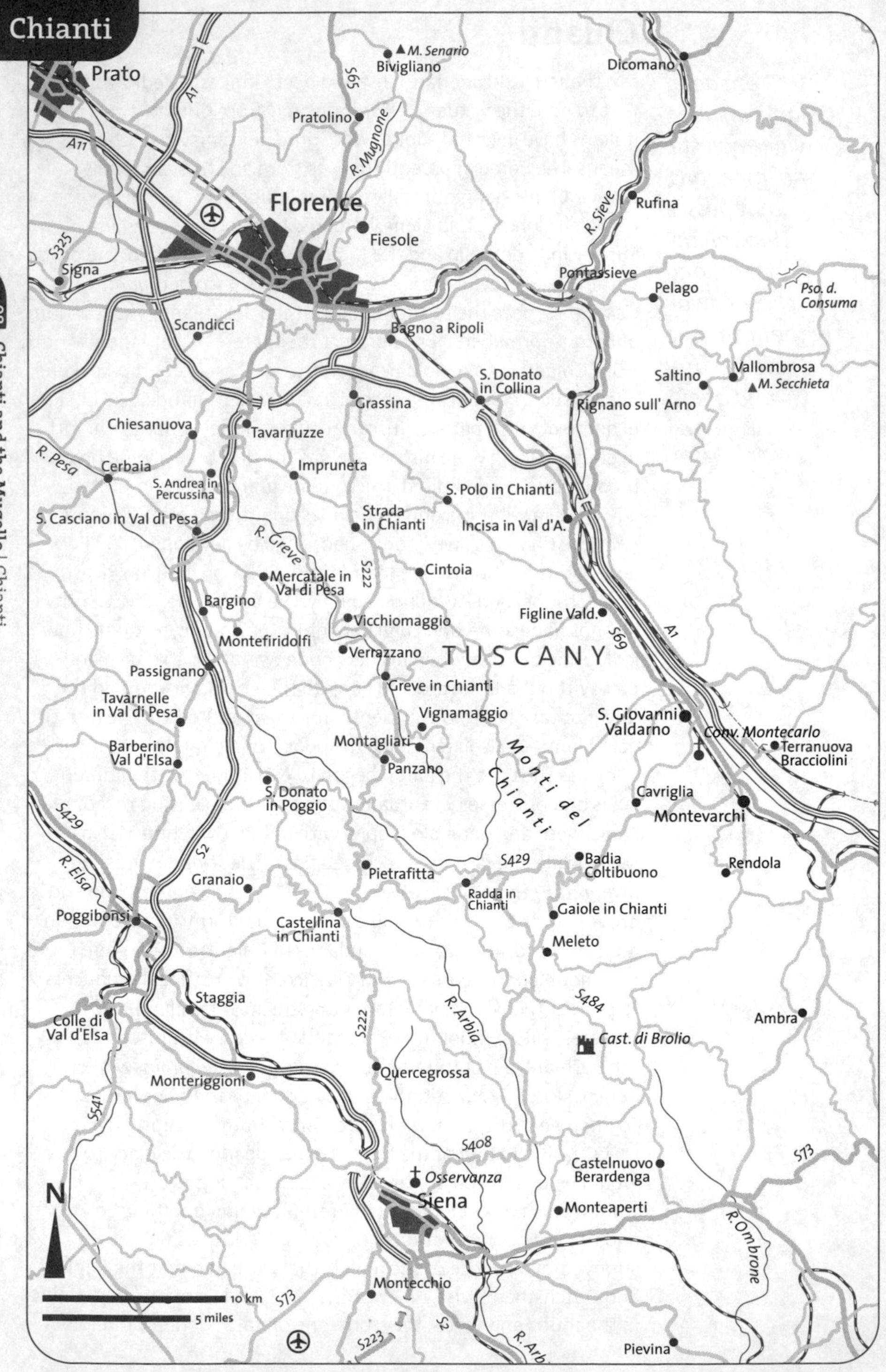

Prato
M. Senario
Bivigliano
Dicomano
A1
S65
Pratolino
R. Mugnone
A11
Florence
R. Sieve
Rufina
S325
Fiesole
Signa
Pontassieve
Pelago
Pso. d. Consuma
Scandicci
Bagno a Ripoli
S. Donato in Collina
Saltino
Vallombrosa
M. Secchieta
Grassina
Rignano sull' Arno
Chiesanuova
Tavarnuzze
R. Pesa
Cerbaia
Impruneta
S. Andrea in Percussina
S. Polo in Chianti
S. Casciano in Val di Pesa
Strada in Chianti
Incisa in Val d'A.
R. Greve
S222
Cintoia
Mercatale in Val di Pesa
Bargino
Figline Vald.
Vicchiomaggio
Montefiridolfi
S69
Verrazzano
TUSCANY
Passignano
Greve in Chianti
Tavarnelle in Val di Pesa
Vignamaggio
S. Giovanni Valdarno
Montagliari
Conv. Montecarlo
Terranuova Bracciolini
Barberino Val d'Elsa
Panzano
Monti del Chianti
S. Donato in Poggio
Cavriglia
S429
Montevarchi
R. Elsa
S2
Badia Coltibuono
Rendola
Pietrafitta
Granaio
Radda in Chianti
Poggibonsi
Castellina in Chianti
Gaiole in Chianti
Meleto
S484
Staggia
R. Arbia
Colle di Val d'Elsa
Ambra
Cast. di Brolio
Quercegrossa
Monteriggioni
S541
S408
S73
Castelnuovo Berardenga
Osservanza
N
Siena
Monteaperti
R. Ombrone
Montecchio
10 km
5 miles
S223
R. Arbia
Pievina

Getting around Chianti

Getting around by **bus** is fairly easy in Chianti, though you may not always find connections between two towns very convenient; from Florence, SITA buses (**t** 055 47821, *www.sitabus.it*) go to Greve (25km/45min), Gaiole (55km/90min), Castellina in Chianti (44km/1hr), Mercatale, S. Casciano in Val di Pesa (17km/25min), Tavarnelle Val di Pesa (29km/40min), Panzano, Strada, and Radda (42km/1hr); CAP buses run frequently from Florence to Impruneta (14km/20min). From Siena TRA-IN buses (**t** 057 204111, *www.trainspa.it*) go to Castellina (20km/25min), Radda (30km/40min), Tavarnelle (38km/50min) and S. Casciano (49km/90min), Tavarnuzze and Strada.

The two main north–south routes through Chianti, the old Roman Via Cassia (SS2) and the Chiantigiana (SS222), rival one another in beauty. An ideal **motoring wine tour** would take in the east–west SS429 between the Badia a Coltibuono and Castellina. The distances aren't very great, though the single-lane winding routes make for fairly leisurely travel.

colonies, wryly nicknamed 'Chianti-shire'. The newcomers brought more money than Chianti's mouldering barons and contessas had seen since the Renaissance; property prices shot to the moon.

But just when this enchanting region was getting ready to nod off, a small band of wine-makers, looking towards Bordeaux and thinking their wines could be just as good, started to break the DOCG rules. Planting Cabernet Sauvignon, Cabernet Franc and Merlot in Chianti was heresy enough, but in the early 1970s two estates began selling with them as *vino da tavola* (although hardly at *vino da tavola* prices): Tenuta San Guido's Sassicaia (75% Cabernet Sauvignon, 25% Cabernet Franc) and Antinor's Tiganello (80% Sangiovese and 20% Cabernet Sauvignon). The Super-Tuscan revolution was born, and Chianti, instead of retiring, has become one of the hottest wine regions in Europe.

Some 800 farms and estates (only a selection of the most historic are listed in this chapter) produce wine in the 70,000 hectares of the Chianti Classico zone, and one of the chief pleasures is trying as many labels as possible – with the different mixtures of grapes, different soils and bottling methods, each should be, or at least strives to be, individual. Nor do estates limit themselves to Chianti; many produce *vinsanto*, a white called Bianca della Lega, and many reds, as well as Chianti's other speciality, a delicate olive oil. Before setting out to any of them, call to check hours.

Western Chianti: Florence to Tavarnelle Val di Pesa

Santa Caterina dell'Antella
open Mon–Sat

Chianti begins 10km to the south of Florence, but on the way there you may want to follow the sign west off the SS222 just past the *autostrada*, to get to **Ponte a Ema** and the prettily sited 14th-century chapel of the Alberti, **Santa Caterina dell'Antella** with its contemporary frescoes on St Catherine's life, one of Spinello Aretino's greatest works.

Further along, at Grassina, there's a turn-off to **Impruneta**, a large town on a plateau noted for its terracotta tiles (including those on Brunelleschi's dome) and pottery, which is very much on sale, especially during St Luke's horse and mule fair in October. The fair takes place in the main piazza, in the shadow of Impruneta's pride and joy, the Collegiata, built to house a miraculous icon of the *Madonna and Child* attributed to St Luke, dug up by a team of oxen in the 10th century. After the Collegiata was bombed in the last war, restorers brought it back to its Renaissance appearance to match its two beautiful chapels, both designed by Michelozzo and richly decorated with enamel terracottas by Luca della Robbia. One houses the icon and the other a piece of the True Cross. In an adjacent chapel is a marble relief, the *Finding of the Icon*, by the school of Donatello; the bronze crucifix in the nave is attributed to Giambologna. The campanile dates from the 13th century, and the fine portico from 1634. Among the many terracotta shops, **Artenova** has creative designs and a good selection of gifts.

Artenova
Via della Fonte 76, t 055 201 1060

Macchiavelli in Exile, and Artistic Links

From the SS222 south of Florence, a byroad leads west from Tavarnuzze (8km) to **Sant'Andrea in Percussina**, long the country fief of the Macchiavelli. Here Niccolò spent his tedious exile, which he described in a letter as whiling away the day in his tavern 'playing at *cricca* and tric-trac, and this gave rise to a thousand arguments and endless exchanges of insults, most of the time there is a fight over a penny... and so surrounded by these lice, I blow the cobwebs from my brain and relieve the unkindness of my fate'. In the evening he would retire to work on *The Prince*. You can still eat and drink in the tavern (*see* opposite) and there's a small museum devoted to his life.

Near Chiesanuova, to the north, the 16th-century **Palazzo al Bosco**, attributed by some to Michelangelo, is a villa built atop a 13th-century structure. The stately, theatrical 15th-century **Villa Tattoli** to the west (on the Chiesanuova–Cerbaia road) features two levels of arcades.

Near Cerbaia, 5km from San Casciano, **Villa Talente** is the former property of the artists who built Orsanmichele in Florence; you can buy Chianti, white wine and olive oil there.

Villa Talente
t 055 825 9484; call for opening hrs

Where to Stay and Eat in Western Chianti

In this part of Chianti, hotels tend to be on the small side and annexed to restaurants.

It's worth knowing that many of the larger wine estates let a few guestrooms or apartments.

For Villa la Massa in Candeli and Centanni in Bagno a Ripoli, *see* p.197 and p.198 respectively.

ⓘ Impruneta >>
Piazza Buondelmonti 29, t 055 231 3729, www.proimpruneta.rtd.it

Impruneta ✉ 50023

B&B Benedetta Bianchi, Via Paolieri 26, t 055 231 2558, *www.bed-breakfast-bianchi.it* (€€). A spacious B&B located just off the main piazza, offering well-furnished rooms and mini-apartments, and boasting lovely views over the hills.

I Falciani, Via Cassia 245, **t** 055 202 0091 (€€). A rustic, casual place full of locals, serving tasty *crostini, ribollita*, a hunters' roast-meat platter in autumn, pizza and home-made pasta. Booking is advised.

Località I Falciani ✉ 50029

Il Ciliegiolo, Via Chiantigiana 22, **t** 055 232 6327 (€€). Sturdy dishes such as *rognone al ginepro* (kidneys with juniper) and *tagliolini* with truffles. Booking is required. *Closed Mon.*

Tavarnuzze ✉ 50029

*****La Vallombrosina**, Via Montebuoni, **t** 055 202 0491, *www.lavallombrosina.it* (€€€). A comfortable option with panoramic views of the Florence hills. Breakfast is included in the rates.

****Gli Scopeti**, Via Cassia 193, **t** 055 202 2008 (€€). Decent accommodation for the budget-conscious.

Sant'Andrea in Percussina ✉ 50029

Albergaccio di Machiavelli, **t** 055 828471 (€€). A restaurant in Machiavelli's own tavern (*see* opposite), literally the 'nasty little inn'. Now owned by the Conti Serristori Wine Company, it serves simple Tuscan meals – try the refreshing *panzanella* in summer – and fine wines from the estate. You can also buy bottles to take home. *Closed Mon and Tues.*

Along the Via Cassia (SS2)

Up-to-date **San Casciano in Val di Pesa**, 17km south of Florence, is the largest and busiest town in Chianti. Long an outpost of Florence, it suffered numerous vicissitudes until its walls were begun by the ill-fated Duke of Athens in 1342. Within these, near the gateway, the **church of Santa Maria del Prato** (1335) has retained its trecento interior and trecento art: a fine pulpit by Giovanni Balducci da Pisa, a pupil of Andrea Pisano, a crucifix attributed to Simone Martini, a triptych by Ugolino di Neri, and framed paintings on the pilasters by Giotto's pupil, Taddeo Gaddi. The **Museum of Sacred Art** includes the *Madonna and Child* that is considered the first work of Ambrogio Lorenzetti.

Museo di Arte Sacra
open summer Sat 9–12 and 5–7, Sun 10–12.30 and 5–7.30; winter Sat 4–7, Sun 10–12.30 and 4–7

Around San Casciano, Florentine merchants and noblemen dotted the countryside with villas, including the late Renaissance **Fattoria Le Corti**, 2km east on the Mercatale road, owned by the princely Corsini family for the past six centuries and selling its own Chianti; and the 17th-century **Poggio Torselli**, just off the SS2, approached through a long avenue of cypresses and surrounded by a lovely garden.

Fattoria Le Corti
t 055 829 9301; call for opening hrs

Mercatale, Bargino and Barberino Val d'Elsa

Mercatale, 5km east of San Casciano, grew up around its *mercato* (market), protected in the old days by the castle of the Florentine bishops but now a ruin fit only to protect the odd lizard.

More muscular, just east on the road to Passo dei Pecorai, is the **Castello di Greve**, bound by four round towers. The Bardi put it up in the 11th century, before they moved to Florence and founded the greatest pre-Medici bank. It sells its Chianti, *vinsanto* and olive oil.

Castello di Greve
t 055 821 101; tastings and lunches by appt

Other villas worth visiting near Mercatale are Villa Caserotta, once property of the Strozzi, and the fortified Villa Palagio, on the Mercatale–Campoli–Montefiridolfi road, adapted from a 14th-century castle. The Mercatale–Panzano road will bring you to **La Torre a Luciana**, an unspoiled medieval hamlet once belonging to the Pitti family.

Castello di Bibbione
t 05 58 24 92 31, www.castellodibibbione.com

The Via Cassia, between San Casciano and Bargino, passes the ancient **castle of Bibbione**, once residence of the Buondelmonte family, who owned much of this territory in the days when they were throwing fat on the Guelph and Ghibelline fires in Florence. It has some apartments to rent.

Near **Bargino**, in the same bellicose spirit, is the impressive fortified hamlet of **Montefiridolfi**, just east of the Via Cassia. This road, meanwhile, rolls south through lovely hills towards **Tavarnelle Val di Pesa**, of mostly 19th-century origin, and medieval **Barberino Val d'Elsa**, with some Etruscan finds in the town hall and a good 10th-century Romanesque church, the Pieve di Sant'Appiano.

From here the Via Cassia continues to **Poggibonsi** (*see* pp.354–55), with a possible detour to **La Paneretta**, a sturdy 15th-century fort amid olive groves, with Baroque frescoes inside.

Where to Stay and Eat along the Via Cassia

Most of the area's accommodation is in this area, as are some of Chianti's best restaurants.

Cerbaia ✉ 50026

La Tenda Rossa, Piazza del Monumento 9/14, **t** 055 826132 (€€€€). A family-run shrine to *haute cuisine*, offering four tasting menus and particularly good home-made pasta. Try the wonderful *cappelletti* soup with dried cod; lamb with lard and peas; and tuna with saffron and basil. The wine list has some superb bottles. Booking is strongly advised. *Closed Sun, Mon lunch and Aug.*

San Casciano in Val di Pesa >
Piazza della Repubblica
t 055 822 9558

Villa il Poggiale >

La Trattoria del Pesce >>

San Casciano ✉ 50026

*****Villa il Poggiale**, Via Empolese 69, **t** 055 828311, *www.villailpoggiale.it* (€€€). A lovely Renaissance villa overlooking a cypress-bordered lawn, with elegant rooms, some with four-posters, and a good pool. Great value, it feels like a grand but unstuffy private country home. Breakfasts (included) are hearty. Half board is available, or there are self-catering apartments.

*****Antica Posta**, Piazza Zannoni 1/3, **t** 055 822313, *www.coltman.com/antica* (€€). Simple but comfortable rooms and a restaurant (€€€€–€€€) offering inviting Tuscan flavours: try the home-made potato dumplings with tomato sauce; grilled *filet mignon* with balsamic vinegar sauce; and fresh cream pudding in a wild berry sauce. *Closed Tues.*

Nello, Via IV Novembre 64, **t** 055 820163 (€€). Fresh seafood (try the spaghetti with cod and octopus), plus Tuscan staples such as *ribollita* pasta with *funghi porcini* and beef braised in Chianti Classico, and a good wine list. *Closed Wed eve and Thurs.*

Bargino ✉ 50024

***Bargino**, Via Cassia 122, **t** 055 824 9055 (€). Seven rooms in a garden along the old Roman road, with an excellent fish restaurant, **La Trattoria del Pesce** (€€). Breakfast is included.

Mercatale ✉ 50026

***Hotel Paradise**, Piazza V Veneto 28, **t** 055 821327, *www.hotelparadise.it* (€€). Simple rooms with TVs and kettles.

Il Salotto del Chianti, Via Sonnino 92, **t** 055 821 8429 (€€). A well-established spot on the local culinary scene – the *ravioli con formaggio, pappardelle alla lepre* and wild boar are extraordinary, and the courgette cake with flowers and ricotta, and *rotolino* filled with aubergines and prawns are recommended. *Closed lunch and Wed.*

Tavarnelle ✉ 50028

Ostello del Chianti, Via Roma 137, **t** 055 805 0265, *www.ostellodelchianti.it* (€). A pleasant youth hostel.

Osteria di Passignano, Loc. Badia a Passignano, **t** 055 807 1278 (€€€). The abbey-fief of the Antinori clan, who have been making wine for more than 600 years and produced the first Super-Tuscans (*see* p.203). You can try them in this wonderful restaurant, which offers seasonal menus designed to bring out the best in the wines. *Closed Sun.*

La Gramola, Via delle Fonti 1, **t** 055 8050321 (€€). A pleasantly rustic restaurant in the heart of the town, with a seasonally changing menu: try ravioli with pumpkin and local truffles, vegetable lasagne, and peppery Impruneta beef stew.

Barberino Val d'Elsa ✉ 50021

Barberino Val d'Elsa >>
Via Cassia 31a, t 055 807 5622, www.barberinovaldelsa.net; closed Nov–Mar

****Primavera**, Via della Repubblica, **t** 055 805 9223, *www.hotelprimavera-chianti.it* (€€). A pleasant, simple hotel. Rooms have bath and TV, and there's parking.

San Donato in Poggio ✉ 50028

Villa Francesca, Strada Monestiero 12, **t** 055 807 2849 (€€). A good place to come for tasty roasts, risotto with *porcini*, and *bistecca*. Wine and oil are produced here too. *Closed Mon–Wed, and Thurs and Fri lunch.*

Central Chianti: Along the Chiantigiana (SS222)

From Florence the scenic Chiantigiana (SS222) passes the Ugolino golf course (*see* p.170) and offers its first tempting detour at Petigliolo: turn left after 4km for the Ivy-covered **Santo Stefano a Tizzano**, a Romanesque church built by the Buondelmonti, not far from an 11th-century castle-villa, the **Castello di Tizzano**, where you can buy Riserva, *vinsanto naturale* and prizewinning olive oil.

Castello di Tizzano
t 055 495380; call for opening hrs

The same road continues for 2km to **San Polo in Chianti**, the centre of Tuscany's iris industry, celebrated in an iris festival in May. On a hill from San Polo you can see a lonely building once belonging to the Knights Templar; an equally ancient church, San Miniato in Robbiana, was reconsecrated in 1077 by the bishop of Fiesole, according to a still legible inscription. San Polo's **Antico Toscano** is a wine shop with offerings from all over the region.

Strada, 14km from Florence along the Chiantigiana, is thought to take its odd name from an old Roman road. In the Middle Ages, the road to the south, towards the Valdarno, was protected by the **Castello di Mugano**, one of the best-preserved in the region. The rolling countryside is the dominant feature until **Vicchiomaggio**, with its distinctive castle where Leonardo da Vinci once stayed. This is now the British-run **Fattoria Castello di Vicchiomaggio**, offering own-label Chianti, *vinsanto*, olive oil and honey, and plush rooms.

Fattoria Castello di Vicchiomaggio
t 055 854079, www.vicchiomaggio.it

New Yorkers will recognize the name of nearby **Verrazzano** at once, thanks to Giovanni da Verrazzano, a captain who, in the service of François I of France, discovered New York harbour and

Castello di Verrazzano
t 055 854243; tastings with a week's notice

Castello di Uzzano
t 055 854 4851; tastings with 24hrs' notice

Manhattan island in 1524. He disappeared on his second voyage to Brazil but surely smiles down on the bridge named in his honour. His birthplace, the **Castello di Verrazzano**, sells wines and olive oils.

East of the Chiantigiana, 1.5km north of Greve, is the 13th-century **Castello di Uzzano**, built by the bishop of Florence and gradually converted into one of Chianti's most impressive villa estates.

Greve in Chianti and Around

Macelleria Falorni
Piazza Matteotti 69/71, t 055 853029

The biggest **wine fair** in Chianti occurs in September in medieval **Greve** (population 10,800), seen as the region's capital. On the banks of the river, it is celebrated for its charming, arcaded, funnel-shaped **Piazza del Matteotti**, studded with a statue of Verrazzano, for its specialized wine shops (*see* opposite), and for the **Macelleria Falorni**, one of the region's most famous butchers, acclaimed for its cured hams and *finocchiona* salamis flavoured with fennel seeds. In the church of **Santa Croce** is a triptych by Lorenzo di Bicci and a painting by the 'Master of Greve'. In a nearby hamlet, **Cintoia**, the little church of Santa Maria a Cintoia has a beautiful 15th-century panel attributed to Francesco Granacci.

The ancient village and castle of **Montefioralle**, 1km west of Greve, is where the townspeople lived in the bad old days. Now restored, it is an interesting place to poke around, with its intact octagonal walls, old towerhouses and Romanesque churches: Santo Stefano, housing early Florentine paintings, and the porticoed Pieve di San Cresci a Montefioralle, just outside the walls.

A minor road west passes the ruined castle of **Montefili**, built in the 900s as the eastern outpost of one of Chianti's most powerful religious institutions, the **Badia a Passignano**, a fortified complex now partly occupied by a restaurant (*see* p.210). The old abbey church, **San Michele**, has paintings by Ghirlandaio, Alessandro Allori and Domenico Cresti (better known as Passignano) and a bust of San Giovanni Gualberto, founder of the Vallombrosan order, who arrived here in the mid 11th century. Most buildings date from the 14th century, with a few 17th- and 19th-century remodellings.

Just east of Greve, the beautiful **Vignamaggio** villa was built by the Gherardini family, whose most famous member, Lisa, was born here. She married Francesco del Giocondo before posing for the world's most famous portrait. Used as a location for Kenneth Branagh's film, *Much Ado About Nothing*, it's now a hotel (*see* p.210).

Panzano, an agricultural centre 6km south of Greve on the Chiantigiana, played an important role in the Florence-Siena squabbles but retains only part of its medieval castle. Its butcher, Dario Cecchini, is famous for protesting when 'beef on the bone' was banned in 2001. He holds court in his shop at Via XX Luglio 11 on the outskirts of town on Sunday mornings, playing loud music and reciting Dante. Panzano is best known for its embroidery, and for the **Pieve di San Leolino**, 1km south, with its pretty 16th-century portico on a 12th-century Romanesque structure; inside is a triptych by Mariotto di Nardo. Another Romanesque church south of Panzano, Sant'Eufrosino, just off the SS222, enjoys especially fine views.

Fattoria Montagliari
t 0555 852014; call for opening hrs

Near Panzano, the **Fattoria Montagliari** sells a wide variety of its own wines, grappa, olive oil, cheese, salami, honey and so on. **Pietrafitta**, 9km further south and 4km from Castellina, is a lovely hamlet hidden in the woods.

Castellina in Chianti and Around

27 Castellina in Chianti

One of Chianti's most charming hilltop villages, **Castellina** (population 2,700) was fortified by Florence as an outpost against Siena, and for centuries its fortunes depended on who was on top in their endless war. It was lost to a combined Sienese-Aragonese siege in 1478, though after the fall of Siena itself in 1555 both cities lost interest in Castellina. Today it looks much as it did in the quattrocento: the circuit of walls is almost intact, with houses built into and on top of them. The **Rocca**, or fortress, is in the centre, its mighty donjon now home to the mayor; the covered walkway, Via delle Volte, is part of the 15th-century defensive works. Less historic but worth visiting is the **Bottega del Vino Gallo Nero**, which sells wines and olive oils. Visitors can explore the **Ipogeo Etrusco di Montecalvario**, a restored 6th-century BC Etruscan tomb.

Bottega del Vino Gallo Nero
Via della Rocca 13

West of Castellina on the SS429, **Granaio** has one of Chianti's most renowned wineries, the **Melini wine house**, established in 1705.There are also splendid old farmhouses and villas around Castellina, nearly all formerly fortifications along Chianti's medieval Maginot line, such as the **Villa La Leccia** southwest of Castellina, and the **Castello di Campalli** near **Fonterutoli**, an ancient hamlet south on the Chiantigiana. In the 13th century Florence and Siena often met here to work out peace settlements; none lasted long. Since 1435 the **Fattoria di Fonterutoli** has produced wine in traditional oak casks, including Chianti and Bianco della Lega, as well as lavender products, honey and Tuscany's finest *extra-vergine*.

Fattoria di Fonterutoli
t 0577 740476; call for opening hrs

Further south, **Quercegrossa**, 10km from Siena but now practically a suburb of it, was the birthplace of quattrocento sculptor Jacopo della Quercia. A road forks northeast for Vagliagli, site of the medieval **Fattoria della Aiola** selling wines, grappa, oil, honey and vinegar.

Fattoria della Aiola
t 0577 322615; call for opening hrs

17 Wine-tasting in and around Greve

Wine-tasting in and around Greve

Bottega del Chianti Classico, Via Cesare Battisti 4, **t** 055 853631. Wine/oil sales.

Castello di Querceto, Via A. François 2, just outside Greve, **t** 055 85921. A wide variety of wines, including Sangiovese aged in *barriques*, and olive oil. Tastings require one week's notice.

Enoteca del Chianti Classico, Piazzetta S. Croce 8, **t** 055 853297.

Fontodi, Via S. Leolino, on Chiantigiana, near Sant'Eufrosino, **t** 055 852005. Wine aged in *barriques*, Chianti, Bianco della Lega and oil. One week's notice.

ⓘ **Greve in Chianti >**
*Viale G. da Verrazzano 59, **t** 055 854 6287, www.chiantiechianti.it*

★ **Villa le Barone >**

★ **La Cantinetta di Rignana >>**

Where to Stay in and around Greve

Greve ✉ 50022

Villa Vignamaggio, Via Petriolo 5, 5min drive from Greve on Panzano road, **t** 055 854 4661, *www.vignamaggio.it* (€€€). A historic villa (*see* p.208) with tennis facilities and a pool. Some of the accommodation is in the grounds. There's a minimum 2-night stay.

*****Giovanni da Verrazzano**, Piazza Matteotti 28, **t** 055 853189, *www.verrazzano.it* (€€€–€€). Elegant rooms overlooking the pretty main square, with breakfast included in the rates, plus a restaurant (*see* below)

*****Del Chianti**, Piazza Matteotti 86, **t** 055 853763, *www.albergodelchianti.it* (€€). Comfortable, stylish rooms with baths and all comforts, near the centre, with a pool and garden.

Panzano ✉ 50022

****Villa le Barone**, Via S. Leolino 19, **t** 055 852621, *www.villalebarone.it* (€€€€). The 16th-century villa of the Della Robbia family, who still own it, just south of Greve. It's a lovely, intimate hotel, whether you need a base for visiting the region or a place to lounge – there's a pretty garden, an outdoor pool and a tennis court. Kids are very welcome. There's a minimum 3-night stay, and rates include breakfast and dinner. *Closed Nov–Mar.*

Villa Rosa, Via San Leolino 59, **t** 055 852577, *www.resortvillarosa.it* (€€€). A pleasant, relaxed place on the road between Panzano and Radda, with a shady terrace and a hillside pool with beautiful views. Two of the rooms have private terraces.

Monte S. Michele ✉ 50020

Villa San Michele, Via Casole 40, **t** 055 851034 (€). A hostel with two apartments, double rooms and dorms, plus a very good guests' restaurant. *Closed Nov–Mar.*

Castellina ✉ 53011

******Tenuta di Ricavo**, 3km north of town, **t** 0577 740221, *www.ricavo.com* (€€€€€–€€€€). An entire medieval hamlet of stone houses, wonderfully isolated in the pines, with a large garden and a pool. It's ideal for families. Breakfast is included in the rates, and there's a restaurant offering Chianti specialities. *Open April–Oct.*

******Villa Casalecchi**, **t** 0577 740240, *www.villacasalecchi.com* (€€€€–€€€). A comfy if rather sombre old house among trees and vineyards, with some elegant rooms full of antiques and others not so elegant, plus 3 apartments. It also has a large pool, a traditional restaurant and enchanting views over the hills. *Closed Nov–Mar.*

*****Salivolpi**, Via Fiorentina, just outside town, **t** 0577 740484, *www.hotelsalivolpi.com* (€€). A smart place combining an old-fashioned atmosphere with modern comforts, set in two old farmhouses, with a garden and pool. Breakfast is included.

Eating Out in and around Greve

Greve ✉ 50022

Osteria di Passignano, Via Passignano 33, Badia a Passignano, **t** 055 807 1278 (€€€€–€€€). One of the best country restaurants in the area, set in the old wine cellars of a monastery (*see* p.208) on the famous Antinori wine estates just south of Florence. The atmosphere is rustically elegant, the creative food rooted in Tuscan and Italian traditions. Try *pici* with pigeon, red wine and bay leaf; or herb-crusted veal cutlet with potatoes and pumpkin flowers. It's essential to book. Ask about cookery courses. *Closed Sun, Jan and 2wks Aug.*

La Cantinetta di Rignana, Via Rignana, Greve, **t** 055 852601 (€€€). A trattoria in idyllic countryside between Greve and Badia in Passignano (to the south), with a panoramic terrace. Try home-made ravioli with butter and sage, pork steaks, or stewed beef with wine and peppers. Reservations are advisable. *Closed Tues.*

Bottega del Moro, Piazza Trieste 14r, **t** 055 853753 (€€). A simple, central trattoria serving typical Tuscan dishes such as onion soup and grilled rabbit.

Giovanni da Verrazzano, Piazza Matteotti 28, **t** 055 853189 (€€). One of Greve's most charming restaurants, furnished with antiques and boasting a lovely terrace overlooking the piazza. The main meat dishes are especially good – try *nana in sugo* (duck in wine sauce), turkey with olives, the mixed grill or the *pappardelle* with wild boar. *Closed Sun eve and Mon.*

Montefioralle ✉ 50022

Taverna del Guerrino, Via di Montefioralle 39, **t** 055 853106 (€€). A rustic place in a panoramic garden, offering simple Tuscan classics, including *panzanella, ribollita* and sausage and beans *all'uccelletto*, and wines from the local *fattoria*. *Closed Mon and Tues, and Wed in winter.*

Spedaluzzo ✉ 50027

La Cantinetta, Chiantigiana 93, **t** 055 857 2000 (€€). Good home-made pasta and country specialities such as stuffed rabbit, pigeon, stuffed artichokes and grilled meats. Try the fabulous sausages with truffles, the *ribollita* and the grilled meat. *Closed Mon, and 3wks in Feb/Mar.*

Località Lucolena ✉ 50020

Borgo Antico, Via Case Sparse 115, **t** 055 851024 (€€). A place worth visiting for its tomato or bean *bruschetta*; *pappardelle* with wild boar or duck; little salami with truffles and other excellent salami and hams; and renowned Florentine beefsteak. It also has some rooms to let. *Closed Tues.*

Panzano ✉ 50022

Montagliari, Via di Montagliari 28, **t** 055 852184 (€€). A restaurant decorated in the style of an old farmhouse, with tables in the panoramic garden. Try the *pappardelle* with wild boar sauce or the guinea fowl with *vinsanto* sauce. Booking is required. *Closed Mon.*

Castellina ✉ 53011

Albergaccio di Castellina, Via Fiorentina 63, on road to San Donato, **t** 0577 741042 (€€€). Creative fare such as lamb with saffron, and mushroom and chestnut soup, plus grilled meat and fish dishes. Booking is strongly recommended. *Closed Wed and Thurs lunch, Sun, last 2wks Nov, and 1st week Dec.*

Antica Trattoria La Torre, Piazza del Comune 1, **t** 0577 740236 (€€). A popular family-run place with a cosy atmosphere, serving tasty rice or *pici* with *porcini, ribollita*, cheeses, Tuscan hams and salami, and more. *Closed Fri.*

Pietrafitta Ristoranti in Chianti, Loc. Pietrafitta 41, t 0577 741123 (€€). An American-owned place with an Australian chef, offering good regional and international dishes, including imaginative Italian-Med food. Try the *Fiorentina* steak, grilled lamb or gnocchi with sheeps'-cheese fondue. *Closed Thurs and Feb.*

ⓘ **Castellina in Chianti >>**
Via Ferruccio 40, t 0577 774 1392

★ **Antica Trattoria La Torre >>**

Monti del Chianti: Radda and Gaiole

East of Castellina lies the more rugged region of the Monti del Chianti. Here in the ancient capital of the Lega del Chianti, **Radda in Chianti** (population 1,650), the streets follow a medieval plan, radiating from the central piazza and its stately, heraldry-encrusted Palazzo Comunale, and a 15th-century fresco *Madonna, St Christopher and St John the Baptist* in the atrium. Just outside town is the Franciscan **Monastero**, a pretty 15th-century church.

Two medieval villages are to be found nearby: **Ama**, with its castle, 8km to the south, near the attractive Romanesque church of San Giusto; and **Volpaia**, 7km north, with another ancient castle and walls, and an unexpected 'Brunelleschian' church called La Commenda. Also near Radda is the **Fattoria Vigna Vecchia**, where you can stock up on Chianti, grappa, *vinsanto* and olive oil, and enjoy tastings (with three days' notice).

Fattoria Vigna Vecchia
t 0577 738090; call for opening hrs

On the way to Gaiole, 10km east of Radda, is the ancient **Badia a Coltibuono**, one of Chianti's gems. Set among centuries-old trees and gardens, the abbey is believed to have been founded in 770, passing to the Vallombrosan order in the 12th century. The Romanesque church, San Lorenzo, dates from 1049. The monastery was turned into a splendid villa, owned in the 19th century by the Poniatowski, one of Poland's greatest noble families, and now occupied by a wine estate, **Fattoria Badia a Coltibuono**. You can visit the cellars and Italianate garden, and it has a restaurant (*see* opposite).

Fattoria Badia a Coltibuono
t 0577 744801; open May–Oct Mon–Sat 2.30–6.30

Gaiole in Chianti (population 4,780) is an ancient market town: the **Agricoltori Chianti Geografico**, which sells Chianti, Vernaccia di San Gimignano, *vinsanto* and olive oil, is the HQ of a local cooperative; and the **Enoteca Montagnani** specializes in Chianti Classico. Gaiole is also a good base for visiting the impressive castles between the Arno and Siena. Just to the west are the walls and imposing donjon of the well-preserved 13th-century **Castello di Vertine**, one of the most striking sights in Chianti.

Agricoltori Chianti Geografico
Via Mulinaccio 10, t 0577 749489

Enoteca Montagnani
Via B Bandinelli 9

East of Gaiole is the ancient fortified village of **Barbischio**, and 3km south on the SS408 is the impressive medieval **Castello di Meleto** with its sturdy cylindrical towers. From here the road continues 4.5km up to the mighty **Castello di Castagnoli**, guarding a fascinating little medieval town in a commanding position.

Most majestic of all is the Iron Baron's isolated **Castello di Brolio** some 10km south of Gaiole along the SS484, high on a hill with views for kilometres around. Donated to the monks of the Badia in Florence in 1009, by Matilda of Tuscany's father Bonifacio, it passed to the Ricasoli in 1167. In 1478 the castle was bombarded for weeks by the Aragonese and Sienese, who later demolished it so that 'the walls levelled with the earth'. Florence rebuilt it, and in the mid 19th century Baron Ricasoli converted it into a splendid fortified residence, while experimenting with the modern formula for Chianti. You can sample the famous wines and olive oil and visit the cellars 10km south at the **Cantine Barone Ricasoli**. The **Fattoria dei Pagliaresi** near Castelnuovo Berardenga, between S. Gusmè and Pianella, offers older wines as well as new, and olive oil.

(3) Castello di Brolio
open summer daily 9–12 and 3–6, winter Sat–Thur 9–12 and 2.30–4.30 (Sat and Sun only Dec and Jan); adm

Cantine Barone Ricasoli
t 0577 7301; call ahead

Fattoria dei Pagliaresi
t 0577 359070; call for opening hrs

To the south, Castelnuovo Berardenga is an agricultural centre with the remains of a 14th-century castle. From here it's 16km to **Monteaperti**, where Florence almost went down the tubes. To continue south, *see* 'Monte Oliveto Maggiore and Around', p.374.

Where to Stay and Eat in the Monte del Chianti

(i) Radda >
Piazza Ferrucci 1, t 0577 738494

Radda ✉ 53017

****Relais Vignale, Via Pianigiani 9, t 0577 738300, *www.vignale.it* (€€€€€–€€€€). Well-equipped rooms furnished with antiques in a charming old house with fine views and an outdoor pool for hotter days, plus an excellent restaurant 300m down the road. Buffet breakfasts are included in the rates. *Closed Jan–Mar.*

La Locanda, Loc. Montanino, Volpaia, **t** 0577 738833, *www.lalocanda.it* (€€€€€–€€€€). A little hotel on a wooded hill, in restored stone farm buildings, with a pool and good food. Breakfast is included.

Podere Terreno, 5km north of Radda on road to Volpaia, **t** 0577 738312, *www.podereterreno.it* (€€€). A working wine farm and *agriturismo*, with simple rooms (breakfast included) and a relaxed atmosphere – meals (half board is available) are served at a communal table in a cluttered living room.

***Il Girarrosto**, Via Roma 41, **t** 0577 738010 (€). Double rooms, some with bath, and a restaurant (€€) offering local cuisine. *Closed Wed.*

Antica Trattoria Botteganova, Via Chiantigiana 29, **t** 0577 284230 (€€€). Fish and meat in interesting combinations. The *tagliolini* with lemon, paprika and little squid is recommended. Come at lunch to eat for half the price. *Closed Sun.*

Il Vignale, Via XX Settembre 23, **t** 0577 738094 (€€€). A spot popular with locals for its refined Tuscan cooking using organic produce. *Closed Thurs.*

Badia a Coltibuono, next to old abbey of same name between Radda and Gaiole, **t** 0577 749424 (€€€). A *menu degustazione*, or tempting à la carte dishes such as risotto whisked with salt cod, tomato and olive pesto sauce; and guinea fowl roasted with lard, chestnuts and sausage. *Closed Mon.*

Il Carlino d'Oro, Via Brolio, San Regolo, **t** 0577 747136 (€). A small, family-run trattoria in an idyllic setting. Make sure to book ahead at weekends. Try the excellent bean soup, *pappardelle* with hare sauce, and deepfried chicken and rabbit, and outstanding home-produced wine. *Closed winter exc Sat and Sun lunch.*

Gaiole ✉ 53013

Castello di Tornano, Loc. Lecchi, **t** 0577 746067, *www.castelloditornano.it* (€€€€€). A fortified farmhouse and castle with a 1,000-year-old tower commanding views of steep wooded hills. The castle and tower house luxurious double rooms and suites with original antiques; outbuildings have been converted into rustically styled self-catering apartments for 2–4. There is a restaurant, pool and tennis court. Breakfast is included.

Relais Borgo San Felice, Castelnuovo Berardenga, Loc. Borgo San Felice, **t** 0577 3964, *www.relaischateaux.fr/borgofelice* (€€€€€). A lovely renovated hilltop hamlet with rooms dotted around various buildings, surrounded by vines of the famous San Felice estate. There is an excellent restaurant, a gym, a pool and a tennis court. Breakfast is included, and half/full board is available. *Closed Nov–Mar.*

****Castello di Spaltenna**, **t** 0577 749483, *www.spaltenna.it* (€€€€). A fortified monastery just by Gaiole. The delightful rooms have all comforts plus stunning views over the valley or courtyard. There is also an indoor pool, a sauna, a gym, a tennis court, billiards and a beauty centre. The restaurant in the ancient refectory serves both traditional and creative Tuscan dishes. *Closed mid-Jan–Mar.*

Brolio ✉ 53013

Castello di Brolio, **t** 0577 7301, *www.ricasoli.it* (€€€€€). A chic farmhouse to let at this famous site (*see* opposite).

Osteria del Castello, **t** 0577 747277 (€€€). A delightful restaurant with an Irish chef who has a creative take on Tuscan cuisine. Booking is strongly recommended. *Closed Thurs.*

The Mugello

Over the years, as their ambitions became less discreet, the Medici concocted a pretty story of how they were descended from knights of Charlemagne. In truth they came down to Florence from the Mugello, the hilly region just to the north – as did Giotto and Fra Angelico. As far back as Boccaccio's time, the Mugello was considered the loveliest region of the Florentine *contada*, and its

Getting around the Mugello

The Mugello lies east of the A1 and north of Pontassieve. It has two **exits off the A1**: at Barberino (28km from Florence) and Roncobilaccio (47km from Florence) near the Passo della Futa. The two main roads north from Florence, the **SS65** (Via Bolognese) to the Medici villas and Passo della Futa and the **SS302** to Borgo San Lorenzo (28km), are pretty drives. North of the river Sieve, mountain roads make for slow travelling – allow at least 2hrs to get from Florence to Firenzuola (51km), more to Marradi (64km).

You can also loop through the Mugello by **train** (**t** 892021, *www.trenitalia.com*) from Florence, passing through Pontassieve, Dicomano, Vicchio, Borgo San Lorenzo, San Piero a Sieve, and Vaglia.

SITA **buses** (**t** 055 47821, *www.sitabus.it*) are more scenic and just as infrequent; check times before setting out (most pass through the junction at San Piero). Better still, hire a car.

---

bluish-green hills are dotted with elegant weekend and summer retreats, rather smarter than the typical stone *fattorie* of the Chianti. The Florentines come here whenever they can, and if you find yourself stewing with them in the traffic gridlocks approaching Piazza della Libertà, know that all you have to do is turn up the Via Bolognese or Via Faentina and in 10 minutes you'll be in a cool, enchanting world immersed in green.

North of Florence altitudes rise appreciably towards the central Apennine spine that divides Tuscany from Emilia-Romagna. Tucked in these hills lies the Mugello basin, a broad valley along the Sieve and its tributaries that, in the Miocene era, held a lake. Most of the

The Mugello

towns of the Mugello are here, surrounded by a sea of vines; olive groves cover the slopes but soon give way to cool, deep forests of pines, chestnuts and oaks, dotted with small resorts. Like any fashion-conscious Florentine, the Mugello changes colours with the seasons, though it's strikingly beautiful any time of year.

The Original Medici Villa

Following Via Bolognese (SS65) north, past the gardens of **Pratolino**, one of the last Medici villas (*see* p.194), it's a panoramic and winding 30km to two of the very first. On the way, a slight detour east (from Pratolino or Vaglia) ascends to **Monte Senario** (820m) where, in 1233, seven Florentine noblemen founded the mendicant Servite Order, living in grottoes and building simple cells in the woods. The Servites later built Santissima Annunziata in Florence. Rebuilt in the 16th century, the monastery here has amazing views over the Arno valley and Mugello.

North, towards San Piero a Sieve, is a turn-off west on an untarred road for the Medici **Castello di Trebbio**, a family estate remodelled in 1461 by Michelozzo into a fortified villa with a tower. It has a formal Italian garden you can look around.

A bit further up looms the even grander **Villa Cafaggiolo**, favoured by Cosimo il Vecchio and Lorenzo il Magnifico, who spent as much of the summer as possible in its cool halls. Cosimo had Michelozzo transform this ancient family seat into an imposing castellated villa, its entrance protected by a bulging tower with an incongruous clock. It has apartments for rent (*www.villagaggiolo.it*).

East, a minor road leads up to the wooded **Bosco ai Frati**, with a simple porticoed church also by Michelozzo; inside is a fine crucifix by Donatello, and another attributed to Desiderio da Settignano.

Beyond Cafaggiolo, towards Barberino, is the huge artificial **Lago di Bilancino**. The lake, which is dammed (the dam controls the water of the Sieve river), occupies nearly 5 sq km, has a beach with loungers and parasols, and is good for sailing, windsurfing, fishing and canoeing. Bars, restaurants and other facilities are springing up.

To the Passo della Futa

Just off the *autostrada*, the largest town on the west rim of the Mugello basin is **Barberino di Mugello**, spread under the **Castello dei Cattani**. Its 15th-century Palazzo Pretorio is emblazoned with coats of arms; the open Loggie Medicee is another work by Michelozzo. On the SS65, 5km away at Colle Barucci, is one of the Mugello's grandest estates, the **Villa delle Maschere** ('of the masks').

Passo della Futa

Continue 14km north to appreciate the breathtaking views from the **Passo della Futa** (903m), a pass on the principal Apennine watershed; below, the whole Mugello extends like a relief map. In 1944, the pass was the Germans' strong point on the Gothic Line.

Beyond the pass the road winds under the craggy **Sasso di Castro** (1,276m); at La Casetta turn off for Firenzuola (*see* below) or hotfoot it over the mountains for dinner in Bologna, culinary capital of Italy.

Scarperia and Around

At the major crossroads of the SS503 north and the SS551 along the Sieve, **San Piero a Sieve** is a busy little town defended by a mighty Medici citadel, the **Fortezza di San Martino**, designed by Buontalenti in 1571. Its Romanesque parish church, with a façade from 1776, contains a remarkable octagonal baptismal font in polychrome terracotta, by Luca della Robbia.

Scarperia

From here it's 4km to **Scarperia**, the most charming town in the Mugello, perched high above the valley. Florence fortified it in 1306, and laid out its simple rectangular plan, with one long main street. The **Palazzo dei Vicari**, from 1306, is so heavily decorated with stone and ceramic coats of arms it resembles a page from a postage stamp album. Its atrium and upper halls have 14th- and 15th-century frescoes, the earliest ones by the school of Giotto. The **oratory of the Madonna di Piazza** has an attractive Renaissance front and a cinquecento fresco of the *Madonna and Child*, attributed to Iacopo del Casentino; the church dedicated to Our Lady of the Earthquakes has a fresco that some attribute to Filippo Lippi.

Palazzo dei Vicari
open 16 Sept–31 May Sat, Sun and hols 10–1 and 3–6.30; 1 June–15 Sept Wed, Thurs and Fri 3.30–7.30, Sat, Sun and hols 10–1 and 3.30–7.30

The *palazzo* houses the **Museo dei Ferri Taglienti**, a small museum of knife-making and cutting tools. From the 16th century, Scarperia supplied the duchy of Tuscany with knives, forks and scissors, as well as daggers and swords. By 1900 there were 46 thriving firms, though machine-made competition has reduced this. Firms still making knives, and selling bone- or horn-handled cutlery (at high prices), include **Conaz** (Via Roma 8), **Saladini** (Via Solferino 15), **Berti** (Via Roma 37) and **Giglio** (Via delle Oche). Scarperia is now better known for the **Autodromo Internazionale del Mugello**, a 5km track built by Florence's Auto Club in 1976, fairly well hidden in the hills east of town.

Museo dei Ferri Taglienti
open same hrs as Palazzo dei Vicari; adm

Autodromo Internazionale del Mugello
www.mugellocircuit.it

The Mugello's most fascinating historical relic, 4km northwest of Scarperia, is the 11th-century parish **church of Sant'Agata**, restored after an earthquake in 1919, with an unusual apse and a pulpit from 1175, decorated with white and green marble intarsia designs and animals. The chapel to the right of the altar houses Bicci di Lorenzo's painting, *The Mystical Marriage of St Catherine*.

Sant'Agata
open daily 7.30–5

Firenzuola, 22km north of Scarperia, is famous for its production of 'Pietra Serena', the pale grey stone seen in buildings all over Tuscany. A small holiday resort, cool even in August, it was devastated in the Second World War and rebuilt along the lines of the original streetplan between the Porta di Bologna and Porta di Firenze. Four kilometres west, in **Cornacchiaia**, is a church believed to date back to Carolingian times.

Borgo San Lorenzo and Vicchio

Borgo San Lorenzo (population 16,300) on the Sieve is the boom town of the Mugello, partly due to its fast-train link to Florence. It's surrounded by new residential neighbourhoods with gardens full of little chameleons. The main sights are the Romanesque churches: **San Lorenzo**, with an unusual hexagonal campanile built in 1263; and, 3km north, the parish **church of San Giovanni Maggiore**, with a belltower square at the base but octagonal on top, and a lovely 12th-century pulpit in marble intarsia.

To the north the road divides into the SS477 to **Palazzuolo sul Senio** and the SS302 to **Marradi**, also small resorts; Palazzuolo has a small **ethnographic museum** in the 14th-century Palazzo dei Capitani, and hosts an annual festival in July (*see* p.59)

Museo della Civiltà Contadina ed Artigiana
t 055 844 6114; open Mar–June and Sept–Dec Sun 3–6; July and Aug daily 4–7; but call ahead

Sleepy little **Vicchio**, east of San Lorenzo, was the birthplace of the Blessed Fra Angelico (Giovanni da Fiesole, 1387–1455) and often home from home for Benvenuto Cellini. Its **Museo Comunale Beato Angelico** has detached frescoes, Etruscan finds from nearby Poggio alla Colla, and a 13th-century holy-water stoup.

Museo Comunale Beato Angelico
t 055 844 8251; open Sat and Sun 10–12 and 4–7, plus Thurs 10–12 in summer; adm (combined with Casa di Giotto)

The nearby hamlet of **Vespignano** was the birthplace of Giotto di Bondone (1267–1337). The simple stone cottage where the father of Renaissance painting is said to have been born has been well restored as the **Casa di Giotto**. According to tradition, Cimabue discovered Giotto near the old (now restored) bridge over the Enza, where the young shepherd was sketching his sheep on a stone.

Casa di Giotto
t 055 843 9224; open winter Sat and Sun 10–12 and 3–6, summer Tues by appt, Thur, Sat and Sun 10–12 and 3.30–6.30, adm (also allows entry to Museo Comunale Beato Angelico)

The Valdisieve

The lower Sieve valley is mostly industrial: **Dicomano** can boast an interesting fresco by the school of Piero della Francesca but little else besides a big Saturday-morning market and the junction for the SS67, which climbs east into a pretty range of mountains, the Alpi di San Benedetto. **San Godenzo**, 10km up the SS67, is the largest village, site of an 11th-century Benedictine abbey; its plain church has a raised presbytery and a polyptych by the school of Giotto.

From San Godenzo a road continues up to the birthplace of Andrea del Castagno, now called **Il Castagno d'Andrea** ('Andrew's chestnut'; 1,022m), a small holiday village. Wind a further 18km up to **San Benedetto in Alpe**, with a 9th-century Benedictine abbey that sheltered Dante (*Inferno*, Canto XVI, 94–105). Here you can hire horses to visit the enchanting **Valle dell'Aquacheta** with its waterfall.

In the old town of **Portico di Romagna** 11km further north, the Portinari family, including the beautiful Beatrice, spent their summers – their house still stands in the main street.

Deeper into Romagna lie fascinating medieval **Brisighella**, the ceramic city of **Faenza**, and **Ravenna,** filled with ravishing Byzantine mosaics from the time of Justinian and the site of Dante's real tomb.

Castello di Nipozzano
t 055 27141; open Mon 2.30–6.30; Tues–Fri 10.30–1 and 2.30–6.30; Sat 10.30–1

Museo della Vite e del Vino
t 055 839 7932; open mid-April–Oct Wed–Sat 10–1 and 2–7; mid-Mar–mid-April Wed–Sat 9–1 and 2–6; but call ahead; adm

Rufina, 10km south of Dicomano, is dominated by the 16th-century Villa Poggio Reale, producing Chianti Rufina and Pomino wines. Continuing east along the SS70 beyond Pontassieve, turn left after a few kilometres for **Castello di Nipozzano**, one of the great Frescobaldi wine estates, producing prizewinning oak-aged red wines. For white wines, climb into the hills to the north to **Castello di Pomino**, another Frescobaldi property. **Poggio Reale** has a small **wine museum**.

From **Pontassieve** the scenic SS70 leads up to the dramatic **Passo della Consuma** (1,022m) then descends into the Casentino (*see* p.400).

Where to Stay and Eat in the Mugello

Nearly all Mugello hotels are in the countryside, so you need a car.

Bivigliano ✉ 50030

****__Giotto Park Hotel__, Via Roma 69, **t** 055 406608, *www.giottoparkhotel.it* (€€€). A small, restful, comfy villa, and a cheaper *dipendenza*, in a garden with a tennis court. *Closed Nov–Feb.*

ⓘ Borgo San Lorenzo >
Via P. Togliatti 45, t 055 845271, www.mugellotoscana.it

Borgo San Lorenzo ✉ 50032

***__Locanda degli Artisti__, Piazza Romagnoli 2, **t** 055 845 5359, *www.locandartisti.it* (€€). A neat, central little guesthouse; breakfast is included.

Ristorante degli Artisti, Piazza Romagnoli 1, **t** 055 845 7707 (€€). An elegant spot for Mugello cooking, with a pretty courtyard terrace. *Closed Wed.*

Marradi ✉ 50034

Palazzo Torriani, Via Fabroni 58, **t** 055 804 2363, *www.palazzotorriani.it* (€€€€€). A beautiful 16th-century *palazzo* in the centre, with 3 very comfy self-catering flats, one of which can be rented as two separate bedrooms. Breakfast is included, meals are available on request, and there are cookery courses. *Closed Jan–mid-Mar.*

★ Il Giorgione >>

Scarperia ✉ 50038

__Hotel Cantagallo__, Viale Kennedy 17, **t 055 843 0442, *hotelcantagallo@libero.it* (€€€). A tidy, quiet little hotel overlooking a shady garden, with a pool.

Teatro dei Medici, Loc. La Torre 14, **t** 055 845 9876 (€€). An old house that once belonged to the Medici; book ahead in summer for country *antipasti*, good pasta dishes and wild game in season. *Closed Mon.*

Palazzuolo sul Senio ✉ 50035

***__Locanda Senio__, Borgo dell'Ore 1, **t** 055 8046019, *www.locandasenio.it* (€€€). Ancient buildings furnished with antiques. The food is excellent (breakfast is included; the restaurant serves mushroom, truffle and wild boar), and there is a pool and small spa.

Vicchio ✉ 50039

Villa Campestri, Via de Campestri 19, **t** 055 849 0107, *www.villacampestri.it* (€€€€). An elegant Tuscan villa in a 300-acre park on a hill, with a pool with a view, exquisite rooms, a good restaurant, and a riding school.

Antica Porta di Levante, Piazza Vittorio Veneto 5, **t** 055 840050 (€€). Creative Tuscan cuisine, including *tagliolini* with Mugello black truffles. There's a vine-covered terrace and a few rooms to let. *Closed Mon, 2wks Jan and summer exc Sat lunch (*Enoteca *open all year).*

La Casa di Caccia, Loc. Farneto, **t** 055 840 7629 (€€). An isolated old hunting lodge north of Vicchio, with stunning views. Try ravioli with *scamorza* cheese. Book at weekends. *Closed Tues.*

Sagginale ✉ 50032

Il Giorgione, between Borgo San Lorenzo and Vicchio, **t** 055 849 0130 (€€). A family-run restaurant at the back of a shop, serving excellent rustic food – try rolled, stuffed rabbit.The owner has a small, cheaper *bottega*. *Closed Thurs.*

Ponte a Vicchio ✉ 50039

Casa del Prosciutto, Via Ponte a Vicchio, **t** 055 844031 (€). A grocer-cum-trattoria specializing in local dishes, including potato-stuffed *tortelli*. *Closed eves, Mon and Tue, and Jan and July.*

The Valdarno, Prato and Pistoia

Half the people in Tuscany inhabit this strip between Florence and the sea. It's the hard-working, prosaic part of the region, full of factories and garden nurseries that churn out truly impressive quantities of motor scooters, bricks, fruit trees, straw hats, wool scarves, rail cars, raincoats, rooftiles and rose bushes.

There are two ways across it, both pretty crowded. To the south lies the Arno valley, to the north the modern A1 superstrada, *passing Prato and Pistoia, estimable art towns with proud histories. Between the routes are some charming hills to explore, the Monte Pisano and Monte Albano, where the star attraction is Leonardo's hometown of Vinci.*

09

Don't miss

1. A museum of Leonardo's inventions
   Vinci **p.224**
2. Tiger-striped medieval churches
   Pistoia **p.236**
3. The grandest of Italy's Belle Epoque spas
   Montecatini Terme **p.245**
4. Italy's flower capital
   Pescia **p.248**
5. Baroque gardens and a labyrinth
   Castello Garzoni **p.249**

See map overleaf

Valdarno, Prato and Pistoia

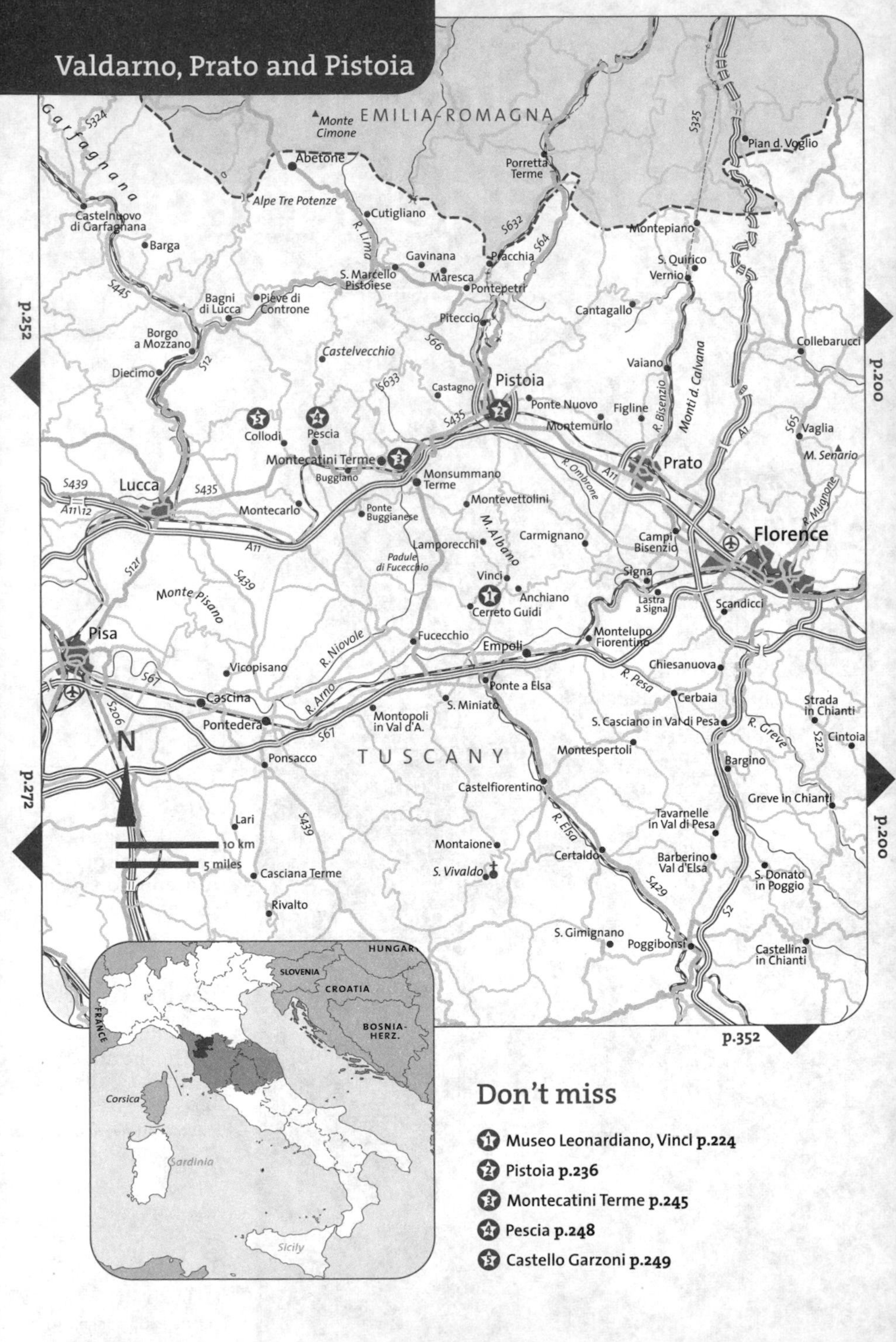

p.252
p.200
p.272
p.200
p.352

Don't miss

1. Museo Leonardiano, Vinci p.224
2. Pistoia p.236
3. Montecatini Terme p.245
4. Pescia p.248
5. Castello Garzoni p.249

Down the Arno to Pisa

Florence to Empoli

The old Florentine satellite town of **Scandicci** (6km west of the city), once in the business of renting villas to foreigners such as Dylan Thomas and DH Lawrence (who finished *Lady Chatterley's Lover* here), has since found more profit in industry. Most towns along the Arno specialize in certain products; in **Lastra a Signa** it's straw goods, sold in numerous village shops. Lastra retains its 14th-century walls and the **Loggia di Sant'Antonio**, all that survives of the hospital founded by Florence's silk guild in 1411; many believe Brunelleschi was the architect, and that the work was a prototype of Florence's Spedale degli Innocenti, funded by the same guild.

Just outside Lastra, the church of **San Martino a Gangalandi** has a beautiful semicircular apse with *pietra serena* articulation by Alberti. In **Signa**, the next village, the Romanesque **San Lorenzo** has a remarkable 12th-century marble pulpit and trecento frescoes.

After Signa the road and river continue 12km through a gorge before coming to **Montelupo Fiorentino**, celebrated since the Renaissance for its terracottas and delicately painted ceramics. Its ceramics fair at the end of June also features Renaissance music and costumes, demonstrations and exhibitions, and its **Museo Archeologico e della Ceramica** has examples from nearly every period, and a display on the lower Valdarno's prehistory. Shops here sell more recent ceramic creations. The old **castle** was built in 1203 by the Florentines, during the wars against Pisa; the church of **San Giovanni Evangelista** contains a lovely *Madonna and Saints* by Botticelli and his assistants.

Museo Archeologico e della Ceramica
*Via Baccio Sinaldi 45, **t** 0571 51352; open Tues–Sun 10–6; adm; joint adm available with Museo della Collegiata* (see *p.222*) *and Museo Leonardiano* (see *p.224*)

On the outskirts of Montelupo, you can see Buontalenti's **Villa Ambrogiana** (1587) from the outside; it houses a mental hospital. From Montelupo a road leads southeast 20km to the town of San Casciano in Val di Pesa, in Chianti (*see* p.205).

Empoli

The modern market town of Empoli, 32km from Florence, witnessed a turning point in Tuscan history: in 1260, the Ghibellines of Siena, fresh from their great victory over Florence at Monteaperti, held a parliament in Empoli to decide the fate of their arch enemy. Everyone was for razing Florence to the ground, and waited for the approval of their leader, Farinata degli Uberti. The Uberti were Florentine gangster nobles famous for their hatred of their fellow citizens, and Farinata surprised all when he announced that, even if he had to stand alone, he would defend Florence for as long as he lived. The Sienese let their captain have his way, and lost their chance of ever becoming *numero uno* in Tuscany.

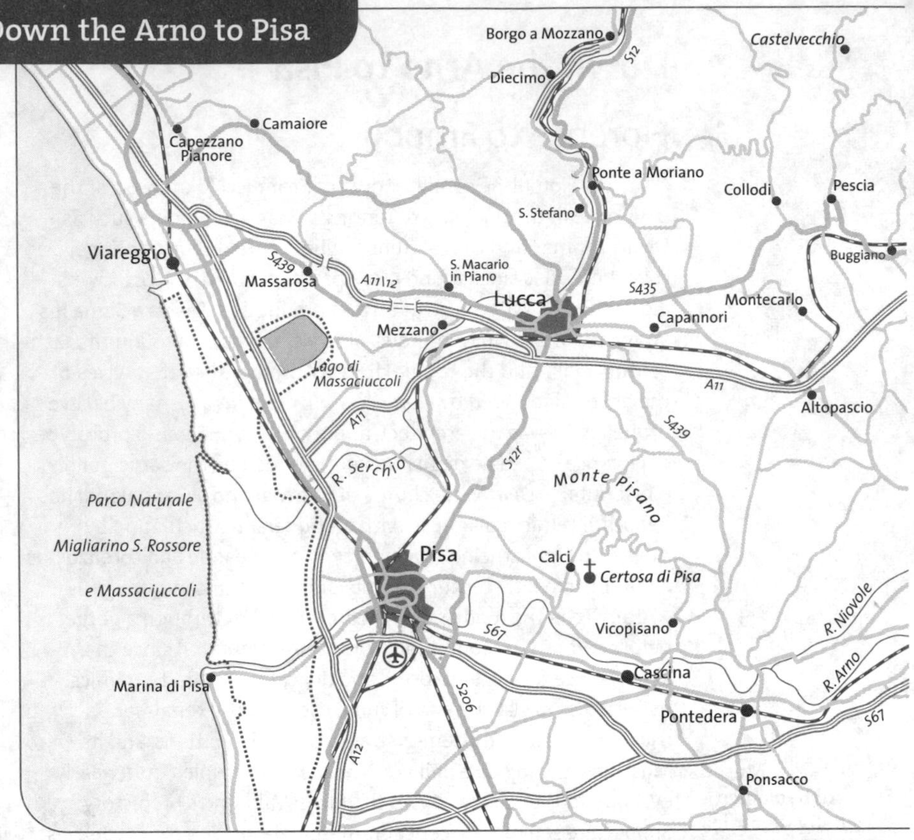

The prosperous new Empoli (population 45,000) produces green glass and raincoats. You'll find little to recall the days of Farinata, until you reach the piazza named after him; here is the palace where the parliament convened, across from the gem of a Romanesque church, the **Collegiata Sant'Andrea**, with its green and white marble geometric façade in the style of Florence's San Miniato. The lower portion dates from 1093; the upper had to wait until the 18th century, but it harmonizes extremely well.

Museo della Collegiata

Museo della Collegiata
Collegiata's cloister; open Tues–Sun 9–12 and 4–7; adm; joint adm available with Museo Archeologico e della Ceramica (see p.221) and Museo Leonardiano (see p.224)

Empoli has its share of 13th- and 14th-century Florentine art, much of it in the small but choice **Museo della Collegiata**. The most celebrated work is Masolino's *Pietà* fresco, with its poignant faces; upstairs are an elegant relief of the *Madonna and Child* by Mino da Fiesole and his brother Antonio's painted tabernacle of St Sebastian. Lorenzo Monaco contributes a long-eyed *Madonna and Saints*; Lorenzo di Bicci's scene of San Nicola da Tolentino shielding Empoli from a rain of plague arrows is a quattrocento view of the city. There is a rare series of frescoes by Masolino's master, Starnina, as well as two saints by Pontormo, born nearby, and the fine

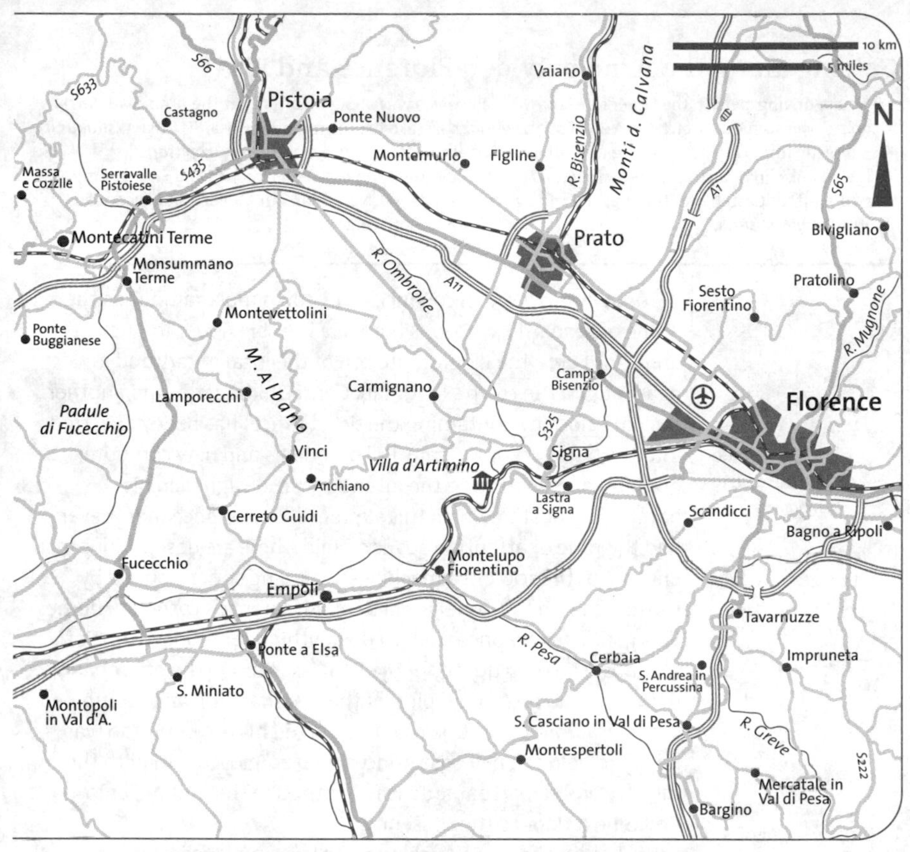

Tabernacle of the Holy Sacrament by Francesco Botticini and his son Raffaello, with a good predella. The upper loggia has works by Andrea della Robbia, and the suspended wooden wings of the donkey that flies down on a wire from the church tower on *Corpus Domini* (a papier-mâché donkey has replaced the original one).

Church of Santo Stefano
open Tues–Fri 9–12 by appt with Museo della Collegiata (see *opposite*)

Empoli's **Santo Stefano church**, restored after damage during the Second World War, has more beautiful frescoes by Masolino and a marble *Annunciation* by Bernardo Rossellini.

Around Empoli

Northwest of Empoli, in the Monte Albano, lies the little old hilltown of **Cerreto Guidi**, former property of the counts of Guidi, taken over by Florence in 1237. It is known these days for its Chianti Putto, and for the **Villa Medicea**, rebuilt for Cosimo I by Buontalenti in 1564 and relatively simple as Medici villas go, but approached by the 'Medici bridges', a grand double ramp of bricks. In 1576 Cosimo I's daughter Isabella was murdered here by her husband Paolo Orsini for her infidelities; look carefully to see the unhappy couple among the scores of Medici portraits in the villa.

Villa Medicea
open Tues–Sun 8.15–7

Getting along the Arno between Florence and Pisa

If you're **driving**, persist: the Florentine sprawl finally gives way at Signa; after that the Arno road (S67) becomes even scenic in stretches. LAZZI **buses** (*www.lazzi.it*) take the main route to Pisa; SITA (*www.sitabus.it*) goes directly from Florence to Castelfiorentino or Certaldo; for Vinci, use COPIT (*www.copitsap.it*).

At least once an hour, **trains** (*www.trenitalia.com*) follow the Arno between Florence and Pisa; at Empoli they turn off for Castelfiorentino, Certaldo, Poggibonsi and Siena. Note that San Miniato and Fucecchio share a railway station; local buses commute from there to both centres.

From Cerreto it's 5km to **Vinci**, a tiny town most famous as the home of Leonardo, who was born in a humble house in Anchiano on 15 April 1452, the illegitimate son of the local notary and a peasant girl. The town's landmark Conti Guidi castle (and another building close by, containing the ticket office) has been converted into the **Museo Leonardiano**, full of models and new computer graphics demonstrating the inventions he designed in his notebooks, most of which this supreme 'Renaissance man' never had the time or attention span to build. There are descriptions in English for the 100 or so machines, including some inspired by those invented by Brunelleschi to build Florence's cathedral dome. This gentle fellow once said, 'I'll do anything for money' – one of the most startling quotes of the Renaissance. On the other hand, nothing could be more typical of the age than brilliance combined with immorality; while he often neglected his art, Leonardo was happy to help the bellicose princes who employed him with their military problems. Leonardo was baptized in the font in Santa Croce, next door to the museum.

Museo Leonardiano
open daily 9.30–7; adm; joint adm available with Museo Archeologico e della Ceramica (see p.221) and Museo della Collegiata (see p.222)

It's 3km southeast to **Anchiano** and the simple restored stone house where Leonardo was born, the **Casa Natale di Leonardo**.

Casa Natale di Leonardo
open Mar–Oct daily 9.30–7, Nov–Feb daily 9.30–6

Vinci ›
Via delle Torri 11, t 0571 568012, www.terredelrinascimento.it (also serves Empoli)

Where to Stay and Eat from Florence to Empoli

For Paggeria Medicea and Da Delfina in Artimino, *see* p.197 and p.198.

Santa Maria a Marciola ✉ 50018

Fiore, Via di Marciola 112, near Scandicci, **t** 055 768678 (€€). A handy spot if you're leaving or approaching Florence, with delicious crêpes, grilled steak, game, *bistecca* and so on, and a lovely garden with pine-clad slopes. *Closed lunch Mon–Fri.*

Vinci ✉ 50059

*****Alexandra**, Via dei Martiri 38, **t** 0571 56224, *www.hotelalexandravinci.it* (€€€). Vinci's one hotel, quiet and comfortable, with some apartments as well as rooms.

Antica Cantina di Bacco, Piazza Leonardo da Vinci 3, **t** 0571 568041 (€). A cosy wine bar with a pretty terrace. *Closed Mon.*

Empoli ✉ 50053

*****Sole**, Piazza Don Minzoni 18, **t** 0571 73779 (€€). A good bargain, by the station, with baths in all rooms.

Cucina Sant'Andrea, Via Salvagnoli 43, **t** 0571 73657 (€€€). A trattoria on the remains of the city walls, with creative versions of local dishes: pigeon terrine, courgette flan, risotto with artichokes, wild boar and game, and fish. *Closed Mon, 1 wk Dec/Jan, and all Aug.*

La Panzanella, Via dei Cappucini 10, **t** 0571 922182 (€€). An old-fashioned trattoria by the station, offering an unusual artichoke soup, wonderful things with porcini, and fish. *Closed Sat, Sun in summer, and 2wks Aug.*

South of Empoli

San Miniato

Just southwest of Empoli, the Elsa flows into the Arno near **San Miniato** (population 23,000), a hilltown that grew up at the crossroads of the Via Francigena (the main pilgrimage route from France to Rome) and the Florence–Pisa road. On a clear day the view takes in everything from Fiesole to the sea. Its strategic location made it the Tuscan residence of the emperors, from Otto IV to Frederick II; Matilda of Tuscany was born here in 1046, and in the 12th century it was an important imperial fortress, protecting the crossroads and levying tolls on travellers and merchandise.

Of the citadel, only two towers survive: the present campanile of the cathedral and the taller 'Torrione', in the shady Prato del Duomo that crowns San Miniato, with its peculiar chimney-like structures. It was from the top of this tower that Frederick II's secretary and court poet Pier della Vigna, falsely accused of treason, leapt to his death, to be discovered by Dante in the forest of suicides, as described in the *Inferno* XIII. Also in the Prato del Duomo are the 12th-century **Palazzo dei Vicari dell'Imperatore** and the **Duomo** itself, with a Romanesque brick façade, incorporating pieces of sculpted marble and 13th-century majolica that catch the light at sunset. Most of the art inside is Baroque, save a fine 13th-century holy-water stoup; most earlier artworks from the region are in the **Museo Diocesano d'Arte Sacra**, left of the cathedral. Among the prizes are the fresco of the *Maestà* by the 'Maestro degli Ordini' from Siena, a bust of Christ attributed to Verrocchio, Neri di Bicci's *Madonna con Bambino* and a *Crucifixion* by Filippo Lippi. The Prato del Duomo hosts the **national kiteflying contest** on the first Sunday after Easter.

Museo Diocesano d'Arte Sacra
open Tues–Sun 10–12.30 and 3–6 (6.30 in summer); adm

The Piazza del Popolo's 14th-century church of **San Domenico** has minor works by Masolino, Pisanello and the Della Robbias. Bernardo Rossellino carved the fine 15th-century tomb of Giovanni Chiellini, Florentine founder of San Miniato's Hospital of Poor Pilgrim Priests; it's modelled after Rossellino's famous tomb of Leonardo Bruni in Florence's Santa Croce. The beautiful church of **San Francesco** has fresco fragments by a follower of Masolino. Napoleon came in 1797, to visit relatives in the **Palazzo Bonaparte**.

In the surrounding countryside are rich caches of white truffles, sought fervently in autumn for the big market on the last Sunday in November. Many of what seem to be plain-looking Romanesque churches around San Miniato are 1900s tobacco-curing barns.

Castelfiorentino and San Vivaldo

Some 12km south along the Valdelsa from San Miniato, **Castelfiorentino** (population 18,000) is another old hilltown, much rebuilt after damage in the Second World War. Its 18th-century

Museo di Arte Sacra Santa Verdiana
open Sat 4–7, Sun and hols 10–12 and 4–7; guided tours by appt, call t 057 164096; adm

Biblioteca Comunale
Via Tilli 41, open June–mid-Sept Mon, Tues and Thurs 3.30–8, Wed and Fri 9–1; rest of year Mon–Fri 2.30–7.30; adm

Cappelle del Sacro Monte di San Vivaldo
guided tours April–Sept Sun and hols 5pm, Oct–Mar Sun and hols 3.30, or by appt on **t** *0571 699252*

church of **Santa Verdiana** houses the **Museo di Arte Sacra Santa Verdiana**, with excellent trecento paintings, including a *Madonna* attributed to Duccio da Buoninsegna, another by Francesco Granacci, and a triptych by Taddeo Gaddi. The **Biblioteca Comunale** has frescoes by Benozzo Gozzoli that were originally in the Tabernacle of the Madonna della Tosse, 'the coughing Madonna', in a nearby village, and also from the Cappella della Visitazione.

One of the more unusual sights in Tuscany, the **monastery of San Vivaldo**, lies southwest of Castelfiorentino, beyond the village of Montaione. Vivaldo, a hermit from San Gimignano, lived in a hollow chestnut tree where he was found dead in 1301, still in the attitude of prayer. A Franciscan community grew up in his footsteps, and in 1500, when the monastery was being rebuilt, one member, Fra Tommaso da Firenze, designed a 'New Jerusalem' in the monastery's wooded hills, with 34 **chapels** representing the sites of Christ's Passion. To render the symbolic journey more realistic for pilgrims, the 34 chapels combined polychrome terracottas by Giovanni della Robbia and other artists, set in frescoes – Pope Leo X granted a fat indulgence to anyone who did the whole route. Today only 18 survive.

Certaldo

Certaldo (population 16,000), former seat of Florence's deputy, or vicarate of the Valdelsa, is synonymous with Giovanni Boccaccio, who spent the last 13 years of his life in the old town, Castello Aldo, which could be a set for the *Decameron*. He died here in 1375 and is buried in **Santi Michele ed Iacopo**, under an epitaph he penned.

Museo Palazzo Pretorio
open summer daily 10–7; winter Tues–Sun 10.30–4.30; adm

Everything here is of good, honest brick, from pavements to *palazzi*, of which the most striking is the 14th-century castellated **Palazzo Pretorio**, studded with the arms of the former vicars. Inside is a beautiful courtyard and a **museum** with Etruscan artefacts, frescoes and, in the annexed church and cloister, Gozzoli's *Tabernacle of the Punished*, not one of his more cheerful works. The walls of the old jail bear the forlorn graffiti of past prisoners.

From Certaldo a pretty road leads south to **San Gimignano** (*see* pp.356–60), about 13km away.

ⓘ San Miniato >
Piazza del Popolo 3, **t** *0571 42745, www.cittadisanminiato.it*

ⓘ Certaldo >>
Viale Fabiani 5, **t** *057 165 6721, www.comune.certaldo.fi.it*

Where to Stay and Eat South of Empoli

San Miniato ✉ 56027

*****Miravalle**, Piazza Castello 3, **t** 0571 418075, *www.albergomiravalle.com* (€€€). Frederick II's 12th-century imperial palace, with rooms furnished in a rustic Tuscan style, and views over the Arno valley. It has a restaurant (half board available).

Il Canapone, Piazza Bonaparte 5, **t** 0571 418121 (€€). A simple place serving local truffles in season – in soup (with *porcini*) on spaghetti, in risotto or with veal *scaloppine*; in spring there's risotto with asparagus. *Closed Mon.*

Certaldo ✉ 50052

****Il Castello**, Via della Rena 6, **t** 0571 668250, *www.albergocastello.it* (€€€–€€). A small hotel and restaurant (half/full board available). *Closed Nov.*

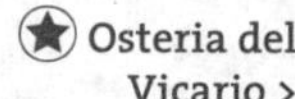

Osteria del Vicario >

***Osteria del Vicario, Via Rivellino 3, t 0571 668228 (€€). A beautiful former monastery boasting a garden and Romanesque courtyard. The guestroons are simple, with terracotta floors; breakfast is included in rates. The restaurant (€€€) serves creative local fare, including red tuna. *Restaurant closed Wed.*

Dolci Follie/La Saletta, Piazza Boccaccio, **t** 0571 668188 (€€–€). An establishment combining a fancy *pasticceria*, a wine bar and a fine little restaurant where you can come to enjoy the likes of onion soup with three cheeses, and *taglierini* with pesto, prawns and little tomatoes. The wine list is good.

Empoli to Pisa

Padule di Fucecchio
open all year; guided nature tours in spring by Centro di Ricerca, Documentazione e Promozione del Padule di Fucecchio, t 800 645303

There is no huge reason to stop in the lower Valdarno, although **Fucecchio** has good panoramic views, and the **Padule di Fucecchio**, said to be Italy's biggest inland swamp, has excellent bird-watching.

Downriver lies industrial **Pontedera**, where Piaggio produces most of Italy's motor scooters. You may wish to make a detour south along the SS439 to Volterra (*see* pp.361–68), by way of **Ponsacco** and the four-towered **Villa di Camugliano**, built by Alessandro and Cosimo I, an example of Medici real estate speculation. Between here and Volterra roll the Pisan Hills, some of the quietest, most rural countryside in Tuscany. Alternatively, from Ponsacco, head southwest to tiny **Lari**, with the remains of a Medici fortress, and for your rheumatism, to **Casciana Terme**, famous for its cures In Roman times, rebuilt by the Pisans in the 14th century.

Vicopisano, north of the Arno, defended the eastern frontier of Pisa from Lucca's ambitions. Its impressive *castello* was remodelled by Brunelleschi after the Florentine conquest of Pisa; vineyards now surround its walls and towers. Across the bridge, **Cascina** still has most of its medieval walls and Roman grid plan, and three churches: **San Casciano**, an unusual 12th-century Romanesque church with blind arches and fine sculptural details; Romanesque **San Benedetto a Settimo**, with a 14th-century alabaster altarpiece of Irish origin; and **San Giovanni Evangelista**, built by the Knights of St John, with restored trecento Sienese frescoes.

Further west lies the Certosa di Pisa (8km; *see* p.293) and Pisa itself (14km; *see* p.281).

Where to Stay and Eat from Empoli to Pisa

Fucecchio ✉ 50054

***La Campagnola, Viale Colombo 144, **t** 0571 260786, *www.lacampagnola.it* (€€). Basic, very plain rooms.

Le Vedute, Via Romana-Lucchese 121, **t** 0571 297 7201 (€€€). A good seafood restaurant in the countryside, with a veranda. *Closed Mon.*

Montopoli in Val d'Arno ✉ 56020

***Quattro Gigli, Piazza Michele 2, **t** 0571 466 878, *www.quattrogigli.it* (€€). An inn with a pool and garden. The restaurant (€€€), beyond a display of ceramics, serves imaginative dishes, some based on centuries-old recipes, such as tripe with eggs and saffron. Booking is advisable. *Closed Mon, Sun eve in winter, and 2wks Aug.*

Prato

Prato is only 18km from Florence but a world away in atmosphere; this is a city that works for its living, where the population has doubled since the Second World War to 145,000, making it the third largest in Tuscany after Florence and Livorno. And a vibrantly, joyously proletarian city it is, fond of Henry Moore, comic books, avant-garde theatre and heavy-metal bars, full of people wanting you to sign petitions or buy encyclopaedias, all proud to live in 'the Manchester of Tuscany'. Living in Florence's shadow for 1,000 years has not dampened its spirits; as in the days of Francesco di Marco Datini, immortalized in Iris Origo's book *The Merchant of Prato*, this city still earns its keep from the manufacture of textiles, especially the recycling of wool and rags. In the Renaissance, Prato made enough profit from these rags to hire the greatest artists of the day to embellish its churches and palaces.

History

In the 9th century Prato was known as Borgo al Cornio. Outside it was a meadow, or *prato*, the site of the market and fortifications, which gradually became so important that the town took the name. It was first ruled by the Alberti, one of the region's more ambitious feudal families, who conquered lands from the Maremma to the Mugello. In 1107 Countess Matilda personally led a combined Tuscan army against Prato to humble the Alberti; then, in 1140, the Pratesi rid their counts of most of their power and ran their city as a free *comune*. In 1193, at the height of the city's power, it even snatched some of Florence's own *contado*. By this time Prato had also become one of the most important manufacturers of woollen goods in Europe, and was so wealthy that the university of Paris created a college for students from Prato.

Florence could not countenance so near and ambitious a rival, and in 1350, on charges of fomenting rebellion in the Valdelsa, it besieged Prato. An honourable peace was made; the next year Florence cemented its hold by purchasing Prato for 17,500 florins from its nominal overlord, the Angevin Queen of Naples.

Despite the ignominy of being bought, Prato functioned more as Florence's ally than its possession, retaining a certain amount of local autonomy. The late 14th century was the day of Francesco di Marco Datini, the Merchant of Prato, one of the richest men in Europe and history's first recorded workaholic businessman. However, though he built his palace in his home town of Prato, the big profits were to be had in Florence, and he spent most of his time there. Under the influence of Savonarola's preaching, Prato joined Florence in rebelling against Medici rule but was soon to play the role of whipping boy when the Spaniards, at the

Getting to and around Prato

Prato is best reached by LAZZI **bus** (*www.lazzi.it*) from Florence (25mins), Pistoia (25mins) or Bologna (55mins). Buses departing from Prato (CAP/*www.capautolinee.it* or Lazzi buses to Florence every 30mins, with connections to the Mugello; Lazzi buses to Pistoia, Montecatini, Lucca, Pisa and Viareggio) set out from Piazza Ciardi or the Stazione Centrale; all pass through Piazza San Francesco.

It also easily reached by **train**. It has two stations: the main Stazione Centrale across the Bisenzio river, and Stazione Porta al Serraglio, just north of the walls and closer to the centre, on the Florence–Pistoia line (not all trains stop here).

Prato has two exits on the *autostrada* **A11** between Florence and Pisa (from Florence get on at Peretola). The centre is closed to traffic: Piazza Mercatale is a convenient place to **park**.

---

instigation of the Medici pope Leo X, sacked the city with unheard-of brutality. Since then, Prato's history followed that of its imperious neighbour – until a few years ago, when Prato and its hinterlands become a province in their own right – one of Italy's newest, and smallest.

The Castello dell'Imperatore

Castello dell'Imperatore
open Apr–Sept Wed–Mon 9–1 and 4–7; Oct–Mar Wed–Mon 9–1; adm.

Most people, whether arriving in Prato by car or bus or at the Stazione Centrale, approach the walled core of the city through the Piazza San Marco, which is embellished with a white puffy 1974 sculpture by Henry Moore. Viale Piave continues to the defiantly Ghibelline swallowtail crenellations of this castle, built in 1237 by Frederick II, Holy Roman Emperor and heir to the Norman kingdom in southern Italy and Sicily.

Frederick, unlike his grandfather Frederick Barbarossa, never spent much time in Tuscany, preferring his more civilized dominions in Apulia and Sicily, where he could discuss poetry, philosophy and falconry (in Arabic or Latin) in the company of his court scholars. When he did come, it was in magnificent progress featuring dancing girls, elephants and the Muslim imperial bodyguard. His Tuscan taxpayers were not impressed; nor did they much appreciate his tolerant, syncretistic approach to religion. The popes excommunicated him twice. He built this castle here because he had to, not so much to defend Prato but to defend his imperial *podestà* from the Pratesi, and perhaps impress locals with its design – its clean lines must have seemed very sharp and modern in the 13th century.

This Castello dell'Imperatore is quite intentionally a work of art. The design, by the Sicilian architect Riccardo da Lentini, is perfectly in tune with the south Italian works of the 'Hohenstaufen Renaissance' of Frederick's reign, and as such provides a reminder of a rare age when artistically the south was keeping up with northern Italy, and often a little in advance. There isn't much inside the castle these days, though the city often uses it for special exhibitions. Usually it is possible to walk up along its walls for a bird's-eye view of Prato.

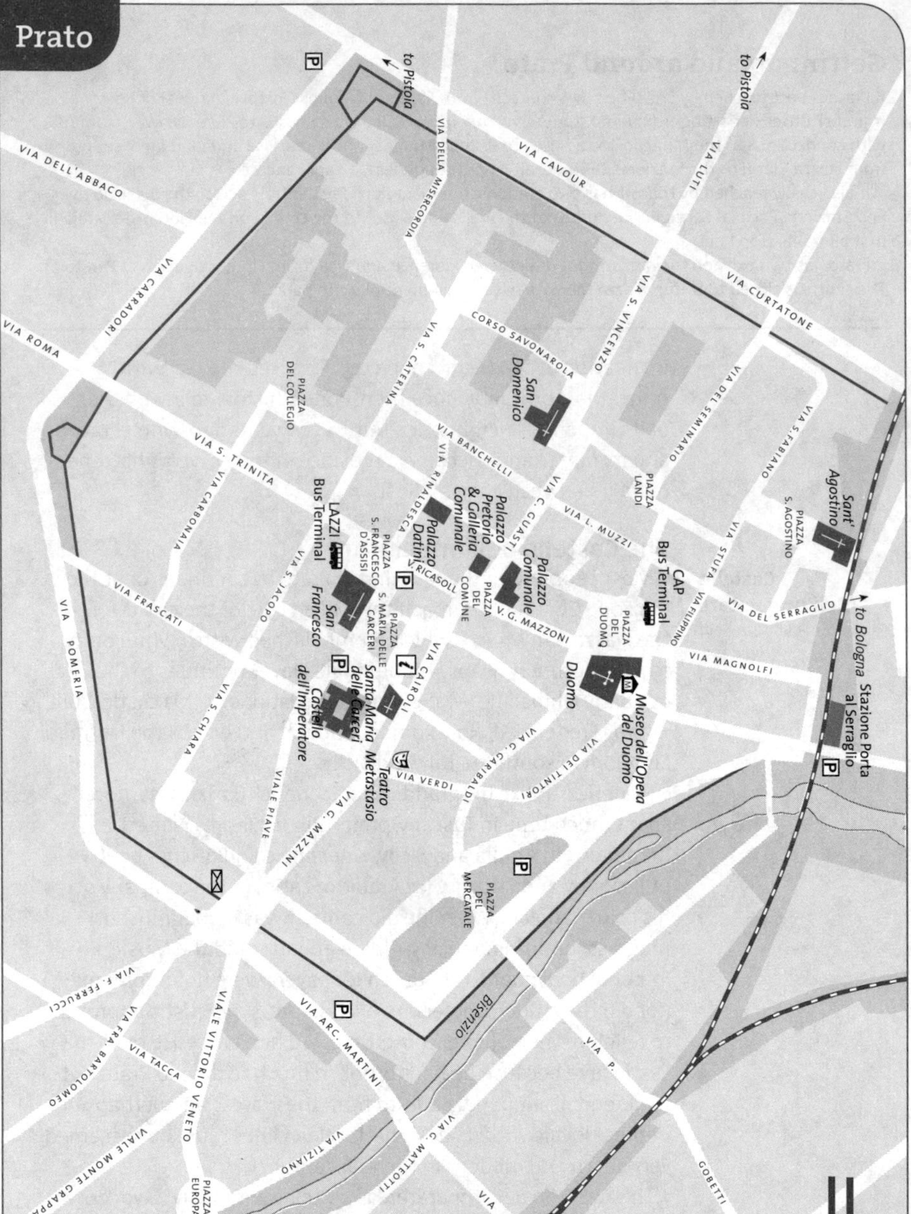

Prato
250 metres
250 yards
N
to Pistoia
to Pistoia
to Bologna
to Florence
Stazione Porta al Serraglio
Train Station
Stadio Comunale
Sant' Agostino
Piazza S. Agostino
San Domenico
CAP Bus Terminal
LAZZI Bus Terminal
Museo dell'Opera del Duomo
Duomo
Piazza del Duomo
Palazzo Comunale
Palazzo Pretorio & Galleria Comunale
Piazza del Comune
Palazzo Datini
Piazza S. Francesco d'Assisi
San Francesco
Piazza S. Maria delle Carceri
Santa Maria delle Carceri
Castello dell'Imperatore
Teatro Metastasio
Piazza Landi
Piazza del Collegio
Piazza del Mercatale
Piazza della Stazione
Piazza Europa
Bisenzio
Via Luti
Via Curtatone
Via S. Fabiano
Via del Seminario
Via Stufa
Via del Serraglio
Via Filippino
Via Magnolfi
Via S. Vincenzo
Via L. Muzzi
Via Cavour
Corso Savonarola
Via C. Guasti
Via V. G. Mazzoni
Via Banchelli
Via Rinaldesca
V. Ricasoli
Via della Misericordia
Via S. Caterina
Via Cairoli
Via dei Tintori
Via G. Garibaldi
Via Verdi
Via G. Mazzini
Viale Piave
Via S. Jacopo
Via S. Trinita
Via Carbonaia
Via S. Chiara
Via Frascati
Via Carradori
Via dell'Abbaco
Via Roma
Via Pomeria
Via P.
Gobetti
Via N. Machiavelli
Via G. Matteotti
Via Arc. Martini
Via Tiziano
Viale Vittorio Veneto
Via Tacca
Via F. Ferrucci
Via Fra. Bartolomeo
Viale Monte Grappa
Via Firenze

Santa Maria delle Carceri

Next to the castle is the unfinished black and white marble façade of Santa Maria delle Carceri, begun in 1485 by Giuliano da Sangallo. Brunelleschian architecture was always a fragile blossom, as is clearly shown by the failure of this sole serious attempt to transplant it outside the walls of Florence. It was an audacious enterprise: Sangallo, a furiously diligent student of Vitruvius and Alberti, attempted to create a building based entirely on philosophical principles. Order, simplicity and correct proportion, as in Brunelleschi's churches, were to be manifest, with few frills allowed. Sangallo, favourite of Lorenzo il Magnifico, proved to be a better theorist than architect: Santa Maria was a clumsy tombstone for the sort of theoretical architecture that was a fad in the 1400s, one more often expressed in paintings than actual buildings. The interior is better, with a plain Greek cross in the Brunelleschian manner with a decorative frieze and *tondi* of the four Evangelists by Andrea della Robbia. The church's name – *carceri* means prisons – refers to a local miracle, a speaking image of the Virgin painted on a nearby prison wall.

Behind the church is the grand 1820's **Teatro Metastasio**, home to some of the most innovative theatre in Italy and frequent concerts.

Piazza San Francesco and Datini

From Santa Maria delle Carceri you can see the apse of Prato's huge brick **church of San Francesco**, dating from the end of the 13th century and embellished in front with white and green marble stripes. Inside, on the left wall is the tomb of Gemignano Inghirami, one of Europe's crack lawyers of the quattrocento, the design attributed to Bernardo Rossellino (1460s); near the altar is the **tomb slab of Francesco di Marco Datini** (1330–1410) by Niccolò di Piero Lamberti. Off the elegant Renaissance cloister is the entrance to the **Cappella Migliorati**, beautifully frescoed in 1395 by Niccolò di Pietro Gerini, one of the period's finest draughtsmen; here he depicts the lives of saints Anthony Abbot and Matthew.

Palazzo Datini
Via Mazzei 33; open Mon–Sat 9–12 and 4–6

Niccolò also frescoed the nearby **Palazzo Datini**, the showplace palace built in the 1390s by the Merchant of Prato. If there were an Accountants' Hall of Fame, Francesco di Marco Datini would be in it; he helped invent that dismal science. The 150,000 documents, ledgers (all inscribed: 'For God and Profit') and private letters stored in the archives in this palace formed the basis for Iris Origo's fascinating account of his life and times.

The Piazza del Comune and Around

Just north lies Prato's charming civic centre, the **Piazza del Comune**, with a 19th-century **statue of Datini** with bronze reliefs of the merchant's life, and a pretty fountain by Tacca, nicknamed

'Il Bacchino', or Little Bacchus (1659). The **Palazzo Comunale**, behind the portico, retains only traces of its medieval heritage; drop in to see its **Sala di Consiglio** with its coffered ceiling, two quattrocento frescoes and portraits of the grand dukes. In the grand **Sala dell'Udienza** with its fine wood ceiling is Bernardo Daddi's *Story of the Holy Girdle*, a predella telling of Prato's most famous relic, the Virgin Mary's belt. According to tradition she gave it to Doubting Thomas, from whom it was passed down until it became part of the dowry of a woman who married Michele, a knight from Prato during the First Crusade. Michele returned to Prato and hid the precious relic under his mattress; angels lifted him off, and the girdle was given into the care of the cathedral. In the same hall are fine 14th-century works by Giovanni di Milano, Michele di Firenze, Lorenzo Monaco, and a *tondo* attributed to Luca Signorelli.

The rugged **Palazzo Pretorio** is entirely medieval, a relic of the days when Prato governed itself without any help from the Medici; the stair on the façade leads up to the **Galleria Comunale 'Alberti'**, with a good collection of mostly Florentine art. There's a tabernacle by Filippino Lippi, painted for his mother and restored after damage in the war. In an adjoining room is *Noli me tangere* by Battistello, a follower of Caravaggio; this curious work portrays Christ wearing a fedora at a rakish angle, doing a quick dance step to evade the Magdalene's touch.

Galleria Comunale 'Alberti'
open by appt on **t** *057 461 7359*

For a celebration of Prato's medieval and modern textile industry, visit the **Museo del Tessuto**, which has a unique collection of fabrics and looms (some 6,000 pieces) dating from 5th century AD to today. It is housed in a stunning 19th-century textile mill.

Museo del Tessuto
Via Santa Chiara 24; open Mon–Fri 10–6, Sat 10–2, Sun 4–7; for guided tours call **t** *057 461 1503; adm exc Sun*

Cathedral of Santo Stefano

Duomo di Santo Stefano
open July-Sept daily 7.30–12.30 and 4–7.30; rest of year Fri 7–12.30 and 3–6.30, Sun and hols 7–12.30 and 3-8; guided tours of chapel (including Lippi frescoes) Sat 10, 11, 4 and 5, and Sun 10 and 11, by appt with tourist office (see p.234); adm

In the centre of Prato rises its cathedral, like a faded beauty who has never really recovered from the blow of a broken engagement. The building was begun with great promise in the 13th century, and added to on and off over the next 200 years, but with ever-dwindling passion and money. The best features are an exotic, almost Moorish campanile, a rather dirty Andrea della Robbia lunette of the *Madonna and St Stephen* over the door, and a big clock on the half-striped façade, where the rose window ought to be. But above all there's the circular **Pulpit of the Sacred Girdle**, projecting from the corner of the façade – something beautiful and special that the Pratesi look at every day as they walk through the *piazza*. Michelozzo designed it in 1428 and Donatello added the delightful reliefs of dancing children and *putti* along the lines of his *cantoria* in Florence's cathedral museum (the originals are now housed in the Museo dell'Opera). The Holy Girdle (*see* above) is publicly displayed here on Easter Day, 1 May, 15 August, 8 September and Christmas Day.

The interior continues the motif of green and white stripes in its Romanesque arcades and ribs of the vaulting. The **Chapel of the Sacred Girdle**, left as you enter, is protected by a screen, and the inside is covered with frescoes by Agnolo Gaddi on the legend of the girdle, and adorned with a beautiful marble statue, the *Madonna and Child*, by Giovanni Pisano. In the left aisle is a masterful **pulpit** carved by Mino da Fiesole and Antonio Rossellino, with harpies around the base. Filippo Lippi's celebrated frescoes on the *Lives of Saints John the Baptist and Stephen* (1452–66) are undergoing long-term restoration. While painting these, his first major work, Lippi fell in love with a brown-eyed novice, Lucrezia Buti, who according to tradition posed for his magnificent *Herod's Banquet*, either as the melancholy Salome or as the figure in the long white dress, second from right; Fra Filippo placed himself among the mourners for St Stephen, third from right, in a red hat. The less lyrical frescoes in the next chapel are by Uccello and Andrea di Giusto. There's a lovely, almost Art Nouveau, candelabra on the high altar by Maso di Bartolomeo (1440s), closely related to his work in Pistoia cathedral.

Museo dell'Opera del Duomo
open Mon and Wed–Sat 9.30–12.30 and 3–6.30, Sun 9.30–12.30; undergoing long-term restoration/ enlargement, with only 2 rooms open; most important works now in Museo di Pittura Murale (see below)

The **Museo dell'Opera del Duomo** is next door in the cloister, one side of which retains its 12th-century geometric marble decorations and rambunctious capitals. The tragic star of the museum is the original pulpit of the Sacred Girdle, with Donatello's merry *putti* made lepers by car exhaust. Lippi's *Death of San Girolamo* was painted to prove to the bishop that he was the man to fresco the cathedral choir. Other works include his son Filippino's *St Lucy*, blissfully ignoring the knife in her throat, and another full-length portrait, of Fra Jacopone di Todi, believed to be an early work by Uccello. More dancing *putti* adorn the *Reliquary of the Sacred Girdle* (1446) by Maso di Bartolomeo, stolen but recovered at the Todi antiques fair.

Walking through Prato

Most of Prato's old streets are self-effacing Tuscan. Some areas suffered bomb damage in the war, notably the great pear-shaped **Piazza del Mercatale** on the banks of the Bisenzio. This was long the working core of the city, surrounded by porticoes and workshops; it remains the site of Prato's big market and fairs. A few faded, peeling, porticoed buildings remain, overlooking the river that has laundered the products of Prato's main industry for eight centuries.

Museo di Pittura Murale
open Mon and Wed–Sat 10–6, Sun and hols 10–1; adm

Sunday is a good day to visit sturdy brick **San Domenico** on the west side of town: a large Gothic church begun in 1283 and completed by Giovanni Pisano, one side lined with arcades. The adjacent convent, home of painter Fra Bartolomeo and Pratese address of Savonarola, holds the **Museo di Pittura Murale** with its collection of detached frescoes from surrounding churches; it also tends to hold works from other museums undergoing reorganization. There are charming quattrocento graffiti court scenes from the Palazzo Vaj, a sinopia from the cathedral attributed to Uccello, and Niccolò di Piero Gerini's *Tabernacle of the Ceppo*. Filippo Lippi painted the *Madonna del Ceppo* for the Ceppo offices in the Palazzo Datini; it portrays the tycoon himself, with four fellow donors who contributed less and thus get portrayed as midgets.

Just north, **San Fabiano** at Via del Seminario 30 has an enchanting pre-Romanesque mosaic pavement depicting mermaids, birds and dragons biting their own tails; north again, 15th-century **Sant'Agostino** contains Prato's most ridiculous painting, the *Madonna della Consolazione* (attributed, naturally, to Vasari), who does her consoling by distributing belts from heaven.

Centro per L'Arte Contemporanea Luigi Pecci
Viale della Repubblica, open Tues–Sat 10–7; adm

Despite its artistic treasures, Prato doesn't sit on its Renaissance laurels. The ambitious **Centro per L'Arte Contemporanea Luigi Pecci** in the suburbs has a collection of modern works from artists around the world, temporary exhibitions by important artists, and concerts. After the popularity of Henry Moore's big lump by the station in the 1970s, Prato has also accumulated outdoor abstract sculpture in a big way. Two that stand out, if only for their breathtaking pretentiousness, are Barbara Krueger's billboard *Untitled* (Viale da Vinci), and Anne and Patrick Poirier's *Monumentum Aere Perennis*, in the grounds of Centro Luigi Pecci.

ⓘ Prato >
Piazza Santa Maria delle Carceri 15, **t** *0574 24112, www.prato.turismo.toscana.it (closed Sun)*

Shopping in Prato

Prato makes its living from fine fabrics (including cashmere) and clothes, and people from all over Tuscany come for the discount factory outlets.

Angorelle, Via Vella, **t** 0574 467275. Cashmere and mohair.

M-Wear-Milior, Via Pistoiese 755D, **t** 0574 818288. Women's clothing and accessories.

Maglificio Denny, Via Zarini 261, **t** 0574 592350. Cashmere/wool/cotton knits.

Maglificio Pratesi, Via Baccheretana 83, Seano, **t** 055 870 5467. Clothing for adults and kids.

Tessiture Cecchi & Cecchi, Via delle Calandre 53, Calenzano, **t** 055 887 8196. Cashmere, wool and silk items.

Where to Stay in Prato

Prato ✉ 50047

Prato's hotels mostly cater for businessmen but can be a good bet in summer when Florence is packed.

***__Flora__ —

*****Flora**, Via Cairoli 31, near S. Maria dei Carceri, **t** 0574 33521, *www.hotelflora.info* (€€€). Old-fashioned but decent rooms with VHS players (there's a small video library). Check the website for special offers.

*****Villa Santa Cristina**, Via Poggio Secco 58, **t** 0574 595 951, *palaceprato@libero.it* (€€€). A relaxing spot over the river in the hills east of Prato, with a garden, pool and restaurant. Breakfast is included. *Restaurant closed Sun.*

*****Hotel Giardino**, Via Magnolfi 2, **t** 0574 26189, *www.giardinohotel.com* (€€€–€€). A well-modernized friendly hotel with a pleasant bar, reading room and private garage (€11/day). Breakfast is included.

*****San Marco**, Piazza San Marco 48, **t** 0574 21321, *www.hotelsanmarcoprato.com* (€€). A simple, comfortable place situated between the Stazione Centrale and the Castello, convenient if you arrive by train.

*****Villa Rucellai**, Via di Canneto 16, 4km northeast of town, **t** 0574 460392 (€€). A delightful, good-value B&B in a

Renaissance villa, with a pool. Rooms are very simple but well furnished, and breakfast is included. Though surrounded by Prato's industrial sprawl, its formal gardens and wonderful atmosphere (it's filled with the family's books, pictures and furniture) make it an oasis. The farm produces wine, oil, honey and jams.

****Toscana**, Piazza Ciardi 3, **t** 0574 28096, *www.hoteltoscana.prato.it* (€€). Newly renovated rooms on a quiet square on the far side of the Stazione Porta al Serraglio.

Eating Out in Prato

Prato ✉ 50047

The food is reason enough to stay in Prato, especially if you like fish.

Enoteca Barni, Via Ferucci 22, **t** 0574 607 845 (€€€). Simpler, cheaper lunch menus and more interesting choices at night, in an elegant setting. Try lobster cake, asparagus soufflé with foie gras sauce, red mullet with basil, black olives and tomato, and lamb in a herb crust. Booking is advised. *Closed Sat lunch, Sun eve and Aug.*

Osvaldo Baroncelli, Via Fra Bartolomeo 13, **t** 0574 23810 (€€€). A small place with an innovative chef and good-value set menu. A la carte options include *fricassée* of salt cod, and Tuscan bean and spelt soup with fish and frizzled leeks. The *sedano alla pratese* (celery with meat) is highly recommended, and there is a fabulous array of Italian and French cheeses and an excellent wine list. *Closed Sat lunch and Sun.*

Il Pirana, Via Valentini 110 (south of Viale Vittorio Veneto, between Stazione Centrale and Piazza San Marco), **t** 0574 25746 (€€€). An elegant place, hidden behind reflecting glass windows, serving some of the best seafood in inland Tuscany: try prawns with pears and *pecorino* cheese, and hagfish with vegetables. *Closed Sat lunch, Sun and Aug.*

Mattei, Via Ricasoli 20 (€). A *biscotteria* and bar dating back to 1858 and selling the best *biscotti* (or *cantucci*) *di Prato* around, packaged in distinctive bright blue bags. *Closed Mon.*

Osteria Cibbé, Piazza Mercatale 49, **t** 0574 607509 (€). A small, family-run *osteria* with marble-topped tables in a brick-vaulted room, serving delicious rustic food such as *pan cotto* ('cooked bread') and *pappa al pomodoro*, and *finocchiona* and other Tuscan salami. *Closed Sun.*

La Vecchia Cucina di Soldano, Via Pomeria 23, **t** 0574 34665 (€). An unpretentious family-run trattoria serving traditional dishes on red-checked tablecloths. Meat is the speciality: wild boar, roe deer, sheep and *sedano alla pratese* (*see* above). *Closed Sun.*

★ **La Vecchia Cucina di Soldano >>**

North of Prato: the Val di Bisenzio

Prato's river begins some 40km up in the Apennines, and along its valley runs the SS325, a secondary highway towards Bologna. This valley was long the fiefdom of the Alberti counts, whose fortifications dot its sides. **Vaiano**, the first town on the main route, has a Romanesque abbey church and green-striped campanile as its landmark; just beyond are the ruins of the Alberti's **Rocca di Cerbaia** (12th century). The highway continues to **San Quirico**, with another ruined Alberti castle up above.

From San Quirico's neighbour to the west, Cantagallo ('Cock's crow'), a lovely walking path leads up to the **Piano della Rasa**, a panoramic valley with an **alpine refuge**, in little over an hour. Further north on the SS325, at the small resort of **Montepiano**, the waters destined for the Tyrrhenian and Adriatic split and go their

Rifugio Alpino
open April–Oct

own ways. There is another ancient abbey here, the Vallombrosan **Badia di Santa Maria**, with good 13th- and 14th-century frescoes. From the abbey begins another fine walking path up to **Alpi di Cavarzano** (1,008m), and from there, it is another hour or so's walk up to the highest peak in the region, **Monte La Scoperta** (1,278m).

Figline and Montemurlo

The old road between Prato and Pistoia passes **Figline di Prato**, a medieval village known for its terracotta vases. It has a 14th-century parish church with contemporary mural paintings, including a 'primitive' *Last Supper* and a *St Michael* with a finely detailed background; a small museum contains other 'primitives'.

Montemurlo, on its hill over the plain of Prato, is also medieval; in 1537 its castle, a stronghold of the Guidi counts, was the Alamo for the anti-Medici republican oligarchs of Florence, led by Filippo Strozzi, defeated here once and for all by the troops of Cosimo I. The old walled town is interesting, with an impressive, rather stylish **Rocca** for its crown, approached by a Mannerist ramp. The Romanesque church of 'Beheaded John' (**San Giovanni Decollato**) has a pretty campanile and some good art in its Baroqued interior, including a miraculous Byzantine crucifix and a 16th-century painting by Giovanni da Prato illustrating its story.

Pistoia

Pistoia

You know Pistoia (population 94,000) is near when the road plunges into a Lilliputian forest of umbrella pines and cypresses in tidy rows. These are Italy's most extensive ornamental nurseries, a gentle craft that thrives in the rich soil at the foot of the Apennines. But Pistoia wasn't always content to cultivate its own garden; this is the place that gave us the word 'pistol' – which originally referred to the surgical knives made in the city but came to mean daggers, and finally guns.

...Proud you are, envious, enemies of heaven, Friends to your own harm and, to your own neighbour, The simplest charity you find a labour

'Invective against the People of Pistoia', a sonnet by Michelangelo

Today it specializes in light rail trains, mattresses, cymbals and baby trees. Very untouristy, it has an almost perfectly intact historic centre, and some fine art behind its part Pisan, part Florentine medieval walls, reflecting its position between the two great rivals.

History

Pistoia's fellow Tuscans have looked askance at her ever since Roman times, when the city was called *Pistoria* and saw the death struggle of the Catiline conspiracy, the famous attempted coup against the Roman Republic in 62 BC, which ended when the legions tracked down the escaped Catiline and his henchmen near

Getting to and around Pistoia

Pistoia lies along the **A11**, and at the foot of two important routes north over the Apennines, the **SS64** towards Bologna and the **SS633** to Abetone.

COPIT **buses** (*www.copitspa.it*) for Vinci and Empoli (37km/2hrs – a beautiful, twisting road over the Monte Albano), Cutigliano (37km/1hr 45min), Abetone (50km/2hrs 30mins), the zoo, Montecatini (16km/30min), and other destinations in Pistoia's little province depart from Piazza San Francesco. LAZZI buses (*www.lazzi.it*) depart for Florence (35km/1hr), Prato, Lucca (43km/90mins), Montecatini, Viareggio and Pisa (65km/2hrs) from Viale Vittorio Veneto, near the train station.

There are frequent **trains** (*www.trenitalia.com*) along the main Florence–Lucca line from the station, just south of the city walls at the end of Via XX Settembre

Cars are banned from most of the centre (in theory) but there's plenty of parking around the Fortezza di Santa Barbara in the southeast corner of the walls.

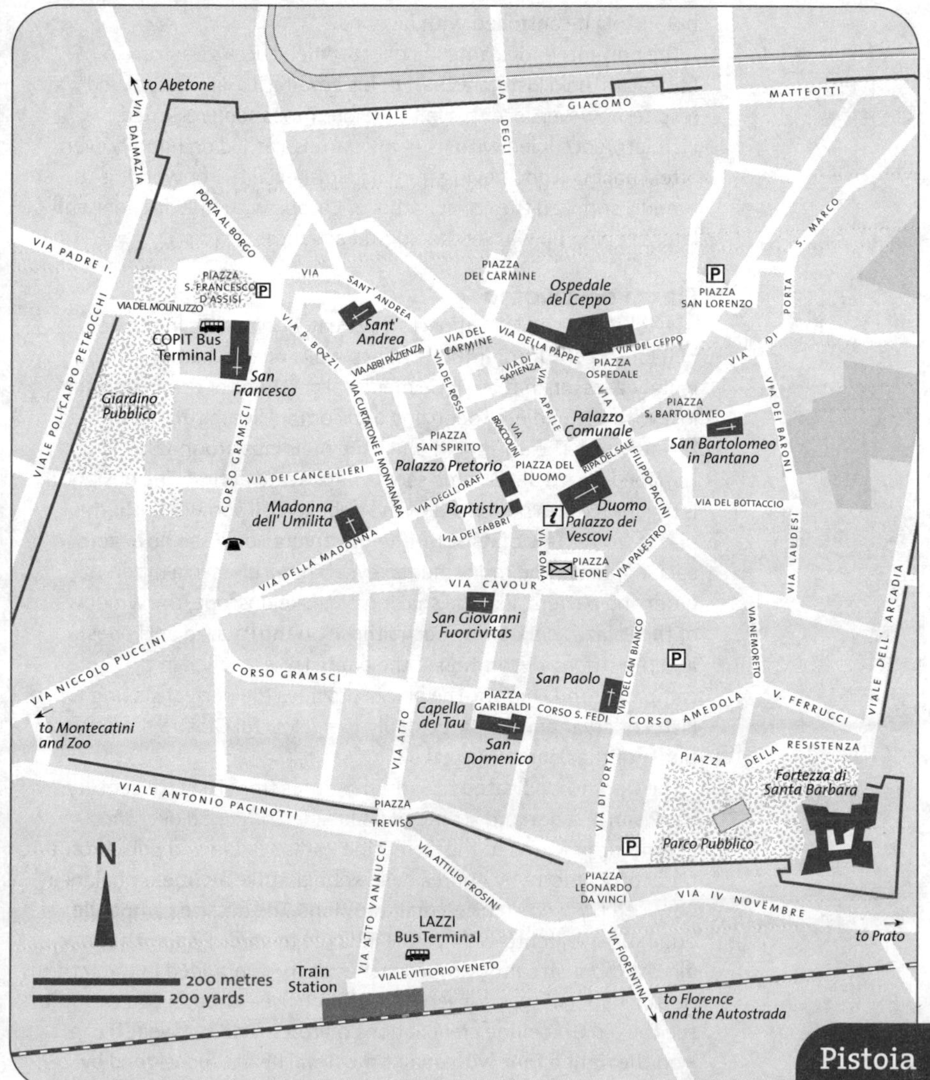

Pistoia. Its position on the Via Cassia helped it prosper under the Lombards, who elevated it to a royal city. In 1158 Pistoia became a *comune*, and was seen as enough of a threat for Florence and Lucca to gang up against it twice. In the 13th century Pistoia's evil reputation gave it credit for having begun the bitter controversy between Black and White Guelphs that so obsessed Florence; Dante, himself a victim of that feud, made sure that in writing the *Divina Commedia* he never missed an opportunity to curse and condemn the fateful city. In 1306 Florence exacted revenge by capturing Pistoia, and as usual it adapted its politics to the nature of its conquest: Prato it made an ally, Pisa it held with fortresses, but Pistoia it controlled with factions.

The only interlude came in 1315–28, when Lucca's Castruccio Castracani held Pistoia as part of his empire; it was a shortlived respite, however: after his fall the Florentines soon returned. Pistoia, preoccupied with its own quarrels, carried on happily ever after, making a good living from its old speciality, ironworking. It proudly supplied the conspirators of Europe with fine daggers, and later, keeping up with technological advances, pistols.

Piazza del Duomo

Pistol-Pistoia no longer packs any heat, but it packs in the heart of its 16th-century diamond-shaped walls one of the finest squares in Italy, a lesson in the subtle medieval aesthetic of urban design, lost with the endless theorizing and compulsive regularity of the Renaissance. The arrangement of the buildings around the L-shaped Piazza del Duomo seems haphazard at first. The design is meant to be experienced from street level; if you walk into the piazza from a few of its surrounding streets, you'll see how from each approach the monuments reveal themselves in a different order and pattern, like the shaking of a kaleidoscope; the windows of the Palazzo del Comune echo those on the Palazzo del Podestà, and the striped decoration of the baptistry is recalled in the campanile and Duomo. The piazza provides the perfect setting for Pistoia's great annual party in July, the colourful Giostra dell'Orso (Joust of the Bear; *see* p.243).

The **Duomo**, dedicated to San Zeno, dates from the 12th century; the Pisan arcades and stripes of its façade, combined over the geometric patterns of the Florentine Romanesque and polychrome terracotta lunette by Andrea della Robbia, strike an uneasy balance between the two architectural traditions. The outsize **campanile**, originally a watchtower, tips the balance towards Pisa, with exotic, almost Moorish candy-striped arches at the top, added in the 14th century when it was converted to church use – though you can still see the old Ghibelline crenellations on top. Inside is a wealth of art – on the right a **font** with quaint medieval heads, redesigned by

Benedetto da Maiano, the **tomb of Cino da Pistoia** (1337), a close friend of Dante, shown lecturing to a class of scholars, and a 13th-century painted crucifix by Coppo di Marcovaldo. The most precious treasure is in the **chapel of St James**: a fabulous altar made of nearly a ton of silver, comprising 628 figures, begun in 1287 and added to over the next two centuries; among the Pisan, Sienese and Florentine artists who contributed to this shining *tour de force* was Brunelleschi, who added the two half-figures on the left before devoting all his talents to architecture.

Cappella di San Jacopo
ask sacristan to view; adm

Some of the oldest art, fine medieval reliefs of the Last Supper and Gethsemane, have been relegated to the dim and ancient crypt. By the altar are a fine painting by Caravaggio's pupil, Mattia Preti, and Maso di Bartolomeo's bronze candelabra. On the left the **chapel of the Sacrament** has a bust of a Medici archbishop attributed to Verrocchio, who also added the statues of Faith and Hope to the weeping angels on the **tomb of Cardinal Forteguerri**, just left of the main entrance.

Next to the Duomo. the partly striped, partly brick **Palazzo dei Vescovi** was mangled by remodellings over the centuries. The tourist office is here; restorations undertaken to install it uncovered some Etruscan *cippi* (gravestones), and the foundations of Pistoia's original cathedral. The Etruscan finds, plus relics of Roman Pistoia, are arranged in an '**archaeological itinerary**' in the Palazzo's basement, and the old cathedral is now included in the **Museo San Zeno**, with some paintings and a fine reliquary by Lorenzo Ghiberti.

Museo San Zeno
t *057 336 9272; open by appt Tues, Thurs, Fri and 2nd and 4th Sun of month 10–1 and 3–5*

Across from the Duomo is Pistoia's octagonal zebra of a baptistry, properly named **San Giovanni in Corte**. Built over the site of a Lombard-era royal palace (the *corte*), it was finished in 1359, to a design by Andrea Pisano. It is one of the few outstanding Gothic buildings in Tuscany, embellished with fine sculptural details. The interior has a remarkable conical ceiling of brick and a beautifully decorated font from 1226, designed by Lanfranco da Como. Piazza della Sala, behind the baptistry, has a medieval well topped by a Florentine *Marzocco*.

San Giovanni in Corte
open Tues–Sat 10–12.30 and 3–6, Sun 9.30–12.30

The Piazza del Duomo's other two palaces are civic in nature. The 14th-century **Palazzo Pretorio** on the west side has a decorated courtyard and an old stone bench where the judges sat, often condemning malefactors to a unique punishment – they were ennobled. Not that Pistoia wanted to reward them; rather, to become noble meant losing one's rights as a republican citizen. The tower near here is known as the tomb of Catiline, who, according to tradition, was secretly buried here.

On the other side of the piazza stands the elegant **Palazzo Comunale**, begun in 1294,and prominently embellished with the usual Medici balls and the more unusual black marble head, believed to be that of a Moorish king captured by a captain from

Museo Civico
t 057 337 1296; www.comune.pistoia.it/museocivico; open summer Mon–Sat 10–6, Sun 9.30–12.30; winter Mon–Sat 10–5, Sun 9.30–12.30; adm

Pistoia on a freebooting expedition to Mallorca. Besides the town council and offices, the *palazzo* houses the **Museo Civico**, with an excellent collection of great and odd paintings. Many works (especially the large historical canvases of assassinations and plots against the tyrannical Medici) were donated by the local Puccini family, whose warts'n'all portraits are a highlight. Other Pistoiese patrons were uncommonly fond of the *Sacra Conversazione*– a group portrait of saints around the Madonna – and there are good ones by Mariotto de Nardo, Beccafumi, Lorenzo di Credi and Pistoia's own Gerino Gerini (1480–1529), a follower of Raphael. From the 15th-century 'Maestro delle Madonne di Marmo' there's a sweetly smiling marble relief of the Madonna and child; then two fancy St Sebastians with flowing curls, who precede the *Madonna della Pergola*, by local painter Bernardino di Antonio Detti (1498–1554), whose flaccid charwoman of a Madonna holds a child with a large fly on his chubby arm before a crazy quilt of iconography.

On the mezzanine is the documentation centre of 20th-century Pistoiese architect Giovanni Michelucci, with a comprehensive collection of models and drawings, as well as photos of his buildings and the media reaction to them. One example of his work is the large, angular Santa Maria Novella station in Florence; another is the restaurant in the Parco Collodi (see p.250).

Plod up another flight of stairs for some lurid paintings from the 17th–19th centuries, with enough historical canvases of murder and mayhem to suggest the local taste for violence lingered on for some time, at least within the confines of art. There are two mythological paintings swathed in Caravaggiesque darkness by Cecco Bravo; a 17th-century *Young Woman with a Flower*, bathed in ghostly light; a sensuous, pouting St Sebastian, disdainfully plucking arrows from his chest; an absurd allegory of Medici rule in Pistoia, with putti scattering the family's lily symbol like flowers over the city; and a Magdalene fondly patting a skull.

Museo Rospigliosi
open Mon–Sat and 2nd Sun of month 10–1 and 3–6; joint adm with Museo Diocesano

Museo Diocesano
open Tues–Fri 10–1 and 4–7, Sat 4–7; joint adm with Museo Rospigliosi

Just off Piazza del Duomo on Ripa del Sale, the 16th-century Palazzo Rospigliosi houses two small museums, the **Museo Rospigliosi**, with its original furniture and paintings *in situ*, the latter mostly by Pistoiese artist Giacinto Gimignani, and the **Museo Diocesano**, with crosses and reliquaries of the early Middle Ages.

Ospedale del Ceppo and Sant'Andrea

In medieval Tuscany, it was customary to collect alms in a hollowed log (*ceppo*) left in a public place, to be distributed to the poor at Christmas. *Ceppo* became synonymous with the word 'charity', as in Datini's foundation in Prato, and even earlier here in Pistoia, when the **Ospedale del Ceppo** was founded in the 13th century. Still at the same address just north of the Palazzo Comunale (though not for much longer – plans are to move all facilities to a new hospital outside the walls), the building was given a fine arcaded porch in the 1500s, in the style of the Spedale degli Innocenti in Florence. And, as in Florence, the Della Robbias were called upon to provide the decoration, in this case the usually insipid Giovanni, who with the help of his workshop and other artists created not only the typical Della Robbian *tondi* but a unique terracotta frieze that spans the entire loggia in Renaissance Technicolor, with scenes of the acts of mercy and theological virtues. Inside is the small **Museo dei Ferri Chirurgici** about Pistoia's old iron industry, especially surgical knives. You can visit one of the city's wrought-iron 'laboratories', **Bartoletti** at Via Sestini 110.

Bartoletti
open Mon–Sat; call **t** *0573 452784 for times*

Sant'Andrea
open daily 8–12.30 and 3.30–6

A short walk west of the hospital on Via Sant'Andrea is the 12th-century **church of Sant'Andrea**, with a Pisan façade and, over the door, a charming bas-relief of the Journey of the Magi, dated 1166, and a pair of ghastly, leering lions. The real jewel is inside: Giovanni Pisano's hexagonal **pulpit** (1297), exquisitely carved in stirring high relief with scenes of the *Nativity*, *Massacre of the Innocents*, *Adoration of the Magi*, *Crucifixion* and *Last Judgement*, with sibyls in the corners and pedestals in the forms of the four Evangelists – one of the masterpieces of Italian Gothic. Sant'Andrea contains three other crucifixions: Giovanni Pisano's wooden crucifix in the right aisle, a medieval version over the main altar, portraying Christ crowned and dressed in a kingly robe, and in the right nave a large, rather mysterious painting of the saint crucified on a tree.

San Francesco and the Madonna dell'Umilità

Pretty striped churches circle the centre of Pistoia like zebras on a merry-go-round. The two plain ponies in the lot lie to the west. The large **San Francesco al Prato** in Piazza San Francesco d'Assisi, plain and Gothic like most Franciscan churches, has notable 14th-century frescoes, especially in the chapel left of the altar. On the side of the church are an ancient olive tree and a memorial to assassinated PM Aldo Moro, a contrast with the piazza's Fascist-era war monument.

South along Corso Gramsci is Pistoia's main theatre, the 1694 **Teatro Manzoni**; further south, on Via della Madonna, is Pistoia's great experiment in High Renaissance geometry, the octagonal, unstriped **Basilica della Madonna dell'Umilità** begun in 1518 by local architect Ventura Vitoni, a pupil of Bramante who graced it with an imposing barrel-vaulted vestibule. In the 1560s Vasari was called upon to crown Vitoni's fine start, adding a dome so heavy the basilica has been threatening to collapse ever since.

San Giovanni Fuoricivitas and San Domenico

South of the Piazza del Duomo (Via Roma to Via Cavour) lies tiny **Piazza San Leone**, the ancient Lombard centre of Pistoia; its stubby tower belonged to the nastiest Pistoian of all, a 13th-century noble thug and church robber named Vanni Fucci whom Dante found in one of the lower circles of Hell, entwined in a serpent, cursing and making obscene gestures up at God. Around the corner of Via Cavour, the 12th-century **San Giovanni Fuorcivitas** claims the honour of being the most striped church in all Christendom, its green and white flank an abstract pattern of lozenges and blind arches. The gloomy interior holds a dramatic pulpit (1270) by Fra Gugliemo da Pisa, a pupil of Nicola Pisano, a holy-water stoup supported by caryatids by Giovanni Pisano and a white, glazed terracotta group of the Visitation by Luca or Andrea della Robbia.

Piazza Garibaldi, also south, is adorned with a equestrian statue of Garibaldi and **San Domenico**, begun in the late 13th century, with a splendid Baroque organ from 1617 and the Renaissance tombs of Filippo Lazzari, by the Rossellino brothers, portraying the deceased lecturing to his pupils (one of whom is yawning), and of Lorenzo da Ripafratta, with a fine effigy. In 1497 Benozzo Gozzoli died of the plague in Pistoia and is buried somewhere in the cloister of San Domenico; you can see a fresco he began of the *Journey of the Magi* nearby. Though the monastery is still in use, you can ring to see the frescoes in the chapterhouse, among them good Sienese works and a *Crucifixion* with its sinopia, from the mid 13th century.

Cappella del Tau
open Mon–Sat 9–2

Even more interesting are the frescoes across the street in the little **Cappella del Tau**, so named after the blue T its priests wore on their vestments. The vividly coloured scenes of Adam and Eve and assorted saints are attributed in part to Masolino. The convent of the chapel has become the **Fondazione Marino Marini**, tracing the career of this Pistoiese artist, who died in 1980, in both paint and sculpture; it includes the bronze *Young Girl*, who recalls the antique tradition not only in her facial features but also her truncated arms. Next to it, at No.72, over the pretty window, note the coat of arms with dancing bears, recalling the Giostra dell'Orso. There's another good Gothic façade on **San Paolo**, a block east, with broader stripes and a statue of St James on the top, attributed to Orcagna.

Fondazione Marino Marini
t 057 30285; open Mon–Sat 10–5; adm

On the east side of town, built on marshy land in the 8th century and sinking into the ground ever since, **San Bartolomeo in Pantano** (St Bart in the Bog) has an attractive, partially completed façade, and contains a carved marble lectern of 1250 by Guido da Como.

The Zoo and the Medici

Giardino Zoologico di Pistoia
Via Pieve a Celle, t 057 391 1219; open Mon–Fri 9–6.30, Sat, Sun and hols 9–7; adm exp

La Magia in Quarrata
t 0573 7710; open by appt

The newest stripes in Pistoia may well be on the zebras in the **Pistoia Zoo**, 4km northwest of the city, and one of the best in the country; though the Medici kept big menageries, modern Italians don't usually care for zoos. Thirteen kilometres southeast, off the SS66, is yet another Medici villa, **La Magia in Quarrata**, begun in 1318. Its grand hall has 18th-century frescoes, and in 1536 Charles V and Alessandro de' Medici met here. Concerts are hosted in summer.

ⓘ Pistoia > bishop's palace, Piazza del Duomo, t 0573 21622, www.turismo.pistoia.it

Shopping in Pistoia

On Wed and Sat, a huge market takes over the city centre; it's hard to find a parking place at these times.

Post office: Via Roma 5, **t** 057 399 5300.

Events in Pistoia

Giostra dell'Orso (Joust of the Bear), 25 July. The culmination of a month of concerts, fairs and exhibits. The Joust began in the 14th century, pitting 12 knights against a bear dressed in a checked cloak. The bear has been replaced by two wooden dummies, but the pageantry remains the same.

Where to Stay in Pistoia

Pistoia ✉ 51110

Pistoia is better attuned to business travellers than pleasure-seekers; you may prefer to stay in nearby Montecatini Terme (*see* p.247).

*****Il Convento**, Via S. Quirico 33, Pontenuovo, 5km east of town, **t** 0573 452651, *www.ilconventohotel.com* (€€€). A former convent with views over Pistoia, a pool and one of the city's best restaurants. Breakfast is included.

Tenuta di Pieve a Celle, Via Pieve a Celle 158, **t** 0573 913087, *www.tenutadipieveacelle.it* (€€€). A stylish *agriturismo* next to the zoo, in a farmhouse converted with taste and style, with a fine pool. The setting is peaceful (minus the odd animal roar) and the farm produces oil. Guests can order dinner.

★ Villa Vannini >

Villa Vannini, about 6km north of town, **t** 0573 42031, *www.volpe-uva.it* (€€€–€€). A delightful if fading villa among fir trees, with hill walks on the doorstep, elegant, comfortable, good-value rooms (breakfast included) and a fantastic restaurant.

*****Leon Bianco**, Via Panciatichi 2, **t** 0573 26675, *www.hotelleonbianco.it* (€€). A dated but reasonable option with views over the campanile and free Wifi access. Breakfast is included.

*****Hotel Patria**, Via Crispi 8, **t** 0573 25187, *www.patriahotel.it* (€€). A cheerful choice near San Domenico, serving bacon and eggs for breakfast, or a buffet (included).

*****Piccolo Ritz**, Via Vannucci 67, **t** 0573 26775 (€€). A modern place near the station, suffering a little from noise. Cheaper rooms share facilities.

****Firenze**, Via Curtatone e Montanara 42, **t** 0573 23141, *www.hotel-firenze.it* (€€). The least expensive option, near Piazza del Duomo and a bit woebegone.

Eating Out in Pistoia

Pistoia ✉ 51110

Pistoia has many simple trattorias and pizzerias, and several places with more sophisticated local cuisine.

Rafanelli, Via Sant'Agostino 47, Sant'Agostino, **t** 0573 532046 (€€). Local dishes, including risotto with *porcini*, wild boar with olives and grilled meats. *Closed Sun eve, Mon, 1wk Jan, and Aug.*

★ La BotteGaia >>

La BotteGaia, Via del Lastrone 17, **t** 0573 365602 (€€). A wine bar/restaurant tucked away behind the baptistry, occupying a beautiful vaulted room and lovely terrace. It serves snacks (cheeses and meats, *bruschette* and salads) and full meals from a short but ever-changing menu. The excellent-value *menu degustazione* features such delights as celery soup with *pecorino*, leek flan, pesto lasagne, duck breast with wild fennel, and foie gras. There are some 600 wines to choose from, and a jazz soundtrack. *Closed Sun lunch, Mon and 2wks in Aug.*

Trattoria dell'Abbondanza, Via dell'Abbondanza 10, **t** 0573 368037 (€€). A cheery trattoria near the Duomo, with delicious rustic food: *porcini* soup, salt cod *alla livornese*, *maccheroni* in duck sauce... Booking is advised for evenings. *Closed Wed, Thurs lunch and 2wks in Oct.*

Bar Pari, Via CE Montenara 15, outside town (€). A bar with a simple rear dining room serving up vast portions of tasty fare such as ravioli in walnut sauce, at the lowest prices in town.

San Jacopo, Via Crispi 15, **t** 0573 27786 (€). A pleasant trattoria serving top-quality traditional food (fish and meat) on crisp white tablecloths; try *ribollita*, potato *tortelli*, octopus, or rabbit with olives. The desserts are delicious. *Closed Mon and Tues lunch.*

The Mountains of Pistoia

North of Pistoia rises a fairly unspoiled stretch of the central Apennines, luxuriantly forested and endowed with lovely mountain escape routes, deep green in summer and ski white in winter. Main routes include the beautiful Bologna road (SS64; the 'Porrettana'), which follows the Bologna–Pistoia railway through the sparsely settled mountains, and the lovely parallel SS632, less encumbered with traffic. The main mountain resorts up to Abetone are along the SS66 and SS12, as easily reached from Lucca as from Pistoia.

Due north of Pistoia, 10km along a byroad towards Piteccio, is the ancient hamlet of **Castagno**, now a unique open-air art gallery. Its lanes are embellished with 20th-century frescoes on the 12 months; modern statues pose in the nooks and crannies; and Castagno's ancient church and oratory dedicated to St Francis, both with interesting frescoes, have been restored. A 4km backtrack takes you to the main SS66; at Pontepetri (20km) the SS632 veers north to the formerly popular little mountain resort of **Pracchia**.

Most visitors continue along the SS66 for the newer summer–winter resorts by way of the lovely state forest of Teso, at the fine old villages of **Maresca** and **Gavinana**. The latter is notorious in Florentine history for the defeat of its army by the imperial forces of Charles V, a battle that cost the lives of both commanders. The Florentine leader, Francesco Ferrucci, was knifed in the back, and has his own little museum in the main piazza.

The SS66 continues to **San Marcello Pistoiese**, 29km away from Pistoia, the 'capital' of the mountains, in a lovely setting where, since 1854, inhabitants have launched a hot-air balloon each year on 8 September, as a farewell to summer. You can walk over the 219m **suspension bridge of Mammiano** all year, however. **Cutigliano**, a growing winter resort 7km north, has 27km of ski trails and a cable car up to its highest peak, Doganaccia (1,175m). In the village itself, the **Palazzo Pretorio** bristles with the coats of arms of its former governors.

Near the northern border of Tuscany, through a lush and ancient forest, lies **Abetone** (1,400m), one of the most famous resorts in the central Apennines. Named after a huge fir tree, it grew up in the late 18th century, when grand duke Pietro Leopoldo built the road to the duchy of Modena, designing it not to pass through the detested Papal States (the modern province of Bologna). Two milestones at Abetone mark the old boundary. The closest ski resort to Florence, it is highly developed, with 35km of trails, a cable car and 23 chairlifts; in summer its cool climate, pools and other facilities make it popular, especially at weekends. In other seasons, rain is not exactly unknown.

Where to Stay and Eat in the Mountains of Pistoia

Nearly all hotels in this pretty but neglected corner of Tuscany are bargains; the ski resort of Abetone is the place for something fancier. In the mountains, many open only in the ski season and July and August. The tourist office has a list of good-value holiday villas near the towns and alpine refuges in the mountains.

ⓘ Abetone >> *Piazza Piramidi, t 0573 60231, www.abetone.com*

San Marcello Pistoiese ✉ 50128

ⓘ San Marcello Pistoiese > *Via Marconi 28, t 0573 621289, www.comunesanmarcello.it*

***Il Cacciatore**, Via Marconi 87, **t** 0573 630533, *www.albergoilcacciatore.it* (€€). A pleasant, quiet choice offering half and full board.

★ La Vecchia Cantina >>

La Vecchia Cantina, Via Risorgimento 4, Maresca, **t** 0573 64158 (€€). Seasonal menus and dishes rooted in local traditions, including risotto with *porcini*, emmer soup, rabbit with olives and polenta, and quail wih onions. *Closed Tues in winter and 3wks in Jan.*

Cutigliano ✉ 50124

ⓘ Cutigliano > *Via Roma 25, t 0573 68029, www.comune.cutigliano.pt.it*

***Hotel Miramonte**, Piazza Catalina 12, **t** 0573 68012, *www.hotelmiramonte.it* (€€). A quiet option with a pleasant garden and a restaurant serving genuine Tuscan cuisine.

L'Osteria, Via Roma 6, **t** 0573 68272 (€). Top-class mountain food served in the centre of town, at bargain prices; try wild boar ham, *polpettone* (meatloaf) with mushroom sauce, and grilled mushrooms. *Closed Tues lunch, Mon.*

Abetone ✉ 51021

***Regina**, Via Uccelleria 5, **t** 0573 60007 (€€€–€€). A decent choice on a quiet street, offering half and full board. *Closed May, July and mid-Sept–Nov.*

****Il Granduca**, Via Brennero 289, **t** 0573 60067, *www.hotelgranduca.info* (€€). The most upmarket choice in the area, run by a ski school, with superb views. Full board is available. *Closed May, June and Sept Nov.*

Ostello Renzo Bizzari, Via Brennero, Cosuma, **t** 0573 60117 (€). The youth hostel, also offering inexpensive meals. *Closed Apr–June and Sept–Nov exc by request.*

La Capannina, Via Brennero 256, **t** 0573 60562 (€€). Rustic decor and typical country recipes, including good soups and pasta dishes. There are rooms too. *Closed Mon and Tues outside high season, 2wks May and 2wks Oct.*

Da Pierone, Via Brennero 288, **t** 0573 60068 (€€). A rustic family-run place for plain traditional cuisine. *Closed Thurs, 2wks June and 2wks Oct.*

The Valdinievole

Montecatini Terme

3 Montecatini Terme

West of Pistoia lies the Valdinievole, the 'Valley of Mists', a land obsessed with water, though mostly of the subterranean, curative variety, available in Italy's most glamorous thermal spa, Montecatini (population 21,500). Leonardo da Vinci's first known drawing was of a view towards Montecatini from Lamporecchio, near his home town of Vinci (*see* p.224), and it is believed that his lifetime fascination with canals, locks, currents and dams and the misty, watery backgrounds of his most famous paintings come from a childhood spent in the Valdinievole. He even designed a fountain for the baths of Montecatini in one of his notebooks, which after 380 years is now being built of Carrara marble as his monument.

Even in these days of holistic medicine, preventive medicine, herbal cures and pharmaceutical paranoia, the Montecatini tourist board despair that Anglo-Saxons from both sides of the Atlantic

Getting to Montecatini Terme

Montecatini is easily reached by **train** (*www.trenitalia.it*) from Florence (51km/90mins), Pistoia (16km/25mins) and Lucca (27km/45mins). The station, **t** 0572 78551, is on Via Toti, as is the LAZZI (*www.lazzi.it*) **bus** terminal, which has hourly daytime services to Florence, Lucca, Pisa, Viareggio and Montecatini Alto, plus six buses daily to Collodi via Pescia.

---

refuse to believe that soaking in or drinking mere water can do anything as beneficial for them as imbibing a pitcher of Chianti. After all, the Romans spent the plunder accumulated from conquering the world on ever more fabulous baths. But taking the waters, no matter how hot, radioactive, or chock-full of minerals, is only half the cure; the other is relaxation – the chance to stroll through gardens, listen to a little music, linger in a café, indulge in a bit of the old *dolce far niente*. In Montecatini you can do just that, surrounded by Belle Epoque nostalgia from the days when the spa seethed with dukes, politicians, literati and actresses.

Parco delle Terme

Parco delle Terme
baths open May–Oct (New Excelsior all year); day ticket/subscription from central office in Viale Verdi 63, **t** *800 132538 or* **t** *0572 7781; adm*

A short stroll from the station, past Montecatini's trendy boutiques, cafés, cinemas and some of its 200 hotels up to Viale Verdi, takes you to the town's mineral water Elysium, the immaculately groomed Parco delle Terme, where the high temples of the cult dot the shaded lawn. The Lorraine grand dukes, spa-soaks like their Habsburg cousins, were behind the development of Montecatini's springs, and many of the baths, or *terme,* are neoclassical pavilions – monumental, classical and floral architecture that lent itself to the later Liberty-style embellishments of the 1920s.

Take in some of these Art Nouveau fancies in Montecatini's Municipio, on Viale Verdi opposite the park, or in the most sumptuous and ancient of its nine major bathing establishments, **Tettuccio**. In the 1370s a group of Florentines attempted to extract mineral salts from the spring and built a little roof (*tettuccio*) over it; though they failed, it was soon discovered that the water had a good effect on rotten livers – one of the first to come here was Francesco Datini, Merchant of Prato, in 1401. By the 18th century Tettuccio was in a state of ruin, and grand duke Leopold I had it splendidly rebuilt. His façade remains. The interior was redone by Montecatini's greatest architect, Ugo Giovanozzi, in the 1920s, and embellished with paintings by Italy's Art Nouveau master Galileo Chini, and ceramic pictures by Cascella in the drinking gallery; there's an elegant café, fountains, a reflecting pool and rotunda, a writing hall, music rooms, a little city within a city – all adorned with scenes from an aquatic Golden Age of languid nymphs.

Other establishments, each with their special virtues, are nearby – the Palladian-style arcade of the **Regina** spring; the **Terme Leopoldine**, another grand ducal establishment, boasting mud baths housed in a temple-like building that is dedicated to Aesculapius, god of health; the half neo-Renaissance, half modern **New Excelsior baths**; the pretty Tuscan rustic **Tamerici**, in its lush garden; the **Torretta**, with its phoney medieval tower and afternoon concerts in the loggia.

During Digestion

Montecatini Golf and Country Club
t 0572 640692, www.montecatinigolf.com

La Toretta
t 0572 78161

Grotta Maona
open April–Oct; call tourist office (see below) for more details

Just behind the Parco delle Terme is **Le Panteraie**, a wooded park with a swimming pool, where deer roam freely. You can play a round at the **Montecatini golf course**, among olive groves and cypresses, or a game of tennis at the central courts of **La Toretta**. Alternatively, try to win back your hotel bill at the trotting races at the **Ippodromo**. The **Kursaal**, with cinema, nightclub and games, is a popular meeting place.

One of the prettiest trips is on the funicular up to **Montecatini Alto**, the original old hilltown, with breathtaking views over the 'Valley of Mists' and a charming little piazza with a small theatre; nearby you can visit the stalactites in the **Grotta Maona**.

ⓘ Montecatini >
Viale G Verdi 66, t 0572 772244, www.montecatiniturismo.it (closed Sun and May–mid-Aug)

★ Il Salotto di Gea >>

Where to Stay in Montecatini Terme

Montecatini Terme ✉ 51016

Italy's choicest spa has than six hotels that claim the title 'Grand' and a half-dozen others that only decline to for discretion's sake. Full board (not counting breakfast) is the rule in most places; some may relax this outside high season (make sure to ask).

The **APIA hotel association**, Via V Foscolo 19, **t** 0572 904344, helps with bookings.

*******Grand Hotel & La Pace**, Via della Torretta 1, **t** 0572 9240, *www.grandhotellapace.it* (€€€€€). A hotel renowned throughout Europe for its Belle Epoque charm, with a pool, tennis court, elegant restaurant and other luxuries. *Closed Nov–Mar.*

*******Grand Hotel Bellavista**, Viale Fedeli 2, **t** 0572 78122, *www.panciolihotels.it* (€€€€). Luxurious rooms, golf and tennis facilities, indoor and outdoor pools, a sauna, health club and beauty farm, and a bar and restaurant. Check the website for special offers. *Closed Nov–Feb.*

*****Belvedere**, Viale Fedeli 10, **t** 0572 70251, *www.gallinganihotels.it* (€€€). One of the more charming choices, with rooms with all comforts, an indoor pool, tennis courts and friendly service, next to the Parco delle Terme. Breakfast is included.

Villa Pasquini, Via Vaccherecia, Massa e Cozile, 8km from Montecatini, **t** 0572 72205, *www.villapasquini.it* (€€€). A charming, friendly choice, in lush gardens with a beautiful terrace. Some rooms have frescoes, and there's a good restaurant. Breakfast is included.

******Grand Hotel Plaza e Locanda Maggiore**, Piazza del Popolo 7, **t** 0572 75831, *www.hotelplaza.it* (€€). The hotel said to have been Verdi's favourite, near the station, with a pool. Breakfast is included.

*****Corallo**, Viale Cavallotti 116, **t** 0572 78288, *www.golfhotelcorallo.it* (€€). A refined little place with a pool and garden, on a quiet sidestreet near the park. Half and full board are available; the restaurant serves Tuscan and Mediterranean cuisine.

Il Salotto di Gea, Via Talenti 2, **t** 0572 904318, *salottodigea@inwind.it* (€€). A delightful alternative to some of the more overblown hotels here, in the heart of the old town. Rooms are decorated with unfussy good taste, breakfast is served on the piazza in summer, and the restaurant offers tempting warm octopus salad, spaghetti with mullet roe, and aubergine ravioli with pesto.

Eating Out in Montecatini Terme

Montecatini Terme ✉ 51016

Most visitors dine in their hotel, but there are other options .

★ Enoteca Giovanni >

Enoteca Giovanni, Via Garibaldi 27, **t** 0572 71695 (€€€€). Impeccable haute cuisine by a master chef: try filled courgette flowers, risotto with pigeon and squash, or the sea bream or sea bass. *Closed Mon.*

Ristorante il Cucco, Via Salsero 3, **t** 0572 72765 (€€€€–€€€). The place to come for elaborate Tuscan meat and seafood dishes, including raw prawns, cod *alla livornese* with polenta, and grilled octopus. *Closed Tues, and Wed lunch.*

Cucina da Giovanni, Via Garibaldi (€€€). Simple but good food, including *pappa al pomodoro, ribollita* and grilled meats.

La Torre, Piazza Giusti 8, **t** 0572 70650 (€€). A wine bar/restaurant located up in the old town, serving good main dishes such as gnocchi with mushrooms, *ribollita* and more. It's a good place for snacks too, along with a fine selection of wines, and you can also buy products to take away.

Around Montecatini Terme

Monsummano and Serravalle

Narrow lanes crisscross the Valdinievole landscape, offering a wealth of tempting excursions. About 5km to the east of Montecatini, its sister spa, **Monsummano Terme**, specializes in vapour baths in natural grottoes. The first was discovered by accident in 1849, when the Giusti family moved a boulder and found the entrance to a stalactite cave. The **Grotta Giusti**, 99m deep, has three small lakes fed by hot springs. These caves, including the steamy **Grotta Parlanti**, are only open to visitors seeking serious thermal treatment.

Grotta Parlanti
open May–Oct, call **t** *0572 953071 for times*

Monsummano hasn't rested on its vapours, transforming itself into one of Italy's biggest shoe-making towns; similarly to Montecatini, it has an old antecedent atop a hill, **Monsummano Alto**, today all but abandoned but with a pretty Romanesque church, a ruined castle and splendid views. Another panoramic view may be had from **Montevettolini**, 4km from Monsummano, site of a villa built by Ferdinando I in 1597.

Continuing in an easterly direction from Montecatini, the old fortress that you will see at **Serravalle Pistoiese** 'locks the valley' between the Apennines and Monte Albano. Its old Lombard tower and 14th-century additions saw not-inconsiderable action during Tuscany's days of inter-urban hooliganism.

Pescia and Around

To the west of Montecatini is another attractive old hilltown, **Buggiano Castello**. For those who imagine that frescoes went out of fashion years ago, there's San MIchele in nearby Ponte Buggianese, freshly frescoed in stark colours by Pietro Annigoni.

The colours are even more dazzling in **Pescia** (population 20,000),

Italy's capital of flowers, a title that it snatched from San Remo on the Riviera. Some 3 million cut flowers are sent off every summer's day from Pescia's enormous market; besides the gladioli, it is celebrated by gourmets for its tender asparagus and *fagioli*. Pescia also has several interesting monuments, beginning with the 14th-century church of **San Francesco**, containing Bonaventura Berlinghieri's 1235 portrait of St Francis with scenes from his life, considered one of the most authentic likenesses of the saint; make sure you also take look at the *Crucifixion* by Puccio Capanna in the sacristy. The **Duomo** was rebuilt in the 1600s but has a fine Romanesque campanile sporting a little cupola, and a late terracotta triptych by Luca della Robbia. On long, narrow Piazza Mazzini stands the imposing **Palazzo del Vicario**; in nearby **Sant'Antonio**, dating from the 1360s, look up the 'Ugly Saints', a 13th-century wooden *Deposition from the Cross*.

The green, hilly region of prosperous villages that lie to the north of Pescia in the upper Valdinievole has been dubbed 'Little Switzerland'. In its cheerful core, some 12km from Pescia, stands one of the most bizarre churches in the whole of Italy, the 12th-century **Pieve di Castelvecchio**, decorated with grinning and grimacing stone masks.

Collodi and Pinocchio

Just west of Pescia is **Collodi**. As a child, Florentine writer Carlo Lorenzini (1826–90) often visited his uncle, who worked in the castle, and he took the name Collodi as his own when he published his *Adventures of Pinocchio*. In his honour the town built the **Parco di Pinocchio**, with a bronze statue of the character by Emilio Greco and a piazza of mosaics with scenes from the book by Venturino Venturi, as well as other figures, all in the angular style of the late 1950s and early 60s; there's also a lawn maze, a museum dedicated to the book, a playground and other amusements for the kids.

Parco di Pinocchio
t 0572 429342; open daily 8.30–sunset; adm

Adults can try to work their way through a much older labyrinth located in the magnificent restored hillside gardens of the **Castello Garzoni**, designed in the 17th century by Ottaviano Diodati of Lucca and considered one of the finest late Italian gardens, with fountains and statuary. The castle 'of a hundred windows' has a few grand rooms plus the kitchen where young Carlo sat and dreamed up Pinocchio.

Castello Garzoni
open mid-Mar–Oct daily 9–sunset; rest of year daily 8–12 and 2–5.30; adm

Where to Stay and Eat in Monsummano Terme

Monsummano Terme ✉ 51015

****__Grotta Giusti__, Via Grotta Giusti 171, **t** 0572 51165, *www.grottagiustispa.com* (€€€€€–€€€€). The villa of the family of poet Giuseppe Giusti, near the vaporous grottoes. Now a very comfortable hotel, it's filled with antiques, rich fabrics, marbles and so on. Rates include all spa treatments. Half or full board is obligatory in high season (Aug–Sept, Christmas, Easter). The restaurant serves Tuscan specialities. *Closed late Dec–Feb.*

Montevettolini ✉ 51015

Villa Lucia, Via dei Bronzoli 144, **t** 0572 617790, *www.villaluciaoftuscany.com* (€€€€). An English-style B&B in a delightful setting on a hillside, with a garden and pool, plus some apartments. The farm produces oil.

San Michele, Piazza Bargellini 80, **t** 0572 617 547 (€). A café-bar-restaurant with great wine list, a tempting array of antipasti (smoked salmon, caviar, carpaccio with truffles), and the likes of spaghetti with lobster. *Closed Mon.*

Pescia ✉ 51017

***__Villa delle Rose__, Via del Castellare 21, just outside town, **t** 0572 4670, *www.rphotels.com* (€€€). Comfortable modern guestrooms and a pleasant garden and swimming pool. Breakfast is included in rates.

Cecco, Via Forti 84, **t** 0572 477955 (€€). Fine dining on seasonal dishes such as emmer soup, spaghetti with *ovoli* mushrooms, turbot and grilled rabbit. *Closed Mon.*

Monte a Pescia, Via del Monte Ovest 1, Monte a Pescia, just outside Pescia, **t** 0572 476887 (€€). A rustic restaurant in a tiny hilltop hamlet with a terrace overlooking the Valdinievole. Highlights are the gnocchi, the grilled meats and the delicious desserts. *Closed Wed, lunch exc Sun, and Oct.*

Collodi ✉ 51014

All'Osteria del Gambero Rosso, Via San Gennaro 2, Parco Collodi, **t** 0572 429 364 (€€€). A restaurant in the grand Parco Collodi, in a building designed by Giovanni Michelucci – one of Italy's greatest 20th-century architects. Tuck into good emmer soup, *cioncia alla pesciatina* (a hot soup of meat and vegetables) and Florentine steak. *Closed Mon eve, Tues and Nov.*

Lucca, the Garfagnana and Lunigiana

Tuscany's northernmost corner is full of treats, starting with utterly urbane Lucca, birthplace of Puccini and home to an unusual set of medieval churches, a Roman amphitheatre turned into a piazza and a unique elevated promenade on top of the city walls. Yet a hop and skip north, the mountainous micro-regions of the Garfagnana and Lunigiana are among Tuscany's best kept secrets; here you can relax in the sleepy spa of Bagni di Lucca where romantic poets once lazed, explore the Cave of the Wind, or scratch your head over the statue-steles of Pontremoli.

10

Don't miss

1. **A luminescent and tender tomb**
   Lucca cathedral **p.258**
2. **A church splendid as a cathedral**
   San Michele in Foro, Lucca **p.259**
3. **The spa where roulette was born**
   Bagni di Lucca **p.265**
4. **Rugged scenery and stout castles**
   The Lunigiana **p.268**
5. **Mysterious statue-menhirs**
   Pontremoli **p.269**

See map overleaf

Lucca, the Garfagnana and Lunigiana

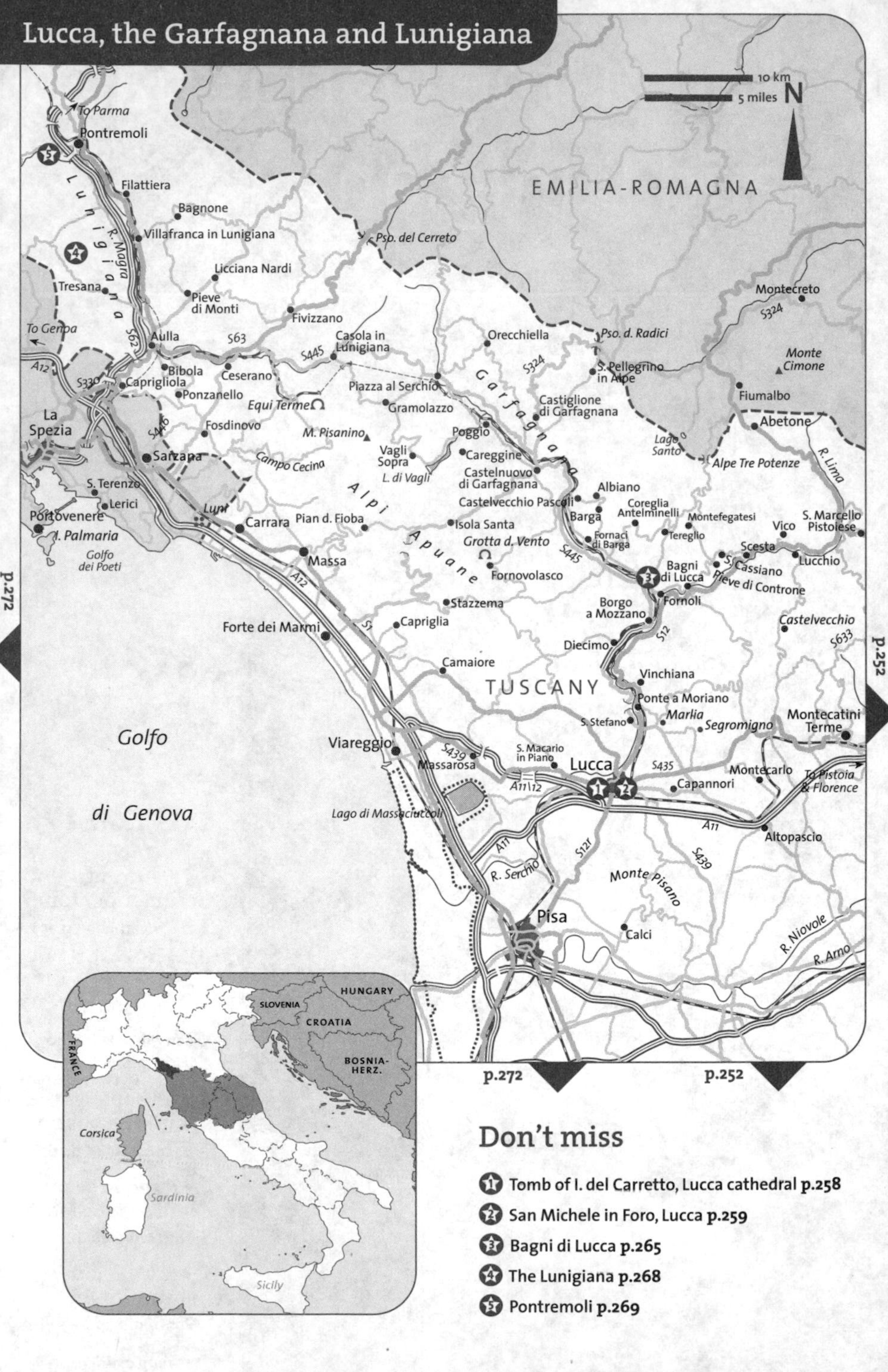

Don't miss

1. Tomb of I. del Carretto, Lucca cathedral **p.258**
2. San Michele in Foro, Lucca **p.259**
3. Bagni di Lucca **p.265**
4. The Lunigiana **p.268**
5. Pontremoli **p.269**

Lucca

Nowhere in Lucca will you see the face of a Philistine.

Heine, *Travels in Lucca*

Of all Tuscany's great cities, Lucca (population 92,500) is the most cosy, sane and domestic, a tidy gem of a town within famous walls that seem more like garden walls than something that would keep the Florentines at bay. The old ramparts and surrounding areas, once the outworks of the fortifications, are full of lawns and trees; on the walls, where the city's soldiers once patrolled, citizens ride their bikes, walk their dogs and admire the views.

Like paradise, Lucca is entered by way of St Peter's Gate. Inside you'll find neat, well-preserved Romanesque churches and medieval towers that destroyed Ruskin's romantic notion that a medieval building had to be half-ruined to be beautiful – a revelation that initiated his study of architecture. Nor do Lucca's numerous Liberty-style shop signs show any sign of rust; even the mandatory peeling ochre paint and green shutters of the houses seem part of some great municipal housekeeping plan. Bicycles have largely replaced cars within the walls. At first glance it seems too bijou, but after its long and brave history it's earned the right to a little quiet.

The tourist hordes leave Lucca alone for the most part, although it does get a surprising number of Americans, many of whom are descendants of Lucchese who went to the States after the collapse of the old silk industry. Today the city is one of Europe's top paper producers, although the new mills (non-stinky) are far from the beautiful bijou centre.

History

Lucca's rigid grid of streets betrays its Roman origins; it was founded as a colony in 180 BC as *Luca*, and it was here in 56 BC that Caesar, Pompey and Crassus met to form the ill-fated First Triumvirate. It was converted to Christianity early on by St Peter's disciple Paulinus, who became first bishop of Lucca. The city did especially well in the Dark Ages; in late Roman times it was the administrative capital of Tuscany, and under the Goths repulsed the murderous Lombards; its extensive archives were begun in the 8th century, and many of its churches were founded shortly after.

By the 11th and 12th centuries Lucca emerged as one of the leading trading towns of Tuscany, specializing in the production of silk, which was sold by colonies of merchants in the East and West, who earned enough to make sizable loans to Mediterranean potentates. A Lucchese school of painting developed, and beautiful Romanesque churches were erected, influenced by nearby Pisa. Ghibellines and Guelphs, then Black and White Guelphs, made nuisances of themselves here as they did everywhere else, and Lucca often found itself pressed to maintain its independence from Pisa and Florence.

Getting to and around Lucca

The **train** station (**t** 0583 892021) is just south of the walls on Piazza Ricasoli, with lots of trains on the Viareggio–Pisa–Florence line. **Buses** leave from Piazzale Verdi, just inside the walls on the western end: LAZZI (**t** 0583 584876, *www.lazzi.it*) goes to Florence, Pistoia, Pisa, Prato, Bagni di Lucca, Abetone, Montecatini and Viareggio; CLAP (**t** 0583 541239, *www.clapspa.it*) to towns within Lucca province, including Collodi, Marlia, and Segromigno, as well as the Serchio valley.

Get around Lucca like a Lucchese by hiring a **bicycle** from Poli (**t** 0583 493787) or Bizzarri (**t** 0583 496031), both in Piazza Santa Maria.

In 1314, at the height of the city's wealth and power, the Pisans and Ghibellines finally seized it. But Lucca had a trump card: Castruccio Castracani, an ambitious noble who lived for years in exile – part of it in England. When he heard the bad news he set forth to rescue his home town. Within a year he had chased the Pisans out and seized power, leading Lucca into its most heroic age, capturing most of western Tuscany to form a Luccan empire, subjugating even Pisa and Pistoia. After routing the Florentines at Altopascio in 1325, Castracani was planning to snatch Florence too, but he died of malaria just before the siege was to begin. Bickering between the powerful local families soon put an end to Lucca's glory days, though in 1369 the city convinced Emperor Charles IV to grant it independence as a republic, albeit a republic ruled by oligarchs such as Paolo Guinigi, who was the sole big boss between 1400 and 1430.

But Lucca continued to escape being gobbled up, surviving even after the arrival of the Spaniards – perhaps not so much thanks to its great walls as to its relative insignificance. Amazingly, after the rreaty of Cateau-Cambrésis, Lucca and Venice were the only truly independent states in Italy. And, like Venice, the city was an island of relative tolerance and enlightenment in the Counter-Reformation, its walls proving stout enough to deflect the Inquisition.

In 1805 Lucca's independence came to an end when Napoleon gave the republic to his sister Elisa Baciocchi; it was given later to Maria-Louisa, daughter of Spain's Charles IV, who became Lucca's favourite ruler and earned a statue in the main Piazza Napoleone. Her son sold it to Leopold II of Tuscany in 1847, just in time for it to join the Kingdom of Italy.

The Walls

Lucca's lovely bastions evoke the walled rose gardens of chivalric romance, enclosing a smaller, more perfect cosmos. They owe their charm to Renaissance advances in military technology. Prompted by the start of the Wars of Italy, Lucca began to construct the walls in 1500. The councillors wanted up-to-date fortifications to counter advances in artillery, and their (unknown) architects gave them state-of-the-art examples, a model for the new style of fortification soon to transform the cities of Europe. Being Renaissance Tuscans, the architects also gave them a little more elegance than was strictly necessary. They were never severely tested.

Today, with the outer ravelins, fosses and salients cleared away, Lucca's walls are just for decoration; under the peace-loving duchess Maria-Louisa they were planted with a double row of plane trees to create a 4km elevated garden boulevard offering a bird's-eye view over Lucca. They are among the best preserved in Italy. Of the gates, the most elaborate is the 16th-century **St Peter's gate**, near the station, its portcullis intact, with Lucca's motto of independence, LIBERTAS, inscribed over the entrance. One of the best ways to explore the walls is by bike (*see* opposite).

Duomo

Duomo di Lucca
open summer daily 9.30–7; winter daily 9.30-5; adm to sacristy (joint adm available with Museo della Cattedrale and San Giovanni e Santa Reparata;see p.258 for both)

Through St Peter's Gate (Porta San Pietro), and then to the right, Corso Garibaldi leads to Lucca's cathedral, perhaps the outstanding work of the Pisan style outside Pisa, begun in the 11th century and completed only in the 15th. Above the singular porch, with three different-sized arches, are three levels of colonnades, with pillars arranged like candy sticks; behind and on the arches are exquisite 12th- and 13th-century reliefs and sculpture. Look for the *Adoration of the Magi* by Nicola Pisano, for the column carved with the Tree of Life, with Adam and Eve crouched at the bottom and Christ on top, and a host of fantastical animals and hunting scenes, the months and their occupations, mermaids and dragons (*see* Pienza, p.379), and a man embracing a bear, even *Roland at Roncevalles*, all by unknown masters. There is also a medieval maze on the right side of the portico, which you can trace with your finger. At the back the splendidly ornate apse and transepts are set off by the green lawn.

The dark interior offers an excellent introduction to Lucca's one great artist, **Matteo Civitali** (1435–1501), who was a barber until his mid-30s. He deserves to be better known, but everything he made is still in Lucca. His most famous sculpture is the octagonal **Tempietto** (1484), a marble tabernacle in the middle of the left aisle, containing Lucca's most precious holy relic, the world-weary *Volto Santo* (Holy Image), a cedar-wood crucifix said to be a true portrait of Jesus, sculpted by Nicodemus, an eyewitness to the crucifixion. Saved from the iconoclasts, it was set adrift in an empty boat and floated to Luni, where the bishop was instructed by an angel to place it in a cart drawn by two white oxen; where the oxen should halt, there should the image remain. They lumbered to Lucca, where the *Volto Santo* has remained. Its likeness appeared on the republic's coins, and there was a devoted cult of the image in medieval England; Lucca's merchant colony in London cared for a replica in old St Thomas's, and, according to William of Malmesbury, King William Rufus always swore by it,

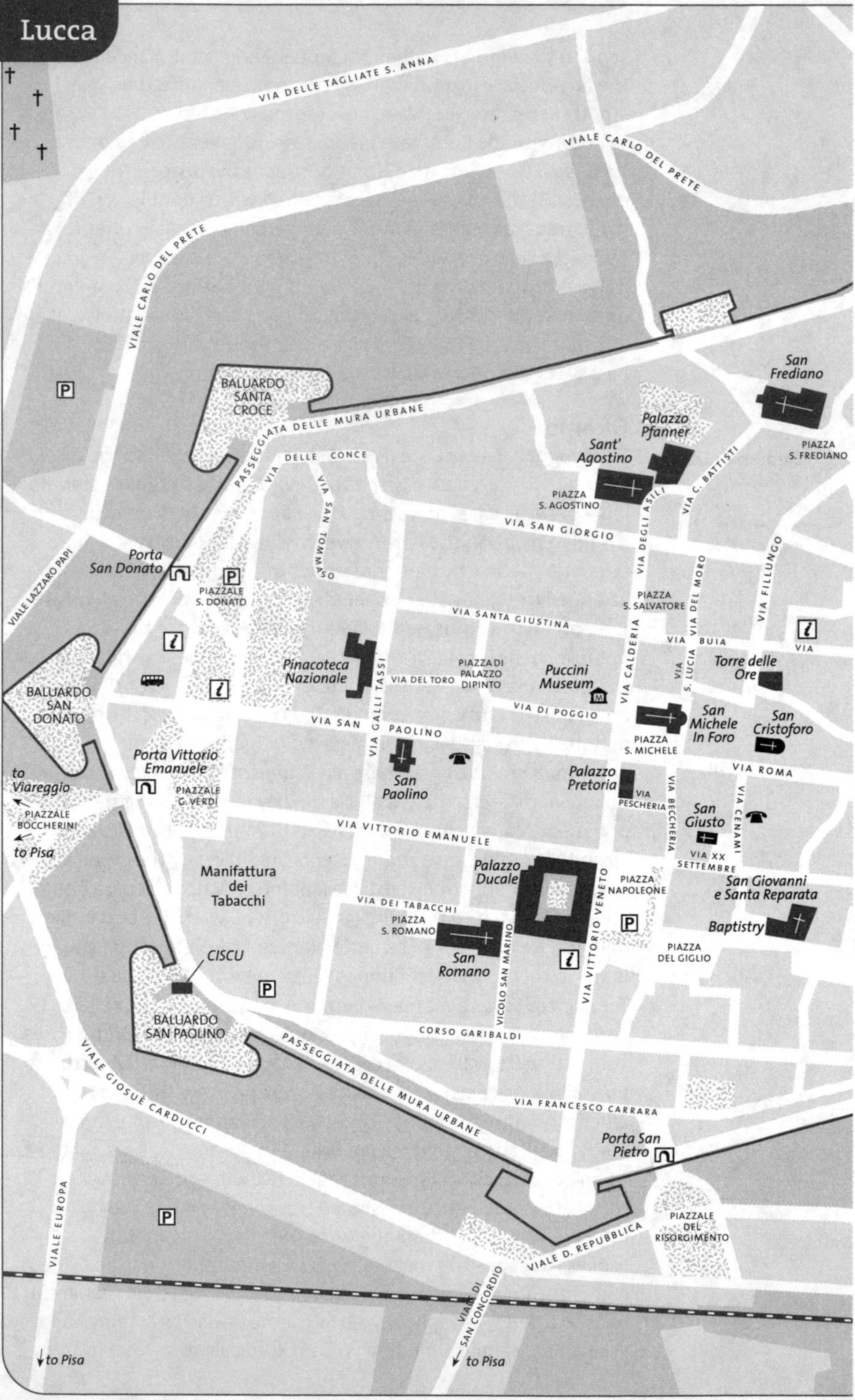

Lucca

VIA DELLE TAGLIATE S. ANNA
VIALE CARLO DEL PRETE
VIALE CARLO DEL PRETE
BALUARDO SANTA CROCE
PASSEGGIATA DELLE MURA URBANE
San Frediano
Palazzo Pfanner
Sant' Agostino
PIAZZA S. FREDIANO
PIAZZA S. AGOSTINO
VIA DELLE CONCE
VIA SAN TOMMASO
VIA C. BATTISTI
VIA SAN GIORGIO
VIA DEGLI ASILI
VIALE LAZZARO PAPI
Porta San Donato
PIAZZALE S. DONATO
PIAZZA S. SALVATORE
VIA DEL MORO
VIA FILLUNGO
VIA SANTA GIUSTINA
VIA BUIA
VIA
BALUARDO SAN DONATO
Pinacoteca Nazionale
VIA GALLI TASSI
VIA DEL TORO
PIAZZA DI PALAZZO DIPINTO
Puccini Museum
VIA CALDERIA
VIA S. LUCIA
Torre delle Ore
VIA DI POGGIO
VIA SAN PAOLINO
San Michele In Foro
San Cristoforo
PIAZZA S. MICHELE
Porta Vittorio Emanuele
to Viareggio
PIAZZALE G. VERDI
San Paolino
Palazzo Pretoria
VIA PESCHERIA
VIA ROMA
VIA BECCHERIA
VIA CENAMI
PIAZZALE BOCCHERINI
to Pisa
VIA VITTORIO EMANUELE
San Giusto
VIA XX SETTEMBRE
Manifattura dei Tabacchi
Palazzo Ducale
PIAZZA NAPOLEONE
San Giovanni e Santa Reparata
Baptistry
VIA DEI TABACCHI
PIAZZA S. ROMANO
San Romano
VICOLO SAN MARINO
VIA VITTORIO VENETO
PIAZZA DEL GIGLIO
CISCU
BALUARDO SAN PAOLINO
CORSO GARIBALDI
PASSEGGIATA DELLE MURA URBANE
VIALE GIOSUÈ CARDUCCI
VIA FRANCESCO CARRARA
Porta San Pietro
VIALE EUROPA
PIAZZALE DEL RISORGIMENTO
VIALE D. REPUBBLICA
VIALE DI SAN CONCORDIO
to Pisa
to Pisa

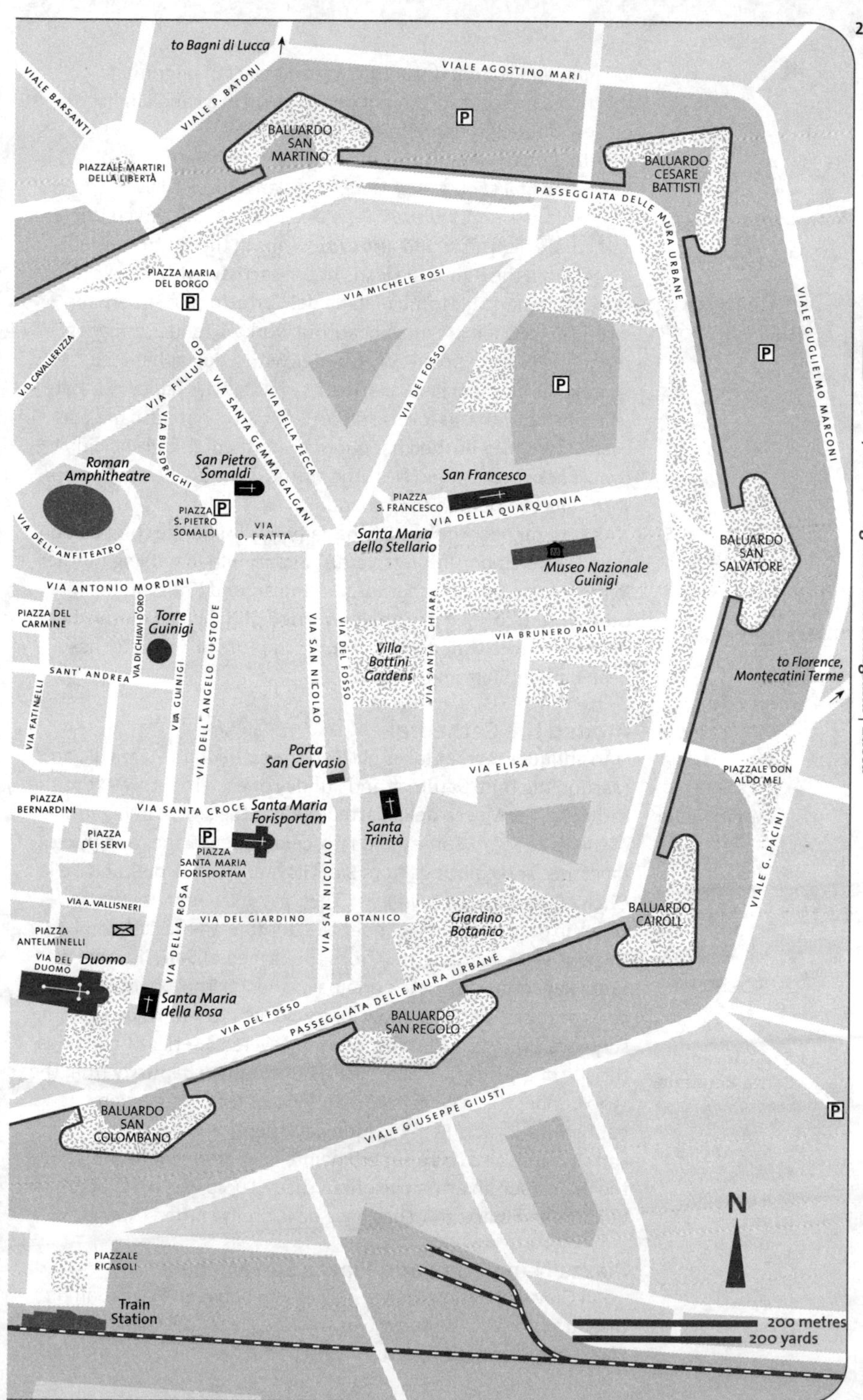
to Bagni di Lucca
VIALE AGOSTINO MARI
VIALE BARSANTI
VIALE P. BATONI
BALUARDO SAN MARTINO
PIAZZALE MARTIRI DELLA LIBERTÀ
BALUARDO CESARE BATTISTI
PASSEGGIATA DELLE MURA URBANE
PIAZZA MARIA DEL BORGO
VIA MICHELE ROSI
V. D. CAVALLERIZZA
VIA FILLUNGO
VIA SANTA GEMMA GALGANI
VIA DELLA ZECCA
VIA DEI FOSSO
VIALE GUGLIELMO MARCONI
VIA BUSDRAGHI
Roman Amphitheatre
San Pietro Somaldi
San Francesco
PIAZZA S. FRANCESCO
VIA DELLA QUARQUONIA
PIAZZA S. PIETRO SOMALDI
VIA D. FRATTA
VIA DELL'ANFITEATRO
Santa Maria dello Stellario
Museo Nazionale Guinigi
BALUARDO SAN SALVATORE
VIA ANTONIO MORDINI
PIAZZA DEL CARMINE
VIA DI CHIAVI D'ORO
Torre Guinigi
VIA DELL' ANGELO CUSTODE
VIA SAN NICOLAO
VIA DEL FOSSO
VIA SANTA CHIARA
VIA BRUNERO PAOLI
Villa Bottini Gardens
SANT' ANDREA
VIA GUINIGI
VIA FATINELLI
to Florence, Montecatini Terme
Porta San Gervasio
VIA ELISA
PIAZZALE DON ALDO MEI
PIAZZA BERNARDINI
VIA SANTA CROCE
Santa Maria Forisportam
Santa Trinità
PIAZZA DEI SERVI
PIAZZA SANTA MARIA FORISPORTAM
VIALE G. PACINI
VIA A. VALLISNERI
VIA DEL GIARDINO
BOTANICO
Giardino Botanico
BALUARDO CAIROLI
PIAZZA ANTELMINELLI
VIA DELLA ROSA
VIA DEL DUOMO
Duomo
Santa Maria della Rosa
VIA DEL FOSSO
PASSEGGIATA DELLE MURA URBANE
BALUARDO SAN REGOLO
BALUARDO SAN COLOMBANO
VIALE GIUSEPPE GIUSTI
N
PIAZZALE RICASOLI
Train Station
200 metres
200 yards

'*per sanctum vultum de Lucca*'. Long an object of pilgrimage, the image goes out for a night on the town in a candlelight procession each 13 September.

Further up the left aisle a chapel contains Fra Bartolomeo's *Virgin and Child Enthroned*. Here, too, is an altarpiece by Giambologna, *Christ with SS. Peter and Paul*. Civitali carved the cathedral's high altar, and also two tombs in the south transept. A door from the right aisle leads to the **sacristy**, with Lucca's real icon, the remarkable **tomb of Ilaria del Carretto** (1408), perhaps Jacopo della Quercia's most beautiful work – a tender, effigy of the young bride of boss Paolo Guinigi, with a dog at her feet, waiting for his mistress wake. The city has always had a love-hate relationship with this lovely statue. Right after her husband was overthrown they hustled her out of the cathedral, and she didn't come back for centuries. Near the statue is a *Madonna Enthroned with Saints* by Domenico Ghirlandaio.

Tomba di Ilaria del Carretto

A side altar near the sacristy has a typically strange composition from the Venetian Tintoretto, a *Last Supper* with a nursing mother in the foreground and cherubs floating around Christ. In the centre, often covered up, is a fine section of the inlaid marble floor; on the entrance wall, a 13th-century sculpture of St Martin has been brought in from the façade.

Around the Cathedral

An **antiques market** takes place in the cathedral's Piazza di San Martino the third Saturday and Sunday of each month. Next to the cathedral, the **Museo della Cattedrale** has the crown and garments of the *Volto Santo*, some good 13th-century reliquaries and pyxes, tapestries and paintings from San Giovanni (*see* below), and Della Quercia's *St John the Evangelist*. The upstairs windows afford a close-up of some of the wonderful sculpture on the cathedral.

Museo della Cattedrale
open April–Oct daily 10–6; Nov–Mar Mon–Fri 10–3, Sat, Sun and hols 10–6; adm (joint adm available with sacristy, see above, and San Giovanni e Santa Reparata)

Across Piazza San Martino from the cathedral, **San Giovanni e Santa Reparata** was Lucca's original cathedral. The exterior has only parts of an 1187 portal to show for its old distinction; inside are some surprises. Excavations in the 1970s uncovered a series of buildings: the site of a 5th-century basilica, a huge, square **baptistry** from the 1300s, under this a walk-in Roman font for total immersion baptisms, and later Romanesque pavements and a bishop's chair. San Giovanni also has a superb painted coffered ceiling and, above the main door, an attractive organ case – Lucca was a city of organ builders and many churches have beautifully crafted examples.

San Giovanni e Santa Reparata
open summer daily 10–6; winter Sat, Sun and hols 10–6 or by appt; adm (joint adm available with sacristy, and Museo della Cattedrale)

Piazza Napoleone and Piazza San Michele

San Giovanni lies on the Via del Duomo between Piazza San Martino and Lucca's shady twin squares, **Piazza del Giglio** and **Piazza Napoleone**, the focus of the Lucchesi evening *passeggiata*.

The architectural hotchpotch of a palace on Piazza Napoleone, formerly seat of the republican council, has been called the **Palazzo Ducale** ever since it was used by Lucca's queen for a day, Elisa Bonaparte Baciocchi. In the 16th century, Ammannati had a go at it, and the courtyard preserves signs of his Mannerist handiwork. One of Matteo Civitali's most beautiful works, the tomb of San Romano, is in the rarely opened church of **San Romano**, behind the Palazzo.

Via Vittorio Veneto leads from Piazza Napoleone into Piazza San Michele, with a church many people mistake for Lucca's cathedral. Built about the same time, and with a similar Pisan façade, it is almost as impressive. The full name, **San Michele in Foro**, stems from its location on what was Roman Lucca's forum. The ambitious façade rises high above the level of the roof, to make the building look even grander. Every column in the Pisan arcading is different; some doubled, some twisted like corkscrews, inlaid with mosaic Cosmati work, or carved with fanciful figures and beasts. The whole is crowned by a giant statue of the Archangel – note the bracelet on his arm, set with real jewels. On the corner of the façade is a Madonna by Civitali; the graceful, rectangular campanile is Lucca's tallest and loveliest.

(2) San Michele in Foro
open daily 7.40–12 and 3–6

Inside are a glazed terracotta *Madonna and Child* attributed to Luca della Robbia, a striking 13th-century *Crucifixion* over the high altar and a painting of plague saints by Filippino Lippi. Giacomo Puccini began his musical career as a choirboy in San Michele – he didn't have far to go, as he was born across the street, in the house that is now the little **Puccini museum**, with manuscripts, letters, mementos, and odds and ends of the composer, plus the piano he used to compose *Turandot*. Don't miss the statue of Puccini lounging ever so suavely in nearby Piazza di Palazzo Dipinto.

Casa Natale e Museo di Giacomo Puccini
Via di Poggio 30, entrance at Corte San Lorenzo 9; closed for restoration at time of writing; call **t** *0583 469225 for update*

West of San Michele

Now the state tobacco factory has been moved out of town, the quarter west of San Michele no longer smells of Toscanelli cigars; what will become of the factory was still being debated at the time of writing. Via San Paolino (the Roman *decumanus major*) leads to the **church of San Paolino**, where little Puccini played the organ to earn pin-money. It contains two beautiful works: a 13th-century French *Madonna and Child* brought back by Lucchese merchants from Paris, and an anonymous quattrocento Florentine *Coronation of the Virgin*, with Mary hovering over a city of pink towers; unusually she is crowned by God the Father instead of Christ.

The **Pinacoteca Nazionale** is in the 17th-century Palazzo Mansi. Most of the art, as well as the rich furnishings, dates from the 17th century. Portraits by Pontormo and Bronzino hang in the Prima Sala after the large hall: the Salone has a dark, damaged Veronese, and a *Miracle of St Mark Freeing the Slave* by a follower of Tintoretto,

Pinacoteca Nazionale
Via Galli Tassi; open summer Tues–Sat 8.30–7.30, Sun 8.30–1; winter Tues–Sat 9–7, Sun 9–1; adm

showing the saint dive-bombing from heaven to save the day. There is also a set of neoclassical reliefs from the Palazzo Ducale of the *Triumphs of Duchess Maria Luisa*. The 1600s frescoes are more fun, especially the *Judgement of Paris*, which Venus wins by showing a little leg. And the rococo bedroom is amazing.

East of San Michele

Medieval **Via Fillungo** and its surrounding lanes make up the shopping district, a tidy grid of straight, narrow alleys where Lucca's contented cheerfulness seems magnified. Along Via Fillungo you can trace the old loggias of 14th-century palaces, now bricked in, and the ancient **Torre delle Ore** (Tower of Hours), which since 1471 has striven to keep the Lucchesi on time, and perhaps now suggests that it's time for a coffee in Lucca's historic **Caffè di Simo** at Via Fillungo 58.

Torre delle Ore
for opening hrs ask at tourist office, see p.262; adm (joint adm available with Torre Guinigi, see opposite)

At Via Fillungo's north end is the tall church and taller campanile of **San Frediano**, built in the early 1100s and shimmering with the colours of the large mosaic on its upper façade, showing Christ and the Apostles in elegant flowing style. The 11th-century bronze Arabian falcon at the top is a copy – the original is in a safe. The palatial interior houses Tuscany's most remarkable baptismal font, the 12th-century *Fontana lustrale* carved with reliefs, and behind it, a lunette of the *Annunciation* by Andrea della Robbia. In the second chapel on the left are Aspertini's excellent frescoes on the *Miracles of San Frediano* and the *Arrival of the Volto Santo*. The last chapel on the left has an altarpiece and two tomb slabs by Jacopo della Quercia and his assistants. The bedecked mummy is St Zita, patroness of maids and ladies-in-waiting; even in England maids belonged to the Guild of St Zita. The Lucchesi are very fond of her; on 26 April they bring her body out to caress.

Palazzo Pfanner
*Via degli Asili, open Mar–Oct daily 10–6; Nov–Feb by appt on **t** 0583 954029; adm*

Next to San Frediano, the **Palazzo Pfanner** has an 18th-century garden attributed to Filippo Juvarra (where Jane Campion filmed *Portrait of a Lady* in 1996), a fine staircase, a collection of silks made in Lucca, and 17th–19th-century costumes. In the other direction, skirting Via Fillungo, narrow arches lead to the **Roman amphitheatre**. Only outlines of its arches are traceable in the outer walls, and within the inner ring only the form remains – the marble was probably carted off to build San Michele and the cathedral – but the outline is perfectly preserved. The foundations of the grandstands support a perfect ellipse of medieval houses. Duchess Maria Louisa cleared out the old buildings in the former arena, and now, where gladiators slugged it out, boys play football and the less active while away time in cafés and shops round the piazza.

The streets in this quarter have scarcely changed in 500 years. Along Via Sant'Andrea and narrow Via Guinigi are some resolutely medieval palaces, including that of the Guinigi family. Their lofty

Torre Guinigi
open May–Aug daily 9am–11pm, April, Sept and Oct daily 9–9, Nov and Dec daily 10–6, Jan daily 10–5, Feb daily 9.30–6, Mar daily 9–7.30; adm (joint adm available with Torre del Ore, see opposite)

stronghold, the **Torre Guinigi** next to their palace, is one of Lucca's landmarks, with seven holm oaks sprouting from the top – the best example of that quaint Italian fancy. It's worth the stiff climb up 230 steps for the views over the city and the Apuan Alps.

The East Side

Roman Lucca ended near the Guinigi palace. When a new church was built in the early 12th century, it was outside the gate, hence the name of **Santa Maria Forisportam**, a pretty church in the Pisan style with blind arcades, in Via Santa Croce. It has two paintings by the often esoteric Guercino. Beyond it is the best-preserved gate of 1260, the **Porta San Gervasio** giving on to the former moat, now a picturesque little canal running along Via del Fosso. Just across the canal from the gate is **Santa Trinità**, home of Civitali's *Madonna della Tosse* (Our Lady of the Cough), a bit too syrupy sweet, but perhaps that helped the cure. Nearby on Via Elisa is the entrance to the **Villa Bottini gardens**, a rare green oasis within the walls.

Santa Trinità
if closed ask for key in convent next door

At the northern end of Via del Fosso stands a 17th-century column dedicated to another Madonna, and to the east is the **church of San Francesco**, a typical 13th-century Franciscan preaching church with the tombs of Castracani and Lucchese composer Luigi Boccherini – he of the famous *minuet* – and some detached frescoes of the Florentine school. Beyond San Francesco stands the palatial brick Villa Guinigi, built in 1418 by the big boss Paolo Guinigi in his glory days. Now the **Museo Nazionale Guinigi**, its ground floor houses Etruscan and Roman finds from ancient Lucca. Upstairs, Room XI has a lovely *Annunciation* by Civitali. The painting gallery contains intarsia panels from the cathedral, each with scenes of Lucca as seen from town windows, some trecento works by the Lucca school and a charming quattrocento *Madonna and Child* by the 'Maestro della Vita di Maria'. Other rooms contain oversized 16th-century canvases, some by Vasari.

Museo Nazionale Guinigi
open Tues–Sat 8.30–7, Sun 8.30–1; adm

Villas around Lucca

In 16th-century Lucca, as elsewhere in Italy, trade began to flounder, and merchants turned to the joys of property, where they could decline genteelly in a little country palace and garden. For the Lucchesi, the preferred site for these was the soft, rolling country to the north and northeast of the city. Some of these villas or their grounds are open for visits. In Segromigno, 10km from Lucca towards Pescia, is the charming, mid-16th-century but often modified **Villa Mansi**, embellished with a half-Italian (geometric) and half-English (not geometric) garden by the Sicilian architect Juvarra. Nearby in Camigliano, the even more elaborate **Villa Torrigiani**, also begun in the 16th century, was known for its

Villa Mansi
open Tues–Sun 10–6; adm exp

Villa Torrigiani
*villa and park open Mar–mid-Nov Wed–Mon 10–1 and 3–sunset; in winter call ahead, **t** 0583 928041; adm exp*

fabulous parties and entertainments. Set in a lush park of pools and trees, it has 16th–18th-century furnishings. Elisa Bonaparte Baciocchi combined a villa and a summer palace to make her country retreat, now called the **Villa Pecci-Blunt ex-Villa Reale** in Marlia. Only the park and the Giardino Orsetti are open, but they are worth the trip. Three other villas, **Bernardini**, **Grabau** and **Oliva**, have opened in the area; the tourist office (*see* below) has details.

Villa Pecci-Blunt ex-Villa Reale
t 0583 92841; open Mar–Nov daily 10–1 and 3–7 (or 5 outside daily saving time); tours by appt; adm exp

The Lucchese Plain

East and west of Lucca, medieval swampland has been reclaimed to form a rich agricultural plain. One feature is its 'courts' – farm hamlets not constructed around a central piazza but with houses in neat rows. At one time there were 1,100 such courts on the plain.

Among the highlights of the area is curious **Castello di Nozzano** just to the west, built by Matilda of Tuscany on a hill, its pretty tower now incongruously topped by a large clock. To the east, one of the first villages, **Capannori**, is the head town of several courts and has a couple of interesting Romanesque churches, especially the 13th-century **Pieve San Paolo**, around which a small village incorporated itself, using the campanile for defence. The most imposing monument nearby is the 19th-century **Acquedotto del Nottolini**, which is also visible from the *autostrada*.

Southeast of Bagna di Lucca is the pretty hilltop village of **Castelvecchio**, its tall houses forming an effective circular wall. **Altopascio**, on the Lucca–Empoli road, was built around an 11th-century hospice run by an obscure chivalric order, the Hospitaller Knights of the Order of Altopascio, who originally rescued travellers from the swamps. Only the campanile of their church remains in the village today. **Montecarlo** gives its name to a very good dry white wine produced in the immediate area.

Where to Stay in Lucca and Around

Lucca and Around ✉ 55100

Book ahead; there simply aren't enough rooms (especially inexpensive ones) in Lucca to meet demand.

*******Locanda l'Elisa**, Via Nova per Pisa, Massa Pisana, **t** 0583 379 737, *www.locandalelisa.it* (€€€€€). A French-style 18th-century villa in a glorious garden. The one double room and four suites are luxuriously appointed, and there is a swimming pool and a conservatory restaurant (€€€) mixing tradition with modern trends. *Closed Jan.*

******Ilaria**, Via del Fosso 26, **t** 0583 47615, *www.hotelilaria.com* (€€€€€–€€€€). An elegant choice with comfortable rooms (breakfast included) and a car park.

******Alla Corte degli Angeli**, Via degli Angeli 23, **t** 0583 469204, *www.allacortedegliangeli.com* (€€€€). An upmarket modern B&B with attractive, comfy rooms with Jacuzzis.

*****Universo**, Piazza del Giglio 1, **t** 0583 493678, *www.universolucca.com* (€€€€). A delightful green-shuttered hotel, slightly frayed, in the centre. Ruskin slept here, paving the way for nearly everyone who followed him to Lucca. The restaurant serves fine food.

ⓘ **Lucca >**
*Palazzo Ducale, Cortile Carrara, **t** 0583 919941, and Piazza S. Maria, **t** 0583 919931, www.luccatourist.it (closed Sun)*

★ **Locanda l'Elisa >**

***La Luna, Corte Compagni 12, t 0583 493634, www.hotellaluna.com (€€€). A cosy place in a quiet part of the centre, with a private garage and a free Internet point.

***Piccolo Hotel Puccini, Via di Poggio 9, t 0583 55421, www.hotelpuccini.com (€€). A small central hotel, comfy but lacking air-con.

**Diana, Via del Molinetto 11, t 0583 592202, www.albergodiana.com (€€). Some of the best inexpensive rooms in Tuscany, some with a bath; those in the annexe are even better.

**Villa Casanova, Via Casanova, Balbano, just outside city, t 0583 548429 (€€). Simple rooms (including breakfast), a pleasant garden, a tennis court, a pool and a restaurant; full or half board are available.

Affittacamere S. Frediano, Via degli Angeli 19, **t** 0583 469630, *www.sanfrediano.com* (€€). Spotless, well-furnished rooms (not all with private bath) near the Anfiteatro, with breakfast included. A nearby car park has special rates for guests.

Da Elisa alle Sette Arti, Via Elisa 25, **t** 0583 494539, *www.daelisa.com* (€). A good-value guesthouse with airy rooms with shared facilities in the town centre, with use of a kitchen. Breakfast is taken in a neighbouring bar.

Locanda Buatino, Borgo Giannotti 508, **t** 0583 343207 (€). Five simple but welcoming rooms with shared facilities, above a restaurant of the same name (*see* below) just outside the city walls to the north.

Eating Out in Lucca and Around

Lucca and Around ✉ 55100

La Buca di Sant'Antonio, Via della Cervia 3, **t** 0583 55881 (€€€). An inn dating back to 1782, offering the likes of home-made *pappardelle* with rabbit, and pork with onions. *Closed Sun eve and Mon.*

★ Giglio >

Giglio, Hotel Universo, Piazza del Giglio, **t** 0583 494058 (€€€). Lucca's best seafood restaurant. Try the spaghetti with crab pulp or the grilled seabass. *Closed Tues eve, Wed and 2wks Aug.*

Da Giulio in Pelleria, Via Conce 45, **t** 0583 55948 (€€€). Sophisticated twists on 'peasant' fare, including *farinata*, spelt and bean soup, and tripe. Booking is recommended. *Closed Sun and Mon.*

★ La Mora >>

La Mora, Via Sesto di Moriano 1748, Ponte a Moriano, 15min drive north of Lucca, **t** 0583 406402 (€€€). An old posthouse serving perhaps the best food in the province, in a rather formal dining room or more informally in summer, under a pergola. The seasonal menu features more seafood than the average Lucchese restaurant, and exquisite *fritto misto* as well. *Closed Wed.*

Vipore, Pieve Santo Stefano 4469, near Lucca, **t** 0583 394065 (€€€). An old farmhouse with views over the fertile plain of Lucca, serving good fresh pasta and meat dishes such as *pappardelle* with rabbit. *Closed Mon, and Tues lunch.*

Vineria I Santi, Via dell'Anfiteatro 29a, **t** 0583 496124 (€€). A restaurant/wine bar with a pretty terrace. Snack on cheeses, salamis and hams or go for something more substantial from the daily menu: perhaps grilled *tomino* (goats' cheese) with pear and walnuts or a fabulous salad. *Closed Wed.*

Buatino, Via Borgo Giannotti 508, **t** 0583 343207 (€€). Good-value, excellent meals in lively surroundings, including *zuppa di farro*, roast pork, and salt cod with leeks, plus live jazz. *Closed Sun.*

Da Leo, Via Tegrimi 1, **t** 0583 492236 (€€). A chaotic place near Piazza San Salvatore, full of locals and tourists, serving good *panzanella* (cold bread soup with tomato and basil) and veal with tuna sauce. *Closed Sun.*

Mecanate, Via della Chiesa, Gattaiola, 4km from Lucca (follow signs from Lucca Ovest *autostrada* exit), **t** 0583 512167 (€€). A little Slow Food place (with slow service) in an old hayloft. Try the delicious *tortelli* filled with meat and cinnamon. *Closed Mon.*

Gli Orti di Via Elisa, Via Elisa 17, **t** 0583 491241 (€). A cheerful trattoria with a great risotto, pizzas, pastas, salads and so on. *Closed Wed, and Thurs lunch.*

Caffè di Simo, Via Fillungo 58 (€). A classic turn-of-the-19th-century *gran caffè*.

The Garfagnana and the Lunigiana

The rugged northern finger of Tuscany encompasses the region's 'Alps', the tall and jagged **Alpi Apuane**, which like the real Alps wear brilliant white crowns, though not made of snow – that's marble up there, the 'tears of the stars', the purest and whitest in Italy. Historically the land is divided into two mini-regions: along the bank of the Serchio river, between the Apuan Alps and the Apennines, is the **Garfagnana**; while the region north of the village of Piazza al Serchio is the **Lunigiana**, former hinterland of the ancient Roman port of Luni.

The Garfagnana and Lunigiana are relatively undiscovered, and threaten to dispel many people's typical image of Tuscany; the mountains are too high, the valleys are too narrow, and you're more likely to find yourself amidst pine forests than vineyards and olive groves. However, a spell in this striking mountain scenery can be what you need when cathedrals or art galleries begin to pall.

The Garfagnana

For many years the chief export of the Garfagnana has been Italians; the green hills and mountains, the narrow valley of the Serchio, between the Apennines and the Apuan Alps, the stone villages perched on slopes that look so picturesque on postcards never provided a sufficient livelihood for their inhabitants. The chief staple of the district until recently was flour made from chestnuts, and chestnut groves still cover much of the region.

Lucca to Bagni di Lucca

North of Lucca, the first tempting detour off the SS12 is to one of many Romanesque churches in the region, **San Giorgio di Brancoli**, near Vinchiana, as notable for its lovely setting as its 12th-century pulpit. **Dìecimo**, across the river, has a name that survives from Roman times – it lies 10 Roman miles (18km) from Lucca. Its main landmark is the mighty Romanesque campanile of the 13th-century church of **Santa Maria**, stark against the surrounding hills.

Borgo a Mozzano, 4km upstream, is famous for its beautiful little humpback bridge, with arches in five different shapes and sizes, dedicated to the Magdalene, or to the Devil. According to legend, he built it one dark stormy night in exchange for the first soul to cross – the villagers outwitted him by sending a dog over in the morning. The real builder was the slighty less lethal 11th-century countess Matilda, who also endowed the villages around Borgo with a number of solid Romanesque parish churches. Inside Borgo's church you can see a wooden *San Bernardino* by Civitali.

Getting to and around the Garfagnana

CLAP **buses** (*www.clapspait.*) from Lucca serve Bagni di Lucca (27km/40min), Barga (37km/1hr), and Castelnuovo di Garfagnana (50km/90mins).

Lucca **train** station (*www.trenitalia.com*) is just south of the walls on Piazza Ricasoli. Trains on the scenic Lucca–Aulla line go up the Serchio valley, but the stations for Bagni di Lucca and Barga are quite a distance from their centres and don't always have bus links, so you're better off taking the bus from the start.

If you're **driving** from the south, the most convenient way into these mountains begins at Lucca; the SS12 and SS445 follow the river Serchio.

---

3 Bagni di Lucca

North, just above the confluence of the Serchio and the Torrente Lima, lie the long, narrow riverside hamlets that make up **Bagni di Lucca**, Lucca's once-grand old spa, first mentioned in the days of countess Matilda. In the early 1800s, under the patronage of Elisa Bonaparte Baciocchi, it enjoyed high society's favour for the time it took to build one of Europe's first official gambling casinos (in 1837; roulette was invented here), an Anglican church in an exotic Gothic Alhambra style, and an unusual 1840 suspension bridge, the **Ponte alle Catene**, before sinking into obscurity. In its heyday, Byron, Browning, Shelley and Heine came to take the sulphur and saline waters. These days it's a sleepy but charming little place with pretty villas, elegant thermal establishments that spring into action every summer and a miniature pantheon.

Up the Lima Valley

From Bagni di Lucca, the SS12 leads to San Marcello Pistoiese and the ski resort of Abetone (*see* p.244), following the lovely valley of the Lima. A byroad from Bagni leads to picturesque, rugged stone hamlets such as **Pieve di Controne** and **Montefegatesi**, which only appear on the most detailed maps; from Montefegatesi, an unsealed road continues to the dramatic gorge of **Orrido di Botri** at the foot of the Alpe Tre Potenze (1,939m). As the byroad winds back towards the SS12 at Scesta, it passes **San Cassiano**, site of a fine 13th-century Pisan-style church with a delicately carved façade.

To Barga and the Cave of the Wind

The Garfagnana proper begins where the Lima river flows into the Serchio at Fornoli. In the 14th century this area was ruled by the kinsmen of Castruccio Castracani, based at **Coreglia Antelminelli**, high above the Serchio and the main SS445 (you need to turn off at Piano di Coreglia). Coreglia Antelminelli's church contains a magnificent 15th-century processional cross, and it is also home to the **Museo della Figurina di Gesso e dell'Emigrazione**, devoted to the Garfagnana's traditional manufacture of plaster figures.

Museo della Figurina di Gesso e dell'Emigrazione
open summer Mon–Sat 9.30–12.30, Sun 10–1 and 3–6; winter Mon–Sat 9.30–12.30; adm

North, the hilltown of **Barga** (population 11,000) stands above its modern offspring, Fornaci di Barga on the main SS445. Barga was astute enough to maintain independence until 1341, when it linked its fortunes with Florence. At the top of town its **cathedral**, begun in 1000 on a terrace, has a panoramic view over the rooftops, green velvet hills and bare mountains scoured with white marble. Built of a blonde stone called *alberese di Barga*, its square façade is discreetly decorated with a shallow pattern, charming reliefs and two leering lions; on the side the campanile is incorporated into the church; over the portal is a relief of a feast scene with a king and dwarfs. There's yet another dwarf inside, supporting one of the red marble pillars of the **pulpit** by idiosyncratic 13th-century Como sculptor Guido Bigarelli. The other pillars required a pair of lions, one grinning over a conquered dragon, one being both stroked and stabbed by a man. Less mysterious are the naive reliefs around the pulpit itself, startlingly sophisticated versions of familiar scriptural scenes. In the choir note the venerable polychrome wood statue of St Christopher (early 1100s) and a choir screen with strange medieval carvings, including a mystic mermaid.

Museo Civico
open June–Sept daily 10–12.30 and 2.30–5; adm

Next to the cathedral, the **Palazzo Pretorio** has the small **Museo Civico** and the 14th-century **Loggetta del Podestà**; down the stairs towards the dungeon are Barga's old corn measures – a medieval Trading Standards Office. The rest of Barga is a photogenic ensemble of archways and little *palazzi* piled on top of each other, with walls, gates and a ravine planted with kitchen gardens. Things get lively in July and August with the classes and performances of **Opera Barga** in the old Dei Differenti Theatre, founded in 1600.

Grotta del Vento
t 0583 722 024; open daily for 1hr guided tours at 10, 11, 12, 2, 3, 4, 5 and 6, 2hr tours April–Oct daily 11, 3, 4 and 5, rest of year Sun and hols 11, 3, 4 and 5; adm exp; come in the morning to avoid the crowds; sometimes only part of cave is visited

From Barga, take a 17km detour to Fornovalasco in the Apuan Alps to see Tuscany's best cave, the **Grotta del Vento**, with fat stalactites, bottomless pits and abysses, and subterranean lakes and streams, set in a barren, eerie landscape.

Castelnuovo di Garfagnana and Around

Hanging over the Serchio, 11km north of Barga, is **Castelnuovo di Garfagnana**, the region's lively 'capital', guarded by its **Rocca**. Its famous commander, Ludovico Ariosto, author of the epic poem of chivalry and fantasy, *Orlando Furioso*, was employed by the Este dukes of Ferrara to chase bandits and collect tolls here in the 1520s, but didn't take to it. 'I have too much pity,' he wrote. It's a handy base for excursions into its often wild surrounds. Northeast, a tortuous mountain road traverses about 20km of magnificent scenery to the **Foce delle Radici** (the pass into Emilia-Romagna) and **San Pellegrino in Alpe**, with superb views, an ancient monastery and a good little museum, the **Museo Etnografico Campagna**.

Museo Etnografico Campagna
t 0583 649072; open April and May Tues–Sun 9–12 and 2–5; June and Sept Tues–Sun 9.30–1 and 2.30–7; July and Aug daily 9.30–1 and 2.30–7; Oct–Mar Tues–Sun 9–1 and 2–5; adm

West of Castelnuovo a scenic road leads over the Apuan Alps to Carrara and the coast, through the desolate Turrite Secca, relieved by the romantic oasis of **Isola Santa** (13km) – a tiny, slate-roofed village on a lake, a hideout for medieval renegades, now home to a few old folks and a sheep who lives behind the altar of the church.

North of Castelnuovo the road enters Garfagnana Alta, one of the least-known corners of Tuscany. Just north of town lies the **Parco Naturale dell'Orecchiella**, with eagles, mouflons, deer and a botanical garden; pick up a map at the visitor centre in Orecchiella.

At Poggio, back on the Serchio, is a turn-off for the **Lago di Vagli**. Creating this lake submerged the village of Fabbriche; the campanile still sticks stubbornly out of the water. There are more stunning views from **Vagli Sopra**, village of old marble quarries and an 18th-century road, deteriorated into a footpath, that leads into the Valle di Arnetola. Towering over all is **Monte Pisanino** (1,945m), tallest of the Apuan Alps; the road up to the summit and the alpine refuge of Donegani, passing the lakelet of Gramolazzo, begins at **Piazza al Serchio**, leaving the Serchio and the Garfagnana behind.

ⓘ Barga >>
Via di Mezzo 47, **t** *800 028497, www.comune.barga.lu.it*

ⓘ Bagni di Lucca >
Via del Casinò Municipale 4, **t** *0583 805745, www.serchionet.it/bagnidilucca (closed Sun)*

ⓘ Castelnuovo di Garfagnana >>
Via Cavalieri di Vittorio Veneto, **t** *0583 641007 (closed Sun)*

Where to Stay and Eat in the Garfagnana

Cooking here is graced by Ligurian and Emilia-Romagna influences. Treats include great pasta, *torte di erbe* (vegetable pies), chestnut puddings and *pattona* (chestnut biscuits).

Bagni di Lucca ✉ 55022

Bagni di Lucca is wonderfully genteel, with quiet, modest Victorian hotels.

*****Corona**, Via Serraglia 78, **t** 0583 805151, *www.coronaregina.it* (€€€). A very comfy option in a 19th-century palace. The restaurant serves imaginative dishes such as nettle *tagliolini* with lobster and basil; half and full board are available.

*****Regina Park Hotel**, Viale Umberto I 157, **t** 0583 805508, *www.coronaregina.it* (€€€). A Renaissance *palazzo* in the centre, under the same ownership as the Regina. A lovely *loggia* overlooks the ample grounds. Breakfast is included, and half and full board are available. *Closed mid-Oct–Easter.*

***Roma**, Via Umberto I 110, **t** 0583 87278 (€). A small, old-fashioned place where Toscanini, Puccini and Caruso stayed, with a shady garden. About half the rooms have a bath.

Circolo dei Forestieri, Loc. Ville, Piazza Varraud, **t** 0583 86038 (€€). A good place for *filetto al pepe verde* and crêpes *ai funghi*. *Closed Mon.*

Da Vinicio, Via del Casino 3, **t** 0583 87250 (€). A chaotic, popular pizzeria also serving good roast pigeon and seafood, with tables by the river.

Barga ✉ 55051

******Il Ciocco in Castelvecchio**, Pascoli, 6km north of town, **t** 0583 7191, *www.ciocco.it* (€€€). A huge resort hotel with apartments and chalets as well as rooms with panoramic views and marble baths. There's also a restaurant, bars, a tennis court and a heliport. Full board is available.

*****Villa Libano**, Via del Sasso 6, **t** 0583 723774, *www.hotelvillalibano.com* (€). A lovely place in a courtyard, with a restaurant and Apuan Alps views.

Terrazza, Piazza San Michele, Albiano, 5km north of town, **t** 0583 766155 (€). Specialities of the region, plus some rooms (full board available). *Closed Wed.*

Castelnuovo di Garfagnana ✉ 55032

*****Da Carlino**, Via Garibaldi 13, **t** 0583 644270 *www.dacarlino.it* (€€). A rustic old place with an Alpine feel. Rooms are comfy, and the excellent restaurant serves home-made and organic produce, including wild boar with polenta, plus pizzas baked in a wood oven (half/full board available).

Osteria Vecchio Mulino, Via Vittorio Emanuele 12, **t** 0583 62192 (€). An atmospheric wine bar with wines, cold meats and cheeses set out on wooden boards at long tables, plus great flans and marinated vegetables. Oil and honey are sold. *Closed Mon.*

La Cezagetta, Capanne di Careggine, **t** 0583 667005 (€). A chalet-style place serving bargain rustic feasts. Try the cod fritters. *Closed Mon.*

The Lunigiana

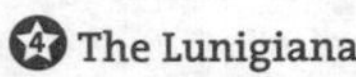

Even less populous and less visited than the Garfagnana, the **Lunigiana**, separating Liguria and Emilia-Romagna from the rest of Tuscany, has traditionally been a tough nut for would-be governors. The Romans of Luni (founded in 180 BC to contain the fearsome Ligurians) found it wild; even in the 7th century, missionaries were bashing ancient idols. This rugged territory of chestnut forests is crowded with the castles of would-be rulers and other toll-collecting gangsters. In the early 1900s the Lunigiana was a stronghold of rural anarchism, and in 1944 its partisans made it one of the bigger free zones in the north. Since then life has been fairly tranquil; rocky, forested landscapes, ruined castles (many bombed in the last war) and simple Romanesque churches form the main attractions.

Piazza al Serchio to Aulla

Parco delle Grotte
t 0187 422598; open July–mid-Sept 10.30–7; June and mid-Sept–Dec by appt; adm

Beyond **Piazza al Serchio**, the first town of consequence along the SS445 is fortified **Casola in Lunigiana** (20km); just beyond, a road veers south for **Equi Terme**, a tiny spa with the medieval town perched spectacularly on a rock above the new town. It's less known these days for its waters than for its splendidly sited **Parco delle Grotte**, where you can visit natural caves such as La Buca ('The Pit'), a caves museum and an archeopark, with reconstructed Palaeolithic and Neolithic settings. Our ancestors apparently socialized with bears (or ate them), judging by the bones found here.

Fivizzano to the north belonged to the Malaspina of Massa until the Medici snatched it and fortified it as a grand ducal outpost. The main square, **Piazza Medicea**, has a grand fountain paid for by Cosimo III, a few Florentine-style palaces, and the 13th-century parish church with the inevitable Medici balls on the front.

There are two interesting Romanesque chapels in the vicinity, **Santa Maria Assunta**, 3km towards Pognana, in a lovely isolated setting, and 12th-century **San Paolo a Vendaso**, with carved capitals inside, on the SS63 towards the Passo di Cerreto.

Castello di Fosdinovo
t 0187 68891; open for guided tours summer Wed–Mon 10–12 and 4–6; winter Wed–Mon 9–11 and 3–5; adm

From Ceserano, just south of the SS445, the SS446 heads southwest over the mountains to Sarzana, passing **Fosdinovo**, where the **Malaspina castle** that hosted Dante in 1306 is one of the most beautiful and majestic in the Lunigiana. Inside is a collection of arms and ornaments found in local tombs.

Aulla

Museo di Storia Naturale
t 01867 400252; open summer Tues–Sun 9–12 and 4–7; winter Tues–Sun 9–12 and 3–6; adm

Aulla grew up at the Lunigiana's hotly contested crossroads, guarding access into the Magra valley. The powerful, 16th-century **Fortezza della Brunella** was built by the Genoese, who bought Aulla in 1543; Napoleon gave it to his sister Elisa in Lucca; it now contains a **natural history museum**. Nearby are the citadels of two

Getting to and around the Lunigiani

If you're approaching from the north, **trains** and *autostrade* from Genoa (A12) and Parma (A15) merge near Aulla. From here there are frequent trains to Massa-Carrara, Viareggio and Pisa, Pontremoli or Lucca. From Lucca, trains to Aulla take more than 2hrs (85km) and to Pontremoli 2hrs 30mins (108km).

CAT **buses** (*www.catspa.it*) serve the Lunigiana, with Aulla as the main depot; there are services to Massa and Carrara, and to Bagnone, Filattiera, Fivizzano, Fosdinovo, Licciana Nardi, Pontremoli and Villafranca.

---

other rivals for the town – the bishop of Luni's **Caprigliola**, a fortified village inaccessible to cars (6km southwest on the SS62), and the Malaspinas' fortified hamlet of **Bibola** and their ruined **Ponzanello**, both due south of Aulla. The Malaspina also fortified the strategic road to the pass, northeast at **Licciana Nardi**, and especially at **Bastia**, 4km further on.

From Aulla you can tuck down into Liguria and the **Italian Riviera** to visit the 'Gulf of the Poets' (Gulf of La Spezia), named after Byron, who swam across it, and Shelley, who last lived in San Terenzo near the Pisan town of **Lerici**. On the gulf's western shore (in Liguria) lies enchanting old **Portovenere**, named after the goddess of love. Near Carrara are the excavations of ancient Luni (*see* p.275).

North of Aulla is **Villafranca in Lunigiana**, along the Via Francigena, the pilgrimage route from France; here you can visit the 16th-century **church of San Francesco** and an **ethnographic museum** devoted to rural life in the Lunigiana, especially the chestnut industry.

Museo Etnografico
open summer Tues–Sun 9–12 and 4–7; winter Tues–Sun 9–12 and 3–6; adm

Pontremoli

Stretched lazily along the river Magra and the Torrente Verdi is Pontremoli (population 11,000), chief town of the Lunigiana and the northernmost in Tuscany. It's full of wonderful Belle Epoque details – lampposts, shopfronts and interiors, even the marble street names. The Liberty-style **Caffè Fratechi Aichta** in Piazza della Repubblica, has old carved wood cabinets and counters. In 1322 Guelph and Ghibelline quarrels led Castruccio Castracani to build a fortress, Cacciaguerra ('drive-away war'), in Pontremoli's centre to keep the two parties apart until they made peace. Of this noble effort only the **Torre del Campanone** and what is now the campanile of the **Duomo** survive. The Duomo itself has a fine, ballroom interior with glittering chandeliers. Over the Torrente Verdi, the **church of San Francesco** has a lovely polychrome relief of the Madonna and Child attributed to Agostino di Duccio. Between the centre and the station, the oval 18th-century church of **Nostra Donna** is a rare example of Tuscan rococo.

Museo delle Statue-stele della Lunigiana
open May–Sept Tues–Sun 9–12 and 3–6, Oct–Apr Tues–Sun 9.30–12.30 and 2.30–5.30; adm

The gloomy 14th-century Castello del Piagnaro is home to a small **museum of statue-*steles***, large and carved, by an unknown culture that flourished in the Lunigiana between the 3rd millennium BC and 2nd century BC. The *steles*, rather like menhirs with personality, include stylized warriors with daggers or axes, and women with little knobbly breasts. They are displayed in semi-darkness, adding to their mystery. The oldest (3000–2000 BC) have a U for a face and a head hardly distinguishable from the trunk; the middle period (20th–8th century BC) sport anvil heads and eyes; the last group (7th–2nd century BC) are mostly warriors, with a weapon in each hand, just as Virgil described the Gauls who invaded Lazio. They were often found near sources of water, and some scholars think they may have symbolized the heavens (the head), the earth (the arms and weapons) and the underworld (the lower third, buried in the ground). Some had their heads knocked off – a sure sign that the pope's missionaries in the 8th century were doing their job. Curiously, in the nearby hamlet of Vignola, a folk memory survives of the destruction of idols; during the patron saint's festival they make little wooden idols strangely similar to Pontremoli's statue-*steles* and burn them to celebrate the triumph over the pagans.

In 1471 the Virgin made an appearance 1.7km south of Pontremoli, and to honour the spot the **church of Santissima Annunziata** was built with a lovely marble **Tempietto** by Jacopo Sansovino, a quattrocento fresco of the Annunciation by Luca Cambiaso, an elegant triptych of uncertain hand or date, and some fun trompe-l'œil frescoes by a Baroque painter from Cremona named Natali.

★ **Da Bussè >>**

★ **Osteria Caveau del Teatro >>**

ⓘ **Fivizzano >**
*Piazza Garibaldi 10, **t** 0585 927111, www.aptmassacarrara.it (closed Oct–May); Fivizzano is also home to the Consorzio Lunigiana Turistica information centre, at Via Roma, **t** 0585 926925, www.tdl.it*

ⓘ **Pontremoli >**
*Piazza della Repubblica, **t** 0187 833701, www.tdl.it*

Where to Stay and Eat in the Lunigiana

Equi Terme ✉ 54022

***La Posta**, Via Provinciale 15, **t** 0585 97937 (€€). A friendly little place with attractive guestrooms and a bright restaurant. *Closed Jan and Feb, and Tues in winter.*

Bagnone ✉ 54021

I Fondi, Via della Repubblica 24, **t** 0187 429086 (€€). Good, solid country cooking. In summer you can eat in the garden overlooking the river. Booking is advisable.

Fivizzano ✉ 54013

****Il Giardinetto**, Via Roma 151, **t** 0585 92060 (€). A delightful, old-fashioned place, with simple but comfy rooms and a little garden. The restaurant (€€) was established in 1882. Booking is required. *Closed Mon.*

Pontremoli ✉ 54027

*****Golf Hotel**, Via Pineta 32, **t** 0187 831573, *www.golfhotel.it* (€€). A modern option in a pine wood outside town, with very comfortable rooms, suites and apartments, plus a restaurant (half board and full board are available).

Da Bussè, Piazza del Duomo 31, **t** 0187 831371 (€€). An age-old restaurant offering the likes of lasagne with chestnut flour, rabbit casserole, and *involtini* in tomato sauce. *Closed Mon–Thurs eves and Fri.*

Osteria Caveau del Teatro, Piazza Santa Cristina, **t** 0187 833328 (€€). An elegant yet cosy cellar restaurant serving *testaroli pontremolesi* (a local pasta) with pesto, and a variety of other unusual treats. Booking is advisable. An adjoining 17th-century tower has a few lovely rooms named after musicians.

Trattoria del Giardino da Bacciottini, Via Riccl Armani 13, **t** 0187 830120 (€€–€). An old-town spot serving some of the best cod in the area. *Closed Sun eves and Mon.*

La Manganella, Via Garibaldi 20, **t** 0187 830653 (€). One of the Lunigiana's most authentic trattorias, serving mushrooms every way under the sun. *Closed Mon.*

The Tuscan Coast

The Etruscan Riviera, Tyrrhenian shore, Tuscany by the sea: whatever you call it, this coastline is an acquired taste. Most of it is flat, straight and dull – with the exception of the backdrop of marble mountains – with wide, usually crowded, sandy beaches. The most beautiful and fashionable part, the Argentario, is expensive. Elba, the largest island, is ruggedly beautiful but a busy Euro-holiday destination. Highlights are the characterful resort of Viareggio, Torre del Lago with its opera festival, Livorno and its seafood restaurants, the mellow old maritime republic of Pisa, Carrara, where you can learn about marble in the Apuan Alps, and the Maremma, where you can learn about Italian cowboys and discover lovely old Massa Marittima.

11

Don't miss

1. Art Nouveau splendour
   Viareggio p.279
2. A 'Field of Miracles'
   Pisa p.282
3. Nature walks and birdlife
   Monti dell'Uccellina park p.313
4. Spanish forts and posh resorts
   Monte Argentario p.315
5. A Gaudi-esque tarot garden
   Capalbio p.320

See map overleaf

The Tuscan Coast

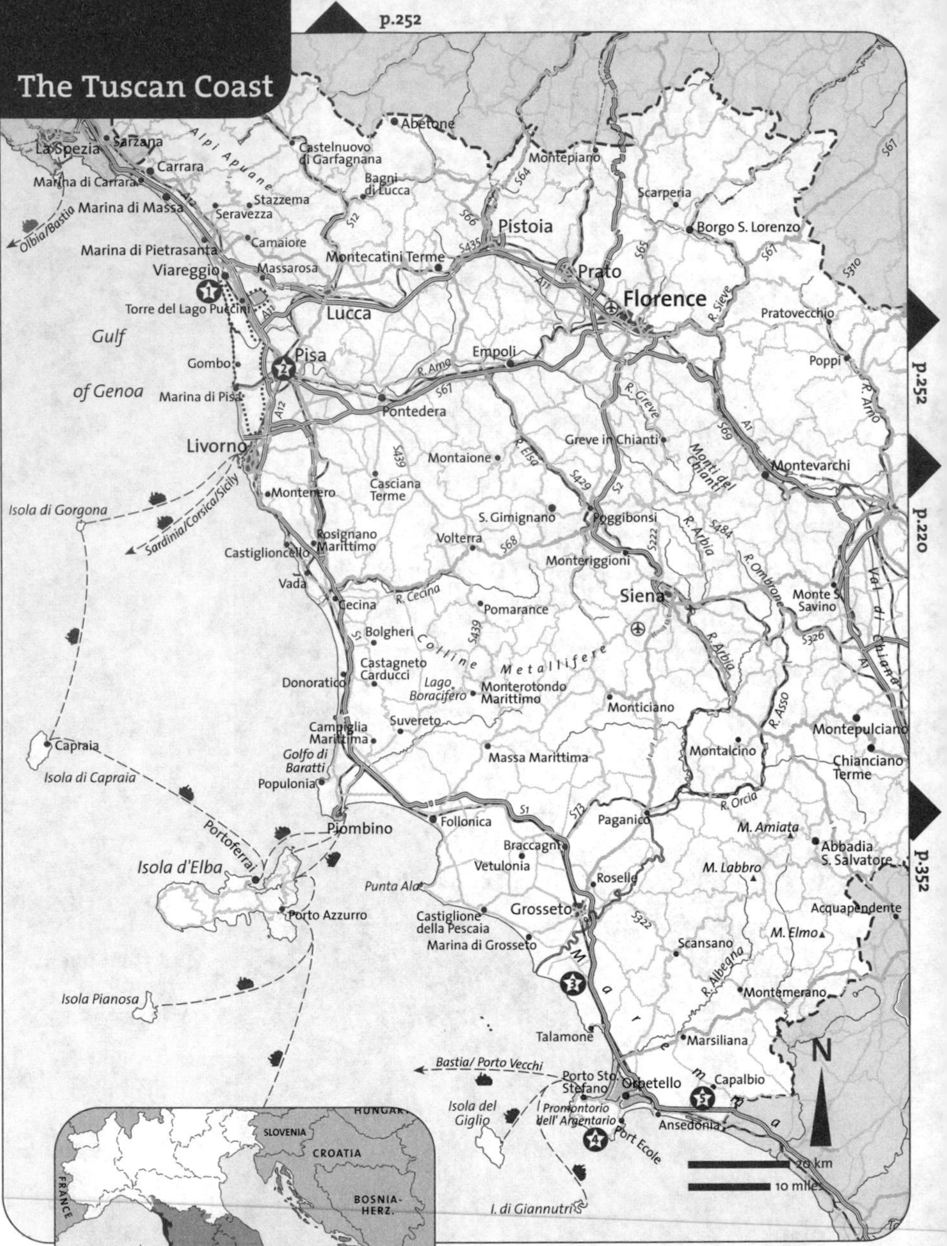

p.252

La Spezia
Sarzana
Carrara
Marina di Carrara
Marina di Massa
Alpi Apuane
Abetone
Castelnuovo di Garfagnana
Bagni di Lucca
Stazzema
Seravezza
Camaiore
Marina di Pietrasanta
Viareggio
Massarosa
Torre del Lago Puccini
Montepiano
Pistoia
Montecatini Terme
Scarperia
Borgo S. Lorenzo
Prato
Florence
Lucca
Gulf of Genoa
Gombo
Pisa
Marina di Pisa
Empoli
Pontedera
Pratovecchio
Poppi
Livorno
Montaione
Greve in Chianti
Monti del Chianti
Montevarchi
Casciana Terme
Montenero
Isola di Gorgona
Sardinia/Corsica/Sicily
Olbia/Bastia
S. Gimignano
Poggibonsi
Rosignano Marittimo
Castiglioncello
Volterra
Monteriggioni
Vada
Cecina
Pomarance
Siena
Monte S. Savino
Val di Chiana
Bolgheri
Colline Metallifere
Castagneto Carducci
Donoratico
Lago Boracifero
Monterotondo Marittimo
Monticiano
Campiglia Marittima
Suvereto
Montalcino
Montepulciano
Chianciano Terme
Capraia
Isola di Capraia
Golfo di Baratti
Populonia
Massa Marittima
Follonica
Paganico
M. Amiata
Abbadia S. Salvatore
Piombino
Portoferraio
Isola d'Elba
Braccagni
Vetulonia
Punta Ala
M. Labbro
Roselle
Porto Azzurro
Castiglione della Pescaia
Grosseto
Acquapendente
Marina di Grosseto
Scansano
M. Elmo
Isola Pianosa
Montemerano
Maremma
Talamone
Marsiliana
Bastia/Porto Vecchi
Porto Sto. Stefano
Orbetello
Capalbio
Isola del Giglio
Promontorio dell'Argentario
Ansedonia
Port Ecole
I. di Giannutri
N
20 km
10 miles

p.252
p.220
p.352

Slovenia
Croatia
Bosnia-Herz.
France
Corsica
Sardinia
Sicily

Don't miss

1. Viareggio **p.279**
2. Pisa's 'Field of Miracles' **p.282**
3. Monti dell'Uccellina park **p.313**
4. Monte Argentario **p.315**
5. The Tarot Garden, Capalbio **p.320**

North of Livorno: The Coast and Inland

Riviera della Versilia: Carrara to Viareggio

Carrara

In the centre of dynamic, up-to-date Carrara (population 69,000) is a garden square, Piazza Gramsci, with an unusual fountain: a large, snow-white sphere of marble that revolves hypnotically, glistening with water, as the Apuan Alps tower in the background, streaked with the white quarries from which the sphere was 'liberated'. Carrara actually means marble; its name is believed to come from 'kar', the Indo-European for stone. The Romans were the first to extract it 2,000 years ago; they drove wooden wedges soaked in water into natural cracks in the stone; when the wedges swelled the marble broke off and was rolled away on iron balls and sent to Rome to become Trajan's column or Apollo Belvedere.

The same techniques were being used when Carrara began its revival in 1502, when Pope Julius II sent Michelangelo to find marble for his tomb. These mountains are haunted by the memory of the 'divine' sculptor, in his old clothes and smelly goatskin boots, going to the most inaccessible corners to discover new veins of perfect white stone. Michelangelo thought quarrying just as serious an art as sculpture; he loved to spend time here with his rock, and he claimed with his usual modesty to have 'introduced the art of quarrying' to Carrara. Marble has also made the Carraresi traditionally a breed apart – though their official past is dominated by the rule of godfatherish noble clans such as the Malaspina and Cybo-Malaspina, the undercurrents were always fiercely independent, leaning strongly towards anarchism.

Some of Carrara's marble went into its one outstanding monument, the **cathedral**, a distinctive Romanesque church begun in the 11th century with marble stripes and an arch of marble animals, and later embellished with an exquisite 14th-century rose window of marble lace, and marble art and statues inside, including a huge bowl in the baptistry. In the little piazza is a bulky sculpture by Florentine hack Bandinelli, generally known as

Beachlife, Tuscan-style

The sea along the Tuscan coast isn't as clean as it might be, and the closer you get to the mouth of the Arno and Livorno the less savoury it becomes. For a spell on the beach, you may find Tuscany's archipelago of seven islands more congenial – the sea is cleaner and the coast and beaches prettier.

Unless you go to the smallest islands, Italian beach culture is hard to escape here. Much of the shore is privately owned and you have to pay to access a veritable wall of deckchairs and beach umbrellas, packed as densely as possible; behind this there's inevitably a busy road, where the traffic is mainly vans with loudspeakers and motorcycles; behind the busy road is another wall of hotels, and perhaps a few pine woods. As always, you'll find it more pleasant and less frenzied outside July and August.

Getting around North of Livorno

Transport is very easy along the coast, especially by **bus**. CAT (**t** 800 570530, *www.catspa.it*) links the Marinas of the coast with Massa and Carrara, and the towns of the Lunigiana; CLAP (**t** 800 602525, *www.clapspa.it*) links Forte dei Marmi and Viareggio with Lucca; LAZZI (**t** 055 351061, *www.lazzi.it*) connects the coast with Lucca, Montecatini, Pistoia and Florence.

There are regular **trains** along the coastal line, which hugs the shore except at the mouth of the Arno and the Maremma. Trains to Massa or Carrara leave you between the beach and the centre, but CAT bus links to either are frequent. The stations at Pietrasanta and Camaiore are inland, not at the marinas.

By **car** you can whip through the dull stretches on the A12, or follow the Via Aurelia (SS1), the main Roman route, though both keep their distance from the sea.

North of Livorno

the Giant, though it is supposed to be *Andrea Doria in the Guise of Neptune*. Next to Piazza Gramsci, on Via Roma 1, is the **Accademia delle Belle Arti**, in a medieval castle converted into a palace in the 16th century by Alberico Cybo-Malaspina, Marchese di Massa, whose descendants ruled Massa and Carrara until they died out in 1829, when the state joined the duchy of Modena until unification. The courtyard has sculptures from Luni and the *Edicola dei Fantescritti*, a Roman tabernacle from the Fantescritti quarry, with bas-reliefs of Jove, Hercules and Bacchus, arm-in-arm like old chums, surrounded by graffiti by Giambologna and other sculptors who visited the quarries.

Marble Quarries and Roman Ruins

Carrara exports 0.5 million tonnes of different marbles a year, but there is little danger of it running out soon (though locals will gravely tell you there are only a few cubic kilometres of good stone left). The **quarries** surrounding Carrara are an unforgettable sight; usually they extend straight up to the sky, forming a blinding white scar down the mountain, with a narrow access road zigzagging perpendicularly to the top. Signs from the centre of Carrara direct you to the quarries, or **Cave di Marmo – Colonnata** (8km, founded as a colony of Roman slaves and famous for *lardo di Colonnata*, a fat bacon salted in marble vats), **Fantiscritti** (a Roman quarry still in use) and **Ravaccione** (with fine mountain views). The **Museo Civico del Marmo** has remarkable photos of the marble-workers of a century ago and the surreal world of the quarries; halls of polished slabs introduce the amazing variety of marbles and travertines from the area, and the rest of the world; and there's marble art and a room of modern marble to prove it's not limited to churches.

Museo Civico del Marmo
Viale XX Settembre (main road between Carrara and train station); open May, June and Sept Mon–Sat 10–6; July and Aug Mon–Sat 10–8; Oct–April Mon–Sat 9–5; adm

The Apuan Alps, only a few kilometres from the sea, give this coast a certain majesty. The beach at **Marina di Carrara** is divided in two by the marble port, which sends the big blocks all over the world; in July and August the port-resort puts on a large show of marble arts and crafts.

Just north, on the border of Liguria near Marinella, is the site of Roman **Luni**, built as a bulwark against the fierce Ligurians. The city survived until the Middle Ages; the power-hungry bishopric of Luni survived until 1929, when it was combined with that of La Spezia. You can see a large amphitheatre, forum, houses, temples and so on; the **Museo Nazionale di Luni** has marble statuary, coins, jewellery, portraits and more, as well as a display of modern techniques used in the excavation of the site, which can be toured with a guide.

Museo Nazionale di Luni
open Tues–Sun 8.30–7.30 (amphitheatre Tues–Sun 10.30–3.30); adm

East off the SS446, 20km in the mountains, **Campo Cecina** has an extraordinary panoramic view over the marble quarries. The city of Carrara has an alpine refuge here; it's a good base for exploring the trails across the Apuan Alps (the tourist office has maps).

Massa

Massa (population 66,200), nearly the same size as Carrara and co-capital of the province, was the principal seat of the Cybo-Malaspina dukes. They were never great builders or patrons, except when it came to their own digs – the polychrome 17th-century **Palazzo Cybo-Malaspina**, on central Piazza degli Aranci, with its orange trees and obelisk, and, up the hill, the **Castello Malaspina**, an 11th-century castle with Renaissance additions, including a beautiful, ornate courtyard, loggias and frescoed rooms.

Castello Malaspina
Via della Rocca; open Tues–Sun 9.30–12.30 and 4–7.30; adm

From Massa there are other marble quarries to visit, near **Pasquilio** 11km east, a balcony with views over the gulf of La Spezia; in the same area, the **Pian della Fioba**'s botanical garden features the flora of the Apuan mountains, more stunning views, and another alpine refuge open all year.

Marina di Massa, which is situated on a drained marsh, is a lively proletarian resort with lots of pine trees; its neighbour, **Cinquale**, the 'Marina' of the old hilltown of Montignoso, is smaller and prettier; between it and Forte dei Marmi you'll find a long stretch of free beach. Near Montignoso stand the picturesque ruins of the **castle of Aghinolfi**, a Lombard outpost that was constructed in AD 600 by King Agilufo.

Castello Aghinolfi
open summer Tues–Sun 4.30–7.30, winter Sun 3–5.30; adm

Around Forte dei Marmi

Forte dei Marmi, one of the larger, smarter resorts, full of very chic shops, bars, clubs and restaurants, is a playground for the rich and famous. Founded in 1788, when Grand Duke Leopoldo constructed the fortress and seaport in order to serve the marble quarried from Seravezza, it has an old loading pier that is now a promenade. In the 1860s the first holiday villas were built alongside the white sandy beach. Don't miss excellent market on Piazza Marconi on Wednesday mornings.

Marina di Pietrasanta to the south isn't quite so upmarket, but in its **Parco della Versiliana** you will find the last section of the coastal forest, lush with parasol pines, holm oaks and myrtles. This was a favourite haunt of Gabriele D'Annunzio; in summer La Versiliana arts festival includes concerts, plays and ballets, put on in its small outdoor theatre. **Lido di Camaiore**, the last resort before Viareggio, caters mainly for families, and has an elevated garden terrace along the beachfront.

Inland from Forte dei Marmi is the marble town of **Seravezza**, where Michelangelo lived in 1517 during his marble pilgrimage to Monte Altissimo; it's rich in statue stone known as *statuario*. Not long after, Duke Cosimo I commissioned Ammannati to build the **Villa Medicea** with its Mannerist courtyard. The **cathedral** contains works by Florentine goldsmiths, including a crucifix attributed to one of the Pollaiuolo brothers; 5km away, the **Pieve alla Cappella** has a fine rose window, the 'Eye of Michelangelo'.

Pretty **Stazzema** has a Romanesque church and stunning views. Quarries nearby produce the blue and white streaked 'flowered' marble used in the Medicis' Princes' Chapel. Among the mountains is the curious **Monte Forata** (1,212m), with a hole near its summit.

Pietrasanta

Pietrasanta is a mellow old town rich in marbly traditions, patronized by well-heeled Italian holidaymakers and home to a sub-culture of foreign artists attracted by its proximity to one of the world's greatest sources of marble and by the facilities around it, from marble studios to bronze foundries. Henry Moore and Mitoraj, among others, have been temporary residents.

The town's walls date from 1255, though its regular street plan suggests a Roman origin. Life centres around Piazza del Duomo with its Florentine *Marzocco* on a pillar (1514) and the **Duomo di San Martino**, begun in 1256, with a rose window carved from a single block of marble. There's more marble inside, plus a bronze crucifix by Tacca and a 13th-century fresco by the school of Giotto. It shares the piazza with the **Palazzo Pretorio** and **Sant'Agostino** (14th century) with an attractive minimalist Pisan façade. From here a road leads up to the citadel, or **Rocca Arrighina**, built in the 1300s by Castruccio Castracani and lit up at night, which often hosted emperors on their way to Rome. Or turn right from the main gate for the central market building, its parking area adorned with an erotic statue of a woman *en déshabille* pulling a young bull after her. There is often a sculpture exhibition in the pretty piazza or cloisters of Sant'Agostino. **Cosmave** can give information about the work of local artists.

Cosmave
t 0584 791297

The Mountains Beyond Pietrasanta

From Pietrasanta a road heads inland to **Valdicastello Carducci** (birthplace of poet Giosuè Carducci) passing the 9th-century **Pieve di Santi Giovanni e Felicità**, the oldest church in the Versilia, with 14th-century frescoes. The road winds up into the mountains giving lovely views, particularly at **Capezzano** and **Capriglia**.

Camaiore (from the Roman *Campus Major*; population 31,000) is an industrial town on the road to Lucca, with two Romanesque churches – the **Collegiata**, **Santi Giovanni e Stefano** (with a stately belltower and Roman sarcophagus for a font), and **Badia dei Santi Benedettini**, 8th-century with 11th-century additions. In Via IV Novembre, the **Museo d'Arte Sacra** has good Flemish tapestries.

Museo d'Arte Sacra
open summer Tues, Thurs and Sat 4–7.30, Sun 9–12; winter Thurs and Sat 3.30–6, Sun 10–12

A road from Camaiore leads up to **Monteggiori**, with more fine views. Other destinations include **Pieve a Elici**, near Massarosa, with a fine Romanesque church, 12th-century **San Pantaleone**. From here a minor road continues up through chestnut groves to **Montigiano**, one of the best balconies in the Apuans.

ⓘ **Carrara >**
Viale Galileo Galilei 40, t 0585 857288, www.aptmassacarrara.it

ⓘ **Pietrasanta >>**
Piazza Statuto, t 0584 283284 or t 0584 284877, www.pietrasantaemarina.it

ⓘ **Marina di Pietrasanta >>**
Via Donizetti 14, t 0584 20331

★ **Enoteca Marcucci >>**

ⓘ **Marina di Massa >**
Viale Vespucci 24, t 0585 240063

ⓘ **Forte dei Marmi >**
Via Franceschi 8b, t 0584 80091

Where to Stay and Eat

At many hotels in coastal resorts, half board is obligatory in high season (mid-July–mid-Aug). There are lots of campsites along the public beach between Massa and Carrara marinas.

Carrara ✉ 54033

Most good places to eat are outside town. Look out for Candia, the white wine eked from Carrara's mountain terraces, and for local speciality *lardo* – pork-fat lard preserved in salt and rosemary in marble vats

******Michelangelo**, Corso F Rosselli 3, **t** 0585 777161, *hm.carrara@tin.it* (€€). Modern rooms, most with baths, a restaurant and parking facilities.

Da Venanzio, Piazza Palestro 3, Colonnata, **t** 0585 758062 (€€€). A place among the quarries, serving a wonderful risotto with mushrooms. *Closed Thurs, and Sun eve.*

Locanda Apuane, Colonnata, **t** 0585 768017 (€€). Delicious *antipasti, tordelli* (meat, spinach and ricotta-filled ravioli), potato cake and local *panizza*. *Closed Mon, Sun eve, Jan.*

Roma, Piazza Battisti, **t** 0585 70632 (€€). A favourite for simple Tuscan cooking in the town centre, including *osso buco* with peas, and *scaloppine* with mushrooms. *Closed Sat lunch.*

Marina di Massa ✉ 54037

Ostello Apuano, Viale delle Pinete 237, **t** 0585 780034, *ostelloapuano@hotmail.com* (€). A youth hostel. Rates include breakfast. *Closed Oct–mid-Mar.*

Forte dei Marmi ✉ 55042

Forte is expensive, but many places offer big reductions in June and Sept.

*******Augustus**, Viale A Morin 169, **t** 0584 787200, *www.augustus-hotel.it* (€€€€€). A lovely villa in large grounds, with elegant rooms (breakfast is included). Facilities include a pool, private beach and two restaurants, one on the lido. *Closed mid-Oct–Apr.*

*****Hotel Franceschi**, Via XX Settembre 19, **t** 0584 787114, *www.hotelfranceschi.it* (€€€€€). A lovely villa in a shady garden. Many of the comfy bedrooms have a balcony, and breakfast is included. The restaurant (€€€) is excellent; try the speciality of *pesce in pane* (whole fish baked in a bread crust). Prices almost halve out of season. Ask about balloon trips over town.

*****Hotel Mignon**, Via G Carducci 58, **t** 0584 787495, *www.hotelmignon.it* (€€€). Bright and airy rooms (breakfast included), a garden, a pool, saunas, a solarium and a fitness centre a couple of blocks from the sea. The restaurant serves local and international cuisine.

Da Lorenzo, Via Carducci 61, **t** 0584 874030 (€€€€). Beautifully and imaginatively prepared seafood such as steamed octopus. Be sure to reserve. *Closed Mon exc July and Aug, mid-Dec–Jan, and lunch July and Aug.*

Pietrasanta ✉ 55045

This is one of the best places to stay in the area, and full of great eateries.

******Albergo Pietrasanta**, Via Garibaldi 35, **t** 0584 793727, *www.albergopietrasanta.com* (€€€€€). An upmarket hotel in a 17th-century *palazzo*, with contemporary Italian art in public rooms and bedrooms. Rooms and suites have original frescoes too, and breakfast is taken in a conservatory or pretty courtyard garden.

*****Palagi**, Piazza Carducci 23, **t** 0584 70249, *www.hotelpalagi.com* (€€€). Comfy rooms, some with wooden beams, outside the old town walls, plus a solarium and private parking.

Enoteca Marcucci, Via Garibaldi 40, **t** 0584 791962 (€€€). More a restaurant with a fabulous wine list than a wine bar, very popular among the rich and famous (book ahead). Highlights include anchovies with lemon. *Closed lunch, Nov and Mon in winter.*

Da Sci, Vicolo Porta a Lucca 3, **t** 0584 790983 (€€). A simple trattoria serving vegetable flans, grilled veg, *pappa al pomodoro* and more. Booking is advisable for dinner. *Closed Sun.*

Camaiore ✉ 55043

Locanda delle Monache, Piazza XXIX Maggio 36, **t** 0584 989258, *www.lemonache.com* (€€). An excellent hotel and restaurant in a former convent. Half board is available.

Emilio e Bona, Loc. Candalla, Via Lombrici 22, just outside town, **t** 0584 989289 (€€). Excellent dishes, many featuring meat, mushrooms and truffles. *Closed Mon, and Tues lunch.*

Viareggio to the Parco Naturale Migliarino San Rossore e Massaciuccoli

Viareggio

Viareggio

Up until the 1820s **Viareggio** (population 59,000), Tuscany's biggest seaside resort, was little more than a fishing village, named after the medieval royal road, the 'Via Regia' between Migliarino and Pietrasanta. After the 14th-century battles with Pisa, Genoa and Florence, this village was the republic of Lucca's only port. Fortifications were built – Forte del Motrone (lost in 1441), the **Torre del Mare** and **Torre Matilde** near the canal. Lucca's beloved duchess Maria Louisa drained the swamps, developed the shipyards and fishing and resort industries, and laid out the neat grid of streets; by the 1860s the first cabanas and beach umbrellas had arrived, and by 1900 Viareggio was booming.

Torre del Mare/ Torre Matilde
open by request; ask at tourist office *(see p.280)*

Playful, intricate wooden Art Nouveau buildings lined its promenade, the Passeggiata Viale Regina Margherita. A massive fire in 1917 led to major rebuilding in the 1920s; the most important buildings were designed by Galileo Chini and the eclectic Alfredo Belluomini. Chini (1873–1956), one of the founders of Italian Art Nouveau, or the Liberty Style, was especially known for florid ceramics. He also designed stage sets for the New York Metropolitan Opera's premieres of his friend Puccini's operas: *Turandot*, *Manon Lescaut* and *Gianni Schicchi*, as well as the throne room of the King of Siam (1911–14). With Belluomini he produced what has become the symbol of Viareggio, the colourful **Gran Caffè Margherita**, in a kind of Liberty-Mannerism, as well as the **Bagna Balena** and what is now the **Supercinema**, all located on the Passeggiata. You can compare their work with the 1900 **Negozio Martini**, the only wooden building to survive the 1917 fire. Chini and Belluomini also designed a number of hotels (*see* p.280), as well as Puccini's villa on Piazza Puccini and the buildings at Piazza D'Azeglio 15 and Viale Manin 20.

Viareggio's famous **Carnival**, which began in the 1890s, has grown to rival the much older ones of Rome and Venice, and in pure frivolity it surpasses them all. At the centre of the action are large papier-mâché floats, often lampooning public figures and politicians. If you can't make the huge parade that takes place on *Martedi Grasso* (Shrove Tuesday, and also on the four previous Sundays), you can see the floats all year round at the **Cittadella del Carnivale** near the Aurelia in the northwest of the town. This vast modern workshop and performance space is also the setting for concerts (mostly jazz and rock) in summer. Viareggio also has an open-air **fleamarket** around Piazza Manzoni on the fourth Saturday and Sunday of each month.

Cittadella del Carnivale
Via Maria Goretti; visits by appt on **t** *0584 51176; closed for much of winter while floats being made*

Museo Pucciniano
buses from Piazza D'Azeglio; open Mar and April Tues–Sun 10–12.30 and 3.30–5.30; May–Oct Tues–Sun 10–12.30 and 3–6.30; Dec–Feb 10–12.30 and 2.30–5; adm

Festival Pucciniano
Piazzale Belvedere Puccini, Torre del Lago, **t** *0584 359322, www.puccinifestival.it; adm*

Parco Naturale Migliarino
open summer Tues, Thurs, Sat and Sun 9.30–11.30 and 3.30–5.30, winter Tues, Thurs, Sat and Sun 9.30–11.30 and 2–4; for guided tours call **t** *050 530101 or* **t** *050 533751*

Torre del Lago and Puccini

Puccini spent most of his later years in his villa at **Torre del Lago** 6km south of Viareggio. Now the **Museo Pucciniano**, it is on the banks of Lake Massaciuccoli, where he could practise his 'second favourite instrument, [his] rifle' on passing coots. The villa has its original furnishings, old photos, the piano on which Puccini composed many operas, his rifles and other mementos. The maestro, along with his wife and son, is buried in the adjacent chapel.

In July and August the **Torre del Lago opera festival** presents famous and more obscure works by the composer. The stage is built out on the lake and spectators sit on the lakeside – beware the mosquitoes.

Most of Lake Massaciuccoli and the *macchia* (marshlands) and beaches to the south are part of the **Parco Naturale Migliarino San Rossore Massaciuccoli** (reached by boat from Torre del Lago, or drive to tiny Massaciuccoli). The wild beaches from Viareggio and Torre del Lago, with low dunes and pine forest, are free and undeveloped.

ⓘ Viareggio >
Viale Carducci 10, and at station in high season, **t** *0584 962233, www.aptversilia.it*

★ Plaza e de Russie >

Where to Stay and Eat in Viareggio

Viareggio ✉ 55049

There are lots of hotels along the beach, especially inexpensive ones.

******Plaza e de Russie**, Piazza d'Azeglio 1, **t** 0584 44449, *www.plazaederussie.com* (€€€€). An elegant option with marble and Murano glass in the public rooms and a lovely rooftop breakfast room and restaurant where you can enjoy Mediterranean cuisine. Half and full board are available.

******Grand Hotel Excelsior**, Viale Carducci 88, **t** 0584 50726, *www.excelsiorviareggio.it* (€€€). One of the most extravagant Chini-Belluomini ventures, built in 1923. The public rooms preserve their original decor. Breakfast is included, and there's a restaurant and a babysitting service. *Closed Nov–Mar.*

****Apollo**, Viale Carducci 76, **t** 0584 407 2823, *www.hotelapolloviagreggio.com* (€€). A Liberty villa by the seafront, with original Belle Epoque features. Bedrooms are spartan but have baths and sea views, and there's a garden and a restaurant .

****Al Piccolo Hotel**, Via Duilio 16, **t** 0584 51014, *alpiccolohotel@cheapnet.it* (€€). An old villa a few blocks from the sea, now a modest hotel offering half and full board. *Closed winter.*

Da Romano, Via Mazzini 122, **t** 0584 31382 (€€€€). An elegant restaurant with an interior garden, offering creative cooking and delicious seafood such as squid stuffed with vegetables and shellfish. Book ahead. *Closed Mon, Tues lunch in July and Aug, 1wk in Jan, and 1wk in July.*

L'Imbuto, Via Fratti 308, **t** 0584 48906 (€€€). A lively, informal place for innovative fish dishes such anchovies with fried green tomatoes. Booking is advisable. *Closed Mon.*

L'Oca Bianca, Via Coppino 409, **t** 0584 388477 (€€€). A restaurant overlooking the yacht harbour, and a cheaper adjoining *taverna*. Try the squid in basil sauce. *Closed lunch Mon–Sat, Tues in winter.*

Piccolo Tito, Lungomolo del Greco, **t** 0584 962016 (€€€). A lively, popular restaurant overlooking the canal. No-nonsense fish dishes include Catalan lobster. There are pizzas too.

Al Porto, Via Coppino 118, **t** 0584 383878 (€€€). A stunning restaurant overlooking the port, with wonderful home-made tagliatelle in San Pietro sauce, seabass cooked in salt, and more. *Closed Sun eve and Mon in winter; Sun and Mon lunch in summer.*

La Darsena, Via Virgilio 150, **t** 0584 392785 (€€). A hugely popular place for *bavette* (pasta) with anchovies, fried squid and more. *Closed Sun.*

Pisa

Pisa (population 104,000) is at once the best-known and most mysterious Tuscan city. Its most celebrated attraction has become a symbol for all Italy; even the least informed recognize the 'Leaning Tower of Pizza'. Tour buses disgorge thousands of people into the Field of Miracles every day, to spend a couple of hours 'doing' the sights before heading back to Florence, Elba or Rome. At night even the Pisani make a mass exodus into the suburbs, as if they sense that the city is too big for them – not physically, but in terms of unfulfilled ambitions, of past greatness nipped in the bud.

In 1100, Pisa was 'the city of marvels', the 'city of 10,000 towers' – or so it seemed to the awed writers of that century, who, at least outside Venice, had never seen such an enormous, cosmopolitan city in Christian Europe since the fall of Rome. Its population stood at 300,000. Pisan merchants travelled all over the Med, bringing back new ideas and styles in art, as well as riches. Pisa contributed much to the rebirth of Western culture: Pisan Romanesque, with its stripes and blind arcades, which had such a wide influence in Tuscany, was inspired by the Moorish architecture of Andalucía; Nicola Pisano, first of a long line of great sculptors, is as important to the renaissance of sculpture as Giotto is to painting.

Pisa has put all its efforts into one fabulous spiritual monument, while the rest of the city wears an undemonstrative, almost anonymous face. It is a subtle place, a little sad and rundown perhaps, but strangely seductive if you give it a chance. After all, one can't create a Field of Miracles in a void.

History

Pisa used to like to claim it began as a Greek city, founded by colonists from Elis. Most historians won't accept anything earlier than around 100 BC, when a Roman veterans' colony was settled here. Records of what followed are scarce, but Pisa, like Amalfi and Venice, must have had an early start in building a navy and establishing trade connections. By the 11th century, the effort had blossomed into opulence; it had acquired a small empire, including Corsica, Sardinia and, for a while, the Balearics. Around 1060, work began on the great cathedral complex and many other buildings, inaugurating the Pisan Romanesque.

In 1135 Pisa captured and sacked Amalfi, its greatest rival. The First Crusade, when Pisa's archbishop led the entire fleet in support of the Christian knights, was an economic windfall for the city. And when the Pisans weren't fighting the Muslims of Spain and Africa, they were learning from them: much medieval Arab science, philosophy and architecture came into Europe through Pisa. Pisa's architecture, the highest development of the Romanesque in Italy,

Getting to and around Pisa

Pisa's **international airport**, Galileo Galilei (t 050 849300, *www.pisa-airport.com*) 3km to the south, is 10mins from Piazza Stazione (in front of the main station south of the Arno) by bus no.5. It also has a station with a few daily trains to the centre and a special train service to Florence (1hr, every 1–2hrs daily). **Car hire** companies at the airport include Hertz, **t** 050 43220, *www.hertz.it*, Maggiore, **t** 050 42574, *www.maggiore.it*, Easycar, **t** 3939 403761, *www.easycaritalia.it*, and Auto Europa, **t** 050 506883, *www.autoeuropa.it*.

Pisa has three **train stations** (**t** 892021, *www.trenitalia.com*): some coastal trains stop at San Rossore, near Campo dei Miracoli, and some trains from Florence stop at Pisa Aeroporto (*see* above), but it's best to plan trips through the Stazione Centrale south of the Arno, where all trains call.

Intercity buses depart from near Piazza Vittorio Emanuele II, the big roundabout just north of the central station: CPT buses (*www.cpt.pisa.it*) for Volterra, Livorno and the coastal resorts (to the west on Via Nino Bixio, **t** 800 012773) and LAZZI buses (*www.lazzi.it*) to Florence, Lucca, La Spezia (on Via d'Azeglio, **t** 050 46288). Many of these buses also stop at Piazza D Manin, just outside the walls at the cathedral.

The Natural Park Migliarino San Rossore Massaciuccoli can be reached by city bus no.11 from Piazza Vittorio Emanuele.

Pisa lends itself well to **bikes**; you can hire one at A Ruota Libera, Via Galli Tassi 6, near the Leaning Tower.

saw its influence spread from Sardinia to Puglia in southern Italy; when Gothic arrived in Italy, Pisa was one of the few cities to take it seriously, and the city's accomplishments in that style rank with Siena's. In science, Pisa contributed a great if shadowy figure, the mathematician Leonardo Fibonacci, who either rediscovered the principle of the Golden Section or learned it from the Arabs, and also introduced Arabic numerals to Europe. Pisa's scholarly tradition was crowned in the 1600s by its most famous son, Galileo Galilei.

Pisa was always a Ghibelline city, the greatest ally of the emperors in Tuscany if only for expediency's sake. But the real threat eventually came from the rising mercantile port of Genoa. After years of constant warfare, the Genoese devastated the Pisan navy at the battle of Meloria (an islet off Livorno) in 1284. All chance of recovery was quashed by an even more implacable enemy: the Arno. Pisa's port was gradually silting up, and when the cost of dredging became greater than the traffic could bear, the city's fate was sealed. The Visconti of Milan seized the economically enfeebled city in 1396, and nine years later Florence snatched it from them.

Excepting 1494–1505, when the city rebelled and kept the Florentines out despite an almost constant siege, Pisa's history as a key locale ended. The Medici dukes did the city one big favour, in supporting the university and even removing Florence's university to Pisa. In the last 500 years of Pisa's pleasant twilight, this institution has helped the city stay alive and vital, and in touch with the modern world; one of its students was nuclear physicist Enrico Fermi.

Field of Miracles (Campo dei Miracoli)

Almost from its conception, the **Field of Miracles** was the nickname given to medieval Italy's most ambitious building programme. Too many changes were made over two centuries to tell exactly what the original intentions were, but of all the unique things about the complex, the location is most striking. Whether their reasons had to do with aesthetics or land values, Pisans built their cathedral on a broad expanse of green lawn at the northern edge of town, just inside the walls. The cathedral was begun in 1063, the famous Leaning Tower and the baptistry in the middle 1100s, at the height of Pisa's fortunes, and the Campo Santo in 1278.

The Leaning Tower is not the only strange thing in the Field of Miracles. The more time you spend here, the more you notice: little monster-griffins, dragons and such, peeking out of every corner of the oldest sculptural work, or the big bronze griffin on a column atop the cathedral apse (a copy) and a rhino by the door, Muslim arabesques in the Campo Santo, perfectly classical Corinthian capitals in the cathedral nave and pagan images on the pulpit. The elliptical cathedral dome, in its time the only one in Europe, shows that the Pisans had not only the audacity but the mathematical skills to back it up. You may notice that the baptistry too is leaning – about 1.5m in the opposite direction to the tower. And the cathedral façade leans outwards about 30cm; it's hard to notice but disconcerting if you see it from the right angle. This could hardly be accidental. So much in the Field of Miracles gives evidence of a very sophisticated, strangely modern taste for the outlandish. Perhaps the medieval master masons in charge here simply thought that plain perpendicular buildings were becoming just a little trite.

Baptistry

Battistero
open April–Sept daily 8–8; Oct daily 9–7; Nov–Feb daily 10–5; Mar daily 9–6; adm; joint adm available with cathedral, Campo Santo, Museo delle Sinopie and/or Museo del Duomo.

This is the biggest of its kind in Italy. Its original architect, Master Diotisalvi ('God save you'), saw the lower half done in the Pisan-style stripes-and-arcades. A second colonnade was intended, but as the Genoese gradually muscled Pisa out of trade routes, funds ran short. In the 1260s, Nicola and Giovanni Pisano redesigned and completed the upper half in a harmonious Gothic crown of gables and pinnacles. They also added the dome over Diotisalvi's original prismatic dome, still visible from inside. Both domes were among the largest attempted in the Middle Ages.

Inside, the austerity of the simple, striped walls and heavy columns of grey Elban granite is broken by two superb works of art. The great **baptismal font** is by Guido Bigarelli, the 13th-century Como sculptor who made the crazy **pulpit** in Barga (*see* p.266). Its 16 exquisite marble panels are finely carved in floral and geometric patterns of inlaid stones, an almost monochrome variant on the Cosmati work of medieval Rome and Campania. Nicola Pisano's pulpit (1260) was one of that family's first, and established the form for their later pulpits, the columns resting on fierce lions, the relief panels crowded with intricately carved figures in New Testament episodes – a style that seems to owe much to the reliefs

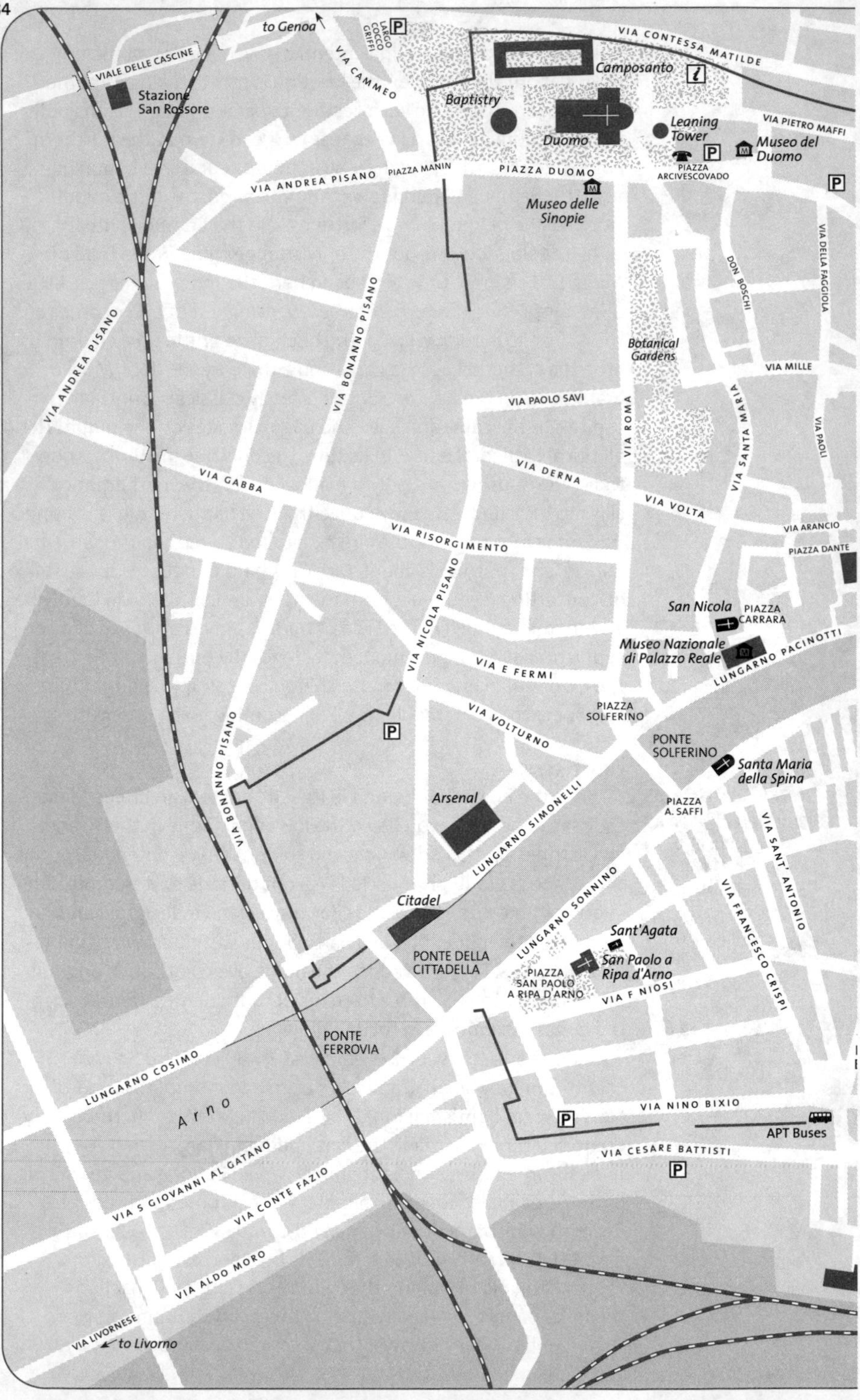

to Genoa
LARGO COCCO GRIFFI
VIA CONTESSA MATILDE
Camposanto
VIALE DELLE CASCINE
Stazione San Rossore
VIA CAMMEO
Baptistry
Leaning Tower
Duomo
VIA PIETRO MAFFI
Museo del Duomo
PIAZZA ARCIVESCOVADO
VIA ANDREA PISANO
PIAZZA MANIN
PIAZZA DUOMO
Museo delle Sinopie
DON BOSCHI
VIA DELLA FAGGIOLA
VIA ANDREA PISANO
VIA BONANNO PISANO
Botanical Gardens
VIA MILLE
VIA PAOLO SAVI
VIA ROMA
VIA SANTA MARIA
VIA PAOLI
VIA DERNA
VIA GABBA
VIA VOLTA
VIA ARANCIO
VIA RISORGIMENTO
PIAZZA DANTE
VIA NICOLA PISANO
San Nicola
PIAZZA CARRARA
Museo Nazionale di Palazzo Reale
LUNGARNO PACINOTTI
VIA E FERMI
PIAZZA SOLFERINO
VIA VOLTURNO
VIA BONANNO PISANO
PONTE SOLFERINO
Santa Maria della Spina
Arsenal
LUNGARNO SIMONELLI
PIAZZA A. SAFFI
VIA SANT' ANTONIO
Citadel
LUNGARNO SONNINO
VIA FRANCESCO CRISPI
Sant'Agata
PONTE DELLA CITTADELLA
PIAZZA SAN PAOLO A RIPA D'ARNO
San Paolo a Ripa d'Arno
VIA F NIOSI
PONTE FERROVIA
LUNGARNO COSIMO
Arno
VIA NINO BIXIO
APT Buses
VIA CESARE BATTISTI
VIA S GIOVANNI AL GATANO
VIA CONTE FAZIO
VIA ALDO MORO
VIA LIVORNESE
to Livorno

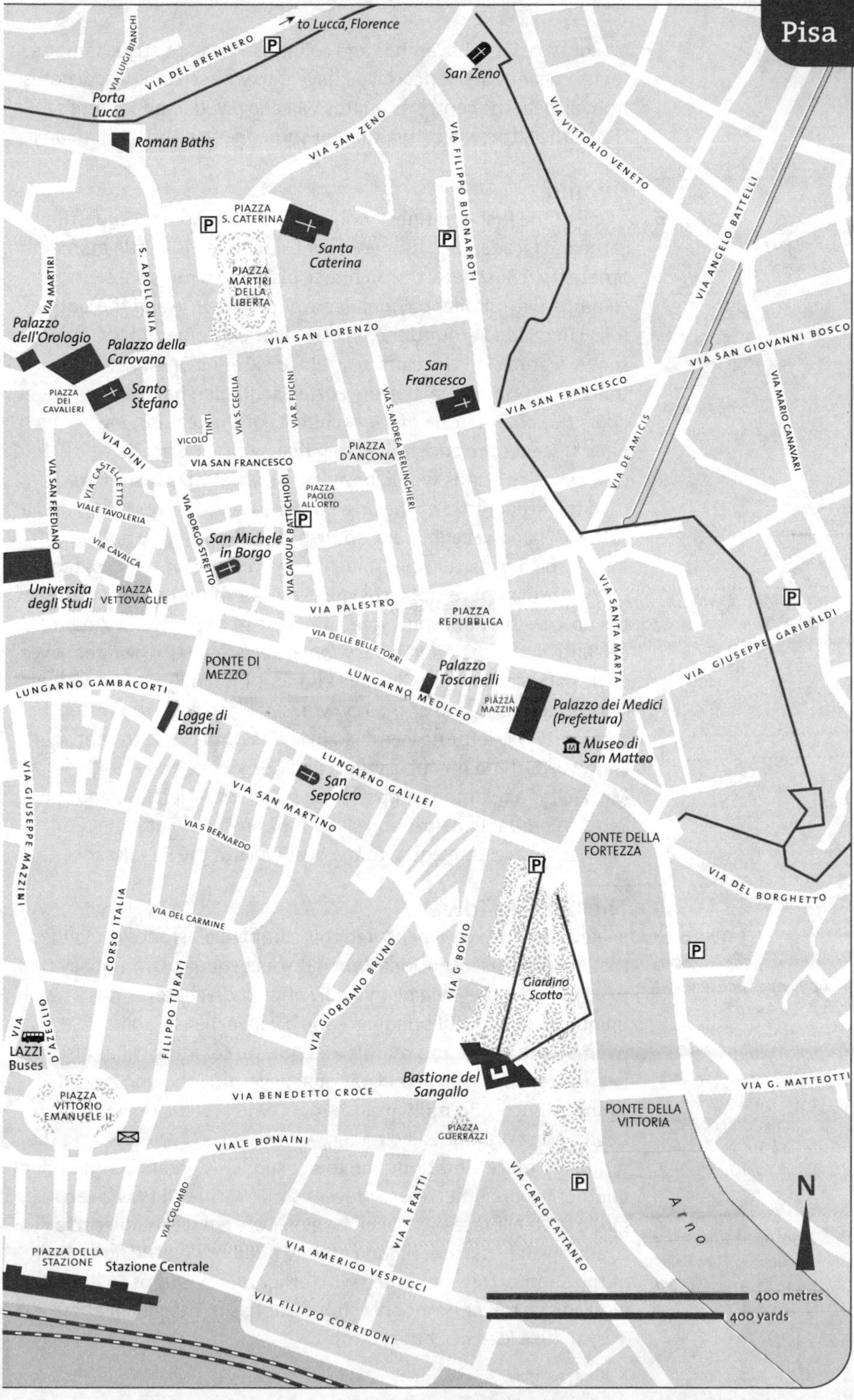

to Lucca, Florence
Via del Brennero
Via Luigi Bianchi
Porta Lucca
Roman Baths
San Zeno
Via San Zeno
Via Filippo Buonarroti
Via Vittorio Veneto
Piazza S. Caterina
Santa Caterina
Piazza Martiri della Liberta
S. Apollonia
Via Martiri
Via Angelo Battelli
Palazzo dell'Orologio
Palazzo della Carovana
Via San Lorenzo
Piazza dei Cavalieri
Santo Stefano
San Francesco
Via San Giovanni Bosco
Via San Francesco
Via Mario Canavari
Via De Amicis
Via S. Cecilia
Via R. Fucini
Via S. Andrea Berlinghieri
Vicolo Tinti
Via Dini
Piazza d'Ancona
Via San Francesco
Via Castelletto
Via San Frediano
Viale Tavoleria
Via Borgo Stretto
Via Cavour
Battichiodi
Piazza Paolo all'Orto
San Michele in Borgo
Via Cavalca
Universita degli Studi
Piazza Vettovaglie
Via Palestro
Piazza Repubblica
Via Santa Marta
Via delle Belle Torri
Via Giuseppe Garibaldi
Ponte di Mezzo
Lungarno Gambacorti
Lungarno Mediceo
Palazzo Toscanelli
Piazza Mazzini
Palazzo dei Medici (Prefettura)
Museo di San Matteo
Logge di Banchi
Lungarno Galilei
San Sepolcro
Via San Martino
Via S Bernardo
Ponte della Fortezza
Via del Borghetto
Via Giuseppe Mazzini
Corso Italia
Via del Carmine
Via G Bovio
Via Giordano Bruno
Filippo Turati
Giardino Scotto
Via D'Azeglio
LAZZI Buses
Bastione del Sangallo
Via Benedetto Croce
Via G. Matteotti
Piazza Vittorio Emanuele II
Ponte della Vittoria
Viale Bonaini
Piazza Guerrazzi
Via Carlo Cattaneo
Via Colombo
Via A Fratti
Arno
N
Piazza della Stazione
Stazione Centrale
Via Amerigo Vespucci
400 metres
400 yards
Via Filippo Corridoni

on Roman triumphal arches and columns. The baptistry is famous for its uncanny acoustics; if you have it to yourself, sing a few notes from as near the centre as guards will allow you to go. If there's a crowd the latter will be waiting for someone to bribe them to do it.

Duomo

Duomo
open April–Sept daily 10–8; Oct daily 10–7; Nov–Feb daily 10–5; Mar daily 10–6; adm; joint adm available with baptistry, Campo Santo, Museo delle Sinopie and/or Museo del Duomo.

One of the first and finest works of the Pisan Romanesque, the cathedral façade, with four levels of colonnades, is a little more ornate than Buscheto, the architect, planned in 1063. These columns, with similar colonnades around the apse and the Gothic frills later added around the unique elliptical dome, are the only showy features on the calm, restrained exterior. On the south transept, the late-12th-century **Porte San Ranieri** has fine bronze doors by Bonanno, one of the architects of the Leaning Tower. The biblical scenes are enacted among real palms and acacia trees; the well-travelled Pisans would have known what they looked like.

On the inside, little of the original art survived a fire in 1595, and a coffered Baroque ceiling and some poor painting were added during the reconstruction. Some fine works remain: a few patches of the Cosmati pavement; the great mosaic of *Christ Pantocrator* in the apse by Cimabue; and some portraits of the saints by Andrea del Sarto in the choir and his *Madonna della Grazia* in the right nave.

The **pulpit** (*c.* 1300), by Giovanni Pisano, is his family's acknowledged masterpiece, and one of the key works of Pisan sculpture. After the 1595 fire it was left unassembled in crates until the 20th century. It shows a startling mix of classical and Christian elements. St Michael, as a telamon, supports the pulpit with Hercules and the Fates, as prophets, saints and sibyls look on. The relief panels, full of expressive faces, are equal to the best work of the Renaissance.

The Leaning Tower

La Torre
www.opapisa.it; open April–mid-June and 2nd half Sept dail 8.30–8.30; mid-June–mid-Sept daily 8.30am–11pm; Oct daily 9–7; Nov–Feb daily 9.30–5; Mar daily 9–6; max. 30 people at a time, with guide; book well in advance; 300 steps to top; no under-8s, 8–12 year-olds must be hand-held by adult, 12–18 year-olds must be accompanied by adult; adm exp

The architects who measured this campanile's stones concluded that its lean was intentional when it was begun in 1173, but say this to a Pisan and they will be mortally offended. Whatever, it is a unique and beautiful building – and a very expensive bit of whimsy, with some 190 marble and granite columns. It has also been expensive to local and national governments, who have had to shore it up – $80 million since 1990, when rescue operations began. Most dramatically, in 1995, while workers were freezing the ground to mute vibrations, the tower suddenly groaned and tipped another few millimetres; to prevent similar scares it was given a girdle of steel braces, attached by a pair of 22m steel cables to a counterweight system hidden among buildings on the north end of the Campo. This, combined with other moves, seems to have worked; the tower is not only stable but has righted itself about 40.5cm (to a lean of about 4.5m).

Campo Santo

Campo Santo
open April–Sept daily 8–8; Oct daily 9–7; Nov–Feb daily 10–5; Mar daily 9–6; adm; joint adm available with baptistry, cathedral, Museo delle Sinopie and/or Museo del Duomo

This remarkable cloister is as unique in its way as the Leaning Tower. Basically, the cemetery is a rectangle of gleaming white marble, unadorned save the blind arcading around the façade and the beautiful Gothic tabernacle of the enthroned Virgin Mary over the entrance. With its uncluttered, simple lines, the Campo Santo seems more like a work of our own times than the 1300s.

The cemetery began, according to legend, when the battling archbishop Lanfranchi, who led the Pisan fleet into the Crusades, came back with boatloads of soil from the Holy Land for extra-blessed burials. Over the centuries an exceptional hoard of frescoes and sculpture accumulated here. Much went up in flames in July 1944, when an Allied incendiary bomb set the roof on fire. Many priceless works of art were destroyed and others, including most of the frescoes, were damaged beyond hope of being perfectly restored. The biggest loss, perhaps, was the set of frescoes by Benozzo Gozzoli – including the *Tower of Babylon*, *Solomon and Sheba*, *Life of Moses* and the *Grape Harvest*; in their original state they must have been as fresh and colourful as his famous frescoes in Florence's Medici Palace.

Even better known, and better preserved, are two 14th-century frescoes by an unknown artist (perhaps Buffalmacco, described by Boccaccio in the *Decameron*): the *Triumph of Death*, a memento of the century of plagues and trouble in which Death (in Italian, feminine: *La Morte*) swoops down on frolicking nobles; and the *Last Judgement*, with the damned variously cooked, wrapped in snakes, poked, disembowelled, banged up and chewed on. These are some of the best paintings of the trecento.

Museo delle Sinopie
closed for restoration at time of writing; normally open April–Sept daily 8–8; Oct daily 9–7; Nov–Feb daily 10–5; Mar daily 9–6; adm; joint adm available with baptistry, cathedral, Campo Santo and/or Museo del Duomo

Another curiosity is the *Theological Cosmography* of Piero di Puccio, a vertiginous diagram of 22 spheres of the planets and stars, angels, archangels, thrones and dominations, cherubim and seraphim, and so on; in the centre, the small circle trisected by a T-shape was a common medieval map pattern for the known earth. The three sides represent Asia, Europe and Africa, and the three lines the Mediterranean, the Black Sea and the Nile.

Other Museums

Museo del Duomo
Piazza Arcivescovado; open April–Sept daily 8–8; Oct daily 9–7; Nov–Feb daily 10–5; Mar daily 9–6; adm; joint adm available with baptistry, cathedral, Campo Santo and/or Museo delle Sinopie

Opposite the cathedral, the **Museo delle Sinopie** contains the pre-painting sketches on plaster of the frescoes lost in the Campo Santo fire. Many are works of art in their own right, and, though faint, give an idea of how the frescoes once looked.

Near the Leaning Tower, the **Museo del Duomo** in the old chapterhouse boasts descriptions in English in each room. The first rooms contain the oldest works – beautiful fragments from the cathedral façade and altar; two Islamic works, the strange, original bronze **griffin** from the top of the cathedral, believed to have come from Egypt in the 11th century, and a 12th-century bronze basin with an intricate decoration. Statues by the Pisanos from the baptistry were brought in from the elements too late; worn and bleached, they resemble a convention of mummies. Sculptures in the next room survived better: Giovanni Pisano's grotesque faces, his gaunt but noble *St John the Baptist* and the lovely *Madonna del Colloquio*, so named because she speaks to her child with her eyes.

In the next room are fine works by Tino di Camaino, including the tomb of San Ranieri and his sculptures from the tomb of Emperor Henry VII, sitting among his court like some exotic oriental potentate. In Room 9 you'll find works by Nino Pisano, and in Rooms 11–12, the cathedral treasure. Giovanni Pisano's lovely ivory *Madonna and Child* steals the show, curving to the shape of the elephant's tusk; there's an ivory coffer and the cross that led the Pisans on the First Crusade.

Upstairs are some extremely large angels used as candlesticks, intarsia and two rare illuminated 12th- and 13th-century scrolls ('exultet rolls'), perhaps the original visual aids; the deacon would unroll them from the pulpit as he read so the congregation could follow the story with the pictures. Remaining rooms have Etruscan and Roman odds and ends (including a good bust of Caesar) and prints and engravings of the original Campo Santo frescoes made in the 19th century. The courtyard has a unique view of the Leaning Tower, which seems to be bending over to spy inside.

North Pisa

With the cathedral on the edge of town, Pisa has no real centre, but Pisans are very conscious of the division made by the Arno; every June neighbourhoods on either side of it fight it out on the Ponte di Mezzo in the *Gioco del Ponte*, in a medieval tug-of-war where opponents try to push a big decorated cart over each other.

From the Field of Miracles, Via Cardinale Pietro Maffi leads eastwards to ruined **Roman baths** near the Lucca Gate. Also in the neighbourhood are **San Zeno**, in a corner of the walls, with some parts as old as the 5th century, and **Santa Caterina**, a Dominican church with a beautiful, typically Pisan façade, and, inside, an *Annunciation* and a sculpted Saltarelli tomb by Nino Pisano, and a large 1340s painting of the *Apotheosis of St Thomas Aquinas*, with Plato and Aristotle in attendance and defeated infidel philosopher Averroës below, attributed to Francesco Traini.

One long street near the Campo dei Miracoli begins as Via della Faggiola, leading into the **Piazza dei Cavalieri**. Duke Cosimo I started what was probably the last crusading order of knights, the Cavalieri di Santo Stefano, in 1562. The crusading urge ended long before, but the duke found the knights a useful tool for placating the anachronistic fantasies of the Tuscan nobility – most of them newly titled bankers – and for licensing out freebooting expeditions against the Turks. Cosimo had Vasari build the **Palazzo della Carovana** for the order, demolishing the old Palazzo del Popolo, symbol of Pisa's lost independence. Vasari gave the palace an outlandishly ornate *graffito* façade; it now holds the Scuola Normale Superiore, founded by Napoleon in 1810.

Next door, **Santo Stefano**, the order's church, is also by Vasari, though the façade was by a young Medici dilettante; inside are some war pennants the order's pirates captured from the Muslims in North Africa. Also on the piazza, the **Palazzo dell'Orologio** was built around the 'Hunger Tower' (right of the big clock), famous from Dante's story in the *Inferno* of Ugolino della Gherardesca, the Pisan commander walled in here with his sons and grandsons after his fickle city began to suspect him of intrigues with the Genoese. The **university**, founded by his family in 1330 and still one of Italy's most important, is just south of here, while Via dei Mille leads west to the **botanical gardens**, created under Cosimo I in 1544, for the university; the institute, in the grounds, has an extraordinary façade covered with shells and mother-of-pearl.

Orto Botanico di Pisa
open by appt Mon–Sat 8.30–1; call **t** *050 221 5367*

From Piazza dei Cavalieri, Via Dini takes you south into the twisting alleys of the lively market area, around **Piazza Vettovaglie** ('victuals square') where every morning except Sunday the city's ancient mercantile traditions are renewed. Tucked in the main street, old arcaded **Borgo Stretto**, is one of the most gorgeous façades in the city, belonging to **San Michele in Borgo**, a 10th-century church redone in the 14th century, with three tiers of arcades. Much of the interior collapsed during the bombing raids of 1944.

Off to the east, Via S. Francesco leads to the **church of San Francesco** – Gothic, with a plain marble façade but some good paintings – a polyptych over the altar by Tommaso Pisano, frescoes by Taddeo Gaddi, Niccolò di Pietro Gerini (in the chapterhouse) and, in the sacristy, *Stories of the Virgin* by Taddeo di Bartolo (1397). The unfortunate Count Ugo and sons are buried in a chapel near the altar.

Museo Nazionale di San Matteo

Museo Nazionale di San Matteo
Lungarno Mediceo; open Tues–Sat 9–7, Sun 9–2; adm; joint adm available with Museo Nazionale di Palazzo Reale (see *p.290*)

An old convent that also served as a prison now holds much of the best Pisan art from the Middle Ages and Renaissance: works by Giunta Pisano, believed to be the first artist ever to sign his work (early 1200s), excellent 1300s paintings by Pisans and other schools from the city's churches; a polyptych by Simone Martini, paintings by Francesco Traini, Taddeo di Bartolo, Agnolo Gaddi, Antonio Veneziano and Turino Vanni; sculptures by the Pisanos; and medieval ceramics brought from the Middle East by Pisan sea-dogs.

In Room 7, after all the trecento works, the Early Renaissance comes as a startling revelation, as it must have been for the people of the 15th century: here is Neri di Bicci's wonderfully festive *Coronation of St Catherine* bright with ribbons, a *Madonna* from the decorative Gentile da Fabriano, a sorrowful *St Paul* by Masaccio, with softly moulded features and draperies, an anonymous *Madonna with Angel Musicians*, and a beautifully coloured *Crucifixion* by Gozzoli, which looks more like a party than an execution. The last great work is Donatello's gilded bronze reliquary bust of *San Lussorio*, who could pass for Don Quixote.

Along the Lungarno

Pisa's **Prefettura** is housed in the lovely 13th-century stone, brick and marble Palazzo Medici, once a favoured residence of the magnificent Lorenzo. Nearby is the beautiful 16th-century **Palazzo Toscanelli** (once attributed to Michelangelo), where Byron lived in 1821–2 and wrote six cantos of *Don Giovanni*. Behind it, picturesque **Via delle Belle Torri** has 12th- and 13th-century houses interspersed with modern constructions that fill in the gaps left by bombs.

Museo Nazionale di Palazzo Reale
entrance at Lungarno Pacinotti 46; open Mon–Fri 9–2.30, Sat 9–1.30; adm; joint adm available with Museo Nazionale di San Matteo (see p.289)

Further down the Lungarno, the former Palazzo Reale, begun in 1559 by Cosimo I, has a new life as the **Museo Nazionale di Palazzo Reale**, an annexe to the Museo di San Matteo, housing old armour that gets dusted off every June for the *Gioco del Ponte*, and some 900 other pieces from the 15th–17th centuries. There are plans for a section with paintings, sculptures and collectables (mostly 15th–18th-century) from the Medici and Lorraine archducal hoards.

Just behind the Palazzo Reale is Pisa's other famous belltower, belonging to 12th-century **San Nicola**, designed by Nicolò Pisano. Cylindrical at the bottom, octagonal in the middle and hexagonal on top, it has exactly the same kind of tilt as the Leaning Tower – it was built to lean forward before curving back towards the perpendicular. Ask the sacristan to show you the famous spiral stair inside, claimed by Vasari to have inspired Bramante's Belvedere stair in the Vatican. The church contains a fine *Madonna* by Traini, a wooden sculpture, also of the Madonna, by Nino Pisano, and a painting from the quattrocento of St Nicholas of Tolentino shielding Pisa from the plague (fourth chapel on the right).

Pisa South of the Arno

After the Campo dei Miracoli, what most impresses Pisa's visitors is its languidly curving stretch of the Arno – an exercise in Tuscan gravity, with the river lined with mirror-image lines of blank-faced yellow and tan buildings, all the same height, with no remarkable bridges or any of the picturesque quality of Florence. Its uncanny monotony is broken by only one landmark, but it is something special: **Santa Maria della Spina**, sitting on the bank opposite the Palazzo Reale like a precious Gothic jewel box. Although its placement on the Lungarno Gambacorti is perfect, it was built at the mouth of the Arno, where it suffered so many floods that it was on the point of vanishing in 1871, when it was dismantled and rebuilt by the city on this new site. Although it's an outstanding achievement of Italian Gothic, it wasn't originally Gothic at all. Partially rebuilt in 1323, its new architect – perhaps one of the Pisanos – turned it into an extravaganza of pointed gables and blooming pinnacles. All of the sculptural work is first-class, especially the figures of Christ and the Apostles in the 13 niches facing the streets. The chapel takes its name from a thorn of Christ's crown of thorns, a relic brought back from the Crusades. Inside the luminous zebra interior, the statues of the Madonna and Child, St Peter and St John are by Andrea and Nino Pisano.

Just down from Santa Maria della Spina, the **church of San Paolo a Ripa del Arno** has a beautiful 12th-century façade similar to that of the cathedral. It stands in a small park, and is believed to have been built over the site of Pisa's original cathedral; perhaps building cathedrals in open fields was an old custom. Behind it, the unusual and very small 12th-century chapel of **Sant'Agata** has eight sides and an eight-sided prismatic roof like an Ottoman tomb.

Down the Arno, the monotony is briefly broken again by the arches of the 17th-century **Logge di Banchi**, the old silk and wool market, at the Ponte di Mezzo and at the head of Pisa's main shopping street, the Corso Italia. A bit further down is another octagonal church, **San Sepolcro**, built for the Knights Templar by Diotisalvi.

Behind it, picturesque **Via San Martino** was Pisa's old casbah, the main street of the Chinizica, the medieval quarter of Arab and Turkish merchants. At No.19 a Roman relief was incorporated into the building, known since the Middle Ages as Kinzica, after a maiden who saved Pisa when the Saracens sailed up to the famous Golden Gate, medieval Pisa's door to the sea.

At the east end of the Lungarno is a shady park, **Giardino Scotto**, in the former Bastion Sangallo. Shelley lived nearby, in the Palazzo Scotto (1820–22), where he wrote *Adonais* and *Epipsychidion*.

ⓘ **Pisa >**
*Piazza Duomo 1, **t** 050 560464, Piazza Vittorio Emanuele II 16, **t** 050 42291, and airport, **t** 050 503700, www.pisaturismo.it*

Festivals in Pisa

Gioco del Ponte, Ponte di Mezzo, last Sun in June. A 13th century tug-of-war held on the bridge, with costumes, processions and music (*see* p.288).

Regatta and lights festival of San Ranieri, 16–17 June. An event when the banks of the Arno glimmer with tens of thousands of candles.

San Sisto, 6 Aug. Folklore displays.

Old Maritime Republics boat race. A contest between old sea rivals Pisa, Venice, Genoa and Amalfi, hosted by Pisa every four years (next one 2010)

Shopping and other Activities in Pisa

Pisa abounds in tacky souvenirs, especially around the Campo dei Miracoli, including light-up Leaning

Towers in all sizes. For boutiques, head down Via Oberdan and Corso Italia.

You can **horseride** at the Cooperativa Agrituristica in Via Tre Colli in Calci, and **swim** in the pool in Via Andrea Pisano.

Where to Stay in Pisa

Pisa ✉ 56100

Many of the moderate hotels are around the central train station. Inexpensive hotels, spread throughout town, are often full of students, particularly around the start of the university term, so book ahead.

*******Relais dell'Orologio**, Via della Fagiola 12–14, **t** 050 830361, *www.hotelrelaisorologio.com* (€€€€€). An elegant option in the 13th-century home of the owner's ancestors. Bedrooms are rather small but the swish public rooms make up for it.

★ Ristoro dei Vecchi Macelli >>

******Grand Hotel Duomo**, Via S. Maria 94, **t** 050 561894, *www.grandhotelduomo.it* (€€€€). An unexciting choice near the Campo dei Miracoli, with a restaurant serving national and international cuisine. Breakfast is included in the rates.

*****Di Stefano**, Via Sant'Apollonia 35, **t** 050 553559, *www.hoteldistefano.it* (€€€). A good central choice; rates, which are much lower for rooms without baths, include breakfast.

*****Giardino**, Piazza Manin, **t** 050 562101, *www.hotelilgiardino.pisa.it* (€€€). A smart little hotel just outside the walls off Piazza dei Miracoli. Rooms are modern and quite stylish (breakfast is included), and there is a pleasant terrace.

★ Royal Victoria >

*****Royal Victoria**, Lungarno Pacinotti 12, **t** 050 940111, *www.royalvictoria.it* (€€€). An atmospheric 1839 hotel overlooking the Arno; guests have included Dickens and Ruskin. Rooms (still in a 1930s style) have antiques. Breakfast is included, and rooms minus baths are nearly half the price.

*****Verdi**, Piazza Repubblica 5, **t** 050 598947, *hotelverdi@sirius.pisa.it* (€€€). A good choice in a well-restored palace in the centre. Breakfast is included.

Villa Kinzica, Piazza Arcivescovado 2, **t** 050 560419, *www.hotelvillakinzica.it* (€€€). Fairly basic and rather worn bedrooms from which you can practically touch the Leaning Tower. Breakfast is included; staff are friendly.

***Helvetia**, Via Don Boschi 31, **t** 050 553084 (€€). A clean budget option, with some ensuite rooms.

Youth hostel, Via Pietrasantina 15, **t** 050 890622. A hostel 1km from the Campo dei Miracoli (no.3 bus), with cooking facilities.

Eating Out in Pisa

Pisa ✉ 56100

Pisa is a good place for walks on the wild side of the Tuscan kitchen – eels, *baccalà*, tripe, wild mushrooms, 'twice-boiled soup' and dishes waiters can't satisfactorily explain. There are also a good many unpretentious trattorias, many near the university.

Ristoro dei Vecchi Macelli, Via Volturno 49, **t** 050 20424 (€€). A gourmet stronghold on the north bank of the Arno, near Ponte Solferino, with especially good fish. Booking is a must. *Closed Wed and 2wks in Aug*.

Cagliostro, Via del Castelletto 26–30, **t** 050 575413 (€€). An extraordinary restaurant /*caffè*/*enoteca*/art gallery/ nightclub and general trendy hang-out, known for its good cheeses and mainly 'Tuscan Creative' food. *Closed Tues*.

Osteria dei Cavalieri, Via San Frediano 16, **t** 050 580858 (€€). Several fixed-price menus featuring seafood, meat and veggie dishes, and good game. The spaghetti with octopus and clams is recommended. Book for Saturday evenings. *Closed Sat lunch and Sun*.

Il Nuraghe, Via Mazzini 58, **t** 050 44368 (€€). A trattoria offering Tuscan and Sardinian specialities, including octopus, and ravioli with ricotta cheese. *Closed Mon*.

La Mescita, Via D Cavalca 2, **t** 050 544294 (€€). A monthly-changing menu and a huge wine list in the heart of the Vettovaglie market area. *Closed Mon, and lunch Tues–Thur*.

Osteria La Grotta, Via San Francesco 103, **t** 050 578105 (€€). A cosy place situated in an impressive old wine cellar, with a regularly changing menu of comforting, very traditional dishes. *Closed Sun*.

Re di Puglia, Via Aurelia Sud 7, Loc. Mortellini, **t** 050 960157 (€€). A converted farmhouse 1km from the Pisa Sud *autostrada* exit, famous for its home-produced organic meat and vegetables, much of which is cooked over an open grill. *Closed Mon and Tues, and lunch Wed–Sat.*

Pasticceria Federico Salza, Borgo Stretto 46, **t** 050 580144 (€). Pisa's most elegant bar/*pasticceria*, with tables under Borgo Stretto's portico – great for watching the world go by. Come for morning coffee, a light lunch, a delicious afternoon pastry or an evening aperitif. *Closed Mon.*

Trattoria S. Omobono, Piazza S. Omobono 6, **t** 050 540847 (€). A rustic trattoria in a little square just off the main market place, with good risotto with porcini, *spaghetti alla marinara*, *stoccafisso* (stockfish) with potatoes, and fish *fritto misto*. It's always very crowded, so come early to get a table. *Closed Sun.*

Vineria di Piazza, Piazza delle Vettovaglie 13 (€). Tables right in the market, where you can enjoy simple but very tasty food such as bean soup with *pioppini* mushrooms, and risotto with radicchio and gorgonzola. *Closed lunch, Sun and 2wks in Aug.*

Around Pisa

A couple of kilometres upriver to the east is 'Pisa's second leaning tower', the campanile of the Romanesque **San Michele degli Scalzi**, built between 1152 and 1171. Under the slopes of Monte Pisano, **Calci** has a good 11th-century church and an eroded giant of a campanile

Certosa di Pisa
open Tues–Sat 8.30–6.30, Sun 8.30–12.30; natural history collections summer Tues–Fri 10–7, Sat, Sun and hols 10am–midnight; winter Tues–Sat 9–6, Sun and hols 10–7; adm

In a prominent site overlooking the Arno, the ornate **Certosa di Pisa** was founded in 1366 but completely Baroqued in the 18th century, in a kind of 1920s Spanish-California exhibition style with three fine cloisters. There are some lavish pastel frescoes by Florentine Baroque artist Bernardo Poccetti and his school, plus a giraffe skeleton, stuffed penguins, Tuscan minerals and even wax intestines – all part of the university's **natural history collections**, founded originally by the Medici.

Towards the coast, 6km from Pisa, is the beautifully isolated **basilica of San Piero a Grado**. According to tradition it was founded in the first century by St Peter himself, and in the Middle Ages it was a popular pilgrimage destination. It was first documented in the 8th century but the current buildings are 11th century, embellished with blind arcades and ceramic *tondi*. Like many early churches and basilicas, it has an apse on either end, though of different sizes; the columns were brought in from various ancient buildings. The altar stone, believed to have been set there by St Peter, was found in excavations that uncovered the remains of several previous churches. Frescoes in the nave by a 14th-century Lucchese, Deodato Orlandi, tell the *Story of St Peter* with effigies of the popes up to the turn of the first millennium AD (John XVIII). The retreating German army blew up the campanile.

In 1822, a strange ceremony took place on the wide, sandy beach of **Gombo**, near the mouth of the Arno, described in morbid detail by Edward Trelawny: 'the brains literally seethed, bubbled, and boiled as in a cauldron, for a very long time. Byron could not face this scene, he withdrew to the beach and swam off to the *Bolivar*.' Such was Shelley's fiery end, after he drowned sailing from Livorno. Gombo, and Pisa's other beaches, the **Marina di Pisa** and **Tirrenia**, are often plagued by pollution, although Marina di Pisa makes a pretty place to stroll, with its Liberty-style homes and pine forests.

The Livorno Coast and Tuscan Islands

Livorno

...There is plenty of space; it is a fully registered cemetery with an attendant keeper. So, if any of you have the intention of retiring to this very interesting part of Tuscany you will be well taken care of!

Horace A. Hayward on the British cemetery in Livorno

From its founding in 1577, the English spent so much time in this city and grew so fond of it, they renamed it. It's time the bizarre anglicization, Leghorn, be put to sleep. The city that Duke Cosimo founded to replace Pisa's silted-up harbour is named Livorno. It hasn't much in common with other Tuscan cities: instead of frescoes, it has perhaps the best seafood on the Tyrrhenian coast; instead of rusticated *palazzi* and marble temples, it has canals, docks and a very lively citizenry famous for freethinking and tolerance; and instead of winding country lanes, there are big white ferries to carry you off to the Tuscan Islands, Corsica or Sardinia.

History

The site had always been a safe harbour, and in the Middle Ages there was a small fortress here. The Pisani briefly considered making a port here in the 1300s, when it was becoming clear that Pisa's own port would fill up with the sands of the Arno. Eventually the fortress fell into the grasp of the Genoese, who sold it to Florence in 1421. Cosimo I, in his attempts to build Tuscany into a modern state, first saw the advantage of having a good port to avoid trading at the mercy of the Spaniards and Genoese. Cosimo expanded the fortress, but it was not until the reign of his successors, Francesco and Ferdinando, that Livorno really got off the ground. The first stone was laid on 28 March 1577, and a regular gridiron city soon appeared, designed by Buontalenti, and surrounded by fortresses and canals.

Almost from the start there was an English connection. Sir Robert Dudley, Queen Elizabeth's favourite, son of the Earl of Leicester, left England in 1605 after failing to prove his legitimacy in the Star Chamber court. Dudley built warships for the grand dukes, fortified the port of Livorno and drained the coastal swamps, making the region healthy and inhabitable. In 1618, Livorno was declared a free port – free not only for trade but for the practice of any faith and for men of whatever nationality. It was a brilliant stroke, designed to fill out the population of this very rough and dangerous new town, and it is, to the credit of the Medici dukes, an act of tolerance

Getting to and around Livorno and its Coast

Livorno train station is on the edge of the city, with plenty of services to Pisa and Florence and along the Tyrrhenian coast. Some trains to Pisa go on to Lucca–Pistoia–Florence. There are some connections to Volterra, with a change down the coast at Cecina. The station is about 2km from the city centre; take bus no.1 (most other city buses also pass through the centre, but routes are circuitous).

Buses for all villages in Livorno province (the strip of coast down as far as Follonica) leave from Piazza Grande. LAZZI buses (**t** 055 363041, *www.lazzi.it*) for Florence depart from Scali A Saffi, on the Fosse Reale, just off Piazza Cavour.

Livorno is the main port for **ferries** to Corsica and Sardinia, with Corsica Ferries (**t** 0586 881380, *www.corsicaferries.com*) and Moby Lines (**t** 0586 899950, *www.mobylines.it*). Some ferries call at Elba.

---

almost unthinkable in the Catholic Mediterranean of the 1600s. Before long, Livorno was full of persecuted Jews, Greeks, English Catholics, Spanish Muslims and loose ends from around Europe. The only safe trading port in a sea full of Spaniards acquired thriving communities of English and Dutch merchants. In the 1700s progressive, tolerant Livorno was a substantial city, a breath of fresh air in the decadent Mediterranean and a home from home for British travellers. Shelley wrote *The Cenci* here, as well as 'To a Skylark'; he bought his fatal sailing boat in Livorno's port.

Livorno declined a little once the same low tariffs and trading advantages became available in other Mediterranean ports. The Austrian dukes, especially Leopold II, helped keep it ahead of its rivals; still, true to its traditions, the city contributed greatly to the mid-century revolutionary movements and the wars of the Risorgimento. After unification it was still a lively place, full of many nationalities; it also began to make cultural contributions to the new Italy – the operatic composer Mascagni, the painter Modigliani, and several other artists of the Macchiaioli school. The Second World War hit Livorno harder than anywhere in Tuscany, but the city rebuilt itself quickly. Long before other ports, Livorno realized the importance of container shipping. As the Mediterranean's first big container port, Livorno today has become the second city of Tuscany, and Italy's second-largest port after Genoa.

Four Moors, Inigo Jones and the American Market

Though the streets are usually brimming, a combination of north Tuscan austerity and an excess of dreary architecture make Livorno a disconcertingly anonymous city. The **port**, however, is a busy, fascinating jumble of boats, cranes, docks and canals. Close to the port entrance, the **Fortezza Vecchia** conceals the original Pisan fortress and an 11th-century tower built by Countess Matilda. Piazza Micheli, Livorno's front door to the sea, is decorated with its only great work of art, the **Quattro Mori** by Carraran sculptor Pietro Tacca (1623). The monument's original design became somewhat mangled, and Tacca's brilliant figures now sit in chains under a silly

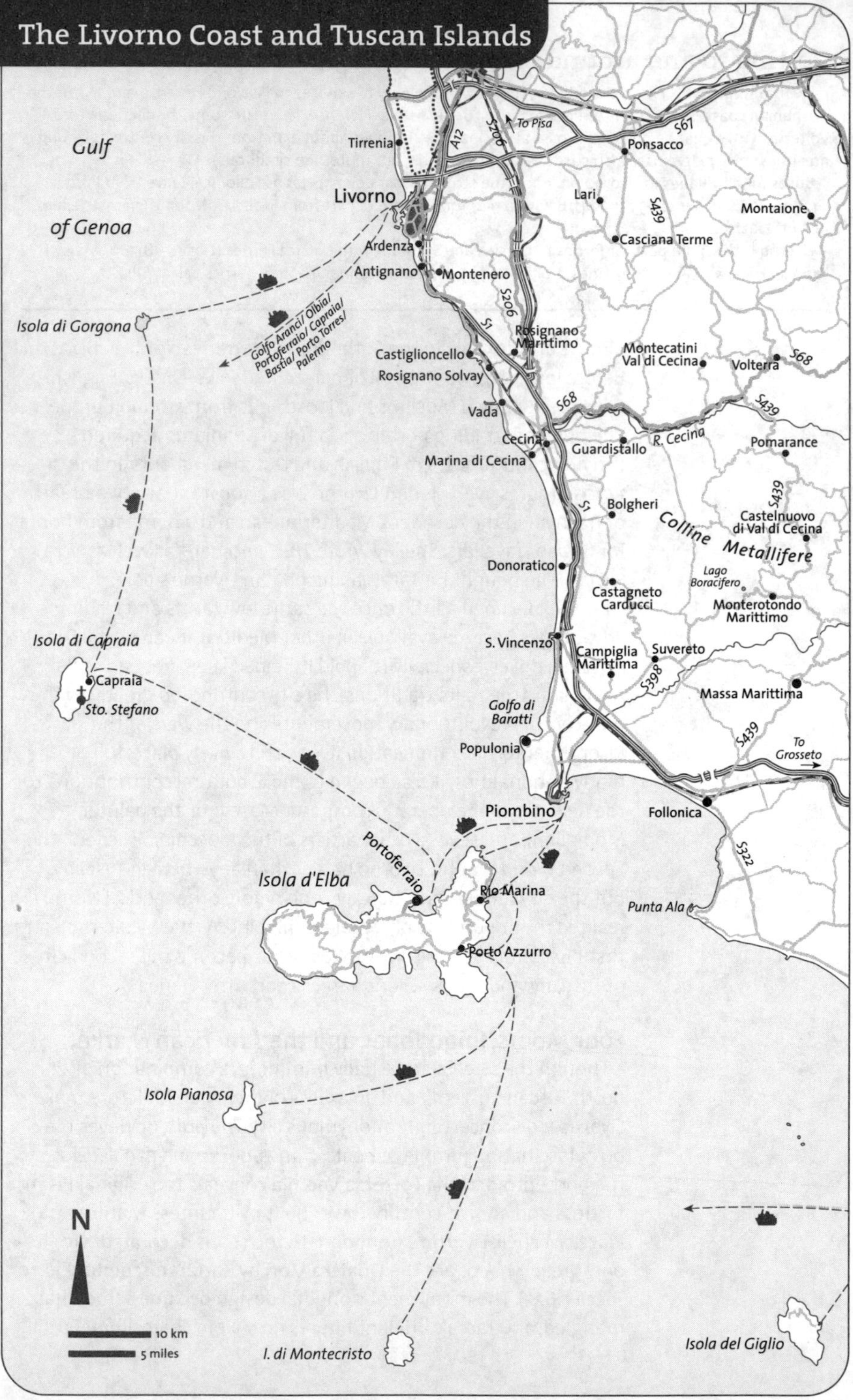

The Livorno Coast and Tuscan Islands

Gulf of Genoa
To Pisa
S206
A12
S67
Tirrenia
Ponsacco
Livorno
Lari
S439
Montaione
Casciana Terme
Ardenza
Antignano
Montenero
S206
Isola di Gorgona
Golfo Aranci/ Olbia/ Portoferraio/ Capraia/ Bastia/ Porto Torres/ Palermo
S1
Rosignano Marittimo
Castiglioncello
Rosignano Solvay
Montecatini Val di Cecina
Volterra
S68
Vada
S68
S439
Cecina
Marina di Cecina
Guardistallo
R. Cecina
Pomarance
S1
Bolgheri
S439
Colline Metallifere
Castelnuovo di Val di Cecina
Donoratico
Lago Boracifero
Castagneto Carducci
Monterotondo Marittimo
Isola di Capraia
S. Vincenzo
Campiglia Marittima
Suvereto
Capraia
S398
Sto. Stefano
Massa Marittima
Golfo di Baratti
Populonia
S439
To Grosseto
Piombino
Follonica
Portoferraio
Isola d'Elba
S322
Rio Marina
Punta Ala
Porto Azzurro
Isola Pianosa
N
10 km
5 miles
I. di Montecristo
Isola del Giglio

earlier statue of Duke Ferdinando I. The four Moors are a symbol of Sardinia, but the statue's intent was to commemorate the successes of the great Tuscan pirates, the Order of Santo Stefano, against North African shipping.

From here, the arcaded **Via Grande** leads into the centre; every original building on this street was destroyed in the bombings of 1944. **Piazza Grande** has the **cathedral**, designed on a bad day by Inigo Jones in 1605; the present building is a post-war reconstruction. Jones took a little bit of Livorno home with him: his plan for Covent Garden (originally arcaded all round, without the market) is a copy of this piazza, with St Paul's in place of the cathedral.

Via Grande continues to ghastly **Piazza della Repubblica**, a treeless, paved-over section of the **Fosso Reale**, the curving canal that surrounded the original city. Just north, the sprawling, brick **Fortezza Nuova** is on an island in the canal, landscaped as a park and a popular resort for the Livornese on Sundays. Nearby, on Via della Madonna, three adjacent churches, Greek Orthodox, Catholic and Armenian (all recycled for other uses) make a fitting memorial of Livorno's career as a truly free city. On the other side of Piazza della Repubblica, Piazza XX Settembre is the site of the Saturday **American market**, so called for the vast stores of GI surplus sold here after the war, and still a street market for clothes and odd items.

Little Venice and the Museo Civico

Just off Piazza della Repubblica is a neighbourhood unlike any outside Venice; in fact, it's known as 'Nuova Venezia', or 'Piccola Venezia', and for picturesque tranquillity it may even outdo its famous precursor. On a few blocks square, **Little Venice** is laced with quiet canals that flow between the Fortezza Nuova and the port, lined with sun-bleached tenements hung with laundry. The pseudo-Baroque **Santa Caterina** church is typical of the ungainly, functional buildings of early Livorno. In late July or August restaurants stay open late for the *Effetto Venezia*, a 10-day festival with evening shows and concerts and *cacciucco* (*see* p.298) stalls.

Leading east towards the train station from Piazza della Repubblica, **Viale Carducci** is Livorno's *grand boulevard*. It passes the **Cisternone**, a neoclassical palace built to house the waterworks Leopold II had constructed in the 1830s.

Along the coast south of the centre, Viale Italia leads past the **Terrazza Mascagni**, a grandiose overlook on the sea. A few streets inland, in a park called the Villa Mimbelli, the **Museo Civico Giovanni Fattori** has a good collection of works by the Macchiaioli, Italy's late 19th-century Impressionists and one work by Modigliani plus a wealth of paintings that lead up to his art. Other painters represented include Ulivi Liegi, Mario Puccini, that rare blossom Lodovico Tommasi and Livorno's own Giovanni Fattori, one of the

Museo Civico Giovanni Fattori
3rd floor of city library; open Tues–Sun 10–1 and 4–7; adm

leading figures of the Macchiaioli. Together, they make a natural progression from the Biedermeier art of the 1860s – including stirring scenes of Italian volunteers leaving for the front – to the sweet haziness of the Belle Epoque 1890s.

South of Terrazza Mascagni, Viale Italia continues past the **Italian naval academy** (you may glimpse one of the exquisite old sailing ships the navy uses for training), then through neighbourhoods full of surprisingly blatant neogothic and Art Nouveau villas from the 1890s, on the way to **Ardenza**, with its seafront park and marina.

The English Cemeteries and Montenero

Cimiteri Inglese
Via Pisa and Via Adua, next to Anglican Church; to visit ask at Archiconfraternità della Misericordia on Via Adua

For a sentimental journey into Livorno's cosmopolitan past, visit the **English cemeteries**. Crotchety old Tobias Smollett, who never stopped crabbing about Italy and never quite got around to leaving it, is interred here, along with numerous members of the British trading community and quite a few Americans. Many of the tombs (dating back to 1670) are truly monumental, some with inscriptions from Scripture or Shakespeare; some are charmingly original.

Villa delle Rose
open by request of owner Signor Di Valentina at No.57

Many members of the British community, including Byron and Shelley, passed their time up on the suburban hill of **Montenero** to the south. Byron and Shelley spent six weeks in 1822 at **Villa delle Rose**, a fascinating romantic ruin. There is a charming, old-fashioned funicular railway to the top, where there's been a sanctuary and pilgrimage site since an apparition of the Virgin Mary in the 1300s. The present church, full of *ex votos*, is the work of 18th-century architect Giovanni del Fantasia; there are also a small museum, an ancient pharmacy and some caves, the Grotte del Montenero.

ⓘ Livorno >
Piazza Cavour 6 (2nd floor), **t** *0586 204611; there are also 2 summer (June–Sept) booths at port, on Porto Mediceo,* **t** *0586 895320, www.livorno.turismo.toscana.it, www.costadeglietruschi.it*

Where to Stay in Livorno

Livorno ✉ 57100

As this is a port, there's an abundance of inexpensive hotels, many across the piazza from the train station or around the port and Via Grande. Some are dives; Corso Mazzini, a few blocks south of the Fosso Reale, has some good ones.

*****La Vedetta di Montenero**, Via della Leccetta 5, suburb of Montenero. **t** 0586 579957, *www.hotellavedetta.it* (€€€€). A modern hotel overlooking the sea, with comfortable rooms and a restaurant (half board and full board available). *Restaurant closed May–Sept.*

*****Gran Duca**, Piazza Micheli 16, *t* 0586 891024, *www.granduca.it* (€€€). Livorno's most interesting hotel, built into a section of the walls right on the piazza near the harbour. Inside it's modern; some rooms overlook the Quattro Mori and the port. Breakfast is included in rates, and you can stay half or full board: the restaurant specializes in fresh fish.

****Giardino**, Piazza Mazzini 85, **t** 0586 806330, *www.parkingiardinohotel.it* (€€). Ensuite rooms near the port.

Eating Out in Livorno

Livorno ✉ 57100

The main reason to coming to Livorno is to eat seafood. Livornese ways of preparing it, especially, *cacciucco*, the famous fish stew, are now much copied throughout Tuscany, but restaurants here are generally better value. After a rich meal, try a *bomba livornese*, with equal quantities of coffee and rum.

Ciglieri, Via Ravizza 43, Ardenza, **t** 0586 508194 (€€€€). An elegant, intimate, highly regarded restaurant serving high-quality fish dishes such as spaghetti with clams, dried tomatoes and basil, and stuffed seabass with mushrooms. For dessert, don't miss the chocolate ravioli filled with *gianduja*. *Closed Wed.*

La Barcarola >

La Barcarola, Viale Carducci 39, **t** 0586 402367 (€€€€–€€€). A big, noisy place near the train station, set up in 1935 and serving up the likes of gnocchi with prawns, smoked salmon ravioli, squid *au gratin*, and shellfish soup. *Closed Sun and Aug.*

Da Oscar, Via Franchini 78, Ardenza. **t** 0586 501258 (€€€). A longstanding favourite in a seaside suburb, serving good grilled fish in a garden in summer. Booking is advisable. *Closed Mon and 3wks in Jan.*

La Chiave, Scali delle Cantine 52, **t** 0586 829865 (€€). A restaurant renowned for its seafood: spaghetti with clams, smoked mullet roe and courgettes, oysters, caviar, and risotto with crustacea flavoured with gin. It's small, so book ahead. *Closed Wed, lunch, and mid-Aug–mid-Sept.*

Da Motorino, Via Oberdan 30, **t** 0586 896485 (€€). A spartan trattoria with a brusque owner, one of the best places to eat *cacciucco* in town (you need to book it in advance). The Livornese mullets are also good. Booking is essential. *Closed Mon.*

Vecchia Livorno, Via Scali delle Cantine 34, **t** 0586 884048 (€€). A lively trattoria in the *centro storico*, serving interesting variations on traditional dishes. The baked sea bream, squid rings and fish *fritto misto* are good; note that you have to book the *cacciucco* in advance. Reservations are highly advisable. *Closed Tues.*

Cantina Nardi, Via L. Cambini 6, **t** 0586 808006 (€). A pleasant wine bar serving lunch at a few tables, with the menu chalked up on a board. Try the deepfried cod and fish soups. *Closed eves, Sun and 2wks in Aug.*

Livorno's Coast

LIvorno's canny tourist office calls this shore the 'Etruscan Riviera', conjuring up the irresistible idea of Etruscans lounging in beach chairs the way they do on funerary urns. Beyond Antignano, the shoreline becomes jagged and twisting, dotted with beaches that are usually more than well exploited, including **Castiglioncello**, a pretty corner with narrow beaches packed with Italians all summer. **San Vincenzo** is an awful, booming resort, but it does have kilometres of good beaches on either side – perhaps your best chance on this strip of coast for a little seaside peace and quiet.

Next is the half-moon **Golfo di Baratti**, with tranquil beaches and some Etruscan tombs from the once-mighty town of **Populonia**. Modern Populonia has an impressive medieval castle and a small **archaeological museum**; ask there about visiting the ruins of the Etruscan city and tombs, which include a so-called 'arsenal' where the Etruscans turned Elban iron into armaments. **Piombino**, at the tip of this stubby peninsula, mercilessly flattened during the war, and mercilessly rebuilt, is the major port for Elba.

Museo Archeologico del Territorio di Populonia
t 0565 29436; call for opening hrs

Towns of interest up in the hills include **Bolgheri**, centre of a DOC wine area (Bolgheri is a little-known dry white wine); **Castagneto Carducci**, a pretty strawberry-growing town; and **Suvereto**, a seldom-visited medieval village with an arcaded Palazzo Comunale and the 12th-century Pisan church of San Giusto.

Where to Stay and Eat on Livorno's Coast

ⓘ **San Vincenzo >** *Via Aliata 1, t 0565 701533*

San Vincenzo ✉ 57027

Gambero Rosso, Piazza della Vittoria 72, **t** 0565 701021 (€€€€). One of Italy's top restaurants, renowned not only for its fish but also for its delicate crustacea, pasta, pheasant and pigeon with foie gras. Try the *zuppa di ceci* with shellfish, the fish ravioli, the seabream with artichokes, or the squab casserole, or order the *menu degustazione*. It's a wonderful place to eat and watch the sun set over the sea. *Closed Mon, Tues, Nov and Dec.*

Bibbona ✉ 57020

Podere Le Mezzelune, Loc. Mezzelune 126,**t** 0586 670266, *www.lemezzelune.it* (€€€€). A little 19th-century house situated near Cecina, with charming owners, antique furnishings, an open fire to snuggle up beside in the colder months and a shady terrace to sit out on on hot days.

Donoratico ✉ 57022

Enoteca Maestrini, Via Aurelia 1 (on SS1), near Castagneto Carducci, **t** 0565 775209 (€). A wine bar serving light dinners, local cheeses and home-made desserts. *Closed Mon and Sept.*

The Tuscan Islands

The Tuscan archipelago is a broad arch stretching from Livorno to Monte Argentario; Elba is its only large and heavily populated member. Fate has not been kind to these islands as a whole: with deforestation, Saracen and Turkish pirates, and finally the Italian government, not much is left. Two islands are still prison camps, another is a nature reserve where no one can stay overnight.

Capraia

Capraia, 65km from Livorno, measuring about 10 x 5km and home to about 400 people, is the third largest of the Tuscan islands. Like Elba, it is mountainous, but it has fewer trees; most of the island is covered with scrubby *macchia*. In Roman times Capraia seems to have been a private estate, and the ruins of an extensive villa can be seen. In the days of the Empire, the island was occupied by Christian monks. The setting was perfect for withdrawal and contemplation but it also prevented Church authorities from keeping a close watch on the colony, and the monks slipped into unorthodoxy and loose behaviour; an armed mission from Pope Gregory the Great forced them back in line in the late 6th century.

When Saracen pirates began to infest the Tyrrhenian Sea, Capraia, like most of the group, became deserted. The Pisans thought it important enough to repopulate and fortify in the 11th century. Genoa eventually gained control, as she did in Corsica only 32km away. This proximity gave Capraia its one big moment in history; in 1767 the revolutionary forces of Corsican nationalist leader Pasquale Paoli, and the weakness of the Genoese, resulted in, of all things, an independent Capraia, which learned to support itself by piracy. French occupation put an end to that four years later.

Getting to and around the Tuscan Islands

There's a daily trip from Livorno to **Capraia**, plus a daily (16 June–30 Sept) afternoon run to **Portoferraio, Rio Marina** and **Porto Azzurro** on **Elba**, run by TOREMAR (Via Calafati 6, Livorno, **t** 0586 896113, *www.toremar.it*).

Gritty Piombino is the main point of departure for ferries to **Elba**. Any train down the Tyrrhenian coast will take you as far as Campiglia Marittima station; from there the FS operates a regular shuttle train to Piombino (don't get off at the central station; the train continues to the port). TOREMAR (**t** 0586 896113; on Elba at Calata Italia 23, Portoferraio, **t** 0565 960131; in Piombino at Piazzale Premuda, **t** 0565 31100) run services on this route too, as do Moby Lines (Piazzale Premuda, Piombino, **t** 0565 9361, *www.mobylines.it*). The most frequent passage is the 1hr Piombino–Cavo–Portoferraio trip; there are also TOREMAR hydrofoils that go from Piombino to Rio Marina (45mins) and on to Porto Azzurro (1hr 20mins) or Portferraio (1hr). Services to Elba can be as frequent as every half-hour in July, down to two or three a day in winter. Moby Lines connects Piombino to Portoferraio and Livorno to Bastia and Olbia.

Elba has just room enough for an **airport** (**t** 0565 976011, *www.elbaisland-airport.it*), and there are plenty of flights in summer – mainly to Germany, Switzerland and Austria. There's also an infrequent service to Pisa, Florence and Milan.

An efficient **bus** service goes to every corner of Elba frequently. Portoferraio is the hub of the system, with buses leaving and returning to the terminal by the Grattacielo, facing the harbour.

There are plenty of **car hire** agencies in Elba's main towns. You can hire **scooters and bikes** everywhere too, and the tourist office (*see* p.308) has itineraries for bike/mountainbike trips around the island.

The main draw is Capraia's natural setting, deep-sea diving and marine grottoes. The northern quarter has long been an agricultural penal colony, and the civilian population Is almost entirely concentrated in the port and only town, **Capraia Isola**, where the Baroque church and convent of **Sant'Antonio**, used as a barracks in the last century, is crumbling and abandoned. On the outskirts are the ruins of the **Roman villa**, apocryphally the abode of Augustus' profligate daughter Julia, and an 11th-century Pisan chapel dedicated to the **Vergine Assunta**. Overlooking it all is the impressive fortress of **San Giorgio**, begun by the Pisans and completed by the Genoese. The well-preserved **watchtower** at the port was built by the Genoese Bank of St George. On the eastern side of town, the beach under the cliffs has an interesting tower built by the Pisans, connected to the cliff by a natural bridge.

From Capraia Isola a road leads southwest across the island, passing another Pisan church, **Santo Stefano**, built on the ruins of a 5th-century church used by the early monks and destroyed by the Saracen pirates. Near Monte Pontica is a sacred cave, the **Grotta di Parino**, used as a place of meditation by the monks. The road ends at a lighthouse on the west coast. Just south is a sea-cave, the **Grotta della Foca**, where Mediterranean seals are reported to still live. At the southern tip of the island is another Genoese watchtower, the **Torre dello Zenobito**.

Capraia can be reached by a daily boat from Livorno, of which it is administratively part. The same goes of nearby Gorgona, where the boat stops to drop off new prisoners and supplies on the way to Capraia; you, however, can't alight there (there's nothing to see anyway, except maquis and a handful of olive trees).

Elba

Able was I ere I saw Elba
The Napoleonic palindrome

When the government closed the steel mills on Elba after the war, local authorities sought to make up lost income by promoting tourism. They have been singularly successful: it is one of Europe's most popular holiday playgrounds, with nearly 2 million visitors a year, making its 30,000 inhabitants prosperous once more.

It's a comfortable, unglamorous place attracting families, especially Germans, who have bought up most of the southern coast. There is no single big, crowded tourist ghetto but plenty of quiet, small resorts around the coast. In an unspectacular way, however, Elba is beautiful. Pink and green predominate – pink for the granite outcrops and houses, green for the heavy forests. Like its neighbour Corsica, it is a chain of mountains rising out of the sea, the tallest to the west, grouped around Monte Capanne (1,080m). For a mineralogist, it's a dream – besides iron ore, dozens of common and rare minerals are found here, from andalusite to zircon. For most people, however, Elba's big draw is beaches and mild climate – it hardly ever rains. The coastline, all bays and peninsulas, is more than 150km long, and there are beaches everywhere, large and small, sand or pebbles. Even in August, there's plenty of Elba-room for all.

History

Elba is close enough to the Italian mainland to have been inhabited from the earliest times. When Neanderthals were tramping through the neighbourhood about 50,000 years ago, Elba may still have been linked to the peninsula. Later peoples, a seemingly unending parade, colonized the island after 3000 BC,

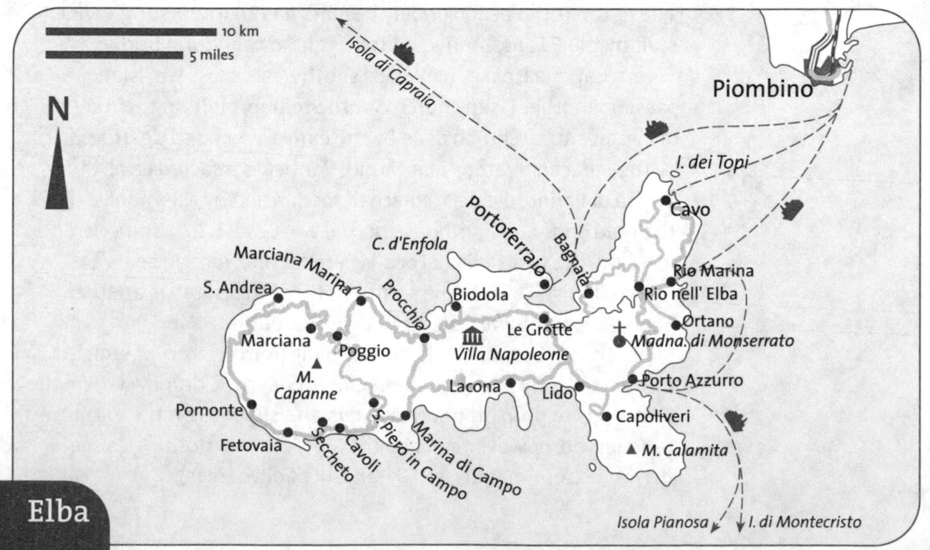

drawn by the treasure hoard of metals. In the Copper Age they mined its copper; in the Bronze Age they alloyed the copper into bronze. The copper gave out just in time for the Iron Age; Elba had vast deposits of this as well. Competition was fierce: the Etruscans and Greeks fought over the island and established colonies of miners to extract the iron, but archaeologists have been unable to find evidence of permanent settlements.

For Rome, expanding across the Italian peninsula in the 4th century BC, Elba was an important prize. After conquering the island at the end of the century, the Romans founded towns to consolidate their hold. From then on, whenever Roman legions ran their swords through Teutons, Persians, Gauls, Carthaginians or each other, they were usually made from Elban iron. The mines and forges, then as now, were concentrated on the eastern third of the island, while the beautiful beaches everywhere else became a holiday spot for wealthy Romans, as demonstrated by the archaeological remains of large villas discovered near Portoferraio.

The fall of Rome brought invasions, disorder, depopulation and pirates; the Lombards in the 6th century, under the murderous Gummarith, subjugated the island with their usual bloodshed; Saracens and adventurous barons from Italy fought for the scraps. By the 11th century Pisa had complete control, as the island lay across its most important trade route. It held Elba for almost 500 years, constructing fortresses at Luceri and Volterraio and exploiting the mineral resources. At the time the capital was called *Ferraia*, of which the modern capital of Portoferraio was only the port. Nowadays not a trace remains of the medieval city; archaeologists are still trying to locate its site.

From the 13th century, Genoa contested Pisa's possession. In the 16th century, Duke Cosimo I saw his opportunity and seized it for Florence. He built Portoferraio and the walls around it but soon had to contend with the growing power of Spain in the western Med, and after inconclusive skirmishes Elba was partitioned between Tuscany and Spain. Spain built the town and fortress of Porto Azzurro as a counter to Portoferraio, an arrangement that lasted through the 18th century, despite French efforts to grab the island.

Portoferraio

Portoferraio (population 11,000) is the capital, and indeed the only city of Elba. The massive walls built by Cosimo remain, though Portoferraio has spilled west along the bay. Here the ferries dock at the Calata Italia, where the visitor's introduction to Elba is the hideous **Grattacielo** (skyscraper), a 10-storey pile of peeling paint built in the 1950s, which contains a tourist office, most of the ferry offices, and the bus terminal. Follow Calata Italia and its various pseudonyms beneath the walls, next to the old U-shaped harbour.

On the far side rises the **Torre del Martello**, from which in the old days a chain was stretched across the harbour in times of danger. The main gate of the city is the **Porta a Mare** at the base of the U, over which can be seen the inscription of Duke Cosimo reminding us, with the usual Medicean vanity, how he constructed the whole town 'from the foundations upwards'; the new town had originally been dubbed Cosmopolis.

Directly inside the Porta a Mare is **Piazza Cavour**. Portoferraio is a big natural amphitheatre; from the piazza the town slopes upwards in all directions towards the walls on the high cliffs. North of the piazza, Via Garibaldi leads up to the main attraction, Napoleon's house, the **Villa dei Mulini**, yellowing, unloved, unchanged since Napoleon had it built according to his simple tastes; inside are furnishings, books and other paraphernalia, including the flag with three golden bees he bestowed on the Elbans and political cartoons mocking him. The gardens, equally uncared for, offer fine views over the walls. On either side, two Medici fortresses dominate the highest points in the city: **Forte Falcone** to the west, and **Forte Stella**.

Villa dei Mulini
open daily 9–7; adm; joint adm available with Villa di San Martino (see opposite)

Forte Falcone
open summer Wed–Mon 10–1 and 3.30–7.40, rest of year Wed–Mon 10–1; adm

Forte Stella
open summer daily 10–6; adm

On the way down Via Garibaldi are two parish churches: the **Holy Sacrament**, which has a copy of Napoleon's death mask, and the **Misericordia**, which on 5 May holds a procession to commemorate Napoleon's death, with a replica of his coffin. The **town hall**, which

Napoleon on Elba

During the Napoleonic wars, Elba was occupied for a time by the English, and Portoferraio was unsuccessfully besieged for more than a year by Napoleon's troops in 1799. Napoleon finally annexed it in 1802, with no premonitions that the 1814 Treaty of Fontainebleau would put a temporary end to the First Empire and send him there.

Napoleon chose Elba, from the variety of small Mediterranean outposts offered him, for 'the gentleness of its climate and its inhabitants'. Also, perhaps because on clear days he could see his own island of Corsica. No one, however, seems to have consulted the Elbans themselves on the matter, and they can be excused for the cold indifference with which they received their new ruler, who arrived on 4 May 1814 with some 500 of his most loyal officers and soldiers and a British Commissioner charged with keeping an eye on him. But he soon won the hearts of the Elbans, by being the best governor they had ever had. New systems of law and education were established, the last vestiges of feudalism were abolished, and what would today be called economic planning was begun; he reorganized the iron mines and started work on Elba's modern network of roads.

Not that Napoleon ever really took his stewardship seriously. Remaking nations and institutions was a reflex by then; he'd done it all across Europe for 20 years. It was the return to France that occupied his attention. The atmosphere was thick with intrigues and rumours, and secret communications flowed incessantly between Napoleon and his partisans on the Continent. On 20 February 1815, just nine months after his arrival, the Elbans and the embarrassed British watchdog awakened to find the emperor missing. The 'Hundred Days' had begun. Later, after Waterloo, a smaller, gloomier and more distant island would be found to keep Napoleon out of trouble.

Elba was returned to Tuscany, and soon after it joined the new Kingdom of Italy. It was hit hard by the World War II; Portoferraio and environs were bombed in 1943–4, first by the Allies, then the Germans. In 1944, in one of the most disgraceful episodes of the war, Elba was 'liberated' by Free French and African troops, with more murder, pillage and rape than had been seen in the Med since the days of the pirates.

was originally a bakery for Cosimo's troops, was the boyhood home of Victor Hugo, whose father was the French military commander in Elba. There's a **Roman altar** in the courtyard.

Two blocks west, the tiny but surprisingly grand **Teatro dei Vigilanti**, was rebuilt by Napoleon from an abandoned church. East of Via Garibaldi, **Piazza della Repubblica** is the throbbing heart of Portoferraio, with its crowded cafés, 18th-century **cathedral** (not a cathedral at all these days) and nearby market.

Museo Civico Archeologico
opn Fri–Wed 10–1 and 4–7.40 but afternoon hours may vary in winter; adm

Outside the walls, on the eastern side of the port, a converted salt warehouse is now home to the **Museo Civico Archeologico**, which displays items from the Roman patrician villas, one of which was discovered here.

Around Portoferraio

Most of Portoferraio's hotels and restaurants are in the modern extension outside the walls. There are pebble beaches on the north side (**Le Ghiaie**) and under the walls near Forte Falcone (**Le Viste**). One of the two roads from the capital leads along the northern coast to the small resorts of **Acquaviva** and **Viticcio**, and to **Capo d'Enfola**, a lovely headland rising sheer out of the sea, barely connected to the rest of the island. The second road runs south to the junction of **Bivio Boni**, where it branches east and west. Nearby is a thermal spa at **San Giovanni**, and the ruins of a Roman villa at **Le Grotte**, on the south shore of the gulf of Portoferraio, more interesting for its view than its scant remains. There are beaches here, at Ottone, Magazzini and **Bagnaia**, the latter the site of the simple, beautiful 12th-century **church of Santo Stefano**, the best Pisan monument in the archipelago.

Villa Napoleone di San Martino
open Tue–Sun 9–7; adm; joint adm available with Villa dei Mulini, *see opposite*

At **Acquabona** you can shoot some bogeys at one of Elba's two golf courses (nine holes), or continue west from Bivio Boni to the resort at **Biodola Bay** and the **Villa Napoleone di San Martino**. The emperor soon tired of life in Portoferraio and built this as his country retreat. In later years the husband of his niece (daughter of Jérome) bought it and added a pretentious neoclassical façade with big Ns pasted everywhere; it's now another Napoleonic museum, with a little art gallery including a *Galatea* by Canova.

Eastern Elba

Rio nell'Elba is the old mining centre, although it's as pleasant and pastel as any other Elban town, set in the hills overlooking the eastern coast. Archaeological sites, the scanty remains of mines and Etruscan mining camps dot the surrounds. There are many undeveloped beaches on the western side of Rio's peninsula, including Nisporto and Nisportino. The road between Portoferraio and Rio passes the steep hill of **Volterraio**, and you can make the long climb to the 11th-century Pisan castle perched on the summit.

Museo dei Minerali dell'Elba e dell' Arte Mineraria
Palazzo Comunale; open April–June, Sept and Oct Tues–Sun 9.30–12.30 and 3.30–6.30; July and Aug Tues–Sun 9.30–12.30, 4.30–7.30 and 9–11pm; adm

Parco Minerario
visits April–June, Sept and Oct daily at 10am; July and Aug daily at 6pm; for guided visits, call **t** *0565 962088*

Rio Marina, as its name implies, is the port for Rio nell'Elba. Here, the **mineralogical museum** has displays of the island's unusual rocks and minerals – few places on earth have such a variety. Devoted rock-hounds should continue to the **Parco Minerario** in an old mine. Rio Marina has a busy harbour, its many small fishing boats bobbing under the vigilant eye of an octagonal Pisan watchtower. The eastern side of this peninsula, like the western side, has fine beaches where you can sometimes escape the crowds – Ortano, Porticciolo, Barbarossa among others.

Porto Azzurro and Capoliveri

South of Rio, the road passes through some difficult terrain towards **Porto Azzurro**, built by the Spaniards and now a large holiday town, with a beach. Until 1947 it was called Porto Longon. The fortress, built in 1603 to withstand the Austrians and French, was converted into a famous Italian calaboose that hosted many political prisoners and criminal celebrities.

Several other beaches nearby include a bizarre one at **Terrenere**, where a yellow-green sulphurous pond festers near the blue sea in a landscape of pebble beach and ancient mine debris. In season, day excursions run from Porto Azzurro to the island of Montecristo.

Just north of Porto Azzurro is the **sanctuary of Monserrato**, a famous shrine with a 'Black Madonna' icon. The Spanish governor built this here in 1606 because the mountain (Monte Castello) reminded him of the odd mountain of Monserrat near Barcelona. Similar Black Madonnas are revered from Portugal to Poland; over the centuries the oxidization of yellow paint has darkened them.

South of Porto Azzurro is another Spanish fortress at **Capo Focardo**, on a large oval-shaped peninsula consisting of Monte Calamita and the rough hill country around it. On this peninsula is **Capoliveri**, one of the oldest inhabited sites on the island. The town takes its name from the Roman *Caput Liberi*, which may refer either to the worship of Liber, an Italian equivalent of Dionysus (this has always been a wine-growing area) or to the free men (*liberi*) who lived here – in Roman times, Capoliveri was a refuge for any man who could escape to it. It has had a reputation for independence ever since, giving a bad time to the Pisans, the Spanish, and even Napoleon. Today it is peaceful, with fine views from its hilltop over the surrounding countryside and sea, though much of its scenic coast is privately owned.

South, near the coast, is the **sanctuary of the Madonna delle Grazie**, with a *Madonna and Child* by the school of Raphael, miraculously saved from a shipwreck. The coast west of Capoliveri is marked by two lovely broad gulfs, **Golfo Stella** and **Golfo di Lacona**, separated by a steep, narrow tongue of land. Both are developed resorts, with centres at Lacona and Lido Margidore.

Western Elba

Fortezza di Marciana
t 0565 901215; open usually Easter–Oct mornings and 6pm–11pm; adm; joint adm available with archaeology museum

Museo Civico Archeologico
t 0565 901215; open usually Easter–Oct mornings and 6pm–11pm, adm; joint adm available with Fortezza

Impianto di Risalita (cable lift)
daily mid-April–Oct 10–12.15 and 2.30–4.45; €10 return

Beyond Biodola, the scenic corniche road west from Portoferraio passes through the resorts of **Procchio** and **Campo all'Aia**; the former is larger and one of the more expensive resorts on Elba. **Marciana Marina**, 7km west, is another popular resort, with a 15th-century Pisan watchtower, the **Torre Saracena**. This is the port for **Marciana**, the oldest continuously inhabited town on Elba. In the 14th and 15th centuries, when life near the coast wasn't safe, Marciana was the 'capital' of the feudal Appiani barons, the most powerful family on the island. Today, high in the forests on the slopes of Monte Capanne, it is surprisingly beautiful, with narrow streets, stone stairs, archways and belvederes. Sections of the old city wall and gate are still intact, and the old Pisan **fortress** hangs over the town.

The palace of the Appiani may be seen on a narrow *vicolo* in the oldest part of town. Marciana's **archaeology museum** has some prehistoric and Roman objects found in the area. In season, a **cable lift** climbs to the summit of Elba's highest peak, **Monte Capanne** (1,019m), with stupendous views over Corsica, the Tuscan archipelago and the mountains of Tuscany itself.

Three churches outside Marciana are of interest: the ruined Pisan **San Lorenzo**, the **sanctuary of San Cerbone**, who escaped here from the troublesome Lombards (later his body was buried in a rainstorm, so they wouldn't see), and the 11th-century **sanctuary of the Madonna del Monte**, one of the island's most important shrines, with a Madonna painted on a lump of granite. Pagan Elbans may have worshipped on this site as well, as did Napoleon for two weeks, after a fashion, with his Polish mistress, Maria Walewska.

Another mountain village is **Poggio**, just east, with a natural spring where Elbans bottle their *acqua minerale* – called Napoleone, of course. It's very good, but the Elbans keep it all to themselves.

On the rugged coast west and south of Marciana are more beaches and resorts: **Sant'Andrea**, **Patresi**, **Chiessi**, **Pomonte**, lovely **Fetovaia**, **Seccheto** and **Cavoli**. Seccheto has ancient granite quarries from which the stone was cut for the Pantheon in Rome.

Elba's pocket-sized plain, the **Campo nell'Elba**, stretches 7km east of Marciana, extending from Procchio to Marina di Campo and separating the western mountains from the central range. Elba's airport is here – it's the only place they could put it. Two old towns lie on the edge of the plain: **Sant'Ilario in Campo** and **San Piero in Campo**. San Piero's parish church of San Niccolò has interesting frescoes; it was built on the ruins of an ancient temple to Glaucus.

Halfway between the towns are the ruins of the Pisan church of **San Giovanni**, with a watchtower you can view from outside. On the coast is **Marina di Campo**, Elba's first resort, with the largest beach. The harbour watchtower was built by the Medici.

Pianosa and Montecristo

Two other members of the Tuscan archipelago are included in Livorno province: one you won't want to visit, and the other you usually can't. **Pianosa** is the black sheep of the chain. Its name, taken from the Roman *Planasia*, explains why – it's as flat as a pool table. Like Gorgona, Pianosa's unhappy fate was to serve as a prison island. There are some substantial ruins of a Roman villa, from the days when Pianosa was the playground of Cornelius Agrippa, Emperor Augustus' great general, but to see them you need special permission from the prison authorities in Rome.

Tiny **Montecristo**, the tip of an ancient volcano 40km south of Elba, and the hunting preserve of King Vittorio Emanuele III, is now a nature reserve. Private boats and day-trips organized from Porto Azzurro on Elba may dock at Cala Maestra, but visitors must stay on the cove and its beach; the mountain, ruins of a medieval monastery and royal villa (now the custodian's house) are out of bounds. In Roman times this was an important religious site, *Mons Jovis*, with a famous temple of Jupiter; not a trace remains. The early Church wasted no time Christianizing the place, renaming it Montecristo. None of *The Count of Monte Cristo* is really set here; like the Count himself, seeing the place on a map is probably as close to it as Alexandre Dumas ever got.

Where to Stay on the Tuscan Islands

ⓘ **Capraia >** *Via Assunzione, Capraia Isola,* **t** *0586 905138, www.prolococapraiaisola.it*

Capraia ✉ 57032

The tourist office in Capraia Isola will provide a list of accommodation – a decade or so ago, this consisted of one hotel and two tiny *pensioni*; today, by a miracle of 21st-century Eurotourism, these have all grown into three-star hotels, and two have more sprouted to join them.

ⓘ **Elba >** *Grattacielo building, Calata Italia 26, Portoferraio, across from ferry dock,* **t** *0565 914671/2, www.aptelba.it*

Elba ✉ 57037

There are more than 150 hotels on the island, especially mid-priced resorts for families, but this a big package-tour destination, so you must book ahead. Many hotels require half board in high season (mid-June–mid-Sept). Lots stay open all year, offering substantial off-season discounts.

Prices tend to be slightly lower at Cavo, on the east coast, which has plenty of campsites and holiday apartments. The same is true of most beaches on the southeastern peninsula around Capoliveri. Among the resorts to the west, there are some smart places near Procchio, more modest hotels at Sant'Andrea and Pomonte, and a few that are blissfully out of the way.

For self-catering accommodation, see *www.tuscany-charming.it*.

******Villa Ottone**, at Ottone, **t** 0565 933042, *www.villaottone.com* (€€€€€). A 19th-century villa with its white-sand beach, with a shady garden and a tennis court. Full board is available.

The Hermitage, Loc. Biodola, Portoferraio, **t** 0565 9740 (€€€€). A sprawling resort hotel by a white-sand beach, with lots of facilities for families, including a tennis court. Rooms are quite luxurious, and all have a patio or balcony. Breakfast and dinner are included in the rates. *Closed mid-Oct–Easter.*

*****Hotel Ilio**, Capo Sant'Andrea 24, **t** 0565 908018, *www.ilio.it* (€€€). A whitewashed modern villa and its outbuildings, with pretty bedrooms with rattan furniture. Breakfasts (included) are huge, and evening meals excellent (half board is obligatory April–mid-Oct).

L'Ape Elbana, Salità de' Medici 2, Portoferraio, **t** 0565 914245 (€€). The oldest hotel on the island, where Napoleon's guests were entertained. All rooms are ensuite, and half and full board are available.

La Conchiglia, Cavoli, **t** 0565 987010, *www.laconchigliacavoli.it* (€€). A small family-run hotel with air-con. There's a good restaurant; in high season it's full board only.

La Voce del Mare, Naregno beach, **t** 0565 968455, *www.hotelvocedelmare.it* (€€). One of many pleasant hotels on the beach, with its own private stretch of sand. Half board is required, or you can opt for full board. There are also apartments let by the week, and some rooms have kitchenettes.

Eating Out on the Tuscan Islands

Piombino (mainland)

Ristorante Terrazza, Piazza Premuda, **t** 0565 226135 (€€). Somewhere to wait for the ferry, above the bar in the port, with delicious *spaghetti alle vongole* and grilled fish, and a picture window with a good view of Piombino's steel mills. Pizzas are also served.

Elba ✉ 57037

Elba's DOC wines, Elba Rosso and Elba Bianco, complement any meal.

Osteria del Noce >

Osteria del Noce, Via della Madonna 27, Marciana Alta, near Poggio, **t** 0565 901284 (€€€). An *osteria* in a hilltop village, with fabulous views to the sea. You sit at tables carved from old wine barrels to eat dishes marrying the flavours of Elba, Liguria and Sardinia; anchovies marinated in lemon juice, mussel and bean soup, spaghetti with pesto, and oven-baked fish of the day. Booking is essential. *Closed Oct–Mar.*

Rendezvous, Piazza della Vittoria, Marciana Marina, **t** 0565 99251 (€€€). A place famous for serving an odd dish of baked potato stuffed with seafood but also offering good seafood soup and spaghetti with seafood. *Closed Wed in winter, Jan, Feb and Nov.*

Chiasso, Via Nazario Sauro 20, Capoliveri, **t** 0565 968709 (€€). The place to try stuffed fresh anchovy spaghetti with fish roe, *risotto al nero di seppia* (with cuttlefish in its own ink) and a fabulous octopus soup with onions and potatoes. *Closed Tues, and lunch mid-Oct–mid-Apr.*

La Ferrigna, Piazza della Repubblica 22, Portoferraio, **t** 0565 914129 (€€). One of the most popular places in town, offering an exquisite spaghetti with seafood and an Elban version of Livornese *cacciucco* (which you must order in advance). There are tables on the convivial piazza. *Closed Tues out of high season, and mid-Nov–mid-Feb.*

Osteria Libertaria, Calata Matteotti 12, Portoferraio, **t** 0565 914978 (€€). A traditional *osteria* serving local seafood: try mussel and clam soup; spaghetti with clams, or *cozze alla marinara* (mussels with lemon and oil). Come early if you want a seat in the garden or one of two tables on the pier, with great views. *Closed Mon.*

Tavernetta, Lungomare Vitaliani 42, Porto Azzurro, **t** 0565 95110 (€€). One of many seafood places on the beach in southern Elba, built over the sea. *Closed Thurs.*

Solemar, Loc. Lacona, just outside Capoliveri, **t** 0565 964248 (€). A pleasant trattoria with the best pizzas on Elba. Booking is advisable. *Closed Mon in winter.*

South of Piombino

The Maremma

In a sense, this flat, lonely stretch of coast really belongs to Italy's south. History has been unkind to the Maremma, domain first of the Etruscans, later of the anopheles mosquito. Like many southern

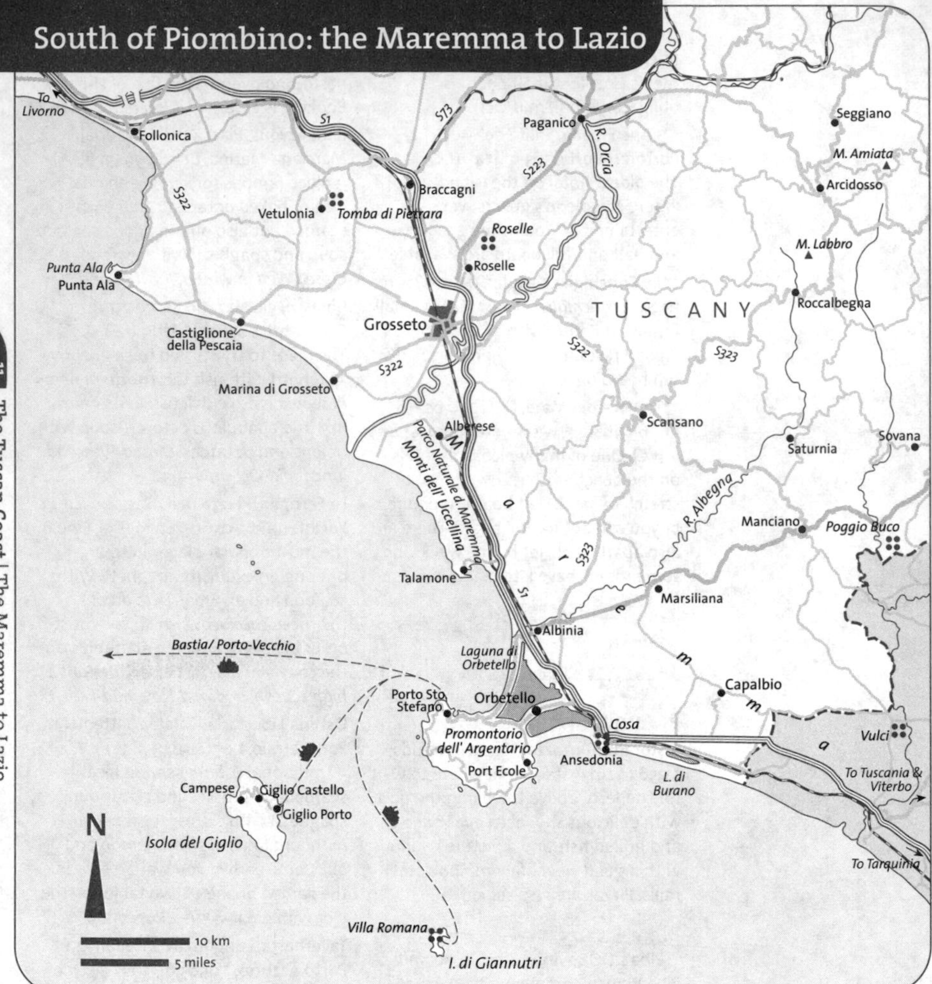

coastal regions, the Maremma was a prosperous agricultural region until Roman times. The Romans gave it its name: the 'maritime' zone (as in names such as Massa Marittima), gradually mangled into Maremma.

Historians sometimes give the Romans too much credit for capable governance; their grasping, bureaucratic state slowly corroded and eventually destroyed the Italian economy. Many centuries of Roman misgovernment – impossible taxes, cheap imported grain and especially, in this case, neglect of the Etruscans' system of drainage canals – doomed the Maremma to a slow death. When the canals failed, much of the land was abandoned and reverted to swamps, breeding the malarial mosquitoes that made the Maremma of the Middle Ages a place of suffering and death, inhabitable only by the *butteri*, tough

Tuscan cowboys who tended the herds in the abandoned marshy pastures. A considerable body of folklore has grown up around the *butteri*; the Maremma's proudest moment came in the last century when some of them went to Rome and defeated Buffalo Bill and his travelling Wild West show in a test of cowboy know-how.

The first work of reclamation began with the Austrian grand dukes. The Italian Kingdom that followed forgot all about the Maremma, and it was not until after World War II that the task was completed. The Maremma today is back on its feet, a new region and a little rough around the edges but prosperous once more.

Follonica and Punta Ala

After Piombino, the coast bends eastwards into a broad arc, the Golfo di Follonica. There are some wonderful beaches between Piombino and Follonica, notably La Sterpaia, which partly backs on to a nature reserve.

Since the Second World War, new resort towns have been popping up like toadstools all along the Tuscan coast. One of the biggest and least likeable is **Follonica**, 21km east of Piombino, partially redeemed by the long pine groves that follow its crowded beaches. Follonica has some other enchantments, notably the **Museum of Iron and Cast Iron**, in an 1830s foundry where Elban iron was once smelted. There is also **CARAPAX**, the European Centre for the Protection of Turtles and Tortoises, who study turtles, save endangered ones and reintroduce them into the wild. Visitors can look at the turtle clinic and nursery, and see exotic species. The centre is also working to reintroduce the stork to Italy, and has a colony of them in Italy's biggest aviary.

Museo del Ferro e della Ghisa
open summer Wed 8.30–1.30 and 5–8, Fri and Sat 8.30–1.30 and 5–11pm, Sun 5–11pm; winter Wed and Sun 4.30–7.30, Fri and Sat 9–12 and 4.30–7.30; or call **t** *0566 59391 or* **t** *0566 59380*

CARAPAX
t *0566 902387, www.carapax.org; open April–20 June daily 9.30–6; 21 June–20 Sept daily 9–7; 21 Sept–31 Oct daily 9–5 (feeding time 9am)*

On the promontory that closes the gulf, 14km south, **Punta Ala** is a modern, entirely synthetic resort built in the suburban style of the Costa Smeralda. It's an attractive location, with a fine sandy beach and views around the gulf, and it attracts a well-heeled clientele with diversions rare in Tuscany, such as golf (at the Golf Hotel, Via del Gualdo) and polo (at the Polo Club).

Castiglione della Pescaia, attached to an attractive, ancient fishing village to the south, is much less exclusive. The beach isn't great, but the town on its hill, with trees and ivy-covered walls, is one of the more pleasant detours on this coast. The Spanish left a 16th-century castle, and the church of San Giovanni has an tower that could pass for a minaret. From the harbour, Navimaremma offers summer island cruises; ask at the tourist office (*see* p.314).

Grosseto

Under the prevailing prosperity, the natural Tuscan sense of order and propriety has slowly been asserting itself in this place that we described, in the original edition of this book, as 'a city of

Getting to and from Grosseto

Seven **trains** a day (**t** 892021, *www.trenitalia.com*) leave Grosseto for Siena, via Roccastrada and Buonconvento (some continue to Florence). There are also services along the coastal line for Livorno, or Orbetello and Rome.

GRIFORAMA (**t** 0564 25215, *www.griforama.it*) runs **buses** from Grosseto to Siena (7 a day) and every town in Grosseto province, including 2 a day to Massa Marittima (*see* Hilltowns West of Siena), and 5 daily to Arcidosso and Pitigliano (*see* Southern Tuscany). Buses leave from the train station.

Art Nouveau buildings and perverse teenagers, a city conducive to hallucinations, its streets alive with swirls of dust and flying plastic bags.' Instead of punk music, there are dance and chamber music concerts and scholarly conferences, and Italy's Most Improved Town, always a likeable place, grows steadily more normal, even pleasant – though you still can't buy a decent slice of pizza.

Via Carducci leads from the station towards the fearful hexagon of walls that enclose Grosseto, passing Mussolini's contribution to the city, the circular Piazza Fratelli Rosselli, or **La Vasca** (which can mean 'tub' or 'toilet bowl'). Here the starring role is played by an exuberant **Mussolini post office**, with heroic statuary in travertine. The main gate is only a block away. Cosimo's walls are perfectly preserved, done in tidy, reddish brick festooned with Medici balls.

Much of the old city looks very Spanish; the Art Nouveau pharmacies and shoe shops along the main street, Corso Carducci, contribute to the effect, as does the arcaded Piazza del Duomo, very like a Spanish *Plaza Mayor*. The **Duomo** (1190–1250) suffered grievously from overambitious restoration in the 1840s; the façade looks like a Hollywood prop. Inside is a genuinely lovely painting, Matteo di Giovanni's *Madonna delle Grazie* (1470). Around the side of the Duomo is an interesting sundial, and the piazza has an allegorical monument to the Maremma's benefactor, the Lorraine Grand Duke Leopold II; the woman he is raising up represents the suffering Maremma, and the snake he's crushing is Malaria.

Museo Archaeologico e d'Arte della Maremma
t 0564 488750; open summer Tues–Sun 10–1 and 5–8; Nov–Feb Tues–Fri 9–1, Sat and Sun 9.30–1 and 4.30–7; Oct and April Tues–Sun 9.30–1 and 4.30–7

Around the corner in Piazza Baccarini, two museums, collectively called the **Museo Archaeologico e d'Arte della Maremma**, show you something of life in this region before there ever was a Grosseto. Thousands of years ago, Grosseto and most of its plain were underwater; by the time of the Etruscans, the sea had receded, leaving a large lake on the plain. Two wealthy Etruscan cities, Vetulonia and Roselle (*see* opposite), stood on the hills above the lake, and they contributed most of the items here: cinerary urns with scenes from Homer, architectural fragments and delicate terracottas, some with bits of their original paint. Up on the third floor, the **Pinacoteca** has some good Sienese art, including an amazing, very Byzantine *Last Judgement* by 13th-century artist Guido da Siena.

Pinacoteca
open summer Tues–Sun 10–1 and 5–8; Nov–Feb Tues–Fri 9–1, Sat and Sun 9.30–1 and 4.30–7; Oct and April Tues–Sun 9.30–1 and 4.30–7

Just north of the museum, San Francesco has an early work by Duccio di Buoninsegna, the crucifix above the high altar, and some good 13th-century frescoes. From here you can walk around the

Medicean walls. After Italian unification, the bastions were landscaped into beautiful semi-tropical gardens; some are still well kept, others have decayed into spooky jungles.

The liveliest parts of Grosseto are the shopping streets around Piazza del Mercato; nearby, just outside the walls, mornings see a large, almost picturesque street market.

Roselle and Vetulonia

You learn more about these two Etruscan towns from the Grosseto museum (*see* opposite) than seeing the ruins, but a visit can be fun. **Roselle**, 7km north of Grosseto, survived Roman rule better than many other Etruscan cities, but by the 5th century it was almost abandoned. The bishops of Roselle hung on until 1178, when the seat was transferred to Grosseto. Like many other Etruscan towns, Roselle is a high plateau and is surrounded by more than 3km of walls. A Roman road leads up to the complex, where there are still a few foundations, remains of the baths, the imperial forum and the outline of the amphitheatre, a medieval tower, and necropoli. North of the site are the ruins of a **Roman villa** with parts of its original mosaic floor paving. The last occupant operated a forge here to melt down bronze statues.

Domus dei Mosaici
open daily 9–dusk

Vetulonia, 17km from Grosseto, above the Via Aurelia west of Braccagni, lives on in its worthy successor, Massa Marittima (*see* pp.368–70). On the site itself, a miniature hilltown survives, in rugged but lovely countryside with occasional views over the Tyrrhenian and the islands. Like Roselle, it lasted until the Middle Ages, and was probably destroyed in a 14th-century revolt against its Pisan overlords. Bits of old Vetulonia can be seen in the **Aree Archeologiche** (signposted) and nearby **museum**. The scanty ruins are more Roman and medieval than Etruscan, but the periphery has some interesting tombs (also signposted): the massive **Tomba della Pietrera** and the unique **Il Diavolino** (7th century BC). Both have a long corridor under a tumulus, with an arched burial chamber in the centre; the Diavolino has an window to the sky.

Aree Archeologiche and Museo Archeologico
open summer daily 9–7.30; winter daily 9–5.30; joint adm.

3 Monti dell'Uccellina
Visitor centre: Alberese, west of coastal Via Aurelia/SS1 (regular shuttle service from car park), **t** *0564 407098; open daily 8am–1hr before sunset; adm; guided tours in English in summer, or private guides available for about €12/hr; visitors limited to 500/day; call ahead at busiest times (Easter, 29 April–1 May, July and Aug); no cars or dogs; bring good shoes and some water*

Monti dell'Uccellina: The Maremma Nature Park

One effect of the Maremma's history of abandonment is a lovely, unspoiled coast. In the 1950s and 1960s developers followed the DDT where they could, but the government set aside a few of the best parts. The **Monti dell'Uccellina**, a ragged chain of hills south of Grosseto, largely covered with umbrella pines, is an important stop for migratory birds between Europe and Africa, hence the name.

For such a small area (roughly 5x15km), the park has a lot to see: nine old defence towers, dozens of caves and the ruins of an 11th-century monastery, **San Rabano**, that belonged to the Knights of Malta. It retains its campanile and some early medieval stone carvings. Where the park meets the sea is a strip of fabulous beaches. Despite the park status, some people still make their living here, herding cattle, cutting cork oak and gathering pine nuts for Italy's pastry cooks. The landscape ranges from swamps to heather and scented *macchia* to pine groves, and the fauna includes wild horses, deer and boar, along with the *uccellini* themselves – herons, eagles and falcons, ospreys and kingfishers, every sort of duck, and that most overdressed of waterfowl, the *cavaliere d'Italia*. Some peripheral areas can be toured on horseback, and **Il Rialto** at Albarese can fix you up with a steed, plus bikes and canoes.

Il Rialto
t 0564 407 1020

Nine walks have been laid out in the park, lasting 2–6 hours, and visitors are expected to keep to them. One walk begins from a separate park entrance at Talamone, further south, and doesn't connect to the others. Note that in summer some areas can only be visited by guided tour.

Talamone

The Sienese Republic never really had a port, gravely hampering foreign trade. Now and then it tried to make one out of Talamone, a fishing village at the tip of the Monti dell'Uccellina, but the little harbour couldn't be kept clear – a continuing embarrassment for the republic; even Dante dropped a jibe about foolishly 'hoping from Talamone'. Garibaldi had better luck: when in 1860 he and his 'Thousand' chose to stop here rather than Sardinia, they avoided the orders for their arrest sent by the treacherous Count Cavour; Garibaldi also found a cache of weapons in Orbetello, which came in handy during the conquest of Sicily.

The walled village on its rock has become a discreet, laidback resort with a small marina. Above, a 16th-century Spanish castle sits like an abstract modern sculpture, set to house a new museum devoted to nature in the Monti dell'Uccellina.

Where to Stay and Eat in the Maremma

ⓘ Castiglione della Pescaia >
Piazza Garibaldi, harbour, t 0564 933678, www.col-castiglionegr.it

Castiglione della Pescaia ✉ 58043

Castiglione lacks appealing beaches but has a good choice of inexpensive hotels. Most insist on half or full board mid-July–mid-Sept.

****Rossella**, Via Fratelli Bandiera 18, **t** 0564 933832, *www.albergorosella.it* (€€€). Good rooms, most with a balcony, plus a solarium and a restaurant with a terrace, serving Tuscan specialities. Breakfast is included, and half board is compulsory June–mid-Sept.

Ristorante Miramare, Via Vittorio Veneto 35, **t** 0564 933524 (€€€). An excellent seafood restaurant offering seasonal dishes such as prawns with beans, or pumpkin tart. There are also some comfy rooms and flats (€€).

Osteria nel Buco, Via del Recinto 11, **t** 0564 934460 (€€). A cosy trattoria with good food and occasional live music. Sample the exquisite soups, grilled fish and meat, and excellent Pecorino cheese. *Closed Mon exc July and Aug, lunch Tues–Sat.*

ⓘ Grosseto >>
Viale Monterosa 206, t 0564 462611, www.lamaremma.info

Grosseto ✉ 58100

The Consorzio Albergatori (**t** 0564 415446) might be able to help in the unlikely event you can't find a room.

****Bastiani Grand Hotel, Via Gioberti 64, t 0564 20047, *www.hotelbastiani.com* (€€€€). An elegant city-centre hotel in a gracious 1890s *palazzo*, with a restaurant. Breakfast is included.

***Leon d'Oro, Via San Martino 46, t 0564 22128 (€€). An option with a decent restaurant (full board available) and private parking. The guestrooms without baths are much cheaper. *Closed Sun.*

Buca di San Lorenzo, Via Manetti 1, t 0564 25142 (€€€). A restaurant dug into the Medicean walls, serving local cuisine based on seasonal produce. *Closed Sun, Mon, 3wks in Jan and 2wks in July.*

Da Remo, Rispescia Stazione, a few km south of Grosseto, just off Aurelia, t 0564 405014 (€€€). Fish brought directly from the daily market: try the spaghetti with prawns and lemon. *Closed Wed and mid-Oct–mid-Nov.*

Il Canto del Gallo, Via Mazzini 29, t 0564 414589 (€€). A tiny trattoria in the centre of the old town, with an owner who advises you on what to eat and prepares it personally. Game is a speciality. Booking is essential. *Closed lunch and Sun.*

La Taverna Etrusca, Vetulonia, t 0564 949601 (€€). A good trattoria at the top of town, plus some guestrooms and a lovely pool.

Monte Argentario

In the last decade or so, this curiosity of the Tuscan coast has grown popular. It has much going for it: attractive old towns, a genuine Mediterranean feeling and matching scenery. Long ago, **Monte Argentario** was an island, the closest of the Tuscan archipelago to the shore. No one can explain how it happened, but the Tyrrhenian currents gradually built up two symmetrical sandbars connecting the rugged, mountainous island to the mainland. In between, there was a peninsula with the Etruscan, then Roman city of Orbetello; the Romans built a causeway on to Argentario that split the natural lagoon in half. It is said that sailors named the Argentario in classical times, noticing the bright flashes of silver from the olive trees that still cover its slopes.

Most books describe Porto Santo Stefano and Porto Ercole as 'exclusive'. The Argentario does attract its share of the high life, particularly the yachting crowd from Rome, and it's pricier than other resorts, but the peninsula has not become an overcrowded beach Babylon like Elba. The beaches are not special, and Tuscany's art and other attractions are far. On balance, though, the Argentario is a contender for the best place for a seaside holiday in the region.

Orbetello

Go to the northern tip of the peninsula of Orbetello (population 13,500), near the causeway, and look over the water; below the modern breakwater are bits of ancient wall in huge irregular blocks – the sole remnants of Etruscan Orbetello, probably the biggest port on the Etruscan coast, and defensible enough to give the city a minor historical role over the centuries. The Byzantines held out longer here than anywhere else on this coast; the city then fell into the hands of the Three Fountains Abbey in Rome, who handed it to

Getting around the Monte Argentario

Orbetello is the centre for public transport around the Argentario, with a bus station just off Piazza della Repubblica. There are regular **buses** for Porto Ercole, Porto S. Stefano, Grosseto and the **train** station, about 2km east of town, on the Grosseto–Rome coastal line, plus daily buses to Capalbio and Pitigliano.

---

the pope – until 1980 the pope was also bishop of Orbetello. After the treaty of Cateau-Cambrésis in 1559, Orbetello became capital of a new province – the Spanish military *Presidio*, from which imperialist Spain could menace both Tuscany and the Pope, ruled by a viceroy directly responsible to the King. The *Presidio* lasted only until 1707 but had a strong impact on the area's buildings and its people.

Orbetello was briefly a resort but passed this role on to Porto Ercole and Porto Santo Stefano; its most recent flash of glory was in the 1930s ,when Mussolini made it Italy's main seaplane base. Fascist hero Italo Balbo began his famous transatlantic flight from the lagoon in 1933, landing at the opening of the Chicago World's Fair.

Confined on its peninsula, with its palm trees and sun-bleached Spanish walls, this is a charming town, where buses barely squeeze through the main gate. Viale Italia, the main street, runs down the centre of the peninsula; just north on Piazza della Repubblica, is the **cathedral** with a sculpted portal and rose window from 1376.

Laguna di Orbetello
Visitor Centre: coast road between Orbetello and Albinia, **t** *0564 820297; open for guided tours Oct–April (outside nesting period) Thurs, Sat and Sun 10 and 3; adm*

Orbetello's lagoons, on average about 90cm deep, are partly used for fish farms, but most of the north half has been declared a **WWF nature reserve**. Like the Monti dell'Uccellina, the area is a breeding ground for marine birds, and also storks and a species of eagle, not to mention the stilt plover, bee-eater and lesser hen harrier.

Porto Ercole and Porto Santo Stefano

Over the causeway from Orbetello on to Monte Argentario, you can go north or south to begin the *gita panoramica*, the 24km road that circles the island (it offers some exceptional views, but it's not surfaced the whole way and you won't get round without a Jeep).

South, **Porto Ercole** wraps itself around a yacht-filled harbour, guarded by Spanish fortresses. Forte Stella and Forte San Filippo were probably the last word in 16th-century military architecture, with low, sloping walls and pointed bastions draped over the cliffs; today they are an ominous, surreal sight. San Filippo is the more interesting, though you can't visit – it's been converted to holiday flats. Above the souvenir shops and seafood restaurants of the harbour is a fine old town, entered through a Gothic gate built by the Sienese. Piazza Santa Barbara has the dignified 17th-century palace of the Spanish governor, and a view over the harbour. Caravaggio was buried in the church of Sant'Erasmo in 1609 after dying of malaria in a tavern nearby, on his way back from Malta to Rome, where he'd hoped the pope would pardon him for a murder committed years before.

Beyond Porto Ercole, the coast road twists and turns under the slopes of Il Telegrafo, Argentario's highest peak (635m). One feature of the *gita panoramica* is the many defence towers, some built by the Sienese, others by the Spaniards.

On the northern side of the Argentario, **Porto Santo Stefano** makes a matching bookend for Porto Ercole. Larger than its sister town, this also began as a sleepy fishing village. Now the fishing boats are elbowed off to the side of the port by speedboats, shiny yachts and the Giglio ferries, and the old town is lost in the agglomeration of hotels and villas on the surrounding hills. However, it remains less exclusive than Porto Ercole and more of a real community than an exclusive yachting port. There are really two harbours: the first, larger one has the ferries and fish markets; the yachts – some real dreadnoughts – call at the western harbour.

The spits of land joining Argentario to the mainland are made up of two long beaches, the Giannella and the Feniglia. The latter is backed by a beautiful protected pine forest (a nature reserve) with a path along it. You can hire bikes and ride the 7km of its length, branching on to the beach at various points. The Giannella is backed by the main road but faces west, so you get lovely sunsets.

ⓘ **Orbetello >** *Piazza della Repubblica,* **t** *0564 860447*

★ **San Biagio Relais >**

★ **I Pescatori >**

Where to Stay and Eat in the Monte Argentario

Orbetello ✉ 58035

*****Hotel Relais Presidi**, Via Mura di Levante 34, **t** 0564 867601, *www.ipresidi.com* (€€€€). Lagoon views, a restaurant and a beautiful American bar. Most rooms have balconies.

***San Biagio Relais, Via Dante 34, **t** 0564 860543, *www.sanbiagiorelais.com* (€€€€) A classy hotel in an elegant *palazzo* in the centre, with comfortable rooms and suites, a gym and fitness centre, and a restaurant. There's a minimum two-night stay in high season. Rates include breakfast.

***Piccolo Parigi**, Corso Italia 169, **t** 0564 867233 (€€). A delightful, very friendly spot with a Mediterranean feel. Breakfast is included.

Osteria del Lupacante, Corso Italia 103, **t** 0564 867618 (€€). Wonderful fresh seafood, including risotto with shrimps and pine nuts, and mussels with Marsala wine. *Closed Tues in winter, and 3wks Dec/Jan.*

I Pescatori, Via Leopardi 9, **t** 0564 860611 (€€). A simple restaurant run by the local fishermen's cooperative, serving only fish caught in the lagoon, on plastic plates from a self-service counter. Try *bottarga d'Orbetello* (tuna eggs), smoked eels, or grilled lake fish. *Closed lunch, Mon–Thurs eves in winter.*

Porto Ercole ✉ 58018

******Il Pellicano**, Sbarcatello (cove near Porto Ercole), **t** 0564 858111, *www.pellicanohotel.com* (€€€€€). A Relais et Châteaux hotel popular with yachtsmen and Italian TV stars, with a beach, a pool, watersports, tennis and two fish restaurants, plus golf nearby. Half board is obligatory mid-June–Sept.

******Torre di Calapiccola**, **t** 0564 825111, *www.torredicalapiccola.com* (€€€€€). An apartment complex perched spectacularly above the sea, with a beach, a pool and lots of activities. *Closed late-Oct–Mar.*

*****Don Pedro**, Via Panoramica, **t** 0564 833914, *www.hoteldonpedro.it* (€€€). An option above the town, some way from the nearest beach, with a fish restaurant. Breakfast is included and half board available. *Closed Nov–Mar.*

***La Conchiglia**, Via della Marina 22, **t** 0564 833134 (€€). One of the few moderate places on Argentario proper, comfortable, with breakfast included.

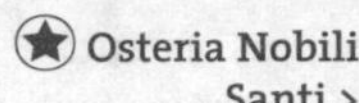 Osteria Nobili Santi >

Osteria I Nobili Santi, Via dell'Ospizio 8, **t** 0564 833015 (€€€). Elegant fish dishes in an elegant setting; try the *maltagliati* with squid and tomatoes. Booking is advisable. *Closed Mon, and lunch Tues–Sat in summer.*

ⓘ Porto Santo Stefano >
Piazzale S. Andrea, t 0564 814208

Porto Santo Stefano ✉ 58019

***Filippo II**, Loc. Poggio Calvella, **t** 0564 811611, *www.filipposecondo.it* (€€€€€). Plush suites and apartments with a restaurant, close to beaches.

***La Caletta**, Via Civinini 10, **t** 0564 812939, *www.hotelcaletta.it* (€€€€). Pleasant rooms overlooking the sea; rates include breakfast. Half and full board are available.

Alfiero, Via Cuniberti 12, **t** 0564 814067 (€€). A simple hotel by the harbour. Rates include breakfast.

Dal Greco, Via del Molo 1, **t** 0564 814885 (€€€). An elegant place on the harbour, serving great spaghetti with lobster. *Closed Tues in winter.*

I Due Pini, Loc. La Soda, on coast road into Porto Santo Stefano, **t** 0564 814012 (€€€). A stunning beachside setting for some of the best seafood in the area, including *spaghetti al nero di seppia*. There's live music at night.

Da Orlando, Via Breschi 3, **t** 0564 812788 (€€). A relaxed, lively place facing the islands. Try seabream, black seabass or lake bass. *Closed Wed.*

Giglio and Giannutri

Giglio

Giglio is the largest Tuscan island after Elba (about 21km by 8km). It is also second in population, with about 1,600 souls, almost all in its little villages: Giglio Porto, Giglio Castello and Giglio Campese. Like many Italian islands, Giglio suffered from deforestation and abandonment of the land in the 18th and 19th centuries. Though much of it remains green and pretty, large expanses are now almost barren. In latter years, however, a switch in environmental consciousness has occurred – there's no camping, no noise, no riding over the wildflowers, and no collecting rocks.

Giglio means 'lily', and the lily is the island's symbol, though it has nothing to do with its name. The Romans called it *Aegilium* or *Gilium*. Under them, Giglio, like most Italian islands, was a resort for the very wealthy. Pisa, Aragon and various feudal families held it in the Middle Ages. Duke Cosimo seized it for Tuscany in the 16th century but did little to protect it against its great danger, pirates. But the Giglians had the holy right arm of San Mamiliano to protect them. This 6th-century Sicilian bishop, fleeing Arian heretics, became a hermit on Montecristo. When he died, a divine signal alerted fishermen from Elba, Giglio and even Genoa, who arrived and began to fight over the remains. In the true tradition of Christian brotherhood they struck a deal and cut Mamiliano in three. Giglio got the arm, which proved its worth by chasing away Turkish pirates in 1799. On other occasions it wasn't so helpful. The redoubtable pirate Barbarossa carried off most of the population in 1534, and his understudy Dragut came back for the rest in 1550.

Giglio Porto, the island's metropolis, has red and green lighthouses, and pink and beige houses straggling up the hills. There are two beaches south of the town, at **Cala delle Canelle** and **Cala delle**

Getting to and around Giglio and Giannutri

Porto S. Stefano is the port for **Giglio** (1hr); **ferries** are run by TOREMAR (**t** 0564 810803, *www.toremar.it*) and Maregiglio (**t** 0564 812920, *www.maregiglio.it*), both in Porto S. Stefano. Boats run at least twice dally (more in summer). The **train** station (**t** 892021, *www.trenitalia.com*) for Porto S.Stefano, along the main Livorno–Rome line, is Orbetello Scalo; buses meet the trains to carry passengers to the port. On Giglio, **buses** run fairly regularly from the ferry dock to Giglio Castello and Giglio Campese.

Giannutri can be reached regularly only in July and August, on a daily boat from Porto S. Stefano.

Caldane, one to the north at **Punta Aranella**; all are more or less developed. In the town itself is the world's smallest beach, tucked behind the houses on the left side of the port.

From Giglio Porto a difficult mountain road leads up to **Giglio Castello**, the only secure refuge in pirate days, and until recently the only real town. The fortress itself was begun by the Pisans and completed under the grand dukes. The picturesque town inside, all medieval alleys and overhanging arches, has plenty of gulls and swallows, a few German tourists, and a small Baroque church with an odd tower and the famous arm of San Mamiliano.

From Giglio Castello, a road leads south past **Poggio della Pagana**, the island's highest peak (498m), to Punta del Capel Rosso, at the southern tip, then back along the coast to Giglio Porto. The main road from Giglio Castello continues on to **Giglio Campese**, a growing resort with an old watchtower and a large sandy beach.

Giannutri

Giannutri, the southernmost of the Tuscan islands, is a rocky crescent about 5km long, with little water and no fertile ground, and little history to speak of. The ancient Greeks knew it as *Artemisia*, the Romans as *Dianium*; perhaps the associations with the moon goddess came from the crescent shape. In Roman times it was an estate of the noble Ahenobarbus family; there are the substantial ruins of a **Roman villa** (1st century AD) near Cala Maestra, a popular destination among day-trippers from Porto Santo Stefano in summer. Though Giannutri has no permanent population, there is a tourist village and some holiday cottages near the well-protected bay, **Cala Spalmatoio**, on the eastern coast.

Where to Stay and Eat on Giglio

ⓘ **Giglio >**
Via Provinciale 9, Giglio Porto, t 0564 809400, www.isoladelgiglio.biz (summer only)

Giglio ✉ 58012

*****Campese**, Via della Torre 18, Giglio Campese, **t** 0564 804003, *www.hotelcampese.com* (€€€€). A good, modern beach hotel (half/full board).

****Pardini's Hermitage**, Cala degli Alberi, **t** 0564 809034, *www.hermit.it* (€€€€). A little hotel in a quiet cove, reached by boat. There are sports and nature activities, or just lie back and enjoy the sea and mountains. It's full or half board only in summer. The farm produes oil, wine, milk and meat. *Closed mid-Oct–Mar*.

*****Arenella**, Via Arenella 5, **t** 0564 809340, *www.hotelarenella.com* (€€€). An option near the beach, with a pretty garden, a sauna, Turkish bath and gym, and a good restaurant. Rates include breakfast.

***Demo's, Via Thaon De Revel 31, t 0564 809235, *www.hoteldemos.com* (€€€). A hotel right in the port, in a 1960s Miami Beach style. Breakfast is included, and there's a restaurant serving fish and seasonal specialities.

**La Pergola, Via Thaon De Revel 30, t 0564 809051 (€€). A cosy little option; breakfast is included.

Da Maria, Via Casamatta 12, Giglio Porto, **t** 0564 806062 (€€€). A family-run trattoria with excellent seafood. *Closed Wed in winter and 3wks in Jan.*

La Margherita, Via Thaon De Revel 5, Giglio Porto, **t** 0564 809237 (€€). One of the most popular seafood restaurants around the harbour, with a terrace on the beach. Booking is recommended. *Closed Mon.*

Da Santi, Via Marconi 20, Giglio Porto, **t** 0564 806188 (€€). An old-fashioned restaurant in the old town, run by a former ship's cook. Try the octopus, and sample local white wine, rarely on sale. It's tiny, so book ahead. *Closed Mon outside high season, and Feb.*

Capalbio and the Tarot Garden

Back on the coast south of Orbetello, almost nothing is left of **Ansedonia**, destroyed by the Sienese in 1330: there's a beach, a few hotels, and an unusual Etruscan attempt to stop Cosa's harbour silting up – deep channels hewn from solid rock. Climb up to **Cosa**, settled by Romans in the 3rd century BC to keep an eye on the restless Etruscan cities – and maybe accelerate their decline by draining off trade. Cosa was sacked by Visigoths in the 5th century, but the ruins and small museum give a fair idea of the Roman city,.

Lago di Burano
tours Sept–April Sun at 10 and 2.30; summer by advance booking on **t** *0564 898829; adm*

Before the Via Aurelia (SS1) passes into Lazio, it skirts another World Wildlife Fund project, a nature reserve at the **Lago di Burano**. Though small, the lagoon attracts the same birds as the Monti dell'Uccellina and Orbetello lagoons; including, in summer, perhaps the only cranes left on the Italian mainland.

Tarot Garden
turn off SS1 to Capalbio then right just before 1st petrol station; www.nikidesaintphalle.com; open April–mid-Oct daily 2.30–7.30; for group visits (min. 15 people) 1st Sat of month winter, adm exp (free to groups in winter)

Capalbio, 6km inland, is one of the loveliest villages in southern Tuscany – a circular hilltop enclave built around a castle. Head a few kilometres east for the unsignposted **Tarot Garden**, the project of French artist Niki de Saint-Phalle (who died in 2002), known for her works at the Pompidou Centre in Paris, and *nanas,* here colossal, humorous figures scattered over Europe. In this garden, created for meditation, monumental sculptures represent the 22 key arcana of the Tarot – mad, brilliant works harking back to Gaudí.

Over the Border

There are a few attractions on the way to Rome. The wealthiest Etruscan cities were here, so the finest painted tombs are on the north Lazio coast at **Tarquinia** and **Cervetri**. Inland are the remains of Etruscan **Vulci**; the fortress of Castello dell'Abbadia holds an Etruscan museum, and an Etruscan bridge spans the gorge.

Tuscania has two unusual early medieval churches in the style of medieval southern Italy. Further inland is a chain of lakes, including tranquil **Lake Vico**, and the city of **Viterbo**, once home to the popes.

Siena

Draped on its three hills, Siena is the most beautiful city in Tuscany, a flamboyant medieval ensemble of palaces and towers cast in warm, brown, Siena-coloured brick. Its soaring skyline, dominated by the blazing black and white banner of a cathedral and the taut needle of the Torre di Mangia, is its pride, yet the Campo, the very centre, is only four streets away from olive groves and orchards. The contrast is part of the city's charm: dense brick urbanity, neighboured by a fine stretch of long Tuscan farmland that fills the valleys within the city's walls.

Here art went hand-in-hand with a fierce civic desire to make Siena a world of its own, and historians go so far as to speak of 'Sienese civilization' when summing up the achievements of this unique little city.

12

Don't miss

1. The face of Siena's history
   Palazzo Pubblico p.332
2. A treasure-box cathedral
   Duomo p.335
3. An innovative museum complex
   Ospedale di Santa Maria della Scala p.341
4. A temple of Sienese art
   Pinacoteca Nazionale p.343
5. An Italian wine showcae
   Enoteca Nazionale p.347

See map overleaf

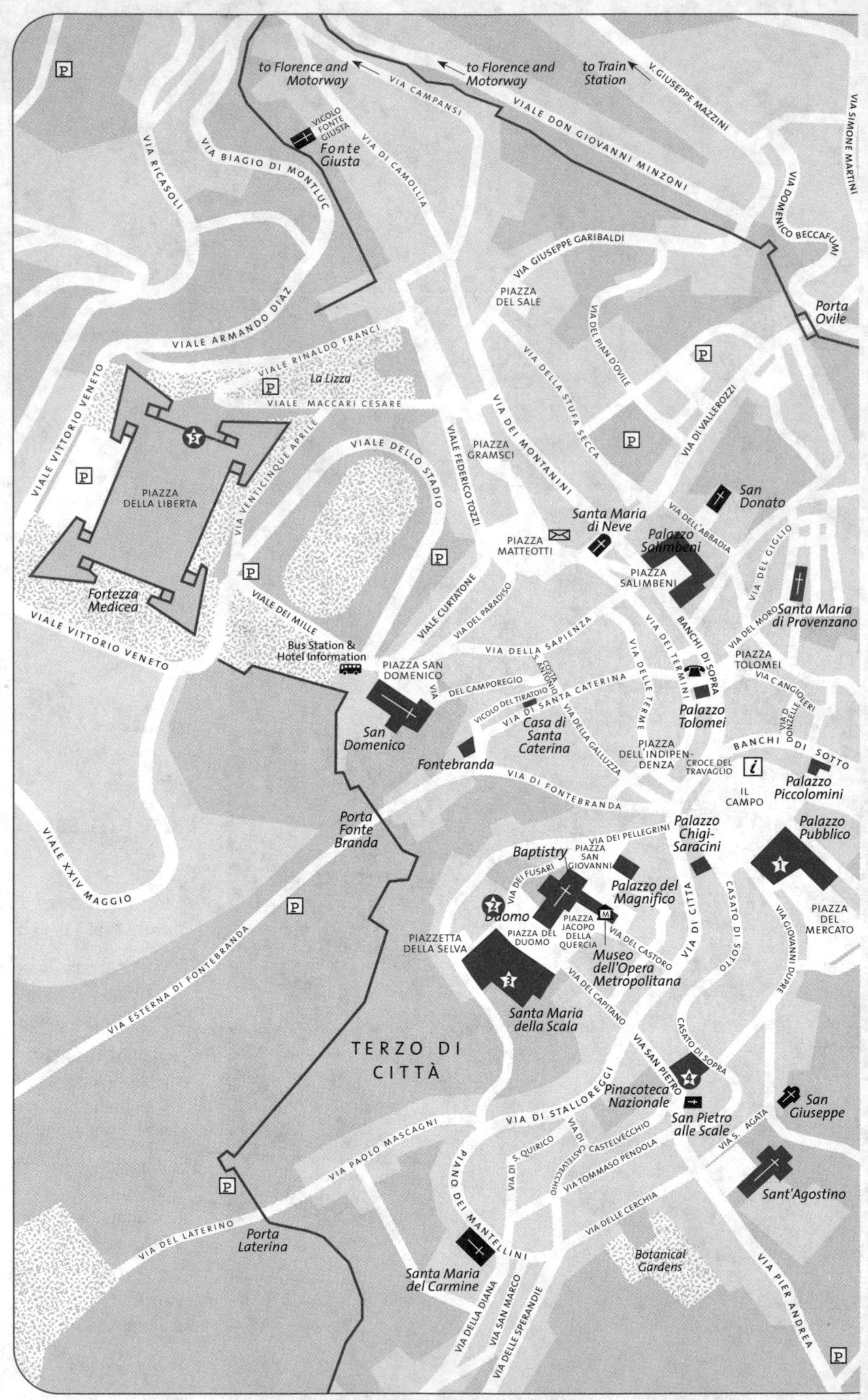

to Florence and Motorway
to Florence and Motorway
to Train Station
V. GIUSEPPE MAZZINI
VIA SIMONE MARTINI
VIA CAMPANSI
VIALE DON GIOVANNI MINZONI
VICOLO FONTE GIUSTA
Fonte Giusta
VIA DI CAMOLLIA
VIA BIAGIO DI MONTLUC
VIA RICASOLI
VIA DOMENICO BECCAFUMI
VIA GIUSEPPE GARIBALDI
PIAZZA DEL SALE
Porta Ovile
VIALE ARMANDO DIAZ
VIALE RINALDO FRANCI
La Lizza
VIALE MACCARI CESARE
VIA DEL PIAN D'OVILE
VIA DELLA STUFA SECCA
VIA DI VALLEROZZI
VIALE VITTORIO VENETO
VIA VENTICINQUE APRILE
VIALE DELLO STADIO
VIALE FEDERICO TOZZI
PIAZZA GRAMSCI
VIA DEI MONTANINI
PIAZZA DELLA LIBERTA
San Donato
Santa Maria di Neve
VIA DELL'ABBADIA
Palazzo Salimbeni
PIAZZA MATTEOTTI
PIAZZA SALIMBENI
VIA DEL GIGLIO
Santa Maria di Provenzano
Fortezza Medicea
VIALE DEI MILLE
VIALE CURTATONE
VIA DEL PARADISO
VIA DEL MORO
VIALE VITTORIO VENETO
Bus Station & Hotel Information
VIA DELLA SAPIENZA
BANCHI DI SOPRA
VIA DEI TERMINI
PIAZZA TOLOMEI
PIAZZA SAN DOMENICO
COSTA S. ANTONIO
VIA DELLE TERME
VIA C. ANGIOLIERI
VIA DEL CAMPOREGIO
VIA DI SANTA CATERINA
VICOLO DEL TIRATOIO
Palazzo Tolomei
VIA D. DONZELLE
San Domenico
Casa di Santa Caterina
VIA DELLA GALLUZZA
PIAZZA DELL'INDIPENDENZA
BANCHI DI SOTTO
Fontebranda
CROCE DEL TRAVAGLIO
Palazzo Piccolomini
VIA DI FONTEBRANDA
IL CAMPO
Porta Fonte Branda
Palazzo Chigi-Saracini
VIA DEI PELLEGRINI
Palazzo Pubblico
Baptistry
PIAZZA SAN GIOVANNI
VIALE XXIV MAGGIO
VIA DEI FUSARI
Palazzo del Magnifico
CASATO DI SOTTO
VIA DI CITTÀ
Duomo
PIAZZA JACOPO DELLA QUERCIA
PIAZZA DEL MERCATO
VIA GIOVANNI DUPRÉ
PIAZZETTA DELLA SELVA
PIAZZA DEL DUOMO
VIA DEL CASTORO
Museo dell'Opera Metropolitana
VIA ESTERNA DI FONTEBRANDA
VIA DEL CAPITANO
Santa Maria della Scala
TERZO DI CITTÀ
CASATO DI SOPRA
VIA SAN PIETRO
Pinacoteca Nazionale
San Giuseppe
VIA DI STALLOREGGI
San Pietro alle Scale
VIA PAOLO MASCAGNI
VIA DI CASTELVECCHIO
CASTELVECCHIO
VIA DI S. QUIRICO
VIA TOMMASO PENDOLA
VIA S. AGATA
PIANO DEI MANTELLINI
Sant'Agostino
VIA DEL LATERINO
Porta Laterina
VIA DELLE CERCHIA
Botanical Gardens
Santa Maria del Carmine
VIA DELLA DIANA
VIA SAN MARCO
VIA DELLE SPERANDIE
VIA PIER ANDREA

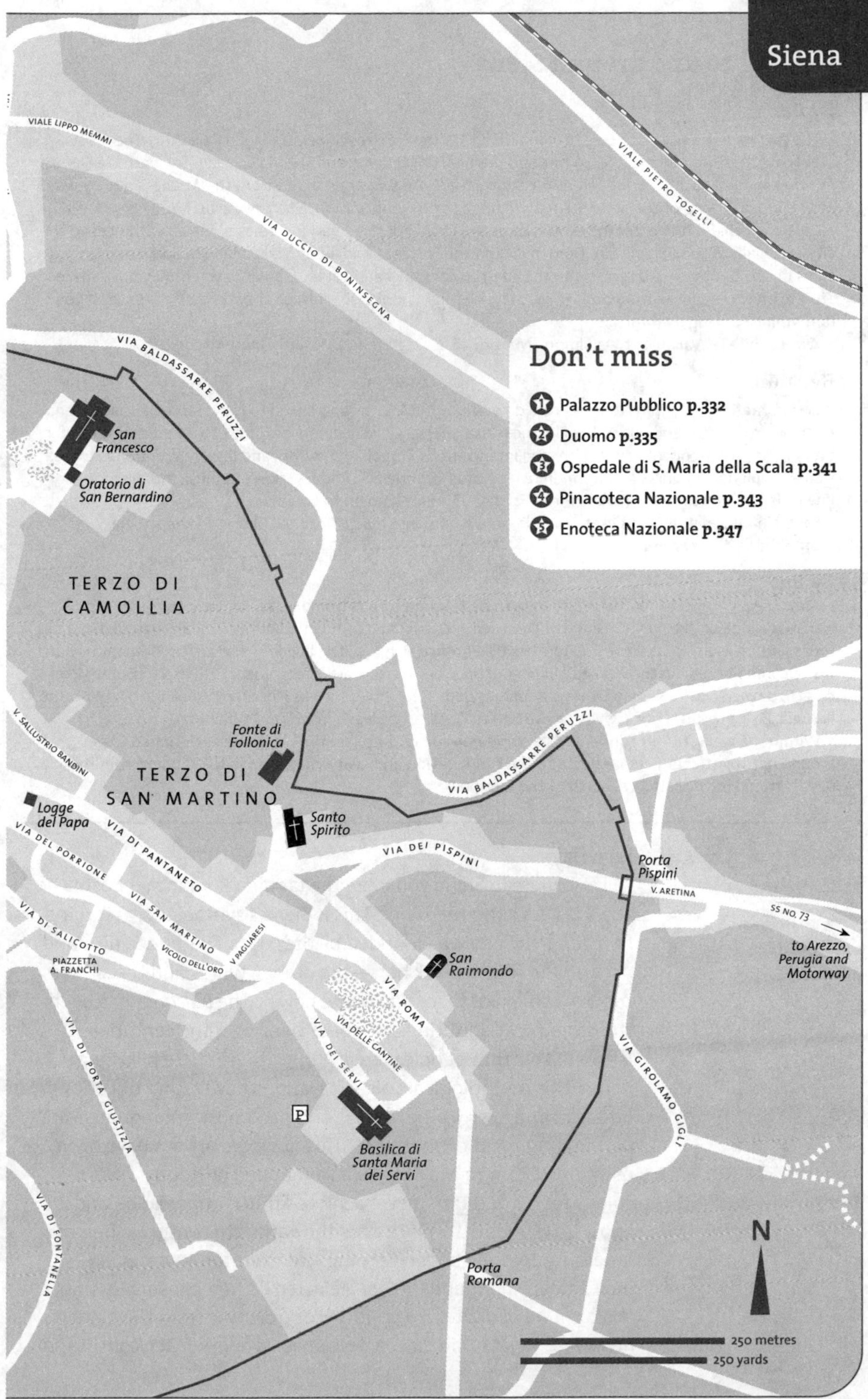

Don't miss
1 Palazzo Pubblico p.332
2 Duomo p.335
3 Ospedale di S. Maria della Scala p.341
4 Pinacoteca Nazionale p.343
5 Enoteca Nazionale p.347
VIALE LIPPO MEMMI
VIALE PIETRO TOSELLI
VIA DUCCIO DI BONINSEGNA
VIA BALDASSARRE PERUZZI
San Francesco
Oratorio di San Bernardino
TERZO DI CAMOLLIA
Fonte di Follonica
TERZO DI SAN MARTINO
V. SALLUSTRIO BANDINI
Logge del Papa
Santo Spirito
VIA DEL PORRIONE
VIA DI PANTANETO
VIA DEI PISPINI
Porta Pispini
V. ARETINA
SS NO. 73
to Arezzo, Perugia and Motorway
VIA SAN MARTINO
VIA DI SALICOTTO
VICOLO DELL'ORO
V. PAGLIARESI
PIAZZETTA A. FRANCHI
San Raimondo
VIA ROMA
VIA DELLE CANTINE
VIA DEI SERVI
VIA DI PORTA GIUSTIZIA
VIA GIROLAMO GIGLI
P
Basilica di Santa Maria dei Servi
VIA DI FONTANELLA
Porta Romana
N
250 metres
250 yards

Getting to and around Siena

By Car

The fastest route from Florence to Siena (68km) is the toll-free Superstrada del Palio (1hr). The most scenic are the Chiantigiana (SS222) through the heart of Chianti, and the Via Cassia (SS2); both weave amidst the hills. Both take 2hrs. From the south, there are two approaches from the A1: the SS326 by way of Sinalunga (50km) or the more scenic, winding SS73 by way of Monte Sansovino (44km).

Cars are forbidden to enter the centre; there are clearly defined **parking areas** along all entrances to the city, especially around Piazza San Domenico and the Fortezza and along Viale dello Stadio. Computerized signs on the approaches direct you to the city-run car parks and garages, and tell you if they have spaces. They're pretty expensive, especially if you stay overnight; look out for free car parks along the way if you don't mind walking a bit further.

Avis **car hire** is available at Via Simone Martini 36, **t** 0577 270305, *www.avisautonoleggio.it*.

By Train

Siena's **station** is 1.5km from the centre down Viale G. Mazzini, and linked to it by frequent buses. Siena's main line runs from Empoli (on the Florence–Pisa line) to Chiusi (Florence–Rome). There are trains roughly every hour, with frequent connections to Florence from Empoli (97km/1hr), and less frequent ones to Pisa from Empoli (125km/2hrs), and from Chiusi towards Umbria and Rome (65km to Chiusi, 1hr). A secondary line runs towards Grosseto (70km/1hr) – 8 a day, of which 3 go on to Orbetello.

For train information and tickets, call **t** 892021 (*www.trenitalia.it*), or try Il Carroccio agency, Via Montanini 73, **t** 0577 226964.

By Bus

Almost every town in southern Tuscany can be reached by bus from Piazza San Domenico, the big transport node on the western edge of Siena, with tourist and hotel info booths. A board has all departure times and the exact location of the stop; the ticket office is in the little building next to San Domenico church.

The company serving the whole of Siena province is TRA-IN, Viale F. Tozzi, just north of San Domenico, **t** 0577 204111, *www.trainspa.it*, Other companies depart for cities such as Florence (about 1hr; also to Rome, Perugia, Pisa, etc.; SITA, **t** 055 47821, *www.sitabus.it*). All buses leave from San Domenico.

Within the walls, TRA-IN runs a service using *pollicini* or 'Tom Thumbs': little buses designed to get around narrow streets. Regular buses to the train station and everywhere else in the modern suburbs depart from Piazza Matteotti, north of the Campo.

History

Everywhere in Siena you'll see the familiar Roman symbol of the she-wolf suckling the twins. This is Siena's symbol too; according to legend, the city was founded by the sons of Remus, Senius and Ascius. One rode a black horse, the other a white, and the simple *comunal* shield of black and white halves (the *balzana*) has been the other most enduring symbol of Siena over the centuries. It is most likely that people were living on these three hills long before this mythological pair; excavations have found traces of Etruscan and even Celtic habitation. The almost impregnable site, dominating most of southern Tuscany, would always have been of interest. Roman-era *Sena Julia*, refounded by Augustus as a colony for his veterans, never achieved much importance, and we know little about the place until the early 12th century, when the emerging *comune* began keeping written records. In 1125, an increasingly independent Siena elected its first consuls. By 1169, the *comune* had wrested political control away from the bishop, and some 10 years later Siena developed its own written constitution.

The political development of the city is complex, with good reason. Twelfth-century Siena was a booming new city: having control over its rich countryside, supplying some of the best wool in Italy, helped start an important cloth industry, and a small silver mine, acquired from Volterra in the 1160s, provided seed capital for what became one of the leading banking towns of Europe. Like so many other Italian cities, Siena was able early on to force its troublesome rural nobles to live within its walls, where they built scores of tall defence towers, fought pitched battles in the streets and usually kept the city divided into armed camps; in the narrowest part of the city, the *comune* once had to lay out new streets parallel to Via Camollia because of one particularly boisterous nobleman whose palace most Sienese were afraid to pass. Yet Siena was never completely able to bring its titled hoodlums under control. The businessmen made the money, and gradually formed their city into a sophisticated self-governing republic, but the nobles held on to many of their privileges for centuries, giving an anachronistically feudal tinge to Siena's life and art.

Like its brawling neighbours, medieval Siena enjoyed looking for trouble; in the endless wars of the 13th century, they never had to look far. Originally a Guelph town, Siena changed sides early to avoid being in the same camp with arch-rival Florence. With Pisa, Siena carried the Ghibelline banner through the Tuscan wars with varying fortunes. Its finest hour came in 1260, when a Florentine herald arrived with the demand that Siena demolish its walls and deliver up its large population of Ghibelline exiles from Florence; if they didn't, the armies of Florence and the entire Guelph League – 40,000 men – were waiting outside to raze the city to the ground. The Sienese determined to resist. They threw the keys of the city on the altar of the as yet unfinished cathedral, dedicating Siena to the Virgin Mary (a custom they have repeated ever since when the city is endangered, most recently just before the battle for liberation in 1944). In the morning they marched out to the **battle of Monteaperti** and beat the Florentines so badly they captured their *carroccio*.

After the battle, Siena had Florence at her mercy and, naturally, was anxious to level the city and scatter the ground with salt. One of the famous episodes in the *Inferno* relates how the Florentine exiles, who made up a large part of the Sienese forces, refused to allow it. Unfortunately for Siena, within a few years Florence and the Tuscan Guelphs had the situation back under control and Siena never again came so close to dominating Tuscan affairs. Yet the city was a constant headache to Florence for the next three centuries.

When things were quiet at the front, the Sienese settled for bashing each other. The constant stream of anti-Siena propaganda in Dante isn't just Florentine bile; medieval Siena earned its reputation for violence and contentiousness. The impressive forms and rituals of the Sienese Republic were a façade concealing endless pointless struggles between the factions of the elite. Early on, Siena's merchants and nobles divided themselves into five *monti*, syndicates of self-interest that worked like political parties only without any pretence of principle. At one point, this Tuscan banana republic had 10 constitutions in 27 years, and more often than not its political affairs were settled in the streets. Before the Palio, Siena's favourite civic sport was the *Gioco del Pugno*, a 300-a-side fistfight in the Campo. Sometimes tempers flared and the boys would bring out the axes and crossbows.

Siena's Golden Age

For all its troubles and bad intentions, Siena often ran city business disinterestedly and with intelligence. An intangible factor of civic pride always made the Sienese do the right thing when something important was at hand, such as battling the Florentines or selecting a new artist to work on the cathedral. The battle of Monteaperti was a disappointment territorially but inaugurated the most brilliant period of Sienese culture, and saw the transformation of the hilltop fortress town into today's beautiful city.

In 1287, under pressure from the Guelphs and their Angevin protectors, Siena actually allied itself with Florence and instituted a new form of government: the '**Council of the Nine**'. Excluding nobles from office, as Florence would do six years later, the Rule of the Nine lasted until 1355, and gave Siena a more stable regime than at any other period. Business was better than ever. The city's bankers came to rival Florence's, with offices in all the trading

Ancient Rivals

Few rivalries have been more enduring than that between Florence and Siena. Long ago, while Florence was off at university busily studying her optics and geometry, Lady Siena spent her time dancing and dropping her scarf for knights at the tournament. Florence thought she had the last laugh in 1555, when Duke Cosimo and his black-hearted Spanish pals wiped out the Sienese Republic and put this proud maiden in chains. It's frustrating enough today, though, when Florence looks up in the hills and sees Siena, an unfaded beauty with a faraway smile, sitting in her tower like the Lady of Shalott.

For two towns built by bankers and wool tycoons, they could not have less in common. Siena may not possess an Uffizi or a David, but nor does it have to bear the marble antimacassars and general stuffiness of its sister on the Arno, nor her smog, traffic, tourist hordes and suburban squalor. Florence never goes over the top. Siena loves to, especially around the race of the Palio, the wildest party in Tuscany, a worthy successor to the fabulous masques and carnivals, bullfights and bloody free-for-alls of the Sienese Middle Ages. In fact, Florence has clicked its tongue at Siena since the time of Dante, who refers sarcastically in his *Inferno* to a famous club, the *Brigata*, made up of 12 noble Sienese youths who put up 250,000 florins for a year of nightly feasting; every night they had three sumptuously laid tables, one for eating, one for drinking and the third to throw out the window.

But there's more to Siena than that. This is a city with its own artistic tradition (*see* p.26); in the 1300s, Sienese painters gave lessons to the Florentines. Always more decorative, less intellectual than Florence, Siena fell behind in the quattrocento, but by then the greatest achievement of Sienese art was nearing completion – Siena herself.

centres and capitals of Europe. A sustained peace, and increasing cultural contacts with France and Naples, brought new ideas and influences into Siena's art and architecture, in time to embellish massive new building programmes such as the **cathedral** (begun in 1186 but not substantially completed until the 1380s) and **Palazzo Pubblico** (1295–1310). Beginning with Duccio di Buoninsegna (1260–1319), Sienese artists explored new concepts in painting and sculpture and, through the 1300s, contributed as much as or more than the Florentines in laying the foundations for the Renaissance. Contemporary records show an obsession on the part of bankers and merchants with decorating Siena and impressing outsiders.

At its height, in the early 14th century, Siena ruled most of southern Tuscany. The very pinnacle of civic pride and ambition came in 1339, with the fantastical plan to expand the still-unfinished cathedral into the largest in Christendom. The walls of that effort, a nave that would have been longer than St Peter's in Rome, stand as a monument to the event that snapped off Siena's career in full bloom. The **Black Death** of 1348 carried off a third of the population – a death toll perhaps no greater than in some other Italian cities, but it struck Siena at a moment when its economy was vulnerable, and started a decline that continued for centuries. Economic strife led to political instability, and in 1355 a revolt of the nobles, egged on by Emperor Charles IV, then in Tuscany, overthrew the Council of the Nine. In 1371, seven years before the Ciompi revolt in Florence, the wool workers staged a genuine revolution. Organized as a trade union of sorts, the **Compagnia del Bruco** seized the Palazzo Pubblico and instituted a government with greater popular representation.

The decades that followed saw Siena devote more and more of its diminishing resources to buying off the marauding mercenary companies that infested much of Italy. By 1399 the city was in such dire straits it surrendered independence to **Giangaleazzo Visconti**, tyrant of Milan, who was attempting to surround and conquer Florence. After his death, Siena reclaimed its freedom. Political confusion continued through the century, with only two periods of relative stability. One came with the pontificate (1458–63) of Pius II, the great Sienese scholar **Aeneas Silvius Piccolomini**, who exerted a dominating influence over his native city while he ruled at Rome. In 1487, a nobleman named **Pandolfo Petrucci** took over the government; as an honest broker, regulating the often murderous ambitions of the *monti*, he and his sons kept control until 1524.

The Fall of the Republic

Florence, always waiting in the wings to swallow Siena, had its chance in the 1500s. The real villain of the piece, however, was not Florence but that most imperious emperor, **Charles V**. After the fall of the Petrucci, factional struggles resumed immediately, with frequent assassinations and riots, and constitutions changing with the spring fashions. Charles, who had bigger prey in his sights, cared little for the fate of the perverse little republic; he feared, though, that its disorders, religious tolerance and wretched finances were diseases that might spread. In 1530, he took advantage of riots in the city to install an imperial garrison. Yet even the emperor's representatives, usually Spaniards, could not keep Siena from sliding further into anarchy and bankruptcy several times, largely thanks to Charles's war taxes. Cultural life was stifled as the Spaniards introduced the Inquisition and the Index. Scholars and artists fled, while poverty and political disruptions meant that Siena's once-proud university ceased to function.

In 1550, Charles announced he was going to build a fortress within the city walls, for which the Sienese were going to pay. Realizing that the trifling liberty still left to them would soon be extinguished, the Sienese ruling class began intrigues with Charles' great enemy, France. A French army, led by a Piccolomini, arrived in July 1552. Inside the walls the people revolted and locked the Spanish garrison in its own new fortress. The empire was slow to react but, inevitably, in late 1554, a huge force of imperial troops, along with those of Florence, entered Sienese territory. The siege was prosecuted with remarkable brutality by Charles's commander, the **marquis of Marignano**, who laid waste much of the Sienese countryside, tortured prisoners and even hired agents to start fires inside the walls. After a brave resistance, led by a republican Florentine exile, **Piero Strozzi**, and assisted by France, Siena was starved into surrender in April 1555. Two years later, Charles's son Philip II sold Siena to Duke Cosimo of Florence and the republic was consumed by the new Grand Duchy of Tuscany.

If nothing else, Siena went out with a flourish. After its capture, some 2,000 republican bitter-enders escaped to make a last stand at Montalcino. Declaring 'Where the *Comune* is, there is the City', they established the world's first republican government-in-exile. With control over much of the old Sienese territory, the '**Republic of Siena at Montalcino**' held out against the Medici for four years.

With independence lost and a ruined economy, Siena withdrew. For centuries there was no recovery, little art or scholarship, and no movements towards reform. The aristocracy, decayed into a parasitic *rentier* class, made its peace with the Medici dukes early on; in return for their support, the Medici let them keep much of their power and privileges. The once-great capital of trade and finance shrank rapidly into an overbuilt farmers' market, its population dropping from a 14th-century high of 60–80,000 to around 15,000 by the 1700s. This explains largely why medieval and Renaissance Siena is so well preserved – nothing happened to change it.

By the Age of Enlightenment, with its disparaging of everything medieval, the Sienese seem to have forgotten their own history and art, so it is no surprise that the rest of Europe forgot them too. During the first years of the Grand Tour, no self-respecting northern European so much as considered visiting Siena. It was not until the 1830s that it was rediscovered, with the help of literati such as the Brownings, who spent several summers here, and later that truly Gothic American, Henry James. The Sienese were not far behind in rediscovering it themselves. The civic pride that had lain dormant for centuries yawned and stretched like Sleeping Beauty and went diligently back to work.

Before the 19th century was out, everything that could still be salvaged of the city's ancient glory was refurbished and restored. More than ever fascinated by its own image and eccentricities, and more than ever without any kind of economic base, Siena was ready for its present career as a cultural attraction, a tourist town.

Orientation: *Terzi* and the *Contrade*

The centre of Siena (population 59,000) , the site of the Palio and, importantly to the Sienese, the 'farthest point from the world outside', is the piazza called **Il Campo**. The city unfolds from it like a three-petalled flower along three ridges. It has been a natural division since medieval times, with the oldest quarter, the **Terzo di Città**, to the southwest; the **Terzo di San Martino**, to the southeast; and the **Terzo di Camollia**, to the north.

Siena is tiny, covering little more than 2.5 square kilometres. The density, and especially the hills, make it seem much bigger when you're walking. There are no short cuts across the valleys between the three *terzi*. There are few cars in the centre, but taxis and motorbikes will occasionally try to run you down.

Contrade

The Sienese have taken the *contrade* – the 17 neighbourhoods into which Siena is divided – for granted for so long that their history is almost impossible to trace. Like the *rioni* of Rome, the *contrade* were the original wards of the ancient city – not merely geographical boundaries but self-governing entities; the ancients with their long racial memories often referred to them as the city's 'tribes'. In Siena, the *contrade* survived and prospered through classical times and the Middle Ages, maintaining the city's traditions and sense of identity through the dark years after 1552. Incredibly, they're still here now, unique in Italy and perhaps all Europe. Once Siena counted more than 60 *contrade*. Now there are 17, each with a sort of totem animal for its symbol, ranging from a snail to a dragon. Sienese and Italian law recognize these as legally chartered communities.

The Palio

The thousands of tourists who come twice a year to see the Palio, Siena's famous horse race around the Campo, probably think the Sienese are doing it purely for their benefit. Yet, like the *contrade* that contest it, the Palio is an essential aspect of Sienese culture, as significant to the city today as it was centuries ago. Here are the plain facts on Italy's best-known annual festival.

The oldest recorded Palio was run in 1283, though no one knows how far the custom goes back. During the Middle Ages, besides the horse races there were violent street battles, bloody games of primeval rugby and even bullfights. (Bullfights were also common in Rome and there's an argument to be made that Italy is actually the place where the Spaniards got the idea, back in the 16th and 17th centuries when Spain's own medieval passion for such things was all but forgotten.) At present, the course comprises three laps around the periphery of the Campo, although in the past the race has been known to take in some of the city's main streets.

The *palio* (Latin *pallium*) is an embroidered banner offered as a prize to the winning *contrade*. Two races are held each year, on 2 July and 16 August, and the *palio* of each is decorated with an image of the Virgin Mary; after political violence, the city's greatest passion has always been Mariolatry. The course has room for only 10 horses per race, so some of the 17 *contrade* are chosen by lot each race so they all have a fair chance. The horses, too, are selected by lot, but the *contrade* select their own jockeys.

Though the race itself lasts only 90 seconds, an hour or two of pageantry precedes it; the famous flag-throwers or *alfieri* of each participating *contrada* put on dazzling shows, while the medieval *carroccio*, drawn by a yoke of white oxen, circles the Campo, bearing the prized *palio* itself.

The Palio is no joke; baskets of money ride on each race, not to mention the sacred honour of the district. To obtain divine favour, each *contrada* brings its horse into its chapel on race morning for a special blessing (and if a little horse manure drops during the ceremony, it's taken as a sign of good luck). The only rule stipulates that you can't seize the reins of an opponent. There are no rules against bribing opposing jockeys, making alliances with other *contrade* or ambushing jockeys before the race.

The course around the Campo has two right angles. Anything can happen; recent Palii have featured not only jockeys but *horses* flying through the air at the turns. The Sienese say no one has ever been killed at a Palio. There's no reason to believe them. They wouldn't believe it themselves, but it is an article of faith among the Sienese that fatalities are prevented by special intervention of the Virgin Mary. The post-Palio carousing, while not up to medieval standards, is still impressive; in the winning *contrada* the party might go on for days on end, while the losers shed bitter tears.

No event in Italy is as infectiously exhilarating as the Palio. There are two ways to see it, either from the centre of the Campo, packed tight and always very hot, or from an expensive (€130–260) seat in a viewing stand, but book well in advance if you want one of these. Several travel agencies offer special Palio tours (*see* pp.69–70); otherwise make sure you book by April.

Today a *contrada* functions as a combination of social-and-dining club, neighbourhood improvement association, religious confraternity and mutual assistance fund. Each *contrada* elects its own officials annually in May. Each has its own chapel, museum and fountain, its own flag and colours, and its own patron saint, who pulls all the strings he can in Heaven twice a year to help his beloved district win the Palio.

Sociologists, not only in Italy, are becoming ever-more intrigued by this ancient yet very useful system, with its built-in community solidarity and tacit social control. (Siena has almost no crime and no social problems, except a lack of jobs.) The *contrade* probably function much as they did in Roman or medieval times, but it's surprising just what up-to-date, progressive, adaptable institutions they can be, and they are still changing today. Anyone born in a *contrada* area, for example, is automatically a member; besides their baptism into the Church, they receive a sort of 'baptism' into the *contrada*, conducted in the pretty new fountains constructed all over Siena in recent years as centrepieces for the neighbourhoods.

The best place to learn more about the *contrade* is one of the 17 little *contrada* museums; the tourist office (see p.348) has a list of addresses (most ask visitors to contact them a week in advance), plus details of the annual *contrada* festivals and other shows and dinners they are wont to put on; visitors are always very welcome.

Walking in Siena

If you keep your eyes open while walking the backstreets of Siena, you'll see the city's entire history laid out for you in signs, symbols and scores of other clues. Little ceramic plaques with the *contrada* symbol appear on buildings and street corners, not to mention flags in the neighbourhood colours, bumper stickers on cars and fountains, each with a modern sculptural work, usually representing the *contrada*'s animal.

Look for the coats of arms of nobles above doorways; aristocratic, archaic Siena has more of these than almost any Italian city. In many cases, they are still the homes of the original families, and often the same device is on a dozen houses on one block, a reminder of how medieval Siena was largely divided into separate compounds, each under the protection (or intimidation) of a noble family. One common symbol is formed from the letters IHS in a radiant sun: Siena's famous 15th-century preacher, San Bernardino, was always pestering nobles to forget their contentiousness and vanity, and proposed that they replace their heraldic symbols with the monogram of Christ. The limited success his idealism met with can be read on the buildings of Siena today.

They don't take down old signs in Siena. One, dated 1641, informs prostitutes that the Most Serene Prince Matthias (the Florentine governor) forbids them to live on his street (Via di Salicotto). Another, a huge 19th-century marble plaque on the Banchi di Sotto, reminds passers-by that 'in this house, before modern restorations reclaimed it from squalidness, was born Giovanni Caselli, inventor of the pantograph'. A favourite, found on Via del Giglio, announces a stroke of the rope and a 16-lira fine for anyone throwing trash in the street, with proceeds to go to the accuser.

The Campo

There is no lovelier square in Tuscany, and none more beloved by its city. The Forum of ancient *Sena Julia* was on this spot, and in the Middle Ages it evolved into its present fan shape. The Campo was paved with brick as early as 1340; the nine sections into which the fan is divided are in honour of the Council of the Nine, rulers of the city at the time. Thousands crowd over the bricks every year to see the Palio run on the periphery.

For a worthy embellishment to their Campo, the Sienese commissioned for its curved north end the **Fonte Gaia** from Jacopo della Quercia, their greatest sculptor, who worked on it from 1408 to 1419, creating the broad rectangle of marble with reliefs of Adam and Eve and allegorical virtues. It was to be the opening salvo of Siena's Renaissance, an answer to the baptistry doors of Ghiberti in Florence (for which Della Quercia himself had been a contestant). What you see now is an uninspired copy from 1868; the badly eroded original is up on the loggia of the Palazzo Pubblico.

The republic always made sure each part of the city had access to good water; medieval Siena created the most elaborate engineering works since ancient Rome to bring the water in. Fonte Gaia, and others such as Fontebranda, are fed by underground aqueducts that stretch for miles across the Tuscan countryside. Charles V, when he visited the city, is reported to have said that Siena is 'even more marvellous underground than it is on the surface'.

The original Fonte Gaia was completed in the early 1300s; there's a story that soon after, some Sienese citizens dug up a beautiful Greek statue of Venus signed by Praxiteles himself. The delighted Sienese carried it in procession through the city and installed it on top of their new fountain. With the devastation of the Black Death, however, the preachers were quick to blame God's wrath on the indecent pagan on the Fonte Gaia. Throughout history, the Sienese have been ready to be shocked by their own sins; in this case, with their neighbours dropping like flies around them, they proved only too eager to make poor Venus the scapegoat – they chopped her into little bits, and a party of Sienese disguised as peasants smuggled the pieces over the border and buried them in Florentine territory to pass the bad luck on to their enemies.

Palazzo Pubblico

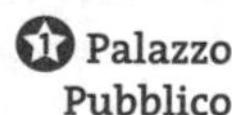

Palazzo Pubblico

Torre di Mangia
open mid-Mar–June, Sept and Oct daily 10–7; July and Aug daily 10am–11pm; Nov–mid-Mar daily 10–4; adm; joint adm available with Musei Comunali, *see opposite*

If the Campo is like a Roman theatre, the main attraction on stage since 1310 has been the brick and stone **Palazzo Pubblico**, the enduring symbol of the Sienese Republic and still the town hall. Its façade is the face of Siena's history, with the she-wolf of Senius and Ascanius, Medici balls, the IHS of San Bernardino, and squared Guelph crenellations, all in the shadow of the **Torre di Mangia**, the graceful, needle-like tower Henry James called 'Siena's Declaration of Independence'. At 101m, the tower was the second-tallest raised in medieval Italy (behind the campanile in Cremona). At the time, the cathedral tower on its hill dominated Siena's skyline; the Council of the Nine wouldn't accept that the symbol of religious authority or any of the nobility's fortress-skyscrapers should be taller than the symbol of the republic, so its Perugian architects, Muccio and Francesco di Rinaldo, made sure it would be hard to beat. There was a practical side to it, too. At the top hung the *comune*'s great bell, which had to be heard in every corner of the city tolling the hours and announcing the curfew, or calling citizens to assemble in case of war or emergency. One of the first bell-ringers gave the tower its name: fat, sleepy Mangiaguadagni ('eat the profits'), Mangia for short; there is a statue of him in one of the courtyards. Climb the tower's endless staircase for the definitive view of Siena – on the clearest days, you'll see about half of the medieval republic's territory. At the foot of the tower, the marble **Cappella della Piazza**, with its graceful rounded arches, stands out clearly from the Gothic earnestness of the rest of the building. It was begun in 1352, in thanks for deliverance from the Black Death, but not completed until the mid 15th century.

Musei Comunali
open mid-Mar–Oct daily 10–7; Nov–mid-Mar daily 10–6.30; 26 Nov–mid-Feb daily 10–5.30; 23 Dec–6 Jan daily 10–6.30; adm; joint 2-day adm available with Palazzo delle Papesse, *see p.335,* *and Ospedale di Santa Maria della Scala,* *see p.341*

Most of the Palazzo's ground floor is still city offices, but the upper floors house the city museum, the **Musei Comunali**. Here the main attraction is the state rooms done in frescoes, a sampling of the best of Sienese art throughout the centuries. First, though, come the historical frescoes in the **Sala del Risorgimento**, done by A.G. Cassioli in 1886: the meeting of Vittorio Emanuele II with Garibaldi, his coronation, portraits, epigrams of past patriots and an 'allegory of Italian Liberty', all in a colourful, photographically precise style. Next, on the same floor, the **Sala di Balia** has frescoes depicting the life of Alessandro VII, vigorous battle scenes by the Sienese Spinello Aretino (1300s) and the *Sixteen Virtues* by Martino di Bartolomeo. The adjoining **Anticamera del Concistoro** has a lovely *Madonna and Child* by Matteo di Giovanni. In the **Sala del Concistoro**, Gobelin tapestries adorn the walls, while the great Sienese Mannerist Beccafumi contributed a ceiling of frescoes in the 1530s celebrating the political virtues of antiquity; that theme is continued in the **vestibule to the chapel**, with portraits of ancient heroes from Cicero to Judas Maccabeus, all by Taddeo di Bartolo. These portrayals, plus more portraits of the classical gods and goddesses and an interesting view of ancient Rome, bear witness to a real fascination with antiquity even in the 1300s. Intruding among the classical crew is a king-sized St Christopher covering an entire wall; before setting out on a journey, it was good luck to catch a glimpse of this saint, and in Italy and Spain he is often extra large so you won't miss him. In a display case in the hall, some of the oldest treasures of the Sienese Republic are kept: the war helmet of the Captain of the People, and a delicate **golden rose**, a gift to the city from the Sienese Pope, Pius II.

The chapel (**Cappella del Consiglio**) is surrounded by a lovely wrought-iron grille by Jacopo della Quercia; when it is open, you can see more frescoes by Taddeo di Bartolo, an altarpiece by

Il Sodoma and exceptional carved wood seats by Domenico di Nicolò (*c.* 1415–28). In the adjacent chamber (**Sala del Mappamondo**), only the outline is left of Lorenzetti's cosmological fresco, a diagram of the universe including all the celestial and angelic spheres, much like the one in the Campo Santo at Pisa. Above it is a very famous fresco by Simone Martini (*c.* 1330), showing the redoubtable *condottiere* **Guidoriccio da Fogliano** on his way to attack the castle of Montemassi, during a revolt against Siena. Also by Martini is an enthroned Virgin or *Maestà*, believed to be his earliest work (1315).

The Allegories of Good and Bad Government

When you enter the **Sala dei Nove** (or Sala della Pace), meeting room of the Council of the Nine, you understand at a glance why they ruled Siena so well. Whenever one of the councillors had the temptation to skim some cream off the top, or pass a fat contract over to his brother-in-law, or tighten the screws on the poor by raising the salt tax, he had only to look up at Ambrogio Lorenzetti's great frescoes to feel like a worm. There are two complementary sets, with scenes of Siena under good government and bad, and allegorical councils of virtues or vices for each. Enthroned Justice rules the good Siena, with such counsellors as Peace, Prudence and Magnanimity; bad Siena groans under the thumb of one nasty piece of work, sneering, fanged Tyranny and his cronies: Pride, Vainglory, Avarice and Wrath, among others. The good Siena is a happy place, with buildings in good repair, well-dressed folk dancing in the streets, and well-stocked shops. Bad Siena is almost a mirror image, only the effects of the Tyrant's rule are plain to see: urban blight, crime in broad daylight, buildings crumbling, and business bad for everybody – a landscape that for many of us modern city-dwellers will seem all too familiar. Lorenzetti finished his work, probably the most ambitious secular painting attempted up to that time, around 1338. Fittingly, Good Government has survived more or less intact, while Bad Government has not aged so well and parts have been lost.

In the next room is Guido da Siena's large *Madonna and Child* (mid 1200s), the earliest masterpiece of the Sienese school. If you're not up to climbing the tower, take the long, unmarked stairway by the Sala del Risorgimento up to the **loggia**, with the second-best view over Siena and disassembled pieces of Della Quercia's reliefs from the Fonte Gaia, worn and damaged.

Around the Campo

Part of the Campo's beauty lies in the element of surprise; one usually enters from narrow arcades between the medieval palaces that give no hint of what lies on the other side. Two of Siena's three main streets form a graceful curve around the back of the Campo;

where they meet the third, behind the Fonte Gaia, is the corner the Sienese call the **Croce del Travaglio** (a mysterious nickname: the 'Cross of Affliction'). Here, the three-arched **Loggia della Mercanzia**, in a sense Siena's Royal Exchange, was where the republic's merchants made their deals and settled their differences before the city's famed commercial tribunal. The Loggia marks the transition from Sienese-Gothic to early Renaissance style – begun in 1417, it was probably influenced by Florence's Loggia dei Lanzi. The five statues of saints on the columns are the work of Antonio Federighi and Vecchietta, the leading Sienese sculptors after Della Quercia.

The three streets that meet here lead directly into the three *terzi* of Siena. All three are among the city's most beautiful, in particular the gracefully curving **Banchi di Sotto**, main artery of the Terzo di San Martino. Just beyond the Campo, this street passes Siena's most imposing *palazzo privato*, the **Palazzo Piccolomini**, done in the Florentine style by Rossellino in the 1460s. This palace houses the old **Sienese state archive** – not a place you might consider visiting but for the presence of the famous *Tavolette della Biccherna* (the account books of the Biccherna or state treasury). From the 1200s, the republic commissioned the best local artists to decorate the covers of the *tavolette*, portraying such prosaic subjects as medieval citizens coming to pay their taxes, city employees counting their pay and earnest monks trying to make the figures square. Among other manuscripts and documents are Boccaccio's will.

Palazzo Piccolomini
state archive open Mon–Sat 10–12.30 and 3–6; adm

Terzo di Città

Southwest from the Croce del Travaglio, Via di Città climbs up to the highest and oldest part of Siena, the natural fortress of the Terzo di Città. Among the palaces that it passes is the grandiose **Palazzo Chigi-Saracini**, home to internationally important music school, the Accademia Musicale Chigiana, and a large collection of Sienese and Florentine art .

Palazzo Chigi-Saracini
open to public limited times of year; call **t** *0577 246928 for info*

Next door is yet another reminder of the Piccolomini, the **Palazzo delle Papesse**, now home to the **Centro Arte Contemporanea**, with permanent and changing exhibitions of modern works. The Piccolomini family, along with the Colonna of Rome and Correr of Venice, was one of the first to really exploit the fiscal possibilities of the papacy; Aeneas Silvius (Pius II) built this palace, also designed by Rossellino, for his sister, Caterina.

Centro Arte Contemporanea
t *0577 22071; Via di Città 126; open Tues–Sun 11–7; adm; joint 2-day adm available with Musei Comunali,* see *p.333**, and Santa Maria della Scala,* see *p.341*

The Duomo

Duomo
open summer daily 10–12.45 and 4–6.30, winter Mon–Sat 10–12.45, Sun 10–12.45 and 3.30–6; adm

All approaches from Via di Città to Siena's glorious cathedral, spilling over the highest point in the city, are oblique. Easiest, perhaps, is Via dei Pellegrini, which winds around the back, past the unusual crypt-baptistry tucked underneath (*see* p.341), up the steps to the Piazza del Duomo, and through a portal in a huge, freestanding wall of striped marble arches, a memorial to that incredible ill-starred 1339 rebuilding plan confounded by the Plague. The cathedral the Sienese had to settle for may not be a transcendent expression of faith, and it may not be a landmark in architecture, but it is one of the most delightful, decorative ornaments in Christendom.

Begun around 1200, and one of the first Gothic cathedrals in central Italy, it started in the good medieval tradition as a communal effort, not really a project of the Church. There doesn't seem to have been much voluntary labour – even in the Middle Ages, Italians were too blasé for that – but every citizen with a cart was expected to bring two loads of marble from the quarries each year, earning him an indulgence from the bishop. One load must have been white and the other black for, under the influence of Pisa, the Sienese built themselves one thoroughly striped cathedral – stripes darker and bolder than Pisa's or even Pistoia's. The campanile, with its distinctive fenestration, narrowing in size down six levels, rises over the city like a giant ice-cream parfait. Most of the body of the church was finished by 1270; 14 years later, Giovanni Pisano was called in to create the sculpture for the lavish **façade**, with statues of biblical prophets and pagan philosophers. The upper half was not begun until the 1390s and the glittering mosaics in the gables are, like Orvieto's, the work of Venetian artists of the late 19th century.

The Cathedral Interior: the Marble Pavement

This is a virtual treasure box, fit to keep a serious sightseer busy for an entire day. Inside the main portal, the ferociously striped pilasters and Gothic vaulting, a blue firmament painted with golden stars, draw the eye upwards. The most spectacular feature, though, is at your feet – the marble pavement, where the first peculiar figure smiling up at you is **Hermes Trismegistus** (*see* p.338), legendary Egyptian father of alchemy, depicted in elegant *sgraffito* work of white and coloured marble. In fact, the entire floor of the cathedral is covered with almost 12,000 square metres of virtuoso *sgraffito* in 56 scenes, including portraits, mystical allegories and Old Testament scenes. Like the Biccherna covers in the Palazzo Piccolomini, they were a tradition carried on over centuries. Many of Siena's best artists worked on them, from 1369 into the 1600s; Vasari claimed that Duccio di Buoninsegna himself first worked in this medium, though he has none among the pictures here.

Even in a building with so many marvels – the Piccolomini Library, Nicola Pisano's pulpit, Duccio's stained glass, works by Donatello, Della Quercia, Pinturicchio, Michelangelo, Bernini and many others – this pavement takes pride of place. The greatest limitation of

Siena Cathedral

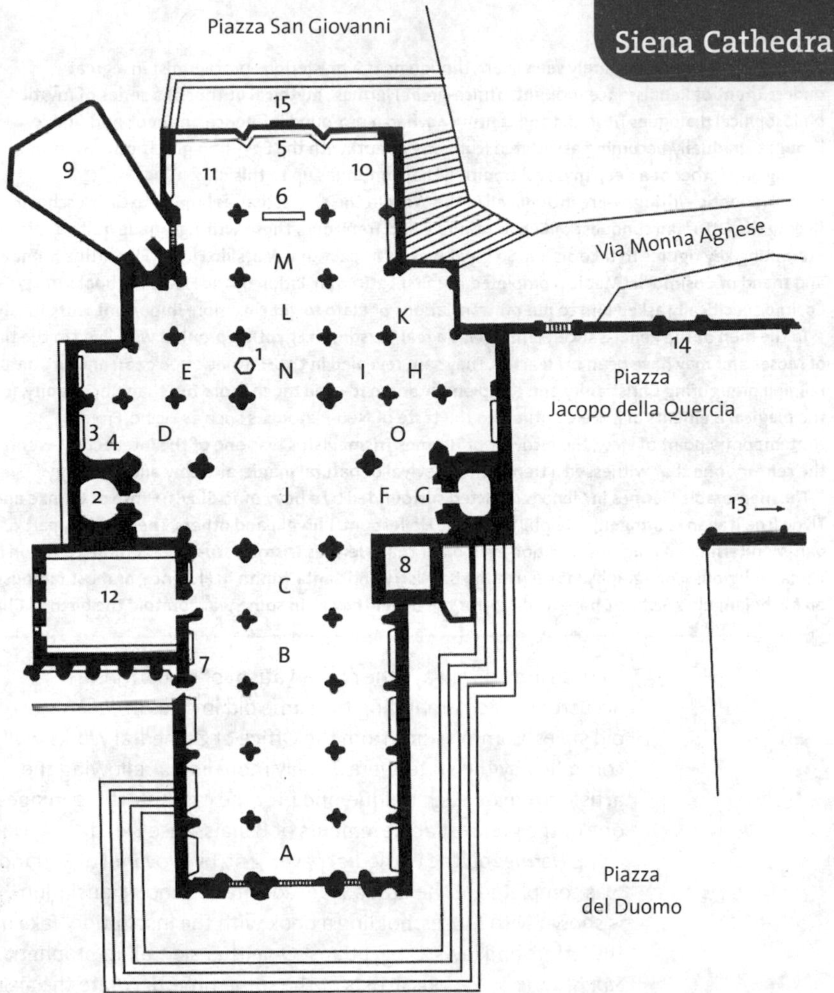

1 Pisano's Pulpit
2 Chapel of San Giovanni Battista
3 Tomb of Cardinal Pecci (Donatello)
4 Tomb of Cardinal Petroni (Tino da Camaino)
5 Stained glass of Duccio
6 High altar
7 Piccolomini altar (Della Quercia, Michelangelo)
8 Campanile
9 Sacristy
10 *Cantorie*
11 Choir
12 Piccolomini Library
13 To cathedral museum
14 Cathedral extension
15 Baptistry (lower level)

A *Hermes Trismegistus*
B *Allegory of Virtue*
C *Wheel of Fortune*
D *Massacre of the Innocents*
E *Judith Liberating Bethulia*
F *Seven Ages of Man*
G *Allegories of Faith, Hope and Charity*
H *Story of Absalom*
I *Emperor Sigismund on his Throne*
J *Sacrifice of Elias, Execution of the False Prophets*
K *Samson and the Philistines*
L *David the Psalmist*
M *Sacrifice of Abraham*
N *Moses Receives the Commandments*
O *Story of Jephta*

Hermes Trismegistus

Hermes Trismegistus is rarely seen in art, though he is a mysterious protagonist in a great undercurrent of Renaissance thought. 'Thrice-great Hermes', mythical author of a series of mystic philosophical dialogues from the 2nd century AD, had a profound influence on Greek and Arabic thought, gradually becoming associated (correctly or not) with the Egyptian god Thoth, inventor of writing and father of a deep mystical tradition that continues up to this day.

The Hermetic writings were introduced in the West In the 1400s, thanks largely to Greek scholars fleeing the Ottoman conquest of Constantinople and Trebizond. These writings made quite a splash, prompting key figures to take action. So great was its impact that Marsilio Ficino, Florentine humanist and friend of Cosimo de' Medici, completed the first Latin translation of the Hermetic books in 1471 – Cosimo specifically asked him to put off translations of Plato to get this more important work finished!

To the men of the Renaissance, Hermes was a real person, an Egyptian prophet who lived in the time of Moses and may have been his teacher. They saw, revealed in the Hermetic books, an ancient, natural religion prefiguring Christianity and complementary to it – and much more fun than Christianity, for the magical elements in it were entirely to the taste of Neo-Platonists such as Ficino. From a contemporary point of view, the recovery of Hermes Trismegistus was one of the intellectual events of the century, one that witnessed a tremendous revival of natural magic, alchemy and astrology.

The memorable Hermes in Siena is depicted surrounded by a bevy of 10 Sibyls: those of Cumae and Tivoli (the Italian contingent), Delphi, Libya, the Hellespont, Phrygia and others. These ladies, part of a pan-Mediterranean religious tradition even older than Hermes Trismegistus, are far more common in Tuscan religious iconography (as seen in the Baptistry and Santa Trínita in Florence, or most famously, on Michelangelo's Sistine Chapel ceiling), for the belief they all in some way foretold the birth of Christ.

Sienese art was always the conservatism of its patrons, accustomed to demanding the same old images in the same old styles. Commissions from the Office of Cathedral Works, controlled by the state, were usually more liberal, allowing the artists to create such unique, and in some cases startling images, one of the greatest achievements of Renaissance Siena.

The *Hermes* on the cathedral pavement, by Giovanni di Stefano, was completed in the 1480s, a decade after Ficino's translation; he is shown with Moses, holding a book with the inscription 'Take up thy letters and laws, O Egyptians'. On either side, all 10 prophetic *Sibyls*, done by various artists at the same time, decorate the aisles. Nor are Hermes and the sibyls the only peculiar thing on this floor. Directly behind him begins a series of large scenes, including a *Wheel of Fortune*, with men hanging on it for dear life, another wheel of uncertain symbolism, and emblems of Siena and other Tuscan and Latin cities. Oddest of all is a work by Pinturicchio, variously titled the *Allegory of Virtue* or *Allegory of Fortune*; on a rocky island full of serpents, a party of well-dressed people has just landed, climbing to the summit, where a figure of 'Socrates' accepts a pen from a seated female figure, and another, 'Crates', empties a basket of gold and jewels into the sea. Below, a naked woman with a gonfalon has one foot in a boat, the another on land.

Many of the best scenes, under the crossing and transepts, are covered to protect them. The visionary works of Alessandro Franchi – the *Triumph of Elias* and other events in that prophet's life – and

Domenico Beccafumi's *Sacrifice of Elias* and the *Execution of the False Prophets of Baal*, are usually uncovered for a couple of months in late summer (September and October; call the tourist office for confirmation). Works uncovered all year include *The Seven Ages of Man* by Antonio Federighi, *Scenes From the Life of Moses* by Beccafumi, Matteo di Giovanni's *Massacre of the Innocents* (a favourite subject in Sienese art), and, best of all, the beautifully drawn *Judith Liberating the City of Bethulia*, a collaboration of Federighi, Matteo di Giovanni and Urbano da Cortona.

Elsewhere in the Cathedral

Perhaps the greatest attraction above floor level is the great 1280s Carrara marble **pulpit** by Nicola Pisano. He started it directly after finishing the one in Pisa; one of the assistants he brought to help with the work was the young Arnolfo di Cambio. The typical Pisano conception is held up by allegorical figures of the seven liberal arts – more sibyls, prophets, Christian virtues and saints tucked in odd corners, and vigorous, crowded relief panels from the Passion as good as the ones in Pisa. Nearby, in the left transept, the **chapel of San Giovanni Battista** has frescoes by Pinturicchio and a bronze statue of St John the Baptist by Donatello, who also contributed the **tomb of Giovanni Pecci**, a 1400s Sienese bishop.

Some of the **stained glass** in the cathedral is excellent, especially the earliest windows, in the apse, designed by Duccio, and the rose window with its cornucopia. Over the high altar is a bronze **baldachin** by Vecchietta, and in the north aisle the **Piccolomini altar** includes four early statues of saints by Michelangelo, and one by Torrigiano, the fellow who broke Michelangelo's nose and ended up in exile, working in Westminster Abbey. There is also a *Madonna* by Jacopo della Quercia.

Be sure to keep an eye out for details, such as the tiny, exquisite heads of the popes that decorate the clerestory wall. The Office of Works never settled for anything less than the best, and even such trifles as the holy water fonts, choir stalls, iron grilles and candlesticks are works of genuine artistic merit.

Libreria Piccolomini
entrance off left aisle, near Piccolomini altar; open Mar–May Mon–Sat 10.30–7.30, Sun 1.30–5.30; June–Aug Mon–Sat 10.30–8, Sun 1.30–6.30; Sept and Oct Mon–Sat 10.30–7.30, Sun 1.30–7.30; Nov–Feb Mon–Sat 10.30–6.30, Sun 1.30–5.30; adm

Piccolomini Library

This is the room with the famous frescoes by Pinturicchio, built to hold the library of Aeneas Silvius, the greatest member of Siena's greatest noble family, eventually to become Pope Pius II. The very definition of a Renaissance man, he was probably the greatest geographer of his age – his works were studied closely by Columbus – plus a poet, diplomat and historian, founder of Pienza and important patron of artists and humanist scholars. During his busy clerical-political career, he worked fitfully to reform the Church of Rome and the constitution of his native city.

In 1495, 31 years after his death, Cardinal Francesco Piccolomini, who became Pope Pius III, decided his celebrated uncle's life would make a fine subject for a series of frescoes. He gave the job to Pinturicchio, his last major commission; among his assistants was the young, still impressionable Raphael – anyone who knows his *Betrothal of the Virgin* will find these paintings eerily familiar. The 10 scenes include Aeneas Silvius' attendance at the court of James I in Scotland – a Scotland with a Tuscan fantasy landscape – where he served with an embassy. Later he is shown accepting a poet laureate's crown from his friend Emperor Frederick III and presiding over the meeting of Frederick and his bride-to-be, Eleanor of Aragon. Another fresco has him canonizing St Catherine of Siena. The last, poignant one portrays a view of Ancona, and its cathedral up on Monte Guasco, where Pius II went in 1464, planning a crusade against the Turks. While waiting for the help promised by the European powers, help that never came, he fell ill and died.

Art historians and critics, following the sniping biography of the artist by Giorgio Vasari, are not always kind to Pinturicchio. As with Gozzoli's frescoes for the Medici Palace in Florence, the consensus seems to be that this is a less challenging sort of art or perhaps just a very elevated approach to interior decoration. Certainly Pinturicchio seems extremely concerned with the latest styles in court dress and coiffure. However, the incandescent colour, fairytale backgrounds and beautifully drawn figures are irresistible. These are among the brightest, best-preserved of quattrocento frescoes; the total effect is that of a serenely confident art, concerned above all with beauty for beauty's sake, even when chronicling the life of a pope.

Aeneas Silvius' books have been carted away, but one of his favourite things remains: a marble statue of the *Three Graces*, a copy of the work by Praxiteles much studied by artists of the 1400s.

Around the side of the cathedral, off the right transept, Piazza Jacopo della Quercia is the name the Sienese have given to the doomed nave of their 1330s **cathedral extension**. All around this square, heroic pilasters and arches rise, some incorporated into the walls of later buildings.

Museo dell'Opera Metropolitana

Museo dell'Opera Metropolitana
t *0577 83048; open Mar–May, Sept and Oct daily 9.30–7; June–Aug daily 9.30–8; Nov–Feb daily 10–5; adm*

This museum, built into what would have been one of the cathedral transepts, is the place to inspect the cathedral façade at close range. Most of the statues on it are modern copies, replacing works of great sculptors such as Nicola Pisano, Urbano da Cortona and Jacopo della Quercia. The originals have been moved into the museum for better preservation, and there you can look the cathedral's remarkable marble saints in the eye. There are also architectural fragments and leftover pinnacles, and bits of the marble pavement that had to be replaced. On the first floor, a collection of Sienese paintings includes Duccio di Buoninsegna's masterpiece, the *Maestà* that hung behind the cathedral's high altar from 1311 to 1505. It's painted on both sides, with the main composition a Sienese favourite: the enthroned Virgin flanked by neat rows of adoring saints – with expressive faces and fancy clothes against a glittering gold background. Among the other paintings and sculptures are works by Pietro and Ambrogio Lorenzetti, Simone Martini, Beccafumi and Vecchietta.

On the top floor is the *Madonna dagli Occhi Grossi* ('of the Big Eyes') by an anonymous 1210s artist, a landmark in Sienese painting, and the original cathedral altarpiece. A hoard of golden croziers, reliquaries and crucifixes from the cathedral treasure includes another lovely golden rose from the Vatican – probably a gift from Aeneas Silvius. A stairway leads to the top of the **Facciatone**, the 'big façade' of the unfinished nave, with a view over the city.

Baptistry

Battistero
open Mar–May, Sept and Oct daily 9.30–7; June–Aug daily 9.30–8; Nov–Feb daily 10–5; adm

Outside the unfinished cathedral nave, a long, steep set of stairs leads down around the back of the church to Piazza San Giovanni. In this lower but prominent setting, the Office of Works architects squeezed in a baptistry, perhaps the only one in Italy directly under a cathedral apse. Behind its unfinished 1390s Gothic façade, this contains yet another impressive hoard of art. It's hard to see anything in this gloomy cellar, though; bring plenty of coins for the lighting machines. Frescoes by Vecchietta, restored to death in the 19th century, decorate much of the interior. The crown jewel is the king-sized **baptismal font** with some of the finest sculpture of the quattrocento. Of the gilded reliefs around the sides, *Herod's Feast* is by Donatello, the *Baptism of Christ* and *St John in Prison* by Ghiberti. The first relief, with the *Annunciation of the Baptist's Birth*, is the work of Jacopo della Quercia, who also added the five statues of prophets above. Two of the statues at the corners of the font, representing the virtues Hope and Charity, are also by Donatello.

Ospedale di Santa Maria della Scala

3 Ospedale di Santa Maria della Scala
Piazza Duomo 2, t 0577 224811; open Mar–Nov daily 10.30–6.30; adm; joint 2-day adm available with Musei Comunali, *see p.333**, and Palazzo delle Papesse,* *see p.335*

Opposite the old cathedral façade, one entire side of the piazza is occupied by the **Ospedale di Santa Maria della Scala**. Believed to have been founded in the 9th century and for centuries one of the largest, finest hospitals in the world, it is now an exciting museum.

According to legend, the hospital had its beginnings with a pious cobbler, Sorore, who opened a hostel and infirmary for pilgrims on their way to Rome. Sorore's mother, it is said, later had a vision here of babies ascending a ladder (*la scala*) into heaven and being received into the arms of the Virgin Mary; consequently, a foundling hospital was soon added. Meticulous attention to the health of its citizens was always one of the most praiseworthy features of Siena; even in the decadence of the 1700s, advances in such things as inoculation were made here. In the 14th century, it insisted on such revolutionary practices as the washing of hands by doctors and nurses, meals adapted to each patient's illness, and the use of iron beds (to prevent the spread of bed bugs). To encourage donations, laws were passed allowing wealthy Sienese to deduct gifts from their taxes (remember, this was the 14th century) and not a few left huge sums in their wills; after the plague of 1348, the hospital was up to its ears in gold.

The Sienese say that their new museum, which is dedicated to all the arts and the city's history, will end up as one of the largest in the world, but don't ask when it will be finished; the point of this innovative exercise is that it will never be finished. The complex is conceived as a *cantiere didattico*, a kind of 'educational construction site', where the process of museum-building itself is part of the attraction. That said, many of the permanent exhibits should be place in the next few years, along with shops, temporary exhibits and restoration workshops.

For now, it's worth the price of admission just to see the big frescoes in the **Sala dei Pellegrini**, the hospital's main reception hall. Another pioneering fresco cycle devoted to a secular subject, like those in the Palazzo Pubblico, this is a tribute to old Siena's advanced, humanistic outlook; all the scenes are devoted to the history of the hospital, including the vision of Sorore's mother and everyday views of the hospital's activities. In the best, Domenico di Bartolo shows how Sienese art was still keeping up with the Florentines in 1441 with his *Reception, Education and Marriage of a Daughter of the Hospital*; care of abandoned children, the *getatelli* ('little ones thrown away'), was one of the hospital's important functions. Other frescoes, by different Sienese artists, portray in loving detail the caring for the sick, the distribution of alms to the poor, and the paying of the wetnurses. They provide an insight into a side of old Siena you might not have thought existed.

There's also a collection of precious golden reliquaries and other church paraphernalia, some from medieval Constantinople, in refurbished chambers cheerfully marked *isolamento dei contagiosi*. Other original features include the **Cappella del Sacro Chiodo**, with damaged frescoes by Vecchietta, the elaborate **Cappella SS. Annunziata**, and the spooky **Cappella di Santa Caterina**, beginning with a leering skull and ending with an altarpiece by Taddeo di Bartolo. Old views and relics of the hospital are displayed in many of the long hallways; in some of the oldest, you see how the façade was covered with frescoes, by Pietro and Ambrogio Lorenzetti.

Museo Archeologico
open summer daily 10–6, winter 10.30–4.30; joint adm with Santa Maria della Scala

Another part of the complex houses the **Museo Archeologico**, with an Etruscan and Roman collection.

The Piazza della Selva and around

The ancient quarter of steep narrow streets to the north of the cathedral is the *contrada* of the *Selva* (forest) – Rhinoceros country. In its heart, Piazza della Selva, one of the most charming of the new *contrada* fountains has a bronze statue of the neighbourhood's Rhino symbol. Leaving the cathedral in the opposite direction, south down Via del Capitano, leads you into the haunts of the Dolphin and Turtle (*Onda* and *Tartaruga*).

Pinacoteca Nazionale
open Mon 8.30–1.30, Tues–Sat 8.15–7.15, Sun and hols 8.15–1.15; adm

Where the street meets Via di Città, it changes its name to Via San Pietro, passing the 14th-century Palazzo Buonsignori, one of the most harmonious of the city's noble palaces, now home to the **Pinacoteca Nazionale**, the temple of Sienese art, with a representative sampling of this inimitable city's style. The collection is arranged roughly chronologically, beginning on the top floor with Guido da Siena and his school in the mid 13th century (Room 2) and continuing through an entire room of delicate, melancholy Virgins by Duccio and his followers, before reaching a climax with Duccio's luminous if damaged *Madonna dei Francescani* in Room 4. Madonnas and saints fill room after room, including important works by Siena's greatest 14th-century artists. One of the most famous is Simone Martini's *Madonna and Child*; the story goes that this *Madonna* was a great Palio fan. When everyone had gathered in the Campo for the event, she would wander out in the empty streets and tiptoe over for a look. One day, she lingered too long and had to run home, losing her veil in her haste. She has yet to find it, and according to the Sienese, weeps sweetly during the Palio, probably because she can't get through the Pinacoteca's security system.

Other *Madonnas* that stand out are those of Pietro and Ambrogio Lorenzetti (*Madonna Enthroned* and the *Annunciation*; Room 7) and Taddeo di Bartolo (*Triptych*; Room 11), with their rosy blooming faces and brilliant colour – a remarkable counterpoint to the relative austerity of contemporary painting in Florence. Evident in many of these paintings is Sienese civic pride; the artists take obvious delight in including the city's skyline and landmarks in the background of their works – even in Nativities.

Sienese Renaissance painters are well represented, often betraying the essential conservatism of their art and resisting the new approaches of Florence: Domenico di Bartolo's 1433 *Madonna* in Room 9; Nerocchio and Matteo di Giovanni of the 1470s (Room 14); Sano di Pietro, leading painter of the 1440s (Rooms 16–17). The first floor displays some of Il Sodoma's most important works, especially the great *Scourging of Christ* in Room 31 (1514); in Room 37 the *Descent into Hell* is one of the finest works by Siena's greatest Mannerist, Beccafumi.

Around the Terzo di Città

Next to the Pinacoteca, **San Pietro alle Scale** contains *The Flight into Egypt*, an altarpiece by Rutilio Manetti, the only significant Sienese painter of the Baroque era, a follower of Caravaggio. **San Giuseppe**, off the end of Via San Pietro, marks Siena's uneasy compromise with the new world of the 1600s. One of the city's first Baroque churches, it was nevertheless built not in Baroque marble or travertine but good Siena brown brick. This is the church of the *Onda* (Dolphin) district; the *contrada*'s fountain is in front.

Around the corner, gloomy **Sant'Agostino** conceals a happier rococo interior of the 1740s by Vanvitelli, the Dutchman (born Van Wittel) who was chief architect for the kings of Naples. Most of the building dates back to the 13th century, however, and there are surviving bits of trecento frescoes and altarpieces all around.

Further west, the *contrada* of the Chiocciola (Snail) centres on **Santa Maria del Carmine**, a 14th-century church remodelled by Baldassare Peruzzi in 1517; inside is a painting of *St Michael* by Beccafumi and a rather grimly Caravaggiesque *Last Judgement* by an anonymous 16th-century artist.

Terzo di San Martino

Beginning again at the Croce del Travaglio and Palazzo Piccolomini (*see* p.335), Banchi di Sotto leads into the quiet eastern third of the city, passing the **Logge del Papa**, a Renaissance ornament given to Siena by Aeneas Silvius Piccolomini in 1462. The most intriguing parts of this neighbourhood are on the hillside behind Piazza del Mercato: old streets on slopes and stairs in the *contrada* of the *Torre* (Elephant). Although they haven't won a Palio in decades, they have a fine fountain with their elephant-and-tower emblem on pretty Piazzetta Franchi.

One of the most typical streets in this part of town is **Via dell'Oro**, an alley of overhanging medieval houses much like the ones in the Palazzo Pubblico's frescoes of Good and Bad Government (*see* p.334). **Via Porta Giustizia** leads you on a country ramble within the city's walls, along the valley that separates the Terzo San Martino from the Terzo di Città.

Among noteworthy churches in this Terzo are **Santo Spirito** on Via dei Pispini, with further frescoes by Il Sodoma in the first chapel on the right; and **Santa Maria dei Servi**, south on Via dei Servi in the *contrada* of *Valdimontone* (Ram). Here, in the north transept, is one of the earliest, finest Sienese nativities, the altarpiece in the second north chapel, by Taddeo di Bartolo. Good paintings include a *Madonna* by Coppo di Marcovaldo and the *Madonna del Popolo* by Lippo Memmi. An interesting comparison can be made between two versions of that favourite Sienese subject, the *Massacre of the Innocents*: one from the early trecento by Pietro Lorenzetti, another from 1491 by Matteo di Giovanni.

Società Esecutori Pie Disposizioni
Via Roma 7, t 0577 284300; open Mon and Fri 9–1, Tues and Thurs 3–5.30, but call ahead

Nearby, the **Società Esecutori Pie Disposizioni** has an **oratory** and a small but good collection of Sienese art. This Terzo also has two of the best surviving city gates, the **Porta Romana** at the end of Via Roma, and the elegant **Porta Pispini** on the road to Perugia, with traces of a *Nativity* by Sodoma.

Terzo di Camollia

Leading north from the Campo, the **Via Banchi di Sopra**, lined with the palaces of the medieval Sienese elite, forms the spine of this largest and most populous of the *terzi*. The first important palace is also one of the oldest: that of the Tolomei family, a clan of noble bankers who liked to trace their ancestry back to the Greek Ptolemies of Hellenistic-era Egypt. The **Palazzo Tolomei**, begun in 1208, is the soul of Sienese Gothic; it gave its name to Piazza Tolomei in front, the space used by the republic for its assembly meetings before the construction of the Palazzo Pubblico.

A few blocks down Banchi di Sopra, **Palazzo Salimbeni** on Piazza Salimbeni was the compound of the Tolomeis' mortal enemies; their centuries-long vendetta dragged Sienese politics into chaos on more than a few occasions. With the two adjacent palaces on the square, the Salimbeni is home to the **Monte dei Paschi di Siena**, founded by the city as a pawnshop in 1472, now a remarkable savings bank with a medieval air that has a tremendous influence over everything that happens in southern Tuscany, and branches as far away as Australia – they also have a good art collection, sometimes open to the public along with special exhibitions.

East of these palaces, in the neighbourhood of the *Giraffa* (Giraffe), is one of the last important churches built in Siena, the proto-Baroque **Santa Maria di Provenzano** (1594), at the end of Via del Moro. This particular Virgin Mary, a terracotta image said to have been left by St Catherine (see p.346), has had one of the most popular devotional cults in Siena since the 1590s; the annual Palio is in her honour.

The quiet streets behind the church, Siena's red-light district in Renaissance times, lead to **San Francesco**, begun in 1326, one of the city's largest churches. After a big fire in the 17th century, this great Franciscan barn was used as a warehouse and barracks. Restoration began in the 1880s and the 'medieval' brick façade was completed only in 1913. The interior is still one of the most impressive in Siena, a monolithic rectangle with vivid stained glass and good transept chapels in the Florentine manner. A little artwork has survived, including traces of frescoes by both Lorenzettis (north transept).

Oratorio di San Bernardino
open mid-Mar–Oct daily 10.30–1.30 and 3–5.30; adm

Next to San Francesco is the equally simple **Oratorio di San Bernardino**, begun in the late 1400s in honour of Siena's famous preacher and graced with his heart. Its upper chapel, a monument of the Sienese Renaissance, has frescoes by Beccafumi, Il Sodoma and the almost-forgotten High Renaissance master Girolamo del Pacchia.

The areas west of San Francesco, traditionally working class, make up the *contrada* of *Bruco* (Caterpillar); their fountain is by the steps on Via dei Rossi. On the wall of the house opposite is an odd marble relief of a woman peering at a pomegranate from behind half-closed curtains. Caterpillars are everywhere. Bruco's name recalls the Compagnia del Bruco, the trade union that initiated the revolt of 1371, temporarily reforming Siena's faction-ridden government. The workers paid a terrible price; while the revolution was underway, some young noble provocateurs started a fire that consumed almost the entire *contrada*. Today it is the unluckiest of the 'unlucky' neighbourhoods; it hasn't won a Palio since 1955.

St Catherine, St Dominic and the Goose

Unlike the poor caterpillar, the equally proletarian *Oca* (Goose) seems the best organized and most successful *contrada*. On occasion during the Napoleonic Wars, with Tuscan and city governments in disarray, the *Oca*'s men took charge of the city.

Santuario e Casa di Santa Caterina
Vicolo di Tiratoio; open daily 9–12.30 and 3–6

The *contrada* stretches down steeply from Banchi di Sopra to the western city walls. At its centre, the **Santuario e Casa di Santa Caterina** includes the home of Caterina Benincasa (*see* box below) and her father's wool-dyeing workshop; each room is converted into a chapel, many with 15th- and 16th-century frescoes by Sienese artists. The adjacent oratory is now the *Oca*'s *contrada* chapel (note the goose in the detail of the façade).

The Goose's Most Famous Daughter

Caterina Benincasa was the last but one of 25 children born to a wool-dyer, in 1347. At an early age the visions started; by her teens,she had turned her room into a cell, and, while she never became a nun, she lived like a hermit, a solitary ascetic in her own house, sleeping with a stone for a pillow. After she received the stigmata, like St Francis, her reputation as a holy woman spread across Tuscany; popes and kings corresponded with her, and towns sent for her to settle their disputes. In 1378 Florence was under a papal interdict, and the city asked Catherine to plead its case at the papal court at Avignon. She went, but with an agenda of her own – convincing Pope Gregory XI to move the papacy back to Rome where it belonged. As a woman, and a holy woman to boot, she was able to tell the pope to his face what a corrupt and worldly Church he was running, without ending up dangling from the top of a palace wall.

Talking the pope (a French pope, mind you) into leavlng the civilized life in Provence for turbulent, barbaric 14th-century Rome is only one of the miracles with which Catherine was credited. Political expediency probably helped more than divine intervention – much of Italy, including anathemized Florence, was in revolt against the absentee popes. She followed them back and died in Rome in 1380, aged only 33. Canonization came in 1460, and in the 19th century she was declared co-patron of Italy (along with St Francis) and one of the Doctors of the Church. She and St Teresa of Avila are the only women to hold this honour – given in acknowledgement of their inspired devotional writings and their practical, incisive letters encouraging church reform.

Via Santa Caterina, the main street, slopes down towards the city walls and **Fontebranda**, a simple pointed-arched fountain of the 13th century that was an important part of Siena's advanced system of fountains and aqueducts. **San Domenico**, on the hill above Fontebranda, fails to impress close up from the bus depot on Piazza San Domenico, but from Fontebranda the bold Gothic lines of its apse and transepts give a great insight into the straightforward, strangely modern character of much Sienese religious architecture. Inside, the church is as big and empty as San Francesco; among the relatively few works of art is the only existing portrait of St Catherine, on the west wall, painted by her friend Andrea Vanni. In this church, scene of so many incidents from the saint's life, you can see her head in a golden reliquary. But the real attraction is the wonderfully hysterical set of murals by Il Sodoma in the **Cappella Santa Caterina**, representing the girl in various states of serious exaltation.

The open, relatively modern quarter around San Domenico offers a welcome change from the dark and treeless streets of this brick city, in a shady park, **La Lizza**, and the green spaces around the **Fortezza Medicea**. Though the site is the same, this is not the hated fortress Charles V compelled the Sienese to build in 1552; as soon as the Sienese chased the imperial troops out, they razed it to the ground. Cosimo I forced its rebuilding after annexing Siena, but to make the bitter pill easier to swallow, he employed a Sienese architect, Baldassare Lanci, and let him create what must be the most elegant and civilized, least threatening fortress in Italy. The Fortezza, a long, low rectangle of Siena brick profusely decorated with Medici balls, seems more like a setting for garden parties or summer opera than anything that was designed to intimidate a sullen populace.

The Sienese weren't completely won over; right after Italian reunification, they renamed the central space of the fortress **Piazza della Libertà**. The grounds are now a city park, and the vaults of the munition cellars the **Enoteca Nazionale**, the 'Permanent Exhibition of Italian Wines'. Almost every variety of wine Italy produces can be bought here, by the glass or bottle, and there's an annual *Settimana dei Vini* of regional wines (first half of June).

57 Enoteca Nazionale
open Mon noon–8pm, Tues–Sat noon–1am; adm

To the east of the fortress, beyond the Lizza and city stadium, lie the twin centres of modern Siena, **Piazza Gramsci**, the terminus for most city bus lines, and **Piazza Matteotti**.

Continuing north towards the Camollia Gate, you pass the little Renaissance church of **Fonte Giusta**, just off Via di Camollia on Vicolo Fontegiusta. Designed in 1482 by Urbano da Cortona, it has a fresco by Peruzzi (another sibyl) and a magnificent tabernacle over the main altar; there is also a whalebone, left, according to local legend, by Christopher Columbus.

Porta Camollia, in the northernmost corner of Siena, underwent the Baroque treatment in the 1600s. Here is the famous inscription 'Wider than her gates Siena opens her heart to you'. Old Siena was never that sentimental. The whole thing was added in 1604 – undoubtedly under the orders of the Florentine governor – to mark the visit of Grand Duke Francesco I, who wasn't really welcome at all.

Peripheral Attractions

From Porta Camollia, Viale Vittorio Emanuele leads through some of the modern quarters outside the walls. Beyond the gate it passes a column commemorating the meeting of Emperor Frederick III and his bride-to-be Eleanor of Aragon in 1451 – the event captured in one of the Pinturicchio frescoes in the Piccolomini Library (*see* p.335). Next looms a great defence tower, the **Antiporto**, erected just before the Siege of Siena and rebuilt in 1675. Further down, the **Palazzo dei Diavoli** (1460) was the headquarters of the Marquis of Marignano during the siege.

There isn't much on the outskirts of the city – thanks largely to Marignano, who laid waste lovely and productive lands for kilometres around. Some 2km east (take Via Simone Martini from the Porta Ovile), in the hills above the train station, the **basilica and monastery of L'Osservanza** has been restored after serious damage in the last war. Begun in 1422, a foundation of San Bernardino, it retains much of its collection of 13th- and 14th-century Sienese art.

West of the city, the road to Massa Marittima passes through the hills of the Montagnola Sienese, an important centre of monasticism in the Middle Ages (*see* San Galgano, p.370). Near **Montecchio** (6km), the hermitage of **Lecceto**, one of the oldest in Tuscany, has been much changed but retains some Renaissance frescoes in the church and a 12th-century cloister. Close by, the hermitage of **San Leonardo al Lago** is mostly in ruins but the 14th-century church survives, with masterly frescoes (*c*. 1360) by Pietro Lorenzetti's star pupil, Lippo Vanni. Just outside the village of **Sovicille** 13km away is a 12th-century Romanesque church, the **Pieve di Ponte alla Spina**.

Abbazia di Torri
open Mon–Fri 3.30–6

The village of **Rosia** (17km) has another Romanesque church. Just south is the Vallombrosan **abbey of Torri**, with much from its 1200s foundation, and a rare three-storey cloister with three types of column.

Tourist Information in Siena

ⓘ Siena >
Piazza del Campo 56, **t** *0577 280551, www.siena.turismo.toscana.it or www.terresiena.it.*

The tourist office sells 7-day **joint tickets** to the many of Siena's attractions (winter, €13; summer, €16).
Post office: Piazza Matteotti 37, **t** 0577 214295 (*closed Sun*).

Shopping in Siena

Siena is blissfully short of designer boutiques and tourist trinkets. The backstreets have lots of unpretentious artisan workshops, almost all so unconcerned with the tourist industry they don't bother hanging out a sign.

Antica Drogheria Manganelli, Via di Città 71–73, **t** 0577 280002. A gourmet treasure trove with its original wooden shelving, crammed with regional foods and wines.

Ceramics: Via di Città 94. A wealth of interesting pieces.

La Fattoria Toscano, Via di Città 51. Gastronomic goodies.

Libreria Senese, Via di Città 62–64. Siena's best bookshop.

Morbidi, Via Banchi di Sopra 73/75. Picnic treats: cheeses, hams, salamis, prepared dishes, wines and breads.

Vetrate Artistiche Toscane, Via Galluzza 5, off Piazza Indipendenza. Stained-glass creations (mostly portable) in a distinctive modern style. The artist gives informal talks about his work.

Market Days

There are markets round the Fortezza and Via XXV Aprile on Wednesdays.

Where to Stay

Siena ✉ 53100

Much of Siena's best accommodation is outside the walls or in the country and needs to be booked well in advance. If you come without a reservation, head to the **Hotel Information Centre**, Via Madre Teresa di Calcutta 5, **t** 0577 288084, *www.hotelsiena.com* (*closed Sun*).

Luxury (€€€€€)

*****La Certosa di Maggiano**, Strada di Certosa 82, 1km southeast of city, near Porta Romana, **t** 0577 288180, *www.certosadimaggiano.com*. One of the most remarkable establishments in Italy, in a restored 14th-century Carthusian monastery, with a pool, tennis courts, beauty treatments, an excellent restaurant serving local cuisine (see p.350; half and full board available by request), a library to make antiquarians dream, a quiet chapel and cloister, and a salon with backgammon and chess.

*****Grand Hotel Continental**, Via Banchi di Sopra 85, **t** 0577 56011, *www.ghc.royaldemeure.com*. Rooms with fine fabrics and antiques, public rooms with original frescoes, a covered courtyard with a winter garden, and a sumptuous restaurant and wine bar.

***Park Hotel**, Via Marciano 18, **t** 0577 290290, *www.parkhotelsiena.it*. A 16th-century building by Peruzzi, on the hill that dominates Siena, with pool, a tennis court, a beauty centre, and Sienese cuisine.

Relais La Suvera, Pievescola, just north of city, **t** 0577 960300, *www.lasuvera.it*. A medieval fort in the Chianti hills, converted into a villa for Pope Julius II, then into a luscious country hotel. Rooms are packed with heirlooms, and there's a pool, wellness centre, restaurant and delightful bar-terrace.

Luxury–Very Expensive (€€€€€–€€€€)

****Villa Scacciapensieri**, Strada Scacciapensieri 10, 3km north of city, **t** 0577 41441, *www.villascacciapensieri.it*. A quiet country house with spacious rooms, glorious sunset views over Siena, a pool and a good restaurant.

Hotel Garden, Via Custoza 2, about 1km from city, **t** 0577 47056, *www.gardenhotel.it*. A renovated 1700s villa in a big garden, with antiques and original frescoes, plus three annexes. There is a pool, a good restaurant, an American bar and a reading room.

Very Expensive (€€€€)

***Duomo**, Via Stalloreggi 38, **t** 0577 289088, *www.hotelduomo.it*. A friendly, comfortably old-fashioned place with some rooms overlooking the Duomo and the Sienese hills.

***Palazzo Ravizza**, Pian dei Mantellini 34, near Porta Laterina just inside walls, **t** 0577 280462, *www.palazzoravizza.it*. An elegant 19th-century *palazzo* with a lovely rear garden and a restaurant.

Expensive (€€€€)

***Antica Torre**, Via di Fieravecchia 7, **t** 0577 222255, *www.anticatorresiena.it*. Siena's most popular small hotel, in a restored 16th-century tower, with marble floors, antiques and beams.

Villa Liberty, Viale V. Veneto 11, **t** 0577 44966, *www.villaliberty.it*. An elegant 'Liberty-style' villa near San Domenico, in a peaceful garden, with free Internet access in rooms, two of which have private terraces. Breakfast is included.

Moderate (€€)

Many of Siena's 2- and 3-star hotels are round the entrances to the city, but there are some closer to the centre.

★ Relais La Suvera >>

★ Palazzo Ravizza >>

★ Osteria Le Logge >>

★ Osteria La Chiacchiera >>

****Canon d'Oro**, Via Montanini 28, **t** 0577 44321, *www.cannondoro.com*. A hotel near the bus station, friendly and good value (breakfast is included).

****Il Giardino**, Via Baldassare Peruzzi 35, near Porta Pispini, **t** 0577 285290, *www.hotelilgiardino.it*. A option highly recommended by readers, with good views and a pool. Breakfast is included.

****Piccolo Hotel Etruria**, Via delle Donzelle 3, **t** 0577 288088, *www.hoteletruria.com*. A friendly, clean spot with rooms in the annexe opposite and two flats, plus a restaurant.

****Piccolo Hotel Il Palio**, Piazza del Sale 18, **t** 0577 281131, *www.piccolohotelilpalio.it*. Simple but comfy rooms in a quiet location a little way from the centre.

Eating Out in Siena

Siena's eateries tend to serve simple dishes, washed down with something from three of Italy's greatest wine-producing areas (Chianti, Brunello of Montalcino, and Vino Nobile of Montepulciano), between which the city sits. The favourite pasta dish is *pici* – thick south Tuscan spaghetti served with a sauce of ground pork, pancetta, sausages, chicken breasts and tomatoes cooked with Brunello wine. As a university town, Siena is also a good place for snacks and fast food; try *ciaccino*, a variation on pizza.

The real speciality is sweets; visitors often find they have no room for a meal after repeated slices of *panforte*, a heavy but indecently tasty cake laced with fruits, nuts, orange peel and secret Sienese ingredients or *panpepato*, containing pepper.

Gastronomic tastings focusing on various regions of Italy are held at the Enoteca Nazionale (*see* p.347).

Very Expensive (€€€€)

Il Canto, La Certosa di Maggiano, Strada di Certosa 82, **t** 0577 288180. Part of a luxury hotel (*see* p.349), offering modern haute cuisine served with some pomp – try gnocchi with lemon and cumin. *Closed Tues, Wed lunch, 1wk Dec, and 9 Jan–9 Feb.*

Expensive (€€€)

Antica Trattoria Botteganova, Strada Chiantigiana 29, few km northeast of Siena on SS408 to Montevarchi, **t** 0577 284230. Earthy meat dishes or more delicate fish options: try *tagliolini* with lemon and squid. *Closed Sun.*

Compagnia dei Vinattieri, Via delle Terme, **t** 0577 236568. A basement restaurant/*enoteca* with a vast choice of wines stored in a 14th-century cellar. There are snacks or excellent main dishes such as *tagliolini* with Tuscan herbs. *Closed Tues in winter.*

Da Enzo, Via Camollia 49, **t** 0577 281277. A traditional restaurant with a long, varied menu. *Closed Sun.*

Osteria Le Logge, Via del Porrione 33, **t** 0577 48013. One of the city's most pleasant places to eat; try spinach and ricotta ravioli with salmon, and chocolate *millefoglie*. *Closed Sun.*

Osteria di Castelvecchio, Via Castelvecchio 65, **t** 0577 49586. The old stables of one of Siena's oldest *palazzi*, with modern decor. It's a good place for veggie dishes. *Closed Tues.*

Expensive–Moderate (€€€–€€)

Guido, Vicolo Pier Pettinaio 7, **t** 0577 280042. A traditional restaurant with a medieval feel. Booking is advised.

Al Marsili, Via del Castoro 3, **t** 0577 47154. Great Sienese fare, including green gnocchi with duck sauce and tomatoes. Book ahead. *Closed Mon.*

Moderate (€€)

Osteria di Ficomezzo, Via dei Termini 71, **t** 0577 222384. Siena's oldest *osteria*, serving simple lunches and more inventive dishes for dinner. *Closed Sun.*

La Torre, Via Salicotto 17, **t** 0577 287548. A fun, lively place popular among students, offering good home-made *pici*, *ossobuco* and Florentine steak. *Closed Thurs.*

Inexpensive (€€€€)

Il Grattacielo, Via dei Pontani 8, **t** 0577 289326. A popular student hangout serving simple cold meals and good wines. *Closed Sun.*

Osteria La Chiacchiera, Via Costa di Sant'Antonio 4, **t** 0577 280631. A tiny, friendly, trattoria serving excellent local dishes, including *tegamata* (pork casserole). There are outdoor tables for summer dining. Book ahead.

Pizzeria Carlo e Franca, Via Pantaneto 138, **t** 0577 284385. Antipasti, pizzas and *panini* not far from the centre. *Closed Wed.*

Hill Towns West of Siena

In the late Middle Ages, this dramatically diverse, often rugged countryside was a border region, culturally and politically, its people alternately subject to the strong pull of Florence and Siena. Its towns do not have that much in common: Poggibonsi is almost all new; Volterra goes back to the Etruscans. San Gimignano has its famous skyline of medieval skyscrapers, while parts of the Metal Hills show outlandish silhouettes of cooling towers from the geothermal power plants. San Gimignano and Volterra, both beautiful cities containing remarkable works of art, are the main attractions. Massa Marittima, often overlooked, has one of the finest cathedrals in Italy. Beyond that there is a doll-sized walled city, bubbling sulphurous pits, alabaster souvenirs, a Roman theatre, lonely moors and a sword in a stone (not King Arthur's but someone else's).

13

Don't miss

See map overleaf

Hill Towns West of Siena

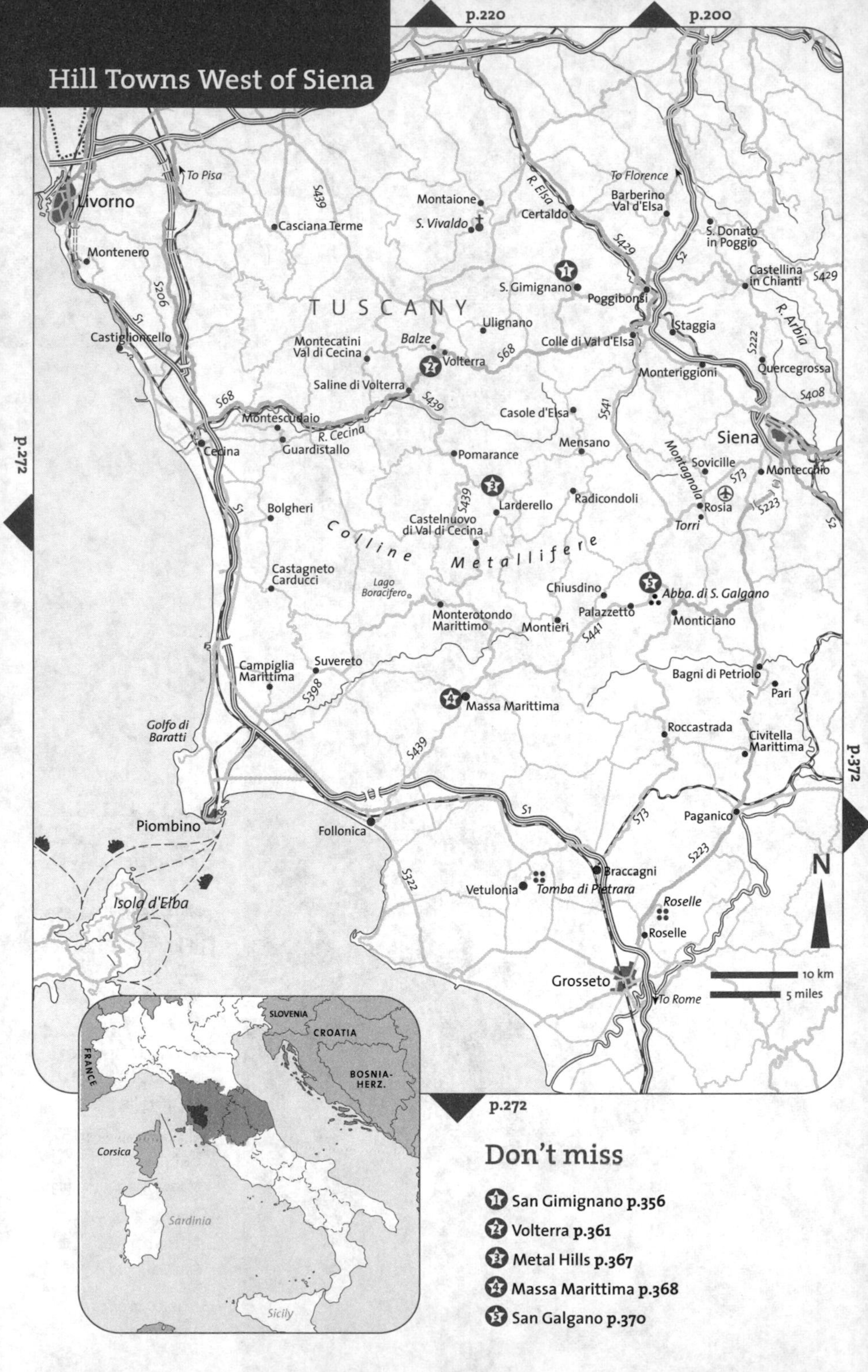

Don't miss

1. San Gimignano p.356
2. Volterra p.361
3. Metal Hills p.367
4. Massa Marittima p.368
5. San Galgano p.370

Monteriggioni, Colle di Val d'Elsa and Poggibonsi

Monteriggioni

The SS2 passes a genuine curiosity 11km north of Siena: the tiny fortified town of Monteriggioni. For much of Siena's history, this was its northernmost bastion, often in the frontlines in the wars with Florence after construction in 1219. Now it sits like a crown on its roundish hill, a neat circle of walls with 14 towers and just enough room for two oversized piazzas, a few houses and gardens, and the inevitable bars and restaurants. In late July the town hosts a re-enactment of medieval life with food, drink, music and dance.

Some 3km further towards Colle di Val d'Elsa is a turn-off left for the 12th-century abbey of Santi Salvatore and Cirino, better known as the **Abbadia dell'Isola**. The Cistercians began it in 1101 on an 'island' in the marshes, hence the name. The stark Romanesque building has a restored fresco by Taddeo di Bartolo and a Renaissance altarpiece.

Colle di Val d'Elsa

Colle di Val d'Elsa (population 16,300), a striking, ancient town on a steep hill, has an impressive silhouette from the right angle – it's quite long but only three blocks wide at most. Though probably as old as the Etruscans, Colle became prominent in the 12th century, as a safe, fortified stronghold attracting many migrants from the surrounding plains. In later centuries, it was known for wool, paper and ceramics manufacture; today, it's Italy's largest producer of fine glass and crystal, and has lots of shops selling it. There is also the **Museo del Cristallo** in a 19th-century crystal factory in the 'new' town (down the hill). The Collegiani will never allow the world to forget that their town was the birthplace of Arnolfo di Cambio, who built Florence's Palazzo Vecchio and began its cathedral.

Museo del Cristallo
Via dei Fossi, **t** *0577 924135; open Tues–Sun 10–12 and 4–7.30; adm*

Down on the plain below the citadel, the modern district surrounds the arcaded **Piazza Arnolfo di Cambio**. Via Garibaldi or Via San Sebastiano take you up to old Colle, but for a proper introduction you need to come on the road from Volterra, passing through a grim Renaissance bastion, the **Porta Nuova**, designed by Giuliano da Sangallo, then across the medieval-Renaissance suburb, the **Borgo**. Between the Borgo and the old town, called the **Castello**, is a picturesque narrow bridge and the **Palazzo di Campana** (1539, by Giovanni di Baccio d'Agnolo); the arch in its centre is the elegant gateway to the town.

Via del Castello runs straight up the centre, with narrow medieval alleys on both sides. Here you'll find the **cathedral**, built in 1603 (Colle only got its own bishop in 1592) with a Victorian-era façade, plus a few Renaissance palaces, and some museums. Beside the

Getting around Monteriggioni, Colle di Valle d'Elsa, Poggibonsi

The **main routes** between Florence and Siena – the Via Cassia (SS2) or the parallel Superstrada del Palio – have exits for Colle di Val d'Elsa (27km/35mins from Siena, 49km/1hr from Florence) and Poggibonsi, 7km further north on SS68.

Poggibonsi is a major **bus** junction, with easy connections to Florence, Siena, San Gimignano, Volterra and Colle di Val d'Elsa (TRA-IN buses if you're coming from Siena, SITA from Florence).

Poggibonsi is also on the Empoli–Siena **train** line, with a branch or bus beyond to Colle (15mins).

Museo Archeologico/ Museo Civico/ Museo d'Arte Sacra
open May–mid-June Tues–Sun 10.30–12.30 and 4.30–7.30; mid-June–Sept Tues–Sun 10.30–12.30, 4.30–7.30 and 9–11pm; Oct–April Tues–Fri 3.30–5.30, Sat, Sun and hols 10–12 and 3.30–6.30; adm

cathedral, in the Palazzo Pretorio, the small **Museo Archeologico** displays Etruscan objects; there is a small picture collection in the nearby **Museo Civico**. The **Museo d'Arte Sacra** in the old episcopal palace has Sienese and Florentine paintings and frescoes commissioned by some jolly 14th-century bishop – scenes of the hunt and from the Crusades, believed to be by Ambrogio Lorenzetti.

Near the end of Via del Castello, the Collegiani claim an old tower-fortress as the **house of Arnolfo di Cambio**. Arnolfo's father, a gentleman and architect, probably came to Colle di Val d'Elsa from Lombardy in the 1230s, bringing the great tradition of the Lombard master masons to Tuscany. He may have received his initiation into the new (for Italy) Gothic style from studying works in Siena or the new Cistercian abbey at San Galgano. He worked for Nicola Pisano on the Siena cathedral pulpit, and for Giovanni Pisano on the Fonte Maggiore in Perugia, and probably moved to Florence in the 1270s.

South of Colle

Many of the villages in the hills retain their simple Romanesque churches from the 11th–12th centuries, beginning with the isolated **Badia a Coneo**, a Vallombrosan foundation of the 1120s (5km from Colle on an unpaved lane off the road to Casole). At **Casole d'Elsa** (15km south, with a local bus servie), a town that took hard knocks in the last war, is an interesting **Collegiata church** begun in the 12th century, with Sienese frescoes, two fine, late 14th-century sepulchres by Gano da Siena, and terracottas by Giovanni della Robbia. Casole's Sienese **Rocca** held out into the 16th century, long after the rest of the Valdelsa flew the Florentine flag.

South from Casole, the road winds through pleasant, green countryside leading up to the Colline Metallifere, the 'metal hills'. You can seek out more Romanesque churches in **Mensano** (7km) and **Radicondoli** (15km; the **church of San Simone**).

Poggibonsi

If you spend enough time in Tuscany, sooner or later you are bound to pass through Poggibonsi (population 25,700), a major knot on the SS2, SS429 and Superstrada del Palio roads linking Siena to Florence and Pisa. These days, residents of the pretty tourist towns of central Tuscany are not above having a laugh at the expense of this homely, hard-working industrial centre. Poor Poggibonsi! Founded only in 1156, the original *Poggiobonizzo* grew rapidly. By 1220, it was probably one of the largest cities in Tuscany, with some 15,000 people; in that year, Emperor Frederick II declared it a *Città Imperiale* with special rights and privileges. Ghibelline politics and its imperial favour, however, proved Poggiobonizzo's undoing. In 1270, San Gimignano and Colle di Val d'Elsa, with the Florentines and the troops of Charles of Anjou, besieged and conquered the city then razed it. Some of the poorer citizens stayed behind, refounding it as a market village on the plain. Poggibonsi was wrecked again in the battles of 1944, but has since grown to become the biggest town between Florence and Siena.

There isn't much to see; the 14th-century Palazzo Pretorio and the collegiate church on the main street recall something of the appearance of pre-war Poggibonsi. Close by, the **Castello della Magione** is a small complex from the 1100s; the Romanesque chapel and outbuildings form a little closed square, a fortified pilgrims' hospice that is said to have been built by the Templars. Above the town, an unfinished fortress begun by Lorenzo de' Medici covers much of the original city of Poggiobonizzo.

Just 2km south of town, near the SS2, is the austerely Franciscan **basilica of San Lucchese**; inside are good frescoes, some by Taddeo Gaddi and Bartolo di Fredi. Unsurprisingly, this strategically important corner of Tuscany is scattered with castles, including the 13th-century **Castello della Rochetta**, once home to famous *condottiere* Sir John Hawkwood, and the romantically ruined **Rocca di Staggia** (5km south of Poggibonsi on the SS2), built by the Florentines in the 1430s – a counterpart to Sienese Monteriggioni a few kilometres further on.

ⓘ Colle di Val d'Elsa >>
Via Campana 43, t 0577 922791

ⓘ Monteriggioni >
Piazza Roma, t 0577 304810, www.prolocomonteriggioni.it

★ Il Pozzo >

Where to Stay and Eat in Monteriggioni, Colle di Val d'Elsa, Poggibonsi

Monteriggioni ✉ 53035

This little castle village is a good lunch stop if you're heading from Florence to Siena, or from Siena out to the west.

Hotel Monteriggioni, Via Imagio 4, **t** 0577 305009, *www.hotelmonteriggioni.net* (€€€€). A hotel occupying two old stone houses,with a garden and a tiny pool. Breakfast is included in rates.

Il Pozzo, Piazza Roma 2, **t** 0577 304127 (€€€). A place serving simple but well-prepared dishes such as *pici* with basil, ravioli with truffles, and stuffed pigeon. *Closed Sun eve, Mon, and 7 Jan–Feb.*

Colle di Val d'Elsa ✉ 53034

*****Arnolfo**, Via Campana 8, **t** 0577 922020, *www.hotelarnolfo.it* (€€). A simple but comfortable option.

*****Villa Belvedere**, Loc. Belvedere, about 1km east of town, near Siena highway, **t** 0577 920966, *www.villabelvedere.com* (€€). A pretty villa with simple rooms (breakfast included), a big garden, a pool, a good restaurant with a terrace overlooking San Gimignano, and a cookery school.

Arnolfo, Via XX Settembre 52, **t** 0577 920549 (€€€). One of the very best restaurants in Italy, in a Renaissance palace. Among seasonal treats are red prawns marinated in ginger, *tagliolini* with flowering courgettes, and lamb in red wine sauce. *Closed Tues, Wed, mid-Jan–Feb, and 2wks July and Aug.*

Osteria di Sapia, Via del Castello 4, **t** 0577 921453 (€€). A elegant *osteria* in the old town, serving creative variations on the Tuscan theme, such as pork tenderloin with peaches and *vinsanto*. There is a lovely terrace, and live jazz some evenings. *Closed Mon, and lunch Nov–Feb.*

Fattoria di Mugnano, Mugnano, 7km along Colle–Volterra road, **t** 0577 959023 (€). An old farm among olive groves, with a delightful restaurant offering local and Sicilian cuisine, wine, grapes and olive oil for sale, and a few spartan rooms. *Closed Thurs.*

L'Oste di Borgo, Via Gracco del Secco 58, **t** 0577 922499 (€). A very pleasant spot with marble-topped tables in a wood-panelled room and a terrace. Try *crostoni* with various sauces, pasta or a salad. *Closed Wed.*

Poggibonsi ✉ 53036

***__Alcide__, Via Marconi 67a, **t** 0577 937501, *www.hotelalcide.com* (€€). Rooms with air-con, breakfast included; there's a minimum 3-day stay. The restaurant (€€€), open since 1849, is renowned for its fish dishes. *Closed Sun eve, Mon.*

San Gimignano

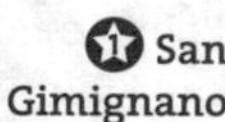

In the miniaturist landscape of this corner of Tuscany, Italy's best-preserved medieval city is an almost fantastic landmark. Seen from Poggibonsi or the Volterra road, its medieval towers, some more than 50m tall, loom over the surrounding hills. Almost every city in central Italy once looked like this; more than just defensive strongholds in the incessant family feuds, the towers served as status symbols for the families and the cities themselves, a visible measure of power and prosperity. By the 16th century, most of Italy's towers had succumbed to age, decay and the efforts of the urban *comuni*, which pruned and destroyed these symbols of truculent nobility at every opportunity. Oddly, this did not happen in San Gimignano, famous even in the 1300s as the '*città delle belle torri*'. Originally there were at least 70 towers (in a town half a square kilometre in size). Only 15 remain, but in conjunction with the beautiful streets, churches and public buildings they give you the impression the town has been sealed in a time capsule since the Middle Ages – if you imagine away the gaggle of trinket shops.

History

According to legend, the town was originally called Castel della Selva. When the Gothic army of Totila passed through during the 550s, the townsfolk for some reason prayed to an obscure saint named Gimignano, a martyred bishop of Modena, for salvation from a near-guaranteed sacking. Gimignano came through in style, looming down from the clouds clad in golden armour to scare away the besiegers.

Although it must have been an important and prosperous place, San Gimignano does not cut much of a figure in the medieval chronicles. The city was an independent republic from the early 1100s until 1353, when it came under the rule of Florence. It participated in the Guelph-Ghibelline strife, and in all the other

Getting to and around San Gimignano

San Gimignano **train** station 11km from town is an infrequent stop on the Empoli–Siena line. **Buses** to the town usually coincide with the trains, but from Siena or Florence you're better off taking the bus, which leaves you right at the Porta San Giovanni, the main entrance to the town. TRA-IN buses from Siena (38km/45mins – the same bus that goes to Colle di Val d'Elsa) are very frequent, though for most you need to change in Poggibonsi. Several daily SITA buses arrive from Florence (54km/1hr 15mins), and there are 4 buses a day to nearby Certaldo.

San Gimignano is 11km west of Poggibonsi, 13km south of Certaldo or 14km from Colle di Val d'Elsa, each route more scenic than the last. Within the walls, San Gimignano is usually closed to traffic; the main **car park** is outside Porta San Giovanni. Get a pass from the police to park at one of the hotels inside.

troubles of the period, though it is probably best remembered as the home town of poet Folgore di San Gimignano (c. 1250), famous for his lovely sonnets to the months of the year.

San Gimignano has the air of a false start, a free *comune* that could build a wall and defend itself yet lacked the will or the money to make itself into a Siena or a Florence. When it lost the wealth or the fierceness that briefly made it a player on the Tuscan stage, the city crystallized into its medieval form – perfect preparation for its role as a tourist town. Today San Gimignano has a population of some 7,700. On a good day in July or August, it may see several times that in day-trippers. Even during the Renaissance, the town was a resort for Florentines: Dante, Machiavelli and Savonarola spent time here, and artists such as Ghirlandaio and Gozzoli were happy to come for a small commission.

Don't let the prospect of crowds keep you away. San Gimignano handles them gracefully; its fine art, elegant medieval cityscapes and the verdant rolling countryside right outside its gates make this one of the smaller towns of Tuscany most worth seeing.

Piazza del Duomo and the Palazzo del Popolo

From the southern gate, Porta San Giovanni, the street of the same name leads towards the centre, passing the little churches of **San Giovanni**, built by the Knights Templar, and **San Francesco**, with a good Pisan-Romanesque façade, now deconsecrated and converted into a wine shop. Another ancient gate, the Arco dei Bacci, leads into the triangular **Piazza della Cisterna** and the adjacent **Piazza del Duomo** – a superbly beautiful example of asymmetrical, medieval town design. Piazza della Cisterna contains the town's well and some of its towers.

Local Wine

San Gimignano has its own DOCG wine, La Vernaccia di San Gimignano, a dry, light yellow white with a pungent bouquet and slightly bitter aftertaste. It is generally drunk with fish and as an aperitif, try it with typical San Gimignano dishes such as liver, tripe, rabbit and *panzanella*. Made only from the hills around San Gimignano and around since antiquity, it gets a mention in Dante's *Purgatory*: Pope Martin IV apparently drowned eels in Vernaccia before roasting them over a charcoal fire.

On Piazza del Duomo, two stout, Gothic public buildings with Guelph crenellations and lofty towers compete with the Collegiata church for your attention. The **Palazzo del Podestà**, with its vaulted *loggia*, was begun in the 1230s by Emperor Frederick II at the height of imperial power. Above it stands the Torre della Rognosa, with a small cupola; at 51m it once marked the height limit for private towers – the *podestà* didn't want anyone putting him in the shade. Later, when the *comune* wrested effective self-government from the emperors, it built an even taller tower for the **Palazzo del Popolo** across the piazza; the 54m Torre Grossa was completed about 1300 and the rest of the Palazzo about 20 years later.

Museo Civico
open Mar–Oct daily 9.30–7.30; Nov–Feb daily 10–5.30; adm

Underneath this tower, an archway leads into the charming, thoroughly medieval **Cortile**, or courtyard, with bits of frescoes (one by Il Sodoma) and the painted coats of arms of Florentine governors from after 1353. A stairway leads up to the **Museo Civico**, with an excellent collection of art by Florentine and Sienese masters. One of the oldest is a remarkable painted crucifix by Coppo di Marcovaldo (c. 1270) that predates (and some might say surpasses) the similar, more famous crucifixes of Giotto. There are also two sweet *Madonnas* by Benozzo Gozzoli, a pair of *tondi* by Filippino Lippi portraying the *Annunciation,* and a big, colourful enthroned *Virgin* by Pinturicchio, famous for the Piccolomini chapel in Siena. Taddeo di Bartolo's paintings depict the story of San Gimignano; he is pictured calming the sea, exorcizing a devil inhabiting the daughter of Emperor Jovian, and succumbing to the flesh while saying Mass (he has to pee, but as he sneaks out of the church a winged devil attacks him; he has a crucifix to hand, and drives it away). To the San Gimignanese, the biggest attraction of the museum is the Sala del Consiglio, or **Sala di Dante**, where the poet spoke in 1299 as an ambassador of Florence, seeking to convince the *comune* to join the Guelph League. The frescoes on its walls include more works by Gozzoli, a glittering company of angels and saints in the *Maestà* of the Sienese artist Lippo Memmi, and some trecento scenes of hunting and tournaments.

Torre Grossa
open Mar–Oct daily 9.30–7.30; Nov–Feb daily 10–5.30; adm

After this, contemplate a climb up the **Torre Grossa** –there are several hundred steps but the view is worth the effort.

The Collegiata

Collegiata
closed for long restoration; call tourist office (see p.360) for latest information

The name Piazza del Duomo is misleading: San Gimignano no longer has a cathedral. Instead it has a **collegiata**, begun in the 12th century and enlarged in the 15th, that would make an impressive seat for any bishop. It turns a blank brick façade to the world, but the interior is a lavish imitation of Siena cathedral, with its tiger-striped arches and vaults painted with golden stars. Its walls outshine the larger cathedral, with first-class frescoes of the 14th and 15th centuries, mostly by artists from Siena, including Old

Testament scenes done by Bartolo di Fredi in the 1360s. New Testament pictures by Barna da Siena (about 1380) cover the south wall; on the west wall, over the entrance, is a well-punctured *Saint Sebastian* by Gozzoli and the most perverse *Last Judgement* in Italy, by Taddeo di Bartolo – you may think you have seen the damned suffering interesting tortures and indignities before, but this is the first time delicacy forbids us to describe one.

Around the Town

Just to the left of the Collegiata is a lovely small courtyard where musicians sometimes play on summer weekends. Here, on the wall of the baptistry, is a fine fresco by Domenico Ghirlandaio, an *Annunciation* that has survived reasonably well for being outside for 500 years. The town's three other museums are here: the **Museo Archeologico**, the **Museo Etrusco**, with a small collection of local archaeological finds, and the **Museo d'Arte Sacra**, with some good painted wood statues from the late Middle Ages.

Museo Archeologico/ Museo Etrusco/ Museo d'Arte Sacra
open April–Dec Sat–Thur 11–6; adm

From Piazza del Duomo, It's not too difficult a climb to the **Rocca**, a ruined 1350s fortress offering one of the best views of this towered town. In summer it's the site of an outdoor cinema.

Down Via di Castello, at the east end of town, the **oratory of San Lorenzo in Ponte**, unused, has quattrocento Florentine frescoes and of 16th–18th-century finds from Santa Fina hospital's pharmacy.

The busiest and finest street heads north from Piazza del Duomo: Via San Matteo, lined with shops and modest Renaissance palaces. It begins by passing the three truncated **Salvucci towers**, once the fortified compound of the Ghibelline Salvucci, one of the town's most powerful families (the towers of their enemies, the Guelph Ardinghelli, are on the west side of Piazza della Cisterna).

In the quiet streets on the north side of town is the **church of Sant'Agostino**, famous for a merry series of frescoes by Gozzoli on the *Life of St Augustine*. Many are faded and damaged, but not the charming panel where the master of grammar drags sullen little Augustine off to school. Another well-preserved scene shows the saint in Rome, with most of the city's ancient landmarks visible in the background. There is a haunting altarpiece (1483) by Piero Pollaiuolo, with an anticipatory touch of the El Greco to it.

Around much of the town, the countryside begins right outside the wall. Pleasant walks or picnics can be had in any direction, with a few landmarks to visit along the way: the **Fonti**, arched, medieval well-houses much like Siena's, are just outside the Porta dei Fonti, south of San Jacopo. The **Pieve di Cellole**, a pretty 12th-century church, is in a pleasant, peaceful setting 4km west of the Porta San Matteo; its harmonious serenity amid the cypresses inspired Puccini's opera *Suor Angelica*. Ruined castles and monasteries around town each offer a view of the town's remarkable skyline.

ⓘ **San Gimignano >**
Piazza del Duomo 1, t 0577 940008, www. sangimignano.com

★ **Antico Pozzo >>**

Tourist Information in San Gimignano

Ask at the tourist office about the *biglietto cumulativo* (€7.50), which covers the 4 museums and the tower of Palazzo del Popolo.

You can explore the surrounding countryside on horseback with Il Vecchio Maneggio (Sant'Andrea 22, Ulignano, **t** 0577 950232, *www. ilvecchiomaneggio.com*) 5km along the road to Certaldo, which is also an *agriturismo* offering guestrooms (€) and selling its own wine, saffron, olive oil and honey.

Shopping in San Gimignano

Ceramics are everywhere here; some of the local work is quite good and inexpensive. Other specialities are a formidable white wine, Vernaccia (*see* p.357) and a sweet called *mandorlato*, like the *panforte* of Siena. Many local vineyards sell bottles of Vernaccia, including Cantine Baroncini, Casale, **t** 0577 940600.

Just within Porta San Giovanni is a 13th-century church now converted to a shop for local wine, olive oil and other farm products.

Linea Oro, Via San Giovanni. Pretty things in alabaster from Volterra.

La Stamperia, Via San Matteo 88. Original prints, including views of Tuscan towns and countryside.

Via San Matteo 85. One of the best shops for alabaster, located north of Piazza del Duomo.

Where to Stay and Eat in San Gimignano

San Gimignano ✉ 53037

There's a dearth of inexpensive hotels here; ask the tourist office for a list of the score of **rooms to let**. In summer, the **Hotel Association**, just inside the gate on Via S. Giovanni, **t** 0577 940809, can help.

*****Le Renaie**, Loc. Pancole, about 7km north of town towards Certaldo, **t** 0577 955044, *www.hotellerenaie.com* (€€€€€–€€€€). An attractive modern building, with a garden, outdoor pool, tennis court, fitness centre, free spa, and bikes. Breakfast is included.

*****Antico Pozzo**, Via San Matteo 87, next to main square, **t** 0577 942014, *www.anticopozzo.com* (€€€). A stylish hotel with wonderful views from rooms at the top of the 1500s building. Several rooms have delicately frescoed ceilings, and there's Wifi internet access. Look for special offers on the website.

*****Leon Bianco**, Piazza della Cisterna, **t** 0577 941294, *www.leonblanco.com* (€€€). An excellent hotel with Internet access and breakfast on a terrace with superb views in summer.

Dorando, Vicolo del Oro 2, **t** 0577 941862 (€€€€). Authentic re-creations of Renaissance and Medieval cuisine , highly praised by our readers. Try the tagliatelle with lobster, ricotta, tomatoes and basil; *pici* with rabbit sauce, herbs, olives and tomatoes; or roasted seabass with lemon and tomatoes. *Closed Mon in winter*.

Le Terrazze, Hotel La Cisterna, Piazza della Cisterna, **t** 0577 940328 (€€). A highly recommended option serving local cuisine since 1918, with panoramic views. Highlights are the hand-made pasta and the grilled mushrooms and meats. Booking is advisable, and rooms are available, with or without full board. *Closed Tues, and Wed lunch*.

Osteria del Carcere, Via del Castello 13, **t** 0577 941905 (€€). A tiny restaurant where you can enjoy the likes of *crostoni* with sausage and garlic, *ribollita*, and *porcini* and bean soup, and a good selection of local cheese. *Closed Wed, and Thurs lunch*.

Osteria delle Catene, Via Mainardi 18, **t** 0577 941966 (€€). Good regional food such as guinea fowl with wine and juniper. *Closed Wed*.

Enoteca Gustavo, Via San Matteo 29, **t** 0577 940057 (€). A good winebar for a glass of local Vernaccia and a snack; try *crostoni* with artichokes and *pecorino*, *bruschetta*, and the hams and cheeses. *Closed Tues*.

Gelateria di Piazza, Piazza della Cisterna, **t** 0577 942244 (€). Wonderful ice cream in a myriad of flavours. *Closed Nov–Feb*.

Volterra

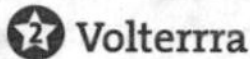

On a good day in spring or summer, sunshine illuminates Volterra's elegant streets and *piazze* full of locals, and holidaymakers come to buy alabaster cups and lampshades. A cloudy, windy day may remind you of fate and of the Etruscans, who arrived here some 2,700 years ago. They founded Volterra, like so many of their other cities, on top of a steep hill with a flat top; from afar, you see only a silhouette looming over an eerie, empty landscape. The soil around Volterra (population 12,796) is a thin clay, not much good for vines or olives. Few trees grow here. It makes good pasture land – it's not as barren as it looks, but it's disconcerting enough among the green woods and well-tended gardens of this part of Tuscany.

History

Etruscan **Velathri**, one of the largest, most powerful cities of the Dodecapolis, grew up in the 9th or 8th century BC from an even earlier settlement of the Villanovan culture, making it one of Italy's oldest cities. What has kept this hill continuously occupied for so many centuries is easily explained: sulphur, alum, salt, alabaster, lead and tin. The town is at the centre of one of the richest mining regions in Italy. In Etruscan days there was iron too, and the people of Velathri did a thriving trade with the Greeks and Carthaginians.

Velathri reached the height of its prosperity in the 5th and 4th centuries BC, leaving three great circuits of walls; the largest is more than 8km long, enclosing an area three times the size of the present city. The Romans captured it sometime in the 3rd century and Velathri began to decline. Along with most of Etruria, the city chose the populist side in the Social Wars, and was punished with a siege and sacking by Sulla in about 80 BC. Yet Roman *Velaterrae* remained an important town. It was the home of Saint Linus, successor to St Peter and the second pope.

Though many of the mines were giving out, Volterra survived the Dark Ages intact. The Lombards favoured it; for a time it was their capital. Medieval Volterra was ruled by its bishops, increasingly in conflict with the rising middle class. An independent *comune* was established late in the 12th century, a good Ghibelline town that participated in most of the factional wars of the period, before finally coming under the nominal control of Florence in 1361.

The Florentines were content with an annual tribute until the 'affair of the alum' in the 1470s, that wonderfully Italian ruckus that caused Pope Sixtus IV to plot the murder of Lorenzo de' Medici, excommunicate him and finally declare war on him. Lorenzo had taken over a syndicate to mine here for alum, a key material in dyeing cloth, on which the popes had a monopoly from their mines at Tolfa. Besides alarming the pope, Lorenzo caused the

Getting to and around Volterra

Volterra is 81km/2hrs 30mins southwest of Florence by way of Colle di Val d'Elsa and the winding SS68; it's 50km/1hrs 30mins west of Siena; and 61km/2hrs southeast of Pisa by way of Cascina and the SS439.

It isn't the easiest town to reach if you don't have a **car**. The only **train** service gets as far as Saline di Volterra, 10km southwest; this is an infrequent branch line to Cecina, 30km to the west on the coast south of Livorno. Some trains continue on from Cecina to Pisa. Buses connect the Saline station with Volterra, but not always when you need them.

Buses leave from Piazza Martiri della Libertà just inside the walls. You can get timetables and tickets at the tourist office. There are plenty of buses direct to Pisa and Montecatini Terme, 4 a day to Florence and Siena via Colle Val d'Elsa, and a few to Poggibonsi and San Gimignano; 3 a day go to Livorno via Cecina; 2 daily go to Massa Marittima (usually with a change at Monterotondo).

There are car **parking** spaces and underground garages outside the walls and at the gates. There are also some street parking spaces inside; you can usually sneak your car into one near your hotel in the evening (check out the situation on foot beforehand).

Volterrans to revolt when they realized he wanted to keep production down and prices high without letting any profit trickle down to them. Lorenzo eluded the pope with some difficulty (*see* pp.92–4), then hired the mercenary captain Federico da Montefeltro – the famous broken-nosed Duke of Urbino, patron of artists and scholars – to subdue the Volterrans. This he did with a brutality quite unbecoming to the 'ideal Renaissance prince'. Lorenzo wept crocodile tears over Volterra; after extinguishing the city's independence once and for all, he offered it the magnificent sum of 2,000 florins in damages.

Fortunately for the Volterrans, the mining business was picking up again. Between 1400 and 1800, many pits abandoned since Roman times reopened. In particular, Volterra became Europe's largest centre for the mining and working of alabaster, a craft tradition that is still the city's biggest business today.

A Little Archaeology

From Florence or Siena, the entrance to Volterra is the eastern gate, the **Porta a Selci**, with a moving tribute to the *partigiani* of Volterra killed in 1944–5. Inside, Via Don Minzoni is home to the

Volterra's *Pietra Candida*

The craft of carving alabaster in this region, which dates back to at least 800 bc, has revived dramatically in the last 200 years, and Volterra is full of small workshops, and even a few large firms, that turn the stone into vases, figurines, ashtrays and anything else serviceable or collectable. Many alabaster-workers are genuine artists, turning out one-of-a-kind pieces at high prices; others produce vast numbers of attractive little baubles costing from €3. Try:

Artisans' Cooperative (Cooperativa Artieri Alabastro), Piazza dei Priorl.
Via Porta all'Arco 45. Some of the most original creations in town.
Via Porta all'Arco 26. Unusual miniatures.
Via di Sotto 2. Simple, elegant vases and lamps.
Via Antonio Gramsci, Via di Sotto 20 and 53. Interesting shops.
Via Guarnacci 26, Via di Sotto. Splashy modern work in coloured alabaster.

For crafts of a different kind, head for **Via Don Minzoni 54**, where Auro Bongini makes dolls'-house furniture from local olive wood in a 19th-century style; call in advance (**t** 0588 88040).

Museo Etrusco Guarnacci
open mid-Mar–Oct daily 9–7; 5 Nov–mid-Mar daily 9–2; adm (inc adm to other Volterra museums)

Museo Etrusco Guarnacci, the repository for finds from the Velathri necropolises. More than 600 sculpted alabaster, travertine or terracotta cinerary urns make up the core collection. Exhibits are arranged in chronological order, except the original Guarnacci collection, grouped by subject matter. These tend to be conventional – an Etruscan family would ask the artist for a scene from Greek mythology, from the Trojan War perhaps, or something like the death of Actaeon. Perhaps the artist already had one in stock. One rule of Etruscan art is its lack of rules. Expect anything: some of the reclining figures of the dead atop the urns are brilliant portraiture; others could be the first attempts of a third-grade craft class. All, holding the little cups or dishes they carry down into Hades, look as serene and happy as only a defunct Etruscan can. As always, the Etruscans do their best to make you laugh. One terracotta, the *Urna degli Sposi*, portrays a hilariously caricatured couple who look as if they are about to start arguing over whose turn it is to do the dishes. Another Etruscan joke is the *Ombra della Sera* (evening shadow), quite a celebrity around Volterra: a small, carefully detailed bronze of a man with a quizzical expression and spidery, grotesquely elongated arms and legs. There are also prehistoric finds, Roman mosaics from the baths, artefacts discovered in the theatre, and some fine Etruscan jewellery.

The museum lies a stone's throw from Piazza XX Settembre, home to the bus terminal; from here Via Gramsci leads towards the centre. Climb any of the alleys south of the museum to reach Volterra's **Parco Archeologico**, located just inside the walls. There isn't really much that's archaeological about it – some Etruscan foundations and a huge ancient cistern, the *Piscina Romana* – but it does boast a lush English garden of manicured lawns and shady groves unlike anything else in Tuscany.

Parco Archeologico
open mid-Mar–Oct daily 10.30–5.30; Nov–mid-Mar Sat, Sun and hols 10–4; adm

Above the park stretches an exceptionally long, elegant castle, the **Fortezza Medicea**, which was begun in 1343 and completed by Lorenzo de' Medici in 1472. You can't get inside; it's been a prison almost from the day it was built – perhaps the fanciest in this nation of fancy calabooses.

Piazza dei Priori

This is a fine little republican piazza, surrounded by plain, erect *palazzi* that discreetly call your attention to the sober dignity of the *comune*. The **Palazzo dei Priori**, which was constructed in 1208, is said to be the oldest such building in all of Tuscany, and to have served as the model for Florence's Palazzo Vecchio and many others. Across the square, the simple **Palazzo Pretorio** is almost as old. Next to it, the rakishly leaning **Porcellino tower** takes its name from the little pig sculpted in relief near the base, barely visible after seven centuries.

The Cathedral and the Etruscan Arch

Just right of the Palazzo dei Priori, a bit of green and white striped marble façade peeks out between the palaces: this is the back of the archiepiscopal palace, around the corner in **Piazza del Duomo**. Quiet and dowdy, this square contrasts with the well-built Piazza dei Priori, a lasting memory of the defeat of Volterra's medieval bishops by the *comune*. Its octagonal **baptistry**, begun in 1283, has its marble facing completed only on one side. Within is a fine early 1500s baptismal font by Andrea Sansovino, a Mino da Fiesole altar, and a holy-water dish carved from an Etruscan boundary stone.

The plain **cathedral** façade has a good marble doorway. This forlorn mongrel of a building was begun in the Pisan-Romanesque style in the 1200s and worked on fitfully for two centuries. The campanile went up in 1493; the interior was redone in the 1580s, when the blatant Medici coat of arms was placed over the high altar. The *duomo*'s works of art are few but of an exceptionally high quality, beginning with the painted coffered ceiling from the 16th century. Fittingly, as this is Volterra, some of the windows are made of thin-sliced alabaster, a stone also used in the intricate, Renaissance **tabernacle** by Mino da Fiesole over the high altar. The chapels on either side have excellent Tuscan woodcarving: a 15th-century piece, the *Madonna dei Chierici*, attributed to local artist Francesco di Domenico Valdambrino off to the left, and to the right a polychromed *Deposition* with five separate, full-sized figures, ranking among the best of 13th-century Pisan sculpture.

Another chapel to the right contains fragments of unusually good anonymous trecento frescoes of the *Passion of Christ*, much ahead of their time in composition, in the figures and the folds of the draperies – even Giorgio Vasari might have liked them. In the left aisle, the *pergamo* (**pulpit**) is one of the lesser-known works of the Pisani, less spectacular than the ones in Pisa, Siena and Pistoia but still showing something of the vividness and immediacy of the best Pisan sculpture. Guglielmo Pisano did the fine relief of the *Last Supper*. The pulpit's supporting columns rest on two lions, a bull and one unclassifiable beast, all by Bonamico Pisano.

In the oratory, off the left aisle near the entrance, behind a 16th-century wooden statue group of the *Adoration of the Magi*, is a small fresco said to be by Benozzo Gozzoli, though perhaps because of its deterioration or early date it lacks Gozzoli's usual charm. Close by, in the archiepiscopal palace, the small **Museo d'Arte Sacra** displays sculpture and architectural fragments, and a Della Robbia terracotta of St Linus, Volterra's patron.

Museo d'Arte Sacra
open mid-Mar–Oct daily 9–1 and 3–6; Nov–mid-Mar 9–1; adm

From the Duomo, retrace your steps towards Piazza dei Priori and turn down Via Porta all'Arco to find the quaintest old relic in Volterra, the **Arco Etrusco**. The Etruscans built the columns at least;

the arch above them was rebuilt in Roman times. Set into this arch are three primeval black basalt sculpted heads from the original gate, *c.* 600 BC, believed to represent the Etruscan gods Tinia (Jupiter), Uni (Juno) and Menvra (Minerva). Nearly 3000 years of wind and rain have worn them into great black knobs – carved out of the *voussoirs*, they resemble nothing so much as garden slugs.

Just off Piazza dei Priori, the intersection of Via Roma and Via Buonparenti, is one of the most picturesque corners of Volterra, with venerable stone arches and tower houses such as the 13th-century Casa Buonparenti. Via Buonparenti leads into Via dei Sarti, where the elder Antonio da Sangallo's restored Palazzo Solaini holds the city's art collection.

The Pinacoteca

Pinacoteca
open mid-Mar–Oct daily 9–7, 5 Nov–mid-Mar daily 9–2; adm (inc adm to other Volterra museums)

This small but choice collection includes a fair amount of trecento Sienese painting, including a glorious altarpiece of the *Madonna and Child* by Taddeo di Bartolo. To complement the remarkable 14th-century wood sculptures in the Duomo, it also has two figures portraying the *Annunciation* by Francesco di Valdambrino. Neri di Bicci was a quattrocento Florentine, but his *St Sebastian* here looks entirely Sienese – probably at the request of the customer. Among other Tuscan works are a shiny altarpiece by Ghirlandaio, and two by Luca Signorelli (or his workshop): a *Madonna and Saints* and an *Annunciation*. The prize of the collection Is the Rosso Fiorentino *Deposition*, dated 1521 and perhaps his greatest work in all Italy. Even out in the boondocks of Volterra, it attracts considerable attention from art scholars, being one of the thresholds from the Renaissance into Mannerism, with all the precision and clarity of the best quattrocento work yet also an intensity that few works had ever achieved. *The Descent from the Cross* is a starkly emotional subject; in Rosso's work it is terror and disarray, a greenish Christ and a small, nearly hysterical crowd dramatically illuminated against a darkening deep blue sky. You'll find little that this painting has in common with Rosso's contemporaries, not even with his fellow madman Pontormo (who did his own, quite different, *Deposition* in Florence's Santa Felicità) – but, oddly, it could almost be mistaken for a work of Goya.

San Francesco and the Roman Theatre

Another of Volterra's gems is a few minutes' walk west of here – follow Via San Lino past backstreets of alabaster workshops to **San Francesco**. Here the attraction is off to the right of the altar: the **chapel of the Holy Cross**, completely frescoed in 1410 by a Florentine artist whose name seems to be Cenni di Francesco di Ser Cenni – a rare soul, indeed, with a sophisticated, wonderfully reactionary, medieval sense of composition and his own ideas about Christian iconography, in a bold style in places almost like modern poster art. *The Legend of the Cross* frescoes generally follow those of Gaddi at Santa Croce in Florence (*see* p.156), and there are also scenes of *St Francis*, the *Passion*, and the *Massacre of the Innocents*, many with fantasy city backgrounds.

Palazzo Incontri-Viti
Via dei Sarti 46, north of Palazzo Pretorio; t 0588 84047, open Mar–Nov daily 10–1 and 2.30–6.30; rest of year by appt; adm

Back towards the centre, the vast facade of the 16th-century **Palazzo Incontri-Viti** is attributed to Bartolomeo Ammannati. It was built for Attilo Incontri, minister to the grand duke of Tuscany; recently the Vitis, wealthy alabaster merchants, started opening 12 of their lavish rooms to the public, filled with heirlooms going back to the 15th century. In 1964 Visconti shot his film *Vague Stelle dell'Orso* here. Near the top of Via dei Sarti, the church of San Michele has a Pisan Romanesque facade.

Teatro Romano
open mid-Mar–Oct daily 10.30–5.30; Nov–mid-Mar Sat, Sun and hols 10–4; adm

From here Via Guarnacci leads down outside the walls to Viale Francesco Ferruci, home to a lively outdoor **market** on Saturday, and to ancient Velaterrae's large **Roman theatre**. Enough marble slabs and columns have survived of this for the archaeologists to reconstruct part of the stage building – an impressive testimony to the past importance of the city.

The *Balze*

Leaving Volterra by the San Francesco gate, you pass the Borgo San Giusto and its ruins of the 12th-century Pisan-Romanesque **church of Santo Stefano**. The road to Pisa exits through the outer **Etruscan walls**, barely more than foundations but traceable for most of their length around the city and easily visible here.

Some 2km beyond, decorating the moors, are the *balze*: barren clay-walled gullies that may have begun as Etruscan mining cuts. They've a life of their own; medieval chronicles report them gobbling up farms and churches around the city, and no one has yet found a way to stop their inexorable growth. In the 1700s they tried to atone for their appetite, revealing some of the most important Etruscan necropolises yet discovered, and contributing urns to the Guarnacci Museum. Now even the necropolises are all but gone, though on the edge of one cliff you can see the **Badia**, an 11th-century Camaldolensian abbey, half-devoured.

The Val di Cecina and the Metal Hills

There are few attractions in the romantically empty Volterran hills. Take the SS68 west from Volterra along the Cecina valley to Guardistallo to reach a rolling valley with pines and cypresses in just the right places – a good Tuscan backdrop for any Renaissance painting. **Montecatini Val di Cecina**, in the hills to the north, is quiet and medieval, with a 12th-century castle. Further west, a big wine area extends around **Montescudaio** (Montescudaio, red and white, is a distinguished if lesser-known dry variety with a DOC label).

Metal Hills

The most unusual road from Volterra, the SS439, leads south over the **Colline Metallifere** towards Massa Marittima and the coast. These 'metal hills', along with the iron mines of Elba, did much to finance the gilded existence of the Etruscans. Several mines operate today, though driving through the hills you see little but oak forests and olive groves.

Larderello, self-proclaimed 'World Centre of Geothermal Energy', is the north boundary of volcanic Italy; that extinct volcano, Monte Amiata, and the ancient crater lakes of Umbria and Lazio are not far away. This far north, the only manifestations of a subterranean nature are benign little geysers and gurgling pools of sulphurous mud. Larderello is a growing town; huge ugly cooling towers of the type that signify a nuclear power plant anywhere else can be spotted wherever there is a geothermal source worth tapping. Near the centre is a strange, postmodernist 1950s church by Michelucci, architect of Florence's rail station, and the **Museo della Geotermia**, explaining this overheated little town's career.

Museo della Geotermia
t 0588 07724, open mid-Mar–mid-Sept Mon–Fri 9–12 and 1.30–5.30, Sat and Sun 10–12 and 1.30–6.30; mid-Sept–mid-Mar Mon–Fri 8–12 and 1.30–4.30, Sun 9–12 and 1.30–5.30

After Larderello, almost as far as Monterotondo, the landscape is uncanny. It smells bad, too; geysers and steam vents (*soffioni*) whistle and puff by the roadside, while murky pits bubble up boric salts amidst yellow and grey slag piles. Follow the yellow signs of the *itinerario dei soffioni* to see the best of it. Despite the sulphur and borax, the cooling towers and occasional rusting hulks of old mining equipment, the Metal Hills are quite winsome, especially south of Larderello (still on the SS439) around the medieval village of Castelnuovo di Val di Cecina, surrounded by chestnuts and the Ala dei Diavoli ('Devils' Wing') pass at the crest of the hills.

Monterotondo Marittimo, further south, has more than its fair share of subsurface curiosities; nearby Lago Boracifero is Italy's centre for borax mining. In some places, the ground is covered with strange webs of steam pipes, built since the *comune* discovered its unique resource could power almost everything in town for free.

Where to Stay and Eat in Volterra

Volterra >
Via Turazza 2, t 0588 86150, www.provolterra.it; Palazzo dei Priori 19–20, t 0588 87257, www.volterratur.it

Volterra ✉ 56048

*****Villa Nencini**, Borgo S. Stefano 55, **t** 0588 86386, *www.villanencini.it* (€€€€). A 16th-century house with beautiful views, a lovely outdoor pool. and a restaurant and *enoteca*, just north of the centre. Breakfast is included; half/full board is available.

L'Etrusca, Via Porta all'Arco 37, just off Piazza del Popolo, **t** 0588 84073, *letrusca@libero.it* (€€). Apartments with kitchenettes, for two or three people. Guests may use the pool at the sister establishment Sant'Elisa (*see* p.368).

*****Nazionale**, Via dei Marchesi 11, **t** 0588 86284, *www.albergonazionalevolterra.it* (€€). A pleasant, comfy old hotel within the town walls. Rates include breakfast; half/full board is available (the restaurant serves Tuscan food).

******San Lino**, Via San Lino 26, near Porta San Francesco, **t** 0588 88053, *www.hotelsanlino.com* (€€). Tastefully remodelled rooms in an old cloister (buffet breakfast included), a garden, a sun terrace, a pool, an internet and private parking.

Many restaurants here specialize in roast boar and so on – medieval fare in keeping with the spirit of the place.

Del Duca, Via di Castello 2, **t** 0588 81510 (€€€). A standout restaurant offering the likes of *ribollita* with wood pigeon and Volterra truffles, plus a vegetarian menu. *Closed Tues, 2wks Jan/Feb, and 2wks Nov.*

Il Porcellino, Vicolo delle Prigioni 9, **t** 0588 86392 (€€€). Lots of different set menus, combining seafood and Tuscan favourites with local treats such as boar with olives. Booking is advisable. *Closed Tues, and Oct–Mar.*

Il Sacco Fiorentino , Piazza XX Settembre 18, **t** 0588 88537 (€€). A place named after Lorenzo de' Medici's massacre of the citizens of Volterra in 1472, serving *pappardelle* with *mallegato* (a kind of salami) and more. *Closed Wed, mid-Jan–Feb, and 2wks June/July.*

Sant' Elisa, about 3km from town on SS68, **t** 0588 80034 (€€). A favourite with Volterrans, in an old farmhouse, serving very local cuisine, including *pappardelle* with deer sauce. There are a few guestrooms too. *Closed Tues.*

La Vecchia Lira >>

La Vecchia Lira, Via G. Matteotti 19, **t** 0588 86180 (€€). A jolly lunchtime self-service *tavola calda* with especially good mains (try the rabbit with artichokes or the duck stewed in chocolate and pine nuts), and a regular restaurant in the evenings.

Massa Marittima

This lovely, rugged area is part of the coastal Maremma district only in name; even in Roman times it was considered part of the 'maritime' province. And for just as long, it's been making its living from the mines, though today its 10,000 people are not enough to fill the space within its medieval walls. It may be small, but its brief prosperity left it beautiful. Come to admire the second city of the Sienese Republic, a lesson in urban refinement within a small place, and its exquisite cathedral, a great Tuscan medieval monument.

This town appeared as a free *comune*, the Repubblica Massetana, around 1225, just coinciding with a dizzying period of prosperity owing to its discovery of new silver and copper deposits nearby. This wealth proved fatally attractive to Massa's bigger neighbours: Pisa and Siena fought over it for a century, and it finally fell to the latter in 1337. Soon after, the mines gave out, putting Massa into centuries of decline. Malaria was a problem from the 1500s, and not until the Lorraine dukes drained the wet places and reopened some of the mines did things start looking up.

The Duomo

This is quite a sight, rising incongruously on its pedestal, its effect heightened by its setting above and at an angle to Massa's **Piazza Garibaldi**, a true *tour de force* of medieval town design. The rebuilding of an earlier cathedral began around 1200 and finished in 1250, though some additions were made; note the contrast between the original Pisan-Romanesque style, with blind arches and lozenges, and the Sienese campanile, added about 1400. Its best features include Gothic windows, capitals and the carvings of animals protecting humans on the façade and the left side.

Getting to Massa Marittima

Massa is 22km off the coastal Via Aurelia at Follonica and worth the diversion if you're passing; direct from Siena it's a not particularly captivating 65km/1hr 20min drive on the SS73 (passing San Galgano) and the SS441.

There are 3 or 4 **buses** a day from Volterra (change at Monterotondo), 5 to nearby Follonica, and frequent buses and **trains** from there to Grosseto (Massa is in Grosseto province), plus 2 a day to Florence and Siena, and one direct to Grosseto. Information and tickets are available from Agenzia Massa Veterensis opposite the Duomo. Most buses stop on Via Corridoni, behind and a little downhill from the Duomo.

The interior, under massive columns with delicate capitals, each different, has a few trecento and quattrocento frescoes. On the left are a luminous *Madonna* by Duccio (1318) and unique reliefs from the original 11th-century church: staring priests and apostles in vigorous, cartoon-like style. On the right hangs the *Nativity of Mary* by that most peculiar Sienese artist, Rutilio Manetti (d. 1639): woebegone ladies and a jellicle cat attend a pug-nosed, thumb-sucking, very unbeatific baby Mary. Nearby is a fine font with reliefs by Giraldo da Como (*c.* 1250) and a Renaissance tabernacle added in 1447. A wooden crucifix by Giovanni Pisano hangs over the high altar; in the Gothic apse is the *Ark of San Cerbone* with more reliefs (1324) on the life of Massa's patron saint.

Museo Archeologico/ Pinacoteca
Piazza Garibaldi; open April–Oct Tues–Sun 10–12.30 and 3.30–7; Nov–Mar Tues–Sun 10–12.30 and 3–5; adm

Torre del Candaliere
open April–Oct Tues–Sun 10–1 and 3–6; Nov–Mar Tues–Sun 11–1 and 2.30–4.30; adm

Museo di Arte e di Storia della Miniera
Piazza Matteotti; open April–Oct Tues–Sun 3–5.30; rest of year by appt on **t** *0566 902289; adm*

Museo della Miniera
open for frequent guided tours, in English by request, summer Tues–Sun 10–5.45; winter Tues–Sun 10.15–4.30; call **t** *0566 902289 for exact times; adm*

Up and Down Massa

Next to the cathedral , the 1230 **Palazzo del Podestà** holds Massa's uninspiring **Museo Archeologico** (the Medici dukes carried the best finds to Florence) and the small **Pinacoteca**, in which the best work is a *Maestà* by Ambrogio Lorenzetti, aglow with rosy faces, flowers and golden trim. Note the angel with the distaff and spindle in the centre – a sure sign the local wool guild paid for the painting.

Piazza Garibaldi is lively, often crowded with Teutons perching on the steps of the **Duomo** or swigging beer in the café-pizzerias. Via Libertà leads into the older quarter, a nest of arches and alleys that has barely changed over centuries. Like Siena, Massa is divided into three *terzi*; this is the *terzo* of **Civitavecchia**. Via Moncini climbs to the **Città Nuova**, a 14th-century suburb behind unusual Sienese fortifications; the street ends at Piazza Matteotti, with the 1330 **Torre del Candaliere** (Torre dell'Orologio), linked to the fortifications by the **Senese arch**, a slender walkway; it's a beautiful ensemble, created more for show than any military consideration. Up Corso Diaz, **Sant'Agostino church** (1313) has works by Rutilio Manetti.

No visit is complete without a trip to a mining museum; the **Museo di Arte e di Storia della Miniera** is very small; the **Museo della Miniera**, on Via Corridoni, leads into nearly 1km of tunnels, with exhibits to show how the job was done from medieval days. Ask politely at the library and you might get to see the city's treasure, the 1310 *Codice Minerario Massetano*, modern Europe's first code of laws concerning mining rights.

ⓘ Massa >
Via Parenti 22, t 0566 902756, www.coopcollinemetallifere.it, www.aptmassacarrara.it

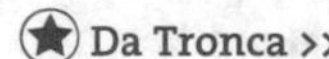

Where to Stay and Eat in Massa Marittima

Massa Marittima ✉ 58024

Massa's hotels are often full.

****Duca del Mare**, Via D. Alighieri 1/2, **t** 0566 902284, *www.ducadelmare.it* (€€). A modern building in a lovely setting with a garden and rural views, with a pool and a trattoria. A buffet breakfast is included, and half board is available. Archery, mountainbiking and horseriding can be arranged.

****Girifalco**, Via Massentana 25, **t** 0566 902177, *www.ilgirifalco.com* (€€). A simple but comfy choice with an excellent restaurant using home-produced meat, veg and oils. Breakfast is included, and half board is available

Da Bracalì, Loc. Ghirlanda, **t** 0566 902318 (€€€€). Haute cuisine variations on local dishes – try pumpkin flowers with lobster. Book ahead. *Closed Mon, Tues, and Wed and Thurs lunch.*

Taverna del Vecchio Borgo, **t** 0566 903950 (€€€). Great *pici* with *porcini*, or boar with olives. *Closed Sun eve, Mon and mid-Feb–mid-Mar.*

Da Tronca, Vicolo Porte 5, **t** 0566 901991 (€€). A trattoria with delicious cod *alla Maremmana* and other local fare. *Closed lunch, Wed and mid-Dec–Feb.*

San Galgano and the Sword in the Stone

Abbazia di San Galgano
2km north of Palazzetto; open daily 8am–11pm

The SS73 from Massa to Siena skirts the southern Colline Metallifere, through lands that saw a great medieval flowering of monasticism. The monks left one of the most unusual, least-visited sights in Tuscany – the ruined Cistercian **abbey of San Galgano**. Galgano Guidotti, from nearby Chiusdino, was a dissolute soldier who had a vision of St Michael on Montesiepi, ordering him to change his ways. Thrusting his sword into a rock to symbolize his new life, he became a holy hermit; ensuing miracles ensured his canonization in 1181. The community he founded, associated with the Cistercian Order, played a vital role in the community for centuries, draining swamps, building mills and starting a small textile industry. The Republic of Siena found them indispensable architects, administrators and accountants. With its French architects eager to initiate Italians in the glories of the Gothic style, the order began its great **abbey church** in 1218. Today only the lovely travertine columns and pointed arches remain, with the sky as roof and green lawns as carpet. Surviving parts of the monastery are in the care of Olivetan nuns.

After Galgano's death, St Michael appeared on a hill above the abbey to command his followers to build the **Cappella di Montesiepi** over the sword in the stone; this curious round chapel, one of very few in Italy, was begun in 1185. The sword is still there, protruding from its rock in the centre. A reminder of a branch of medieval mysticism hardly well understood, it's a curious place – on one of our visits, a beautiful woman in black entered, carrying a silver sword, and went to a side room with the caretaker. Note the human hands in a glass box, supposedly bitten off by wolves. The altar has a cross of the type often seen on buildings of the Knights Templar; the ceiling dome, patterned in 22 concentric stripes, may represent the heavenly spheres of medieval cosmology.

Southern Tuscany

Not counting the coastal Maremma around Grosseto, the old territories of the Sienese Republic make a coherent landscape, of rolling hills mostly given over to farming and pastures. It isn't as garden-like as some other parts of Tuscany, though vineyards and avenues of cypresses are not lacking. Hill towns poke above the horizon – Montepulciano, Pienza and Castiglione d'Orcia. At times, it seems the whole region is laid out before you, bounded on one side by the hills around Siena, on the other by the cones of Monte Amiata and Radicofani. In the little tourist offices they remark that not many English or Americans pass through, missing beautiful countryside, among the best food and wine in Tuscany, and delightful towns with reminders of the Renaissance and Middle Ages.

14

Don't miss

1. An élite Renaissance monastery
Monte Oliveto Maggiore p.374

2. Pope Pius II's Renaissance city
Pienza p.379

3. *Vino nobile* and fine art
Montepulciano p.381

4. Underground mysteries
Chiusi p.387

5. Idyllic skiing and hiking
Monte Amiata p.390

See map overleaf

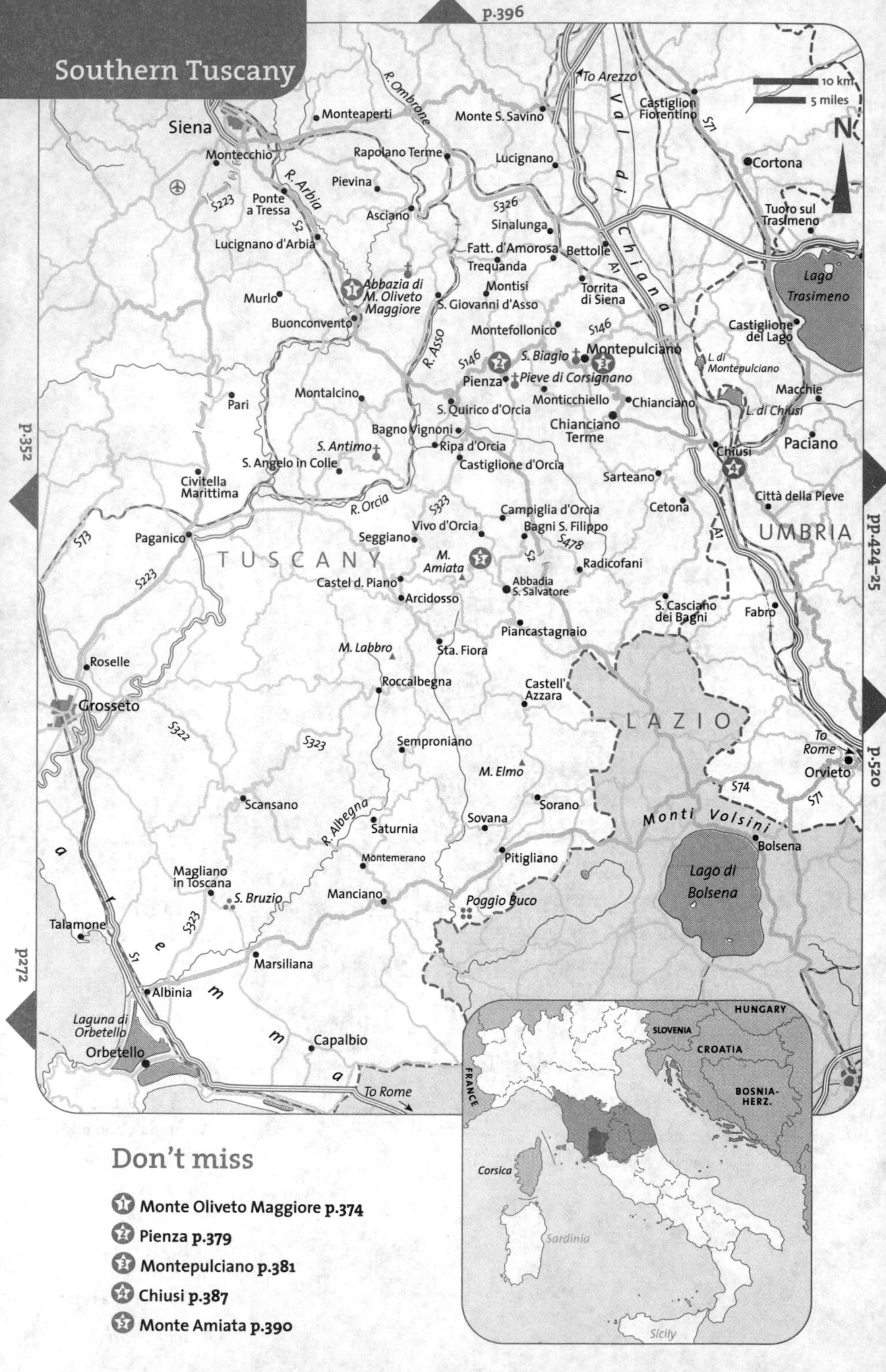

Don't miss

1. Monte Oliveto Maggiore **p.374**
2. Pienza **p.379**
3. Montepulciano **p.381**
4. Chiusi **p.387**
5. Monte Amiata **p.390**

Asciano and the *Crete*

The SS326 from Siena heads east, its main purpose to get you to Cortona (*see* pp.418–22) then Umbria. Before leaving Siena province, it passes the village of **Monteaperti**, where the Sienese won their famous victory over Florence in 1260, and **Rapolano Terme** (27km), a small spa retaining some of its medieval walls. Besides the hot springs there is a surplus of natural gas in the area, some of it pumped from wells and some leaking out of the ground – take care not to drop a match.

Museo d'Arte Sacra/ Museo Etrusco
Corso Matteotti 122; open Mar–Oct Tues–Sun 10–1 and 3–7; Nov–Feb Thurs–Sat 10–1 and 3–5.30, Sun 10–1 and 2.30–6; adm

Via del Canto 11
to visit ask at pharmacy on Corso Matteotti

Asciano, 10km south of Rapolano, has walls built by the Sienese in 1351 and a good collection of Sienese art. Its **Museo d'Arte Sacra** and the **Museo Etrusco** are in the same building, **Palazzo Corboli**. The house at **Via del Canto 11** has some Roman mosaics.

Southeast of Siena, the valleys of the Ombrone and the Asso enclose the country of the *crete*. Like the *balze* of Volterra, the *crete* are uncanny monuments to the power of erosion. The countryside around Asciano is dotted with them, exposing chalk cliffs where the soil above has eroded; they often appear in the backgrounds of 14th- and 15th-century Sienese and Florentine paintings (similar eroded chalk hills are called *biancane*). This sheep country suffered a great deal after the Second World War, when many local men left to seek work in the cities. Today, immigrants from Sardinia make up a sizable minority of the population, born shepherds trying to get the business back on its feet.

Old **Sinalunga**, on its hill, is next (22km east); the main square is named after Garibaldi, to commemorate his arrest here in 1867 on the orders of King Vittorio Emanuele, afraid his volunteers were about to attack Rome. **Torrita di Siena**, an old Sienese border fortress 6km southwest of the junction with the A1 from Florence to Rome, owes its name to the tall towers of its walls (some remain).

ⓘ **Buonconvento >>**
Piazzale Garibaldi 2, t 0577 807181 (closed Mon)

ⓘ **Asciano >**
Corso Matteotti 18, t 0577 719510

Where to Stay and Eat in Asciano and the *Crete*

In this quiet corner, villages may only have one real hotel, or none. But there are plenty of farmhouse *agriturismo* rooms; follow signs, or ask at tourist offices. Some restaurants and private homes, too, let rooms – ask around.

Asciano ✉ 53041

La Pievina, Loc. La Pievina near Asciano on Laurentana road, **t** 0577 718368 (€€€). A very friendly place specializing in sea fish, fowl and veggie dishes. The owners also let a house in the centre. *Closed Mon, Tues, and lunch exc Sun.*

Buonconvento ✉ 53022

****Albergo Ristorante Roma**, Via Soccini 14, **t** 0577 806021 (€). The closest rooms to Monte Oliveto Maggiore: simple and old-fashioned, with breakfast included. The very good restaurant serves traditional fare.

Sinalunga ✉ 53048

******Locanda dell'Amorosa**, Loc. L'Amorosa, 2km south of Sinalunga, **t** 0577 677211, *www.amorosa.it* (€€€€€). A truly special place (book far ahead) – a medieval hamlet with a manor house, frescoed church, 16 beautiful rooms, an outdoor pool and a restaurant (€€€). *Closed Mon; restaurant Tues lunch.*

Monte Oliveto Maggiore and Around

South of Siena, the SS2 wends towards Rome, roughly following the Roman Via Cassia and medieval pilgrims' path to Rome, the *Via Francigena*. It passes **Lucignano d'Arbia** (16km), a charming, tiny village with a medieval church, and **Buonconvento** (27km), a gritty industrial town that hides a miniature walled medieval centre. The walls, no longer very proper or military, are peppered with windows of the houses built against them. There are two fine gates either end of the main street, and, in the middle, the 14th-century parish church with an altarpiece by Matteo di Giovanni.

In the broken, jumbled hills south of Asciano, austere green meadows alternate with ragged gullies and bare white cliffs. At the centre of these *crete*, in the bleakest and most barren part, is a grove of tall, black cypresses around the **monastery of Monte Oliveto Maggiore**. Gentlemen from Siena's merchant elite founded it, including Giovanni Tolomei and Ambrogio Piccolomini, jaded merchants and sincere Christians who retired here in 1313 to escape the fatal sophistication of the medieval city. Their Olivetan Order was approved by the pope only six years later. With such wealthy backers, the monastery became a sort of elite hermitage for central Tuscany. An ambitious building programme in the 1400s made it a marvel of Renaissance clarity and rationality, expressed in simple structures and good Siena brick.

17 Monte Oliveto Maggiore
9km from Buonconvento on SS451; **t** *0577 718567; open daily 9.15–12 and 3.15–5 (until 6 in summer)*

The beautiful, asymmetrical **gatehouse**, which is decorated with a Della Robbia terracotta, makes for a fitting introduction. Inside, the well-proportioned brick **abbey church** (which was finished in 1417) has an exceptional set of wooden intarsia **choirstalls** by the master of the genre, Fra Giovanni da Verona – it's among the best work of this kind in Italy. Note also the unusual dome with an octagon of interlocking arches, an Islamic Andalucian design that made its way here via Spanish Christian churches and the chapel of the Castel Nuovo in Naples.

The monastery's greatest treasure is the **great cloister**, with 36 frescoes of scenes from the life of St Benedict (whose original rule Tolomei and the Olivetans were trying to restore). All 36 are currently being restored. The first nine are by Luca Signorelli, with formidable ladies and bulky, white-robed monks in his distinctive balloonish forms and sparing use of colour. The rest are by Il Sodoma (1505–8) – some of his best painting, ethereal scenes of Pre-Raphaelite ladies and mandarin monks, with blue and purple backgrounds of ideal landscapes and cities. Mr Sodomite himself appears in the scene '*Come Benedetto risaldò lo capistero che era rotta*' ('How Benedict repaired the broken sieve'); he's the dissipated fellow on the left, with the white gloves. He also painted in his pet badgers, of which he was very fond.

Unlike so many great Tuscan art shrines, Monte Oliveto, which is isolated in the Sienese hills, retains some of its original aloof dignity. Though Napoleon suppressed the monastery in 1810, a group of talented brothers still works here, restoring old books. They're vowed to silence, but the monkish gift shop outside sells home-made wine and honey, as well as other products from the monasteries around Tuscany.

In the *crete* around Monte Oliveto, the village of **San Giovanni d'Asso** (8km southeast) is built around a Sienese fortress; the church of San Pietro in Villore is from the 12th century, with an ambitious, unusual façade. From here, unsignposted byroads lead east to **Montisi** (7km) and **Trequanda** (12km), two fine villages, seldom visited because they're hard to find; the latter has a 13th-century castle and Romanesque church. You might even find **Sant'Anna in Camprena**, between Montisi and Pienza, an ambitious medieval monastery complex that time forgot – until the location scouts from *The English Patient* arrived. The place is now being fitfully restored, and if you liked Il Sodoma's work in Monte Oliveto, stop here to see another of his frescoes, portraying Christ with children, small dogs and fantasy Roman monuments.

Montalcino and Around

On a lofty hill inhabited since Etruscan times, swathed in vineyards and olive groves, walled **Montalcino** (population 5,400) dominates the serene countryside 14km south of Buonconvento. Its major attraction is liquid – Brunello di Montalcino, a dark pungent red proudly holding its own among Italy's finest wines.

Every year at the Palio in Siena, a procession of representatives from all the towns that once were part of the republic takes place. The honour of leading the parade belongs to Montalcino, for its loyalty and for the great service that it rendered in 1555 after the fall of Siena (*see* p.327). During the siege, diehard republicans escaped from Siena to the impregnable fortress of Montalcino, where they established the 'Republic of Siena at Montalcino', holding out against the Medici until 1559. Today, Montalcino is a friendly, resolutely sleepy town.

Within the Walls

Piazza Cavour in home to the modest **archaeology museum**, set in a former hospital pharmacy with detached frescoes by a student of Il Sodoma. Via Mazzini leads west to Piazza del Popolo and the attractive **Palazzo Comunale**, begun in the late 13th century, with a slender tower that apes the Torre di Mangia in Siena (*see* p.332). Nearby, **Sant'Agostino** is a simple Sienese church containing some original frescoes from the 1300s.

Getting to Montalcino

There are regular **buses** from Siena (41km/1hr), a few involving a change at Buonconvento, near the SS2 crossroads for Montalcino. Buses stop at Piazza Cavour at the east end of town; you can get tickets at the bar on the piazza. There are no convenient buses to Sant'Antimo.

Museo Civico e Diocesano d'Arte Sacra
open Tues–Sun 10–1 and 2–5.40; adm

The **diocesan and civic museum** round the corner has Sienese paintings and polychromed wood statues, including *Madonnas* by three great Sienese artists (Martini, Pietro Lorenzetti and Il Vecchietta), and some of the earliest successes of Sienese art, an illuminated Bible and painted crucifix, both from the 12th century. Besides some minor works of the 14th–15th-century Sienese masters, there's a collection of local majolica from the same period.

Rocca
open summer daily 9–8; winter daily 9–6; adm to go up on walls

Just down Via Ricasoli, at the east end of town, the impressive 14th-century **Rocca** was the centre of the fortifications that kept the Spaniards and Florentines at bay. This citadel was the last stronghold of the Sienese and a symbol of all the medieval freedoms of the Italian cities blotted out in the reactionary 1500s. Near the entrance is a plaque with a poem from the 'Piedmontese Volunteers of Liberty', extolling Montalcino's bravery in 'refusing the Medici thief'. Now a city park, the Rocca contains the last battle standard of the Sienese Republic and an ***enoteca***, where you can acquaint yourself with Montalcino's venerable Brunello and other local wines, such as Moscadello and Rosso di Montalcino.

Following the town walls on the north side, you pass through neighbourhoods largely made up of orchards and gardens. The **cathedral**, on Via Spagni, was mostly rebuilt in the 1700s. Follow that street past the Baroque church of the Madonna del Soccorso, and you come to the city park, the 'Balcony of Tuscany', with views over Siena and beyond.

Sant'Antimo

Sant'Antimo
about 10km south of Montalcino; open daily 6.45am–9pm (Mass sung Mon–Sat 9.15am and 7pm, Sun 11am and 6.30pm); adm

One of the finest Romanesque churches in Tuscany, Sant'Antimo originally formed part of a 9th-century Benedictine monastery founded, according to legend, by Charlemagne. The present building, begun in 1118, incorporates parts of the Carolingian works, including the crypt. This half-ruined complex, reached by a long, winding avenue of cypresses, could easily serve as the set for *The Name of the Rose*. An important monastic community flourished here, and there are still some monks; they'll sell you a CD of their Gregorian chant, which you can hear them sing at Mass. The church is exquisite, with its elegant tower and rounded apse. Some of the stone inside, on the capitals and elsewhere, is luminous alabaster from Volterra. The sophistication of the architecture is impressive – in particular, the Byzantine-style women's gallery, and the ambulatory behind the apse with its radiating chapels.

ⓘ **Montalcino >**
Costa del Municipio 8,
t 0577 849331

Tourist Information in Montalcino

A few of the **vineyards** that produce the famous Brunello di Montalcino are on the road south for Sant'Antimo. Two welcome visitors: the Azienda Agricola Greppo (**t** 0577 848087) and the Cantine dei Barbi (**t** 0577 841111). Call ahead for both.

Besides wine, Montalcino is known for its honey, and in early September hosts the **national honey fair**.

★ **Boccon Divino >>**

Where to Stay and Eat in Montalcino

Montalcino ✉ 53024

****La Vecchia Oliviera**, Porta Cerbaia, **t** 0577 846028, *www.vecchiaoliviera.com* (€€€€). A former olive press by the old gate into the town, with pretty, elegant rooms and a pool with a Jacuzzi, overlooking the hills.

***Dei Capitani**, Via Lapini 6, **t** 0577 847227, *www.deicapitani.it* (€€€). An old *palazzo* with rooms and little apartments furnished in the Arte Povere style, wonderful views, a small pool and (a rarity here) a car park.

***Bellaria**, Via Osticcio 19, **t** 0577 849326, *www.hotelbellariamontalcino.com* (€€). A farmhouse a short walk from town in a pine wood. Some of the simple but comfortable rooms, and the pool, have fabulous views.

***Il Giglio**, Via Soccorso Saloni 5, **t** 0577 848167, *www.gigliohotel.com* (€€). Rustically styled rooms and apartments and a Tuscan restaurant. Rates include breakfast.

Boccon Divino, Loc. Colombaio Tozzi 201, **t** 0577 848233 (€€€). Some of the best food in the area, including a great onion soup and *scottiglia* (stew with hot peppers). Booking is advisable. *Closed Tues.*

Osteria Osticcio, Via Matteotti 23, **t** 0577 848271 (€€). A pleasant wine bar with magnificent views, serving meats, cheeses, *crostini* and salads. Try the fabulous Brunello wine. *Closed Sun.*

Locanda Sant'Antimo, Via Basso Mondo 6, Castelnuovo dell'Abate, **t** 0577 835615 (€). A good pizzeria plus rooms (€€). *Closed Tues.*

Il Pozzo, Piazza del Pozzo 2, Loc. S. Angelo in Colle, **t** 0577 844015 (€). Good-value traditional meals, including wild boar in Brunello wine sauce. *Closed Tues, and 2wks Aug.*

The Val d'Orcia

San Quirico d'Orcia, which is a humble agricultural centre where the SS146 from Pienza joins the SS2, still has some of its medieval walls. Once on the pilgrim route of the Via Francigena, it was endowed with hospices and hospitals to accommodate pilgrims en route to Rome. The magnificent **Collegiata**, rebuilt in the 12th century over an 8th-century church, has an exceptional façade of local travertine and three portals from the 1200s, sculpted with lions and telamons, the finest of their kind in the area. Just behind it is the somewhat forbidding 17th-century **Palazzo Chigi** – a grand presence for such a tiny town. Since its restoration, the frescoed rooms are open to visitors.

Palazzo Chigi
open by appt on
t 0577 898247

There are a couple more attractive churches here: **Santa Maria di Vitaleta**, with a Gothic façade and an enamel *Annunciation* by Andrea della Robbia on the high altar, and the pretty little 11th-century **Santa Maria Assunta**. There's also the **Horti Leonini**, a lovely garden designed in the late 15th century by Diomede Lioni, as a resting place for pilgrims.

Horti Leonini
open daily
dawn–sunset

There are a couple of points of interest nearby: **Ripa d'Orcia**, a hamlet with a stately castle (now a hotel), 7km south, and **Bagno Vignoni**, a small spa town just south off the SS2, where the piazza has a *vasca termale* built by Lorenzo de' Medici, who came for the waters. If you long for a bathe, you can get day tickets for the hot springs at the Hotel Posta Marcucci (*see* opposite).

Before the modern SS2 was built, the old Via Francigena traversed the valley of the Orcia, passing a patch of castles and fortified towns that began in the early Middle Ages. **Castiglione d'Orcia** (9km south of San Quirico) is as medieval-looking a town as you could ask for (though its cobbled piazza and fountain are from the 1600s), with two parish churches. The ruined fortress overlooking the town was built by the Aldobrandeschi family, who controlled much of southern Tuscany as late as the 1200s.

Just outside to the north, a pretty road winds up through olive groves to **Rocca d'Orcia**, another well-preserved medieval village clustered below its impressive castle, the **Rocca di Tentatenno**, which is used to host art exhibitions. Another 15km to the south of Castiglione lies **Vivo d'Orcia**, which began life as a Camaldolensian monastery in 1003; when the monastery withered the village grew, leaving only the attractive Romanesque **Cappella dell'Ermicciolo** in the woods above the town.

Bagni San Filippo, 8km east of Vivo, may be the world's smallest thermal spa, with its phone booth, handful of old houses and small hotel. It takes its name from San Filippo Benizi, a holy hermit of the Middle Ages who hid here when he heard there was a movement to elect him pope. Gouty old Lorenzo Il Magnifico came here, too, though he didn't leave any embellishments such as the piazza in Bagno Vignoni. You can swim in the natural terraced pools of **the Fosso Bianco**, a glistening limestone formation – a sort of stone waterfall – created by the flowing sulphurous waters.

Radicofani

Some wonderfully rugged countryside lies in the valley of the Orcia, east of this chain of villages, especially along the roads approaching **Radicofani**, a landmark of southern Tuscany, with its surreal, muffin-shaped hill topped by a lofty tower. The ruined fortress around it, originally built by Pope Adrian IV (the Englishman Nicholas Breakspear), served in the 1300s as HQ for legendary bandit Ghino di Tacco, solid citizen of Dante's *Inferno* and subject of a story in the *Decameron* (Day 10, Number 2), about how he imprisoned the Abbot of Cluny in this tower.

The elegant loggias on the main road, just outside town, belong to the 17th-century Palazzo La Posta, once the only good hotel between Siena and Rome; most of the famous on the Grand Tour stopped on their way through.

Festivals in the Val d'Orcia

Incontri in Terra di Siena, t 0578 69101, *www.lafoce.com*. A chamber music festival in late July, based at La Foce, home of writer Iris Origo, on the Monte Amiata road from Chianciano.

Festival del Val d'Orcia. A month (late July–Aug) of music, theatre and dance.

Where to Stay and Eat in the Val d'Orcia

Bagno Vignoni ✉ 53027

La Locanda del Loggiato, Piazza del Moretto 30, **t** 0577 888925, *www.loggiato.it* (€€€). A B&B on the first floor of a lovely medieval house, with rustically elegant rooms; breakfast is included. A wine bar takes over the breakfast room in the evenings.

Hotel Posta Marcucci, Via Ara Urcea, **t** 0577 887112, *www.hotelpostamarcucci.it* (€€). A hillside option with a thermal pool and terraces with amazing views over the Val d'Orcia, plus a tennis court. The restaurant is a bit dull but does have a veggie menu.

Osteria del Leone, Piazza del Moretto, **t** 0577 887300 (€€€–€€). Very good home-made *pici* with garlic, risotto with pear and *provola* chese, rabbit in orange sauce, and more. Book ahead. *Closed Mon, and 4wks Nov/Dec.*

San Quirico d'Orcia ✉ 53027

Hotel Palazzo del Capitano, Via Poliziano 18, **t** 0577 89028, *www.palazzodelcapitano.com* (€€€). An elegant 15th-century *palazzo* in the medieval heart of town, with tasteful rooms (breakfast included), an outdoor pool and an excellent restaurant in the old bakery. *Restaurant closed Nov–Feb.*

Radicofani ✉ 53040

La Palazzina, Loc. Le Vigne, **t** 0578 55771, *www.fattorialapalazzina.com* (€€€). A 200-year-old villa just outside the village, with a pool, and a minimum 3-night stay in high season. Superb home-made pasta is on the menu.

ⓘ **San Quirico >>** *Via Dante Aligheri 33, t 0577 897211 (closed Oct–Easter)*

ⓘ **Radicofani >>** *Via R. Magi 57, t 0578 55684*

★ **La Palazzina >>**

Pienza

㉗ **Pienza**

Some 50km south of Siena on the SS2 is a perfect, tiny core of Renaissance order and urbanity, surrounded by a village of about 2,500 souls. Pienza is delightful, if touristy. Like Monte Oliveto Maggiore, it's a jewel among archetypal Tuscan landscapes.

During a period of political troubles, common in Renaissance Siena, the great family of the Piccolomini exiled itself temporarily in one of its possessions, the village of Corsignano. Aeneas Silvius Piccolomini (*see* p.339) was born there in 1405; later, as Pope Pius II, he determined to raise his birthplace into a city. No historian has discovered a compelling economic or military reason for a new town here. Bernardo Rossellino designed it, with help from Pius; the pennies of the faithful paid for it; and Pius named it after himself: Pienza. Perhaps fortunately, after the first wave of papal patronage, Pienza was nearly forgotten. The grid of streets that was to extend over the Tuscan hills never materialized, and only the central piazza with a new cathedral and a Piccolomini palace was completed.

Pienza's Piazza Pio II

Piazza Pio II, heart of Rossellino's design scheme, is simple and decorous; it displays the chief buildings of the town without any of the monumental symmetry of the later Renaissance, relying on proportion to tie it all together. Such a square shows how, despite all its paintings of ideal buildings and streetscapes, the early Renaissance still followed the 'picturesque' urban design of the Middle Ages; Piazza Pio was made to be a stage set for daily life or the background of a painting.

Rossellino designed an elegant façade for the **cathedral** (1462), capturing the spirit of the times by omission – there is no hint it belongs to a Christian building, though the Piccolomini arms and papal keys are carved on the pediment. The interior, equally elegant, is tame Gothic – as if this bold Renaissance architect were a slightly embarrassed humanist who believed only Gothic suited a church. Rossellino also carved a marble altar and baptismal font in the lower church; there are also altarpieces by other leading Sienese artists. Nothing in this cathedral has been changed, or even moved, since it was completed; Pius' papal bull of 1462 forbade it. See it while it lasts: the cathedral, built on the edge of a slight cliff, has been subsiding almost since it was built, and occasionally sulphurous fumes seep from the floor. No one has discovered a way to shore it up permanently, and though restoration work has been done it could collapse, at least partially, at any time.

Next door, the columned **well**, a favourite sort of Renaissance urban decoration, is also by Rossellino. So is the restored **Palazzo Piccolomini**, a rehash of the more famous Palazzo Rucellai in Florence, the design of which follows Alberti. The best bit is the rear, where a three-storey loggia overlooks a 'hanging garden' on the cliff edge. The interior and the gardens are open to visitors.

Palazzo Piccolomini
open summer Tues–Sun 10–12.30 and 3–6; winter Tues–Sun 10–12.30 and 4–7; adm

Behind the Palazzo Piccolomini, the **church of San Francesco** predates the founding of Pienza; the 14th–15th-century frescoes inside include one attributed to Luca Signorelli. The **Museo Diocesano di Pienza**, in the sumptuously restored 15th-century Palazza Borgia, has objects from nearby churches, several paintings (some by Signorelli) and Flemish tapestries.

Museo Diocesano di Pienza
Corso Rossellino; open mid-Mar–Oct Wed–Mon 10–1 and 3–7; rest of year Sat and Sun 10–1 and 3–6; or by appt on **t** *0578 749905; adm*

Few people visit the 11th-century **Pieve** of old Corsignano, 1km west of town. This unusual church, where Aeneas Silvius was baptized, has some even more peculiar carvings over its entrance. Mermaids, or sirens, turn up with some frequency in Romanesque *tympana* and capitals, in Tuscany and Apulia especially, as well as many other places in Italy and France. Here there are several – one spreading its forked tail to display the entrance to the womb, flanked by others, and a dancer and a musician, with dragons whispering in their ears. Such symbols are steeped in medieval mysticism but are not entirely inaccessible to the modern imagination. It has been claimed that they betray the existence of an ecstatic cult, based on music and dance and descended from the ancient Dionysian rituals.

Ask at the tourist office (*see* opposite) about **guided tours** of Pienza.

Shopping in Pienza

Corso Rossellino, leading from the centre of the village to Porta Murello and the bus terminus, has trendy ceramics and leatherwork workshops, antiques shops, and health food stores selling the good local honey and preserves. Pienza's delicate variety of *pecorino*, maybe Italy's best sheep's cheese, is available in different strengths depending on how long it has been aged.

Where to Stay and Eat in Pienza

Pienza ✉ 53026

If you're on a budget, ask the tourist office for their list of private houses with **rooms to let**.

La Saracina, about 7km from Pienza on road to Montepulciano, **t** 0578 748022, *www.lasaracina.it* (€€€€€). Rooms, suites and an apartment in an old farmhouse with lovely gardens, a pool and a tennis court, in the countryside. Breakfast is included.

******Il Chiostro**, Corso Il Rossellino 26, **t** 0578 748400, *www.relaisilchiostrodipienza.com* (€€€€). An old cloister in the centre. just off Piazza Pio II, with stylish, modernized rooms, beautiful gardens, a small pool, and a good restaurant. *Closed mid-Jan–mid-Mar.*

*****Corsignano**, Via della Madonnina 9, **t** 0578 748501, *www.corsignano.it* (€€€). A comfy modern option with an Internet corner, restaurant and bar.

La Pergola, Via dell'Acero 2, just outside town on road to San Quirico, **t** 0578 748051 (€€€). An uninspiring building housing an excellent restaurant serving local cuisine, including an excellent *panforte*, in a garden in summer. *Closed Mon.*

Latte di Luna, Via S. Carlo 2/4, **t** 0578 748606 (€€). A place popular with locals for its roast pork and rabbit. Note that credit cards aren't accepted. *Closed Tues, and 3wks in July.*

Sperone Nudo, Piazza di Spagna 3/5, **t** 0578 748641 (€€). A great lunch stop; try *pici* with boar, tagliatelle with *porcini*, tripe, and nut cake. *Closed Mon.*

★ **La Pergola >>**

ⓘ **Pienza >**
Piazza Dante Alighieri 18,
t 0578 748359

Montepulciano

③ **Montepulciano**

Another graceful hill town lies south of Siena, also with a distinguished past and best known for wine. Montepulciano is larger (population 14,500) and livelier than Montalcino, with fine buildings and works of art. Old Montalcino was a home from home for the Sienese, while Montepulciano usually allied itself with Florence. Its Vino Nobile was praised by connoisseurs more than 200 years ago and can contend with Italy's best today.

Inhabitants of Montepulciano (Roman *Mons Politianus*) are called *Poliziani*, after its most famous son – Angelo Ambrogini, or Poliziano, one of the first Renaissance Greek scholars, and an accomplished poet and critic and scholar at the court of Lorenzo de' Medici and tutor to his children. Botticelli's mythological paintings may have been inspired by his *Stanze per la Giostra*. Today's Poliziani are a genteel, cultured lot still given to poetic extemporization and singing. The *Bruscello*, a partly improvised play on medieval and Renaissance themes in music and verse, acted by the townspeople in the Piazza Grande each August, is the town's biggest festival. A second August festival, the *Bravio delle Botti*, requires no poetry but plenty of sweat, as neighbourhood teams race up the steep main street pushing huge barrels.

Getting to and around Montpulciano

Montepulciano is 12.5km/20mins east of Pienza on the SS146, 66km/90mins from Siena, and 16km/30mins west of the Chiusi exit on the A1.

The **train** station (Florence–Rome line), way out in the countryside, is irregularly served by buses to town, and only local trains tend to stop. It's better to use the station at **Chiusi-Chianciano**, which has bus links up to Chiusi town, to Chianciano Terme, Montepulciano and occasionally Pienza.

Montepulciano bus station is just outside the Porta al Prato, the main gate into the city. There are very regular buses to Chianciano Terme–Chiusi–Chiusi station; slightly fewer to Pienza; and one each in the morning and afternoon for Siena (via Pienza and San Quirico). There are also daily connections to Abbadia San Salvatore, Montalcino, Perugia and Arezzo. There is an LFI bus info booth (**t** 0575 39881, *www.lfi.it*) in the train station at Chiusi; outside, besides the buses mentioned above, there are rather infrequent LFI links to Cortona, Arezzo, Perugia, Orvieto and Città della Pieve.

If you aren't up to climbing up to the top of Montepulciano, the LFI runs a handy **minibus** service up the Corso to Piazza Grande.

Palazzi and Pulcinella

Entering the city through the **Porta al Prato**, you encounter a stone column bearing the *Marzocco*, a symbol of Montepulciano's long attachment to Florence. Though nominally under Florentine control, the city was allowed a sort of independence up to the days of Cosimo I. The main street, called here Via di Gracciano nel Corso, winds in a circle up to the top of the city (if you follow it all the way, you'll walk twice as far as you need to, and think Montepulciano is a metropolis). This stretch is lined with noble palaces: No.91 and No.82 are the work of the late Renaissance architect Vignola, famous for the Farnese Palace in Caprarola (*see* p.547). Up at No.73, **Palazzo Bucelli** has the most unusual foundation in Italy, made almost entirely of Etruscan cinerary urns, filled with cement and stacked like bricks, many retaining their sculpted reliefs. Montepulciano was once Etruscan, though the urns probably came from Chiusi.

Piazza Michelozzo, where the street begins to ascend, is named after the Florentine architect of **Sant'Agostino church**, with an excellent, restrained Renaissance façade, similar to the cathedral in Pienza but more skilfully handled. Michelozzo also contributed the terracotta reliefs over the portal. Across the piazza, note the figure atop the old **Torre del Pulcinello**: to anyone familiar with Naples,

Vino Nobile and Other Vinous Delights

Montepulciano and its environs are full of *cantine*, each full of people ready for long discussions on the virtues of this famous wine, which after two years carries the bouquet of unknown autumn blooms, a perfume that confounds melancholy; its colour is a mystery of faith.

A **wine tour of Montepulciano** begins with the Cantine Cantucci, on Piazza Grande, where they might show you the salon with frescoes by Baroque artist Andrea Pozzo. The Cantina Gattavecchia, next to Santa Maria at the south end of town, has a 1500s *cantina*; don't neglect the venerable cellar built into the embankment beneath Piazza Grande, next to the Teatro Poliziano.

Vino nobile isn't the only variety of wine made in these parts. There is a version of Chianti – Chianti Colli Senesi, a creditable white Valdichiana and the sweet dessert Vinsanto. On evenings when quantity means more than quality, try any of the mass-produced Montepulciano reds; more honourable plonk is hard to find.

this white *Commedia dell'Arte* clown banging the hours on the town bell will be an old friend. It is said a Neapolitan bishop was exiled here for indiscretions back home; when he returned, he left this bit of Parthenopean culture as a souvenir to thank the Poliziani. Along the main street, you pass a dozen or so more palaces, reminders of the city's aristocratic past. There is one florid Baroque interior, in the **Gesù church** by Andrea Pozzo. Further down, the street curves around the medieval ***fortezza***, now partly residential, in the oldest part of town with its fascinating ancient alleys.

Piazza Grande

These days, when even the stalwart citizens of hill towns are too spoiled to walk up hills, the old centres of towns sometimes become quiet and out-of-the-way. So it is in Montepulciano, where **Piazza Grande** is city's highest point. On one side, Michelozzo added a rusticated stone front and tower to the 13th-century **Palazzo Comunale** to create a lesser copy of Florence's Palazzo Vecchio. Opposite is a Renaissance well in front of the **Palazzo Contucci**, built by the elder Antonio da Sangallo. On the west side, a tremendous pile of bricks, a sort of tenement for pigeons, proclaims the agonizing unfinishability of the preposterous **cathedral**, begun in 1592 and housing a single transcendent work of art: atop the marble Renaissance altar adorned with *putti* stands an *Assumption of the Virgin* by Taddeo di Bartolo, one of the greatest of 14th-century Sienese paintings. Set in glowing, discordant colours – pink, orange, purple and gold – this is a very spiritual Madonna, attended by a court of angel musicians. Don't miss the *predella* panels beneath, each a serious, inspired image from the Passion, including one panel of the *Resurrection* that can be compared to Piero della Francesca's more famous version in Sansepolcro.

Museo Civico/ Pinacoteca Crociani
Via Ricci; open April–Oct Tues–Sun 10–1 and 3–6 (until 8 in summer); Nov–Mar Sat and Sun 10–1 and 3–6; adm

The **Museo Civico/Pinacoteca Crociani** unite several collections. On the first and second floors are some Della Robbia terracottas from the dissolved convent that was downstairs, and the Crociani collection of paintings. The old collection, with a *Crucifixion* from Filippino Lippi's workshop, an *Assumption* by the Sienese Jacopo di Mino, an odd work by Girolamo di Benvenuto – baby Jesus as an *objet d'art* – and, even more peculiar, an inexplicable *Allegory of the Immaculate Conception* by one Giovanni Antonio Lappoli (d. 1552), has additions from other collections in Montepulciano. There's also an archaeological section at ground level, including the contents of five locally discovered Etruscan tombs previously housed in the Uffizi. Artefacts include Bucchero ware, ceramics and bronzes dating from the 5th to the 2nd century BC.

Continue down Via Ricci for the church of **Santa Lucia**, with a small *Madonna* by Luca Signorelli in a chapel to the right.

Antonio da Sangallo's San Biagio

One of the set pieces of Renaissance architecture was the isolated temple – a chance to create an ideal building in an uncluttered setting, often on the edge of a city. Giuliano da Sangallo's Santa Maria delle Carceri in Prato was the first and worst, followed by Bramante's San Pietro in Montorio in Rome and the Tempio della Consolazione in Todi (Umbria). Montepulciano's example is south of the city (a long walk downhill and back), near the road junction for Chianciano. A stately avenue of cypresses, each over a small marker commemorating a local soldier who died in the First World War, leads to the masterpiece of Antonio da Sangallo, long in the shadow of his less talented brother Giuliano. **San Biagio**, a central, Greek cross church of creamy travertine, stands in a small park. As with so many other Renaissance churches, it has more architecture than Christianity in its design – a consciously classical composition with an adaptation of the 'Tuscan' order on the ground level, Ionic on the second and Corinthian on the upper storeys of the campanile, gracefully fitted into one of the corners of the Greek cross. The interior, finished in marble and other expensive stone, is equally symmetrical, rational and impressive. Over the handsome altar, a Latin inscription proclaims '*Hinc deus homo et home Deus. Immensum Concept – Aeternum Genuit*' (Hence God is Man, and for humanity, the created Eternity). The beautiful canon's house, with its double loggia, is also by Sangallo.

Around Montepulciano

Among beautiful villages on the hills around Montepulciano, **Montefollonico** (8km northwest) has a frescoed church and Palazzo Comunale, both 13th-century. **Monticchiello**, 7km southwest on a back road towards Pienza, hangs languorously on its hilltop; it too has a 13th-century church, with a rose window, an altarpiece by Pietro Lorenzetti and Sienese frescoes (late 14th century).

ⓘ **Montepulciano >**
Via Gracciano nel Corso 59a, off Piazza Grande, **t** *0578 757341, www.prolocomontepulciano.it*

Shopping in Montepulciano

Besides Vine Nobile (*see* p.382), Montepulciano has jams, preserves, honey, *pecorino* cheese, ham or boar salami and other farm specialities to offer – the ideology of natural food has become as popular here as in the trendiest neighbourhoods of New York. You'll find them in almost any grocer's.

There are also some very good antique stores on the backstreets, together with craft workshops, especially woodcarving.

Where to Stay and Eat in Montepulciano and Around

Montepulciano ✉ 53045

There are lots of *agriturismos* in the surrounding countryside, and hundreds of rooms just south at Chianciano Terme (*see* p.386).

The best restaurants are outside town. Alternatively, any of the back roads off the SS146 will lead you at some point to an ideal spot for a picnic on those fine local products.

***Borghetto**, Borgo Buio **t** 0578 757535, *www.ilborghetto.it* (€€€). Pleasant rooms, some with great views over the edge of town, plus Internet access.

Marzocco >

***Marzocco, Via G. Savonarola 18, **t** 0578 757262, *www.albergoilmarzocco.it* (€€). An airy family-run establishment next to the *Marzocco* itself, with spacious rooms (breakfast included) and large panoramic terraces.

***Il Riccio**, Via Talosa 21, **t** 0578 757713, *www.ilriccio.net* (€€). Tasteful rooms (breakfast included) in a renovated medieval *palazzo*, with a pleasant rooftop terrace.

La Chiusa >

La Chiusa, Via Madonnina 88, Montefollonico, **t** 0577 669668 (€€€€). The best restaurant in southern Tuscany, though its reputation has wobbled in recent years, in an old *frantoio* or olive press, with panoramic views back towards Montepulciano. Highlights are the tagiatelle with truffles, lamb's liver with wine sauce, duck with wild fennel, and *pannacotta*. The wine list is short but well chosen. Some suites and rooms (€€€€€) are available. *Closed Tues.*

La Grotta, Loc.S Biagio 15, **t** 0578 757607 (€€€). A restaurant the shadow of the dramatic San Biagio, serving traditional Tuscan dishes with a creative twist, such as squash tart with aubergines in balsamic vinegar, gnocchi in rabbit sauce, and boar with spinach. *Closed Wed, Jan and Feb.*

Osteria Borgo Buio, Via di Borgo Buio 10, **t** 0578 717497 (€€). An excellent *osteria* offering the likes of tagliatelle with sardines, tomatoes and pine nuts, ravioli filled with *pecorino* cheese, pear and nuts, lamb with herbs, potatoes and aubergines, and grilled Fiorentina steak. *Closed Sun.*

Caffé Poliziano, Corso, **t** 0578 758615 (€). Montepulciano's old-fashioned *gran caffè*.

Monticchiello ✉ 53020

L'Olmo, just below Montichiello, **t** 0578 755133, *www.olmopienza.it* (€€€€). A beautifully restored stone posthouse with gardens and a swimming pool overlooking the Val d'Orcia. Bedrooms are comfortable and sophisticated; there are also suites and apartments. Breakfast is included, and dinner is available on request. *Closed mid-Nov–April.*

La Porta, Via del Piano 3, **t** 0578 755163 (€€). An excellent *osteria/enoteca* with wonderful views over Pienza and the valley from its panoramic terrace. Standout dishes are the *pici* with *cacio* cheese and pepper, *ribollita*, *pappa al pomodoro*, stuffed guinea fowl, and cod. *Closed Thurs, and 10 Jan–5 Feb.*

Chianciano Terme

'*Chianciano – Fegato Sano*' is the slogan you see everywhere in Chianciano Terme (population 7,500): on the signs that welcome you, on the municipal buildings, even on the garbage trucks: 'Chianciano, for a healthy liver'. And after rotting yours on too much Montepulciano wine, how convenient it is to have a spa close at hand to flush it out. The waters here were known to the Etruscans but have only been exploited in a big way in the last half century or more. There is an old walled town, Chianciano Vecchio, with a medieval clocktower and the **Museo d'Arte Sacra**; at the gate is the bus station and info booth.

Museo Civico Archeologico delle Acque
open April–Oct Tues–Sun 10–1 and 4–7; Nov–Mar Sat and Sun 10–1 and 4–7; or by appt on **t** *0578 30471; adm*

In a former granary situated just outside the old town you'll find the **Museo Civico Archeologico delle Acque**. Here you can see a collection of mainly Etruscan and Roman exhibits that have been excavated in the environs since 1986. Reconstructed tombs built in the hollows, which were originally carved out to hold wine barrels,

Getting to Chianciano Terme

For details of Chiusi-Chianciano **train** station and of local **buses**, see p.382.

contain finds from the excavation of the Tolle Necropoli at nearby La Foce. These items are arranged more or less as they were discovered at the site.

Beyond, modern Chianciano stretches for kilometres down Viale della Libertà, passing hundreds of hotels, gardens with clipped lawns, and 1950s bathhouses in a clean, modern style. Besides liver repair, Chianciano has mineral mud packs for acne, hot aerosol douches and plenty of other treatments for every ailment, mistrusted by British visitors but medically respected.

Around Chianciano: La Foce and Castelluccio

La Foce
gardens open Wed 3pm–dusk; **t** *0578 69101*

To the southwest of Chianciano lies **La Foce**, a large estate on the hills overlooking the Val d'Orcia. Its strategic position on the Via Francigena has long attracted settlers; excavations brought to light a burial place from the 7th century BC. The villa was built in the late 15th century as a hostel for pilgrims and merchants, and bought by Antonio and Iris Origo in 1924, when it was barren and poverty-ridden. They spent their lives regenerating the area; they set up a school, day clinic and nursery, and an orphanage during the war. English landscape architect Cecil Pinsent designed the delightful **gardens**. Iris Origo's autobiographical books *Images and Shadows* and *War in the Val d'Orcia* make fascinating reading.

Nearby, on the road to Montepulciano, the medieval **Castelluccio** is also part of the estate. As well as exhibitions, it holds concerts during the summer, as a venue for the **Incontri in Terra di Siena** music festival (*see* p.379).

ⓘ Chianciano Terme >
Piazza Italia 67, **t** *0578 671122*

Where to Stay and Eat in Chianciano Terme

Chianciano Terme ✉ 53042

Even if you aren't here for thermal torture, Chianciano can be useful in summer when hotels everywhere else are booked solid. The Azienda Autonima di Cura, Viale Roma 6, can help with accommodation.

La Foce, Strada della Vittoria 61, **t** 0578 69101, *www.lafoce.com* (€€€€€). Several farmhouses turned into upmarket self-catering apartments with plenty of antiques, sleeping 2–14. Each has use of a swimming pool and a private garden, and meals are available on request.

La Rosa del Trinoro, Castriglioncello del Trinoro, on road between La Foce and Sarteano, **t** 0578 265 529 (€€€€). A restaurant in a tiny, otherworldly hamlet with wonderful views. Come for risotti with *porcini* and prawns in balsamic vinegar, home-made *pici* in rabbit sauce, lamb with herbs, beans and pepper, and exquisite chocolate desserts. There are also some pleasant guestrooms (€€). *Closed Mon, and lunch Tues–Fri.*

L'Oasi, Loc. La Foce (just below La Foce on road to Monte Amiata), **t** 0578 755 077 (€€). A useful, rustic, family-run bar/restaurant with a children's playground and a summer garden, serving home-made pizzas, pastas and more. *Closed Wed.*

Chiusi and Around

If anyone ever read you Macaulay's rouser *Horatio at the Bridge*, you'll remember the fateful Lars Porsena of Clusium, leading the Etruscan confederation and their Umbrian allies to attack Rome in brave days of old. Thanks to Horatio, Rome survived and made a name for itself; here you can see what happened to Clusium – or *Camars*, as the Etruscans called it. Most of its 9,500 citizens live in the new districts by the railway station, but the hill town on the site of Lars Porsena's capital still thrives.

Archaeological Museum

Museo Archeologico Nazionale di Chiusi
open daily 9–8; adm

From those brave days of old, Chiusi retains at least this excellent museum, beautifully laid out and well labelled. As with so many Etruscan collections, the main attraction is the large number of cinerary urns, and as usual, the Etruscans produced a bewildering variety of styles and themes. Large urns with thoughtful reclining figures are common, as well as mythological battle scenes with winged gods. Not all the tombs contained the well-known rectangular urns; some Etruscans chose to be buried in 'canopic' jars, surmounted by a terracotta bust of the deceased.

Camars was a wealthy town, and excavations at its necropolises unearthed a large amount of Greek pottery – note the urn with Achilles and Ajax playing at dice, and the Dionysian scenes with sexy maenads and leering satyrs. Many Etruscan imitation vases are on display; it's easy to believe local talent could have done as well as the Greeks, had they had thinner paintbrushes. Don't miss the glittering hoard of barbaric trinkets from 6th–7th-century Lombard tombs discovered on the Arusa hill just outside town.

Etruscan Tombs and Tunnels

If you're interested in seeing some of the Etruscan tombs (5th–3rd century BC) in which various items in the archaeological music were found, ask the museum guards, who arrange tours (in fact, they'll probably ask you first). These are the only good painted tombs in Tuscany; the best, the **Tomba della Scimmia**, contains paintings of wrestlers and warriors, in addition to the monkey that gives the tomb its name. The **Tomba della Pellegrina** and **Tomba del Granduca** are also interesting, as is the **Tomba Bonci Casuccini**, in a different necropolis east of town.

The Cathedral

Cattedrale di San Secondiano
open daily 9–8, adm

Across from the museum, Chiusi's cathedral is the oldest in Tuscany, though only parts – the recycled Roman columns in the nave – go back to the original 6th-century building. The rest was rebuilt in the 12th century and again in the 19th. At first glance, the

Getting to Chiusi

For details of Chiusi-Chianciano **train** station and of local **buses**, see p.382.

mosaics that cover the walls inside seem astounding, an unknown chapter in Early Christian art. Then you notice they have a touch of Art Nouveau about them and realize they aren't mosaics at all, but skilfully sponged-on squares of paint, a crazy masterpiece of mimicry completed in 1915.

Museo della Cattedrale/ Labirinto di Porsenna
open June–mid-Oct daily 10–12.45 and 4–6.30; mid-Oct–May Mon–Sat 10–12.45 and Sun 10–12.45 and 3.30–6; adm

The small **cathedral museum** has Roman fragments and beautiful 15th-century illuminated choirbooks. You can also climb the campanile and descend into the mysterious **network of tunnels and galleries** underlying the town, bits of which go back to the Etruscans. Whatever their original purpose, some were converted into catacombs by Early Christian communities; there's also an underground cistern from Roman times.

Around Chiusi: Lakes, Sarteano and More *Crete*

Just northeast of Chiusi, on the border between Tuscany and Umbria, pretty **Lago di Chiusi** and the **Lago di Montepulciano** are the smallest in the chain of lakes that begins with Lago Trasimeno. Lago di Chiusi is good for a picnic if you're headed from Florence to Rome or Orvieto on the *autostrada*.

Sarteano is a smaller resort spa, situated 9km to the south of Chianciano or Chiusi, attached to a fine old hill town with Renaissance palaces, a squarish medieval fortress, and the church of **San Martino in Foro**, with an *Annunciation* that is one of the best works of the Sienese Mannerist Beccafumi. A small, delightful Etruscan museum – the **Museo Civico Archeologico** – occupies the impressive Palazzo Gabrielli; note the wonderful funerary accoutrements and striking urns containing bones and other anthropomorphic paraphernalia.

Museo Civico Archeologico di Sarteano
t 0578 269261 open Tues–Sun 10–noon and 4–7

Another 6km south of Sarteano, off the ruggedly scenic SS321, you'll find **Cetona**, a small, untouristy gem with a growing population of discerning foreign residents who have rejected Chianti country and all it implies. The Palazzo Comunale is home to the **Museo Civico per la Preistoria del Monte Cetona**, documenting archaeological discoveries since the 1920s, including a massive bear some believe to be 50,000 years old.

Museo Civico per la Preistoria del Monte Cetona
*Via Roma 37, **t** 0578 237632; open June–Sept Tues–Sat 9–1 and 3–7, Sun and hols 9.30–12.30; Oct–May Tues–Sun 9.30–12.30*

Take the road to Sarteano, and after 6km or so you reach the **Parco Archeologico Naturalistico di Belvedere**, with remains from one of the most important Bronze Age sites in Italy. On the approach to Sarteano, visit the 14th-century ex-convent of Santa Maria a Belvedere, inhabited by the same community who run the upmarket La Frateria di Padre Egidio (*see* opposite), and housing frescoes attributed to Petruccioli and Andrea di Giovanni.

The SS478 from Sarteano towards Monte Amiata passes one of the loneliest, most barren regions of *crete* en route to the Val d'Orcia (*see* p.377). The road south from Cetona takes you on a beautiful, winding drive skirting Monte Cetona, punctuated by dramatic views as you pass through woods and olive groves towards **San Casciano dei Bagni**, a pretty spa town on the borders of Umbria and Lazio. There are a couple of ancient churches and a castle; the hot springs are just to the south. The resort's heyday was in the Renaissance, when Grand Duke Ferdinand built a villa here and developed the spa; the baths have been restored and the Medici villa transformed into a luxury hotel (*see* below).

Where to Stay and Eat in and around Chiusi

ⓘ Chiusi >
Pro Loco, Piazza Duomo 1, t 0578 227 667

Chiusi ✉ 53043

Le Anfore, Via Chiusi 30, just outside town on road to Sarteano, **t** 0578 265521, *www.balzarini.it* (€€€). A beautifully restored farmhouse with good-value family accommodation (breakfast included), a pool, a tennis court, horseriding and a restaurant.

★ La Locanda di Anita >>

*******La Fattoria**, Loc. Saccianese 48, Conciarese al Lago, **t** 0578 21407, *www.la-fattoria.it* (€€). An old farmhouse with lake views, a garden, good rooms and a great restaurant. *Closed Mon.*

Da Gino, Via Cabina Lago 42, **t** 0578 21408 (€€). A place on the lake shores, specializing in fresh lake fish and home-made pasta. *Closed Wed.*

La Solita Zuppa, Via Porsenna 21, **t** 0578 21006 (€€). A friendly *osteria* up in the old town, with four or five daily soups and home-made pasta. *Closed Tues, and mid-Jan–mid-Mar.*

★ Zaira >

Zaira, Via Arunte 12, **t** 0578 20260 (€€). Speculative 'Etruscan cuisine', popular with Italians in the know. It's a harmless fancy; try rabbit in lemon sauce. *Closed Mon in winter.*

Sarteano ✉ 53047

Residenza Santa Chiara, Piazza Santa Chiara, **t** 0578 265412, *www.conventosantachiara.it* (€€). A pleasant old building with a shady garden, simple rooms (plus a suite and an apartment) and a great restaurant.

La Giara, Viale Europa 2, **t** 0578 265511 (€€). Popular Tuscan fare and pizzas from a wood-burning oven. *Closed Mon.*

Osteria Da Gagliano, Via Roma 5, **t** 0578 268022 (€€). A simple osteria; try anchovies with pesto. *Closed Tues.*

Cetona ✉ 53040

********La Frateria**, Convento di San Francesco, **t** 0578 238015, *www.lafrateria.it* (€€€€€). The most unusual hotel in the area, in a 13th-century monastery founded by St Francis, tranquil yet lavish. There's an excellent if overpriced restaurant (€€€€). *Closed Jan; restaurant closed Mon.*

La Locanda di Anita, Piazza Balestrieri 6, **t** 0578 237075, *www.lalocandadianita.it* (€€€).Beautiful rooms and a suite, and a pretty terrace for summer breakfasts (included). **L'Osteria Vecchia**, under the same management, serves good food.

S. Casciano dei Bagni ✉ 53040

********Fonteverde**, Loc Terme 1, **t** 0578 58023, *www.fonteverdespa.com* (€€€€€). A spa hotel in and around a Medici villa, on the site of the restored thermal baths. Half board is required. Packages including beauty treatments.

*******Sette Querce**, Viale Manciati 2, **t** 0578 58174, *www.settequerce.it* (€€€€). A delightful all-suite hotel (some have kitchenettes), with spa treatments and a beauty centre.

La Fontanella, Via Roma 6, **t** 0578 58300, *www.albergolafontanella.com* (€€€). Bright, comfy rooms and an excellent restaurant (€€–€). *Restaurant closed Tues.*

Da Daniela, Piazza Matteotti 7, **t** 0578 58041 (€€€). Interesting variations on local themes, including *tortelli* stuffed with pigeon meat *Closed Wed in winter, and 10 Jan–10 Feb.*

Monte Amiata and Around

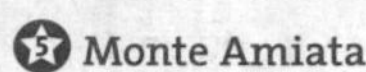

Monte Amiata, the rooftop of southern Tuscany, is an extinct volcanic massif with a central peak 1,722m high. With no real competition close by, it has become a skiing and hiking centre – the closest to Rome, and as such, popular in summer and winter. The presence of Europe's second-largest mercury mine (a complex that has been putting dinner on the table for Abbadia San Salvatore since the Middle Ages) does not detract from the area's natural beauty. The lower, uncultivated slopes are covered in chestnut and beech trees, while higher up are beautiful mature forests where the leaves catch the early frosts and change colour marvellously in the autumn.

Abbadia San Salvatore

A thousand years ago you might have heard of this town, home of the most important monastic centre in Tuscany and a fair-sized city in its own right. History passed Abbadia San Salvatore by a long time ago; today it makes a modest living as a mountain resort, gateway to Monte Amiata.

Abbadia (population 7,900) appears modern at first, but just behind Viale Roma a narrow gateway leads into the grey, quiet streets of the small **medieval centre**, as complete and unchanged as any medieval quarter in Tuscany. Note the symbols carved into many doorways: coats of arms, odd religious symbols (a snake, for example) or signs such as a pair of scissors that declare the original owner was a tailor. The **abbey church** is a few blocks north in Via del Monastero; in the Middle Ages this must have been open countryside. According to legend – there's even a document telling the story, dated the Ides of March, 742 – the Lombard King Rachis was on his way to attack Perugia when a vision of the Saviour appeared to him. Rachis not only founded the monastery but retired to it as a monk. Historians consider the whole business a convenient fabrication, but by 1000, the abbey had achieved considerable wealth and influence, ruling over a large piece of territory and waging occasional wars with the bishop of Chiusi.

In 1036, the present church was begun; this excellent Romanesque work may seem plain to us, but it was undoubtedly one of the grandest sights in Tuscany when it was new. Behind the twin-steepled façade, it is surprisingly long; the eastern end has a raised chancel, which leads to a series of arches over the altar and choir. Here frescoes by Nasino, an early-1700s artist, tell the story of King Rachis. His **crypt**, located under the chancel, was the original 8th-century church. The proportions are thoroughly Byzantine, with some stone vaulting and oddly carved columns and capitals, no two of which are alike.

Getting to and around Monte Amiata

There's a 'Monte Amiata' **train** station on an infrequent branch line from Siena, but it's some 40km on the northern side of the massif, near Castiglione d'Orcia. It's much easier to get a **bus** from Siena, Chiusi or Grosseto. Buses stop on Viale Roma in the centre of Abbadia San Salvatore (tickets/timetables available in the toyshop behind the information booth); a few go daily to Buonconvento and Siena (79km/2hrs 30mins), Montepulciano–Chiusi (48km/90mins); and 9 a day go from Abbadia to Arcidosso (25km/1hr) and Castel del Piano on the western side of Amiata.

Note that Arcidosso and the other towns on the west slope are in Grosseto province; almost all buses there go on to Grosseto. There are also at least 2 daily COTRAL (*www.cotralspa.it*) or SIRA buses (*www.sirabus.it*) through Castel del Piano, Arcidosso and Abbadia San Salvatore to Viterbo and on to Rome.

Around Amiata

South of Abbadia San Salvatore, **Piancastagnaio** is a smaller mountain resort. It has a **castle** of the Aldobrandeschi (with a small museum), a 17th-century palace and, as its name implies, lots of chestnut trees. Chestnuts and chestnut flour were the staple food around Amiata; restaurants still sometimes offer chestnut polenta.

On the panoramic route around Amiata, **Seggiano**, 20km northwest of Abbadia, has an unusual 16th-century church with a square cupola, the Madonna della Carità. South another 7km is **Castel del Piano**, with an old centre, Belle Epoque parks and boulevards.

Arcidosso, 4km south, is the largest town (population 4,500) on the Grosseto side of Amiata, with a stately Aldobrandeschi fortress, and one church outside the town, the triple-apsed Santa Maria in Lamula, begun in the 900s and redone in the 12th century. It's best known for the strange career of David Lazzaretti, a millenarian prophet gunned down by the *carabinieri* during a disturbance in 1878. His movement combined reformed religion and plain rural socialism. Before his murder, his followers had started to create a sort of commune on **Monte Labbro**, 10km south. The tower, bits of buildings and remains of the church they built on Monte Labbro still stand, and the faithful occasionally hold 'Giurisdavidical' services there.

Roccalbegna, 20km south on the SS323, has an Aldobrandeschi castle, and some Sienese art in SS. Pietro e Paolo and nearby Oratorio del Crocifisso. Its landmark is one very conspicuous rock: a looming conical mass called simply 'La Pietra'. The Aldobrandeschi also built at **Santa Fiora**, a pleasant town 7.5km south of Arcidosso, with Della Robbia terracottas in its three churches.

Parco Faunistico del Monte Amiata
open Tues–Sun dawn–sunset; **t** *0564 966867*

Just south of Arcidosso, on the northern slopes of Monte Labbro, is a nature reserve, the **Parco Faunistico del Monte Amiata**. Hiking trails offer a look at various kinds of deer, mountain goats, and maybe wolves – there is a project to reintroduce them.

Amiata's summit, decorated with an obligatory iron crucifix lies about halfway between Abbadia and Arcidosso; roads reach almost to the top. The skiing area is here, too, at **Vetta Amiata**.

ⓘ **Abbadia San Salvatore >>**
Via Adua 25, t 0577 775811, www.amiataturismo.it.

ⓘ **Arcidosso >>**
Piazza Castello 1, t 0564 968010

ⓘ **Castel del Piano >>**
Via G. Marconi 2, t 0564 951026

★ **Albergo Ristorante Silene >>**

Activities in and around Monte Amiata

One of the few good **skiing** areas close to Rome, Monte Amiata can get busy. Facilities include ski schools (**t** 0577 789740 and **t** 0564 959004). For snow news and info, call Abbadia San Salvatore tourist office.

It's also perfect for cross-country skiing and **hiking**, with a network of hiking trails marked as far as Castiglione d'Orcia. Ask tourist offices for the *Cartografia dei Sentieri* map.

Where to Stay and Eat in and around Monte Amiata

Monte Amiata ✉ 53021

*****La Capannina**, Vette Amiata, **t** 0577 789713, *www.albergocapannina.it* (€€). A cosy place near the summit, offering half and full board. Its restaurant is one of the best in the area. *Closed Oct exc weekends, Nov–15 Dec, Easter–May.*

*****Rifugio Cantore**, '*Secondo Rifugio 10*', along road from Abbadia, **t** 0577 789704, *www.hotelcantore@libero.it* (€€). Pleasant facilities near the summit, open all year (to cater for summer mountaineers too), and offering half-board accommodation.

Abbadia San Salvatore ✉ 53021

This is popular for winter skiing but also as a cool summer retreat.

Relais San Lorenzo, Loc. San Lorenzo, **t** 0577 785003, *www.relaissanlorenzo.it* (€€€). An old building on the slopes, with ample grounds, an outdoor pool, comfy rooms and apartments with fridges, and an excellent restaurant. Half and full board are available.

****San Marco**, Via Matteotti 19, **t** 0577 778089 (€€–€). Clean, comfy rooms and a restaurant (€) serving a *menu fisso*. Half and full board are available.

Arcidosso ✉ 58031

*****Aiuole**, Loc. Aiuole, **t** 0564 967300 (€€€). Good-value rooms and a good restaurant serving the likes of *tortelli* with nettles, and pheasant with chestnuts (half/full board available). *Closed Mon in winter, and Sun eve.*

Castel del Piano ✉ 58033

*****Contessa**, at Prato della Contessa, **t** 0564 959000, *www.hotelcontessa.it* (€€€). A hotel in a lovely setting on the slopes, organizing nature walks, cultural tours and more, and offering seasonal menus (full board available).

Albergo Ristorante Silene, Loc. Pescina 8, **t** 0564 950805 (€€). A provider of beds and food (€€€) since 1830. Don't miss the boar with chocolate.

The Lost Corner of Tuscany

The inland reaches of Grosseto province form the largest stretch of territory in Italy north of the Abruzzo without any well-known attractions. Part of the Etruscan heartland, these towns have been poor and usually misgoverned since – by the Romans, the noble Aldobrandeschi, the popes and the Tuscan dukes. Some don't even consider it part of Tuscany, and in many ways it has more in common with the haunted expanses of northern Lazio over the border.

Sorano

This grim town clings tenaciously to its rock between two lovely wooded canyons. Bits of it have been crumbling into the valleys for centuries; many houses were destroyed in a landslide 85 years ago. It is still inhabited, but more houses have been abandoned as younger people move away for work. On the road to Sovana is a strange rock formation, the **Mano di Orlando** ('Hand of Roland').

Sovana and the *Vie Cave*

Sovana, perched on a ridge 10km west, with a population of about 190, has almost perfectly preserved its 13th- or 14th-century look . An important Etruscan city, it thrived as the family HQ of the Aldobrandeschi in the 11th century. This clan, controlling much of southern Tuscany and northern Lazio, had a political role on a European level. The zenith of its influence came with the election to the papacy of one of its members in 1073, Gregory VII.

There is some interesting Early Christian and medieval sculpture in the 12th-century **church of Santa Maria** in the centre, including a remarkable 9th-century *ciborium* in bold barbaric arabesques and floral motifs, along with Renaissance frescoes. The **Duomo**, just outside the village, has an octagonal dome from the 900s, a crypt 200 years older, and sculptural work on the façade that may have been recycled from a pagan temple.

The ***Vie Cave***, signposted all around this area, are sacred ways of the Etruscans, carved for part of their length out of the tufa, often lined with tombs. In many cases they follow modern roads, as with the pretty road from Sovana to Saturnia. Here you can stop to see the **Tomba della Sirena**, with a pediment carved with a much-eroded fork-tailed mermaid – possibly the original of the mermaids on the Pieve di Corsignano and elsewhere around Tuscany.

Not far away Is the elaborate 3rd-century BC **Tomba Ildebranda**, which once had the façade of a Greek temple, though little of the colonnade survives. It resembles the rock-cut tombs of the same era common in Lycia, on the south coast of Turkey, built by people who may have been the Etruscans' cultural cousins.

Pitigliano

Just 8km away is an ominous-looking place that could be Sorano's twin, perched along the edges of the cliffs; underneath are holes in the cliff faces, once Etruscan tombs, now stables or storehouses. Piazza della Repubblica has the 14th-century **Palazzo Orsini**, stronghold of the powerful Roman family that aced the Aldobrandeschi out of many holdings in south Tuscany. The castle has a small **museum of Etruscan finds**, and an analemmic sundial with a Latin inscription reminding us the hours are 'for work, not for play'.

Remains of Jewish ghetto and synagogue
open Mar–May, Oct and Nov Sun–Fri 10–12.30 and 3–6; June–Sept Sun–Fri 10–12.30 and 3–6.30; Dec–mid-Jan Sun–Fri 10–12.30 and 3–5.30; adm

Pitigliano has a picturesque medieval centre, and a 16th-century **aqueduct**. The alleys around Vicolo Manin, where parts of **synagogue** still stand, once formed Pitigliano's **Jewish ghetto**; the centuries-old community was decimated in 1945. Other Jewish relics can be visited on the International Day of Jewish Culture, usually the first Sunday in September.

On the cliffs underneath the town, along the road for Sovana, is a Christian **cave chapel** (c. 400 AD). They claim it's the oldest in Italy.

Saturnia

Little Saturnia, 25km west of Sovana, sits all alone above the Val d'Albegna. One of Italy's most ancient centres, it claims to be the first city founded there – by the god Saturn, in the Golden Age. Fragments of pre-Etruscan walls can be seen, and aerial photos have discerned traces of an older city beneath the Roman level. There are hot springs, still used, and ruins everywhere, including an Etruscan necropolis (north) and **Poggio Buco** (road to Pitigliano).

West on SS323, the walled city of **Magliano in Toscana** has a Sienese-style Palazzo dei Priori, and the church of San Giovanni Battista, with a Renaissance façade. Its best-known attraction is the **Ulivo della Strega** ('witches' olive'), a gnarled tree more than 1,000 years old, said to be the site of ritual dances in pagan days, and still haunted. It's just outside the Porta San Giovanni, near the Romanesque **Annunziata church** with its Sienese frescoes.

ⓘ Saturnia >>
Pro Loco, Piazzale Benvenuto di Giovanni, t 0564 601237, www.proloco-saturnia.it

ⓘ Pitigliano >
Piazza Garibaldi 51, off main piazza, t 0564 617111

Where to Stay and Eat in and around Sovana

The region produces some good but little-known wines, notably Morellino di Scansano, a severe dry variety with a beautiful deep red colour, and also a delicious, crisp Bianco di Pitigliano.

Sovana ✉ 58010

***__Hotel della Fortezza__, Piazza Cairoli 5, **t** 0564 632010, *www.sovanahotel.it* (€€€€). Antiques-filled rooms (breakfast included) with fab views in the 11th-century Orsini fortress.

***__Scilla__, Via del Duomo 5, **t** 0564 616531, *www.sovanahotel.it* (€€€). A good hotel offering half and full board in its restaurant (€€), serving Maremmana dishes. Breakfast is included. *Closed Tues.*

***__Taverna Etrusca__, Piazza Pretorio, **t** 0564 616183, *www.sovanahotel.it* (€€€). Good rooms, breakfast included, above a restaurant (€€) serving the likes of nettle and ricotta soup.

Pitigliano ✉ 58017

__Corano__, Loc. Corano, SS74 just outside town, **t 0564 616112, *www.hotelcorano.it* (€€). Modern rooms, a pool and a restaurant (with half and full board).

__Guastini__, Piazza Petruccioli 4, **t 0564 616065 (€€). A recently renovated, central option, with a restaurant offering the likes of *pappardelle* with boar.

Il Tufo Allegro, Vicolo della Costituzione, **t** 0564 616192 (€€€). A wonderful restaurant in a great setting carved out of tufa. Hearty dishes include lamb with artichoke sauce. *Closed Tues, mid-Jan–mid-Feb and 2wks July/Aug.*

Hostaria del Ceccottino, Piazza San Gregorio, **t** 0564 614273 (€€). A good place for boar *scottiglia* and *ribollita*. *Closed Thurs in winter.*

Saturnia ✉ 58050

****__Hotel Terme di Saturnia__, Strada Provinale della Follonato, **t** 0564 600111, *www.termedisaturnia.it* (€€€€€). The top spa resort in Tuscany, exploiting waters famous since Etruscan times, with airy rooms in a large park, four thermal pools, a re-created Roman bath, state-of-the-art health and beauty treatments, and a new 18-hole golf course.

Villa Clodia, Via Italia 43, **t** 0564 601212, *www.hotelvillaclodia.com* (€€€). Good rooms, great views, a sauna, a fitness room, a pool and mountainbike loan.

Locanda Laudomia, Poderi di Montemerano, 7km south of Saturnia, **t** 0564 620013, *locandalaudomia@tiscali.it* (€). Pretty rooms in the country, some ensuite, and a good restaurant.

Montemerano ✉ 58050

Da Caino, Via Canonica 3, **t** 0564 602817 (€€€€). An elegant restaurant for such a small village; try ravioli with tomatoes and oil or cod carpaccio. There are some rustic rooms. *Closed Wed.*

Arezzo and its Province

Between Florence and Umbria lies a lovely region of nature and art, most of which is included in the province of Arezzo. Watered by the newly born Arno and Tiber rivers, it occupies a keystone position in Italy, not only geographically but as amazingly fertile ground for 'key' Italians: Masaccio and Cosimo Il Vecchio's humanist Greek scholar and magician, Marsilio Ficino, were born in the Arno valley; Petrarch, Michelangelo, Piero della Francesca, Paolo Uccello, Luca Signorelli, Andrea Sansovino, Vasari, satirist Aretino, Guido Monaco (inventor of the musical scale), Pietro da Cortona and the Futurist Gino Severini were born in Arezzo or its province. Its strategic location means battlefields and castles dot the countryside, yet here, too, is St Francis' holy mountain of La Verna.

15

Don't miss

See map overleaf

Arezzo Province

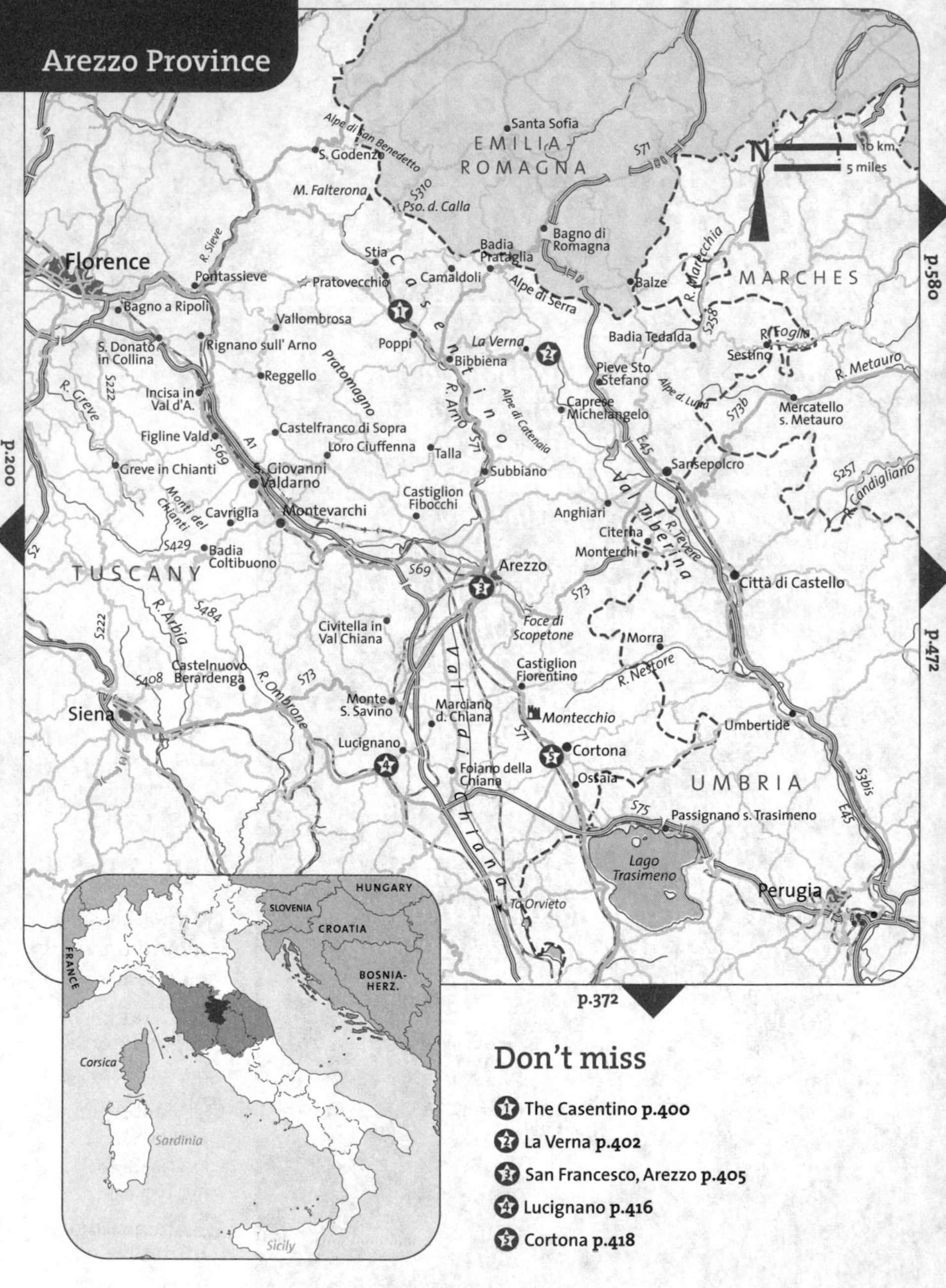

p.580
p.200
p.472
p.372

Don't miss

1. The Casentino **p.400**
2. La Verna **p.402**
3. San Francesco, Arezzo **p.405**
4. Lucignano **p.416**
5. Cortona **p.418**

There are two possible routes between Florence and Arezzo: the quick one, following the trains and Autostrada del Sole down the Valdarno, or the scenic route, through the Passo della Consuma or Vallombrosa, taking in the beautifully forested areas of Pratomagno and the Casentino.

The Valdarno and Casentino

Florence to Arezzo

If a Tuscan caveman ever yearned for the ideal Neolithic home, he would have wanted to live in what is now the Arno valley. In the Pliocene Age, the valley was a lake, a popular resort of ancient elephants, and farmers are not surprised when their ploughs collide with fossils. The typically Tuscan towns of the Valdarno, however, are hardly fossilized. On the contrary, it is a highly industrialized region: lignite and felt hats stand out in particular, but factories and power lines seem to go up all the time.

Besides the *autostrada*, the main valley routes are the old SS69 and the beautiful 'Strada dei Sette Ponti' following the old Etruscan road of 'Seven Bridges' from Saltino by Vallombrosa to Castiglion Fibocchi, along what was the upper shore of the ancient lake, between the Valdarno and the Pratomagno ridge. Along it are areas strikingly eroded into pyramids, around Pian di Scò and Castelfranco. By public transport the Valdarno's peripheral attractions are harder to reach; buses from Arezzo to Loro Ciuffenna and Castelfranco di Sopra stick to the Strada dei Sette Ponti.

The most scenic route from Florence to the Valdarno follows the A1 down to Incisa (23km), though it's worth turning off at Torre a Cona for **Rignano sull'Arno**, with sculptures by Mino da Fiesole and Bernardino Rossellino in the church of San Clemente, and for **Sanmezzano** (2km across the Arno). Here a medieval castle was converted into a Medici villa and in the 19th century purchased by the Ximenes d'Aragona family, who gave it a Spanish-Moorish fantasy facelift. Downriver, at **Incisa Valdarno**, Petrarch spent his childhood. There's an old bridge off which, the Italians claim, Lucrezia Borgia jumped in 1529, fleeing the Prince of Orange, despite the fact that she had died in childbirth 10 years earlier.

Figline Valdarno (population 15,000), 5km south, was the birthplace of Ficino in 1439. The historic centre has preserved the loggia of the old Serristori hospital, the Palazzo Pretorio, and the **Collegiata di Santa Maria**, containing among its works of art a beautiful painting of the *Madonna with Child and Angels* by the 14th-century 'Maestro di Figline' and a fresco by the school of Botticelli.

San Giovanni Valdarno

San Giovanni (population 19,500), though one of the most industrial towns in the region, is also one of the most interesting. The Florentines fortified it in the 13th century against the warlike Aretini and sent Arnolfo di Cambio to lay out the streets and fortifications, and design the handsome arcaded **Palazzo Comunale**; its arches are echoed by the buildings opening on to the piazza

and covered with escutcheons left by Florentine governors. The oft-restored **Basilica di Santa Maria delle Grazie** (1486) has a rich 17th-century interior, though most paintings have been removed to the adjacent **Museo della Basilica**: a *Madonna, Child and Four Saints* attributed to Masaccio (1401–28), an *Annunciation* by Jacopo di Sellaio, Baroque paintings by Giovanni di San Giovanni (born here; 1592–1636), and a fresco of a local miracle, in which a grandmother is able to give milk to her starving grandchild (14th century). Best is Fra Angelico's *Annunciation*, in deep, rich colours, seemingly a model for the *Annunciation* in Florence's San Marco, though here Adam and Eve are off to the left, fleeing the Garden of Eden. Earlier frescoes adorn the Gothic **church of San Lorenzo**.

Museo della Basilica
open summer Mon, Tues and Thur–Sat 10.30–12.30 and 4–7, Sun 4–7; winter Mon, Tues and Thur–Sat 10.30–12.30 and 3.30–6.30, Sun 3.30–6.30; adm

Some 2.5km south of San Giovanni is the Renaissance **Convento di Montecarlo**. From here the road continues up to the Monti del Chianti by way of **Cavriglia**; the hills around are scarred with open lignite mines. Cavriglia is also a natural park, where modern deer and buffalo roam with other animals from around the world.

The Valdarno also offers a look at older species of animal, especially the *elephas meridionalis*, in the **Museo Paleontologico** in **Montevarchi**, a major marketing centre of the region, famous for

Museo Paleontologico
open Wed–Sat 9–12.30 and 4–6, Sun 10–12; adm

hats and chickens. In its ancient core, trace the oval medieval street plan. In the centre, the old **Collegiata di San Lorenzo** had a facelift in the 18th century. Within it is an unusual reliquary 'of the holy milk', brought from a cave in the Holy Land where the Holy Family is said to have rested and where a fountain of milky water flows; a small museum holds a quattrocento **Tempietto** covered inside and out with Andrea della Robbia's cherub friezes.

Along the Road of Seven Bridges

East of the Arno, the panoramic Strada dei Sette Ponti passes several medieval towns en route to Arezzo. **Reggello** (8km east of Sanmezzano) stands amid its famous olive groves; some streets retain their medieval arcades, and the 12th-century parish **church of San Pietro a Cascia** has good, early Romanesque columns with carved capitals depicting lively scenes.

Castelfranco di Sopra, 12km south, was another Florentine military town laid out by Arnolfo di Cambio. Northeast, at **Pulicciano**, are pyramidical forms, or *balze*, like those at Volterra (*see* p.366). **Loro Ciuffenna** has picturesque medieval corners, a Romanesque bridge and tower, and a triptych by Lorenzo di Bicci in **Santa Maria Assunta**.

Best of all is the tiny 12th-century parish church of **Gropina** (from the Etruscan *Kropina*), 2km away, a fine example of rural Romanesque. Though it was referred to in the 8th century, the current church was built in the early 1200s. Dominated by its huge campanile, its façade is simplicity itself; the three naves and semicircular apse have never been altered. The columns are carved with primitive tigers, eagles and so on; the round marble **pulpit** is a bizarre relic of the Dark Ages, carved with archaic figures raising their arms over a marble knot; over them is a kind of totem pole, geometrical and floral decorations, and a siren with a snake whispering in her ear.

ⓘ **San Giovanni Valdarno >**
Palazzo d'Arnolfo, Piazza Cavour 3, **t** *055 9121123*

Where to Stay and Eat from Florence to Arezzo

San Giovanni Valdarno ✉ 52027

*****Hotel Masaccio**, Lungarno Don Minzoni 38, **t** 055 912 3402, *www.hotelmasaccio.it* (€€). Rooms with all comforts (breakfast included), a garden and a restaurant with Tuscan cuisine.

Giovannino, Piazza della Libertà 24, **t** 055 912 2726 (€€). A family-run place serving Tuscan fare. *Closed Wed.*

La Lanterna, Via Lavagnini 11, **t** 347 6742443 (€€). A simple restaurant offering the best local cuisine: try *tagliata* with *porcini* and truffles, and Chianina meat. *Closed Wed and Aug.*

Montevarchi ✉ 52025

*****Delta**, Via Diaz 137, **t** 055 901213, *www.hoteldelta.it* (€€). A fair option with parking and a restaurant. Breakfast is included.

L'Osteria di Rendola, Via di Rendola, Loc. Rendola 88, **t** 055 970 7491 (€€€). Wonderful creative Tuscan dishes such as tuna in tartare sauce with baby vegetables, and gorgonzola cheese *tortelli* with peaches. *Closed Thurs lunch, Wed, and Nov–Feb.*

Terranuova Bracciolini ✉ 52028

Il Canto del Maggio, Loc. Penna Alta, near Loro Ciuffenna, **t** 055 970 5147 (€€€). A delightful restaurant in a stone house with a pretty garden, in a

Hosteria Costachiara >>

tiny hamlet. Meals are served under the olive trees in summer. Among standout dishes are Florentine-style *strozzapretti*, *pepose dei fornaciai*, and home-made chocolate cake. Adjacent buildings house a wine bar and apartments to let. *Closed Mon, Tues Oct–May, lunch exc Sun, and Nov.*

Hosteria Costachiara, Viale Le Ville 129 (signed from Valdarno *autostrada* exit), **t** 055 944318 (€€€). A wonderful, family-run country restaurant where you can enjoy the likes of *pappardelle* with wild boar sauce and *pici* with pigeon. There are rooms in a nearby *locanda*. *Closed Mon eve and Tues.*

The Pratomagno and Vallombrosa

The Strada dei Sette Ponti skirts the west of the **Pratomagno**, a wrinkled, forested mountain ridge. Its highest peak, Croce di Pratomagno (1,592m), is due north of Loro Ciuffenna; winding roads from Loro go through tiny mountain hamlets, while the Loro–Talla route crosses over into the Casentino.

Further north, the two routes from Florence into the Casentino take in fine, wooded scenery. The SS70 over the **Passo della Consuma** (1,025m) is a favourite Italian rest stop; the secondary route passes through **Vallombrosa**, famous for its abbey founded by San Giovanni Gualberto of Florence, and HQ of his Vallombrosan order. The abbey underwent several remodellings in the 15th and 17th centuries and is mainly of interest for its splendid position.

Saltino, 1km away, is a small summer resort, an excellent base for a walk or a drive. One of the loveliest routes leads up to the Monte Secchieta (1,449m), with views over most of north-central Italy; in winter, skiing facilities spring up. For a longer outing, follow the **Panoramica del Pratomagno**, crossing nearly the entire Pratomagno to join the Strada dei Sette Ponti near Castiglion Fibocchi.

The Casentino: North to South

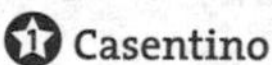
Casentino

The **Casentino**'s blue mountains, pastoral meadows and velvet valleys have long been Tuscany's spiritual refuge. Since the 18th century, travellers have trickled into the area, attracted initially by its famous monasteries, then charmed by one of the most beautiful and peaceful regions in Tuscany. The Arno, such a turgid, unmannerly creature in its lower reaches, is a fair, sparkling youth near its source at **Monte Falterona** (1,658m); one of the classic excursions is to take the trail up and spend the night, to witness the sunset over the Tyrrhenian Sea and dawn over the Adriatic.

Stia (population 3,000), the first town the Arno meets, is pretty and medieval, centred about large porticoed Piazza Tanucci and **Santa Maria Assunta**. The 17th-century façade hides a fine Romanesque interior, with some curious primitive capitals, a triptych by Lorenzo di Bicci and a *Madonna* by Andrea della Robbia. Wool – the thick, heavy, bright *lana del Casentino* – is the main

Getting around the Casentino

A **car** is the only convenient way of seeing all the sights of the Casentino, but you might enjoy getting around on the LFI **narrow-gauge train** line (**t** 0575 28414, *www.lfi.it*) that goes through Stia, Poppi, Bibbiena and Subbieno on its way to Arezzo (about 17 trains daily).

---

industry; in the old days, Stia was the market for the Guidi counts, whose ruined **Castello di Porciano** guarded the narrow Arno Valley from the 10th century.

Castello di Porciano
open mid-May–mid-Oct Sun 10–12 and 4–7; rest of year by appt on **t** *055 400517; donations appreciated*

Just north of Stia is the **sanctuary of Santa Maria delle Grazie**, a 14th-century church containing frescoes, works attributed to Luca della Robbia, and a painting by Lorenzo di Niccolò Gerini. This road continues into the Mugello (*see* p.213); the SS310 from Stia skirts Monte Falterona towards the **Passo la Calla** and Emilia-Romagna. Near the pass, the Alpine pasture **Burraia** (15km from Stia) is ideal for a cool summer picnic.

Down the Arno, **Pratovecchio** was the birthplace of Paolo Uccello in 1397; he would still recognize its narrow, porticoed lanes. Just 2km from the centre is the most beautiful Romanesque church of the Casentino, **Pieve di Romena**, founded in 1152 and retaining its original lines in spite of several earthquakes and subsequent repairs. The façade is plain but the apse has two tiers of blind arcades, pierced by narrow windows. Inside, the capitals are decorated with a medieval menagerie. Among the works of art is a 1200s *Madonna* by the Maestro di Varlungo.

Pieve di Romena
open by appt with custodian, **t** *0575 583725*

Nearby, the Guidis' **Castello di Romena** was one of the most powerful in the Casentino, with three sets of walls and 14 towers (reduced to three), and wide-ranging views. It houses a small **archaeological museum and armour collection**. Dante mentioned it in the *Inferno*. The writer knew this region well; at 24, he fought with the Guelphs against the Ghibellines of Arezzo and their allies at the **battle of Campaldino** (1289), just south of Pratovecchio. The victory made Florence the leading power in Tuscany; from there it went on to conquer Pisa and Arezzo. A column commemorating the battle was erected near the crossroads in 1921.

Castello di Romena
open by appt on **t** *0575 58633; adm*

Poppi and Camaldoli

Between 1000 and 1440, the Casentino was ruled by the Guidi counts, whose headquarters were at **Poppi** (population 5,700). From many kilometres around, you can see their stalwart **Castello**, which was modelled on the Palazzo Vecchio in Florence. The best-preserved medieval castle in the region, it has a magnificent courtyard and stairs that zigzag with a touch of Piranesi. Ask the custodian to show you the grand hall with 1400s Florentine frescoes, the chapel with restored frescoes by Taddeo Gaddi, and the commanding views from the tower.

Castello
open mid-Mar–June daily 10–6; July–Oct daily 10–7; Nov–mid-Mar Thurs–Sun 10–5

The centre of Poppi has ancient porticoed lanes winding around a small domed chapel; at the end of the main street is the Romanesque church of **San Fedele**, with a 13th-century *Madonna and Child*. Shops selling local copperware line the main street of lower Poppi, and there's the little **Zoo Fauna Europea** for kids.

A beautiful road runs northeast through the forest of Camaldoli, part of the Parco Nazionale delle Foreste Casentinesi, with wild deer and a huge variety of trees. It's ideal for walking. The road leads to the hermitage and monastery of **Camaldoli**, founded in 1012 by St Romualdo, a Benedictine monk. He was given this forest by Count Maldolo (hence 'Camaldoli') to found a community of hermits, similar to those of the Early Christians. A conflict arose, for the piety of the hermits soon attracted pilgrims and visitors who interfered with their solitary meditations. Romualdo's founded another monastery lower down, with a more relaxed rule, to entertain visitors and care for the forest domains. The Camaldolese are self-sufficient vegetarians whose rule orders them to plant at least 5,000 new trees every year. Little remains of San Romualdo's original foundation, save portions of the 11th-century cloister, the rich library and the 16th-century pharmacy, where the monks sell their balsams, herbal remedies and liqueurs. Part of the monastery is now a ***foresteria*** with simple accommodation and meals.

Foresteria
t 0575 556013

Some 3km further up, a beautiful hour's walk, is the **Eremo**, with 20 cottages set in an amphitheatre of pines, each with its own chapel and walled kitchen garden, where the hermits live in silence and solitude, meeting only on certain feast days and in the church, which was decorated inside by Vasari and has two marble tabernacles by Desiderio da Settignano. The church and St Romualdo's cell are open to visitors, but you may not go past the gate to the hermits' cottages.

Badia Prataglia, 10km from Camaldoli, is the region's most popular secular retreat – a summer resort spread out among the trees and hills, with beautiful walks along streams and waterfalls.

Bibbiena and La Verna

As chief town of the modern Casentino, **Bibbiena** is enveloped in sprawl and lacks Poppi's quaint charm, though in its heart it retains its old Tuscan feel. Few buildings stand out – a good Renaissance palace, **Palazzo Dovizi**, and the **church of San Lorenzo**, with some excellent polychrome terracottas by Andrea della Robbia.

From Bibbiena, the S208 crosses east into a range of hills bravely called the Alpe di Catenaia, which divides the Arno from the Tiber valley, to the famous Franciscan monastery of **La Verna**, high on a bizarre rocky outcrop, which, according to one of St Francis's visions, had been rent and blasted into its wild shape at the moment of the Crucifixion. The land was given to Francis in 1213

27 La Verna

by another pious nobleman, Count Orlando, and the saint at once built some mud huts here for a select group of his followers. He found La Verna a perfect spot for meditation and came to his holy mountain on slx occasions. During the last, on 14 September 1224, he became the first person ever to receive the stigmata – an event pictured in the frescoes of Assisi and elsewhere – after which he could only walk in extreme pain.

The churches, chapels and convent at La Verna are simple and rustic, though the main church, the chapel of Stigmata and St Francis's tiny **church of Santa Maria degli Angeli** are decorated by the most transcendently beautiful blue, green and white terracottas that Andrea della Robbia ever made, especially the *Annunciation*. You can also visit the **Sasso Spicco**, Francis's favourite retreat under a huge boulder, and **La Penna** (1,283m), on a sheer precipice, with views of the Arno and Tiber valleys.

Where to Stay and Eat in the Casentino

ⓘ **Stia >**
Pro Loco, Piazza Tanucci 65, t 0575 504106

Stia ✉ 52017

*****Albergo Falterona**, Piazza Tanucci 85, **t** 0575 504569, *www.albergofalterona.it* (€€). Upmarket rustically styled rooms in the *centro storico* (23 has frescoes).

****La Foresta**, Via Roma 27, **t** 0575 504650, *laforestahotel@hotmail.com* (€€). Basic, comfy rooms, some ensuite.

Ristorante Filetto, Piazza Tanucci 28, **t** 0575 583631 (€€). *Pappardelle* with wild boar, excellent stewed game and other hearty fare. *Closed Sat in winter.*

Poppi ✉ 52010

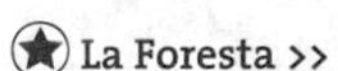

*****Casentino**, Piazza Repubblica, **t** 0575 529090, *www.albergocasentino.it* (€€). A good option opposite the castle, with rates includIng breakfast. The popular restaurant, set in the old castle stables, offers *tortellini*, ravioli, game, truffles and mushrooms.

****Campaldino**, Via Roma 95, **t** 0575 529008, (€€). An inn established in 1800, offering simple rooms (breakfast included). The restaurant uses lots of mushrooms, game, Florentine steak and grilled pork (half/full board available). *Closed Wed, and 1st 3wks July.*

*****Il Rustichello**, Via del Corniolo 14, **t** 0575 556020 (€€). A small modern resort hotel, great for families. with tennis, mini-golf and woodland walks. The restaurant (€€€) serves great pasta dishes from Emilia-Romagna, grilled meats and Casentino cheeses. Half and full board are available.

Pratovecchio ✉ 52015

La Tana Degli Orsi, Via Roma 1, **t** 0575 583377 (€€). One of the more interesting places to eat and drink in this remote area; it's a restaurant/*enoteca* (the name translates as 'The Bears' Den'), so you can enjoy a bottle and a snack, or a full meal. Highlights are potato *tortelli* with prawns, pigeon with panfried radicchio, and deer in Chianti sauce. Note that you can't pay by credit card. *Closed lunch, Tues, Wed, 10 days in early July, and Nov.*

Camaldoli ✉ 52010

***La Foresta**, Via Nazionale 13, **t** 0575 559009, *laforesta@inwind.it* (€). Spartan bedrooms with their original wood-panelled ceilings, rustic wood floors and rickety 1930s furniture. The restaurant serves up wholesome local food. Half and full board are available.

Passo della Consuma ✉ 52010

*****Miramonti**, **t** 055 830 6566, *www.hotelmiramonti-ar.it* (€€). A modern hotel with a spectacular setting at the top of the Passo della Consuma (1,058m). Bedrooms are functional but the grounds are lovely and there is a tennis court. The restaurant is a popular truck stop serving a cracking mushroom risotto.

Arezzo

Strategically located on a hill at the convergence of the Valdarno, Casentino and the Valdichiana valleys, ancient Arezzo (population 92,000) was one of the richest cities of the Etruscan Dodecapolis. Nor is modern Arezzo a loser in the money game – it has one of the biggest jewellery industries in Europe, with hundreds of small firms stamping out gold chains and rings, and bank vaults full of ingots. Its second most notable industry, one that fills the shops around its main Piazza Grande, is furniture-making and marketing antiques; on the first weekend of each month, the entire square becomes an enormous curiosity shop.

Arezzo is a bit of a curiosity shop itself. It had only a brief, though remarkable, bask in the Renaissance sunshine, though in the Middle Ages it was a typical free *comune*, a Ghibelline rival to Florence and a city of great cultural distinction. Around the year 1000, it gave birth to Guido Monaco (or Guido d'Arezzo), inventor of musical notation and the musical scale; in the 13th century, it produced Margarito, or Margaritone, an important painter in the transition from the Byzantine to the Italian styles. In 1304 Petrarch, the 'first modern man', was born here into a banished Florentine

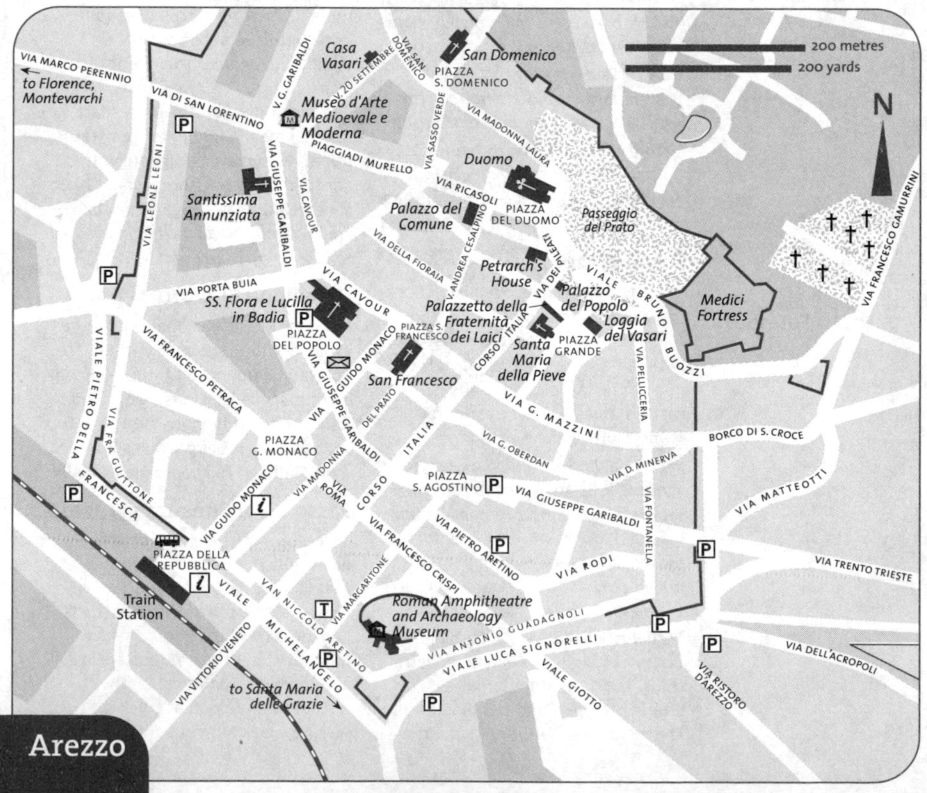

Arezzo

Getting to Arezzo

The **train** is the easiest way to reach Arezzo from Florence (75km/90mins), Perugia (73km/90mins) and Cortona (32km/45mins). The station is at the southern end of town, where Via Guido Monaco meets the old city walls.

There are **buses** from Cortona and other towns in Arezzo province, as well as Siena (7 a day) and Florence (4 a day). The station is opposite the train station on Viale Piero della Francesca, **t** 0575 382647/382651.

Black Guelph family; his Arezzo contemporary was Spinello Aretino, one of Tuscany's trecento masters. Arezzo was at its most powerful in the early 1300s, when it was ruled by a remarkable series of warrior bishops. One died in the battle of Campaldino; another, the fierce Guido Tarlati, ruled the city from 1312 to 1327. He expanded its territory, built new walls, settled internal bickerings, renewed warfare with Florence and Siena, and was excommunicated. After Bishop Guido came the deluge – his brother sold the city for a brief period to Florence, family rivalries exploded, the plague carried away half the population and, to top it all, in 1384 French troops of Louis d'Anjou sacked the city and brought it to its knees, refusing to move on until Arezzo paid 40,000 florins. Florence came up with the ransom money, in effect purchasing Arezzo's independence. Henceforth an economic backwater, on the fringe of the Renaissance, it produced two leading personalities: Giorgio Vasari and Pietro Aretino, the uninhibited writer and poet whose poison pen allowed him to make a fortune by not writing about contemporary princes and popes – the most genteel extortionist of all time.

If you arrive by train or bus, Via Guido Monaco leads up to the old centre by way of a stern statue of musical monk Guido, and passes on the left one of Italy's prettiest post offices, with an ornate ceiling, before ending in Piazza San Francesco, site of Arezzo's star attraction.

San Francesco

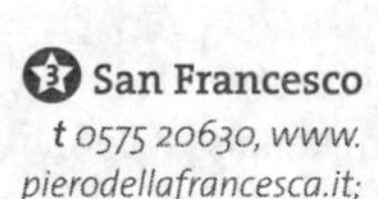

San Francesco
t 0575 20630, www.pierodellafrancesca.it; open summer Mon–Fri 9–7, Sat 9–6, Sun 1–6; winter Mon–Fri 9–5.30, Sat 9–5, Sun 1–5.30; booking compulsory; adm

This dowdy barn of a Franciscan church contains Piero della Francesca's frescoes on the popular pseudo-classical/Christian subject of the *Legend of the True Cross* (*see* p.156), the most riveting cycle of frescoes of the 1400s and the gospel of Renaissance painting. Piero literally wrote the book on the new science of artificial perspective, yet as strictly as these frescoes obey the dictates of the vanishing point, they make no concessions to realism; simplified and drawn with geometrical perfection, Piero's beings are purely spiritual creatures. It is intriguing that Piero and Uccello, the two artists most obsessed with perspective and space, created the most transcendent art; few compositions are as haunting as Piero's *Dream of Constantine*, a virtuoso demonstration of lighting, colouring and perspective, the angel swooping down from the upper left-front of the scene – and yet all is uncannily still; the soldiers stand guard, woodenly unaware; the sleeping emperor's attendant gazes out with a bored expression. Note, too, the *Annunciation* in which Gabriel announces both the birth and death of her son to Mary.

That these frescoes exist at all is nothing short of a miracle. The walls have been damaged by an earthquake, struck by lightning, burned twice and shot at by Napoleon's troops, who scratched the eyes of the figures. To keep the church standing after so much abuse, the first restorers injected tons of cement into the walls, which, combined with humidity, nearly ruined the frescoes. Although they were cleaned in the 1960s, no attempt was made to protect them from further damage. Now, after nearly two decades of complex work, they are fully restored and, hopefully, saved. During restoration, it was discovered that the 'night' the art historians always referred to in Piero's *Dream of Constantine* is not night after all but a magnificent dawn hidden beneath layers of dirt. So much for the most famous nighttime painting in the history of art.

Piazza Grande

Few *piazze* in Italy have the eclectic charm of Arezzo's Piazza Grande, perfect backdrop for both the *Giostra del Saracino* in early September and the monthly antiques fair. For the former, the town sports from the four quarters of Arezzo don 13th-century costume to re-enact an event first documented in 1593, a celebration of the feats of arms against Saracen pirates who menaced the Tyrrhenian coast in the 16th century and penetrated inland as far as Arezzo. Revived in 1932, it begins with a parade of costumes and flag-tossing by the *sbandieratori*, followed by a test of individual prowess between eight knights, two representing each quarter, who tilt against a wooden figure, 'Buratto, King of the Indies', for the prize of a golden lance.

Fiera Antiquaria
1st Sat and Sun of month but call tourist office (see p.410) to check if making a special trip

The **Fiera Antiquaria** attracts hundreds of 'antiques' vendors from all over the country, selling everything from Renaissance ceramics to 1950s junk. The piazza and surrounding streets are also lined with antique shops. On one side of the piazza you'll find the **Loggia del Vasari**, a large building that Giorgio Vasari designed for his hometown in 1573, with the idea of replicating a Greek *stoa*, with little shops, workshops, and expensive bars and restaurants under the portico.

Vasari also designed the clocktower of the **Palazzetto della Fraternità dei Laici**, an ornate building, half Gothic and half by Renaissance master Bernardo Rossellino. It looks like a town hall but is really the home of a lay brotherhood that was founded in the 1200s. The Palazzo del Popolo exists only in ruins, behind Vasari's loggia on Via dei Pileati. Like Pisa's, it was destroyed by the Florentines after they captured the city.

Santa Maria della Pieve

Perhaps most impressive on Piazza Grande is the round, Romanesque arcaded apse of Arezzo's great 12th-century church, Santa Maria della Pieve; it turns its back on the piazza, directing its unusual Pisan-Lucchese façade towards narrow Via dei Pileati, where it's hard to see well. Each tier of arches is narrower than the previous one, in a unique rustic style with no two columns or capitals alike. The campanile 'of a hundred holes' has so many neat rows of double-mullioned windows it resembles a primitive skyscraper. Under the arch of the front portal, note the restored early medieval *Reliefs of the Twelve Months*: April with her flowers, February with his pruning hook, and the pagan two-headed god Janus for January. The dim interior has an early Romanesque relief of the *Three Magi* on the entrance wall and decorated capitals in the nave. As in many early churches, the presbytery is raised above the low crypt, the most ancient part of the church, with primitive capitals – human faces mingling with rams, bulls and dragons. On the left wall is another primitive relief of the *Nativity* and *Christ's Baptism*; above in the choir is a beautiful polyptych by Pietro Lorenzetti (1320), featuring the *Madonna and Saints* modelling the latest Tuscan fashions and fabrics.

Below Santa Maria descends Corso Italia, Arezzo's main evening parade; above, Via dei Pileati continues into the oldest quarter of the city, passing by way of **Petrarch's house**, a replacement for the original bombed in the last war; it stands near the picturesque 14th-century Palazzo del Pretorio, decked with coats of arms of imperial and Florentine governors.

Casa del Petrarca
open Mon–Fri 10–12 and 3–5; Sat 10–12; booking required on **t** *057 524700*

The Duomo

From Piazza Grande, narrow streets lead up to the **Passeggio del Prato**, an English-style park with lawns, trees, a café and a big white elephant of a Fascist monument to Petrarch. Arezzo slopes gradually upwards from the train station, ending abruptly here; the cliffs on the edge of the Prato have memorable view over the mountains towards Florence and Urbino. Overlooking the park is a half-ruined 1500s Medici fortress

At the other end is the back of the **Duomo**, with a lovely Gothic belltower from the 19th century. The cathedral, built in bits and pieces over two and a half centuries (1276–1510), has a nondescript façade but several great works of art in its dimly lit Gothic naves. Its stained-glass **windows**, created by the greatest 16th-century master, Frenchman Guillaume de Marcillat, seem almost like illuminated frescoes by Gozzoli or Luca Signorelli. The magnificent marble Gothic high altar is dedicated to San Donato, and there are some impressive tombs – the first of Pope Gregory X (1205–76) with a canopy and 4th-century sarcophagus, holding the mortal dust of the pope who holds the record for taking the longest to be elected; the enclave, in Viterbo, lasted from 1268 to 1271, and only ended when the Viterbans starved the cardinals into deciding. The second, even more impressive, is the 1327 **tomb of Bishop Guido Tarlati**, an early predecessor of the heroic sculptural tombs of the Renaissance, perhaps designed by Giotto. The tomb is divided into three sections, with a relief resembling a miniature theatre and a Ghibelline eagle on top; below lies the battling bishop's effigy; and below that, 16 fine relief panels tell the story of his life, battles and good works. Beside it is Piero della Francesca's fresco of the Magdalene holding a crystal pot of ointment.

Museo del Duomo
open Thurs–Sat 10–12; adm

The **Museo del Duomo** contains detached frescoes by Spinello Aretino and his son Parri di Spinello, a terracotta depicting the *Annunciation* by Bernardo Rossellino and paintings by 13th-century master Margarito d'Arezzo, Signorelli and Vasari.

Diagonally opposite the cathedral is Arezzo's Ghibelline **Palazzo del Comune** with its distinctive tower; from here Via Ricasoli descends past the **birthplace of Guido Monaco** (with a plaque of Guido's do-re-mi) to the art museum.

Museo d'Arte Medioevale e Moderna

Museo d'Arte Medioevale e Moderna
open Tues–Sat 9–7; Sun and hols 9–1; adm

Here you can get to know local medieval and Renaissance artists not often seen elsewhere. The collection – in a medieval palace remodelled in the Renaissance, perhaps by Bernardo Rossellino – is arranged chronologically. The courtyard has medieval columns and capitals, a fine sculpted horse's head and gargoyles. The two rooms on the **ground floor** contain sculptural details from the cathedral façade and a fine 10th-century *pluteo* carved with peacocks.

Among works on the **first floor** are a stylized Byzantine *St Francis* by Margarito d'Arezzo, painted just after the saint's death, and an *Enthroned Virgin* by Guido da Siena, studded with chunky, plasticky gems. Next come detached frescoes by Spinello Aretino, the city's greatest trecento artist, and his son Parri di Spinello (1387–1453), whose ghostly battle scene *Sconfitta di Massenzio* was found in the Badia after the war. Another native of Arezzo, Bartolomeo della Gatta, painted the plague saint Rocco praying to liberate the city from the Black Death. Also on the first floor is a fresco attributed to Signorelli; a huge busy canvas by Vasari of *Esther's Wedding Banquet*; a collection of small Renaissance bronzes; beautiful ceramics from Urbino, Deruta and Montelupo; and a plate by Master Giorgio of Gubbio with his secret red (*see* p.482).

On the **second floor** are a strange painting by Angelo Cacoselli (d. 1652), the *Maga*, of an enchantress with her animals, a few 18th-century Neapolitan *presepi* figurines, and some splashy Mannerist canvases by Vasari, Allori and the great Rosso Fiorentino.

Vasari, Cimabue and More Vasari

Casa del Giorgio Vasari
Via XX Settembre 55; open Tues–Sat 9–6.30, Sun 9–1.30; adm

Around the corner from the Museo d'Arte Medioevale e Moderna you'll find the **Casa del Giorgio Vasari**. Vasari was so fond of his own brand of spineless Mannerism, he wasn't about to leave it all for Duke Cosimo aned decorated his own house with the same fluff. Mediocrity attracts mediocrity; besides the frescoes there are several rooms of nondescript paintings, of which three stand out: the most repugnant *St Sebastian* committed to canvas, a terracotta portrait of Galba, one of Rome's ugliest mugs, by Sansovino, and a painting by a follower of Santi di Tito, of *Christ and the Apostles* dining in the 17th-century equivalent of a greasy spoon.

From Vasari's house, Via San Domenico takes you to 13th-century **San Domenico**, with a simple asymmetrical exterior and a fine stone Gothic chapel (1360s) on the right wall. The main altar has a crucifix by Cimabue (c. 1265); the chapel to the left has a fine triptych of the Archangel Michael by the 'Maestro del Vescovado'.

Via Garibaldi from the art museum returns to the centre by way of **Santissima Annunziata**, Arezzo's late response to the Florentine Brunelleschi, begun by Bartolomeo della Gatta in the 1490s and completed by Antonio da Sangallo; the fourth altar has a painting by Pietro da Cortona and in the choir is a stained-glass window by Marcillat. Further up, off Via Porta Buia, is **Santissime Flora e Lucilla in Badia**, a 13th-century church with an unusual interior remodelled by Vasari. He also designed the two-sided altar, with reliefs from the Gospel of St Matthew on the front and St George slaying the dragon on the back. Over the presbytery the impressive cupola is a masterful fake by 17th-century trompe-l'œil master Andrea Pozzo. At the entrance is a good fresco of St Lawrence by della Gatta; the fine cloister is by Giuliano da Maiano, a student of Brunelleschi (entrance at No.2, Piazza della Badia).

On the southern edge of Arezzo, near the station on Via Margaritone, the remains of a small **Roman amphitheatre** have become a quiet city park. The restored Olivetan monastery, built on a curve over the amphitheatre's foundations, houses the **Museo Archeologico**. Not much has survived of the thriving Etruscan and Roman city of Arretium, but there are some mosaics and sarcophagi, Etruscan urns and Greek vases, examples of the Roman era red *corallino* vases and an excellent portrait of a rather jaded-looking, middle-aged Roman worked in gold.

Museo Archeologico
open daily 8.30–7.30; adm

Santa Maria delle Grazie

It's 15-minute walk from Viale Mecenate through Arezzo's car-clogged southern suburbs to see the simple but exceptionally pretty Renaissance church of Santa Maria delle Grazie, finished in 1444, and given a jewel of a porch by Benedetto da Maiano in 1482.

With its subdued, delicate decoration, and round arches braced with slender iron bars, this could be the archetypal creation of early Renaissance architecture – it calls to mind the backgrounds of any number of Tuscan paintings. The interior has an early Renaissance delight to match, a colourful terracotta altarpiece full of coloured fruit and putti by Andrea della Robbia, surrounding Parri di Spinello's *Madonna della Misericordia* (1430).

La Foresteria >>

Arezzo >
Piazza della Repubblica 28, in front of train station, **t** *0575 377678, www.apt.arezzo.it*

Antica Osteria L'Agania >>

Where to Stay in Arezzo

Arezzo ✉ 52100

****__Hotel Patio__, Via Cavour 23, **t** 0575 401962, *www.hotelpatio.it* (€€€€). An 18th-century palace with rooms in the style of countries visited by travel writer Bruce Chatwin – China, India, Africa, Morocco and so on. Breakfast is included, and there's an American-style bar/restaurant in the basement.

****__Minerva__, Via Fiorentina 4, **t** 0575 370390, *www.hotel-minerva.it* (€€€). Pleasant rooms west of the city walls in ugly modern suburbs, convenient if you're travelling by car (with parking). A buffet breakfast is included, and there's an excellent restaurant (€€) and a Turkish bath and fitness centre.

***__Continentale__, Piazza Guido Monaco 7, **t** 0575 20251, *www.hotelcontinentale.com* (€€€). A fine, older hotel, with comfortable rooms (breakfast included) and a lovely roof terrace.

***__Casa Volpi__, Via Simone Martini 29, a few km southeast of city, **t** 0575 354364, *www.casavolpi.it* (€€). A pleasant old villa set above the road, with comfortable bedrooms with antiques, a large garden with panoramic terraces, and an excellent evening restaurant serving local dishes home-made from prime ingredients (half/full board offered).

__Truciolini__, Via G. Ferraris 29, **t 0575 984104, *www.truciolini.it* (€€). A good-value option with parking and its own restaurant, serving the likes of good ravioli filled with potatoes, grilled lamb, and chicken breast with lemon. Breakfast is included, and half and full board available.

*__Toscana__, Via Perennio 56, near Porta San Lorentino, **t** 0575 21692 (€). Simple rooms outside the centre, most ensuite.

La Foresteria, Via Bicchieraia 32, **t** 0575 370474, *www.foresteriaarezzo.com* (€). Simple but stylish rooms with shared facilities but beautiful frescoes (in most) in a former Benedictine convent approached via a lovely cloister. Meals are served in the refectory, and there's a TV room, Internet point and garden.

Ostello Villa Severi, Via Francesco Redi 13, near Porta San Lorentino (bus no.4 from station), **t** 0575 299047, *www.peterpan.it/ostello* (€). A hostel with a lovely garden and a guests' restaurant (half board and full board available).

Eating Out in Arezzo

Bacco e Arianna, Via Cesalpino 10, **t** 0575 299598 (€€). A restaurant in a 14th-century *palazzo*, offering the likes of meat with black cabbage and *crostone* with cannellini beans. The wines come from the *enoteca* round the corner. *Closed Mon, and Jan.*

Buca di San Francesco, Via S. Francesco 1, **t** 0575 23271 (€€). A tourist favourite with a medieval atmosphere and tasty Tuscan fare; try *tagliolini* in broth. *Closed Mon eve, Tues, and July.*

Da Guido, Via Madonna del Prato 85, **t** 0575 23760 (€€). A cosy trattoria. *Closed Sun (exc 1st Sun of month).*

Osteria La Capannaccia, Loc Campriano 51c, **t** 0575 361759 (€€). Specialities of the Aretine countryside, including great *minestra di pane*, plus Colli Aretini wines. *Closed Sun eve, Mon and Aug.*

Antica Osteria L'Agania, Via Mazzini 10, **t** 0575 295381 (€). A rustic option, excellent value and hence very popular. Try the Chianana meat.

Torre di Gnicche, Piaggia San Martino 8, near Piazza Grande, **t** 0575 352035 (€). A tiny wine bar with snacks, daily soups, and dishes of the day. *Closed Wed, 3wks Jan, and 1wk July.*

The Valtiberina and the Valdichiana

The Valtiberina

The Valtiberina, or upper valley of the Tiber, is a luminous patchwork filled with glowing pasturelands and pine and beech woodlands, birthplace of Michelangelo and Piero della Francesca.

Arezzo to Sansepolcro

While Michelangelo took fresh air and stone-flavoured milk from his native place, Piero della Francesca carried the light and luminous landscape along the Tuscan-Umbrian frontier with him through his career, and left more behind in his native haunts than Michelangelo.

From Arezzo, it's a pretty 41km drive to Sansepolcro, especially along the SS73, which ascends through the Foce di Scopetone (with panoramic views back towards the city) then continues 17km to the short turn-off for **Monterchi**. Dedicated to Hercules in Roman times, this town is a tiny medieval triangle; don't miss the curious underground passageway around the apse of the parish church, dating back to the Middle Ages but of uncertain purpose. Monterchi is most famous for Piero della Francesca's extraordinary fresco, the **Madonna del Parto** (1445), perhaps the first (and last?) portrayal of the Virgin in the ninth month of pregnancy, a mystery revealed by twin angels who pull back the flaps of a tent empty but for Mary, weary and melancholy, one eyelid drooping, one hand on her hip, the other on her swollen belly, almost painful to see.

Madonna del Parto
former schoolhouse, Via della Reglia (well signposted from all directions); open Tues–Sun 9–1 and 2–7 (until 6 in winter); adm

Anghiari (population 6,200), between Monterchi and Sansepolcro, is a fine old town on a balcony over the Valtiberina. Once a property of Camaldoli and later of the Tarlati family, it was the site of a 1440 victory of the Florentines over the Milanese – a decisive victory in corking up Visconti ambitions over Tuscany and the rest of Italy, and a nearly bloodless one, the epitome of Renaissance Italy's civilized chessboard wars; only one man died, and that was an accident. Leonardo da Vinci chose it as his subject matter in the Battle of the Frescoes in Florence's Palazzo Vecchio – one of the Renaissance's greatest unhappenings, though the cartoons left behind by the master were often copied and became one of the inspirations of Florentine Mannerism.

Anghiari's Renaissance Palazzo Taglieschi houses the **Museo delle Arti e Tradizioni Popolari dell'Alta Valle del Tevere**, with exhibits relating to traditional crafts of the Upper Tiber Valley.

Museo delle Arti e Tradizioni Popolari dell'Alta Valle del Tevere
Via Mameli 16; open Tues–Sat 8.30–7, Sun 9–1.30; adm

Sansepolcro

Sansepolcro (population 15,500), the largest town of the Valtiberina, is famous for lace, pasta (the Buitoni spaghetti works are just outside the city) and Piero della Francesca. The painter was

Getting around the Valtiberina and Valdichiana

CAT **buses** (**t** 800 223010, *www.catspa.it*) from Arezzo serve this area efficiently, if not especially frequently. Buses from Sansepolcro station (just outside the walls) go to Città di Castello, Caprese Michelangelo (26km/45mins), Arezzo (38km/1hr), Florence and Pieve Santo Stefano.

Sansepolcro is the terminus of Umbria's FCU **light rail line**, which slowly trundles you down to Città di Castello (16km/25mins), Umbertide, Perugia, Todi and Terni.

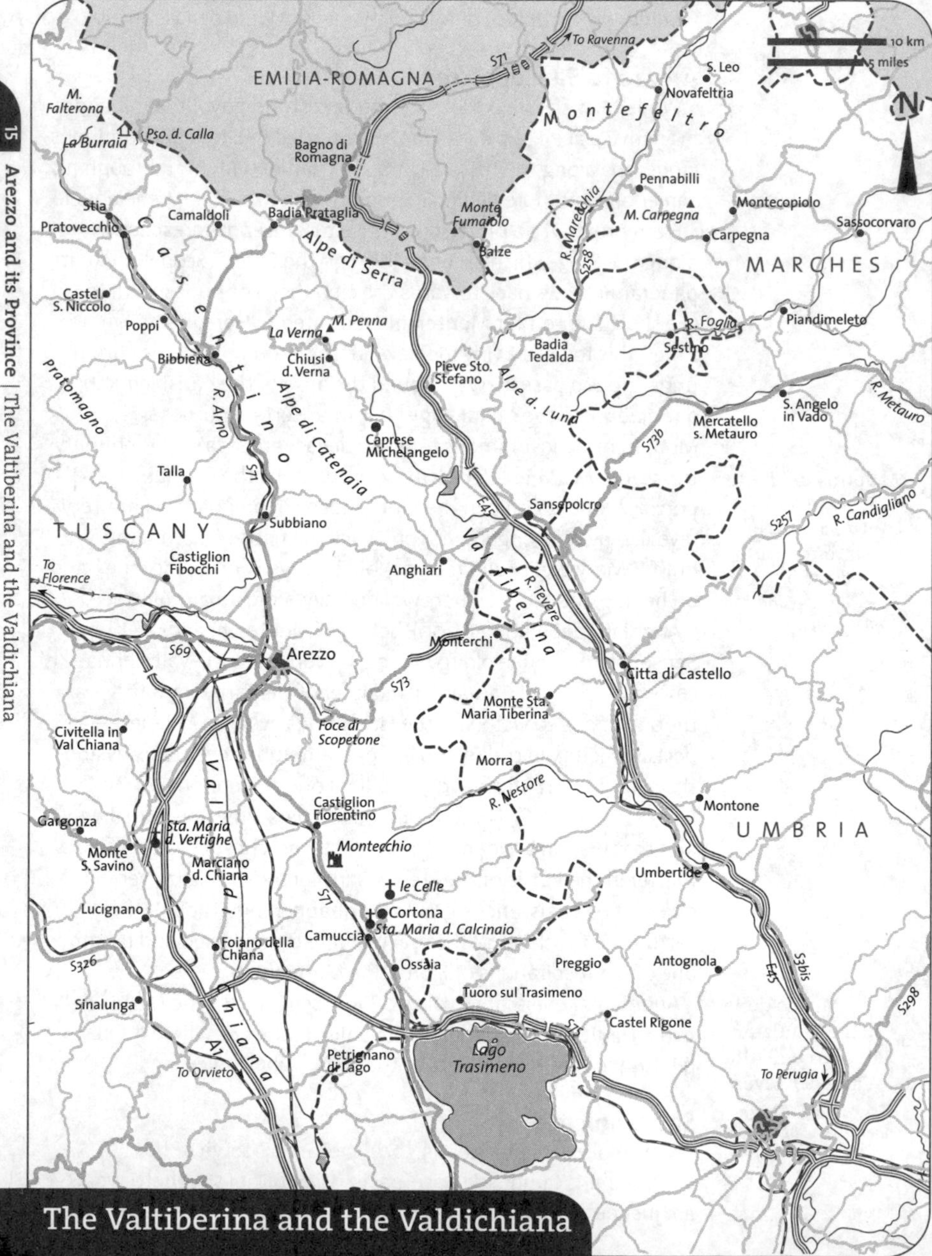

The Valtiberina and the Valdichiana

born here c.1410–1420 and given his mother's name (his father died before his birth). Although he worked in the Marches, Arezzo and Rome, he spent most of his life in Sansepolcro, painting and writing books on geometry and perspective until he went blind at the age of 60. Piero may have had a chance to discuss his theories with a younger son of Sansepolcro, mathematician Luca Pacioli (born 1440), who wrote his *Divina Proporzione* with some help from Leonardo da Vinci (he also gets credit for the first book on accounting).

Sansepolcro was founded around the year 1000, and like Anghiari belonged to the monks of Camaldoli until the 13th century. The historic centre, with its crew-cut towers, has plenty of character. It is enclosed within well-preserved walls, built by the Tarlati and given a Renaissance facelift by Giuliano da Sangallo. **Piazza Torre di Berta** is the centre of town, where on the second Sunday of September crossbow-men from Gubbio challenge home archers in the *Palio della Balestra*, an ancient rivalry.

Museo Civico
open daily 9.30–1 and 2.30–6 (until 7.30 in summer); adm

Strung out along Via Matteotti are many of the city's surviving 14th–16th-century palaces, notably the Palazzo delle Laudi and the 14th-century palace housing the **Museo Civico**. Here are Piero's masterpiece, the *Resurrection*, an intense, almost eerie depiction of the solemnly triumphant Christ stepping out of his tomb surrounded by sleeping soldiers and a land more autumnal than springlike, plus two of Piero's early works, the *Misericordia Polyptych*, a gold-background altarpiece dominated by a serene, giant goddess of a Madonna, sheltering under her cloak members of the confraternity (note the black hood on one) who commissioned the picture, and a damaged fresco of San Giuliano. Other works are by his greatest pupil, Luca Signorelli, Pontormo, Santi di Tito, Mannerist Raffaellino del Colle, and the 16th-century Giovanni de' Vecchi, also of Sansepolcro, whose *Presentation of the Virgin* is interesting for its unusual vertical rhythms. You can see a 16th-century scene of Sansepolcro in the *Pilgrimage of the Company of the Crucifix of Loreto*, a relic of the days of the Black Death – as are the wooden panels of *Death* (one showing a fine strutting skeleton).

Near the museum is Gothic **San Francesco**, with a fine rose window and portal. The **Duomo**, on Via Matteotti, was built in the 11th century but has been much restored. Among the art is a fresco by Bartolomeo della Gatta and a polyptych by Matteo di Giovanni; note the huge rose window made of alabaster. Another church, **San Lorenzo**, has a *Deposizione* by Rosso Fiorentino.

Up the Tiber: Caprese Michelangelo

Signor Buonarroti, a minor noble of Florence, was *podestà* in tiny Caprese, 26km northwest of Sansepolcro, when his wife gave birth to little Michelangelo. As was the custom, the baby was sent into the countryside to be nursed by a mason's wife. 'If my brains are any good at all, it's because I was born in the pure air of your Arezzo countryside,' Michelangelo later told Vasari. 'Just as with my mother's milk, I sucked in the hammer and chisels I use for my statues.'

Casa del Podestà *open April, May and Oct Mon–Fri 10.30–5.30, Sat and Sun 10.30–6.30; June, July and Sept Mon–Fri 9.30–6.30, Sat and Sun 9.30–7.30; Aug daily 9.30–7.30; Nov–Mar Mon–Fri 11–5, Sat and Sun 11–6; adm*

He only returned once to the Valtiberina, to select sturdy firs to float down the Tiber for the scaffolding in the Sistine Chapel, but Caprese does not let any chance slip by to remind us of its most famous son, even changing its name to Caprese Michelangelo. The artist's purported birthplace, the restored 14th-century **Casa del Podestà**, is a museum with photos and reproductions of his works.

From here it's not far into the Alpe di Catenaia and La Verna (*see* pp.402–403).

Caprese to Sestino

East of Caprese the countryside is the biggest attraction; between **Pieve Santo Stefano** (Roman *Sulpitia*, mostly rebuilt after the Second World War) and **Badia Tedalda** (a small resort) lie the rolling Alpe della Luna, the 'Mountains of the Moon'.

Sestino (from the Roman woodland god Sextius), Tuscany's easternmost *comune* on the border of the Marches, was ruled by the Montefeltro dukes of Urbino until 1516. It has been the area's agricultural centre since antiquity and has many medieval buildings. Near its little Romanesque parish church, the **Antiquarium** has the headless *Venus of Sestino* and other local finds. The 8th-century church shows the influence of Ravenna, Byzantine capital of the west; its 13th-century altar sits on a Roman boundary stone.

Antiquarium *open daily 9.30–12 and 3–6*

Sestino is Tuscany's easternmost village; if you like this area, you cross the border into the Marches – specifically, the lovely upland region called the Montefeltro above the Renaissance city of Urbino.

Where to Stay and Eat in the Valtiberina

ⓘ **Anghiari >** *Corso Matteotti 103, t 0575 749279*

★ **Fiorentino >>**

Anghiari ✉ 52031

Locanda al Castello di Sorci, San Lorenzo, near Anghiari, **t** 0575 789066 (€). A country beanery in a former tobacco barn, in a beautiful setting. Guests eat an incredible-value set menu that includes wine, and the likes of *ribollita*, risotto with mushrooms, polenta, and *tagliolini* with mushrooms. *Closed Mon.*

ⓘ **Sansepolcro >** *Via Matteotti 8, t 0575 740536*

Sansepolcro ✉ 52037

****__La Balestra__, Via del Montefeltro 29, **t** 0575 735151, *www.labalestra.it* (€€). Comfortable modern rooms and one apartment, parking and a good restaurant where you might enjoy pasta and chickpeas, *tortellini* with white truffles, and grilled lamb. Breakfast is included; half or full board are available.

***__Fiorentino__, Via L. Pacioli 56, near main gate, **t** 0575 740350, *www.albergofiorentino.com* (€€). The town inn since the 1820s, with basic rooms (buffet breakfast included), a garage, and Sansepolcro's best restaurant, serving great Italian onion soup and other local specialities, and a wide assortment of local cheese. *Closed Fri.*

Il Convivio, Via Traversari 1, **t** 0575 736543 (€€). A restaurant in a Renaissance *palazzo*, offering interesting dishes from the Valtiberina, including *tagliolini* with Fossa cheese. *Closed Tues and early Feb.*

Locanda La Pergola, Via Tiberina 17, Pieve Santo Stefano, 16km north of Sansepolcro on La Verna road, **t** 0575

797053 (€). An inn restored in a classy country style. A couple of the basic rooms share facilities. The restaurant serves superbly cooked country food, including ravioli freshly made daily with local ricotta. *Closed Wed.*

****Orfeo**, Viale Diaz 12, **t** 0575 742061 (€). Basic ensuite rooms.

Enoteca Guidi, Via Pacioli 44, **t** 0575 736587 (€€). A cosy wine bar with a rear dining room serving spaghetti with *speck*, *porcini* and rocket, risotto with asparagus and prawns, and Chianina meat with Parmesan and lemons. There are also a few rooms. *Closed Sun lunch, Wed and Sat.*

Caprese Michelangelo
✉ 52033

*****Fonte della Galletta**, up in Alpe Faggeto above Caprese Michelangelo **t** 0575 793925 (€). A pleasant little mountain hotel and restaurant set in a lovely forested landscape, with simple ensuite rooms (breakfast included). The restaurant (€€) uses the freshest local ingredients – chestnuts, wild mushrooms, truffles, game, mountain hams – to create tasty fare. Try the home-made pasta dishes, grilled meats and *semifreddo al croccante*. *Closed Mon and Tues.*

South of Arezzo: the Valdichiana

The flat Valdichiana south of Arezzo is the largest, broadest valley in the Apennines, surrounded by hills and old towns. The Etruscans, headquartered at Cortona, were the first to drain its marshlands, making it their breadbasket – so rich, it is said, that even after Hannibal's troops pillaged on their way to Lake Trasimeno, there was still more than enough to feed the army and its elephants. By the Middle Ages, however, the valley had reverted to a swamp, forcing the inhabitants back into the hills. And so it stayed, until the beginning of the 19th century, when the Lorraine grand dukes initiated a major land reclamation scheme. Now, once again, prosperous farms are the main feature of the Valdichiana. The equally prosperous-looking cattle are a prized breed called the Chianina, descendants of the primal herds whose fossils were discovered in the vicinity.

Monte San Savino and Lucignano

But there is more to the Valdichiana than farms and *bistecca alla fiorentina* on the hoof. On both sides of the valley are some of the most beautiful villages in this part of Tuscany. Cortona is the most famous, but there are others, including **Monte San Savino** (21km from Arezzo, on the west side of the valley), birthplace of Andrea Contucci, better known as Andrea Sansovino (1460–1529), artistic emissary of Lorenzo de' Medici to Portugal and one of the heralds of the High Renaissance; his Florentine pupil Jacopo adopted his surname and became chief sculptor and architect in Venice in its Golden Age. Spread out on a low hill, this is an attractive town with a melange of late medieval and fine Renaissance palaces. Andrea Sansovino left several works to his hometown: an attractive portal on the **church of San Giovanni**, terracottas (with others by the Della Robbias) in the little **church of Santa Chiara** in Piazza Jalta,

Getting around the Valdichiana

LFI **trains** (**t** 0575 28414, *www.lfi.it*) head south from Arezzo for Monte San Savino and Lucignano, and Sinalunga (*see* p.373), with links to Chiusi and Siena.

and the lovely **cloister of Sant'Agostino** (13th-century, with a small rose window by Guillaume de Marcillat). Sansovino, or Antonio da Sangallo the Elder, designed the beautiful, harmonious **Loggia dei Mercanti** with its grey Corinthian capitals in the early 1500s; Antonio da Sangallo gets credit for the simple, partly rusticated **Palazzo Comunale**, originally the home of the Del Monte family, whose money paid for most of Monte San Savino's Renaissance ornaments. Foremost among the medieval monuments, the **Palazzo Pretorio** was built by the Perugians. The city walls are the work of the Sienese.

On a cypress-clad hill 2km east, **Santa Maria della Vertighe**, built in the 12th century and restored in the 16th, houses a rare 13th-century triptych by Margarito d'Arezzo and 14th-century works by Lorenzo Monaco. Some 7km west is pretty **Gargonza**, with its mighty tower dominating a tight cluster of houses on a wart of a hill, the whole of which is now a hotel (*see* opposite).

47 Lucignano

Cheerful little **Lucignano**, to the south of Monte San Savino,is unique among Italian hilltowns for its street plan – it is laid out in four concentric ellipses, like a kind of maze, with four picturesque little *piazze* in the centre. One piazza is dominated by the Collegiata with a theatrical circular stair, another by the 14th-century **Palazzo Comunale**, now the **Museo Civico**, with a good collection of 13th–15th-century Sienese works, a *Madonna* by Signorelli and, most famously, a 14th-century masterpiece of Aretine goldsmiths, the delicate reliquary *Albero di Lucignano*. There are more good Sienese paintings in the **church of San Francesco**. Outside the centre are a 16th-century Medici fortress and the **Madonna delle Querce**, a Renaissance temple sometimes attributed to Vasari, with a Doric interior.

Museo Civico
open summer Tues–Thurs, Sat and Sun 10–1 and 2.30–6; winter Tues, Thurs, Fri 10–1 and 2.30–5.30, Sat and Sun 10–1 and 2.30–6

Marciano della Chiana, 6km northeast, is another old fortified village with an impressive main gate that also does time as clock and belltower. **Foiano della Chiana**, just south, is encompassed by newer buildings, but in its **collegiata** has a good *Coronation of the Virgin* by Signorelli and a terracotta by Andrea della Robbia. Between Marciano and Foiano is the curious octagonal **church of Santa Vittoria**, built by Ammannati for Cosimo I.

Castiglion Fiorentino

East, on the last hill overlooking the Valdichiana plain, fortified **Castiglion Fiorentino** was Castiglion Aretino until the Florentines snatched it in 1384. Another old Etruscan settlement, with medieval streets, it nevertheless had more than a nodding acquaintance with the Renaissance. Like many a larger town, it has an ornamental geometric temple below the walls, the octagonal **Madonna della Consolazione**, untampered with since 1607. Then there's the 16th-century **Loggiato Vasariano**, overlooking the countryside from the old market square. The 1860 plebiscite that brought Tuscany into the kingdom of Italy made a big impression here: the **Palazzo Comunale** opposite has a marble plaque recording not only the precise vote but the exact day, hour and minute of the count.

Pinacoteca Civica
open Tues–Sun 10–12.30 and 4–6.30; adm

Just behind and above the Palazzo Comunale, Castiglion's ancient heart, the Cassero (from the Roman *castrum*), has the Palazzo Pretorio and the church of Sant'Angelo, the latter home to the small **Pinacoteca Civica**. Its prizes are a French Renaissance gilded silver reliquary bust of Sant'Orsola, a pair of 13th-century crucifixes, the *Stigmata of St Francis* by Bartolomeo della Gatta, a *Portrait of St Francis* (1280) by the workshop of Margaritone di Arezzo, and the 15th-century *Probatica Piscina*, an uncommon subject (Jerusalem's sheep pond, with curative waters) by Jacopo de Sellaio. The **Collegiata**, rebuilt in the 19th century, has kept its art: *Enthroned Madonnas* by Della Gatta, an *Adorazione* by Lorenzo di Credi, and, in the adjacent **Pieve Vecchia** Signorelli's fresco of the *Deposition*. The Gothic 13th-century **church of San Francesco** has a cloister, some frescoes and a wooden *Crucifixion* sculpted by Giambologna.

Dilapidated castles are all around Castiglion, most impressively at **Montecchio**, 4km south, with its tall honey-coloured tower and walls, visible all over the Valdichiana. In the 1400s it was the stronghold of *condottiere* Sir John Hawkwood (*see* p.108).

Where to Stay and Eat in the Valdichiana

ⓘ **Monte San Savino >**
Piazza Gamuzzini 3, t 0575 849418, www.promontesansavino.it

Monte San Savino ✉ 52048

*****Sangallo**, Piazza Vittorio Veneto 16, t 0575 810049, *www.hotelsangallo.it* (€€€€). A fine hotel. Breakfast is included but there's no restaurant.

******Castello dei Gargonza**, 8km from Monte San Savino, just off SS73, t 0575 847021, *www.gargonza.it* (€€€). An entire walled village, medieval in atmosphere, with rooms, apartments/ houses and a pool, surrounded by forest. Local specialities are served at the popular restaurant (€€). *Closed Tues, Feb and Nov.*

ⓘ **Castiglion Fiorentino >**
Corso Italia 111, t 0575 658278

Castiglion Fiorentino ✉ 52043

Relais San Pietro in Polvano, Loc. Polvano 3, t 0575 650100, *www.polvano.com* (€€€€). A family-run hotel in a peaceful setting, with a charming little pool. There are no TVs and small children are discouraged. Italian cuisine is served on a fabulous panoramic terrace, and breakfast is included in the rates.

*****Park**, Via Umbro-Casentinese 88, t 0575 680288, *www.parkhotelarezzo.com* (€€). A big, modern hotel with a pool, gym and restaurant for guests.

Antica Trattoria la Foce, Via della Foce 30, t 0575 658187 (€€). Authentic local food such as *agnolotti* with truffles and smoked swordfish with tomatoes, plus pizza. *Closed Mon, Tues–Fri lunch.*

Lucignano ✉ 52046

La Rocca, Via Giacomo Matteotti 15, t 0575 836775 (€€). A place in the delightful *centro storico*, serving *pan di lepre* (with rabbit), roast duck and more since 1903. *Closed Tues and Jan.*

Cortona

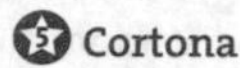

High above the Valdichiana plain on terraced slopes of olives and vines, Cortona (population 27,000) is one of the crown jewels of Tuscan hilltowns. Some 600m above sea level, sweeping down a spur of Monte Sant'Egidio, it has crooked, cobbled streets that climb precipitously to the Medici fortress – even halfway up, between the houses, you can see Lake Trasimeno in Umbria and mounts Amiata and Cetona near Siena. Three Cortonese became celebrated artists: Luca Signorelli (1441/50–1523); Baroque painter Pietro Berrettini (1596–1669), better known as Pietro da Cortona, master of the rooms in the Pitti Palace; and Futurist-Impressionist mosaicist Gino Severini (1883–1966); all left works in their hometown.

According to Virgil and popular tradition, Cortona is nothing less than the 'Mother of Troy and Grandmother of Rome' – founded by Dardanus who, according to legend, was fighting a neighbouring tribe when he lost his helmet (*corythos*) on the hill, giving the name *Corito* to the city that grew up on the spot. He later went to Asia to found Troy and give his name to the Dardanelles. There may be a grain of truth in this myth. The Etruscans claimed to have come from Western Anatolia (around 900 BC), and inscriptions very similar to Etruscan have been found on the Greek island of Lemnos, near Troy; artefacts from the Iron Age found in Anatolia and Tuscany suggest cultural affinities. Cortona was an important Etruscan city, one of the Dodecapolis and one of the largest in the north; ragged Etruscan stonework is visible in the foundations of its walls. These stretch over 3km of the perimeter, but still cover only two-thirds of the area of the original Etruscan fortifications.

As a medieval *comune*, Cortona held its own against Perugia, Arezzo and Siena, while internally its Ghibellines and Guelphs battled until the Ghibellines won out. When that was settled, the ruling family, the Casali, spent the 14th century bumping each other off. This ended in 1409, when King Ladislas of Naples captured the city, selling it to Florence at a handsome profit.

Cortona's heart, **Piazza della Repubblica**, is a striking asymmetrical square. Dominant here is the **Palazzo Comunale** (13th century), with a tower from 1503 and monumental steps. Just behind is the 13th-century Palazzo Casali, impressive home of the city's murderous lordlings, now the seat of the Etruscan Academy, a cultural organization founded in the 17th century by the local nobility.

Palazzo Casali: Museo dell'Accademia Etrusca

Museo dell' Accademia Etrusca
open April–Sept daily 10–7; Nov–Mar Tues–Sun 10–5; adm

Through the Palazzo Casali's attractive courtyard awaits the Museo dell'Accademia Etrusca, a fascinating collection begun by the Academy in 1727, encompassing bronzes (note the two-faced god Selvans); Greek vases, attesting to the city's wealth and trading

Getting to Cortona

Cortona is just off the main Florence– Arezzo–Rome **train** line. The nearest station is Camucia, 5km west; if you're coming up from Umbria, the station is Terontola, 10km south. Both stations have frequent LFI **buses** (*www.lfi.it*) up to Cortona. There are also LFI train connections to Arezzo (34km/50mins), Castiglion Fiorentino, Foiano della Chiana and Castiglione del Lago on Lake Trasimeno (22km/30mins); schedules for both buses and trains, and tickets for the former, are available in the office in Via Nazionale, near the bus terminus and car park in panoramic Piazzale Garibaldi, or call **t** 0575 398813.

---

contacts of long ago; Egyptian mummies and a doll-like Egyptian funeral barque; and Cortona's most famous relic, a 5th-century BC Etruscan bronze chandelier with 16 lamps, found in a nearby field. Each lamp is a grotesque squatting figure, uncircling a ring of stylized waves and dolphins, and in the centre an archaic gorgon.

There is a fine collection of paintings, the oldest being a Roman portrait of the *Muse Polyhymnia*. Others include works by Pietro da Cortona, *Two Saints* by Niccolò di Pietro Gerini, a 12th-century Tuscan mosaic of the Madonna, a fine polyptych by Bicci di Lorenzo, a *Madonna* by Pinturicchio, and another by Signorelli, who portrays her in the company of the saintly protectors of Cortona, with a -nasty-looking devil squirming at their feet. One room is dedicated to Francesco Laperelli (1521–70) from Cortona, who built the walls of Valletta for the Knights of Malta; also ivories, globes of the earth and sky from 1714, costumes, the library founded by the Etruscan Academy in 1727, ceramics and a fine Roman alabaster *Hecate*, queen of the night. There's also a recreation of the inside of the Etruscan tumulus, the **Secondo Melone di Sodo**, excavated in 1991 (*see* p.421). Part of its unique platform altar, sculpted with a man stabbing a lion while it bites off his head, is displayed too.

Behind the civic museum signs point back to the **Duomo**, an 11th-century church unimaginatively rebuilt in 1560, probably by Giuliano da Sangallo; inside is a mosaic by Gino Severini. Across the piazza in the deconsecrated church of Gesù is the excellent diocese museum.

Museo Diocesano

Museo Diocesano
open April–Oct Tues–Sun 10–7; Nov–Mar Tues–Sun 10–5; adm

This has two masterpieces: Luca Signorelli's *Deposition*, with scenes of the *Crucifixion* and *Resurrection* (the latter inspired by his master Piero della Francesca) with an excellent predella, and a beautiful, luminous *Annunciation* by Beato Angelico, who came to Cortona to paint this solemn angel gently whispering his tremendous message; it has another exceptional predella. Note how the frame echoes the Corinthian columns of the loggia. Other works include a 14th-century crucifix by Pietro Lorenzetti, a triptych by Il Sassetta, a fine Sienese *Madonna* by the school of Duccio di Buoninsegna, and a 2nd-century AD Roman sarcophagus with reliefs of the Battle of Lapiths and Centaurs that was closely studied by Donatello and Brunelleschi. Note the churche's fine coffered wooden ceiling.

Up and Down Cortona

Below Piazza del Duomo is one of Cortona's most picturesque lanes, medieval Via Jannelli (or del Gesù), where some houses have *porte del morto* ('doors of the dead'), more common in medieval Umbria than in Tuscany. Other picturesque streets to look out for are Via Ghibellina, Via Guelfa and Via Maffei, with its town palaces.

You'll need your climbing shoes if you want to see the other monuments, though **San Francesco** is only a short walk up from Piazza della Repubblica. St Francis's controversial lieutenant Brother Elias was a native of Cortona and founded this little church at an interesting angle in 1245; it retains its original façade and one side. Both Brother Elias and Luca Signorelli are buried here, and on the left wall is a fine fresco of the *Annunciation*, last work of Pietro da Cortona. On the high altar is a slice of the Holy Cross brought back from Constantinople by Brother Elias, housed in an ivory reliquary that Byzantine emperor Nicephoras Phocas carried into battle against the Saracens in the 960s, as described in the Greek inscription on the back.

From here handsome Via Berrettini continues up to Piazza Pozzo and Piazza Pescaia and the medieval neighbourhood that surrounds **San Nicolò**. This handsome little Romanesque church, which was built by an anachronistic architect in the 1440s, was the seat of San Bernardino da Siena's Company of St Nicholas, for whom Luca Signorelli painted a magnificent standard of the *Deposition* still hanging by the altar.

You can reach the loftiest church of them all, the pretty 19th-century neoromanesque **Santuario di Santa Margherita**, from San Nicolò; the views become increasingly magnificent. The original church was built by Santa Margherita (1247–97), a beautiful farmer's daughter and mistress of a young nobleman; upon his sudden death, she got religion, became a Franciscan tertiary and founded a convent and hospital where she cared for the sick. Her remains are in a silver urn on the altar; her fine but empty Gothic sarcophagus on the left wall is by Angelo and Francesco di Pietro. Right of the altar are standards and lanterns captured from the Turks in 18th-century sea battles, donated by a local commander.

Just above, the overgrown **Medici fortress** of 1556 occupies the site of the old Etruscan acropolis. Descend from Santa Margherita to the centre by way of Via Santa Margherita and the **Via Crucis**, which are made up of mosaic shrines by Gino Severini; they were commissioned in 1947 by the people of Cortona to thank their patron saint for sparing their city from the war.

As in many Etruscan and Roman towns, Cortona's gates are orientated to the four points of the compass. The northern **Porta Colonia** has an Etrusco-Roman arch and is near some well-preserved remains of the Etruscan walls; from here, it's a 15-minute walk to the late, tall Renaissance **church of Santa Maria Nuova**, partly by Vasari and one of the more serene works to come out of the Counter-Reformation, designed in a Greek cross and crowned by a dome. Outside the southern **Porta Berarda**, at the end of Via Nazionale, Gothic **San Domenico** has an elegant interior presided over by a grand triptych by Lorenzo di Niccolò Gerini (1402) given to the Dominicans by Lorenzo de' Medici; in the apse there's a *Madonna with Angels* by Signorelli.

Nearby you'll find a a good stretch of Etruscan wall and the beginning of the Passeggiata Pubblica through Cortona's shady public gardens, the **Parterre**, where you can enjoy more grandstand views over the Valdichiana.

Around Cortona

In the Renaissance, it was fashionable in Tuscany and Umbria to decorate the outskirts of a town with a perfectly symmetrical church – exercises in geometry and divine order visible from all four sides. By the 16th century, this was impossible to do in built-up town centres. Cortona has one of most graceful of these ornamental set pieces, **Santa Maria delle Grazie al Calcinaio**, 3km down the road to Camucia. Built in 1485–1513 by Sienese architect Francesco di Giorgio Martini, this Latin cross topped with an octagonal drum has a harmonious interior in Brunelleschian dark and light accents, luminous and airy and pure, with colour provided by fine stained glass by Guillaume de Marcillat.

Santa Maria delle Grazie al Calcinaio
rarely open; ask at tourist office (see p.422)

Ancient tombs pepper the plain. One of the most evocative of them, the Hellenistic **Tanella di Pitagora**, is signposted from the crossroads near Santa Maria delle Grazie. Named after Pythagoras – apparently the ancients confused Cortona with Croton in Calabria, where the philosopher lived – the 3rd-century BC hypogeum is surrounded by cypress trees and has an unusual vault over its rectangular funeral chamber.

Tanella di Pitagora
open by appt on **t** *0575 630415*

Northwest of Cortona is the 7th-century BC Melone di Camucia, an Etruscan tumulus with two large chambers and corridors. Nearby, at Il Sodo ('the hard-boiled egg'), are two large 6th-century BC tumuli with massive walls 200m in perimeter, the **Meloni del Sodo**. You can visit the first; *tumulo II*, with its five mortuary chambers, yielded the treasures and altar in Cortona's museum and is still being excavated.

Meloni del Sodo
guided tours by appt 1 day in advance, **t** *0575 630415*

Beyond Santa Maria Nuova, the road continues 3.5km along the slopes of Monte Sant'Egidio to the **Convento delle Celle**, which was founded by St Francis in 1211 in a beautiful setting. Little has changed; its simple rustic buildings have preserved their Franciscan spirit better than many others – the humble founder's cell retains the saint's stone bed.

Locanda del Molino >>

Cortona >
Via Nazionale 42,
t *0575 630352*

La Grotta >>

Festivals and Events in Cortona

National antique furniture market, Aug–Sept.

Copperware show and market: A showcase for a local hand-made speciality, April.

Umbria Jazz Festival: Concerts throughout July in the public gardens.

Sagra di Bistecca (beefsteak festival): a huge outdoor grill of the Valdichiana's chief product, 15 Aug.

Under the Tuscan Sun Festival: A music festival attracting international performers, plus food and wine events, films, talks and seminars, Aug.

Activities in Cortona

Just off the mountain road above Torreone, among the chestnut woods at Tornia, is the 'Priest's Hole', a quiet **swimming** pool (donations requested).

Horses can be hired from Unione Popolare Sport Equestre, Loc Ossaia, Montanino di Cortona, **t** 0575 67500.

Where to Stay in Cortona

Cortona ✉ 52044

Lodgings can be scarce: Cortona hosts a language school and a University of Georgia art programme (June–Oct).

****Il Falconiere**, San Martino a Bocena, 3km from town, **t** 0575 612679, *www.ilfalconiere.com* (€€€€€). Refined, frescoed rooms (breakfast included) with Jacuzzi , two pools and a first-class restaurant (€€€€) with a splendid terrace. Ask about cookery courses. *Closed Wed in winter.*

***Oasi**, Via Contesse 1, **t** 0575 630354, *www.hoteloasi.org* (€€€€). A restored monastery with a warm welcome, lovely gardens and a Tuscan Renaissance restaurant. *Closed Nov–Easter.*

****San Michele**, Via Guelfa 15, **t** 0575 604348, *www.hotelsanmichele.net* (€€€). An elegant Renaissance palace with painted friezes, ancient hearths and old waxed floors. Breakfast is included but the garage is €11/day.

****Residence Borgo San Pietro**, Loc. San Pietro a Cegliolo, 4km north of town, **t** 0575 604348, *www.hoteltuscany.net* (€€). Upmarket apartments sleeping 2–4 in a lovely 17th-century farmhouse and outbuildings, with a pool, gym and garage. There's a minimum 3-night stay Nov–Mar and 1wk the rest of the year. *Closed early Jan–early Mar.*

***San Luca**, Piazza Garibaldi 1, **t** 0575 630460, *www.sanlucacortona.com* (€€). Simple rooms, many with great views; breakfast is included.

Locanda del Molino, Loc. Montanare, **t** 0575 614192, *www.locandadelmolino.com* (€€). A converted stone mill house with an excellent restaurant.

***Athens**, Via S. Antonio 12, **t** 0575 630508 (€). Very basic lodgings high up in the old town; all but one room share facilities. *Closed Dec–mid-Mar.*

Ostello San Marco, Via Maffei 57, 3km up from Piazza Garibaldi, **t** 0575 601392, *www.cortonahostel.com* (€). One of Italy's best hostels, organizing Italian courses and archaeology tours. *Closed mid-Oct–mid-Mar.*

Eating Out in Cortona

Local treats are *salumeria* and beef steaks from the Valdichiana, and local *bianchi vergini* ('white virgins') wines.

Da Tonino, Piazza Garibaldi, **t** 0575 630500 (€€€). Cortona's most elegant restaurant, serving wonderful *antipastissimo* (different *antipasti*). Booking is advisable. *Closed Mon eve in winter, and Tues.*

Osteria del Teatro, Via Maffei 3, **t** 0575 630556 (€€). A 15th-century *palazzo* by the theatre; try duck breast with artichokes. *Closed Wed, and 2wks Nov.*

La Grotta, Piazzetta Baldelli 3, **t** 0575 630271 (€€). An intimate restaurant locals try to keep secret, with a pretty courtyard. Try grilled Chianina meat. *Closed Tues, 7 Jan–12 Feb, and 1wk July.*

Miravalle, Frazione Torreone 6, **t** 0575 62232 (€€). Simple cuisine, great views.

Dardano, Via Dardano 24, **t** 0575 601944 (€). A simple trattoria popular with locals; try *pici contadine* (with vegetables and mushrooms). *Closed Wed, and Jan and Feb.*

La Saletta, Via Nazionale 26/28, **t** 0575 603366 (€). A wine bar serving regional snacks, soups, lovely sandwiches and the odd pasta dish.

Perugia, Lake Trasimeno, Assisi

Perugia, capital of Umbria, is one of Italy's greatest art cities, an intensely atmospheric place sheltering some of Europe's most authentic medieval streets. What's more, Perugians have their own 'riviera' a hop and skip to the west, on the gentle shores of Lake Trasimeno with its bijou islands and mighty castles; Perugino was born just south of the lake in Città della Pieve and made these bluish green landscapes his own. To the east, in view of Perugia's balconies, is lovely cream and pink Assisi, home of St Francis and Italy's finest collection of trecento painting.

16

Don't miss

1 Modern jazz and medieval arches
Perugia **p.425**

2 Colourful ceramics
Deruta **p.446**

3 Islands and lakeside villages
Lago Trasimeno **p.447**

4 Perugino's hometown
Città del Pieve **p.453**

5 The restored Basilica of St Francis
Assisi **p.459**

See map overleaf

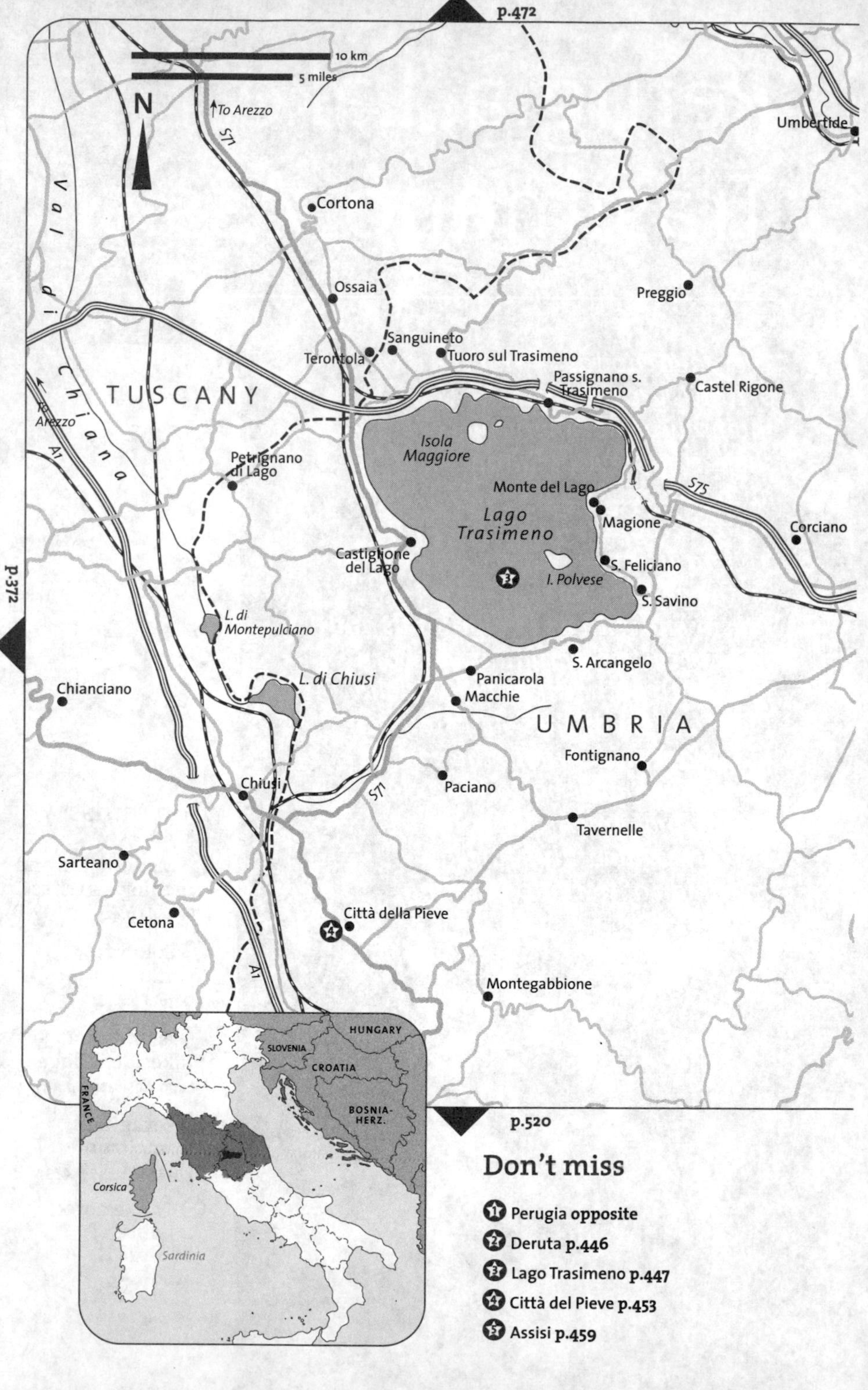

Don't miss

1. Perugia **opposite**
2. Deruta **p.446**
3. Lago Trasimeno **p.447**
4. Città del Pieve **p.453**
5. Assisi **p.459**

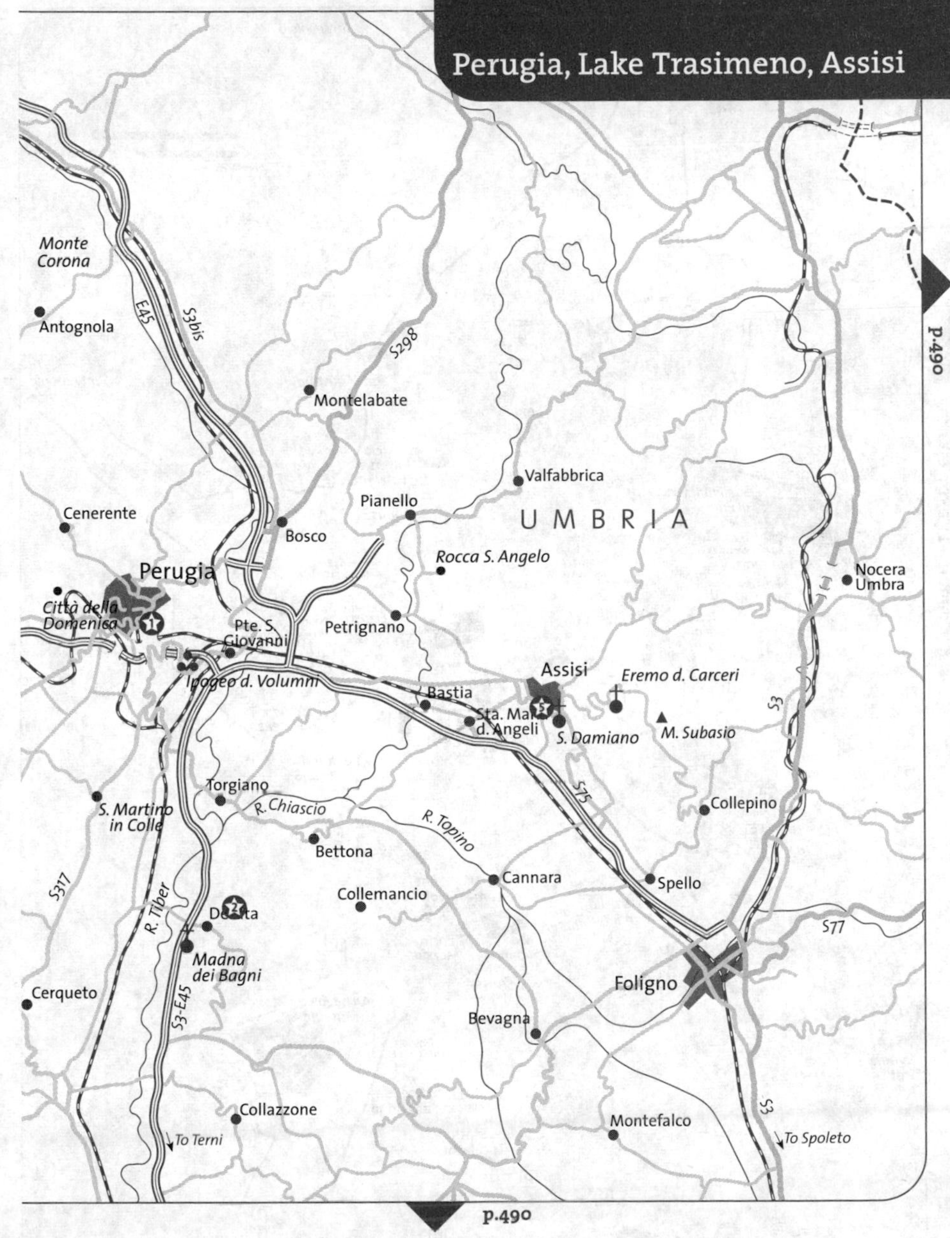

1 Perugia

Perugia

What a town for assassinations!
H. V. Morton

Balanced on a commanding hill high over the Tiber, Perugia (population 155,000) is a fascinating medieval acrobat able to juggle adroitly several roles: that of an ancient hilltown, a magnificent *città d'arte*, a bustling university centre and a slick cosmopolitan city famous for chocolates. It is a fit capital for

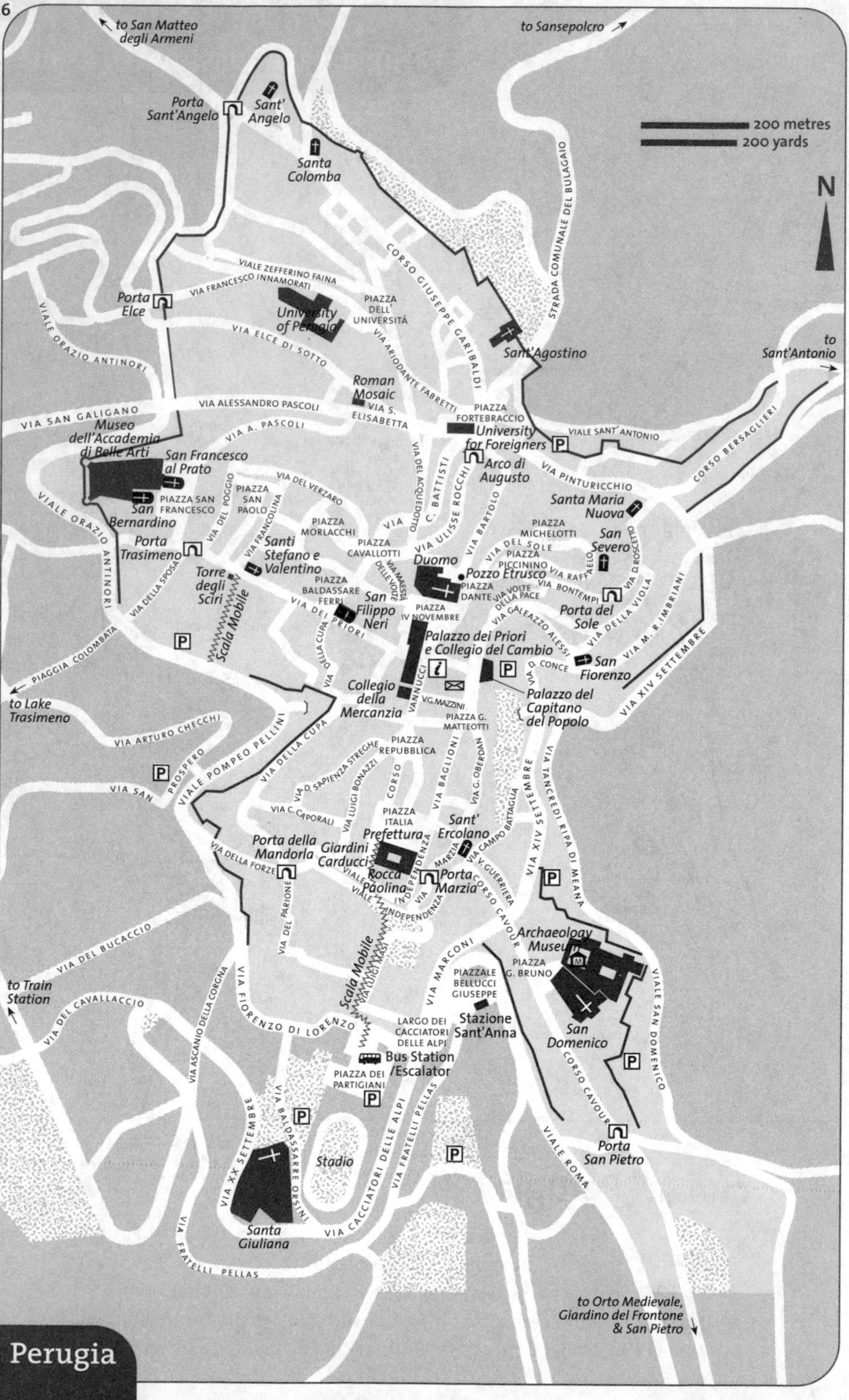

Perugia

to San Matteo degli Armeni
to Sansepolcro
200 metres
200 yards
N
Porta Sant'Angelo
Sant' Angelo
Santa Colomba
Strada Comunale del Bulagaio
Corso Giuseppe Garibaldi
Viale Zefferino Faina
Via Francesco Innamorati
Porta Elce
University of Perugia
Piazza dell' Universitá
Via Elce di Sotto
Viale Orazio Antinori
Sant'Agostino
to Sant'Antonio
Via Ariodante Fabretti
Roman Mosaic
Via Alessandro Pascoli
Via San Galigano
Via S. Elisabetta
Piazza Fortebraccio
Via A. Pascoli
Museo dell'Accademia di Belle Arti
University for Foreigners
Viale Sant' Antonio
Corso Bersaglieri
San Francesco al Prato
Arco di Augusto
Via del Acquedotto
Via C. Battisti
Via Ulisse Rocchi
Via Pinturicchio
Piazza San Francesco
San Bernardino
Via del Verzaro
Piazza San Paolo
Via del Poggio
Via Francolina
Piazza Morlacchi
Via Bartolo
Santa Maria Nuova
Viale Orazio Antinori
Porta Trasimeno
Santi Stefano e Valentino
Piazza Cavallotti
Via Maestà delle Volte
Duomo
Piazza Michelotti
Via del Sole
Piazza Piccinino
San Severo
Via Raffaello
Via D. Roscetto
Torre degli Sciri
Scala Mobile
Via della Sposa
Pozzo Etrusco
Piazza Dante
Via Volte della Pace
Via Bontempi
Porta del Sole
Via della Viola
Via M. R. Imbriani
Piazza Baldassare Ferri
San Filippo Neri
Via dei Priori
Piazza IV Novembre
Via Galeazzo Alessi
Via della Cupa
Palazzo dei Priori e Collegio del Cambio
San Fiorenzo
Via XIV Settembre
Piaggia Colombata
Via D. Conce
to Lake Trasimeno
Collegio della Mercanzia
Vannucci
V.G. Mazzini
Piazza G. Matteotti
Palazzo del Capitano del Popolo
Via Arturo Checchi
Viale Pompeo Pellini
Via della Cupa
Piazza Repubblica
Via D. Sapienza Streghe
Via Luigi Bonazzi
Corso
Via Baglioni
Via G. Oberdan
Via XIV Settembre
Via Tancredi Ripa di Meana
Via San Prospero
Via C. Caporali
Piazza Italia
Prefettura
Sant' Ercolano
Via Campo Battaglia
Porta della Mandorla
Giardini Carducci
Via della Forze
Rocca Paolina
Viale Indipendenza
Via Marzia
Porta Marzia
Via V. Guerriera
Corso Cavour
Via del Parione
Via del Bucaccio
Archaeology Museum
Piazza G. Bruno
Viale San Domenico
Via Marconi
Scala Mobile
Via Luigi Masi
Piazzale Bellucci Giuseppe
to Train Station
Via del Cavallaccio
Via Ascanio della Corgna
Via Fiorenzo di Lorenzo
Largo dei Cacciatori delle Alpi
Stazione Sant'Anna
San Domenico
Corso Cavour
Bus Station /Escalator
Piazza dei Partigiani
Via XX Settembre
Via Baldassare Orsini
Via Fratelli Pellas
Via Cacciatori delle Alpi
Stadio
Porta San Pietro
Viale Roma
Santa Giuliana
Via Fratelli Pellas
to Orto Medievale, Giardino del Frontone & San Pietro

Getting to and around Perugia

By Air

Perugia's airport, Sant'Egidio-Perugia (**t** 075 592141, *www.airport.umbria.it*), 12km east of the city towards Assisi, has Ryanair flights (*see* p.63) from London Stansted, plus connections with Milan (Malpensa; with Alitalia and Interstate), Rome (Fiumicino; with Interstate) and Reggio Calabria (with Interstate) and, from June to September, Olbia in Sardinia (with Air Vallee).

By Train

As Perugia is on a hill, its 2 train stations are some distance from the centre. Regular city buses (nos.6, 7, 8 and 9) link the FS station with Piazza G. Matteotti or Piazza Italia in the centre; the more convenient FCU station (S. Anna, **t** 075 575 4038) is a short walk from Piazza dei Partigiani and the escalators to the centre.

The main FS station, on Piazza V. Veneto, is about 3km from the centre in the lower suburb of Fontivegge; it has trains (**t** 892021, *www.trenitalia.com*) for Florence (154km/2hrs 30mins) and Arezzo (78km/90mins), via the Terontola junction on the northern shore of Lake Trasimeno; for Siena (147km/3hrs 30mins) another change is required, at Chiusi (a pain – the FS replaced several routes with direct buses). Another line passes through Assisi (26km/25mins), Spoleto (47km/70mins), Foligno and Terni on the way to Rome (3hrs), while the route to Ancona (3hrs) via Foligno stops at Nocera Umbra, Gualdo Tadino, Gubbio, Genga and Fabriano.

For other places in Umbria, the narrow-gauge Ferrovia Centrale Umbria (FCU), **t** 075 575401, *www.fcu.it*, is handy. Its main station here is Stazione Sant'Anna, halfway up the hill, off Piazza dei Partigiani. The FCU goes north to Città di Castello (45km/1hr) and Sansepolcro (60km/1Vhrs), south to Todi (41km/1hr) and Terni.

By Bus

Perugia's bus station is near the FCU station in Piazza dei Partigiani, linked to Piazza Italia by steps and escalators. APM buses, **t** 075 573 1707, *www.apmperugia.it*, serve villages in Perugia province (roughly the northern two-thirds of Umbria). There are about 12 a day to Santa Maria degli Angeli (for Assisi), 5 carrying on to Spello and Foligno; others to Deruta and Todi; Torgiano and Bettona; Gubbio; Gualdo Tadino; the towns of Lake Trasimeno; one to Orvieto; and 5 a day to Città della Pieve and Chiusi (on the Florence–Rome line).

SSIT (**t** 075 573 1707; *www.spoletina.com*) has one or more buses a day to Nocera Umbra, Spoleto, and Norcia and Cascia. SULGA (**t** 075 5009641, *www.sulga.it*) has direct links to Rome and Fumicino airport; SENA (**t** 800 930 960, *www.sena.it*) goes to Siena, Ascoli Picero and the coast of the Marches; CONTRAM (**t** 800 037737, *www.contram.it*) to Macerata and Civitanova Marche, and Freccia dell'Appennino (**t** 800 930 960, *www.sena.it*) go down the coast of the Marches to San Benedetto del Tronto and Porto Ascoli.

By Car

Most of the city is closed to traffic, peripheral garages and car parks are few and usually charge by the hour. Car parks nearest the centre, at Piazza Italia, Piazza Pellini, the Mercato Coperto and Piazza dei Partigiani, are connected to the centre by elevator or escalator.

Small local car-hire firms may give better rates but tend not to be as flexible over pick-ups and drop-offs. The main operators are at the airport; some are at the train station too: AVIS, **t** 075 692 9346, *www.avisautonoleggio.it*, Hertz, **t** 075 500 2439, *www.hertz.it*, Maggiore, **t** 075 500 7499, *www.maggiore.it*, Europcar, **t** 075 692 0615, *www.europcar.it*.

For a taxi, call Radio taxi, **t** 075 500 4888.

On Foot

Perugia's difficult topography has been mastered with ingenuity – stairs, elevators or escalators to carry you from one part to another. Many are on the edges, where beautiful parks have been strung along the cliffs to take advantage of unusable land – Perugia has one of the highest densities of green areas in Italy.

Umbria, with splendid monuments from the Etruscan era to the late Renaissance stacked next to one another; its gallery contains the region's finest art. Yet it is haunted by sinister shadows. Four medieval popes died in Perugia. One did himself in – stuffing himself with Lake Trasimeno eels – but for the other three the verdict was poison. And then there were the Baglioni, the powerful family that ruled the city for a time, so dangerous they nearly exterminated themselves. Yet creativity and feistiness went hand-in-hand, and the Umbrian capital has contributed more than its share to Italian culture and art; the biggest annual event is a jazz festival. Just as remarkable as the people is the stage they act on: the oldest, most romantically medieval streets and squares in Italy.

Perugia suffered in the political changes of the 1500s but claims the singular privilege of having been a part of the Papal States. Art, scholarship, trade and civic life quickly withered, and the town's penchant for violence was rocked to sleep under a warm blanket of Hail Marys. Now, a little more than 100 years after liberation, its people are famed for their politeness, urbanity and good taste; Perugians dress more sharply than Florentines for half the money and effort. They make their living from chocolates and ladies' shoes, and teaching Italian language and culture to foreigners. Maybe a few centuries under the pope was just what they needed.

History

Gubbio, Perugia's longtime rival, liked to claim it was one of the first cities founded by Noah's sons after the flood. To top that, one of Perugia's medieval chroniclers records that Noah himself, at the age of 500 or so, pitched his tents on Perugia's mountain. That would have been news to the Etruscans, who had settled *Pieresa* by the 5th century BC and probably much earlier. Pieresa was the easternmost city of the Dodecapolis, and maintained its freedom until the Roman conquest of 309 BC.

Never entirely happy under Roman rule, the city staged several revolts. In the years after Caesar's assassination, it chose the wrong side with catastrophic results; Octavian's troops besieged it for seven months, and when after the capitulation an Etruscan diehard committed suicide rather than surrender, his funeral pyre started a conflagration that took the rest of the city with him. Some years later, Octavian, by then **Emperor Augustus**, rebuilt the city and renamed it after himself – *Augusta Perusia*.

Almost nothing is known of the city in the Dark Ages. Totila the Goth took it from the Byzantines around 545, after a (probably apocryphal) siege of seven years, but the Exarchs of Ravenna were still, with the Lombards, fighting for it 50 years later. Among the constantly changing alliances of medieval Italian states, Perugia found itself out of the turbulent mainstream, with no large and dangerous neighbours and a potential ally (when it suited Perugia) of pope, emperor or any Tuscan cities. As a result, the Perugians were almost always able to manage their own affairs. Mostly they spent their time subjugating neighbours: Lake Trasimeno towns in 1130, Città di Castello not long after, then Assisi and Spello. Foligno, another bitter enemy, fell in 1282.

Almost always a Guelph city, Perugia maintained a special relationship with Florence and the popes – it had allies, certainly, but friends never. Even fierce, factional cities such as Florence and Siena were careful to walk wide of this wildcat that was constantly molesting its neighbours when not itself convulsed in civil wars. Siena had its annual festive punch-up, the *Gioco del Pugno*, but the Perugians enjoyed spending their holidays at the *Battaglia de' Sassi*, the 'Battle of Stones', in Piazza del Duomo, usually causing a dozen or so fatalities each year. In religion, besides being a graveyard for popes, Perugia gave a cold shoulder to most of the early reformers. Even St Francis, who before he became a preacher spent a year in a Perugian dungeon, couldn't make the city mend its ways. However, the medieval mass psychosis of the **Flagellants** began with the hallucinations of a monk here in 1265.

Perugia belonged to the papal dominions from the days of Charlemagne. Few popes, though, were able to exercise much control over such a volatile city. After 1303, the priors of the 10 major guilds established their rule, though noble families such as the **Oddi** and the **Baglioni** remained extremely influential. In the 1360s–70s, when **Cardinal Albornoz** was raising armies and building castles to reassert papal authority over central Italy, Perugia revolted. Pope Urban VI paid a visit in 1387 to make up – a wild dove perched on his shoulder as he entered, taken as a good omen. Unfortunately, the rebellion only took the lid off a cauldron of conflicting ambitions that was ready to boil over, and Perugia's three big factions – the nobles, *raspanti* (the wealthy merchant class) and commoners – leapt at each other's throats. In 1393, with the connivance of the pope, a noble named **Biondo Michelotti** seized power. Five years later (again the pope was involved), Michelotti was murdered on his wedding day by the abbot of San Pietro. In the resulting confusion, Giangaleazzo Visconti of Milan grabbed the city for a time (1400–2); there followed a period under the rule of King Ladislas of Naples (1408–14).

After Ladislas, celebrated Perugian *condottiere* **Braccio Fortebraccio** ('Arm Strongarm', the Popeye of the Renaissance, whose arms picture a bouquet of spinach and a helmet), won the city by defeating another *condottiere*, Carlo Malatesta of Rimini, at the battle of Sant'Egidio. Fortebraccio, soon master of all Umbria and 'Prince of Capua', had king-sized ambitions and potent friends – according to contemporary gossip he owned a crystal with a genie inside who gave him good advice. After conquering most of the Marches, Fortebraccio had dreams of ruling a united Italy, but his luck ran out in 1424, when he died at the hands of another Perugian during the siege of L'Aquila in Abruzzo. In the aftermath, Pope Martin V took control of Perugia, though he wasn't able to stop the increasingly bloody fighting between the noble clans.

In 1488 the Oddi were exiled and the Baglioni became rulers of Perugia. This family, with their good looks, pet lions and tendency to fratricide, blazed through Perugia's history. In 1520 the Medici pope Leo X tricked **Gianpaolo Baglioni**, last family tyrant of Perugia, into coming to Rome, where he was murdered. The remaining Baglioni found employment as *condottieri* around Italy. One, Malatesta Baglioni, distinguished himself by betraying Florence to the Medici and Charles V in the siege of 1530. Another, Rodolfo, murdered a papal legate to avenge the death of his uncle, giving **Pope Paul III** an excuse to intervene.

It had become customary for popes reasserting their authority to make a formal visit to Perugia; contemporaries record Paul, father of the Inquisition and one of the kinkiest, most corrupt of all popes, requiring all nuns in the city to queue up and kiss his feet. As part of his campaign to put an end to Perugia's independence, Paul raised the salt tax in 1538, a year after promising not to. The Perugians revolted again, initiating the '**Salt War**', but were crushed by a huge papal force of mercenaries and Spaniards. Government was handed over to officials entitled Preservers of Ecclesiastical Obedience; its trade ruined and its streets full of monks, nuns and Jesuits, Perugia began a precipitous economic decline not be reversed until the Risorgimento. To this day, Perugians, indeed all Umbrians, eat bread made without salt, an unappetising hangover from the salt rebellion (Umbrians swear it tastes better).

The next major event was the Napoleonic occupation: troops sent the hordes of monks and nuns packing but also packed much of Perugia's art – some of the best Peruginos included – back to the Louvre. In 1859, during the disturbances of the Risorgimento, Perugia rebelled once more against the pope. Pius IX sent his **Swiss Guard** to quell them – some 2,000 Switzers forced the city, burning, looting and butchering citizens. The liberation a year later was greeted with delirium. King Vittorio Emanuele's army had to protect the retiring Swiss Guards from massacre by the Perugians.

A Vanished Fortress and Underground Perugia

For a dramatic approach to Perugia: leave your car in Piazza dei Partigiani and ascend on a series of *scale mobile* (escalators), via a Perugia that for more than 300 years was lost to view and almost forgotten. Only days after the end of the Salt War, Paul III found a way to intimidate the Perugians into obedience until Judgement Day while obliterating the Baglioni family at the same stroke. The quarter of town he demolished for his famous **Rocca Paolina** was the stronghold of the Baglioni, including all their palaces, 138 houses they owned and seven churches. Most buildings were not razed, however, because Paul's architect, Antonio da Sangallo the Younger, needed them to give the new fortress a level foundation.

The 16th century may have been the age of the Renaissance, but in Italy it was also the era of grudges; Paul III came to Perugia seven times over the next three years to make sure the fortress was sufficiently repressive, and to crown it had the Rocca inscribed with large letters: *Ad repellandam Perusinorum audaciam* ('To curb the audacity of the Perugians'). From the beginning, Perugians looked on it as a loathsome symbol of oppression, of the grisly terror of the 1500s. No enemy ever attacked it, and through the centuries of papal rule its only real use was as a prison – one from which few ever found their way out. In the general revolutionary year of 1848, a pick was ceremoniously handed to Count Benedetto Baglioni to begin its longed-for demolition. This was far from complete when the papal forces returned, but as soon as Perugia was liberated from the Swiss Guard in 1860, the Piemontese general Pepoli signed a decree giving the Rocca to the Perugians and they gleefully tore down the rest.

In a way, it's a pity that the Rocca no longer stands: old paintings and prints depict a startlingly modern building designed by one of the best Renaissance architects. At the bottom of the top escalator you'll be at the medieval street level, among the brick palaces of the Baglioni, all roofed over by the arches and vaults of Sangallo. There are many corners to explore, which are often used for special exhibitions and shows, including stretches of the **Rocca Paolina bastions**, where you can peek out through the pope's gun-slits over peaceful Viale Indipendenza below. At the top of the escalators, where the main fortress stood, the Perugine built the neoclassical Piazza Italia and bulky 1870s Prefettura; behind it, the balustrades of the Giardini Carducci afford wonderful views over the suburbs and distant countryside.

Rocca Paolina bastions
open daily 8–7 (exhibitions Mon–Fri 2.30–6.30, Sat and Sun 10.30–1 and 2.30–6.30); adm to exhibitions

Just below Piazza Italia, off Via Sant'Ercolano, the exterior entrance to the bastions is worth a look. This is the **Porta Marzia**, the best surviving piece of Etruscan architecture anywhere that isn't a tomb. Antonio da Sangallo reassembled it here after destroying Perugia's original walls. The five sculpted panels, now almost eroded, probably represented five gods, although the Perugians have a strange old story that they are a Roman family who died from eating poisonous mushrooms.

It's all in the Detail

Make sure you take time to notice the atmospheric street names while wandering around Perugia, including Via Curiosa ('Curious Street'); Via Perduta ('Lost Street'); Via Piacevole ('Pleasant Street') and Via Pericolosa ('Dangerous Street'). And look out for medieval details – carved symbols and coats of arms. One local peculiarity is the narrow Porta del Morte, 'Death's Door', used only to carry out the dead, and bricked up the rest of the time – where death has once passed, the superstition went, he might pass again. Or so the story goes; in most houses these doors were the only access to the upper floors, with ladders inside that could be pulled up in emergencies.

Corso Vannucci and Piazza IV Novembre

Perugia's truly elegant main street begins in Piazza Italia: the pedestrianized Corso Vannucci is named after Pietro Vannucci, who, after all, was named Perugino after Perugia. Locals stroll along it every evening in central Italy's liveliest passeggiata.

The Corso ends in magnificent, time-worn Piazza IV Novembre, once the setting for the 'War of the Stones' and countless riots and street battles, and still the heart and soul of Perugia. The old town hall, symbol of the *comune*, upstages the cathedral; the two stare at each other over Italy's most beautiful medieval fountain, the 24-sided polygonal pink and white **Fontana Maggiore**, designed in the 1270s by Fra Bevignate. The occasion was the construction of Perugia's first aqueduct since Roman times, and the priors commissioned Nicola Pisano and his son Giovanni to sculpt the 48 double relief panels around the lower basin. Twelve of these portray that favourite medieval conceit, the *Labours of the Months*, each accompanied by its zodiacal sign; in-between are scenes from Roman legend, Aesop's fables, and saints' lives, personifications of the sciences and arts – altogether, a complete, circular image of the medieval world. Above them, the twelve-sided upper basin has concave panels filled with 24 saints and figures from Perugia's history, most by Giovanni Pisano, with three water nymphs to keep them company. The more you look, the more you see the subtlety and dynamism of Fra Bevignate's design, particularly the way the panels of the lower basin are never congruent but pull the eye along.

Palazzo dei Priori

Surveying the piazza, high on the wall of the **Palazzo dei Priori**, perch a Guelph lion and Perugia's totem, the famous brass griffin, an emblem visible at least once on every street. The scrap iron dangling beneath it is said to be chains and bolts from the gates of Siena, captured after a famous victory at Torrita in 1358 (this isn't true – the real war trophies, whatever they were, disappeared 200 years ago; these chains simply held them up). This stern, Gothic, asymmetrical complex, crowned with toothsome crenellations and pierced by beautiful, narrowly spaced windows, looks as new as when it was begun in 1297. Two later building phases left an elegant, slightly curved, elongated building along Corso Vannucci.

Sala dei Notari
open June–Sept daily 9–1 and 3–7; rest of year Tues–Sun 9–1 and 3–7

The whole of the first floor of the Piazza IV Novembre section is occupied by the **Sala dei Notari**, a remarkable room divided into bays by huge round arches, with interesting early-13th-century frescoes of Old Testament scenes along the top by a student of Pietro Cavallini. The other frescoes, painted in the 19th century, are the coats of arms of all the *podestà* and *capitani del popolo* who served Perugia from 1293 to 1443.

Through the elaborate **main door** (1326) of the Palazzo dei Priori, round the corner on Corso Vannucci, with its lunette featuring statues of Perugia's patron saints, Louis of Toulouse, Lawrence and Ercolanus, the **Galleria Nazionale dell'Umbria** has the finest, largest collection of Umbrian (and many other) paintings anywhere, displayed with explanations in English. The mezzanine floor was left unsound by the earthquake, but the masterpieces are all accessible, displayed chronologically and thematically. The first rooms contain some striking early works, among them sculptures for a public fountain by **Arnolfo di Cambio** (1281) and others from the Fontana Maggiore by **Nicola and Giovanni Pisano**, which were replaced by copies. There's a pre-Giotto *Crucifixion* and other works of the **Maestro di San Francesco** from the 1270s. Nor are all the best works Umbrian – the Sienese, in particular, are well represented, with a fine polyptych by Vigoroso da Siena (*c.* 1290) and a sweet *Madonna* by **Duccio di Buoninsegna**.

Galleria Nazionale dell'Umbria

t 075 572 1009 or t 800 223300; open daily exc 1st Mon of month 8.30–7.30 (16 June–15 Sept Sat 8.30–11); adm

Mesmerizing rooms of trecento and early quattrocento gold-ground *Madonnas* and *Annunciations* (by Ambrogia Maitani, Meo di Guido da Siena, Ottaviano Nelli, Peccio Capanna) culminate in **Beato Angelico**'s *Guidalotti Polyptych*, his pupil **Benozzo Gozzoli**'s *Pala della Sapienza Nuova* and **Piero della Francesca**'s *Polyptych of Sant'Antonio* (1465–70), painted for a Franciscan convent. Piero himself assembled works from two distinct periods to fulfil the wishes of the buyers, who thought the project was dragging on. The *Annunciation* shows the painter at his height, creating an eerie stillness out of mathematical purity – either side of Gabriel and the Virgin, rows of arches recede into a blank wall.

From the International Gothic wizards of the Marches come **Gentile da Fabriano**'s *Virgin and Child* (1408), painted for Perugia's San Domenico – note how the wood of the Virgin's throne is alive and budding – and a *Madonna del Pergulato* (1445) by **Giovanni Boccati da Camerino**, master of angelic choirs, *putti*, flowers and perspective tricks. The best Perugians of the same period, **Benedetto Bonfigli** and **Bartolomeo Caporali**, show perhaps less spirituality, but fancier clothes and a lilting lyricism. Bonfigli also contributes the sharp, meticulously drawn **Cappella dei Priori** frescoes (1454–80), dedicated to two of Perugia's three patrons: the older frescoes, late Gothic in style, are on the life of St Louis of Toulouse; the unfinished later frescoes, showing a more mature, Renaissance handling of space, on St Ercolanus. They also feature the best portraits of Perugia itself, bristling with towers – at the time it had around 500, astonishing even for such a belligerent city.

The next section has two Perugian painters of the next generation, **Pinturicchio** and **Perugino**. Both, when young, worked on the *Miracles of San Bernardino of Siena* (1473), eight small panels with charming imaginary town settings. Though he refused to participate in the High Renaissance, Pinturicchio rarely fails to charm; his nickname, 'Rich Painter', derives from his use of gold and gorgeous colours, seen here in his *Pala di Santa Maria dei Fossi*. Perugino maintained an ideal classical vision, touched with the 'sweetness' mastered by Raphael. At worst, he can be painfully unconvincing ('I'll give them their Virgin and Saints,' you imagine him grumbling as he dabbed on another rolling eyeball). The gallery has about a dozen of these, many almost entirely by his assistants; there's an *Adorazione* featuring the most disdainful Magi ever, as well as Perugino at his finest, in the *Polyptych of Sant'Agostino*.

The mezzanine floor, up a spiral staircase, displays long galleries of numb gigantic canvasses from the 16th to 18th centuries (a particularly good one is by **Pietro da Cortona**, the ultimate idealized *Nativity*). The wooden horse was a model for an equestrian monument to Orazio Baglioni. On the first floor, you can look through the glass door to the **Sala del Malconsiglio** (Bad Counsel), so-called because in the 1360s the priors decided here to release some prisoners – English mercenaries from Sir John Hawkwood's company. The next year, Hawkwood's men defeated Perugia at the battle of Ponte San Giovanni. The Perugians learned their lesson; they were never nice to anyone again. It contains the original bronze lion and griffin from the façade of the palace; over the door (on the inside) is an early lunette by Pinturicchio.

Collegio del Cambio
*Corso Vannucci 25, **t** 075 572 8599; open Mon–Sat 9–12.30 and 2.30–5.30, Sun 9–1; joint adm with Capella di San Giovanni Battista and Collegio della Mercanzia, see opposite*

In the third and final annexe (1443) to the enormous Palazzo dei Priori, Perugino received a major commission in 1499 to decorate the **Collegio del Cambio**, the headquarters of Perugia's moneychangers' guild. Money-changing, or banking, was not quite reputable owing to Biblical injunctions against usury, and the first challenge was to come up with an appropriate decorative scheme. The city's leading humanist, Francesco Maturanzio, proposed an array of Christian, Classical and secular virtues for the walls and planetary gods for the ceiling. Perugino dressed them in the haute couture of the time, creating one of the finest pure Renaissance rooms in Italy. Among these beautiful figures, he painted an unflattering self-portrait in the middle of the left wall, tight-lipped and stern and sceptical, over an inscription added by the grateful Perugini 'If the art of of painting had been lost, he would have rediscovered it. If it had never been invented, he would have done so.' Perugino's pupil Raphael probably served as the model for the figure of the *Prophet Daniel*. The ceiling was later decorated with grotesques, not long after Raphael set the fashion for them in Rome with the discovery of Nero's Golden House; the magnificent woodwork is by Domenico del Tasso and Antonio Bencivenni da Mercatello (1493–1508), and the gilded terracotta statue of *Justice* (the moneychangers' guild arbitrated in financial disputes) is by Benedetto da Maiano.

Cappella di San Giovanni Battista
t 075 572 8599; open Mon–Sat 9–12.30 and 2.30–5.30, Sun 9–1; joint adm with Collegio del Cambio, see opposite, and Collegio della Mercanzia

Collegio della Mercanzia
Corso Vannucci 15 bis; **t** *075 573 0366, open Mar–Oct and 20 Dec–6 Jan Tues–Sat 9–1 and 2.30–5.30, Sun 9–1; 1 Nov–19 Dec and 7 Jan –28 Feb Tues, Thurs and Fri 8–2, Wed and Sat 8– 4.30, Sun 9–1; joint adm with Collegio del Cambio, see opposite, and Cappella di San Giovanni Battista*

Duomo di San Lorenzo
t 075 572 4853; open Mon–Sat 7–12.45 and 4–7.45, Sun and hols 4pm–5.45pm

The frescoes on the *Life of St John the Baptist* in the bankers' chapel, the **Cappella di San Giovanni Battista**, are by another Perugino student, Giannicola di Paolo; the adjacent **Collegio della Mercanzia** was the seat of the merchants' guild, one of the oldest and most important in Perugia; the Sala di Udienza is richly decorated with 15th-century carvings, panelling and inlays, perhaps by craftsmen from northern Europe.

The Cathedral of San Lorenzo

For all the attention they lavished on their Palazzo dei Priori, the Perugians never seemed much interested in their Duomo. After laying the cornerstone in 1345, they didn't add a stone for a decade. A century later, when the building was substantially completed, a papal legate tore part of it down to use the stone for his palace. For the façade, they once stole half a marble facing destined for the cathedral at Arezzo, but not long after the Aretini whipped them in battle and made them give it back. The cathedral's finest hour, perhaps, came during a fit of civic strife in 1488, when the Baglioni, fighting the Oddi, seized the building, turning it into a fortress, complete with cannon protruding from its Gothic windows. So much blood was spilled that the cathedral had to be washed out with wine and reconsecrated.

Despite its lack of a proper façade, this building seems just right for its position on lovely Piazza IV Novembre. The side facing the Fontana Maggiore has a geometrical pattern employing the warm pink marble quarried near Assisi. Next to it a bronze statue commemorates pleasure-loving Julius III, the only pope the Perugians ever liked. The unfinished pulpit on the façade was built for the charismatic revivalist San Bernardino of Siena, who preached to vast crowds in the piazza, finally persuading them to stop the *Battaglia de' Sassi* in 1425; Perugia, he claimed, was his favourite town, and judging by the church the Perugians gave him (*see* p.437), he was their favourite saint. The best feature of the façade, however, is the elegant travertine **Loggia di Braccio Fortebraccio**, added by the *condottiere* in 1423.

The Baroqued interior is determinedly unimpressive, supported by columns badly painted to simulate marble. In the first chapel on the right, the tomb of Bishop Baglioni (d. 1451) by Urbano da Cortona stands across from a saccharine *Descent from the Cross* by 16th-century painter Federico Barocci of Urbino. In the **Cappella del Sacramento**, by Galeazzo Alessi, Perugia's top 16th-century architect, hangs Luca Signorelli's luminous *Pala dI Sant'Onofrio* (1484), one of his earliest and best works, showing the Madonna enthroned with saints and a potbellied angel tuning a lute. The presbytery has beautiful intarsia choir stalls by Gianiano da Mairano and Domenico del Taso (1486–91).

On the left, near reliefs of the *Eternal Father* and *Pietà* by Agostino di Duccio, is the **Cappella del Santo Anello**, housing the Perugians' prized relic – the wedding ring of the Virgin Mary. Many stories have grown around this big onyx stone that, like a 1970s mood ring, changes colour according to the moral character of the wearer. A Perugian woman stole the ring from Chiusi in the Middle Ages and townspeople have never stopped worrying that the Chiusini might try to get it back: they keep it in 15 nested cases under 15 locks, spread the keys out among 15 notable, trustworthy citizens, and only take it out of the box on 29–30 July. The relic indirectly inspired Raphael's *Betrothal of the Virgin*; Raphael picked up the idea from a painting by Perugino that hung in this chapel before Napoleon spirited it off to France – the emperor had a weakness for doe-eyed Virgins and Perugino was one of his favourite painters.

Behind the cathedral, the cloister of the Canonica witnessed five conclaves of cardinals between 1124 and 1305. It contains the **Museo Capitolare della Cattedrale**, with a little art, some reliquaries and hymnals. If it's noon, the campanile bells above you will make sure you know it.

Museo Capitolare della Cattedrale
t 075 572 4853; open Tues–Sun 10–1 and 2.30–5.30; adm

Perugia's West End: Down Via dei Priori

On the Corso Vannucci side of the Palazzo dei Priori, a little archway leads into Via dei Priori and Perugia's quiet, lovely west end. The first sight is **San Filippo Neri**, rebuilt by Roman architect Paolo Marucelli from an earlier church in the 1630s, with façade awkwardly squeezed and only visible in its entirety from across the small square. Perugians still call this impressive pile the Chiesa Nuova; it's surely the showiest Baroque building in Umbria. Its interior, full of florid paintings, seems to be made of dirty ice cream, an echo of Rome out in the provinces. You can also see the high altarpiece of the *Immaculate Conception*, completed by Pietro da Cortona. The medieval Via della Cupa descends from here under a series of arches to the Etruscan walls and gate, **Porta della Mandorla**.

Further down Via dei Priori is charming **Santi Stefano e Valentino**, a vaulted medieval church: the altarpiece is a fine *Madonna* by 16th-century Perugian Domenico Alfani. Next, in the shadow of the 46m **Torre degli Sciri** (13th century), Perugia's tallest surviving tower fortress, Santa Teresa degli Scalzi was an ambitious Baroque project that was never finished. In the little piazza by the **Porta Traslmena**, built in the Middle Ages on Etruscan foundations, the church of the **Madonna della Luce** has a good Renaissance façade, a round fresco of *God the Father* by Giovanni Battista Caporali and another of the *Madonna and Saints* by Tiberio d'Assisi. The church commemorates a miracle: a barber, playing cards by his shop, swore so hard after losing a hand that a wooden Madonna in a nearby shrine shut her eyes and didn't open them for four days.

Piazza San Francesco

Turning right at the Madonna della Luce, the street opens into the green lawn of **Piazza San Francesco**, originally outside the walls. San Francesco al Prato (1230), once the finest and most richly decorated church in Perugia, suffered a partial collapse in a mudslide in 1737 and a thorough looting by Napoleon's soldiers; the elegant façade remains, in patterns of pink and white stone. Part of it is now open to the elements.

Next door, the **Oratorio di San Bernardino** commemorates the 15th-century Franciscan from Siena who made such an impression on the Perugians; 'Little St Bernard' must have been a crafty preacher to affect these pirates. The oratory was begun in 1461, the year after the saint's canonization, and placed on this site because Bernardino always stayed at the convent of San Francesco when visiting. Agostino di Duccio (1418–81), that rare Florentine sculptor who decorated the Malatesta temple of Rimini, was commissioned to do the façade, turning the little chapel into Umbria's greatest temple of pure Renaissance art. Framed in rich pink and green marbles, Agostino's reliefs are exquisite: beatific angel musicians, scenes of miracles from the life of the saint and allegorical virtues: Mercy, Holiness and Purity on the left; Religion, Mortification and Penance on the right. One of the panels on the lower frieze portrays the original Bonfire of Vanities, held in front of the cathedral after a particularly stirring sermon from Bernardino – which may have given Savonarola in Florence the idea. Inside, the chapel altar is a late Roman sarcophagus, perhaps that of a Christian; it seems to tell the story of Jonah and the whale and was the tomb of the Beato Egidio of Assisi (d. 1262), the third person to follow St Francis. The Oratory also has two works from the church of San Francesco: one of Benedetto Bonfigli's gonfalons, depicting the Madonna sheltering Perugia from the plague (1464), and a copy of Raphael's *Deposition*, now in Rome's Galleria Borghese.

Museo dell' Accademia di Belle Arti
closed for restoration at time of writing: ask at tourist office (see p.443) for latest info

Just behind, the convent of San Francesco holds the **Museo dell'Accademia di Belle Arti**, displaying a huge collection of plaster models, starring Canova's *Three Graces*; there are also prints, and typically academic 18th- and 19th-century paintings.

Old Streets Around the Cathedral

Around the back of Perugia's cathedral you'll find a half-vertical cityscape of dark, grim buildings and overhanging arches, some incorporating bits of Gothic palaces and Etruscan walls – a set no film director could possibly improve upon. And they are as old as they look. Many arches originally supported buildings over the street; medieval Perugia must have seemed like one continuous building, linked by arches and passageways.

An Etruscan Well and the Arch of Augustus

Pozzo Etrusco
t 075 573 3669; open April and Aug Wed–Mon 10–1.30 and 2.30–6.30; May–July, Sept and Oct Wed–Mon 10–1.30 and 2.30–6.30; Nov–Mar Wed–Mon 10.30–1.30 and 2.30–5; adm (ticket also valid for San Severo, see p.440, Museo delle Porte e delleMura Urbiche, and Porta Sant'Angelo, see p.439)

At Piazza Dante 18, marvel at an example of ancient engineering, the 3rd-century BC **Pozzo Etrusco**, a monumental 35m-deep well and cistern (if the debris at the bottom is ever excavated, it may prove deeper). According to estimates, it held 95,000 gallons of water, enough to supply all of Etruscan *Perusia*. Via Ulisse Rocchi, leading down steeply to the northern gate, used to be called Via Vecchia and is the oldest street in town; Perugians have been treading it for at least 2,500 years.

The old north gate is formed of another fabulous relic of the city's past, the **Arco di Augusto**. The huge stones of the lower levels are Etruscan; above rises a perfectly preserved Roman arch built during the emperor's refounding of Augusta Perusia. The city's new name is inscribed with typical Imperial modesty: 'Augusta' in very large letters, 'Perusia' in tiny ones. The portico on the Roman bastion, making this gate one of the most beautiful in Italy, was added in the 16th century. The arch faces Piazza Fortebraccio and the 18th-century Palazzo Gallenga Stuart, home of the **Università per Stranieri** (*see* p.76), founded in 1921 for the study of Italian language and culture and attended by students from all over the world.

Another little walk, beginning back in Piazza IV Novembre, is down **Via Maestà delle Volte**, one of the most picturesque medieval streets in Perugia, covered with arches that once supported a large Gothic hall. It leads down to **Piazza Cavallotti**, where Roman houses and a road were discovered just under the pavement.

The University and Borgo Sant'Angelo

Another itinerary through this ancient district begins behind the cathedral and take you into a jumble of medieval arches and asymmetrical vaults that lead down to Via Battisti. Near it, a long stairway descends through the Roman-Etruscan walls to the **Borgo Sant'Angelo**, Perugia's medieval suburb, once the centre of popular resistance to the Baglioni and the popes; it's now home to the city's famous university. Walk over the **Acquedotto**, which in the Middle Ages supplied water from Monte Pacciano to the Fontana Maggiore; much later, it was converted into a long stone footbridge over the housetops to the precincts of the **university**, founded in 1307 and still one of the most prestigious in Italy. The central university buildings are now on Via Ariodante Fabretti, in an Olivetan monastery liquidated by Napoleon in 1801. In the **Institute of Chemistry** on Via Pascoli you can see a 2nd-century **Roman mosaic** of Orpheus charming the wild animals with his lyre.

Dipartimento di Chimica
open Mon–Fri 8–7.45

Beyond the university, Corso Garibaldi runs north through Borgo Sant'Angelo, passing bulky pink-and-white checked **Sant'Agostino**, with its set of extravagantly carved choirstalls by Baccio d'Agnolo, from designs by Perugino. The fresco over the altar is by Giannicola di Paolo, a student of Perugino, but the real prize, a five-part altarpiece by the master himself, was looted by Napoleon. Its panels are scattered across France, save the *Madonna*, who took a cannonball on the nose in Strasbourg during the Franco-Prussian war. Further up Corso Garibaldi is a plaque commemorating the meeting of St Francis and St Dominic, founders of the two great preaching orders of the Middle Ages, both in Perugia to visit Pope Honorius III; contemporary accounts say they embraced and went their separate ways, without more than a word or two.

One of the many convents in this area is **Santa Colomba** at Corso Garibaldi 191 (ring the bell); its most famous nun, the Blessed Colomba of Rieti (1467–1501), was so wise that the magistrates of Perugia often consulted her; her cell has a lovely painting of *Christ Carrying the Cross* by Lo Spagno and mementos of her life.

At the end of Corso Garibaldi, one of the highest points in the city was graced in ancient times by a circular temple, dedicated to Venus or Vulcan. In the 5th century Christians converted it into a church, the **Tempio di San Michele Arcangelo**, replacing the outer circle of columns with a plain stone wall. Many legends grew up around this singular church in the Middle Ages – some writers referred to it as the 'pavilion of Roland'. Today, with tons of Baroque frippery cleared away, it has something like its original appearance. Some scholars doubt there really was a temple here: the 16 beautiful Corinthian columns do come in a wild variety of styles and heights and some were undoubtedly brought from other buildings. Still, this oldest church in Umbria casts its quiet spell.

Tempio di San Michele Arcangelo
t 075 572 2624; open Tues–Sun 10–12 and 3.30–6.30 (until 7 in summer)

The tall **Porta Sant'Angelo** behind the church, a key point in Perugia's medieval defences, was built by Lorenzo Maitani in 1326 next to a castle tower added by Braccio Fortebraccio. Beyond it, enjoy a rare patch of countryside that has remained unchanged over the centuries; here the **church of San Matteo degli Armeni** has good restored 13th-century frescoes.

Porta Sant'Angelo
t 075 41670; open April and Aug daily 11–1.30 and 3–6.30; May–July, Sept and Oct Wed–Mon 11–1.30 and 3–6.30; Nov–Mar Wed–Mon 11–1.30 and 3–5; joint adm with Pozzo Etrusco, see p.438, and San Severo, see p.440

On Perusia's Acropolis

Yet another excursion from the cathedral and Piazza Dante would be up Via del Sole, through another ancient part of the city to **Piazza Michelotti**, an attractive spot and the highest point in Perugia. Long before the Rocca Paolina, the popes built their fortress here; and, like the work of Paul III, this castle was destroyed by the Perugians. In the rebellion of 1375 the people besieged it; after bribing Sir John Hawkwood, the paid protector of the papal legate, they knocked down the walls with the aid of a fearsome homemade catapult called the *cacciaprete* (priest-chaser). Today it is surrounded by peaceful 17th-century houses.

San Severo
t 075 573 3864; open April and Aug daily 10–1.30 and 2.30–6.30; May–July, Sept and Oct Wed–Sun 10–1.30 and 2.30–6.30; Nov–Mar Wed–Sun 10.30–1.30 and 2.30–5; joint adm with Pozzo Etrusco, *see p.438**, and Porta Sant'Angelo,* *see p.439*

From here, an arched lane leads to **San Severo**, founded in 1007 by Camaldolese monks; the story goes that this high ground was ancient *Augusta Perusia*'s acropolis, and the church was built over the ruins of a Temple of the Sun. One chapel survives the Baroque remodelling of the 1750s and contains a celebrated fresco of the *Holy Trinity and Saints*, one of Raphael's very first solo efforts; underneath are more saints by his master Perugino, ironically painted a couple of years after Raphael's premature death when Perugino was in a noticeable artistic decline.

Via Bontempi leads around to another Etruscan gate, the **Porta del Sole**. Two churches near here, **San Fiorenzo** in Via Alessi and 14th-century **Santa Maria Nuova** on Via Pinturicchio (at the bottom of Via Roscetto), both have one of Benedetto Bonfigli's bizarre gonfalons – painted banners intended to be carried during mournful *misericordia* processions in the streets, invoking God's mercy during plagues, famines or the frequent attacks of communal guilt to which Perugians were always subject. The one in Santa Maria Nuova (1472) is badly damaged but shows a vengeful Christ raining down thunderbolts of plague on sinful Perugia, while the Virgin, SS. Benedict and Scholastica, and the Blessed Paolo Bigazzini try to placate his wrath.

East of Santa Maria Nuova, Corso Bersaglieri continues out to the gate of Porta Sant'Antonio, where the **church of Sant'Antonio** has a frescoed *Crucifixion* recently attributed to Raphael.

To San Domenico

The streets southeast of the cathedral, while not quite as dramatic, are just as ancient and intractable as those to the north and west. If you care to climb a bit, a tour of this area will take you to such sights as the **Via delle Volte della Pace**, an ancient vaulted tunnel of a street just east of the cathedral, where Perugians signed their peace treaties (with fingers crossed behind their backs). One of the few breathing spaces in the crowded district is elongated **Piazza Matteotti**, former marketplace and field for burning witches, parallel to and below Corso Vannucci. In the old days it was called Piazza Sopramura, being actually built on top of a section of the Etruscan-Roman walls. The west side is shared by the post office and a Perugian institution, a brightly decorated kiosk with an eccentric owner who sells nothing but bananas. Opposite stand the 17th-century Gesù church and two splendid 15th-century buildings: the **Palazzo del Capitano del Popolo**, and the **Palazzo dell'Università Vecchia**, built between 1453 and 1515 and used as the quarters of the university until 1811.

From Piazza Matteotti, Via Oberdan descends to Perugia's oddest church, **Sant'Ercolano** (1326), a tall octagon constructed on the old walls with a gigantic pointed arch in each facet, a double Baroque stair, a train-station clock and lace curtains in the upstairs window; the interior, which is in good if rotting Baroque, has a Roman sarcophagus for its altar.

From here, the city extends along a narrow ridge, following Corso Cavour to another colossal, ambitious, woefully unfinished church, **San Domenico**. Designed by Giovanni Pisano, it was rebuilt in 1632 by Carlo Maderno when the vaulting caved in, though one wall and the apse are original; the latter has the second-largest stained-glass window in Italy after Milan cathedral, dated 1411. The light streaming through is the main feature of the interior, but there is also the fine *Tomb of Pope Benedict XI* by a student of Arnolfo di Cambio. Poisoned figs did Benedict in a year after his election, during a visit in 1304, but surprisingly, the Perugians had nothing to do with it; prime suspects after the nun who served them to him included the Florentines and King Philip the Fair of France. The fourth chapel on the right holds a beautiful marble and terracotta dossal (1459) by Agostino di Duccio.

The Museo Archeologico Nazionale dell'Umbria

Museo Archeologico Nazionale dell'Umbria
t 075 572 7141; open Mon 2.30–7.30, Tues–Sun 8.30–7.30; adm

Housed behind San Domenico, in an equally grandiose yet unfinished convent, this displays excellent material from prehistoric and Etruscan Umbria. The prehistoric collection will get you in touch with Palaeolithic, Neolithic and Bronze Age Umbria, while a large part of the historic collection comes from the Etruscan cemeteries around Perugia: an incised bronze mirror (an Etruscan speciality, 3rd century BC); intricate gold filigree jewellery; sarcophagi; a famous stone marker called the *Cippus Perusinus*, with one of the longest Etruscan inscriptions ever found (151 words); and bronzes, armour and weapons. Among the funeral vases and urns is one portraying a hero who looks like a dentist about to examine a monster's teeth; another shows a procession, perhaps of a victor. Roman finds include inscriptions in honour of Augustus, rebuilder of Perugia, and a beautiful sarcophagus sculpted with the myth of Meleager.

San Pietro

From San Domenico, Corso Cavour leaves the city at the elegant **Porta San Pietro** (1473),which was designed by Agostino di Duccio with help from Polidoro di Stefano. Changing its name to Borgo XX Giugno, the street continues to the end of the ridge, past the university's **Orto Medievale** at No.74, a botanical garden where each plant has a symbolic meaning, to an 18th-century park, the **Giardino del Frontone**.

Orto Medievale
t 075 585 6432; open Mon–Fri 8–5 (until 6 in summer)

Facing it is the Benedictine **church of San Pietro**, which was founded in the 10th century and retains substantial parts of its original structure. This is the most gloriously decorated church in the whole of Perugia, with nearly every square centimetre inside covered with frescoes and canvases. During the sack by the Swiss Guards in 1859, the monks of San Pietro shielded the leaders of the revolt from the papal bloodhounds – the story goes that they cut down their bell ropes by night and used them to lower the fugitives down the cliffs to safety. The twelve-sided belltower is one of Perugia's landmarks. The façade has a rare fresco of the *Trinity*, which is a feminine word in Italian and is here represented by a three-headed woman. The basilican interior dates from the early 1500s and has a carved, gilded ceiling. Among acres of painting are the large canvases in the nave by a Greek student of Veronese, L'Alisense. Two paintings in the right aisle have been attributed to Perugino's pupil Eusebio da San Giorgio, a *Madonna and Two Saints* and a *St Benedict*.

The **Cappella di San Giuseppe** has some fine 16th-century works, the sacristy paintings of *Five Saints* by Perugino, all that remains of yet another altarpiece looted by Napoleon, as well as a *Portrait of Christ* by Dosso Dossi, and a bronze crucifix by Algardi. The best works, however, have to be the extraordinary 1520s choirstalls, which were sculpted and inlaid by Bernardino Antonibi of Perugia, Nicola di Stefano of Bologna and Stefano Zambelli of Bergamo. A pretty door in the choir gives on to a little balcony with a memorable view over Assisi and Spello. The left aisle boasts a *Pietà* by Fiorenzo di Lorenzo.

There's a tabernacle attributed to Mino da Fiesole in the **Cappella Vibi**; the nearby **Cappella Ranieri** has a *Christ on the Mount* by Guido Reni, *St Peter and St Paul* attributed to Guercino, and a *Judith* by Sassoferrato, who was also responsible for the several Raphael and Perugino copies in the church. Beyond the **Cappella del Sacramento**, with paintings by Vasari, is an *Adoration of the Magi* in the nave by Eusebio da San Giorgio and a *Pietà* by Perugino.

On the Outskirts of Perugia

Santa Giuliana
t 075 575051; closed for renovation at time of writing

Ipogeo dei Volumni
t 075 393329; open July and Aug daily 9–12.30 and 4.30–7; rest of year daily 9–1 and 3.30–6.30; adm; max. 7 people at a time, max. visit 5mins

Leaving Perugia, Via XX Settembre down to the train station passes 13th-century **Santa Giuliana**, with a delicate pink and white façade and beautiful campanile, one of Perugia's landmarks. Attributed to Gattapone, it is one of the few medieval churches in Perugia to survive essentially intact, with frescoes from the 1200s and 1300s and a cloister from 1375, now a military hospital.

Near Ponte San Giovanni, east of Perugia, signs lead to one of the best-preserved Etruscan tombs anywhere, the **Ipogeo dei Volumni**. Sheltered by a modern yellow building next to a gritty bypass and train tracks, it can be hard to find: the most painless way is from Perugia by taxi. Dating from the 2nd century BC, the hypogeum is characteristically shaped like an Etruscan house, with an underground 'atrium' under a high gabled roof carved in the rock, surrounded by small rooms, the main one holding the travertine urns containing the ashes of four generations of the family. The oldest, that of a man named Arnth, is a typical Etruscan tomb with a representation of the deceased on the lid; that of his descendant, the 1st-century AD Pulius Voluminius, demonstrates Perugia's rapid Romanization. Unlike most Etruscan tombs, the Volumni has unusual high reliefs in stucco, rather than paintings.

ⓘ **Perugia >**
Loggia del Lanari, Piazza Matteotti 18, **t** *075 577 2686, and Via Mazzini 6,* **t** *075 572 8937, www.umbria 2000.it or http://turismo.comune.perugia.it*

Tourist Information in Perugia

Post office: Piazza Matteotti, **t** 0755 736977, *www.poste.it*.

Churches: open 8–12 and 4pm–sunset unless otherwise noted.

Market Days in Perugia

Food market: Pian di Massiano, Sat mornings.

Mercato della Terrazza, near Kennedy escalator, off Piazza Matteotti, daily. The city's market with a view, selling clothes and shoes.

Entertainment, Events and Festivals in Perugia

The main Perugian evening occupation remains the ***passeggiata*** down Corso Vannucci, with a stop for a bite at Bar Ferrari (No.43), full of Perugia's famous chocolate *Baci* and other confections, or a refreshing ice cream at the Gelateria Veneta (No.20), before loitering in Piazza IV Novembre. For **live music** in every possible shade, from jazz to traditional Turkish and tango, try Il Contrappunto, Via Scortici 4/a, **t** 075 573 3667 (Tues, Thurs and Sat).

Numerous **outdoor performances**, including concerts and films, cater to the large student population in summer. See the monthly *Viva Perugia: What Where When* for the latest happenings.

If you're travelling with children, Perugia has a large **funfair** plus Umbria's modest but sincerely meant answer to Disneyland, **Città della Domenica**, just west of the city (**t** 075 505 4941, *www.cittadelladomenica.com; open 10–7 daily April–Sept; Sat and Sun Oct–Mar; adm exp*), with a miniature Africa, serpentarium and bumper cars.

Festivals

Umbria Jazz Festival, tickets from booth in Piazza della Repubblica, *www.umbriajazz.com*, July. An excellent event that has drawn such luminaries as Stan Getz and Wynton Marsalis.

Teatro in Piazza festival, July and Aug. Performances in the city's cloisters and squares.

Tenera è la notte, July–Sept. Music in and around the city.

Sagra Musicale Umbra, Sept. Sacred music in Perugia's churches.

Marcia della Pace, 2nd Sun in Oct. The march for peace, when thousands of Italians walk the 10km from Perugia to Assisi.

Eurochocolate Festival, mid-Oct. Tastings, events, exhibits and courses on sweets and chocolate.

Fiera dei Morti, Pian di Massiano, 1st wk Nov. The oldest fair in central Italy.

Where to Stay in and around Perugia

Perugia ✉ 06100

The tourist office can provide you with a list of nearby rooms to rent, B&Bs and *agriturismi*.

Luxury–Very Expensive (€€€€€–€€€€)

*****Brufani Palace**, Piazza Italia 12, **t** 075 573 2541, *www.brufanipalace.it*. Elegant rooms, a splendid indoor pool, fine countryside views, an attractive courtyard and a private garage.

Very Expensive (€€€€)

****Giò Arte e Vini**, Via R. d'Andreotto 19, **t** 075 573 1100, *www.hotelgio.it*.

A memorable hotel dedicated to the noble art of wine-drinking, a short drive out of town. Each room has rustic Umbrian furniture, including a display case filled with bottles of wine; guests are encouraged to taste them and buy from the amply stocked cellars on departure. In the restaurant the sommelier chooses 3 wines each evening; for a surprisingly modest fee, diners can quaff to their heart's content. Dishes include tripe with potatoes, and wild boar with spelt polenta.

******Locanda della Posta**, Corso Vannucci 97, **t** 075 572 8925, *novelbet@tin.it*. An old place that once played host to Goethe, centrally located, with an ornate exterior, pleasant, renovated rooms and a garage.

******Perugia Plaza**, Via Palermo 88, **t** 075 34643, *www.umbriahotels.com*. A large, prestigious hotel in greenery at the foot of the city, with a pool, sauna and fitness centre. Breakfast is included, and there's an excellent restaurant (€€) with very reasonable fixed-price menus. *Closed Mon*.

******La Rosetta**, Piazza Italia 19, **t** 075 572 0841, *www.umbriaonline.com/larosetta*. A deservedly popular option with cosy, quiet rooms from different periods, all with Internet access, a garden, and a celebrated restaurant.

Expensive (€€€)

*****Fortuna**, Via Bonazzi 19, just off Corso Vannucci, **t** 075 572 2845, *www.umbriahotels.com*. A place more comfy than charming, with a private garage.

Moderate (€€)

****Aurora**, Viale Indipendenza 21, **t** 075 572 4819, *albergoaurorapg@virgilio.it*. Rather spartan rooms, most ensuite, a minute's walk from the station.

****Priori**, Via dei Priori 40, **t** 075 572 3378, *www.hotelpriori.it*. A refurbished building in the historic centre, plus a suite in a 15th-century palace nearby. A buffet breakfast is included in rates.

Inexpensive (€)

***Etruria**, Via della Luna 21, **t** 075 572 3730. A simple place just off Corso Vannucci, with panoramic views. Some rooms are ensuite.

Centro Internazionale Accoglienza per la Gioventù, Via Bontempi 13, **t** 075 572 2880, *www.ostelloperugia.it*. A hostel by the Duomo, with bunks. You don't need a youth hostel card. It's cash only. *Closed 15 Dec–15 Jan*.

Sant'Ercolano, Via del Bovaro 9, **t** 075 572 4650, *www.santercolano.com*. Tidy ensuite rooms in a quiet 17th-century building in the *centro storico*. Its friendly owners know the city well.

Cenerente ✉ 06070

******Castello dell'Oscano**, 9km northwest of Perugia, **t** 075 584371, www. *oscano.com* (€€€€€–€€€€). A Neo-Renaissance establishment with antique-furnished rooms, a pool in a large park, and two restaurants, plus wine-tasting and cookery courses.

Bosco ✉ 06080

******Relais San Clemente**, Passo dell'Acqua, Loc. Bosco, 10km east on road to Gubbio, **t** 075 591 5100, *www.relais.it* (€€€€). A 14th-century Benedictine abbey with lovely grounds, a pool, tennis and volleyball courts, luxurious, stylish rooms and a very good restaurant. Breakfast is included; half/full board are available.

Torgiano ✉ 06089

*******Le Tre Vaselle**, Corso Garibaldi 48, **t** 075 988 0447, *www.3vaselle.it* (€€€€€–€€€€). A luxurious hotel in an old *palazzo* and neighbouring houses, on the edge of the village of Torgiano (*see* opposite), surrounded by vineyards and olive groves. It offers babysitting, a pool, a whirlpool, a sauna, a fitness suite... the list goes on. The restaurant, **Le Melograne** (€€€€), is among the top in Umbria but can have off days; it serves local fare with a creative twist.

Eating Out in Perugia

Perugia ✉ 06100

Some of the best restaurants are in the hotels listed p.443–44; try Perugia Plaza, La Rosetta and Giò Arte e Vini.

Expensive (€€€)

Antica Trattoria San Lorenzo, Piazza Danti 19a, **t** 075 5721956. An elegant place in the centre, serving traditional fare with a creative spark: *maltagliati* with rabbit *alla cacciatore*, *pappa al pomodoro* with cod and cauliflower, and more. There's live jazz some evenings. Book ahead. *Closed Sun*.

★ Antica Trattoria San Lorenzo >>

Il Falchetto, Via Bartolo 20, **t** 075 573 1775. Umbrian specialities served in a medieval atmosphere near the cathedral, including home-made pasta with spinach and ricotta, risotto with *porcini*, prawns with brandy, and veal fondue. *Closed Mon and 15–30 Jan.*

Osteria del Gambero, Via Baldeschi 17, **t** 075 573 5461. A quattrocento *palazzo* offering good variations on Umbrian themes, including *porcini* soup and duck with vegetables and broad bean sauce. *Eves only, closed Sun, and part of Jan and June.*

Osteria del Gufo, Via della Viola 18, right by San Fiorenzo, **t** 075 573 4126. A seasonal menu that never lacks flair. Try *maltagliati* in a vegetable sauce, plus some ethnic dishes such as couscous, in a garden in summer. *Closed Sun, Mon, lunch and Aug.*

Il Paiolo, Via Angusta 11, **t** 075 572 5611. A Renaissance *palazzo* with good-value, tasty food, such as *taglierini* with smoked salmon, home-made *ravioloni* with *porcini*, and pork chop in apple vinegar. Pizzas are the real forte, though – try *del paiolo*, with truffles. *Closed Wed, and 1st half Aug.*

★ Del Borgo >>

Expensive (€€)

La Bocca Mia, Via V. Rocchi 36, **t** 075 572 3873. A place near the Etruscan Arch, with a reputation for desserts, not usually an Umbrian forte – the *pannacotta* and plumcake are especially good. Beforehand, try home-made *strangozzi* with truffles, spelt soup, or roast pork. *Closed Sun, Mon lunch, and 1–25 Aug.*

Da Cesarino, Piazza IV Novembre 4/5, **t** 075 572 8974. An old favourite serving reliable home-made pasta, traditional meat dishes and pizzas. *Closed Wed and Jan.*

Porta del Sole, Via delle Prome 11 (extension of Via del Sole), **t** 075 572 0938. Good Neapolitan-style pizzas, served in a garden in warmer months. *Closed Mon and lunch.*

Inexpensive (€)

Il Cantinone, Via Ritorta 6, just left of cathedral, **t** 075 573 4430. Simple fare such as *spaghetti all'amatriciana*, beans and sausage, plus good *secondi* with meat, including *filetto tartufato* – fillet steak with a black truffle sauce. *Closed Tues.*

Ceccarani, Piazza Matteotti 16, **t** 075 572 1960. Perugia's best bread, baked 30 ways.

Del Borgo, Via della Sposa 23/27, **t** 075 572 0390. A picturesque trattoria and *norcineria* (charcuterie specialist) with an exquisite array of *salumi* served with *torta al testo*. *Closed lunch.*

Sandri, Corso Vannucci, **t** 075 572 4112. One of the prettiest pastry shops in the whole of Italy, with a frescoed ceiling and divinely artistic confections. *Closed Mon.*

Around Perugia: Torgiano, Deruta and Corciano

Torgiano

Museo del Vino
Corso Vittorio Emanuele;
t 075 988 0200;
open daily 9–1 and 3–7;
cantina *by appt on* **t** *075 988 661; adm*

Traditionally under Perugia's influence, Torgiano, situated 15km south of the capital, is practically synonymous with wine and the Lungarotti family; from the late 1970s, Dr Giorgio Lungarotti has made this minute DOC-growing area internationally famous. The Lungarotti foundation runs an excellent **wine museum**, in the cellars of the 17th-century Palazzo Baglioni. Displays labelled in English as well as Italian trace the history of wine, techniques, rules and regulations; it also has a history of wine jars and vessels, a beautiful display of majolica, from Deruta, Faenza and Montelupo, and a wine library, with books going back to the Renaissance. For accommodation in Torgiano, *see* opposite.

Deruta

 Deruta

If there's room in your case, buy a plate in the tiny hilltown of Deruta (population 7,500), 5km south of Torgiano. Along with Gubbio, Deruta has been Umbria's centre for ceramics and majolica since the 13th century, and still has 200 ceramic workshops. Its location, on the fringe of Perugia's *contado*, brought it some hard knocks from Perugia's enemies over the centuries. During the height of its fame in the 1500s, Deruta was sacked twice, by Cesare Borgia and Braccio Baglioni, but it picked itself up.

Maioliche Sberna
t 075 971206; call for opening hrs

Museo Regionale della Ceramica
Largo San Francesco; t 075 971 1000; open April–Sept daily 10–1 and 3.30–7; Oct–Mar Wed–Mon 10–1 and 3.30–7; joint adm with Pinacoteca

There are dozens of ceramics shops, particularly in the lower part of town. One of the biggest is **Maioliche Sberna**, where you can watch ceramics being made and painted in the workshop. Admire works of past artisans in the **Museo Regionale della Ceramica**, in a former convent: examples from Deruta's golden age in the early 1500s, church floor tiles, devotional plaques and a majolica font.

Pinacoteca
t 075 971 1000; open Sat and Sun 10–1 and 3.30–7; joint adm with Museo della Ceramica

In Piazza dei Consoli (note the miniature copy of Perugia's Fontana Maggiore, minus the reliefs), the 14th-century **church of San Francesco** has patches of Sienese and Umbrian frescoes, while the medieval Palazzo Comunale holds the **Pinacoteca**, with paintings and a gonfalon by Nicolò Alunno, painted on both sides. There's also a detached fresco by Fiorenzo di Lorenzo, one of his best works, of the *Plague Saints Rocco and Romano standing over Deruta* (1478).

Madonna dei Bagni
open by appt on t 075 973455

Another church, **Sant'Antonio Abate**, has a fresco by Bartolomeo Caporali of the *All-Protecting Virgin*, who also features in the **Madonna dei Bagni**, 3km south along the SS3bis in Frazione Casalina. This is full of quaint ceramic votive plaques made in the 17th and 18th centuries, showing pratfalls, sinking ships and exorcisms, all with happy endings thanks to the Madonna.

Closer to Perugia, to the west of the Tiber, a country chapel outside **San Martino in Colle** has a fresco of the *Madonna and Child*, restored and attributed to Pinturicchio.

Corciano: Town of Cashmere

On its hill midway to Lake Trasimeno, pretty Corciano is protected by a nearly intact castle and 13th-century walls. Controlled by Perugia into the 15th century, it has small-scale versions of all the essential buildings of a *comune*, neatly labelled with a ceramic plaques, which gives it a slight museumish air. To visit the small museums here, call the **Comune di Corciano** several days ahead.

Comune di Corciano
t 075 518 8254/5

Pink-and-white striped **San Francesco** was founded after St Francis' visit in 1211 (the Corcianese got a headstart on his church, sure he was going to be canonized). Perugino left one of his finest late works, the *Assumption* altarpiece (1513) in 13th-century **Santa Maria**; it also has one of Bonfigli's strange gonfalons, dedicated to the *Madonna della Misericordia*, here defending Corciano.

Pieve del Vescovo
t 075 505 8611, open for pre-booked visits last Fri of month

The big castle just north of Corciano at **Pieve del Vescovo** was restored in the late 1500s by Galeazzo Alessi, as a residence. There's an even more impressive work by the same architect just north of the main road: the **Villa del Cardinale**, built for Cardinal Fulvio Della Corgna, now owned by the state (there are plans to open it to the public). It has a very imposing gate and a lovely Renaissance garden.

Corciano is best known, these days, for its cashmere factory outlets. One of the most famous designers, Brunello Cucinelli, has a boutique in Solomeo near Corciano, a village he is slowly restoring.

Lake Trasimeno

Lago Trasimeno

The fourth largest lake in Italy, Trasimeno (45km in circumference) has a subtle charm. Sleepy, placid and shallow, almost marshy in places, and large enough to create its own soft micro-climate, it shimmers like a mirror embedded in gentle rolling hills covered with olives and vineyards. The Etruscans of *Camars* (Chiusi) coveted the lake for its fish and the fertility of its shores, and around the time of their famous king Lars Porsena, the bad guy in Macaulay's *Horatio at the Bridge*, they founded Perugia to control it. In the 12th and 13th century, wars were fought for its eels. Napoleon took one look at it and wondered how to drain it.

Hans Christian Andersen, drawing on his own travels, put Trasimeno in one of his fairytales, *The Galoshes of Fortune* – how beautiful it was, but how poor the people were (in the 1830s), and how wretched their lives among the swarms of biting flies, mosquitoes and malaria. A postwar dose of American DDT wiped out the latter, and the lake has since become a modest resort – the Umbrian Riviera. Never one to fully cooperate with humanity, Trasimeno, once prone to flooding, is now doing its best to become a peat bog. A few fishermen skim over its waters, seeking eels, tench, shad and carp. Ducks, cormorants and kingfishers love it, and waterlilies float among the reeds. And, as the tourist office reminds visitors, some 20% of the world's artistic heritage listed by UNESCO lies within two hours of its quiet shores.

Magione and Trasimeno's East Shore

From Perugia it's 30km to Trasimeno; snub the *autostrada* to visit **Magione**, a little industrial centre known for its copper- and brassware. Like any place within Perugia's radius, it spent much of the Middle Ages fighting: there's a ruined 13th-century **Torre dei Lombardi**, and on the edge a striking **Castello dei Cavalieri di Malta** of 1420, built by Bolognese architect Fieravante Fieravanti and still owned by the Knights of Malta, now based in Rome. The knights had inherited an 11th-century Templar hospital here, of which a few

Castello dei Cavalieri di Malta
t 075 843547; open in summer for guided tours, call for times

Getting to and around Lake Trasimeno

Lake Trasimeno lies 37km south of Arezzo, 13km south of Cortona, 69km east of Siena, and 30km west of Perugia. By **car**, you can approach it along the A1 from the north; take the Val di Chiana exit for the spur of the *autostrada* that skirts the northern shore en route to Perugia. Coming from the south, taking the Chiusi exit off the A1 will bring you out near the SS71 to Castiglione del Lago.

Perugia is the main **bus** terminus for the area; connections from Cortona and Siena are less frequent. A fairly frequent bus service runs around the north shore (Tuoro– Passignano–Magione–San Feliciano–San Savino–Perugia) and around the southern shore (Perugia–Magione–S. Arcangelo– Panicarola–Macchie–Castiglione del Lago). Contact APM buses (**t** 075 506781, freephone **t** 800 512141, *www.apmperugia.it*).

Train travel can be a bit awkward: Castiglione del Lago is a stop on the main Florence–Rome line but not for fast trains (*Intercity* and *Eurostar*), so check before setting out. Florence–Perugia *Regionale* trains and Rome–Perugia *Interregionale* and *ES* trains also pass through. On the main Florence–Rome line, you can change at Terontola for Perugia and the north-shore towns of Tuoro sul Trasimeno and Passignano; coming from Siena, change at Chiusi for Castiglione.

You can hire **bikes** in Castiglione from Marinelli, Via B. Buozzi 26, **t** 075 953126, in Passignano from Eta Beta Modelismo, Via della Vittoria 58, **t** 075 829401, or in Tuoro from Balneazione Tuoro, Loc. Punta Navaccio, **t** 334 979 4208 (mobile), April–Sept, or from Marzano, Via Console Flaminio 59, **t** 075 826269.

Castiglione, Tuoro and Passignano, the lake's ports, are linked by **boat** to one another as well as to Isola Maggiore and Isola Polvese. Connections are frequent in summer but only once or twice daily in winter; for times, call **t** 075 827157 or ask at tourist offices (*see* pp.452–53).

traces remain. Their church, **San Giovanni**, was damaged in the last war, and rebuilt and frescoed in a traditional manner by Perugian futurist Gherardo Dottori in 1947. On the main road, the little 13th-century **church of the Madonna delle Grazie** has a lovely fresco of the *Madonna Enthroned* by Andrea di Giovanni da Orvieto.

Long before the knights, this was the birthplace of missionary Fra Giovanni di Pian di Carpine ('of the hornbeam plain', as the area under Magione was known), sent in 1245 by Innocent IV to convert the Mongols; though his preaching failed to make an impact, he returned from Karakorum after 20 years and wrote the *Historia Mongolorum*, the first eyewitness account of China and the Far East, which was much studied by later missionaries and Marco Polo. Some scholars suspect the Venetian merchant never visited Kubla Khan but cribbed much of his *Travels* from Fra Giovanni.

Three of Trasimeno's prettiest beaches are between Magione's lakeside *frazioni*. One of these *frazioni*, **Montecolognola**, high on a hill blanketed with olives, has another castle built in the late 13th century by the beleaguered residents of Magione, and lovely views over the lake. Montecolognola's parish church has 14th- to 16th-century frescoes, another of 1947 by Gherardo Dottori and a pretty majolica altarpiece made in Deruta.

Further south are picturesque **Monte del Lago**, near the impressive but ruined **Castello di Zocco** (1400) with its five towers and **San Feliciano**. The latter village is home to the fascinating little **Museo della Pesca**, dedicated to the lake's fishermen, and enjoys magical sunsets over the water and **Isola Polvese**, the largest of Trasimeno's three islands, reached in summer by boats from San Feliciano. The large village that stood on Polvese was abandoned in

Museo della Pesca
t 075 847 9261; open Feb–Oct daily 10.30–1 and 4–7; adm

the 17th century because of malaria; today, only the 14th-century castle and an older monastery still stand. Now owned by the province, Polvese has olive groves, lush vegetation and hundreds of nesting birds; a path encircles it and takes about an hour to walk, and there's a little beach and summer snack bar.

Oasi la Valle
t 075 847 6007; open June–Sept daily 9–1 and 4–8; Oct–May Tues–Sun 9–1 and 3–6; guided tours for a min. of 6 by advance booking; adm

South of San Feliciano, the **Oasi la Valle**, run by an environmental group, is the most important bird-watching area on Trasimeno, hosting an impressive number of migratory visitors, especially in spring. It's here that the Romans dug a 7km underground emissary to drain the lake when levels reached the flood stage, diverting it through streams and into the Tiber; a second emissary was built in 1423 by Braccio Fortebraccio. Leonardo da Vinci, who visited in 1503, suggested diverting its flow into the Tiber, Arno and Chiana. As the shore grew swampier, his proposal received serious consideration, until yet another emissary was dug here in 1896. You can walk along it, and a museum on the site tells the whole soggy story.

The North Shore: Castel Rigone, Passignano and Isola Maggiore

To the north of Magione, a road ascends to **Castel Rigone**, a dramatically poised fortress hilltown that was founded in 543 by Rigone, lieutenant of Totila the Goth. It has spectacular views over the lake and a delightful Renaissance church, the restored **Madonna dei Miracoli**, which was built in 1494 by Perugia as a votive for the Virgin who spared the city from a plague. In the form of a Latin cross, it has a doorway with a relief by a student of Michelangelo, Domenico Bertini da Settignano (who, like most Renaissance artists, had a nickname – Topolino or 'Mousey' – the same as the Italian for Mickey Mouse). It has a fine interior and a gilded high altar by Bernardino di Lazzaro, a chapel with *ex votos* dedicated to the miraculous Madonna, and a sweet statue of St Anthony Abbot and his pet pig.

The lake's busiest resort, **Passignano sul Trasimeno** is on its own promontory midway between Perugia and Cortona. In the 1930s this was the HQ of the Società Aeronautica Italiana, which made zippy seaplanes and boats, until it was bombed in the war. Within Passignano's walls is an attractive old quarter around the 14th-century castle; below lies a beach with windsurf hire. Near the cemetery, the **Pieve di San Cristoforo** dating from the 11th century has restored frescoes from the 1300s; 1.5km northeast, the **Madonna dell'Olivo** is an elegant Renaissance church with a beautiful high altar and a fresco attributed to Bartolomeo Caporali. The town is at its liveliest for the **Palio delle Barche** on the third Sunday of July, when young Passignanesi dressed in medieval costume carry their boats shoulder-high through the streets and launch them on to the lake for a race.

Passignano is the nearest port to **Isola Maggiore** (20mins), Trasimeno's second-largest island, with a charming 15th-century village inhabited by fishermen and women famous for lace-making. In 1211, St Francis came to the then-deserted island to spend Lent alone. He made a lasting impression by throwing back a pike a fisherman had given him, only to be followed doggedly across the lake by his grateful 'Brother Fish' until the saint blessed him. Francis took only two loaves of bread to sustain himself, and when the fisherman returned to the island to pick him up, he was amazed to see that only one loaf had been half eaten in 40 days.

A footpath encircles the island, passing the Franciscan convent, built to commemorate the saint's visit and converted in the late 19th century into a neogothic folly by Senator Giacinto Guglielmi from Rome, now crumbling gently into a romantic ruin (a village custodian shows people round). The 13th-century **church of San Michele Arcangelo** has frescoes and an excellent *Crucifixion* by Bartolomeo Caporali (*c.* 1460).

Tuoro sul Trasimeno

West of Passignano, Tuoro sul Trasimeno grew up in the late Middle Ages near the **Castello di Montegualandro**, a haven for citizens while their town was attacked by every army crossing the

The Battle of Trasimeno

Tuoro's first battle was the worst. Two years into the Second Punic War, Hannibal was on a winning streak, having defeated the Romans on the rivers Ticino and Trebbia – victories that had rallied the local Gaulish and Ligurian tribes to his banner. As it made its way south towards Rome, this swollen army got bogged down in the disease-ridden marshland of the Arno, at the cost of thousands of troops and all the exasperated elephants who had survived the march over the Pyrenees and Alps. Meanwhile, the Roman Senate sent Consul Gaius Flaminius, a bold populist politician (builder of the Via Flaminia), and an army of 25,000 to destroy the Carthaginians once and for all. With Flaminius in pursuit through the Valdichiana, Hannibal led his army, reduced to 40,000, to Trasimeno. Finding a perfect place for an ambush just west of Tuoro, in a natural amphitheatre closed off by the lake (the water level was considerably higher then), he arranged his troops in the hills, determined to risk all to defeat the Romans and convince the restive Etruscan cities to join him.

Believing Hannibal was at least a day's march in front, Flaminius failed to send scouts ahead; the morning of 24 June 217 BC was foggy and, according to chroniclers, he ignored a number of auguries pointed out by his Etruscan soothsayers. He marched straight into Hannibal's trap, along the narrow shore passage at Malpasso. In a panic, unable to get into battle formations, 15–16,000 legionaries (including Flaminius) were drowned or slaughtered within hours; those who got away found a safe haven in Perugia. The blood of the dead, which legend says ran in a river for three days, is recalled in the name of the hamlet Sanguineto, their whitened bones in the hamlet of Ossaia (from *ossa*, bones). Hannibal slew all the Roman prisoners but freed the various Italic tribes, hoping to gather support.

After Trasimeno, the Roman military machine grimly threw even more legions to their death against Hannibal at Cannae, before changing strategy and giving the Carthaginians the run of southern Italy for 15 years, harassing Hannibal while refusing to fight him before ultimately defeating him in Africa. The long-term effects of the war are felt to this day: as small farmers fled, they lost their income and had to sell their land to pay their debts. Snapped up cheap by a few rich men, it marked the beginning of the feudal *latifondo* system that condemned the once prosperous south of Italy to grinding poverty.

Italian peninsula or heading south to Rome. Visit the battlefield by car or foot, along the signposted **Percorso Storico Archeologico della Battaglia**, dotted with viewing platforms; along the way explanatory notes and maps help bring the Roman disaster to life. Near the first platform, note the pretty portal of the Romanesque **Pieve di Confini**. Tuoro has decorated its lake shore with Pietro Cascella's **Campo del Sole** (1985–89), a contemporary 'solar temple' garden of 27 pillars in locally quarried sandstone, each about 3.6m high and sculpted by a different artist, arranged in a wide spiral like a forest of idols to a preposterous god.

La Dogana near here was the Customs House between the Papal States and the Grand Duchy of Tuscany, and has plaques to the famous folk who passed this way.

Castiglione del Lago

Among the silvery olive groves that soften the west shore juts the picturesque promontory of Castiglione del Lago (population 13,500), setting for the lake's biggest town, a cheerful, mostly modern place dating back to the Etruscans. Emperor Frederick II destroyed it for being an ally of Guelph Perugia, then ordered Fra Elia Coppi to lay out a new town, neatly in six streets, served by three gates and three squares. Afterwards, it kept siding with Cortona, causing no end of friction with Perugia until 1490, when it came once and for all under the Baglioni family, who in their brief period of glory hosted here such luminaries as Machiavelli and Leonardo da Vinci. Eventually the town was recovered by the popes; one, Julius III, gave it to his sister. In 1550, her son, celebrated *condottiere* Ascanio della Corgna and husband of Giovanna Baglioni, became the first in a series of dukes to rule the lake as an independent duchy, until 1648, when it passed into the Grand Duchy of Tuscany before returning to the popes the next century.

Palazzo Ducale
open 21 Mar–April daily 9.30–1 and 3.30–7; May and June daily 10–1 and 4–7.30; July and Aug daily 10–1.30 and 4.30–8; Sept and Oct daily 10–1.30 and 3.30–7; Nov–20 Mar Sat, Sun and hols 9.30–4.30; adm

During Castiglione's ruritanian interlude, the great architect Vignola designed the ducal Palazzo della Corgna or **Palazzo Ducale**. Many rooms retain their fetching late Renaissance frescoes by Niccolò Pomarancio and the Roman school; one scene shows the battle of Trasimeno, another the battle of Lepanto, in which Ascanio distinguished himself. Like the great *condottiere* Federico da Montefeltro (*see* p.484), Ascanio was something of a humanist and so had his study decorated with frescoes on the Life of Caesar. From the palace, a covered walkway, fortified in case of surprise attack, allowed direct access to the mightiest of all the castles on the lake, the pentagonal Rocca del Leone designed in 1247 by Friar Elia Coppi with a sturdy triangular keep and four outer towers.

Also worth seeing, in the 19th-century **church of the Maddalena**, is a lovely painting of the *Madonna and Child with SS. Anthony Abbot and Mary Magdalene* (1500), by Eusebio da San Giorgio.

The South Shore

Much of this shore is patterned by vines producing the grapes that go into Colli del Trasimeno, a local DOC wine. In **Panicarola**, the most famous producer was Ferruccio Lamborghini, who declared an ambitious intention to make wines as fine as his sports cars – his father had been a farmer, and the first motors young Ferruccio built were for his tractors. He died in 1993, before quite succeeding, but you can still buy a Lamborghini to call your own.

ⓘ Tuoro sul Trasimeno >>
Pro Loco, Via Ritorta 1, t 075 825220, www.proloco tuorosultrasimeno.it

★ I Capricci di Merion >>

★ Relais Il Cantico della Natura >

★ Da Sauro >

Tourist Information around Lake Trasimeno

Ask at Castiglione del Lago tourist office about **joint tickets** to the main attractions of Castiglione del Lago, Città della Pieve and Isola Maggiore.

In addition to Castiglione del Lago and Tuoro, there are **summer tourist offices** at Isola Maggiore, Magione, Rossignano and San Feliciano.

Market Day: Weds, Castiglione del Lago.

Sailing: Club Velistico, Viale Brigata Garibaldi 3a, Castiglione del Lago, **t** 075 953035; and Loc. Darsena, Passignano, **t** 075 829 6021.

Waterskiing: Scuola Federale Sci Nautica, Punta Navaccia, Via Navaccia 4, Tuoro sul Trasimeno, **t** 075 826357. (closed Nov–Feb).

Sci Club Trasimeno, Castiglione del Lago, **t** 075 965 2836.

Where to Stay and Eat around Lake Trasimeno

Montesperello di Magione ✉ 06063

Relais Il Cantico della Natura, t 075 841699, *www.ilcanticodellanatura.it* (€€€). A 42-hectare organic *agriturismo* in an ancient olive grove, with orchards and woods with lake views. Rooms have canopy beds. Walk, mountainbike or ride horses over the hills, swim in the pool, and enjoy hearty meals.

Isola Maggiore ✉ 06060

***Da Sauro**, Via Guglielmi, **t** 075 826168, *www.hoteldasauro.it* (€€€€). The best place in Umbria to get away from it all, gracious and uncomplicated, with basic but comfortable rooms. The island's only hotel, it has a private beach on the lake and a beautiful garden. The brilliant restaurant (€€) specializes in fish from the lake: eels, carp and more, along with traditional Umbrian dishes. Breakfast is included, and half and full board are available.

Tuoro sul Trasimeno ✉ 06069

I Capricci di Merion, Via Pozzo 21, **t** 075 825002, *www.caprricidimerion.it* (€€€), A few delightful antiques-filled rooms in a Liberty-style *palazzo* built for harp-playing Lady Merion by her lover. Surrounded by vines and olive trees, the saltwater pool has a double hydro-massage. The restaurant is excellent.

San Feliciano ✉ 06060

***Da Settimio**, Via Lungalago Alicato 1, 7km south of Magione, **t** 075 847 6000, *dasettimio@tiscali.it* (€€). Peaceful ensuite rooms and a simple restaurant in a lakeside hamlet.

Rosso di Sera, Via Fratelli Papini 81, **t** 075 847 6277 (€€). An *osteria* serving delicious lake fish and land dishes. Try the seasonal soups, *bollito* and mustard, rock bass, pigeon with leek cake, and eels. *Closed Tues, lunch exc Sun, and 20 days in Jan.*

Castel Rigone ✉ 06060

****Relais La Fattoria**, Via Rigone 1, **t** 075 845322, *www.relaislafattoria.com* (€€€€). Pretty 1600s farm buildings with a pool, luxury rooms and a restaurant serving good *filetto di persico* (perch) and *spaghetti al sugo di Trasimeno* (with a sauce of mixed lake fish); half and full board are available. There is horse-riding and golf nearby. *Restaurant closed 3wks Jan.*

L'Acquario, Via Vittorio Emanuele 69, **t** 075 965 2432 (€€). A classy place featuring pike, carp, eel and tench in imaginative ways, plus good meat dishes – the fat home-made *pici* with goose is excellent.

Passignano sul Trasimeno ✉ 06065

***Villa Paradiso, Via Fratelli Rosselli 5, **t** 075 829191, *www.bluhotels.it* (€€€€). A large, comfortable option with a rustic feel, boating a pool, a kids' area and a restaurant.

***Lido, Via Roma 1, **t** 075 827219, *www.umbriahotels.com* (€€€). Well-equipped rooms on the water, a pool with hydromassage, a solarium, a garden, and a restaurant on a terrace with a lake view, specializing in fish (half board is available). Breakfast is included, and there's a minimum 3-night stay. *Closed Nov–Feb.*

*Del Pescatore, Via San Bernadino 5, **t** 075 829 6063, *www.delpescatore.com* (€€). Holiday apartments refurbished in 2006, furnished in a country style, with iron beds. The attractive trattoria serves lake fish and more; try eel with green beans, and roast carp. *Closed Tues.*

*Florida, Via 2 Giugno 2, **t** 075 827228 (€). Good simple ensuite rooms and a welcoming atmosphere.

Da Luciano, Via Lungolago 3, **t** 075 827210 (€€€). A lakeside restaurant serving fish for more than 40 years. Booking is strongly advised. *Closed Wed and 3wks Jan.*

Il Fischio del Merlo, San Donato 17a, **t** 075 829283 (€€). Creative cuisine based on seafish and Chianina meat in a lovely rustic room. Booking is advisable. *Closed Tues and 3wks Nov.*

Castiglione del Lago ✉ 06061

***Duca della Corgna, Via Buozzi 143, **t** 075 953238, *www.hotelcorgna.com* (€€). A comfy, relaxing option in a wood, with ensuite rooms and a pool. There's a summer restaurant (with half board).

***Miralago, Piazza Mazzini 5, **t** 075 951157, *www.hotelmiralago.com* (€€). A small, basic but comfortable choice with pretty lake views. Half board is available. *Closed Jan and Feb.*

***Trasimeno, Via Roma 174, **t** 075 965 2494, *www.hotel-trasimeno.it* (€€). Basic rooms, a pool, and a fish restaurant.

La Cantina, Via Vittorio Emanuele 69, **t** 075 965 2463 (€€). Smoked eel, carp wrapped in *porchetta* (a typical local dish) and pizzas. Local products are sold. *Closed Mon in winter.*

ⓘ **Castiglione del Lago >>**
Piazza Mazzini 10,
***t** 075 965 2484,*
www.lagotrasimeno.net

South of Lake Trasimeno

These hills and their towns are known for their magical views over Lake Trasimeno and their souvenirs of Perugino, who made this loveliness part of his artistic vocabulary. Italian writers have often commented that Città della Pieve looks more Sienese than Umbrian – the Tuscan border and interesting towns such as Chiusi and Montepulciano are only a few kilometres away.

Città della Pieve

Città della Pieve

From Castiglione del Lago, it's 27km to handsome red-brick Città della Pieve (population 6,500). Etruscans and Romans were here; in the Middle Ages it became *Castrum Plebis*, then *Castel della Pieve*. Perugia considered it within the western borders of its turf and in the 1320s built the square fortress to defend it. In 1503, Cesare Borgia sacked it, then, typically, had colleagues, the Duke of Gavina and Piero Orsini, strangled for conspiring against him. Later it was ruled by Ascanio della Corgna and his heirs until 1601, when the Church picked it up and Clement VIII made it a bishopric, changing its name to Città della Pieve. It's best known as the birthplace of **Perugino** (Pietro Vannucci, *c.* 1446–1523), who, to Vasari, committed the sin of not being born in Tuscany. If there is anything to the Vasari's *Lives of the Artists*, Perugino was perhaps the most bitter artist of the Renaissance. Born into a desperately poor family, he was transformed by success into an untrusting miser, riding from job to job with saddlebags full of money he was afraid to leave anywhere else. About midpoint in his career, he became an atheist, yet he cranked out two decades of richly rewarded, often vacuous, Madonnas and religious scenes with lyrical soft-tinted Trasimeno backgrounds, before dying, unconfessed and unabsolved – very rare then – rejecting a future with the angels he depicted for others.

Oratorio di Santa Maria dei Bianchi
open by appt on t 0578 299375

He left several paintings in his home town; the greatest is a lovely fresco of *The Adoration of the Magi* (1504), painted for a charitable confraternity in the **Oratorio di Santa Maria dei Bianchi**, just within the walls. It portrays the birth of the Saviour in an Arcadian spring, with the view from Città della Pieve towards Lake Trasimeno in the background and an elegant Renaissance garden party – a world that seems hardly to need a redeemer. Two letters from Perugino on display show he demanded 200 florins for his work but settled for much less, partly as he was painting for his fellow citizens.

Duomo
open daily 9.30–7

Via Vannucci leads uphill to the cluster of monuments in Piazza Plebiscito. The undistinguished **Duomo** was built in the 1600s to replace the far older **SS. Gervasio e Protasio**, the *pieve* (parish church) that gave the town its name; 9th-century sculptural work is embedded in the façade. There are more works by Perugino, as well a crucifix attributed to Pietro Tacca. The second chapel has one of Domenico Alfani's finest works, the *Madonna and Child and Saints*.

Palazzo della Corgna
t 0578 299375; open May–Sept daily 9.30–1 and 4–7.30; Oct–Apr Sat, Sun and hols 10–12.30 and 3.30–6; adm

Next door is the lofty **Torre del Pubblico**, built in the 12th century but heightened in 1471; in the same piazza are the trecento **Palazzo dei Priori** and **Palazzo della Corgna**, designed in 1551 by Perugian architect Galeazzo Alessi; inside are good 16th-century frescoes by Pomarancio and Salvio Savini and a little sandstone obelisk, brought here from the convent of San Francesco. Near the piazza is what locals claim is the narrowest lane in Italy, **Vicolo Bacciadonne** ('Kiss-the-Women Lane'; you're almost compelled to do so, to get past).

Santa Maria dei Servi
often locked; custodian at Santa Maria dei Bianchi has key

Oratorio di San Bartolomeo
open daily 10–12 and 4–7

Just off Piazza Pretorio is the brick **Palazzo Bandini**, remodelled in the 16th century by Galeazzo Alessi; carry on to the Porta Romana and **Santa Maria dei Servi**, frescoed by Perugino with a famous *Deposition* of 1517, damaged when monks erected a *cantoria* in front. The Porta Romana is linked by walls to the Perugian **Rocca**, built by Ambrogio and Lorenzo Maitani in 1326. Opposite is 13th-century **San Francesco**, redone in the 18th century, now a popular shrine to Fatima. It has two good paintings, Domenico Alfani's *Virgin and Saints* and a *Pentecost* by Niccolò Pomarancio. Next door, the **Oratorio di San Bartolomeo** has a large fresco of the *Crucifixion* (1342) by Sienese painter Jacopo di Mino del Pellicciaio, surrounded by weeping angels, hence its nickname, *Pianto degli Angeli*.

Panicale and Around

Panicale is famous for its enchanting, and strategic, view over Trasimeno, which in the Middle Ages made it sought by Chiusi and Perugia; even so, in 1037, it became an independent *comune*, one of Italy's first. In the 14th century it produced sweet early Renaissance master Tommaso Fini (or Masolino da Panicale), who painted with Masaccio in Florence; it also produced Giacomo Paneri, a fierce and brutal *condottiere* known as Boldrino di Panicale.

An old walled town built on a natural terrace 'in a spiral', Panicale has pretty squares. The asymmetrical Piazza Umberto I is home to a charming fountain of 1473 and the 14th-century **Palazzo Pretorio**, with peculiar carvings and coats of arms. Nearby is the late-18th-century stuccoed **Teatro Cesare Caporali**, restored in 1991. Further up, the handsome semi-fortified Baroque **Collegiata di San Michele** has an *Adoration of the Shepherds* by Gian Battista Caporali (1519).

Teatro Cesare Caporali
tours of theatre and San Sebastiano by arrangement with tourist office (see p.456)

San Sebastiano
tours of church and Teatro Cesare Caporali by arrangement with tourist office (see p.456)

Panicale's most important treasure is in **San Sebastiano**, just outside the walls. Here Perugino left one of his finest frescoes: a formal, dream-like *Martyrdom of St Sebastian* (1505), a geometrical composition with antique ornamentation, with four superbly costumed and codpieced archers powerfully poised to shoot the saint; in the background is a faithful rendition of Panicale's lovely lake view. The same church contains Perugino's *Madonna*, a detached fresco from the church of Sant'Agostino.

Just west, **Paciano** is a well-preserved medieval village on a spur of Monte Petrarvella, wrapped in 14th-century walls, towers and gates. The **Confraternità del Santissimo Sacramento** has a fresco of the *Crucifixion* (1425) by the first reputed teacher of Perugino, Francesco di Castel della Pieve. Another church, **San Giuseppe**, keeps the communal gonfalon from the workshop of Benedetto Bonfigli (c. 1480). Outside the walls, the **Madonna della Stella** (1574) is a simple Renaissance church with frescoes by Scilla Pecennini.

Confraternità del Santissimo Sacramento
t 075 830120, ask over road at No.12 to visit

Near the lignite-mining village of **Tavernelle**, just off the SS220, the tiny *frazione* of **Mongiovino Vecchio** has a well-preserved castle overlooking a stately domed Renaissance temple, the **Sanctuario di Mongiovino**. Begun in 1513, this is an early but characteristic shrine to Mary. With its fine octagonal cupola, it has been attributed to Michelangelo or Bramante; a more likely candidate is Rocco di Tommaso from Vicenza, who made the finely sculpted doorways. Inside are cinquecento frescoes by Niccolò Pomarancio and the Flemish painter Heinrich van den Broek (aka Arrigo Fiammingo).

Perugino died of the plague in nearby **Fontignano** in 1523; his tomb, and the fresco he was working on when he died, an almost primitive *Madonna and Child*, are in the **Annunziata**, the parish church, plus a photo of another fresco he made for the church, the *Adoration of the Shepherds*, now in the National Gallery in London.

Annunziata
ask at tourist office, t 075 600276, about guided tours

ⓘ **Panicale >>**
Piazza Umberto I,
t 075 837 8017.

ⓘ **Città della Pieve >**
Piazza del Plebiscito 1,
t 0578 299375,
www.prolocopieve.it

Shopping South of Lake Trasimeno

Market Day: Sat, Città della Pieve.

Where to Stay and Eat South of Lake Trasimeno

Città della Pieve ✉ 06062

***__Al Poggio dei Papi__**, Loc. San Litardo, just outside town, **t** 0578 297030, *www.alpoggiodeipapi.com* (€€). A comfy, modern hotel with a restaurant, an Olympic-size pool, a gym and a tennis courts. Rooms are rustically styled. Half and full board are available.

Da Bruno, Via Pietro Vannucci 90–92, **t** 0578 298108 (€). A restaurant serving good, unpretentious food. *Closed Mon.*

Panicale ✉ 06064

Vannucci, Via Icilio Vanni 1, **t** 0578 298063, *www.hotel-vannucci.com* (€€€). A revamped option, now quite luxurious, with a sauna, a Jacuzzi and a pool that opened in the private walled garden in spring 2007.

***__Le Grotte di Boldrino__**, Via V Ceppari 43, **t** 075 837161, *www.grottediboldrino.com* (€€). A sweet little hotel with 19th-century furnishings, home to the best restaurant in town, serving gourmet Italian dishes and specialities based on lake fish (half board available).

Assisi

Less than half an hour east of Perugia and visible for kilometres around, Assisi (population 26,000) sweeps the flanks of Monte Subasio in a broad curve, like a pink ship sailing over the green sea of a valley. This is Umbria's most famous town and one of its loveliest, but there's more to it than St Francis. Occupied from the

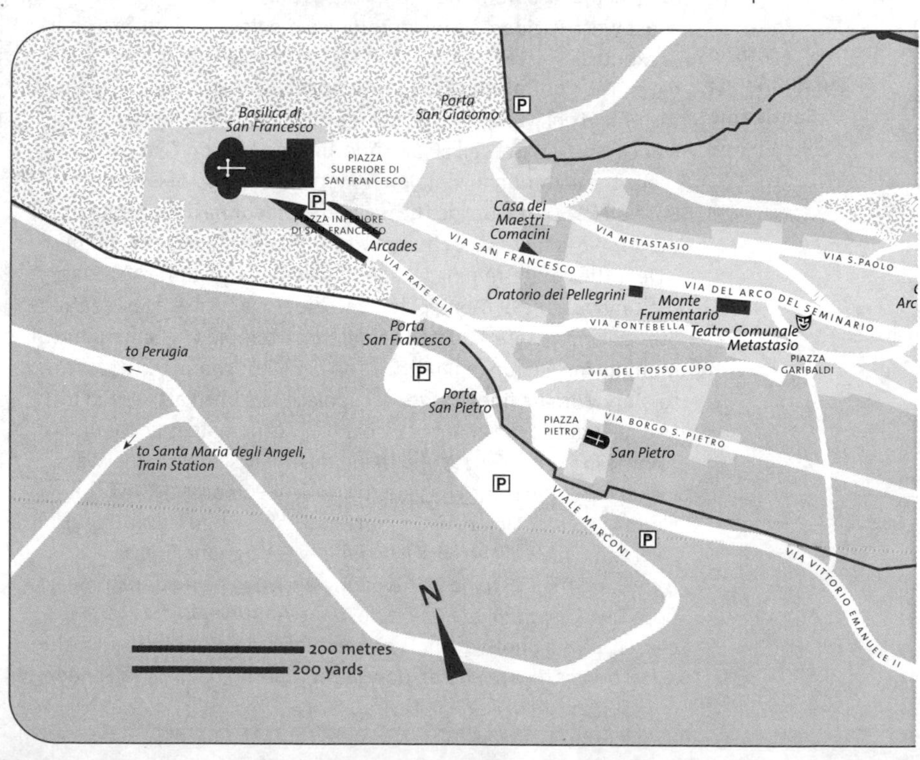

Iron Age, it emerged as an ancient Umbrian town in the 6th century BC, one that maintained its cultural distinction into the 1st century BC. As wealthy Roman *Asisium*, it produced the poet Sextus Propertius and first heard of Christianity from St Rufino in 238.

Part of the Lombard duchy of Spoleto, the city came into prominence again in the Middle Ages as another of Umbria's battling *comuni*, one firmly on the side of the Ghibellines, though in 1198 it rebelled against the duke of Spoleto and defied its nominal lord, Emperor Frederick Barbarossa.But Assisi saved most of its bile for incessant wars with arch-rival Perugia; St Francis in his chivalry-obsessed youth had joined in the fighting. The 13th century, which saw his great religious revival, was also the time of Assisi's greatest power and prosperity, leaving behind a collection of beautiful buildings any Italian city could be proud of, and one of Europe's greatest hordes of 13th- and 14th-century frescoes in the Basilica di San Francesco.

Although Cardinal Albornoz nominally put Assisi under the Church's thumb and rebuilt the Rocca Maggiore to keep it there, the city was controlled by various *signori* until the early 16th century, when the papal pall descended like a curtain at the end of a play. Even pilgrimages declined dramatically after the Council of Trent began the Counter-Reformation. Another pall that fell over Assisi was taste. In 1786, Goethe, on his way to view the Temple of

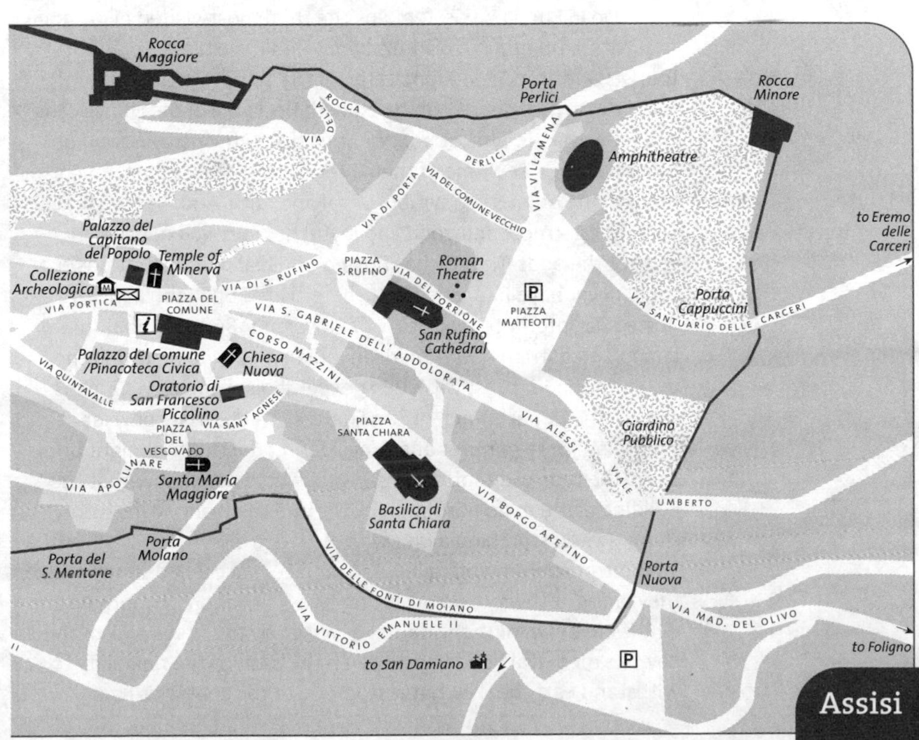

Getting to and around Assisi

Assisi is a 23km/30min **train** ride (**t** 892021, *www.trenitalia.it*) from Perugia or Foligno, where you have to change from Rome (177km/2hrs 30mins) or Terni. The station is on the plain, a block from the suburban Basilica of Santa Maria degli Angeli, and there are regular linking buses every 20mins to Piazza Unità d'Italia.

There are also convenient **buses** direct from Perugia, Bettona and Gualdo Tadino (APM, **t** 075 573 1707, freephone **t** 800 512141, *www.apmperugia.it*); Rome and Florence (SULGA, **t** 075 30799, *www.sulga.it*); 1 a day from Norcia and Cascia (SSIT, *www.spoletina.com*); and several from Bevagna, Montefalco, Foligno and Spello (APM or SSIT). The bus stops are in Piazza Matteotti, Largo Properzio, Piazza Unità d'Italia, S. Maria degli Angeli and Piazza Garibaldi.

There are 3 **car parks** on the fringes of town: in Piazza Unità d'Italia below the Basilica of San Francesco, at the Porta Nuova at the east end of town, and an underground lot at Piazza Matteotti, by the Duomo. A series of little buses, the A and B, do the run between Piazza del Comune and Piazza Matteotti every 20mins or so (tickets sold at newsstands, bars and tobacconists).

There is **car hire** by Hertz, Via V. Veneto 4, **t** 075 500 2439, *www.hertz.it*; **bike hire** by Angelucci Cicli, Via Becchetti 31, **t** 075 804 2550, *www.angeluccicicli.it*.

Minerva, walked past the Basilica of St Francis, dismissing it as 'a Babylonian tower'. Nevertheless, it was Francis who in the long term made all the difference to Assisi (*see* p.42). Pilgrimages began again in the 19th century with the revival of interest both in the saint and the artists who decorated his shrine – Ruskin, who went into ecstatic overdrive at the medieval purity of the frescoes and used to dream he was a Franciscan friar, was the locomotive drawing the first train of English-speakers.

Though now surpassed by the new shrine of the miracle-working Padre Pio in Puglia, Assisi remains the third most-visited pilgrimage site in Italy. On any given summer day, you'll see coachloads of tourists and stands peddling ceramic friars and plastic medieval torture instruments, intermingled with flocks of serene Franciscans and enthusiastic, almost bouncy nuns from Africa or Missouri or Bavaria, having the time of their lives visiting a place that, much more than Rome, is the symbol of a living faith. And it's true that something simple and good and joyful has survived in Assisi in spite of the odds. The city has hosted unusual demonstrations that could never have happened anywhere else – Pope John Paul II's hosted his interfaith World Day of Prayer in 1986, with Tibetan lamas, Zoroastrians and American Indian medicine men, and the 1988 Umbria Jazz Festival, when gospel choirs from New Orleans sang in the upper church of San Francesco – the friars only let them sing for 15 minutes at a time, fearing the rhythm might bring down the roof and Giotto's frescoes, but providence saw that the building came to no harm, and by the end the Franciscans were clapping and stomping along with everyone else.

Where gospel singing failed, earthquakes succeeded. In 1997 they brought the roof down, killing two friars and two journalists who were examining the damage caused by the first shock of the day. The medieval builders had given the basilica the flexibility to withstand earthquakes, but restorers over the centuries had been too lazy to haul out the rubble that they had created, and it accumulated, tons of it, in the essential breathing space between the pricelessly frescoed ceiling vaults and the walls; ultimately, the weight proved too great.

The upper church reopened in 1999 after extensive restoration and structural reinforcements. To ensure that a similar disaster never happens again, the foundations have been reinforced to withstand earth tremors of 12 on the Richter Scale. The two arches that collapsed have been repaired but are blank. Technicians are still painstakingly piecing the frescoes back together; much of what they are working with is just fine rubble, but two are now back in place, the other frescoes in the nave were virtually unscathed and the façade has been beautifully restored.

The *palazzi* on the east side of Piazza del Comune were all badly damaged. Piazza S. Ruffino and around are practically invisible beneath scaffolding and tarpaulin – the Assisi skyline is dotted with cranes. In fact, visitors in the next few years will see the city, and to a lesser extent the whole region, in better condition than ever. As a result of the quake, even buildings that were not damaged have been restored, as it was deemed a good time to do the work and funds were there.

The social effects of the quake have not been addressed with such vigour, however, and many feel that, for the sake of tourism, art has been given precedence over people (*see* pp.47–48).

Basilica of San Francesco

I would give all the churches in Rome for this cave.

Hippolyte Taine (19th-century French critic)

Basilica Patriarcale di San Francesco

t 075 819001, www.sanfrancescoassisi.org; open Easter–Nov daily 6am–6.45pm (upper basilica 8.30–6.45); Nov–Easter daily 6am–6pm (upper basilica 8.30–6); Info office, Piazza San Francesco, t 075 819 0084, open Mon–Sat 9–12 and 2–5.30, Sun 2–5; no shorts/bare shoulders

Though the medieval popes were mistrustful of the spontaneous, personal approach to faith preached by Francis and his followers, they realized that this powerful movement would be better off within the Church than outside. In transforming the Franciscans into a respectable, doctrinally safe arm of Catholicism, they had the invaluable aid of Francis's successor, Brother Elias, Vicar-General of the Order, a worldly, businesslike, organization man, epicurean and friend of Emperor Frederick II. Elias's methods caused the first split within the Franciscans, between those who enjoyed the growing opulence of the new dispensation and those who tried to keep to the poverty preached by their founder.

This monumental building complex, begun the day after Francis's canonization in 1228, when Pope Gregory IX laid the cornerstone, was one of the biggest causes of contention. Nothing could have been further removed from the philosophy and intentions of Francis himself; on the other hand, nothing could have been more successful in perpetuating his memory and his teaching than this great treasure house of art. The popes paid for it with a great sale of special indulgences across Europe, and the basilica belongs to the Vatican (though thanks to a clause in the Lateran Treaty of

Basilica of San Francesco: Lower Church

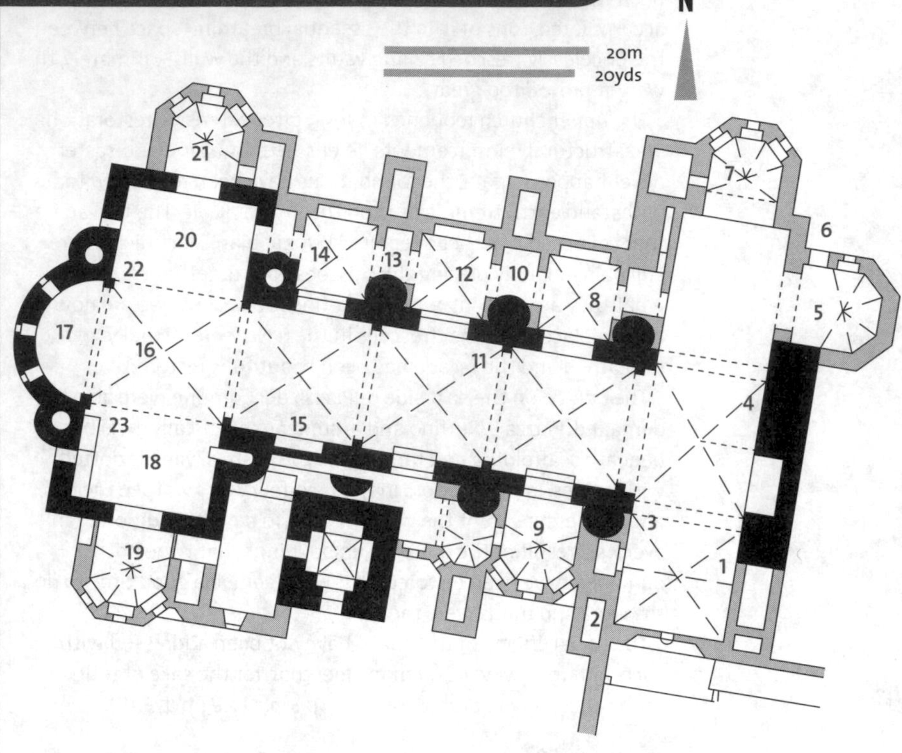

1 Cerchi Tomb with big porphyry vase (13th century)
2 Cappella di San Sebastiano, frescoes by Girolamo Martelli (1646) and the *Madonna della Salute*, the only known work by 15th-century painter Ceccolo di Giovanni
3 *Madonna with Saints* by Ottaviano Nelli (1422)
4 Tomb of John Brienne, Latin Emperor of Constantinople (and friend of St Francis)
5 Cappella del Sacramento, with two 14th-century tombs
6 Cemetery cloister
7 Cappella di Santa Caterina, frescoes by Andrea de' Bartoli of Bologna (1360s)
8 Cappella di Santo Stefano, frescoes by Dono Doni (1574)
9 Cappella di San Martino by Simone Martini (c. 1320)
10 Cappella di San Lorenzo, frescoes by Andrea de' Bartoli
11 Stairs to the crypt
12 Cappella di Sant'Antonio di Padova, frescoes by Cesare Sermi (1610), early-14th-century stained glass
13 Cappella di San Valentino, with a pavement tomb of Friar Ugo of Hartlepool, one of the first English Franciscans (d. 1302)
14 Cappella della Maddalena, frescoes by Giotto and assistants (c. 1309)
15 *Coronation of the Virgin* by Puccio Capanna (1337), over a Cosmati work pulpit
16 The *Quattro Vele* (*Poverty*, *Chastity*, *Obedience* and the *Glory of St Francis*)
17 *The Last Judgement* by Cesare Sermei (1623)
18 Frescoes of the *Passion* by Pietro Lorenzetti (*c.* 1320)
19 Cappella di San Giovanni Battista, triptych by Lorenzetti (*c.* 1320-30)
20 Frescoes by Cimabue, Giotto, Martini, Lorenzetti
21 Cappella di San Nicola, frescoes by Giotto and assistants
22 Steps to the chapterhouse
23 Stairs to terrace and treasury

1929, renewed in 1989, the state is responsible for the upkeep – including all earthquake repairs). There's a story that Brother Elias supplied the design – the lower basilica does have an amateurish, clumsy form. The beautiful campanile dates from 1239; the completed basilica was consecrated by Innocent IV in 1253. Behind it, visible for kilometres around, on huge buttressed vaults, is the enormous convent built by Sixtus IV in the 15th century. Now a missionary college, it, too, was damaged by the quake, though part of it is being used as a fresco hospital.

The Lower Church

With its low dark vaults, this seems at first to be a simple crypt, though once your eyes adjust to the light, you see they are covered with magnificent 13th- and 14th-century frescoes (bring plenty of coins and a torch to illuminate them). The first chapel left of the frescoed nave contains magnificent frescoes, stained glass and other decorations on the *Life of St Martin* by Simone Martini, painted around 1322; the third chapel on the right contains frescoes on the *Life of Mary Magdalene*, attributed to Giotto (1314). Italians are convinced that the frescoes in the lower and upper churches are the climax of Giotto's early career; most foreign scholars believe Giotto never painted them. Whatever the case, Martini's 'International Gothic-style' poses are a serious artistic challenge to the great precursor of the Renaissance. This master of line and colour creates a wonderful narrative of St Martin's life; the Gaulish soldier and wastrel who ended up as a bishop and gave half his cloak to a beggar seems a perfect foreshadowing of St Francis.

Giotto is also credited with the four beautiful allegorical frescoes over the high altar, *Poverty*, *Chastity*, *Obedience* and the *Glory of St Francis*. Note the striking *Marriage of St Francis with Lady Poverty*. In the left transept are frescoes by Pietro Lorenzetti of Siena, among the best in the basilica, especially the lovely *Madonna della Tramontana* ('of the sunset') *with St Francis and St John*, a *Crucifixion* (badly damaged) and a *Descent from the Cross*. In the right transept is a work considered Cimabue's masterpiece, the *Madonna and Saints*, with a portrait of St Francis (1280), believed to be an accurate likeness; the serious-looking female saint nearby, by Simone Martini, is believed to be St Clare.

In the **crypt** lie the bones of St Francis and four of his closest followers, which were discovered in 1818; Brother Elias, worried that the Perugians would steal the saint's body, hid it behind tonnes of stone. His fears were not unfounded; when Francis was coming back from La Verna to die, the Perugians were waiting to kidnap him along the road; Brother Elias had the foresight to direct Francis on a longer route.

Museo-Tesoro della Basilica
open April–Oct Mon–Sat 9.30–5.30; Nov–Mar by appt; adm

From the transepts, stairs lead up to a terrace and the **Museo-Tesoro della Basilica**, containing anything not pillaged or pinched from the treasury through the centuries – a beautiful Venetian cross, a French ivory *Madonna* from the 13th century, a Flemish tapestry with St Francis, and more. In 1995 the contents of the former 'secret sacristy' were put on display in another room: Pope Honorius III's *Bull approving the Order's Rule* (1223), the saint's tunic, cowl, girdle and sandals, an ivory horn given to Francis by the Sultan of Egypt, which he blew to assemble his followers, the 'Laud to the Creator' and 'Benediction of Brother Leone' on parchment, in the saint's hand, and a chalice and paten used by Francis and his followers.

The Upper Church

The Upper Church on its emerald lawn, airy and vibrant, contains two major series of medieval frescoes; the quake left them cracked and broken in places but more or less intact, and work continues on the fragmented parts. The lower set of 28 panels on the *Life of St Francis* is by Giotto or his school; the upper, with *Old and New Testament scenes*, is usually attributed to Cimabue's followers and Roman painters Pietro Cavallini and Jacopo Torriti. Giotto amazed his contemporaries with his ability to illustrate physical and spiritual essentials with simplicity and drama. The scenes begin with *St Francis Honoured by the Simple Man*, who lays down his cloak and foretells the saint's destiny (note Assisi's Temple of Minerva in the background); Francis returns his clothes to his father, who in his anger has to be restrained; Pope Innocent III has a dream of Francis supporting the falling Church; the demons are expelled from Arezzo by Brother Sylvester; Francis meets the Sultan of Egypt; he creates the first Christmas crib, or *presepio*, at Greccio; he preaches to the birds, then to Pope Honorius III; he appears in two places at once and receives the stigmata from a six-winged cherub; finally, he dies, bewailed by the Poor Clares, and is canonized.

The transepts were painted with frescoes by Giotto's master, Cimabue, though the works had oxidized into negatives of their former selves even before the quake; what can be salvaged will, and some kind of Cimabue clones will refill the rebuilt transepts, good enough to give most of us non-experts a feel for what was lost, perhaps even of the *Crucifixion*, a faded masterpiece of 1277 that still radiated some of its original drama and feeling.

To the Piazza del Comune

San Pietro
t 075 812311; open summer daily 8–12 and 3–5; winter daily 8–12 and 2–6

Entering Assisi along the main road from the car park, you may have noticed the Romanesque-Gothic façade of **San Pietro**, with three rose windows, just inside the gate of the same name. This Benedictine church was built in the 1200s, although Assisi's chroniclers date the original building to Palaeochristian times.

Museo degli Indios dell'Amazzonia
t 075 812280; open Easter–14 Jan daily 10–12 and 3–6; donations welcome

From the tidy lawn of the Upper Church, Via San Francesco, the main street, leads into the *centro storico*, passing fine medieval houses and the rather unexpected **Museo degli Indios dell'Amazzonia**, with ethnographic items collected by Capuchin missionaries in the Amazon. In the same building, Amazonian fish and plants are on show as the **Mostra Etnologica**.

Pinacoteca
t 075 812033; open 16 Mar–6 July and Sept–15 Oct daily 10–1 and 2.30–6; 7 July–Aug daily 10–1 and 2.30–7; 16 Oct–15 Mar daily 10–1 and 2–5; joint adm with Museo e Foro Romano (see below)

Palazzo Vallemani, on the left, houses the **Pinacoteca**, with detached frescoes, including a scene of 13th-century knights from the Palazzo del Capitano del Popolo that probably caught the fancy of the young Francis, and others by Tiberio d'Assisi; there's also a rather sleepy collection of Umbrian paintings, including a *Madonna della Misericordia* by L'Alunno.

Oratorio dei Pellegrini
t 075 812267; open Mon–Sat 9–12 and 4–6

At No.11, the **Oratorio dei Pellegrini** is a 15th-century gem, all that survives from a pilgrims' hospice, frescoed on the façade and altar wall by Matteo da Gualdo. The frescoes on the walls are by another Umbrian, Pierantonio Mezzastris (1477), with scenes of miracles on the road to Compostela and the life of St Anthony Abbot (with the friendly camels). The Oratorio is currently home to works from the **Museo Comunale di Nocera Umbra**, closed by the earthquake.

At No.3, the portico belonged to **Monte Frumentario**, built in the 13th century as a hospital, one of Italy's first, later converted into a granary. Next to it, a 16th-century **fountain** still warns that the penalty for washing clothes here is one *scudo* and confiscation of laundry. Via San Francesco then passes through an arch from the city's Roman walls and continues as the Via del Arco del Seminario, named for the former missionary college on the left. Further up, the 19th-century **Teatro Comunale Metastasio** is now a cinema.

Museo e Foro Romano
Via Portica 1, t 075 813053; open daily 10–1 and 2.30–7; joint adm with Pinacoteca (see above)

Near here is the **Museo e Foro Romano**, in the crypt of the now-vanished church of San Niccolò (1097); it has a small collection of urns, statues and bits of Roman frescoes. The collection was founded in 1793 by the local Accademia Properziano del Subasio and hasn't changed much. A passage leads from the museum into the ancient **Roman forum** (or the sacred area of *Asisium*), excavated in the 19th century, under the modern Piazza del Comune. Here you can see bases of statues, a platform that may have been an altar, an inscription to the Dioscuri, steps to the temple of Minerva and the remains of a fountain.

Piazza del Comune

Tempio di Minerva
t 075 812268; open daily 7–7

Long Piazza del Comune, medieval centre of Assisi, is embellished with 13th-century buildings of the old *comune*: the lofty **Torre del Popolo** and the **Palazzo del Capitano del Popolo**, the **Palazzo del Podestà** (now the Palazzo del Comune) and a genuine Roman **temple of Minerva** from around the 1st century BC, with Corinthian columns and travertine steps. Goethe came to Assisi to see this and nothing else. It has the best-surviving Roman temple front on the Italian peninsula, as good as any ruin in Rome for helping your imagination conjure up the classical world. But only the pronaos and façade remain; inside is some eccentric Baroque belonging to the church of Santa Maria della Minerva.

Chiesa Nuova
t 075 812339; open summer daily 6.30–12 and 2.30–5; winter daily 6.30–12 and 2.30–6

Left of the palazzo, the **Chiesa Nuova** was constructed in 1615 by Philip III of Spain on property owned by St Francis's father. In an adjacent alley, the **Oratorio di San Francesco Piccolino** is believed to mark the saint's birthplace.

Upper Assisi: the Cathedral, the Castle and Around

Cattedrale di San Rufino
t 075 812283; open Aug daily 7–6, rest of year daily 7–1 and 2.30–6

Most visitors labour under the impression that the Basilica of St Francis is Assisi's cathedral: the real **Cattedrale di San Rufino** is up Via di San Rufino from Piazza del Comune. Set over a piazza (another candidate for the Roman forum), it has a huge campanile and the finest Romanesque façade in Umbria, designed by Giovanni da Gubbio in 1140 and adorned with fine rose windows and the robust medieval carvings of animals and saints that Goethe so disdained. In the central lunette, God the Father sits enthroned in the circle with San Rufino on the right and Mary, nursing the infant Christ, on the left. The three monumental figures in the rectangular niche above appear to hold up the church. Inside is the porphyry font where Saint Francis and Saint Clare were baptized, as well as Emperor Frederick II, born nearby in Jesi, in the Marches. The holy water must have had a special essence in it. Both Francis and Frederick were profoundly influenced by the East and were among the first poets to write in vernacular Italian rather than Latin. The interior was restored in the 16th century, when the beautiful carved wooden choir was added.

Museo Capitolare
t 075 812712; open (inc crypt) Mar–Oct daily 10–1 and 3–6; adm

Off the right nave is the small **Museo Capitolare**, with Romanesque capitals, codices, frescoes, paintings by Matteo da Gualdo and a beautiful triptych by L'Alunno (1470). You can explore the ancient **crypt**, dating from an earlier, 11th-century church, with a few frescoes and a 3rd-century Roman sarcophagus decorated with reliefs of the myth of Endymion, where St Rufino was buried. Don't miss the barrel-vaulted Roman cistern under the campanile, with an inscription in the Umbrian dialect. The Umbrii worshipped springs, and this is believed to have been a sacred fountain.

Rocca Maggiore
t 075 815292; open Aug daily 9–sunset; rest of year daily 10–sunset; adm

From the cathedral, it's a bracing walk up to the **Rocca Maggiore**, the well-preserved castle, built in 1174 and used by Conrad von Luetzen (who cared for the orphan Emperor Frederick II). Destroyed and rebuilt on several occasions, once by Cardinal Albornoz, it has great views of Assisi, the Valle Umbra, the Rocciciola (an inaccessible fortress built by Albornoz) and the surrounding countryside.

East of the cathedral, you can visit more of Roman *Asisium* – the **theatre** in Via del Torrione, by the cathedral, and the remains of the **amphitheatre**, off Piazza Matteotti and Via Villamena. The

Porta Perlici near the amphitheatre dates from 1199 and there are some well-preserved 13th-century houses on the Via del Comune Vecchio. The **Giardino Pubblico**, with its pavilions and fishponds, is a fine place to have a picnic. *Asisium* had up-to-date plumbing; you might be able to pick out the Roman drain between the amphitheatre and the Giardino Pubblico, built to carry off water after the amphitheatre was flooded for mock sea-battles.

Basilica di Santa Chiara

Basilica di Santa Chiara
southeast of Piazza del Comune by way of Corso Mazzini, t 075 812282; open daily 7–12 and 2–6.45

Saint Clare's basilica, built in 1265 , is a pink-and-white striped beauty with a lovely rose window, supported by huge flying buttresses added a century later that not only keep it from falling over but create a memorable architectural space below. It stands on the site of the old church of San Giorgio, where Francis attended school and where his body lay for two years awaiting completion of his own basilica. The shadowy **interior** has frescoes in the transepts by followers of Giotto, damaged and hard to see; by the altar are scenes from Clare's life by the late 13th-century Maestro di Santa Chiara. On the right, the **Oratorio del Crocifisso** contains the famous *Crucifix of San Damiano* (*see* p.466), a 13th-century triptych by Rinaldo di Ranuccio and reliquaries of St Clare, with some of her garments and golden curls. The adjacent **Cappella del Sacramento** has fine Sienese frescoes; these two chapels were part of San Giorgio. Clare's body, rediscovered in 1850 under the high altar, shrivelled and darkened with age, lies like a never-kissed Snow White in a crystal coffin, down in the neogothic crypt.

Piazza Vescovado and Around

Santa Maria Maggiore
t 075 813085; open Easter–Nov daily 8–7; Nov–Easter daily 8–6

From Santa Chiara, Via Sant'Agnese leads down to Piazza Vescovado and the **church of Santa Maria Maggiore** (1163), with a pink-and-white checked façade. This was Assisi's first cathedral, built on the site of the Roman temple of Apollo, traces of which are

The Patron Saint of TV

Born in 1194, Chiara Offreduccio was 17 when she ran away from her wealthy, noble family to become a disciple of St Francis at the Porziuncola. By 1215, she was abbess of a Franciscan Second Order, the Poor Clares or Clarisse, based on the primitive rule of St Francis. Whatever the later church mythology, rumours were never lacking that there was more to her relationship with Francis than practical piety. Gentle and humble, she once had a vision of a Christmas service in the Basilica of St Francis while at San Damiano, more than 1km away – a feat that led Pope Pius XII in 1958 to declare her the patron saint of television.

Like Francis, Clare lived on alms and is reputed to have twice saved Assisi from the army of Frederick II. Her rule of poverty was only confirmed by Pope Innocent IV while she lay on her deathbed, two days before she died in 1253. She was canonized two years later but, as in the case of Francis, her desire for her followers to live in absolute poverty was denied when Pope Urban IV approved a new Rule for her Order (1264). Still, it did offer something of an alternative for women in an age where many were forced into arranged marriages or convents if there wasn't enough dowry to go around; two Umbrian women who followed in Clare's footsteps were the great 13th-century mystics, the Blessed Angela of Foligno and St Clare of Montefalco.

House of Sextus Propertius
visitors need permission from Soprintendenza Archeologica in Perugia, **t** *075 57411*

visible in the 9th-century crypt. Nearby, the reputed **house of Sextus Propertius**, Roman poet of love (46 BC–AD 14), was found, with wall paintings. Between here and Piazza Unità d'Italia, Via Fontebella has wrought-iron dragons and a pretty fountain.

Around Assisi

San Damiano

San Damiano
t *075 812273; sanctuary open summer daily 10–12 and 2–6 (vespers 7pm); winter daily 10–12 and 2–4.30 (vespers 5pm)*

Many of the key events of Francis's life took place in the countryside around Assisi. San Damiano is a short drive or a pleasant 2km walk from Santa Chiara down Via Borgo Aretino, through the Porta Nuova. It was in this simple, asymmetrical Benedictine priory (1030) surrounded by olives and cypresses that the Crucifix bowed and spoke to Francis in 1205, commanding him to 'rebuild my church'. Francis took the injunction literally and sold his father's horse and cloth to raise the money – the priest at San Damiano refused to take it, so Francis threw it out of the window and returned to restore the church with his own hands. He brought Clare to San Damiano in 1212, when restoration was complete, and here she and her followers passed their frugal, contemplative lives (forbidden to beg, they nearly starved). Sitting in the garden on one of his visits, Francis composed his superb *Cantico della creature*, the 'Canticle of All Things Created', in 1224.

The church is entered through the Cappella di San Girolamo, with a fine fresco by Tiberio d'Assisi of the *Madonna and Child, with SS. Francis, Clare, Bernardino and Jerome* (1517); the next chapel has a large wooden crucifix of 1637 by Fra Innocenzo da Palermo. Frescoes in the church record the events that happened here (one shows the saint's father chasing him with a stick when he found out he had sold his property). The crucifix over the altar is a copy of the original, now in Santa Chiara. In the convent are a fresco of the *Crucifixion* by Mezzastris, the room where St Clare died in 1253, and the tiny cloister with frescoes by Eusebio da San Giorgio (1507) of the *Annunciation* and *St Francis Receiving the Stigmata*.

In 1870, when the Papal States were united to the new Kingdom of Italy, Lord Ripon, a Catholic convert, bought San Damiano to stop it becoming state property and let it to the friars on the condition they did nothing to restore it. Lord Lothian, who inherited it, returned it to the Franciscans in 1983.

The Eremo delle Carceri and Monte Subasio

Eremo delle Carceri
t *075 812301; open daily 8–sunset; guided tours 9, 11.30, 2.30 and 5.30*

Another Franciscan shrine more true to the spirit of the saint than the great art-filled basilicas is the peaceful **Eremo delle Carceri**, in a beautiful setting on the edge of a ravine, deep in the woods along the road up Monte Subasio, a spectacular walk or drive 4km east of Assisi (leave via the Porta dei Cappuccini). This 'Hermitage of the Prison' was Francis's retreat, where he and his followers strove to live like the first Umbrian saints, walking through the woods and meditating. In 1426 Bernardino of Siena founded the small convent here where a handful of friars still live a traditional Franciscan existence on the alms they receive.

By the little triangular courtyard are two small chapels, the **Cappella di San Bernardino**, with tiny stained-glass windows, and the **Cappella di Santa Maria delle Carceri**, with a fresco of the *Madonna and Child and St Francis* by Tiberio d'Assisi. A steep stair leads down to the **Grotto di San Francesco**, with one of the saint's beds hollowed from the rock, and the very old ilex down in the ravine, where the birds are said to have flocked to hear him preach, as a faded fresco on the cave recounts.

From the Eremo delle Carceri it's 7.5km up the Collepino road to the distinctive bald summit of **Monte Subasio** (1,289m), centre of a regional park, with superb views over the high Apennines to the east and a network of walking paths. In summer you can continue a further spectacular 10km over the mountains on an unpaved road to the medieval village of **Collepino**, above Spello (*see* p.493).

Santa Maria degli Angeli

The real centre of early Franciscanism was the oratory called the Porziuncola ('the little portion'), where angels were wont to appear, down on the plain near the train station. Francis, in return for the use of the oratory, owed a yearly basket of carp from the Tescio river to the Benedictines, which is still faithfully paid by the Franciscans. In 1569, a monumental basilica, **Santa Maria degli Angeli**, by Galeazzo Alessi, was begun to shelter the Porziuncola. Only completed in 1684, it is an excellent piece of nostalgic Baroque, though it was mostly reconstructed after an 1832 earthquake; the grandiose façade was only added in 1927.

Basilica Patriarcale di Santa Maria degli Angeli
t 075 80511; open summer daily 6.15am–8pm; winter Mon–Fri 6.15–1.30 and 2–7.45, Sat and Sun 6.15am–7.45pm

Within the austere interior, the Porziuncola stands out, with frescoes that were touched up in the 19th century. The rugged stone of the original chapel can be seen inside (it may be as old as the 6th century), plus darkened 1393 frescoes of St Francis's life by Ilario da Viterbo, his only known work. Remains of the original Franciscan monastery have been partly excavated under the high altar; here St Clare took her vows of poverty as the spiritual daughter of Francis. St Francis died 'naked on the bare earth' in the convent's infirmary, now the **Cappella del Transito**, with unusual frescoes by Umbrian painter Lo Spagna, along with a statue of St Francis by Andrea della Robbia.

The garden contains the roses Francis is said to have thrown himself upon while wrestling with severe temptation, staining their leaves red with blood, only to find that they lost their thorns

Museo della Porziuncola
t 075 805 1430; open summer Thurs–Tues 9–12 and 3.30–6.30; winter Thurs–Tues 9–12.30 and 3–6.30

Museo Etnografico Universale
Via de Gasperi; open Mon–Fri 9–12 and 3–6, Sat 9–12

on contact with his body. Still thornless, they bloom every May. Francis's cell has been covered with the frescoed Cappella del Roseto; there's also an old pharmacy and a **museum** containing a portrait of St Francis by an unknown 13th-century master, another attributed to Cimabue, and a *Crucifix* (1236) by Giunta Pisano; there's also a **Museo Etnografico Universale**, with items relating to Franciscan missionary work.

West of Assisi

Bastia Umbria and Around

A prosperous industrial centre, **Bastia Umbria** began as an island, the *Insula Romana*, before the valley was drained. Once surrounded by walls, it was a hot potato contested by Perugia and Assisi. Its unattractive environs fend off most visitors, but the *centro storico* has a pretty 14th-century church with a triptych by L'Alunno and frescoes by Tiberio d'Assisi and students of Bartolomeo Caporali.

North of Bastia and the village of **Petrignano** (famous for its animated *presepio* at Christmas), the valley of the Chiascio is guarded by the splendidly sited **Rocca Sant'Angelo**; nearby, the **Convento di Santa Maria della Rocchicciola** (ring bell next to church for sister to let you in) has frescoes by Bartolomeo Caporali and Lo Spagna, and a crucifix by Matteo da Gualdo. .

Bettona

Southwest of Assisi, Bettona is a compact, nearly elliptical hilltown wrapped in olive groves. It was big enough to have a long history as Vettona, an Etruscan city – it is the only Umbrian town east of the Tiber with Etruscan origins – and later as a Roman *municipium*. At the north end of the walls, the huge golden stones of the original Etruscan fortifications (4th century BC) are visible, and 1km west is thee simple, barrel-vaulted **Ipogeo Etrusco** (key held at Vigili Urbani at Municipio in Piazza Cavour) from the 2nd century BC, with funerary urns *in situ*.

Pinacoteca Comunale
t 075 987306; open Mar–May, Sept and Oct daily 10.30–1 and 2–6; June and July daily 10.30–1 and 3–7; Aug daily 10.30–1 and 3–7; Nov–Feb Tues–Sun 10.30–1 and 2.30–5; adm

Up in Bettona itself, central Piazza Cavour has a fountain and the 14th-century **Palazzo del Podestà**. Within this and an adjoining palazzo is the **Pinacoteca Comunale** with two minor paintings by Perugino, detached frescoes by Fiorenzo di Lorenzo and Tiberio d'Assisi, Dono Doni (*Adoration of the Shepherds* with a predella on the *Life of San Crispolto*, first bishop of Bettona), ceramics from Deruta and wooden chests. Ask here to visit the **Oratorio di Sant'Andrea** in the same piazza, with a fresco of the *Passion* by Giotto's school; opposite, **Santa Maria Maggiore** has a gonfalon by Perugino and works by L'Alunno, currently in the museum while the church is being restored. For accommodation here, *see* p.470.

ⓘ **Assisi >**
Piazza del Comune 12, t 075 812534 (closed Sun); Largo Properzio, t 075 816766. (closed Wed and Nov–Easter), www. umbria2000.it

Tourist Information in Assisi

Post office: Largo Properzio 4, **t** 075 813114, *www.poste.it*.

Churches: open daily 7–12 and 2–sunset unless otherwise stated. All churches and major sights are open but the slow restoration of frescoes continues and many buildings are still clad in scaffolding.

Festivals in Assisi

Calendimaggio, *www.calendimaggiodiassisi.it*, 1st Thurs–Sat in May. Assisi's medieval May Day celebrations, commemorating Francis's troubadour past with song, dance, torchlight parades, lovely costumes and contests between lower and upper Assisi.

Easter week. Religious celebrations, including a mystery play on the Deposition from the Cross (Holy Thursday), and processions through town (Good Friday and Easter Sunday).

Antiques fair, *www.assisiantiquariato.it*, April and May.

Festa del Perdono (Feast of Forgiveness), Porziuncola, 1–2 Aug. Indulgences given out in commemoration of St Francis, who had a vision of Christ asking him what would be most helpful for the soul, and suggested offering forgiveness to anyone who crossed the threshold of the chapel.

St Francis's Day, 3–4 Oct. Religious ceremonies, singing and dancing.

Marcia della Pace, 2nd Sun Oct. A peace walk begun in 1963, from Perugia to Assisi.

Shopping in Assisi

Assisi overflows with little ceramic friars, crossbows, local ceramics and glass, and textiles, and there are serious art galleries too.

Enoteca Hispellum, Corso Cavour 35, **t** 0742 651766. A place to sample and buy a vast selection of local cheeses, wines, biscuits, honeys, jams, sauces and spreads.

Market Day

Saturday, Piazza Matteotti.

Where to Stay in and around Assisi

Assisi ✉ 06081

Book ahead for Calendimaggio (*see* above), Easter, July and August. There's a hotel booking service at Via Cristofani, **t** 075 816566, *caa@krenet.it* (*closed Sat and Sun*). Or the tourist office has a long list of rooms in religious or private houses.

Luxury (€€€€€)

Fontebella, Via Fontebella 25, **t** 075 *812883,wwwfontebella.com*. A 17th-century *palazzo* with quite elegant rooms with modern bathrooms (breakfast included), a restaurant, a garden and a garage.

Very Expensive (€€€€)

★ **Le Silve >>**

****__Le Silve__, Armenzano, 10km from centre on Monte Subasio , **t** 075 801 9000, *www.lesilve.it*. A 10th-century former hostel combining antique furnishings with all modern comforts, including a pool and sauna. There's a restaurant serving home-made Umbrian fare; half and full board are available. *Closed Dec–Feb*.

****__Subasio__, Via Frate Elia 2, **t** 075 812206, *www.hotelsubasio.com*. A traditional, formal hotel linked to the Basilica of St Francis by a portico, counting among its past guests the King of Belgium and Charlie Chaplin. Many of the recently renovated rooms have views over the countryside from vine-shaded terraces, and there's a private garage and an attractive medieval-vaulted restaurant. Breakfast is included in the rates.

Very Expensive–Expensive (€€€€–€€€)

***__Dei Priori__, Corso Mazzini 15, **t** 075 812237, *www.assisi-hotel.com*. A gracious, well-restored 18th-century *palazzo* off the main piazza, with a restaurant. Breakfast is included, half and full board are available.

Expensive (€€€)

***__Giotto__, Via Fontebella 41, **t** 075 812209, *www.hotelgiottoassisi.it*. Very pleasant, modern rooms near the basilica, a restaurant, a splendid garden, and a garage. Breakfast is included, and full board available.

*****Il Palazzo**, Via San Francesco 8, **t** 075 816841, *www.hotelilpalazzo.it*. A 13th-century building in the centre, with simple rooms with antiques.

*****Umbra**, Via degli Archi 6, **t** 075 812240, *www.hotelumbra.it*. A charming family-run inn near Piazza del Comune, with a walled garden. Rooms can be small, but many have balconies. The restaurant serves creative cuisine grounded in Umbrian tradition. *Restaurant closed Sun.*

Moderate (€€)

****Country House**, Via di Valecchie 41, 1km from west gate of Assisi, **t** 075 816363, *www.countryhousetreesse.com*. Lovely rooms with antiques, most ensuite. Evening meals can be prepared for guests, and there's a splendid pool, a solarium and garden terraces, plus parking.

****Ideale per Turisti**, Piazza Matteotti 1, **t** 075 813570, *www.hotelideale.it*. A decent little hotel close to the amphitheatre, with a garden in which to enjoy good breakfasts in summer.

****Pallotta**, Via S. Rufino 4, **t** 075 812307, *www.pallottaassisi.it*. Basic rooms in a medieval palace, plus a trattoria. Parking can be difficult.

****San Giacomo**, Via S. Giacomo 6, **t** 075 816778, *www.hotelsangiacomoassisi.it*. A reliable, welcoming option in the historic centre, with a restaurant.

****Sole**, Corso Mazzini 35, **t** 075 812373, *www.assisihotelsole.com*. A large hotel with some ensuite rooms and a good restaurant. *Closed Wed.*

Inexpensive (€)

****Cenacolo Francescano**, Via Piazza d'Italia 70, **t** 075 804 1083, *www.hotelcenacolo.com*. A large pilgrimage houses with basic ensuite rooms near the train station. It has a private chapel, parking and a restaurant.

***Anfiteatro Romano**, Via Anfiteatro Romano 4, **t** 075 813025, A good, quiet little place near Piazza Matteotti, with a restaurant. One room is ensuite.

Brigolante Guest Apartments, Costa di Trex 31, 6km from centre at foot of Mt Subasio, **t** 075 802250, *www.brigolante.com*. A working farm with apartments sleeping 2–4, with washing machines. Guests get a basket of local produce and can buy fresh meat, veg, eggs and cheese. Lets are by the week.

Il Morino, Via Spoleto 8, Bastia Umbria, 2km west of town, **t** 075 801 0839, *www.ilmorino.com*. A guesthouse on a working farm. Two of the basic rooms have balconies with views. Bikes are loaned and reasonably priced dinners served (half/full board available).

St Anthony's Guest House, Via G. Alessi 10, **t** 075 812542. One of the most pleasant religious houses, run by American sisters. Breakfast is included, good cheap lunches are available. Note the 11pm curfew. *Closed Nov–Feb.*

San Gregorio ✉ 06086

*****Castel San Gregorio**, Via S. Gregorio 16, 12km northwest of Assisi, **t** 075 803 8009 (€€). Rooms in a restored 13th-century castle with a garden. Half and full board are available.

Bettona ✉ 06084

Relais La Corte Di Bettona, Via Caterina 2, **t** 075 987114, *www.relaisbettona.com* (€€€). Unexpected contemporary style in sleepy Bettona (*see* p.468), in a former medieval hospital for orphans. The good restaurant (€€) serves Umbrian dishes with the odd twist; half board is available

Eating Out in and around Assisi

Assisi ✉ 06081

Expensive (€€€)

San Francesco, Via S. Francesco 52, **t** 075 812329. Fine cuisine and views from a veranda overlooking the basilica; try *strangozzi* with truffles. *Closed Wed and 1–15 July.*

Moderate (€€)

Il Medio Evo, Via Arco dei Priori 4, **t** 075 813 068. Local and global fare in a medieval setting. Try guinea fowl with grapes. *Closed Wed, Jan and 3wks July.*

Inexpensive (€)

La Bottega della Pasticceria, Via Portica 9. Strudels, chocolate and nut breads

La Stalla, Via Eremo delle Carceri 8, Fontemaggio, **t** 075 812317. A lovely country trattoria on the way to the Eremo delle Carceri (*see* p.466). The good hearty fare at very reasonable prices includes polenta with sausages. *Closed Mon exc Easter and summer.*

Northern Umbria

Route SS3bis and Umbria's private railway, the FCU, follow the upper Tiber valley into a green landscape of tobacco farms, olive groves and rolling hills, enclosed by large stretches of forest and mountains – some of the most underpopulated countryside in Italy. To the west near Tuscany, is arty Città di Castello; to the east stern, grey Gubbio is a drop of pure Umbrian essence up in the rugged mountains. In-between are frescoes by Signorelli at Morra, a garden maze at Castello Bufalini in San Giustino, and lovely hilltowns such as Monte Santa Maria Tiberina, Citerna and Montone. The mountains along the border of the Marches, meanwhile, form one of Umbria's beautiful natural parks.

17

Don't miss

1. **Expressive junk-based art** — Collezione Burri, Città di Castello p.475
2. **Renaissance moated gardens** — Castello Bufalini, San Giustino p.479
3. **A race between wax saints** — Gubbio p.483
4. **Awesome views** — Monte Ingino p.485
5. **Meadows and beech forests** — Parco Naturale del Monte Cucco p.486

See map overleaf

Northern Umbria

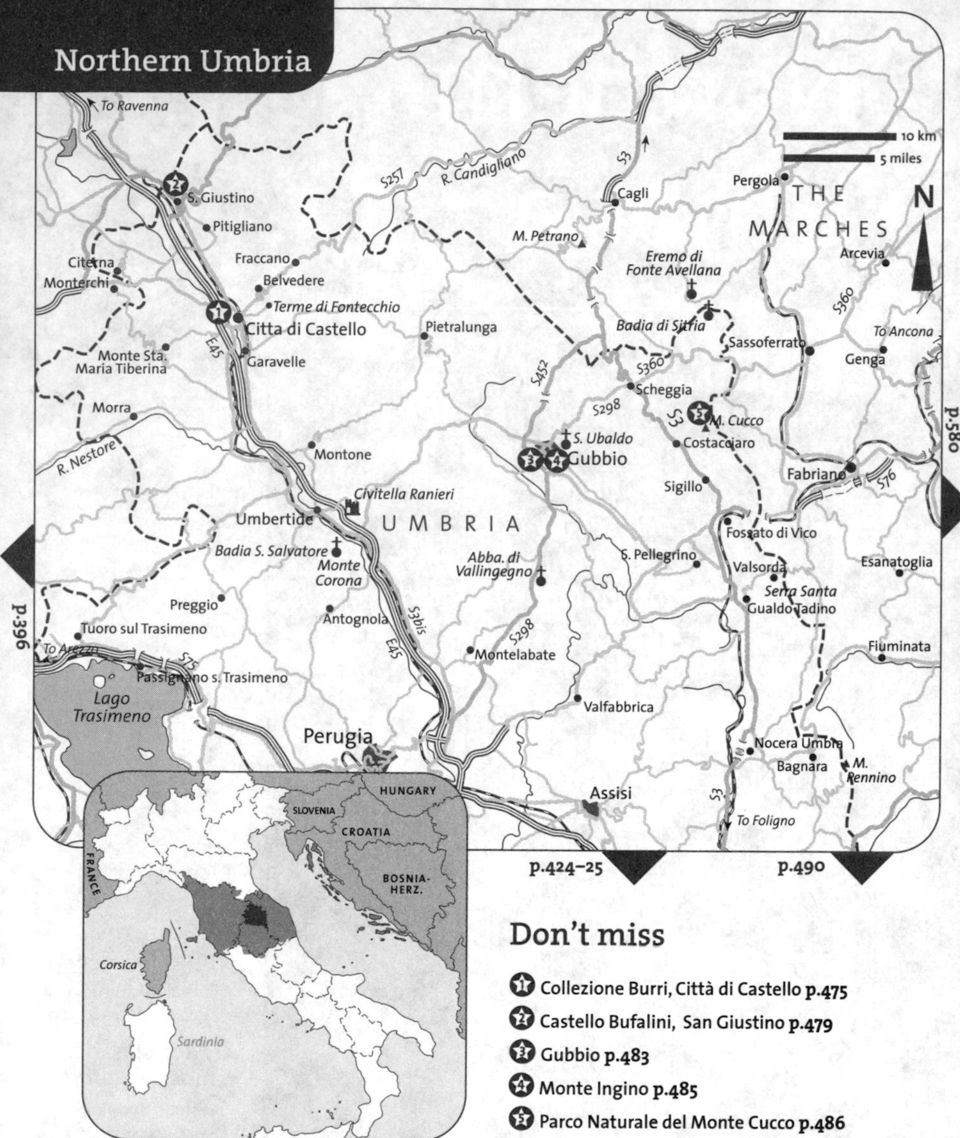

p.396
p.580
p.424–25
p.490

Don't miss

1. **Collezione Burri, Città di Castello p.475**
2. **Castello Bufalini, San Giustino p.479**
3. **Gubbio p.483**
4. **Monte Ingino p.485**
5. **Parco Naturale del Monte Cucco p.486**

Umbertide and Around

Approaching Umbertide from Perugia, the most important town between the SS3bis and the road to Gubbio Is **Montelabate**, where large **Santa Maria** (1325) has an 11th-century crypt and good frescoes, a *Madonna and Saints* by Bartolomeo Caporali and a *Crucifixion* by Fiorenzo di Lorenzo. **Civitella Benazzone** has the restored medieval **Abbazia Celestina** and a parish church with paintings by Benedetto Bonfigli and Domenico Alfani.

Midway between Perugia and Città di Castello, **Umbertide** (population 14,000) on the Tiber was an Etruscan and Umbrian trading post. Known as *Pitulum* by the Romans, then Fratta until 1863, it changed its name in its enthusiasm for the new Kingdom of Italy, in honour of Umberto, son of Vittorio Emanuele II. It's sprawling and industrial, with a small *centro storico* that survived allied bombs. The main landmark, the **Rocca**, with fat crenellated towers, was built by the Perugians in the 1300s and houses the **Centro per L'Arte Contemporanea**, with temporary exhibitions. There are three churches in Piazza San Francesco, outside the original walls. **Santa Croce** is a small museum with an excellent *Deposition* (1515) by Luca Signorelli and Niccolò Pomarancio's *Madonna and Child and Angels* (1577). Next door, **San Francesco** has good, if damaged 17th-century frescoes.

Centro per L'Arte Contemporanea
open summer Tues–Sun 10.30–12.30 and 4.30–7.30; winter Tues–Sun 10.30–12.30 and 4–7; adm

Santa Croce
open Fri–Sun and hols 10.3–1 and 4–6.30; adm

At the foot of **Monte Corona** (693m), 3km south of town, the **Badia di San Salvatore** was founded by wandering hermit saint Romualdo in 1008 for his Camaldolesian monks. Remodelled in the 18th century, and partly un-remodelled in the 20th, it has an unusual campanile that doubled as a defensive tower. The bare stone interior has traces of 14th-century frescoes and the nave is supported by an interesting hotchpotch of capitals and columns.

Montone

Northeast of Umbertide is fortified Montone, founded in the 9th century. Its strategic position over the Tiber valley made it fought over by Perugia, Città di Castello and Gubbio. Gothic **San Francesco** (1305) has fine frescoes, including a *St Anthony Abbot* by Bartolomeo Caporali. Its convent houses the **Museo Comunale** and **Museo Etnografico**, containing Caporali's *Madonna del Soccorso*, with a charming scene of Montone, and works by local 16th-century artist Vittorio Cirelli, including a fantastical *Immaculate Conception*. The ethnography collection has artefacts from East Africa.

Museo Comunale/ Museo Etnografico
t 075 930 6535; open Fri–Sun 10.30–1 and 3–6; adm

Up the valley is the *condottiere* Braccio Fortebraccio's castle, the restored **Rocca d'Aries**. Further up the narrow road northeast is **Pietralunga**, a medieval village and good base for exploring the mountains and forests, and communing with boars, foxes and more.

Morra

Tobacco is king west of the Tiber. Morra, on the banks of the torrential Nestore, is the village to aim for. The story goes that Luca Signorelli, a native of nearby Cortona, fell in love when passing through in 1508 and decided to stay awhile, picking up the commission to fresco the 15th-century **Oratorio di San Crescentino**, on a hill outside town. The master worked with assistants, but his hand is easily identifiable in the *Flagellation*, *Crucifixion* and *Christ between Two Angels* (look out for the trademark bottoms).

Oratorio di San Crescentino
open daily 9.30–2 and 2.30–7; adm; knock at modern house next door for custodian

ⓘ **Umbertide >**
Piazza Caditi del Lavoro 23 (in car park below Rocca), t 075 941 7099, www.comune.umbertide.pg.it

ⓘ **Montone >>**
Pro Loco, Via San Francesco 1, t 075 930 6427, www.montone.info

Where to Stay and Eat in and around Montone

Umbertide ✉ 06019

******Rio**, SS. Tiberina, **t** 075 941 5033, *www.hotelrio.org* (€€€). Comfortable modern rooms (breakfast included in rates), a classy restaurant and landscaped grounds.

****Moderno**, SS. Tiberina, **t** 075 941 3759, *hotelmoderno@hotmail.com* (€€). Comfortable if basic rooms and a restaurant (half board is available).

****Capponi**, Piazza 25 Aprile 19, **t** 075 941 2662, *www.hotelcapponi.com* (€). A simple central option with a restaurant serving good-quality dishes at very reasonable prices. *Restaurant closed Sun.*

Montone ✉ 06060

Ristorante Erba Luna, Piazza Fortebraccio 4, **t** 075 930 6405 (€€€). Sophisticated versions of traditional Umbrian cuisine on the main square, with views out over the valley. *Closed Tues.*

Città di Castello

Set on a plateau overlooking the Tiber valley, Città di Castello (population 38,000), the most important city in northern Umbria, started as *Tifernum* and prospered under the early Roman Empire, when as *Tifernum Tiberinum* it controlled much trade in the upper Tiber valley. Totila and his Goths knocked it flat; the Early Christian bishops rebuilt it into a fortress town called *Castrum Felicitatis* ('Happy Castle'). In the 1400s and 1500s, under the enlightened tyranny of the Vitelli family, the city hired some of the best Renaissance artists (Raphael among them). In the 20th century, it was the birthplace of one of Italy's best-known postwar artists, Alberto Burri, who has left it an impressive collection of his works. Though bombed in war, Città di Castello has recovered well; today, the Tifernati make their living from textiles, printing and tobacco.

The Duomo and its Museum

Within its Renaissance walls, Città di Castello is a neat rectangle, still roughly following the streetplan of ancient *Tifernum*. The **Duomo**, with exactly one-half of a harmonious Baroque façade, was rebuilt in 580, and several more times. Much of what you see is from the 1400s, though parts of the original Romanesque cathedral remain – especially the 11th-century round campanile, inspired by the ancient towers of Ravenna (and just as tilted). Two handsome Gothic reliefs decorate the north portal. Inside, the single nave has a panelled wooden ceiling: the best painting is a mystical, dramatic altarpiece of the *Transfiguration* in the fourth chapel by Florentine Mannerist Rosso Fiorentino, who took refuge here when he fled the sack of Rome in 1527. Much of the rest of the decoration is by local artists: one, 17th-century Giovanni Battista Pacetti (Lo Sguazzino or 'Splashy'), painted a view of his hometown in the third chapel. The lower church was the ancient crypt and contains the bodies of Città's patrons, saints Florido and Amanzio.

Getting to and around Città di Castello

Città di Castello has a station on the FCU Sansepolcro–Terni **train** line, or take the FS train to Arezzo then the bus. There are also daily **buses** to Urbino, Gubbio and Perugia.

Parking within the walls can be a nightmare; there are some car parks outside the walls – the free one to the north on Viale Nazario Sauro (Parcheggio Enrico Ferri) is close to an **escalator** taking you up into town.

Museo del Duomo
t 075 855 4705; open Tues–Sun 9.30–1 and 2.30–7; adm

The rarest prize in the excellent **Museo del Duomo** is the **treasure of Canoscio** – beautiful 6th-century liturgical silver, probably hidden by the priest when Totila and the Goths came, and found 1,400 years later in 1932. The enamelled and gilded 12th-century altar frontal, showing Christ, the Evangelists and scenes from the Life of Christ, is said to have been donated by Pope Celestine II. There's a beautifully worked 14th-century crozier and 15th-century paintings, including a *Madonna* by a follower of Signorelli; a rich collection of liturgical items, two angels attributed to Giulio Romano and a small *Madonna and Child* and *St John the Baptist* by Pinturicchio.

Near the Duomo

Torre Civica
open Tues–Sun 10–12.30 and 3–6.30; adm

Laboratorio e Collezione Tela Umbra
t 075 855 9071; open Tues–Sat 10–12 and 3.30–5.30, Sun and hols 10.30–1 and 3–5.30; adm

In Piazza Gabriotti by the Duomo is the trecento sandstone **Palazzo dei Priori** (or Comunale) by Angelo da Orvieto, handsome but unfinished. The **Torre Civica** from the same century once held the medieval prisons and has magnificent views over the valley.

From a 14th-century **loggia**, Corso Cavour leads past the covered market, with an 18th-century print shop on top and a pretty 1890s Art Nouveau bank. Civic life focused on Piazza Matteotti, which is overlooked by the very austere **Palazzo del Podestà** with double clocks on the façade, also by Da Orvieto. In Piazza Costa, cloth is woven on traditional looms at the **Laboratorio e Collezione Tela Umbra**, founded in 1908 by Baron Leopoldo Franchetti. The adjacent **museum** tells the history of weaving.

Collezione Burri

Collezione Burri
Via Mazzini, t 075 855 4649, www.fondazioneburri.org; open Tues–Sat 9–12.30 and 2.30–6, Sun 10.30–12.30 and 3–6; adm

Alberto Burri (1915–95) was a doctor who ended up a prisoner of war in Texas in 1943; there he turned to art to express the carnage he had witnessed, using whatever he could find. On his return to Italy, he continued to explore the evocative power of discarded materials and junk, most famously his sacking soaked in red paint that resembled giant bandages, and his carefully composed pieces of twisted metal and charred wood. Burri was one of the great precursors of Abstract Expression and junk art in the USA, and of Italian Arte Povera; in later years he explored colour and other materials. This collection in the quattrocento Palazzo Albizzini is comprised of numerous works from 1943 to 1983.

Seccatoi Tabacchi
open Tues–Sat 9–12.30 and 2.30–6; Sun 10.30–12.30 and 3–6; adm

Burri's large-scale works are exhibited in the tobacco-drying shed he used as a studio, the **Seccatoi Tabacchi**, to the south of town in Via Francesco Pierucci.

The North End of Town

The ruling Vitelli family could not have enough palaces; the Collezioni Burri is near their largest spread, the elegant **Palazzo Vitelli a Porta Sant'Egidio** built in 1540 by Giorgio Vasari. It has a beautiful façade facing a huge garden, and an interior lavishly frescoed by Cristoforo Gherardi (Il Doceno) and Prospero Fontana; it's now owned by a bank and used for concerts.

Also along Via Albizzini is 13th-century **San Francesco** with its 18th-century interior. Vasari designed the elaborate Cappella Vitelli and painted the altarpiece; both are outdone by the fancy wrought-iron grille by local craftsman Pietro di Ercolano. There's a majolica of *St Francis receiving the Stigmata* by the Della Robbia workshop, and a German-made wooden polychrome *Pietà* from the 1400s. The **Betrothal of the Virgin** (1504), Raphael's early masterpiece, was painted for this church, but Napoleon put it in the Brera; Città di Castello grudgingly shows a copy. In the adjacent piazza is an 1860 monument celebrating the end of the Papal States.

Biblioteca Comunale/ Museo Civico
***t** 075 855 5687; open Mon, Tues, Thurs and Sat 9–12.45 and 3–6.45, Wed and Fri 9–1*

Via San Bartolomeo heads north, passing a smaller Palazzo Vitelli on the way to the **Biblioteca Comunale** and **Museo Civico**. This contains fossils from the Pleistocene era, when the Tiber was a lake, and a small archaeological collection. Around Via XI Settembre are three convents of closed orders of the Clarisse; at No.21, the nuns at **Santa Veronica** will show on request their pretty cloister and a small museum dedicated to their order and to St Veronica Giuliani (d. 1727), who lived here for 50 years in a state of almost continuous mystical experience. Nearby, the non-conventual **church of Santa Maria delle Grazie** has a fresco of the *Transition of the Virgin* by Ottavino Nelli and a highly venerated painting of the *Madonna della Grazie*, by Giovanni di Piemonte, a collaborator of Piero della Francesca; it's shown only twice a year (2 February and 26 August).

The Pinacoteca Comunale

Pinacoteca Comunale
*Via della Cannoniera 22 (from behind Duomo, take Via di Modello/Via C. Battisti south), **t** 075 852 0656; open Tues–Sun 10–1 and 2.30–6.30; adm*

This contains Città di Castello's only surviving Raphael, a half-ruined processional standard of 1503, but there are plenty of other attractions, beginning with the building itself. The Palazzo Vitelli alla Cannoniera (one of five Vitelli *palazzi* in town) was built in the 1520s by Antonio da Sangallo the Younger and Pier Francesco da Viterbo, decorated with *sgraffito* by Giorgio Vasari – a lovely façade, facing the inner gardens. The 16th-century frescoes inside are the work of Cola dell'AmatrIce (on the stairs, celebrating the glory of the Vitelli family) and Doceno.

The star of the early paintings is a beautiful restored 14th-century *Maestà* by an anonymous painter known as the Master of Città di Castello. Nearby hangs a fine *Madonna and Child* by Spinello Aretino. The next room has another *Madonna* by the Sienese

Andrea di Bartolo, as well as some early choirstalls; after that there's a residual Gothic Venetian view of the same subject by Antonio Vivarini. Lorenzo Ghiberti, master of Florence's baptistry doors, puts in a rare guest appearance with an equally Gothic-style golden reliquary of St Andrew (1420). The other highlight in this room is a Florentine *Madonna and Two Angels* by Neri di Bicci. In the next room is a *Coronation of the Virgin* from the workshop of Domenico Ghirlandaio; the *Head of Christ* is usually attributed to Giusto di Gand, a Flemish painter who worked in Urbino. The ensuing room has the Raphael standard, followed by altarpieces by local boy Francesco Tifernate and five marquetry sacristry cupboards. Many of these rooms contain frescoes by Doceno and reproductions of other works he produced during his stay. The most powerful painting in the museum is a *San Sebastiano* by Luca Signorelli and his workshop – a fascinating work with fantasy Roman ruins and a surreal treatment of space. There's also a good comical kitsch piece, an anonymous *Quo Vadis?*, a strange Virgin by an unknown follower of Pontormo.

The sculpture collection includes early medieval woodcarving, or mixtures of painting and wooden sculpture, especially the altarpiece of the *Crucifixion with the Virgin Mary and the Magdalene*, the Sun and Moon – the wooden crucifix has disappeared, but the work is strangely suggestive without it. Here, too, is a fine 14th-century Sienese relief on the Baptism of Christ and works by Della Robbia.

San Domenico

The first street left of the museum, Largo Muzi, leads up to the huge preaching church of San Domenico, finished in 1424. The façade was never finished but it has a handsome door on the left ; the gloomy interior has good 15th-century frescoes and choirstalls. Signorelli's *San Sebastiano* used to hang in the Renaissance chapels by the altar, along with Raphael's *Crucifixion*, which is now in the National Gallery in London; it's replaced here by a copy.

ⓘ Città di Castello >
Via Sant'Antonio 1, t 075 855 4817, and Piazza Matteotti, t 075 855 4922, www.umbria2000.it and www.cdcnet.net

Tourist Information in Città di Castello

It's worth noting that entrance to any museum within Città di Castello gets you a discount on admission to others, so you should make sure to keep your ticket.

Market Days

Food and general market, Thurs and Sat, Piazza Gabriotti.

Fleamarket, third Sun of month, Piazza Matteotti and surrounding streets.

Where to Stay in Città di Castello

Città di Castello ✉ 06012

****Tiferno**, Piazza R. Sanzio 13, **t** 075 855 0331, *www.hoteltiferno.it* (€€€€). A plush option occupying a 17th-century palace, with comfortable rooms (a buffet breakfast is included in rates), a billiards room, a garage, and one of the best restaurants in town, where you can feast on the likes of ravioli with shrimp in orange sauce or pigeon with grapes.

***Europa, Via V.E. Orlando 2, t 075 855 0551, *www.gita.it* (€€€). A newly upgraded option in town, with pleasant rooms. Rates include breakfast, and half and full board is offered. Note that rates nearly halve outside high season.

***Hotel delle Terme, Fontecchio, t 075 852 0614, *www.termedifontecchio.it* (€€). A large, pleasant hotel offering all modern comforts, thermal treatments, a fine open-air pool, a restaurant, and a pizzeria with a beautiful terrace. Breakfast is included and half board is available.

**Umbria, Via Sant'Antonio 6, t 075 855 4925, *www.hotelumbria.net* (€). Modest rooms in the centre, with half or full board if you wish.

Eating Out in Città di Castello

This is one place in Umbria with good bread; try *pane nociato* with walnuts.

Il Bersaglio, Via V.E. Orlando 14, just outside walls, **t** 075 855 5534 (€€). Game, truffles, mushrooms and local wines. *Closed Wed and 2wks July.*

Amici Miei, Via del Monte 2, **t** 075 855 9904 (€€). Good salmon with chard, and wild boar with beans and sage. *Closed Wed and 2wks Nov.*

Ristorante da Meo >>

Ristorante da Meo, Fraccano, on SS257 10km east of town, **t** 075 855 3870 (€€). A limited but excellent menu of the day often featuring game, white truffles and mushrooms. *Closed Wed.*

Around Città di Castello

Centro Tradizioni Popolari
Villa Cappelletti; t 075 855 2119; open summer Tues–Sun 8.30–12.30 and 3–7; winter Tues–Sun 8.30–12.30 and 2–6; adm

Just 2km south of Città di Castello, at **Garavelle**, the **Centro Tradizioni Popolari** is a fascinating folk museum in an Umbrian farmhouse, furnished as it would have been a century ago, with blacksmith's forge, oil press, wine cellars and farm instruments.

Just east, Città di Castello has its own spa, the **Terme di Fontecchio**, where Pliny the Younger came to take the alkaline sulphurous waters. The current spa (Mar–Dec) dates from the 19th century. There's fine scenery along the SS257, especially 5km east of Città di Castello at the hill of **Belvedere**, site of the **Santuario della Madonna del Belvedere**, an octagonal domed Baroque church with a quirky façade and a venerated terracotta *Madonna and Child*.

West of Città di Castello, **Monte Santa Maria Tiberina** is a lovely medieval hilltown in a sublime lofty setting. Once inhabited by the Etruscans, the vllage was made an independent marquisate for the Del Monte family by Emperor Charles IV in 1355. A favour to the French earned them the right to call themselves the Bourbon del Monte; they ruled their little Ruritania until 1798, when Napoleon, who had no patience for anachronisms, especially with the name Bourbon on, snatched it away. Today, fewer than 150 souls live here, but you can see what remains of the Del Monte family's medieval castle and some of their tombs in the parish church.

Citerna

Head west from Città di Castello along the SS221 towards Arezzo to reach this gem of a hilltown that has aged like fine wine. On the border of Tuscany, peacefully set over the Tiber valley on a densely wooded hill, **Citerna** was a Roman town, rebuilt by the Lombards, fought over by its neighbours and restored after a quake in 1917. One unusual feature is the partly vaulted medieval passageway circling much of the lower town. Further up, **San Francesco**, rebuilt in 1508, is the chief repository of art, with a late, rather worn fresco by Luca Signorelli and helpers, the *Madonna and Child, St Francis and St Michael*. The altars are decorated with Della Robbia ceramics that seeped over the Tuscan border, and there are fine altarpieces by Raffaellino del Colle, the *Christ in Glory* and the *Madonna and St John the Evangelist*, plus a *Deposition* by Pomarancio.

San Francesco
if locked ask at Via Garibaldi 27 just down from church

Casa Prosperi
ask at bar on piazza for someone with a key

San Michele Arcangelo
ask at same bar for key

The nearby **Casa Prosperi** has an extraordinary carved 16th-century fireplace. Up past pretty Piazza Scipioni, the dark 18th-century **church of San Michele Arcangelo** has more colourful Della Robbia work, a *Crucifixion* by Pomarancio and a bell from a church destroyed in the quake, signed and dated 1267. In the last war, Citerna's castle on top of the town was blown up by the Germans, leaving the walls and brick tower, which offer a spectacular view as far as La Verna in Tuscany, where St Francis received the stigmata. A fountain by the walls commemorates the saint, who visited in 1224.

San Giustino

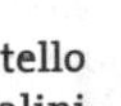 **Castello Bufalini**
open July–Oct Sat and Sun 10.30–12.30 and 3–6.30; guided tours by appt on t 075 852 2655

Further up the Tiber valley, San Giustino has the lovely **Castello Bufalini**, begun in the 1200s as a fortress by the *comune* of Città di Castello, which gave it in 1487 to the noble Bufalini family, to finish (and pay for) the impressive walls and star-shaped moat. A century later, when war seemed unlikely, Giulio Bufalini converted it into an seigneurial villa, on plans by Vasari, with a loggia and courtyard. He also planted one of the most beautiful Italian gardens in Umbria inside the moat, with a maze, geometric hedges, fountains and parterres. In 1989, the Bufalini donated the castle to the State; the gardens and ground floor, with rooms of antiques frescoed by 16th-century painter Cristofano Gherardi, are being restored.

Gubbio

In a way, Gubbio (population 33,000) is what Umbria has always wanted to be: stony, taciturn and mystical, a tough mountain town that fought its own battles until destiny and the popes caught up with it, and also a town of culture, one with its own school of painters. For a city more than 2,500 years old, it still seems like a frontier town, an elemental place that sticks in the memory, with its green mountainside, rushing stream, straight rows of rugged grey-stone houses. On its windy slopes, the hard-edged brilliance of the Italian Middle Ages is clear and tangible.

Gubbio is also one of the few Italian hilltowns that a stick-in-the-mud geologist might recognize. Everyone has heard of the theory that the dinosaurs became extinct after a large meteor struck the

Getting to and around Gubbio

Around 10 daily APM **coaches** (**t** 800 512141, *www.apmperugia.it*; Fontevegge station, **t** 075 501 0485, Fossato di Vico station, **t** 075 919230) follow the beautiful SS298 to Perugia (40km/1hr) from the central Piazza Quaranta Martiri (where schedules are posted). There are also buses to the closest **train** station, 20km southeast at Fossato di Vico, on the FS Foligno–Ancona line to Rome and a Città di Castello–Arezzo–Florence line. The bus and train info office at Via della Repubblica 13, **t** 075 922 0066, sells bus tickets.

earth 65 million years ago and raised so much dust that it blocked out the sun. Some of the strongest evidence for the theory was discovered just outside Gubbio, in the Camignano valley towards Scheggia, where there's a layer of sedimentary rock dense with the rare minerals of meteorites. It's thin but chronologically correct, and thick enough to have done the dirty deed.

History

Gubbio was a city of the ancient Umbrii, perhaps even their political and religious centre. In Roman times, it flourished as *Iguvium* and, according to legend, was where Rome exported its lunatics, which has left a lingering influence on the populace. Mad or not, the Eugubini, as the natives are known, certainly weren't stupid; when unsolicited visits by the Goths, Huns and Avars left the place a mess, the survivors moved their town to a more defensible site on the nearby hillside.

The chronicles paint a picture of a tough, querulous medieval *comune*. In the 1150s, 12 Umbrian cities under Frederick Barbarossa combined to attack it; the city was saved by its bishop, later Sant' Ubaldo, who persuaded the emperor to grant it independence. The chroniclers also claimed for Gubbio a population of 50,000 – probably double the real figure but still quite large for a medieval town. As in every other city, there was continuous conflict between the *comune* and ambitious nobles. One of them, Giovanni Gabrielli, became *signore* of the town in 1350, but only four years later Cardinal Albornoz and his papal army snatched it away. In 1387 it fell to Urbino's dukes of Montefeltro, who ruled it well until their line became extinct in 1508. Gubbio remained part of the duchy of Urbino until 1624, when it became part of the Papal States.

In 1206–7 St Francis found it plagued by wolves; one was ravaging the countryside and terrorizing the populace. Ignoring fears for his safety, he went and had a word with the wolf, brought it to town and made it promise to stop terrorizing Gubbio in exchange for regular meals – an agreement sealed with a shake of the paw. The wolf kept the bargain and is immortalized in a bas-relief over the door of a church on Via Mastro Giorgio. A few years ago, in another church, workmen discovered the skeleton of a giant wolf under a slab. In recent years some of its descendants have been sighted after a long absence, in the forests of northern Umbria.

In 1943, after the Italian surrender, Umbria was occupied by the Germans, who were harried by partisans, based in the mountains above Gubbio. Though most of Umbria fell relatively quickly to the British and Commonwealth forces as they advanced north after the liberation of Rome on 4 June, the fighting was intense and progress slow in the north. Meanwhile, a number of vicious reprisals on innocent villagers took place around Gubbio, while the Germans took positions and pounded the allies; the battle for Gubbio took three weeks, only ending on 25 July.

All of Gubbio's churches are now open, except San Domenico. The earthquake damage in 1997 was relatively minor compared to that of 1982, which left 1,500 homeless.

Gubbio, From the Bottom Up

Teatro Romano/ Antiquarium
t 075 922 0992; open April–Sept daily 8.30–7.30; Oct–Mar daily 8.30–sunset

Most people approach Gubbio from the west, passing open pastureland – once the centre of Roman *Iguvium*. In the middle stands a large, well-preserved 1st-century AD **Roman theatre and antiquarium** used for summer performances of classical Greek and Roman drama and Shakespeare. From here, you get the best view of Gubbio: stone houses climb the slope in neat parallel rows, and the tall Palazzo dei Consoli on its vast platform dominates the centre.

San Francesco
visits by appt on t 075 927 3460

Gubbio proper is entered via big green **Piazza Quaranta Martiri**, named for the 40 citizens gunned down on this spot by Nazis in reprisals for partisan activities. On the west end of the square, behind its unfinished façade, mid-13th-century **San Francesco**, with an octagonal campanile and a distinctive Gothic design with a triple apse, is the work of Perugian architect Fra Bevignate. Inside are good frescoes, especially the damaged series on the *Life of the Virgin* in the left apse, painted in 1408–13 and one of the greatest works by Gubbio's greatest painter, the International Gothic master Ottaviano Nelli. There is also a copy of Daniele da Volterra's *Deposition* on the third altar; right of the altar are 14th-century frescoes on the *Life of St Francis*. The oldest frescoes from the 1200s are high up in the main apse. In the restored cloister are bits of polychrome Roman mosaics found in Gubbio and more frescoes.

On the other side of the piazza you can see the **Loggia dei Tiratoio** (Weaver's Loggia), an arcade dating from 1603 under which newly woven textiles could be stretched to shrink evenly – it's one of few such loggias to survive.

Piazza Grande and the Palazzo dei Consoli

From Piazza dei Quaranta Martiri, Via Piccardi ascends past picturesque medieval lanes on the banks of the Camignano, a rushing torrent in spring and winter. Many of the houses and modest *palazzi* date back to the 13th century, here and there adorned with carved doors or windows, or 'Death's doors' as in

Perugia. At the top is the magnificent **Piazza Grande** (or Piazza della Signoria), occupying a balcony hovering over a steep drop, with a stunning view of the town.

King of the piazza is the beautiful, huge **Palazzo dei Consoli**, one of Italy's most remarkable public buildings, begun in 1332 by Gubbio's master architect Gattapone, with a bit of help from Angelo da Orvieto. Supported on the hill by a remarkable substructure of arches, it's graced with an elegant loggia, a slender campanile, square Guelph crenellations and asymmetrically arranged windows and arches. It faces the **Palazzo Pretorio** (now the *municipio*) designed by the same architect to make the piazza a set-piece.

Museo Civico
t *075 927 4298; open daily 10–1 and 3–6; adm*

The **Palazzo dei Consoli**, now the **Museo Civico**, boasts treasures from the 16th century BC to the 19th century AD. On the first floor, the vast barrel-vaulted Sala dell'Arengo, where assemblies were held, is cluttered with fascinating archaeological odds and ends, tombstones, sarcophagi and crossbows. There's a Roman inscription – Governor Gnaeus Satirus Rufus bragging how much he spent to embellish the town – and a collection of seals and coins from the days when Gubbio minted its own. One unique treasure, the bronze **Eugubine tablets** have by far the most important inscriptions ever found in the Umbrian language, discovered in the 15th century near the Roman theatre. Partly written in the Etruscan alphabet and partly in the Latin, these codes of religious observances and rituals for Gubbio's priests are also a rare survival of a religious how-to textbook, with details on sacrifices (including human enemies) and how to read the future in a liver or in the flight of birds.

Medieval Gubbio made its living from ceramics; in the 16th century, this tradition produced a real artist, **Mastro Giorgio Andreoli**, who discovered a beautiful ruby and golden glaze for majolica plates (you'll notice the absence of red in most painted ceramics; it's very hard to do). Mastro Giorgio's secret died with him, and it was long one of Gubbio's deepest regrets that it had not a single example of his work to show. When it became known that Sotheby's had a plate by Mastro Giorgio to auction in 1991, the townspeople purchased it by public subscription. With another piece bought in 1996, it is displayed in the loggia; they show the *Fall of Phaeton* and *Circe*, and keep company with ceramic works made over the centuries, including red terracotta pharmaceutical jars.

Pinacoteca
open daily 10–1 and 3–6

The **Pinacoteca**, on the *piano nobile*, is as quirky and charming, though there are few first-rate pieces: a 13th-century diptych in a Byzantine portable altar; painted crucifixes; a detached 17th-century fresco on *St Francis and the Wolf*; a *Tree of Jesse* by a cinquecento Gubbio artist; the quattrocento *Madonna del Melograno* by Pier Francesco Florentini; a *Flight into Egypt* by Rutilio Manetti; and an anonymous 1600s work, *Last Night of Babylon* – one of the best crazy paintings in Italy. Some rooms remain in their 1500s state.

Museo Archeologico
open daily 10–1 and 3–6

The lower floor of the *palazzo* houses the **Museo Archeologico**, with an Umbrian and Roman collection of bronzes and ceramics, other architectural odds and ends, and a Byzantine sarcophagus.

To the Duomo and Palazzo Ducale

From Piazza Grande, stepped **Via Galeotti**, one of the city's most resolutely medieval lanes, leads up to the winding Via Ducale and Gubbio's Duomo. On the way, note the old cellar under the cathedral housing the **Botte dei Canonici**, a house-sized 1500s barrel that once held 40,000 litres of wine – a masterpiece of the cooper's art, made without nails. On top, the 14th-century **Palazzo dei Canonici** houses the **Museo Diocesano**, with a damaged 14th-century fresco of the *Crucifixion* and a beautiful 16th-century Flemish cope, magnificently embroidered and presented to the cathedral by Pope Marcellus II, a native of Gubbio.

Museo Diocesano
t 075 922 0904; open summer daily 10–7; winter daily 10–6; adm

The 13th-century **Duomo**, refitted with a simple front in the 1400s, is remarkable for the unusual pointed wagon stone vaulting of the nave, a Eugubine speciality, and for its stained-glass windows. Local talent is well represented in the side chapels; in the presbytery is a *Nativity* attributed to one of Pinturicchio's talented students, Eusebio di San Giorgio. The high altar is a Roman sarcophagus. Note the 16th-century choirstalls, painted to resemble intarsia by Benedetto Nucci, and the 1556 carved throne (real) by Girolamo Maffei.

Corse dei Ceri

From the Duomo, you can walk up and up to the sanctuary of Sant'Ubaldo, following the route run in the **race of the Ceri** (*see* below), but it's much easier to take the *funivia* (*see* p.485)

The Corsa dei Ceri

Some exceedingly medieval festivals fill Gubbio's solemn streets with colour and exuberance. On the last Sunday in May, crossbow-men from Sansepolcro compete in the *Palio della Balestra* dating back to 1461, with a procession, flag-throwing and music. An even older custom is the Good Friday procession and a representation of the Passion, performed at the little church of Santa Croce della Foce just outside the walls, with medieval chants and music played on wooden instruments called *battistrangoli*.

Oldest of all is the *Corsa dei Ceri*, every 15 May, the eve of the feast of patron saint Sant'Ubaldo. First documented a couple of years after Ubaldo saved the city from Emperor Frederick and his Umbrian allies, over centuries it has taken on the trappings of a pagan celebration that may have predated the bishop's heroism. The *ceri* (candles) are three octagonal wooden towers 4m high. On May 15, following Mass, wax saints representing the three guilds of Gubbio are brought out of the church of the Muratori and taken in a procession to the *ceri* in Piazza Grande, where they are affixed to the top of the 'candles' and taken round town by their colourfully costumed teams. This is followed by a fish banquet in the Palazzo dei Consoli. At 4.30pm there's another procession in which the *ceri* are baptized with a jug of water. The race begins at 6 in Piazza Grande; 10 bearers hoist the supports of their respective *cero* on their shoulders and race pell-mell through the crowds up Via XX Settembre, Via Colomboni and Via Appennino to Porta del Monte, where they rest before continuing to the mountain-top church of Sant'Ubaldo. Then the saints are returned to their home with a candlelit procession.

In 1943 during the German occupation, all-women teams carried the *ceri* (each weighs around 200kg) up to Sant'Ubaldo, out of pride and to spite the Nazis. Since the war, the *ceri* have become the

Palazzo Ducale
Via Federico da Montefeltro, **t** *075 927 5872; open Tues–Sun 8.30–7; adm*

Opposite the cathedral, the **Palazzo Ducale** was designed in the 1470s for that great patron of artists and humanists, the *condottiere* Federico da Montefeltro, Duke of Urbino, by Sienese architect Francesco di Giorgio Martini. Gentlemanly Federico was a paragon among Renaissance rulers; he took a paternalistic interest in the welfare of his subjects and frequently travelled to keep an eye on things. He also liked to lodge in style and built at least a dozen palaces in the northern Marches as homes from home. His Gubbio address was one of the most stylish – a compact version of his famous palace in Urbino. The elegant, serene little courtyard in particular evokes its great model, with *pietra serena* details and the initials FD (Federico Duca). The palace was stripped of its furnishings before it was purchased by the State in 1957, but some fireplaces remain, along with fine stairways, windows and original terracotta flooring, one wooden ceiling, a few 15th-century intarsia doors and photos of the beautiful intarsia work of the little *studiolo* or ducal study, made by Giuliano da Maiano, now in New York. Some rooms have detached frescoes and paintings. Downstairs, examine the plumbing and old kitchen, foundations of a Lombard palace from the 10th century. Upstairs, the loggia has a handsome frieze in *pietra serena* and lovely views onto the Palazzo dei Consoli.

Gubbio's West End

From Piazza Grande, Gubbio's main street, Via dei Consoli, leads past ceramic shops to the very medieval western quarter. Near Piazza Giordano Bruno, the **Bargello** (1302), the first public building here, was a police station and governor's office; its round 16th-century **Fontana dei Matti** (Fountain of the Mad) was Gubbio's main water source and has the power to make you *loco* if you run around it three times. Here, too, is **San Domenico**, an earlier Romanesque church taken over by the Dominicans in the 1300s. After an 18th-century remodelling, only bits of the trecento frescoes remain, along with an exceptional Renaissance intarsia reading stand.

Vias Vantaggi and Gabrielli lead from here to the 13th-century **Palazzo del Capitano del Popolo**, a no-nonsense Romanesque structure with a privately run **museum of torture instruments**. Nearby is one of the equally austere city gates, **Porta Metauro**, and a medieval tower fortress belonging to the Palazzo Gabrielli. **Santa Croce della Foce**, just outside the gate, is the site of the medieval Good Friday representation of the Passion.

Just inside Porta Metauro is the entrance to the **Parco Ranghiasci-Brancaleoni**, which sweeps up under the town walls to the Palazzo Ducale. Laid out as an English garden in 1841 by Francesco Ranghiasci, it was restored by the *comune* and offers the greatest possible contrast to the grey-stone streets of the city. It has a pretty covered bridge, neoclassical pavilions, big shady trees and a café.

The East End

Porta Romana
t 075 922 1199; open daily 9–1 and 3.30–7.30; adm

At the east end of town, the 13th-century **Porta Romana** is now a museum devoted to medieval gates, with a collection of old keys and a drawbridge mechanism, as well as a collection of Gubbio ceramics, which includes some from the workshop of Mastro Giorgio. Near the gate, two 13th-century churches contain works by Ottaviano Nelli. The deconsecrated **Santa Maria Nuova** has his joyous, worldly *Madonna del Belvedere* and frescoes by his followers. Just outside the gate, **Sant'Agostino** has more frescoes by Nelli and his pupils: the *Life of St Augustine* in the triumphal arch and apse and, on the fifth altar on the right, *Sant'Ubaldo and Two Saints*. The *funivia* here ascends to Monte Ingino (*see* below).

Santa Maria Nuova
*visitors need permission from Soprintendenza Archeologica in Perugia, **t** 075 57411*

Back within the Porta Romana, the **Arco di San Marziale** marks the site of the ancient Umbrian gate. Via Dante leads down to a giant 18th-century tabernacle of Sant'Ubaldo at the crossroads with Corso Garibaldi. Nearby, the **Palazzo Accoramboni** was the birthplace in 1557 of Vittoria Accoramboni. By age 16 she was not only married but having an affair with Duke Paolo Giordano Orsini, who killed her husband to marry her (twice), before she was killed aged 28 by Orsini ruffians. Papal involvement and other sordid details made it juicy enough for the London stage – John Webster's play on Vittoria's life, *The White Devil*, appeared in 1608.

From Corso Garibaldi, Via V. Armanni descends to **San Pietro**, with four Corinthian columns on the façade and a Renaissance interior. The first altar has a *Martyrdom of St Bartholomew* by Sienese painter Rutilio Manetti; the fourth has a *Visitation* by Giannicola di Paolo; the fifth was decorated by Raffaellino del Colle. In the left transept is a 13th-century wooden statue of the *Deposition*.

Chiesa della Vittorina
open Tues–Sun 9–12 and 4–7

Funivia
*t 075 927 3881; **April and May** Mon–Sat 10–1.15 and 2.30–6.30, Sun and hols 9.30–1.15 and 2.30–7; **June** Mon–Sat 9.30–1.15 and 2.30–7, Sun and hols 9–7; **July and Aug** Mon–Sat 8.30–7.30, Sun and hols 8.30–8; **Sept** Mon–Sat 9.30–1.15 and 2.30–7, Sun and hols 9.30–1.15 and 2.30–7.30; **Oct** Sun and hols 10–1.15 and 2.30–6; **Nov–Feb** Thurs–Tues 10–1.15 and 2.30–5; **Mar** Mon–Sat 10–1.15 and 2.30–5.30, Sun and hols 9.30–1.15 and 2.30–6*

Below San Pietro is the **Porta Vittoria**: if you follow Via della Piaggiola from here, you pass **Santa Maria della Piaggiola**, with an ornate Baroque interior used for concerts; there's a *Madonna and Child* by Ottaviano Nelli on the altar, repainted. Another Baroque church just over the bridge to the right, **Santa Maria del Prato** (1662), is a copy of Borromini's San Carlino alla Quattro Fontane in Rome.

If you continue along Via della Piaggiola, it's about 2km to the spot where Francis met with the wolf on Via Frate Lupo: the isolated **Chiesa della Vittorina** was built in the 13th century and the charming interior has another odd nave with pointed Gothic vaults and early frescoes, undisturbed by remodelling in the 1500s. A bronze statue (1973) of the saint and wolf marks the encounter.

Monte Ingino

Monte Ingino

You can make the stiff climb up **Monte Ingino** to the **sanctuary of Sant'Ubaldo** from the cathedral, but you'll make life much easier for yourself if you take the **funivia** from the Porta Romana instead. On display within the five-naved church, besides the ashes of the patron saint who saved Gubbio from the emperor, are the three *ceri* (*see* p.483). There's a café and restaurant too, and you can walk a bit further up for even more spectacular views from the **Rocca** (888m). At Christmas time, the entire slope of Monte Ingino is illuminated, using 12km of electric cable, to form 'the world's largest Christmas tree'.

Excursions from Gubbio

Around Gubbio you can expect long stretches of empty space punctuated by an occasional half-ruined castle, monastery or the plainest of mountain villages. **Castel d'Alfiolo**, 6km to the south of Gubbio on the SS219, was converted from a family fortress to a Benedictine abbey in the 1100s; most of the buildings were redone in the 16th century, but the chapel and the main building conserve good stone carving from the 1200s.

Parco Naturale del Monte Cucco

To the east of Gubbio, the SS298 passes through a lovely gorge with old watermills on the way to the **Parco Naturale del Monte Cucco** on the border of the Marches. This is a popular spot with the Eugubini on summer weekends, with pretty mountain meadows and beech forests around Pian di Ranco; it's also one of the best places in Umbria in which to go hang-gliding, and in winter people head up for the cross-country skiing. Descendants of Francis's Brother Wolf still roam on **Monte Cucco** (1,566m), one of Umbria's highest peaks. One of its flanks, Monte Cucco conceals one of the deepest subterranean systems in the world (922m) – the 20km-long **Grotte di Monte Cucco**, which is reached by a long iron stair (although it's currently off-limits to the public). The remains of gigantic prehistoric cave bears have been found here, and the innermost, darkest chambers are inhabited by a singular race of blind brown flies.

Grotte di Monte Cucco
closed to public; for guided tours of other caves, contact CENS, **t** *075 917 0400 or* **t** *075 917 0601, www.cens.it*

This mountainous region had a special pull on holy men of the 10th and 11th centuries. San Romualdo, a nobleman turned monk and the founder of the Order of the Camaldolese Benedictines, had a mystical vision of his vocation on Monte Sitria; the site is marked by the handsome Romanesque church of the **Abbazia di Santa Maria di Sitria**, above **Scheggia**, the last Umbrian town on the Via Flaminia. Romualdo, though a great wanderer who founded abbeys as far as the Pyrenees, was also the moving spirit behind the **Monastero della Fonte Avellana**, which is found off the SS360, just over the border in the Marches, in an isolated mountain setting. Founded in 979, this was an important centre of learning during the Middle Ages (Dante was one of many famous visitors). Almost nothing here has changed since the 12th century. Perhaps unique in all Italy, it preserves the *scriptorium* in which codices and manuscripts were copied.

Monastero della Fonte Avellana
open Mon–Sat 9–11.30 and 3–5, Sun 3–4

ⓘ **Gubbio ›**
Piazza Oderisi 6,
t *075 922 0693 or*
t *075 922 0790,*
www.umbria2000.it

★ **Taverna del Lupo ››**

★ **Villa Montegranelli ›**

★ **La Fornace di Mastro Giorgio ››**

Shopping in Gubbio

Market day is Tuesday, in Piazza Quaranta Martiri.

Gubbio's artist-artisans still turn out some of the most beautiful **ceramics** in Italy, hand-painted in colourful, original floral designs, including plates in all sizes. On Via dei Consoli alone, try Fabbrica Ranimi, Fabbrica Mastro Giorgio, and No.44. Gubbio also has a longstanding tradition in **wrought-iron** work, harder to carry home.

Where to Stay in Gubbio

Gubbio ✉ 06024

Advance bookings are essential in July and August.

Luxury–Very Expensive (€€€€€–€€€€)

****__Park Hotel ai Cappuccini__, Via Tifernate, **t** 075 9234, *www.parkhotelaicappuccini.it*. An award-winning Franciscan monastery outside town, with a cloister and chapel, a pool, sauna and fitness centre, and an Umbrian restaurant.

Very Expensive (€€€€)

****__Relais Ducale__, Via Galeotti, **t** 075 922 0157, *www.mencarelligroup.com*. Three historic buildings in the medieval heart, linked by a lift. Rooms are sumptuous with beautiful views of town. It has a garage on the edge of town, accessed by a shuttle service.

Expensive (€€€)

***__Bosone__, Via XX Settembre 22, **t** 075 922 0688 *www.mencarelligroup.com*. A picturesque *palazzo* off Piazza Grande, with a meal service (half and full board available) and a garage.

***__Villa Montegranelli__, Loc. Monteluiano, 4km from town, **t** 075 922 0185, *www.villamontegranellihotel.it*. An 18th-century villa overlooking town, with original features, including the *piano nobile* and private chapel, plus a garden and babysitting. The great restaurant serves Umbrian and Puglian fare (half/full board available).

Dei Consoli, Via dei Consoli 59, **t** 075 922 0639, *www.urbaniweb.com*. A simple option with a restaurant offering creative cuisine grounded in tradition (half/full board available).

Moderate (€€)

***__Beniamino Ubaldi__, Via Perugina 74, **t** 075 927 7773, *www.rosatihotels.com*. Functional rooms in a seminarians' college just outside the walls, with a bar and restaurant (half/full board available), Internet access, parking, and a babysitting service.

***__Gattapone__, Via G. Ansidei 6, **t** 075 927 2489, *www.mencarelligroup.com*. A pleasant choice in the medieval centre, with a garden and garage. Half and full board are offered.

***__San Marco__, Via Perugina 5, **t** 075 922 0234, *www.hotelsanmarcogubbio.com*. Modern comforts in a former convent, with a pretty garden terrace and a restaurant serving Umbrian cuisine. Breakfast is included and half and full board available.

__Oderisi__, Via Mazzatinti 2, **t 075 922 0662, *www.rosatihotels.com*. Good, well-furnished if basic rooms.

*__Locanda del Duca__, Via Piccardi 1, **t** 075 927 7753, *locandadelducaditraversi@tin.it*. Simple rooms, some with bath, overlooking the river. The restaurant, which specializes in duck and lamb, has outdoor tables. Half/full board are available. *Restaurant closed Wed.*

Eating Out in Gubbio

Taverna del Lupo, Via Ansidei 21a, **t** 07 927 4368 (€€€). Excellent, traditional fare such as truffled *bresaola* in lemon sauce, and steak with Parmesan and truffles, served in a medieval setting with a name recalling the legend of St Francis. *Closed Mon Oct–July.*

All'Antica Frantoio, Via Cavour 18, Largo Bargello, **t** 075 922 1780 (€€). Umbrian cuisine served in a 13th-century oil mill, plus wood-oven pizzas. *Closed Mon and 15–20 days Jan/Feb.*

Alla Balestra, Via della Repubblica 41, **t** 075 927 3810 (€€). Unusual dishes such as *fondutina con tartufo*, plus home-made pasta, pizza, and meat, truffles and mushroom dishes. *Closed Tues.*

Federico da Montefeltro, Via della Repubblica 35, **t** 075 927 3949 (€€). Memorable mushroom- and truffle-based dishes. *Closed Thurs, Feb and Aug.*

La Fornace di Mastro Giorgio, Via Mastro Giorgio 2, **t** 075 922 1836 (€€). A local classic in the workshop where the master ceramicist created his famous ruby glaze, serving esoteric Umbrian specialities. *Closed Tues, Wed lunch Nov–May and 3wks Jan.*

Funivia, Monte Ingino, **t** 075 922 1259 (€). Fabulous views on clear days, accompanying delicious stuffed pigeon and other good-value treats. *Closed Dec–Feb exc Christmas holidays, and Wed exc summer.*

San Francesco e Il Lupo, Via Cairoli 24, **t** 075 927 2344 (€). Local products, *porcini* and truffles, or pizza. *Closed Tues, 10 days in Jan and 10–25 July.*

Down the Via Flaminia

The Via Flaminia (SS3) was a Roman road of conquest; even in the Dark Ages, the Goths and Lombards kept it in repair as a highway linking Ravenna, Spoleto and Rome. Somewhere between Scheggia and Gualdo Tadino, the deciding battle in the Greek-Gothic War took place in 552. The Goths, led by Totila, were coming up from the south and were met here by the freshly arrived Byzantine forces under eunuch general Narses, nearly 80 years old. The Goths were outnumbered; Totila did all he could to stall battle until reinforcements arrived, to the extent of ordering his most skilled horsemen to put on a display of dressage to entertain the Byzantines. But Narses was not fooled. His troops outflanked the Goths; Totila was mortally wounded, and though enough Goths fled to fight one last showdown with the Greeks near Cumae, their show was over.

Gualdo Tadino

A stern old town under the steep slopes of Monte Serra Santa, Gualdo has taken big blows from earthquakes. In the main **Piazza dei Martiri della Libertà** is the **Duomo** with a good façade and rose window of 1256 and three doors, with an inscription mentioning restoration after the 1751 quake; the 16th-century fountain on its side is attributed to Antonio da Sangallo. The 13th-century **Palazzo del Podestà**, remodelled in Baroque times, houses the **museum of emigration**; the quakes have caused many to flee this region. Here, too, is the former **church of San Francesco**, a copy of the basilica in Assisi, with a luminous interior and frescoes by Matteo da Gualdo, a local boy of the late quattrocento. The **Rocca Flea**, home to the **Museo Civico**, has ceramics, including Renaissance lustreware (Gualdo has made it for centuries), archaeological finds and the town's art: a sumptuous polyptych by Niccolò Alunno, a *Coronation of the Virgin* by Sano di Pietro and more Matteo da Gualdo. In September, townspeople from the four quarters, or 13th-century 'gates', don their medieval glad rags to play the *Giochi de le Porte* – archery and slingshot competitions and donkey races.

Museo Regionale dell'Emigrazione
t 075 914 2445, open Tues–Sat 10–1 and 4–6.30

San Francesco
closed for restoration at time of writing

Museo Civico
open April–June Thurs–Sun 10.30–1 and 3–6; July–Sept Tues–Sun 10.30–1 and 3.30–7; Oct–Mar Sat and Sun 10.30–1 and 2.30–5; adm

There's fine walking country above Gualdo: take the road 8km east to **Valsorda**, a resort 1,015m up and the base for the pilgrimage walk to the 12th-century **sanctuary of Santissima Trinità** on Monte Serra Santa, now part of Monte Cucco park.

The Valle Umbra

Between Assisi and Spoleto spreads one of the largest patches of open country in the region. The sunny Valle Umbra, or Vale of Umbria , encompasses the valleys of the Teverone and the Topino (Little Mouse River) and has much in common with parts of southern Tuscany; the magnificent landscape seems almost consciously arranged by some geomantic artist to display each olive grove, vineyard, city and town to the best advantage. One Grand Tourist, the Abbé Barthélemy, wrote of the area, 'It is the most beautiful countryside in the world. I do not exaggerate.'

18

Don't miss

See map overleaf

The Valle Umbra

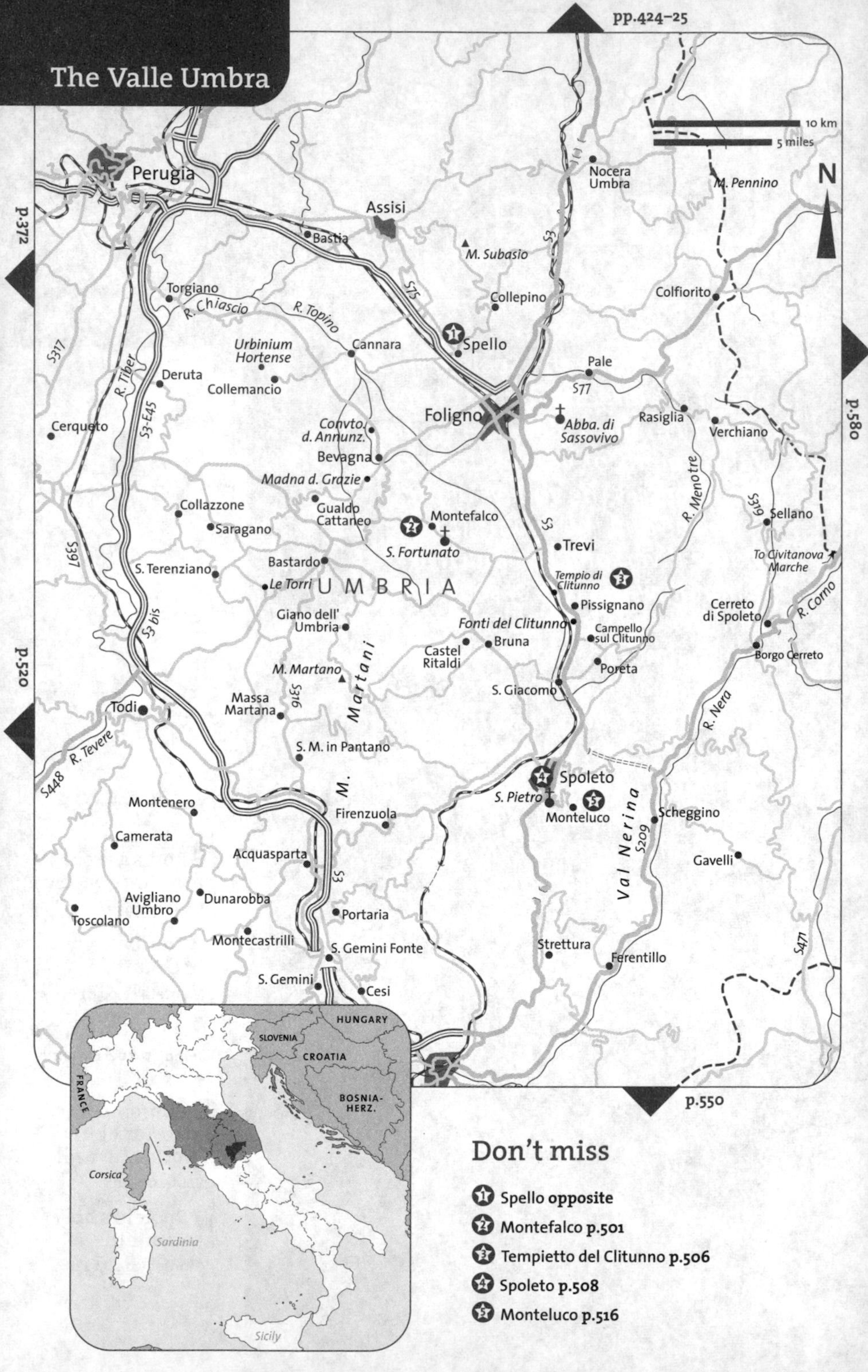

Don't miss

1. Spello **opposite**
2. Montefalco **p.501**
3. Tempietto del Clitunno **p.506**
4. Spoleto **p.508**
5. Monteluco **p.516**

This area is littered with fascinating Roman and Lombard relics, thanks to that vital ancient thoroughfare, the Via Flaminia (SS3), the two branches of which joined in the remarkable but often overlooked town of Foligno before heading north to Gualdo Tadino. Besides some of Umbria's most beautiful hilltowns, Spello, Montefalco and Trevi, the Valle Umbra is home to that unique relic of the Dark Ages called the Tempietto del Clitunno, and to glorious Spoleto, a genuine capital in those times, one of the most fascinating art towns in Italy, and now one of the trendiest, thanks to its famous Festival of the Two Worlds. For tourist information for the whole of this area, see *www.valleumbra.com*.

Spello

Lovely medieval Spello (population 8,000) could be Assisi's little sister, dressed in the same pink and cream Umbrian stone, lounging on the same sort of gentle hillside under Mount Subasio, overlooking the Valle Umbra. It has a similar history, first as an Umbrian settlement, then as the Roman city with a fancy name, *Splendidissima Colonia Iulia Hispellum*, or just *Hispellum* for short. The Lombards destroyed it, then made it part of the duchy of Spoleto. In the Middle Ages, as a *comune*, Spello fought to keep free of Assisi, the same way Assisi resisted domination by the Perugians. This earned it a thumping from Frederick II, and when he was dead Spello was swallowed up by Perugia. There's so much to see in nearby Assisi that relatively few tourists find their way up here, but like most little sisters, Spello has charms of her own.

Pinturicchio *et al*

Spello has three excellently preserved Roman gates, including the main entrance to town, the **Porta Consolare**, with three arches and three worn statues from the time of the Roman republic, placed here in the 1600s after their discovery by the amphitheatre; in the Middle Ages, it was incorporated into the walls and given a tower.

From the gate, Via Consolare winds up into the centre, following the old Roman main street, passing an open chapel, the **Cappella Tega**, with faded Renaissance frescoes by L'Alunno. Where Via Consolare becomes Via Cavour stands Spello's chief monument, late-13th-century **Santa Maria Maggiore**, with its original Romanesque campanile and some 11th-century carving incorporated into its 17th-century façade. The interior was renovated at the same time, when it was given its fancy stuccoes and a hotchpotch of Baroque altars. The two holy-water stoups are ancient Roman columns, and there are two late, mediocre frescoes by Perugino on the pilasters either side of the apse, an excellent pulpit with grotesques of 1545 sculpted by Simone di Campione,

Santa Maria Maggiore
t 0742 301792; open summer daily 8.30–12.30 and 3–7; winter daily 8.30–12.30 and 2.30–6

Getting to Spello

Spello is linked by **train** (station 1km from town) and **bus** to Assisi, Perugia and Foligno.

---

and fine inlaid choirstalls (1520), as well as a *baldacchino* by Tommaso di Rocco. Best of all is the **Cappella Baglioni**, commissioned in 1500 by Troilo Baglioni, scion of Perugia's gangster family, and brilliantly frescoed by Pinturicchio (you need €1 coins for the lighting). The three scenes, *Annunciation*, *Nativity* and *Dispute in the Temple*, are delightful, full of colour and incident, and include Pinturicchio's self-portrait hanging under the *Annunciation*. The floor is made of painted ceramics from Deruta (1516). More by Pinturicchio can be seen in the **Cappella del Sacramento**.

Pinacoteca Civica
t 0742 301497, Tues–Sun 10.30–1 and 3–6.30; adm

The adjacent Palazzo dei Canonici contains the **Pinacoteca Civica**, a repository for art from Spello's churches: there's woodcarving from the 13th–14th centuries, including a fine *Madonna and Child* (1240) by an anonymous Umbrian sculptor; gold and silver work (a beautiful enamelled silver cross of 1398 by Perugian goldsmith Paolo Vanni); a portable diptych by Cola Petruccioli from the 1390s and Umbrian paintings by L'Alunno and his circle. Marcantonio Grecchi's *Madonna and Child with St Felice Vescovo and the Blessed Andrea Caccioli* includes a fine view of early 17th-century Spello.

Sant'Andrea
open Mon–Sat 8–12.30 and 3–7, Sun 3–7

There's yet more Pinturicchio (he spent 1501 in Spello) in nearby 13th-century **Sant'Andrea**: a large *Madonna, Child and Saints* to the right of the crossing he painted with another Perugino student, Eusebio di San Giorgio. There are also 13th–16th-century frescoes, and a high altar with a crucifix attributed to a follower of Giotto.

Souvenirs of Roman *Hispellum*

Walking the narrow, cobbled streets, hidden archways and stairways of Spello is a joy, though they're a bit steep. Off the rather anonymous Piazza della Repubblica, the Romanesque **San Lorenzo** (*c.* 1160) has an unusual façade full of bits from Roman and early medieval buildings and some curious paintings within by a 16th-century artist from Brussels, Frans van de Kasteele. From here, ambitious climbers can continue up Via di Torre Belvedere to the top of Spello for the **belvedere** over the Vale of Umbria. There are ruins of the 14th-century **Rocca**, built by the indefatigable Cardinal Albornoz. The small **Roman arch** nearby was the entrance to *Hispellum*'s acropolis.

A circumnavigation of Spello's walls will show you the two other Roman gates: the **Porta Urbica** (near the Porto Consolare, close to a well-preserved stretch of walls dating back to the 1st century AD), and, best of all, the **Porta Venere**, a beautiful, almost perfectly preserved monumental gate from the time of Augustus, flanked by a pair of tall cylindrical towers.

Outside the Walls of Spello

The Porta Venere is plainly visible from the road to Assisi and Perugia. Look the other way and you'll see the overgrown ruins of the **Roman amphitheatre**, perhaps more impressive when viewed from the belvedere in the city than ground level; it seated 15,000.

Just north of Spello is the charming, resolutely asymmetrical 12th-century Romanesque **church of San Claudio**. Already in bad shape in 1997, it was almost entirely destroyed by the quake and is still being restored. Just beyond, amid a lovely Italian garden, the **Villa Fidelia** was built in the 1500s but has been fiddled with; it contains the **Collezione Straka-Coppa**, with late Renaissance, Baroque and early-20th-century art, including a few big names (including a 16th-century *Madonna and Child* by Vincenzo Catena of Venice, Italy's first amateur painter), as well as silver and ceramics.

Villa Fidelia
Via Flamina 72, **t** *0742 301866; open April–June and Sept Thurs–Sun 10.30–1 and 3.30–6; July and Aug daily 10.30–1 and 4–7; Oct–Mar Sat and Sun 10.30–1 and 3–6; adm*

Beyond the 18th-century Porta Montanara 1km northeast of town, the cemetery **church of San Girolamo** (1474), has a portico and interior decorated by students and followers of Pinturicchio. Another road continues to the slopes of Monte Subasio and the walled medieval village of **Collepino**. Above town, Romanesque **San Silvestro**, founded by St Romualdo in 1025, has an interesting crypt and an altar carved from a Roman sarcophagus. From here, an unpaved road goes over Subasio to the Eremo delle Carceri (*see* p.466).

West of Spello: Cannara and Urbinum Hortense

The fertile plain of Foligno, along the banks of the Topino, was greatly appreciated in ancient times. Cannara was founded as a satellite of the large Roman town of Urbinum Hortense to the west but has survived the centuries in better nick; it is famous for its red onions (subject of a local festival) and its unique Vernaccia di Cannara, a sweet red dessert wine. There are two churches with good paintings of the *Virgin, Child and Saints* by Nicolò Alunno: one in San Matteo (1786), the other in San Giovanni. The *municipio* has fresco fragments and other finds from Urbinum Hortense.

West of Cannara, in a beautiful setting, tiny walled **Collemancio** has a Romanesque church and Palazzo del Podestà in its core. From the public garden, a road leads up 0.5km to the ruins of Urbinum Hortense. Mentioned by Pliny the Younger, this has been partially excavated to unearth a temple, baths and a basilica.

Festivals in Spello

Bruschetta festival, Feb.

Corpus Domini, 1st half June. An *infiorata* (flower carpets bedeck the town; best early mornings).

Festa dell'Olivo, early Dec. A festival celebrating local olive oil production.

Where to Stay and Eat in and West of Spello

Spello ✉ **06038**

****La Bastiglia**, Via dei Molini 17, **t** 0742 651277, *www.labastiglia.com* (€€€€). A charmingly restored mill

ⓘ Spello >
Piazza Matteotti 3, **t** *0742 301009, www. comune.spello.pg.it*

with pleasant rooms, a beautiful terrace and views, Internet access, babysitting, parking, and good restaurant (€€). *Closed Wed.*

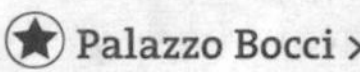

Palazzo Bocci >

****Palazzo Bocci**, Via Cavour 17, **t** 0742 301021, *www.palazzobocci.com* (€€€€). An frescoed 17th-century building with elegant rooms, a hanging garden and a restaurant, **Il Molino**, just opposite, at Piazza Matteotti 6/7 (**t** 0742 651305). Under a vaulted ceiling, try characterful dishes featuring Norcia truffles, ceps, pulses and game. *Closed Tues and 10–24 Jan.*

***Del Teatro**, Via Giulia 24, **t** 0742 301140, *www.hoteldelteatro.it* (€€€). A quiet, cheerfully furnished hotel near the Teatro Comunale, with well-equipped, comfy rooms (breakfast included), wonderful views from the breakfast verandah, and parking.

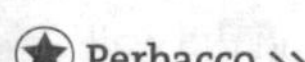

Perbacco >>

***Altavilla**, Via Mancinelli 2, **t** 0742 301515, *www.hotelaltavilla.com* (€€). Well-furnished rooms, a beautiful pool, a terrace and a restaurant with local cuisine (half/full board available).

***Il Cacciatore**, Via Giulia 42, **t** 0742 651141, *www.ilcacciatorehotel.com* (€€). Comfy rooms, most with splendid valley views, and a very popular restaurant serving beautifully prepared home-made pasta and other dishes at good prices. *Closed Mon and Nov.*

Il Portonaccio, Via Centrale Umbra 46, **t** 0742 651313, *www.albergoilportonaccio.it* (€€). Decent rooms and room-service breakfasts.

La Cantina, Via Cavour 2, **t** 0742 651775 (€€). Seasonal dishes, BBQ meats and home-made pasta. *Closed Wed.*

Cannara ✉ 06033

Casa delle Volpi, Vocabolo Ducale 50, **t** 0742 720361 (€). Self-catering lodgings outside town, with a garden and views to Assisi. Breakfasts and dinners can be provided; cookery evenings are hosted. There's a minimum 1-week stay.

Perbacco, Via Umberto I, **t** 0742 720492 (€€). *The* place to try Cannara's onions, especially in the delicious onion soup. Ask for directions when you book.

Foligno

In Foligno (population 54,000), which ranks as Umbria's third city, the locals are wont to point out the exact centre of a billiard table in the centre of a bar in the centre of town, which is in the centre of Umbria, which is in the centre of Italy, which is in the centre of the Mediterranean, whose name means 'the middle of the world'. In September 1997, Foligno was in the middle again, this time of an earthquake. The whole world watched as its medieval Torre Comunale collapsed; the Folignati wept and vowed to rebuild it 'where it was, as it was' – the battle cry of major Italian restoration projects. A few townspeople are still living in containers but most are back in their homes or new houses. The tower will take longer, and many *palazzi* are still under scaffolding, but most churches have now reopened.

Even before the disaster, not many people stopped for Foligno; in a sense, the centre has also been a victim of its post-war prosperity, and the ring of factories and modern suburbs that surrounds it is enough to discourage most travellers. But to pass by is to miss one of the most distinctive Umbrian towns, neither as archaic nor as cute as Assisi but memorable in its own way, a minor medieval capital with a pinch of grandeur and an air of genteel dilapidation and hopelessness that the tremors have aggravated.

Getting to and around Foligno

Foligno, 36km/30mins from Perugia and 158km/2hrs 30mins from Rome, is one of the main **rail** junctions for eastern Umbria. **Buses** link it to Colfiorito, Montefalco, Bevagna, Trevi and Spoleto; FS bus services connect it to Assisi, Perugia and Siena 3 times a day. The bus station is on Viale Mezzetti.

There is underground **car parking** near Porta Romana, handy for the tourist office. You can hire **bikes** at Baltistelli, Via XX Settembre 88, **t** 0742 344059.

History

Foligno was the ancient Roman *Fulginum*, near the junction of the branches of the Via Flaminia. This key location brought Christianity early to Foligno, thanks to St Felicianus, martyred in the 3rd century. In spite of its location on a plain, the city never disappeared in all the troubles that followed the crack-up of the Roman Empire: it survived attacks by the Saracens and Magyars to spring back up in the 12th century as a free *comune* with strong Ghibelline tendencies. St Francis was a frequent visitor; not long afterwards, it was the home of the Blessed Angela (1248–1309), a mystic whose direct communion with God and visions were recorded by her spiritual director in her autobiographical *Book of Divine Consolation*.

The Blessed Angela was 12 when the man suspected of being the Antichrist, the Emperor Frederick II, with his exotic Saracen army and dancing girls, held his parliament in Foligno, in defiance of the pope who had excommunicated him. This got the Folignati into trouble after his death, and the period of wars and civil disorders that followed resulted in the Trinci family assuming power in 1305. Their rule, which saw Foligno dominating Assisi, Spello, Montefalco, Bevagna and Trevi, lasted until 1439, when in a moment of upheaval Pope Eugenius IV sent in an army under Cardinal Giovanni Vitelleschi. Vitelleschi's family hated the Trinci and had no qualms about executing the last lord and his followers and instituting direct papal rule.

There was one bright spot before the town nodded off, when German printers brought their presses to Foligno in 1470, only six years after the first books were printed in Italy; the first printed edition of Dante's *Divina Commedia* – also the first printed book in the Italian language – came out in Foligno the following year.

Piazza della Repubblica

Piazza della Repubblica marks the centre of Foligno, with the Duomo facing the **Palazzo Comunale** – a rare architectural catastrophe. This was a genuine 12th-century monument, until someone pasted a neoclassical façade on it in the early 1900s, mercifully disguised by scaffolding at present. The tower survived with its original lantern with Ghibelline crenellations as one of Foligno's proudest landmarks, before it collapsed in the quake.

The Folignati can't leave well alone; in the 18th century they commissioned Luigi Vanvitelli, court architect to the Kingdom of Naples, and the town's own Giuseppe Piermarini, designer of La Scala in Milan, to modernize their already grandiose **Duomo**. Fortunately, they didn't tamper with the two façades on either side of the L-shaped piazza: the **east front** (1133) is pink and white in Perugian style, with some 1900s Venetian mosaics and other modern improvements, but the original **south front** remains, featuring one of the finest portals in Umbria (1201). It's also one of the least orthodox, a strange testament to the syncretic religious and philosophical currents of that age. The reliefs include figures of the zodiac, a medieval bestiary and long panels with geometric patterns and grapevines. Frederick II appears left of the door, one of only two existing likenesses in Italy. Two porphyry lions hold up the doorway, and at the top of the arch, barely visible, is a Muslim star and crescent. There are more fantastical animals above the portal and a good rose window. The portal was brand-new when young Francis of Assisi came here in 1205 and sold his father's stock of cloth and a packhorse to raise money for the restoration of San Damiano (*see* p.466). He wouldn't, however, recognize the Duomo's interior, where the Cappella dell'Assunta is all that remains of the 12th-century original. The best art is in the sacristy: a painting of the *Madonna and St John* by Alunno and busts of Bartolomeo and Diana Roscioli, recently attributed to Bernini.

Palazzo Trinci
t 0742 357989; open Tues–Sun 10–7; adm

At the western end of the piazza, the much-altered **Palazzo Trinci**, still has its elegant original Renaissance courtyard behind a neoclassical façade. Nearly all the interior dates from the period of Foligno's greatest *signore*, Ugolino III Trinci (ruled 1386–1415), who commissioned a precocious humanistic cycle of late Gothic frescoes, by Gentile da Fabriano and others, for the second floor. They are an early example of the reawakening of interest in the classical past, especially notable for being far from the centre of action in Florence. The frescoes were undergoing restoration for years before the quake and emerged unscathed. The palace **chapel** has frescoes on the *Life of Mary* (1424) by Ottaviano Nelli of Gubbio, who also painted the heroic Roman figures in the Sala dei Giganti. Frescoes in the loggia show the founding of Rome: most curious of all is a half-completed fresco and *sinopia* (preparatory sketch), *Rhea Silvia Being Buried Alive*; Rhea was the Vestal Virgin who gave birth to Romulus and Remus. The **Sala delle Arti Liberali e dei Pianeti** has allegorical figures of the liberal arts represented by women seated on thrones, and allegories of the planets. The corridor, which gave the Trinci access to the Duomo, has frescoes of ancient heroes and the *Seven Ages of Man*. Ugolino also collected ancient art: there's a rare high relief of the games in the Circus Maximus, busts of the emperors and a statue of Cupid and Psyche.

Pinacoteca Comunale
open Tues–Sun 10–7; joint adm with Palazzo Trinci and other sights

Museo Multimediale dei Tornei delle Giustre e dei Giochi
t 0742 357697; open Tues–Sun 10–7

The building also houses the **Pinacoteca Comunale**, with an *Annunciation* attributed to Gozzoli, works by Pierantonio Mezzastris of Foligno and detached trecento frescoes. The newest museum, the **Museo Multimediale dei Tornei delle Giustre e dei Giochi**, also in Palazzo Trinci, has multimedia displays on Foligno's medieval pageant and similar jousts and tournaments elsewhere.

Down Via Gramsci

Palazzo Trinci is only the first of a long line of Folignati palaces along Via Gramsci. Most of the noble residences were built in the 1500s and can now be seen restored after the earthquake and the preceding hundreds of years of neglect. The one nearest Palazzo Trinci, the 16th-century **Palazzo Deli**, is by far the most beautiful.

Santa Maria Infraportas
open Mon–Sat 9–12 and 4–6, Sun 9–12

San Domenico
t 0742 344563; open for musical events Tues–Sat 10am–12.30pm

Nunziatella
t 0742 357989; open Tues–Sat 10–1 and 4–7

Foligno's other churches are well endowed with art: **San Niccolò** in Via Scuola d'Arti e Mestieri has works by Foligno's own Niccolò di Liberatore, known as Alunno; in Piazza San Domenico, **Santa Maria Infraportas** is one of Foligno's oldest churches, with unusual 12th-century windows and portico, and frescoes by Mezzastris and others; the large, deconsecrated **San Domenico** has good trecento frescoes, currently hidden by scaffolding.

There are more Renaissance palaces along Via Mazzini and Via Garibaldi, its northern extension, where the oratory known as the **Nunziatella** has a fresco by Perugino.

ⓘ Foligno >
Corso Cavour 126, t 0742 354459 or t 0742 354165, www.umbria2000.it, www.comune.foligno.pg.it

Tourist Information in Foligno

As in Assisi, the earthquake has left many buildings unstable, with many places still under restoration.

Foligno is one of Umbria's **gliding and hang-gliding** centres (Aeroclub, Via Cagliari 22, **t** 0742 670201). Or you might like to **horse-ride** (Centro Ippico CO.GI.VE, Fraz. Verchiano, **t** 0742 632846).

Market Days

Markets take place on Tuesday and Saturday on Via Nazario Sauro.

Festivals in Foligno

Giostra della Quintana, *www.quintana.it*, 14–15 June, or nearest weekend. A 17th-century custom with knights from 10 districts jousting, plays in 300-year-old Umbrian dialect, a historic cooking competition, games, a fair, parades, outdoor taverns and so on.

Rematch of Giostra, 14–15 Sept.

Where to Stay and Eat in Foligno

Foligno ✉ 06034

*****Le Mura**, Via Bolletta 29, **t** 0742 357344, *www.albergolemura.com* (€€). A comfortable modern hotel on the northwest of town, with Internet access and a restaurant serving good *strangozzi* with pepper, tripe, lamb and veal (half and full board offered). *Closed Tues.*

*****Villa Roncalli**, Viale Roma 25, just south of centre, **t** 0742 391091 (€€). A stylish 17th-century villa with a shady garden, a pool, bike loan, a garage, comfy rooms, and the city's finest restaurant (€€€) serving Umbrian dishes with gourmet flair, including ravioli and pigeon *allo spiedo*. Half board is available. *Closed Mon, 2wks Aug and 2wks Jan.*

****Albergo Valentini**, Via F. Ottaviani 19, near station, **t** 0742 353990 (€€). A pleasant family-run choice with parking and bike loan.

Il Bacco Felice >>

Da Remo, Via Filzi 10, near station, **t** 0742 340522 (€€). A classic choice in a Liberty-style villa, four generations strong, serving typical Umbrian cuisine such as tasty *strangozzi* and roast kid simmered in Montefalco's Sagrantino wine. There's a garden for summer. *Closed Sun eve, Mon and Aug.*

Osteria del Teatro, Via Petrucci 6, **t** 0742 350745 (€€). An atmospheric, romantic restaurant in a 15th-century palace, with a vaulted ceiling, theatre posters, lovely wine cellars and a garden. The courgette fritters, deepfried sage, pumpkin ravioli and lamb and beef are recommended. *Closed Mon, Jan and Aug.*

Il Bacco Felice, Via Garibaldi 73, **t** 0742 341019 (€). A cosy *enoteca* serving cheeses and other snacks to accompany the good choice of bottles.

Barbanera, Piazza della Repubblica, **t** 0742 350672 (€). An old *drogheria* with a wonderful old counter offering light snacks, coffees or *aperitivos*. *Closed Mon.*

Up the Menotre Valley

Directly east of Foligno, follow the valley of the little Menotre river into the mountains, a beautiful but seldom-visited corner of Umbria that extends to the border with the Marches. This area was the worst hit by the quake. The collapsed buildings in villages have been cleared, but it will take a few years for the scaffolding, rubble and cranes to be removed. The villages are largely abandoned. Many families moved to Foligno or even Rome and most likely will not come back. While the state gave immediate compensation to victims, it has been slower to invest in rebuilding homes. In some cases, containers have been replaced by wooden chalets, and there is some new building outside the old villages. But overall, the area is very demoralized. The villagers had little before, and what little they had they lost. Modest roadside stalls sell the lentils, chick peas, red potatoes and onions indigenous to the region.

Abbazia di Sassovivo
closed for restoration at time of writing

The SS77 from Foligno follows the valley but, just after crossing the Via Flaminia, a side road to the right (signposted Casale) heads 5km to the **Abbazia di Sassovivo**, an 11th-century Benedictine abbey with a remarkable cloister. The main road twists up into the mountains, passing interesting caves and a pretty waterfall on the Menotre at **Pale**, 8km from Foligno, a village wedged between the rocks. Paper has been milled here since the 13th century.

On the heights, just before the Marches border, the mountains level out to form the broad meadow or *valico* of **Colfiorito**, where the lofty green marshlands, 730m above sea level, are a favourite spot for migrating birds; other parts of the *valico* are used for growing beans and lentils. Most of the hamlets around its rim have been abandoned since the quake. The rugged roadside 11th-century church, **Santa Maria di Pistia**, has porticoes on two sides to accommodate the country fairs held here in the Middle Ages.

A side road turns off before Colfiorito (24km), heading south into pristine mountain scenery around **Rasiglia**, where the **Santuario della Madonna delle Grazie** has walls covered with well-preserved, colourful quattrocento frescoes, many painted as *ex votos*.

Bevagna

Under the Martani hills, on the original westerly route of the Via Flaminia, Roman *Mevania* has survived as Bevagna (population 2,400), a quiet, unspoiled, friendly town, where the main crops are flax and wine. Though low-key, it has some artistic gems. During its period as a free *comune* in the Middle Ages, before being taken over in 1371 by the Trinci family of Foligno, it built two of Umbria's best Romanesque churches. The quake left a number of people homeless; nearly all are back in their homes. It also damaged the churches, though there are fewer external signs of damage than elsewhere.

Piazza Silvestri

Bevagna's pride and joy is perfect Piazza Silvestri, a medieval and theatrical *pièce de résistance* that shows that the Bevanati tried hard to keep up with their bigger neighbours. It has a Corinthian column, a fountain and the impressive Gothic **Palazzo Comunale** of 1270, restored after an earlier earthquake in 1832, with a charming little theatre inside. An archway connects it to the delightful **church of San Silvestro**, built by architect Maestro Binello (who signed his work) and being restored with the help of funds raised by Prince Charles. The simple façade incorporates bits of Roman buildings, an 1195 inscription to Emperor Henry VII and a frieze over the door. The interior is essentially Romanesque, and like many 12th-century buildings it features a raised presbytery, leaving room for twin pulpits (or *ambones)*, now vanished, on either side of the steps and a small crypt beneath. The real surprise is the style of the capitals – they're in the Egyptian order, representing papyrus leaves the way Ionic and Corinthian capitals recall the leaves of the acanthus. Such columns are common in this area, but their presence has never been explained: maybe they were copied from the ruins of some Roman-era temple to Isis or Serapis. They are slightly curved, in *entasis* to look straight.

Across the piazza, the late-12th-century **church of San Michele Arcangelo** has a few Egyptian capitals recycled from older buildings. Binello and Rodolfo built this about the same time as San Silvestro and to the same interior plan. St Michael and his dragon figure prominently on the façade, with some re-used Roman friezes, a Cosmatesque arch, and a menagerie of cows, cats and such, similar to the portal in Foligno (by the same architects). The crypt under the raised presbytery is supported by Roman columns. There are also two processional statues of Bevagna's patron saint Vincenzo, one of wood and the other of silver.

Santi Domenico e Giacomo
open 11–12.30 and 3.30–6.30

The third church on the piazza, **Santi Domenico e Giacomo**, has a Baroque interior with what must be the biggest alabaster window in Italy behind the altar. Of the original decoration, little remains

Museo della Città
t 0742 360031; open April, May and Sept daily 10.30–1 and 2.30–6; June and July daily 10.30–1 and 3.30–7; Aug daily 10.30–1 and 3–7.30; Oct–Mar Tues–Sun 10.30–1 and 2.30–5; adm; circuito cittadino *ticket includes museum, theatre and mosaics,* *(see below)*

but a radiant trecento *Virgin of the Annunciation* in the choir; there are also works by Bevagna-born artist Il Fantino ('the Jockey', Ascensidonio Spacco, d. 1646).

From here, Corso Matteotti follows the route of the old Via Flaminia, passing an 18th-century pharmacy and a *municipio* of the same period, home to the **Museo della Città**, with Roman artefacts and coins, busts and architectural fragments found in and around town, medieval manuscripts, a model of the Santuario della Madonna delle Grazie (*see* below), and works by Dono Doni and Il Fantino and an *Adoration of the Magi* by Corrado Giacinto.

The Rest of Town

Mosaic Romano
t 0742 360031, or ask at tourist office (see below)

There are more remnants of Roman *Mevania* a few blocks further up the Corso, at Via Crescimbeni, where a **Roman temple** was partly conserved when its columns were bricked in long ago. Nearby, at Via Porta Guelfa, is a **marine mosaic** with a big lobster, seahorses and Tritons, once part of the 2nd-century baths. A crescent of houses traces the curve of the **amphitheatre**, in Via dell'Anfiteatro, and a house at the end, in Via Dante Aligheri, has a fine **Roman frieze**.

At the highest point in town, 13th-century **San Francesco** holds the stone on which Francis stood when he preached to the birds at Pian d'Arca, north of here. Steps lead down to Piazza Garibaldi and Bevagna's best-preserved medieval gate, **Porta Cannara**.

Around Bevagna

Convento dell'Annunziata
closed for restoration at time of writing; call **t** *0742 361234 for latest information*

Santuario della Madonna delle Grazie
open daily 8–12 and 4–sunset

More bits of Roman *Mevania* can be seen off the old Via Flaminia to Foligno (the SS316): the fossil-like imprint of another amphitheatre in a field and two ruined tombs. Just north of Bevagna, the **Convento dell'Annunziata** has more works by Il Fantino and a pretty terracotta altarpiece of the *Annunciation*. A path from the convent leads down to a spring-fed lake.

Southwest of Bevagna is yet another 16th-century shrine to the Virgin Mary, the **Santuario della Madonna delle Grazie**, designed by Valentino Martelli with a comely octagonal dome and a pretty view.

ⓘ Bevagna >
Piazza Silvestri 1, **t** *0742 361667, www.bevagna.it*

★ L'Orto degli Angeli >

Festivals in Bevagna

Mercato delle Gaite, mid-June. A neo-medieval fair in which the 4 districts (*gaite*) vie to dress more authentically, and stalls sell food and drink.

Where to Stay and Eat in Bevagna

Bevagna ✉ 06031

L'Orto degli Angeli, Via D. Alighieri 1, **t** 0742 360130, *www.ortoangeli.it* (€€€€€). Modern comforts in a medieval atmosphere in the town centre. The Antonini Angeli Nieri Mongelli family home, it is filled with family antiques and pictures, and contains both a 2nd-century temple to Minerva (forming one wall of the restaurant) and the ruins of a Roman theatre (part of the delightful hanging garden). A 'residence' contains some luxurious guesthouses. There's also a restaurant (€€€) where you can enjoy Umbrian classics with a creative twist. *Closed Tues.*

***Palazzo Brunamonti, Corso Matteotti 79, t 0742 361932, *www.brunamonti.com* (€€€). An old *palazzo* with 16 comfortable bedrooms with Internet access, and frescoed public rooms. *Closed 9–31 Jan.*

Il Chiostro di Bevagna, Corso Matteotti 107, **t** 0742 361987, *www.ilchiostrodibevagna.com* (€€). Simple but very charmingly furnished rooms with modern comforts, set in the frescoed cloister of the former Dominican convent.

El Rancho, Via Flaminia 53, **t** 0742 360105, *www.elrancho.it* (€€). Basic rooms and a beautiful pool amidst trees, plus a restaurant offering tempting local dishes and products at down-to-earth prices, with the emphasis on truffles and wild boar. You can eat outside in fine weather. *Closed Mon.*

Da Nina, Piazza Garibaldi 6, **t** 0742 360024 (€€). A simple but attractive lunch stop with a daily-changing menu featuring lots of truffles. *Closed Tues.*

Montefalco

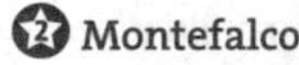

Only 7km from Bevagna but much higher in the hills, Montefalco (population 5,500) is another unspoilt gem. Dubbed the '*Ringhiera* (balcony) *d'Umbria*', the town offers splendid 360° views over to Assisi and Perugia and down the entire Valle Umbra as far as Spoleto. Another nickname, '*il lembo di cielo caduto in terra*' ('heaven's hem fallen to earth'), refers to its reputation as a factory for saints, extraordinary even by Umbrian standards; the celestial hosts count eight former Montefalconesi.

Until 1240 it was known as Coccorone; when Frederick II destroyed it and rebuilt it as a Ghibelline town, he named it after his imperial eagle. It later became part of the domain of the Trinci family, then part of the Church's; today, it is practically synonymous with its fine Sagrantino wines and woven textiles.

San Francesco

Appropriately, the town of heaven's hem is capped by a monk's tonsure: the central, circular, partially arcaded **Piazza del Comune**, from which streets radiate down like spokes. One, Via Ringhiera Umbra, takes in the lovely Clitunno valley while descending to Montefalco's pride and joy: the frescoes in the deconsecrated 14th-century **San Francesco**, now a **museum**. Benozzo Gozzoli spent two years here (1450–52), painting the apse with the Life of St Francis. Montefalco's Franciscans did not let him put in many of his usual fancies, though there are a few moppet children grinning out from the corners. He does, however, indulge in his favourite cityscapes, including views of Montefalco (where Francis visited after preaching to the birds around Bevagna) and Arezzo (where he cast out the devils). Panels along the bottom of the apse show portraits by Gozzoli of great Franciscans – a distinguished company of saints, popes and philosophers, including Duns Scotus. The cycle makes a fascinating contrast to the earlier, much better frescoes in Assisi, but Gozzoli's rather facile, charming and sentimental figures

San Francesco
t 0742 379598; open Mar–May, Sept and Oct daily 10.30–1 and 2–6; June and July daily 10.30–1 and 3–7; Aug daily 10.30–1 and 3–7.30; Nov–Feb Tues–Sun 10.30–1 and 2.30–5; adm

Getting to Montefalco

There are 2 **trains** a day to/from Foligno, and SSIT **buses** (**t** 0743 212208, *www.spoletina.com*) to Montefalco from Bastardo, Bevagna and Perugia once a day, and from Foligno and Spoleto several times a day.

clearly struck a deep chord in the mid 15th century, because they were a model for a good deal of later Umbrian painting. Gozzoli also frescoed the first chapel, a triptych with the *Madonna and Saints and Crucifix*. The other Renaissance fresco here is by Perugino, a restored run-of-the-mill *Nativity* with Lake Trasimeno. The aisles contain fine trecento painting, including a vivid and unique *Temptations of St Anthony*; there is a fond painting by Tiberio d'Assisi of a local favourite and exemplar of spiritual first aid, the *Madonna del Soccorso*, in which Our Lady is about to whack a devil with a big club when he comes to snatch a child whose exasperated mother had exclaimed 'May the Devil take you!'

The **Pinacoteca**, also in the church, has an 18th-century statue of Foligno's Quintana Saracen, another *Madonna del Soccorso*, a *Madonna and Child* by the school of Melozzo da Forlì, and a lovely painting, *SS. Vincent, Illuminata and Nicolas of Tolentino*, by Antonizzo Romano; another section has an ancient marble statue of Hercules found in the town, a medieval lion and a Renaissance river god.

The Rest of Town

Sant'Agostino/ Sant'Illuminata
opening hrs depend on priest

Two other churches have frescoes by 14th–16th-century Umbrian painters – **Sant'Agostino** and **Sant'Illuminata**. Montefalco retains medieval walls, including two gates: **Porta Sant'Agostino**, with a fresco of the *Virgin and Saints*, and **Porta Federico II**, with the eagle.

Outside the Walls of Montefalco

Santa Chiara da Montefalco
open daily 9.30–11.30 and 3.30–5.30

Just outside the Porta Federico II, 17th-century **Santa Chiara da Montefalco**, built around a much earlier chapel of Santa Croce, has lovely frescoes of 1333 on the life of Saint Clare of the Cross (*c.* 1268–1308), a follower of St Francis, famous for her charity; after she died, her heart was found to be branded with the sign of the cross.

San Fortunato
open daily 9.30–12 and 3.30–5

The Franciscan **convent of San Fortunato**, just over 1km southeast of Montefalco's Porta Spoleto, enjoys a beautiful setting and still shelters a handful of friars; the thick ilex forest that surrounds it was planted as insulation against winter winds. The church, which is dedicated to Fortunatus (d. 400), a priest who was famous for his charity to the poor, was founded over a Roman basilica in the 5th century, rebuilt during the 16th and later Baroqued inside, although it preserves some interesting fresco fragments by Gozzoli: a lunette over the door, an *Adoration of the Child* and the *Enthroned St Fortunatus*. The cloister uses Roman columns and has a chapel frescoed by Tiberio d'Assisi on the *Life of St Francis*.

Where to Stay and Eat in Montefalco

ⓘ **Montefalco >** *Via Ringhiera Umbra 1*, **t** *0742 379598, www.montefalco.it (closed Sun Nov–Feb)*

Montefalco ✉ 06036

This is perhaps best known for Sagrantino and Rosso di Montefalco red wines, both sold in shops around town and used widely in its cuisine.

****Villa Pambuffetti**, Viale della Vittoria 20, **t** 0742 379417, *www.villapambuffetti.com* (€€€€€). A 19th-century villa owned by a local noble family, with 15 rooms with antiques, a park with huge trees and an outdoor pool, and beauty treatments. Half board is available.

Ringhiera Umbra, Corso G. Mameli 20, **t** 0742 379166, *www.ringhieraumbra.com* (€€). Basic rooms near Piazza del Comune, some ensuite, and a restaurant serving local cuisine (half/full board available).

Coccorone, Vicolo Fabbri 7, off central square, **t** 0742 379535 (€€€). An elegant, understated place with tempting home-made tagliatelle, *papardelli* and *strangozzi*, and beef cooked in Sagrantino wine sauce. *Closed Wed in winter*.

Il Falisco, Via XX Settembre 14, **t** 0742 379185 (€€). Local specialities such as beef fillet cooked in Sagrantino wine, and good gnocchi. It's tiny, so get here early. *Closed Mon*.

Enoteca Federico II, Piazza del Comune, **t** 0742 378902 (€). A pleasant spot to come for a snack and a glass of wine on the piazza. *Closed Wed*.

Around Montefalco: Into the Monti Martani

At Montefalco begins a range of hills and lofty plateaux known as the Monti Martani, separating the Valle Umbra from the Tiber. This lies well off the tourist trails. Places such as **Gualdo Cattaneo**, west of Bevagna, knew their peak of importance under the Lombards (the name Gualdo comes from the German *wald* or wood). Its big cylindrical castle dates from 1494 – the work of Pope Alexander VI, built after his fiery son Cesare Borgia stormed through the area to show the Umbrians who was boss. When Gualdo's church was rebuilt in 1804, stonework from its 13th-century predecessor was preserved on its façade; the crypt is original as well. The apse has a fine *Last Supper* by Bevagna's early-17th-century master Fantino.

A pretty drive west of Montefalco is a market town bearing the unfortunate name of **Bastardo**, the gateway to other forgotten castles: **Le Torri** (a poor man's San Gimignano), Renaissance **Barattano** and a Lombard fort at **Saragano**.

Southeast of Bastardo, amid olive groves on the slopes of the Monti Martani, the walled village of **Giano dell'Umbria** is one of several in the area founded by Norman knights granted the land after fighting as mercenaries for Pope Gregory VII in the 1080s – the whole area extending to Castel Ritaldi was known as Normandia in the Middle Ages. Originally it consisted of two fortified villages, and it has two 13th-century churches on the same piazza but only a single Palazzo Pubblico; until the 1300s, Giano managed to remain independent in spite of being circled by all the local sharks. Of the churches, the Pieve has a Baroque interior and a restored painting by Andrea Polinori of the *Madonna and Child* (1620) who keeps company with a much-venerated *Madonna and Child* painted 300 years earlier.

Just north of Giano, the red-stone **Abbazia di San Felice** was founded by some of Umbria's early coenobitic monks. In the 8th century, the Benedictines moved in and rebuilt it, and since 1815 it has been reoccupied by a congregation dedicated to mission work. The Romanesque church, from the 12th century, has a handsome portal topped by a three-light window and an impressive apse with a gallery. Under the raised presbytery, the crypt has quaint old Roman and early medieval capitals and an ancient sarcophagus, holding the remains of the martyred bishop of Martana. San Felice's frescoed cloister is especially pretty.

Castel Ritaldi (14km south of Montefalco) has a castle from the 1200s. Just outside is the **Pieve di San Gregorio**, built in 1140, with a charming pink and white sculpted façade with elaborate interwoven designs inhabited by little monsters; it has been restored by funds raised in New York. Nearby **Bruna** has a Renaissance church in the shape of a trefoil, **Santa Maria della Bruna** (1510).

Trevi and the Tempietto del Clitunno

No small town in Umbria makes a grander sight than Trevi (population 7,400), a nearly vertical village that's reminiscent of Positano on the Amalfi coast, hung on a steep and curving hillside draped with olive groves above the Via Flaminia. It has no connection with the fountain in Rome except that both were at the intersection of three roads or *tre vie*. Trevi, part of the duchy of Spoleto and seat of a bishop, was destroyed by the Saracens and Magyars. Briefly an independent *comune*, its strategic position made it a prize fought over by Perugia and Foligno. Joining the Papal States in 1439 brought it prosperity, at least in the short run, as well as the fourth printing press in Italy in 1470. These days, like its sister hilltowns, it may look medieval but it dallies on the wild side of the international avant-garde.

Two Churches, Two Art Museums

Trevi's credentials as a free *comune* in the Middle Ages are in its small but proud **Palazzo Comunale** in Piazza Mazzini, built in the 14th century, with later additions. From here, the stepped Via Beato Placido Riccardi leads up past the Piazza della Rocca, lined with quattrocento palaces; further up stands the domed cathedral, **Sant'Emiliano**. Emiliano, an Armenian monk, served in the 4th century as bishop of Trevi, and has been solemnly celebrated every 27 January since the Middle Ages with a procession of the Illuminata. His church has three Romanesque

Getting to Trevi

There are **buses** to Trevi from Foligno several times a day (**t** 0743 212208, *www.spoletina.com*). There are also **trains**, from Spello, Assisi and Perugia several times a day, and from Spoleto, Terni, Narni and Rome, but you have to get a bus down the hill from the station.

---

apses and a 15th-century portal, with the good bishop and a pair of lions carved in relief. The interior was redone in the 19th century but contains a beautiful altar of 1522, carved by Rocco di Tommaso.

Trevi Flash Art Museum
t 0742 381021; open Tues–Sun 3–7; adm varies by exhibition

Next door, the **Palazzo Lucarini** hosts the **Trevi Flash Art Museum**, a joint endeavour between *Flash Art* magazine and the *comune*, with works by contemporary Umbrian, Italian and foreign artists.

For older stuff, make your way to **San Francesco**, a huge mid-14th-century church with original frescoes, on the site where Francis's preaching was drowned out by the braying of an 'indomitable ass'. 'Brother ass, do hush and let me preach to these people,' Francis said, and the animal 'put its head down on the ground and knelt, and remained silent until Francis had finished, much to the wonder of the people'. It has Renaissance tombs, a Roman sarcophagus with the remains of St Ventura (d. 1310) and one of Lo Spagna's finest works, the *Assumption with SS. Jerome, John the Baptist, Francis and Anthony of Padua*, where the Virgin ascends to heaven over Foligno. This was first in the chapel of the San Martino monastery (*see* below).

Museo Civico/ Raccolta d'Arte di San Francesco
t 0742 381628; open April, May and Sept Tues–Sun 10.30–1 and 2.30–6; June and July Tues–Sun 10.30–1 and 3.30–7; Aug daily 10.30–1 and 3–7.30; Oct–Mar Fri–Sun 10.30–1 and 2.30–5; adm

Museo della Civiltà dell'Olivo
t 0742 381628; open April, May and Sept Tues–Sun 10.30–1 and 2.30–6; June and July Tues–Sun 10.30–1 and 3.30–7; Aug daily 10.30–1 and 3–7.30; Oct–Mar Fri–Sun 10.30–1 and 2.30–5; adm includes visit to San Francesco church

Access to the church is via its enormous convent, home to the **Museo Civico** or **Raccolta d'Arte di San Francesco**. There are good paintings by local artists, including an *Incoronazione di Maria* by Lo Spagna and scenes of the *Life of Christ* from polyptychs by Giovanni di Corraduccio, a charming 15th-century painter from Foligno. The convent is also home to the **Museo della Civiltà dell'Olivo**. Trevi is famous for its olive oil: its conical hill is wrapped with majestic olive trees, including specimens believed to be well over 1,000 years old (especially the so-called Olivo da Sant'Emiliano, 3km south at Bovara). Olives, introduced by the Greeks in the bay of Naples, reached Umbria by the 5th century BC; like many Greek things, they were quickly adapted by the Etruscans and the rest is history.

Around Trevi

San Martino
open daily 8–12 and 4–sunset

Though the town has many churches, the best two are just outside. From Piazza Garibaldi, outside the gate to the *centro storico*, Via Ciuffelli leads to the 14th-century Capuchin monastery and **church of San Martino**. Over the door is a lunette by Tiberio d'Assisi, whose *St Martin and the Beggar* is inside; the other prize painting is Pierantonio Mezzastris' *Madonna*.

South of Trevi, in an olive grove, is the votive **church of the Madonna delle Lacrime**, built in 1487 to house a weeping statue of the Virgin – the first of many churches that went up during the great Marian renewal, inspired by the sermons of San Bernardino. The church, shaped like a Latin cross, has a fine sculpted portal by Giovanni di Gian Pietro of Venice; when the quake damage has been repaired, you'll be able to see the lovely frescoes: the *Adoration of the Magi* by Perugino, an anonymous *Madonna and Child* of 1483 and a *Deposition* by Lo Spagna. Many of the locally prominent Valenti family have impressive tombs from the 1500s and 1600s.

Tempietto del Clitunno
t 0743 275085; open summer daily 9–7, winter daily 9–2; adm

Though the Roman villas and temples that stood in sacred Clitunno (*see* below) are long gone, bits were reassembled in the mysterious little **Tempietto del Clitunno**, on the SS3 just south of Trevi (signposted). Two centuries ago this was believed to be a pagan temple converted to Christian use; Goethe dissented, believing it to be an original Christian work. For once this most misinformed of all geniuses got it right. The most recent studies put the Tempietto somewhere in the 6th century, or even as late as the 8th, making this obscure, lovely building in a way the last work of classical antiquity, Christian enough, but an architectural throwback to a world that was already lost.

The little track below the temple was the original Roman Via Flaminia; travellers between Ravenna and Rome would look up and see the beautiful façade, with its two striking coloured marble columns and ornate pediment in an exotic, half-oriental late Roman style. The entrance, however, is round the side, leading into the portico and from there to the tiny sanctuary decorated with Byzantine frescoes of the 700s: saints Peter and Paul flanking the altar, and, above, two unforgettable, very spiritual angels inspired by the great mosaics of Ravenna, gazing inscrutably out from the depths of the Dark Ages. The dedication remains intact, on the architrave: 'Holy God of the Angels who made the Resurrection'.

The Fonti del Clitunno

Fonti del Clitunno
t 0743 521141; open May–Aug daily 8.30–8; Sept daily 9–1 and 2–7.30; Oct–3 Nov daily 9–1 and 2–6.30; 4 Nov–Dec 10–1 and 2–5; Jan–14 Mar daily 10–1 and 2–4; 15 Mar–Apr daily 9–7; adm

Still on the SS3, 2km south of the Tempietto, is **Fonti del Clitunno**, a famous beauty spot for some 2,300 years. Through the poetry of Virgil and Propertius, all of Rome knew about Clitumnus, its eponymous river god, and the snow-white oxen raised here to serve as sacrifices. It was one of the great sights of the Grand Tour; in the 19th-century, it inspired Giosuè Carducci to write one of his best-known poems, baptizing Umbria green for evermore.

'Salve, Umbria verde, e tu del puro fonte nume Clitumno! Sento in cuor l'antica patrla e aleggiarmi su l'accesa fronte gl'ital iddii.'

'Hail, green Umbria, and you, Clitumno, genius of the pure spring! I feel in my heart the ancient fatherland, and the Italic gods alighting on my fevered brow.'

A score of underground springs rise at the river's source, forming a landscape of astonishing crystal lagoons and islands, planted with weeping willows and poplars. Byron devoted a few stanzas of

Childe Harold's Pilgrimage to the place (Canto 4), but today the proximity of the busy Via Flaminia and the railway keep the springs from being quite the idyllic paradise evoked by the poets; still it comes pretty close if you come on a quiet weekday, late in the afternoon after the coach parties have moved on. Next to the park, part of the lagoon doubles as a delightful picnic ground and a well-stocked trout farm.

The village hanging on the steep slope above, **Campello sul Clitunno**, is built around the 16th-century **Chiesa della Bianca**, with frescoes by Lo Spagna. For a remarkable view over the Valle Umbra, take the steep little road up and up through the terraces of olives to the tiny **Castello** (or Campello Alto), hunkered down in the walls.

South of Clitunno: San Giacomo

After Clitunno, the Via Flaminia passes under a grim square castle in **San Giacomo di Spoleto**, an outpost built in the 14th century by Cardinal Albornoz. Unlike the Cardinal's other Umbrian fortresses, this was later converted into a residential neighbourhood, with tiny lanes lined with little houses. Opposite the castle walls stands the **church of San Giacomo**, founded in the 13th century and redone in the 16th, the date of its beautiful carved doorway and frescoes. The best of these are by Lo Spagna and show miracles accredited to St James the Greater that occurred along the road to Compostela: a young man, unjustly hanged, is discovered still to be alive when his parents return to cut down his body. The parents hurry to tell the judge, who scoffs and says their son is as alive as the roast chickens on his table, whereupon the roast chickens fly away.

ⓘ **Trevi >**
Piazza Mazzini 5, t 0742 781150, www.protrevi.com

Where to Stay and Eat in Trevi

Trevi ✉ 06039

In Oct try Trevi's famous black celery (*sedano nero*); every Thurs morning that month sees a market devoted to it.

***Il Terziere**, Via Salerno 1, **t** 0742 78359, *www.ilterziere.com* (€€€). A fine choice, with lovely views and delicious local cuisine (half/full board available).

****Il Pescatore**, Via Chiesa Tonda 50, Loc. Pigge, **t** 0742 78483, *www.hotelilpescatore.net* (€). A peaceful *pensione* with pleasant ensuite rooms, near a brook. Its excellent restaurant (€€), has an imaginative menu based on fish and truffles, very good value. Full board is offered. *Closed Wed.*

***La Cerquetta**, Via Flaminia 144, Loc. Parrano, **t** 0742 78366, *www.hotelcerquetta.com* (€). Decent ensuite rooms and reliable Umbrian food at very honest prices; full board available. *Closed Sun.*

Campello sul Clitunno ✉ 06042

*****Vecchio Molino**, Via del Tempio 34, Loc. Pissignano, **t** 0743 521122, *www.vecchio-molino.it* (€€€). A former watermill close to the Perugia–Spoleto road but filled with the sound of gurgling water; two streams run through the garden. Bedrooms (breakfast included) are elegantly furnished in a traditional Umbrian style. *Closed Nov–Mar.*

****Fontanelle**, Via d'Elci 1, Loc. Fontanelle, **t** 0743 521091, *www.albergofontanelle.it* (€€). A lovely hotel surrounded by greenery. The bedrooms are basic but ensuite, and they boast panoramic views. The restaurant serves good *bruschette*, *strangozzi* and specialities based on local truffles, and half and full board are available.

****Ravale**, Via Virgilio, Loc. Ravele, Fonti del Clitunno, **t** 0743 521320, *www.ravale.it* (€€). Simple rooms and a restaurant-pizzeria (half and full board offered).

Pettino da Palmario, Loc. Pettino, northeast of town towards Colle Pian Fienile, **t** 0743 276021 (€€). A family-run *agriturismo* with simple but comfy double rooms and 2-person apartments in a rural setting, and a good reputation for its food (€€€). *Closed Tues and Mar.*

Spoleto

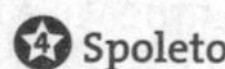

When composer Giancarlo Menotti was dreaming up the Festival of Two Worlds in the 1950s, he spent months travelling across central Italy looking for a pretty town where the best of modern culture could be displayed against a background that recalled the best of the past. Spoleto (population 36,000), a rather austere town of grey stone and cobbled streets, buried in one of the most obscure corners of darkest Umbria, was almost unknown then. But it has a remarkable past; after its prominence in classical times, it became the seat of one of the most powerful states in Italy at the very beginning of the Middle Ages. It remained splendid enough through the golden years of the high Middle Ages and Renaissance to acquire its share of lovely monuments, and then it pricked its finger on a spindle and dozed like Sleeping Beauty. Shelley called it 'the most romantic city I ever saw'.

After its long sleep, Spoleto was ready for Menotti. More than ready, perhaps: even after the musicians pack their instruments, they leave behind a Spoleto full of exhibitions and art workshops, its streets littered with jarring chunks of abstract sculpture. This experimental marriage of trendy art and the medieval hilltown is not always a happy one, but it's done Spoleto no harm.

History

Ancient *Spoletium*, one of the Umbrii's most important cities, was resettled as a Roman colony in 242 BC, only 24 years before an over-confident Hannibal came pounding at the gates, expecting an easy victory after his rout over the legions at Trasimeno (*see* p.450). But *Spoletium* remained loyal to Rome and repulsed the Carthaginians and their allies; Hannibal, who'd planned to go to Rome from there, was discouraged enough to make a fatal detour into the Marches.

Strategically located on the Via Flaminia midway between Rome and the late Imperial capital Ravenna, Spoleto was one of the rare towns to prosper in the twilight of the empire. King Theodoric built it up for the Ostrogoths; Justinian's general, Belisarius, did the same for the Byzantines; the Goths under Totila made it into a fortress, while the Lombards, arriving in 569, made it the base of their power, a duchy that in the 700s controlled most of central Italy.

Getting to and around Spoleto

The Rome–Ancona **train** line follows the Via Flaminia to Spoleto. There are also some 12 trains daily from Perugia (63km/70mins). The station is a bit far from the centre, but there are regular connecting buses. The ticket office is at Piazza Polvani, **t** 0743 48516.

Spoleto has its own intercity **bus** company, Società Spoletina di Imprese Trasporti (SSIT, **t** 0743 212208, *www.spoletina.com*), with connections from Piazza Garibaldi on the west of town to Assisi, Terni, Perugia and nearby villages. Regular buses go to Norcia and Foligno; 1 a day to Rome and to Urbino in the Marches.

Parking in the centre is next to impossible; there's a convenient car park outside Porta Loreto at the west end of the city, a free one in Via Don Bonilli, by the stadium and Roman theatre, and another just south of the city walls along Viale Cappuccini.

Bikes can be hired at Scocchetti Cicli, Via Marconi 82, **t** 0743 44728.For **car hire**, there's: AVIS, Loc. S. Chiodo 164, **t** 0743 46272, *www.avisautonoleggio.it*; and Hertz, Via Cerquiglia 144, **t** 0743 46703, *www.hertz.it*.

In 890, after Charlemagne, Duke Guido III made an armed play for the Imperial Crown, but had to be content with crowning himself King of Italy at Pavia. After Guido and his son Lamberto, the duchy fell into decline, and in the 11th century the popes began to lean on Spoleto, claiming authority through that famous forgery, the 'Donation of Constantine'. Not until 1198, though, was Innocent III successful in capturing the city, and in 1247 it became part of the papal domains once and for all. But not without occasional complications: in 1499 Spoleto was briefly ruled by Lucrezia Borgia, a 19-year-old just married to the second of three husbands by her scheming papal father. By all accounts, Lucrezia ruled well but was sent off two years later to marry a bigger fish – Alfonso d'Este of Ferrara. Under the popes, It became a favourite with the papal nobility, who filled it with palaces and used it to entertain celebrities: chronicles record lavish banquets laid on for Queen Christina of Sweden in 1655 and for Maria Casimira, widow of the hero John Sobieski, in 1699.

Spoleto is only heard from again some three centuries later, thanks to Giancarlo Menotti and the late Thomas Schippers, who bestowed on the town their **Festival of Two Worlds** (*see* p.517).

Remnants of Roman *Spoletium*

Like Perugia, Spoleto is a city of many ages, jammed together cheek-by-jowl in a fascinating collage of time and space. Thanks to the festival, the 20th century gets its say, too: if you arrive in Spoleto by train, you'll be greeted by a huge iron sculpture, the *Teodolapio* by Alexander Calder, a relic of the 1962 festival now used to shade a taxi stand. Buses from the station leave you at central **Piazza della Libertà**, which is also the usual approach if you arrive by car. Just across from the tourist office, the open side of the piazza overlooks the **Roman theatre**, built in the 1st century AD. In the 1950s it was restored as a venue for concerts and ballets during the music festivals; most of the theatre's impressive substructure of arches and tunnels has survived, as well as the

Teatro Romano
open daily 8.30–7.30; joint adm with Museo Archeologico (see p.511)

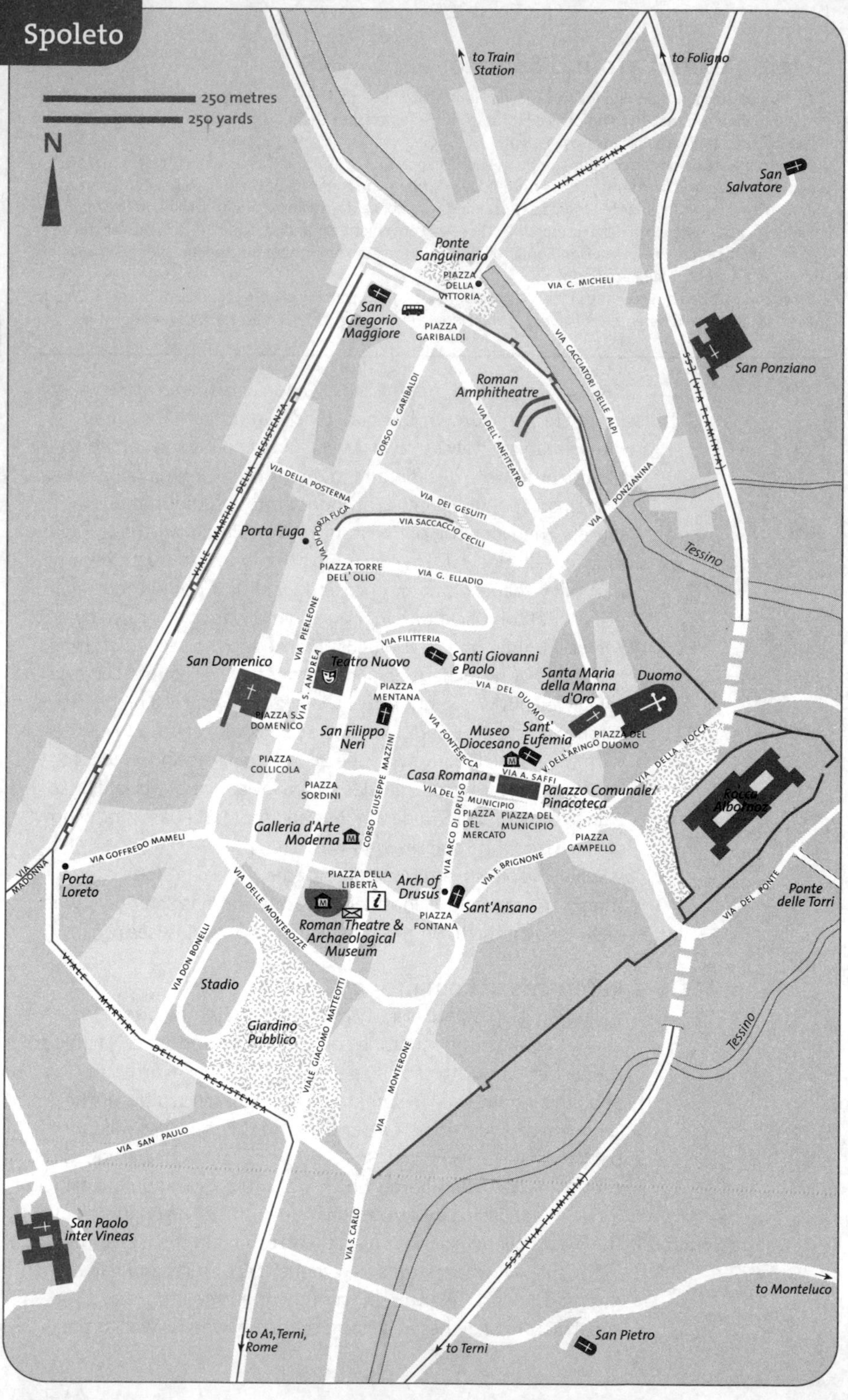
Spoleto
250 metres
250 yards
N
to Train Station
to Foligno
Via Nursina
San Salvatore
Ponte Sanguinario
Piazza della Vittoria
Via C. Micheli
San Gregorio Maggiore
Piazza Garibaldi
Via Cacciatori delle Alpi
SS3 (Via Flaminia)
San Ponziano
Roman Amphitheatre
Corso G. Garibaldi
Via dell' Anfiteatro
Viale Martiri della Resistenza
Via della Posterna
Via dei Gesuiti
Via Ponzianina
Via di Porta Fuga
Via Saccaccio Cecili
Porta Fuga
Tessino
Piazza Torre dell' Olio
Via G. Elladio
Via Pierleone
Via Filitteria
San Domenico
Teatro Nuovo
Santi Giovanni e Paolo
Santa Maria della Manna d'Oro
Duomo
Via S. Andrea
Piazza Mentana
Via del Duomo
Piazza S. Domenico
San Filippo Neri
Via Fontesecca
Museo Diocesano
Sant' Eufemia
Piazza del Duomo
V. dell'Aringo
Via della Rocca
Piazza Collicola
Corso Giuseppe Mazzini
Casa Romana
Via A. Saffi
Palazzo Comunale/ Pinacoteca
Rocca Albornoz
Piazza Sordini
Via del Municipio
Piazza del Mercato
Piazza del Municipio
Via Arco di Druso
Galleria d'Arte Moderna
Via Goffredo Mameli
Piazza Campello
Via Madonna
Porta Loreto
Via F. Brignone
Piazza della Libertà
Arch of Drusus
Sant'Ansano
Ponte delle Torri
Via del Ponte
Via delle Monterozze
Roman Theatre & Archaeological Museum
Piazza Fontana
Via Don Bonelli
Stadio
Giardino Pubblico
Viale Giacomo Matteotti
Via Monterone
Viale Martiri della Resistenza
Tessino
Via San Paulo
SS3 (Via Flaminia)
San Paolo inter Vineas
Via S. Carlo
to Monteluco
to A1, Terni, Rome
to Terni
San Pietro

pretty marble pavement in the *scena*. In the Middle Ages, the stage building was replaced with the formidable church, charming cloister and Benedictine **monastery of Sant'Agata**. The restored convent houses Spoleto's **Museo Archeologico**, with inscriptions and architectural fragments, busts of Julius Caesar and Augustus and other distinguished Romans, and a stone found in a sacred grove dedicated to Jupiter, warning against profaning the place (or chopping wood). The convent refectory has a good cinquecento fresco of the *Last Supper*.

Museo Archeologico
t 0743 223277; open daily 8.30–7.30; joint adm with Roman theatre (see p.509)

East through Piazza Fontana and then left, you pass under the travertine **arch of Drusus and Germanicus**, erected in AD 23 by Tiberius' son (Drusus would have made a good emperor, but he died, and the Roman world got Caligula instead). The arch marked the entrance to the Forum, and on the adjacent modern building is the outline of the columns of a temple, as well as its actual foundations beneath. **Sant'Ansano**, built over a Paleochristian church and a Roman temple, incorporates more ancient fragments, though its original medieval appearance was sacrificed for fashion in the late 18th century. The 11th-century **crypt of San Isacco** has stayed the same, decorated with rare frescoes in the Byzantine style: the *Beheading of John the Baptist*, *Christ in Glory*, the *Last Supper*, and the *Life of St Isaac the Hermit*, a 5th-century Syrian monk who took refuge near Spoleto. The crypt's columns are Roman, the capitals Lombard.

Sant'Ansano
t 0743 40305; open April–Oct daily 7.30–12 and 3.30–6.30; Nov–Mar 7.30–12 and 3–5.30

Via Arco di Druso empties into the Roman forum, now **Piazza del Mercato**, where glistening tomatoes and aubergines compete for your attention with the 18th-century **Fonte di Piazza**, a provincial version of Rome's Trevi Fountain, which incorporates Carlo Maderno's monument to Urban VII of 1626.

Pinacoteca Comunale and the Roman House

While waiting to move into a new home it will share with the forthcoming **textile and antique costume museum**, the **Pinacoteca** is on the first floor of the **Palazzo Rosani-Spada**. Among its highlights are works by Spoleto-born Lo Spagna, including his finest, the Raphaelesque *Madonna, Child and Saints* (1512), painted for the Rocca Albornoz. Another of his commissions, an allegorical *Charity, Mercy and Justice*, was painted for Julius II, although they were hardly that pope's strongpoints; in 1824 the work was adjusted to fit a bust of another pope, Leo XII, a Spoleto native. There are portraits of the Teutonic dukes of long ago and coins from the days of the Lombard duchy, as well as a beautiful crucifix reliquary and painting of Christ in a lavish filigree frame by the Maestro di Sant'Alò, from the late 1200s. There's a bejewelled Byzantine-style icon from the 13th century and frescoes on the *Lives of SS. Peter and Paul*.

Pinacoteca Comunale
Corso Mazzini, t 0743 46434; open mid-Mar–mid-Oct Wed–Mon 10.30–1 and 3–6.30; rest of year Wed–Mon 10.30–1 and 3–5.30; adm

Casa Romana
*Via di Visiale, **t** 0743 224656; open mid-Mar–mid-Oct daily 10–8; mid-Oct–Mar daily 10–6; adm*

The 1st-century BC **Casa Romana** is believed, perhaps fancifully, to have been the house of Emperor Vespasian's mother, Vespasia Polla. The atrium and wellhead, bedrooms, bath and beautiful mosaic floors survive.

Piazza Campello, the Rocca and the Ponte delle Torri

From Piazza del Municipio, Via Saffi climbs up to panoramic **Piazza Campello** with another good fountain, the 17th-century **Mascherone**, with a huge, grotesque face spitting out the water from the Roman and medieval aqueduct. The monument on the square is from 1910, built to honour all the Spoletines who fought to free their city from the Papal States. The symbol of the oppression looms just above: the **Rocca Albornoz**, an impressive, six-towered citadel by Gattapone from Gubbio, commissioned in 1359 by that indefatigable papal enforcer Cardinal Albornoz, who made this his personal HQ. Most of the stone used is at least third-hand: first employed in the Roman amphitheatre, then cannibalized by the Goth Totila for his fortress, then dragged up here. When Spoleto was firmly in the papal pocket, the Rocca became a popular country resort for the popes, frequented in particular by Julius II, accompanied on occasion by Michelangelo, who loved the peace of these hills. Until recently, the Rocca served as a prison (among inmates was Mohammed Ali Agca, would-be assassin of Pope John Paul II); when it is fully restored, there are plans to install a museum dedicated to the duchy of Spoleto, a laboratory for the restoration of books and art, an exhibition and conference area and an open-air theatre. Ruins of a 7th-century **church of Sant'Elia** have been found on the hill, which will become a park; there are beautiful views of Spoleto and the valley below.

Rocca Albornoz
***t** 0743 43707 or **t** 0743 238920; open for 45min guide tours April–mid-June and mid-Sept–Oct daily 10–1 and 3–7; mid-June–mid-Sept daily 10–8; Nov and Dec Mon–Fri 2.30–5, Sat and Sun 10–5; 15–31 Mar Mon–Fri 10–1 and 3–6, Sat and Sun 10–6; adm*

The pedestrian-only **Via del Ponte** from Piazza Campello leads down to one of the greatest engineering works of the 1300s, the spectacular 230m **Ponte delle Torri**, a bridge and aqueduct of 10 towering arches built by Gattapone for Cardinal Albornoz, to guarantee the water supply to the Rocca. It dizzily spans the 79m-deep ravine of the Tessino river far, far below, and was one of the unmissable sights for Grand Tourists, who thought it was Roman; Turner painted a fine picture of it. The bridge does stand on a Roman foundation; you can cross it to the towers that gave it its name, and to Monteluco's San Pietro (*see* p.516). From here, Via del Ponte circles around under the Rocca back to Piazza Campello.

Sant'Eufemia
***t** 0743 231022; open April–Sept Mon–Sat 10–1 and 4–7, Sun 10–6; Oct–Mar Mon and Wed–Sat 10–12.30 and 3–6, Sun 10–6; adm*

Sant'Eufemia and the Museo Diocesano

Behind the Palazzo Comunale on Via Saffi, an archway leads into the small courtyard of the archbishop's palace, facing one of the finest Umbrian Romanesque churches, **Sant'Eufemia**, completed about 1140. It has a plain façade, but its interior in luminescent white stone is remarkable. Fragments of Roman buildings are built into the walls and columns in surprising ways, and it has an anachronistic *matroneum*, the Byzantine-style second-floor gallery where women were segregated during Mass – although this was a common practice in Rome and Ravenna, it's the only *matroneum* in Umbria. The altar, brought from Spoleto's first cathedral, is good Cosmatesque work, with symbols of the four Evangelists surrounding the Paschal lamb.

Museo Diocesano
open April–Sept Mon–Sat 10–1 and 4–7, Sun 10–6; Oct–Mar Mon and Wed–Sat 10–12.30 and 3–6, Sun 10–6

Part of Sant'Eufemia's convent, built over an important and still partly visible 1st-century Roman structure, became the Palazzo Arcivescovile, home of the **Museo Diocesano**. This has works garnered from the diocese, with an array of early painted crucifixes and trecento Madonnas, including a lovely one by the First Master of Santa Chiara di Montefalco. Highlights among later works are an *Adoration of the Child* by Domenico Beccafumi of Siena, the *Madonna delle Neve* by Neri di Bicci and a *Madonna and Child with SS. Montano and Bartolomeo* by Filippino Lippi. One room has an excellent collection of medieval Umbrian sculpture, and there's a fascinating assortment of popular 16th–19th-century *ex votos*.

Via dell'Arringo

Via dell'Arringo, a grand, shallow stairway behind Sant'Eufemia, opens into the Piazza del Duomo. In early medieval times Spoletani gathered here to make communal decisions by acclamation after hearing speeches. It must have been this theatrical ensemble that sold Menotti on Spoleto, with its naturally tiered seating set against the cathedral façade and the Umbrian hills as a backdrop.

Teatro Caio Melisso
t 0743 222209, www.teatrostabile.umbria.it; open for performances

Among the buildings, there's the **Teatro Caio Melisso**, an exquisite little late-19th-century theatre named after the Spoleto-born dramatist and librarian of the Emperor Augustus; the pink-and-white striped **Casa dell'Opera del Duomo** (1419); and an octagonal church, **Santa Maria della Manna d'Oro**, built after 1527 as a votive after the Sack of Rome, with four paintings by Sebastiano Conca. Note the Roman sarcophagus used as a fountain, the memorial to US conductor Thomas Schippers, who loved the view and festival so much he asked to be buried here. Nearby is the 16th-century **Palazzo Racani**, designed by Giulio Romano, with faded *sgraffito* decoration in dire need of restoration.

The Duomo

Duomo
t 0743 44307; open Mar–Oct daily 7.30–12.30 and 3–7; Nov–Feb daily 7.30–12.30 and 3–5

The magnificent cathedral was rebuilt after Emperor Frederick Barbarossa, the most powerful of papal enemies, razed its predecessor to the ground in 1155. Consecrated by the most powerful of medieval popes, Innocent III, in 1198, it has several unusual features. A graceful Renaissance portico (1491) incorporates two pulpits; four rose windows and four circular emblems of the Evangelists adorn its façade, surrounding a gold-ground Byzantine-style mosaic of *Christ Enthroned with Mary and John the Baptist* (1207), signed by Solsternus. The lower middle *rosone* is an exceptional example of the Cosmatesque work imported from Rome – stone or enamel chips in sinuous patterns. The campanile is built from Roman odds and ends.

The Latin cross **interior** was redone in the 1630s, a misguided gift to the city by the Barberini family of Rome: Maffeo Barberini had been cardinal of Spoleto before he was elected Urban VIII in 1623, and his nephew, another cardinal of Spoleto, funded the works and commemorated his uncle with the bronze bust by Bernini inside the central door. Several treasures survived the interior redesigners, including the fine Cosmati pavement in the central nave. Pinturicchio, not on one of his better days, painted the frescoes of the *Madonna and Saints* in the first chapel on the right, his usual amusing detail including St Jerome's lion frisking about the landscape. His pupil Jacopo Siculo painted the frescoes in the next chapel. In the right transept, a Baroque chapel by Giambattista Mola holds the 12th-century *Santissima Icona*, a highly venerated icon from Constantinople donated as a peace offering to Spoleto by Frederick Barbarossa. The chapel has two paintings by the Cavalier d'Arpino, who painted the dome of St Peter's.

In the apse are the exquisite, rich frescoes of the *Life of the Virgin* (1467–69), a masterpiece by Florentine Fra Filippo Lippi, beautifully restored. Not only did Lippi paint larger-than-life figures, he fitted them expertly into the space, through a canny use of perspective and architectural features, including columns and friezes from Spoleto itself. The splendid *Coronation of the Virgin*, in the upper part of the apse, is the best-preserved of the cycle, crowded with the angel musicians and female figures Lippi loved to paint, here in the guise of Sibyls and women from the Old Testament. Lippi portrayed himself (in a white habit with a black hat), his son Filippino (the young angel) and his assistants among the mourners in the central scene of the Virgin's death. The fun-loving monk (he ran off with a nun but was permitted to leave his order and marry her) died in Spoleto while working on the project, and the *Nativity* was finished by his chief helpers, Fra Diamanti and the Umbrian Pier Matteo d'Amelia. When Lippi's great patron Lorenzo de' Medici asked that the artist's body be returned to Florence, the Spoletini refused, claiming they had no notable dead while Florence had a great many. Lorenzo had to be content with commissioning a handsome Florentine tomb for him, now in the right transept.

In the left aisle, the original sacristy was converted into a chapel of reliquaries in the 1560s, with lavish intarsia cupboards made mostly by local craftsmen, although the two with architectural perspectives are by the great Fra Giovanni da Verona; the most important relic is a very rare letter in the hand of St Francis to Fra Leone. Hanging by the first altar on the left is a large and colourful *Crucifix*, dated 1187 and signed by Alberto Sotio, the first Umbrian artist whose name has come down to us.

Lower Spoleto

Galleria Civica d'Arte Moderna
Via Collicola, t 0743 46434; open 16 Mar–14 Oct daily 10.30–1 and 3.30–7; rest of year Mon and Wed–Sat 10.30–1 and 3–5.30, Sun 11–1 and 3–6; adm

Some of the city's contemporary art has gone to the Palazzo Collicola, now the **Galleria Civica d'Arte Moderna**, with works by Italy's 20th-century masters (Pomodoro, Burri, Guttoso, Accardi) and Spoleto's Leoncillo Leonardi (1915–68), who evolved a distinctive, colourful style in highly textured glazed terracotta. The custodian keeps the key for **Santi Giovanni e Paolo**, consecrated in 1178. It has excellent frescoes; on the left wall is a scene, attributed to Alberto Sotio, of the *Martrydom of St Thomas Becket*, canonized five years before (1170).

Via Tobagi leads you to Spoleto's fanciest Baroque church, **San Filippo Neri**, with an ornate façade and lofty dome, by local architect, Loreto Scelli, who studied in Rome. It has a fine Baroque bust of *St Philip Neri* by Bolognese sculptor Alessandro Algardi and paintings by Sebastiano Conca and Gaetano Lapis da Cagli.

Teatro Nuovo
Largo B. Gigli, t 0743 40265

San Domenico
closed for restoration at time of writing

Via Filitteria leads into Via Sant'Andrea, site of the **Teatro Nuovo**, HQ of the Two Worlds festival and older Festival of Experimental Opera. Down the steps, the colourful pink-and-white striped preaching **church of San Domenico** was built in the 13th century; the interior has been restored to its medieval appearance and has a colourful crucifix hanging in the nave, plus other items of interest.

Walk down Via Leone to the tall-towered 13th-century **Porta Fuga** ('Put-to-flight Gate' – as experienced by Hannibal in 217 BC) and along Via Saccoccio Cecili to take in a stretch of Spoleto's **walls**. The Umbrii built the 6th-century BC cyclopean base using huge blocks, heightened by the Romans and all the other Spoletans up to the 15th century. The street ends in Piazza Cairoli; from here, Via dell'Anfiteatro leads past the ruined 2nd-century AD **amphitheatre**, made into a fortress by Totila and still part of a barracks.

On Piazza Garibaldi is 12th-century **San Gregorio Maggiore**; through the gate are the ruins of the Roman **Ponte Sanguinario** (Bloody Bridge), supposedly named after Christians martyred in the amphitheatre but more probably a corruption of the Latin name of a nearby gate, the *Sandapilarius*. It was built in the 1st century BC to carry the new Via Flaminia over the river and rediscovered in 1817.

Outside Spoleto

San Ponziano and San Salvatore

San Ponziano
t 0743 40655; to visit, ring bell of custodian's house near church

From the bridge and Piazza Vittoria, it's a short drive or an unpleasant 15-minute walk on the road under the *superstrada* to the cemetery, passing the 12th-century **San Ponziano**. Ponziano is Spoleto's patron, martyred here in 1169. The façade of his church, once faced with marble, is divided horizontally by a cornice and has a pretty Cosmatesque door and a round window surrounded by symbols of the Evangelists. The interior was redone by Giuseppe Valadier in 1788 but has the original crypt, with an upside-down Roman column, two turning posts (*metae*) from a Roman circus, three ancient sarcophagi and some fresco fragments. In the corridor, embedded like fossils in the wall, are huge Corinthian columns.

San Salvatore
t 0743 49606; open Mar and Oct daily 7–6; May–Sept daily 7–7; Nov–Feb daily 7–5

Even more Roman material went into building the charming 4th-century **San Salvatore**, just down from San Ponziano by the cemetery. Spoleto's oldest church has its façade and apse despite rebuildings and loss of its marble facing; the three doors have fine marble architraves and three curious old windows. The fluted Corinthian columns inside originally supported a Roman temple; the fresco of the jewelled cross in the apse is 8th or 9th century.

Monteluco

Monteluco

Just east of town, beautiful, forested Monteluco is Spoleto's holy mountain. The name is derived from *lucus* (sacred wood), and in Roman times it was forbidden to chop down the trees. In the 5th century, Isaac the Hermit from Antioch founded the first cenobitic community here; the Benedictines and the Franciscans followed.

San Pietro
t 0743 44882; open summer daily 9–6.30; winter daily 9–4.30; in afternoon ring custodian's bell near church

You can get to Monteluco by car, by bus from Piazza della Libertà, or on foot over the Ponte delle Torri (*see* p.512). Near the base of the mountains stands the great Romanesque **church of San Pietro**, with a magnificent 12th-century façade, the last hurrah of the Lombard dukes of Spoleto. The Lombards delighted in portraying real and imaginary animals: here is a fox playing dead to capture some too-curious chickens, battles with lions, oxen, peacocks, eagles, a wolf in monk's clothing, animals devouring one another and the occasional armoured knight; devils contest souls, and St Michael slays his dragon. On the top level are two bulls, statues of St Peter and St Andrew and reliefs of Christ washing St Peter's feet and Christ calling St Peter and St Andrew. An elaborate frieze of vines and plants links allegorical scenes; on the left, the pious could compare the post-mortem destinies of the righteous and the sinful. The interior was Baroqued in 1699.

San Giuliano
visits by appt with monastery of San Francesco, ***t*** *0743 40711*

San Francesco
t 0743 40711 or t 0743 47797; open daily 9–12 and 3–6

A steep, hairpinning road leads up through ilex forests to the lonely 12th-century **church of San Giuliano**, with a façade incorporating 6th-century elements of its predecessor. In the 7th century, anchorites and hermits, refugees from the wars in the Holy Land, settled here and set up monasteries; St Francis, who tried to emulate them, came to meditate here and in 1218 founded the tiny **monastery of San Francesco** near the summit of the mountain, a serene spot overlooking the countryside. Monteluco now has more summer villas and hotels than hermitages but it's still a cool and tranquil place to spend an afternoon.

San Paolo Intervineas

San Paolo Intervineas
1km southwest of Spoleto (take Via San Paolo off Via Martiri della Resistenza); closed for restoration since earthquake; ask at tourist office (see below) for latest information

Founded in Paleochristian times and mentioned in the 6th century by St Gregory the Great, this was rebuilt in the 10th century and again in 1234, when it was consecrated by Gregory IX as a church for a convent of Clarisse. It has a pretty façade with a rose window and frescoed lunette over the door; the interior contains a good series of frescoes from the period, including an account of the Creation, and an old altar.

ⓘ Spoleto >
Piazza della Libertà 7, t 0743 238911, www.umbria2000.it (closed Sun afternoon in winter).

Tourist Information in Spoleto

Post office: Viale G. Matteotti 2, **t** 0743 201521, *www.postei.it*.

The main **market** takes place on Via Cacciatori delle Alpi on Fridays. There's also a sporadic farmers' market on Piazza del Mercato, and an antiques/fleamarket the 2nd Sun of the month.

Festival in Spoleto

Festival dei Due Mondi (Festival of Two Worlds), Piazza del Duomo 8 and Piazza della Libertà (info and tickets), **t** 45028 220320 or freephone **t** 800 565600, *www.spoletofestival.it*, 3wks end June–mid-July. Italy's leading arts festival, with music, theatre and dance.

Where to Stay in and around Spoleto

Spoleto ✉ 06049

If Spoleto is full for the Two Worlds Festival, try Terni (*see* p.563), or ask the tourist office for a list of rooms to let and *agriturismo*, though it's still vital to book ahead. Con-Spoleto, Piazza della Libertà 7, **t** 0743 220773, *www.conspoleto.com*, can help find rooms.

Luxury (€€€€€)

******Albornoz Palace**, Viale Matteotti 4, **t** 0743 221 221, *www.albornozpalace.com*. A refined, stylish option just outside the historic centre, with babysitting, a restaurant (half and full board possible). and parking.

******San Luca**, Via Interna delle Mura 21, **t** 0743 223 399, *www.hotelsanluca.com*. A charming little hotel situated within Spolet's historic centre, boasting a sophisticated 19th-century ambience. Some of the guestrooms have baths with hydromassage.

Palazzo Dragoni, Via del Duomo 13, **t** 0743 222220, *www.palazzodragoni.it*. A beautiful *residenza d'epoca* in a central 16th-century building, retaining much of its original atmosphere, with rooms furnished in an elegant Umbrian style.

Very Expensive (€€€€)

******Dei Duchi**, Viale Matteotti 4, **t** 0743 44541, *www.hoteldeiduchi.com*. An attractive contemporary hotel and restaurant, popular among visiting artists and performers. Half and full board are available.

******Gattapone**, Via del Ponte 6, **t** 0743 223447, *www.hotelgattapone.it*. The most spectacular option: a stone house clinging to the slope near the Rocca and Ponte delle Torri, with good views. Rooms (breakfast included) are spacious and finely furnished, and there's free Internet access, babysitting and a beautiful garden.

Expensive (€€€)

*****Charleston**, Piazza Collicola 10, **t** 0743 *220052,www.hotelcharleston.it*. A pretty 17th-century *palazzo* in the *centro storico*, with comfortable rooms and apartments (let by the week), a sauna, an *enoteca* and two bars.

*****Clarici**, Piazza della Vittoria 32, **t** 0743 223311, *www.hotelclarici.com*. A more modern choice in the lower part of town, decorated with taste, with babysitting and parking.

*****Nuovo Clitunno**, Piazza Sordini 6, **t** 0743 223340, *www.hotelclitunno.com*. A good option close to the centre of town, with a restaurant offering Umbrian cuisine (half and full board are available).

Moderate (€€)

****Il Panciolle**, Via Duomo 4, **t** 0743 45677. Simple rooms and a good restaurant where meat is grilled over an open fire. *Closed Wed.*

Inexpensive (€)

****Due Porte**, Piazza della Vittoria 5, **t** 0743 223666. Basic rooms, a beautiful garden and parking.

Outside Spoleto

Il Barbarossa, Via Licina 12, just outside town walls, **t** 0743 43644, *www.countryhouse-ilbarbarossa.it* (€€€). Guestrooms with all comforts set the middle of an olive grove, plus meals by prior arrangement.

*****La Macchia**, Loc Licina 11, just north of centre off Via Flaminia, **t** 0743 49059, *www.albergolamacchia.it* (€€). A quiet, good-value option with rustic local furniture and a pretty garden. The restaurant specializes in *cucina spoletana*, using lots of mushrooms, truffles and asparagus; half board is available. The owners also let a flat in the nearby Castel San Felice.

*****Michelangelo**, Loc.Monteluco, **t** 0743 47890, *www.michelangelohotel.net* (€€). Large, simple rooms near the top of the town, very friendly staff, and a good restaurant-pizzeria (full board available). *Closed 7 Nov–7 Dec.*

*****Paradiso**, Loc Monteluco 19, **t** 0743 223082, *www.albergoparadiso.net* (€€). Comfortable rooms, a restaurant (half/full board available), a garden, great views, and peace and quiet.

****Ferretti**, Loc Monteluco 20, **t** 0743 49849, *www.albergoferretti.com* (€€). A charming *pensione*, with some of its guestrooms boasting balconies overlooking the pretty piazza.There's a restaurant offering typical local cuisine, and full board is offered.

Pecoraro, Fraz. Strettura 76, Strettura, about 12km down SS3 towards Terni, **t** 0743 229697, *www.ilpecoraro.it* (€). A very pretty, welcoming *agriturismo*, with cosy rooms (breakfast included in rates), a small outdoor pool, a billiards table, horseriding, trekking, canoeing and a very good restaurant offering a wide range of regional dishes and strong home-made grappas (full board available). *Closed 15–30 Nov, 1–15 Feb.*

Eating Out in and around Spoleto

Spoleto ✉ 06049

Expensive (€€€)

Apollinare, Via S. Agata 14, near Roman theatre, **t** 0743 223256. A romantic 13th-century Franciscan convent. Try gnocchi with fried leek and pigeon sauce or smoked eel with lentils. Booking is recommended. *Closed Tues.*

Pentagramma, Via Martani 4, near Piazza della Libertà, **t** 0743 223141. A welcoming former stable owned by Arturo Toscanini's daughter, serving perfectly prepared local dishes such as *strangozzi di Spoleto* (with olive oil, garlic, tomato and basil). Book ahead. *Closed Mon and part of Jan and Aug.*

★ Tartufo >>

Tartufo, Piazza Garibaldi 24, **t** 0743 40236. The black diamonds of the Valnerina in various combinations: try *risotto al tartufo* or guinea fowl with truffles and potatoes (there are non-truffle dishes too). Booking is required. *Closed Sun eve, Mon, 2wks in Feb and 3wks in July.*

Moderate (€€)

★ Del Festival >>

Del Festival, Via Brignone 8, **t** 0743 220993. A pretty place for *millefoglie* with *caciottina* cheese and the like, plus pizza. *Closed Thurs and 1–15 Feb.*

Sabatini, Corso Mazzini 54, **t** 0743 221831. Traditional Umbrian fare. *Closed Mon, 2wks Jan and 2wks Aug.*

Trattoria Pecchiarda, Vicolo San Giovanni 1, off Via Porta Fuga, **t** 0743 221009. Very typical cuisine prepared with organic products. *Closed Tues.*

Inexpensive (€)

Sportellino, Via Cerquiglia 4, **t** 0743 45230. A simple, homely place for try *frittatina* with truffles, *ossobuco* with peas, and more. *Closed Thurs and 10 days in July or Aug.*

Outside Spoleto

Il Capanno, Loc. Torrecola 6, 10km south on Via Flaminia, **t** 0743 54119 (€€€). Umbrian dishes such as *pappardelle* with pigeon ragout. *Closed Mon.*

Palazzo del Papa, Strettura, on SS3, **t** 0743 54140 (€). A trattoria with some of the best home cooking around, plus pizzas. *Closed Wed.*

★ Pecoraro >

The Tiber Valley

South of Perugia, Old Father Tiber flows below the proud medieval eagle's eyrie of Todi then swells to form the Lago di Corbara and takes a sharp left under lofty hills to form the border with Lazio. This corner of Umbria closest to Rome has a character all its own, much of it concentrated in Orvieto, where mementos of Etruscans rub elbows with those of medieval popes and the papal nobility, in the shadow of one of Italy's great cathedrals. Charming Amelia, wrapped in walls built by the ancient Umbrii, is often overlooked. Between the three big hilltowns are vineyards and steep wooded ridges, a score of smaller villages and lovely churches, and a handful of oddities.

19

Don't miss

1. **A medieval civic ensemble**
   Piazza del Popolo, Todi **p.522**
2. **Renaissance perfection**
   Tempio della Consolazione **p.524**
3. **A jewelbox theatre**
   Montecastello **p.525**
4. **The 'golden lily of cathedrals'**
   Orvieto **p.528**
5. **A dream garden**
   La Scarzuola, Montegiove **p.540**

See map overleaf

The Tiber Valley

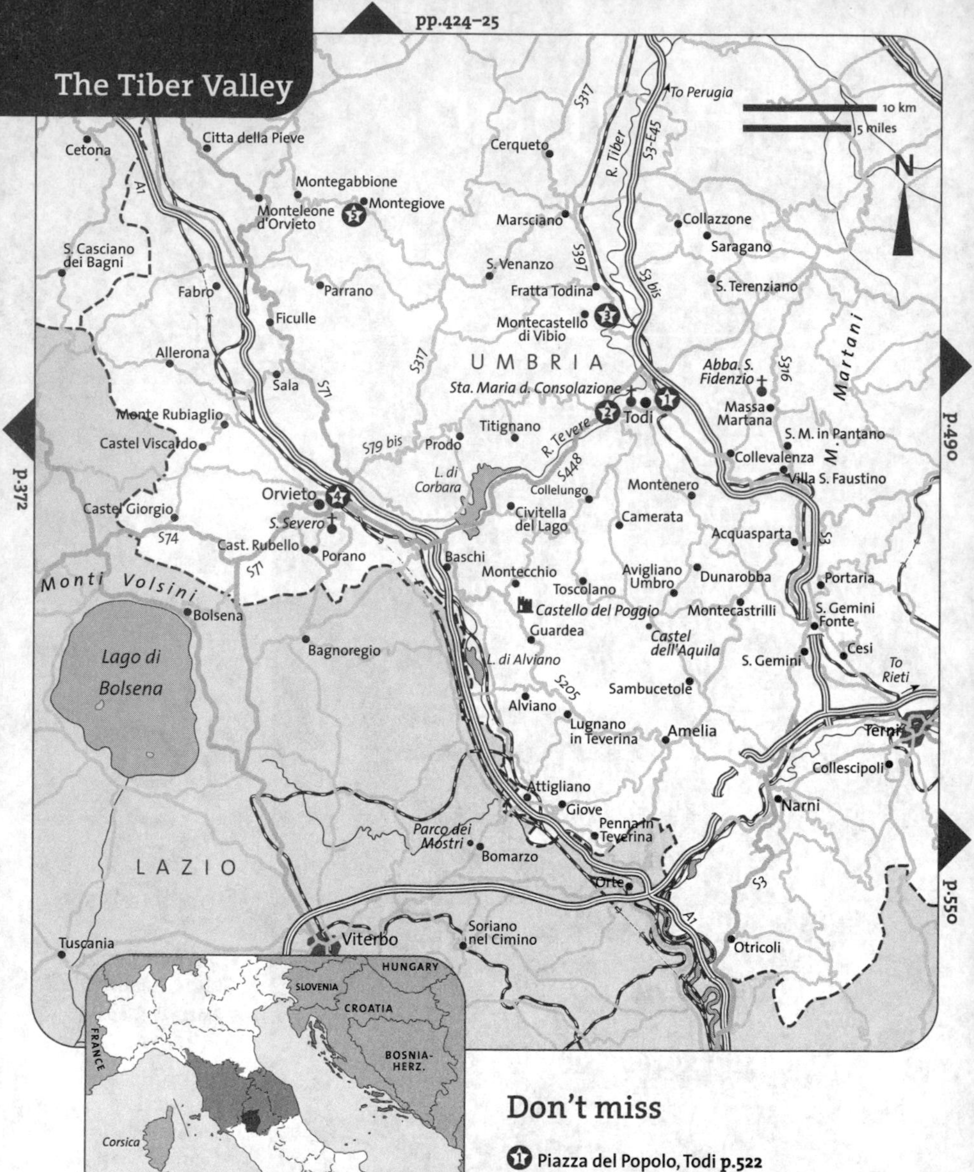

pp.424–25
p.372
p.490
p.550

Don't miss

1. **Piazza del Popolo, Todi p.522**
2. **Tempio della Consolazione p.524**
3. **Montecastello p.525**
4. **Orvieto Cathedral p.528**
5. **La Scarzuola, Montegiove p.540**

Todi

Todi (population 17,200) may be small but it has everything a self-respecting central Italian hilltown needs. There's the hill in a gorgeous setting, a cathedral and medieval public buildings, one

Getting to and from Todi

Todi is linked by **bus** to Terni (33km/45mins; ATC, **t** 0744 492711, *www.atcerni.it*), Perugia (41km/1hr; APM, **t** 800 512141, *www.apmperugia.it*), and Rome (130km/2hrs 30mins), and by the FCU's little **trains** (**t** 075 575401, *www.fcu.it*) to Perugia and Terni. Trains (FS, **t** 892021, *wwwtrenitalia.com*) and coaches (to Perugia, Terni, Rome and Orvieto) come and go from Ponte Rio, **t** 075 894 2092, linked to the centre by city bus.

There's only 1 bus a day between Todi and Orvieto (SULGA, **t** 800 099 661, *www.sulga.it*) , but the route takes in the lovely scenery over the Tiber valley. There are SSIT buses to Spoleto (**t** 074 321 2208 and **t** 0743 212229 for timetables, *www.spoletina.com*).

---

great Renaissance monument, a long and tortuous history, a saint (uncanonized, this time), and a proud *comune* escutcheon, a fierce eagle over the inevitable device 'SPQT'. In the past few years it has consistently been voted the world's most livable-in town by the University of Kentucky, an accolade that has brought American tycoons rushing to buy its villas and castles as holiday retreats, inviting comparisons with the Hamptons. But Todi was always a sophisticated little place, famous for its carpentry and woodworking. In April it hosts one of Italy's major antiques fairs, the Rassegna Antiquaria d'Italia, and in August and September the Mostra Nazionale dell'Artigianato, a national crafts fair.

History

It was the eagle that showed the ancient Umbrii where to build the city they were to call the 'Border' or *Tuter*, above modern Todi, on what is now the Rocca. The border was an uncomfortable one with the Etruscans, who settled lower down around the Piazza del Popolo; one day, the Etruscans became kings of the whole hill when they surprised, slaughtered and enslaved their Umbrian neighbours. As *Colonia Julia Fida Tuder*, dedicated to the war god Mars for its role in the wars against Hannibal, the town prospered through Roman times, and its nearly impregnable site kept the barbarians out; there's no evidence that Todi was ever part of the Lombard duchy of Spoleto, and it's possible that it may have maintained its independence all along.

By the 1200s, Todi had accumulated a little empire, including Terni and Amelia, and its soldiers were kept in trim by constant dust-ups with their peers in Spoleto, Narni and Orvieto. In 1227 their *podestà* was the notorious Mosca dei Lamberti, exiled from Florence after the killing of Buondelmonte dei Buondelmonti (*see* p.41); Dante would consign him to the Eighth Circle of Hell. But above all, Todi took special pride in its good deeds. In 1249 the *comune* founded the Ospedale della Carità, where the poor were treated free – even Florence wasn't to have the like until 1316 – and it produced one of the greatest Italian poets of the Middle Ages in Fra Jacopone (*see* p.523). By the end of the century, the government and the political effectiveness of the free *comune* were failing. The

Atti family established themselves as *signori* during the early 1300s but were pushed out by the Malatesta of Rimini and Francesco Sforza of Milan among others, until eventually, in the 1460s, the pope gobbled up the town definitively for the Papal States.

Piazza del Popolo

Piazza del Popolo

Todi's streets converge on this magnificent 13th–15th-century piazza, centre of civic life since the Etruscans and Romans. In the 15th century, as Todi's existence as an independent city-state came to an end, the square was preserved in aspic, leaving a medieval pageant in grey stone. The sternest building, the **Palazzo dei Priori** (1293–1337), has square battlements with a chunky tower; the **Palazzo del Popolo** (1213), with swallow-tail crenellations, and its adjacent **Palazzo del Capitano** (1290) are all grace by comparison. Linked by a grand Gothic stairway, these make up one of the most remarkable medieval town halls in Italy. These outer stairs emphasized how easy it was for the citizenry to have access to local government, who invariably held their meetings on the first floor. They now provide access to Todi's attic, the **Museo Pinacoteca di Todi** on the fourth floor of the Palazzo del Popolo. This harbours fond civic memories: retired eagles, archaeological pieces, 16th-century scenes of charity by local painter Pietro Paolo Sensini, among portraits of saints and worthies linked to the city, a model of the Tempio della Consolazione from *c.* 1570, a fine *Coronation of the Virgin* by Lo Spagna, and works by a 16th-century so-so painter, Ferraù da Faenza, who spent a lot of time here. Todi is especially proud of a saddle it made for the ailing pregnant Anita Garibaldi.

Museo Pinacoteca di Todi
t *075 894 4148; open Apr–Oct Tues–Sun 10.30–1 and 2.30–6.30; Nov–Mar Tues–Sun 10.30–1 and 2.30–5; adm; beware: stairs can be slippery when wet*

To the right of Palazzo del Capitano stands a cypress that was planted in 1849 in honour of Garibaldi's visit – which was a fleeting one, because the Republic of Rome had just fallen to the French allies of the pope and they were pursuing the hero, his wife and a handful of loyal Garibaldini.

Duomo
t *075 894 3041; open 28 Mar–Oct daily 8.30–12.30 and 2.30–6.30; Nov–27 Mar daily 8.30–4.30; adm to lapidary museum*

On the far side of the Piazza del Popolo, the **Duomo** is at the top of another distinguished flight of steps. Begun in the 12th century and finished 200 years later, it has a handsome flat screen façade, fine rose window and delicately decorated portal. Inside are good capitals, a Gothic arcade by a fourth aisle and a 14th-century altarpiece. Parishioners who turned to gossip during Mass were confronted by a not-too-terrifying vision of the *Last Judgement* by Ferraù da Faenza, a reworking of Michelangelo's in the Sistine Chapel. The large crypt is now a **lapidary museum** with bells, a copy of Todi's patron deity *Mars*, now housed in the Vatican, and fragments of statue groups by the school of Giovanni Pisano.

Left of the Duomo stands the 16th-century **bishop's palace** and the **Palazzo Rolli**, attributed to the younger Antonio da Sangallo; it was home to Paolo Rolli (d. 1765), who translated Milton into Italian.

Down to Porta Perugina

Right of the Duomo, the road twists round, allowing a view of its beautiful apse. Some of Todi's **Etruscan-Roman walls** survive nearby, off Via Mure Antiche. Via Santa Prassede leads down to the pink and white **church of Santa Prassede**, from the 14th century but with a Baroque interior. The early medieval town ended here; beyond, Via Borgo Nuovo descends steeply past the **monastery of San Francesco**, also from the 14th century, with an allegorical fresco on *Salvation* from the same period by the altar. Further down, a round tower marks the 13th-century **Porta Perugina**, offering views over the countryside. The only hitch is walking back up the hill.

San Fortunato and the Rocca

San Fortunato
open April–Oct daily 8.30–12.30 and 2.30–6.30; Nov–Mar daily 8.30–4.30

From Piazza del Popolo, Via Mazzini leads past the **Teatro Comunale** (1872) to Todi's other great monument, **San Fortunato** (1292). In a prominent position at the top of a broad stair, this was one of many churches built during the late-13th-century Franciscan spending spree, when the Order received permission from the popes to administer as well as 'use' the substantial property it received as donations from the pious. In Todi they built on a grand scale, but the façade remains unfinished. According to scurrilous legend, when the Orvietani heard that the Tuderini had commissioned Lorenzo Maitani to decorate it, they had the sculptor murdered to prevent Todi from having a church as good as their cathedral. The late Gothic central portal was completed only in the 1400s and has little figures hidden among the acanthus and decorative bands: there's St Francis receiving the stigmata and the damned in hell with a little salamander, who doesn't seem to mind because salamanders were believed to be fireproof. The statues on either side of the door are of the *Annunciation*; the beautiful angel has been attributed to Jacopo della Quercia. The airy, luminous and remarkably wide Gothic interior, divided into three naves of equal height, is one of the best in central Italy. Large fragments of frescoes decorate many of the chapels, including a *Madonna and Child* (1432) by Masolino da Panicale, his only work in Umbria. The fine wooden choir is by Antonio Maffei of Gubbio (1590). But for the Tuderini the focal point is the **tomb of poet and mystic Jacopone da Todi** in the crypt, the subject of much local if unofficial devotion. With his revolt against Boniface, Jacopone may have blown all hopes of ever being canonized, but Todi regards him as a saint, and in 1906, on the 600th anniversary of his death, erected the bronze statue in the niche at the bottom of San Fortunato's steps.

Next to San Fortunato stands the Palazzo Ludovico Atti, built for the town's *signori* and attributed to Galeazzo Alessi. From the garden right of the church, a lane leads up to the top of the town and the massive round tower of the Rocca, what remains of

Todi's 14th-century citadel; the public gardens and belvedere offer an unforgettable view of the Tiber valley and Tempio della Consolazione. Here, too, is a Roman cistern converted into a chapel, known as the Carcere di San Cassiano for an account that it also at one point served as St Cassian's prison cell.

Piazza Mercato Vecchio and Santa Maria in Camuccia

The most impressive reminder of Roman *Tuder* is in **Piazza Mercato Vecchio**: take the stepped Via San Fortunato down to Via Roma, walk through the handsome medieval **Porta Marzia** (made out of Roman pieces) then turn left. A temple of *Tuder*'s patron Mars stood near here, and in the old market square is a series of imposing arches with a Doric frieze called the **Nicchioni** (niches) from an Augustan-era basilica. Below the piazza is the little Romanesque **church of San Carlo** and the **Fontana Scarnabecco**, which was built in 1241 by a *podestà* from Bologna.

Santa Maria in Camuccia
open summer daily 8–1 and 3–8; winter daily 8–1 and 3–5

Return to the Porta Marzia, continue down Via Roma and turn right for **Santa Maria in Camuccia**, a 13th-century church with Roman columns by the door; inside is the 12th-century wooden statue of the *Virgin and Child* known as the *Sedes Sapientiae* (Seat of Wisdom). From here, you can walk down to the Tempio della Consolazione (if you don't mind the slog back up the hill); you can also reach it by car on the ring-road around Todi.

Tempio di Santa Maria della Consolazione

(2) Tempio di Santa Maria della Consolazione
open April–Oct Wed–Mon 9–1 and 2.30–6; Nov–Mar Wed–Mon 10–12.30 and 2.30–6

This is the most ambitious attempt in Umbria to create a perfect Renaissance temple, and it is a beautiful ornament for Todi, an ivory-coloured essay in geometric forms, isolated amid wooded slopes and farmlands. Dedicated to an apparition of the Virgin, it was begun by the unknown Cola da Caprarola in 1508 but shows the influence of the great Roman architect Bramante, who may indeed have helped with the design. Scholars attempting to unravel the building's origins found only more puzzles, as a picture of the temple was discovered among the architectural sketches of Leonardo da Vinci from 1489.

Begun in 1508, the church was not completed until 99 years later. By that time, every celebrity architect of the late Renaissance had stuck his oar in, including many who worked on St Peter's: Antonio da Sangallo the Younger, Baldassare Peruzzi, Vignola and Sanmicheli among others. In 1589 Perugian architect Valentino Martelli designed the drum and dome. But unlike St Peter's in Rome, the Tempio's purity of form, geometrically harmonious restraint, patterns of semicircles and triangles and careful proportions of the fine dome and four apses (three polygonal and one semicircular) emerged as if the work of a single architect. Four

Tudertini eagles guard the corners of the terrace and the classical interior, in the form of a Greek cross, is white, spacious and serene, with Baroque statues of the 12 Apostles and an elaborate altar with a 15th-century fresco of the *Madonna della Consolazione*.

Convento di Montesanto

Convento di Montesanto
Viale Montesanto; call ***t*** *075 894 8886 for opening hrs*

Another sacred site outside Todi's walls is the 13th–14th-century fortified Convento di Montesanto 1km below the Porta Orvietana. A famous Etruscan bronze statue of Mars (probably made in Orvieto) was found here in what may have been an Etruscan temple. The great lime tree by the entrance is one of the oldest in Italy, planted in 1428 by San Bernardino of Siena. The church contains a massive 16th-century fresco of the *Nativity*, and another by Lo Spagna, and has lovely views over the Tempio della Consolazione.

Around Todi

North of Todi: Montecastello and the Smallest Theatre in the World

Montecastello

Todi's lovely surrounds are dotted with minor attractions. If you have to choose one, make it **Montecastello di Vibio**, 10km northwest, a walled medieval hilltown high over the Tiber valley, home to an American art school. When Montecastello became its own master under Napoleon, the village's nine leading families decided to commemorate the Revolution by pooling their money to build the delightful (now restored) **Teatro della Concordia**, a mini-version of La Scala, with its boxes, decorations and 99 seats.

Teatro della Concordia
t *075 878 0737; open Mar and Oct Sat, Sun and hols 10–12.30 and 3–6; Apr–Sept Sat, Sun and hols 10–12.30 and 4.30–7.30; Nov–Feb Sat 3–6, Sun and hols 10–12.30 and 3–6*

Beyond Montecastello

Just north of Montecastello, the little hilltown of **Fratta Todina** was a bone of contention between Perugia and Todi before it became a favourite country retreat of the rich families of Todi; it has a handsome Franciscan convent, La Spineta.

There's a 12th-century castle 7km further north in the industrial sprawl of **Marsciano**, built by its *signori* the Bulgarelli, who gave their fief to Perugia rather than let it fall into the talons of Todi. North again is part of a fresco of *St Sebastian and the Plague Saints* by a young Perugino (1478), in the parish church of **Cerqueto**.

On the other side of the Tiber from Marsciano, charming **Collazzone** is a near-intact walled medieval hilltown that was once a Perugian outpost. Like Todi, it enjoys a lovely setting among olive groves and forests, so perhaps Jacopone, who spent his last years here in the monastery of San Lorenzo, wasn't too homesick. The monastery was restored by Todi's bishop Angelo Cesi and now serves as Collazzone's town hall.

South, similarly charming **San Terenziano** has a handsome Palazzo Cesi and a pink Romanesque church outside the centre; don't miss the crypt with its funny old capitals.

East of Todi: Massa Martana and Around

These days, pilgrims tend to ignore the Tempio della Consolazione and Montesanto, preferring the hideous **Santuario dell'Amore Misericordioso**, situated 6km east of Todi in **Collevalenza**. Founded in 1955 by Mother Speranza Alhama Valera (d. 1983), it was so popular it had to be enlarged 10 years later.

East a further 10km is **Massa Martana**, behind a 10th-century gate and 13th-century walls; it was founded as *Vicus ad Martis*, a waystation along the western branch of the Via Flaminia. Massa was the epicentre of the first earthquake – in May 1997 – of the many that would shake Umbria for the next two years, and it will be a long time before its *centro storico* and its houses, town hall and theatre are repaired. Like Orvieto, the town is built on a *rupe*, or spongey bluff made of tufa, which adds to the restoration difficulties; it requires major infrastructure work and buttressing as well as the more obvious repairs to walls and roofs. Just outside the centre, a late Renaissance church, the octagonal **Santa Maria della Pace** is a minor jewel, with an interior reminiscent of the Tempio della Consolazione.

Abbazia Santi Fidenzio e Terenzio
closed for restoration at time of writing

To the west of Massa, in a beautiful setting, the pink and white 11th-century **Abbazia Santi Fidenzio e Terenzio** was constructed over the tomb to Umbria's first saints, who came from Syria to spread the Good Word and were martyred under Diocletian. The campanile stands on a 12-sided pedestal of tufa blocks, which was cannibalized from a Roman structure; if it ever reopens, you wil be able to admire an unusual crypt and Lombard reliefs, and a marble pulpit dating from the 1200s.

Santa Maria in Pantano
key held at house next door

South of Massa, **Santa Maria in Pantano** was built in the 7th or 8th century out of a Roman structure along the Via Flaminia. The oldest section is the apse; the adjacent campanile was converted from a medieval defensive tower. Inside there are Roman bits and a Roman altar, columns erected in the 12th century and frescoes from the 14th century and earlier; it also has a beautiful wooden Christ on the cross, halfway down the nave.

Abbazia di San Faustino
key held next door

Catacomba di Villa San Faustino
*open Tues, Thurs, Sat and Sun 9–1; book with tourist office on **t** 075 889371*

Further south, the little walled town of **Villa San Faustino** is synonymous in Umbria with its bottled mineral water. Just outside the walls, the **Abbazia di San Faustino** was also built using Roman stone, this time in the 12th century. It's an old, mysterious place, set among other buildings cobbled together over the centuries. One was a Paleochristian funerary chapel built over **catacombs** dating back to the 4th century AD and decorated with Christian symbols, the fish and lamb.

(i) Todi >
*Comprensorio del Tuderte, Piazza Umberto I 6, **t** 075 894 3395 or **t** 075 894 5416*

Where to Stay in and around Todi

Todi ✉ 06059

Ask at the tourist office for a full list of *agriturismi* around Todi.

****Bramante**, Via Orvietana 48, **t** 075 894 8381, *www.hotelbramante.it* (€€€€€). A 13th-century convent just outside town, in a lovely setting, with half/full board in its restaurant. The decor and service need an overhaul.

Relais Todini, on road to Collevalenza di Todi, **t** 075 887521, *www.relaistodini.com* (€€€€€). A 14th-century *palazzo* with a pool, tennis court, gym, restaurant and lovely views. The park houses camels, kangaroos, zebras and penguins, and there are horses or carriages to ride, and boating lakes. Choose from rooms, suites, studios and apartments.

****Fonte Cesia**, Via L. Leoni 3, **t** 075 894 3737, *www.fontecesia.it* (€€€€). Stylish rooms in an 18th-century building. Full board is available.

***Villa Luisa**, Via A. Cortesi 147, **t** 075 894 8571, *www.villaluisa.it* (€€€). A pleasant place with a beautiful pool surrounded by trees, elegant rooms, room service and a restaurant (half and full board available).

★ Poggio d'Asproli >

Poggio d'Asproli, Loc. Asproli 7, 15mins from Todi, **t** 075 885 3385, *poggiodasproli@email.it* (€€€). A quirky 16th-century convent filled with the artist-owner's works, with a pool and meals by request. Music and theatre evenings take place in summer.

San Lorenzo Tre, Via S. Lorenzo 3, **t** 075 894 4555, *lorenzotre@tin.it* (€€€). A *residenza d'epoca* in a *palazzo*, with most rooms ensuite.

L'Arco, Loc. Fossaccio 19, Cordigliano, **t** 075 894 7534, *www.umbria-villa.it* (€€). A luxurious villa for up to 9, with a lovely pool. *Closed Oct–April.*

Castello di Porchiano, Porchiano, **t** 075 885 3127, *www.agriturismotodi.it* (€€). An *agriturismo* with ensuite rooms with a medieval atmosphere, studios and 2-bed apartments. *Closed Feb.*

Poponi, Via delle Piagge 26, **t** 075 894 8233, *www.argoweb.it/agriturismo_poponi* (€€). Simple rooms, most with shared facilities. *Closed mid-Jan–mid-Feb.*

Montecastello di Vibio ✉ 06057

***Il Castello**, Piazza G. Marconi 5, **t** 075 878 0560, *www.hotelilcastello.it* (€€€). A charming 15th-century building with a pool, solarium and restaurant with half/full board. *Closed Jan; restaurant Tues Dec–Mar.*

Collazzone ✉ 06050

Relais il Canalicchio, Canalicchio di Collazzone, **t** 075 870 7325, *www.relaisilcanalicchio.com* (€€€€). A medieval hilltop idyll decorated *à la* English country home, with a pool, a sauna, a gym, mountainbikes, tennis, billiards, a library and a cigar room. The great restaurant uses produce from the owners' farm.

Eating Out in Todi

Local specialities include pigeon, lamb and *porchetta*, and fat home-made spaghetti called *ombricelli*, served *alla boscaiola* (with tomatoes, piquant black olives and hot peppers). The dry white wine Grechetto di Todi dates back to the Roman Republic.

Antica Osteria de la Valle, Via Ciuffelli 19, **t** 075 894 4848 (€€). An atmospheric bar with a daily menu of home-made fare, including a good *antipasto della casa* featuring cheese fondue flavoured with truffles, rustic pâté and *bruschette*. *Closed Mon.*

Italia, Via del Monte 27, **t** 075 894 2643 (€€). A typical family trattoria using local ingredients; try the speciality *capriccio* (a bit like lasagne). *Closed Fri.*

Jacopone (Da Peppino), Piazza Jacopone 3, **t** 075 894 2366 (€€). Umbrian specialities served by friendly staff. *Closed Mon and 2wks July.*

★ La Mulinella >>

La Mulinella, Loc. Pontenaia, 3km from centre, **t** 075 894 4779 (€€). A reliable favourite with a fine view towards Todi from its garden. Try *bruschetta* with mushrooms and gnocchi in duck sauce. Booking is advisable. There are a few rooms too. *Closed Wed and 1–15 Nov.*

La Torre, Via Cortesi 57, **t** 075 894 2694 (€). Sophisticated fare such as risotto with pigeon and *linguini* with crab, followed by home-made ice cream. *Closed Tues and 1–15 Nov.*

Orvieto

Orvieto (population 20,700) owes much of its success to an ancient volcano. First this created the city's magnificent pedestal – a 325m sheer-cliffed *mesa*, straight out of the American southwest – then it enriched the hillsides with a special mix of volcanic minerals that form part of the secret alchemy of Orvieto's famous white wine. Though new buildings crowd the outskirts of Orvieto's unique crag, the medieval town on top, crowned by its stupendous cathedral, looks much the same as it has for the last 500 years.

History

Attracted by Orvieto's incomparable natural defences, the Etruscans settled it early and named it *Velzna* (or *Volsinium* as the Romans pronounced it). It was one of the 12 cities of the Etruscan confederation, and it fought frequently with the Romans until they laid it waste in 280 BC. Velzna/Volsinium must have been a wealthy place; historians record the Romans carrying home 2,000 statues after the sack. The Etruscans left and founded a new *Volsinium* on the shores of Lake Bolsena, leaving behind their old city (*Urbs Vetus*, hence 'Orvieto'). Orvieto in the Middle Ages was an important stronghold of the Papal States – primarily for popes who could take refuge here when their polls went down with the fickle Romans.

The Duomo

Duomo
t 0763 341167; open Mar and Oct daily 7.30–12.45 and 2.30–6.15; April–Sept daily 7.30–12.45 and 2.30–7.15 Nov–Feb daily 7.30–12.45 and 2.30–5.15

The 13th century may have been an age of faith but it certainly wasn't an age of fools. The popes were having trouble putting over the doctrine of transubstantiation, an archaic, genuinely pagan survival that many in the Church found difficulty accepting. But then the necessary miracle occurred, during a visit to Orvieto by Pope Urban IV in the 1260s. A Bohemian priest named Peter, on his way to Rome, was asked to celebrate Mass in Bolsena, just to the south. Father Peter had long been sceptical about the doctrine of the Host becoming the body of Christ, but during this Mass the Host itself answered his doubts by dripping blood on the altar linen. Peter took the linen to show to the Pope, who declared it a miracle and instituted the feast of Corpus Christi. St Thomas Aquinas, also visiting Orvieto at the time, was asked to compose a suitable office for the new holy day, while Urban IV promised Orvieto (rather unfairly to poor old Bolsena) a magnificent new cathedral to enshrine the bloodstained relic. The cornerstone was laid by Pope Nicholas IV in 1290 and the nave was built in the Romanesque style, probably to a design by Arnolfo di Cambio, builder of Florence cathedral. In 1300 the plan was changed into Gothic by local architect Giovanni di Uguccione, who replaced the stone vaults with an open truss roof. When the walls began to

Getting to and around Orvieto

Orvieto, at least its lower version, Orvieto Scalo, is on the main **train** line between Rome (121km/2hrs) and Florence (152km/2hrs); from Perugia it's 86km and just over 1hr.

It is also linked by ATC **coach**, **t** 0763 301224, *www.atcternit.it*, with Amelia, Narni, Terni, Viterbo in Lazio, etc. The once-daily trip to Todi (48km/2hrs) down the SS79 bis is magnificently scenic. All coaches stop by the *funivia* at the railway station.

There are **car parks** at Piazza Cahen and the ex-Campo della Fiera under the cliff; from here take a lift up to the church of San Giovanni, or bus C to Piazza della Repubblica. It may be easier to park free by the station; from here bus 1 makes the steep trip up a couple of times a day, or take the scenic *funicolare* (every 10–15mins) from the station to Piazza Cahen next to the Rocca and Etruscan temple, then shuttle bus A directly to the cathedral, or bus B around the *centro storico* (save your tickets for a discount at the Museo Faina).

For **car hire**, try Avis, Viale I Maggio 46, Orvieto Scalo, **t** 0763 393007, *www.avisautonoleggio.it*, or Hertz, Via Sette Martiri 32f, Orvieto Scalo, **t** 0763 301303, *www.hertz.it*. For **bike and motorbike hire**, try: Gulliver, Strada del Piano 6a, Orvieto Scalo, **t** 0763 302969, or Ciclo e Trekking Natura e Avventura, Via dei Tigliza, Orvieto Scalo (near the station), **t** 0763 301649 (Mar–Oct), which also runs **bike tours** in the countryside.

sway in 1305, architect and sculptor Lorenzo Maitani of Siena was summoned to remedy the situation. He built four lateral flying buttresses and made the apse square to stabilize the building, then designed the façade. The grateful Orvietani made him a citizen and let him choose his assistants. Subsequent architects included his son, followed by such luminaries as Nicolò and Meo Nuti, Andrea and Nino Pisano, Andrea Orcagna and Michele Sammicheli. Ippolito Scalza of Orvieto oversaw the works for 50 years.

The result is one of Italy's greatest cathedrals, visible for kilometres around, with a stunning, sumptuous 52m façade resembling a giant triptych. This Is Maitani's masterpiece, the 'golden lily of cathedrals' or 'the greatest polychrome monument in the world,' as Burckhart called it, designed as an architectural and decorative whole, the simple geometric forms and gables emphasized to make them strong enough to take the lavish detail. Colour it certainly has, especially when the late-afternoon sun inflames the dazzling Technicolor **mosaics** that fill every flat surface, though artistically there's not much to say about them – all were replaced after the façade was struck by lightning in 1795, except the restored *Nativity of Mary* (1364) over the south door. The magnificent **rose window** (1360) by the great Florentine artist Orcagna is surrounded by 16th-century statues of the Apostles.

Close up, the richness and beauty of the sculptural detail is simply breathtaking. It is said that 152 sculptors worked on the cathedral, but it was Maitani himself who contributed the best work – the remarkably designed and executed (with his son Vitale, and Nicolò and Meo Nuti) **bas reliefs** (1320–30) on the lower pilasters that recount the story of the *Creation* to the *Last Judgement*. This Bible in stone captures the essence of the stories with vivid drama and detail – the *Last Judgement*, in particular. Maitani also cast the four bronze symbols of the Evangelists, the ox, eagle, man and winged lion, all ready to step right off the

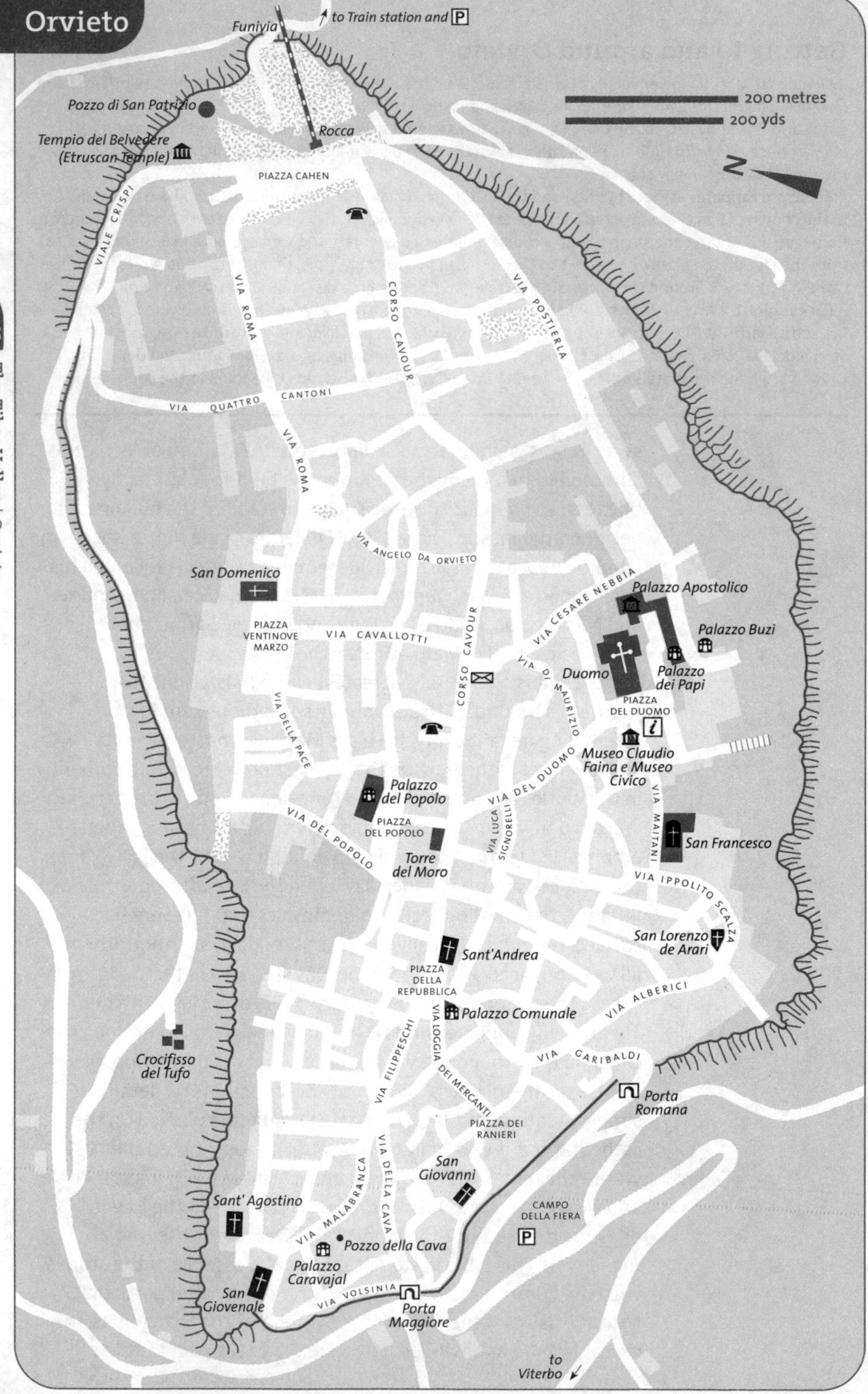
Orvieto
to Train station and P
Funivia
Pozzo di San Patrizio
Tempio del Belvedere
(Etruscan Temple)
Rocca
200 metres
200 yds
N
PIAZZA CAHEN
VIALE CRISPI
VIA ROMA
CORSO CAVOUR
VIA POSTIERLA
VIA QUATTRO CANTONI
VIA ROMA
VIA ANGELO DA ORVIETO
San Domenico
PIAZZA
VENTINOVE
MARZO
VIA CAVALLOTTI
CORSO CAVOUR
VIA CESARE NEBBIA
Palazzo Apostolico
Palazzo Buzi
VIA DI MAURIZIO
Duomo
Palazzo
dei Papi
PIAZZA
DEL DUOMO
VIA DELLA PACE
Museo Claudio
Faina e Museo
Civico
VIA DEL DUOMO
Palazzo
del Popolo
PIAZZA
DEL POPOLO
VIA DEL POPOLO
Torre
del Moro
VIA LUCA
SIGNORELLI
VIA MAITANI
San Francesco
VIA IPPOLITO SCALZA
San Lorenzo
de Arari
Sant'Andrea
PIAZZA
DELLA
REPUBBLICA
Palazzo Comunale
VIA ALBERICI
VIA GARIBALDI
VIA LOGGIA
DEI MERCANTI
VIA FILIPPESCHI
Crocifisso
del Tufo
Porta
Romana
PIAZZA DEI
RANIERI
San
Giovanni
VIA DELLA CAVA
VIA MALABRANCA
Sant' Agostino
CAMPO
DELLA FIERA
P
Pozzo della Cava
Palazzo
Caravajal
San
Giovenale
VIA VOLSINIA
Porta
Maggiore
to
Viterbo

cornice of the façade, and the bronze angels in the lunette over the central portal. The bronze doors, portraying the *Works of Mercy* (1965) are by Emilio Greco. The 16th-century sibyls on the corners of the façade were sculpted by Fabiano Toti and Antonio Federighi.

In contrast with the soaring vertical lines of the façade, the cathedral's sides and little rounded chapels are banded with horizontal zebra stripes of yellow tufa and grey basalt. On the right (south side) is the oldest door, the Porta di Postierla. On the left, the Porta del Corporale had three statues by Andrea Pisano in its lunette; along with Pisano's *Madonna* from the Duomo, these are being stored by the Museo dell'Opera del Duomo (*see* p.534).

One of the best times to come to Orvieto is after Easter, when you can witness the Pentecost **Festa della Palombella**, a tradition founded by the Monaldeschi in 1404: a steel wire is suspended from the roof of the church of San Francesco (*see* p.536) to a wooden tabernacle on the porch of the cathedral, and on the stroke of noon a white dove tied with red ribbons on an iron wreath-like contraption gets the ride of its life hurtling down to the tabernacle, greeted by a round of firecrackers to symbolize the flames of the Holy Spirit that lit up over the heads of the Apostles. The dove is later presented to the last couple to have been wed in the cathedral, who are charged to keep it as a pet until the end of its natural days. Another high day after Easter, **Corpus Christi**, occasions a procession of the *Corporale* in its glittering reliquary through town, accompanied by Orvietani in their trecento finery.

The Interior

Filtered through stained-glass and alabaster windows, the muted light adds to the serene beauty of the striped Romanesque nave, divided into three by fine columns and capitals and rounded arches, topped in turn by a clerestory. The lack of clutter – much of the art is stowed away in the Museo dell'Opera del Duomo (*see* p.534) – reveals the lovely proportions and the subtle asymmetries that give the interior its unique dynamism. Note how neither the five semicircular chapels on each wall nor the windows are centred between the arches of the aisles, nor the upper clerestory windows. The floor rises gently up to the altar, and each striped column is slightly shorter as you approach, producing a magical effect as you walk down the nave.

Look for Gentile da Fabriano's delicate fresco of the *Madonna and Child* (1426) by the left door, near the baptismal font of 1407. Many of the side chapels have remains of votive frescoes. In the left transept is a *Pietà* (1579) by Ippolito Scalza, its figures carved from a single block of marble. Beyond is the **Cappella del Corporale**, built *c.* 1350 to house the famous relic and decorated by Sienese masters: the frescoes of the *Miracle of Bolsena* and *Crucifixion* by Ugolino di

Prete Ilario (1360s) and, in a niche in the right wall, the exquisite *Madonna dei Raccomandati* (1339) by Lippo Memmi, brother-in-law of Simone Martini. The altar, with Gothic tabernacle by Nicola da Siena and Orcagna, shelters the venerated blood-stained linen. To the left, encased, is the silver gilt **Reliquario del Corporale** (1338), echoing the façade of the cathedral and decorated with 12 enamelled scenes from the Life of Christ by goldsmith Ugolino di Vieri of Siena. In the nave, the magnificent **organ**, built in 1584 is the second largest in Italy. The restored **choir frescoes** are by Ugolino di Prete Ilario and other Sienese painters, the intarsia **stalls** by another Sienese, Giovanni Ammannati, and the **stained glass** by Giovanni di Bonino from Assisi (1334). To the right is Ippolito Scalza's last work, an *Ecce Homo* (1608). In the little south transept, the **altar of the Magi** was sculpted by a young Sammicheli, before he became Venice's great military architect.

Cappella di San Brizio

Cappella di San Brizio
*t 0763 342477; open **Mar and Oct** Mon–Sat 8–12.45 and 2.30–6.15, Sun and hols 2.30–5.45; **April–June** Mon–Sat 8–12.45 and 2.30–7.15, Sun and hols 2.30–5.45; **July–Sept** Mon–Sat 8–12.45 and 2.30–7.15, Sun and hols 2.30–6.45; **Nov–Feb** Mon–Sat 8–12.45 and 2.30–5.15, Sun and hols 2.30–5.45; buy tickets at tourist office; only 26 people admitted at a time*

This contains one of the finest and most powerful fresco cycles of the Renaissance, but its genesis was hit and miss. In 1408, the Monaldeschi financed the construction of the Cappella Nuova, which became known as Cappella di San Brizio after the pretty 14th-century altarpiece of the *Madonna di San Brizio*. In 1447 they hired Fra Angelico to fresco it; he began with the ceiling vaults, completing two scenes near the altar – the serene *Christ in Judgement* and the *Prophets* – while his pupil Benozzo Gozzoli contributed the hierarchies of angels. Then the pope summoned Fra Angelico to Rome and he died before returning to finish.

Years later, Perugino was commissioned to complete the work, but he left after a few days. Finally, in 1499, Luca Signorelli of Cortona, a student of Piero della Francesca and already sufficiently famous to have painted a fresco in the Sistine Chapel, was hired to complete the vaults. The patrons liked what they saw and commissioned him to fresco the walls. Signorelli made the end of the world his theme, and worked on the project until 1504. This chapel is, in many ways, the stylistic and psychological precursor of Michelangelo's *Last Judgement* in the Sistine Chapel; Signorelli's remarkable draughtsmanship and foreshortening, his dynamic male nudes inspired by Antonio Pollaiuolo and what he learned from Piero about simplifying nature and architecture into essential geometrical forms give the frescoes tremendous power.

The six scenes in the Cappella di San BrIzio are iconographically taken from the *Divine Comedy* and St Augustine's *City of God*. The first, the *Preaching of the Antichrist*, is a rare subject and evokes the confusion and turmoil in Florence after the Dominican preacher Savonarola was burned at the stake in 1498. If you look in the crowd attending the Antichrist (whose words are prompted by the Devil), you can see Dante's beaky profile and red hat as he stands with Petrarch and Christopher Columbus – symbolic of the beginning of the modern era – while in the background, around the Temple of Solomon, chaos and catastrophe are at work in the last throes of the Middle Ages. Far left of the Antichrist, the artist portrays himself and Fra Angelico dressed in black, watching the anarchy with a quiet detachment that seems almost chilling. Signorelli's mistress jilted him while he painted this, so he put her in the scene as the prostitute taking money. Overhead St Michael keeps the Antichrist from ascending to heaven.

Next to this is the *End of the World*, where a prophet foretells doomsday: the sea floods, the earth shakes, the stars fall from the firmament and the darkened sky is shot with streaks of fire. In the next scene, Signorelli gives us the *Resurrection of the Dead* in unforgettable, literal detail as the corpses and skeletons pull themselves out of the curiously glutinous earth and form new coats of flesh, though the fellow on the right merrily conversing with six skeletons adds a humorous touch. This is one of the most powerful nude studies of the quattrocento, only surpassed by the next scene, *The Damned Consigned to Hell*, a crowded writhing *Inferno*; even the cruel devils, one per person, are more or less human, except for their metallic colours, horns and shaggy hips (Signorelli made sure to put his mistress here, too, caught in the embrace of a flying devil). The *Blessed* in the next scene get to go to Paradise with the lovely angels (parts of this fresco, concealed by the 18th-century altar, can be seen by way of video), while the final scene shows the *Coronation of the Chosen*.

Below the frescoes Signorelli painted medallions of Cicero, Homer (though since the restoration, he's been identified as Statius), Dante, Virgil, Ovid, Lucan and pre-Socratic philosopher Empedocles (right of the entrance). He also painted the scenes from the *Divine Comedy* and myth in the *tondi*, and the *Deposition*, where one mourner is Pietro Parenzo, who served Orvieto as *podestà* in the 13th century and was killed by heretics.

Piazza del Duomo

The cathedral shares the piazza with Ippolito Scalza's handsome **Palazzo Buzi** (1580), the deteriorating neoclassical church, **San Giacomo Maggiore**, and other *palazzi* housing Orvieto's five museums.

Musei Archeologici Claudio Faina e Civico
t 0763 341511; open April–Sept daily 9.30–6; Oct–Mar Tues–Sun 10–5; guided tours 11 and 3; adm

Opposite the cathedral, the 19th-century Palazzo Faina contains two of these, the **Musei Archeologici Claudio Faina e Civico**. The ground floor, the **Museo Civico**, has terracotta decorations from the Belvedere temple – male figures, a warrior, a horse and the goddess Artemis that show a strong Greek influence. The *Venus of Cannicella*, an Archaic Greek statue made of Naxos marble from the 6th century BC, was found in Orvieto's oldest tombs; a giant warrior's head from the same period came from the Crocifisso del Tufo. A 4th-century BC sarcophagus is decorated with gruesome scenes from the Trojan War, of Achilles sacrificing Trojan prisoners to Patroclos, and Neoptolemos killing Polyxena, Priam's daughter, on Achilles' tomb. The **Museo Claudio Faina**, one of Italy's top private archaeological collections, garnered in the last century by the Faina counts and donated to the city in 1954, fills the two upper floors and is rich in finds from Orvieto's necropoli: 3,000 ancient coins, Etruscan gold, an excellent collection of vases and bronzes, a beautiful selection of the black and red figure Attic vases imported by wealthy Etruscans, *bucchero* ware, and an Etruscan sarcophagus with traces of its bright paint. Ask about the special kid's booklet (in English and Italian) with information and a quiz, and about concerts held in the garden in summer

The south side of the cathedral was the heartbeat of papal Orvieto. The austere, crenellated tufa **Palazzo Soliano** was begun by Boniface VIII in 1297, who didn't think the slightly older Palazzo Apostolico (*see* below) was up to snuff. It was finished in the 1500s and contains the **Museo dell'Opera del Duomo**, with works that filled the cathedral – statues by grand masters such as Arnolfo di Cambio and Andrea Pisano, grand statues by little-known hands, especially the colossal *Apostles*, and two early Baroque figures of the *Annunciation* by Bernini's teacher, Francesco Mocchi. Paintings include a *Crucifixion* by Spinello Aretino, a *Madonna* by 13th-century master, Coppo di Marcovaldo, a *Self-portrait* and a *Magdalene* by Signorelli (like the one painted by his master Piero, in Arezzo), a reliquary of San Savino's head by Ugolino di Vieri and, most lovely of all, two richly coloured *Madonnas* by Simone Martini. There are two beautiful sketches on parchment of the cathedral façade, one by Maitani, and an older one attributed to Arnolfo di Cambio. The ground floor houses the **Museo Emilio Greco**, with a large collection of works from 1947 to the 1980s, donated by the sculptor.

Museo dell'Opera del Duomo

t 0763 343592; open April–June, Sept and Oct daily 10–6; July and Aug daily 10–1 and 3–7; Nov–Mar Wed–Mon 10–5; guided tours by appt; adm (joint ticket with Cappella San Brizio; see p.532)

Museo Emilio Greco

t 0763 344605; open April–Sept daily 10.30–1 and 2.30–6; Oct–Mar daily 10.30–1 and 2–5.30; adm; combined ticket available with Pozzo della Cava, see p.536, and Pozzo di San Patrizio, see p.537

Adjacent, the restored 13th-century **Palazzo Apostolico** (or Palazzo Papale), begun by Urban IV and finished in 1304, holds the **Museo Archeologico**, with an excellent collection of Etruscan bronzes, vases (including some fine Greek ones), mirrors, bronze armour and a fresco of an Etruscan butcher's stand. Best of all are two painted 4th-century BC tombs from Settecamini, reconstructed here, representing scenes of the banquet all good Etruscans expected to find when they went into the underworld. Those in the first tomb, of the Leinie, show scenes of the kitchen, as servants (all carefully named) prepare the meat. On the opposite wall the banquet takes place, presided over by the gods of the underworld, Pluto in a wolfskin cap and spear decorated with a serpent, and Persephone, holding a sceptre topped by a bird. The dead guest of honour arrives in a chariot with a demon.

Museo Archeologico

t 0763 341039; open 2 Aug–15 Sept Sun–Fri 8.30–7.30, Sat 8.30am–11pm; rest of year daily 8.30–7.30; adm

Città Sotterranea
t 0763 344891, www. orvietounderground.it; tours Feb Sat and Sun 11, 12.15, 4 and 5.15; rest of year daily 11, 12.15, 4 and 5.15 (call **t** *0763 334 0688 for tours in English or extra tours); adm*

From the tourist office at Piazza del Duomo 24, tours depart for **Orvieto Underground**, a shadow, alternative city that residents of the *rupe* excavated from within their obliging tufa, an underground labyrinth of galleries (or *grotte*) containing wine cellars, silos, wells, cisterns, ovens, aqueducts, little religious shrines, medieval rubbish pits, dovecotes and more.

Piazza del Popolo and Around

In contrast to its heavenly cathedral (Pope John XXIII said that on Judgement Day the angels would bear it up to Paradise), the rest of Orvieto is a solid medieval town, dotted with *palazzi* built for Roman and local bigwigs by many of the architects who worked on the cathedral. **Corso Cavour** has been Orvieto's main street since Etruscan times, and where it meets Via del Duomo towers the 42m **Torre del Moro**, built in the 12th century and affording a sublime view over the city. The big bell, decorated with 24 symbols of Orvieto's guilds, was cast in 1316; the cathedral builders timed their workday by it. Next to it, the **Palazzo del Sette** (1300) was built for the seven magistrates elected by the guilds to govern the *comune*.

Torre del Moro
t 0763 344567; open Mar, April, Sept and Oct daily 10–7; May–Aug daily 10–8; Nov–Feb daily 10.30–1 and 2.30–5; adm

One block north, in Piazza del Popolo, the **Palazzo del Popolo**, a tufa palace begun in 1250, has mullioned windows and an open loggia in the Lombard style. Turned into a prison and warehouse by the popes, it is now a conference centre. The restoration uncovered the sacred area of an Etruscan temple, a medieval aqueduct and a cistern. Also in the piazza, Palazzo Simoncelli is the site of the **Museo delle Ceramiche Medioevali Orvietane**; Orvieto was an important centre for ceramic production in the Middle Ages.

Museo delle Ceramiche Medioevali Orvietane
ask at tourist office, see p.538, for opening hrs

From here, Via della Pace leads back to a piazza with the **church of San Domenico**, built in 1233, just after St Dominic's canonization, making it the first ever Dominican church. St Thomas Aquinas taught at the former monastery here and is recalled with several mementos in the **Cappella Petrucci**, built by Sammicheli below the church. None of these claims to fame spared the church from amputation of its naves in 1934 to make room for a barracks.

Four Churches and a Palazzo

From the Torre del Moro, Corso Cavour winds down through 16th-century *palazzi* and medieval buildings to **Piazza della Repubblica**, Orvieto's main square and site of the Etruscan and Roman forums. Here is 12th-century **Sant'Andrea** with its unusual 12-sided campanile, pierced by mullioned windows and topped by bellicose crenellations. The mosaic pavement of a 6th-century church was discovered beneath Sant'Andrea; an even lower level has an **Etruscan street and buildings**. Decorated with 14th-century frescoes, Sant'Andrea was the most important church in Orvieto before the construction of the cathedral and basks in the memory

Resti Etruschi
sacristan of church has key to excavations

of the events that took place within its walls: here Innocent III proclaimed the Fourth Crusade, and here in 1281, Charles of Anjou and his glittering retinue attended the coronation of Martin IV.

Piazza della Repubblica's 13th-century **Palazzo Comunale**, hidden behind a late Renaissance façade, is the starting point for exploring Orvieto's most picturesque medieval streets, such as Via Loggia dei Mercanti, lined with *tufa* houses; at its end, beyond Piazza dei Ranieri, octagonal **San Giovanni** was first built in 916 and rebuilt in 1687; it has a 14th-century detached fresco of the *Madonna* from the original church and a handsome cloister used for exhibitions. At this point, Orvieto's pedestal is almost sheer; a narrow lane follows along the edge down and around to the oldest corner of the town and delightful **San Giovenale**, begun in 1004, with a fortified tower, 12th–15th-century frescoes and charming bits of ancient sculpture. The big adjacent Gothic **church of Sant'Agostino**, with its handsome door, has been restored as an exhibition space.

To Porta Maggiore

Picturesque Via Malabranca leads back to the centre by way of the 16th-century **Palazzo Caravajal** by Ippolito Scalza, with its handsome portal and an inscription in Spanish informing passers-by that the house was built for the comfort of the owner's friends. Here, too, is the 15th-century **Palazzo Filippeschi** (or Pietrangeli), the most beautiful in Orvieto. Florentine rather than Roman in style, it has such a lovely courtyard and portico that it has been attributed to Bernardo Rossellino. From here, Via della Cava descends to the old gate, **Porta Maggiore**; at the restaurant at Via della Cava 26, you can peer into the depths of the **Pozzo della Cava**, a deep public well excavated by the Etruscans and used from 1428 to 1546.

Pozzo della Cava
t 0763 342373; open Tues–Sun 8am–8pm; other times by appt; adm; joint ticket available with Pozzo di San Patrizio, see p.537, and Museo Emilio Greco, see p.534

San Lorenzo and San Francesco

The 13th-century Romanesque **church of San Lorenzo de Arari**, reached by Via Ippolito Scalza from Corso Cavour (or on Via Maitani from the Piazza Duomo) was named for its venerable altar (*ara*), supported by a cylindrical Etruscan altar, the whole protected by a lovely 12th-century stone *ciborium*. The Byzantine-style frescoes in the apse add an ancient feel, especially the elongated figures and staring eyes of *Christ Enthroned with Saints*. Other frescoes, from the 1330s and restored with more goodwill than skill, depict the *Life of St Lawrence*, who retains his sense of humour even while being toasted on the grill ('Turn me over, I'm done on this side,' he said). In the Middle Ages, when no body part was too kinky to stick in a reliquary, some churches claimed to have vials of his melted fat.

Nearby, in Piazza dei Febei, the 13th-century preaching **church of San Francesco** has been much changed over time. Its size came in handy for important events – it was here that Boniface VIII canonized St Louis of France in 1297. Inside you can see a wooden *Crucifixion* attributed to Maitani or a close follower and some 14th-century frescoes in the sacristy.

The Citadel, a Temple and St Patrick's Well

Orvieto's northeastern end and funicular terminus, **Piazza Cahen**, is dominated by the ruins of the **Rocca**, a citadel built in 1364 by Cardinal Albornoz. The people of Orvieto, always willing to host a pope or two (33 spent extended periods in the city), showed their appreciation of this direct attempt at papal domination by destroying it in 1390; only the walls, a gate and a tower survive, now encompassing a garden of umbrella pines. Views from the ramparts stretch from the shallow Paglia river to the Tiber valley.

Next to the citadel is the massive podium of an Etruscan temple, the 5th-century BC **Tempio del Belvedere**, made of travertine: it had a double row of columns in front, a *pronaos*, and three *cellae* – a perfect example of the typical Etruscan-Italic temple described by Vitruvius. The podium was rediscovered by accident in 1828 and fragments of its terracotta decoration are in the Museo Civico.

Pozzo di San Patrizio
Valle Sangallo, **t** *0763 343768; open April–Sept daily 10–7; Oct–Mar daily 10–6; adm, joint ticket available with Museo Emilio Greco, see p.53, and Pozza della Cava, see p.536; bring a sweater as it is cold and damp at bottom*

Much of the temple's stone was cannibalized for the building of a nearby well, the ingenious **Pozzo di San Patrizio**, designed in the 1530s by Antonio da Sangallo the Younger, and the most celebrated of all Orvieto's subterranean wonders. Its name comes from St Patrick's well in Ireland, where according to legend, Patrick found Paradise after passing through the depths of Hell. The well was built on the orders of calamitous Medici pope Clement VII. After surviving the sack of Rome – and sneaking out of the city disguised as a greengrocer – Clement became paranoid about the security of the papal person. He commissioned this unique work of engineering to supply Orvieto in the event of a siege; to reach the spring, Sangallo had to dig the equivalent of seven storeys. To haul the water to the surface, he built two spiral stairs of 248 steps in a brick double helix – one for the water-carriers and their donkeys going down, another for going up, meeting at a narrow bridge at the base. The stairs are lit by 72 windows on the central shaft. Despite the labour that went into its construction, the well was never needed. But it didn't harm the Church as much as another decision hapless Clement made during his stay – his refusal to annul Henry VIII's marriage to Catherine of Aragon.

Around Orvieto

The base of Orvieto's bluff is pocked with Etruscan tombs excavated off and on for centuries; back in the finders-keepers age of archaeology, many of the most beautiful finds went to the Louvre and the British Museum. Unlike Perugia's impressive Ipogeo dei Volumni, few of these have any decoration; the tombs resemble

Crocifisso del Tufo
t 0763 343611; open April–Sept daily 8.30–7.30; Oct–Mar daily 8.30–5; adm

streets of low houses, sparsely furnished with a pair of benches where the urns of the departed were arranged. The most impressive is the 6th-century BC **Crocifisso del Tufo**, on the SS71 north of Orvieto; go by foot from the Porta Maggiore, where the austerity of its large tufa blocks are relieved by moss and grassy roofs. Excavations began in the 1800s and continue slowly. More than 100 rectangular chamber tombs have been found, one per nuclear family, sharing walls, each with a little entrance with the family and given names inscribed on the lintel. Originally they were closed with a stone door. Piles of clay and earth sealed the roofs, which would be topped with a *cippus* – the head of the warrior in the Museo Civico was one of these. By the unique wealth of inscriptions found here, it seems Velzna was unusually multicultural for an Etruscan town – the oldest burials were of Greek origin; other families have Latin, Umbrian and even Gothic names.

Still on the SS71, about 2.5km south from the Porta Romana, the 12th–13th-century Benedictine **abbey of Santi Severo e Martirio** (renovated in the 19th century and now partly a hotel, La Badia; *see* below) retains much of its original work – a Cosmatesque pavement and some trecento frescoes, as well as another dodecagonal campanile similar to the peculiar one at Sant'Andrea.

Castel Rubello
open by request; custodian lives nearby

Further south in Loc. Porano is the painted Etruscan **tomb of the Hescanas** near **Castel Rubello**. Just over the border in Lazio, medieval **Bagnoregio** is piled on a smaller version of Orvieto's tufa pedestal.

ⓘ Orvieto >
Piazza del Duomo 24, t 0763 341772 and t 0763 341911, www.orvienet.it, www.umbria2000.it, www.comune.orvieto.tr.it

Tourist Information in Orvieto

Ask at the tourist office about the **Carta Orvieto Unica** (€12.50), which admits you to various sights, and gives you a free round-trip on the *funicolare* plus minibus A or B or 5hrs' parking in the Campo della Fiera and lifts to the centre. It's also sold in museums and in booths in car parks.

Tourist information is also available from **Consorzio Orvieto Promotion**, Piazza dell'Erba 1/A, **t** 0763 393453, *www.orvietoturismo.it*, a consortium of hotels, restaurants, and more.

Post office: Largo Ravelli, **t** 0763 398311.

Where to Stay in Orvieto

★ Palazzo Piccolomini >>

Orvieto ✉ 05018

There are plenty of *agriturismi* in the Orvieto area; ask at the tourist office for their list.

Very Expensive (€€€€)

******La Badia**, Loc. La Badia 8, 5km south on Bagnoregio road, **t** 0763 301959, *www.labadiahotel.it*. An old abbey with lovely views up to the *tufa*-crowned citadel. Rooms are elegant, and there's an outdoor pool, a tennis court, a restaurant (half and full board available) and parking.

Expensive (€€€)

******Aquila Bianca**, Via Garibaldi 13, **t** 0763 341246, *www.hotelaquilabianca.it*. An old-fashioned, central choice, with spacious rooms, Internet access, a restaurant and a garage. Rates are at the lower end of this price range.

******Maitani**, Via Maitani 5, **t** 0763 342011, *www.hotelmaitani.com*. Comfy rooms opposite the cathedral, with Internet access and parking.

******Palazzo Piccolomini**, Piazza dei Ranieri 36, **t** 0763 341743, *www.hotelpiccolomini.it*. A gorgeous medieval palace in the historic centre, with half/full board in its restaurant.

******Villa Ciconia**, Via dei Tigli 69, north along SS71, **t** 0763 305582, *www.hotelvillaciconia.com*. A 16th-century villa in an oasis of green in the ugly sprawl of Orbetello Scalo. There's a beautiful pool, parking and a frescoed restaurant (half and full board available) serving fine food.

*****Duomo**, Vicolo di Maurizio 7, **t** 0763 341887, *www.orvietohotelduomo.com*. Basic rooms (at the lower end of this category), plus a garage.

Moderate (€€)

*****Valentino**, Via Angelo da Orvieto 30/32, **t** 0763 342464, *www.valentinohotel.com*. Simple but comfortable rooms in a 16th-century house near the old church of San Domenico, with a garage.

*****Virgilio**, Piazza Duomo 5, **t** 0763 341882, *www.hotelvirgilio.com*. A trecento building just across from the cathedral, with ensuite rooms.

Inexpensive (€)

****Pergoletta**, Via Sette Martiri 5, **t** 0763 301418, *alberto.mon@libero.it*. Rooms with or without bath, a restaurant (half and full board available) and a garage.

****Picchio**, Via G. Salvatori 17, **t** 0763 301144, *www.bellaumbria.net/hotel-picchio*. Simple rooms with parquet flooring and good baths, plus an Internet point and private garage.

****Posta**, Via Luca Signorelli 18, **t** 0763 341909, *www.orvietohotels.it*. Rooms off Corso Cavour in the historic centre, most with shared facilities, plus a garage and a patch of garden.

Eating Out in Orvieto

Besides wine (see p.541), specialities are *cinghiale in agrodolce* (sweet and sour boar) and *gallina ubriaca* ('drunken chicken'). Beware that tourists have helped keep some mediocre venues in business – choose with care.

If you book at a restaurant in the historic centre, you can park for free in Via Roma: restaurants have vouchers for your dashboard.

★ I Sette Consoli >

I Sette Consoli, Piazza Sant'Angelo 1A, **t** 0763 343911 (€€€€). The best local ingredients cooked with imagination: try lasagne with broccoli and sausage. *Closed Sun eve in winter and Wed.*

Le Grotte del Funaro, Via Ripa Serancia 41, **t** 0763 343276 (€€€). An elegant restaurant in tufa caves, with solid Umbrian cuisine. Book ahead. *Closed Mon exc July/Aug; 1wk Jan; 1wk July.*

Osteria dell'Angelo, Piazza 29 Marzo 8a, **t** 0763 341805 (€€€). Local products prepared with flair: try gnocchi with tomatoes and tuna. *Closed Sun eve, Mon and Tues lunch and 1–15 Aug.*

L'Asino d'Oro, Vicolo del Popolo 9, **t** 0763 344406 (€€). Excellent, innovative fare such as saltcod in tomato sauce, and charming service. *Closed mid-Jan–mid-Mar and mid-Oct–mid-Nov.*

Etrusca, Via Lorenzo Maitani 10, **t** 0763 344016 (€€). Great traditional food; try *umbrichelli* with white or black truffles.

Maurizio, Via Duomo 78, t 0763 341114 (€€). Inspired Umbrian home-made pasta and other dishes with game, mushrooms and truffles. *Closed Tues and 1st half Jan.*

Zeppelin, Via G. Garibaldi 28, **t** 0763 341447 (€€). Excellent lunches and dinners, plus residential cooking courses where you can learn to cook treats such as *umbrichelli* with wild boar sauce. There's a veggie menu.

La Volpe e L'Uva, Via Ripa Corsica 1, **t** 0763 341612 (€). A busy place with unusual *secondi*: try eels with peppers and onions. *Closed Mon, Tues and Jan.*

Wine-tastings

Consorzio per la Tutela dei Vini Doc Orvieto e Rosso Orvietano, Corso Cavour 36, **t** 0763 343790, *www.consorziovinidiorvieto.it*. Information.

Antinori, Castello della Sala, Loc. Sala, Ficulle, **t** 0763 86051. A place famous for its Cervara; visits are by appt.

Barberani, Loc. Cerreto (Lago di Corbara), Baschi, **t** 0763 341820. Weekend visits by appointment.

Cantina Foresi, Piazza Duomo 2, **t** 0763 341611. The best place to taste and buy.

Cooperativa Vitivinicola per la Zona di Orvieto, Vini Cardeto, Via Constanzi 51, **t** 0763 300594. Visits Tues–Fri except hols and harvest, but call first.

Tenuta Le Velette, Le Velette, near Orvieto Scalo, **t** 0763 29090. Visits by appt (exc Sun).

Cantina Monrubio, Loc. Le Prese, Monterubraglio, **t** 0763 626064. No visits weekends, hols or harvest.

Hills, Lakes and Gardens around Orvieto

North of Orvieto

The rather empty territory in the hills north of Orvieto isn't one of Umbria's better-known regions – which may be part of its appeal. One possible destination, along the winding SS71 to Città della Pieve, is walled medieval **Ficulle**, founded by the Lombards and long home to potters who make earthenware wine pitchers (*panate*), oil containers (*ziri*) and bean pots (*pignatte*), which you can buy. All houses here have little terracotta numberplates by the doors. The Collegiata was designed by Ippolito Scalza, while the little **church of Santa Maria Vecchia**, outside the walls, has 15th-century frescoes and preserves an ancient *cippus* from a *mithraeum*.

Castello della Sala
open for visits Mon–Fri exc Aug; advance booking needed on **t** *0763 86051*

La Scarzuola
2hr guided visits for groups of 8 or more by appt with Convento della Scarzuola e Città Buzziana, **t** *0763 837463; adm exp*

The Marchesi Antinori, who make the finest Orvietos, live 6km south at the imposing, beautifully preserved **Castello della Sala**, built by the Monaldeschi in the 1300s; it has a Gargantuesque cylindrical tower, linked to the square castle by a covered gallery.

North, near Montegiove, up a signposted unpaved road through a forest, lies **La Scarzuola**. In 1956, architect Tomaso Buzzi (1900–81) purchased a 13th-century Franciscan convent and its grounds to create this garden based on the lovely woodcuts and descriptions in the celebrated *Hypnerotomachia Polifili* (Polyphilus' 'Dream of the Strife of Love'), a nearly incomprehensible philosophical romance on love, beauty and architecture written by Dominican friar Francesco Colonna and published in Venice in 1499. The result is a series of ruins and stage sets that are meant to be viewed by following a special itinerary: there's even a transparent pyramid (predating the one at the Louvre) and a musical staircase.

East and South of Orvieto: Lakes Corbara and Alviano

Between Orvieto and Todi, a dam stops up the Tiber to form the **Lago di Corbara**, Umbria's second largest lake, with good fishing. Both Orvieto–Todi routes are scenic: the slower SS79bis passes **Prodo**, with its pink medieval castle, and the turn-off for **Titignano**, a 16th-century fortified villa connected to a hamlet; the more southerly SS448 passes along the lake shore and **Civitella del Lago**, known for its restaurant (*see* p.542). The convent by the lake was founded by St Francis in 1218 on land donated by the Baschi family and rebuilt in 1703. Nearby, at the confluence of the Paglia and the Tiber, stands their fief, **Baschi**, a hilltown with a medieval centre enjoying spectacular views. Below lie the ruins of the ancient Roman port of *Palianum*, from where Orvieto's wine (*see* opposite) was shipped to Rome. Baschi's **church of San Nicolò**, designed by Ippolito Scalza (1584) has a lovely triptych by Sienese painter Giovanni di Paolo and a Murano chandelier.

Orvieto's Wine, in Legend and in a Glass

When Signorelli drew up his contract to fresco the Cappella di San Brizio, he added a clause 'that he be given as much as he wanted of that wine of Orvieto'. Fuelled on the stuff, he never painted better.

First made by the Etruscans and Romans, and shipped down the Tiber at *Palianum*, near Baschi (where archaeologists have found large caches of amphorae), the wine legendarily saved the city from the barbarians, who partook so generously of the golden nectar they found in the city's temples that all locals had to do was gather up the drunks in the middle of the night and give them the old heave-ho.

Refined over the centuries, Umbria's most famous wine is grown in 16 designated areas in the provinces of Terni and Viterbo, and consists of a careful mixture of grapes, with Tuscan Trebbiano and Verdello dominant. Light straw-coloured Orvieto DOC comes in four varieties: dry (Orvieto *secco*), which predominates because of the market, the more authentic moderately dry (*abboccato*, often served with appetizers), medium-sweet (*amabile*) and sweet (*dolce*), made like a Sauternes from noble rot (*muffa nobile*). If made in the oldest growing zone, right near Orvieto, it's called Classico.

Castello del Poggio
t 0744 903379; open 2nd Sat and 3rd Mon of month 9–12.30

From Baschi, the SS205 climbs high over the valley of the Tiber, taking in splendid scenery on the way to **Montecchio** and the 15th-century **Castello del Poggio**. On a wooded hill, with beautiful views over lakes Corbara and Alviano, the *castello* is reached by a hard-to-find road from the village of Guardea. This peaceful area was busy in the Greek-Gothic wars; the castle was founded by the Byzantines and occupied by the Normans when they took over the Greek lands of southern Italy; it was restored by Antonio Sangallo the Younger and is now being restored again, as a cultural centre and residence.

Museo di Alviano
t 07444 905028; open Tues–Fri 4–7; adm

South, just off the SS205 at medieval **Alviano**, St Francis hushed the swallows drowning out his preaching. Alviano has a perfectly preserved **castle** (1495–1506) built by *condottiere* Bartolomeo d'Alviano. Its fine Renaissance courtyard affords access to the **Museo di Alviano**. A scion of the Liviani family, Bartolomeo was employed by the Republic of Venice and gave such satisfaction he was made lord of the Venetian city of Pordenone. In 1651 his castle was purchased by grasping Olimpia Pamphili, sister-in-law of Pope Innocent X; in 1920 her family donated it to Alviano, which uses it as a town hall. On the round tower, note the Medusa head designed to ward off enemies. The **chapel** in the castle courtyard is frescoed with scenes of St Francis and the swallows; in the old storage cellars is the **Museo della Civilità Contadina**, dedicated to farm tools from the good old days. Alviano's charming **parish church** (1505) has kept most of its original features, and has Umbria's only fresco (the *Madonna and Saints*) by the painter Pordenone. The commission came from Pentesilea Baglione, widow of the *condottiere*; she is the elderly woman on the right. The church also contains one of Niccolò Alunno's finest paintings, the *Madonna in Gloria* (1480s).

Oasi di Alviano
entrance at Madonna del Porto, on Mutano–Scalo–Baschi road; t 0744 903715; open Sept–mid-May Sun and hols 10–sunset; other times by guided tours by appt; adm

The Tiber has been dammed near here to create another small artificial lake, the **Lago di Alviano**; its banks are nothing to look at now, but come back in a century or so. The surrounding marshes are a nature reserve, the **Oasi di Alviano**, with hides from which you can watch herons, bitterns and ducks.

Where to Stay and Eat around Orvieto

Ficulle ✉ 05016

La Casella >

La Casella, near Parrano, **t** 0763 86684 or **t** 0763 86588, *www.lacasella.com* (€€€). An *agriturismo* in a 1,000-acre forest. Rooms (breakfast included) are in 12 stone houses in an old hamlet, and there is riding (including tuition), a pool with hydromassage, tennis, volleyball and 5-a-side football facilities, mountainbikes, an antique billiards table, an Internet point and a good restaurant (half and full board available). In summer the moonlit rides followed by a candlelit dinner in the forest are popular.

Titignano ✉ 05010

Fattoria di Titignano, Loc. Titignano, **t** 0763 308000, *www.titignano.com* (€€). A simple guesthouse on a working farm producing wine and oil. The rooms (breakfast included) and self-catering apartments are in the main house or in cottages in the grounds, and there's a pool. The restaurant (€; half and full board available) serves wonderful rustic food, including superlative roasts; non-residents must book ahead. Ask about tasting and Italian courses.

Baschi ✉ 05023

*****La Penisola**, Pian delle Monache 138, Lago di Corbara on SS448, **t** 0744 950521/2/3, *www.albergolapenisola.it* (€€€). A handsome complex of three old farmhouses in its own grounds on the shore of Lake Corbara, with comfy rooms in a traditional Umbrian style (breakfast included), all with a private garden or terrace. There's also a pool and a restaurant specializing in giant *bistecca alla fiorentina* (half and full board offered).

Pomurlo Vecchio, Loc. Pomurlo Vecchio (5km east of Baschi on Montecchio road), **t** 0744 950190, *www.pomurlovecchio-lecasette.it* (€€). An *agriturismo* on a 350-acre farm producing wine, oil, fruit, honey and jams, and offering horseriding. There are 2 apartments in the house – actually a tower – and 14 very simple doubles (breakfasts included) in outbuildings. The good restaurant uses produce from the estate; half and full board is available.

Vissani, on SS448 Todi–Baschi towards Civitella del Lago, **t** 0744 950206 (€€€€). A restaurant gourmets rank among Italy's top five – an almost passionately religious inner sanctum of *cucina altissima* serving such marvels as risotto in red wine sauce with cinnamon, quail casserole with grape flan, and seabass with lettuce, mushrooms, spelt and blueberries. Booking is required. *Closed Wed, Thurs lunch, Sun eve and Aug.*

Montecchio ✉ 05020

Semiramide, Via Pian dell'Ara, Melezzole, **t** 0744 951008 (€€). A fine place in lovely woods above Montecchio, offering the likes of tagliatelle in chicken sauce, roast chicken or lamb, and ravioli in tomato and basil sauce, at fair prices in a family atmosphere. *Closed Tues and 3wks Sept.*

Amelia

Authorities as important as the Elder Pliny and Cato claimed *Ameria* was among the oldest cities in Italy – perhaps founded in the 12th century BC, three centuries prior to Rome. It didn't take advantage of its headstart, but it was an important Roman *municipium* by 90 BC, and it gave its name to the Via Armerina, linking Perugia and Todi to southern Etruria. When it became a *comune* in the Middle Ages, its sympathies lay with the Ghibellines, even after it was officially incorporated into the Papal States. In 1571 the town was excommunicated after refusing to pay a war tax the popes had levied to raise money to fight the Turks.

Getting to and around Amelia

Amelia is on the ATC **bus** routes from Terni, Orvieto and Orte. Less frequent buses from Amelia go on to Lugnano in Teverina, Attigliano and Alviano.

Cars are forbidden in the centre on weekdays; there are car parks outside the Porta Romana with a minibus link into the centre.

In a beautiful setting on the ridge dividing the valleys of the Tiber and Nera, modern Amelia (population 11,200) is far enough off the busy *autostrada* to Rome to retain its tranquillity, at least in its *centro storico*; the surroundings are gritty and prosperous. Once there, reward yourself with one of the town's famous candied figs, made with cocoa and almonds.

The Walls, San Francesco and the Archeological Museum

The great age that was attributed by the Romans to Amelia is most tangible today in its **Mura Poligoni**, the 5th-century BC Cyclopean walls that were constructed by the Umbrii without using mortar. A section remains substantially intact, 3.5m thick in places and standing some 7.5m high, near the Renaissance **Porta Romana**. These walls are about all that survived after the Goths devastated the town in 548, though parts of the Roman town can stIll be seen in bits and pieces of ancient masonry and columns in some houses; sections of Roman street paving have been revealed along Via della Repubblica.

Museo Archeologico
Palazzo Boccarini, Piazza Augusta Vera 10, **t** *0744 978120; open April–June and Sept Tues–Sun 10.30–1 and 4–7, July and Aug Tues–Sun 10.30–1 and 4.30–7.30; Oct–Mar Fri–Sun 10–1 and 3–6; adm*

Near the Porta Romana, the **Museo Archeologico** has a restored bronze statue of Germanicus, father of Caligula, found near the town in 1963 and displayed for years in the Museo Nazionale Archeologico in Perugia, which eventually agreed to its return. Also on display are relics of the Umbrii in Amelia and the **Pinacoteca**'s collection of paintings.

Just off Via della Repubblica, Piazza Vera opens up with the town war memorial and the **church of San Francesco** (or SS. Filippo e Giacomo), built in 1287 and remodelled inside in the 18th century. The one chapel that was left alone houses six fine Renaissance tombs of the Geraldini family, one of which (Matteo and Elisabetta) is by Agostino di Duccio, exquisite if somewhat worse for wear. The best-known member of the family, Alessandro Geraldini (1455–1525), lobbied in the court of Ferdinand and Isabella for Columbus' voyage and was rewarded by being appointed Bishop of Santo Domingo, the first in the New World.

To Piazza Marconi and the Duomo

Continuing up Via della Repubblica, take the narrow stepped alley that leads under the arch on the left to reach Amelia's most impressive palace, the **Palazzo Farrattini** (1520), which was designed by Antonio da Sangallo the Younger as a smaller version of the famous Palazzo Farnese in Rome; inside it incorporates two Roman mosaics.

Via della Repubblica continues up steeply past some more Renaissance *palazzi* to the **Arco della Piazza**, which was made up in the Middle Ages of Roman fragments and a frieze. Through here is Amelia's charming old main square, rectangular **Piazza Marconi** with its original paving, more proud Renaissance palaces, and the **Loggia dei Banditori**, from which public proclamations were read. **Palazzo Petrignani** has frescoed Mannerist and Baroque rooms, some of them by Zuccari .

Palazzo Petrignani
visits by appt on t 0744 976219

From here, Via Duomo ascends steeply towards the cathedral, passing pretty Via Pellegrino Carleni as it rises into the medieval part of town. At the summit, the **Duomo** was almost completely rebuilt in 1640 with a brick façade. The handsome dodecagonal **campanile** was built in 1050 as a Torre Civica, reusing Roman stones and a portion of another frieze. The cathedral features a worn Romanesque column where Amelia's patron saint Firmina is said to have been bound and tortured to death under Diocletian in 303. It also contains reliefs by Agostino di Duccio's followers in the tomb of another Bishop Geraldini (1476), in the first chapel on the left. Another Duccio, the great Sienese Duccio di Buoninsegna, painted the cathedral's finest painting, an *Assumption*, but you have to come in May or between 15 and 20 August to see it on display. In the right transept is a *Last Supper* by Francesco Perini of Amelia (1538), and in the Oratorio del Sacramento are two restored paintings by Niccolò Pomarancio. The octagonal chapel in the right aisle is said to be the work of Antonio da Sangallo. Here there are also two Turkish flags captured in the battle of Lepanto in 1571 – most peculiar for a town excommunicated for refusing to contribute its share to the Christian cause. There are lovely views from the nearby belvedere.

Duomo
open daily 10–12 and 4–6.30

Sant'Agostino to Piazza Matteotti and the Roman Cisterns

Sant'Agostino
open mornings

From the Duomo, Via Geraldini descends to the **church of Sant'Agostino**, which boasts a good, squarish Gothic façade that was rebuilt in 1477, a beautiful ogival doorway and a large rose window. The interior was enthusiastically Baroqued and frescoed by Francesco Appiani in 1747–62. The first altar to the right contains a *Vision of St John at Patmos* by Pomarancio. Of the older church, only the pavement remains, but work in the sacristry has revealed some very curious *sinopie* dating from the 11th century. A *sinopia* is the rough sketch made for a fresco in red earth pigment: these show saints, floral patterns and stars in the vault that were never completed.

From here, Via Poserola descends to a little 13th-century gate, passing the large **convent of San Magno**; the church has a rare old organ of 1680, restored and used for concerts.

Heading in the opposite direction, Via Garibaldi passes some medieval alleys and takes you into Piazza Matteotti, the home of Amelia's delightful **Palazzo Comunale**. Fragments of Roman *Ameria* decorate its courtyard and a *Madonna with Saints* presides in the **Sala Consiliare**, painted by Pier Matteo d'Amelia (d. 1508), who, through art history sleuthing, has been identified with the *Master of the Gardner Annunciation*. In 1996, a steep staircase was built to allow access to the remarkable vaulted **Roman cisterns** beneath, which are capable of holding more than 4,000 cubic metres. Constructed for emergencies in the 1st century BC, they comprise 10 chambers into which rainwater was channelled; another channel was employed to release the waters periodically in order to keep them fresh.

Sala Consiliare
open by request Mon–Fri 10–12

Cisterna Romana
*open April–Sept Sat 4.30–7.30, Sun and hols 10.30–12.30 and 4.30–7.30; Oct–Mar Sat 3–6, Sun and hols 10.30–12.30 and 3–6; or call Associazone I Poligonali, **t** 0744 978436, to arrange a visit; adm*

Amelia has an especially delightful theatre, the **Teatro Sociale**, near Piazza Matteotti. Built in 1783 on the model of La Fenice in Venice, its boxes and stalls are well preserved. Notice how some of the boxes are equipped with cupboards to store food; in the late 18th century only a magnificently sung aria had the power to make an audience shut up or stop eating.

Teatro Sociale
t 0744 976219/20; performances Nov–May; rest of year guided tours by appt

The surrounding hills are famous for their figs and wine: for the latter, visit the **Cantina dei Colli Amerini** near Amelia at **Fornole**. On the first Sunday in October, the wine is miraculously made to pour from Amelia's fountains.

Cantina dei Colli Amerini
t 0744 989721; open Mon–Sat 9–1 and 3.30–6

Around Amelia

Lugnano in Teverina

Lugnano in Teverina (population 1,650), which lies 11km northwest of Amelia, is a walled town set on a ridge that long served as a bone of contention between the *comuni* of Amelia, Orvieto and Todi; in 1503 it was sacked by Cesare Borgia. Nowadays it attracts a few Romans and foreigners for summer-holiday *villeggiatura*. The enormous **Palazzo Pennone** that was built in the 1500s by wealthy cardinals has been converted into the town hall, with a little **antiquarium** on the first floor, where you can see fragments of frescoes and mosaics from a 1st-century BC Roman villa unearthed at Poggio Gramignano. Excavations began in 1988 in collaboration with the University of Tucson, Arizona. Among finds was an infant cemetery that may be unique – dozens of babies died from malaria and were buried in a series of amphorae; their skeletons (still in the vessels) can be seen among the artefacts in the antiquarium.

Antiquarium
*open by appt on **t** 0744 902321*

Lugnano's main attraction is one of the finest, most exotic Romanesque churches that you'll ever see, the 12th-century **Collegiata di Santa Maria Assunta**. This has a striking roof and columned portico or *pronaos*, which was added in 1230 reusing older columns on a design derived from the ancient Roman basilica. The shallow arches above bear a few traces of their once-glorious Cosmati decoration, and there is a fine large window in the form of a double wheel. On the wall left of the portico, a curious three-headed figure represents the Trinity. The barrel-vaulted interior, not remodelled to everyone's taste, retains its fine proportions. Like so many churches of the period, the presbytery at the end of the central nave is raised over the crypt. The pavement is beautifully worked and there are fine carved capitals along the nave; the third one to the left shows a scene of a Byzantine-style Mass and a man with a snake coming out of his mouth, symbolic of evil, almost like an editorial comment on the Great Schism. There are finely carved *ambones* (twin pulpits) and *transennas* from the original choir, with bas-reliefs showing St Michael killing the dragon and two men exchanging the kiss of peace, and a rare *ciborium* restored in 1937. The apse has a fine tripytch of the *Assumption* by Nicolò Alunno, and Mannerist painter Livio Agresti from Forlì checks in with a surprising *Beheading of John the Baptist* of 1571, in the chapel to the right.

South of Amelia: Penna in Teverina, Giove and a Dip into Lazio

To the southwest of Amelia, towards the Tiber and the big road and railway junction at Orte, you'll find **Penna in Teverina**, a charming old fortified town with houses built directly into the walls. It was disputed by Rome's eternal Punch and Judy factions, the Colonna and Orsini families, until the Colonna got tired of the show and sold it to the Orsini, who constructed a Palazzo Orsini in town with a fine 19th-century Italian garden attached (now privately owned). Other relics of the same era are the Mammalocchi, allegorical herms in travertine standing at the entrance to villas on the road to Amelia.

To the north of Penna are a pair of crumbling medieval villages, **Giove** and **Attligliano**. Giove was smashed in 1503 by the troops of Cesare Borgia, who dismantled the walls and castles; what was left was reconstructed in the next century as the imposing and elegant **Palazzo Ducale** overlooking the Tiber; it was built by the Mattei, a great Roman family, and is still in the hands of their heirs. Members of great Roman families can be on the lazy and decadent side; one of the original features of this palace is the proto-parking garage ramp spiralling up to the first floor, big enough for horse-drawn carriages.

Most of the truly remarkable sights in these parts are situated over the border in **Lazio**, especially the **Monster Park** in the woebegone village of **Bomarzo** – a mad garden full of colossal cinquecento sculptures that brings the neurosis of late Renaissance Italy to the surface.

Just south, the pretty Cimini hills shelter fine towns such as **Soriano nel Cimino** and **San Martino al Cimino**, and beautiful, unspoiled **Lake Vico**, an ancient volcanic crater. **Caprarola**, nearby, sits in the shadow of one of the greatest, strangest and most arrogant of all Renaissance palaces, the Farnese, built with papal booty by Perugia's arch enemy Paul III.

North of Amelia

Much of the countryside lying north of Amelia towards Todi is *terra incognita*, with hamlets standing abandoned. Yet in Roman times this area was important enough for a road, the Via Falisca Armerina – traces of this and a Roman bridge can be seen by **Sambucetole**, and the modern hamlet lies in the shadow of the abandoned medieval town.

Further north the road passes the tower of the medieval **Castel dell'Aquila**, then forks: to the west, surrounded by forests, is the unusual circular walled village of **Toscolano**, once owned by Todi (note the eagle over the gate), now used as the summer base for the Centro Europeo Toscolano, dedicated to the renewal of popular Italian music, among other things. Just outside the centre, the **chapel of the Santissima Annunziata** contains restored frescoes attributed to Pier Matteo d'Amelia.

A scenic road continues north to **Collelungo**, which was the last outpost of the Monaldeschi on the frontier of Todi. Inside its restored church you can see a Lombard-era altar and some frescoes dating from the late 1200s.

The east fork of the road from Castel dell'Aquila leads to **Avigliano Umbro** with its castle-like water tower. To the north, little **Dunarobba** with its big 16th-century castle stood on the banks of the prehistoric Lago Tiberino that filled the Tiber valley to the brim. During the 1980s, diggers in a quarry nearby came upon 40 specimens of the 200,000-year-old ancestors of the sequoia that once stood on the lake shores. The mighty trunks of this **Foresta Fossile**, some standing 7.5m high, were so well preserved that they were still upright in thick clay. They are the most important palaeobotanical finds in the region; a research centre has been set up to study them.

Foresta Fossile
open for guided tours every hr mid-April–June and Sept–mid-Oct Fri–Sun and hols 10–1 and 3.30 6.30; July and Aug Tues–Sun 10–1 and 4–7; or by appt with Pro Loco in Avigliano Umbro, **t** *0744 940348; adm*

The surrounding countryside is truly lovely, whether you decide to heard northwards to Todi or east towards **Montecastrilli**, a traditional fortified Umbrian hamlet that was an outpost of Todi for several centuries.

Where to Stay and Eat in and around Amelia

ⓘ Amelia > *Via della Rimembranza 8, t 0744 981453, www.umbria2000.it (closed summer Sun and Mon afternoon, winter Sat and Mon afternoon); and Pro Loco, Piazza A. Vera 8, t 0744 982559, http://web.tiscali.it/proloco.amelia*

Amelia ✉ 05022

*****Scoglio dell'Aquilone**, Via Orvieto 23, **t** 0744 982445, *scogliodellaquilone@tiscali.it* (€€). A quiet place in the woods, with comfortable rooms with panoramic views and a restaurant (half/full board offered).

Parco degli Ulivi, Strada Statale Amerina 27, on road into Amelia, **t** 0744 982681 (€€€). Umbrian cuisine plus pizzas in a little natural park. A highlight is the *spaghetti alla Spoletina*. On Tues, Thurs and Fri there's fresh fish ifyou order ahead. In summer you can enjoy use of a swimming pool. *Closed Wed.*

Lugnano in Teverina ✉ 05020

Podere Ceoli, Vocabolo Ceoli 117, **t** 0744 347448, *podere_ceoli@yahoo.it* (€€). An atmospheric little *affittacamere* in the countryside, with 2 self-catering apartments, a beautiful pool and horses. Weekly stays are better value.

Ostello Casa Laboratorio Vallenera, Casale di Vallenera, **t** 0744 902674, *www.vallenera.it* (€). The youth hostel, offering full board if you wish.

La Frateria dell'Abate Loniano, Loc. San Francesco 6, just outside Lugnano, **t** 0744 902180 (€€). An atmospheric restaurant in the restored 13th-century refectory of a former convent, serving traditional seasonal fare based on organic produce. *Closed Wed.*

The Valnerina

The clear Nera, one of the main tributaries of the Tiber and the region's special river, flows across the southern edge of Umbria. Nera *means 'black' in Italian, but the name derives from Naharkum, a tribe of the Umbrii, the valley's mysterious first-known inhabitants. 'There would be no Tiber if the Nera did not give it to drink,' is an old Umbrian saying; the Umbrians have know deep in their hearts that the ancient Romans learned all their simple and honest virtues from their ancestors. Much of the Valnerina is still an Italian secret, though its black truffles and saints have global reputations, and its superb, often dramatic natural beauty is now protected as a natural park.*

20

Don't miss

1. **Mountains and a romantically ruined bridge**
   Narni p.550
2. **Europe's highest waterfall**
   Cascata delle Marmore p.562
3. **Byzantine-style frescos**
   San Pietro in Valle p.565
4. **A dream landscape**
   Piano Grande p.576
5. **Boar salami and basilicas**
   Norcia p.572

See map overleaf

The Valnerina

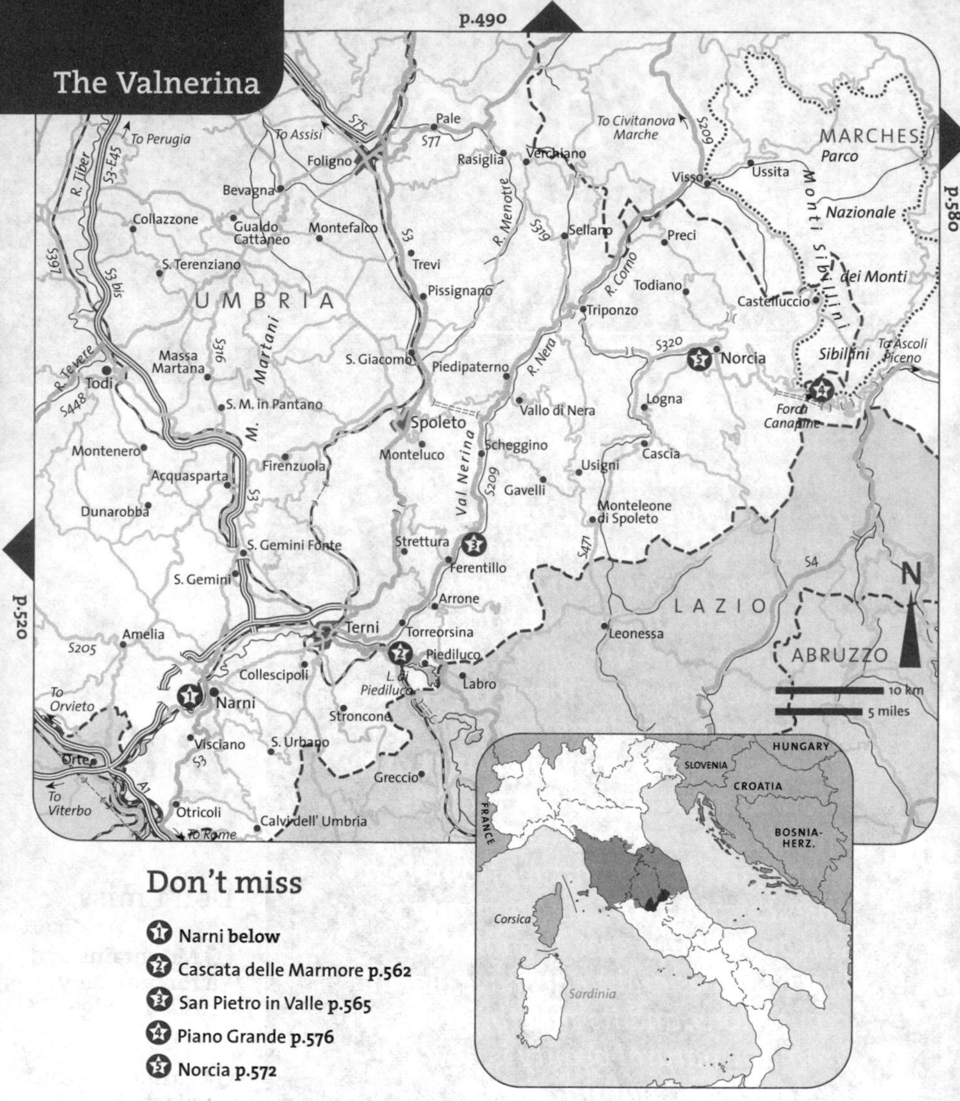

Don't miss

1. **Narni** below
2. **Cascata delle Marmore** p.562
3. **San Pietro in Valle** p.565
4. **Piano Grande** p.576
5. **Norcia** p.572

Narni, Terni and Around

Narni

1 **Narni**

Once an important stop on the Via Flaminia, Narni (population 21,000) is a fine old hilltown in a dramatic position, guarding the steep gorge as you enter the Valnerina. Originally the Umbrian *Nequinum*, it renamed itself *Nahar* or *Narnia* after the river when it changed its allegiance to Rome in 299 BC. Pliny wrote of its unassailable defences, the emperor Nerva was born here in AD 32, and the city can also claim a pope, John XIII (965–72), as well as a great *condottiere*, Gattamelata (1370–1443), who went on to fame

Getting to and around Narni

Narni is easily reached by **train** from Rome (89km/1hr), Terni, Spoleto or Assisi on the main Rome–Ancona line; it is 15km from the main Florence–Rome rail and *autostrada* junction at Orte. Frequent buses link the station and the city on the hill.

ATC **buses**, **t** 0744 492711, *www.atcterni.it*, also departing from the train station, connect Amelia, Terni, Otricoli and surrounding hamlets.

---

and fortune in Venice. However, many people never bother to breach the modern industry and electrocarbon plant at Narni Scalo in the river valley to discover the fine town within – which, *pace* Foligno, is in reality the closest to the geographic centre of Italy.

To Piazza Garibaldi

The sight in Narni that most engaged the Grand Tourist of the past two centuries, the romantically ruined **Ponte d'Augusto** (27 BC), is now just visible from the bridge at lower, industrial Narni Scalo, or from the train window as you approach from the south. This

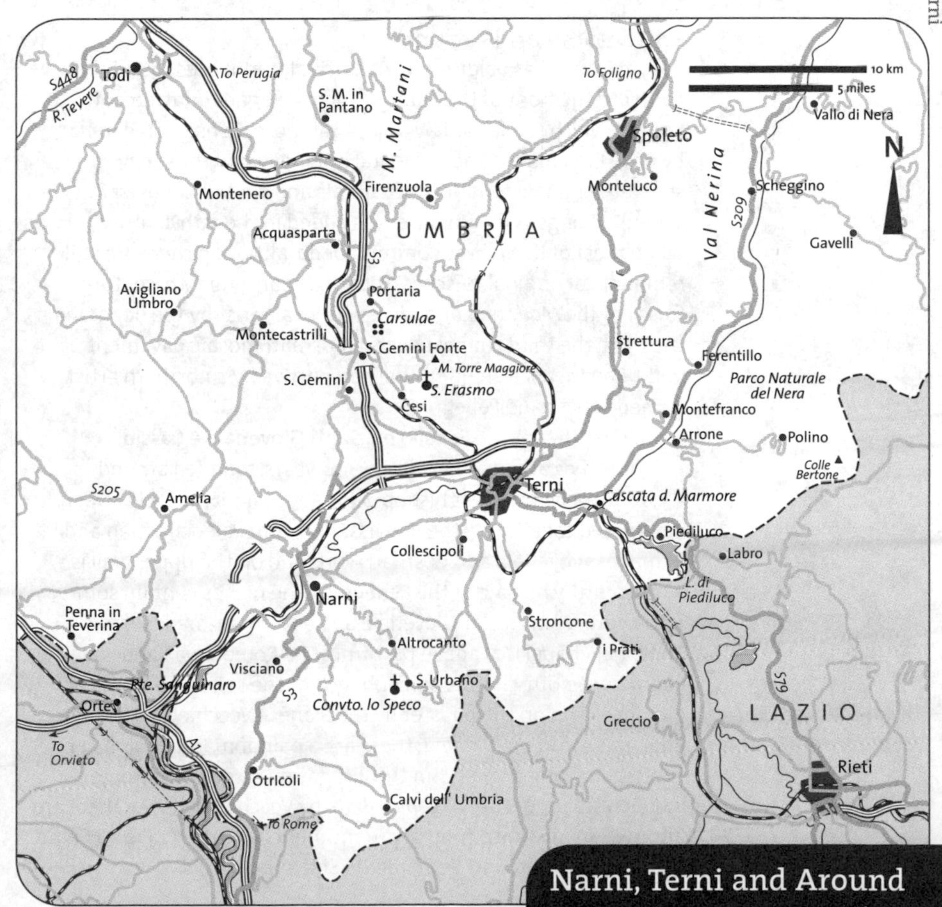

Narni, Terni and Around

lofty massive arch in the river is all that survives of a bridge famous even in Roman times for its size – it stretched 130m and stood 27m high – built to carry the newer Via Flaminia towards Terni and Spoleto. It fell into ruins in the Middle Ages, and until 1855 it had two arches and a much more picturesque setting. If it looks familiar, you may have seen Corot's famous painting in the Louvre.

Many of Narni's old city gates are intact, especially the eastern **Porta Ternana**, with its twin round towers built by Sixtus IV where the Via Flaminia entered Narni proper. This bustling ancient road served the city well through history, except in 1527, when the brutal mercenary troops of Charles V, having sacked Rome, were marching home and stopped to sack and pillage Narni as well. The Flaminia (here called Via Roma) leads to Narni's main crossroads: the busy, colourful, irregularly shaped **Piazza Garibaldi**, overlooked by the side door of the cathedral and a neoclassical palace. The whole square was originally a Roman *piscina*, and steps from the restored 15th-century fountain descend into a 12th-century cistern.

The Duomo and Around

From Piazza Garibaldi, main Via Garibaldi squeezes round the corner to the front of the Duomo and its elegant quattrocento portico, which is adorned by a classical frieze. Consecrated in 1145 by Pope Eugenius III, the cathedral originally had three naves, separated by a wide variety of capitals and columns reused from other buildings. A fourth nave was added in the 15th century, when most of its art was commissioned, although there are still remnants of original frescoes. There's a charming 15th-century fresco of the *Madonna and Child* by a local artist by the door. On the right, the third chapel boasts a Cosmati mosaic pavement and a Renaissance architectural perspective by a northern artist named Sebastiano Pellegrini.

The next chapel, the **Sacello dei Santi Giovenale e Cassio**, predates the cathedral by almost 800 years, founded around the tomb of Narni's first bishop, San Giovenale. Its marble screen was pieced together in the Renaissance from Paleochristian and Romanesque reliefs and Cosmati work, and on the upper wall is a 9th-century mosaic of the Redeemer. The niches contain some 15th-century statues of Giovenale and a German-made *Pietà*. The inner chapel is made in part from the Roman wall and contains the 6th-century sarcophagus of the saint; there's a picture of him on the pilaster by the Sienese Vecchietta. The high altar was completed in 1714; there are a pair of marble pulpits and choirstalls from 1490 and, in the left nave, a large polychrome wooden statue of *Sant'Antonio Abate* by Vecchietta (1474). There are also two Renaissance funerary monuments to the left; Pietro Cesi's has been attributed to Bernardo da Settignano.

Pinacoteca
Palazzo del Vescovile; open Tues–Sun 9–1 and 2–7; adm

Opposite the Duomo, in little Piazza Cavour, is the **Pinacoteca**, with an *Annunciation* by Benozzo Gozzoli. Tucked behind Piazza Cavour is the **Roman arch**, reworked into a medieval gate.

Right of the cathedral, off Via Garibaldi, the Via del Campanile leads to the sturdy Roman base of the cathedral's **belltower**; the upper section was added in the 1400s and adorned with colourful ceramic plates. The 14th-century **church of San Francesco** near the top of the next street to the left is on the site of an oratory founded in 1213 by St Francis. It burnt down in a fire in 1998, but its fine façade remains and the interior is being restored.

Piazza dei Priori

Via Garibaldi, the main street since Roman times (note the pretty 19th-century restored Teatro Comunale), widens to form Piazza dei Priori, centre of Narni's civic life in the Middle Ages. Here sits the **Palazzo del Podestà** (14th–15th centuries), now seat of the *comune*, an old tower melded with three medieval towerhouses and decorated with four bas-reliefs depicting a joust, a lion and dragon, the beheading of Holofernes, and a hunt with falcons. The palace shows some cracks from Narni's very own earthquake in 2000, which left 250 homeless. In the **Sala Consigliare** hangs Narni's finest painting, a magnificent *Coronation of the Virgin* (1486) by Florentine Domenico Ghirlandaio, in a lovely frame with a *predella* showing *St Francis Receiving the Stigmata*, a *Pietà* and *St Jerome*.

Sala Consigliare
open Fri–Sun 10–1 and 3–7

The circular **fountain** dates from 1303. Opposite is the medieval **Casa Sacripanti**, with more reliefs, and the **loggia** and **clocktower** of the once-massive 14th-century Palazzo dei Priori, built by Matteo Gattapone, all that survived the sack of Charles V's *Landsknechten* in 1527; the pulpit was used for reading public proclamations.

Santa Maria in Pensole
*visits April–Oct Sat 3–6, Sun 10–1 and 3–6, Nov–Mar Sun 11–1 and 3–5, by appt with Associazione Culturale Subterranea, **t** 0744 722292; adm*

At the end of the piazza, **Santa Maria in Pensole** (1175) has a beautiful Romanesque façade fronted by a handsome portico made with columns borrowed from older buildings and three beautiful doors with elaborate marble decoration. Other reused columns line the three naves, many of which have charming capitals. The church was built over the vaults (*in pensole*) of an 8th-century Benedictine church and a Roman cistern once believed to be a temple of Bacchus. Opposite are two attractive palaces: the 17th-century **Palazzo Bocciarelli** and 16th-century **Palazzo Scotti**.

The iron fixtures in the walls, here and all around Narni, hold torches for the May medieval pageant of San Giovenale (*see* p.557), one of the most colourful festivals of the Umbrian calendar.

San Domenico

San Domenico
open daily 11–1 and 3–7

Further down tower- and palace-lined Via Mazzini, the deconsecrated 12th-century pink and white **church and campanile of San Domenico**, now the public library, has a door adorned with worn medallions of the 12 apostles, and 13th- to 16th-century fresco fragments inside. On the east end is a wall memorial (1494) near a tabernacle by the workshop of Agostino di Duccio; on the left side are faint frescoes by the Zuccari family and the tusk of a prehistoric elephant found on the banks of the Nera in 1988.

The Dominicans' convent, demolished in the 1950s, was replaced by the **Giardino di San Bernardo**, with ruins of a lofty tower and an great view towards the Romanesque abbey of San Cassiano over the narrow gorge of the Nera. Near Narni the river turns robin's-egg blue from the copper and lime deposits in the soil. The Associazione Culturale Subterranea discovered an earlier church under the apse of San Domenico, dating from the 1100s with frescoes, another Roman cistern and a prison cell with 18th-century graffiti left by poor souls imprisoned by the Dominican-run Inquisition; the ensemble is called the **Sotterranei della Chiesa di San Domenico**.

Sotterranei della Chiesa di San Domenico
open April–Oct Sat 3–6, Sun 10–1 and 3–6, Nov–Mar Sun 11–1 and 3–5

Lower Narni, and the Rocca

At the end of Via Mazzini, in Piazza Marzio, is the 15th-century well, the **Pozzo della Comunità**; from here follow the 15th-century walls along Via della Mura, or cut down the steps of Vicolo degli Orti to the most picturesque bit, around the tall tower of the **Porta della Fiera**. Via Gattamelata continues back to the centre, passing the so-called **house of Gattamelata** (No.113). The 'Honeyed Cat' (Erasmo da Narni) was born here in 1370 to a baker, and became such a successful, reliable and honest *condottiere* for Venice that he received the highest honour that the usually stingy Republic bestowed on anyone: a paid funeral and an equestrian statue by Donatello, the first since Roman times and one of Padua's gems.

Via Gattamelata continues to **Sant'Agostino**, its severe façade decorated with a faded fresco in a niche, attributed to Antoniazzo Romano. The interior has good quattrocento frescoes, a *Crucifixion* by the school of Antoniazzo Romano and a *Madonna* by Pier Antonio d'Amelia, a fine Renaissance wooden crucifix and a lofty carved ceiling holding a 16th-century painting on the *Triumph of St Augustine* by Carlo Federico Benincasa of Narni.

From Piazza Garibaldi, Via del Monte winds up through a picturesque medieval neighbourhood to the restored four-square **Rocca Albornoz** that dominates all views of Narni from the plain of Terni, built in the 1370s by the indefatigable Cardinal Albornoz.

About 3km east of town you can see inside the narrow tunnel of the **Ponte Cardona**, part of a 1st-century Roman aqueduct .

Rocca Albornoz
open Wed–Sun 10.30–12.30 and 3.30–6; adm

Ponte Cordona
visits by appt with tourist office (see p.557)

South of Narni

South of Narni, the ancient Via Flaminia (SS3) continues towards the Rome of the Caesars, now just a back road in an obscure corner of Umbria. At about the 83km mark, it passes through a small plain with rugged cliffs near the road, an ancient holy site, **Grotte d'Orlando** (Roland's Cave). Badly worn Roman reliefs can be made out on the rocks and there are remains of an altar, 'Roland's Seat'.

On a steep slope below the hamlet of **Visciano**, southwest of Narni off the Otricoli road, is a lovely 11th-century church dedicated to Santa Pudenzia, surrounded by trees, with an exceptionally tall slender campanile. The portico has two Roman columns with fine capitals and some other Roman bits embedded in the walls. The polygonal apse is similar to those in Ravenna. Where the road branches off for Calvi, you'll see scanty remains of another Roman bridge, the **Ponte Sanguinario**.

The first Umbrian town a Roman would find along the Via Flaminia was **Otricoli** (16km from Narni), a town of the Umbrii destroyed by the Romans in the Social War in the 1st century BC. It was rebuilt down on the then-navigable Tiber as the city and port of *Ocriculum*. When this became swampy in the Middle Ages, the inhabitants moved back up to their hill, and what was once a thriving city became by the 18th century a wretchedly poor village. The rest of Otricoli is concentrated in a walled hilltown with medieval streets of cannibalized Roman stone. The constantly rebuilt and reworked parish church of Santa Maria seems to have something from every century somewhere, from Roman columns within to a 19th-century campanile.

Resti della Città Romana di Ocriculum
always open

The **ruins of Ocriculum** are located 1.6km below town, overlooking the Tiber. Excavations began under Pope Pius VI in 1776, enriching the Vatican Museum with an enormous head of Jupiter and other pieces, but little has happened since, and many ruins, including the big baths, a theatre, amphitheatre, funerary monuments and a section of the original Via Flaminia, are overgrown and crumbling from exposure.

Fine oak forests and scenery surround **Calvi dell'Umbria** (south of Narni, 11km east of Otricoli), the southernmost *comune* of Umbria, prosperous until the plague crippled it in 1527. It was the home of Bernardo da Calvi, a follower of St Francis martyred in the first Franciscan mission to Morocco; the church of San Francesco is built on land Bernardo donated to Francis. Calvi's pride, however, is the 16th-century *presepio* of unusually large terracotta figures in the church of Sant'Antonio.

Convento del Sacro Speco
guided tours daily 8–11.30 and 3–4.45; churchyard and cloisters open daily 8–11.30, 3–5 and 6–7.30; some parts closed for restoration

To the southeast, 13km from Narni beyond Altrocanto and Sant'Urbano, the **Convento del Sacro Speco** was founded in 1213 by St Francis, who often sojourned in a nearby cave; the legend goes that once when he fell ill here, an angel comforted him with some sweet violin music. It was reconstructed during the 1300s and is one of the most evocative Franciscan monuments in all Italy. In recent years, it has been reoccupied by friars living according to the saint's First Rule.

San Gemini, Carsulae, Acquasparta and Cesi

North of Narni, the SS3bis to Todi passes two towns known for their waters since the Etruscans. The first, **San Gemini**, keeps its spa a few kilometres to the north; the old centre remains the essential Umbrian hilltown, despite being wrecked on two occasions, by the Saracens in 882, and the Imperial mercenary army of the Constable of Bourbon in 1527, practising for the Sack of Rome. There's a handy car park near the 1291 **church of San Francesco**, with a carved portal and doors from the 14th century and 15th–17th-century frescoes.

San Francesco
open daily 9–7.30

In the medieval centre (take narrow Via Casventino), in Piazza Palazzo Vecchio, the restored 12th-century **Palazzo Pubblico** has an external stairway and encompasses an older defensive tower converted into a campanile in the 1700s; here, too, is the 13th-century **Oratorio San Carlo**, with a striking, fresco-covered *ciborium*. Further along, the curiously shaped **church of San Giovanni Battista** started out in the 12th century as an octagon; it has a Romanesque door on its left side, with scant remnants of its Cosmati decoration and an inscription of 1199. Near San Gemini's 18th-century **gateway** stands its **cathedral**, with a tarted-up 19th-century interior.

San Nicolò
open summer Fri–Sun 3–6; winter Fri–Sun 10–1 and 3–5; ask keeper for key

Outside the gate, in a pretty garden, the **church of San Nicolò** was built as a dependency of the once-mighty abbey of Farfa near Rieti and is now privately owned; the frieze and lions on its portal are copies of the originals, now in the Metropolitan Museum in New York. The columns within have fine sculpted capitals, several from Carsulae (*see* below), and among its 13th-century frescoes, most of which are detached, is the only known work of Rogerino da Todi.

Carsulae
***t** 0744 334133; open April–Sept daily 8.30–7.30; Oct–Mar daily 8.30–5.30; adm*

The spa, **San Gemini Fonte**, is in a pretty park full of old oaks, where you can try the carbonated diuretic waters (May–October). Near here, under the steep green hills, are the remains of Imperial era **Carsulae**, a Roman city abandoned and never rebuilt after a quake in the 800s. In its day, *Carsulae* was famous for its waters and wines. From the handsome gate built by Trajan (a favourite spot for wedding photos), you can follow a stretch of the original Via Flaminia, dotted with funerary monuments, among them two large, well-preserved tombs and a head of Claudius. There are the remains of a residential district, a theatre and an amphitheatre; in the pink marble forum are the bases of twin temples that may have been dedicated to the heavenly twins, the Dioscuri, and the basilica used as a council house or Curia. One temple was rebuilt in the 11th century to become a little chapel of **Santi Cosma e Damiano**.

North of San Gemini, the village of **Portaria** is known for its restaurants and for possessing one of the oldest postboxes in Italy (1674, under the clocktower). Further north, **Acquasparta** (Latin *Ad Aquas Partas*) is another quiet spot in which to sort out your digestive problems, recommended by no less than St Francis;

Amerino and Furapane waters are bottled here. In the centre is the **Palazzo Cesi**, from 1565, owned by the University of Perugia, with has Renaissance frescoes and a beautiful courtyard filled with ancient inscriptions. Here Roman prince Federico Cesi established a country branch of the scholarly Accademia dei Lincei he founded in Rome in 1609; his friend Galileo came out to visit for a month in 1624. Though the Accademia died with the prince, the idea caught on across Italy and most towns of any consequence managed to create a little academy. Normally peaceful and very typical of the region, the town alarms its neighbours every summer by hosting, of all things, a German lieder-singing competition.

Palazzo Cesi *visits by appt on* **t** *075 5851*

From Acquasparta, you can follow a mountain road, the SS418, across to Spoleto – just don't think you've somehow got lost in Tuscany when you see signs for Arezzo. There are pleasant picnic spots along the way, overlooking deep-set **Lake Arezzo**, and nearby a Romanesque church with an unusual portico at **Firenzuola**.

On the last craggy slope of the Monti Martani, 6km east of San Gemini Fonte, **Cesi** thrived between the 12th and 16th centuries, though it lies under a much older town. The entrance, through the Porta Ternana, leads into the medieval centre and the church of **Santa Maria Assunta** (1515–25), with a trecento wooden sculpture of the *Virgin and Child*, and underneath, a room that belonged to a former church on the site, frescoed with a *Crucifixion* of 1425 by Giovanni di Giovannello of Narni. Outside the second gate, the **Porta Tudertina**, is the handsome **church of Sant'Andrea**, built of Roman stones from Carsulae, as well as another impressive 16th-century Palazzo Cesi. A road twists up Monte Eolo to the site of the ancient town, with remains of the 6th-century BC walls and splendid views. **Sant'Erasmo**, a 12th-century church with a pretty window, stands near the remains of the medieval fortress. An unpaved road continues to the top of **Monte Torre Maggiore** (1,121m).

ⓘ **Narni >** *Piazza dei Priori 3,* **t** *0744 715362, www.narni.it*

Festival in Narni

Festival of San Giovenale, last wk April and 1st wk May. Medieval pageantry at its brightest, with a torchlit costumed procession the night before the Corsa dell'Anello, in which knights from the town's 3 neighbourhoods compete to pierce a ring suspended over the street with their lances.

Where to Stay and Eat

Narni ✉ 05035

Podere Costa Romana, SS. Flaminia, Strada per Itieli, **t** 0744 722495, *www.poderecostaromana.com* (€€€–€). A beautifully restored stone farmhouse on a wooded hillside just outside Narni, with rustic apartments sleeping 2–5, with all comforts and panoramic views. There's a big garden and a pool overlooking the hills. Choose from B&B (mininum 2-night stay) and self-catering (minimum 1wk)

*****Dei Priori**, Vicolo del Comune 4, **t** 0744 726843, *www.loggiadeipriori.it* (€€). A medieval palace in the centre, with very comfortable rooms and suites (breakfast included) and a restaurant that has long been popular for dishes such as pasta with onions, tomatoes and peppers (half/full board available). *Closed Mon.*

Il Cavallino, Via Flaminia Romana 220, road to Terni, **t** 0744 761020 (€). A good, old-fashioned little inn with simple rooms and a restaurant offering local cuisine. *Closed Tues, part of July, and Dec.*

Monte del Grano 1696, Strada Guadamello 328, Loc. San Vito, 15km south of Narni on SS3bis, **t** 0744 749143 (€€€). A typical Umbrian trattoria specializing in meat dishes and with an excellent cheese selection. At the time of writing a change of ownership was imminent. *Closed Mon, lunch Tues–Fri, and Jan.*

San Gemini ✉ 05029

*****Locanda di Carsulae**, Via Tibernia 2, Loc. Fonte, on SS3bis, **t** 0744 630163, *www.gruppobacus.com* (€€). Simple rooms with private baths and a restaurant and *enoteca* (half and full board available).

****Duomo**, Piazza Duomo 4, **t** 0744 630015 or **t** 0744 630005, *www.gruppobacus.com* (€€). Basic ensuite rooms in the centre of town, breakfast included, plus a restaurant specializing in meat and truffle dishes (half/full board offered).

Terni

Sprawling, mouldering, modern – you may not want to spend long in southern Umbria's capital, but at least muster some respect for Terni's accomplishments. In 1867, as the city closest to the geographical centre of Italy, it was intended to be the nation's capital (this was before Rome was wrested from the occupying French), but the idea flew like a penguin. If Italy's politicians couldn't appreciate Terni's location, far from the country's vulnerable coasts and frontiers, the military did. Its location on the river Nera, and the vicinity of the Cascata delle Marmore, Europe's highest waterfall, sealed its destiny: in the 1870s the beautiful thundering waters were diverted for cheap hydroelectric power, and Italy's first steel mill went up to build ships for its navy to pester Africa, pushing Umbria to lurch belatedly into the Industrial Revolution (even though Italy has no iron ore to speak of; the mill has never made a profit, but it's still there on the east end of town).

Centro di Documentazione sul Patrimonio Industriale
t 0744 428753; July and Aug Mon 9–12 and 4–7, Tues–Fri 4–7; rest of year Mon, Tues and Thurs 9–12 and 4–7, Wed and Fri 4–7, Sat and Sun 9–12; adm

The **Industrial Heritage Documentation Centre** offers guided tours on themes such as 'The City Factories' and 'The Culture and Conditions of a Worker's Life'. Before World War I, Terni employed a third of Umbria's workforce, and what was an insignificant medieval town before Unification became Umbria's second city after Perugia, the Manchester of Italy. In the 1920s Terni scientists created the first practical plastic. Terni also has the State arms factory (the rifle that killed John Kennedy was made here); these three industries together were enough of an attraction in the last war for Allied air forces to smash the place. They also keep Terni ardently Communist, the heart of Red Umbria, and a fun place to be on 1 May for a parade of humorous floats made by towns in the province.

For the past few years, Terni has hosted an Easter holiday instalment of the Umbrian Jazz Festival, with an emphasis on gospel and spirituals. It has taken a new pride in its industrial past:

Getting to and around Terni

The SS209 from Terni to Visso is the main route of the upper Valnerina; you can reach Norcia and Cascia by turning off at Sant'Anatolia di Narco or Triponzo (the latter offers prettier routes). Both towns have frequent SSIT buses (*www.spoletina.com*) to Spoleto. From Terni, ATC **buses, t** 0744 492711, *www.atcterni.it*, leave from the park near the station to go to Narni, the Cascata delle Marmore (bus 21), Piediluco (bus 24), Arrone, Ferentillo, Spoleto, Orvieto, Viterbo and Scheggino; another bus picks up passengers along the SS209 daily to Rome.

Terni is the terminus of the FCU **train** line (*www.fcu.it/www.trenitalia.com*) through Todi, Perugia and Città di Castello to Sansepolcro, **t** 0744 59741, and a stop on the FS's Rome– Ancona line, though from Rome you often have to change at Orte; travelling from Assisi and the east usually requires a change at Foligno.

For **bike hire**, contact Blob Service, Via G. di Pergamo 66, **t** 0744 287686, *www.cuoreverde.com*.

the mills, now employing 3,000 and specializing in stainless and other speciality steels, have been tarted up. Major intersections and piazze are decorated with imposing rusty chunks of raw industrial art. And as Italian film-makers grow estranged from the high costs and confabulations of Rome and Cinecittà, they are falling into the seductive clasp of Terni: cheap, spacious and just over an hour's drive from the capital. Some of Italy's best special effects gizmos and wizardry are concentrated in the increasingly important **Centro Multimediale di Terni**, which lent its support to Roberto Benigni's *Pinocchio* and *Life is Beautiful*, much of which was shot in the suburb of Papigno.

St Valentine's City

During the building of the steelworks, bulldozers uncovered an important Iron Age necropolis, and the mysterious Umbrii Naharkum were here around 7th century BC. Terni's name derives from their *Interamna Nahars* (from *inter amnes*, 'between two rivers', namely the confluence of the Nera and the torrential Serra). *Interamna* was conquered by the Romans in the 3rd century BC, and grew into a major station along the newer, easterly route of the Via Flaminia. It was traditionally considered the birthplace of the historian Tacitus, although scholars now quibble that Terni's was a more meagre Tacitus, Claudius Tacitus, one of the many Roman emperors for a day.

More certainly identified with the city is its first bishop, the martyred St Valentine, beheaded in 273. Several stories attempt to explain how he became the patron saint of lovers: one claims he miraculously united a 4th-century Romeo and Juliet, a Christian and a pagan (who converted after matrimony); another that his feast day coincided with the traditional mating day of Umbrian birds. He was buried in a cemetery 2km south of the centre, where the first chapel was built; in the 17th century this was rebuilt rather modestly as the **Basilica di San Valentino**. Valentine's mummified head was stolen in 1986 but found three years later, unharmed, wrapped in newspaper under a park bench at the Cascata delle

Marmore. Until then, the city seemed unaware of its patron's fame abroad. Now. on 14 February. it hosts the traditional Mass, market and fireworks, a full range of international chocs and schlock, and a jewellery exhibition and prize for the best piece dedicated to St Valentine. An 'Act of Love' prize is solemnly awarded by the city to a person or organization who has performed one (in 1996 it was dedicated to the memory of Itzhak Rabin), and modern lovers have an all-night Latino dance party.

In the Heart of the City of Love

Much of the rest of Terni has relatively little to show in spite of a history of more than 2,500 years. The post-war rebuilding, however, was left in the expert hands of architect Mario Ridolfi (d. 1984) who, after working on the reconstruction of Rome, moved here and laid out Terni's more pleasant residential districts, filling in the gaps left by the bombs. Of Roman Terni only part of the **amphitheatre** (32 AD) remains, in the south of the city near the pretty public gardens, where gladiators once tussled to the death before a crowd of 10,000, and pensioners now play *bocce*.

Pinacoteca Comunale
*Palazzo Gazzoli, Via del Teatro Romano 16, **t** 0744 59421; open Tues–Sun 10–1 and 4–7; adm*

The **Pinacoteca Comunale** has a lot of paintings by Anonymous (a strange 16th-century *Circumcision*; a portrait of *St Charles Borromeo*, a light of the Counter-Reformation here almost caricatured, with an enormous nose; and, in the same Counter-Reformation vein, a nightmarish scene of Franciscan martyrdoms in the Low Countries). The highlight is a *Marriage of St Catherine* from 1466 by Benozzo Gozzoli, inspired by Beato Angelico, and there is also a triptych of the *Madonna, Child and Saints* by Pier Matteo d'Amelia, a gonfalon from Siena and a *Crucifixion* painted by L'Alunno, a triptych by the late 14th-century Maestro della Dormitio di Terni, and small works by Chagall, Picasso, Carrà, Severini, Mirò, Kandinsky and Léger. Best of all, there's a large collection of works by Terni's own **Orneore Metelli** (1872–1938), a shoemaker who spent his evenings painting, as Bernard Berenson said, the most naive of naive art. The two rooms of his paintings alone make a trip to this industrial city worthwhile, with their disarming, colourful scenes of Terni, its steel mill and its surroundings, of shoemakers, of Mussolini's motorcade, of Dante, and even of the Venus of Terni.

Duomo
open daily 9–12 and 3.30-7

Nearby, the **Duomo**, which was founded in the 6th century, rebuilt in the 12th and redone in the 17th, has a handsome portico and a pair of original portals, the front one topped with a 12th-century frieze. The interior has an elaborate high altar and a *Circumcision* by Livio Agresti. The 10th-century crypt, with its Roman columns and altar, was restored in 1904. In the cathedral square is a fountain and Terni's most elegant palace, the **Palazzo Bianchini-Riccardi**, both 16th-century.

From here, Via Aminale leads around to Terni's old main street, **Via Roma**, where a number of *palazzi* survived the bombing; a towerhouse marks the crossroads. Turn left here into Piazza Europa; at the south end is the massive **Palazzo Spada** (1546) by Antonio da Sangallo the Younger, perhaps his least inspired effort (some scholars have absolved him from all responsibility), now used as the town hall. To its right is the charming round **church of San Salvatore**, the oldest building in Terni, from the 5th century, which may have been a Roman temple to the Sun. In the 12th century, a nave and some frescoes were added.

San Salvatore
open daily 9–12 and 4–6

From Piazza Europa, Via Cavour leads past the severe medieval **Palazzo Mezzancolli** back to Via Febbraio; off this is the Knights of St John's 12th-century **church of Sant'Alò**, with a pretty exterior, incorporating Roman and medieval fragments. Turn off on to Via Fratini, follow it north to Via Noblini and turn left for 13th-century **San Francesco**. Its landmark campanile with colourful ceramic edgings (1345) is by Angelo da Orvieto; in the Cappella Paradisi, are the Dominican friar Bartolomeo di Tommaso's fascinating restored 15th-century frescoes based on Hell, Purgatory and Paradise as described in the *Divine Comedy*.

San Francesco
open daily 8–11.30 and 3.30–7.30

Piazza della Repubblica is the starting point for modern Terni's main thoroughfare, **Corso Tacito**, which passes through the piazza of the same name, where there's a fountain by Mario Ridolfi (1932) with mosaics of astrological signs. From Piazza della Repubblica the Corso Vecchio passes other signs of medieval Terni, around to **San Pietro in Trivio**, a church that was built in the 14th century and rebuilt in the 1700s and again after the war, yet somehow retains some original frescoes. Nearby **Palazzo Carrara** is a 17th-century reconstruction of a medieval palace; its Iron Age artefacts found under the steel mills are now in the **Museo Archeologico**. Another church along Corso Vecchio, **San Lorenzo**, has Terni's oddest interior, with one short and one tall nave, and a good 16th-century painting on the *Martyrdom of San Biagio*. Opposite are a set of medieval towerhouses, the **Case dei Castelli**.

San Pietro in Trivio
open daily 8–12 and 3.30–7.30

Museo Archeologico
Via Lungonera Savoia
t 0744 22801; open Tues–Sun 10–1 and 4–7; adm

San Lorenzo
open daily 9–12.30 and 4–7

Santa Maria del Monumento is west near the cemetery, 1.5km along the extension of Via Cavour (Viale di Porta Sant'Angelo); partly built from a Roman funerary monument, it was enlarged in 1474. Inside, frescoes depict the legend of the golden apples, and there is an early 16th-century *presepio*.

Santa Maria del Monumento
open daily 8.30–9.30am

Around Terni

Overlooking Terni to the southwest is medieval hilltop **Collescipoli**. Long a defensive outpost of the city, it is now being engulfed in urban sprawl. Among its churches, **Santa Maria Maggiore** has a handsome Renaissance door and one of the most beautiful Baroque interiors in Umbria, and an unusual painting on the *Death of St Joseph*. There are some popular votive frescoes and a *Coronation of the Virgin* (1507) painted by Evangelista Aquili in the church of **San Nicola da Bari**. The **church of Santo Stefano** has an odd belltower, a *Crucifixion* and an inscription from 1093.

The pretty, old walled village of **Stroncone** lies at the crossroads 8km south of Terni, leading to a series of alpine meadows and chestnut forests called **I Prati**. Here there are grand views over Terni's plain from the highest point, **Cimitelle** (840m).

The Cascata delle Marmore and Lago di Piediluco

Terni, appropriately enough as the city of St Valentine, has its own Niagara Falls for honeymooners: the 126m green and misty **Cascata delle Marmore**. Falling in three stages, this is one of Europe's tallest, most beautiful waterfalls – when it's running. Surprisingly, the Cascata is an artificial creation, albeit an ancient one. In 271 BC Curius Dentatus, conqueror of the Sabines, dug a channel to drain the marshlands of Rieti, diverting the river Velino into the Nera. Although the falls are usually swallowed up by hydroelectric turbines, the thundering waters are let down at regular times, and illuminated after dark. The surrounding area is open for picnics except in December and January.

27 Cascata delle Marmore
top and bottom of falls easily reached by bus from Terni 6km west, www.marmore.it; falls let down on following schedule: ***Jan****: Sat and Sun 12–1 and 3–4;* ***Feb****: Sat and Sun 11–1 and 3–5;* ***Mar****: Mon–Fri 12–1 and 4–5, Sat and Sun 11–1 and 4–9;* ***April****: Mon–Fri 12–1 and 4–5, Sat and Sun 10–1 and 4–9;* ***May****: Mon–Fri 12–1 and 4–5, Sat and Sun 10–1 and 3–10;* ***June–Aug****: Mon–Fri 11–1, 4–6 and 9–10pm, Sat and Sun 10–1 and 3–10;* ***Sept****: Mon–Fri 12–1, 4–5 and 8–9pm, Sat and Sun 10–1 and 3–10;* ***Oct****: Fri 3–5, Sat–Sun 11–1 and 3–7;* ***Nov and Dec****: Sat and Sun 12–1 and 3–4; adm*

There are two places from which to view the falls – from the Belvedere Inferiore below on the SS209 (with a large car park, a tourist pavilion and a dozen *porchetta* vans, just beyond the tunnel) or from the Belvedere Superiore, in the village of Marmore. A path through the woods connects the two, although it's steep, muddy in the off season, and much nicer to walk down than up (the path at the bottom begins 100m downstream from the falls). There are some pleasant places to swim near the bottom, but you can't use them when the falls are on (the siren sounds 15 minutes before the falls are turned on to warn swimmers).

For guided canoeing and rafting down the Corno and Nera rivers, contact **Centro Canoa e Rafting Le Marmore**.

Centro Canoa e Rafting Le Marmore
t 330 753420, www.raftingmarmore.com

Up near Marmore, lovely **Lago di Piediluco** zigzags in and out of wooded hills, crowned by a 12th-century fortress. There are a couple of beaches but the water is cold and a bit dirty, and has dangerous undercurrents. There are other diversions; the lake has become the capital of sport rowing in Italy and the site of international competitions. On its shores, the medieval village and modest resort of **Piediluco**, named after a sacred Roman grove of trees (*lucus*), has a fine late-13th-century church, **San Francesco**, up a flight of steps. The bricked-up door has a striking frieze decorated with knots and lions; inside are 16th-century frescoes, among them a *Madonna and Two Saints* by Marcantonio di Antoniazzo. The stoup was a Roman capital and there's a Roman statue of a lady in a niche. Above the church is a ruined castle (1364) by Cardinal Albornoz.

High above the east shore of the lake is lovely **Labro**, former nest of noblemen on the run, now colonized by Belgians after a Belgian architect bought and restored the village. Below the lake, the Arrone road passes **Villalago**, which has an outdoor theatre for summer events and lovely grounds for picnicking.

Shopping in Terni

Post office: Piazza Solferino, **t** 0744 546711, *www.poste.it*

Market day: Wed, off Piazza Briccialdi, near the stadium.

Where to Stay in and around Terni

ⓘ **Terni >** *Via C. Battisti, t 0744 423047, www.umbria2000.it (closed Sun)*

Terni ✉ 05100

This is a good base for the Valnerina if you're relying on public transport.

*****Garden**, Viale Bramante 6, **t** 0744 300041, *www.gardenhotelterni.it* (€€€). Terni's prettiest hotel, near the motorway exit, with plant-filled balconies, a pool, a sauna and rooms with all the usual mod cons (breakfast included). There's also babysitting, an Internet point and a restaurant (half/full board available).

*****Hotel de Paris**, Viale Stazione 52, **t** 0744 58047, *www.hoteldeparis.it* (€€). A decent option right by the station. Breakfast is included in the rates and there's a restaurant.

******Valentino**, Via Plinio il Giovane 5, **t** 0744 402550, *www.hotelvalentinoterni.it* (€€). A central option with comfy modern rooms (breakfast included), all air conditioned (important here in summer), and one of Terni's classiest restaurants, La Fontanella (*see* below). Half and full board is possible. There's also Internet access and babysitting.

*****Allegretti**, Strada dello Staino 7b, **t** 0744 426747, *hotelallegretti@virgilio.it* (€). Comfy ensuite rooms with balconies amidst greenery.

*****Brenta II**, Via Montegrappa 51, **t** 0744 273957 (€). Ensuite modern rooms in a shady neighbourhood near the Nera and Corso del Popolo. There's an Internet point.

*****Vecchia Osteria**, Loc. Valle Spolentina, just below Villalago, **t** 0744 369111, *www.vecchiaosteria.it* (€). A recommended alternative to staying in town, up at Lake Piediluco, with simple rooms in a traditional Umbrian style, with iron beds. The restaurant (€€) serves seasonal local fare. *Closed Mon, and lunch in winter.*

Eating Out in and around Terni

Viparo, the local aperitivo, has all the charm of flat rum and cola.

Terni ✉ 05100

La Fontanella, Valentino hotel, Via Plinio il Giovane 3, **t** 0744 402550 (€€€). Tasty and imaginative dishes featuring fresh, natural ingredients.

Lu Somaru, Viale Cesare Battisti 106, **t** 0744 300486 (€€). A popular choice for Umbrian specialities. *Closed Fri.*

Villa Graziani, Via Villavalle 11, Papigno, 4km from centre, **t** 0744 67138 (€€). An 18th-century place once graced by Byron, offering seasonal cuisine (you have to pre-order fish dishes). *Closed Sun eve, Mon and 2nd half Aug.*

La Piazzetta, Via Cavour 9, **t** 0744 58188 (€). Marinated fish *antipasti*, lamb *cacciatora* with potatoes and so on. *Closed Sun and 2wks Aug.*

Stroncone ✉ 05039

Taverna di Portanova, **t** 0744 60496 (€€€). A family-run spot in an old cloister, with good *scottadito*, grilled meats, soup and pizzas. *Closed Wed, lunch exc Sun, 1wk Jan, 1st half Aug.*

Piediluco ✉ 05038

Tavoletta, Vocabolo Forca 4, off SS79, **t** 0744 368196 (€€). A lakeside venue with a seasonal menu based largely on its fish: try trout with peppers. *Closed Mon, and some wks June–Oct.*

★ **Peppe Scappa >>**

Peppe Scappa, Vocabolo Algerini 7, over lake on Arrone road, **t** 0744 368416 (€€). Some of the tastiest and best-priced Umbrian cuisine in the area, and great valley views. *Closed Mon.*

Up the Valley and Into the Mountains

The further you head up the Valnerina, the more wild and beautiful the scenery becomes, and the tastier the truffles. The Parco Naturale del Nera begins at the Cascata delle Marmore. This part of Umbria had just about finished repairs, after tremors in 1979, when the 1997 earthquake caused fresh damage and closed a number of roads; most have since reopened, but the road from S. Anatolia di Narco to Monteleone di Spoleto is closed after Caso. Some villages are still undergoing repairs.

Arrone and Ferentillo

After the Cascata delle Marmore, the SS209 passes beneath the pretty townlets of **Torreorsina** and **Casteldilago** before arriving at the more substantial and picturesque market village of **Arrone**, spilling over its isolated rock. In the centre, the **church of Santa**

The Upper Valnerina

Maria has remarkably good frescoes, including a *Life of the Virgin*, by Vincenzo Tamagni and Giovanni di Spoleto, inspired by Lippo Lippi's work in Spoleto's Duomo. The *Madonna della Misericordia* (1544) by Jacopo Siculo is to the right of the main altar, and there's a *Supper at Emmaus* by Caravaggio's school. In the apse left of the altar is a Renaissance terracotta of the *Madonna Suckling the Child, Between Two Saints*.

In the old days, Arrone and its neighbours indulged in fierce warfare. The *signori* of Arrone, who built the landmark tower on top of the town (with a tree growing out of it), were bitter enemies of the lords of Polino. A pretty 10km drive along a winding road, passing under the great white arch of a Mussolini-built aqueduct, the Ponte Canale, at **Rosciano**, brings you to **Polino**, Umbria's tiniest *comune*. It, too, has its feudal tower, as well as a monumental Baroque fountain and a road up to the **Colle Bertone** (1,223m), a modest winter sports resort and summer picnic area.

The biggest rivals of the lords of Arrone were the powerful abbots of **Ferentillo**, the next town up the Valnerina, guarded by twin 14th-century citadels on rocks that dominate the narrow valley like matching bookends; their sheer walls are as popular now with rock-climbers as Arrone's aqueduct is with rubber-banded leapers. In Precetto, the oldest quarter, the **crypt of Santo Stefano** contains **mummies**, accidentally preserved by a microfungus in the soil, complete with brown papery skin and organs, hair, whiskers, teeth and even eyeballs in some cases, and displayed in shiny glass cases. Among them are Chinese newlyweds who came here more than 100 years ago on a pilgrimage to Rome and got cholera; two French prisoners hanged in the Napoleonic wars; a woman who died of bubonic plague, a lawyer stabbed 27 times and one of his murderers, and an eagle, placed here as an experiment and perfectly mummified in less than a year. The nonchalant housewives who give the tours add to the surreal pleasure.

Santo Stefano
t 0743 54395; open daily Mar and Oct 9.30–12.30 and 2.30–6.30; April–Sept 9–12.30 and 2.30–7.30; Nov–Feb 10–12.30 and 2.30–5; adm

San Pietro in Valle

3 San Pietro in Valle
church open summer daily 9.30–6; winter daily 10–12, but call ahead, t 0744 780316; custodian's house clearly marked on road up to abbey

The former Benedictine abbey of Ferentillo, San Pietro in Valle, is 4km up the valley on the lovely slopes of Monte Solenne. You won't find a more charming abbey to visit, or stay in – it's been converted into a *residenza d'epoca*. Founded *c.* 710 by the duke of Spoleto, Faraoldo II, it is on the site of a Syrian hermitage from the 6th century, and has an ornate 12th-century campanile embedded with 8th-century fragments, in a style more common to Rome than Umbria.

The church is full of rare treasures. The nave is covered with restored **frescoes** from 1190, a rare and important early example of the Italian response to the Byzantine style – here already moving away from the stylized hierarchy to a more natural 'Latin style' where figures are individuals rather than types; the only comparable frescoes of the period are in the Roman church of San Giovanni a Porta Latina. The left wall has Old Testament scenes (note *Adam Naming the Animals* and *Noah*), and there are New Testament scenes on the right. The high **altar** (*c.* 740) is a rare example of Lombard work, sculpted front and back, with a self-portrait of the sculptor, signed Ursus Magester. The apse contains good 13th-century frescoes, with a pretty *Madonna* by the school of Giotto. At the back is a cylindrical altar said to be Etruscan. Among the stone fragments on the wall is a real rarity – a bas-relief of a monk with oriental features, believed to be one of the two Syrian monks who set up a hermitage here. The side door is usually open so you can peek into the charming two-storey **cloister**, built in the 12th century, where the hotel rooms are; the two 11th-century figures guarding the door of the church are Peter and Paul.

The views extend across the valley to the abandoned citadel of **Umbriano**, legendary first city of Umbria. If you walk up there, be sure to make a lot of noise to scare off any unexpected vipers. It makes an unforgettable place for a picnic.

Up the Valnerina: Scheggino to Triponzo

Scheggino, next town up the valley, occupies both banks of the Nera and is laced with tiny canals full of trout and a rare species of crayfish (*gamberettini*) imported from Turkey; it is also the fief of Italy's truffle tycoons, Paolo and Bruno Urbani, who thanks to the foresight of their grandfather Carlo control about 70% of the Valnerina's black gold. Scheggino has 12th-century walls that famously repelled notorious brigand Girolamo Brancaleoni in 1522. There are late frescoes by Lo Spagna in the apse of the **church of San Nicolò**, along with a *Madonna del Rosario* by Pierino Cesari and other late-16th-century works.

On the left bank of the Nera, 3km from Scheggino, **Sant'Anatolia di Narco** is another bailiwick of the black truffle. In the 19th century, a necropolis of Naharkum going back to the 8th century BC was discovered here, making it one of the oldest of all Umbrii sites. Today fewer than 600 people live within its 14th-century walls. Its glory days as a medieval *comune* are recalled in an archway with a relief of a knight, all that survives of the 13th-century Palazzo del Comune. Nearby, the medieval **church of Sant'Anatolia** has been restored since the quake, revealing fragments of early frescoes. Just outside the west gate, the Porta di Castello, the pretty church of **Santa Maria delle Grazie** has a façade of 1572 and popular votive frescoes, as well as a beautiful fresco in the presbytery of the *Madonna and Child* by the 15th-century Master of Eggi.

Sant'Anatolia
if locked, ask at house next door for key

Santa Maria delle Grazie
under restoration but keyholder for Sant' Anatolia will show you to priest's house for key

Just up from Sant'Anatolia, medieval **Castel San Felice** is a pretty little hamlet on its hill, restored after 1979. The delightful 12th-century **abbey church of San Felice in Narco** is on an unpaved road

San Felice in Narco
t 0743 613427; key held at Via Orichelle 34

at the foot of the village; there is a great picnic spot just beyond it, by the little bridge over the Nera. The façade has an intricate rose window surrounded by Evangelist symbols, sculpted columns and capitals, Cosmatesque decoration and reliefs on the life of St Felice, who moved here with his father Mauro from Palestine in the 5th century. Locals were having serious problems with a dragon; with the help of an angel, Felice dispatched it and performed other miracles. When he died, Mauro built an oratory over his grave. The interior is equally beautiful, with a pair of *transennae* with Cosmatesque remains and some early-15th-century frescoes. The crypt contains the ancient sarcophagus of St Mauro and St Felice.

High over the left bank of the Nera, walled medieval **Vallo di Nera** has fortified walls, twisting steep cobbled streets, covered alleys, little piazzas and stone houses, all immaculately restored, and two churches with frescoes. One is the 13th-century **Santa Maria**, with a Gothic portal and frescoes by Cola di Pietro from Camerino and Francesco di Antonio, painted in 1383; other frescoes are votive and feature some delightful pigs. Even better are the beautifully coloured frescoes in pink and white **San Giovanni Battista** at the top of the village; these, on the *Life of the Virgin* (1536), are by Pinturicchio's assistant, Jacopo Siculo.

Santa Maria
key from house through gate left of church, by fountain

San Giovanni Battista
key kept next door, or ask any local

This upper part of the Valnerina has been less remote since the opening of a road and tunnel from Spoleto to Piedipaterno, replacing the old narrow winding road. The next village, **Borgo Cerreto**, lies at an important crossroads and has a late-13th-century Franciscan church, **San Lorenzo**, badly damaged in the earthquake and still being restored. Above it, on a high hill, tiny **Ponte** overlooks the confluence of the Tissino and the Nera. In the 9th century, this village was a major Lombard stronghold ruling both Cascia and Norcia. The views are lovely, and the **Pieve di Santa Maria Assunta** (1201) has a beautifully carved rose window with symbols of the Evangelists and a *telemon* on its tall façade, and a fine apse decorated with hanging arches and funny little heads. The handsome restored interior contains ancient fragments, a fine pavement and some damaged frescoes by the Umbrian school. From here, it is a steep but pretty walk up to the ruined castle.

Pieve di Santa Maria Assunta
custodian's house in Via Nortosce

Across the valley and just off the main road, **Cerreto di Spoleto** sits high on its spur, offering splendid views towards Ponte. This was the birthplace of the humanist and Latin poet Giovanni Pontano (1426–1503), better known as Pontanus. While he was attending university in Perugia, his family's home in Cerreto was burned down, so he went to live with relatives in Naples, advising the court and running the literary academy that was later to take his name, the Accademia Pontana. Cerreto has a number of fine *palazzi*, as well as a pretty main piazza with a 15th-century **Palazzo Comunale** and fountain; just beyond is the tall 15th-century **Torre**

Civica. The churches here were all damaged in 1997 and some of them are still clad in scaffolding, though most of the restoration is now complete. **San Giacomo** on the edge of the hill has beautiful 15th-century frescoes.

Triponzo, last Umbrian village in the Valnerina, was the epicentre of the 1979 quake but is now inhabited again. The road continues on to Pontechiusita, and from there, you can pick up the road to Preci and Norcia (*see* pp.572–76).

Towards Monteleone di Spoleto and Cascia from Sant'Anatolia

Santa Maria delle Grazie/ Santa Cristina
ask in village for keys to both churches

A spectacular mountain road rises east of Sant'Anatolia di Narco to the hamlet of **Caso**, with interesting churches: **Santa Maria delle Grazie** with some frescoes by the school of Lo Spagna; and, outside the village, Romanesque **Santa Cristina**, with frescoes dating from the 14th–16th centuries.

San Michele Arcangelo
key kept next to door

Further along, the road (which was closed at the time of writing) rises and rises to **Gavelli** (1,152m), a tiny village on the cliff, home to the 15th-century **church of San Michele Arcangelo**, beautifully frescoed by Lo Spagna and his school. The remote hamlet of **Usigni**, signposted off the main road, has a remarkable 17th-century Roman-Baroque church, **San Salvatore**, attributed to Bernini. It was commissioned by Fausto Poli, who was born here and became a cardinal in the court of Urban VIII; he is best remembered for promoting the beatification of St Rita.

Further south, high above the Corno valley, remote little **Monteleone di Spoleto** has a pretty setting that has been inhabited for centuries: a large 6th-century BC cemetery on the road from Usigni, discovered in 1902, yielded a wooden chariot of Etruscan manufacture, decorated with magnificent bronze reliefs of the life of Achilles (now in the Metropolitan Museum in New York). Monteleone was ruled by Spoleto until 1559 but suffered earthquakes in 1703 and 1979. In the upper, semi-deserted part of town, a couple of fine quattrocento *palazzi* and a porticoed **Palazzo dei Priori** are testimony to its former importance. Here, too, is the massive 13th-century church and **convent of San Francesco**, with a beautiful Gothic door. The restored interior has a fine high altar, an 18th-century painted ceiling decorated with symbols of the Madonna and fascinating remains of 15th-century frescoes, especially a magnificent *Christ in Majesty*. The arcaded cloister has more frescoes, as does the lower church, with a good one of *St Anthony Abbot and the Animals*.

For stupendous views over much of southern Umbria, take the remote SS471 south through the mountains to Leonessa in Lazio and follow the signs west to Labro, Lake Piediluco and the Cascata della Marmore near Terni.

Activities in the Upper Valnerina

Fiume Corno, **t** 348 351 1798, *www.raftingumbria.it*. Rafting, kayaking, hiking and mountainbike tours in the Valnerina.

Valnerina Verticale Sport, Piazza Vittorio Emanuele 9, Ferentillo, **t** 0744 780003. Rock-climbing at various levels around Ferentillo, Montefranco and Arrone.

Where to Stay and Eat in the Upper Valnerina

Arrone ✉ 05031

★ **Rossi** >

/***Rossi**, Loc. Isola 7, on SS209, **t** 0744 388372, *www.rossihotelristorante.it* (€). Modern ensuite rooms (breakfast included), a magnificent pool and one of the best local restaurants (€€), offering tasty river shrimps and more, served in a pretty garden in summer. Book ahead for the deservedly popular Thursday seafood feasts. *Closed Fri.*

Locanda Paradiso, Via del Colle Buonacquisto 9, **t** 0744 368526 (€). A few simple rooms with baths, and a restaurant for reliable pizza and other basic fare.

Ferentillo ✉ 05034

ⓘ **Ferentillo** > *Comune, Via della Vittoria, t 0744 780521, www.comune.ferentillo.tr.it and Pro-Loco, t 0744 780990 (closed mornings)*

★ **Del Ponte** >>

Abbazia San Pietro in Valle, Case Sparse 4, Loc. Macenano, **t** 0744 780129, *www.sanpietroinvalle.com* (€€€). Well-furnished, comfortable rooms, some with frescoes, in the old monks' quarters of a former abbey (breakfast included). There's also a solarium, sauna, Internet point and restaurant serving typical local fare. *Closed Nov–Mar.*

*****Fontegaia**, on SS209 near town, **t** 0744 388621, *www.hotelfontegaia.it* (€€). Comfortable rooms, a kids' area and beautiful gardens for dining al fresco. The restaurant, popular with locals for special occasions, offers lots of game and truffles cooked in creative ways. *Closed Mon, and Tues–Thurs lunch.*

*****Monterivoso**, Via Case Sparse 5, Loc. Monterivoso on mummy road (*see* p.565), **t** 0744 780772, *www.monterivoso.it* (€). A converted mill with simple rooms with great views, a lovely garden and a good restaurant (half/full board available).

Piermarini, Via Ancaiano 23, **t** 0744 780714 (€€). Wonderful local dishes; try rabbit with lentils and sage, and duck breast in balsamic vinegar with radicchio. *Closed Sun eve and Mon.*

Vecchio Ponte, Via Circonvallazione 3, by river, **t** 0744 380016 (€€). Good mixed *bruschette*, river shrimps with bread, shrimps with oil and truffles, and pizza at weekends. *Closed Wed.*

Ai Tre Archi, on SS. Valnerina 29km, **t** 0744 780004 (€). Good workaday pasta dishes, such as *gnocchi al sugo di pecora*, and pizza, plus four simple rooms. *Closed Mon.*

Pizzeria Collestatte, Collestatte, up mountain from Montefranco towards Spoleto (signposted at pass) (€). Delicious pizzas smothered in rocket, and views over the lower Valnerina.

Scheggino ✉ 06040

****Del Ponte**, Via Borgo 15, **t** 0743 61253, *www.bellaumbria.net/hotel-delponte* (€). A charming hotel on the Nera, with mainly ensuite rooms and delicious meals (€€) based on river shrimps, trout and truffles. *Closed Mon.*

Sant'Anatolia di Narco ✉ 06040

****Tre Valli**, Strada Valnerina, **t** 0743 613385 (€). A place offering simple rooms and typical Umbrian cuisine (half/full board available).

Cascia

The narrow SS471 running north from Monteleone takes you to the top of Cascia (population 4,000), a hilltown that sees more pilgrims than truffles; more, in fact, than any Umbrian town except Assisi. Santa Rita, the 'Saint of Impossibilities', was born near here

Getting to Cascia

The Società Spoletina, **t** 0743 212211, *www.spoletina.com*, runs **buses** from Norcia, Spoleto, Terni, Foligno and Perugia to Cascia.

in 1381 but had to wait until 1900 to be canonized, then hold on until the inauspicious period of 1937–47 for her sanctuary. Poor Rita! After a wretched marriage to a roughneck, who was killed by his enemies, she persuaded her two sons not to take vengeance; when they died soon afterwards of disease, she became a nun, only to develop such a foul-smelling sore on her forehead that none of the sisters would come near her. Then she received the Stigmata and spent the rest of her life in pain.

Cascia itself has similarly known more than its fair share of bad luck. Originally Roman *Cursula*, it was wiped out by an earthquake and refounded on a different site. That didn't stop other earthquakes from periodically destroying it, in 1599, 1703 and 1979. The Lombards and Saracens sacked it in the three digit years. Afterwards, Cascia was a freewheeling *comune* like the others, sometimes under Spoleto's sway, sometimes under that of the Emperor or the Trinci family in Foligno. When it came under the Church with the rest of Umbria in 1516, it rebelled but was quickly put in its place.

Basilica di Santa Rita da Cascia
http://www.santaritadacascia.org; open Mar daily 7–6.30; April daily 6.30am–7.30pm; May–Sept daily 6.30am–8pm; Oct daily 6.30am–7pm; Nov–Feb daily 7–6; ***Monastero t*** *0743 76221; open for guided tours April daily 8–4; May–Sept daily 8–6; Oct daily 8.30–4.30; Nov–Mar daily 10–4*

The Basilica of Santa Rita

This proto-Disney castle with a pseudo-Byzantine interior and ghastly frescoes has been described as the most vulgar basilica in all Christendom. Rita's dried-up body is on display in a glass coffin, surrounded by votive offerings from the Terni and Rome football clubs; every year tens of thousands of unhappily married women and victims of bad luck come here to pray for relief. The art inserted into the basilica, the high altar by Giacomo Manzù, doesn't really stand a chance.

The **Monastero di Santa Rita**, left of the basilica, marks the spot where she spent here 40 years as a nun, the 15th-century cloister, her cell and miraculous rose bush.

Museo Comunale di Palazzo Santi
Via G. Palombi, ***t*** *0743 751 010; 18 Mar–April Sat, Sun and hols 10.30–1 and 3–6; May, June and 1–18 Sept Fri–Sun and hols 10.30–1 and 3–6; Aug and 24 Dec–6 Jan daily 10.30–1 and 3–6; 19 Sept–6 Nov Sat and Sun 10.30–1 and 3–6; adm, inc Sant'Antonio Abate*

The Rest of Town

Other spots around Cascia receive less devotion but offer a good deal more substance in the art department. The **Museo Comunale di Palazzo Santi**, which is located within a 17th-century palace, has an archaeological collection and a number of works of art that were taken from the town's churches, including some beautiful early medieval wooden sculpture. You can also see a lovely carved doorway and rose window on the Gothic **church of San Francesco** in nearby Piazza Garibaldi; it's worth venturing inside for the frescoes dating from the 15th and 16th centuries, a fancy Baroque pulpit, the Gothic choirstalls and the last painting by Niccolò Pomarancio, an *Ascension* (1596).

There are some more good frescoes, together with a pretty 14th-century statue of the *Virgin and Child*, in the nearby **Collegiata di Santa Maria**, a large church that was founded in 856 but reconstructed several times; one of the Romanesque lions that held up a porch is now a fountain, while the other peers out from a niche over the door.

Sant'Antonio Abate
open same hrs as Palazzo Santi (see opposite)

Below Piazza Garibaldi, the austere **church of Sant'Antonio Abate** forms part of the Museo Comunale. Despite frequent earthquake repairs over the course of centuries, it preserves in the apse a delightful 14th-century fresco cycle on the *Life of St Anthony Abbot*, which has been attributed to the Maestro della Dormitio di Terni. The nun's choir contains another fine fresco cycle, on the *Passion of Christ* (1461) by Nicola da Siena. Most beautiful of all is the painted 15th-century wooden statue of the *Archangel Raphael with Tobias* by Antonio Rizzo's workshop.

Around Cascia

Above Cascia (you need to follow signs for Monteleone) you can see the ruins of its 15th-century **citadel**, which was destroyed by the papal army after the town's revolt. Below this, the pink and white 14th-century **Convento di Sant'Agostino** has more good 15th-century frescoes.

The last site on the Rita trail is the saint's birthplace, at **Roccaporena**, 6km to the west of Cascia in the Corna valley. The setting, under a mighty rock that has been renamed the Scoglio della Preghiera (Cliff of Prayer) is exactly the kind of slightly otherworldly place in which you might expect a saint to be born. Rita's house was transformed into a church in 1630 by Cardinal Fausto Poli, chief promoter of her beatification; a little chapel crowns the big rock like a cap.

ⓘ Cascia >
Piazza Garibaldi, t 0743 71147, www.umbria2000.it (closed Sun afternoon)

Where to Stay and Eat in Cascia

Cascia ✉ 06043

******Cursula***, Via Cavour 3, **t** 0743 76206, *www.hotelcursula.com* (€€). Pleasant and comfortable rooms with typical Umbrian furniture, breakfast included, and Umbrian fare in the restaurant (half/full board offered).

****Centrale**, Piazza Garibaldi 36, **t** 0743 76736 (€). Ensuite rooms in a handy location, breakfast included.

****Mini Hotel La Tavernetta**, Via Palombi, **t** 0743 71387, *www.minihotellatavernetta.com* (€). A family-run choice offering clean, comfortable ensuite rooms (with breakfast included in rates) and a restaurant (€€) where you can enjoy good *pappardelle* with wild boar, tagliatelle with mushrooms, grilled *pecorino* cheese, sausages with lentils, and mixed grills. Of the three tasting menus on offer, one is wholly vegetarian. Half and full board are available. *Closed Tues*.

Norcia and the Monti Sibillini

Here in its southeast corner, in the shadow of the Monti Sibillini, Umbria achieves its highest heights and widest open spaces. Norcia, in ancient times the northernmost of all Sabine towns, stands battered yet proud on its high plain, famous for its saint and its butchers. Because of the frequent earthquakes, an 18th-century law limited buildings to two storeys and the result is a town unlike any other in Umbria.

Norcia

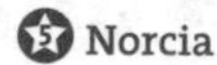

Old Norcia (population 4,900) or, as the gate reads, VETUSTA NURSIA, can seem bright and cheerful or morose and gloomy, barricaded like a Foreign Legion outpost in its 14th-century walls on the edge of the lofty **Piano di Santa Scolastica**, with mountains on all sides. Virgil called it *Frigida Nursia*, so one can imagine when he visited. But the last Roman emperor was still warm in his grave when this old, cold town offered the world St Benedict (480–543), father of Western monasticism.

During the Middle Ages, Norcia was a *comune* to be reckoned with. Nor was it long before the Nursini lost their early reputation for sanctity; they were known at various times for witchcraft (there was a sorcerers' college here in the Middle Ages, when *nursino* or *norcino* became synonymous with 'wizard'), as well as for its pork butchers and surgery. Practitioners of both of the latter were renowned for their expert knife work – after all, in the days when doing autopsies on cadavers was illegal, the famous surgeons of Preci (*see* p.575) practised on pigs. To this day, Norcia is synonymous with *prosciutto* (which is taken from both domestic pork and wild boar) and for having the best *norcinerie* in Umbria, as well as some fine cheeses.

As a sideline, the Nursini were also experts in the art of keeping male voices unnaturally pure and sweet – the parents of a boy with operatic potential would bring him to Norcia, where he would be drugged with opium and put in a very hot bath until he was quite insensible, when the dirty deed was done (the ducts leading to the testicles were severed so the organs would eventually shrivel and disappear). Too bad for the lad whose voice never made the grade, but those who did became the darlings of society and quite wealthy besides. Some were such charming prima donnas that Casanova wasn't the only one to keep falling in love with them. One of the last 'graduates' of Norcia, Domenico Mustafa (d. 1912), was director of the Sistine Chapel choir and stayed long enough to cut the only recording by a *castrato*.

Getting to Norcia

Società Spoletina (**t** 0743 212211, *www.spoletina.com*) runs **buses** to Norcia from Spoleto, Cascia, Perugia, Terni, Foligno, Rome and Ascoli Piceno in the Marches.

Piazza San Benedetto

Norcia's history has been plagued by earthquakes: the one of 1328 destroyed the medieval city, and others in 1703, 1730, 1859 and 1979 all took their toll. However, the city escaped any damage in the 1997 earthquake.

The city's chief monuments are situated on the rounded Piazza San Benedetto, which is presided over by a stern statue of St Benedict dating from 1880. Directly behind stands the 13th-century Gothic **Basilica di San Benedetto**, with a charming portal, framed by statues of Benedict and Scholastica and painted angels, with a Madonna on top and a rose window. On the side of the church, a portico shelters 16th-century grain measures and ends at a sturdy campanile. The interior, remodelled in the 18th century, with unexceptional paintings and restored for the 2000 Jubilee, seems unduly modest for the shrine to the Patron Saint of Europe. In the crypt you can study the ruins of a late Roman house, which tradition says belonged to Europroprio Anicio and Abbondanza Reguardati, parents of twins Benedict and Scholastica, the first Western monk and nun.

The handsome **Palazzo Comunale**, also in the piazza, boasts a 13th-century campanile and portico of 1492, and a **Cappella dei Priori** containing a 15th-century silver reliquary of St Benedict. Next door and in the nearby streets are the boar and truffle gastronomic shops – Norcia's real attraction for Italians.

Castellina
t 0743 817030; open June daily 10–1 and 4–7.30; rest of year Tues–Sun 10–1 and 4–6

Museo Civico Diocesano
t 0743 817030; open June daily 10–1 and 4–7.30; rest of year Tues–Sun 10–1 and 4–6; adm

The other side of the piazza is occupied by the square **Castellina**, built over the ruins of an ancient temple. Designed in 1554 for Pope Julius III by his favourite architect Vignola, its upper floor houses the **Museo Civico Diocesano**, with pretty and precious things, including a late-12th-century painted *Crucifixion* with the two Marys on either side of Christ, a not uncommon Romanesque conceit; there were originally two others but they fell off. Another remarkable *Cross*, signed Petrus, was made half a century later. There's a life-sized *Deposition* group in wood from Ruccataniburo, from the late 1200s, high reliefs of the *Madonna and Child*, and paintings of the same by Antonio da Faenza (whose architectural training shows in his use of perspective) and others in the Salone, under its handsome panelled ceiling, along with a *Risen Christ* by Nicola da Siena. Another room has stone sculptures by Giovanni Dalmata (1469) from an altarpiece formerly in San Giovanni, and further on are two terracotta statues of the *Annunciation* by Luca della Robbia. The loggia is dedicated to detached frescoes.

Next to the Castellina is Norcia's **Duomo**, built by Lombard masons in 1560 and remodelled in the 1700s; the massive campanile was rebuilt in 1859. The 17th-century chapel of the Madonna della Misericordia shelters a venerated 16th-century fresco, *Madonna between SS. Scholastica and Benedict*.

Elsewhere in Norcia

From the Castellina, Via Battisti leads to the 14th-century Gothic **church of San Francesco**, with a rose window and handsome portal; insider are 16th-century frescoes and a fine painting by Jacopo Siculo, *Coronation of the Virgin*. Opposite is the building, now a restaurant, that held the public pawn shop, the Monte di Pietà, founded in 1466. Norcia's straight main street, Corso Sertorio, runs just east; the town's rebuilt **Teatro Civico** is in Piazza Vittorio Veneto, at the north end of the Corso by the handsome 19th-century **Porta Romana**. Just outside, the **Cripto Portico Romano Museo Archeologico** displays finds from the area.

Teatro Civico
t 0743 816022

Cripto Portico Romano Museo Archeologico
open June daily 10–1 and 4–7.30; rest of year Tues–Sun 10–1 and 4–6

From Corso Sertorio, Via Gioberti leads to 15th-century **San Giovanni**, with its belltower built into the walls. This is one of the most important churches in Norcia, with a good interior and art, but it has long been closed. From nearby Piazza Carlo Alberto with its fountain, turn down Via Umberto to see the most curious building in Norcia, the square limestone **Tempietto**, built on the street corner by local stonemason Vanni Tuzi in 1354. No one is sure what it was used for, but it has pretty reliefs. Via Umberto continues past here to Via Anicia, where a left turn takes you to the 13th-century Gothic **church of Sant'Agostino**, with an ogival portal and a frescoed lunette from 1368 and good 15th- and 16th-century frescoes inside. The **Oratorio di Sant'Agostinuccio**, further up Via Anicia, belongs to a local confraternity and has a charming interior covered in fine woodwork of the early 1600s.

Sant'Agostino
open in summer

The **cemetery church of Santa Scolastica**, 3km south, was built not long after the lifetime of the holy twins, according to tradition on the site of their mother's house. Largely rebuilt in the 17th century, it has a late-14th-century fresco cycle on the *Life of St Benedict*.

North of Norcia: the Valcastoriana

North of Norcia, the rugged Valcastoriana is one of the most remote Umbrian valleys, making it a favourite residence for hermits in the early Middle Ages; in addition to its natural beauty, it has a fine collection of small churches, villages and an important abbey, all of which have suffered in recent quakes. The east of the valley is now part of Monti Sibillini National Park.

The road from Norcia (follow signs for Visso) rises through pines to a 1,008m pass, the **Forca d'Ancarano**. Descending into the Valcastoriana it passes the delightful, beautifully restored and

Santa Maria Bianca
signposted right; pick up key at nearby house

maintained church of **Santa Maria Bianca**, rebuilt and added to over the centuries. Early Romanesque capitals support a 15th-century loggia, and there's a funny old campanile. Inside is an ancient font, and the high altar shelters the eponymous *Madonna* (1511), a marble in high relief attributed to the Florentine Francesco di Simone Ferrucci; votive frescoes adorn the walls.

Sant'Andrea
key at Via Entedia 15

The valley road continues towards Campi; before it, on the right, is a sign for **Campi Castello**, a tiny hamlet with a pretty public wall fountain. Its handsome church, **Sant'Andrea**, has a prominent portico that acts as a belvedere over the valley. Two sweet lions guard the Gothic door; a hotchpotch of votive paintings and colourful gilded wooden altars lines the attractive 16th-century interior. **Campi Basso**, back on the main road, is equally proud of its **church of San Salvatore**, with a lovely old asymmetrical façade with a pair of rose windows; inside are fine frescoes by Giovanni and Antonio Sparapane (1464) and an old immersion baptismal font.

Abbazia di Sant'Eutizio
t 0743 99659 or t 0743 231635; open April–Aug Mon and Wed–Sat 10–12.30 and 3.30–7, Sun 10–6; Sept–Mar Sun and hols by appt; if closed, try custodian at 1st door on left inside abbey, or ask at bar

North beyond Piedivalle is the sign for the **Abbazia di Sant'Eutizio** up in its own sub-valley. In the early Middle Ages, Sant'Eutizio owed much of its success to its remoteness: according to St Gregory the Great, it was founded by hermits Eutizio and Spes in the late 400s, who were visited by the young St Benedict. It became an abbey under Benedictine rule, and between the 800s and 1200s prospered under the dukes of Spoleto who, along with emperors and popes, gave it large grants of land, so that by the first millennium it owned more than 100 villages and churches. It had a famous library (with Umbria's oldest examples of vernacular Italian from the 11th century) and an infirmary renowned for the skill of its doctors, a skill handed to Preci when the Benedictines were barred from practising surgery. The abbey enjoys a beautiful setting, hugging the steep wooded mountain, with its campanile high on a rock over the cloister. The Romanesque **church** with its rose window and handsome portal was rebuilt in 1190 by a Master Petrus, who gave it a majestic interior, with a single nave culminating in a lofty presbytery over the crypt. A fine funerary monument to St Eutizio stands behind the altar, attributed to Rocco da Vicenza (1514), and the intarsia choirstalls are 16th-century. The abbey was restored after the 1997 quake as a hostel for pilgrims of the 2000 Jubilee; from the courtyard, you can visit the grottoes where the first hermits lived.

Preci, up the road, was badly damaged in the quakes of 1979 and 1998, and much remains structurally unsound. A small fortified village rebuilt after an attack by Norcia in 1528, it has proud palaces built by its famous surgeons, who learned the art from the Benedictines and passed it down through generations into the 18th century. They had very sharp knives and tools and specialized in eye operations: when Queen Elizabeth I of England needed a cataract operation in 1588, Cesari Scacchi of Preci was summoned. The **museum** displays some surgical instruments from Preci's school, and a jumble of wooden sculpture, paintings (some from earthquake-damaged churches in the area), archaeological bits and pieces and ancient crafts.

From **Preci**, you can circle back to the Valnerina by way of Triponzo, or return to Norcia via the more remote but wonderfully scenic Valle Oblita, where only a handful of people live year-round, at **Abeto** and **Todiano**, both home to handsome *palazzi* and churches holding important Baroque canvases attesting to their former importance, when the inhabitants made their fortunes as itinerant pork butchers in Tuscany.

The Piano Grande and Castelluccio

Since 1993 all of the territory to the east of Norcia has been encompassed in the majestic **Monti Sibillini National Park**, which Umbria shares with the Marches. A protected area covering some 70,000 hectares, it is off the tourist track, remote and wildly beautiful. You can see some of the most spectacular scenery along the narrow road from the church of Santa Scolastica south of Norcia (*see* p.574), which winds a magnificent 21km up to **Forca Canapine** (1,540m), high enough to support a modest ski station in winter, with a refuge and hotel.

On the same Forca Canapine road, 18km from Norcia, a road descends into one of the most poetic landscapes you'll fine in all these pages, affording the best possible ending to a journey in Umbria. This is the sublime **Piano Grande**, a karstic basin, former glacial lake and now an extraordinary meadow measuring 16 square kilometres, surrounded by bare rolling hills and mountains that look as if they are covered with velvet during late spring, when the entire meadow explodes into swathes of wildflowers that go on and on for kilometres, reaching their peak in June. It is a rarefied dream landscape (one used by Franco Zeffirelli in his Franciscan film *Brother Sun, Sister Moon*), large enough to distort distances; the flocks that produce Norcia's famous cheese graze here, and its fields produce the tiny lentils of Castelluccio, which come in three colours and are among the tastiest and rarest in Italy.

A long straight road crosses the Piano Grande, then rises to the lentil village of **Castelluccio**, which at 1,452m is the highest and loneliest settlement in all Umbria. Castelluccio had around 700 inhabitants in 1951 and now has just 40 or so; not so long ago, it was often cut off by the winter snows, a problem that has now been alleviated by ploughs. It is also the one old village in Umbria with no pretence to charm, but it does attract hikers, hang-gliders and cross-country skiers.

The Rooftop of Umbria: the Monti Sibillini

Castelluccio lies near an important crossroads under the dark, legendary **Monti Sibillini** (*see* p.637), the most dramatic mountains in the Apennines. To the east of Castelluccio a secondary road skirts the slopes of **Monte Vettore** (2,476m), the tallest in the Sibillini, covered with snow for much of the year. Its summit (the usual approach is from the east, from the hamlet of Foce near Montemonaco in the Marches) is one of the very few places on the Italian peninsula where both the Adriatic and Tyrrhenian seas are visible, at least on a clear day.

Tourist Information in and around Norcia

Monte Sibillini National Park has an information office at Casa del Parco, Norcia, Via Solferino 22, **t** 0743 817090, *www.sibillini.net* (closed afternoons).

ⓘ Norcia ›
Piazza Garibaldi, t 0743 71147, www.norcia.net

Market Day in Norcia

There's a market every Thursday, and a truffle fair each February.

Events and Activities in and around Norcia

Feast of St Benedict, 20–21 Mar. A crossbow tournament between six *quaite* or districts of town.

For **outdoor activities**, contact:

Associazione Piangrande, Castelluccio, **t** 0743 817 279. Mountainbike excursions and horse-trekking.

Cooperativa Monte Patino, Via Foscolo 2, Norcia, **t** 0743 817487. Hiking trips, mountainbiking and horse-trekking.

Prodelta, Via delle Fate 3, Castelluccio, **t** 0743 821156. A paragliding and hang-gliding school.

Rafting Centre Monti Sibillini, c/o Ristorante dei Cacciatori, Biselli di Norcia, **t** 0742 23146.

Where to Stay and Eat in and around Norcia

Norcia ✉ 06046

*****Grotta Azzurra**, Via Alfieri 12, **t** 0743 816513, *www.bianconi.com* (€€€). An attractive inn dating back to 1850, with comfortable rooms, a disco and a good restaurant serving a monthly-changing menu of traditional local fare such as lamb with red peppers. Breakfast is included in rates; half and full board are available. *Closed Tues.*

*****Nuovo Hotel Posta**, Via C. Battisti 10, **t** 0743 817 434, *www.bianconi.com* (€€). A fine establishment, newly refurbished, with a beautiful garden and a restaurant serving robust Castelluccio lentils, boar salami, *tortellini alla norcina* (with ricotta) and lamb with truffles – topped off, if you dare, by a tumbler of Norcia's nasty *grappa*, which is flavoured with black truffles. Half and full board accommodation are available.

★ Dal Francese ››

Dal Francese, Via Riguardati 16, **t** 0743 816290 (€€€). A place offering bumper meals of mainly truffle-based dishes. Among the highlights are the pasta medley of *tris al tartufo*, the *gnocchi al tartufo* and the *tortellini con crema di tordi* (thrushes) *e tartufi*. *Closed Fri exc in summer, 2wks Jan and 2wks July*.

Restaurant Granaro del Monte, Via Alfieri 12, **t** 0743 816 513 (€€€). Good meats grilled before your eyes over a large open fire, *tagliolini* with black truffles, *pappardelle* with wild boar, and spelt soup. *Closed Tues*.

Castelluccio di Norcia ✉ 06046

To stay in *rifugi* – modest **mountain huts** offering modest meals at modest prices – contact Parco Nazionale dei Monti Sibillini, Largo G.B. Gaola Antinori 1, Visso (Mc), **t** 0737 972711, *www.sibillini.net*.

***Sibilla, t** 0743 821113, *hotelsibilla@hotmail.com* (€). Simple ensuite rooms (breakfast included) and a restaurant (€€; with half/full board). *Closed Tues.*

Il Guerrin Meschino, Via Monte Veletta 22, **t** 0743 821125, *www.guerinmeschino.it* (€). Basic bedrooms and apartments on a working lentil farm.

Taverna Castelluccio, Via dietro la Torre 8, **t** 0743 821100 (€€). The place to come for the best food in town, including Norcia-style *antipasti* and the village's famous lentils in soup or with sausages, plus pizzas. It also has a few reasonably priced rooms. *Closed Wed exc summer.*

The Marches

For those with a fatal attraction for central Italy, the Marches are the new frontier: new emerald landscapes and hilltowns, new discoveries at the table, new surprises from the Renaissance, and fewer tourists to share them with. Prices are lower and the people are friendly to visitors, who are more of a novelty here. Tucked between the Apennines and the sea, this is one of the greenest, prettiest and most civilized corners of Italy, with two lovely Renaissance art towns in Urbino and Ascoli Piceno, lots of beaches, art and scores of fine old rosy brick towns in the valleys that lead to the impressive snowy peaks of the Sibilline mountains.

21

Don't miss

1. The perfect Renaissance palace
Urbino **p.588**

2. High castles
The Montefeltro **p.593**

3. Romanesque churches and beaches
Under Mt Conero **p.616**

4. Rare wildflowers and scenery in the high Apennines
The Monti Sibillini **p.637**

5. A refined travertine town
Ascoli Piceno **p.642**

See map overleaf

The Marches

p.396
p.472
p.550

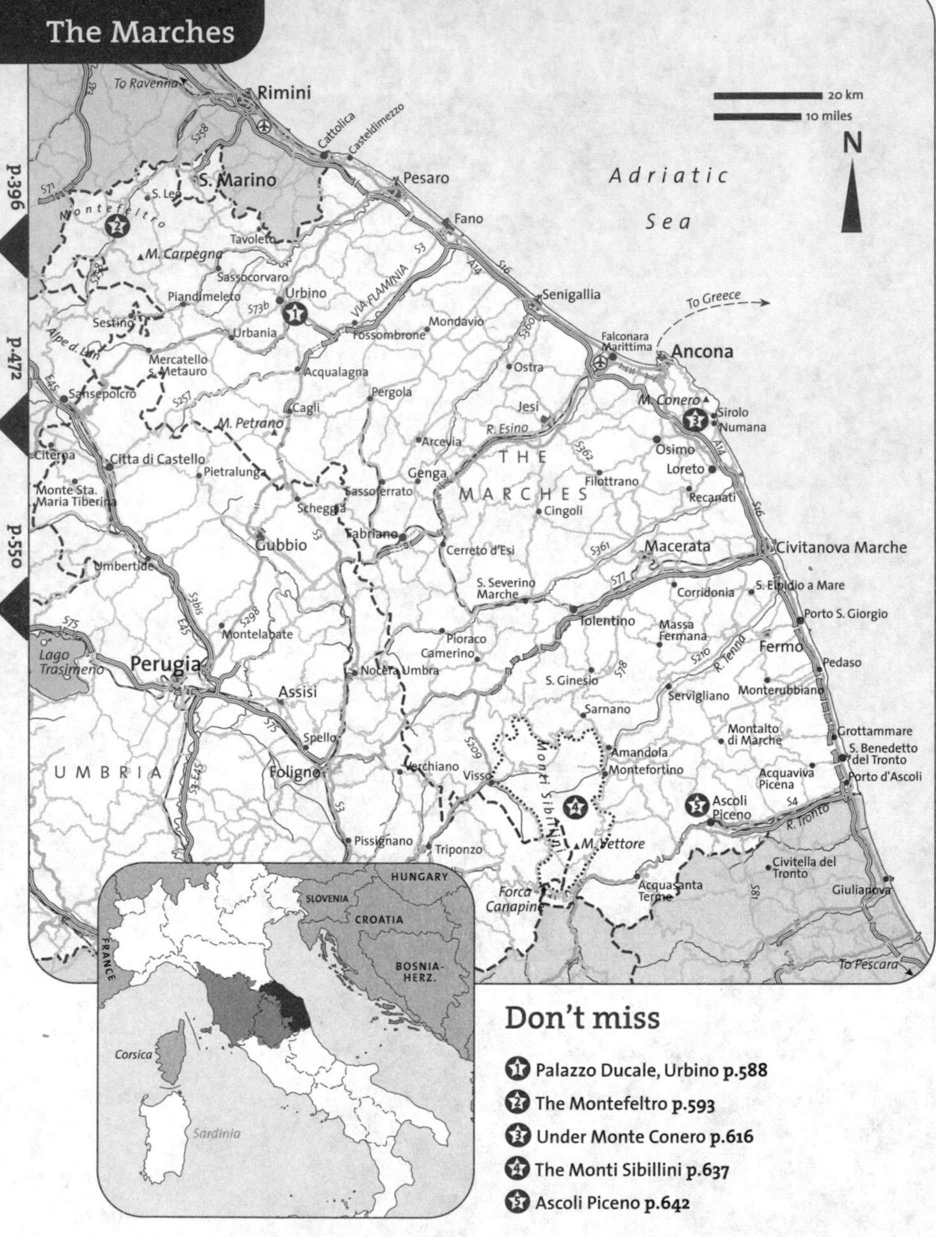

Don't miss

1. **Palazzo Ducale, Urbino p.588**
2. **The Montefeltro p.593**
3. **Under Monte Conero p.616**
4. **The Monti Sibillini p.637**
5. **Ascoli Piceno p.642**

Better a corpse in the house than a man from the Marches at the door
Old Italian saying

What could the inhabitants of this placid little region have done to earn such opprobrium from their countrymen? They aren't so bad, really; the saying comes from the old days when many Marchigiani served across the Papal States as the pope's tax collectors. Since then, their neighbours have more often ignored than insulted this obscure patch of territory along the Adriatic.

In the Middle Ages a *march*, or *mark*, meant a border province in the Holy Roman Empire. These *marche*, bordering on the Papal States, were created by the emperor in 1105 and never found a juicier name besides their generic title, leading one to suspect this Italian region to be lacking in personality. In fact, this has always been the odd bit of central Italy. In ancient times, too, it was a border zone, shared by Umbrii, Gauls, Sabines and the Piceni, a stout-hearted little tribe that had for its totem the *picus*, or woodpecker, the sacred bird of the war god Mars. Unencumbered by art and culture, they occupied much of the central Adriatic; their name lives on in their old capital, Ascoli Piceno. The Romans called it the *Annonaria*, for its annual production of cereals and cattle.

Today, the Marchigiani still have a little identity problem, but it doesn't keep them awake at night. The pope's old taxmen have discovered a talent for business: their region has had one of the highest growth rates in Italy and become a showcase of what Italians like to call their 'new model for capitalism': small firms, often family-run, with a close relationship to their employees and community. They use their natural Italian talent to find something they can make better or more cheaply than anyone else – from shoes to electric guitars – and the results are often spectacular. This will not necessarily be evident to the visitor (just the occasional new power-line ruining a pretty panorama, as in Tuscany), but it has given the region a new pride: its citizens look on it as an updated version of the city-states that made medieval Italy great.

The 1997 earthquake left many people living in containers. Most have now moved into wooden chalets or new housing, which looks permanent. But restoration of churches, *palazzi* and museums has been much slower here than in the media spotlight of Umbria. Many sights are still closed (especially in Fabriano) and city streets are still lined with scaffolding in the worst-hit places.

Northern Marches: The Coast and Inland

The Coast North of Pesaro

If you get as far as Rimini, it's only a short drive down the coast to the northernmost resort in the Marches, **Gabicce Mare**, with 100 hotels. Gabicce calls itself, with a wee bit of exaggeration, the Capri of the Adriatic, for the promontory of Gabbice Monte that closes off its south end; take a good look, as such natural features on the coast are rare from now on. The best views are from the corniche road hugging the coast, passing through **Casteldimezzo** and little medieval **Fiorenzuola di Focara**, with beaches and seafood eateries.

The Northern Marches

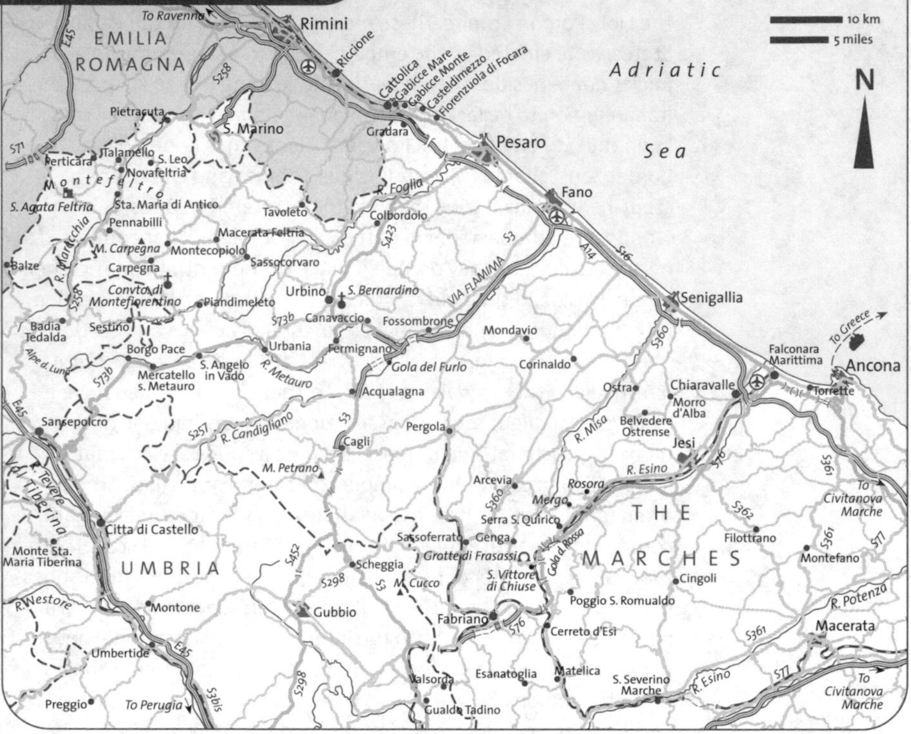

Rocca di Gradara
t 0541 964181; open Mon 8.30–1.15, Tues–Sun 8.30–6.30; last entry 45mins before closing time; adm

Inland, looming over the highway, the frontier of the Marches was defended by the pretty **Rocca of Gradara**, built in the 11th century and rebuilt in the 1300s, when it was hotly contested between the Malatestas and Montefeltros of Urbino. Traditionally, this castle was the scene of the story of Francesca da Rimini and Paolo Malatesta, the tragic lovers consigned to hell by Dante in Canto 5 of the *Inferno*. Being within easy striking distance from Rimini has led the management to exploit the story to the hilt for tour groups, but it's fun if you're in the mood. It has a beautiful little chapel, with a ceramic altarpiece by Luca della Robbia.

Even a small nation is large if it is placed on the rock of truth and radiates the light of justice
John Paul II, during a 1997 pilgrimage to San Marino

The Lilliputian Republic of San Marino

If you drive up through the hills to the top of Monte Titano, you can visit the world's only sovereign and independent roadside attraction. Before Rimini became the Italian Miami Beach, the 50,000 citizens of San Marino made their living peddling postage stamps. Now their streets crowded with day-trippers, they have been unable to resist the temptation to order bright medieval costumes, polish up their picturesque mountain towns and open

Getting to and around San Marino

San Marino, 24km from Rimini, is reached by regular **bus** from Rimini train station (or in summer the Piazza Tripolo or Marina Centro). There's a **funicular** up from Borgo Maggiore to San Marino town that can save parking stress: it runs 8am–9pm July, 8am–1am Aug, 8am–6.30pm rest of year.

---

souvenir stands selling wines, *mistra* – the local aniseed liqueur – ceramics, sweets and tat. Combine this with no sales limit (goods are 20% cheaper than in Italy) and you have a mecca for shoppers.

The famous San Marinesi stamps, though nothing like the exquisitely engraved numbers of 40 years ago, are still prized by collectors and can be bought from the **Officio Filatelico e Numismatico di Stato**. In 1972 the country began to mint its own coins (including gold ones) again after a lapse of decades; nevertheless, the citizens of San Marino, who have one of the highest national average incomes in Europe, are making their living almost entirely from tourism.

The World's Smallest, and Oldest, Republic

According to legend, San Marino (61 sq km, population 27,000) was founded as a Christian settlement on the easily defensible slopes of Mt Titano by a stonecutter, Marinus, fleeing the persecutions of Diocletian in early 4th century. 'Overlooked', as San Marinese put it, by the Empire and various states that followed, the little community had the peace and quiet to evolve its medieval democratic institutions; its present constitution dates from 1243, when the first pair of 'consuls' was elected by a popular assembly. They are now called Captains Regent, but little else has changed in 700 years.

Twice, in 1503 and 1739, the republic was invaded by papal forces, and independence was preserved only by good luck and the intervention of St Agatha, now national co-patron. Napoleon, passing through in 1797, found San Marino amusing and, half-seriously, offered to enlarge its boundaries, a proposal politely declined. The republic felt secure enough to offer refuge to Garibaldi after the Roman revolt of 1849, and as an island of peace during the Second World War distinguished itself by taking in hundreds of thousands of refugees.

San Marino last made the news during the 1970s, when the Communists threatened to win the elections. The San Marino government decided that even emigrants were still citizens, with the right to vote, and thousands of San Marinese descendants in places such as New Jersey were given free holidays at government expense to help tip the election.

Most visitors enter San Marino from Rimini, at the hamlet called Dogana (Customs), though there are no border formalities now. The main road rises through a string of villages: San Marino, no tiny state like the Vatican City, is 12km at its widest. On the slopes of Monte Titano (one of the mountains the mythological Titans piled up to reach heaven and overthrow the gods), **Borgo Maggiore** is the largest town in the republic, with most of the shops and the funicular up to the capital and citadel, also called **San Marino**. This steep medieval village has terrific views over Rimini and the coast, but even here nothing is as old as it looks; in main Piazza della Libertà, the **Palazzo Pubblico**, full of guardsmen with brass buttons and epaulettes, is an 1894 reconstruction. In summer you can see the **changing of the guard**. The Grand Council meets in the Palazzo and the Captains Regent have their offices here; other rooms are full of San Marino memorabilia. The **Museo-Pinacoteca San Francesco** is in the 14th-century convent at Contrada San Francesco 5.

Palazzo Pubblico
t 0549 885370; open Jan–Mar and Oct–Dec daily 8.50–5; April–Sept daily 8am–8pm; adm; ***changing of guard*** *mid-May–Sept daily every hr 8.30–6.30*

Museo-Pinacoteca San Francesco
t 0549 885132; open Jan–Mar and Oct–Dec daily 8.50–5; April–Sept daily 8am–8pm; adm

The medieval tower fortresses on the three peaks give San Marino its silhouette famous to philatelists. The **Rocca Guaita**, was restored in 1500 and used as a prison; the **Rocca Cesta**, on the highest peak of Mount Titano, contains weapons from the 12th to 19th centuries. The **Rocca Montale** is closed to the public.

Rocca Guaita/ Rocca Cesta
t 0549 991369 (Guaita) or t 0549 991295 (Cesta); open Jan–Mar and Oct–Dec daily 8.50–5; April–Sept daily 8am–8pm; adm; joint ticket available

A crop of flaky museums, mainly in San Marino town, has sprouted up to shake loose a few euros from the tourists – collections range from the most obvious stamps, coins and weapons to waxworks and the utterly bizarre Clessidra Atomica, a device that counts the number of atomic bombs being defused at any one time. And when you find you need a fix of Renaissance art or summer beach madness, or both, catch the bus over to Sigismondo Malatesta and Federico Fellini's Rimini.

Where to Stay and Eat in San Marino

ⓘ San Marino town ›
Contrada Omagnano 20, t 0549 882998 from Italy, t 00 378 49 882998 from other countries, www.visitsanmarino.com

San Marino ✉ 47890, t 0549 from Italy; t 00 378549 from elsewhere

San Marino can be cool and fairly quiet in summer, but book early. For hotel bookings, contact Consorzio San Marino, Via Piana 103, t 0549 995031, *www.sanmarino2000.sm*.

******Grand Hotel San Marino**, Viale Onofri 31, t 0549 992400, *www.grandhotel.sm* (€€€€). A modern hotel close to the Rocche, with luxurious rooms (breakfast included), lovely views, a restaurant and a garage.

******Titano**, Contrada del Collegio 31, t 0549 991006, *www.hoteltitano.com* (€€€€). A hotel in the historic centre, retaining much of its 1890s decor but with modern comforts. Breakfast is included. The restaurant terrace has panoramic view. *Closed Jan–mid-Mar.*

*****Panoramic**, Via Voltone 91, t 0549 992359 (€€). Good views and functional ensuite rooms (breakfast included). *Closed Nov–mid-Dec.*

*****Quercia Antica**, junction Via Capannaccia and Via Cella Bella, t 0549 991 257, *www.querciantica.com* (€€). Simple, comfy rooms (breakfast included) just out of the historic centre, with views and a good restaurant.

La Taverna Righi, Piazza Libertà 10, t 0549 991196 (€€€). Refined versions of traditional *passatelli*, seafood and veggie dishes, and fancier ones with foie gras. There's also a bar/*paninoteca*, bistro and ice-cream parlour. *Closed Wed in winter, 2wks Jan and 1wk Aug.*

La Fratta, Salita alla Rocca 14, t 0549 991594 (€€). An old favourite famous for its mushrooms. *Closed Wed April–June, Jan and Feb.*

Pesaro

Under the Byzantines, the five big ports of the central Adriatic were known as the Pentapolis – Rimini, Fano, Senigallia, Ancona and Pesaro, the most pleasant, with a handsome little historic centre.

A Stroll around Rossini's Hometown

Pesaro (population 88,900) is lovely to walk through, both its older quarters and arcaded streets, and the new streets by the beach, full of trees and little 19th-century villas, many in the Liberty style. They include the small but outrageous **Villino Ruggieri**, with a cornice supported by terracotta lobsters designed by Giovanni Brega in 1907. The castle, the **Rocca Costanza**, was built in 1478 by Laurana, designer of the palace at nearby Urbino.

Rocca Costanza
t 0721 387474; closed for restoration at time of writing

The Sforzas of Milan, who ruled Pesaro for a time, sold it to the Della Rovere, family of Julius II, in 1512, right after their acquisition of Urbino. The big crenellated **Palazzo Ducale** in central Piazza del Popolo had been completed by the Sforzas only a couple of years before, though the prettiest thing in the square is the post office, with a terracotta portal of 1395 transferred from a church. In the Sforza years, Pesaro rivalled Faenza as a producer of fine ceramics; you can see lovely examples in the nearby **Pinacoteca e Museo delle Ceramiche**; others come from Urbino, Castel Durante (Urbania), Deruta and Gubbio, including a few superb works by that city's celebrated Mastro Giorgio. Besides the majolica plates there are a few good pictures and one great one, a *Coronation of the Virgin* or *Pala di Pesaro* (1474) by Giovanni Bellini. Pesaro is proud to have given the world the composer Gioacchino Rossini in 1792; his nearby birthplace, the **Casa Rossini**, has mementos.

Palazzo Ducale
t 0721 387474; open for guided tours by appt

Pinacoteca/Museo delle Ceramiche
Piazza Toschi Mosca 29; t 0721 387541; open July and Aug Tues and Thurs 9.30–12.30 and 4–10.30, Wed and Fri–Sun 9.30–12.30 and 4–7; rest of year Tues and Wed 9.30–12.30, Thurs–Sun 9.30–12.30 and 4–7; adm; joint adm available with Casa Rossini

Casa Rossini
Via Rossini 34; t 0721 387357; open July and Aug Tues and Thurs 9.30–12.30 and 4–10.30, Wed and Fri–Sun 9.30–12.30 and 4–7; rest of year Tues and Wed 9.30–12.30, Thurs–Sun 9.30–12.30 and 4–7; adm; joint adm available with Pinacoteca and Museo delle Ceramiche

In nearby Via Mazza, the **Museo Oliveriano** has two Greek bronze ornaments from the 5th century BC, a Roman copy of a statue of a youth from the same period, an elegant 3rd-century Roman sarcophagus and votive offerings, a rare Etruscan-Latin inscription, and the stele of Novilara, with a peculiar relief of a sea battle from an Iron Age civilization similar to the Piceni. In adjacent Piazza Olivieri, you can see Rossini's piano and manuscripts at the **Conservatory** he founded, and during the Rossini festival in late summer you can take in one of his operas (including *William Tell* in its entirety) at Pesaro's grand, five-tiered **Teatro Rossini**, which was inaugurated with *The Thieving Magpie* in 1816.

Museo Oliveriano
t 0721 33344; open July and Aug Mon–Sat 4–7; rest of year Mon–Sat 9–12 by request

Conservatorio di Musica G Rossini
visits by appt on t 0721 33671

Teatro Rossini
Piazza Lazzanini; guided tours by appt on t 0721 387509

North of Pesaro

In the hills towards Gabicce Mare, 2km north, is the 18th-century **Villa Caprile**, with Italian gardens, fountains and a stuccoed gallery. In 1817–19 this was the residence of the Princess of Wales, mother of Queen Victoria; today it hosts the Istituto Tecnico Agrario.

Villa Caprile
open mid-June–mid-Sept daily 3–7; guided tours by appt on t 0721 21440; adm

Getting to and from Pesaro

At least 10 **buses** a day go to Urbino, some via Fano and (usually) Fermignano. All leave from or stop at Pesaro's train station, on Viale Roma, about 500m south of the centre. Bus companies are AMI, **t** 0721 370734, *www.amibus.it*; SAPUM (part of AMI); Capponi, **t** 0721 67980, *www.capponiviaggi.it*; Bucci, **t** 0721 32401, *www.autolineebucci.com*; Davani Arrigo Eredi, **t** 0721 23927, *www.davaniviaggi.it*; SOGET, **t** 0721 371318.

Villa Imperiale
t 0721 69341; guided tours by appt June–Sept Wed; adm exp

Another 3km further on is the **Villa Imperiale**, built for the Sforzas but enlarged by the Della Rovere.

Pesaro >
*Piazzale Libertà 11, t 0721 69341; **Pesaro–Urbino province**: Via Rossini 4, t 0721 359501, www.turismo.pesarourbino.it; **Comune di Pesaro**: Viale Trieste 164, t 0721 34073, or freephone **t** 800 222111 (Marche) and **t** 800 563800 (Pesaro and Urbino province), www.pesaroturismo.com*

Locanda da Ciacci >>

Where to Stay in Pesaro

Pesaro ✉ 61100

There are many one- and two-star places along the beach and on the sidestreets. Viale Trento, parallel to the beach one block from the sea, is scattered with inexpensive 'seasonal' hotels, popular with Italians and backpackers in summer.

****Vittoria**, Via Vespucci 2, **t** 0721 34343, *www.viphotels.it* (€€€€€). One of the 'Hundred Historic Hotels of Italy', in a Belle Epoque villa along the beach strip. Rooms have period beds and hydromassage baths; there's also a pool, a sauna, a billiards room and a restaurant (half/full board available).

****Savoy**, Viale Repubblica 22, **t** 0721 67440, *www.viphotels.it* (€€€€). A modern hotel in a shady spot, with all mod cons, a pool, a sauna and a restaurant (half/full board available).

***Des Bains**, Viale Trieste 221, **t** 0721 34957, *www.innitalia.com* (€€€€). A quite characterful modern hotel. Rates include breakfast, and the restaurant offers full board.

***Villa Serena**, Via San Nicola 6, south of Pesaro, **t** 0721 55211, *www.villa-serena.it* (€€€€). A 17th-century palace in a scenic park, with fireplaces and antiques in the spacious rooms. There's a pool and a restaurant (half/full board available). *Closed 2wks Jan.*

***Abbazia**, Viale Trento 147, **t** 0721 33694, *www.apahotel.it* (€€€). A basic option offering full and half board. *Closed Oct–Easter.*

***Due Pavoni**, Viale Fiume 79, **t** 0721 370 105, *www.hotelduepavoni.com* (€€€). A place offering sea views and a friendly welcome near the *centro storico*. There's the option of full board in the restaurant.

Oasi San Nicola, Via S. Nicola 8, **t** 0721 50849, *wwwoasisannicola.it* (€€€). Good rooms, a pool and a restaurant (half/full board offered) in a quiet location south of town.

***Locanda da Ciacci**, Via Roma 105, Gallo, off SS423, **t** 0722 355030, *www.locandaciacci.com* (€€). An attractive villa with ensuite rooms (breakfast included) in a local style and a farm producing most of the ingredients for the restaurant, which offers *passatelli* and lots of meat, including stuffed pigeon and duck. *Closed 24 and 25 Dec.*

***Principe**, Viale Trieste 180, **t** 0721 30096 (€€). Modern, fairly comfy rooms on the waterfront, plus an excellent, popular restaurant, **Teresa**, offering enticing dishes such as lobster with truffles (half/full board available). *Restaurant closed Nov–Mar.*

Eating Out in Pesaro

The fishy local cuisine includes ravioli with sole fillets, *garagoli in porchetta* (shellfish with olive oil, garlic, rosemary and wild fennel), stuffed cuttlefish and red mullet with *prosciutto*. As for meat, try *olivette alla pesarese* (slices of veal in *prosciutto*, rolled and fried). All go nicely with the local white, Bianchello del Metauro.

Alceo, Strada Panoramica Ardizio 101, **t** 0721 51360 (€€€€). Fresh fish and home-made pasta and desserts served in a friendly atmosphere. Tables outside have sea views. *Closed Sun eve and Mon.*

Lo Scudiero, Via Baldassini 2, **t** 0721 64107 (€€€). The cellar of a 17th-century palace, in which you can enjoy specialities such as *tostarelli* with spinach, tomatoes and *pecorino*, grilled seabass , fish soup, and grilled pigeon. *Closed Sun, 1wk Jan, and July.*

Getting to and around the Montefeltro

There are 4 or 5 Fer **buses** (**t** 0541 25474, *www.fer-online.it*) daily from Rimini station to San Leo, via Pietracuta, Novafeltria and Pennabilli. Salvadori buses link Sassocorvaro to Pesaro. Baschetti buses (**t** 0575 749816, *www.baschetti.it*) take a very pretty route from Arezzo and Sansepolcro to Rimini, via the SS258, over the Alpe della Luna.

If you're **driving** from Urbino, you have a choice of squiggly routes – following the signs to Sassocorvaro, Macerata Feltria and Montecopiolo is the most direct.

Ask at Pennabilli tourist office (*see* p.597) for the map of **walking paths** around the area.

---

2 The Montefeltro

Montefeltro Fortresses

The winding roads leading from Urbino grow increasingly scenic as you approach **Sassocorvaro**, which has been dubbed the 'Sentinel of the Montefeltro' (population 3,500). Built around a spur over the river Foglia, the town has an artificial lake, **Mercatale**, named after the fairgrounds that it drowned. Sassocorvaro is topped by the 15th-century **Rocca Ubaldinesca** ①, an elegant round citadel with bulging towers, one of Francesco di Giorgio Martini's finest designs, commissioned by Duke Federico for one of his top commanders, Ottaviano degli Ubaldini. A spiral stair from the courtyard leads to a little theatre, added in the 1800s, and a museum with exhibits on country life and crafts. There are also copies of some of Italy's greatest paintings, stored here for safety during the Second World War.

Rocca Ubaldinesca
t 0722 76177; open April–Sept daily 9.30–12.30 and 3–7; Oct–Mar Sat and Sun 9.30–12.30 and 2.30–6; adm

There are castles wherever you turn. Though the Montefeltro proper is to the north and west of Sassocorvaro, you may want to take a detour (18km) northeast to **Tavoleto**, a titbit that was snatched from Rimini by Duke Federico in 1462. Although the fortress that defended Tavoleto collapsed in 1865, the fantastical **Castello dei Conti Petrangolini** ②, with its 52m tower and Ghibelline crenellations, bristles proudly intact.

Castello dei Conti Petrangolini
closed to public

Northwest of Sassocorvaro, **Macerata Feltria** inherited the site of *Pitinum Pisaurense*, a Roman foundation of the 3rd century AD crushed in the wars of the 6th. The upper part of town around the Malatesta castle has kept its medieval allure, with its walls, gate and 11th-century **Palazzo del Podestà** and **Torre Civica**, containing a hotchpotch of curiosities, including finds from Pitinum, Renaissance ceramics, a palaeontological collection and some medieval tombs. Macerata Feltria's oldest church is located on the fringe of town: 11th-century **San Cassiano in Pitino**, decorated in the 17th century, with Roman tombs in the garden.

Palazzo del Podestà/ Torre Civica
open June–Sept Tues–Sun4.30pm–7.30pm; Oct–May Sat and Sun 3.30pm–6.30pm; other times, call Giuseppe. Rossi on **t** *0722 74546 or* **t** *0722 73231; adm*

Southwest is **Piandimeleto** (from the Latin *Planus Mileti*), another unspoiled town with a late-15th-century castle, the **Castello dei Conti Oliva** ③, retaining original fireplaces and fittings, and now defender of a pair of **museums** about farm work and the geology of the Marches. The church is worth a look for its 14th-century frescoes and Gothic tombs.

Castello dei Conti Oliva
open by appt on **t** *0722 721528; adm*

North of Piandimeleto and west of Sassocorvaro rises majestic **Monte Carpegna** (1,415m). In 1996 this area, noted for its rare wild orchids, red lilies and falcons, became the **Parco Naturale del Sasso Simone e Simoncello**, named after two of its more prominent mesa-like crags, 'Big and Little Simon', west of Carpegna.

Parco Naturale del Sasso Simone e Simoncello
www.parcosimone.it

From Piandimeleto, stop at the 13th-century **Convento di Montefiorentino**, near Frontino, where the church has a beautiful Renaissance **Cappella dei Conti Oliva**, attributed to Francesco di Simone Ferrucci, and contains the tombs of its patrons.

Convento di Montefiorentino
t *0722 71202; open daily 8–12 and 3.30–6*

Carpegna, 6km north, is the most popular resort on the mountain, built round the vast, late Renaissance **Palazzo dei Principi Carpegna**; also see the little parish church **San Giovanni Battista**, built by travelling Lombard masters in 1182. From Carpegna a road wiggles up to a track just below the summit, for grandiose views across the Montefeltro and San Marino; in winter people come here to ski.

Pennabilli, just to the west, is an important market town under two crags, each of them capped by an 11th-century 'feather' or castle built by the Malatesta, named Penna and Billi. Billi, with a large convent clinging to its slope, now does service as a base for an iron cross, but Penna's castle is in pretty good nick, in the heart of the *centro storico*. Here you'll find a good Renaissance church, the **Santuario della Madonna delle Grazie**, with pretty frescoes, and the **Museo Diocesano** displaying art gathered from the Montefeltro's churches. Pennabilli runs a major antiques exhibition in July but likes new things, too; scattered across town are houses decorated with contemporary art, mostly imitations of famous paintings. Amongst these are the *Path of Sundials*, by contemporary poet Tonino Guerra, and the *Petrified Gardens*, the latter up by the 12th-century tower, standing like an exclamation mark on the next hill, at **Bascio**.

Museo Diocesano
t *0541 928469; open by appt*

Museo di Storia del Calcolo
t 0541 928659 or t 800 553800; open July and Aug daily 10.30–12.30 and 3.30–7.30; rest of year Sat, Sun and hols 10.30–12.30 and 3–6; or by appt; adm

Rocca Fregoso
t 0541 929111; open summer daily 10–1 and 3–7.30; winter daily 10–1 and 3–7; adm

Teatro A. Mariani
t 0541 848022; open by appt

Museo Storico Minerario
t 0541 927576; open Tues–Thurs, Sat and Sun 9–12 and 3–6; adm

Another of Pennabilli's *frazioni*, **Pontemessa**, has the **Museo di Storia del Calcolo**, dedicated to the evolution of calculation, from ancient times to modern computers, with software to play with.

A narrow mountain road runs north of Pennabilli to **Sant'Agata Feltria**, protected by the **Rocca Fregoso** ④, another fantastical castle built by Martini, precarious on its rock. Inside are some Renaissance frescoes, as well as some rather unexpected stained glass from various periods, and Liberty-style Art Nouveau ads and posters. The *municipio* houses a 17th-century wooden theatre, the **Teatro Angelo Mariani**, one of the oldest of its kind in Italy and still used. Sant'Agata comes into its own in autumn, when it holds a white truffle market on four consecutive Sundays, beginning with the second Sunday in October.

Just off the road from Sant'Agata to Novafeltria about 7km northeast, lofty **Perticara** (900m) is tucked under another rocky crag; it once made its living mining sulphur and keeps the now odour-free memory alive in its **Museo Storico Minerario**, containing the reconstruction of a gallery and an extensive mineral collection.

On the slopes of Mount Perticara 2km east, **Talamello** is another old hilltown, where they make a much-loved cheese matured in pits, *formaggio di fossa Ambra di Talamello*, best eaten when it emerges in November and December. The **church of San Lorenzo**, at the highest point of town, has frescoes by Antonio da Ferrara (1473).

Novafeltria is rather dull, but 4km south of it on the Pennabilli road you'll find **Santa Maria Antico**, a sandstone church dating from the 13th century, with a handsome marble lunette of the *Madonna del Soccorso* and another *Madonna* inside, complete with *Bambino*, by Luca della Robbia.

San Leo

The most extraordinary of all Montefeltro's extraordinary castles hangs high over the one and only entrance into San Leo, a road that had to be cut into the living rock. According to legend, San Leo was founded in the 4th century by St Leo of Dalmatia, a companion of Marinus (who founded San Marino). Pepin, father of Charlemagne, donated it to the Church and it briefly served as 'capital of Italy' in the 960s, during the undistinguished reign of King Berengarius II, who after a siege of two years, surrendered both San Leo and Italy to the German emperor Otto, who returned San Leo to the Church. Dante slept here and gave San Leo a mention in *Purgatory*; St Francis also wandered through and preached so convincingly that one of his listeners, the Count di Chiusi, gave him his beloved La Verna as a retreat.

Pieve
open summer daily 9–8; winter daily 9–6

For all that, San Leo is tiny, a huddle of stone houses balanced on the gentle slope of the stupendous crag. Its rough-walled **Pieve** is one of the oldest churches in the whole of the Marches;

the *ciborium* over the altar has an inscription to Christ and the Madonna dating from the year 882, dedicated by Duke Orso, who ruled San Leo for Pope John VIII.

Just above, the Romanesque **Duomo** was built by Lombard masters in 1173 in order to replace a 7th-century church, which was in turn built over a prehistoric shrine; its harmonious interior has some very old capitals, including a few Roman ones; in the crypt are a bas-relief and tomb of St Leo with a 6th-century inscription. The **Palazzo Mediceo** has temporary exhibits, and also houses the **Museo d'Arte Sacra** with artworks from the 14th–18th centuries, including a Botticelli-like *Madonna with SS. Leo and Marino* (1493) by Luca Frosino.

Palazzo Mediceo
t 0541 916306 or t 0541 926967; open Mon–Sat 9–6, Sun 9–6.30

Museo d'Arte Sacra
open daily 9.30–12.15 and 2.30–6.15; adm

Sant'Igne
t 0541 916277; visits by appt

The peaceful 13th-century **church and convent of Sant'Igne**, located 2km away from San Leo, was founded by St Francis on the spot where a miraculous light guided him to shelter when he was lost in the woods at night.

The Rocca di San Leo ⑤

Only one Pope, only one God, only one Fort – San Leo!
A Montefeltro saying

Rocca di San Leo
t 0541 926967 or t 800 553800; open July and Aug daily 9am–11pm; rest of year daily 9–7; adm

In Roman times, the tremendous pinnacle was known as *Mons Feretrius*, referring to Jove's lightning (another castle, on top of nearby Majolo, was blasted to ruins by a thunderbolt in the 1600s). There was probably a temple on top, perhaps of the same Jove Feretro to whom the Roman Consul Marcellus dedicated the corpse of the leader of the Gauls in the 3rd century BC. *Mons Feretrius* gave its name to *Montefeltro*, the old name of San Leo, and in 1158 to the ducal family who relocated to Urbino. In the 15th century, the Urbino dukes commissioned Francesco di Giorgio Martini to replace the old fortifications on the summit with the most spectacular castle in Italy, hung on a breathtakingly sheer cliff. The castle overlooks the whole of the Montefeltro and the three landmark towers of San Marino: in autumn, the region's landmark crags and castles rise over the rolling sea of fog like an enchanted archipelago.

Like the ducal palace at Urbino, Martini's **fortress** is a perfect representative building of the Renaissance: balanced, finely proportioned in its lines, a structure of intelligence and style. However, it proved to be not as impregnable as it looks – in 1523, after a four-month siege, the troops of Lorenzo de' Medici the Younger (made Duke of Urbino by his uncle, Leo X) captured it on a dark and stormy night by using ropes and ladders to scale the west face of the rock – an exploit that Vasari frescoed on to the walls of Florence's Palazzo Vecchio. The Medici were succeeded by the Della Rovere dukes and, when they died out, by the popes, under whom it became a notorious prison, the escape-proof Alcatraz of its day. Inside you can see Renaissance weapons, parts of the prison, the dungeon, charts of various nasty tortures, some

The Rise and Fall of Giuseppe Balsamo

Born into a poor family in Palermo in 1743, Giuseppe Balsamo began his career forging theatre tickets. The rest of his life reads as if concocted by a picaresque novelist on amphetamines. After outlandishly tricking a gullible goldsmith in Palermo with a ghost story, Giuseppe hooked up with a famous Armenian alchemist, Altolas, who took him to Greece, Egypt and Malta, where the Grand Master of the Knights let the two seek the philosopher's stone in his laboratory. Altolas accidently poisoned himself; Giuseppe, thanks to a forged letter, appeared in Rome, supported by the Maltese ambassador in his business of manufacturing love potions. He found a 14-year-old Roman intriguer, Lorenza Feliciani, to marry and, after several unsuccessful machinations, decided there was nothing to do but recreate himself with a new name: Count Alessandro Cagliostro, the greatest magician in Europe, born in Egypt and raised by alchemists, a man who personally assassinated Pompey and gave counsel to Jesus Christ.

After years of travelling around Europe, pimping for Lorenza, staying just ahead of the law or behind bars, and exciting debate as to whether he was a scoundrel, a sage, a prophet or the Antichrist, Cagliostro rocketed to fame and fortune in London in 1776 when he gave a couple the numbers that won them £2,000 in a lottery. All at once people were pounding on his door for his numbers, his elixir of Long Life and his love potions. When the numbers began to lose, Cagliostro retreated to the Continent, where he made a triumphal tour – he became a counsellor to Catherine the Great, healed the blind and crippled in Strasbourg, founded his own Masonic lodge and became the protégé of the cardinal of Rohan in Paris, one of the most powerful men and biggest dupes in France. Rohan was tricked into financing a diamond necklace for Marie Antoinette by a group of swindlers, who took the money and ran; when the queen got the bill, she had Louis XVI toss Rohan and Cagliostro into the Bastille. Ironically, it was the one time Cagliostro was innocent; he was soon acquitted.

Lorenza, however, had thought the gig was up and told the history of the Count's humble origins to a journalist in London. Cagliostro forgave her, and the two returned to Rome and lay low, until Cagliostro caused a sensation in Rome's Masonic Lodge in September 1789 when he hypnotized a girl who accurately predicted the start of the French Revolution. This caught the attention of the Inquisition, and Lorenza, immune to her husband's love potions, confessed that the Count was guilty of Freemasonry. This was enough to get him condemned to death by the Holy Office, a sentence Pope Pius VI commuted in 1791 to solitary confinement for life in the Rocca di San Leo. Cagliostro was placed in a normal cell, but the prison guards were so terrified of his evil eye that he was moved to a tiny, dark, rat-infested pit where he slowly went mad. He died of apoplexy four years later. According to the accounts preserved in San Leo's archives, as an unrepentant heretic he was buried somewhere near the fortress, in unconsecrated ground. When Napoleon showed up a few years later, he freed the pope's prisoners and asked to pay his respects at Cagliostro's grave, but no one could find it.

pieces of modern art, a series of illustrations of Dante's *Inferno*, and the cell where San Leo's most famous prisoner, Cagliostro (*see* box above), spent the last years of his life.

ⓘ **Carpegna >**
*Piazza Conti 1, **t** 0722 77153*

ⓘ **Pennabilli >>**
*Municipio, Piazza Garibaldi, **t** 0541 928659, www.cittapennabilli.it*

Where to Stay and Eat in the Montefeltro

Carpegna ✉ 61021

*****San Michele**, Via Amaducci 51, **t** 0722 77320, *www.hotelsmichele.com* (€€). Basic rooms (full board only) and apartments without TVs, plus a restaurant. *Closed Oct–May.*

*****Ulisse**, Via Amaducci 16, **t** 0722 77119, *www.hotelulisse.it* (€). A modern hotel next to the Palazzo dei Principi, with a swimming pool, mountainbikes and a restaurant (full board required). *Closed 2wks late Nov.*

***Onelia**, Via Amaducci 42/c, **t** 0722 77175 (€). Simple rooms, a restaurant (full board obligatory) and a beautiful garden. *Closed Oct–May.*

Pennabilli ✉ 61016

****Parco**, Via Marconi 14, **t** 0541 928446 (€). A comfy family-run option with a garden and a restaurant (full board obligatory). *Closed Nov–Jan.*

ⓘ **San Leo >>**
Palazzo Mediceo, Piazza Dante 14, **t** *0541 916306*

Piastrino, Via Parco Begni 9, **t** 0541 928569 (€€€–€€). The best food in town, served in a country house with a garden, just outside the *centro storico*. The Northern Marches cuisine features lots of truffles. *Closed Tues.*

Sant'Agata Feltria ✉ 61019

***__Falcon Hotel__, Viale S. Girolamo 30, just outside town, **t** 0541 929090, *www.falconhotel.it* (€€). A glossy modern hotel with a fitness centre, a garden with a view, a restaurant and parking. Breakfast is included; half and full board are offered.

***__Pian del Bosco__, Fraz. Perticara Pian del Bosco, Narafeltria, signposted off road . to Sant'Agata, **t** 0541 927600, *www.piandelbosco.com* (€€). A charming converted farmhouse with a swimming pool, football and tennis courts, a lively pizzeria and a restaurant. Breakfast is included, and half and full board are available.

Antenna >

Antenna, Montebenedetto 32, **t** 0541 929626 (€€). More a bar than a restaurant, offering home-made local cuisine. Call ahead in autumn for the *pièce de résistance* of chestnut-stuffed pheasant. *Closed Mon except July and Aug, and 3wks in Jan.*

San Leo ✉ 61018

Locanda San Leone, Strada Sant'Antimo 102, **t** 0541 912194, *www.locandasanleone.it* (€€€). A few rooms and a farm restaurant (€€; half board availabe) serving local cuisine featuring its own produce. *Restaurant closed Mon–Wed and Jan.*

__Il Castello__, Piazza Dante Alighieri 11–12, **t 0541 916214, *www.hotelristorantecastellosanleo.com* (€€). Comfortable rooms, breakfast included, and an excellent restaurant (half board available).

*__La Rocca__, Via G. Leopardi 16, **t** 0541 916241, *www.paginegialle.it/laroccasanleo* (€€). Simple ensuite rooms (breakfast included) and good home cooking featuring lots of truffles and mushrooms in season. *Secondi* include *pasticciata alla Cagliostro* – beef marinated in wine, with carrots, celery, onions and cloves. *Closed Mon exc July and Aug, and Dec and Jan exc hols.*

Il Bettolino, Via Montefeltro 4, **t** 0541 916265 (€). A bar-pizzeria-restaurant, plus a few guestrooms on the first floor (€€; breakfast included in rates). *Closed Wed.*

South of Urbino

The culture-loving dukes in Urbino had ants in their pants judging by how many *palazzi ducali* they required in their small realm. They took their artists and architects wherever they went, leaving behind some pleasant surprises tucked here and there.

The Upper Metauro Valley: Fermignano and Urbania

Fermignano, 5km south of Urbino, was the hometown of Mrs Bramante and is also believed to have been the birthplace of her High Renaissance architect son Donato, in 1444 (Urbania disputes that honour). Bramante met his much younger fellow Marchigiano Raphael in Rome, and is often credited with designing the architectural setting in Raphael's famous Vatican fresco, *The School of Athens* – a favour Raphael returned by painting Bramante into the scene as the geometer Euclid. In the centre, under a graceful medieval tower and bridge, is a small waterfall on the Metauro river.

In the upper Metauro Valley, just southwest of Urbino, **Urbania** was known as Castel Durante for most of its history; it was renamed in 1636 to flatter Pope Urban VIII, and the name stuck.

Getting to Fossombre and Cagli

Bucci **buses** (t 0721 32401, *www.autolineebucci.com*) from Pesaro serve Fossombrone and Cagli, via Fano, once daily, and there are buses from Urbino to Cagli too.

In the 15th century Castel Durante was famous for its majolica, made in more than 30 workshops, and the town has changed little since. The Porta Cella quarter, in particular, is evocative: a little octagonal temple, mostly destroyed in the last war, is said to have been an early work by Bramante. The **Palazzo Ducale** began as a 13th-century castle and was transformed for Duke Federico by Francesco di Giorgio Martini and Gerolamo Genga into an elegant residence, with a long, arcaded gallery overlooking the Metauro valley. In its heyday it hosted Ariosto, Tasso, Bembo and Cosimo I de' Medici's gallant father, Giovanni dalle Bande Nere; today, it hosts the **Museo Civico** and **Pinacoteca**, with Castel Durante ceramics, a large collection of drawings and engravings, and the remains of Duke Federico's famous library, including terrestrial and celestial globes by the famous geographer Mercatore (1541).

Museo Civico/ Pinacoteca
t 0722 313151; open summer Tues–Sun 10–12 and 3–6; adm

In Via Urbano VIII, the bishop's palace, another building beautifully 'Renaissanced' by Francesco di Giorgio Martini and Gerolamo Genga, contains the **Museo Diocesano** with more treasures: detached 14th-century frescoes, Romanesque capitals, a Paleochristian cross, paintings and more ceramics. The best work, a *Crucifixion* by Pietro da Rimini of 1320, is still in the Baroque **cathedral**. Urbania, like Ferentillo in Umbria, also has naturally preserved **mummies**, next to the **Chiesa dei Morti** beside San Francesco.

Museo Diocesano
t 0722 319555; open summer Tues–Sun 9–12 and 3–6; winter by request; adm

Chiesa dei Morti
t 349 8195469; open daily 10–12 and 3–6

Just outside town on the Sant'Angelo in Vado road, the Montefeltro dukes hunted in the **Parco Ducale**; their villa, begun by Francesco di Giorgio Martini and completed by Girolamo Genga, has ceramics.

Parco Ducale
to visit ask at tourist office, see p.601

Beyond Urbania, in all directions towards the Apennine peaks, villagers dream of the truffles they will find in autumn, like their counterparts over the mountains in Umbria. The October 'Sagra del Tartufo' is the big event of the year in **Sant'Angelo in Vado**, another exceptionally pretty village on the Metauro. Originally called *Tifernum Metaurensis* (to distinguish it from *Tifernum Tiberensis*, nearby Città di Castello in Umbria), it was the home of the Zuccari brothers, late Renaissance painters whose best works are in Rome. The small octagonal **church of San Filippo** has a wooden statue attributed to Lorenzo Ghiberti, who spent time wandering about the Marches in his early 20s, before the great Florentine baptistry door contest changed his life.

From here the SS73bis climbs over the mountains to Sansepolcro and Arezzo, passing the village of **Mercatello**; here one of the earliest Franciscan churches, 13th-century **San Francesco**, is a museum with late medieval works.

San Francesco
t 0722 89593; open by appt

Fossombrone

From Urbino, the SS73bis takes you southeast to the Metauro valley and Fossombrone (population 9,500), a busy workaday town with laundry flapping in the alleys and not a wine bar or olive-oil mill in sight. A Roman foundation that takes its name, *Forum Sempronii*, from famous reformer Sempronius Gracchus, Fossombrone is strikingly built in tiers over the Metauro. It once had pretensions to grandeur: impressive if tattered palaces line the arcaded Corso Garibaldi, including a sometime ducal residence, the Corte Bassa. Near the top of the town, under the citadel, a huge stepped ramp ascends to the **Corte Alta** (you can also drive up), a pint-sized *palazzo ducale* begun by the Malatesta in the 13th century, and sold with the rest of Fossombrone to Duke Federico of Urbino in 1466; the duke, as usual, got Francesco di Giorgio Martini and Girolamo Genga to remodel it according to the style he was rapidly becoming accustomed to. Now seat of the **Museo Civico** and **Pinacoteca Civica**, it has some good Renaissance pavements and ceilings. It also houses a small archaeological museum with busts and fragments of Roman sculpture, ceramics and coins, as well as paintings and etchings by Dürer, Rembrandt and Tiepolo. There's a fine view over Fossombrone's tile roofs, punctured here and there with big cylindrical apses of churches. You can see more art – 19th-century and modern Italian works (De Chirico, Umberto Boccioni, Marino Marini, and so on) – in the **Museo Cesarini**, in the Renaissance Palazzo Pergamino on Via Pergamino 32, outside the centre in the direction of Urbino.

Museo Civico/ Pinacoteca Civica
t 0721 714645; open Sat 3–6, Sun 10.30–12.30 and 3–6; adm to both; joint ticket available with Museo Cesarini

Museo Cesarini
t 0721 714650; open Sat 3–6, Sun 10.30–12.30 and 3–6; adm; joint ticket available with Museo Civico and Pinacoteca Civica

The Gola del Furlo

Southwest 10km of Fossombrone, a little stream, the Candigliano, has spent aeons pounding out a steep gorge, the Gola del Furlo, a wild, rocky landscape that provides a striking contrast to the gently sculpted farmlands beyond. A road has traversed the gorge since ancient times, including a small tunnel cut in the rock by the Consul Flaminius in 217 BC, when he laid out the Via Flaminia; traffic had increased so much by the 1st century AD that a larger tunnel, the 176m **Galleria del Furlo**, was built by Emperor Vespasian. It's still in use. Despite the traffic, the Furlo is home to wildlife, including a few of Italy's rare *aquila reale* (royal eagles; *see* p.637).

Mussolini constructed the tall dam and power plant at the end of the Gola del Furlo; later, passing through during one of his endless trips around Italy in his red Alfa Romeo, he became enamoured of the region and stopped in often for short holidays. To make him feel at home, the local fascists sculpted one of the Furlo's cliffs into the dictator's profile. It can still be seen, from a point near the village of **Acqualagna** – it's a bit hard to make out, since resistance fighters blew his nose off with dynamite after the war. Acqualagna is famous for truffles, both black and white; they are a must-buy for gastronomes.

Cagli and Around

Cagli, 9km south of Aqualagna, is known for craftwork in wrought iron, and has a modest collection of monuments – late Gothic details in the **cathedral and church of San Francesco**, a late Renaissance portal by the Roman architect Vignola on **Sant'Angelo Minore**, a painting by Raphael's dad, Giovanni Santi, in **San Domenico**, and yet another palace of Duke Federico (1463), now the **town hall**. They make a pleasant ensemble in the shadow of the **Torrione**, an elliptical defence tower built for the insatiable Montefeltro dukes by the unflagging Francesco di Giorgio Martini.

A road full of hairpin turns scales **Monte Petrano** (1,120m), which overlooks Cagli from the south, near the border with Umbria; a detour along the side road up to it will bring you out on to some green alpine meadows, full of wildflowers in spring and sheep in summer. The SS3, the Via Flaminia, continues south of Cagli into Umbria – towards Gubbio, with yet another ducal palace (*see* p.484) and the **Parco Naturale di Monte Cucco** and ancient hermitage of **Fonte Avellana** (*see* p.486).

Museo dei Bronzi Dorati e della Città di Pergola
t 0721 734090; open Jan–Mar, Nov and Dec Tues–Sun 10–12.30 and 3.30–6; April–June, Sept and Oct Tues–Sun 10–12.30 and 3.30–6.30; July and Aug daily 10–12.30 and 3.30–7; adm

Pergola (population 7,000), 20km east of Cagli, or south of Fossombrone, is the big town in the area, founded in the 13th century by the lords of Gubbio, who invited everyone in hilltop castles to move down into the little plain. Later part of the duchy of Urbino, it won a gold medal for its bravery in the Risorgimento. It also has a superb set of gilded bronze **Roman statues** (two female figures and two horsemen) from the 1st century AD, found just north in Cartoceto in 1946 and displayed in the **Museo dei Bronzi Dorati e della Città di Pergola** on Largo San Giacomo. Pergola's **cathedral** was built in 1258 but overhauled in the 19th century; only a Gothic reliquary and a 14th-century *Crucifixion* escaped the renovation squads.

Where to Stay and Eat South of Urbino

ⓘ Fermignano >
Via Bramante 9, t 0722 330523, www.proloco-fermignano.it

Fermignano ✉ 61033

*****Bucci**, Via dell'Industria 13, **t** 0722 356050 (€€). A modern, fairly functional option in a quiet location, with simple but comfy rooms, a bar and a private garage.

ⓘ Urbania >
Corso Vittorio Emanuele II 27, t 0722 313140

Urbania ✉ 61049

****Bramante**, Via Roma, **t** 0722 319562, *albergobramante@virgilio.net* (€). A pleasant hotel, always good value.

Big Ben, Corso Vittorio Emanuele 61, **t** 0722 319795 (€€). A 17th-century palace in which you can enjoy dishes featuring *porcini*, truffle and meats, or pizzas or vegetarian recipes, accompanied by a bottle from the good wine list. *Closed Wed, lunch, 2wks Jan and 2wks July or Sept.*

Osteria del Cucco, Via Betto de' Medici 9, **t** 0722 317 412 (€€). An old-fashioned family-run tavern without any sign outside, and wooden tables within. There's no menu, just daily specials. *Closed Sun eve, Mon, 2wks Jan and 2wks July.*

ⓘ **Fossombrone >**
*Via C. Battisti, **t** 0721 740377, and Piazza Dante, **t** 0721 716324*

ⓘ **Cagli >>**
*Via Leopardi 3, **t** 0721 787457*

Fossombrone ✉ 61034

*****Al Lago**, Via Cattedrale 79, Loc. San Lazzaro, **t** 0721 726 129, *www.albergoristoranteallago.com* (€). A pleasant, modern, family-run place in a quiet spot by the bottom of the Gola del Furlo, with a large garden, tennis court, pool and restaurant serving local cuisine (half and full board available). *Closed Christmas; restaurant closed Sat.*

Symposium Quattro Stagioni, Via Cartoceto 38; take *superstrada* to Fano, then follow signs to Calcinelli and Cartoceto, **t** 0721 898320 (€€€€). One of the best restaurants in the region, with a panoramic view and 4 *menu degustazione*. Highlights are the cheese *cappelletti* with asparagus and black truffles, guinea fowl with vegetables, steak with potatoes, truffles and saffron, and white chocolate soufflé. *Closed Sat and Sun eves, Mon and Tues, and Jan.*

Cagli ✉ 61043

Guazza, Piazza Federico da Montefeltro, **t** 0721 787 231 (€€). Unbeatable country lunches involving home-made pasta and fragrant *porcini* mushrooms. Try the local speciality, *fricò* – lamb, chicken and rabbit doused in wine and vinegar and fried with garlic; it's good with the house wine. *Closed eves, all Fri and July.*

Back on the Coast: South from Pesaro

South of Pesaro, the string of Adriatic resorts continues. Fano and Senigallia are not mere seaside playgrounds, however, but also fine old towns, members of the Byzantine/medieval Adriatic Pentapolis.

Fano

Older even than the Romans, Fano (population 54,000) took its name – *Fanum Fortunae* – from a famous temple of the goddess Fortuna. Under Roman rule, it became the most important of the Marches' coastal cities, as the terminus of the Via Flaminia from Rome. Its *centro storico* still looks like the perfect provincial Roman town: the right size, with its grid plan (there's even a copy of a Roman milestone at the meeting of the *cardo* and *decumanus*, modern Via Arco di Augusto and Corso Matteotti) and severe brick buildings.

Palazzo Malatestiano
t 0721 828362; open July and Aug Tues, Thurs and Fri 9–12.30 and 4–7, Wed and Sat 9–12.30, 4–7 and 9pm–11pm, Sun 10–1; rest of year Tues–Sat 9–12.30 and 4–7, Sun 10–1; adm

Today, in central Piazza XX Settembre, a 1500s statue of Fortune (now a copy) decorates the pretty **Fontana della Fortuna**. Behind it is the **Palazzo della Ragione** (1299), an austere Romanesque Gothic hall, linked by an arch with the **Palazzo Malatestiano**, built in the 1420s, when Fano was ruled by Rimini's tyrant Pandolfino Malatesta III, father of bad boy Sigismundo. It has a lovely courtyard with crenellations, mullioned windows and a portico; the elegant loggia, attributed to Jacopo Sansovino, was added in 1544. Inside is a small picture collection, including a fine polyptych (1420) by Venetian Michele Giambono, an *Enthroned Madonna* by Giovanni Santi, a crowded *Annunciation* by a local 16th-century painter, Domenico Sacchetta, works by Renaissance tail-enders Guido Reni and Guercino (including the *Guardian Angel* that inspired Browning's sentimental classic of the same name after a visit in 1848), small bronzes of the ancient Piceni and the original statue of Fortuna.

Santa Maria Nuova
Via dei Pili; open daily 10–12 and 4–6

Santa Maria Nuova, two blocks south, is decorated with stuccoes and altarpieces by Perugino (a lovely *Annunciation* and *Madonna and Saints*) and Giovanni Santi, one with a small predella panel attributed to Raphael, who was there with his father; it's possible this is where he first met his future master. The Romans tell us Vitruvius built a famous basilica in Fana; though time has obliterated all traces of it, the overgrown, roofless ruins of the 14th-century **basilica of San Francesco** offer an evocative replacement, especially where its massive Corinthian columns support the **Portico della Sopressa** – a surprise on the narrow Via S. Francesco. The portico holds the **Arche Malatestiane**: the Renaissance tomb of Pandolfo III Malatesta (1460) attributed to Alberti and, on the left, a more elaborate Gothic model in pink and white marble of his wife Paola Bianca (1421) by Filippo di Domenico.

Fano does preserve a genuine relic of its Roman days, a stately gate of the year AD 2, the **Arco di Augusto**, marking the end of the Via Flaminia. Next to it is the airy **Logge di San Michele** (1495), used for market stalls, and the **church of San Michele** with a relief carved on its façade showing how the arch looked before having its block knocked off with artillery in 1463. The besieging *condottiere* who bombarded it, eventually successfully, was none other than Duke Federico of Urbino, working at that time for the pope; the defender was Sigismondo Malatesta of Rimini. Another corner of the walls is occupied by a 15th-century **Rocca Malatestiana**, built by Pandolfo III, once used as a prison and now hosting special exhibitions.

Fano's **Lido**, modern and a little overbuilt, is one of the better resorts on the Adriatic, but the long, broad beach continues down the coast for kilometres, through the suburbs of Torrette and Marotta, and there's room for all, all the way to Senigallia.

Senigallia

Senigallia (population 41,000), next down the coast, was one of the first resorts. Its long 'velvet beach', one of the best along this coastline, has a recently restored Art Deco *Rotunda a Mare* (1933) on piers and an enormous modern pyramid thingamabob on its north end. Before sun and fun, Senigallia was best known for its duty-free port, the site of an important annual trade fair that attracted some 500 ships from the 12th to the 18th century.

Rocca Roveresca
t 071 662 9348; open summer Mon–Sat 9–1 and 5–10, Sun 9–1; winter Tues–Sat 9–1 and 3–7, Sun 9–1; adm

The centre of town, divided by a canal, has an elegant fortress, the **Rocca Roveresca**, which was built by Laurana for Duke Federico's della Rovere son-in-law in 1480. It has sumptuous Renaissance interiors and was a nasty prison used by the popes. There's a fountain with four lions in the adjacent Piazza Ducale, with yet another down-at-heel 16th-century ducal palace, and, from the same century, the **Palazzo Baviera**, now the town hall, with gloriously stuccoed ceilings.

Prominent next to all this is a vast brick hemicycle of unfulfilled expectations, the **Foro Annonario** (the Roman name for the Marches), a market built in the 19th century after the great trade fair had already ended, as if wishing could somehow bring back the ships. Perhaps Senigallia still believed that producing a pope – Pius IX, or Pio Nono as Italians call him – was equivalent to winning the sweepstakes and dreamed of all the goodies that would trickle down from Rome. Sadly, it was a lousy time to pontificate – though Pio Nono declared the doctrine of papal infallibility in 1869, Rome (as the last vestige of the old Papal States) fell to the Italians the next year, forcing Pius, and all subsequent popes until the Lateran accords, to become 'a prisoner' in the Vatican. The pope's family palace, the **Palazzo Mastai** (behind the *municipio*) has the small **Museo Pio Nono**. The **Collezione Ducati** has examples of nearly every Ducati motorcycle ever produced.

Museo Pio Nono
t 071 60649; open Mon–Sat 9–12 and 4–6

Collezione Ducati
t 071 660 9654; open Mon–Sat 10–12 and 5–7, Sun by appt

You can seek out two bristling walled towns in the hinterland of Senigallia. The first, **Corinaldo** (21km) claims not only some of the best-preserved fortifications in the Marches but also the reliquary with one arm of one of the region's newest saints, Maria Goretti (in her **Casa Natale**, well signposted out of the centre on Via Pregiegna). Maria was a pious illiterate 12-year-old knifed to death in 1902 after refusing the advances of a young swain. When canonized in 1950, she had nearly 50 miracles under her small belt, and her parents and murderer were among the crowd attending the Vatican ceremony.

Another 9km bring you to **Mondavio**, the mountain of birds (*Mons avium*), with ancient walls crowned by a **Rocca**, built by Francesco di Giorgio Martini for Duke Federico in 1482; its studied elegance is only emphasized by the queerest-shaped defence tower in all Italy. Within, the **Museo di Rievocazione Storica e Armeria** has arms and armour from the 15th to 18th centuries.

Museo di Rievocazione Storica e Armeria
t 0721 977331; open Mon–Sat 10–12 and 4–6, Sun and hols 9–12 and 3–7; adm

Back on the coast towards Ancona, at the mouth of the river Esino, **Falconara Marittima** is a dull industrial town with a beach, Ancona's airport and a kiddie park, the **Paese dei Bimbi**. The original village, **Falconara Alta**, 2km inland, enjoys fine views, and there's a heavily restored medieval castle up the river.

ⓘ **Fano ›**
Viale Cesare Battisti 10, t 0721 803534, www.turismofano.com (closed Sun afternoon)

Where to Stay and Eat in Fano and Senigallia

Fano ✉ 61032

Fano boasts the cheapest, tastiest seafood in the Marches.

******Augustus**, Via Puccini 2, **t** 0721 809781, *www.hotelaugustus.it* (€€€). A central, family-run hotel with all mod cons, a fitness centre and bike loan. The restaurant serves fish and more creative dishes; half and full board are available. *Restaurant closed Sun and 2wks Dec/Jan.*

*****Angela**, Viale Adriatico 13, **t** 0721 801239, *www.hotelangela.it* (€€). Modern rooms overlooking the beach, plus a seafood restaurant (half/full board offered). *Closed Christmas–New Year; restaurant also closed Mon.*

*****Astoria**, Viale Cairoli 86, **t** 0721 803474, *www.hotelastoriafano.it* (€€). A pleasant hotel on the best part of the beach, with a restaurant (half/full board available), babysitting, a volleyball court and sailing facilities. *Closed mid-Oct–mid-Nov*.

****Mare**, Viale C. Colombo 20, **t** 0721 805667 (€). A homely *pensione* just off the beach, where mamma Anna cooks some of the best and most affordable seafood (€€) in Fano (half/full board available). *Closed Mon*.

Ristorantino Giulio, Viale Adriatico 100, **t** 0721 805680 (€€). A reliable little favourite, serving fresh, tasty seafood in the Marchigiano style: try the fish soup and the *fusilli con le canocchie* (a local shrimp). Book in advance. *Closed Tues and Nov*.

Pesce Azzurro, Viale Adriatico 48, near port, **t** 0721 803165 (€). A self-service restaurant unique in all Italy, founded by the local fishermen's cooperative to promote 'blue fish' – sardines, anchovies, mackerel and other small fish – washed down with local Bianchello del Metauro. *Closed Mon exc eves June–Aug, and Oct–May*.

Uliassi >>

Pesce Azzurro >

Madonnina del Pescatore >>

Senigallia >
Piazza Morandi 2, t 071 792 2725, www.senigalliaturismo.it (closed Sun afternoon in summer, Sun. Mon, and Wed, Fri and Sat afternoon in winter)

Senigallia ✉ 60019

******Duchi della Rovere**, Via Corridoni 3, **t** 071 792 7623, *www.hotelduchidellarovere.it* (€€€€). A stylish hotel with all mod cons, by the park a couple of blocks in from the beach. Breakfast is included, and there's a pool and a restaurant (full board available). *Closed Christmas*.

*****Cristallo**, Lungomare Alighieri 2, by rotunda, **t** 071 792 5767, *www.h-cristallo.it* (€€€). A typical resort hotel with rooms with balconies (breakfast included), a roof terrace for drinks in the sun, and a good restaurant (full board offered).

*****La Vela**, Piazzale N. Bixio 35, **t** 071 792 7444, *www.lavelasenigallia.it* (€€€). Comfortable rooms near the port, breakfast included, plus a garden and a good restaurant (full board offered). *Closed Oct–April*.

Uliassi, Via Banchina di Levante 6, **t** 071 65463 (€€€€). A classy place for creative seafood, including a fabulous fish soup, and 4 tasting menus, based around the speciality here, cod.

Madonnina del Pescatore, Lungomare Italia 11, Marzocca, 7km south, **t** 071 698267 (€€€). Brilliant seafood, both traditional and creative, and some of the best desserts in all the Marches. Try the sushi dishes. Book ahead. *Closed Mon, Easter wk, 1 wk Sept and middle 2wks Nov*.

Osteria Del Teatro, Via Fratelli Bandiera 70, **t** 071 60517 (€€). Simple tasty dishes near Senigallia's Teatro La Fenice. *Closed lunch, Wed and 2wks June*.

Osteria del Tempo Perso, Via Mastai 53, **t** 071 60345 (€€). The place for a change from seafood, including veggie dishes and *maltagliati* with wild boar and peas. *Closed Wed in winter*.

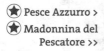

Inland from Falconara: Valle dell'Esino

The Esino is the one of the Marches' most important valleys, with a busy train line and road and clusters of industry. It marked the ancient frontier between the Gauls (north) and Piceni (south), and was busy in the 12th century: in 1126, near the bottom of the valley, 9km inland from Falconara, the Cistercians built one of the first Gothic churches in Italy, **Santa Maria di Castagnola** at **Chiaravalle** – Italian for *Clairvaux*, where St Bernard founded the Order a few years before. Funded by Countess Matilda of Tuscany, the church is as severe as Bernard himself, with only a rose window for decoration.

Jesi

The Valle dell'Esino is named for Jesi (population 40,000, pronounce it 'Yea si'), founded by the Umbrii and called *Aesis* by the Romans, set on a narrow ridge between well-preserved walls, with

Getting to and around the Valle d'Esino

There are several **trains** a day on the Ancona– Rome line, stopping at Jesi, Genga and Fabriano. Crognaletti **buses** (**t** 0731 204965, *www.autolineecrognaletti.it*) go between Ancona and Jesi (at least hourly Mon–Sat, several times on Sun), as well as between Jesi and much of the valley (Mon–Sat).

---

houses built on and over their tops, overlooking the industry that has made Jesi the 'little Milan of the Marches.' The *centro storico*, however, hasn't changed much since the 18th century, after centuries of evolution around a necklace of theatrical squares: in the uppermost, once the Roman forum/market square, Constance de Hauteville, aged 40 and after nine years of marriage to Emperor Henry VI of Hohenstaufen, was on her way home to Sicily on 26 December 1194 when she was unexpectedly assailed by labour pains. She ordered a huge tent to be erected in the square and invited in every matron in town and 19 churchmen to witness the birth and testify to the legitimacy of her son, the future Emperor Frederick II, the medieval *Splendor Mundis*. The discreetly Baroque square was renamed **Piazza Federico II** and the exact spot of the tent marked by an obelisk in 1845, flanked by eight lions from an older fountain. Arch-rival of the popes, Frederick later favoured Jesi and confirmed the town's ancient privileges.

A few clues lead one to suspect that the citizens found their centuries of papal rule a grating experience: the former headquarters of the Inquisition in the piazza wears a plaque in honour of Giordano Bruno, 'Martyr to Free Thought', which was put up by the citizens in 1889. Opposite, a former seminary holds the small **Museo Diocesano**, containing works by Ercole Ramazzani, who was a student of Lorenzo Lotto.

Museo Diocesano
t 0731 56625; open July–Sept Tues, Thurs and Fri 6pm–11pm; rest of year Tues and Sat 10–12, Thurs 4.30pm–7.30pm

In Piazza Colocci, the elegant **Palazzo della Signoria** with its clocktower was begun in 1486 by Francesco di Giorgio Martini and wears Jesi's proud *stemma* over the portal, a giant lion rampant, paws up, ready to box all-comers; the papal keys added later have been carefully effaced. Overlooking the next square, irregular Piazza Indipendenza, is the 16th-century **Palazzo Ricci**, with its striking waffle-iron façade like the Gesù Nuovo in Naples. Near the entrance of the adjacent **Palazzo del Comune** is the engraved text of a letter to Jesi from Stupor Mundis.

Teatro Pergolesi
open for 30min or 1hr guided tours (in English if required) by appt at least 5 days in advance on **t** *0731 215643; adm*

Sale Pergolesiane
t 0731 538355; open Mon, Wed, Fri and Sat 10–1, Tues and Thurs 10–1 and 4–6

Besides the most extraordinary of medieval emperors, Jesi also gave birth to Giambattista Pergolesi in 1710, who started composing at age 16 and died at age 26 but managed in that brief span to produce some perennial favourites of the Italian repertoire: the *Stabat Mater*, the *Frate 'nnammorato* and *La Serva Padrona*. Go through the arch to Piazza della Repubblica to see the fancy late-18th-century **Teatro Pergolesi**. Upstairs next door are the **Sale Pergolesiane**, with odds and ends from the composer's life.

Pinacoteca e Musei Civici
t 0731 538343; open summer Tues–Sun 10–8; winter Tues–Sat 10–1 and 4–7, Sun and hols 10–1 and 5–8; adm; joint ticket available with Pinacoteca and Museo Archeologico

Jesi's real treasure, the **Pinacoteca e Musei Civici**, is in a palace in Via XX Settembre. The Pianetti, the local nobles who built it in 1720, hired Placido Lazzarini to supply the decoration, and he gave them a delightful **Rococo gallery** overlooking the garden, 70m of pink and lavender stuccoes, symbolizing the 'human adventure in time and space' – lobsters, drums, camels, snakes, and just about everything else. Aside Renaissance sculpture, ceramics, archaeological finds and a small modern art gallery, most of the collection is from the same period. The highlight is a set of paintings by Lorenzo Lotto, some of his finest work, including the strange, beautifully lit *Annunciation* (1526) in two panels – Gabriel, his expression uncertain as he alights on earth, and Mary, in terror, even more uncertain – compare it to his more famous *Annunciation* in Recanati (*see* p.625). Other works, all from the same period, include *Santa Lucia in Judgement*, with a good *predella* of scenes from the life of St Lucy; a *Sacra Conversazione*, with the Virgin and Saints, a soft, luxurious work in Lotto's finest style, and a *Visitation* with scattered petals on the floor. Lotto, a tempermental character wandering through the Marches (he was from Venice, until Titian's gang ran him out of town) had a hard time earning a living, perhaps because patrons never knew if they would get something great or mediocre; one wonders if the fallen petals and torn papers so often littering his paintings were the signature of a troubled soul.

San Marco
t 0731 4804; open Mon–Sat 8.30–11.30 and 4–5.30, Sun 9–11.30 and 4.30–5.30

Outside the walls, the 13th-century Benedictine Gothic **church of San Marco** has exceptional early-14th-century frescoes by painters from Rimini, In the manner of Giotto.

Around Jesi

Museo Beltrami
open by appt on t 071 722 1314 or t 071 33037

Museo Utensilia
t 0731 63824; open April–June Sun 10.30–12.30 and 3.30–6.30; July and Aug Fri and Sun 5pm–8pm, Sat 5pm–8pm and 9pm–11pm; Sept–Dec Sun 10.30–12.30 and 3.30–6.30; adm

It's 14km south to **Filottrano**, a fine old brick town with a surprise: the **Museo Beltrami**, where antique carts and wagons share space with Mississippi Indian artefacts, collected by a local man named Giacomo Beltrami in the 1820s, while in exile for having served in the revolutionary government during the Napoleonic Wars.

North of Jesi, a very pretty drive skirts the hills, passing **Belvedere Ostrense** with its crumbling octagonal church, the **Madonna del Sole**, and **Ostra** (18km) a typically pink brick village in its little walls. Nearby **Morro d'Alba** has a well-preserved medieval centre, more picturesque walls and the **Museo Utensilia** of old farm tools.

The Upper Valle dell'Esino to the Grotte di Frasassi

From Jesi, the SS76 winds up through the rolling vineyards that produce the excellent DOC region Verdicchio dei Castelli di Jesi – crisp and clear with green highlights, quaffed young and cold, a great thirst-quencher and just the ticket with seafood, especially the local *brodetto di pesce*. It's powerful stuff: in 410, the Visigoth king Alaric took along several barrels 'to improve his manly vigour' when he passed through: he then sacked Rome. The main castles of the Castelli di Jesi, **Rosora** and **Mergo**, are here on the SS76, before the looming mountains are sliced by another dramatic limestone gorge, **Gola della Rossa**, with the fabulous Grotte di Frasassi (*see* below) on the west end.

If you're not hurrying, you can best take in this beautiful area on a circular route, turning north up the side road just before the entrance to the gorge, to **Serra San Quirico**, a 14th-century village shaped like a ship riding the sheer rocks. Part of its defences include lanes covered by houses, the *copertelle*. From here, the road winds to the medieval village of **Arcevia**, the impregnable 'Pearl of the Mountains' on a crag, with a fortified gate, Palazzo Comunale and tower, and nine other towers. The **church of San Medardo** is surprisingly rich, with a wooden choir of 1490, a majolica altar by Giovanni della Robbia (1512), and a polyptych and *Baptism of Jesus* by Luca Signorelli. Arcevia's public gardens, dedicated to Leopardi, once belonged to a 16th-century villa.

Museo Archeologico Sentinate
*Piazza Matteotti, **t** 0732 956230/1; open Tues, Thurs, Sat and Sun 10.30–12.30 and 4–7; Wed and Fri 10.30–12.30; adm*

Museo d'Arte Sacra
***t** 0732 97211; closed for restoration at time of writing*

Grotte di Frasassi
***t** 0732 97211 (info), **t** 0732 90080 (bookings); open for 70min tours **Mar–July, Sept and Oct** daily 9.20, 11, 12.30, 3, 4.30 and 6; **Aug** daily every 10mins 8–6.30; **Nov, Dec, few days in Jan, and Feb** Mon–Fri 11 and 3, Sat 11, 12.30, 3 and 4.30, Sun 9.30, 11, 12.30, 3, 4.30 and 6; joint adm with Museo d'Arte Sacra di Genga and Museo Speleopaleontologico; temperature inside is about 14°C, so bring a sweater*

From Arcevia, it's 12km west to **Sassoferrato** (population 8,000), a venerable town along the Marena best known for the artist who took its name, Giovanni Battista Salvi, born here in 1609. His deliberately archaic paintings are more reminiscent of Perugino than his own century; the **church of Santa Chiara** has two *Madonnas* by his hand, although his best work resides in Rome.

Mosaics, marbles and other bits excavated from the first town on this site, Umbrii-Roman *Sentinum*, are in the **Museo Archeologico Sentinate**, in the 14th-century Palazzo dei Priori. *Sentinum* witnessed two battles that changed the course of history: the defeat by the Romans of the Gauls and Samnites in 295 BC, securing their possession of central Italy, and one that resulted in the death of Totila in 553, marking the end of the Greek-Gothic wars that ravaged the country.

A panoramic road descends from Sassoferrato to the castle and village of **Genga**, the birthplace of Pope Leo XII (1823–29), who is fondly remembered in the **Museo d'Arte Sacra** in Largo Leone XII. It also has with a quattrocento tryptych, and a *Madonna* from Canova's workshop.

Further down, near Genga train station and the west end of the Gola della Rossa, are a series of magnificent caves, the **Grotte di Frasassi**, the largest karstic complex discovered in Italy, extending over 18km, with a spectacular display of glistening pastel stalactites reflected in calcareous pools; the tour takes in the first 1.6km. The massive **Grotta Grande del Vento**, the 'Cave of the Winds', rising 240m from the ground, was only discovered in 1971.

Museo Speleo-paleontologico
open Mar–July, Sept and Oct daily 10–1 and 1.30–5.30; Aug daily 8–8; Nov–Feb Mon–Fri 12–3, Sat and hols 10.30–12.30 and 1.30–5.30; joint adm with Grotte di Frasassi and Museo d'Arte Sacra di Genga

Grotta del Santuario
open daily dawn–dusk

Near Genga station and a spa with a sulphurous spring, San Vittore Terme is an impressive 10th-century temple showing an unusual combination of Romanesque and Byzantine influences, square in shape, decorated with Lombard blind arcades, a triple apse and corner towers, an octagonal cupola and a huge, squat campanile. The church's former abbey contains the **Museo Speleopaleontologico**, dedicated to the natural history of the caves. There's a rather less spectacular cave, a kilometre's walk uphill, the **Grotta del Santuario**, named for its octagonal domed church by Valadier (1828) with a *Madonna* sculpted by Canova.

Fabriano, City of Paper

Handsome, medieval Fabriano, capital of the upper Esine (population 28,700), was another victim of the 1997 quake; many buildings were left unsound. A lot of scaffolding remains, and many museums and churches are closed. Away from the media spotlight on Umbrian towns such as Assisi, funds have been less readily available and restoration is slow.

Fabriano was one of the first European cities to manufacture paper, at the end of the 12th century – an art that passed from Central Asia to Egypt in the 9th century, and was then introduced into Spain by the Moors, who were making it in Andalucía by the 1150s. Two centuries later, Fabriano is recorded as exporting a million sheets a year, especially to Florence and Venice, leaders in the medieval book trade: today Fabriano's biggest mill, Miliani, rolls out an amazing 965km of paper a day. The watermark (*filigrana*), and various other papermaking techniques were invented here, and, typical of the tenacity of craftwork in many Italian towns, Fabriano still makes its living from the stuff, using modern methods as well as old-fashioned artisan techniques. The most important use for speciality paper is banknotes; besides supplying the Italian treasury, Fabriano paper changes hands each day from Kashmir to the Congo. On the edge of the historic centre, by the public gardens, the San Domenico convent has been restored by the Miliani mill as the **Museo della Carta e della Filigrana** to tell you how it's done. The museum staff hold the key for the **church of San Domenico**, with frescoes from the 1300s, notably those in the chapel of Sant'Orsola.

Museo della Carta e della Filigrana
t 0732 709297; open daily 9.30–7.30; adm

The town centre is a beautiful stage set focused on the arcaded **Piazza del Comune**, with a crenellated **Palazzo del Podestà** (1250), a **Palazzo Comunale** and the **Fontana Sturinalto** (1281–1351), strangely reminiscent of those in Perugia. Opposite is a 19th-century theatre and the 17th-century **Loggia di San Francesco** (shored up with breeze blocks and covered in scaffolding) housing the **Grande Museo**, which has an electronic King Kong, dinosaurs and other life-size 'creatures of horror', plus masks, mysteries, birds, tools, crime, prehistory and memories of old Fabriano.

Grande Museo
t 0732 5726; open Sun and hols 5pm–8pm

Fabriano was home to a school of painting that produced one of Italy's most influential International Gothic artists, Gentile da Fabriano (*c.* 1370–1427), master of the famous *Adoration of the Magi* in the Uffizi, though his major works (frescoes in the Lateran in Rome and the Doge's Palace in Venice) have been lost; if he left anything in Fabriano, it's been lost as well. But there are paintings by other 14th-century members of the school (Allegretto Nuzi, Antonio da Fabriano and Francesuccio di Cecco), along with some detached frescoes and 16th-century Flemish tapestries, in the **Pinacoteca Civica Bruno Molajoli**. While it's being restored, many works are displayed in the **church of San Domenico** and the **Deposito Altrezzato Opera d'Arte**, which also houses works moved from churches after the quake. The Pinacoteca occupies the former **Ospedale di Santa Maria** (1456), with a fine portico facing Piazza della Cattedrale and the glisteningly restored 14th-century **Cattedrale Basilica di San Venanzio**. Rebuilt in 1607, this retains some of its original chapels and its tall polygonal apse; there are frescoes on the *Life of St Lawrence* by Fabriano's Allegretto Nuzi and others in a chapel on the left by Orazio Gentileschi, who worked in the Marches in 1615.

Pinacoteca Civica Bruno Molajoli
t 0732 709223; closed for restoration at time of writing

San Domenico
open Tues–Sun 10–6

Deposito Altrezzato Opera d'Arte
Via Fontanelle, t 0732 709230 or t 0732 709319; open Tues–Sun 10–12.30 and 3–7

Cattedrale Basilica di San Venanzio
open daily 9–12.30 and 4–7.30

Piazza della Cattedrale is one of the prettiest squares in tidy Fabriano. Note the proud 'SPQF' on the fountain and decorative blacksmith's plaque; you'll spot several of these in memory of the ironworking that was Fabriano's stock in trade before paper; these days, Fabriano has branched out again, into household appliances.

Around Fabriano

Weekends, the Fabrianese head to the hills to **Poggio San Romualdo** (936m), 15km east up a hairpinning road, with woodlands, meadows and a handful of places to sleep and eat. The itinerant St Romualdo founded the nearby **Abbazia di San Salvatore in Val di Castro** in 909 – the crypt remains; the church was rebuilt in the 1100s.

The Marches' second Verdicchio-growing region, DOC Verdicchio di Matelica, begins just south of Fabriano. Places to aim for include handsome **Cerreto d'Esi**, southeast of Fabriano, encircled by garden walls with the remains of a Byzantine gate and a leaning silo-shaped tower, supposedly built in the time of Justinian.

Matelica, 7km south (badly hit by the earthquake and still being stabilized), is surrounded by industry but its centre is typically Marchigiano, with the essentials of urban life: a pretty main square, the Piazza Mattei, a civic palace, the **Palazzo Pretorio**, with Roman ruins inside and a clocktower from 1270 (with later touches), a loggia and a 17th-century fountain. The Palazzo Finaguerra holds the **Museo Archeologico**, the prize exhibit of which is a 2,000-year-old Greek marble globe, thought to be a solar clock. Behind the Palazzo Ottoni, home to the **Pinacoteca**, are pretty **Roman mosaics**

Museo Archeologico
open Tues–Sun 10–1 and 3–7; adm

Pinacoteca
open Tues–Sun 10–1 and 3–7

Mosaici Romani
ask for key at tourist office under loggia, t 0737 85671

Enoteca Comunale e Centro Analisi Sensoriale
open Tues, Wed, Fri and Sat 4–7.30; Thurs and Sun 9–1

Museo Piersanti
Via Umberto 11, **t** *0737 84445; open summer Tues–Sun 10–12 and 4–7; winter Sat and Sun 10–12 and 4–6*

from the 1st century AD. The **Enoteca Comunale e Centro Analisi Sensoriale**, under the loggia on Piazza Mattei, lets you local wines or get a chemical analysis of your *cinghiale* sausages. Matelica also has a fine picture gallery, the **Museo Piersanti**, with an exceptional *Crucifixion* by Antonio da Fabriano (1452), and works by Federico Barocci, Guercino and the followers of Raphael; there are other good paintings in the **church of San Francesco**, including a quattrocento triptych by Francesco di Gentile de Fabriano – presumably a relative of the great Gentile.

ⓘ **Jesi >**
Piazza Repubblica 11, **t** *0731 59788, www.comune.jesi.an/proloco (closed Sun)*

ⓘ **Arcevia >>**
Corso Mazzini 105, **t** *0731 9127, www.arceviaweb.it (closed winter)*

★ **Alle Terrazze >>**

ⓘ **Fabriano >>**
Corso della Repubblica 70, **t** *0732 625067, www.fabrianoturismo.it (closed Sun afternoon)*

Where to Stay and Eat in the Valle d'Esino

Jesi ✉ 60035

****__Federico II__, Via Ancona 100, just outside town, **t** 0731 211079, *www.hotelfederico2.it* (€€€€). A luxurious modern option in a lovely garden, with Wifi Internet access, a pool, a restaurant (half board available) and a private garage. As well as rooms (breakfast included), there are a handful of apartments.

***__Italia__, Viale Trieste 28, **t** 0731 4844 or **t** 0731 59004 (€€€). A family-run place a few minutes' walk from the centre towards the station, with simple rooms (breakfast included), Internet access and a good restaurant (full board available). *Restaurant closed Sun.*

***__Mariani__, Via Orfanotrofio 10, **t** 0731 207286, *www.hotelmariani.com* (€€). A quiet, welcoming hotel with Internet access and private parking. Rates include breakfast.

Da Antonietta, Via Garibaldi 19, **t** 0731 207173 (€€). Simple, delicious Italian home cooking, plus takeaways. *Closed eves, Sun and Aug.*

Hostaria Santa Lucia, Via Marche 2/b, **t** 0731 64409 (€€). Seafood specialities and delicious home-made bread. *Closed Mon and 2wks Aug.*

La Rincrocca, Vicolo delle Pace 3 (near Piazza Federico II), **t** 0731 56174 (€€). Mexican, African, Indian and Italian cuisine, served in a garden in summer. *Closed lunch and Mon.*

Tana Liberatutti, Piazza Baccio Pontelli 1, **t** 0731 59237 (€€). A pretty medieval spot with a garden. Try *gnaccheragatti*, a type of pasta in two flavours. *Closed Sun and part of Aug exc by adv booking.*

Serra San Quirico ✉ 60048

__K3__, Via Piedaspri 1, **t 0731 86063 (€). Simple rooms (breakfast included) and good pizzas; full board is available. *Restaurant closed Wed.*

La Pianella, Via Gramsci 31, **t** 0731 880054 (€€€). Tagliatelle in duck sauce, river shrimps, meats grilled over the fire and lots of mushrooms and truffles, in an old pine forest above town. *Closed Mon, July and Nov.*

Arcevia ✉ 60100

***__Alle Terrazze__, Via Rocchi 24, just outside village, **t** 0731 9391 (€€). A lovely setting and great views. Breakfast is included, and there's a hydrotherapy pool, a lovely garden, access to woods. and the town's best restaurant (full board offered). *Restaurant closed Mon.*

Fabriano ✉ 60044

****__Janus__, Piazzale Matteotti 45, **t** 0732 4191, *www.janusgroup.it* (€€€). An ugly but well-equipped modern hotel with Internet access, room service and breakfast included in rates. It's linked to Fabriano's best restaurant, **La Pergola**, serving good *agnolotti* with courgettes and truffles, and a new restaurant-café was due to open as we went to press. Half and full board are offered. *Closed Fri and Sat lunch.*

***__Aristos__, Via Cavour 103, **t** 0732 22308, *hotel.aristos@libero.it* (€€). An old townhouse with simple, pleasant rooms (breakfast included) and free parking nearby. *Closed Aug.*

***__Old Ranch__, Via Piaggia d'Olmo, 3km outside centre, **t** 0732 627610 (€). A handful of modern rooms in a 19th-century villa, run by the same family for decades, plus good local cuisine (€€). *Restaurant closed Tues and July.*

Ancona

Filthy hole: like rotten Cabbage. Thrice swindled.

James Joyce

Just before the city, the mountains once more reach the sea, providing a splendid setting for the mid-Adriatic's biggest port, a crescent-shaped harbour under the steep promontory of Monte Guasco. Here colonists from Syracuse founded the city in the 5th century BC. It was the furthest north the ancient Greeks went in

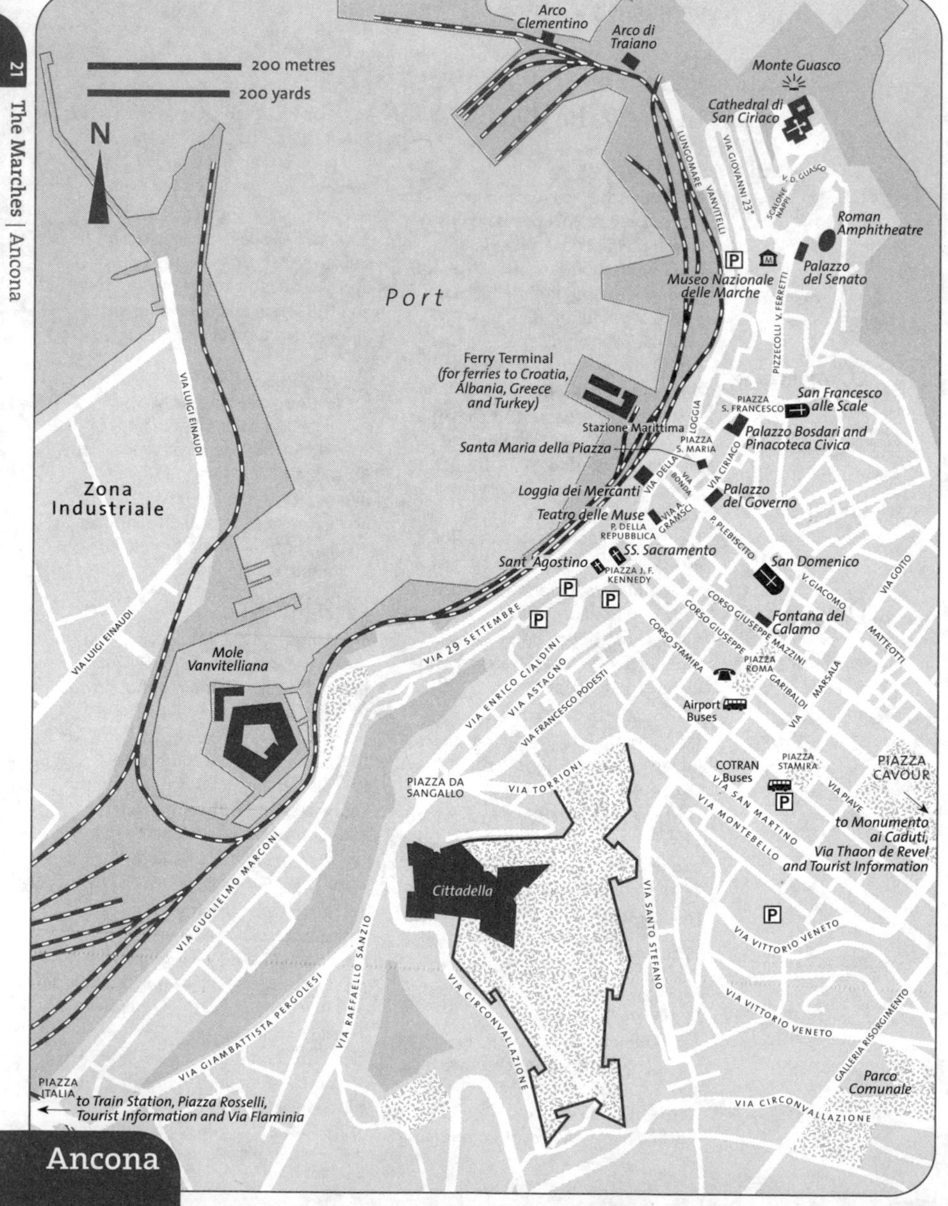

Getting to and around Ancona

By Air

Ancona's **Raffaello Sanzio airport**, 10km north at Falconara, **t** 071 28271 or **t** 071 282 7491, *www.ancona-airport.com*, has daily flights from Rome Fiumicino, Milan Malpensa, London Stansted and Munich. CONERO **buses** (**t** 071 280 2092 or **t** 800 218820, *www.conerobus.it*) run hourly from the airport to Ancona (Piazza Cavour) and Falconara (tickets are sold at *tabacchi* in the airport). There are also regular **trains** from the airport to Ancona, Jesi, Fabriano and Foligna. For airport **taxis**, call **t** 071 918221.

By Rail

Ancona is at the intersection of the Adriatic coast and Ancona–Rome routes, and there are frequent trains in both directions. The **station** is west of the port on Piazza Rosselli (bus no.1 or no.3 to or from Piazza Repubblica near the port). A few trains go on to Ancona Marittima station on the port itself.

Rail info: **t** 892021, *www.trenitalia.com*.

By Bus

RENI buses (**t** 071 804 6504, *www.anconarenibus.it*) to the Conero Riviera via Camerano leave from Piazza Cavour. For the province (Jesi, Recanati, Osimo, Castelfidardo, Loreto, Senigallia, and in summer, Portonovo), CONERO buses (**t** 071 280 2092, *www.conerobus.it*) leave from Piazza Cavour; many also stop at the train station.

By Sea

There are lots of **ferries** for Greece, Albania, Croatia and Turkey; all companies have offices in the Stazione Marittima, but many often open only at sailing times. Frittelli Marittima, Lungomare Vanvitelli 18, **t** 071 5021 1621, *www.frittellimaritime.it*, is a centralized service that will tell you who sails where, and make bookings.

Car Rental

Try: Avis, **t** 071 44241, *www.avisautonoleggio.it*; Hertz, **t** 071 41314, *www.hertz.it*; Maggiore Budget, **t** 071 42624, *www.maggiore.it*.

---

the Adriatic, and the colony wasn't a great success until Roman emperors built it up, especially Trajan, who hired his favourite architect, Apollodoro of Damascus, to lay out the port and town.

After the fall of the Roman Empire, Ancona became the leading city of the Byzantine Pentapolis, and along with the other Adriatic ports was given to the Church by Charlemagne. It recovered from the bad centuries to make a living trading with Dalmatia and the east, though its neverending battles, with Venice on the seas and on land against the emperors, as well as the lords of Jesi, Rimini and Macerata, never allowed it to blossom as a maritime republic in the style of Venice, Pisa or Genoa, though it was independent in all but name. Only in 1532 did the Medici pope Clement VII reassert the authority of the Church, moving in a papal army and constructing a citadel to house them.

The 20th century was murderous. The Austrians bombarded it in 1915, a quake damaged it in 1930, and the British and Americans bombed it again, thoroughly, in 1944. Then came a major flood, a serious earthquake in 1972, and a landslide causing abandonment of parts of the old town. Yet Ancona (population 101,000) has come up smiling. The port is prospering, and though most people live in newer faceless districts to the south and west, the city is devoting its attention to the restoration of the historic centre.

Around the Port

Most of Ancona's monuments survived the recent misfortunes, though many are a little the worse for wear. At its western end, the long curve of the port is anchored by the **Mole Vanvitelliana**, a pentagonal building designed in 1733 by Neapolitan architect Luigi Vanvitelli, court architect of the Bourbons at Naples. Though it looks like a fortress, it really served as Ancona's *lazaretto* or quarantine station; it now hosts temporary exhibitions. At the other end of the port, the tall, graceful **Arco di Traiano** was built in AD 115, in honour of Ancona's imperial benefactor; the sculptural reliefs have disappeared but it is one of the better-preserved in Italy. Nearby, Pope Clement XII had Vanvitelli erect an **Arco Clementino** to himself (1733) as Ancona's papal benefactor (he declared the city a duty-free port).

Teatro delle Muse
t 071 52525 or t 071 207841

At the centre of the port, the elegant 15th-century Venetian Gothic **Loggia dei Mercanti**, the merchants' exchange, is the best souvenir of Ancona's heyday as a free maritime city. Just in from here, the 19th-century **Teatro delle Muse**, restored after bomb damage in 1943, and the **church of Santissimo Sacramento** dominate the Piazza Repubblica. In Piazza Kennedy around the corner, 15th-century **Sant'Agostino** has an elaborate Venetian Gothic portal. Corso Garibaldi leads back to where Ancona's business centre has gravitated, around broad Piazza Cavour. At twilight, walk from here along Via Cialdini to Piazza da Sangallo, just under Clement VII's citadel, to see 'the most beautiful sunset in the world', according to Goethe, who was so overwhelmed by the sun, art and sex that nearly everything he wrote about it in his *Italian Travels* was either mush or wrong.

Santa Maria della Piazza
open daily 7.30–7

To see the oldest quarters, you'll have to climb a little as well, starting up Via Gramsci. Off on a little square to the left, 13th-century **Santa Maria della Piazza** has a great late Romanesque façade with figures of musicians and soldiers and odd animals carved by a 'Master Phillippus'. A window has been installed in the pavement to allow you to see underneath, to the extensive ruins of the church's predecessors, from the 5th and 6th centuries.

San Domenico
open daily 8–12 and 3–7.30

Up and to the right, under the Renaissance decorative arch of the handsome **Palazzo del Governo** (by Francesco di Giorgio Martini; 1484), extends the elongated **Piazza del Plebiscito**, graced with a statue of Clement XII (1738), determined to leave his mark on Ancona, if not on history. At the top of the piazza, ramps and steps lead up to **San Domenico**, built in the 13th century, rebuilt in 1788 and frequently battered and repaired. Step in to see Titian's *Crucifixion* (1558) on the high altar, and Guercino's *Annunciation*, just to the left. Below it, on Corso Mazzini, is the pretty **Fontana del Calamo** with its 13 spouts designed by Pellegrino Tibaldi in 1560.

Pinacoteca Comunale
Via Pizzecolli 17, t 071 222 5041; open Mon 9–1; Tues–Fri 9-7, Sat 8.30–6.30; Sun 3–7; adm

Left of Santa Maria della Piazza, the late Renaissance **Palazzo Bosdari** houses the small **Pinacoteca Comunale**, with a masterpiece of the eccentric Carlo Crivelli: a *Madonna col Bambino* with his trademark apples and cucumbers. Other Madonnas include one in a *Sacra Conversazione* by Lorenzo Lotto and one by Titian, smug on a cloud, and a 16th-century view of Ancona by Andrea Lilli.

Another two blocks up takes you to **San Francesco delle Scale**, theatrically set on a stair, with another charming Gothic portal and, inside, a large lush altarpiece of the *Assumption* by Lotto.

On Monte Guasco

Museo Archeologico Nazionale delle Marche
Via Feretti 6, t 071 202602; open Tues–Sun 8.30–7.30; adm

Further up, Via Pizzecolli becomes Via del Guasco, in an area where bits of decorative brickwork from Roman Ancona's theatre peek out between and under the ruined buildings. This was the area hardest hit by the quake and landslide, and only in 1988 did the **Museo Archeologico Nazionale delle Marche**, in a 16th-century palace, reopen. Its rich archaeological collection includes exceptional Greek vases and metalwork, Etruscan bronzes, gold and amber from Gaulish and Piceni tombs, and an large collection of Roman finds. Also damaged in 1972 was the 13th-century **Palazzo del Senato** round the corner, Ancona's capital when it was self-governing.

Cattedrale di San Ciriaco
accessed via long garden stairway (Scalone Nappi), no.11 bus from Piazza Cavour or Piazza Repubblica, or by car from port; t 071 52688; open summer daily 8–12 and 3–7; winter daily 8–12 and 3–6

Ancona's pink and white 11th-century **Cattedrale di San Ciriaco** crowns Monte Guasco, the ancient Greek acropolis, once home to a famous temple of Venus. Unusually for a church this far north, it shows a strong influence from the Puglian Romanesque. The fancy Gothic porch is by Margaritone d'Arezzo; the sculpted portals and detached campanile were added about 1200. Inside, the marble columns, some crowned with Byzantine capitals, came from the temple of Venus; there's an unusual polygonal cupola and a 12th-century, elaborately carved altar screen in the right transept. The cathedral is dedicated to St Cyriacus, the converted Jew who told St Helen the whereabouts of the True Cross and, in a clever piece of 4th-century propaganda, was said to have been martyred by the virtuous but non-Christian Emperor Julian the Apostate; the saint's perfectly pickled body is in the Rococo casket.

Museo Diocesano
t 071 200391 or t 071 52688; open April–Sept Sun 5–7; winter Sun 4–6; other times by appt

The **Museo Diocesano** has a fine 4th-century Christian sarcophagus, reliquaries and 9th–12th century fragments from the cathedral.

ⓘ Ancona >
Via Thaon de Revel 4, t 071 358991, www.comune.ancona.it (closed Sun afternoons); branches at train station (no tel); port, t 071 201183 (summer) and Piazza Roma, t 320 0196321

Where to Stay in Ancona

Ancona ✉ 60100

The Conero Riviera (*see* p.619) makes for a quieter base .

******Grand Hotel Palace**, Lungomare Vanvitelli 24, by port near Arco di Tralano, t 071 201813, *www.hotelancona.com* (€€€€). The best choice, small and comfy, in a 17th-century palace with a roof garden with stunning port views, a fitness centre and a garage. Breakfast is included. *Closed Christmas–New Year's Day*.

******Grand Hotel Passetto**, Via Thaon de Revel 1, t 071 31307, *www.hotelpassetto.it* (€€€€). A modern, central option with a pool. Breakfast is included.

*****Della Rosa**, Piazza Rosselli 3, **t** 071 41388, *www.hoteldellarosa.it* (€€) Comfortable rooms, some ensuite, near the station.

*****Fortuna**, Piazza Rosselli 15, **t** 071 42663, *www.hotelfortuna.it* (€€). The best option near the station; ask about weekend offers.

****Viale**, Viale della Vittoria 23, almost 1km from centre, **t** 071 201861, *www.hotelviale.it*. (€€) A tranquil spot with its own bar.

****Dorico**, Via Flaminia 8, **t** 071 42761 (€). Simple rooms, most ensuite, near the station.

****Gino**, Via Flaminia 4, **t** 071 42179 , *hotel.gino@tiscalinet.it* (€) Basic rooms, some ensuite, and a restaurant (€€) serving excellent fresh seafood (full/half board available). *Closed Sun.*

Eating Out in Ancona

Don't miss *stoccafisso all'Anconetana* – exquisite dried-cod casserole with tomatoes, potatoes and marjoram. Nearly every port in Italy developed a taste for dried cod in the Middle Ages, when barrel-loads from England and the Baltic passed through in exchange for wine; here it's preferred even to the day's catch from the Adriatic. Another speciality is *brodetto*, a soup with many kinds of fish.

La Moretta >

La Moretta, Piazza Plebiscito 52, **t** 071 202317. (€€€) A longtime favourite with locals for its excellent *stoccafisso all'Anconetana* and *spaghetti agli scampi*. Other highlights are the seabass baked in parchment paper; tagliatelle with oyster sauce; and grilled lamb. Booking is advisable. *Closed Sun.*

La Cantinetta, Via Gramsci, **t** 071 201107 (€€). The place to come for a foretaste of Greece if you're hopping on a ferry, filled with Greek seamen fingering worrybeads. It's famed for its *stoccafisso all'Anconetana* (the best in town), its nightly fish fry, its traditional *vincisgrassi* and its lemon sorbet. *Closed Mon.*

Carloni, Via Flaminia 247, Torrette, north of of Ancona, **t** 071 888239 (€€). A seafood hotspot with reasonable prices, between the sea and the railway tracks (listen to your mussels rattle when trains pass). Standouts are the fish ravioli and the *brodetto. Closed Mon exc Aug.*

Corte, Via della Loggia 5, **t** 071 200806 (€€). An stylish 18th-century palace near the port, with a pretty garden and great cooking. *Closed Sun and Jan.*

Osteria del Pozzo, Via Bonda 2, **t** 071 207 3996 (€€). An elegant spot in the middle of the port, offering good spaghetti with seafood, and *brodetto.* Make sure to book. *Closed Tues and Aug.*

Passetto, Piazzale IV Novembre, **t** 071 33214 (€€). An excellent seafood place with a seaside terrace with panoramic views. *Closed Sun eve, Mon, 3wks Aug.*

Da Irma, Piazza S. Primiano, **t** 071 53110 (€). A classic family-run trattoria offering simple, traditional home-cooking, right by the port. *Closed Tues and 1wk Aug.*

Around Ancona: The Conero Riviera

Under Monte Conero

The arm of the Apennines that stretches down to shelter Ancona's port creates a short but beautiful stretch of Adriatic coast. South of Ancona, the cliffs of **Monte Conero** (572m) plunge into the sea, forcing the railway and coastal highway to bend inland, isolating beautiful beaches and coves only a few kilometres from Ancona; it's now a Parco Naturale and gets very crowded in summer.

Portonovo

From the city, the Conero road between sea and mountain passes after some 7km the cliff of Trave, so-called for a rock formation that resembles a beam (*trave*), dropping sheerly down to the sea.

Getting to the Conero Riviera

For **buses** to the Conero Riviera from Ancona, *see* p.613.

A little further on, a side road to the left leads down to Portonovo, tucked under the cliffs and the most beautiful place for a swim in these parts, with a pebble beach. Besides the beach, three campsites and a little lake, there's a lovely church from the 1030s, once part of a Benedictine abbey, built in the same style as Ancona cathedral. Restored **Santa Maria di Portonovo** is one of the better Romanesque churches in the north; Dante mentions it as 'the House of Our Lady on the Adriatic coast' in the 21st canto of *Paradiso*. Portonovo has a small fortress, the **Fortino Napoleonico** (now a hotel: *see* p.619), and a watchtower built by Pope Clement XII in 1716 – even at that late date, there was worry about pirates. Much earlier, some of the local pirates hung out at the nearby **Grotta degli Schiavi** – *schiavi* in this case meaning Slavs, not slaves: refugees from across the Adriatic. The grotto faces a sheltered cove popular with divers.

Santa Maria di Portonovo
t 071 56307; open summer Tues–Sun 4–7; winter Sun 10–12

South of Portonovo, the road curves inland around Monte Conero proper. A road from Sirolo leads to the mountain's summit and the remains of an 11th-century Camaldolese abbey, **San Pietro**, with interesting capitals, now partly a hotel (*see* p.619). On its inland slopes, Conero is green and luxuriant; in this direction the view takes in a wide stretch of the Apennines, as far south as the highest peak in the range, the Gran Sasso d'Italia in Abruzzo. Somebody, apparently, was enjoying it 100,000 years ago; near the summit archaeologists dug up the oldest traces of human settlement yet discovered in the Marches.

Sirolo and Numana

On the southern slope of Conero are two attractive but often very crowded resorts. **Sirolo** is a medieval village on the cliffs high above the sea, its highest point marked by a 15th-century church and a former Franciscan convent; near its entrance are two holm oaks planted by St Francis in 1215. Sirolo has a beach nearby and the lovely beach of **Due Sorelle**, behind the sea rocks under the stretch of jagged white cliffs called **Sassi Bianchi**.

Merging with Sirolo, **Numana** has Numana Alta, with a beach tucked under the cliff, and Numana Bassa, with a long sandy one and boats out to the swimming holes off the Due Sorelle islets. The Greeks arrived in Numana in the 8th century BC to set up a trading counter with the Piceni, and it grew into an important town, a bishopric from the 5th to the 15th centuries. At its centre, the **Santuario del Crocifisso** is a pilgrimage site for its miraculous icon, a crucifix painted by St Luke and St Nicodemus (a less pious opinion calls it a Byzantine-inspired work from 13th-century

Santuario del Crocifisso
Piazza del Santuario; t 071 933 1026; open daily 9.30–12 and 4–7

Antiquarium
Via La Fenice 4; t 071 933 1162; open Tues–Sun 8.30–7.30; adm

Poland). At the **Antiquarium**, artefacts show the evolution of the Piceni culture. Just inland are pretty rolling hills dotted with oaks and pale pink villas all along the narrow roads, set up by the local wine consortium of DOC Rosso Conero. Robust and characterful, it's based on Montepulciano grapes; Marchetti is a reputed label.

Sweet Music: Castelfidardo and Osimo

South of Ancona, slightly dishevelled **Castelfidardo** is the accordion capital; they say the instrument was invented here in the 1870s. The **Museo Internazionale della Fisarmonica** will fill in any gaps in your knowledge, and in October the town hosts the International Accordion Soloists' Competition. In 1860 Castelfidardo witnessed a comic-opera skirmish: the battle of Castelfidardo, where King Vittorio Emanuele II vanquished the rag-tag legions of the pope and allowed the Piemontese to look heroic in completing Italy's year of unification – after the hard work had been done by Garibaldi and his Thousand. A monument to Piemontese general Cialdini, on a cypress-lined avenue, commemorates the event.

Museo Internazionale della Fisarmonica
Via Mordini, t 071 7808 288; open Mon–Sat 10–12 and 4–7, Sun 10–12; adm

Venerable **Osimo**, 3km up the road, began life as a capital of the Piceni in the 9th century BC and was occupied by the Greeks of Ancona, then by the Romans, who called it *Auximum*. Its neighbours call people from Osimo '*senza teste*' because of the 12 headless Roman statues in the entrance and atrium of the 17th-century **Palazzo Comunale**, overlooking the piazza that once held Osimo's forum. At the highest point in town, the 13th-century Romanesque-Gothic **cathedral of San Leopardo**, dedicated to Osimo's first bishop, has quirky medieval details: a rose window circled with little monsters, a fine *tympanum* carved with the Virgin and Apostles, who seem to be humming, with a figure resembling Jack in the beanstalk on top, and a second door framed by two snakes, slithering up to share an egg. The style of the reliefs over the portals, with the eyes 'holed in', seems to have been copied from the 4th-century Luni marble sarcophagus in the crypt, showing the story of Noah, Jonah and a hunt; there's a 4th-century sarcophagus of St Leopardo too, and a late medieval tomb of St Vitaliano and a wide variety of second-hand capitals holding up the vault. Next door, the 12th-century **baptistry** is now the **Museo Diocesano**, with a remarkably ornate frescoed ceiling of 1629 and a splendid bronze baptismal font by the Jacometti brothers of Recanati.

San Leopardo
t 071 715396; open daily 8–1 and 4–8

Museo Diocesano
t 348 601 7674; open summer daily 10–12 and 4–7, plus Thurs and Fri 9pm–11pm in Aug; winter Sat 4–7, Sun 10–12 and 4–7; adm; guided tours available

Down from Piazza del Comune, in early-17th-century **Palazzo Gallo** (now the Cassa di Risparmio bank), ask to see the Salone delle Feste, frescoed by Pomarancio with the *Judgement of Solomon*. Behind, a huge brick 13th-century Franciscan church acquired Baroque decoration inside when it became the **Santuario di San Giuseppe da Copertino**, dedicated to the flying friar from Puglia (d. 1663) who, as a nearly daily occurrence, would soar from the church door

Museo Civico
t 071 714695; open June–Sept Tues–Sat 5–8, Sun and hols 10–12.30 and 5–8; rest of year Tues–Sat 5.30pm–7pm, Sun and hols 10–12.30 and 5.30–7; adm; free guided tours

over the heads of his parishioners to the altar. One of Italy's most popular 17th-century saints, Giuseppe spent his last years in the **convent** here, which has a little **museum** of his life. One chapel has an elaborate *Enthroned Virgin and Saints* by Antonio Solario.

Below, in Via Fonte Magna, are the remains of a Roman wall and **fountain** or *nymphaeum*. Piazza Dante has the 17th-century **Palazzo Campana**, containing the **Museo Civico**, with a handful of paintings, including the beautiful, retro (for 1464) golden polyptych by the Viviani brothers of Venice (formerly in the Mayor's office).

Where to Stay and Eat on the Conero Riviera

Monte Conero >>

Numana >>
Piazza del Santuario, t 071 933 0612, www.turismonumana.it (closed Oct–Mar)

Internazionale >

Sirolo >
Via Peschiera, t 071 933 0611, www.sirolo.it

Portonovo ✉ 60020

****Fortino Napoleonico**, Via Poggio 166, **t** 071 801450, *www.hotelfortino.it* (€€€€€). An award-winning hotel incorporating a fortress built in the Napoleonic Wars. It's quiet and modern, with its own beach, tennis courts and a pool with hydromassage. The restaurant is one of the Marches' finest; your 8 superb courses might include stuffed olives and scampi, shrimps with fennel and orange, and gnocchi with caviar. Breakfast is included, half/full board available.

****Emilia**, Collina di Portonno, **t** 071 801145, *www.hotelemilia.com* (€€€€). Luxurious minimalism in a lovely setting, with lots of art – artists are invited to stay free in exchange for a painting – plus a pool and a natural terrace. Rates include breakfast, and half board is available. *Closed Nov–Feb.*

***Internazionale**, Via Portonovo, **t** 071 801 001, *www.hotel-internazionale.com* (€€€). A sturdy stone building amidst the trees, with ravishing views above the bay from its guestrooms, a beach of its own and a good restaurant. Breakfast is included; half board is available.

Il Laghetto, near Portonovo's lake, **t** 071 801183 (€€€). Fish specials and a good list of wines, served in a garden with panoramic views in summer. *Closed Mon, mid-Jan–Feb, and Sun lunch Sept–Jan.*

Sirolo ✉ 60020

***Locanda Rocco**, Via Torrione 1, **t** 071 933 0558, *www.locandarocco.it* (€€€). A charming 14th-century inn with stylish rooms (breakfast included). The restaurant serves modern Italian cuisine. *Closed Tues Mar–May and Nov–Feb.*

***Monte Conero**, built round the Badia di San Pietro, **t** 071 933 0592, *www.hotelmonteconero.it* (€€€). A great place to get away from it all, with elegant rooms and suites (breakfast included) in a sublime setting near the top of the headland. There's a pool, a tennis court, a kids' area, parking, and a restaurant (€€) offering full and half board. *Closed Dec–Feb exc New Year.*

Numana ✉ 60026

***Gigli Eden**, Via Morelli 11, **t** 071 933 0652, *www.giglihotels.com* (€€€). Pleasant rooms (breakfast included) and small apartments with great sea views. The huge grounds contain two pools and a tennis court, and there's a secluded private beach, a restaurant (full board offered) and a garage. *Closed Nov–Easter.*

***Majestic**, Via Roma 4, **t** 071 933 0614 (€€€). Simple, comfortable rooms in the centre, within walking distance of the beach, plus a restaurant. *Closed Oct–Mar.*

Teresa a Mare, Via del Golfo 26, **t** 071 933 0623, *www.rivieradelconero.it* (€€€). Simple rooms (breakfast included) and a private beach. Half and full board are offered. *Closed Oct–Easter.*

Il Granaio di Valcastagno, Via Valcastagno 12, **t** 071 739 1580, *www.valcastagno.com* (€€€). A rustic option in the farm buildings of an 18th-century noble's house, with all comforts, including a fitness centre, Turkish bath, solarium, sauna and bar. Room rates include breakfast, or there are apartments for 2–5, with kitchens and gardens. Sailing and riding can be arranged, and there's a garage. There's a minimum week's stay in summer.

ⓘ **Castelfidardo >** *Piazza della Repubblica 6,* **t** *071 782 2987. www.comune.castelfidardo.an.it*

ⓘ **Osimo >** *Via Boccolino 4,* **t** *071 724 9282 or* **t** *800 228800, www.comune.osimo.an.it*

Castelfidardo ✉ 60022

****__Parco__, Via Donizetti 2, **t** 071 782 1605, *www.hotelparco.net* (€€). Comfortable rooms and a suite with Internet connections near the town's pretty park, plus a guests' restaurant.

Osimo ✉ 60027

***__Cristoforo Colombo__, on SS16, 6km east, **t** 071 710 8990, *www.cristoforo-colombo.com* (€€€). Comfy rooms and the best local restaurant, **Cantinetta del Conero** (**t** 071 710 8651), serving good fresh fish (half/full board available), in a beautiful park. *Restaurant closed Sat and 2wks Aug.*

***__La Fonte__, Via Fonte Magna 33, **t** 071 714767, *hotellafonte@libero.it* (€€). A quiet, functional place by the Roman walls, with lovely views and a bar. Half board is offered.

Ostello delle Gioventù, Piazza del Comune 1, **t** 071 723 0037, *www.geosmaver.it/pagine/ostello.html* (€). A recently renovated hostel with clean doubles and singles, most with bath.

The Southern Marches

'Infinite Places': Loreto, Recanati and Around

The tourist offices in these parts have concocted this slogan from one of Leopardi's most famous poems, 'Colle dell'Infinito', which refers to the never-ending panorama of hills from his native Recanati melting in the distance. It is possible to do all four towns in a day, perhaps beginning or ending at the pretty Adriatic resort of Porto Recanati.

Porto Recanati

In 1229, Emperor Frederick II rewarded Recanati's fidelity with a port and long sandy beach, and threw in the **Castello Svevo**; nearly destroyed during an attack by Turkish pirates in 1518, it was reconstructed and still serves as a focal point for Porto Recanati. In 1927, the courtyard of the castle was transformed into the **Arena Beniamino Gigli**, named after the great tenor whose summer villa still stands at Montarice, along the Loreto road; in the summer months this hosts films, plays and opera. One castle tower now holds the **Pinacoteca Moroni** with mainly 19th- and early-20th-century paintings (especially by the *Macchiaioli*), and some minor works by Zurbaran, Ribera, Rosso Fiorentino, Millet, Maratta and Salvator Rosa.

Pinacoteca Moroni *t 071 759 1283; open summer Mon–Fri 4–7; winter by appt*

Just to the south of Porto Recanati, along the SS16, archaeologists are busy excavating the **Roman colony of Potentia**, which dates back to 184 BC and lasted into the 5th century as a bishropic. At the site you can have a look at the remains of a temple, a portico, some houses with frescoed walls and mosaic pavements, a bridge and a noble's tomb.

Potentia **t** *071 759971 or* **t** *071 979 9084; free guided tours Mon and Fri pm*

Getting to Loreto, Recanati and Around

Loreto **train** station (**t** 071 978668) is on the Milan–Bologna–Ancona–Lecce line, though not all trains stop all the time. Buses link the station with the town.

CONERO **buses** (**t** 071 280 2092, **t** 800 218820, *www.conerobus.it*) from Ancona run frequently to Loreto and Recanati via Osimo and Castelfidardo; CONTRAM buses (**t** 0737 63401, **t** 800 037737, *www.contram.it*) link Porto Recanati to Loreto, Recanati and Macerata, along the coast, and there's 1 bus a day linking Loreto to Camerino and Tolentino and Sarnano.

Santa Maria in Potentia
free guided tours Mon and Fri pm

Nearby, the **abbey of Santa Maria in Potentia** is 12th-century, but only its Romanesque apse survives intact; a rest stop for pilgrims to Loreto for hundreds of years, it was given by Napoleon to his sister Pauline and her husband as a villa, and so it has remained.

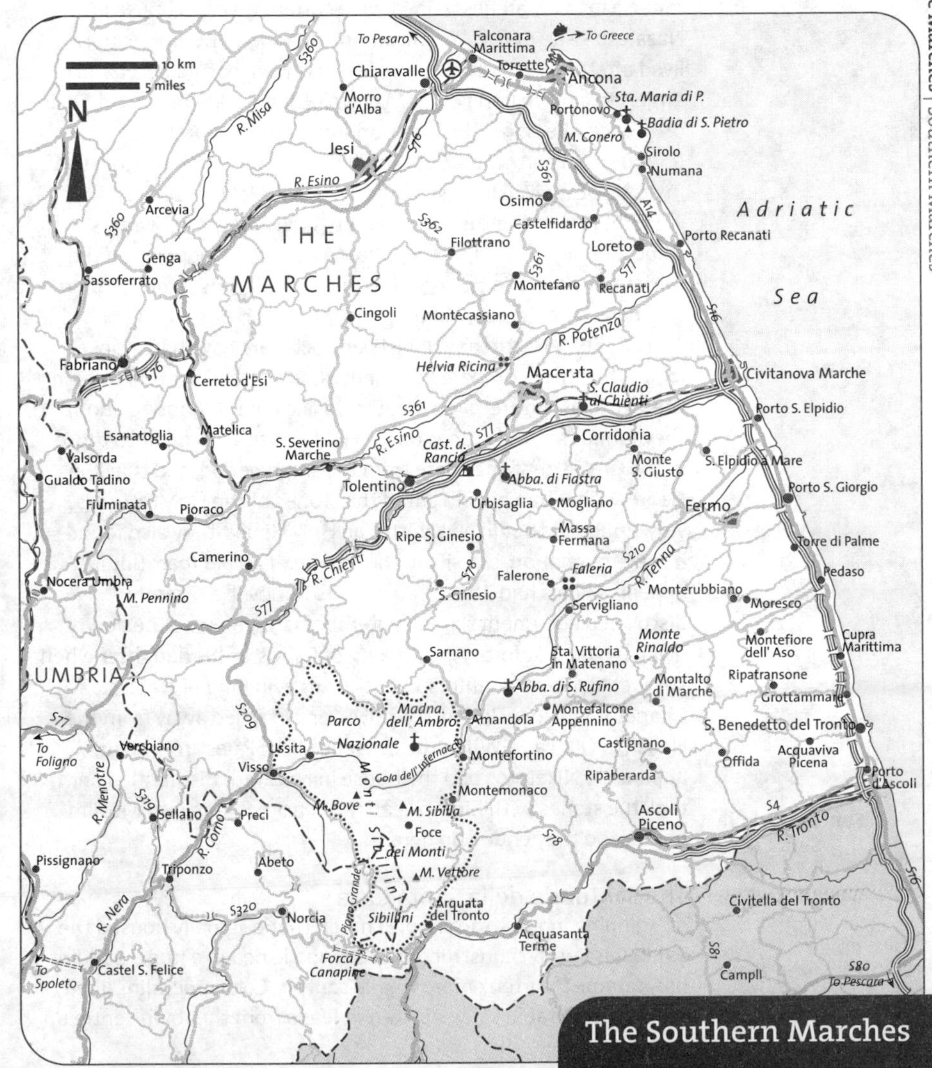

The Southern Marches

Loreto

The inventor of the accordion, the story goes, got his inspiration when an Austrian pilgrim on his way to Loreto left behind a button-box as a gift. This town (population 10,780) has been one of the most popular pilgrimage sites in Europe since the 1300s.

Like Urbino, Loreto is a small but concentrated dose of Renaissance fine art. Its story is a mystery of the faith. During the 1200s, the Church found itself threatened on all sides by heretical movements and freethinkers. The popes responded in various subtle ways to assimilate and control them; creating the Franciscan movement was one, and the encouragement of the cult of the Virgin Mary another. Conveniently enough, a legend of a miracle in the Marches gained wide currency. Mary's house in Nazareth – site of the Annunciation and where the Holy Family lived after their return from Egypt – was transported by a band of angels to a hill in Istria on 10 May 1291, then decided to fly off again on 9 December 1294, this time landing in these laurel woods (*loreti*) south of Ancona. Supposedly the house had bestirred itself in protest over Muslim reoccupation of the Holy Land; the popes were thumping the tub for a new Crusade and Loreto was just coincidentally located on the route to the Crusader ports on the Adriatic. Among the thousands of devout pilgrims to make their way here were Galileo, Montaigne and Descartes.

Since the 1960s, archaeologists and scholars have had a closer look. When they compared the Santa Casa with other buildings in the grotto of Nazareth (now in the Basilica of the Annunciation) they found that the stones of the Holy House are similar to those in the Grotto, that they date from the same period, and that the Hebrew-Christian graffiti cut in the stones of the Holy House is very similar to that in Nazareth. The Holy House, they also found, has no foundation, but sits in the middle of an old road. But it appears angels had little to do with its removal: a recently discovered document dated September 1294 refers to the dowry given by the Nikeforos Angelo, king of Epirus, to his daughter when she wed Philip of Taranto, son of the Angevin King of Naples, Charles II, which included 'the holy stones carried away from the House of Our Lady.' When the Crusaders lost Palestine in 1291, apparently Nikeforos had the house in Nazareth dismantled and took the stones with him to keep them from falling into Muslim hands, and they ended up here.

Santuario della Santa Casa
t *071 970104, www.santuarioloreto.it; open April–Sept daily 6.15am–8pm; Oct–Mar daily 6.45am–7pm (Santa Casa closed 12.30–2.30)*

The Santuario della Santa Casa

Beginning in 1468, the simple church that originally housed the **Santa Casa** was reconstructed and embellished in a huge building programme that took more than a century. Corso Boccalini, lined with the inevitable souvenir stands, leads from the town centre up to the sanctuary, which materializes in all its glory when you turn a corner and enter the enclosed **Piazza della Madonna**, with the church, a great fountain by Carlo Maderno, one of the architects of St Peter's, the **Palazzo Apostolico**, and its elegant **loggia** by Bramante, enclosing the square. This being a papal production, a big bronze statue of Sixtus V, in front of the church doors, dominates the piazza – many of the most important figures in the Roman art world had a hand in the work. In summer this space is often filled up with white trainloads of sick people hoping that Loreto's Madonna may succeed where modern medicine has fallen short.

The sanctuary's understated façade is typical early Roman Baroque, though a little ahead of its time (1587); no one is perfectly sure to whom they should ascribe it, since so many architects were involved. Giuliano da Sangallo built the cupola, almost a copy of Brunelleschi's great dome in Florence, Bramante did the side chapels, and Sansovino and Sangallo the Younger also contributed. One of the best features is the series of reliefs on the bronze doors by the Lombardis and other artists; another is the circle of radiating brick **apses** on the east end, turreted like a Renaissance castle; walk around for a look. Apparently the original architects really did intend the back of the church, overlooking the town walls, to function as part of the fortifications, a bookend to Antonio da Sangallo the Younger's round bastion by Piazza Garibaldi at the far end of town. The only unfortunate part is the ungainly neoclassical **campanile**, topped with a bronze-plated garlic bulb. Luigi Vanvitelli designed it in the 1750s; don't blame him for the proportions; the tower had to be squat and strong to hold the 15-tonne bell.

Chapels line the walls inside, embellished by the faithful from around the world, including the USA and Mexico. The sedate Spanish chapel is one of the better ones, the Knights of Malta's chapel has one of the goriest Crucifixes in all Italy, and the English chapel holds a memory of the lyric poet Richard Crashaw, who served as canon here until his death in the 1640s. A good deal of Loreto's art was swiped by Napoleon, and most of the paintings in the interior are from the last two centuries; the two **sacristies** on the right aisle have fine frescoes by Luca Signorelli and Melozzo da Forlì (with 3D angels, and a beautiful *Christ entering Jerusalem*).

Under the dome is the object of the pilgrims' attention. The **Santa Casa**, a simple brick room with traces of medieval frescoes, contains the venerated black Madonna of Loreto, sculpted out of cedar in 1921, after the original was destroyed in a fire. The house was sheathed in marble by Bramante to become one of the largest and most expensive sculptural ensembles ever attempted. In size and plan it is rather like Michelangelo's original project for the famous tomb of Pope Julius II; its decoration includes beautiful reliefs by Sansovino, Sangallo, Della Porta and others, with scenes from the *Life of Mary*. The reliefs on the back show the airborne house removal that made Loreto's Virgin the patroness of the airline industry; Charles Lindbergh took her image with him (plus a kitten and a ham sandwich) on his historic transatlantic flight.

The **Sala del Tesoro** (1610) off the left nave has a ceiling frescoed with the *Life of Mary* by Pomarancio, who won the (rigged) competition over Caravaggio, only to get his face knifed by a gangster hired by Caravaggio. Napoleon and his troops looted the treasures but many were eventually returned, only to fall victim to a spectacular robbery in 1974.

Museo Pinacoteca
t 071 974 7198; open Tues–Sun April–Oct 9–1 and 4–7; Nov–Mar Tues–Sun 10–1 and 3–6; donation requested

The upper floor of the Apostolic palace houses what the crooks missed, displayed in the **Museo Pinacoteca**, especially the dramatic late paintings by Lorenzo Lotto, who spent his last years in Loreto, took orders and died in 1556. There are some Flemish tapestries from cartoons by Raphael and a superb collection of ceramics, many from the 16th-century workshop of Orazio Fontana.

Just by the basilica is a Polish war cemetery with more than 1,000 graves of men who died on the Adriatic front. The rest of Loreto is devoted to the pilgrim trade and pastry shops (**Pirri** is good) selling almond sweets such as *amaretti di Loreto* and *dolci del Conero*. From the 1600s until the 1940s, a Loreto pilgrim's favourite souvenir was either an envelope containing Holy Dust (i.e. daily sweepings from the Holy House) or a tattoo of the Virgin, but now there's just the usual plaster models, pictures and plastic catapults.

Recanati

South of Loreto, rising above a massive ring of sprawl, Recanati (population 19,300) is a sombre town within brick walls. It was born in the late 12th century, when three Ghibelline lords of surrounding hilltops united to form a single town, an endeavour blessed by Emperor Frederick II. In later years, Recanati was the birthplace of Italy's greatest modern poet, Giacomo Leopardi (1798–1837), and the town has made a discreet industry out of this melancholy soul. His family, still residing in the **Casa Leopardi**, permits visits to the **library** where young Giacomo spent much of his dismal childhood, with original manuscripts and archives. Fans can also study the poet's death mask and first editions in the neighbouring **Centro Nazionale di Studi Leopardiani**. Below, the gardens of the **Colle dell'Infinito** take in the view of Leopardi's famous poem. The Capuchin church by the palace contains a rather unusual 18th-century Madonna, *Our Lady of the Salad*.

Casa Leopardi
Piazzale Sabato del Villaggio, t 071 757 3380; library open summer daily 9–6; winter daily 9.30–12.30 and 2.30–5.30; adm

Centro Nazionale di Studi Leopardiani
t 071 757 0604; open Mon–Fri 10–1 and 4.30–8; Sat 10–1

Recanati's main square, Piazza Leopardi, is presided over by a statue of the poet. The swallowtail crenellations of the **Torre del Borgo** commemorate the town's Ghibelline origins, as does the golden seal that Frederick II conceded to Recanati, housed in the

Pinacoteca
t 071 757 0410; open summer Tues–Sun 9–12 and 3–7; winter Tues–Fri 9–12 and 3–7, Sat and Sun 9–1 and 3–8; adm

Pinacoteca; other highlights are a polyptych and three other works by Lorenzo Lotto, including one of the most original, colourful if silliest *Annunciations* (1528) ever painted – even Mary's cat can't bounce out of the scene fast enough. Another section has the operatic wardrobe and other relics of the tenor Beniamino Gigli (1890–1957). **Gigli's tomb**, a fair-sized pyramid with full *Aida* trappings, lords it over the town cemetery in Viale Dalmazia. Get there through the **Porta Marina**, erected in honour of a visit by Pius VI in 1782, although Napoleon had the papal friezes knocked off prior to his own triumphal entry into Recanati.

Museo Diocesano
t 0737 630400; open Sat and Sun 10–1 and 3–6

North of Piazza Leopardi, Recanati's cathedral was made over in the 1700s, though there are a few interesting paintings, reliquaries and archaeological fragments in the **Museo Diocesano**, within the 14th-century bishop's palace, later a papal prison. The 12th-century **church of Santa Maria in Castelnuovo** retains its campanile façade and a lunette over the door.

Teatro della Rondinella
t 0733 850001; open for performances

Montefano, 11km west, is a hilltown guarded by the **Castello di Montefiore**, built by Recanati in the 15th century, with a tower dominating the landscape for kilometres around. Montefano was the birthplace of Pope Marcello II, whose pontificate may have been one of the briefest – it lasted 22 days in 1555 – but it was long enough to get him a lovely requiem mass from Palestrina and a marble bust on Montefano's **Palazzo Comunale**, which also houses a charming 19th-century **Teatro della Rondinella**, a provincial version of Venice's La Fenice.

ⓘ Porto Recanati >
Corso Matteotti 111, t 071 979 9084, www.portorecanatiturismo.it (closed Sun afternoon)

ⓘ Recanati >
Piazza G. Leopardi 31, t 071 981471 (closed Mon–Wed and Fri afternoon, and Sun)

ⓘ Loreto >>
Via Solari 3, t 071 970276, www.loreto.it (closed Sun afternoon)

★ Villa Tetlameya >>

Where to Stay and Eat in Loreto and Porto Recanati

Porto Recanati ✉ 62017

****__Enzo__, Corso Matteotti 21–23, **t** 071 759 0734, *www.hotelenzo.it* (€€€). Rooms and suites with all creature comforts, including free Wifi, near the port. There's a good restaurant and a garage.

***__Giannino__, Via Cristoforo Colombo 25 (Lungomare Nord), north of centre, **t** 071 979 9141 *www.conerohotelgiannino.com* (€€). Modern seaside rooms with pretty views, in a quiet location. Full board is required in high season; the restaurant serves Mediterranean cusine.

***__Bianchi Vincenzo__, Via Garibaldi 15, **t** 071 979 9040, *www.hotelbianchi.com* (€€–€). A good option for families, with very comfortable suites (some with kitchenettes), studios and apartments, sleeping up to 5. There's also a restaurant. *Closed Christmas wk.*

Il Diavolo del Brodetto, Via E Garolini 10, **t** 071 979 9251 (€€€). The place to eat fresh fish on this stretch of coast, on the seafront. Standouts are the grilled mixed fish and the marinated anchovies. Book ahead. *Closed Mon.*

Fatatis, Via Vespucci 2, **t** 071 979 9366 (€€). Excellent Marchigiano cuisine on a pretty, panoramic terrace, including excellent *brodetto*, plus pizzas. *Closed Mon and 2wks Dec/Jan.*

Loreto ✉ 60025

Hotels in the centre are clean, quiet and respectable, with crucifixes above beds; many are run by religious orders.

****__Villa Tetlameya__, Via Villa Costantina 187, Loreto Archi, **t** 071 978863, *www.loretoitaly.com* (€€€). An elegant 19th-century villa with spacious, comfortable rooms, a beautiful garden, parking and one of the best local restaurants, **Zì Nene**, (€€), serving seafood and historical Marchigiano recipes. Half/full board is available. *Restaurant closed Mon.*

*****Blu Hotel**, Via Villa Constantina 89, **t** 071 978501, *www.hotelbluloreto.it* (€€). Simple but pleasant rooms, including breakfast, plus a restaurant serving Marchigiano cuisine (half board possible).

*****Casa del Clero Madonna di Loreto**, Via Asdrubali 104, **t** 071 974 7218, *madomadiloreto@libero.it* (€). Ensuite rooms, available half or full board.

*****Vecchia Fattoria**, Via Manzoni 19, **t** 071 978976, *lavecchiafattoriasrl@virgilio.it* (€). Decent rooms and a restaurant (€€) popular with locals for weddings and banquets. *Closed Mon.*

****Centrale**, Via Solari 7, **t** 071 970173, *www.algirarrosto.it* (€). A secular hotel with a restaurant (half/full board).

Andreina, Via Buffolareccia 14, **t** 071 970124 (€€). Grilled meats and Marchigiano specialities; try home-made *tagliolini* with truffles, spit-roast piglet, and dumplings in duck sauce. *Closed Tues and last 2wks June.*

The Pocket Province of Macerata

You won't find a more out-of-the-way corner in central Italy. This hilly enclave lacks great attractions (when the provinces of Italy were divided up in 1860, Macerata was involved in a bitter quarrel with the commissioner in charge of fixing the borders, so he took away half of its traditional territory – Loreto, Fabriano and other famous places – in revenge). Still, the towns that remain put up a good front, with stout medieval walls or a Romanesque tower to lure you in. Many villages and towns also have fine works of art in their little museums.

Macerata

High on its hill, Macerata is a pleasant medieval-looking town (population 43,000). The town's major landmark is a huge colonnaded hemicycle and outdoor theatre, the **Arena Sferisterio**, built in the 1820s by local subscription for a game, *pallone a bracciale*, that required a long wall on one side. Played here since the 15th century, it reached its peak of popularity not long after the construction of the Sferisterio, losing out to new sport – football – 'which still excites portions of the Italian population' as a local booklet on Macerata drily put it. But the builders of the Sferisterio endowed it with excellent acoustics, making for one of the grandest opera settings south of Verona; the **Macerata Opera Festival**, founded in 1921 and running from mid-July to mid-August, is one of the most popular summer music events in Italy.

Arena Sferisterio
t 0733 234333; open 10.30–1 and 5–8

Macerata Opera Festival
t 0733 230735, www.sferisterio.it; box office Piazza Mazzini 10; open summer daily 9.30–1 and 4–8; winter daily 10–1 and 5–8

Nearly as many people could fit into **Piazza della Libertà**, decorated with Macerata's proudest monuments: a Tuscan **Loggia dei Mercanti** (1505) built by Papal Legate Alessandro Farnese, future Pope Paul III; the 17th-century **Palazzo del Comune**, with an atrium decorated with statues and inscriptions from *Helvia Ricina* (*see* opposite); and an elegant 18th-century **Teatro Rossi**, created by the great Bibbiena family of theatre designers.

Getting to Macerata and Around

Macerata is on a minor **train** line linking Civitanova Marche and Fabriano. The station down in the suburbs is linked to Piazza della Libertà by **city buses**.

CONTRAM **buses** (**t** 0737 63401, **t** 800 037737, *www.contram.it*) to the province leave from the Giardini Diaz, west from the centre, off Viale Puccinotti. APM, **t** 0733 29351, *www.apmgroup.it*, runs local buses.

Museo Civico e Pinacoteca
t 0733 256361; open Mon 4–7.30, Tues–Sat 9–1 and 4–7.30, Sun 9–1

Museo delle Carrozze
open Tues–Sat 9–1 and 4–7.30, Sun 9–1

Museo Tipologico del Presepio
Via Maffeo Pantaleoni 4, open by request, t 0733 235743

Galleria Palazzo Ricci
Via D. Ricci 1, t 0733 247200; open Tues 4–8, Sat and Sun 10–1 and 4–8

Corso della Repubblica leads down to Piazza Vittorio Veneto, where Macerata's museums occupy an old Jesuit college: the **Museo Civico e Pinacoteca** has another *Madonna* by Crivelli (no cucumbers, but lovely), works by Sassoferrato, Parmigiano, and a curious *Idealized Portraits of Michelangelo as Moses and Raphael as a Prophet* by Taddeo Zuccari, and modern works, especially by the Futurists Cagli and Maceratese painter Ivo Pannaggi. Adjacent is the **Museo delle Carrozze**, with carriages from the 16th to 20th centuries; a Risorgimento collection is being added.

Near the Sferisterio, the privately run **Museo Tipologico del Presepio** has 4,000 Christmas crib figures from the 17th century to the present. In the **Palazzo Ricci gallery** is an excellent collection of modern Italian artists, including Manzu, De Chirico, Carrà, Messina, De Pises, Morandi, Balla, and more by Ivo Pannaggi. The noble Ricci family who owned this palace produced the intriguing Matteo Ricci, born here in 1522, eldest of 11 sons. He became a Jesuit against his father's will and ended up in China, where he spent his last 20 years under the name Li Matou, dressed like a Buddhist monk, reputed to be 'a second Confucius' for his writings and understanding of Chinese culture; the Ming emperor Wan Li made him a court scholar, and on his death in 1610 declared a day of national mourning. Ricci wrote in Chinese as well as Italian: among his works are *The Ten Paradoxes* (still read in China), *A Chinese Map of the World*, *Eight Songs for the Harpsichord*, *Treatise on the Constellations* and the semi-autobiographical *The Entry of the Society of Jesus and Christianity into China*.

Santa Maria degli Vergini (1582), located 2km outside the Porta Picena, is a domed Renaissance church in the form of a Greek cross, boasting a rich stucco interior, a fine *Nativity* by Tintoretto (1587) and a stuffed crocodile.

Around Macerata and West to Cingoli

You could spend an extremely agreeable afternoon on a treasure hunt around Macerata; each village has a little something worth seeking out. About 4km north of Macerata on the SS361 towards Osimo, at **Helvia Ricina**, a Roman town that was decimated by the Visigoths in 408, it's the romantically overgrown ruin of an ancient theatre. If you press on a little further you'll get to **Montecassiano**, where the **church of Santa Maria Assunta** has an elaborate Della Robbia altar of 1527.

Southeast of Macerata, just off the SS485, is a 7th-century church, **San Claudio al Chienti**, built over the ruins of a Roman villa, with a pair of round *campanili*; it was reworked in the 12th century and restored in the 20th, after being used as a farm.

Corridonia, 4km south, on the ancient site of *Paulsulam*, was renamed in 1931 after Filippo Corridoni, a union leader who died in the First World War: there's a monument to him, made of melted Austrian cannons, and a display on his life in the town hall. The

Pinacoteca
t 0733 431832; open by request

Pinacoteca, in an 18th-century parish house, has a *Madonna* by Carlo Crivelli, in a wreath of angels, works by the Vivarini brothers and a painting attributed to Sassetta. At Monte San Giusto, 10km to the east, the **church of Santa Maria Telusiano** has a *Crucifixion* by Lorenzo Lotto (1531).

Abbadia S. Maria di Chiaravalle di Fiastra
t 0733 202190; open July and Aug daily 10–12.30 and 3–6.30; rest of year Sat and Sun 10–12.30 and 3–5.30; ***WWF museum*** *open by request; adm*

Southwest of Macerata on the SS77 and SS78, the **Abbadia S. Maria di Chiaravalle di Fiastra** was founded by Cistercians in 1142; now a bit over-restored and reinhabited by Cistercians since 1985, it retains some 15th-century frescoes. The World Wide Fund for Nature runs part of it as a **museum**, with exhibitions of country life and crafts, local flora and fauna, a working *cantina* and exhibition of archaeological finds from *Urbs Salvia*. Medieval **Urbisaglia** inherited the name and enjoys a panoramic setting with its 14th-century castle; below is the largest archaeological site in the Marches, the **ruins of Urbs Salvia**, including a well-preserved amphitheatre dating from AD 75, a sacred area encircled by a *cryptoporticus* frescoed with hunting scenes, a huge theatre, an aqueduct, a cistern, gates and walls.

Urbs Salvia
to visit contact archeological museum on ***t*** *0733 50107*

Medieval **Mogliano**, which is a centre for weaving wicker furniture, is 9km further southeast; its church, **Santa Maria**, was frescoed in 1548 by Lorenzo Lotto.

In the rather empty land to the west, **Rambona** has a church founded in the 8th century by Lombard queen Ageltrude over the Roman temple of *Ara Bona*; remodelled in the 11th century and frescoed in the 16th, it has Ageltrude's original dedication and some Roman architectural fragments.

Further northwest, in increasingly beautiful country, quiet, noble **Cingoli** (22km from Macerata) is a charming little summer resort with a main piazza reminiscent of a French village, lined with lime trees and bright café terraces. By tradition Cingoli receives the last ray of sun this side of the Apennines. The cathedral has some good painting and a bust of Pius VIII, a native son (1761–1830); the famous views that earned Cingoli's reputation as the '**Balcony of the Marches**' are from behind the apse of San Francesco, while outside the gate, Romanesque **Sant'Esuperanzio** has an attractive portal of 1299, a polyptych by Giovanni Antonio da Pesaro, and a *Christ at the Column* by Sebastiano del Piombo. More art is displayed in the **Pinacoteca**. The tiny **Museo Archeologico** in the

Pinacoteca
Via Mazzini 10, ***t*** *0733 602877; open by request*

Museo Archeologico
t 0733 603399; open April–Sept Mon–Wed and Sun 8.30–1.30, Thurs–Sat 8.30–1.30 and 3–7; Oct–Mar daily 8.30–1.30

Museo Internazionale del Sidecar
Corso da Valcarecce 13, open by appt on **t** *0733 602651*

Palazzo del Comune (with a façade attributed to the great Venetian Tullio Lombardo) has items from prehistoric times up to Roman *Cingulum*, while the **Museo Internazionale del Sidecar** has more than 100 types of sidecar, collected by a dedicated nut.

ⓘ Macerata >
Piazza della Libertà 12, **t** *0733 234807, www.comune.macerata.it, www.terredellinfinito.net (closed Sun afternoon)*

ⓘ Cingoli >>
Via L. Ferri 17, **t** *0733 602444, www.cingoli.sinp.net (closed Oct–May)*

★ Da Secondo >

Where to Stay and Eat in and around Macerata

Macerata ✉ 62100

This is the place to try *vincisgrassi*, a kind of lasagne with a rich sauce of chicken livers, gizzards and brains, mushrooms, ground meat and wine, topped with *béchamel* sauce. Some say the name comes from the Austrian General Windischgrätz (from the Napoleonic Wars), who must have liked it a lot; others that it was invented by a Macerata chef in the 18th century to fatten up skinny princes (*princigrassi*).

******Claudiani**, Via Ulissi 8, **t** 0733 261400, *www.hotelclaudiani.it* (€€€). A modern hotel within the walls of an old palace in the historic centre, with elegant rooms and bathrooms and a private garage (extra fee).

*****Da Rosa**, Via Armaroli 94, **t** 0733 232670 (€€). A simple, pleasant place to lay your head, in the centre near Piazza della Libertà, with a trattoria/pizzeria of the same name at No.17 (**t** 0733 260124), serving good home-made pasta and desserts. *Restaurant closed Sun and Christmas.*

****Arena**, Vicolo Sferisterio 16, **t** 0733 230931, *www.albergoarena.com* (€€). A perfectly decent little option right next to the Sferisterio; room rates include breakfast.

Da Secondo, Via Pescheria Vecchia 26, **t** 0733 260912 (€€). Macerata's finest restaurant, in the centre with a terrace. Besides *vincisgrassi*, there's a famous *fritto misto* of lamb and vegetables and a wonderful hot chocolate cake, to accompany lovely views. Book ahead. *Closed Mon and part of Aug.*

Osteria dei Fiori, Via Lauro Rossi 61, **t** 0733 260142 (€). A good, popular eating choice situated between the Sferisterio and Piazza della Libertà. Recommended dishes include the gnocchi with pumpkin and *porcini*, the wild boar with vegetables, and the tagliatelle with chestnuts. *Closed Sun, mid-Aug–mid-Sept and Christmas.*

Montecassiano ✉ 62010

******Villa Quiete**, Valle Cascia 5, 3km south of Montecassiano, **t** 0733 599559, *www.gestionihotels.it* (€€€€). An 18th-century country house set in beautiful grounds amidst industrial sprawl, with rooms furnished with antiques and decorated with masterful simplicity. There's also a babysitting service and a very good restaurant (half/full board available).

******Recina**, Valle Cascia, on S77, **t** 0733 598639, *www.recinahotel.it* (€€€). Comfortable rooms and suites, a garden and a restaurant with panoramic views over the hills to the sea; half and full board available.

Cingoli ✉ 62011

*****Diana**, Via Cavour 21, **t** 0733 602313, *www.hoteldianacingoli.it* (€€). A family-run place in an 18th-century palace in the historic centre, with simple rooms and a restaurant with half and full board. *Closed Feb and Oct.*

*****Miramonti**, Via dei Cerquatti, **t** 0733 604106, *www.hotelmiramonticingoli.it* (€€). A cosy modern option with lovely views over the sea and Apennines, a tennis court, parking and a restaurant (half and full board offered).

*****Antica Taverna alla Selva**, Via Cicerone 1, San Vittore, 12km north, **t** 0733 617119, *www.tavernaallaselva.it* (€). A country inn on the banks of the Musone, with a good restaurant (half/full board offered), a lovely garden and private parking. *Closed Wed and Jan.*

La Terrazza, Via Fra Bevignate 65, **t** 0733 603957 (€€). Marchigiano meat and fish staples.

Le Cascatelle, Fraz. Villa Pozzo, **t** 0733 616129 (€). A pleasant place to eat on the road to Cingoli's lake, by a bubbling river, offering good mixed grills and salads. *Closed outside high season.*

The Chienti Valley

Up the valley from Macerata is a stately array of hilltowns; here, you'll find the region's finest trecento frescoes (in Tolentino), a small version of Urbino, with a Renaissance dukedom and university (Camerino), and a museum of plaster mushrooms (Pioraco), along with lovely mountain scenery towards the Umbrian border.

Tolentino

One of the larger Marchigiano hilltowns (population 18,350), Tolentino is prosperous and modern on the outside, with a walled medieval centre. It is known for two Nicholases: Niccolò da Tolentino, a *condottiere* who earned an equestrian fresco in Florence's cathedral by Andrea del Castagno, and a miracle-working Augustan preacher, San Nicola da Tolentino (1245–1305), one of whose special concerns is souls in Purgatory.

Santuario di San Nicola
t 0733 976311; open daily 9–12 and 3–7

The latter's **Santuario di San Nicola**, one of the most popular pilgrimage destinations in central Italy, has an impressive portal (1430s) by Florentine Nanni di Bartolo, in a restrained Baroque façade with a big smiling sun. Inside, the Baroqued nave has an ornate gilded casement ceiling by Filippo di Firenze (1603–28); there's an *Annunciation* by Guercino in the first chapel to the right, while right of the high altar is the **Cappella dei Santi Braccia** (Chapel of the Holy Arms) – these parts of the saint were taken off for juju when he died, and kept here in reliquaries until his body, hidden for six centuries, was rediscovered during excavations in 1932; note the 19th-century 3D view of heaven in the dome, the iron coffer that once held Nicola's arms, and a votive painting of him putting out a fire in the Doge's Palace in Venice.

In the late 13th century, a noble lady paid for the construction of an oratory, now called the **Cappellone**, where an artist known only as the 'Maestro di Tolentino' (Berenson attributed them to Giuliano da Rimini), working between 1310 and 1325, covered the walls in Giotto-style frescoes: richly coloured, intense, inspired work that bears comparison with the best trecento painting in Tuscany, with the four Evangelists, each coaching a Doctor of the Church amongst the stars in the ceiling, and on the walls a band dedicated to the life of Mary, Jesus and San Nicola – painted more than a century before he was canonized in 1446. In the centre is the saint's stone sarcophagus, over his reconstructed remains in the modern crypt.

Around the **cloister**, wreathed in wisteria, are a series of **museums** displaying ceramics (Italian and foreign) and art from Tolentino's churches – including 14th-century nativity figures, a *Madonna* by Simone de Magistris, a fascinating collection of painted *ex votos*, each detailed in a catalogue by the entrance – and a giant *presepio*, a spooky diorama of the life of St Nicholas.

Tolentino's central Piazza della Libertà a block up is decorated with fine palaces and a fascinating **clocktower** that tells you the phases of the moon, canonical hour and day. Upstairs in the 16th-century **Palazzo Sangallo** (by Antonio da Sangallo the Younger) is the world's first **museum of caricatures**, with satirical cartoons from ancient times to the present. Tolentino also hosts a biennial 'international festival of humour in art' (October in odd-numbered years). In 1797 Napoleon stayed in the **Palazzo Bezzi-Parisani** off the next piazza to the north, where he signed the peace treaty of Tolentino, returning the Papal States to the Pope; the room, kept as it was that fateful day, houses the small **Museo Napoleonico**.

Museo Internazionale della Caricatura
open Tues–Sun 10–1 and 3–6; adm

Museo Napoleonico
Via della Pace 20; t 0733 969797; closed for restoration at time of writing

Down Corso Garibaldi from Piazza della Libertà, Tolentino's **cathedral** was begun in the 8th century and has a campanile from 1100, but was palatially restored in the 1820s, with alabaster windows and chandeliers. The wooden statue of the dead Christ (1200) is carried in Tolentino's Good Friday processions. Just to the left of the altar, the sarcophagus of the town's patron, San Catervo (*c.* 350) is a masterpiece of Palaeochristian art, showing the Good Shepherd, the saints and the Adoration of the Magi, the latter dressed in Phrygian caps. Near the door to the right of the altar, the saint's original mausoleum, built by his wife, was found in 1990 (it's viewable under the glass in the floor), with a 9th-century Byzantine fresco of the *Prudent Virgins*.

Just outside the centre, Tolentino bottles its own mineral water at **Santa Lucia**, a spa and sauna open year-round. The town also owns the brick **Castello della Rancia**, 5km from the centre, a 12th-century farm once belonging to the abbey of Fiastra, transformed into a castle in 1357 with a huge tower and swallowtail crenellations; it houses archaeological finds (Greek and Etruscan ceramics and bronzes), as well as holding exhibitions and special events.

Castello della Rancia
5km from centre on SS77; t 0733 973349; open by appt

Up into the Hills South of Tolentino: San Ginesio and Sarnano

High on its hill, walled **San Ginesio**, 18km south, has views from the Conero and through the Sibillini to the Gran Sasso, the tallest of the Apennines (in the Abruzzo). Its **Collegiata**, in the main piazza, has a peculiar Gothic façade decorated with terracotta lace, and fine quattrocento works by Simone de Magistris, Lorenzo Salimbeni and Pietro Alemanno. Behind is a **picture gallery** in the 15th-century **church of San Sebastiano**, with a lively scene of a battle between San Ginesio and Fermo in 1440, when town rivalries could be dangerous to one's health. San Ginesio's walls still stand; outside the main gate is a large medieval stone pilgrims' hospice.

San Sebastiano
t 0733 656022; picture gallery open summer daily 10–1 and 3.30–7; winter by request

Further south, **Sarnano** has spruced itself up as a small radioactive spa – the waters have been known since Roman times – offering mud, water and aerosol tortures. It has an attractive medieval

Pinacoteca
Palazzo Comunale, Via Leopardi, t 0733 659923; open Mon, Wed and Thurs 10–1 and 4–6.30, Tues and Fri 10–1

centre plus another tiny **Pinacoteca**; look for the exceptional *Last Supper* by Simone de Magistris (*c.* 1600) and a *Madonna* (with cucumber) by Carlo Crivelli's brother Vittore. On top of the medieval town, Piazza Alta has some fine buildings and **Santa Maria Assunta**, with 15th-century frescoes by Niccolò Alunno and Pietro Alemanno.

There are scenic drives in every direction from Sarnano, west towards the mountains or south to Amandola (enchanting: *see* p.636).

San Severino Marche

Pinacoteca Tacchi-Venturi
Via Salimbeni; t 0733 638095; open summer Tues–Sat 9–1 and 4–7; winter Tues–Sat 9–1; adm

Northwest of Tolentino, a road leads to **San Severino Marche** (population 13,000), a town that hasn't risen from its slumbers since Totila the Goth sacked its predecessor *Septempeda* in 545; the oldest parts, in the medieval Castello on Montenero, are almost abandoned but make a brave sight when the two towers are lit at night. In the early 1400s, this was a minor artistic centre, hometown of International Gothic masters Iacopo and Lorenzo Salimbeni. Inspect some of their frescoes at the **Pinacoteca Tacchi-Venturi**, which also has Pinturicchio *Madonnas* and works by Alunno, Girolamo di Giovanni of Camerino, and Carlo Crivelli's brother Vittore, plus a polyptych by the great pre-Renaissance Venetian painter Paolo Veneziano (his only work south of the Veneto) and many others, alongside archaeological finds from Roman *Septempeda* and Piceni tombs from the 6th–4th centuries BC.

The Salimbeni brothers and the Baroque painter Pomarancio also left frescoes in the crypt of 11th-century **church of San Lorenzo in Doliolo** on Via di Piagge, and others in the **church of the Misericordia**, in the elliptical **Piazza del Popolo**, encircled with porticoes. The **Duomo** (10th century, but often remodelled) is a steep hike up in the quiet Castello; the baptistry has frescoes by the Salimbeni.

Museo della Carta e della Filigrana
t 0737 42715; open summer Mon–Sat 10–1 and 3–7; winter Sat and Sun 10.30–12.30 and 4.30–6; adm

Museo dei Fossili/ Museo dei Funghi
t 0733 42142; open summer Tues–Sun 10–1 and 3–7; winter Sat and Sun 10.30–12.30 and 4–6.

West of San Severino, **Pioraco** was a paper-making town; the cloister of 15th-century **San Francesco** in Largo Leopardi has the little **Museo della Carta e della Filigrana**, including a paper-making workshop using 14th-century techniques. The **Palazzo Comunale** has the **Museo dei Fossili** and **Museo dei Funghi**, the latter with models of every mushroom 'personally created by Offerl Spitoni'.

Further to the west you'll find **Fiuminata**, which is lush and green with waterfalls.

Camerino

Camerino (population 7,300) passed the Middle Ages in endless fighting with arch-enemy Fabriano just north (and, like Fabriano, was hit by the quake; there is still some scaffolding, but overall the town is pretty solid). Set on a ridge, it was ruled by the Da Varano dukes from the 14th to 16th centuries, who gave it something in 1355 that the larger, more prosperous Fabriano never had: a **university**, still in business. In main Piazza Cavour, the Da Varano's elegant Renaissance **Palazzo Ducale** has an Urbino-style courtyard and several frescoed halls (now used as a law faculty), and just below, via a 16th-century staircase, the lovely **botanical garden**. The palace shares the square with the **Duomo**, rebuilt in 1832 after a quake in 1799 knocked over its predecessor; the crypt, however, has the beautiful 14th-century **tomb of Sant'Ansovino** (a Carolingian bishop of Camerino) in red and pink marble.

Orto Botanico
t 0737 403084; open Mon–Fri 9–1 and 3–5.

Like Fabriano, Camerino produced a home-grown crop of artists, including quattrocento painter Girolamo di Giovanni, whose works may be seen next to the Duomo in the **Museo Diocesano**, along with a king-size Gian Battista Tiepolo, the *Madonna and St Philip Neri* (1740), paintings by Giovanni Boccati (another native) and a trecento fresco of the *Madonna di Altino*. Down the Corso from here, the Palazzo Comunale incorporates the town's **theatre** (1856); a Roman *cryptoporticus* was discovered under the stage.

Museo Diocesano
t 0737 630 400; open Sat and Sun 10–1 and 3–6

Girolamo di Giovanni's masterpiece, the *Annunciation* and *Deposition* (both on the same panel; 1462) is in the **Pinacoteca**, in the former church complex of San Domenico north of Piazza Cavour. This church saw a brutal murder, ordered by Cesare Borgia in 1502, when good duke Giulio Cesare da Varano and three of his sons were strangled at Mass; two of the youngest escaped and one returned to become duke. Further north, the **church of San Venanzlo** has a fine 14th-century Gothic portal (the rest was rebuilt after the quake).

Pinacoteca
t 0737 402310; open April–Sept Tues–Sun 10–1 and 4–7; Oct–Mar Tues–Sun 10–1 and 3–6; adm for exhibitions

The mountainous Alte Valli del Fiastrone to the south are peppered with castles, towers and fortresses, and there's a striking ruined white 1200s castle just east of Camerino, the **Rocca di Varano**.

Where to Stay and Eat in the Chienti Valley

Tolentino ✉ 62029

ⓘ **Tolentino >**
Piazza Libertà 18, t 0733 972937

******Hotel 77**, Viale B. Buozzi 90, outside centre, **t** 0733 967400, *www.hotel77.com* (€€€). Cosy rooms, a garden, a guests' restaurant (with full board) and parking.

****Milano**, Via Roma 13, **t** 0733 973014 (€). A modest central choice, with a restaurant offering half/full board.

Iuby Park, Contrada Cisterna 55, **t** 0733 969347, *www.iubypark.it* (€). Comfy rooms, some frescoed, in an 18th-century villa amidst Tolentino's sprawl. The restaurant (€€) offers meat, fish and pizzas, and there's a lovely garden.

San Severino Marche ✉ 62027

ⓘ **San Severino Marche >**
Piazza del Popolo 43, t 0733 638414

Il Giardino degli Ulivi, Via Crucianelli 54, Sant'Angelo, near Castelraimondo, off SS361 to Camerino, **t** 0737 642121 (€€€). Charming rooms (breakfast included) on a farm. The restaurant serves delicious traditional fare, and there's a garden and parking. *Closed Jan and Feb; restaurant also closed Tues.*

*****Due Torri**, Via S. Francesco 21, **t** 0733 645419, *www.duetorri.it* (€€). A pretty stone house with a beautiful garden. There's great *vincisgrassi* and good grills in the restaurant (€). *Closed Mon.*

Camerino ✉ 62032

ⓘ **Camerino >>**
Piazza Cavour 19, t 0737 632534

*****I Duchi**, Via V. Favorino 72, **t** 0737 630440, *www.hoteliduchi.it* (€€). A modern, family-run place in the *centro storico*, offering half and full board.

****Roma**, Piazza Garibaldi 6, **t** 0737 632592 (€). Central rooms, some with bath, and a restaurant (half/full board).

Osteria dell'Arte, Via Arco della Luna 4, **t** 0737 633 558 (€€). One of the oldest restaurants in town, with unusual pasta (for instance, with wild fennel or pigeon *ragù*). *Closed lunch exc Sun and Mon, Fri, 2wks Jan, and Feb.*

Around Fermo

After Monte Conero, the Adriatic won't show you another stretch of beautiful coastline until the Gargano peninsula in Puglia. That does not seem to impede the tourist sprawl of humble but growing resorts along the sands, pleasant but unspectacular, and sliced by railways and busy highways: the largest, **Civitanova Marche**, is a big industrial port.

Porto Sant'Elpidio and Porto San Giorgio

If you escape the traffic jams of Civitanova, **Porto Sant'Elpidio** preserves a bit of its old centre, but you're best off heading inland 9km to **Sant'Elpidio a Mare**, which has conserved some pretty things within its walls and seven gates, including the stout 28m **Torre Gerosolimitana** that was built by the crusading Knights of St John in Piazza Matteotti, with 14th-century carvings on one side. Adjacent, the 17th-century **Collegiata** has paintings by Pomarancio and Palma Il Giovane, and, behind the altar, a beautiful 3rd-century BC Roman sarcophagus in Greek marble, with a scene of a lion hunt. Also in Piazza Matteotti, **Maria Santissima della Misericordia** (late 1500s) has a colourful ceiling frescoed by Pomarancio and paintings by Andrea Boscoli, including the latter's beautiful *Marriage of the Virgin* (1603) in the presbytery, as well as two 18th-century organs. Here, too, is the **Palazzo Comunale**, with a façade by Pellegrino Tibaldi, a tryptych by Garofalo and a *Madonna* by Domenichino. Nearby, in the Concento dei Filippini, the **Pinacoteca Civica Crivelli** is home to art by Crivelli.

Pinacoteca Civica Crivelli
*Corso Baccio, **t** 0734 859279; open summer Tues–Sun 5.30–7.30; winter Sat and Sun 4–7; adm according to exhibition*

Museo della Calzatura
***t** 0734 810840; open July–Sept Wed–Sun 4.30–7.30; adm*

Prada Space Outlet
*Via Alpi 97, Montegranaro, **t** 0734 897 8272*

The **Museo della Calzatura** in the Palazzo Montalto traces the local shoemaking industry from medieval clogs and papal slippers to the boots of football heroes, and is a must-see for all devotees of **Prada** shoes, which are manufactured down the road (there's a factory outlet). Luxury shoes are the Marches' biggest industry – there are 2700 factories, mostly small-family run affairs near Sant'Elpidio a Mare (hence the museum). Fermo is even shortly to be its own province as a result of of all this shoe success! The local hero is Diego Della Valle, son of a local cobbler, who founded Tod's in 1978 and is now one of Italy's richest men. His architect wife designed **Tod's** sleek new headquarters in Casette d'Ete above Sant'Elpidio, and there's a factory outlet.

Tod's factory shop
*Corso Garibaldi, Casette d'Ete, Sant'Elpidio a Mare, **t** 0734 871671*

Back down the coast, the next resort south is **Porto San Giorgio**, Fermo's port. It has a rare Saracen tower with battlements (above Villa Pelagallo, built by Napoleon's brother Jerome) and the romantically overgrown **Rocca Tiepolo**, built by Lorenzo Tiepolo, who went on to be elected Doge of Venice. The Festa del Mare on the second Sunday in July is the biggest fish fry in the Marches, with a frying pan nearly 5m across.

Getting to Fermo and Around

Three START **buses** (**t** 800 443040, *www.startspa.it*) run daily from Fermo down the coast to Porta d'Ascoli, then head inland to Ascoli Piceno and Rome. STEAT buses (**t** 800 630715, *www.steat.it*) provide a service from Fermo to Macerata.

Fermo

The old town of Fermo (population 35,000), 6km above Porto San Giorgio, is set against a mountain backdrop. The Piceni town of *Firmum*, later a close ally of Rome, gained importance and lost it several times; in the 10th century, it was the capital of a duchy that included all the southern Marches. Fermo's handsome, brick-arcaded **Piazza del Popolo** has been its drawing room, and between 1398 and 1826,it was also the seat of its university. The Baroque **Palazzo degli Studi** still holds the university's superb library – now the town library – with a beautiful world globe made in 1722.

Pinacoteca
t 0734 284327; open mid-June–mid-Sept daily 10–1 and 4–8, plus Thurs 9pm–11pm in July and Aug; rest of year Tues–Sun 9.30–1 and 3.30–7; adm; joint ticket available with Piscina Epuratoria and science museums

Opposite, another corner of the piazza is closed by the 15th-century **Palazzo Comunale**, with a mildly eerie bronze statue of Pope Sixtus V, by 16th-century sculptor Accursio Baldi, inviting you in to the **Pinacoteca**. Works include a moving *Nativity* by a young Rubens; local records recall a Fermo priest commissioning it in 1608 for the grand sum of 1,700 *scudi*. Other works include the delightful fairytale *Story of St Lucy* by Jacobello del Fiore (1410), a polyptych by Andrea da Bologna and a 15th-century Flemish tapestry of the Annunciation.

Piscina Epuratoria
open mid-June–mid-Sept daily 10–1 and 4–8, plus Thurs 9pm–11pm in July and Aug; rest of year Tues–Sun 9.30–1 and 3.30–7; adm; joint ticket available with Pinacoteca and science museums

Under the Via degli Aceti is a singular relic of Roman times: the **Piscina Epuratoria**, an enormous underground reservoir built in AD 41–61 to both hold and clarify rain and springwater.

Museo di Scienze Naturali/ Museo Polare
t 0734 226166; open mid-June–mid-Sept Mon, Wed and Fri 4–8, Tues, Thurs, Sat and Sun 9–12.30 and 4–8; rest of year Mon–Fri 9–12.30 and 3.30–6.30, Sat and Sun 3.30–7; adm; joint ticket available with Pinacoteca and Piscina Epuratoria

Behind the Palazzo Comunale, Via Perpenti leads down to the Gothic **church of San Francesco**, home to some 15th-century frescoes and a tomb by Andrea Sansovino; further down in Viale Trento, the 18th-century Villa Vitali houses the **Museo di Scienze Naturali** and **Museo Polare**, with stuffed birds, polar flora and fauna, tools and sculptures from Greenland, and photos, all gathered by Silvio Zavatti during his five Arctic expeditions (1959–69). Don't miss the villa's romantic gardens.

At the top of Fermo is **Piazza del Girfalco**. Parasol pines grow where the castle once stood, but the **Duomo**'s still there, begun in 1227 but massively expanded and remodelled during the 1780s. The restorers left the attractive, asymmetrical front rose window and portals alone – note the lobster carved on the left. Inside you can see a fine 1366 tomb, a Palaeochristian sarcophagus in the crypt and, in the sacristy, a superb 12th-century Islamic embroidered silk chasuble that belonged to St Thomas à Becket – they can't really explain how they got it.

Near the south end of Piazza del Popolo, old Roman storehouses contain the **Museo Archeologico** with its Roman artefacts. A pre-Roman collection (before the Piceni, Fermo was the site of a Vilanova culture settlement from the 9th century BC) is on display at the **Palazzo dei Priori**, also in Piazza del Popolo.

Museo Archeologico
t 0734 217140; open mid-June–mid-Sept daily 10–1 and 4–8, plus Thurs 9pm–11pm in July and Aug; rest of year Tues–Sat 10–1 and 3.30–6, Sun 10–1 and 3.30–7; adm

South of Fermo

The hills around Fermo are engraved by the valleys of three small rivers – the Tenna, the Ete Vivo and the Aso to the south. A pretty road heads south for **Monterubbiano** and **Moresco** (16km), picturesque hilltowns above the Aso valley; the latter is supposedly named after the Saracen mercenaries who accompanied 11th-century Norman chieftain Robert Guiscard in his campaigns to boot the Byzantines out of Italy. Its churches have frescoes by a late-16th-century painter, Vincenzo Pagani.

Southwest of Fermo (23km), north off the SS210, a 1st-century BC Roman theatre is used for occasional summer performances at **Faleria** (Roman *Falerio Picenus*); other surviving bits include an aqueduct, tombs, cistern and villas. High above, **Falerone**, the medieval town that replaced it, has a quattrocento merchants' loggia, a clocktower with a tiny museum and a painting by Vittore Crivelli in the **church of San Fortunato**.

Massa Fermana, 8km north of Falerone, must have been a very strategic spot at one point to someone, judging by its massive 14th-century gate, the **Porta di Sant'Antonio**, with loggia and tower. The parish **church of San Lorenzo** houses Carlo Crivelli's oldest work in the Marches, a polyptych of 1468 (no cucumbers and only two apples), and a much later work by his brother Vittore. The *municipio* is home to the **Pinacoteca**, with paintings by Vincenzo Pagani, and a 15th-century wooden choir.

Pinacoteca
t 0734 760126; open Mon–Sat 8–2

South of Faleria, **Servigliano** is a rare old town not on a hill; note how the cemetery just west resembles a mini version of the town.

The scenery becomes increasingly dramatic up the SS210; even more so if you have time to drive south to **Santa Vittoria in Matenano**, then follow the road west to **Montefalcone Appennino** before rejoining the SS210 at **San Martino al Faggio**. Here, the **Abbazia di San Rufino** (13th-century) is built over a 9th–10th-century crypt with early frescoes, holding the remains of St Rufino, a farmboy who could plough thousands of acres in one night. Farmers approach his tomb down on their knees when they have hernias; Rufino is apparently a whizz at curing them.

On the edge of the Monti Sibillini national park, the biggest town in these parts is **Amandola** (population 4,100), formed in the Middle Ages when residents of the surrounding castles banded together. It has a Romanesque bridge, just off the SS210, and, in town, the **church of San Francesco**, with a 13th-century Byzantine-style fresco of *Christ the King*. The convent has the intriguing **Museo della Civiltà**, gathering everything locals used until a few decades ago, down to the kitchen sink. The first week of September sees the sprightly 'International Theatre Festival' in the streets.

Museo della Civiltà
t 0736 840704; closed for restoration at time of writing

The Monti Sibillini

Above Amandola rises the dark, legendary Monti Sibillini, the most striking mountains in the Apennines, wearing snow-capped peaks from late October to late May. The region has been designated a **national park** to protect the flora and fauna thriving there; it is still the haunt of wolves and now of bears, who have migrated up from the Abruzzo. There is the odd wildcat and marten, and about 50 pairs of royal eagles (the entire Italian population of this bird is estimated at 300). In late May and early June they are covered with wildflowers and orchids, some rare.

Parco Nazionale dei Monti Sibillini
t 0737 972754, www.sibillini.net

Further up above Amandola you'll find two small summer resorts, both of which are well served by buses, **Montefortino** and **Montemonaco** (988m). In Montefortino you can visit the small

The Sibyl of the Mountains

One of the most popular medieval Italian romances was *Guerino il Meschino* ('Guerino the Wretch'), written in 1391 by Andrea da Barberino. Guerino, a bold and clever young orphan in search of his parents, meets the Devil in a mountain pass above Norcia. The Devil, playing the role of a pimp, advises Guerino to go up into the mountains and seek out Sibilla, a lovely fairy whose cave is a bower of bliss. The price of her charms, of course, is his soul. Guerino doesn't hesitate, and finds that Sibilla is everything the Devil promises. He also finds out her true identity: she is the Cumean Sibyl from Campania, the most famous of the dozen prophetic wise women honoured by the Church for their predictions of Christ's birth and Passion, thus earning a place on Michelangelo's Sistine Chapel ceiling, on Siena cathedral's inlaid floor, and elsewhere, before the Counter-Reformation put on the brakes.

In the *Aeneid*, the Cumean Sibyl was visited by Aeneas as he went to found Rome, and she offered him a brief tour of Hell; she was later visited by the last king of Rome, Tarquin, coming to purchase the nine Sibylline books of prophesy. When he tried to barter down the price, the Sibyl threw three of the precious books into the fire; when he still tried to bargain, she threw in three more until, in a panic, he paid the original price for the last three. In *Guerino il Meschino*, we learn something else about her: that she had expected God to have chosen her to be the virgin mother of His son and was miffed when He chose Mary, then a nobody. When the new Christianity she had predicted took hold, the Sibyl left her cave in Campania and took refuge in a cave in the mountains that were named in her honour.

Guerino discovers in the nick of time that Sibilla and her ladies turn into monsters on Saturdays, and after spending a year in their pleasant company goes to Rome to seek the Pope's absolution. The humanist Aeneas Silvius (future Pope Pius II) identified Sibilla as the goddess Venus, and the popular tale inspired several variants, all casting their spell of magical eroticism and forbidden knowledge over the Monti Sibillini. The most famous story these days, thanks to Wagner, is *Tannhäuser*.

Soon great numbers of amorous pilgrims and necromancers were making their way to Norcia, the lake and the cave (near Montemonaco), and by the 1490s Rome was threatening to excommunicate anyone who went to visit the Sibyl. So many people continued to defy the pope with their profane pilgrimages that the long corridors descending into the Sibyl's magical realm were filled in during the 17th century, and dynamited in the 19th to keep all the wickedness within from ever escaping. But in Montemonaco they still know where it is, if you're interested.

Pinacoteca
*t 0736 859101; open **April–June** Sat and Sun 10.30–12.30 and 5–7; **3 July–11 Sept** Tues–Sun 10.30–12.30 and 5–7; **12 Sept–31 Oct** Sat and Sun 10.30–12.30 and 5–7; **1 Nov–23 Dec** Sat 3–5, Sun 10.30–12.30 and 3–5; **24 Dec–8 Jan** daily 10.30–12.30 and 3–5; **9 Jan–28 Feb** Sat 3–5, Sun 10.30–12.30 and 3–5; **Mar** Sat 3–5. Sun 10.30–12.30 and 3–7; adm*

Pinacoteca with a polyptych by Pietro Alemanno and a spooky painting of Circe the sorceress dating from the 1700s; from here, a road goes up the pretty valley of the Ambro to the **Santuario della Madonna dell'Ambro**, frescoed in 1610 with pictures of the 12 sibyls by Martino Bonfini.

Medieval Montemonaco, a pretty walled town further up, is even closer to the mountains. You can walk in a couple of hours to the 'cave of the Sibyl' (the lair of Tannhäuser's Venus) or follow the thundering Tenna river up the stark, wild, narrow **Gola dell'Infernaccio**, 'Shabby Little Hell Gorge', a three-hour walk from the road (accessible in summer only).

West of Montemonaco (9.5km), Foce is within trekking distance of the highest peak, **Monte Vettore** (2,475m), snow-covered until June, and its uncanny **Lago di Pilato** (1,949m), receptacle of much of the mountains' weirdness. It lies on the border of Umbria and the Marches (*see* p.549–78) and is a four-hour hike from the road, which is really feasible only in July, August and early September. Bring a map or tag along with some Italians who know the way. The lake is associated with Pontius Pilate, who either threw himself into its waters to drown in remorse or was condemned to death by Tiberius and asked for his body to be placed in a cart and driven by oxen to go where they would, whereupon they dumped his body in this lake. Others say a lake as red as blood formed here at the moment of the Crucifixion (the lake turns red on occasion, thanks to a species of algae). Peaks and crags in these parts are named after Christ and the Devil, and right by the lake is a rock called 'the Policeman' to keep mischief to a minimum. Originally, however, this was the Lake of the Sibyl: amulets and weird carvings were found on its shores, perhaps left by members of Norcia's college of sorcerers, who would trudge up here to baptize their grimoires and so double their powers. No one is sure how the Mountains of the Sibyls got their name; ancient writers record no such oracular priestesses in these parts. Italy, however, is full of stories about them and these mountains supposedly gave birth to the legend of Wagner's *Tannhäuser*.

Where to Stay and Eat in and around Fermo

ⓘ Porto San Giorgio >
Via Oberdan 5, t 0734 67461 (closed Sun, and afternoons exc Tues and Thurs)

Porto San Giorgio ✉ 63017

******David Palace**, Lungomare Gramsci Sud 503, **t** 0734 676848, *www.hoteldavidpalace.it* (€€€). A seaside hotel with a beach and an indoor pool surrounded by a gourmet restaurant offering a number of vegetarian options (full board possible).

*****Rosa Meublé**, Lungomare Gramsci 177, **t** 0734 678485, *www.rosameuble.it* (€€). A quiet, simple option with a beautiful garden and an Internet point. Rates include breakfast.

Damiani e Rossi, Via della Misericordia 1, **t** 0734 674401 (€€). A restaurant offering a daily-changing *menu degustazione*; there's no fish but a variety of vegetarian dishes. *Closed eves exc Sun, Mon and Tues in winter; and Jan.*

Fermo ›
*Largo Calzecchi Onesti, **t** 0734 228738 (closed Fri and Sat afternoon, and Sun)*

Montemonaco ›
*Via Roma, **t** 0736 856462, www.montemonaco.com*

Amandola ›
*Via XX Settembre 9, **t** 0736 848706*

Fermo ✉ 63023

*****Astoria**, Viale Veneto 8, **t** 0734 228601, *www.hotelastoriafermo.it* (€€). A modern option, the comfiest in the centre, with elegant rooms (breakfast included) and a good restaurant (half/full board available).

*****Casina delle Rose**, Piazzale Girfalco 16, **t** 0734 228932 (€€). Grand views and a good restaurant (half/full board offered) near the cathedral.

Servigliano ✉ 63029

*****San Marco**, Via Garibaldi 8, **t** 0734 750761 (€). A reliable stopover with a restaurant (full board offered). *Closed 2wks Jan; restaurant also closed Thurs.*

Montefalcone Appennino ✉ 63029

Da Quintilia Mercuri, Via Corradini 9, **t** 0734 79158 (€€). A tiny place where you can dine really well on the likes of *fritto* of lamb, olives, artichokes, cream and honey. Book ahead. *Closed Wed.*

Amandola ✉ 63021

*****Hotel Paradiso**, Piazza Umberto I 7, **t** 0736 847468, *www.sibillinihotels.it* (€€). A stylish family-run hotel in the centre, in a park with a tennis court. It's home to the town's best restaurant (half/full board available) and has private parking. *Closed Tues.*

Ostello il Chirocefaio, Via Indipendenza 73, **t** 0736 848598 (€). An exceptional hostel with ensuite guestrooms in an old palace. Breakfast is included in rates, and half/full board is available. *Closed mid-Oct–mid-Apr exc groups of 20 or more.*

Montemonaco ✉ 63048

****Hotel Monti Azzurri**, Via Roma 18, **t** 0736 856127, *www.hotelmontiazzurri.com* (€€). Ensuite rooms, breakfast included, and a restaurant (half/full board possible). *Closed 2wks Jan.*

La Cittadella dei Sibillini, Loc. La Cittadella, **t** 0736 856361, *www.lacittadelladeisibillini.it* (€€). A lovely, hospitable place with a pool and a menu of hearty fare such as *linguine* with tripe and polenta with sausages (half/full board are possible). There's a minimum 3-day in high season. *Closed Nov–Feb exc weekends.*

*****Guerrin Meschino**, Via Rocca, Loc. Rocca, **t** 0736 856356, *www.guerrinmeschino.com* (€). An unpretentious but comfortable hotel with a restaurant (half/full board offered).

****La Colombella**, Via Stradone 86, **t** 0736 856155 (€). Reasonable guestrooms, both with and without bath, and a restaurant (half or full board available).

The Riviera delle Palme

The coast down to San Benedetto del Tronto, which has been dubbed the Riviera delle Palme for its thousands of palms, is especially popular with German and Austrian package tours. Inland, more fine hilltowns peer over the sea.

Museo Malacologico Piceno
*Via Adriatica Nord 240, **t** 0735 777550; open April, May and Sept Tues, Thurs, Sat and Sun 3.30–7; June daily 4–8.30, July and Aug daily 4–10.30; Oct–Mar Thurs, Sat and Sun 3–6.30; adm*

Sala de Carolis
*Via Garibaldi 38, **t** 0735 938103; open summer Tues–Sun 4–8; winter Tues–Sun 3–7*

By the Sea

The Riviera delle Palme starts at modest **Cupra Marittima**, where the main attraction besides the beach is the **Museo Malacologico Piceno**, with an enormous collection of seashells, plus displays of buttons, cameos and other shell handicrafts.

Montefiore dell'Aso, 11km inland, has the **Collegiata di Santa Lucia** with paintings by Carlo Crivelli and the carved 13th-century **Portale della Pinnova** in the apse. Montefiore was hometown of Adolfo de Carolis (1847–1928), a friend of Gabriele d'Annunzio, who shared some of the latter's romantic, decadent, nationalist excesses; his woodcuts, engravings and paintings fill the **Sala de Carolis**.

Next down the coast is **Grottammare**, bigger, with a small medieval core. It was the birthplace of Felice Peretti, Pope Sixtus V (d. 1590), who excommunicated Elizabeth I and helped finance the Invincible Armada; there's a portrait in the **church of Santa Lucia**.

Museo Civico C. Cellini
t 0735 99329; open mid-June–Aug Mon–Sat 4–8, Sun 10–1 and 4–8; rest of year Tues–Sun 10.30–12.30 and 4.30–7.30; adm; joint adm available with Pinacoteca

Pinacoteca
Corso Vittorio Emanuele 130, t 0735 99329; open mid-June–Aug Mon–Sat 4–8, Sun 10–1 and 4–8; rest of year Tues–Sun 10.30–12.30 and 4.30–7.30; adm; joint adm available with Museo Civico

A road leads to **Ripatransone** (12km), 'the Belvedere del Piceno', an old, walled town that claims the narrowest alley in Italy, just off Piazza XX Settembre (38cm wide – don't get stuck!), as well as a pair of museums: the **Museo Civico C. Cellini**, in the 17th-century **Palazzo Comunale**, with prehistoric, Etruscan, Greek and Roman finds, and the **Pinacoteca**, featuring Vittore Crivelli, Vincenzo Pagani and others, as well as a big batch of plastercasts. There are some picturesque 15th-century houses in Via Garibaldi and other bits that reward a walk around town, including a Roman amphitheatre discovered outside the walls.

Museo Ittico
t 0735 588850; open summer Tues–Sat 6am–midnight; winter Mon–Sat 9–12 and 4–7

Museo delle Anfore
Via De Gasperi; t 0735 592177; open summer Tues–Sun 6am–midnight; winter Mon–Sat 9–12 and 4–6; adm

Smarter, bigger **San Benedetto del Tronto** (population 42,000), 5km south, started as a Benedictine monastery, grew into a large fishing port and is now a modern resort with white sandy beaches, nightclubs, restaurants and hotels galore, and thousands of palm trees. You get a vague idea of what pre-resort San Benedetto was like in the little streets between the train line and main highway. The **Museo Ittico** by the fishmarket in the port has 3,500 stuffed fish, an aquarium of live ones, and fossils of extinct ones. Near the *municipio* the **Museo delle Anfore** has a collection of 200 Phoenician, Carthaginian, Greek and Roman amphorae.

To the south San Benedetto merges seamlessly into Porto d'Ascoli, marking the end of the Roman Via Salaria and the beginning of the Abruzzo.

Rocca
t 0735 764407; open June and Sept daily 10.30–12.30 and 4–7; July and Aug daily 10.30–12.30, 5–8 and 9.30–11.30pm; Oct–May Sat, Sun and hols 10.30–12.30 and 3–5

Inland from San Benedetto (7km), medieval **Acquaviva Picena** is defended by its **Rocca**, with four big towers, home to a collection of armour; its church of San Rocco has a pretty terracotta frieze.

Pinacoteca
t 0736 888609; open summer daily 10–12.30 and 3.30–7.30; winter Sat and Sun 10–12.30 and 3–7; adm

Further west, hilltop **Offida** (population 5,300) is an ancient place whose name goes back to the Etruscan Ophyte. It overlooks two valleys, is famous for bobbin lace and puts on a good carnival. Its handsome 14th-century **Palazzo Comunale**, on Corso Serpente Aureo (Golden Snake), has a proud Ghibelline tower, a double gallery, a little theatre and the local **Pinacoteca**, with handsome works by Crivelli and his follower Pietro Alemanno (*St Lucy crowned by Angels*, with her eyes in a dish) and Simone de Magistris (*The Three Realms*, 1589).

Outside the centre, Romanesque-Gothic **Santa Maria della Rocca** has beautiful restored trecento frescoes by the Bolognese school. The Roman sarcophagus under the altar has a relief of the Roman god Silvanus; walk around the back for a striking view of the apse.

West and north of Offida are some truly obscure places, such as **Castignano**, its hill dramatically eroding away. A 5th-century BC Piceni *stele* that was found on the site (now in Ascoli's archaeology museum) confirms its age. The 14th-century parish **church of Santi Pietro e Paolo** has frescoes in the crypt by Vittore Crivelli, and a painted terracotta *Addolorata* from Scandinavia on the altar, from the 15th century, showing the Virgin's heart stabbed with knives of sorrow. In 1993 a fresco of the *Last Judgement* was discovered behind a Baroque altar; someone wrote the dates of solar eclipses in the corner in 1485 and 1537. Another church, **Sant'Egidio**, houses the *Ostensorio Reliquario*, one of the masterpieces of Ascoli Piceno's 15th-century goldsmiths.

Museo Diocesano
Piazza Sisto V, **t** *0736 828688; open by request*

Montalto delle Marche is worth a stop for its little **Museo Diocesano**, which is home to one of the most beautiful reliquaries ever made – an exquisite shrine of gold, enamel, gems and cameos that was created in Paris in 1390 and was donated to the town by Pope Sixtus V. The 16th-century Palazzo Comunale is home to a small **Pinacoteca** containing a painting of Sixtus V and some old photographs of the area.

Pinacoteca
t *0736 828015; open Sat and Sun 5.30–7.30*

Further northwest, in **Monte Rinaldo**, you can see an impressive 2nd-century BC **Hellenistic-Roman temple**, its columns re-erected under a modern transparent roof.

Where to Stay and Eat on the Riviera delle Palme

ⓘ **Grottammare >**
Piazza Pericle Fazzini 6, **t** *0735 631087 (closed Mon, Weds and Sat afternoons, and Sun)*

ⓘ **San Benedetto del Tronto >>**
Viale delle Tamerici 5, **t** *0735 592237 (closed Sunday afternoon)*

Grottammare ✉ 63013

****__Parco dei Principi__**, Lungomare De Gasperi 70, **t** 0735 735066, *www.hotelparcodeiprincipi.it* (€€€). A big modern resort hotel, with a pool and a tennis court. Rooms have balconies and panoramic views. Half and full board are offered. *Closed Christmas.*

***__Villa Helvetia__**, Via F. Salvi 1, **t** 0735 631293, *wwwgrottamare.it/villaheletia* (€€). A place with old-fashioned charm. Breakfast is included, and the restaurant serves national and global fare.

***__Roma__**, Lungomare De Gasperi, **t** 0735 631145, *www.hotelromagrottamare.com* (€€). A family-run choice just back from the beach, with a garden and rooms with sea views. Full board is compulsory. *Closed Oct–Mar.*

*__Vagnozzi__**, Via Cilea 109, **t** 0735 632334, *www.pensionevagnozzi.com* (€). A budget option with clean, simple guestrooms over two floors, with private bathrooms, plus a restaurant, a children's area and a TV room. Half and full board are available. *Closed Oct–May.*

Osteria dell'Arancio, Piazza Peretti, Alta Grottamare, **t** 0735 631059 (€€). Excellent local cooking. Book ahead. *Closed lunch and Wed exc July and Aug.*

Locanda Borgo Antico, Via Santa Lucia 1, Alta Grottamare, **t** 0735 634357 (€€). A delicious *menu degustazione* with wine, served outside in summer. *Closed lunch, Tues exc June–Sept, and Nov.*

San Benedetto del Tronto ✉ 63039

****__Bahia__**, Lungomare Europa 98, **t** 0735 81711, *www.hotelbahia.it* (€€€). An ugly modern hotel with an American bar, a gym, a playroom, parking and its own stretch of beach. Half and full board are available. *Closed Nov–Apr.*

***__Miami Beach__**, Viale Europa 40, **t** 0735 82115, *www.hotelmiamibeach.it* (€€). A fair option with a restaurant (half/full board possible) and private beach. *Closed Oct–April.*

Ristorantino da Vittorio, Via Liberazione 31, **t** 0735 81114 (€€€). Delicious seafood in a garden setting near the centre. There's also a café and wine bar, and four elegant rooms. *Closed Mon.*

Lelii, Via Roma 81, t 0735 587320 (€€). One of the best *brodetti di pesce* (local fish stews) plus other seafood at kind prices. *Closed Sun in winter.*

Ascoli Piceno

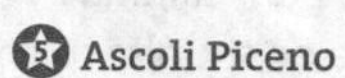

Urbino, at the northern end of the Marches, and Ascoli (population 54,000) at the southern, compete for your attention as almost polar opposites. Urbino gets most of the praise, which partisans of Ascoli may find somewhat unfair. While Urbino was paternalistically led by its enlightened, aesthetic dukes, Ascoli, with its long heritage as a free *comune*, has always had to fend for itself. The difference shows; Ascoli is a beautiful city, but beautiful in a gritty, workaday manner, like Florence. It has taken hard knocks in its 2,500 years, which have no doubt added to its character.

History

Ascoli, as its name implies, began with the Piceni and probably served as the centre of their confederation, united under the sign of their totem woodpecker. To the Romans, *Asculum Picenum* was an early ally after its conquest in 286 BC, but later it proved a major headache. *Asculum* fought Rome in the Samnite Wars and actually initiated the pan-Italian revolt of the Social Wars. The Romans took the city in 89 BC and razed it to the ground for good measure, refounding it soon afterwards with a colony of veterans. The street plan has hardly changed since; it is one of the best examples in Italy of a rectilinear Roman *castrum*.

In the Dark Ages, Ascoli's naturally defensible position between steep ravines helped avert trouble. Its citizens, too, showed admirable determination, defeating Odoacer's Goths on one occasion, the Byzantines and Saracens on others. Despite periods under the rule of Lombards, Franks, Normans and various feudal lords, Ascoli emerged by the 1100s as a strong, free *comune*. Reminders of this glorious period are everywhere: in the 13th-century Palazzo del Popolo, the clutch of tall, noble towers like those of San Gimignano, and in Ascoli's famous festival, the **Quintana**, a jousting contest with rules laid down in the statutes of 1378. With the advent of papal rule in the 15th century, Ascoli lost its freedom immediately and its prosperity gradually, only recovering some of its wealth and importance in the last 100 years.

Piazza del Popolo

Like Rome, Ascoli is built of travertine. Central Piazza del Popolo is one of Italy's most beautiful squares. It's a real town square, too, full of children riding bikes and playing football. This is no grand architectural ensemble, neither monumental nor symmetrical, but the travertine paving shines like marble; the low brick arcades give the square architectural unity and a setting for two fine buildings bearing statues of popes, who keep an eye on the bustling action. The first, the 13th-century **Palazzo dei Capitani del Popolo**, was

Getting to and from Ascoli Piceno

Ascoli is not the easiest place to reach. The only **train** service is a branch off the Adriatic coastline, from San Benedetto del Tronto, with trains roughly once an hour. The station (**t** 0736 341004) is on Viale Marconi in the new town.

START **buses** (**t** 800 443040 or **t** 0736 263053, *www.startspa.it*) for the coast, Fermo and Rome leave from Viale Alcide de Gasperi behind the cathedral; other companies run local services. Details all can be had from: Brunozzi travel agency, Corso Trento e Trieste 56, near Piazza del Popolo, **t** 0736 262128, *www.brunozziviaggi.it*.

---

begun in the 1200s and redone in the late 16th century, after its papal governor set it on fire to discomfit his enemies. It has a façade by Ascoli's best-known architect and artist, Cola dell'Amatrice, and a statue of Paul III over its huge portal; in 1982 excavations revealed buildings dating back to the Roman republic.

San Francesco
open daily 9.30–12.30 and 4–7.30

At the narrow end of the piazza, **San Francesco** (c. 1260) turns its back on the square; the apse and transepts are the best part of the building, an austere ascent of Gothic bays and towers under a low dome added in the late 15th century. Over the south door is a statue of Pope Julius II. The façade, around the corner, isn't much to look at; a flat square of travertine with a plain rose window. It does have a sculpted portal, guarded by a pair of sarcastic-looking lions. Inside are some grand and simple Gothic vaults. The southern end of the façade adjoins the **Loggia dei Mercanti**, built by the wool corporation – a medieval-style manufacturers' cooperative – in the early 1500s.

Northern Quarters and Around the Edges of Town

On the northern side, one of two Franciscan cloisters has become the town's busy, colourful **morning market**. The street in front of San Francesco, **Via del Trivio**, is the centre of activity in Ascoli; follow it north to Ascoli's oldest, prettiest neighbourhoods, on the cliffs above the lovely Tronto valley, which skirts the northern reaches of the town and makes an ideal picnic spot. Parts of the town walls, still visible in places, show the diamond-shaped brickwork (*opus reticulatum*) characteristic of Roman construction. It's here on the northern stretches that you'll find most of the city's surviving towers. Ascoli has as many of these medieval family fortresses as San Gimignano in Tuscany, though they are not as well known; the tallest is the **Torre degli Ercolani** on Via Soderini.

Santi Vincenzo e Anastasio
t 0736 252205; open by request

Piazza Ventidio Basso, the medieval commercial centre, has two good churches with a few 14th-century frescoes: 11th-century **Santi Vincenzo e Anastasio**, with a façade divided into 64 squares that once framed frescoes, still has some Romanesque carvings around the portal; gloomy Gothic 13th-century **San Pietro Martire** has a portal from 1523 by Cola d'Amatrice.

From here, picturesque Via di Solestà, lined with towerhouses, leads to the northern tip of Ascoli; a doughty single-arched Roman bridge, the 1st-century **Ponte di Solestà**, carries traffic across to the

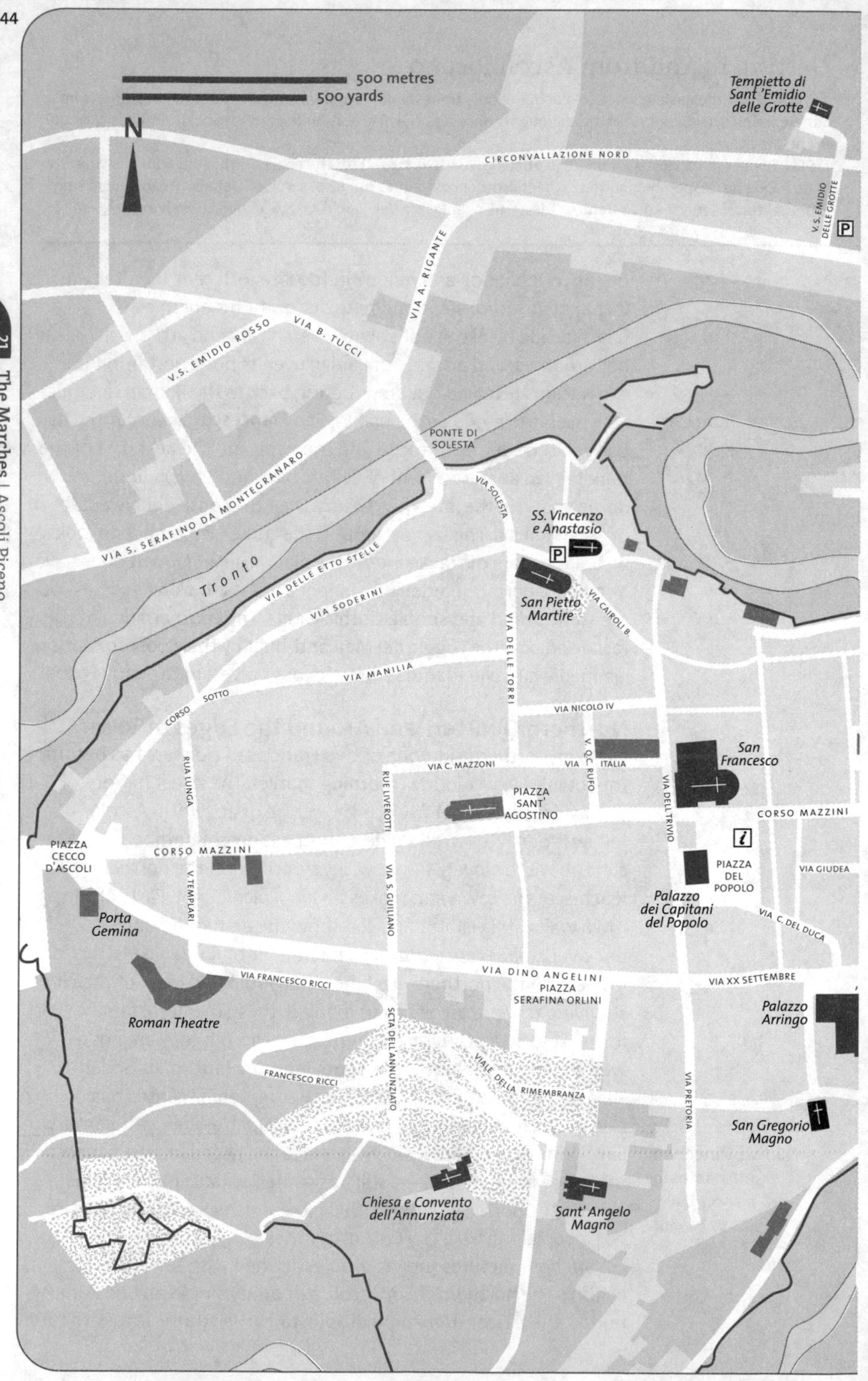
500 metres
500 yards
N
Tempietto di Sant 'Emidio delle Grotte
CIRCONVALLAZIONE NORD
V.S. EMIDIO DELLE GROTTE
VIA A. RIGANTE
V.S. EMIDIO ROSSO
VIA B. TUCCI
PONTE DI SOLESTA
VIA S. SERAFINO DA MONTEGRANARO
VIA SOLESTA
SS. Vincenzo e Anastasio
Tronto
VIA DELLE ETTO STELLE
VIA SODERINI
San Pietro Martire
VIA CAIROLI B.
VIA MANILIA
VIA DELLE TORRI
CORSO SOTTO
VIA NICOLO IV
V. Q.C. RUFO
VIA ITALIA
San Francesco
VIA C. MAZZONI
RUA LUNGA
RUE LIVEROTTI
PIAZZA SANT' AGOSTINO
VIA DELL TRIVIO
CORSO MAZZINI
PIAZZA CECCO D'ASCOLI
CORSO MAZZINI
PIAZZA DEL POPOLO
VIA GIUDEA
V. TEMPLARI
VIA S. GUILIANO
Palazzo dei Capitani del Popolo
VIA C. DEL DUCA
Porta Gemina
VIA DINO ANGELINI
VIA XX SETTEMBRE
VIA FRANCESCO RICCI
PIAZZA SERAFINA ORLINI
Palazzo Arringo
Roman Theatre
SCTA DELL'ANNUNZIATO
VIALE DELLA RIMEMBRANZA
FRANCESCO RICCI
VIA PRETORIA
San Gregorio Magno
Chiesa e Convento dell'Annunziata
Sant' Angelo Magno

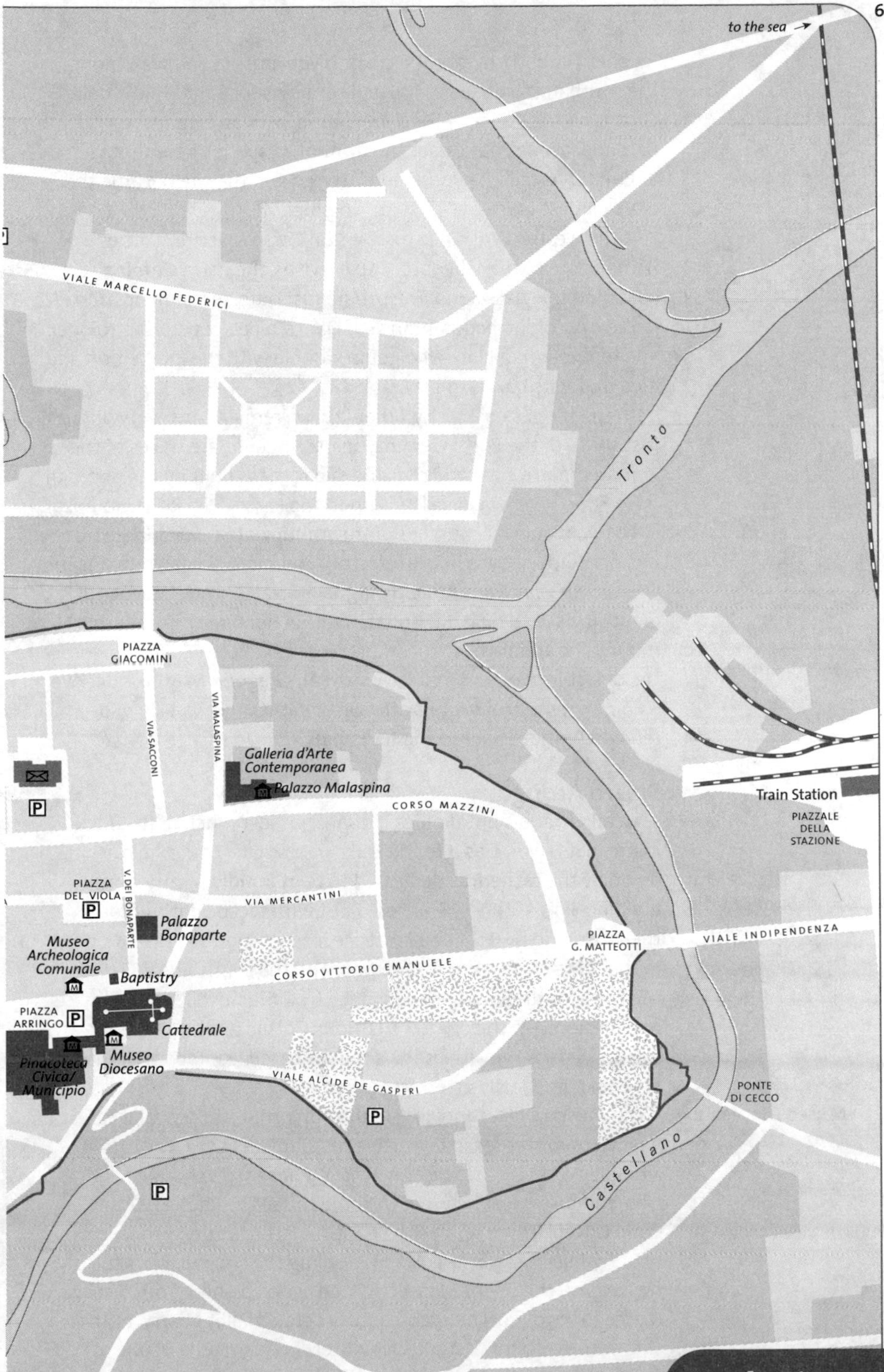

Ascolo Piceno

to the sea →
VIALE MARCELLO FEDERICI
Tronto
PIAZZA GIACOMINI
VIA SACCONI
VIA MALASPINA
Galleria d'Arte Contemporanea
Palazzo Malaspina
CORSO MAZZINI
Train Station
PIAZZALE DELLA STAZIONE
PIAZZA DEL VIOLA
V. DEI BONAPARTE
VIA MERCANTINI
Palazzo Bonaparte
Museo Archeologica Comunale
PIAZZA G. MATTEOTTI
VIALE INDIPENDENZA
Baptistry
CORSO VITTORIO EMANUELE
PIAZZA ARRINGO
Cattedrale
Museo Diocesano
Pinacoteca Civica/ Municipio
VIALE ALCIDE DE GASPERI
PONTE DI CECCO
Castellano
P

northern suburbs without a creak. If you cross it, and walk along the riverbank to the east, you will see signs for Sant'Emidio delle Grotte, on the street of the same name, with an elegant 1623 Baroque façade that closes the front of a cave; it's here that St Emidio, Ascoli's patron, was martyred,and the site became the city's earliest place of Christian worship.

At the western entrance to town, on Corso Mazzini, a little Roman gate of the 1st century AD survives, the **Porta Gemina**, spanning the Via Salaria. The square just outside is named after Cecco d'Ascoli, an acquaintance of Dante, a poet, doctor, astrologer and reputed magician, who got in trouble with the Inquisition and died under its hands in 1327.

On the fringes of the city, other Roman remains are everywhere; just south of the Porta Gemina, on Via Angelini, are traces of the **Roman theatre**, near the remains of a fortress built by the popes in 1564. From here, Via Ricci leads up to the Parco della Rimembranza, with two medieval churches of the **Annunziata** (with a large fresco by Cola dell'Amatrice in the refectory and more Roman remains in the 'Grotte') and **Sant'Angelo Magno**, the latter with frescoes of eight sibyls in the nave, painted in 1712 in honour of the nearby mountains and 10th–11th-century frescoes of the *Old Testament*, the oldest in the city. Finally, there's **San Gregorio Magno**, built over a Roman temple of Vesta, with two columns and walls in *opus reticulatum*, just behind the town hall.

Piazza Arringo

Ascoli's monumental oldest square has lost much of its old lustre in its service as a municipal car park. One end is held down by the **cathedral**, dedicated to **Sant'Emidio**: a 12th-century building similar to San Francesco but with façade dating from the 1530s, also by Cola dell'Amatrice. The interior was tarted up in the 19th century, but in the chapel on the south side you can see the beautiful restored polyptych by Carlo Crivelli, one of his masterpieces; in the crypt is a curious Gothic tomb of a knight; another, left of the altar, shows the deceased leaning forwards on his books, as if lazily attending Mass.

Cattedrale di Sant'Emidio
t 0736 259774; open daily 10–1; adm; guided tours available

The **Museo Diocesano**, within the adjacent bishop's palace, has two rare statues in travertine of Adam and Eve (1300), from a pulpit; works by Cola dell'Amatrice (whose style changed tremendously after he went to Rome to see the Raphaels); a Carlo Crivelli (three apples); a beautiful 15th-century arm reliquary, of St Emidio made in Ascoli and, stealing the show, a room full of frescoes on the *Life of Moses* by a mid-1500s painter from Vicenza, Marcello Fogolino. The 10th-century octagonal **baptistry**, to the side of the cathedral, stands resolutely in the middle of one of Ascoli's busiest streets.

Museo Diocesano
t 0736 252883; open July and Aug daily 10–1 and 3.30–7; rest of year Mon–Fri 9.30–1 and Sat 9.30–1 and 3.30–7; adm

Facing the cathedral, behind the dragons and seahorses in the twin Renaissance fountains, is the 13th-century **Palazzo Arringo**, hidden behind an imposing 17th-century Baroque façade. It holds the **Pinacoteca Civica**, with paintings by Cola dell'Amatrice and other local artists, Simone de Magistris, Pietro Alemanno, Titian, Guido Reni, Van Dyck, Crivelli of course, drawings by Pietro Cortona and Guercino, collections of ceramics and musical instruments, and a 13th-century English-made cope that Pope Nicolas IV (a native of Ascoli) gave to the cathedral in 1288.

Pinacoteca Civica
t 0736 298213; open daily 9–1 and 3–7; adm

Across the square, the **Museo Archeologico** has some bronzes of the ancient Piceni and some of the stones they hurled at the Romans, engraved with curses; there are also Roman mosaics and a plan of the city in Roman times, as well as Lombard jewellery and relics from a medieval necropolis.

Museo Archeologico
Palazzo Panichi, t 0736 253562; open Tues–Sun 8.30–7.30; adm

A walk through the streets north of Piazza Arringo will take you past some of the palaces of medieval Ascoli, with many curious carvings and morally uplifting inscriptions on the old houses; one, the **Palazzo Bonaparte** on Via Bonaparte, was built by a prominent family of the 1500s that local legend claims as the ancestors of the Bonapartes; Napoleon himself said he didn't know if it was true. The 16th-century **Palazzo Malaspina** at Corso Mazzini 224, one of the fancier buildings, houses the **Civica Galleria d'Arte Contemporanea**; its paintings, sculptures and graphic works form a good introduction to Italian modern art, from futurist Gino Severini to Lucio Fontana, a central figure of Arte Povera. Down this long street, you can also visit the **Museo di Storia Naturale**, with exhibits on the natural history of the Marches.

Civica Galleria d'Arte Contemporanea
t 0736 248663; open Tues–Sun 9–1 and 3.30–7.30; adm; reduced adm with ticket for Pinacoteca

Museo di Storia Naturale
Corso Mazzini 39, t 0736 277540; open Mon, Wed, Fri and Sat 10–1, Tues and Thurs 10–1 and 4–6

Where to Stay in Ascoli Piceno

The tourist office has lists of B&Bs or *agriturismi* nearby.

ⓘ Ascoli Piceno >
Piazza del Popolo 1, t 0736 253045, www.comune.ascolipiceno.it (closed Sun afternoon); and Tourist Welcome Centre, Piazza Arringo 7, t 0736 298204 or t 0736 298212

Ascoli Piceno ✉ 63100

******Gioli**, Via Alcide De Gasperi 14, **t** 0736 255550, *www.hotelgioli.it* (€€€). A pleasant modern hotel near the cathedral, with a garden and a private garage. Rates included breakfast. *Closed Christmas.*

*****Marche**, Viale Kennedy 34, about 1.5km east of centre, **t** 0736 45475 (€€). A comfortable modern option with an American bar.

*****Pennile**, Via Spalvieri, **t** 0736 41645, *www.hotelpennile.com* (€€). A quiet modern choice set amidst pines. Guestrooms (with breakfast included in rates) have balconies.

****Cantina dell'Arte**, Rua della Lupa 8, **t** 0736 255620 (€). An old palace with adequate rooms and a restaurant (€€) with abundant servings of local specialities. *Closed Sun.*

***Hotel Pension Le Dune**, Via del Commercio 210/a, **t** 0736 342575, *www.pensioneledune.com* (€€). Simple ensuite rooms.

Ostello dei Longobardi, Via dei Soderini 26, **t** 0736 261862 (€). The youth hostel, in one of the medieval towers on the north of town, with bunkbeds in dorms.

Eating Out in Ascoli Piceno

To most Italians, Ascoli means *olive all'ascolana* – the Marches is the third-biggest producer of olives in Italy, and the groves around Ascoli produce the best, fattest specimens, wonderful stuffed, breaded and fried.

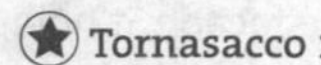

Tornasacco, Piazza del Popolo 36, **t** 0736 254151 (€€€). Olives and other specialities *all'ascolana*, plus tagliatelle with lamb sauce, and very good local cheeses and charcuterie. Don't disdain the *menu turistico* – it offers the best cuisine at the best prices. *Closed Fri, 2wks July, and Christmas/New Year.*

Gallo d'Oro, Corso Vittorio Emanuele 54, **t** 0736 253520 (€€). A longstanding place with good food, a tourist menu with lots of *olive all'ascolana*, *funghi porcini* and *tartufi*, and an *enoteca*. *Closed Sun, and Christmas/New Year.*

C'era una Volta, Via Piagge 336, 6km south on Colle San Marco road, **t** 0736 261780 (€€). Hearty soups, stuffed gnocchi, and olives and lamb cutlet fry. *Closed Tues.*

Caffè Meletti, Piazza del Popolo, **t** 0736 259626 (€). One of Italy's 150 'historical cafés', renowned for its home-made Anisetta liqueur and amaretto. It's a great place for pastries and aperitifs, with original Art Nouveau decor.

LaLiva, Piazza della Viola 13, **t** 0736 259358 (€). A small trattoria with a good menu featuring *olive all'ascolana* and vegetable *fritto misto*. *Closed Tues pm and Weds.*

Dell'Arengo, Via Tamasacco 5, **t** 0736 254711 (€). Another little trattoria with excellent, simple *antipasti*, including salami, cheeses, and steamed beans with tomatoes, and great wines. *Closed Mon.*

Gastronomica Enoteca Migliori >>

Gastronomia Enoteca Migliori, Piazza Arringo 2, **t** 0736 250042 (€). A famous deli and wine bar owned by a huge promoter of local olives, who helped them gain their DOP status.

West towards Umbria

This is the surest year-round route over the Sibillini on the Roman Via Salaria. The mountains outdo any man-made sights, and if you need a break, there's **Aquasanta Terme**, where the Roman legions used to rest. It has a medieval bridge that looks like new and a natural spring where 15 million litres of hot sulphuric water burst out of the ground in a cave – André Gide recommended it highly.

Further up, **Arquata del Tronto** is a lovely village under a 13th-century Rocca. In one of its *frazioni*, **Capodacqua**, is a little octagonal church, **Madonna del Sole**, attributed to Cola dell'Amatrice, who may also have painted the frescoes within.

Beyond Arquata, the spectacular mountain route twists over the **Forca Canapine** pass (1,500m), a balcony over the southern Apennines; in late May, it's covered with purple crocuses, and continues through a mountain meadow, the **Piano Grande** (*see* p.576). The newer route is faster, plunging through a vast tunnel.

Glossary

acroterion: decorative protrusion on the rooftop of an Etruscan, Greek or Roman temple. At the corners of the roof they are called *antefixes*.
ambones: twin pulpits (singular: *ambo*), often elaborately decorated.
ambulatory: aisle round the apse of a church.
atrium: entrance court of a Roman house or early church.
badia: abbey or abbey church (also *abbazia*).
baldacchino: baldachin, a columned stone canopy above the altar of a church.
basilica: a rectangular building, usually divided into three aisles by rows of columns. In Rome this was the common form for law courts and other public buildings, and Roman Christians adapted it for their early churches.
borgo: from the Saxon *burh* of Santo Spirito in Rome: a suburb or village.
bucchero ware: black, delicately thin Etruscan ceramics, usually incised or painted.
Calvary chapels: a series of outdoor chapels, usually on a hillside, that commemorate the stages of the Passion of Christ.
campanile: a belltower.
campanilismo: local patriotism; the Italians' own word for their historic tendency to be more faithful to their hometowns than to the abstract idea of 'Italy'.
campo santo: a cemetery.
cardo: the transverse street of a Roman *castrum*-shaped city.
carroccio: a wagon carrying the banners of a medieval city and an altar; it served as the rallying point in battles.
cartoon: the preliminary sketch for a fresco or tapestry.
caryatid: supporting pillar or column carved into a standing female form; male versions are called *telamones*.
castrum: a Roman military camp, always neatly rectangular, with straight streets and gates at the cardinal points. Later the Romans founded or refounded cities in this form, hundreds of which survive today (Lucca, Aosta, Florence, Pavia, Como, Brescia, Ascoli Piceno, Ancona are clear examples).
cavea: the semicircle of seats inside a classical theatre.
cenacolo: fresco of the *Last Supper*, often on the wall of a monastery refectory.
chiaroscuro: the arrangement or treatment of light and dark areas in a painting.
ciborium: a tabernacle; the word is often used for large, free-standing tabernacles, or in the sense of a *baldacchino* (*see* above).
comune: commune or commonwealth, referring to the governments of the free cities of the Middle Ages. Today it denotes any local government, from the Comune di Roma down to the smallest village.
condottiere: leader of a band of mercenaries in late medieval and Renaissance times.
confraternity: a religious lay brotherhood, often serving as a neighbourhood mutual-aid and burial society, or following some specific charitable work (Michelangelo, for example, belonged to one that cared for condemned prisoners in Rome).
contrapposto: the dramatic, but rather unnatural twist in a statue, especially in a Mannerist or Baroque work, derived from Hellenistic and Roman art.
convento: a convent *or* monastery.
Cosmati work (or *Cosmatesque*): referring to a distinctive style of inlaid marble or enamel chips used in architectural decoration (pavements, pulpits, paschal candlesticks, etc.) in medieval Italy. The Cosmati family of Rome were its greatest practitioners.
crete: found in the pasturelands of southern Tuscany, chalky cliffs caused by erosion. Similar phenomena are the *biancane*, small chalk outcrops, and *balze*, deep eroded ravines around Volterra.

cupola: a dome.
decumanus: street of a Roman *castrum*-shaped city parallel to the longer axis, the central, main avenue called the Decumanus Major.
Dodecapolis: the federation of the 12 largest, strongest Etruscan city states (*see* p.20).
duomo: cathedral.
ex voto: an offering (a terracotta figurine, painting, medallion, silver bauble or whatever) made in thanksgiving to a god or Christian saint; the practice has always been present in Italy.
forum: the central square of a Roman town, with its most important temples and public buildings. The word means 'outside', as the original Roman forum was outside the first city walls.
fresco: wall painting, the most important Italian medium of art since Etruscan times. It isn't easy; first the artist draws the *sinopia* (*see* below) on the wall. This is covered with plaster, but only a little at a time, as the paint must be on the plaster before it dries. Leonardo da Vinci's endless attempts to find clever shortcuts ensured that little of his work would survive.
Ghibellines: one of the two great medieval parties (*see* Guelphs), the supporters of the Holy Roman Emperors.
gonfalon: the banner of a medieval free city; the *gonfaloniere*, or flag-bearer, was often the most important public official.
graffito: originally, incised decoration on buildings, walls, etc.; now means casually-scribbled messages in public places.
Greek cross: in the floor plans of churches, a cross with equal arms. The more familiar plan, with one arm extended to form a nave, is called a *Latin Cross*.
grisaille: painting or fresco in monochrome.
grotesques: carved or painted faces used in Etruscan and later Roman decoration; Raphael and others rediscovered them in the 'grotto' of Nero's Golden House in Rome.
Guelphs (*see* Ghibellines): the other great political faction of medieval Italy, supporters of the Pope.
intarsia: decorative inlaid wood or marble.
loggia: an open-sided gallery or arcade.
lozenge: the diamond shape – this, along with stripes, is one of the trademarks of Pisan architecture.
lunette: semicircular space on a wall, above a door or under vaulting, either filled by a window or a mural painting.
matroneum: elevated women's gallery round the nave of an early church (adopted from the Byzantines in the 6th and 7th centuries).
narthex: the enclosed porch of a church.
naumachia: mock naval battles, like those staged in the Colosseum.
opus reticulatum: Roman masonry consisting of diamond-shaped blocks.
palazzo: not just a palace, but any large, important building (though the word comes from the Imperial *palatium* on Rome's Palatine Hill).
Palio: a banner, and the horse race in which city neighbourhoods contend for it in their annual festivals. The most famous is at Siena.
Pantocrator: Christ 'ruler of all', a common subject for apse paintings and mosaics in areas influenced by Byzantine art.
pietra dura: rich inlay decoration that uses semi-precious stones, perfected in post-Renaissance Florence.
pieve: a parish church.
pluteo: screen, usually of marble, between two columns, often highly decorated.
podestà: in medieval cities, an official sent by the Holy Roman Emperors to take charge; their power, or lack of it, depended on the strength of the *comune*.
polyptych: a painting (usually a panel painting) that is divided into 4 or more sections, or panels.
predella: smaller paintings on panels below the main subject of a painted altarpiece.
presepio: a Christmas crib.
putti: flocks of plaster cherubs with rosy cheeks and bottoms that infested much of Italy in the Baroque era.
quattrocento: the 1400s – the Italian way of referring to centuries (duecento, trecento, quattrocento, cinquecento, etc.).
sbandieratore (or *alfiere*): flag-thrower in medieval costume at an Italian festival.
sinopia: the layout of a fresco (*see* above), etched by the artist on the wall before the plaster is applied. Often these are works of art in their own right.
stele: a vertical funeral stone.
stigmata: a miraculous simulation of the bleeding wounds of Christ, appearing

in holy men such as St Francis during the 12th century, and in Padre Pio of Puglia in our own time.

telamone: *see* caryatid.

thermae: Roman baths.

tondo: round relief, painting or terracotta (plural: *tondi*).

transenna: a marble screen separating the altar area from the rest of an Early Christian church.

travertine: hard, light-coloured stone, sometimes flecked or pitted with black, sometimes perfect. The most widely used material in ancient and modern Rome.

triptych: a painting, especially an altarpiece, in three sections.

trompe l'œil: art using perspective effects to deceive the eye – for example, to create the illusion of depth on a flat surface, or make painted columns and arches seem real.

tympanum: the semicircular space, often bearing a painting or relief, above the portal of a church.

voussoir: one of the stones of an arch.

Language

The fathers of modern Italian were Dante, Manzoni and television. Each did their part in creating a national language from an infinity of regional and local dialects; the Florentine Dante, the first 'immortal' to write in the vernacular, did much to put the Tuscan dialect in the foreground of Italian literature. In the 19th century Manzoni's revolutionary novel, *I Promessi Sposi* (*The Betrothed*), heightened national consciousness by using an everyday language all could understand. Television in the last few decades has been performing an even more spectacular linguistic unification; although the majority of Italians still speak a dialect at home, school and work, their TV idols insist on proper Italian.

Perhaps because they are so busy learning their own beautiful but grammatically complex language, Italians are not especially apt at learning others. English lessons, however, have been the rage for years, and at most hotels and restaurants there will be someone who speaks some English. In small towns and out-of-the-way places, finding an Anglophone may prove more difficult. The words and phrases below should help you out in most situations, but the ideal way to come to Italy is with some Italian under your belt; your visit will be richer and you're much more likely to make some Italian friends.

Pronunciation

Italian words are pronounced phonetically. Every vowel and consonant (except 'h') is sounded. Consonants are the same as in English, except the 'c' which, when followed by an 'e' or 'i', is pronounced like the English 'ch' (*cinque* thus becomes 'cheenquay'). Italian 'g' is also soft before 'i' or 'e' as in gira, pronounced 'jee-ra'. 'H' is never sounded; 'z' is pronounced like 'ts'. The consonants 'sc' before the vowels 'i' or 'e' become like the English 'sh' as in 'sci', pronounced 'shee'; 'ch' is pronouced like a 'k' as in Chianti, 'kee-an-tee'; 'gn' as 'ny' in English (*bagno*, pronounced 'ban-yo', while 'gli' is pronounced like the middle of the word 'million' (Castiglione, pronounced 'Ca-steely-oh-nay').

Vowel pronunciation is: 'a' as in English 'father'; 'e' when unstressed is pronounced like 'a' in 'fate' as in *mele*, when stressed can be the same or like the 'e' in 'pet' (*bello*); 'i' is like the 'i' in 'machine'; 'o' like 'e', has two sounds, 'o' as in 'hope' when unstressed (*tacchino*), and usually 'o' as in 'rock' when stressed (*morte*); 'u' is pronounced like the 'u' in 'June'.

The accent usually (but not always) falls on the penultimate syllable. Also note that, in he big northern cities, the informal way of addressing someone as you, *tu*, is widely used; the more formal *lei* or *voi* is commonly used in provincial districts.

Useful Words and Phrases

For a list of vocabulary relating to Italian **food and drink**, *see* pp.54–56.

General

yes/no/maybe *sì/no/forse*
I don't know *Non lo so*
I don't understand (Italian)
Non capisco (l'italiano)
Does someone here speak English?
C'è qualcuno qui che parla inglese?
Speak slowly *Parla lentamente*

Could you assist me? *Potrebbe aiutarmi?*
Help! *Aiuto!*
Please/Thank you (very much) *Per favore/(Molte) grazie*
You're welcome *Prego*
It doesn't matter *Non importa*
All right *Va bene*
Excuse me *Mi scusi*
Be careful! *Attenzione!*
Nothing *Niente*
It is urgent! *È urgente!*
How are you? *Come sta?*
Well, and you? *Bene, e Lei?*
What is your name? *Come si chiama?*
Hello *Salve* or *ciao* (both informal)
Good morning *Buongiorno* (formal hello)
Good afternoon, evening *Buonasera* (also formal hello)
Good night *Buonanotte*
Goodbye *Arrivederla* (formal), *arrivederci/ciao* (informal)
What do you call this in Italian? *Come si chiama questo in italiano?*
What?/Who?/Where? *Che?/Chi?/Dove?*
Where is/are... *Dov'è/Dove sono...*
When?/Why? *Quando?/Perché?*
How? *Come?*
How much? *Quanto?*
I am lost *Mi sono smarrito(a); mi sono perso(a)*
I am hungry/thirsty/sleepy; I am tired *Ho fame/sete/sonno; sono stanco(a)*
I am sorry *Mi dispiace*
I am ill *Mi sento male*
Leave me alone *Lasciami in pace*
good/bad *buono bravo/male cattivo*
hot/cold *caldo/freddo*
slow/fast *lento/rapido*
up/down *su/giù*
big/small *grande/piccolo*
here/there *qui/lì*

Transport

airport *aeroporto*
bus stop *fermata*
bus/coach *autobus/pullman*
railway station *stazione ferroviaria*
train *treno*
platform *binario*
port *porto*
port station *stazione marittima*
ship *nave*
car *macchina*
taxi *tassì*
ticket *biglietto*
customs *dogana*
seat (reserved) *posto (prenotato)*

Travel Directions

One (two) ticket(s) to Naples, please *Un biglietto (due biglietti) per Napoli, per favore*
one way *semplice/andata*
return (round trip) *andata e ritorno*
first/second class *Prima/seconda classe*
I want to go to... *Desidero andare a...*
How can I get to...? *Come posso andare a...?*
How do I get to the town centre? *Come posso raggiungere il centro città?*
Do you stop at...? *Ferma a...?*
Where is...? *Dov'è...?*
How far is it to...? *Quanto siamo lontani da...?*
What is the name of this station? *Come si chiama questa stazione?*
When does the next ... leave? *Quando parte il prossimo...?*
From where does it leave? *Da dove parte?*
How long does the trip take? *Quanto tempo dura il viaggio?*
How much is the fare? *Quant'è il biglietto?*
Have a good trip *Buon viaggio!*

Driving

near/far *vicino/lontano*
left/right *sinistra/destra*
straight ahead *sempre diritto*
forwards/backwards *avanti/indietro*
north/south *nord/sud*
east *est, oriente*
west *ovest, occidente*
round the corner *dietro l'angolo*
crossroads *bivio*
street/road *strada/via*
square *piazza*
car hire *noleggio macchina*
motorbike/scooter *motocicletta/Vespa*
bicycle *bicicletta*
petrol/diesel *benzina/gasolio*
garage *garage*

This doesn't work *Questo non funziona*
mechanic *meccanico*
map/town plan *carta/pianta*
Where is the road to...? *Dov'è la strada per...?*
breakdown *guasto, panne*
driving licence *patente di guida*
driver *guidatore*
speed *velocità*
danger *pericolo*
parking *parcheggio*
no parking *sosta vietata*
narrow *stretto*
bridge *ponte*
toll *pedaggio*
slow down *rallentare*

Numbers

one *uno/una*
two/three/four *due/tre/quattro*
five/six/seven *cinque/sei/sette*
eight/nine/ten *otto/nove/dieci*
eleven/twelve *undici/dodici*
thirteen/fourteen *tredici/quattordici*
fifteen/sixteen *quindici/sedici*
seventeen/eighteen *diciassette/diciotto*
nineteen *diciannove*
twenty *venti*
twenty-one *ventuno*
thirty *trenta*
forty *quaranta*
fifty *cinquanta*
sixty *sessanta*
seventy *settanta*
eighty *ottanta*
ninety *novanta*
hundred *cento*
one hundred and one *centouno*
two hundred *duecento*
one thousand *mille*
two thousand *duemila*
million *milione*

Days

Monday *lunedì*
Tuesday *martedì*
Wednesday *mercoledì*
Thursday *giovedì*
Friday *venerdì*
Saturday *sabato*
Sunday *domenica*

Time

What time is it? *Che ora è?*
day/week *giorno/settimana*
month *mese*
morning/afternoon *mattina/pomeriggio*
evening *sera*
yesterday *ieri*
today *oggi*
tomorrow *domani*
soon *fra poco*
later *dopo/più tardi*
It is too early *È troppo presto*
It is too late *È troppo tardi*

Shopping, Services and Sightseeing

I would like... *Vorrei...*
How much is it? *Quanto costa questo?*
open/closed *aperto/chiuso*
cheap/expensive *a buon prezzo/caro*
bank *banca*
beach *spiaggia*
bed *letto*
church *chiesa*
entrance/exit *entrata/uscita*
hospital *ospedale*
money *soldi*
newspaper (foreign) *giornale (straniero)*
pharmacy *farmacia*
police station *commissariato*
policeman *poliziotto*
post office *ufficio postale*
sea *mare*
shop *negozio*
tobacco shop *tabaccaio*
WC *toilette, bagno*
men *Signori, Uomini*
women *Signore, Donne*

Useful Hotel Vocabulary

I'd like a single/twin/double room please
Vorrei una camera singola/doppia/ matrimoniale, per favore
with/without bath *con/senza bagno*
for two nights *per due notti*
We are leaving tomorrow morning
Partiamo domani mattina
May I see the room/another room, please?
Posso vedere la camera/un'altra camera?

Is there a room with a balcony?
C'è una camera con balcone?
There isn't (aren't) any hot water/soap/ light/toilet paper/towels
Manca (Mancano) acqua calda/sapone/ luce/carta igienica/asciugamani
May I pay by credit card?
Posso pagare con carta di credito?
Fine, I'll take it *Bene, la prendo*
Is breakfast included?
E' compresa la prima colazione?
What time do you serve breakfast?
A che ora è la colazione?

Further Reading

General

Carmichael, Montgomery, *In Tuscany* (Burns & Oates, 1910).

Goethe, J.W., *Italian Journey* (Penguin Classics, 1982). An excellent example of a genius turned to mush by Italy; good insights, but big, big mistakes.

Hutton, Edward, *Florence, Assisi and Umbria Revisited*, in *Unknown Tuscany*, and *Siena and Southern Tuscany* (Hollis & Carter, 1995). Modern travel classics.

McCarthy, Mary, *The Stones of Florence* and *Venice Observed* (Penguin, 1986). Brilliant evocation of Italy's two great art cities, with an understanding that makes many other works on the subject seem sluggish and pedantic; don't visit Florence without it.

Morton, H.V., *A Traveller in Italy* (Methuen & Co., 1964). Among the most readable and delightful accounts of Italy in print. Morton is a sincere scholar and a true gentleman.

Raison, Laura (ed), *Tuscany: An Anthology* (Cadogan, 1983). An excellent selection of the best by Tuscans and Tuscany-watchers.

Spender, Matthew, *Within Tuscany* (Viking, 1992). Poet Stephen Spender's son, on everything from porcupines to Pontormo's bowel movements.

Williams, Egerton R., *Hill Towns of Italy* (Smith, Elder, 1904). An Englishman goes exploring in Tuscany and Umbria.

Art and Literature

Boccaccio, Giovanni, *The Decameron* (Penguin, 1972). The ever-young classic by one of the fathers of Italian literature. Its irreverent worldliness still provides a salutary antidote to whatever dubious ideas persist in your mental baggage.

Burckhardt, Jacob, *The Civilization of the Renaissance in Italy* (Harper & Row, 1975). The classic on the subject (first published in 1860); the mark against which scholars still level their poison pens of revisionism.

Castiglione, Baldassare, *The Book of the Courtier* (Wordsworth Editions Ltd., 2000)

Cellini, B., *Autobiography of Benvenuto Cellini* (Penguin, translated by George Bull, 1999). Fun reading about the vicious competition of the Florentine art world by a swashbuckling braggart and world-class liar.

Clark, Kenneth, *Leonardo da Vinci* (Penguin, 1993).

Dante, Alighieri, *The Divine Comedy* (plenty of good translations). Few poems have had such a mythical significance for a nation. Anyone serious about understanding Tuscany or Italy and their world view will need more than a passing acquaintance with Dante.

Gardner, Edmund G., *The Story of Florence*, *The Story of Siena*; also **Gordon, Lina Duff**, *The Story of Assisi* and *The Story of Perugia* and **Ross, Janet**, *The Story of Pisa* (J.M. Dent, 1900s). Some of the excellent and highly readable Medieval Towns series.

Ghibert/Linscott, *Complete Poems and Selected Letters of Michelangelo* (Princeton Press, 1984).

Gordon, Lina Duff, *The Story of Assisi* (*see* Gardner, Edmund G. above).

Hale, J.R. (ed), *A Concise Encyclopedia of the Italian Renaissance* (Thames and Hudson, 1981). An excellent reference guide, with many concise, well-written essays. See also *Florence and the Medici: The Pattern of Control* (1977), which describes just how the Medici did it.

Hibbert, Christopher, *Rise and Fall of the House of Medici* (Penguin, 1965). One of the classics – compulsive reading.

Hook, Judith, *Siena* (Hamish Hamilton, 1979). A book a bit weak on art but good on everything else.

Leonardo da Vinci, *Notebooks* (Oxford, 1983).

Levey, Michael, *Early Renaissance* (1967) and *High Renaissance* (1975; both Penguin). Old-fashioned accounts of the period, with a breathless reverence for the 1500s, but still full of intriguing interpretations.

Masson, Georgina, *Frederick II of Hohenstaufen* (Secker & Warburg, 1973).

Murray, Linda, *The High Renaissance* and *The Late Renaissance and Mannerism* (Thames and Hudson, 1977). Excellent introduction to the period; also **Peter and Linda Murray**, *The Art of the Renaissance* (1963).

Origo, Iris, *The Merchant of Prato* (Penguin, 1963). Everyday life in 14th-century Tuscany with the father of modern accounting, Francesco di Marco Datini. Also *Images and Shadows; War in the Val d'Orcia*, about a Tuscan childhood and life during the war.

Petrarch, Francesco, *Canzionere and Other Works* (Oxford, 1985). The most famous poems by the 'First Modern Man'.

Procacci, Giuliano, *History of the Italian People* (Penguin, 1973). An in-depth view from the year 1000 up to the present, and also an introduction to the wit and subtlety of the best Italian scholarship.

Richards, Charles, *The New Italians* (Penguin, 1995). An observant and amusing study of life in Italy during and since the political upheaval and financial scandals of the early 1990s.

Ross, Janet, *The Story of* Pisa (*see* Gardner, Edmund G., opposite)

Symonds, John Addington, *A Short History of the Renaissance in Italy* (Smith, Elder, 1893). A condensed version of the authority of a century ago, still fascinating today.

Vasari, Giorgio, *Lives of the Painters, Sculptors and Architects* (Everyman, 1996). Readable, anecdotal accounts of the Renaissance greats by the father of modern art history.

Index

Main page references are in **bold**. Page references to maps are in *italics*.

10th Edition Published 2007

Cadogan Guides is an imprint of
New Holland Publishers (UK) Ltd
London • Cape Town • Sydney • Auckland

New Holland Publishers (UK) Ltd
Garfield House
86–88 Edgware Road
London W2 2EA

80 McKenzie Street
Cape Town 8001
South Africa

Unit 1, 66 Gibbes Street
Chatswood, NSW 2067
Australia

218 Lake Road
Northcote
Auckland
New Zealand

Cadogan@nhpub.co.uk
www.cadoganguides.com
t 44 (0)20 7724 7773

Distributed in the United States by Globe Pequot, Connecticut

Cover photographs: © Chad Ehlers / Alamy, Gary Yeowell/Getty
Photo essay photographs: © p.1: Gary Yeowell/Getty; © p.2 David Madison/Getty; © p.3 Toyohiro Yamada/Getty; © p.4 CuboImages srl / Alamy; © p.8 Simeone Huber/Getty; © Chad Ehlers / Alamy, Gary Yeowell/Getty © p.9 Peter Horree / Alamy, Mathew Lodge / Alamy; © p.10 Stefano Scata,Altrendo Travel/Getty; © p.11 Gary Yeowell, Kieran Scott, Michael Newton/Getty; © p.12 Denis Waugh; © p.13 CuboImages srl / Alamy, Tino Soriano; © p.14 Simeone Huber; © p.16 David Noton
Maps © Cadogan Guides, drawn by Maidenhead Cartographic Services Ltd
Art director: Sarah Gardner
Editor: Rhonda Carrier
Assistant Editor: Nicola Jessop
Proofreading: Elspeth Anderson
Indexing: Isobel McLean

Printed in Italy by Legoprint
A catalogue record for this book is available from the British Library

ISBN: 978-1-86011-359-8

Please help us to keep this guide up to date. We have done our best to ensure that the information in this guide is correct at the time of going to press. But laws and regulations are constantly changing, and standards and prices fluctuate. We would be delighted to receive any comments. Authors of the best letters will receive a copy of the Cadogan Guide of their choice.

CADOGANguides

ITALY

'Excellently written, bursting with character'

– Holiday Which

Bay of Naples & Southern Italy
Bologna & Emilia-Romagna
Buying a Property Italy
Central Italy
Florence
Flying Visits Italy
Italian Riviera & Piemonte
Italy
Lombardy & the Italian Lakes
Milan
Pick Your Brains About Italy
Rome
Rome Venice Florence
Sardinia
Sicily
Tuscany
Tuscany Umbria & the Marches
Umbria
Venice
Venice Venetia & the Dolomites
Working and Living Italy

CADOGANguides

Working and Living

'Impressively comprehensive'

Wanderlust Magazine

Working and Living Australia • *Working and Living* Canada • *Working and Living* France • *Working and Living* Italy • *Working and Living* New Zealand • *Working and Living* Portugal • *Working and Living* Spain • *Working and Living* USA

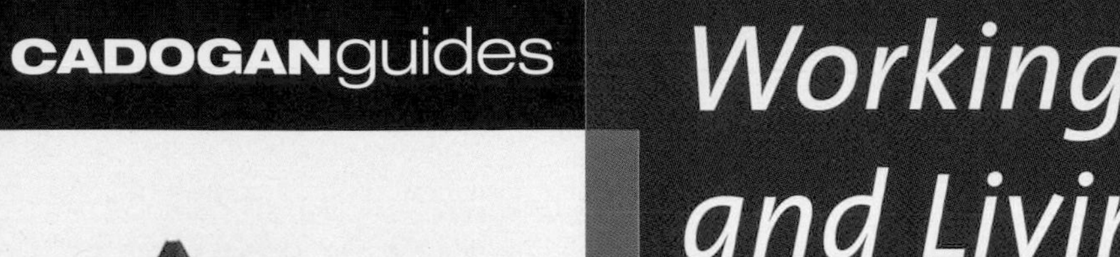

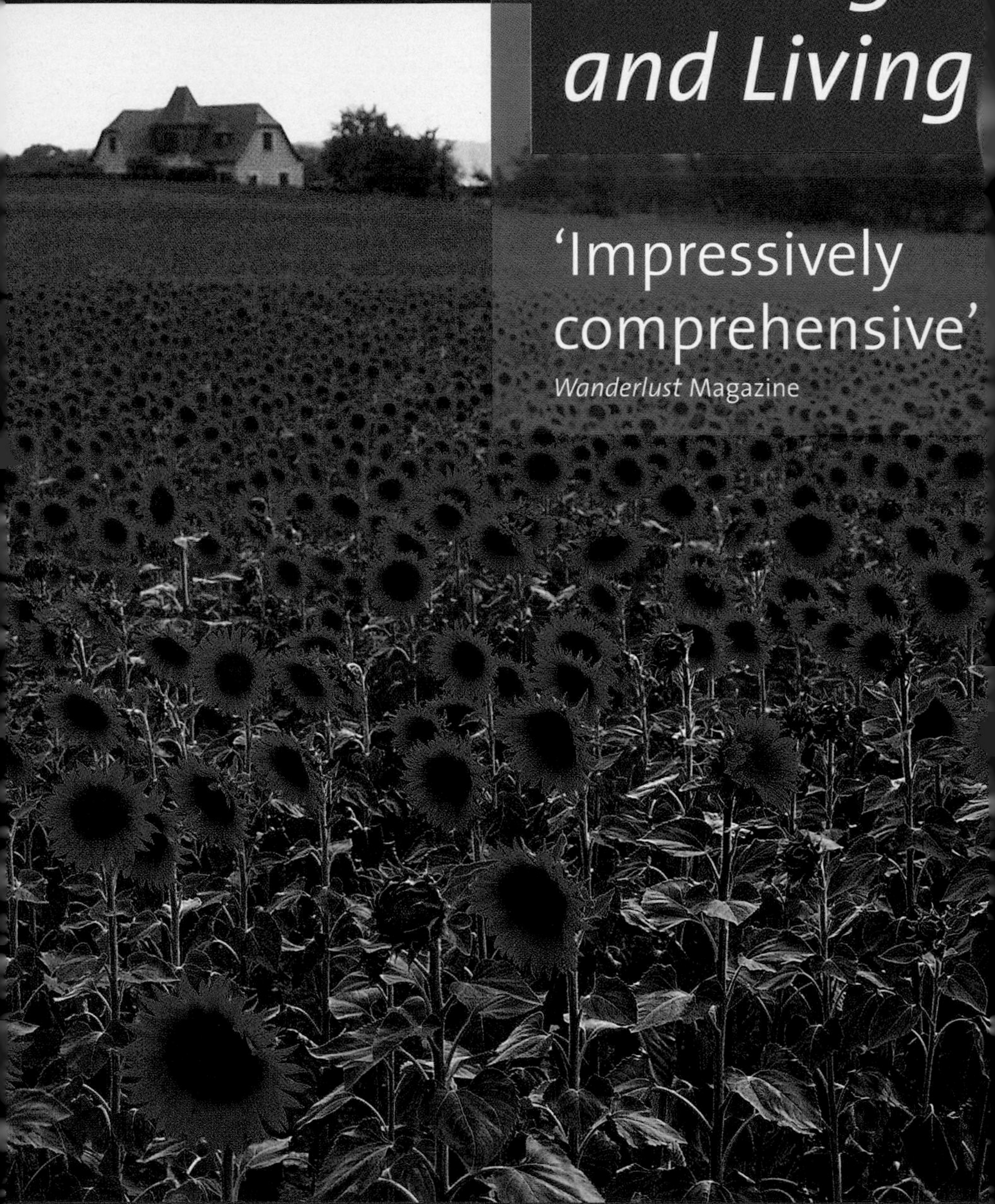

Tuscany, Umbria & the Marches touring atlas

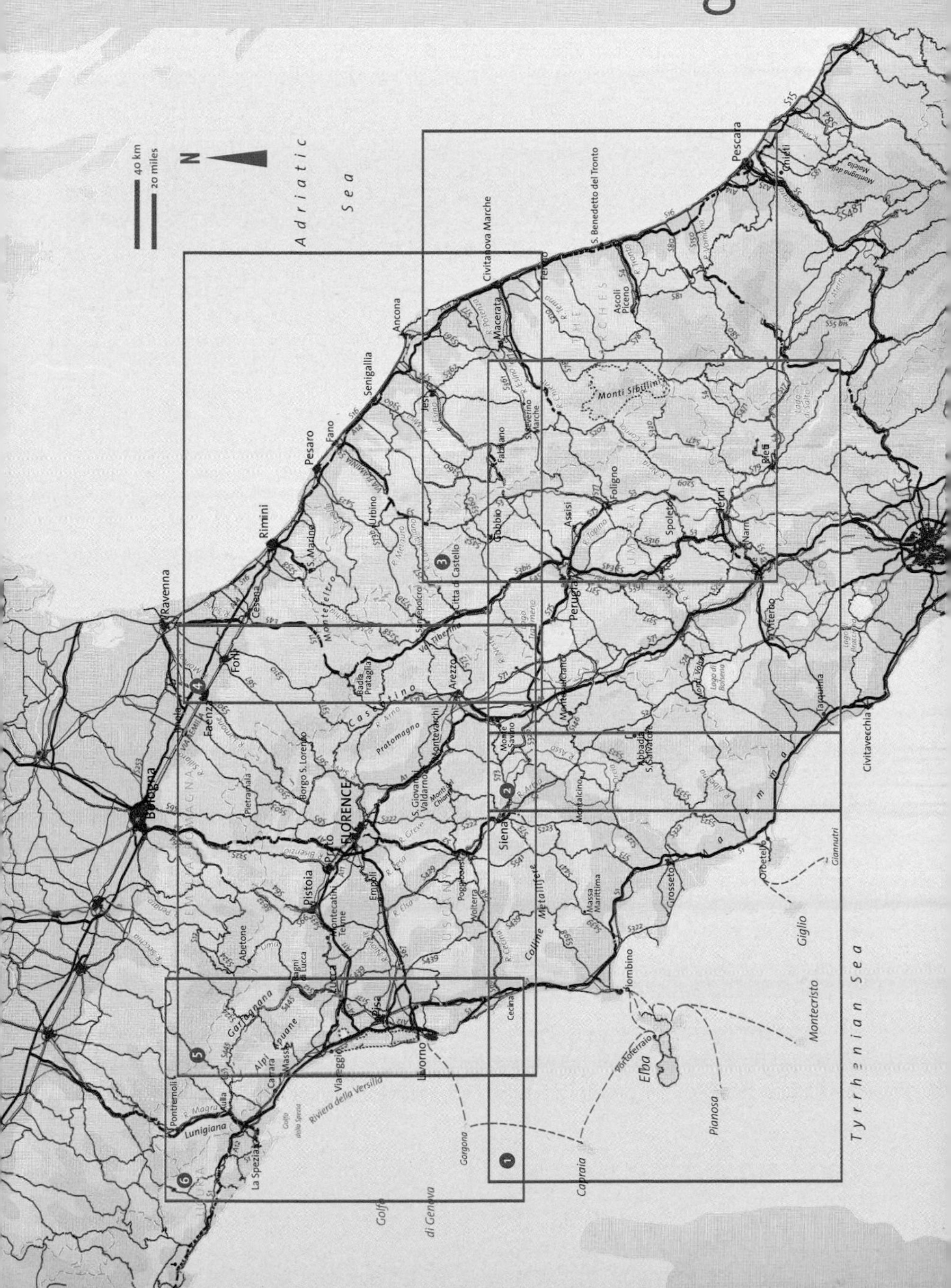

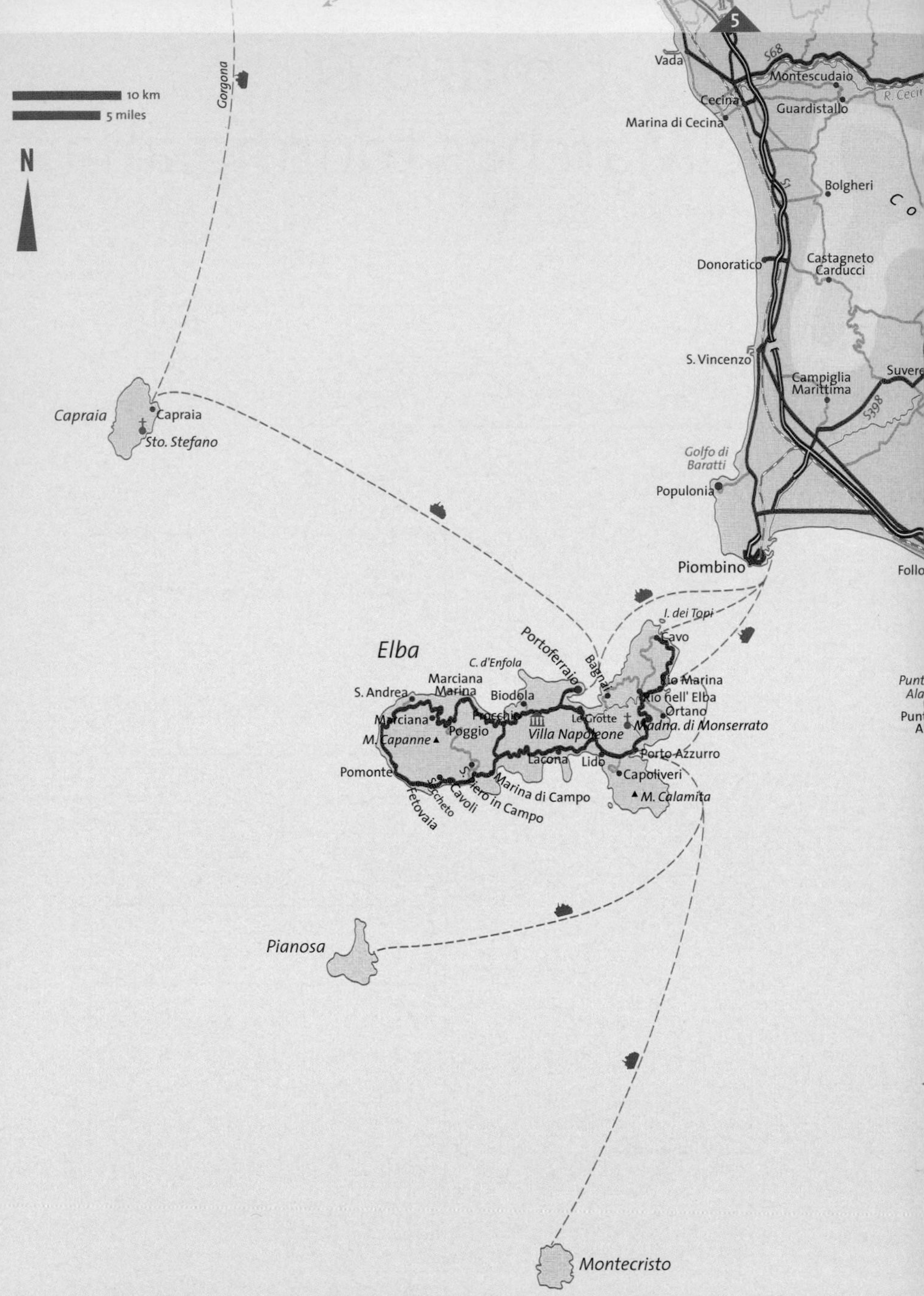

10 km
5 miles
N
Gorgona
Capraia
Capraia
Sto. Stefano
Vada
Montescudaio
Cecina
Guardistallo
Marina di Cecina
R. Cecina
Bolgheri
Donoratico
Castagneto Carducci
S. Vincenzo
Campiglia Marittima
Suvereto
Golfo di Baratti
Populonia
Piombino
Follonica
I. dei Topi
Cavo
Elba
Portoferraio
Bagnaia
C. d'Enfola
Rio Marina
Rio nell' Elba
Ortano
S. Andrea
Marciana Marina
Biodola
Marciana
Procchio
Le Grotte
Madna. di Monserrato
Poggio
Villa Napoleone
M. Capanne
Porto Azzurro
Lacona
Lido
Pomonte
Capoliveri
Marina di Campo
M. Calamita
Cavoli
S. Piero in Campo
Seccheto
Fetovaia
Pianosa
Montecristo
Tyrrhenian Sea

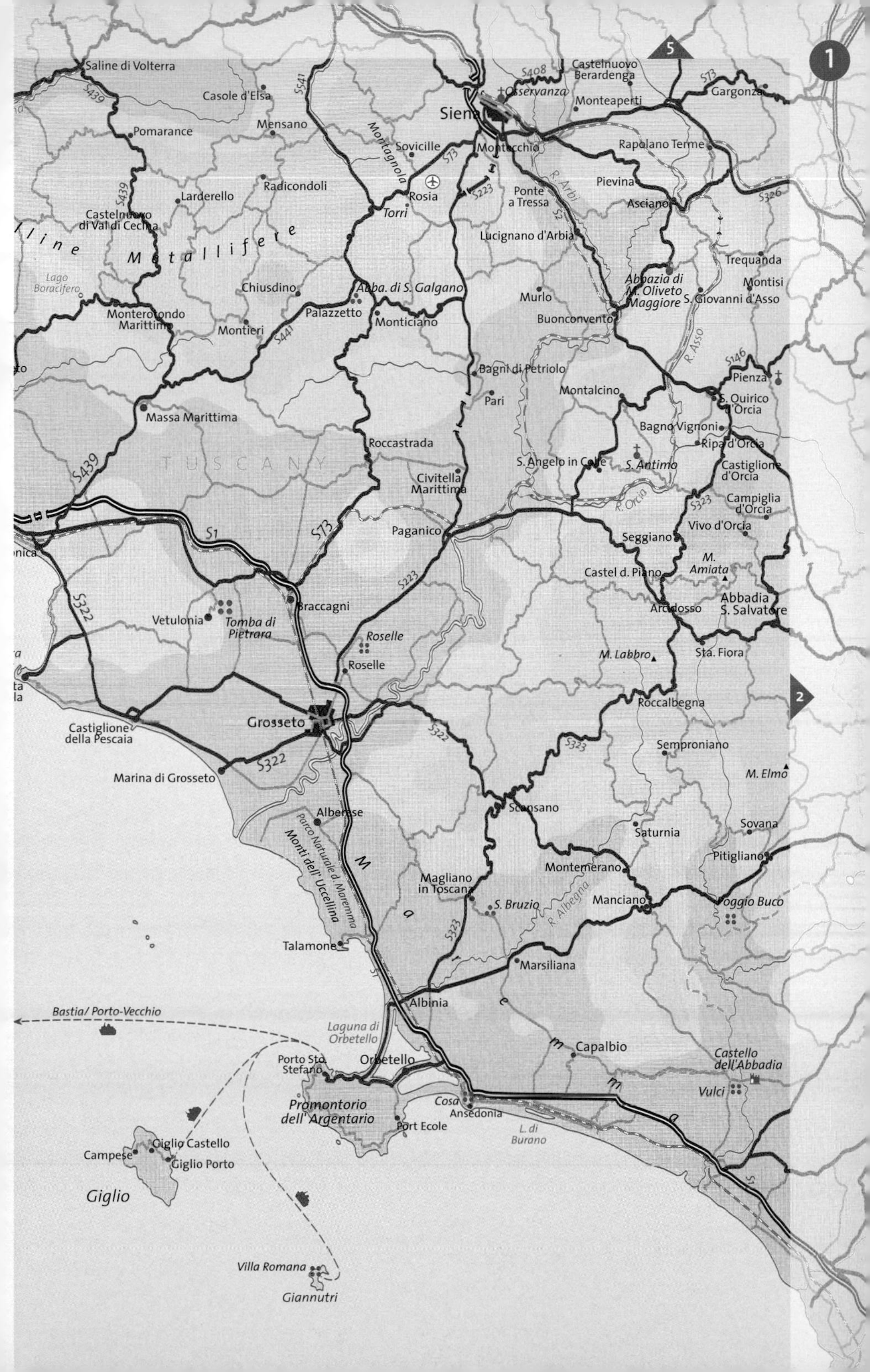

5

1

Saline di Volterra
Casole d'Elsa
S439
S541
S408
Castelnuovo Berardenga
S73
Gargonza
Osservanza
Monteaperti
Siena
Mensano
Pomarance
Montagnola
Sovicille
Montecchio
Rapolano Terme
Radicondoli
Rosia
S223
Pievina
S439
Larderello
Ponte a Tressa
R. Arbia
S326
Asciano
Castelnuovo di Val di Cecina
Torri
S2
Colline Metallifere
Lucignano d'Arbia
Trequanda
Lago Boracifero
Chiusdino
Abba. di S. Galgano
Abbazia di M. Oliveto Maggiore
Montisi
Murlo
S. Giovanni d'Asso
Monterotondo Marittimo
Palazzetto
Monticiano
Buonconvento
Montieri
S441
R. Asso
S146
Bagni di Petriolo
Pienza
Montalcino
S. Quirico d'Orcia
Pari
Massa Marittima
Bagno Vignoni
Roccastrada
Ripa d'Orcia
TUSCANY
S. Angelo in Colle
S. Antimo
Castiglione d'Orcia
S439
Civitella Marittima
R. Orcia
Campiglia d'Orcia
S323
S73
Vivo d'Orcia
S1
Paganico
Seggiano
M. Amiata
Castel d. Piano
S322
S223
Braccagni
Abbadia S. Salvatore
Arcidosso
Vetulonia
Tomba di Pietrara
Roselle
M. Labbro
Sta. Fiora
Roselle
2
Roccalbegna
Grosseto
Castiglione della Pescaia
S322
S323
Semproniano
S322
M. Elmo
Marina di Grosseto
Scansano
Alberese
Parco Naturale d. Maremma
Monti dell' Uccellina
Saturnia
Sovana
Pitigliano
Montemerano
Magliano in Toscana
R. Albegna
Manciano
S. Bruzio
Poggio Buco
S323
Maremma
Talamone
Marsiliana
Albinia
Bastia/ Porto-Vecchio
Laguna di Orbetello
Capalbio
Porto Sto. Stefano
Orbetello
Castello dell'Abbadia
Cosa
Vulci
Ansedonia
Promontorio dell' Argentario
Port Ecole
L. di Burano
Giglio Castello
Campese
Giglio Porto
Giglio
Villa Romana
Giannutri

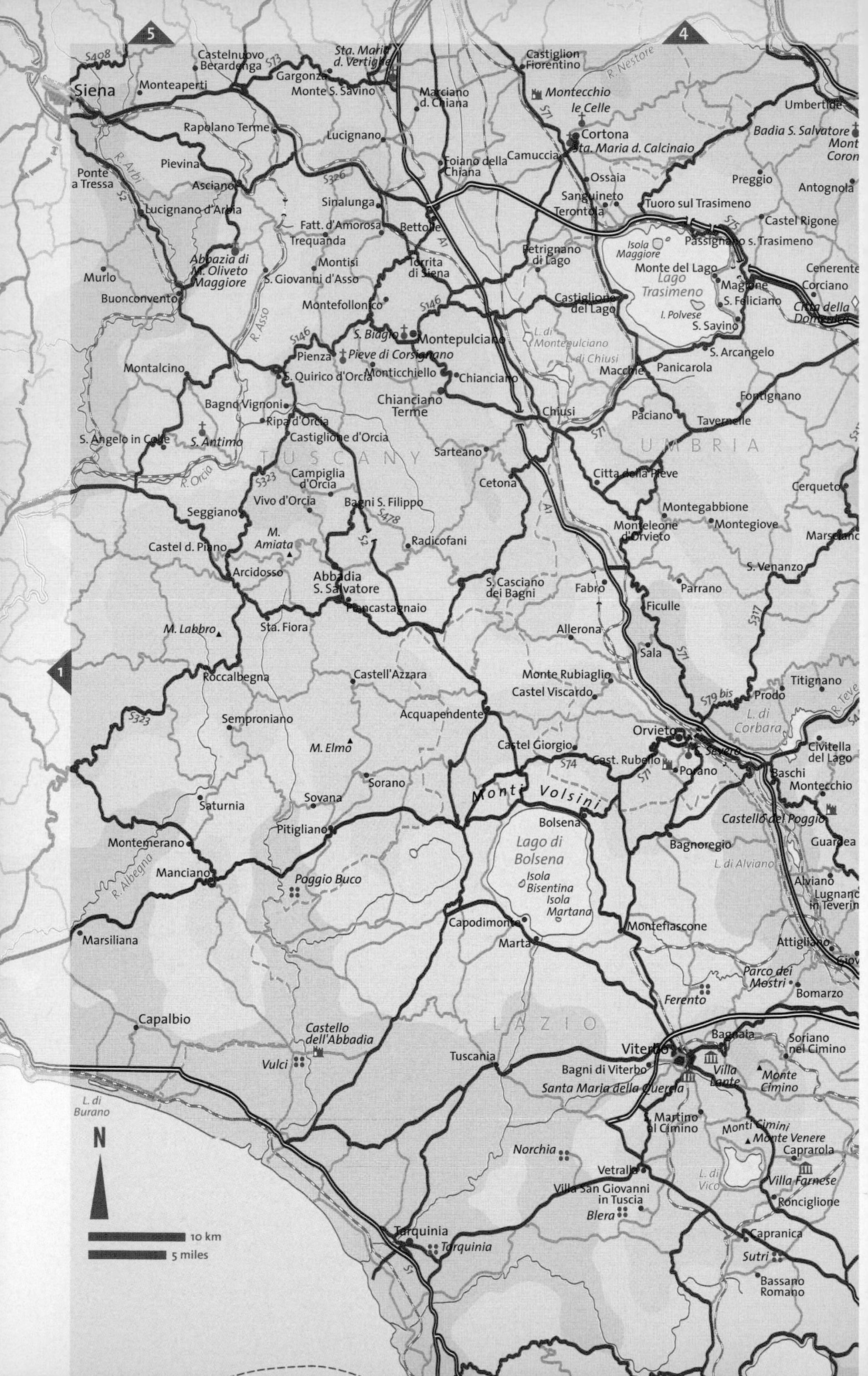
5
4
1
S408
Siena
Castelnuovo Berardenga
S73
Monteaperti
Sta. Maria d. Vertighe
Gargonza
Monte S. Savino
Castiglion Fiorentino
R. Nestore
Marciano d. Chiana
Montecchio
le Celle
S71
Umbertide
Rapolano Terme
Lucignano
Cortona
Sta. Maria d. Calcinaio
Badia S. Salvatore
R. Arbi
Ponte a Tressa
Pievina
Foiano della Chiana
Camuccia
Asciano
S326
Ossaia
Preggio
Antognola
S2
Sinalunga
Sanguineto
Terontola
Tuoro sul Trasimeno
Lucignano d'Arbia
Fatt. d'Amorosa
Bettolle
Castel Rigone
Trequanda
A1
S75
Passignano s. Trasimeno
Isola Maggiore
Abbazia di M. Oliveto Maggiore
Montisi
Torrita di Siena
Petrignano di Lago
Monte del Lago
Cenerente
Murlo
S. Giovanni d'Asso
Lago Trasimeno
Magione
Corciano
Buonconvento
Montefollonico
S146
Castiglione del Lago
S. Feliciano
Città della Domenica
R. Asso
I. Polvese
S. Savino
S146
S. Biagio
Montepulciano
L. di Montepulciano
Pienza
Pieve di Corsignano
L. di Chiusi
S. Arcangelo
Montalcino
S. Quirico d'Orcia
Monticchiello
Chianciano
Macchie
Panicarola
Chianciano Terme
Fontignano
Bagno Vignoni
Chiusi
Paciano
Ripa d'Orcia
Tavernelle
S. Angelo in Colle
S. Antimo
Castiglione d'Orcia
S71
TUSCANY
Sarteano
UMBRIA
R. Orcia
S323
Campiglia d'Orcia
Cetona
Città della Pieve
Cerqueto
Vivo d'Orcia
Bagni S. Filippo
Montegabbione
Seggiano
S478
Monteleone d'Orvieto
Montegiove
M. Amiata
S2
Radicofani
Castel d. Piano
Marsciano
Arcidosso
S. Venanzo
Abbadia S. Salvatore
S. Casciano dei Bagni
Fabro
Parrano
Piancastagnaio
Ficulle
M. Labbro
Sta. Fiora
Allerona
S317
Sala
Roccalbegna
Castell'Azzara
Monte Rubiaglio
Titignano
Castel Viscardo
S79 bis
Prodo
S323
L. di Corbara
R. Tevere
Semproniano
Acquapendente
Orvieto
M. Elmo
Castel Giorgio
S. Severo
Civitella del Lago
S74
Cast. Rubello
S71
Porano
Baschi
Sorano
Montecchio
Monti Volsini
Sovana
Saturnia
Bolsena
Castello del Poggio
Pitigliano
Lago di Bolsena
Montemerano
Bagnoregio
Guardea
L. di Alviano
R. Albegna
Manciano
Poggio Buco
Isola Bisentina
Alviano
Isola Martana
Lugnano in Teverina
Capodimonte
Montefiascone
Marsiliana
Marta
Attigliano
Parco dei Mostri
Bomarzo
Ferento
Capalbio
LAZIO
Castello dell'Abbadia
Bagnaia
Soriano nel Cimino
Viterbo
Tuscania
Vulci
Bagni di Viterbo
Villa Lante
Monte Cimino
Santa Maria della Querela
L. di Burano
S. Martino al Cimino
Monti Cimini
Monte Venere
N
Norchia
Caprarola
Vetralla
L. di Vico
Villa Farnese
Villa San Giovanni in Tuscia
Ronciglione
Blera
10 km
5 miles
Tarquinia
Capranica
Tarquinia
Sutri
S1
Bassano Romano

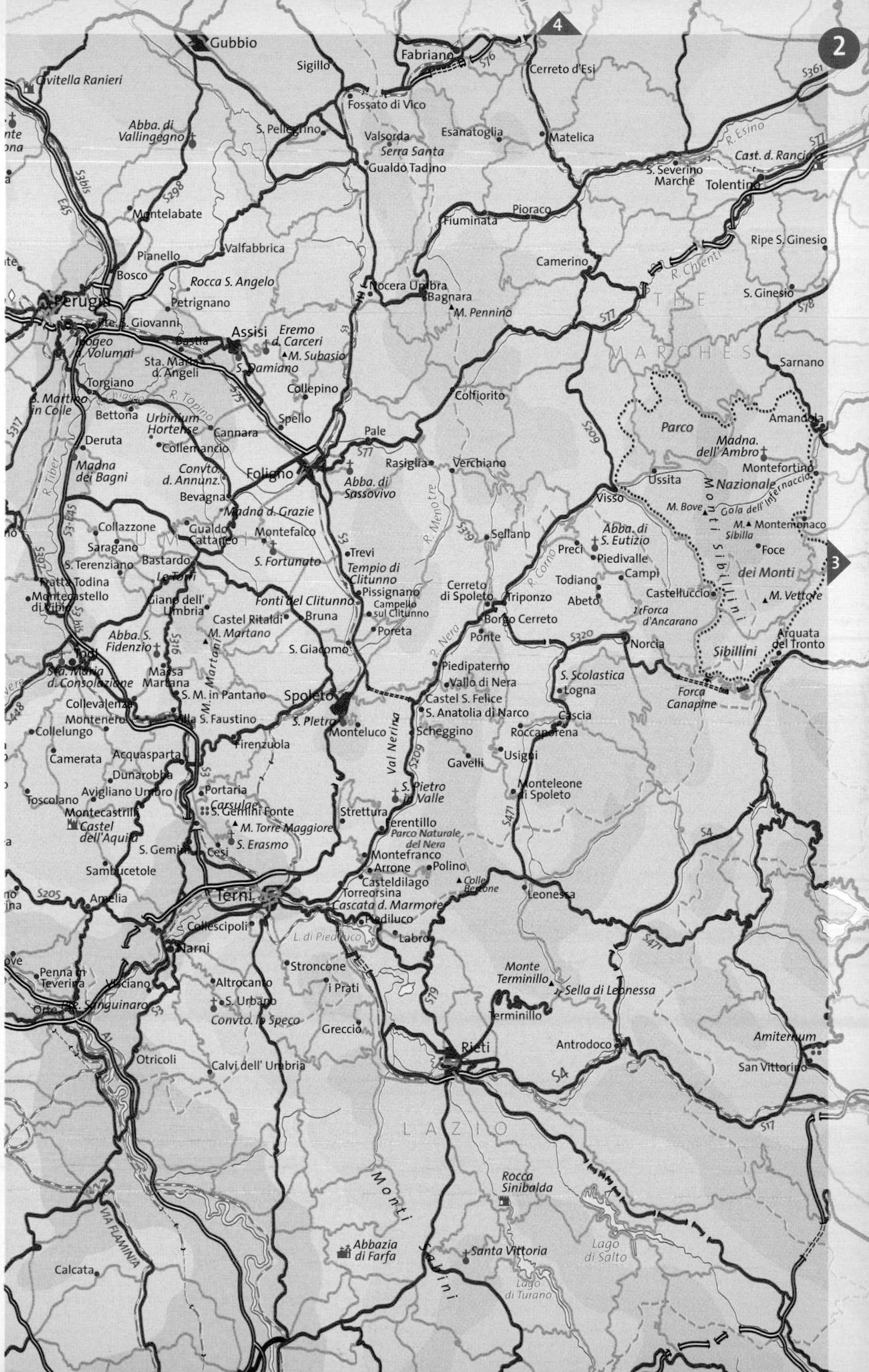

4
2
3
Gubbio
Civitella Ranieri
Sigillo
Fabriano
S76
Cerreto d'Esi
S361
Fossato di Vico
Abba. di Vallingegno
S. Pellegrino
Valsorda
Serra Santa
Esanatoglia
Matelica
R. Esino
S77
Cast. d. Rancia
Gualdo Tadino
S. Severino Marche
Tolentino
S3bis
E45
S298
Montelabate
Pioraco
Fiuminata
Ripe S. Ginesio
Valfabbrica
Pianello
Camerino
R. Chienti
Bosco
Rocca S. Angelo
Nocera Umbra
Bagnara
M. Pennino
S. Ginesio
Perugia
Petrignano
Pte. S. Giovanni
Assisi
Eremo d. Carceri
M. Subasio
Ipogeo d. Volumni
Bastia
Sta. Maria d. Angeli
S. Damiano
S3
S78
THE MARCHES
Sarnano
Torgiano
R. Chiascio
R. Topino
S75
Collepino
Colfiorito
S. Martino in Colle
Bettona
Urbinium Hortense
Spello
S209
Parco
Amandola
S317
Cannara
Pale
Madna. dell' Ambro
Deruta
Collemancio
S77
Rasiglia
Verchiano
Montefortino
R. Tiber
Madna dei Bagni
Convto. d. Annunz.
Foligno
Abba. di Sassovivo
R. Menotre
Ussita
Nazionale
Monti Sibillini
Bevagna
Visso
M. Bove
Gola dell' Infernaccio
Madna d. Grazie
S3-E45
Collazzone
Gualdo Cattaneo
Montefalco
S319
Sellano
Abba. di S. Eutizio
M. Sibilla
Montemonaco
Saragano
S. Fortunato
Trevi
R. Corno
Preci
Piedivalle
Foce
S. Terenziano
Bastardo
Tempio di Clitunno
Campi
dei Monti
La Torri
Todiano
Fratta Todina
S3bis
Montecastello di Vibio
Giano dell' Umbria
Fonti del Clitunno
Pissignano
Campello sul Clitunno
Cerreto di Spoleto
Triponzo
Abeto
Castelluccio
M. Vettore
Castel Ritaldi
Bruna
Borgo Cerreto
Forca d'Ancarano
M. Martano
Poreta
Ponte
Abba. S. Fidenzio
S316
R. Nera
S320
Norcia
Arquata del Tronto
Todi
S. Giacomo
Sibillini
Sta. Maria d. Consolazione
Massa Martana
M. Martani
Piedipaterno
S. Scolastica
Vallo di Nera
Collevalenza
S. M. in Pantano
Spoleto
Logna
Forca Canapine
Castel S. Felice
Montenero
Villa S. Faustino
S. Pietro
S. Anatolia di Narco
Cascia
Collelungo
Monteluco
Scheggino
Roccaporena
Firenzuola
Val Nerina
S209
Camerata
Acquasparta
Gavelli
Usigni
Dunarobba
Monteleone di Spoleto
Toscolano
Avigliano Umbro
Portaria
S. Pietro in Valle
Carsulae
S. Gemini Fonte
Strettura
S471
Montecastrilli
Castel dell'Aquila
M. Torre Maggiore
Ferentillo
S4
S. Gemini
S. Erasmo
Parco Naturale del Nera
Cesi
Montefranco
Sambucetole
Arrone
Polino
Colle Bertone
Casteldilago
S205
Amelia
Terni
Torreorsina
Leonessa
Cascata d. Marmore
Collescipoli
Piediluco
L. di Piediluco
Labro
S471
Narni
Stroncone
Penna in Teverina
Monte Terminillo
Visciano
Altrocanto
i Prati
Sella di Leonessa
Orte
S. Sanguinaro
S. Urbano
S3
Terminillo
Convto. lo Speco
S79
A1
Greccio
Amiternum
Antrodoco
Rieti
Otricoli
Calvi dell' Umbria
San Vittorino
S4
S17
LAZIO
Monti Sabini
Rocca Sinibalda
VIA FLAMINIA
Abbazia di Farfa
Santa Vittoria
Lago di Salto
Calcata
Lago di Turano

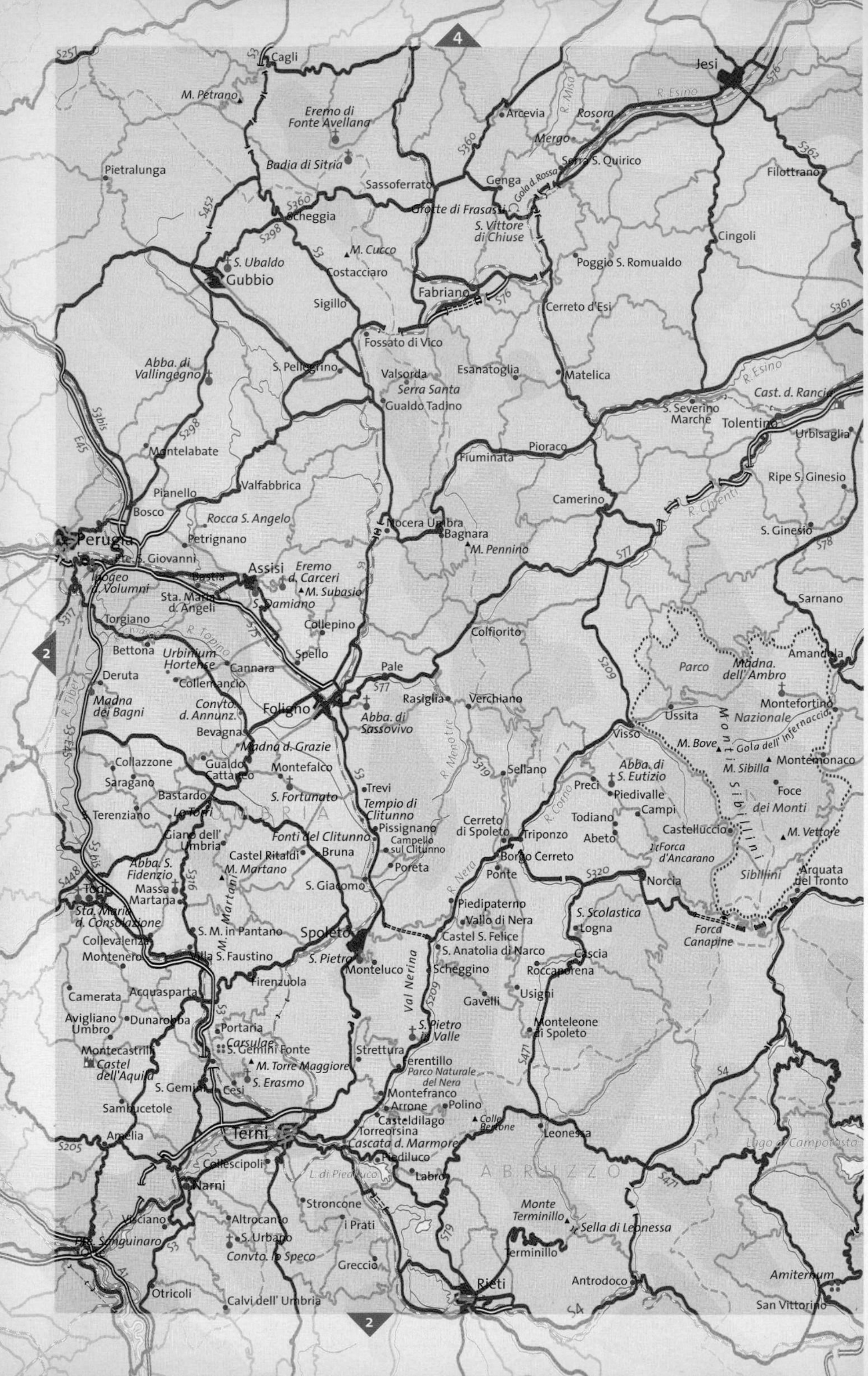
4
Cagli
M. Petrano
Eremo di Fonte Avellana
Badia di Sitria
Jesi
R. Esino
Arcevia
Rosora
Mergo
Serra S. Quirico
Filottrano
Pietralunga
Sassoferrato
Genga
Gola d. Rossa
Grotte di Frasassi
S. Vittore di Chiuse
Scheggia
M. Cucco
Cingoli
S. Ubaldo
Gubbio
Costacciaro
Poggio S. Romualdo
Fabriano
Sigillo
Cerreto d'Esi
Fossato di Vico
Abba. di Vallingegno
S. Pellegrino
Valsorda
Serra Santa
Gualdo Tadino
Esanatoglia
Matelica
R. Esino
Cast. d. Rancia
S. Severino Marche
Tolentino
Urbisaglia
Montelabate
Pioraco
Fiuminata
Ripe S. Ginesio
Valfabbrica
Pianello
Camerino
R. Chienti
Bosco
Rocca S. Angelo
Nocera Umbra
Bagnara
M. Pennino
S. Ginesio
Perugia
Petrignano
Pte. S. Giovanni
Assisi
Eremo d. Carceri
M. Subasio
Ipogeo d. Volumni
Bastia
Sta. Maria d. Angeli
S. Damiano
Sarnano
Torgiano
R. Topino
Collepino
Colfiorito
Bettona
Urbinium Hortense
Cannara
Spello
Amandola
2
Parco
Madna. dell' Ambro
Deruta
Collemancio
Pale
Madna dei Bagni
Convto. d. Annunz.
Foligno
Abba. di Sassovivo
Rasiglia
Verchiano
Montefortino
Nazionale
Monti Sibillini
Ussita
Bevagna
Visso
M. Bove
Gola dell' Infernaccio
Madna d. Grazie
M. Sibilla
Montemonaco
Collazzone
Montefalco
R. Menotre
Sellano
Abba. di S. Eutizio
Saragano
Gualdo Cattaneo
Trevi
Preci
Foce
Bastardo
S. Fortunato
Piedivalle
dei Monti
Tempio di Clitunno
R. Corno
Campi
S. Terenziano
Le Torri
UMBRIA
Cerreto di Spoleto
Todiano
Pissignano
Castelluccio
Giano dell' Umbria
Fonti del Clitunno
Campello sul Clitunno
Triponzo
Abeto
M. Vettore
Castel Ritaldi
Bruna
Forca d'Ancarano
Abba. S. Fidenzio
Poreta
Borgo Cerreto
M. Martano
Ponte
Arquata del Tronto
Massa Martana
S. Giacomo
R. Nera
Norcia
Sibillini
Todi
Piedipaterno
S. Scolastica
Sta. Maria d. Consolazione
Vallo di Nera
Logna
S. M. in Pantano
Spoleto
Castel S. Felice
Forca Canapine
Collevalenza
M. Martani
S. Anatolia di Narco
Cascia
Montenero
Villa S. Faustino
S. Pietro
Monteluco
Val Nerina
Scheggino
Roccaporena
Firenzuola
Camerata
Acquasparta
Gavelli
Usigni
Avigliano Umbro
Dunarobba
S. Pietro in Valle
Monteleone di Spoleto
Portaria
Carsulae
Montecastrilli
S. Gemini Fonte
Strettura
Ferentillo
Castel dell'Aquila
M. Torre Maggiore
Parco Naturale del Nera
S. Erasmo
S. Gemini
Cesi
Montefranco
Sambucetole
Arrone
Polino
Casteldilago
Colle Bertone
Amelia
Terni
Torreorsina
Leonessa
Lago di Campotosto
Cascata d. Marmore
Piediluco
Collescipoli
L. di Piediluco
Labro
ABRUZZO
Narni
Stroncone
Monte Terminillo
Sella di Leonessa
Visciano
Altrocanto
i Prati
Pte. Sanguinaro
S. Urbano
Convto. lo Speco
Terminillo
Amiternum
Greccio
Antrodoco
Rieti
Otricoli
Calvi dell' Umbria
San Vittorino
S4
2
S257
S3
S360
S452
S298
S76
S362
S361
S3bis
E45
S77
S209
S78
S317
S75
S319
S320
S316
S448
S471
S205
S79
A1

10 km
5 miles
N

Sirolo
Numana
Osimo
Castelfidardo
Porto Recanati
Loreto
Montefano
Recanati
ntecassiano
R. Potenza
Helvia Ricina
Macerata
Civitanova Marche
S. Claudio al Chienti
Porto S. Elpidio
Corridonia
THE MARCHES
Monte S. Giusto
S. Elpidio a Mare
Abba. di Fiastra
Adriatic
Porto S. Giorgio
Mogliano
Fermo
Massa Fermana
Torre di Palme
Sea
Falerone
Faleria
Pedaso
Servigliano
Monterubbiano
Moresco
Montefiore dell' Aso
Sta. Vittoria in Matenano
Monte Rinaldo
Cupra Marittima
Ripatransone
Abba. di S. Rufino
Montalto di Marche
Grottammare
Montefalcone Appennino
S. Benedetto del Tronto
Castignano
Offida
Acquaviva Picena
Ripaberarda
Porto d'Ascoli
Ascoli Piceno
R. Tronto
Alba Adriatica
Civitella del Tronto
Acquasanta Terme
Giulianova
Campli
Teramo
Morro d'Oro
Roseto degli Abruzzi
Canzano
Santa Maria di Propezzano
San Clemente al Vomano
Guardia Vomano
R. Vomano
Pineto
Parco Nazionale
Montorio al Vomano
Silvi Alta
Atri
Silvi Marina
Fano Adriano
Santa Maria di Ronzano
Castel Castagna
Montesilvano Marina
Tossicia
Prato Selva
Pietracamela
To Split
Isola del Gran Sasso d'Italia
Prati di Tivo
Pescara
Gran Sasso d'Italia
Castelli
Corno Piccolo
Penne
Francavilla al Mare
Corno Grande
Moscufo
ifugio Duca degli Abruzzi
Loreto Aprutino
Santa Maria del Lago
Campo Imperatore
Fonte Cerreto
Assergi
Gran Sasso
S16 S361 S77 S210 S4 S78 S81 S80 S150 S491 A14 A25

Faenza
Milano Marittima
Cervia
VIA AEMILIA
Forlì
Cesenatico
Terra del Sole
Forlimpopoli
Cesena
Bertinoro
S67
Dovadola
Predappio
Polenta
Predappio Alta
E45
A14
S16
Savignano sul Rubicone
Rimini
EMILIA-ROMAGNA
S310
Riccione
Misano Adriatico
S258
Cattolica
Gabicce Mare
Gabicce Monte
Verucchio
Santa Sofia
Pietracuta
Gradara
S. Marino
Casteldimezzo
Fiorenzuola di Focara
S71
Talamello
S. Leo
Perticara
Novafeltria
Montefeltro
San Piero in Bagno
S. Agata Feltria
Sta. Maria di Antico
Tavoleto
Bagno di Romagna
Pennabilli
Macerata Feltria
R. Foglia
Colbordolo
Monte Fumaiolo
R. Marecchia
M. Carpegna
Montecopiolo
Sassocorvaro
Badia Prataglia
Balze
Carpegna
S423
Alpe di Serra
Convto. di Montefiorentino
5
S258
Urbino
S. Bernardino
La Verna
M. Penna
Badia Tedalda
Piandimeleto
R. Foglia
S73b
Canavaccio
Fossombrone
Sestino
Chiusi d. Verna
Pieve Sto. Stefano
Borgo Pace
Urbania
Fermignano
Alpe d. Luna
S. Angelo in Vado
Alpe di Catenaia
Mercatello s. Metauro
R. Metauro
Gola del Furlo
Caprese Michelangelo
S73b
Acqualagna
S71
Pergola
Sansepolcro
S257
R. Candigliano
S3
Subbiano
Cospaia
Val Tiberina
Cagli
Anghiari
S. Giustino
R. Tevere
Pitigliano
M. Petrano
TUSCANY
Fraccano
Citerna
Eremo di Fonte Avellana
Belvedere
Monterchi
Terme di Fontecchio
Arezzo
Citta di Castello
Pietralunga
Badia di Sitria
S73
Monte Sta. Maria Tiberina
Garavelle
Foce di Scopetone
S452
S360
UMBRIA
Scheggia
Morra
S298
M. Cucco
R. Nestore
S3
S. Ubaldo
Castiglion Fiorentino
Montone
Gubbio
Costacciaro
Montecchio
Civitella Ranieri
Sigillo
S71
le Celle
Umbertide
Fossato di Vico
Cortona
Badia S. Salvatore
Monte Corona
Abba. di Vallingegno
S. Pellegrino
Valsorda
Camuccia
Sta. Maria d. Calcinaio
Serra
Gualdo Tadino
Ossaia
Preggio
Antognola
S3bis
Sanguineto
S298
Terontola
Tuoro sul Trasimeno
E45
S75
Castel Rigone
Montelabate
S3
2
3

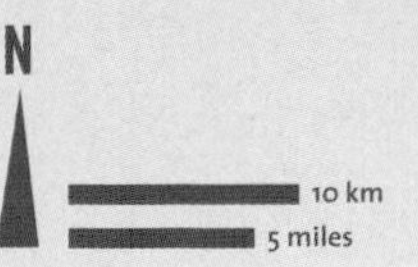

Adriatic

Sea

Pesaro
Fano
S3
A14
S16
Senigallia
To Greece
Mondavio
S360
Corinaldo
Falconara
Marittima
Ancona
Torrette
Chiaravalle
Ostra
Morro
d'Alba
Belvedere
Ostrense
R. Misa
Sta. Maria di P.
Portonovo
Badia di S. Pietro
M. Conero
Sirolo
Jesi
S76
S361
Numana
R. Esino
Arcevia
Rosora
Osimo
THE
Mergo
Castelfidardo
S362
Serra S. Quirico
Porto Recanati
Genga
Gola d. Rossa
Loreto
Filottrano
S361
S77
Grotte di Frasassi
MARCHES
Montefano
Recanati
Vittore
Chiuse
Cingoli
Poggio S. Romualdo
Montecassiano
R. Potenza
Fabriano
S76
Helvia Ricina
Civitanova
Marche
Cerreto d'Esi
S361
Macerata
S. Claudio
al Chienti
Porto S. Elpidio
S77
Matelica
R. Esino
Corridonia
S. Elpidio a Mare
Abba. di Fiastra
Monte
S. Giusto
S. Severino
Marche
Cast. d. Rancia
Tolentino
R. Tenna
Porto S.
Giorgio
Urbisaglia
Mogliano
Pioraco
Fermo

3

Pavullo nel Frignano
S12
Pso. del Cerreto
Montecreto
R. Penaro
S324
Sestola
Casola in Lunigiana
Orecchiella
Pso. d. Radici
S445
Garfagnana
S324
S. Pellegrino in Alpe
Monte Cimone
Piazza al Serchio
Fiumalbo
Castiglione di Garfagnana
Equi Terme
Gramolazzo
Abetone
Porretta Terme
Poggio
Lago Santo
M. Pisanino
Vagli Sopra
Careggine
Doganaccia
Alpe Tre Potenze
L. di Vagli
Alpi Apuane
Castelnuovo di Garfagnana
Albiano
Cutigliano
R. Lima
S632
Castelvecchio Pascoli
Coreglia Antelminelli
Barga
Pian d. Fioba
Gavinana
Pracchia
Isola Santa
Grotta d. Vento
Montefegatesi
Vico
Pasquilio
Tereglio
Scesta
S. Marcello Pistoiese
Maresca
S64
Massa
Fornaci di Barga
Bagni di Lucca
S. Cassiano
Lucchio
Pontepetri
Montignoso
Fornovolasco
Pieve di Controne
Cantagallo
A12
S1
Seravezza
Piteccio
Cinquale
Stazzema
Borgo a Mozzano
Pomoli
Forte dei Marmi
Capriglia
Castelvecchio
Capezzano
S12
S66
Vaiano
Pietrasanta
Valdicastello Carducci
Diecimo
S633
Monteggiori
Castagno
Ponte Nuovo
Marina di Pietrasanta
Camaiore
Capezzano Pianore
Pistoia
R. Bisenzio
Vinchiana
Massa e Cozzile
Figline
S435
Montemurlo
Lido di Camaiore
Ponte a Moriano
Marlia
Collodi
Pescia
Pieve a Elici
S. Stefano
Serravalle Pistoiese
Montecatini Terme
Padule di Fucecchio
Segromigno
R. Ombrone
Viareggio
Massarosa
A11/12
S. Macario in Piano
Buggiano
Monsummano Terme
S435
A11
S439
Mezzano
Capannori
Montevettolini
Ponte Buggianese
Lucca
Montecarlo
Poggio a Caiano
Torre del Lago Puccini
M. Albano
Carmignano
Lago di Massaciuccoli
Lamporecchi
A11
Altopascio
Padule di Fucecchio
Parco Naturale Migliarino S. Rossore e Massaciuccoli
A11
Vinci
Villa d'Artimino
R. Serchio
S12r
Monte Pisano
S439
Anchiano
Lastra a Signa
Cerreto Guidi
Pisa
Calci
Certosa di Pisa
R. Niovole
Fucecchio
Empoli
Montelupo Fiorentino
Gombo
S67
Vicopisano
R. Arno
Ponte a Elsa
R. Pesa
Marina di Pisa
S. Piero a Grado
Cascina
S. Miniato
Pontedera
Montopoli in Val d'A.
S67
A12
S206
Tirrenia
Ponsacco
Montespertoli
Castelfiorentino
Livorno
Lari
R. Elsa
S439
Montaione
Certaldo
S. Vivaldo
Gorgona
Casciana Terme
Ardenza
TUSCANY
S429
Antignano
Rivalto
Montenero
Golfo Aranci/ Olbia/ Portoferraio/ Capraia/ Bastia/ Porto Torres/ Palermo
S206
S. Gimignano
S1
Rosignano Marittimo
Ulignano
Balze
Volterra
Colle di Val d'Elsa
Montecatini Val di Cecina
Castiglioncello
S68
Rosignano Solvay
Saline di Volterra
S439
N
Vada
S68
Casole d'Elsa
S541
Montescudaio
R. Cecina
Cecina
Guardistallo
Pomarance
Mensano
Marina di Cecina
10 km
S439
Radicondoli
Larderello
5 miles
S1
Bolgheri
6
1

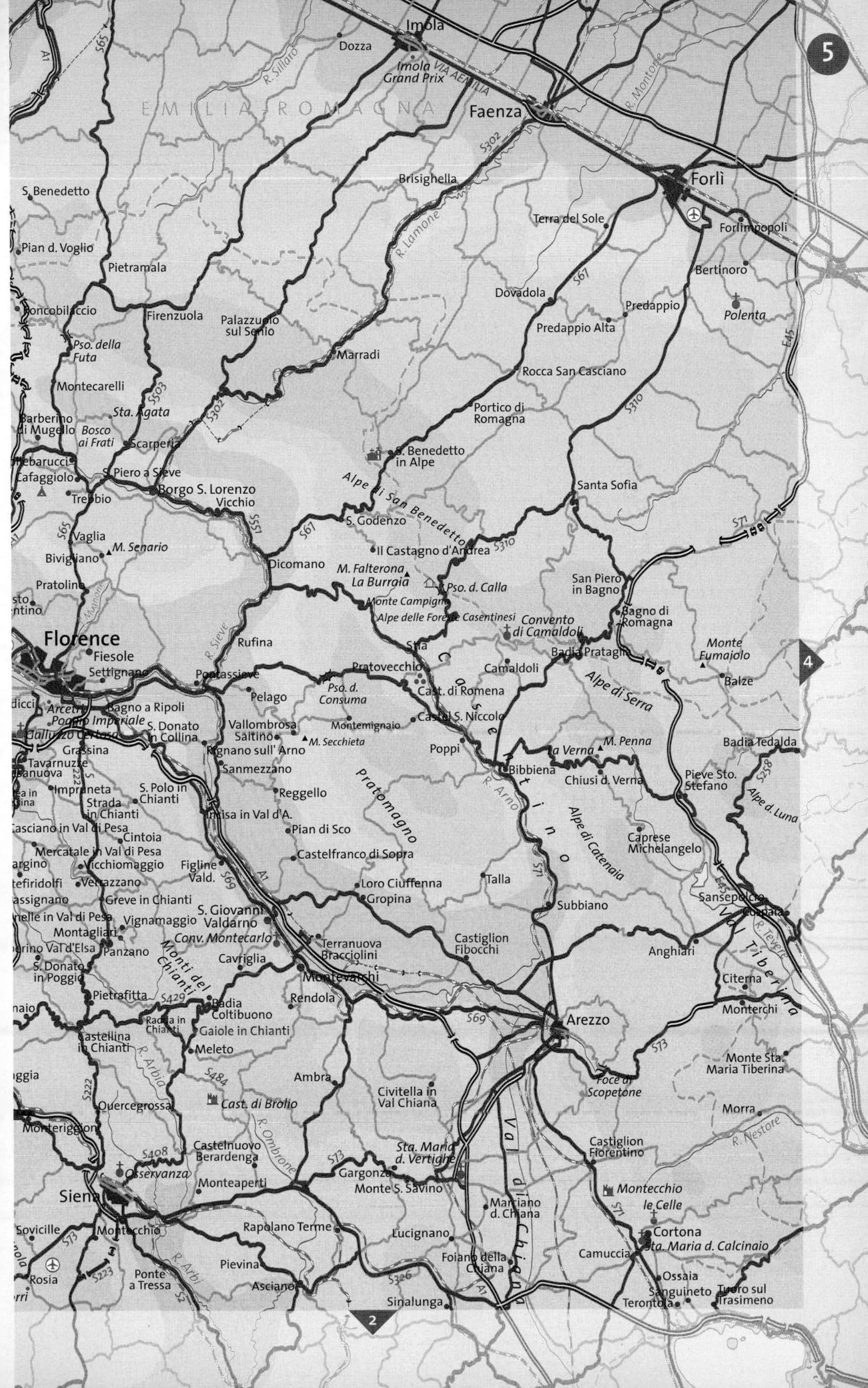
5
Imola
Dozza
R. Sillaro
Imola Grand Prix
VIA AEMILIA
EMILIA-ROMAGNA
Faenza
R. Montone
S302
Forlì
Brisighella
S. Benedetto
R. Lamone
Terra del Sole
Forlimpopoli
Pian d. Voglio
Pietramala
Bertinoro
S67
Dovadola
Predappio
Polenta
Roncobilaccio
Firenzuola
Palazzuolo sul Senio
Predappio Alta
Pso. della Futa
Marradi
E45
Rocca San Casciano
Montecarelli
S503
Sta. Agata
S310
Portico di Romagna
Barberino di Mugello
Bosco ai Frati
Scarperia
S. Benedetto in Alpe
Cafaggiolo
S. Piero a Sieve
Borgo S. Lorenzo
Vicchio
Santa Sofia
Trebbio
Alpe di San Benedetto
S65
Vaglia
S551
S. Godenzo
S71
M. Senario
Il Castagno d'Andrea
Bivigliano
Dicomano
M. Falterona
La Burraia
Pso. d. Calla
San Piero in Bagno
Pratolino
Monte Campigna
Bagno di Romagna
Alpe delle Foreste Casentinesi
Convento di Camaldoli
Florence
R. Sieve
Rufina
Stia
Badia Prataglia
Monte Fumaiolo
Fiesole
Camaldoli
4
Settignano
Pontassieve
Pratovecchio
Balze
Casentino
Alpe di Serra
Pelago
Pso. d. Consuma
Cast. di Romena
Arcetri
Bagno a Ripoli
Poggio Imperiale
S. Donato in Collina
Vallombrosa
Montemignaio
Castel S. Niccolò
Galluzzo
Certosa
Saltino
M. Secchieta
Grassina
Rignano sull' Arno
Poppi
La Verna
M. Penna
Badia Tedalda
Tavarnuzze
Sanmezzano
Bibbiena
S258
Impruneta
S. Polo in Chianti
Reggello
Pratomagno
R. Arno
Chiusi d. Verna
Pieve Sto. Stefano
Strada in Chianti
Alpe d. Luna
Incisa in Val d'A.
Pian di Sco
Alpe di Catenaia
Cintoia
Caprese Michelangelo
Mercatale in Val di Pesa
Vicchiomaggio
Castelfranco di Sopra
Figline Vald.
S69
A1
Verrazzano
Loro Ciuffenna
Talla
Greve in Chianti
Gropina
Sansepolcro
S. Giovanni Valdarno
Subbiano
Val Tiberina
Vignamaggio
R. Tevere
Montagliari
Conv. Montecarlo
Castiglion Fibocchi
Anghiari
Panzano
Monti del Chianti
Terranuova Bracciolini
S. Donato in Poggio
Cavriglia
Citerna
Montevarchi
Pietrafitta
S429
Badia Coltibuono
Rendola
Monterchi
Radda in Chianti
Arezzo
Castellina in Chianti
Gaiole in Chianti
Meleto
S73
R. Arbia
Monte Sta. Maria Tiberina
S484
Ambra
Foce di Scopetone
S222
Civitella in Val Chiana
Quercegrossa
Cast. di Brolio
Morra
Monteriggioni
R. Ombrone
Val di Chiana
R. Nestore
Sta. Maria d. Vertighe
Castiglion Fiorentino
S408
Castelnuovo Berardenga
Osservanza
Gargonza
Monteaperti
Monte S. Savino
Montecchio
Siena
Marciano d. Chiana
le Celle
Sovicille
Montecchio
Rapolano Terme
Cortona
Lucignano
Camuccia
Sta. Maria d. Calcinaio
S223
Ponte a Tressa
R. Arbi
Pievina
Foiano della Chiana
Rosia
S326
Ossaia
Asciano
Sanguineto
Tuoro sul Trasimeno
S2
Sinalunga
Terontola
2

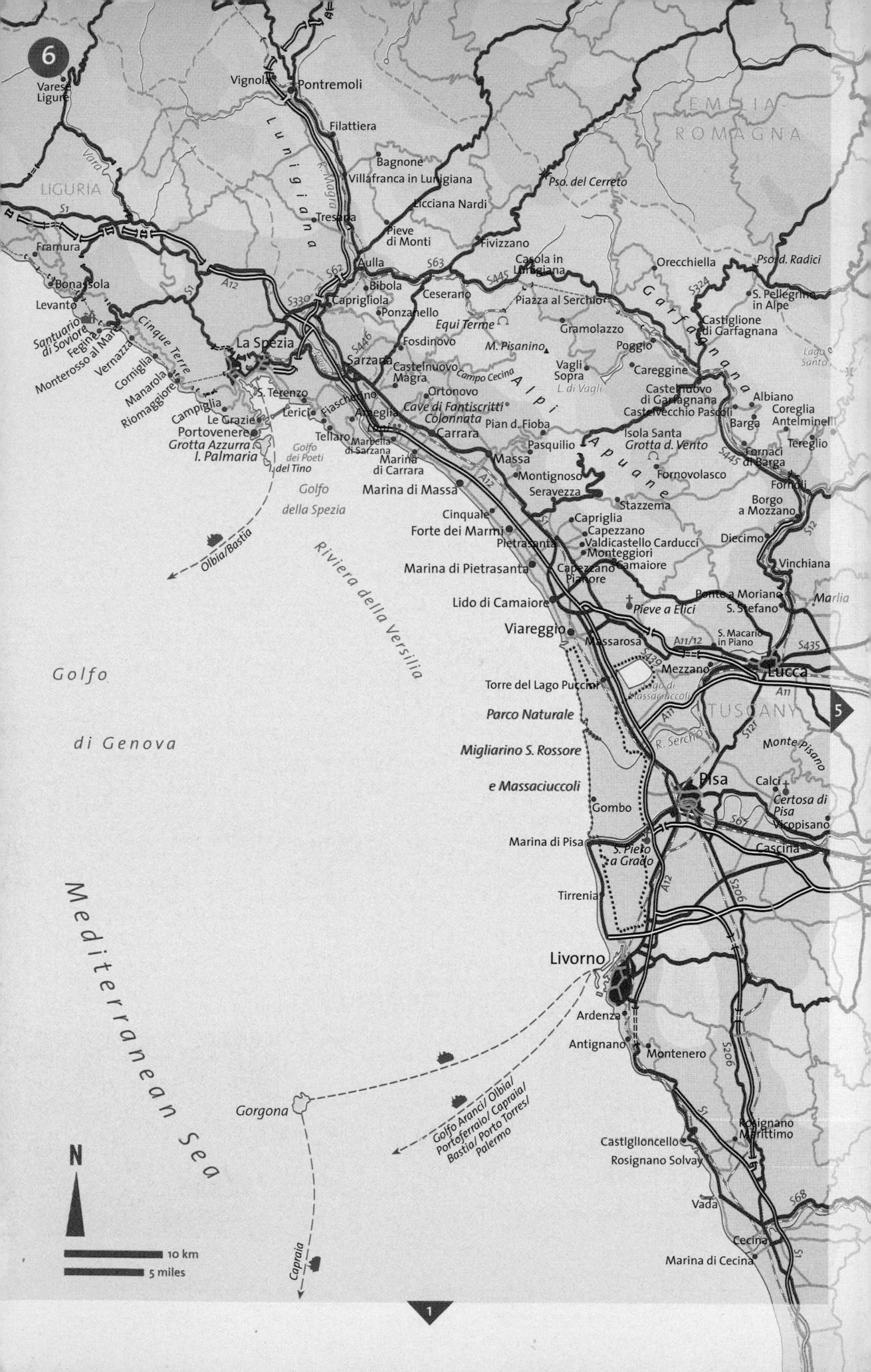
6
Varese Ligure
Vignola
Pontremoli
Filattiera
Lunigiana
R. Magra
Bagnone
Villafranca in Lunigiana
Licciana Nardi
Tresana
Pieve di Monti
Fivizzano
Vara
LIGURIA
S1
Framura
Bonassola
Levanto
Santuario di Soviore
Fegina
Monterosso al Mare
Vernazza
Corniglia
Manarola
Riomaggiore
Cinque Terre
A12
Aulla
Bibola
S62
S63
S330
Caprigliola
Ponzanello
Ceserano
S445
Casola in Lunigiana
Piazza al Serchio
Equi Terme
M. Pisanino
Gramolazzo
La Spezia
S446
Fosdinovo
Sarzana
Castelnuovo Magra
Campo Cecina
Ortonovo
Cave di Fantiscritti
Colonnata
Carrara
S. Terenzo
Lerici
Fiascherino
Ameglia
Luni
Tellaro
Marbella di Sarzana
Marina di Carrara
Campiglia
Le Grazie
Portovenere
Grotta Azzurra
I. Palmaria
Golfo dei Poeti
I. del Tino
Golfo della Spezia
Olbia/Bastia
Massa
Marina di Massa
Montignoso
Seravezza
Cinquale
Forte dei Marmi
Pietrasanta
Marina di Pietrasanta
Lido di Camaiore
Viareggio
Riviera della Versilia
EMILIA-ROMAGNA
Pso. del Cerreto
Orecchiella
Pso. d. Radici
S324
Garfagnana
S. Pellegrino in Alpe
Castiglione di Garfagnana
Lago Santo
Poggio
Vagli Sopra
L. di Vagli
Careggine
Alpi Apuane
Pian d. Fioba
Pasquilio
Castelnuovo di Garfagnana
Castelvecchio Pascoli
Isola Santa
Grotta d. Vento
Albiano
Barga
Coreglia Antelminelli
Fornaci di Barga
Tereglio
S445
Fornovolasco
Fornoli
Stazzema
Borgo a Mozzano
Capriglia
Capezzano
Valdicastello Carducci
Monteggiori
Camaiore
Capezzano Pianore
Diecimo
S12
Vinchiana
Ponte a Moriano
S. Stefano
Marlia
Pieve a Elici
Massarosa
S439
A11/12
S. Macario in Piano
S435
Mezzano
Lucca
Lago di Massaciuccoli
Torre del Lago Puccini
A11
TUSCANY
5
Parco Naturale
Migliarino S. Rossore
e Massaciuccoli
R. Serchio
S12r
Monte Pisano
Pisa
Calci
Certosa di Pisa
Vicopisano
S67
Cascina
Gombo
Marina di Pisa
S. Piero a Grado
A12
S206
Tirrenia
Golfo
di Genova
Livorno
Ardenza
Antignano
Montenero
Mediterranean Sea
Gorgona
Golfo Aranci/ Olbia/ Portoferraio/ Capraia/ Bastia/ Porto Torres/ Palermo
Rosignano Marittimo
Castiglioncello
Rosignano Solvay
S1
S68
Vada
Cecina
Marina di Cecina
Capraia
N
10 km
5 miles
1